Communications in Computer and Information Science 1038

More information about this series at http://www.springer.com/series/7899

Daniel A. Alexandrov · Alexander V. Boukhanovsky ·
Andrei V. Chugunov · Yury Kabanov ·
Olessia Koltsova · Ilya Musabirov (Eds.)

Digital Transformation and Global Society

4th International Conference, DTGS 2019
St. Petersburg, Russia, June 19–21, 2019
Revised Selected Papers

Editors
Daniel A. Alexandrov
National Research University
Higher School of Economics
St. Petersburg, Russia

Andrei V. Chugunov
ITMO University
St. Petersburg, Russia

Olessia Koltsova
National Research University
Higher School of Economics
St. Petersburg, Russia

Alexander V. Boukhanovsky
ITMO University
St. Petersburg, Russia

Yury Kabanov
National Research University
Higher School of Economics
St. Petersburg, Russia

Ilya Musabirov
National Research University
Higher School of Economics
St. Petersburg, Russia

ISSN 1865-0929 ISSN 1865-0937 (electronic)
Communications in Computer and Information Science
ISBN 978-3-030-37857-8 ISBN 978-3-030-37858-5 (eBook)
https://doi.org/10.1007/978-3-030-37858-5

This Springer imprint is published by the registered company Springer Nature Switzerland AG
The registered company address is: Gewerbestrasse 11, 6330 Cham, Switzerland

Preface

The 4th International Conference on Digital Transformation and Global Society (DTGS 2019) was held during June 19–21, 2019, in St. Petersburg, Russia. It became a joint effort of the two leading Russian research institutions: the ITMO University and the National Research University Higher School of Economics (St. Petersburg), as well as the PRIOR - NW Non-Profit Organization, to develop the international platform of interdisciplinary collaboration in the area of Digital Transformation Research, and broadly, of Internet Studies.

The Program Committee received 194 submissions, and after careful evaluation by reviewers and editors (before and after the conference) 65 papers were accepted for this post-conference volume. The submissions fall into several major tracks of the conference:

- E-Polity: issues of e-governance and e-participation, as well as politics online
- E-City: papers related to smart cities, urban governance, and planning
- E-Economy: research on the digital economy, ICT-driven economic practices, and online consumers' behavior
- E-Society: digital culture and education studies, as well as research on Computational Social Science

In addition to the main conference, two international workshops were organized for the second time: the Internet Psychology Workshop, chaired by Prof. Alexander Voiskounsky (Lomonosov Moscow State University), and the Computational Linguistics Workshop, led by Prof. Viktor Zakharov (St. Petersburg State University). The accepted papers from these workshops are also included in this volume.

An innovation of DTGS 2019 became the Young Scholars' Forum – an updated poster session, where students and young academics could present their research and get feedback from peers. The Award Committee, chaired by Dr. Olessia Koltsova (Higher School of Economics), was formed to assess all posters and select the best ones. By the decision of the Award Committee, several posters were accepted to the final volume after the substantial revision and expansion. We hope that the number of young scholars taking part in DTGS will increase.

Furthermore, several insightful keynote lectures were organized at DTGS 2019: "Decision Making using Digital Personalities" by Klavdia Bochenina (ITMO University, Russia), "Fast and Accurate Algorithms for Detection of Spread Source in Large Complex Networks with Single and Multiple Propagation Paths" by Janusz Hołyst (Warsaw University of Technology, Poland), and "The Primacy of Presence: Supporting Psychological Wellbeing with Interactive Technology" by John Waterworth (Umea University, Sweden).

We are grateful to the members of the international Program Committees, the reviewers, and the conference staff. We would like also to thank the session chairs: Yury Kabanov, Olessia Koltsova, and Ilya Musabirov (Higher School of Economics);

Yuri Misnikov, Antonina Puchkovskaya, and Dmitry Trutnev (ITMO University); Radomir Bolgov and Leonid Smorgunov (St. Petersburg State University); and Maxim Bakaev (Novosibirsk State Technological University). We thank our authors for contributing their excellent research to the volume.

We are happy to see the conference developing, and we believe DTGS will continue to contribute to global research on digital transformation.

June 2019

Daniel Alexandrov
Alexander Boukhanovsky
Andrei V. Chugunov
Yury Kabanov
Olessia Koltsova
Ilya Musabirov

Organization

Program Committee

Luis Alvarez Sabucedo	Universidade de Vigo, Spain
Luis Amaral	University of Minho, Portugal
Dennis Anderson	St. Francis College, USA
Francisco Andrade	University of Minho, Portugal
Farah Arab	Université Paris 8, France
Maxim Bakaev	Novosibirsk State Technical University, Russia
Vladimír Benko	Slovak Academy of Sciences, Ľ. Štúr Institute of Linguistics, Slovakia
Nataliya V. Bogacheva	I. M. Sechenov First Moscow State Medical University, Russia
Natalia Bogdanova-Beglarian	St. Petersburg State University, Russia
Irina Bogdanovskaya	Herzen State Pedagogical University of Russia, Russia
Radomir Bolgov	St. Petersburg State University, Russia
Kirill Boyarsky	ITMO University, Russia
Mikhail Bundin	Lobachevsky State University of Nizhni Novgorod, Russia
Sunil Choenni	Research and Documentation Centre (WODC), Ministry of Justice, The Netherlands
Andrei Chugunov	ITMO University, Russia
Olga Filatova	St. Petersburg State University, Russia
Enrico Francesconi	Italian National Research Council, Italy
Floriana Gargiulo	GEMASS-CNRS and University of Paris Sorbonne, France
Carlos Gershenson	National Autonomous University of Mexico, Mexico
Stefanos Gritzalis	University of Piraeus, Greece
André Grow	Katholieke Universiteit Leuven, Belgium
Enrique Herrera-Viedma	University of Granada, Spain
Dmitry Ilvovsky	National Research University Higher School of Economics, Russia
Yury Kabanov	National Research University Higher School of Economics, Russia
Katerina Kabassi	TEI of Ionian Islands, Greece
Argyris Karapetsas	University of Thessaly, Greece
Victor Karepin	National Research University Higher School of Economics, Russia
Nikolay Karpov	National Research University Higher School of Economics, Russia

Egor Kashkin	V. V. Vinogradov Russian Language Institute of RAS, Russia
Sanjeev Katara	National Informatics Centre, Government of India, India
Nikolay Kazantsev	Alliance Manchester Business School, The University of Manchester, UK
Liudmila Khalyapina	Peter the Great Saint-Petersburg Polytechnic University, Russia
Igor Khodachek	Russian Academy of National Economy and Public Administration, Russia
Olga Khodakovskaia	St. Petersburg State University of Culture, Russia
Bozidar Klicek	University of Zagreb, Croatia
Edward S. Klyshinsky	Moscow State Institute of Electronics and Mathematics, Russia
Stefanos Kollias	National Technical University of Athens, Greece
Anastasia Kolmogorova	Siberian Federal University, Russia
Olessia Koltsova	National Research University Higher School of Economics, Russia
Liliya Komalova	Moscow State Linguistic University, Institute of Scientific Information for Social Sciences (RAS), Russia
Natalya Koroleva	Herzen State Pedagogical University of Russia, Russia
Evgeny Kotelnikov	Vyatka State University, Russia
Renaud Lambiotte	University of Oxford, UK
Yanina Ledovaya	St. Petersburg State University, Russia
Sandro Leuchter	Hochschule Mannheim University of Applied Sciences, Germany
Benjamin Lind	Anglo-American School of St. Petersburg, Russia
Yuri Lipuntsov	Lomonosov Moscow State University, Russia
Natalia Loukachevitch	Lomonosov Moscow State University, Russia
William Louw	Coventry University, UK
Mikhail Lugachev	Lomonosov Moscow State University, Russia
Aleksei Martynov	Lobachevsky State University of Nizhny Novgorod, Russia
Athanasios Mazarakis	Kiel University and ZBW, Germany
Julien Mercier	Université du Québec à Montréal, Canada
Elena Mikhailova	St. Petersburg State University, Russia
Yuri Misnikov	ITMO University, Russia
Olga Mitrofanova	St. Petersburg State University, Russia
Sergey Mityagin	ITMO University, Russia
Vladimir Mochalov	IKIR FEB RAS, Russia
Ravil Muhamedyev	International IT University, Kazakhstan
Ilya Musabirov	National Research University Higher School of Economics, Russia
Alexandra Nagornaya	Moscow City Teachers' Training University, Russia

Victor Naumov	Institute of State and Law of the Russian Academy of Sciences, Russia
Olga Nevzorova	Kazan Federal University, Russia
Galina Nikiporets-Takigawa	University of Cambridge, UK, and Russian State Social University, Russia
Prabir Panda	National Institute for Smart Government, India
Polina Panicheva	National Research University Higher School of Economics, Russia
Malgorzata Pankowska	University of Economics in Katowice, Poland
Mário Peixoto	United Nations University (UNU-EGOV), Portugal
Alexander Porshnev	National Research University Higher School of Economics, Russia
Yuliya Proekt	Herzen State Pedagogical University of Russia, Russia
Dmitry Prokudin	St. Petersburg State University, Russia
Antonina Puchkovskaya	ITMO University, Russia
Rui Quaresma	Universidade de Évora, Portugal
Celia Rafael	Escola Superior de Turismo e Tecnologia do Mar, Portugal
Alexander Raikov	Institute of Control Sciences RAS, Russia
Vera Rebiazina	National Research University Higher School of Economics, Russia
Aleksandr Riabushko	St. Petersburg State University, Russia
Manuel Pedro Rodríguez Bolívar	University of Granada, Spain
John Magnus Roos	Centre for Consumer Science, Sweden
Gustavo Rossi	LIFIA UNLP, Argentina
Liudmila Rychkova	Yanka Kupala State University of Grodno, Belarus
Alexander Ryjov	Lomonosov Moscow State University, Russia
Olga Scrivner	Indiana University Bloomington, USA
Svetlana Sheremetyeva	South Ural State University, Russia
Anna Shirokanova	National Research University Higher School of Economics, Russia
Maxim Skryabin	Stepik, Russia
Alexander Smirnov	SPIIRAS, Russia
Polina Smirnova	ITMO University, Russia
Anna Smoliarova	St. Petersburg State University, Russia
Artem Smolin	ITMO University, Russia
Leonid Smorgunov	St. Petersburg State University, Russia
Andrzej Sobczak	Warsaw School of Economics, Poland
Artur Sousa	Polytechnic Institute of Viseu, Portugal
Evgeny Styrin	National Research University Higher School of Economics, Russia
Ilya Surov	ITMO University, Russia
Miroslav Svitek	CVUT, Czech Republic
Roman Tikhonov	National Research University Higher School of Economics, Russia

Irina Tolstikova	ITMO University, Russia
Alice Trindade	Universidade de Lisboa, Portugal
Dmitrii Trutnev	ITMO University, Russia
Costas Vassilakis	University of the Peloponnese, Greece
Linda Veiga	University of Minho, Portugal
Cyril Velikanov	Memorial NGO, Russia
Antonio Vetrò	Nexa Center for Internet and Society (DAUIN, Politecnico di Torino), Italy
Lyudmila Vidiasova	ITMO University, Russia
Alexander Voiskounsky	Lomonosov Moscow State University, Russia
Ingmar Weber	Qatar Computing Research Institute, Qatar
Yanina Welp	University of Zurich, Switzerland
Vladimir Yakimets	Institute for Information Transmission Problems and Russian Academy of National Economy and Public Administration, Russia
Nikolina Zajdela Hrustek	University of Zagreb, Croatia
Victor Zakharov	St. Petersburg State University, Russia
Alina Zakharova	St. Petersburg State University, Russia
Sergej Zerr	L3S Research Center, Germany
Hans-Dieter Zimmermann	FHS St. Gallen University of Applied Sciences, Switzerland
Thomas Ågotnes	University of Bergen, Norway
Vytautas Čyras	Vilnius University, Lithuania

Additional Reviewers

Almazova, Nadezhda
Amreviewer, Amreviewer
Bakhitova, Alina
Balakhontceva, Marina
Bolgova, Ekaterina
Bulygin, Denis
Chunaev, Petr
Chuprina, Daria
Galustov, Kirill
Giannakas, Filippos
Guleva, Valentina Y.
Hvatov, Alexander
Kalloniatis, Christos
Karapetsas, Argyris
Karepin, Viktor
Klimova, Alexandra
Kovalchuk, Sergey
Kuznetsova, Anastasia
Louw, William
Melnik, Mikhail
Menshikova, Anastasia
Menshikova, Nastya
Metsker, Oleg
Novikova, Alexandra
Pashakhin, Sergei
Porshnev, Alexander
Pozdniakov, Stanislav
S. Bargh, Mortaza
Semakova, Anna
Sinyavskaya, Yadviga
Surov, Ilya
Suvorova, Alena
Tsvetkova, Antonina
van den Braak, Susan
Voskresenskiy, Vadim
Zaikin, Oleg

Contents

E-Polity: Politics Online

E-City: Smart Cities and Urban Planning

E-Economy: Online Consumers and Solutions

E-Society: Computational Social Science

E-Society: Humanities and Education

E-Polity: Governance

Fully Informed Classification Systems Simpler, Maybe Better

Ana Fernandes[1], Filomena Carvalho[2,3], Jorge Ribeiro[4], Dinis Vicente[5], João Faria[5], Margarida Figueiredo[6], António Capita[7], José Neves[8(✉)], and Henrique Vicente[8,9]

[1] Departamento de Química, Escola de Ciências e Tecnologia, Universidade de Évora, Évora, Portugal
anavilafernandes@gmail.com

[2] Departamento de Ciências Jurídicas, Escola Superior de Tecnologia e Gestão de Leiria, Instituto Politécnico de Leiria, Leiria, Portugal
filomena.carvalho@ipleiria.pt

[3] Centro de Investigação IJP – Instituto Jurídico Portucalense, Leiria, Portugal

[4] Escola Superior de Tecnologia e Gestão, ARC4DigiT – Applied Research Center for Digital Transformation, Instituto Politécnico de Viana do Castelo, Viana do Castelo, Portugal
jribeiro@estg.ipvc.pt

[5] Escola Superior de Tecnologia e Gestão de Leiria, Instituto Politécnico de Leiria, Leiria, Portugal
dinisvicente98@gmail.com, joaocfaria10@gmail.com

[6] Departamento de Química, Escola de Ciências e Tecnologia, Centro de Investigação em Educação e Psicologia, Universidade de Évora, Évora, Portugal
mtf@uevora.pt

[7] Instituto Superior Técnico Militar, Luanda, Angola
antoniojorgecapita@gmail.com

[8] Centro Algoritmi, Universidade do Minho, Braga, Portugal
jneves@di.uminho.pt, hvicente@uevora.pt

[9] Departamento de Química, Escola de Ciências e Tecnologia, Centro de Química de Évora, Universidade de Évora, Évora, Portugal

Abstract. This paper presents the starting point to adverse event reporting and learning systems designed to describe and prevent unfavorable happenings in *Public Services* organizations. To achieve this goal, the *Eindhoven's Classification Method* was changed to house such incidents. On the other hand, the evolutionary process of the knowledge body of such systems is to be understood as a process of energy devaluation, i.e., their data/information/knowledge will be represented and handled as pure energy transactions, being such procedures and the respective outcomes object of formal proof under a *Proof Theoretical approach to Problem Solving*.

Keywords: Public services · Eindhoven classification method · Knowledge representation and reasoning · Logic programming · Entropy

D. A. Alexandrov et al. (Eds.): DTGS 2019, CCIS 1038, pp. 3–16, 2019.
https://doi.org/10.1007/978-3-030-37858-5_1

1 Introduction

Citizens are better informed and increasingly demanding in terms of the quality of the Public Services (PS) on offer. The development of quality management systems in compliance with the ISO 9001 guidelines ensures their efficiency and helps to increase inner and outer satisfaction [1–3]. An adverse event in this context means failure to perform a prescribed action or the use of a false plan to achieve an intended objective. The most efficient strategy for avoiding adverse events is recognizing their sources, i.e., avoiding the causes can in particular improve the quality of PS. Such causes can be related to practical problems, human relationships, policies, action plans, products, strategies, and/or leaders. People continue to learn from their own mistakes rather than from their successes. However, they do not share the appearance of glitches or what they have learned with them. So, similar mistakes can occur repeatedly and citizens can be harmed by avoidable mistakes. Some studies have suggested that reporting may be a possible solution to this problem. The basic idea of reporting is based on the learning process based on experience. However, it is important to emphasize that the registration of errors is not sufficient to ensure the quality of the services provided. Collecting data is not enough to improve the process. Only an efficient response to adverse events may affect the change. A technical review of the data is essential to identify trends and patterns [4, 5]. One answer to this limitation is the combination of an adverse event reporting system and machine learning methods to identify hazards and risks [6]. Using models to identify causes of adverse events is extremely important to ensuring the exchange of knowledge and experience. Thus, in this paper it is set the formal basis of an adverse event reporting and learning system. It will focus on preventing the causes of adverse events, therefore ensuring performance benchmarking of the organization against a standard, whether absolute or relative to others [7].

2 Computational Model

In order to avoid the occurrence of adverse events, the study of the main causes is obligatory. In order to develop systems that can be used in the PS, special attention should be given to those who describe adverse events, seek to identify their root causes and assess the outcome of the preventive measures taken. The Eindhoven Classification Method (ECM) [4] was chosen once it uses Root Cause Analysis (RCA) methods to classify causes based on previously defined codes. The ECM includes two types of errors, human or active and latent ones. Concerning active faults, the ECM adopts Rasmussen's SRK model, which includes three levels of behavior i.e., the skills-based, the rules-based and the knowledge-based [8]. With respect to latent errors, ECM differentiates between technical and organizational ones [4]. The former one occurs when there are problems with physical components (e.g., equipment, physical installations), while the latter is related to protocols, procedures, or knowledge transfer operations. The starting point in the development of ECM based systems is the recognizing of the sources of a particular adverse event. Thus, in order to attain this end a Causal Tree (CT) was built and RCA techniques applied (Fig. 1), viz.

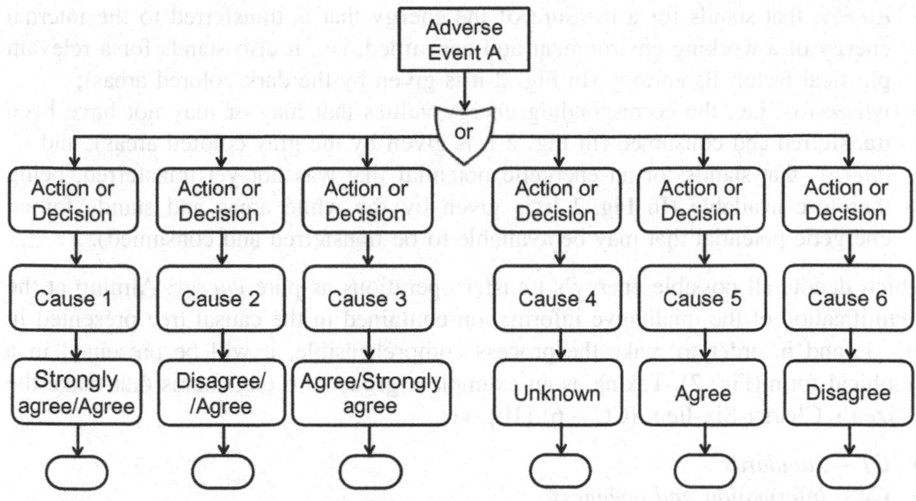

Fig. 1. General structure of the CT for the adverse event A.

Once the root causes have been identified, it is possible to obtain a global picture of the functioning of the system under a hierarchical structure, and put useful and long-term solutions into practice. In Fig. 1 the adverse event A has six possible grounds. It is known that the contribution of causes 5 and 6 to the undesired event are *agree* and *disagree*, respectively (known values), while the contribution of the remaining causes is *unknown*, which sets two different types of unknown values. With regard to causes 1, 2 and 3, it is not possible to determine their precise values, but it is known that their domains are given by the sets {*strongly agree*, *agree*}, {*disagree*, *agree*} and {*agree*, *strongly agree*}, respectively, i.e., an *unknown* value in a finite set of values. With regard to cause 4, it is not possible to assert its contribution to the undesirable event, all values are plausible, i.e., an *unknown* value (not necessarily from a finite set of values).

2.1 Knowledge Representation and Reasoning

The *Knowledge Representation and Reasoning* (*KRR*) practices in use are to be understood as a process of energy devaluation [9], i.e., a data item is to be understood as being in a given moment at a given entropic state as untainted energy that, according to the *First Law of Thermodynamics*, is a quantity well-preserved that cannot be consumed in the sense of destruction but may be consumed in the sense of devaluation. This new understanding may be introduced by splitting a given amount of energy into its parts, viz.

- *exergy*, that stands for a measure of the energy that is transferred to the internal energy of a working environment and consumed, i.e., it also stands for a relevant physical factor, its entropy (In Fig. 2 it is given by the dark colored areas);
- *vagueness*, i.e., the corresponding energy values that may or may not have been transferred and consumed (In Fig. 2 it is given by the gray colored areas); and
- *anergy*, that stands for an energetic potential that was not yet transferred, being therefore available (In Fig. 2 it is given by the white areas and stands for an energetic potential that may be available to be transferred and consumed).

which denote all possible energy's transfer operations as pure *energy*. Aiming at the quantification of the qualitative information contained in the causal tree presented in Fig. 1, and in order to make the process comprehensible, it will be presented in a graphical form (Fig. 2). Taking as an example a group of 6 (six) items that make the Citizen's Charter-Six-Item (CC – 6) [10], viz.

- *C1 – Standards*
- *C2 – Information and openness*
- *C3 –Choice and consultation*
- *C4 –Courtesy and helpfulness*
- *C5 –Putting things right; and*
- *C6 –Value for money*

which aims to raise the standard of public services and to make them more responsive. In order to achieve this goal, it will be used the scale [11, 12], viz.

$$\textit{strongly agree}(4),\ \textit{agree}(3),\ \textit{disagree}(2),\ \textit{strongly disagree}(1),\ \textit{disagree}(2),\ \textit{agree}(3),\ \textit{strongly agree}(4)$$

and the question "How easy would you say agree?" (Table 1).

Table 1. *CC – 6* single citizen answers.

Items	Scale						
	(4)	(3)	(2)	(1)	(2)	(3)	(4)
C1	×	×					
C2					×	×	
C3						×	×
C4				*unknown*			
C5			×				
C6						×	

Leading to → Fig. 2 ← Leading to

How easy would you say ***agree****?*

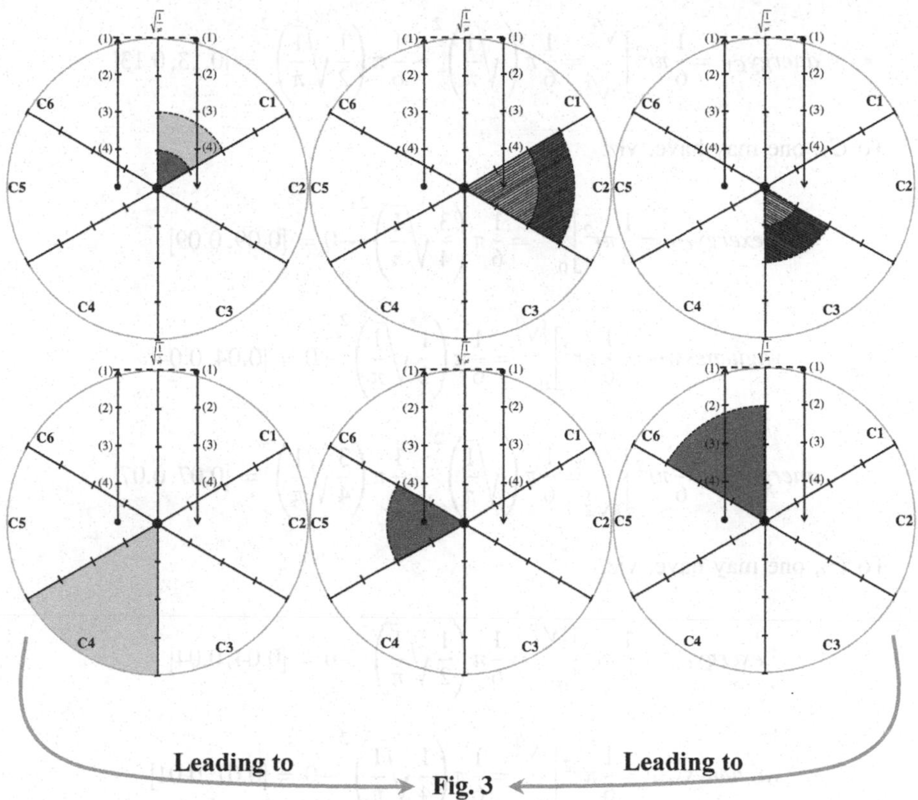

Fig. 2. An assessment of the attained energy with respect to a single citizen answer to *CC-6*.

Considering that the markers on the axis correspond to any of the possible scale options, which may be used from *bottom* → *top* (i.e., from *strongly disagree (1)* to *strongly agree (4)*), meaning that the system will work better once its entropy decreases, or is used from *top* → *bottom* (i.e., from *strongly agree (4)* to *strongly disagree (1)*), indicating that the performance of the system decreases as entropy increases), which is the case with respect to *C1*, whose entropic states as untainted energy are evaluated as follows, viz.

$$exergy_{C1} = \frac{1}{6}\pi r^2\Big]_0^{\frac{1}{4}\sqrt{\frac{1}{\pi}}} = \frac{1}{6}\pi\left(\frac{1}{4}\sqrt{\frac{1}{\pi}}\right)^2 - 0 = [0.01, 0.01]$$

$$vagueness_{C1} = \frac{1}{6}\pi r^2\Big]_{\frac{1}{4}\sqrt{\frac{1}{\pi}}}^{\frac{1}{2}\sqrt{\frac{1}{\pi}}} = \frac{1}{6}\pi\left(\frac{1}{2}\sqrt{\frac{1}{\pi}}\right)^2 - \frac{1}{6}\pi\left(\frac{1}{4}\sqrt{\frac{1}{\pi}}\right)^2 = [0.03, 0.03]$$

$$anergy_{C1} = \frac{1}{6}\pi r^2\Big]_{\frac{1}{2}\sqrt{\frac{1}{\pi}}}^{\sqrt{\frac{1}{\pi}}} = \frac{1}{6}\pi\left(\sqrt{\frac{1}{\pi}}\right)^2 - \frac{1}{6}\pi\left(\frac{1}{2}\sqrt{\frac{1}{\pi}}\right)^2 = [0.13, 0.13]$$

To C_2, one may have, viz.

$$exergy_{C2} = \frac{1}{6}\pi r^2\Big]_{0}^{\frac{3}{4}\sqrt{\frac{1}{\pi}}} = \frac{1}{6}\pi\left(\frac{3}{4}\sqrt{\frac{1}{\pi}}\right)^2 - 0 = [0.09, 0.09]$$

$$vagueness_{C2} = \frac{1}{6}\pi r^2\Big]_{0}^{\frac{1}{2}\sqrt{\frac{1}{\pi}}} = \frac{1}{6}\pi\left(\frac{1}{2}\sqrt{\frac{1}{\pi}}\right)^2 - 0 = [0.04, 0.04]$$

$$anergy_{C2} = \frac{1}{6}\pi r^2\Big]_{\frac{3}{4}\sqrt{\frac{1}{\pi}}}^{\sqrt{\frac{1}{\pi}}} = \frac{1}{6}\pi\left(\sqrt{\frac{1}{\pi}}\right)^2 - \frac{1}{6}\pi\left(\frac{3}{4}\sqrt{\frac{1}{\pi}}\right)^2 = [0.07, 0.07]$$

To C_3, one may have, viz.

$$exergy_{C3} = \frac{1}{6}\pi r^2\Big]_{0}^{\frac{1}{2}\sqrt{\frac{1}{\pi}}} = \frac{1}{6}\pi\left(\frac{1}{2}\sqrt{\frac{1}{\pi}}\right)^2 - 0 = [0.04, 0.04]$$

$$vagueness_{C3} = \frac{1}{6}\pi r^2\Big]_{0}^{\frac{1}{4}\sqrt{\frac{1}{\pi}}} = \frac{1}{6}\pi\left(\frac{1}{4}\sqrt{\frac{1}{\pi}}\right)^2 - 0 = [0.01, 0.01]$$

$$anergy_{C3} = \frac{1}{6}\pi r^2\Big]_{\frac{1}{2}\sqrt{\frac{1}{\pi}}}^{\sqrt{\frac{1}{\pi}}} = \frac{1}{6}\pi\left(\sqrt{\frac{1}{\pi}}\right)^2 - \frac{1}{6}\pi\left(\frac{1}{2}\sqrt{\frac{1}{\pi}}\right)^2 = [0.13, 0.13]$$

To C_4, C5 and C6 the procedures are the same. On the other hand, once a system's performance is a function of its entropic state, the data collected above may be structured in terms of the extent of the so called ***citizen's charter*** (***cc***) predicate, viz.

$$cc : EXergy, VAgueness, System's\ Performance,$$
$$Quality\text{-}of\text{-}Information \rightarrow \{True, False\}$$

whose graphical and formal descriptions in terms of the language of Logic Programming [13] are given below, viz.

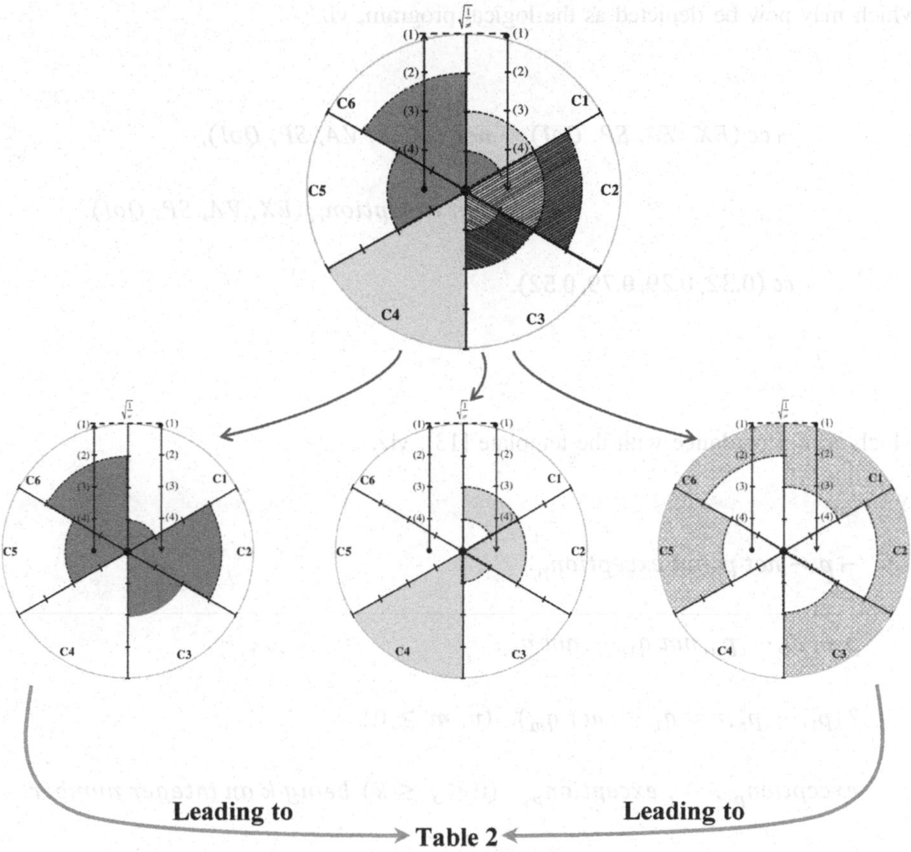

Fig. 3. A graphical view of the *cc* extent obtained according to the answers of a single citizen to the *CC-6*.

Table 2. The *CC* predicate's extent obtained according to the answers of a single citizen to the *CC-6*.

Exergy	Vagueness	System's Performance	Quality-of-Information
0.32	0.29	0.79	0.52

which may now be depicted as the logical program, viz.

$$
\begin{aligned}
&\{\\
&\quad \neg\, cc\,(EX, VA, SP, QoI) \leftarrow not\ cc(EX, VA, SP, QoI),\\
&\qquad\qquad\qquad\qquad\qquad\qquad not\ exception_{cc}(EX, VA, SP, QoI)\\
&\quad cc\,(0.32, 0.29, 0.79, 0.52).\\
&\}
\end{aligned}
$$

which is in accordance with the template [13], viz.

$$
\begin{aligned}
&\{\\
&\quad \neg\, p \leftarrow not\ p, not\ exception_p.\\
&\quad p \leftarrow p_1, \cdots, p_n, not\ q_1, \cdots, not\ q_m.\\
&\quad ?\,(p_1, \cdots, p_n, not\ q_1, \cdots, not\ q_m).\quad (n,\ m \geq 0)\\
&\quad exception_{p_1}, \ \cdots, \ exception_{p_j} \quad (0 \leq j \leq k), being\ k\ an\ integer\ number\\
&\}
\end{aligned}
$$

where the evaluation of *SP* and *QoI* for the different items that make the *CC* – *6* are given in the form, viz.

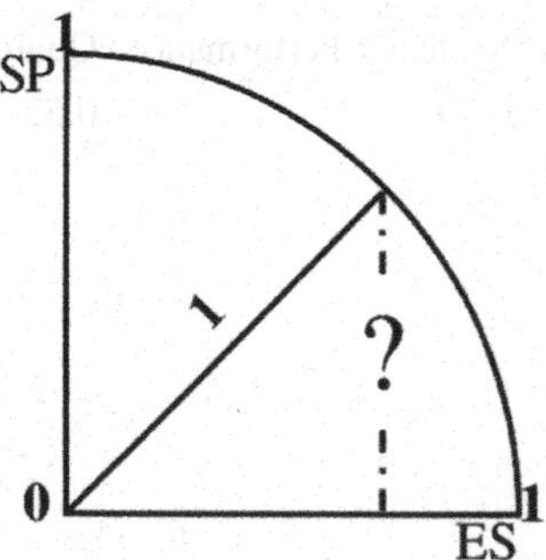

Fig. 4. *SP* evaluation.

- *SP* is figured out using $SP = \sqrt{1 - ES^2}$, where *ES* stands for an *exergy's* value in the worst-case scenario (i.e., $ES = exergy + vagueness$), a value that ranges in the interval [0, 1] (Fig. 4).

$$SP = \sqrt{1 - (0.32 + 0.29)^2} = 0.79$$

- *QoI* is evaluated in the form, viz.

$$QoI = exergy/(exergy + vagueness)$$
$$QoI = 0.32/(0.32 + 0.29) = 0.52$$

3 Case Study

A new version of the ECM with the extensions and adaptations for the PS was conceived, as well as the causal trees for the classification of the adverse events' root causes. Such extensions and adaptations allowed to adequate each category to PS

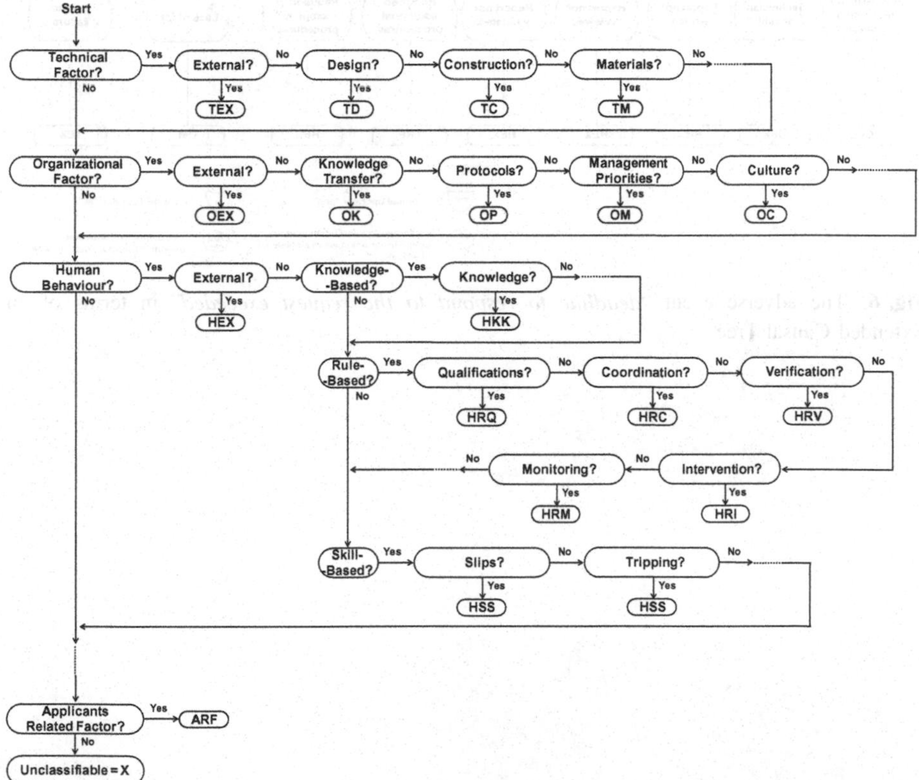

Fig. 5. Flow chart of the Eindhoven Classification Model for the Public Services.

occurrences making the classification easier and more effective. The flow chart of the classification process is depicted in Fig. 5, as well as the codes assigned to classify each type of the adverse events. For instance, the adverse events classified as "*Organizational – Protocols*" (code OP) occur due to failures related to the quality or availability of the internal protocols (e.g., too complex, too simple, unclear, nonexistent).

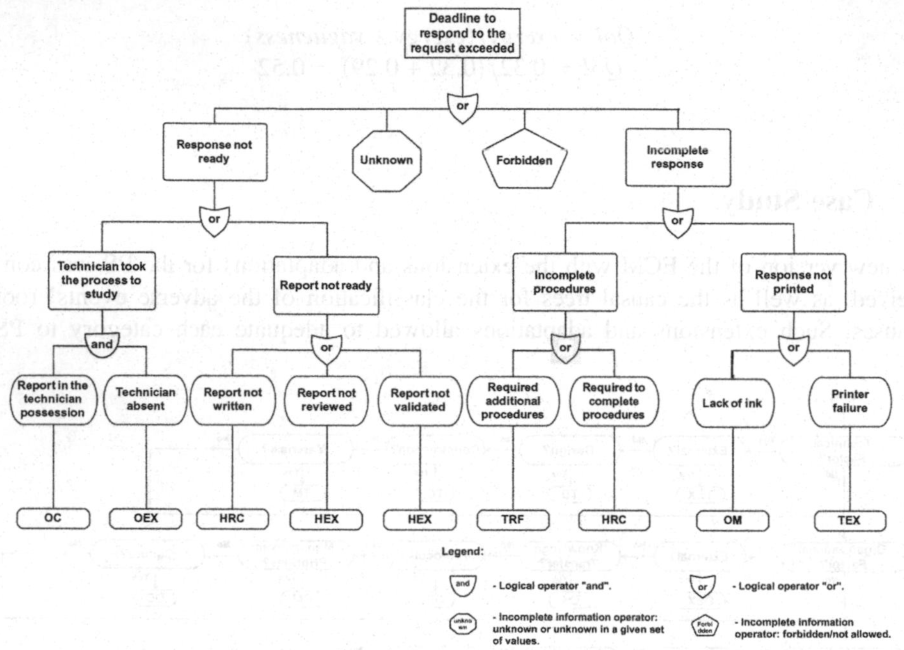

Fig. 6. The adverse event "*deadline to respond to the request exceeded*" in terms of an Extended Causal Tree.

As an example, let one consider the adverse event "*deadline to respond to the request exceeded*" and the correspondent causal tree (Fig. 6). Once this adverse event can arise due to various causes that should be taken simultaneously or separately, *AND/OR*-nodes are used to include such features in the causal tree. In addition, it was used the "*unknown*" and "*forbidden*" operators to describe events for which the event's causes are *unknown/forbidden/not permitted* (e.g., due to internal policies). Thus, considering the information presented in Fig. 6 it is possible to identify all the possible situations, viz.

- *Situation A* – The adverse event "*deadline to respond to the request exceeded*" presents as cause a "*requirement* for *additional procedures*", i.e., its *value* is known;
- *Situation B* – The adverse event "*deadline to respond to the request exceeded*" denotes that the "*report is not ready*". It is not possible to be clear about the cause to bear in mind, but it is known that it can only be "*report not written*", "*report not revised*" or "*report not validated*", whose domain values are {*strongly disagree*, *disagree*}, {*disagree*, *agree*} and {*agree*, *strongly agree*}, respectively, that as a matter of interpretation are assumed to be disjoint; and
- *Situation C* – It is only known that the adverse event stands for "*deadline to respond to the request exceeded*". Here all assumptions are plausible, i.e., one is faced with an "*unknown* or a *forbidden value*".

Thus, the logic program depicted below, built in terms of the extents of predicates *action_or_situation_A, action_or_situation_B, action_or_situation_C* stands for itself, i.e., it denotes a formal description of *Situations A, B* and *C* referred to above. It will allow the use of benchmarking in public organizations, trying to explain the background of the approaches used, providing details on the methods used to solve the problems, alerting to problems and problems encountered, and examining the extent to which benchmarking results were used in decision-making.

The Logic Program that sets A Full Informed Classification System leading to the Excellence in the Provision of Public Services

{

{

action_or_situation_A: *EXergy*, *VAgueness*, *System's Performance*,

Quality-of-Information → {*True*, *False*}

$\neg$ *action_or_situation_A* (*EX*, *VA*, *SP*, *QoI*) ←

not action_or_situation_A (*EX*, *VA*, *SP*, *QoI*)

not $exception_{action\_or\_situation\_A}$(*EX*, *VA*, *SP*, *QoI*)

action_or_situation_A(1, 0, 0, 1)

}

{

action_or_situation_B: *EXergy*, *VAgueness*, *System's Performance*,

Quality-of-Information → {*True*, *False*}

$\neg$ *action_or_situation_B* (*EX*, *VA*, *SP*, *QoI*) ←

not action_or_situation_B (*EX*, *VA*, *SP*, *QoI*)

not $exception_{action\_or\_situation\_B}$(*EX*, *VA*, *SP*, *QoI*)

$exception_{action\_or\_situation\_B}$(0.02, 0.06, 0.99, 0.20)

$exception_{action\_or\_situation\_B}$(0.08, 0.11, 0.98, 0.42)

$exception_{action\_or\_situation\_B}$(0.19, 0.14, 0.94, 0.58)

$$
\begin{array}{l}
\{ \\
\quad action\_or\_situation\_A: EXergy, VAgueness, System's\ Performance, \\
\qquad\qquad Quality\text{-}of\text{-}Information \rightarrow \{True, False\} \\
\quad \neg\, action\_or\_situation\_C\,(EX, VA, SP, QoI) \leftarrow \\
\qquad\qquad not\ action\_or\_situation\_C\,(EX, VA, SP, QoI) \\
\qquad\qquad not\ exception_{action\_or\_situation\_C}(EX, VA, SP, QoI) \\
\quad action\_or\_situation\_C(0, 1, 0, 0) \\
\quad \} \\
\}
\end{array}
$$

4 Conclusions and Future Work

The fully informed classification system is simpler, maybe better, when compared with others. It may be used to assess performance objectively, expose areas where improvement is needed, identify other organizations with processes resulting in superior performance, with a view to their adoption, and to test whether improvement programs have been successful. On the other hand, once it has its root in the Language of Logic Programming where the system's querying is set as theorems to be proved, the answers are object of formal proof. Another advantage is in its modularity, i.e., it offers the possibility of adding new categories and/or sub-categories at any time, without changing the structure or its working mode.

Future work encompasses the development of the *Adverse Events Manager Reports for Public Services* (*AEMR-PS*) module. Such component aims at the analysis of the adverse events recorded by the *Adverse Event Reporting Forms for Public Services* (*AERF-PS*). The *AEMR-PS* will provide automatic reports of the adverse events complemented with charts and statistical information about the events recorded and will contribute to identify trends.

Acknowledgments. This work has been supported by FCT – Fundação para a Ciência e Tecnologia within the Project Scope: UID/CEC/00319/2019.

References

1. International Organization for Standardization: ISO 9001:2015 – Quality Management Systems – Requirements. International Organization for Standardization, Geneve (2015)
2. George, M.: Lean Six Sigma for Service: How to Use Lean Speed and Six Sigma Quality to Improve Services and Transactions. McGraw-Hill, New York (2003)
3. Chong-Fong, Y: Level of Service Quality of SME Laboratory Services on Customer Satisfaction. MBA Thesis, University Sains Malaysia, Penang (2015)
4. van der Schaaf, T.W.: Near miss reporting in the chemical process industry: an overview. Microelectron. Reliab. **35**(9–10), 1233–1243 (1995)
5. World Alliance for Patient Safety: WHO draft guidelines for adverse event reporting and learning systems: from information to action. WHO Document Production Services, Geneve (2005)
6. Vicente, H., Borralho, F., Couto, C., Gomes, G., Alves, V., Neves, J.: An adverse event reporting and learning system for water sector based on an extension of the eindhoven classification model. Water Resour. Manage **29**, 4927–4943 (2015)
7. Cowper, J., Samuels, M.: Performance Benchmarking in the Public Sector: The United Kingdom Experience. Next Steps Team, Office of Public Services, Cabinet Office, United Kingdom (1979)
8. Rasmussen, J.: Outlines of a hybrid model of the process plant operator. In: Sheridan, T.B., Johannsen, G. (eds.) Monitoring Behavior and Supervisory Control, vol. 1, pp. 371–383. NATO Conference Series, Plenum Press, London (1976)
9. Wenterodt, T., Herwig, H.: The entropic potential concept: a new way to look at energy transfer operations. Entropy **16**, 2071–2084 (2014)
10. Luhtanen, R., Crocker, J.: A collective self-esteem scale: self-evaluation of one's social identity. Pers. Soc. Psychol. Bull. **18**, 302–318 (1992)
11. Rosenberg, M.: Society and the Adolescent Self-Image. Princeton University Press, Princeton (1965)
12. Baumeister, R.F., Campbell, J.D., Krueger, J.I., Vohs, K.D.: Does high self-esteem cause better performance, interpersonal success, happiness, or healthier lifestyles? Psychol. Sci. Public Interest **4**, 1–44 (2003)
13. Neves, J.: A logic interpreter to handle time and negation in logic databases. In: Muller, R., Pottmyer, J. (eds.) Proceedings of the 1984 Annual Conference of the ACM on the 5th Generation Challenge, pp. 50–54. Association for Computing Machinery, New York (1984)

Linking Remote Sensing Data, Municipal Statistics and Online Population Activity for Environmental Assessments in Urban Agglomerations

Dmitry Verzilin[1,2,3(✉)], Tatyana Maximova[3], Segey Skorykh[4], and Irina Sokolova[5]

[1] St. Petersburg Institute for Informatics and Automation of the Russian Academy of Sciences, 14th Lin. V.O., 39, St. Petersburg 199178, Russia
modusponens@mail.ru

[2] Lesgaft National State University of Physical Education Sport and Health, St. Petersburg, Dekabristov, 35, St. Petersburg 190121, Russia

[3] Saint Petersburg National Research University of Information Technologies, Mechanics and Optics (ITMO University), Kronverksky pr., 49, St. Petersburg 197101, Russia
maximovatg@gmail.com

[4] Peter the Great St. Petersburg Polytechnic University, Polytechnicheskaya, 29, St. Petersburg 195251, Russia
ssv2k@yandex.ru

[5] St. Petersburg State University, Universitetskayz emb., 7–9, St. Petersburg 199034, Russia
i_sokolova@bk.ru

Abstract. The authors argue that linking in time and space data on search queries and discussions in social networks with remote sensing data and municipal statistics provides valuable information about actual problems in urban agglomeration development. Examples of models for an analysis of such information and model-aided results related to recreational needs and environment pollution confirmed usefulness of linking data for evidence-based policy making in agglomeration development. As a result of the implementation of the models, three goals were achieved: the working ability of the general approach for environmental assessment of agglomerations was tested; new informative results were obtained, characterizing the dynamics of ecological-economic objects of the coastal areas of the Gulf of Finland and the relationship between indicators of the state of these objects; new approaches to integrating data that were not previously used together (remote sensing data, official data from municipal statistics, environmental monitoring data, as well as online population activity data) were tested.

Keywords: Environmental assessments · Environmental monitoring · Key word searchers · Online activity · Smart sensible cities · Smart sensible agglomeration · Social networks

D. A. Alexandrov et al. (Eds.): DTGS 2019, CCIS 1038, pp. 17–28, 2019.
https://doi.org/10.1007/978-3-030-37858-5_2

1 Introduction

During the last fifty years the world has become urbanized. According to UN estimates [24] in 1968, only 36% of the world's population lived in cities, in 2018 this share was 55%, and by 2050 it will be 68%. For Russia, the corresponding figures are higher than the world average: 44% of the urban population in 1968, 74% in 2018, and 83% in 2050. A new spatial development strategy is being discussed in Russia [5] now. The strategy provides priorities for the development of existing and the creation of new urban agglomerations as centers of economic growth. However, the lack of planning for the spatial development of large urban agglomerations led to their unbalanced growth [5]. Nowadays, social and economic disproportions within the agglomerations are intensifying in Russia, and transport and environmental problems are growing. There is an unsatisfactory state of the environment in most of the large urban agglomerations and industrial cities, the tense environmental situation at some large water basins, there is a lack of system thinking for monitoring, controlling and managing the environmental neighborhood of the territory [5].

The concept of a smart sustainable city (SSC) [19, 23] can be used as theoretical basics for developing urban agglomerations. Given the inevitability of urban sprawl to the level of agglomerations, it is advisable, in our opinion, to talk about the concept of balanced development of urban agglomerations. We call it smart sustainable agglomeration (SSA). In accordance with the ideology of the "United for Smart Sustainable Cities" (U4SSC) [23], smart sustainable agglomeration is a concept that aims at a continuous transformational process focused at interaction and collaboration between the government and residents.

There are following problems in evaluating smart sustainable agglomerations. The importance of measuring the state, the needs of the society and its response to changes in the environment is underestimated when making management decisions. There are no tools for analyzing feedback, that is, the reaction of the population to the actions of the authorities. Rapid evaluation of the feedback using statistical data is rather difficult. It takes a long time to collect, aggregate, and analyze data. Moreover, in contrast to a number of foreign countries, there is no official statistical accounting of agglomerations in Russia, and all estimates of limits and number of agglomerations relies on expert opinions. Opinion polls, as sources of data on the reaction of the population to environmental changes, can provide operational information, but they require significant costs. Research question is to find approaches to sharing data from various sources to overcome those problems.

2 Literature Review

City agglomeration is a spatial grouping of settlements, united by industrial, labor, community, recreational, transport, infrastructure links. The problems of spatial development of urban agglomerations and its assessment are widely discussed in the scientific community. Many state and public initiatives are aimed at creating a comfortable urban environment. The following basic questions can be singled out in scientific research of this area: the development of methods for assessing the state of an urban environment; decision-making process in the field of spatial planning and implementation of the concept of smart sustainable city; the relationship between the conditions of the urban environment and the well-being of people.

Series of international standards provide basics for measuring the quality of the urban environment and its comfort for residents. The international standards [9, 10] contain approaches to measuring the development of community's infrastructure (energy, water, transport, waste, information and communication technologies, etc.). They provide indicators and methods for dynamic monitoring of the efficiency of urban services and quality of life. We can compare performance indicators for different cities, as well as check the priorities of urban development.

Series of recommendations of the Telecommunication Standardization Sector of the International Telecommunications Union (ITU-T), which is a specialized agency of the United Nations in the field of information and communication technologies, can be considered as an evolution of the abovementioned standards. The series of ITU-T recommendations in the field of measuring various aspects of smart city development [13, 15–18, 22] contains key performance indicators (KPI) of smart sustainable cities, the basic principles of their choice and the rules for their construction. The recommendations declare that these indicators can also be used to assess agglomerations. In accordance with recommendations [9], the development of SSA should be carried out in economic, social, environmental, managerial, and cultural areas. The environmental sustainability of SSA can be considered in the following six categories: air quality, water and sanitation, noise, environmental quality, biodiversity and energy. The quality of the environment can be assessed by quantitative or qualitative methods for the following aspects: solid waste, electromagnetic fields, green areas and public places. It is recommended [4] to combine the definition of KPI with the use of other assessment methods, such as expert assessments and surveys in order to obtain information on the satisfaction of groups expressing interest.

In the fundamental work [20] a wide range of Smart City initiatives in various countries was analyzed in detail. The majority of initiatives (66%) were implemented by the authorities, 19% by the business sector, 15% by non-governmental organizations. Most of the initiatives were related to planning (60%), and the rest to the implementation (40%). The "top down" initiatives or "under the leadership of the government" were dominant (83%), while only 17% related to "bottom up" citizens' initiatives. The issues of managing a smart sustainable city "from the top down" and "from the bottom up" were considered in publications of domestic researchers.

In [26], an analysis of publications on smart city projects was carried out. The needs and expectations of citizens of St. Petersburg and Russia were analyzed with the aid of content analysis and sociological research. The data obtained indicated the interest of citizens to the problem of a smart city and low readiness to participate in city management through ICT. The problems of electronic participation in management were investigated more deeply in [2, 3]. Electronic participation refers to a two-way process: informational projects led by the government and citizens' initiatives. The contradictory, from the point of view of the optimal decision-making, the nature of electronic participation was analyzed. The factors that adversely affect the process of forming solutions with electronic participation were identified. It was noted that the initiative of the population develops the Internet community, contributing to the emergence of new social norms. Therefore, such an initiative has a strategic advantage over government initiatives that are being enforced.

In [12], a comprehensive critical review of the characteristics of remote sensing systems was given, and the possibilities of their use in two main areas of research were revealed: stratification of the urban environment and sustainable urban development. The paper presented an overview of the main capabilities of remote sensing for the assessment of cities, identified technical problems and limitations in the use of the technology. These problems are related to the integration of data from different sources and the acquisition of characteristics and related information to monitor the growth of a city and its impact on the environment. The authors of [12] distinguish three main areas of research in this field: (1) integration of heterogeneous remote sensing data, first of all for researching or modeling the urban environment as a complex system; (2) developing new algorithms for identifying urban features; (3) improving the accuracy of traditional spectrum-based classification algorithms to account for spectral heterogeneity in urban areas.

Methodological aspects of the processing, synthesis of aerospace information for the purpose of mapping and environmental monitoring of natural resources were described, for example, in [1, 14]. Practical examples of agglomeration assessment with the aid of remote sensing data can be found in [6–8, 11, 27].

A brief analysis of modern methodological and practical approaches to environmental policy planning points out that there is a gap in linking data of official statistics, remote sensing, and behavior of the population in the cyberspace for better understanding of environment-related needs of the society.

3 Theoretical Grounding and Methodology

We study the environmental neighborhood of the agglomeration, containing connected green areas (specially protected natural areas, forest, meadow, wetland eco-systems that do not have protection status, agricultural land, green areas, parks), valuable for preservation and maintenance of biological diversity, natural environmental processes, water and air environment, as well as health and quality of life of the population [5, 19].

To address environmental problems of SSA we supplement remote sensing data and municipal statistics with data on online thematic activity of population [21]. The data on online activity provide real-time information about the attitude of population to environmental problems and initiatives.

To perform environmental assessments in urban agglomerations we developed and used models of three levels. The models of the first level use remote sensing data for evaluation of adverse environmental factors. The main focus of analysis resided in recreational territories attracting population of coastal agglomerations. The models were worked out in details for two main domains: for analysis of long-range water pollution and for degradation of specially protected natural areas with recreational zones. The models describing the first domain produce spatial characteristics (coordinates, area, etc.) of adverse impacts of a port on an aquatic domain and a coastline.

The models describing the second domain use processing of high resolution imagery materials for access to spatial indicators of tourism opportunities: the area of the territory to accommodate tourists in houses, tents, and recreation sites; quantitative indicators for the maximum allowable number of tourists without additional equipment of the territory; the length of tourist routes; area of the territory for various types of recreation; ways and transport routes for delivering tourists; area of disturbed vegetation cover; area of the identified places of unauthorized disposal of waste.

We used the models of the second level to analyze business activities related to the use of environmental assets and activities aimed at preventing and eliminating environmental damage. We calculated relative social, economic, and environmental indicators, determined the trends of their dynamics, and performed a comparative analysis of indicators for different coastal areas.

For that an analysis of monetary flows in environmental assets and economic indicators, flows in physical terms, and stocks in environmental assets in physical terms was performed.

Monetary flows in environmental assets and economic indicators included: agricultural products (at current and constant prices); revenues of the local budget; agricultural tax; payments for using natural resources; fee for a negative impact on the environment; budget expenditures for environmental protection; current (operational) costs of environmental protection, including payment for environmental protection services (at current and constant prices).

Flows in physical terms included: the number of objects with stationary sources of air pollution; the amount of pollutants emitted into the atmosphere from stationary sources; the volume of applied mineral fertilizers (in terms of 100% of nutrients) under crops of agricultural crops in agricultural organizations.

Stocks of environmental assets in physical terms included: total land area of an municipality; total area of built-up land; area of agricultural land of a municipality; total area under crops; livestock and poultry.

The models of the third level include statistical, econometric and environmental models for assessing the elasticity of environmental and socio-economic indicators (sensitivity of indicators to changes in other indicators). To construct cointegration models of time series we used tests for checking stationarity of series and the presence of autocorrelation. Single-factor and multi-factor regression models were obtained. For non-stationary series with upward trends, regression models were considered for cases in which there were obvious causal relationships between the indicators, according to the meaning of the characteristics considered. In these cases, despite the fact that, in accordance with the results of statistical tests, we can speak of a false regression, the obtained regression dependencies were of substantial interest.

In order to construct the models of the third level we used panel data (obtained for different territories at different time points), provided for the models of the first and the second level. We developed an original dynamic model of the load on specially protected natural territories, which included recreation zones.

Models of all three levels were used together, ensuring that constantly updated initial data for calculations were accumulated, including new sources of multi- and hyperspectral data from the Earth remote sensing satellites.

4 Empirical Analysis

4.1 Models and Data

We implemented the abovementioned models of three levels. Single-factor linear and non-linear regression models, multi-factor regression models, a generalized autoregression model with changing coefficients were constructed. Linear and non-linear regression models, multifactor regression models link together indicators of ecological-economic objects in the coastal areas of the Gulf of Finland. Taking into account the socio-economic relations, these areas can be attributed to the St. Petersburg agglomeration and its periphery. We also implemented regression models linking the ecological characteristics with thematic online activity of the population.

As a result of the implementation of the models, three goals were achieved: the working ability of the general approach for environmental assessment of agglomerations was tested (the choice of classes of the applied models was confirmed); new informative results presented below were obtained, characterizing the dynamics of ecological-economic objects of the coastal areas of the Gulf of Finland and the relationship between indicators of the state of these objects; new approaches to integrating data that were not previously used together (remote sensing data, official data from municipal statistics, environmental monitoring data, as well as online population activity data) were tested.

The models of the first level made it possible to evaluate spatial indicators of the tourist capacity of recreational zones and indicators characterizing conditions of the environment at Berezovii Islands reserve through processing of high-resolution shooting materials and hyper-spectral materials.

The second-level models were tested for the analysis of economic activities associated with the use of environmental assets and activities aimed at preventing and eliminating environmental damage. We estimated flows of changes in environmental assets in monetary and physical terms, the cost of environmental damage and costs associated with an exhaustion of environmental assets in areas of the Leningrad Region, the territory of which includes the coastal zone of the Gulf of Finland. We analyzed the indicators for the Vyborgsky, Lomonosovsky, Kingiseppsky municipal districts and the Sosnovyborsky urban district For that we used Petrostat's database (http://www.gks.ru/dbscripts/munst/munst41/DBInet.cgi#1) of municipal indicators of the Leningrad Region. Industrial enterprises were considered as sources of adverse effects on the external environment. Agricultural enterprises were considered as ecological and economic assets and sources of environmental pollution.

4.2 Examples of Trends for Ecological-Economic Indicators

The trends for crop production and animal husbandry in monetary terms at constant 2008 prices are common for coastal agricultural areas: local maximum in 2010 and 2015–2016, a significant decrease in 2017. A significant correlation was found between the values of the series for the Vyborg and Kingisepp regions.

We took notice of a synchronous growth in 2012 in all coastal areas of the values of operational costs for environmental protection per capita in 2008 prices. For coastal areas, indicators differ several times, they are higher in those areas where there are large industrial facilities that have an impact on the environment: the atomic power station in the Sosnovy Bor urban settlement, the port in Ust-Luga in the Kingisepp district, the port in Primorsk in the Vyborg district.

Indicators of average budget revenues per capita from payments for negative impact on the environment and budget expenditures on environmental protection are unevenly distributed over time. There is no correlation between revenues and budget expenditures. There was a decrease in average per capita expenditures on environmental protection. We recognized logarithmic dependencies between the current (operational) costs of environmental protection and the number of objects with stationary sources of pollution for coastal areas. For all areas, with an increase in the number of objects with stationary sources of pollution, the amount of environmental protection costs per organization was reducing (Fig. 1).

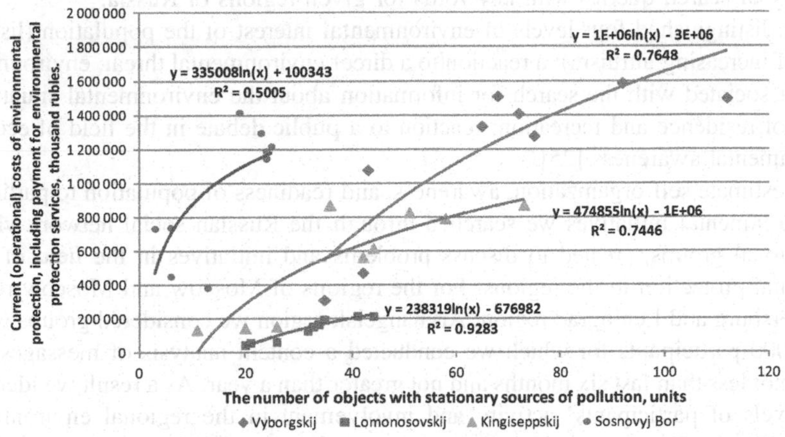

Fig. 1. Logarithmic single-factor regression models describing dependence of the current (operational) costs of environmental protection on the number of objects with stationary sources of pollution (according to http://www.gks.ru/scripts/db_inet2/passport/munr.aspx?base=munst41)

For the case of the absence of upward trends, a two-factor regression model was built, which relates the costs of environmental protection at constant prices with the amount of pollutant emissions from stationary sources and the number of objects with stationary pollution sources (according to Rosstat http://www.gks.ru/scripts/db_inet2/passport/munr.aspx?base=munst41). The value of the Durbin-Watson statistics was in the zone of uncertainty, that is, according to the existing data it was impossible to draw a conclusion about the presence or absence of autocorrelation of residuals. Two-factor regression model:

$$y = -86065 + 3.87x_1 + 6914x_2, \quad (1)$$

where y is the current (operational) expenditure on environmental protection, including payment for environmental protection services, in 2008 prices, thousand rubles; x_1 is the volume of pollutant emissions from stationary sources, tons; x_2 the number of objects with stationary sources of pollution, units.

4.3 Environment-Related Online Activity

A new original approach to the study of public interest in the problem of ecology laid in a comparison of online activity data with environmental monitoring data [21]. We analyzed statistical data on the prevalence of search queries with keywords related to the environmental situation in the regions of residence. In particular, the WordStat service of the Yandex search engine was used. This service provides data on the intensity of search queries with keywords for given regions of Russia.

We distinguished four levels of environmental interest of the population (listed in order of increasing altruism): a reaction to a direct environmental threat; environmental needs associated with the search for information about the environmental situation in places of residence and recreation; reaction to a public debate in the field of ecology; environmental awareness [25].

To estimate self-organization, awareness, and readiness of population to participate in environmental initiatives we searched through the Russian social network vk.com for regional groups, created to discuss problems and initiatives in the field of environmental protection in the regions. For the regions of Moscow and Moscow region; St. Petersburg and Leningrad region; Arkhangelsk region we considered groups with at least 1000 participants for which we conducted a content analysis of messages for a period not less than last six months and not greater than a year. As a result we identified four levels of participants' activity and involvement in the regional environmental policy (Fig. 2). The topics most discussed in the groups were analyzed. There were significant differences between the considered regions both in the structure of the groups and in the topics of discussion. In Moscow and in the Moscow region, sources of an unpleasant odor were discussed and fixed, the 1st-level groups, focused on information exchange, predominate. For groups of St. Petersburg, a characteristic topic of discussion was a separate garbage collection. Also, residents were concerned about the possible construction of waste recycling plants, which, in the absence of a separate waste collection system, will burn a significant proportion of household waste and induce air pollution. The most pronounced were the 3rd-level groups, whose activity is manifested in the organization of environmental events. For the Arkhangelsk region, the main topic was to counter plans of creating new landfills for household waste and importing waste from Moscow and the Moscow region. Here the highest protest activity of the group members was observed. Classification of groups created to discuss problems and initiatives in the field of environmental protection in the region let evaluate the level of self-organization for group members and estimate the degree of environmental awareness. It should be noted that environmental awareness is more developed among the participants of groups from St. Petersburg and the Leningrad Region.

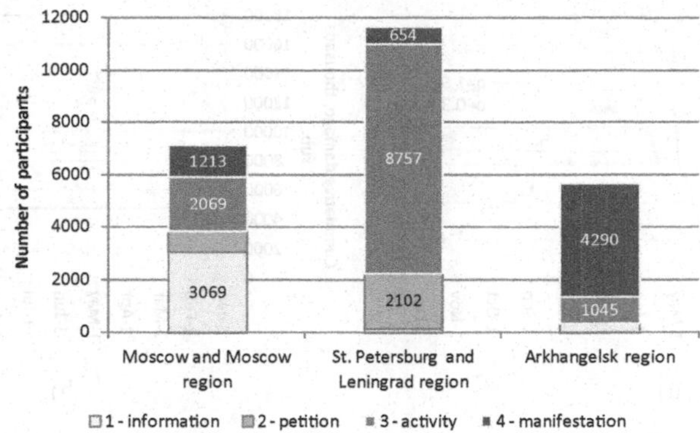

Fig. 2. Target groups in the social network vk.com.

The first level (1 – information) is the presentation of information on local environmental issues and initiatives. Such information included related documents, photo-video materials, links, etc. The second level (2-petition) of activity in the group corresponded to a creation of appeals and petitions to government bodies. The third level (3 – activity) manifested in the organization of environmentally oriented events and actions in support of environmental initiatives. The fourth level (4 – manifestation) is the organization of meetings and protest actions.

4.4 Loads on Specially Protected Natural Territories

We used an original dynamic model (a generalized model of autoregression with changing coefficients) to describe loads on specially protected natural territories, which include recreational zones. To identify the parameters of the model, remote sensing data were used. We implemented a dynamic model of the load on specially protected natural territories for the example of the Berezovii Islands reserve.

For the computational experiment, the observation period was chosen to be one calendar year. Time was measured in days. We applied a finite-difference approximation of the model. Remote sensing data were used for estimating the number of visitors and the visible adverse anthropogenic impacts.

Figure 3(a) and (b) show the simulation results for two cases of the fee for visiting the reserve: q = 0.3 thousand rubles and q = 1.5 thousand rubles.

We can use the model to substantiate scenarios for the development of tourist and recreational activities in protected areas. With a fee for visiting equal to 300 rubles, the fees do not compensate the damage caused, and the accumulated damage increases. By increasing the fee to 1 500 rubles, the damage caused is compensated, the accumulated damage remains constant.

The difference between the numbers of visitors since the middle of the year became insignificant. However, the structure of the contingent of tourists can change by reducing the availability of tourist-recreational services for the disadvantaged population. For more accurate forecasts, it is necessary to attract data from remote sensing of

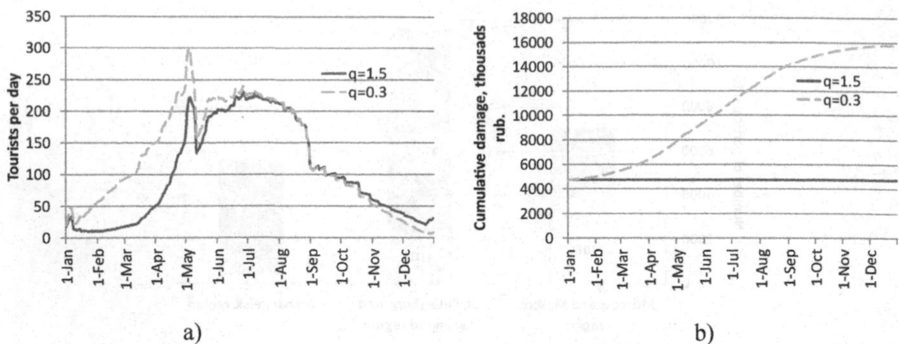

Fig. 3. Model dynamics of the number of visitors to the Berezovii Islands reserve during the calendar year, (a) tourists per day; (b) cumulative damage.

the earth, covering a longer period (up to 10 years), as well as integrated data from social networks and thematic forums.

5 Discussion

Policy making in urban agglomerations should be guided by feedbacks characterizing needs of a society, its reaction to problems and public activities, and its potential in "bottom-up" initiatives. However, there is a lack of mechanism and motivation for the population to participate in decision making, thought its reaction on urgent problems can be rather acute.

An efficient way for real-time analyzing feedbacks lays through collecting data about thematic search queries and discussions in social networks. Such data should be matched in time and space with traditional municipal statistics and remote sensing data.

Various examples show that data on online activity related to recreational needs and environment pollution, on the one hand, can be easily collected and compared with data from alternative sources, and, on the other hand, give valuable information about the problems the people respond to.

As linking remote sensing data, municipal statistics and online population activity appeared to be a promising approach to policy making, it can be transformed into evidence-based decision-making practice with more data and more models.

The proposed approach to identifying the needs of the population can be an addition to the "Active Citizen" internet platforms being developed in Russia for expressing social needs. Analysis of data on online activity of the population when making decisions in government bodies is more operational, flexible and representative in comparison with the tools of the platforms. Such an analysis can be used as an alternative to sociological surveys, as it saves time and money. At the same time, a properly organized sociological survey is more representative, since it allows analyzing the needs of the population who do not use or rarely use social networks and search queries. The proposed approach may be ineffective when intentional mass mailings of biased messages take place.

Acknowledgments. The research described in this paper is partially supported by the Russian Foundation for Basic Research (grants 17-06-00108, 17-08-00797), state order of the Ministry of Education and Science of the Russian Federation №2.3135.2017/4.6, state research 0073–2019–0004 and International project ERASMUS + , Capacity building in higher education, # 73751-EPP-1-2016-1-DE-EPPKA2-CBHE-JP.

References

1. Cabrera-Barona, P.: From the 'Good Living' to the 'Common Good': What is the role of GIScience? Joint Urban Remote Sensing Event (JURSE) (2017). https://doi.org/10.1109/jurse.2017.7924581
2. Chugunov, A.V., Cronemberger, F., Kabanov, Y.: Contextualizing smart governance research: literature review and scientometrics analysis. In: Alexandrov, D.A., Boukhanovsky, A.V., Chugunov, A.V., Kabanov, Y., Koltsova, O. (eds.) DTGS 2018. CCIS, vol. 858, pp. 102–112. Springer, Cham (2018). https://doi.org/10.1007/978-3-030-02843-5_9
3. Chugunov, A.V., Kabanov, Y., Misnikov, Y.: Citizens versus the government or citizens with the government: a tale of two e-participation portals in one city - a case study of St. Petersburg, Russia. In: ACM International Conference Proceeding Series, IET, Vol. Part F128003, pp. 70–77 (2017)
4. Collection Methodology for Key Performance Indicators for Smart Sustainable Cities United 4 Smart Sustainable Cities. https://www.itu.int/en/publications/Documents/tsb/2017-U4SSC-Collection-Methodology/index.html. Accessed 20 Jan 2019
5. Draft Order of the Government of the Russian Federation: On Approval of the Strategy of Spatial Development of the Russian Federation for the Period up to 2025. ConsultantPlus. http://www.consultant.ru/law/hotdocs/54819.html/. Accessed 20 Jan 2019
6. Fanga, Ch., Yub, D.: Urban agglomeration: An evolving concept of an emerging phenomenon. Landscape Urban Plan. **162**, 126–136 (2017). https://doi.org/10.1016/j.landurbplan.2017.02.014
7. Garouani, El.A., Mulla, D.J., Garouani, El.S., Knight, J.: Analysis of urban growth and sprawl from remote sensing data: case of Fez, Morocco. Int. J. Sustain. Built Environ. **6**(1), 160–169 (2017). https://doi.org/10.1016/j.ijsbe.2017.02.003
8. Grigoreva, O., Mochalov, V., Zelentsov, V.: Hyperspectral data processing and adaptive modelling for the natural objects properties detection. In: The 6th International Workshop on Simulation for Energy, Sustainable Development& Environment (SESDE 2018), 17–19 September, 2018, Budapest, Hungary, pp. 7–14 (2018)
9. ISO. ISO-Standard 37120:2018: Sustainable Development of Communities - Indicators for City Services and Quality of Life; ISO: Geneva, Switzerland (2018). https://www.iso.org/standard/68498.html. Accessed 20 Jan 2019
10. ISO/TS 37151:2015(en) Smart community infrastructures - Principles and requirements for performance metrics. ISO: Geneva, Switzerland (2015). https://www.iso.org/ru/standard/61057.html. Accessed 20 Jan 2019
11. Jiang, W., Deng, Y., Tang, Z., Lei, X., Chen, Z.: Modelling the potential impacts of urban ecosystem changes on carbon storage under different scenarios by linking the CLUE-S and the InVEST models. Ecol. Model. **345**, 30–40 (2017). https://doi.org/10.1016/j.ecolmodel.2016.12.002
12. Kadhim, N., Mourshed, M., Bray, M.: Advances in remote sensing applications for urban sustainability. Euro-Mediterr. J. Environ. Integr. **1**, 7 (2016). https://doi.org/10.1007/s41207-016-0007-4

13. Kolm, B.: Global Smart Sustainable City Index (SSC Index): The Global City Ranking. International Telecommunication Union, 26 April 2018. https://www.itu.int/en/ITU-T/ssc/201804/Documents/U4SSC%20BK.pdf
14. Lehner, A., Erlacher, C., Schlögl, M., Wegerer, J. Blaschke T., Steinnocher, K.: Can ISO-defined urban sustainability indicators be derived from remote sensing: an expert weighting approach. Sustainability **10**, 1268 (2018). https://doi.org/10.3390/su10041268
15. Recommendation ITU-T Y.4900/L.1600: Overview of key performance indicators in smart sustainable cities. http://handle.itu.int/11.1002/1000/12627. Accessed 20 Jan 2019
16. Recommendation ITU-T Y.4901/L.1601: Key performance indicators related to the use of information and communication technology in smart sustainable cities http://handle.itu.int/11.1002/1000/12661. Accessed 20 Jan 2019
17. Recommendation ITU-T Y.4902/L.1602: Key performance indicators related to the sustainability impacts of information and communication technology in smart sustainable cities. http://handle.itu.int/11.1002/1000/12662. Accessed 20 Jan 2019
18. Recommendation ITU-T Y.4903/L.1603: Key performance indicators for smart sustainable cities to assess the achievement of sustainable development goals. ITU-T Y-Series Recommendations, 49 p. https://www.itu.int/itu-t/recommendations/rec.aspx?rec=12884&lang=en. Accessed 20 Jan 2019
19. Smart St. Petersburg: The concept of the development of St. Petersburg with the help of technology "smart city". https://www.petersburgsmartcity.ru. Accessed 20 Jan 2019
20. Smart Sustainable Cities – Reconnaissance: Study by Elsa Estevez, Nuno Vasco Lopes, Tomasz Janowski UNU-EGOV-IDRC (2016). 312 p. https://joinup.ec.europa.eu/sites/default/files/document/2016-04/smart_cities_report.pdf
21. Sokolov, B., Verzilin, D., Maximova, T., Sokolova, I.: Dynamic models of self-organization through mass behavior in society. In: Abraham, A., Kovalev, S., Tarassov, V., Snasel, V., Vasileva, M., Sukhanov, A. (eds.) IITI 2017. AISC, vol. 679, pp. 114–123. Springer, Cham (2018). https://doi.org/10.1007/978-3-319-68321-8_12
22. Supplement ITU-T Y-Suppl. 39: ITU-T Y.4900 Series – Key performance indicators definitions for smart sustainable cities. http://handle.itu.int/11.1002/1000/12977. Accessed 20 Jan 2019
23. The "United for Smart Sustainable Cities" (U4SSC). https://www.itu.int/en/ITU-T/ssc/united/Pages/default.aspx. Accessed 20 Jan 2019
24. United Nations, Department of Economic and Social Affairs, Population Division. World Urbanization Prospects: The 2018 Revision, Online Edition. https://esa.un.org/unpd/wup/Publications. Accessed 20 Jan 2019
25. Verzilin, D., Maximova, T., Antokhin, Y., Sokolova, I.: Measurement of public interest in ecological matters through online activity and environmental monitoring. In: Alexandrov, D. A., Boukhanovsky, A.V., Chugunov, A.V., Kabanov, Y., Koltsova, O. (eds.) DTGS 2018. CCIS, vol. 858, pp. 127–143. Springer, Cham (2018). https://doi.org/10.1007/978-3-030-02843-5_11
26. Vidiasova, L., Cronemberger, F., Tensina, I.: The smart city agenda and the citizens: perceptions from the St. Petersburg experience. In: Alexandrov, D.A., Boukhanovsky, A.V., Chugunov, A.V., Kabanov, Y., Koltsova, O. (eds.) DTGS 2018. CCIS, vol. 858, pp. 243–254. Springer, Cham (2018). https://doi.org/10.1007/978-3-030-02843-5_19
27. Wei, Ch., Taubenböck, H., Blaschke, T.: Measuring urban agglomeration using a city-scale dasymetric population map: a study in the Pearl River Delta, China. Habitat International **59**, 32–43 (2016). https://doi.org/10.1016/j.habitatint.2016.11.007

Enhancing Public e-Service Delivery: Recognizing and Meeting User Needs of Youngsters in Estonia

Marili Ruus[1], Ingrid Pappel[2], Valentyna Tsap[2(✉)], and Dirk Draheim[2]

[1] Elevator Startups, Tallinn, Estonia
marili@elevatorstartups.com
[2] Tallinn University of Technology, Tallinn, Estonia
{ingrid.pappel,valentyna.tsap,
dirk.draheim}@taltech.ee

Abstract. The aim of this paper is to investigate the key characteristics that refrain Estonian youngsters from using public e-services and to study whether the level of engagement could be increased by redesigning the current e-service user experience. The technology acceptance model and its derivatives are used as background theoretical concept in combination with the design sprint tool for introducing an improved proactive and engaging e-service. We conduct an empirical study on the basis of interviews and a workshop with the target group. A prototype of an improved e-service is developed and the results of its validation are presented. The research outcomes point to the increasing importance of proactive delivery of public e-services. Moreover, we suggest to consider the benefits of implementing communication bridges between youngsters and governments via online channels.

Keywords: E-services · User experience · Youngsters

1 Introduction

The rapid development of IT solutions has introduced convenient digital services not only into the private sector, but also to the public sector becoming one of the communication channels between the government and citizens [9, 16, 20]. New opportunities as well as obstacles for the implementation of new solutions and communicating the changes to citizens have occurred [14]. Therefore, electronic services come win an expanded accessibility and convenience providing public sector with numerous opportunities for innovation. The success of these projects, however, still depends on the willingness to adopt these solutions [3, 24]. Moreover, when considering the public sector, it cannot be just about digitalizing the existing public services, but reengineering the processes and redesigning service delivery and adjusting them to the IT infrastructure.

The e-governance approaches are now present in all policy areas in Estonia. The Ministry of Economic Affairs and Communications has set a goal to reach e-society - integrate all levels in service delivery by enhancing the collaboration between the

D. A. Alexandrov et al. (Eds.): DTGS 2019, CCIS 1038, pp. 29–40, 2019.
https://doi.org/10.1007/978-3-030-37858-5_3

different public agencies [18]. According to statistics [21], almost all of Estonian public services are accessible online at all times and are widely used: for example, 97% of all tax declarations are submitted by citizens digitally [18].

On the other hand, data shows that the usage of public e-services among the youngsters is still moderate on a general scale, although this particular group is almost constantly connected to the Internet and the technology acceptance rate is high. Yet, only less than 10% of public e-service usage times were performed by the youngsters aged 18–26 in 2017 [5]. Inefficient public service delivery becomes a problem if a fair representation the youth's point of view is not ensured, and their strong engagement in public services and solid foundation for the relationship with the public sector is not established. Hence, there is a strong potential for an increased participation in this demographic group.

Authors proceed as follows. Section 2 gives an overview of the current situation with the state of Estonian e-services. Section 3 explains the methods authors used to carry out the study. In Sect. 4, authors report on the interview outcomes. Section 5 describes the process of using the Design sprint framework and provides insights gained from conducting the workshop and the improved e-service prototype validation. Discussion is presented in Sect. 6 that is followed by conclusions in Sect. 7.

2 Overview of the e-Service Development

The public sector often faces difficulties in identifying the actual needs of the public and how to satisfy those needs by offering governmental services. Some authors find that when duplicating existing public services online is not enough, but rather changes should be done in restructuring the service itself to improve its value that can be delivered through such channel [8].

In case of Estonia, the successful process of digitalizing public services, and transforming the society in a wider sense, was initiated by the private sector - the first e-service was launched in banking. With a quite successful acceptance by users, the government of Estonia saw an opportunity to deliver also the public services via Internet. This served as a motivation to search means for collaboration, setting a foundation of public-private partnership (PPP) in Estonia. An example of a fruitful PPP cooperation is the implementation of early electronic identification means into the states e-infrastructure [10, 13]. Moreover, Estonia has set a focus on improving data sharing and exchange, advocating the quality [22]. This, in total, has been enabled by the wide use of digital authentication and signatures [19].

On the other side, The Digital Agenda 2020 [18] admits that the existing services in Estonia are in need of restructuring, in order to keep up with the constantly evolving user habits and technologies leaving behind out-of-date solutions. To address this point, the Ministry of Economic Affairs and Communications has set the goal of increasing the awareness of public e-services in the adult age group 16 to 74 from 29% in 2012 to 90% by 2020 and reach the rates of higher inclusion and participation [18]. One aspect associated with the satisfaction, according to the Digital Agenda 2020 [18], is the user-friendliness of the services. With the reform, the interests and user needs will be taken into consideration with making the user interfaces of the services available via different channels. The e-inclusion aspect the ministry aims at improving is supposed to be done by developing services and formulating policies together with different stakeholders, including citizens [18].

It is sterling that the Estonian government grasps the necessity of gaining feedback from users. What needs to be ensured is that the 16-year-olds and the 74-year-olds have different expectations and usage habits each of which should be reckoned with by a good public service.

3 Methodology

Qualitative methods have been used to describe and understand the real-life experiences of the subject. Semi-structured interviews were conducted with the target user group (10 people of 18–26 y.o.) and two experts of the e-government service design field that served as a fundamental base and input for the developed technical prototype (Roulston 2010), presented in Sect. 5.

The interview questions were constructed based on the analysis of theories such as Technology Acceptance Model (TAM) and its extension, Unified Theory of Acceptance and Use of Technology (UTAUT) [4, 25]. The researches focus on the matter of acceptance and architecture of public e-services rather on the qualitative aspect [3, 4, 25] or technology perception [15], leaving the notion of understanding the end-user and questions "why" or "how" in the background. Thereby, TAM is incorporated with an aim to set a foundation for the Design Sprint [11, 12, 23], a method for service design - to frame the problem and objectives, used within this research. The main deliverable of the Design sprint is validating or disproving hypotheses in order to decide whether to commit to building the service or not, in addition to answering a set of vital questions, maps, prototyping and structural planning. To successfully deliver the outcome of the Design Sprint, a workshop with the potential target user group (13 participants aged 18–21) was organized. The structure of the workshop has been built based on the authors' experience of leading the Design Sprints, as well as combining the fundamentals of TAM and other different. Introduction of Design Sprint method into the study enriched the outcomes by extracting valuable insights while conducting the research.

Returning back to the data collection, the interviews were divided into three main sections: (i) open ended questions focusing on general e-service usage habits and knowledge of public e-services; (ii) components of theoretical models evaluating acceptance of the public innovation; (iii) facilitating conditions regarding the usage of public e-services. The interviews and the workshop were held in November 2018 in Estonian language.

4 User Needs of Youngsters in the e-Services Domain

This section presents the main points that were drawn from the interview analysis. According to the answers of interviewees, the topic was divided into 3 main categories, where possible relations were examined, in addition to the linkages that were outlined in the description of methodological approach (see Sect. 3).

Firstly, it should be mentioned that the target users are highly active in social media and use mobile phones as their main device. The main communication platforms mentioned during the interviews were Facebook and Instagram.

Secondly, in regard to public e-services, it appeared that the target users' knowledge is low. Three interviewees claimed to have never used public e-services, but later, during the discussion, it became clear they were not connecting some public e-service with the state or its actual connotation. The target users do not associate some e-services with the public sector as the service provider which is an interrelated ecosystem of entities and bodies. In addition to this, in the experts' opinion, youngsters do not associate the offered services with easing the needs they encounter. This can be also explained by the infrequent usage of the services.

The third inference is that although the youngsters realize the potential time savings, they cannot articulate the benefits for themselves, and the general attitude towards e-government services can be described as neutral or even apathetic – different extent of critique of the e-service user-friendliness and confusing user experience were detected in every interview. The main point of confusion is the service on-boarding process: according to the interviewees, the first reaction is to search for information on search engines or use informal sources like peers or parents, and not official sources in the first place. The users are also baffled by the long and legal texts on the websites. The experts find that the current user's pace of life is not supporting the creation of a positive emotion to initiate the continuous relationship between users and service providers.

The fourth aspect is that youngsters actually trust some government-provided services, as for instance, the Mobile ID is widely diffused among the age. This could be identified as a facilitating condition and a lever of encouragement in the acceptance of public e-services.

5 Increasing the Proactivity of e-Services

This section represents practical ideas and suggestions of this paper that are drawn from the empirical analysis described in Sect. 4. To generate a tangible conclusion and a derivation from the analysis, the Design Sprint's 5 stages are carried out.

An application for a driver's license was chosen as a test case. The service was discussed in detail with the target user group in order to gather insights of the existing user experience, reach means of empathy, and set the grounds for redesigning the process of the existing service delivery. This discussion has preceded the Design Sprint procedure.

To provide fundamentals for the Design Sprint, the scope has to be set. The following aspects were considered during the sprint and reflected on a canvas that synthesizes two approaches: Lean UX canvas and Scoping Canvas [2, 7] (Table 1).

Table 1. Adapted canvas for the Design Sprint fundamentals.

Problem/Challenge	Users	Desired outcomes
Low user engagement Low awareness on existing solutions offered by public sector	Youngsters (18-26 y.o.)	Prolong lifecycle of user's journey when using a service (metrics: acquisition; activation; retention; referral)
Hypothesis of a possible solution: service delivery processes integrated into services that the youngsters use in their everyday life by introducing push-delivery system		User benefits: Increased utilization of services that they are eligible for and better knowledge of services they are obliged to use
Goal of Design Sprint		
✓ Prototype of possible solution tested on potential users ✓ List of deliverable proposals for the government ✓ Insight of user perspective (target age group) for the design of Estonian public services ✓ Change the fundamentals of Estonian e-service delivery and user experience		
Lessons to learn		
✓ To understand whether the low usage is caused by undesired and outdated services or the service delivery process does not fit the target users ✓ How to make the existing service user experience more seamless for the target user group and track the points in service delivery where the user potentially drops off		

5.1 Defining the Scope

The main goal of this stage is to empathize with the user in order to solve the challenges listed.

The first part of the Design Sprint requires to map the existing user experience process. An example of user experience in service delivery when applying for a driver's permit is presented in the model in this subsection. Based on the users' point of view the process of applying the driver's permit was selected as the case of evaluation so to illustrate the redundant complexity of service delivery business processes that stand behind actions of public stakeholders.

The service under review is delivered by Estonian Road Administration. The official age for being able to receive the right to drive a car without supervision in Estonia and European Union is 18. In the Road Administration's e-service portal accessed from its webpage, it is possible to apply for or exchange the driver's license, apply for or change the provisional driver's permit, apply for driver's instructor's certificate, and make information inquiries [6]. The e-service portal can be logged in with an ID-card, Mobile-ID or via bank links.

Description of the AS-IS Service Delivery Process. To illustrate the complexity of data sharing and successful cooperation between the institutions in the delivery process, the business process is modelled in this section.

According to the Road Administration protocol, once a person finishes the obligatory driving lessons that precede the examinations in Estonian Road Administration, the driving school sends the data of the graduation certificate electronically to Estonian Road Administration. If the information is received and the person is at least 18 years old, the link to apply for the provisional driver's permit will appear at the home page in the service portal [6].

As the user logs in, an automatic query from Population Register is made to determine the age of the applicant. An underage person cannot perform an administration operation on e-service platform and the application can be filed in the physical office (ibid).

After opening the link, a set of automatic queries to concomitant information systems are made: a query for the medical certificate to Health and Wellbeing Information System Centre's database, an inquiry to Criminal Records database, a request for the picture and signature from Police and Border Guard Board's identity documents database. If all requirements are filled, the application process can be proceeded with, if not, an error message will appear (ibid.)

Then the user can proceed with the application by choosing the time of the examination, the means of the physical driving license delivery and paying the state fee. Once the Road Administration receives the successful payment information from the bank, the time for theory examination will be booked (ibid).

5.2 Ideation: Workshop

To employ the potential users in the design process and enhance the co-creating aspect, the authors held an ideation session in Tallinn School No 21, 12th grade. The 13 participants were aged between 18 and 19. The workshop was held in three sections: overview of this study and general background of e-services and service design methods, validation of conclusions made in the empirical research stage and initiation of ideation session for solving the problem.

In the first two parts of the workshop authors presented a challenge and posed a goal of the session. An open discussion was initiated in the group. The authors used the similar guiding questions as during the interviews. In addition, they presented the User Persona to validate whether the analysis of the interviews is corresponding to the workshop group. The participants agreed on the main conclusions drawn by the authors.

After the discussion, authors asked participants to rank the aspects that refrain them from starting using the public e-services. The list of most crucial aspects to solve during the design process, according to the participants of the ideation session, was the following: (1) target user's low awareness about rights, possibilities and obligations regarding public services; (2) confusing user experience: long, complicated legal text used in service delivery and its obscure algorithm; (3) emotional aspects at Customer Journey starting and end points (for instance, a customer journey starts with a bad emotion, ends with neutral emotion).

The third section of the workshop focused on conceptualizing the ideal service delivery process from a user's point of view.

5.3 Shaping the Solution

In the third stage of the sprint, these constraints are turned into a solution. Based on the outcomes of workshop, authors performed a synthesis of the presented feature list and possible solutions to create positive emotions aiming at continuance while delivering the service of applying for the driver's license. The suggested solution that authors decided to test out was developing a chatbot for Facebook that bridges the users of younger generation with all the Estonian public e-services. The chatbots are used to initiate a dialog with a customer with a purpose to increase data acquisition speed and enhance customer service, allowing the users to forget that they are making inquiries from databases [1]. The rationale that stands behind the choice of a chatbot as an offered solution is that the communication then takes place in users' usual environment which is today the social media platforms.

The AARRR framework [17], a tool that is nowadays applied in the private sector, is used to set goals in a funnel-resembling structure that ensures a steady focus on one of them at a time and suggests metrics to improve the customers journey's lifecycle when using a service or a product (see Fig. 1). This framework was used to facilitate presenting the mechanisms of introducing the offered solution.

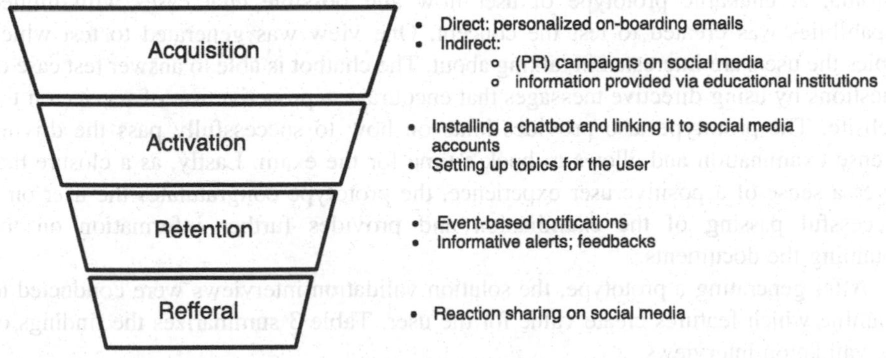

Fig. 1. Suggested AARRR model

Table 2 displays the issues detected during the empirical research and provides potential solutions to address them that were generated during the workshop.

Table 2. Problem-solution list.

Problem indicated	Solution offered
✖ Most of the governmental websites and service delivery portals are optimized only to desktop devices	✓ Use mobile-first approach in the service delivery process
✖ Poor awareness on the public (e-)services	✓Straightforward information channel and onboarding email once a person attains legal adulthood
✖ Infrequent use of (e-)services	✓ Social media applications for raising awareness
✖ Unclear or misleading references to public authorities as service providers of certain e-services	✓ Introduce a chatbot that will guide through the process of choosing the right e-service and the public authority as the service provider
✖ Indirect referral to (e-)service via Google or peers or parents	✓ Onboarding emails and a chatbot for guidance and information provision

5.4 Prototyping and Testing

Authors generated a high-fidelity prototype of the potential solution that is based on empirical research analysis of the target user feedback. The prototype is based on introducing a chatbot into user experience while delivering existing public e-services of Estonia. A clickable prototype of user flow and possible chat cases with limited capabilities was created to test the concept. One view was generated to test which topics the users are interested in talking about. The chatbot is able to answer test case of questions by using directive messages that encourage a proactive use of service on the website. The prototype also provides hints on how to successfully pass the driving license examination and allows to book a time for the exam. Lastly, as a closure that gives a sense of a positive user experience, the prototype congratulates the user on a successful passing of the examination and provides further information on the obtaining the documents.

After generating a prototype, the solution validation interviews were conducted to examine which features create value for the user. Table 3 summarizes the findings of the validation interviews.

Table 3. Validation results.

Type	Content
Positive feedback	Positive feelings about onboarding process and general service delivery; directive features were helpful
Aspects that need improvement	The built-in reaction tool for enhancing e-inclusion; chatbot topic selection view
Questions for future sprints	How to determine the right frequency of chat initiated without becoming burdensome to the user? How to increase the user's hedonic motivations to use public e-services?
Ideas for future sprints	Test of using gamification features and elements as a driver for youth engagement

5.5 Summary of the Design Sprint

To test the outcomes of the empirical research and make practical suggestions to improve the problems identified, Design Sprint was used. In the first stage, the scope of the challenge and sprint was set. The authors used an empirical research as a base to empathize with the end users. In order to describe the current situation in Estonian public e-service, an AS-IS description of the current service delivery process of the application submission for provisional driver's license was given in Sect. 5.1. In the second stage, with a goal to include the potential users in the design process an ideation workshop to generate ideas was conducted. The idea to link the e-service delivery to social media accounts was presented with potential features. In the stage 3, a solution proposal was generated that answered the users' expectations, including the characteristics of personalization, proactive service delivery in a familiar environment and event-based notifications. The focus of stages 4 and 5 was on building a prototype and test it with five potential users to gain feedback. The outcome was that the youngsters were eager to connect their accounts to the government related application. The general assessment of the prototype was positive, and suggestions for improvement were offered.

6 Discussion

For the public sector, technology has become one of the main channels for communication with citizens. Nearly infinite social media usage has set the end-users in the center of the innovation not only in the private sector but also in the public sector - the emphasis has shifted from technological possibilities to satisfying people's needs. Attempts to engage younger generations in using digital public services in Estonia may not be seen as successful so far although the group's technology acceptance rate is the highest among the population. In 2017, as little as 10% of all the services usage was performed by youngsters aged 18–26.

With the rise of attention to the importance of service design in the public sector, the aim of this research was to give possible answers to the question "How to increase youth engagement in public e-services?" Therefore, usage of public e-services from user perspective (in this case, that of the youngsters') was examined, aiming for a qualitative inquiry. Thus, the focus was on finding out which key characteristics play a significant role in youngsters' usage of public e-services with empirical research and to make suggestions how to implement them in the existing service delivery process in Estonia to boost user engagement in the age group of 18–26.

To provide a meaningful insight and to answer the research question, the concepts of technology acceptance and user-centric mindset were studied to establish a fundamental base for the survey. The main characteristics stemming from literature were moulded into a structure of interviews with ten potential users and two experts to identify the problems the current situation is facing.

The main problems that create a bottleneck for increasing service usage among youngsters are the following: firstly, in their everyday life the users are accustomed to proactive services such as social media platforms, and not the existing service portals of public authorities. Secondly, low awareness of the possibilities of the government-provided services to address users' needs. Although youngsters comprehend the time saving aspect, they do not often feel motivated enough to search for the services. Another important facet that was the confusion with the service delivery process and government websites' user-friendliness described mainly as "outdated". What was brought out by the experts is that the services lack the positive emotion creation aspect and fail to involve youngsters to use e-services later when they turn adults. All this results in not forming the habit of or reluctance using public services.

The positive aspects detected were the trust in the safety of government's information technology infrastructure and wide adoption of Estonian identification services, especially the mobile based Mobile-ID.

To generate a possible solution that fulfils the aims to engage more youngsters in using e-governance services, Design Sprint, a practical framework where the ideas of new service design elements have been gathered to solve problems in five stages, was carried out. This method is credited for its success in private sector initiatives accelerating innovations. During these five stages, the challenge was mapped, several means of relieving the pain points were ideated and a focus for a possible solution set that was turned into a prototype tested with the target users to draw conclusions.

It was identified that the youngsters are expecting a personalized service delivered in their natural digital environment using proactive approach, to notify them about all the aspects they need to know in regard to the government service provision.

The proposed solution in this paper is a chatbot in the social media accounts, bridging communication between the government and the youngsters. This allows to communicate with the target users utilizing their natural environment that will assure the continuance of public e-services. The chatbot can act either reactively, which means it is a way to gain information, or proactively, which means it sends notification messages and directs to services on the government websites. Furthermore, it acts as a means of increasing e-inclusion, asking about the youngsters' opinions to involve them in the policy-making process.

This solution is enabled by emerging new technological direction of cloud computing, open source data and Artificial Intelligence, allowing to process data of the single user, change the mobile application user experience scheme on their mobile device and affect the behavior of this user. However, authors do not cover the technical aspects of the offered solution within this paper.

A prototype was generated to test the proposed solution on five test users, using interviews and observations to analyze users' behavior. The feedback was mainly positive on all features, except for the e-inclusion feature, where the 2/5 of users said they are not willing to answer, as they do not feel competent enough, but regardless, had decided to answer anyhow. This may have falsified the outcome of the feature.

With full awareness of the limitations of the given empirical research, this is an attempt to provide an additional insight into using practical service design approaches to place the user in the center.

Due to the provisional stages of introducing such proactive services in the public domain, it is rather early to make assumptions on potential obstacle that may occur during the implementation and on boarding phases. As legal and technical aspects have not been covered within this research for the same reasons, also being outside of the research aims and scope, authors have not analyzed these aspects. The outcomes outlined should be taken as illuminating conjectures and suggestions to be possibly considered by stakeholders in the future as recommendations formulated by means of scientific approach.

7 Conclusion

In this paper, the authors reported on the outcomes of study that aims to understand the reasons behind Estonian youngsters' reluctance to use public e-services. Seeking to answer this question, authors turned to the target users to gain an in-depth perspective on their vision of the problem. This helped to develop an approach for improving the existing e-services that was run as a test on the application for a driver's license permit. By scoping the existing service, user experience and user needs, an ideation session in a form of a workshop was performed. A direct interaction with the target group has allowed to address the existing issues that prevent youngsters to use the services by suggesting a solution. Its prototype was tested by users that were also interviewed to provide insights for the validation of the solution.

The outcomes of the study suggest that the design of the existing public e-services lacks proactivity and user-friendliness, which points to the direction of exploring social networks as the platform and interaction bridge for engagement with the target users and a promising service delivery channel.

The main contribution of this research is the analysis that can serve as an input for governmental representatives and service designers for future design processes to increase the youngsters' user numbers.

References

1. Beaver, L.: The ChatBot Explainer. BI Intelligence (2016). https://www.businessinsider.com/chatbots-explained-why-businesses-should-be-paying-attention-to-the-chatbot-revolution-2016-7. Accessed 29 Nov 2018
2. Board of innovation: Scoping Canvas. https://www.boardofinnovation.com/tools/scoping-canvas/. Accessed 12 Dec 2018
3. Carter, L., Bélanger, F.: The utilization of e-government services: citizen trust, innovation and acceptance factors. Inf. Syst. J. **15**, 5–25 (2005)
4. Davis, F.D., Bagozzi, R.P., Warshaw, P.R.: User acceptance of computer technology: a comparison of two theoretical models. Manag. Sci. **35**, 982–1003 (1989)
5. Estonian Information System Authority. https://ria.ee/. Accessed 04 Dec 2018
6. Estonian Road Administration Homepage. https://www.mnt.ee/eng. Accessed 03 Dec 2018
7. Gothelf, J.: Lean UX Canvas, https://www.jeffgothelf.com/wp-content/uploads/2016/12/LeanUX_canvas_v4.pdf. Accessed 27 Nov 2018
8. Hassan, H., Shehab, E., Peppard, J.: Recent advances in e-service in the public sector: state-of-the-art and future trends. Bus. Process Manage. J. **17**(3), 526–545 (2011)
9. Ilves, T-H., Solvak, M., Vassil, K.: E-voting in Estonia: Technological Diffusion and Other Developments over Ten Years. University of Tartu, p. xii (2015)

10. Kalvet, T.: Innovation: a factor explaining e-government success in Estonia. Electron. Gov. Int. J. **9**(2), 142–157 (2012)
11. Katzan Jr., H.: Design for service innovation. J. Serv. Sci. **8**(1), 1–6 (2015)
12. Katzan Jr., H.: Essentials of service design. J. Serv. Sci. **4**(2), 43–60 (2011)
13. Kitsing, M.: Success without strategy: e-government development in Estonia. Policy Internet **3**(1), 1–21 (2011). Article 5
14. Krimmer, R.: The Evolution of E-voting: Why Voting Technology is Used and How it Affects Democracy – Ph.D. dissertation, Tallinn University of Technology (2012)
15. Linders, D., Liao, C.Z.-P., Wang, C.-M.: Proactive e-Governance: flipping the service delivery model from pull to push in Taiwan. Government Information Quarterly (2015)
16. Madise, Ü., Maaten, E.: Internet Voting in Estonia. E-democracy: a Group Decision and Negotiation Perspective. Springer, Dordrecht (2010). https://doi.org/10.1007/978-90-481-9045-4_17
17. Medium: An introduction to the AARRR framework. http://medium.com/@ginoarendsz/an-introduction-to-the-aarrr-framework-b8570d6ae0d2. Accessed 30 Nov 2018
18. Ministry of Economic Affairs and Communication: Digital agenda 2020 (2013)
19. Pappel, I., Pappel, I., Tepandi, J., Draheim, D.: Systematic digital signing in estonian e-government processes. In: Hameurlain, A., Küng, J., Wagner, R., Dang, T.K., Thoai, N. (eds.) Transactions on Large-Scale Data- and Knowledge-Centered Systems XXXVI. LNCS, vol. 10720, pp. 31–51. Springer, Heidelberg (2017). https://doi.org/10.1007/978-3-662-56266-6_2
20. Pappel, I., Tsap, V., Pappel, I., Draheim, D.: Exploring e-services development in local government authorities by means of electronic document management systems. In: Chugunov, A., Misnikov, Y., Roshchin, E., Trutnev, D. (eds.) EGOSE 2018. CCIS, vol. 947, pp. 223–234. Springer, Cham (2019). https://doi.org/10.1007/978-3-030-13283-5_17
21. Roosna, S., Rikk, R.: e-Estonia: e-Governance in Practice. https://ega.ee/publication/e-estonia-e-governance-in-practice/. Accessed 30 Nov 2018
22. Tepandi, J., et al.: The data quality framework for the Estonian public sector and its evaluation: establishing a systematic process-oriented viewpoint on cross-organizational data quality. In: Hameurlain, A., Küng, J., Wagner, R., Sakr, S., Razzak, I., Riyad, A. (eds.) Transactions on Large-Scale Data- and Knowledge-Centered Systems XXXV, pp. 1–26. Springer, Berlin (2017). https://doi.org/10.1007/978-3-662-56121-8_1
23. Trischler, J., Scott, D.R.: Designing Public Services: the usefulness of three service design methods for identifying user experiences -. Public Manage. Rev. **18**(5), 718–739 (2016)
24. Tsap, V., Pappel, I., Draheim, D.: Key success factors in introducing national e-identification systems. In: Dang, T.K., Wagner, R., Küng, J., Thoai, N., Takizawa, M., Neuhold, E.J. (eds.) FDSE 2017. LNCS, vol. 10646, pp. 455–471. Springer, Cham (2017). https://doi.org/10.1007/978-3-319-70004-5_33
25. Venkatesh, V., Morris, M., Davis, G., Davis, F.: User acceptance of information technology: toward a unified view. MIS Q. **27**(3), 425–478 (2003)

Government as a Platform: Critics of a Technocratic Culture of Public Governance in Digital Era

Leonid Smorgunov(✉)

St. Petersburg State University, Universitetskaya nab., 7/9,
St. Petersburg 199034, Russia
l.smorgunov@spbu.ru

Abstract. The formation of the digital government nowadays belongs to the main directions of reforming public policy and governance. In Russia, the Federal Target Program "Digital Economy" is planned to be implemented with a conjugate transition from electronic to digital government. At the heart of the formation of the digital government is the idea of the state as a platform that allows to effectively implement state functions and services on a new technological basis. The technocratic approach that dominates this idea is accompanied by the conviction that effective public policy and governance is possible almost without a person and public relations. The paper aims to critically analyze the technocratic cultural values of the state as a platform. Adequate answers to the political challenges of the digital government (values of control, centralization, excessive governability, etc.) are possible when integrating a new culture of political opportunities for co-production and the emerging system of state governability through cooperation.

Keywords: Government · Platform · Technocratic approach · Citizen participation · E-government · Consumerism · Cooperation

1 Introduction

Historically, the transformation of public policy in the era of the communicative revolution in the 21st century is already restrained by the traditions laid down by the practice of the implemented e-government, in which considerable attention is paid to services, information and reactive behavior. E-government becomes "narrow" for evolving technology, providing new opportunities for public administration and politics, not only in form but also in content. At the same time, the movement for "e-government 4.0" is gaining momentum, which breaks old habitual forms of interaction between the state and society. Some researchers say that, apparently, it is necessary to abandon the adjective "electronic" in describing the structure and activity of state bodies and to talk either simply about "government 4.0" or to focus on its new mechanisms and the culture of interaction with citizens, using the term "citizen-centric-government" [7, 14]. This transition is connected with the technological and political basis of modern structures of coordination of interaction [5, 20]. In particular, it should be noted the notion of "platform", which acquires not only the importance of an open

D. A. Alexandrov et al. (Eds.): DTGS 2019, CCIS 1038, pp. 41–54, 2019.
https://doi.org/10.1007/978-3-030-37858-5_4

and neutral means of communication, but also a public basis for the formation of political networks.

In the process of transforming e-government from portals to platforms, the political nature of the possible use of the state as a platform was manifested. A narrowly technological approach to platforms allowed only to improve the efficiency of service delivery. A broader interpretation spoke of a change in the ideology of public policy, which began to be characterized by such features as the orientation toward citizens inclusion, the cooperation of the main stakeholders in the development of public decisions, the discursive practice of setting the agenda, and so on. And here "collaboration may now lead to a new role of the state: a state that rather enables and empowers the social creation of value by its citizens. It protects the infrastructure of P2P cooperation and the creation of commons: The state evolves into a manager of a "marketplace", stimulating, enabling and organizing the assets of the country—the abilities and motivations of its citizens—in an efficient manner" [1, p. 188].

The idea of the state as a platform, designed by some scholars [12, 16, 17], received international support. In many countries, it acquired the character of a practical idea and was placed in the basis of appropriate administrative reforms [18]. This idea has support in Russia. However, in our opinion, often its use is based on technological optimism and does not take into account the complex structure of the public state. The platform, of course, is a technologically advanced tool and a base for using large data with various applications for connected governance [8]. However, the platform is not only a technology, but also a convenient basis for representing the state as a ground for civil activity. In this respect, the idea of the state as a platform cannot be effectively realized outside the social and political contexts. This paper draws attention to (1) the idea of the platform in the technological and socio-political sense, (2) describes the use of new technologies in the process of introducing e-government, (3) reveals the main content of the technological view on the idea of the state as a platform and (4) describes some areas of criticism of the technocratic use of this idea. The center is based on the Russian practice of using e-government and the idea of the state as a platform.

2 From Portal to Platform

In the first decade of the existence of electronic governments in the world (conditionally 1995–2005) they were organized into Internet portals. With the emergence of the ideology of "e-government 2.0" began to talk about the fact that the portals no longer provide the government with the whole complex of relations with society and business. They are narrow in their function and government-oriented. Not more portals are more democratic, but Internet platforms based on interactive Web 2.0 technology. In reality, there was a mixture of portals and platforms as a means of modern government activity and cooperation between business and society with the government. There is an international organization called the Open Government Partnership, opengovpartnership.org, which seeks to promote the ideas of a new e-government in the world, creating the basis for national reforms aimed at making governments more open, responsible and sensitive to citizen. It works already as a platform, not a portal, i.e. allows to carry out interaction on the basis of initiative use of electronic applications. This organization was established in September 2011 by representatives of eight countries - Brazil, Indonesia, Mexico, the Philippines, South Africa, the United Kingdom and the United States. Currently, this organization includes 63 countries.

Currently, the functioning of e-government is only partially organized in Internet portals, i.e. complex electronic means that provide for the implementation of a number of government functions and services for citizens. Internet portals provide search and information acquisition, interaction of citizens and organizations with state authorities, holding events for citizens and organizations, and providing public services. Internet platforms are complex electronic tools that provide not only services, but the participation of citizens in the choice of public services and influencing the decision-making process. If we use the direct meaning of the concept of platform as an aggregate of ICT 4.0, oriented to the use of a web application system on one server for interactivity and personal participation, modern public administration includes such technologies under the flag of "e-governance". In this respect, electronic platforms are an open and technically neutral means of ensuring the free exchange of resources. In general, attention is drawn to such political characteristics of electronic platforms as the free structure of political opportunities for participation, the populist orientation of the policy of openness of content, egalitarian involvement, the stimulation of innovation, competitiveness.

E-government 4.0 has characteristics that promote democracy in the broadest sense of the word, including civic participation virtually in the day-to-day activities of the state and in the processes of providing public services. In this respect, e-government becomes the basis for the network interaction of citizens, associations of civil society and business with the state in various areas of public activity. At this stage, the importance of assessing the electronic participation of citizens through the diverse sites of such e-government. As Kay Erickson and Henry Vogt rightly write, "the e-government movement" not only transformed public administration, but also influenced decisively our political self-awareness. New electronic channels seem to create an attractive environment for a new kind of interaction between the government and citizens. New digital forms of policy and management include network-based inputs for organizing all government information and public services in accordance with the needs and interests of certain segments of the population. This approach from the standpoint of "one window" is built on the concept of self-service with the requirement for users to become more active and self-governing " [14, p. 159]. Platforms are technical and information conditions for increasing the self-organization of communities formed in networks. Governability of a network commune is provided by network learning supported by platforms.

3 Russian E-Government Platforms

There are three main stages of Russian public policy in the implementation of new electronic technology in governmental activities and involving citizens in policy-making. The first stage is related to the Federal program "Electronic Russia (2002–2010). This could be named "involving public authorities in electronic space". The second stage is connected to the Governmental program "Information Society

(2011–2020)". This stage is "involving the general population in using electronic public services". The third stage, which overlaps with the second one, is the development of open government in Russia. The third stage is directed to "cooperation of government and society in policy". These three stages or trends in public policy are important for understanding the issue of open government implementation in Russia. These three steps show the process of forming the structure of political opportunities for more active involvement of citizens in public policy. It is particularly important in this context to identify three significant elements for the study of the structure: (1) the transformation of the mentality of instrumental use of new ICT (efficiency of public services) in their use as a means of civic engagement in public policy; (2) expansion of the platforms for citizens to influence the political agenda and their involvement in the process of formation of public decision-making; (3) the formation of the ideology of "open government" with the Russian understanding of mutual responsibility of citizens and the state for public policy.

There are some platforms which realize Russian idea of e-government. On 15 December 2009, *the Single Portal of Public and Municipal Services* (SPPMS) (www.gosuslugi.ru) was launched as a demonstration. The SPPMS provides a uniform point of access for citizens to the corresponding state and municipal services given by public authorities, to give to citizens and business organizations a uniform interface for access to governmental information and to receive public services with the possibility of transition to the Internet site of the authority responsible for granting concrete state service or to an Internet portal of public authorities of the subject of the Russian Federation (a regional portal of the public services). Among them the following services are provided - filing forms for registration of identification documents (passports, driver's licenses), various children's grants, and filling receipts for payment of penalties for infringement of traffic rules. In 2015, 4,200 state and municipal services were available on the Internet. However, according to monitoring by the Ministry of Communications, only about 50% of these services are operating.

To receive a public service the citizens must be registered in the Unified System of identification and authentication (ESIA). In 2015 the number of Russians registered in the Unified System of identification and authentication (ESIA), increased on 7 million. Currently (January, 2016), in the system almost 23,4 million people are registered.

The intensive development of electronic government in Russia was started in 2011 when the platform of "BolshoePravitelstvo" (Big Government) was put on the Internet in a demonstrative version. The 'Big Government' idea was equal to the 'Open Government' (open.gov.ru). The whole system of open government in Russia started to form in 2012, which took a civil-centered approach as the basis of its work. Visitors to the site 10 thousand per month, views more than 40 thousand.

The Portal of Open Data of the RF (data.gov.ru). Here, the Portal focuses on the most current information about the public data of federal authorities, regional authorities and other organizations, places documented data sets, links and metadata of published data sets, information about software products and information services created on the basis of open data. It also publishes normative legal acts regulating the activities of state bodies on disclosure of data, methodical and journalistic resources. Here, communication interfaces have been implemented to interact with organizations that act as owners of socially important data.

Let's show the results of Rosstat's research on the indicator "The proportion of citizens using the mechanism for obtaining state and municipal services in electronic form" (Fig. 1). In Russia in general, 63.4% of citizens in 2017 received electronic public services. The leaders in this indicator in 2017 were the Moscow region (86% of respondents who received state and municipal services in the last 12 months indicated that they did this via the Internet), the Yamalo-Nenets Autonomous Okrug (86%), the Republic of Tatarstan (81%), The Krasnoyarsk Kray (80%), the Republic of Tyva (79%).

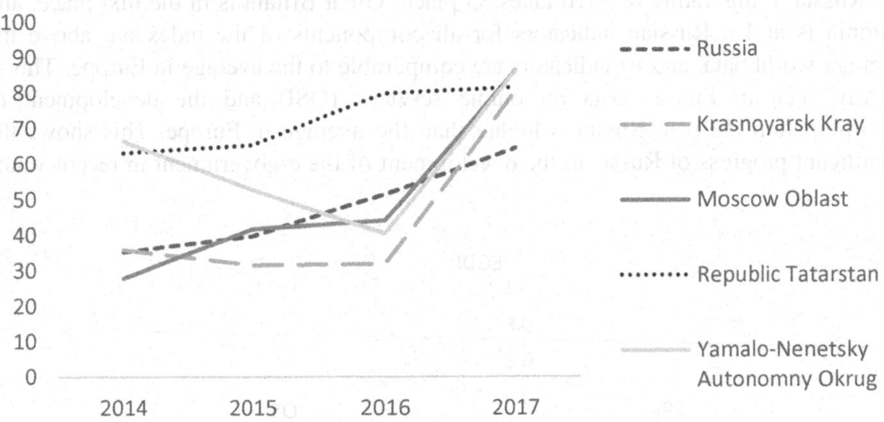

Fig. 1. Percentage of citizens who received electronic public services

To compare the level of e-government development in Russia, we used the indicators of the e-government development index (EGDI) used by the UN for the annual review of the state of the world (see Table 1).

Table 1. E-government development index (UNPAN, 2016)

	Global	Europe	Estonia	Russia	UK
EGDI	0,4222	0,7241	0,8334	0,7215	0,9193
OSI	0,4623	0,6926	0,8913	0,7319	1
TII	0,3711	0,6438	0,7329	0,6091	0,8177
HCI	0,6433	0,836	0,8761	0,8234	0,9402
EPI	0,4625	0,6985	0,8136	0,7458	1

Russia here is compared by three main index indicators, by the index itself and by the index of electronic participation (EPI) with the most developed countries implementing the idea of the state as a platform. This is the UK and Estonia[1]. Also, the state

[1] "In 2013, the UK signed a memorandum of understanding with Estonia, representing 'a commitment by the two countries to work together on developing public services that are digital by default' In

of affairs in Russia is compared with Europe and the average indicators in the world. The E-Government Development Index (EGDI) is a weighted average of normalised scores on the three most important dimensions of e-government, namely: scope and quality of online services (Online Service Index, OSI), status of the development of telecommunication infrastructure (Telecommunication Infrastructure Index, TII) and inherent human capital (Human Capital Index, HCI). Each of these sets of indices is in itself a composite measure that can be extracted and analysed independently [22, p. 133].

Russia in this rating of 2016 takes 35 place. Great Britain is in the first place, and Estonia is at 13. Russian indicators for all components of the index are above the average world data, and its indicators are comparable to the average in Europe. This is clearly seen in Fig. 2. Data on online services (OSI) and the development of e-participation (EPI) in Russia is higher than the average in Europe. This shows the significant progress of Russia in the development of the e-government in recent years.

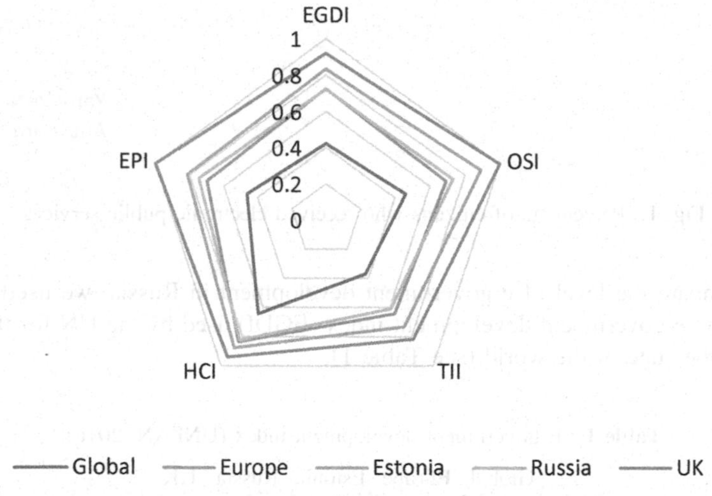

Fig. 2. E-government development index (UNPAN, 2016)

Of course, there are a number of problems with the implementation of the idea of e-government in Russia. First of all, it should be said about the digital inequality that exists in various aspects - generation, regional, social. The greatest digital differentiation is observed between the inhabitants of the city and the village. Although the proportion of users is growing everywhere, but there is no convergence of positions on this indicator between the city and the countryside. There is practically no difference between men and women. Women lag behind men by less than one percent.

(Footnote 1 continued)
2016, accolades finally came the UK's way, with the UK leading the UN rankings for digital government, just as Estonia was slipping down to a middling position" [18, p. 25].

Secondly, it is often said that the development of electronic platforms in Russia should be viewed as an imitation fact that has little effect on real politics and the real interaction of citizens with the state. Of course, some limited use of electronic platforms is available both from officials and from citizens. However, the gradual and expanding use of these platforms indicates a gradual process of learning interaction through electronic mechanisms. Third, there is a certain distrust on both sides of the use of electronic means. It is overcome only by a gradual process of increasing the effectiveness of the provision of public services and the adoption of citizens' initiatives.

4 Russian Idea of a State as a Platform

At present, Russia is implementing the concept of "e-government". However, in April 2016, the World Bank and the Institute for the Development of the Information Society project "Digital Government 2020. Prospects for Russia ", in which it is recommended to develop the concept of "digital government". This document defines a "digital government" as a government, created and operating so that when optimizing, transforming and creating public services, the advantages of digital data are used. The emphasis is on information and data, not on processes and services, as it was in the concept of "e-government" [9]. Many governments now think how to provide application programming interfaces to different intermediaries and to open opportunities for new private and public sector services for reducing costs of government itself and increasing policy effectiveness. This approach has been termed "Government as a Platform" by O'Reilly [12, 13]. "The initial focus on information and communications technology (ICT) was aimed at improving efficiency and productivity, as a precondition for sound fiscal policies. In the longer-term, the use of digital technologies will need to be considered in the broader context in which governments are operating, with users' perspectives increasingly to the fore" [11, p. 9].

Approved by the decree of the President of the Russian Federation of May 9, 2017 No. 203, the Strategy for the Development of the Information Society in the Russian Federation for 2017–2030 defines a list of promising technologies (which includes artificial intelligence, Internet of things, processing of large amounts of data etc.) and, in principle, sets the task of applying them to the government bodies of the Russian Federation. In July 2017, the government program "Development of the digital economy" was adopted, which, although it does not contain a direct section dealing with the digital government, but focuses on the formation of the corresponding public administration.

The Center for Strategic Research, headed by Alexei Kudrin (now the Chairman of the Accounts Chamber of the Russian Federation), has been developing a project of the state as a platform since 2017. In 2018 the Center offered its vision of this process in a special report [19]. In the future, we will use this document and related materials to describe the constituent elements and principles of this public administration model.

Two key characteristics of the "State-as-Platform" are the provision of maximum "human orientation" of the results of governance and provision of services, and at the same time the maximum "human independence" of the processes of rendering services (both in collecting and processing information, and in making decisions).

It is necessary to create a transparent public administration system that will be based on a data-centric and process approach and will provide the following effects:

- "From documents to data": collection, storage, processing and ordering of all necessary data are provided, rules for differentiating access to data (including assigning them to different degrees of secrecy) and protecting data, storing and archiving data, responsibility for the correctness of the data (based on the data lake concept), the priority of trusted data over paper documents was established, complete abandonment of paperwork and the transfer of processes to digital form after their qualitative reengineering;
- state information systems are transferred to a platform that allows to ensure "seamlessness" when using any stored data and functionality on the basis of uniform regulatory rules;
- the decisions made are transparent - first of all, due to the maximum possible disclosure of data, the introduction of automated decision-making technologies and the maximum elimination of the human factor, thereby ensuring the necessary level of trust in the public administration system;
- decisions are made on the basis of real-time data, as well as reliable historical data;
- a digital ecosystem has been created in which citizens and business interact with the state in a multi-channel mode using various mobile devices, providing the necessary convenience and speed, and which, with the relevant speed, allows to expand the opportunities for interaction of citizens and business with the state;
- provides the ability to create independent application/service providers for users;
- established practice of continuous improvement of processes based on feedback from users on the level of satisfaction with the solution of their tasks;
- the costs for the state apparatus are optimized by eliminating unnecessary processes, functions, and the staffing of civil servants.

Accordingly, these ideas a government should start working as an advanced IT company. Proposed basic principles could be the following:

Integrity/controlling: the presence of a single integrated IT architecture (a single IT architect).

Unique/deduplication: identification of unique data and unique services in the zone one business/state agency. Elimination of duplication/erosion of their elements (under a single architectural IT control).

Formalization/algoritmization: bringing services from manual/semi-automated, unclearly formalized unstructured management objects to the unique services with structured unique data (for example, judges will have to render solutions in a strict structured format, available for machine interpretation).

Blockness/efficiency: the implementation of End-To-End processes (services that are complete in their meaning), which are logical workflow of the services and data with maximum reuse of the services and data of adjacent government agencies (absence of duplication of services by public bodies).

Layering/flexibility of governance: a clear division of architecture into a triad of front-line scenarios, back-up scenarios, an interaction between systems. Each of the three components must be holistic (one IT implementation with derived open communication protocols).

Quick development and implementation: development teams work in agile, flexible rules for forming technical assignments, financing, implementation.

As claimed by the developers of this idea "of course, it was important for us to offer a vision image of the future state, in which the state apparatus is small, decision is accepted quickly, there are no intermediaries in the form of state bodies between the person and his data, the possibility of constructing individual trajectories in the development and solution of life situations that a person faces, both in everyday life and in work" [19, p. 3].

5 Critics of Technocratic Approach to a State as a Platform

More or less radical criticism of e-government in general is based on new trends, manifested as in the development of information technology, and in politics and society in this century. Of course, many of these trends have already manifested themselves at the end of the last century, however, their growing importance became clear only today. These tendencies are also characteristic for criticizing the idea of the state as a platform. One can single out the following main directions of the critical approach to the technological theory of the state/government as a platform:

- criticism of the opportunistic nature of the use of ICT in politics and public administration;
- criticism of the consumerism approach to e-government due to the dominance of the ideology of the new public management;
- criticize the prevailing emphasis on information, its storage, dissemination and use in government portals and not take into account that modern public administration is based more on knowledge than information;
- criticism of the liberal/individualistic model of democracy, on which the idea of the state as a platform was based.

All these directions of criticism, of course, are connected with criticism of the optimistic attitude towards the use of new information technologies, which is based on the belief that the technological parameters of development are the determinants of social changes. However, public administration and public policy are social phenomena with their parameters and deterministic relations. We agree with the statement that "government is inherently a social enterprise. The problems of digital government are not entirely technical and often not common to typical businesses and service providers, and little commercial effort can be found addressing the non-technical and uniquely governmental aspects of government needs. In particular, decisions on target constituencies and functionality in government services (such as issues of privacy and trustworthiness) are legal and political, not subject to simple economic or business tradeoffs. Such intertwining of social, legal and technical issues is something that can best be addressed by research efforts targeted specifically at digital government. Therefore, in addition to government's ultimate reliance on utilization of technology, disciplines such as sociology, political science, public administration, business, and law are inextricably involved" [3, p. 7]. Therefore, "the key issues that need to be tackled are about the suitability of technology in government processes rather than developing the right technology" [4, p. 221].

In the process of critically examining the possibilities of new ICTs that have arisen in the course of the post-industrial (fourth) revolution, two main questions arise, to which optimists and pessimists respond in different ways. The first question touches on the problem of the depth of the transformation of technology: How revolutionary are the new ICTs, so that it can be said about their fundamental difference from the previous media and communication? The second question is related to the first and concerns the revolutionizing influence of ICT on political practice and relations: Do new ICTs require new policies and management? Is there something radically new in this process of the Internet?

Criticism, on the one hand, of course, tries to adapt new technologies to old forms and relations. On the other hand, it is recognized that technology affects society in a complex way in a direct and indirect form. And yet, "maybe we need to expand or move beyond our traditional definitions of what constitutes a political one". Technologies could contribute to the development of the nature of political activity and disputes, as proponents of technological optimism write cautiously. The sociotechnical concept of introducing ICT in public administration and politics, of course, a technique put in a social context, and the effectiveness of its use is determined by a complex combination of socio-economic, political, cultural and psychological institutions, attitudes, and attributes, but it is one thing to regard technical innovations as additional and adapt them to the existing system, and the other - to see prospects in the simultaneous change of technology and the surrounding social institutions. "The political approach to DG research addresses the effects of information and technology on transparency, accountability, and citizen and community engagement" [15, p. 3].

In the course of administrative reforms based on the ideology of new public management, this discussion was related to the role of e-government in this process, whether it is an instrument for solving the tasks of reform, or it itself requires reforming public administration. For supporters of the application value of e-government, on the one hand, it is only some additional conceptual and practical means for new public management and reforms based on it. Some reputable experts say that the new public management has had little effect on the interest in new information technologies, and only its actual death as an influential ideology has made it possible to talk about the transition to the era of digital governance (digital-era governance) [10]. The new public management was seen as a global theory of administrative reforms that were implemented in national contexts and which this ideology took little account of. In this respect, the introduction of the state as a platform also claims a global project without taking into account the national and cultural specifics. We agree that "the cultural perspective shows how reforms and change in public organizations trigger an institutionalization process that gradually introduces the 'core informal norms and values'… Hence, a reform is more likely to be successful when its underlying values are better aligned with the values embedded in the existing administrative system" [5, p.5].

The program for introducing the state as a platform focuses primarily on the ideology of new public management with its main idea "to make the government effective and cheap". To a large extent this means that, using e-government, it is possible to provide public services for citizens and businesses more efficiently and less costly. It is no accident that the main task of introducing e-government in many countries was the rapid use of government portals to provide the largest number of services. In general, this task turned out to be feasible, and the possible services using the Internet turned out to be qualitative, cheap and fast, although, naturally, there are difficulties and problems in this process. However, it turned out that the consumerist approach to the e-government suffers from many shortcomings, as well as the ideology of the new state management in general. In general, no one particularly challenged the feasibility of electronic services, it was said that this emphasis is clearly not enough when considering the possibilities of new ICT and the Internet. Especially many among these critics are those who consider the functions of the government to provide services and its relationship with citizens through a socio-political prism. Andrew Chadwick and Christopher May point out the limited nature of the attitude of the government and citizens when the latter act as "clients" of the state. ICTs will increase the provision of services with more accurately targeted communication with citizens and faster responses [to them], but the democratic possibility of such communication is generally ignored. In the center of the managerial model lies the premise that the changes are additional. While ICTs can challenge and provide opportunities for governments (their interactions with the national economy and, more broadly, with civil society), their basic operational logic remains unchanged [6].

The information approach is dominant in the theory and practice of e-government. It is recognized that e-government is an effective means of accumulating government online documents, providing information services to citizens, businesses, disseminating information and sharing it among government departments to improve decision-making and overall management. Modern governments place a huge amount of information on their portals, and this is often considered the main indicator of their information transparency. The use of large data in this regard is considered a breakthrough in increasing the effectiveness of the government.

However, the information paradigm is now in conflict with the principles of a knowledge-based society. The circulation of knowledge implies a different nature of information exchanges. Haridimos Tsoukas summarizes the limitations of the information paradigm for the analysis of organizational knowledge. First, the world, social and natural, is thought to consist of units of information - decontextualized representations - and we tend to explore the world through layers of abstract representations of the world. Secondly, information is viewed through the prism of the "metaphor of the channel": information is supposed to be objective and exist independently of human agents. Thirdly, in an information rich society, social engineering becomes the dominant form of policy making: the world is thought of as rationally managed mainly through the collection, functioning and manipulation of necessary information about it. Hence the paradoxes of the information society: the more information, the less understanding; the more information, the less confidence; the more social engineering, the more problems [21, pp. 20, 21–22]. Therefore, the digital government cannot be conceived only as a platform for providing a multitude of public services in electronic form, i.e. as technology of an impersonal market of services and goods. The state as a platform can only take place in unity with the new deliberative character of the political regime as a whole. "Digital governance can be viewed as a tool for providing citizens with the ability to choose the manner in which they interact with governments. It is a mechanism for ensuring that ICTs are used effectively to improve the flow of information between citizen and government… In general, digital government involves electronic service delivery, electronic democracy, and e-governance (digital support for policymaking and the policy process)" [2, p. 130].

6 Conclusion

The development of the conceptual foundations for the introduction of ICT in the system of public policy and management is carried out as quickly as the technology itself. Theoretical language in the 1990s up to the present time has used various concepts to describe this situation: "online government", "digital government", "network government", "e-government", "mobile government", "electronic government", "government as a platform". If in the initial period this evolution was determined to a large extent by the theories of management, organization, public administration, informatics, in the last ten years political science has been seriously influenced by this process. The result of its influence, recognized by experts of other fields of knowledge, is the conceptual design of the modern movement for the introduction of ICT in public administration and politics in the ideology of e-governance. This ideology is based on new trends in social development - the network society, the communication revolution, the knowledge society, the growing importance of risk and uncertainty in social processes, personalization, etc. Political science in this regard was more sensitive than before to interdisciplinary synthesis with cognitive science, social synergetic, sociological phenomenology, communication science, etc. And the fact that this turned out to be effective is confirmed by the discursive, but still acceptance of the research governments, and international organizations of a new conceptual paradigm of governance and e-government.

An attempt to reduce the use of the idea of the state as a platform to a pragmatic version of an effective mechanism for the provision of public services will have only partial support. This attempt does not take into account the complex nature of the introduction of any technology in the living space of public policy. The brake of reform here, obviously, will be two components of the context of any administrative reform: first, basic cultural values. embodied in the existing system of public administration; secondly, the close connection between the administrative reform and the political regime. The technology of the fourth technical revolution is keeping pace with the need for civic participation and cooperation of the state, civil society and business. Without this context, reform on a purely technological type "state as a platform" is doomed to half of purely commercial success.

Funding. The author disclosed receipt of the following financial support for the research, authorship, and/or publication of this article: This work was supported with a grant from the Russian Foundation for Basic Research (grant 18-011-00756 A "Study of citizens participation and building digital government").

References

1. Al-Ani, A.: Government as a platform: services, participation and policies. In: Friedrichsen, M., Kamalipour, Y. (eds.) Digital Transformation in Journalism and News Media. MBI, pp. 179–196. Springer, Cham (2017). https://doi.org/10.1007/978-3-319-27786-8_14
2. Asgarkhani, M.: The reality of social inclusion through digital government. J. Technol. Hum. Serv. **25**(1–2), 127–146 (2007). https://doi.org/10.1300/J017v25n01_09
3. Arens, Y., Callan, J., Dawes, S.S., Fountain, J., Hovy, E., Marchionini, G.: Cyberinfrastructure and digital government (2003). http://www.digitalgovernment.org/archive/library/pdf/dg_cyberinfrastructure.pdf. Accessed 12 May 2018
4. Aleixo, C., Nunes, M., Isaias, P.: Usability and digital inclusion: standards and guidelines. Int. J. Public Adm. **35**, 221–239 (2012). https://doi.org/10.1080/01900692.2011.646568
5. Castelnovo, W., Sorrentino, M.: The digital government imperative: a context-aware perspective. Public Manag. Rev. (2017). https://doi.org/10.1080/14719037.2017.1305693
6. Chadwick, A., May, C.: Interaction between states and citizens in the age of the Internet: "e-Government" in the United States, Britain, and the European Union. In: Governance: An International Journal of Policy, Administration, and Institutions. Malden, MA, USA, vol. 16, no. 2 (2003)
7. Citizen Service Platform: Strategies to Transform Government in the 2.0 World. Microsoft (2010)
8. Dais, A., Nikolaidou, M., Alexopoulou, N., Anagnostopoulos, D.: Introducing a public agency networking platform towards supporting connected governance. In: Wimmer, M.A., Scholl, H.J., Ferro, E. (eds.) EGOV 2008. LNCS, vol. 5184, pp. 375–387. Springer, Heidelberg (2008). https://doi.org/10.1007/978-3-540-85204-9_32
9. Digital Government 2020: Prospects for Russia (2016). http://documents.worldbank.org/curated/en/562371467117654718/pdf/105318-WP-PUBLIC-Digital-Government-2020.pdf. Accessed 17 May 2018
10. Dunleavy, P., Margetta, H., Bastow, S., Tinkler, J.: New public management is dead – long live digital-era governance. J. Public Adm. Res. Theory **16**(3), 467–494 (2005)
11. OECD Comparative Study: Digital Government Strategies for Transforming Public Services in the Welfare Areas. OECD (2016)
12. O'Reilly, T.: Government as a platform. In: Lathrop, D., Ruma, L. (eds.) Open Government: Collaboration, Transparency, and Participation in Practice. O'Reilly Media, Sebastopol (2010)
13. O'Reilly, T.: What's the Future and Why It's up to Us. Penguin Random House, London (2017)
14. Eriksson, K., Vogt, H.: On self-service democracy: configurations of individualizing governance and self-directed citizenship. Eur. J. Soc. Theory **16**(2), 153–173 (2013)
15. Gil-Garciaa, J., Sharon, S., Pardoa, T.: Digital government and public management research: finding the crossroads. Public Manag. Rev. (2017). https://doi.org/10.1080/14719037.2017.1327181
16. Gillespie, T.: The politics of 'platforms'. New Media Soc. **12**(3), 347–364 (2010)
17. Knox, C.: Public administrators' use of social media platforms: overcoming the legitimacy dilemma? Adm. Soc. **48**(4), 477–496 (2016)
18. Margetts, H., Naumann, A.: Government as a platform: what can estonia show the world? (2017). https://www.politics.ox.ac.uk/publications/government-as-a-platform-what-can-estonia-show-the-world.html. Accessed 12 May 2018

19. Petrov, M., Burov, V., Shkliaruk, M., Sharov, A.: Gosudarstvo kak platforma. (Kiber)gosudarstvo dlia tsifrovoy ekonomiki. Tsifrovaya transformatsia. [State as a platform. (Cyber) state for digital economy. Digital transformation]. Moscow, The Center for Strategic Research (2018)
20. Parker, G., Van Alstyne, M., Choudary, S.: Platform Revolution: How Networked Markets Are Transforming the Economy and - How to Make Them Work for You. W. W. Norton & Company, New York (2016)
21. Tsoukas, H.: Complex Knowledge. Studies in Organizational Epistemology. Oxford University Press, Oxford (2005)
22. United Nations E-Government Survey 2016: E-Government in Support of Sustainable development. United Nations, New York (2016)

Digitalization and Effective Government: What Is the Cause and What Is the Effect?

Elena Dobrolyubova[1(✉)], Elena Klochkova[1,2], and Oleg Alexandrov[3]

[1] Russian Academy of National Economy and Public Administration (RANEPA), Vernadskogo pr. 84, 119571 Moscow, Russia
dobrolyubova@inbox.ru, mrelena_@mail.ru

[2] Plekhanov Russian University of Economics, Stremyanny lane, 36, 117997 Moscow, Russia

[3] CEFC Group, Sadovaya-kudrinskaya 11/1 office 412, 121242 Moscow, Russia
alexandrov@cefc.ru

Abstract. Government digitalization is becoming a mainstream of governance reforms with high expectations in terms of improving public value delivered by governments, raising both efficiency and effectiveness of public administration. Based on cross-country data, this paper presents a quantitative analysis of correlation between government digitalization on the one hand (based on UN E-government and E-participation indices and OECD statistics) and quality of public administration (measured by the WB's governance indicators, Doing Business and WEF data) on the other. The results suggest that while there is statistically significant positive correlation between government digitalization and public administration performance, this relationship is stronger for government effectiveness, control of corruption, and doing business and weaker for e-participation, voice and accountability and efficiency of public spending. The findings suggest that there is direct cause and effect relationship between e-government development index and Doing Business measures. At the same time, surprisingly no direct cause and effect relationship was found between government digitalization and other governance indicators included in this study, such as government effectiveness and control of corruption. Thus, the benefits of businesses from government digitalization so far seem to be more evident than the gains of other beneficiaries. The paper concludes with analysis of some policy implications and recommendations on the directions of further research.

Keywords: Causality · Correlation · Digitalization · Government · Governance indicators · E-government development index · Effectiveness · Efficiency · Performance · Public administration

1 Introduction

Digital transformation is the modern mainstream of social and economic development promising significant digital dividends to citizens and businesses worldwide [35]. The phenomenon of digital transformation gained significant attention in literature [12].

D. A. Alexandrov et al. (Eds.): DTGS 2019, CCIS 1038, pp. 55–67, 2019.
https://doi.org/10.1007/978-3-030-37858-5_5

Though there is still no single approach to defining digital transformation in general or digital transformation of government in particular [27], most authors suggest that digital transformation involves using ICT technology for creating fundamentally new capabilities in business, public government and people's life [20] and radically improving performance or business reach [34].

In the area of public administration, the expectations about the changes digital technologies drive are so high that some researches claim digitalization to be a driver for the new governance concepts of digital era governance [19] or ICT-enabled transformational government [10]. The theory emphasizes the importance of digitalization for optimizing the public value of government services for citizens [1] as well as for raising efficiency of government functions as a result of implementing lean government models [13] with an emphasis on government-as-a-platform solutions [3, 26] where the government organizes the interaction of citizens and other organizations based on a single digital ecosystem.

These theoretical approaches are complemented by the practical ones. Thus, in 2014 OECD Recommendation on Digital Government Strategies digital government is defined as the "use of digital technologies, as an integrated part of governments' modernization strategies, to create public value" [24]. In other words, digital transformation in public administration calls for creating some additional public value as a result of implementing digital technology [16]. This discussion is highly relevant to government policy as many countries have embarked on implementing digital strategies aimed at achieving greater public value. By 2017, digital strategies were developed in 34 OECD countries[1]. This is also relevant for Russia where the *National Program on Digital Economy* aims, inter alia, at using digital technologies for the benefit of people and businesses.

Thus, the theory suggests that digital transformation of government (as the current stage of its digitalization) should lead to improved government performance. But is this the case in practice?

So far, empirical cross-country research on actual influence of government digitalization on public administration performance has been limited. Earlier studies revealed positive association between e-government development and public administration efficiency [29]. Positive interrelation between e-government development and public administration performance is revealed both for democratic countries and autocracies [31]; these conclusions have been confirmed by another recent study [6] which demonstrated strong correlation between some parameters characterizing e-government development, on the one hand, and government performance on the other.

There are also several quantitative studies suggesting that e-government has a positive impact on reducing corruption [7, 18, 30]; some authors argue that more mature e-government might have an impact on economic prosperity and environmental degradation via the impact of e-government maturity on reducing corruption [14].

However, neither of these studies concluded on whether it is the government digitalization (implementing e-government and d-government) which drives performance of public administration, or, vice versa, it is good governance that supports

[1] See: http://www.oecd.org/going-digital/oecd-digital-economy-outlook-paris-2017.htm.

implementing successful digital initiatives in public administration. The quantitative studies on interrelation between e-government and corruption in most cases suggested that causality between digitalization and corruption levels runs both ways [15].

Notably, a broad range of studies suggest that the quality of governance before digitalization (i.e. political support, organizational readiness, managerial capacity – or governance ability in general) is an important success factor for the future e-government initiatives [21, 22, 28]. Another cross-country research suggests that indeed effective governance, ICT investment and competitive telecommunication markets are predictors of online service development and e-participation [9]. Thus, better government effectiveness and efficiency may be considered not as outcomes of digitalization but as factors for successful digital transformation. This paper aims at contributing to this discussion and identifying the areas for further research.

2 Objective and Methodology

2.1 Study Objective

The objective of this paper is to analyze the interrelation between quality of public administration (its effectiveness and efficiency), on the one hand, and the extent of government digitalization – on the other. To achieve this objective, we need to:

1. identify the correlation between the indicators characterizing the quality of public administration and the extent of government digitalization; and
2. assess the casualty between the indicators from these two groups.

The results of the study would help to identify the areas which need further research.

The hypothesis we test in the paper is that greater government digitalization improves the quality of public administration, i.e. makes governments more effective and efficient. Confirmation of such hypothesis would mean that at the current stage of digital transformation in public administration its key objective of creating additional public value (rather than digitalizing for the sake of digitalizing) has been achieved.

2.2 Methodology

For achieving the study objective, we use quantitative analysis based on the latest available cross-country data published by the UN [33], OECD [25], World Bank [36], and WEF [37]. Most data are for 2018 and 2017 (except for the OECD data on the percentage of citizens using Internet for submitting the filled forms through government websites).

The indicators for evaluating the extent of government digitalization include the following:

- UN E-government development index, EGDI (x_1);
- UN Online Service Index (a component of UN EGDI) (x_2);
- UN E-participation index (x_3);

- Percentage of citizens using Internet for submitting the filled forms through government websites (x_4): the indicator reflects the extent of public service digitalization and is estimated by the OECD.

The factors characterizing quality of public administration include:

- World Bank Worldwide governance indicators, such as:
  - Government effectiveness (x_5);
  - Voice and accountability (x_6); and
  - Control of corruption (x_7);
- Efficiency of government spending as measured by the World Economic Forum (x_8);
- Ease of doing business as measured by the World Bank (x_9).

The proposed list of indicators allows for evaluating key quality parameters for public administration, including effectiveness, efficiency, and transparency and accountability. For the purposes of this paper, public administration effectiveness means the extent to which government achieves its goals across all public administration functions and domains, such as service delivery, policy formulation and implementation, regulating business environment and the like. Hence, for measuring public administration effectiveness characteristic, we use WB Government effectiveness index and WB Doing Business index. Public administration efficiency is another government quality characteristic relating to the government ability of using resources (including financial resources) in a way to maximize the value for money. We used WEF Efficiency of public spending data to measure public administration efficiency in this study.

The indicators used for this paper and the expected correlations between them are presented in Fig. 1. Thus, in accordance with our hypothesis (Sect. 2.1), the study expected to find correlation between EGDI (and its online services sub-index) and government effectiveness and efficiency indicators; e-participation index and transparency and accountability indicators; the uptake of e-filing among citizens and government effectiveness and efficiency.

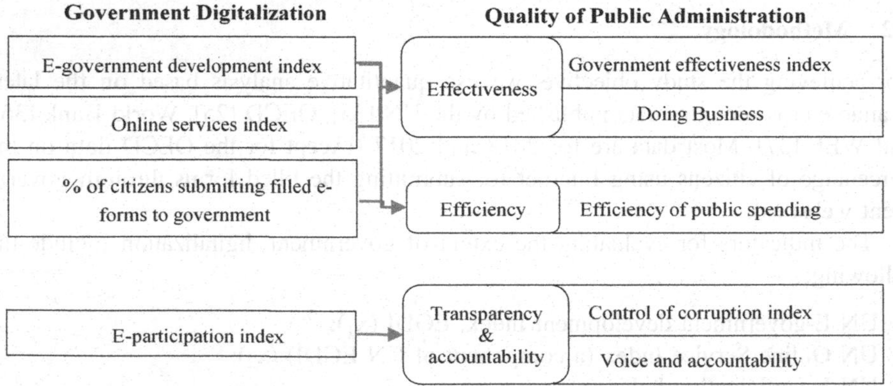

Fig. 1. The system of indicators and expected correlations

74 countries for which the data was available for all the above indicators were included in the analysis. For correlation analysis, Pearson correlation coefficients were calculated.

For performing casualty analysis between the indicators reflecting the extent of government digitalization, on the one hand, and the quality of public administration, on the other, Granger casualty test was used.

3 Key Results

3.1 Correlation Between the Quality of Public Administration and Digitalization

To identify the correlation between the indicators characterizing the quality of public administration and the extent of government digitalization, we performed a correlation analysis based on the dataset of indicators listed in Sect. 2.2. The results of correlation analysis are summarized in Table 1.

Table 1. Matrix of Pearson correlation coefficients

	x_1	x_2	x_3	x_4	x_5	x_6	x_7	x_8	x_9
x_1	1								
x_2	0,779*	1							
x_3	0,718*	0,927*	1						
x_4	0,687*	0,375*	0,379*	1					
x_5	**0,838***	0,600*	0,529*	0,660*	1				
x_6	0,568*	0,355*	0,438*	0,560*	0,625*	1			
x_7	**0,795***	0,531*	0,472*	**0,733***	0,941*	0,671*	1		
x_8	0,416*	0,405*	0,284**	0,556*	0,532*	0,625*	0,503*	1	
x_9	**0,700***	0,495*	0,521*	0,570*	0,712*	0,451*	0,611*	0,339*	1

**results are statistically significant at* $p = 0.01$.

***p = .01 (p value shows that all results are statistically significant).*

The correlation analysis suggests a strong positive correlation between the UN E-government development index (EGDI) (x_1), on the one hand, and some indicators characterizing quality of public administration. The strongest correlation is estimated between EGDI (x_1) and government effectiveness (x_5) (Fig. 2).

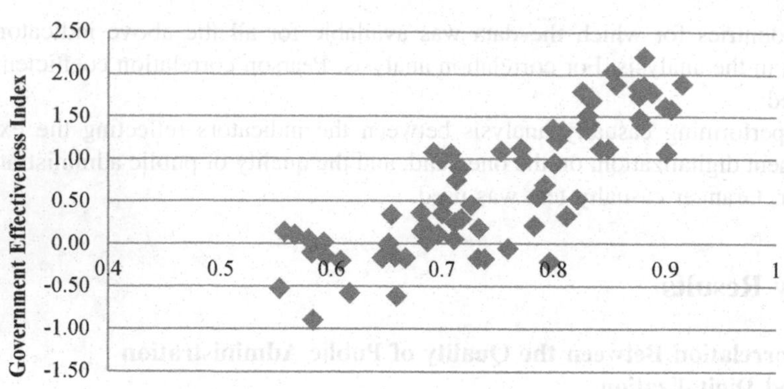

Fig. 2. Correlation between EGDI and WGI government effectiveness

There is also strong positive correlation between EGDI (x_1), on the one hand, and WGI control of corruption index (x_7), on the other. This result confirms the outcomes of some previous studies [15]. Notably, there is also strong correlation between EGDI (x_1) and Doing Business Index (x_9) which suggests that government digitalization is associated with better business climate (Fig. 3).

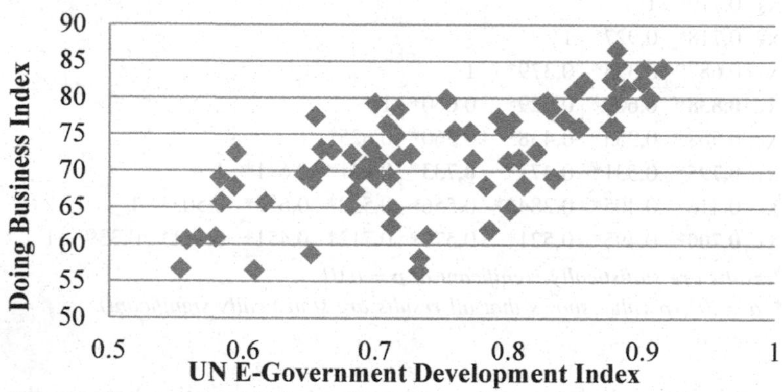

Fig. 3. Correlation between EGDI and Doing Business Index

Other governance indicators included into the study (WGI Voice and Accountability Index (x_6) and efficiency of government spending (x_8) also demonstrate statistically significant correlation with EGDI (x_1) though the strength of this correlation is lower (Table 1).

Noteworthy, the correlation between Online service index (x_2) and all indicators used for measuring public administration quality (x_5 – x_9) is weaker than the correlation between EGDI and the indicators used to measure government effectiveness, efficiency, transparency, and accountability. Such results confirm that it is not only availability of e-interaction with government that matters; government digitalization is in vain in case other components such as infrastructure and skills are missing. Due to comparatively low correlation between Online service index and the indicators characterizing the quality of public administration, we used EGDI for the purposes of further causality analysis.

Strong positive correlation has also been found between the percentage of citizens using Internet for submitting the filled forms through government websites (x_4), on the one hand, and control of corruption (x_7), on the other ($k = 0.733$). This result suggests that using electronic (rather than in-person) interaction with the government authorities has a significant anti-corruption effect.

Noteworthy, the correlation of the UN E-Participation Index with all indicators characterizing the quality of public administration is weaker than the one estimated for the UN EGDI. The weakest correlation was found between e-participation index and the effectiveness of governance spending. The correlation between EGDI and the WGI Voice and Accountability index is also weaker than the one for other WGI components included in this study. Such results suggest that the actual role of digitalization in improving government transparency and accountability may be exaggerated. On the other hand, the importance of voice and accountability for successful government digitalization may also be overestimated.

The study revealed statistically significant correlation between the efficiency of public spending, on the one hand, and some indicators reflecting government digitalization (UN EGDI (x_1) and the percentage of citizens using Internet for submitting the filled forms through government websites (x_4)). Such outcome can be explained by the fact that while digitalization of public services helps optimizing public expenditure [4], the share of such expenses in total budget spending is not that high. Subsequently, other factors which are not related to digitalization affect the efficiency of public spending.

Another explanation for weaker correlation between the efficiency of public spending and digitalization relates to the fact that not all e-government initiatives have resulted in any substantial savings even in the most advanced e-government contexts [23].

While in-depth analysis of regional differences goes beyond the scope of this paper, it should be noted that the strength of correlation between EGDI (x_1) and public administration quality parameters may vary in different groups of countries. For instance, in transition economies of Europe and Central Asia (19 countries in our sample), Pearson correlation coefficient between EGDI (x_1) and Doing Business Index (x_9) is 0.776 which suggests stronger relationship than estimated for the total sample (0.700). At the same time, other correlation coefficients for transition economy group are lower; no statistically significant correlation was found between EGDI (x_1) and efficiency of government spending (x_8) in transition economies. The latter result suggests that transition countries have so far gained less economy from government digitalization.

3.2 Quality of Public Administration and Government Digitalization: Causality Test

For the purposes of the paper, Granger Causality tests were run to determine the casualty between the extent government digitalization (UN EGDI (x_1)), on the one hand, and quality of public administration (indicators $x_5 - x_9$), on the other. Granger causality test assumes that an evolving variable *x* is a cause of evolving variable *y* if predictions of the variable *y* value in the future based on its own past and on the past of variable *x* are better than predictions of *y* based only on its own past values. The results of estimations are summarized in Table 2.

Table 2. Granger causality test between E-government development index and public administration quality indicators: P-values for Null Hypotheses (H_0)

Lag	$x_1 \rightarrow x_5$	$x_5 \rightarrow x_1$	$x_1 \rightarrow x_6$	$x_6 \rightarrow x_1$	$x_1 \rightarrow x_7$	$x_7 \rightarrow x_1$	$x_1 \rightarrow x_8$	$x_8 \rightarrow x_1$	$x_1 \rightarrow x_9$	$x_9 \rightarrow x_1$
2	0.670	0.719	0.134	0.121	0.479	0.558	0.629	0.715	0.068	0.438
3	0.859	0.935	0.070	0.077	0.825	0.447	0,899	0.615	0.003	0.075
4	0.758	0.967	0.205	0.156	0.632	0.633	0,399	0,631		
5	0.538	0.809	0.210	0.184	0.409	0.437	0,543	0,655		
H_0	Accepted	Accepted	Accepted	Accepted	Accepted	Accepted	Accepted	Accepted	Rejected	Rejected

Granger causality test results suggest that, in most cases reviewed, no direct cause-and-effect relationship can be established between the extent of government digitalization, on the one hand, and public administration quality parameters – on the other. Thus, there is no direct causality between UN EGDI, on the one hand, and government effectiveness, voice and accountability, control of corruption, and efficiency of public expenditures, on the other. However, in one instance direct cause and effect relationship was established: with probability of 0.3%, UN EGDI causes the changes in Doing Business index.

4 Discussion of Findings and Conclusion

The results we obtained suggest that there is a statistically significant correlation between the extent of government digitalization (measured based on the UN EGDI) and the parameters of quality of public administration. Notably, for some parameters such as WGI government effectiveness index, control of corruption, and the WB Doing Business index this correlation is strong (k $\geq$ 0.7). These findings support the results of some earlier studies on correlation between governance indicators and digitalization which involved different datasets [6, 7, 30].

However, despite the strong correlation between the government digitalization and public administration performance, the hypothesis that there is a direct cause and effect relationship between the two has been confirmed only partially. Yes, e-government development is a cause for improving business climate as measured by Doing Business Index (with error probability of 0.3%). Simultaneously, Granger test results suggest that there is no direct cause and effect relationship between e-government development and other governance indicators (including WGI indicators and effectiveness of public spending). Thus, public administration performance and e-government development are correlated but the dynamics of these indicators are likely determined by some other external factors.

Overall, several reasons may explain such findings. Firstly, in most countries digital governance is at its early stages of maturity while the positive effects of digital transformation are expected mostly at later stages of the process [8]. While digitalization of G2B interactions is more advanced, the effect of digitalization on businesses is already evident; the positive effects related to other types of interactions (G2C, G2E, G2G) are yet to come. Hence, while the correlation between government digitalization and public administrative quality is evident, more time is needed to reap digital dividends for most stakeholders and for this additional public value to be reflected in the estimates used for measuring governance effectiveness and efficiency.

Secondly, the findings may be at least partially attributed to the limitations of aggregate governance indicators noted in literature and related both to misinterpretations and omissions of data [2] and insufficient accounting for regional specifics [11]. It is therefore highly possible that using regional data sub-sets or data sub-sets based on country income groups and broadening the set of governance indicators based on regional statistics or statistics for other country groups, including citizens perceptions, could allow for formulating more decisive conclusions as to whether it is digitalization that makes governments effective or it is good government that makes digitalization happen. Such analysis is beyond the scope of this paper but appears to be a promising direction for the future studies.

Thirdly, most indicators used for the study are based on changing methodology which limits comparisons over time (see for instance [32]) and, hence, does not allow for using significant time lags for testing causality. As a result, our hypothesis could not be tested based on a long time series data.

Finally, the methodology used by the UN for constructing EGDI does not capture all dimensions of digital governance. For instance, online service index assessment is based on official websites survey and may omit both implementation of other types of digital technologies (i.e. m-government applications, Internet kiosks, big data, cloud computing, etc.) and using digital technologies for other governance purposes not directly related to rendering public services or publishing data (i.e., using ICT for regulation, enforcement, inspections, decision-making, etc.). While the index accounts for ICT infrastructure development it does not account for the uptake of e-services among citizens and businesses. In the countries where the public services are at least partially digitalized but most of the citizens still do not use digital services (do not interact with public bodies in electronic form) as is the case for Russia [5], the EGDI would be high but this result would not translate into raising government effectiveness or efficiency based on implementation of new technologies. Thus, the findings confirm the need for improving the methodology for measuring government digitalization to account for new digital technologies (as identified, for instance, in [17]) and ways of application thereof. To-date there is no alternative indicators which would cover comparable set of countries and could be free from the limitation listed above.

Noteworthy, the results of the analysis conducted suggest that the correlation of the UN E-Participation Index with all indicators characterizing the quality of public administration is weaker than the one estimated for the UN EGDI. These findings correspond to the results of the recent research which demonstrated surprisingly weak correlation between E-Participation index and the indicators used for measuring Civil Society Participation and Direct Democracy [6].

5 Recommendations

The findings of our quantitative analysis have important policy implications. Firstly, the lack of direct cause and effect relationship between government digitalization, on the one hand, and public administration quality on the other, demonstrates that digital government is not a more effective or efficient or transparent government by default. Digitalization does not automatically lead to additional public value. Achieving this additional value calls for transforming government internal and external processes in the interests of the final beneficiaries of such processes – citizens, businesses, other government agencies or government employees. Secondly, since the benefits for businesses from digitalization are more evident (and indeed there is direct causality between e-government development and ease of doing business), achieving digital-driven benefits for citizens requires special attention and efforts. Thirdly, while there is statistically significant correlation between digitalization and efficiency of public spending, it is much weaker than the correlation between EGDI and other governance indicators included in this study. Hence, achieving the savings objective as part of the digitalization effort calls for special efforts, such as introducing transaction costs measurement and monitoring, developing business cases for ICT projects, etc.

As most OECD countries as well as countries from other regions are in the process of digital strategies implementation, the issue of causality between the government digitalization, on the one hand, and quality of government on the other retains its importance. The prospective areas of research include cluster analyses aimed at identifying the factors supporting successful digital transformation and regional and sub-regional studies aimed at identifying cause and effect relationship for various aspects of government digitalization. This work would call for designing additional sets of indicators factoring in the Web 3.0 technologies and measuring not only the extent of digitalization of public services but also other aspects of digital transformation in government. Such prospective indicators should focus not only on infrastructure and other inputs (for instance, digitalized services available) and outputs (i.e., uptake of such services by citizens and businesses) but also on outcomes (the effects which the uptake of digital services has on the society).

References

1. Bannister, F., Connolly, R.: ICT, public values and transformative government: a framework and programme for research. Gov. Inform. Q. **31**(1), 119–128 (2014). https://doi.org/10.1016/j.giq.2013.06.002

2. Bersch, K., Botero, S.: Measuring governance: implications of conceptual choices. Eur. J. Dev. Res. **26**(1), 124–141 (2014). https://doi.org/10.1057/ejdr.2013.49
3. Burov, V., Petrov, M., Shklyaruk, M., Sharov, A.: Gosudarstvo kak-platforma: podhod k realizacii vysokotekhnologichnoj sistemy gosudarstvennogo upravleniya [Government as a platform: approach to implementing high tech system of public administration]. Gosudarstvennaya sluzhba **20**(3), 6–17 (2018). (in Russian)
4. Dobrolyubova, E., Alexandrov, O.: E-government in Russia: meeting growing demand in the era of budget constraints. In: Chugunov, A.V., Bolgov, R., Kabanov, Y., Kampis, G., Wimmer, M. (eds.) DTGS 2016. CCIS, vol. 674, pp. 247–257. Springer, Cham (2016). https://doi.org/10.1007/978-3-319-49700-6_23
5. Dobrolyubova, E., Alexandrov, O., Yefremov, A.: Is Russia ready for digital transformation? In: Alexandrov, D.A., Boukhanovsky, A.V., Chugunov, A.V., Kabanov, Y., Koltsova, O. (eds.) DTGS 2017. CCIS, vol. 745, pp. 431–444. Springer, Cham (2017). https://doi.org/10.1007/978-3-319-69784-0_36
6. Durkiewicz, J., Janowski, T.: Is digitalization improving governance quality? Correlating analog and digital benchmarks. In: Proceedings of the 18th European Conference on Digital Government ECDG 2018, pp. 48–56. Academic Conferences and Publishing International Limited (2018)
7. Garcia-Murillo, M.: Does a government web presence reduce perceptions of corruption? Inform. Technol. Dev. **19**(2), 151–175 (2013). https://doi.org/10.1080/02681102.2012.751574
8. Gartner: 5 Levels of Digital Government Maturity, 6 November 2017. https://www.gartner.com/smarterwithgartner/5-levels-of-digital-government-maturity/. Accessed 15 Dec 2018
9. Girish, J., Gulati, J., Williams, C.B., Yates, D.J.: Predictors of on-line services and e-participation: a cross-national comparison. Gov. Inform. Q. **31**(4), 526–533 (2014). https://doi.org/10.1016/j.giq.2014.07.005
10. Heidelberg, C.A.: Citizens, not consumers. In: Weerakkody, V., Janssen, M., Dwivedi, Y. (eds.) Handbook of Research on ICT-Enabled Transformational Government: A Global Perspective. IGI Global (2009). https://doi.org/10.4018/978-1-60566-390-6
11. Huque, A., Patamawadee, J.: The challenge of assessing governance in Asian states: Hong Kong in the Worldwide governance indicators ranking. Asian J. Polit. Sci. **26**, 1–16 (2018). https://doi.org/10.1080/02185377.2018.1485587
12. Ivančić, L., Vuksic, V., Vugec, Dalia, S.: A preliminary literature review of digital transformation case studies. In: ICMIT 2018: 20th International Conference on Managing Information Technology, vol. 12, no. 9, pp. 737–742 (2018)
13. Janssen, M., Estevez, E.: Lean government and platform-based governance-doing more with less. Gov. Inform. Q. **30**, 1–8 (2013). https://doi.org/10.1016/j.giq.2012.11.003
14. Krishnan, S., Teo, T., Lim, V.: Examining the relationships among e-government maturity, corruption, economic prosperity and environmental degradation: a cross-country analysis. Inf. Manag. **50**(8), 638–649 (2013). https://doi.org/10.1016/j.im.2013.07.003
15. Kossow, N.: Digitising the Anti-corruption sphere: taking stock and looking ahead (2018). https://ecpr.eu/Filestore/PaperProposal/a7770504-e63d-4f96-9a50-9448b15c74c7.pdf. Accessed 08 Feb 2019
16. Lindgren, I., van Veenstra, A.F.: Digital government transformation: a case illustrating public e-service development as part of public sector transformation. In: DGO 2018 Proceedings of the 19th Annual International Conference on Digital Government Research (2018). https://doi.org/10.1145/3209281.3209302

17. Máchová, R., Lněnička, M.: Reframing E-government development indices with respect to new trends in ICT. Rev. Econ. Perspect. **15**(4), 383–412 (2015)
18. Makowski, G.: From weber to the Web… can ICT reduce bureaucratic corruption? In: Paulin, A.A., Anthopoulos, L.G., Reddick, C.G. (eds.) Beyond Bureaucracy. PAIT, vol. 25, pp. 291–312. Springer, Cham (2017). https://doi.org/10.1007/978-3-319-54142-6_16
19. Margetts, H., Dunleavy, P.: The second wave of digital-era governance: a quasi-paradigm for government on the Web. Philos. Trans. R. Soc. **371**(1987) (2013). https://doi.org/10.1098/rsta.2012.0382
20. Martin, A.: Digital literacy and the "digital society". Digit. Literacies Concepts Policies Pract. **30**, 151–176 (2008)
21. Mkude, C.G., Wimmer, M.A.: Strategic aspects for successful E-government systems design: insights from a survey in Germany. In: Janssen, M., Scholl, H.J., Wimmer, M.A., Bannister, F. (eds.) EGOV 2014. LNCS, vol. 8653, pp. 301–312. Springer, Heidelberg (2014). https://doi.org/10.1007/978-3-662-44426-9_25
22. Müller, S., Abildgaard Skau, S.: Success factors influencing implementation of e-government at different stages of maturity: a literature review. Int. J. Electron. Gov. **7**, 136 (2015)
23. National Audit Office: Digital transformation in government (2017). https://www.nao.org.uk/wp-content/uploads/2017/03/Digital-transformation-in-government.pdf. Accessed 08 Feb 2019
24. OECD Recommendation of the Council on Digital Government Strategies (2014). http://www.oecd.org/gov/digital-government/Recommendation-digital-government-strategies.pdf. Accessed 08 Feb 2019
25. OECD Government at a Glance 2017. http://www.oecd.org/gov/govataglance.htm. Accessed 08 Feb 2019
26. O'Reilly, T.: Government as a Platform. Innov. Technol. Gov. Glob. **6**(1), 13–40 (2011)
27. Reis, J., Amorim, M., Melão, N., Matos, P.: Digital transformation: a literature review and guidelines for future research. In: Rocha, Á., Adeli, H., Reis, L.P., Costanzo, S. (eds.) WorldCIST'18 2018. AISC, vol. 745, pp. 411–421. Springer, Cham (2018). https://doi.org/10.1007/978-3-319-77703-0_41
28. Shounak, P.: Where can we improve? A cross-country comparison of factors affecting eGovernment success (2016). https://ssrn.com/abstract=2872178 or http://dx.doi.org/10.2139/ssrn.2872178. Assessed 08 Feb 2019
29. Srivastava, S., Thompson, T.: E-government payoffs: evidence from cross-country data. JGIM **15**, 20–40 (2007)
30. Starke, C., Naab, T.K., Scherer, H.: Free to expose corruption: The impact of media freedom, internet access and governmental online service delivery on corruption. Int. J. Commun. **10**, 4702–4722 (2016)
31. Stier, S.: Political determinants of e-government performance revisited: Comparing democracies and autocracies. Gov. Inf. Q. **32**(3), 270–278 (2015). https://doi.org/10.1016/j.giq.2015.05.004
32. Thomas, M.: Eur. J. Dev. Res. **22**, 31 (2010). https://doi.org/10.1057/ejdr.2009.32
33. UN E-Government Survey 2018. https://publicadministration.un.org/egovkb/en-us/Reports/UN-E-Government-Survey-2018. Accessed 08 Feb 2019
34. Westerman, G., Calmé, J.C., Bonnet, D., Ferraris, P., McAfee, A.: Digital Transformation: A Roadmap For Billion-Dollar Organizations, pp. 1–68. MIT Sloan Management, MIT Center for Digital Business and Capgemini Consulting (2011)

35. World Bank: Digital Dividends. World Development Report (2016) http://documents.worldbank.org/curated/en/896971468194972881/pdf/102725-PUB-Replacement-PUBLIC.pdf. Accessed 15 Jan 2019
36. World Bank: Worldwide Government Indicators (2018). http://info.worldbank.org/governance/wgi/#home. Accessed 30 Jan 2019
37. World Economic Forum: The Global Competitiveness Report 2017–2018. https://www.weforum.org/reports/the-global-competitiveness-report-2017-2018. Accessed 30 Jan 2019

Processing and Analysis of Russian Strategic Planning Programs

Nikita Alekseychuk[1], Veronika Sarkisyan[1], Anton Emelyanov[2], and Ekaterina Artemova[1(✉)]

[1] National Research University Higher School of Economics, Moscow, Russia
echernyak@hse.ru

[2] Moscow Institute of Physics and Technology, Moscow, Russia

Abstract. In this paper, we present a project on the analysis of an extensive corpus of strategic planning documents, devoted to various aspects of the development of Russian regions. The main purposes of the project are: (1) to extract different aspects of goal setting and planning, (2) to form an ontology of goals and criteria of achieving these goals, (3) to measure the similarity between goals declared by federal and municipal subjects.

Such unsupervised Natural Language Processing (NLP) methods as phrase chunking, word embeddings, and latent topic modeling are used for information extraction and ontology construction as well as similarity computation. The resulting ontology should serve in short-term as a helper tool for writing strategic planning documents and in long-term resolve the need to compose strategic planning documents completely by navigating through the ontology and selecting relevant goals and criteria. The resulting similarity measure between federal and municipal goals will serve as a navigation tool for further analysis.

Keywords: Text mining · Topic modeling · Distributional semantics · Governmental strategic planning

1 Introduction

Recently the Russian government has decided to follow the Digital Economy approach. In the coming years, it is expected to achieve synergy between existing government routines (such as issuing a decree) and newly introduced solutions (e.g., Natural Language Processing (NLP)-based classifier for decrees). IT and AI technologies, such as Data Mining (DM), Machine Learning (ML), Deep Learning (DL), Natural Language Processing (NLP), and Text Mining (TM) are becoming widely used in various governmental tasks, including strategic planning, both to analyze collected and stored data and to optimize and automate decision making process in the future.

There are 85 federal subjects in Russia, divided further in municipal formations. The strategic planning of development is organized as follows: the priorities, such as medicine, education, etc., are defined on the state level, further detailed on the federal level. Each municipal formation is responsible for its

D. A. Alexandrov et al. (Eds.): DTGS 2019, CCIS 1038, pp. 68–81, 2019.
https://doi.org/10.1007/978-3-030-37858-5_6

planning, which should follow both state and federal priorities and goals. From a technological standpoint, the planning process results in composing text documents and publishing them online. Each state unit, responsible for strategic planning, composes and publishes each year a new document, devoted to various aspects of strategic planning. Although these documents have a similar structure, to our knowledge they have never been processed or analyzed automatically. We approach the following problems:

1. to extract development goals and criteria, to which extent the goals are reached
2. to create a unified ontology that connects goals and criteria and identifies higher-level goals and higher-level criteria
3. to build a framework and a visualization tool to compare federal goals and criteria with municipal goals and criteria.

For the reader's convenience, we denote short phrases that relate to goals and criteria, to which extent the goals are reached by goals and criteria, concisely.

The remainder is organized as follows. Section 2 reviews related works. Section 3 presents our pipeline of processing strategic planning documents. Next Subsections are devoted to the steps of our pipeline, including short descriptions of distributional semantics and topic models. The last section describes possible future work directions.

2 Related Works

2.1 Processing E-Government Documents

NLP allows to extract and structure information of governmental activity. Baturo and Dasandi [4] used topic modeling to analyze the agenda-setting process of the United Nations based on the UN General Debate corpus [16] consisting of over 7300 country statements from 1970 to 2014. Authors examined which topics were actively discussed during the investigated period, how topics interacted among themselves and related to structural factors such as population size, GDP, level of conflict, etc.

In [20] Shen et al. explored Web data and government websites in Beijing, Shanghai, Wuhan, Guangzhou and Chengdu to do comparative analysis on the development of the five metropolia e-governments. They extracted the first 30 high-frequency e-government words within the topics under study (standardization, communication, informationization, service, and security) with the help of self-made ROST Content Mining System.

Albarghothi et al. [1] introduced an Automatic Extraction Dataset System (AEDS) tool that constructs an ontology-based Semantic Web from Arabic web pages related to Dubai's e-government services. The system automatically extracts data from the website, detects keywords, and finally maps the page to ontology via Protégé tool.

2.2 Processing Petitions

Natural language processing techniques are widely used for the analysis of public opinion and matching it with governmental policies. E-petitions have emerged as a popular tool for expressing public opinion. Therefore there is a need in a tool for aggregating and summating of petition texts.

The concept of e-democracy implicates open communication between government and citizens, which in most cases involves the processing of a large amount of unstructured textual information [18]. Rao and Dey describe the scheme of citizens' and stakeholders' participation in Indian e-governance which allows the government to collect feedback from citizens and correct policies and acts according to it.

In 2009, the second conference on "Working Together to Strengthen Our Nation's Democracy" in the U.S. resulted in decision "to pursue discussions with the White House Office of Public Engagement, supply relevant information, including case material". Under this program, Evangelopoulos and Visinescu [9] had access to the corpus of appeals to the U.S. government, in particular, SMS messages from Africans, sent during Barack Obama's visit to Ghana in July 2009 and data from SAVE Award - initiative, aiming to make the U.S. government more effective and efficient at spending taxpayers' money. For each of the corpus, authors extracted key topics with Latent Semantic Analysis (LSA) to explore trends in public opinion.

Similar online petition portal named e-People exists in the Republic of Korea. In [21] Suh et al. applied keyword extraction algorithms based on $tf - idf$ and K-means clustering to detect and track petitions groups. Additionally, they used radial basis function neural networks to forecast the future trend of petitions.

2.3 Processing Documents in Russian

Several Russian research groups have reported on social studies that are based on using natural language processing or text mining techniques. [14] explore the attitude of news agencies towards the Russian-Ukrainian conflict using topic modeling, [13] use classification algorithms to detect interethnic hostility on social media, following [2], who use topic modeling for mining ethnic-related content from Russian-language blogosphere. Opinion mining and sentiment analysis are in focus, too: for example, the authors of the paper [8] try to predict humor, while in [7] a general-aimed sentiment classification system is developed. Finally, in [10,12] new language resource such as thesauri, aimed at socio-political topics, are built.

3 Our Pipeline

3.1 Raw Data Processing

Raw strategic planning programs can be easily downloaded from the web page of the Strategic Planning Centre (https://strategy.csr.ru) or any other related

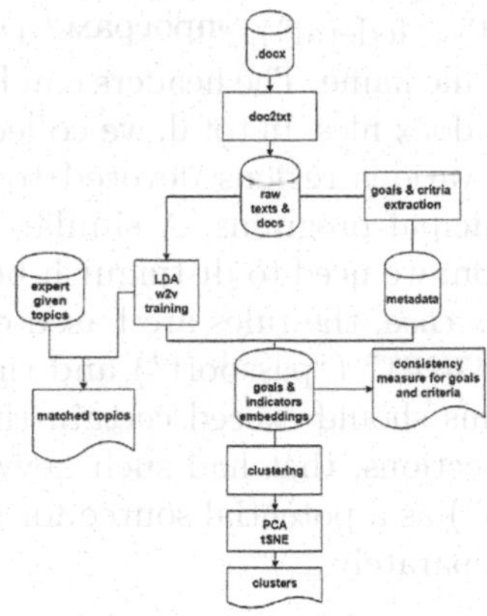

Fig. 1. Our pipeline for processing Strategic Planning Programs

governmental source. The strategic planning programs are distributed mainly in .doc, .rtf or .docx files. The easiest file formats to process are .docx files since they can be easily parsed as XML trees. One of the tools to use for processing .docx files is python-docx package[1] (Fig. 1).

In total, we downloaded around 70K files from the web. Not all of these files should be used for further analysis, since they contain other types of documents, such as financial plans, reports, etc.

The processing of raw data consists of the following steps:

1. convert .rtf and .doc files to .docx files;
2. extract all tables separately from .docx files;
3. extract raw texts separately from .docx files.

We distinguish between tables and texts while processing raw data, since some (but not all) strategic planning programs have special tables, addressed as "program passport" where there are special fields for desired development goals and criteria. The raw texts would be used further not only to extract development goals and criteria but also to train both topic and embedding models and would be addressed as Strategic planning programs corpus.

3.2 Strategic Planning Program Classification

The downloaded corpus consists not only of strategic planning programs. There are other types of documents that fall out of the scope of the current project. This way it is necessary to distinguish between financial plans, reports and desired federal and municipal strategic planning documents. To do this, we developed a simple rule-based classifier that divides a document into three classes: the municipal program, the federal program, and other. The rules included regular expressions that search for relevant keywords and their stems, such as "муниципал"

[1] https://python-docx.readthedocs.io.

("municipal"), "**федеральн**" ("federal"), "**програм**" ("program") in the header of the text and in the actual file name. The headers can be easily found by parsing XML trees, extracted from .docx files. In total, we collected and estimated about 5K federal programs from various regions devoted to various aspects of planning and around 25K municipal programs. A similar rule-based approach was applied to table classification: we need to distinguish between program passport and any other table. In this case, the rules are based on the following features: occurrence of the word "**паспорт**" ("passport") and the shape of the table (the number of rows and columns should exceed certain thresholds). From the raw texts, we extracted those sections, that had such keywords as "**цель**" ("goal") or "**индикатор**" ("criterion") as a potential source for goal and criteria phrases, and stored these sections separately.

3.3 Goal and Criteria Extraction

We extracted goals and criteria from the text in an unsupervised fashion. We noted that goals and criteria are usually formulated according to certain patterns. Let us provide a few examples:

- Goals: "**развитие дорожной сети в Мурманской области**" ("development of the road network in the Murmansk Region"), "**строительство новых больниц**" ("building new hospitals")
- Criteria:
"**количество пострадавших в дорожно-транспортных происшествиях**" ("the number of road traffic casualties"), "**доля смертей от болезней системы кровообращения**" ("the ratio of deaths from circulatory system diseases").

These examples can be generalized using the following formula: trigger word + noun phrase (NP) + location phrase (LP). We manually listed around a hundred trigger words for goals (such as "**увелечение**", "**развитие**", "**модернизация**", "**оптимизация**" ("increasing", "improving", "modernization", "optimization")) and around fifty trigger words ("**доля**", "**объем**", "**количество**", "**степень**" ("ratio", "volume", "number", "degree").

We used context-free parser Yargy[2] for the Russian language to define part of speech patterns for noun phrases, and location phrases and mystem[3] to identify toponyms. Next, we matched program passports and potential goal and criteria sections to the defined formula and extracted the desired goal and criteria phrases. We stripped location phrases. The last step resulted in more than 100K phrases, of which the majority occurred only once because of specific spelling or extraction mistakes. Finally, we lemmatized both the Strategic planning programs corpus and extracted goals and criteria using mystem again.

In the following sections, we describe the further analysis of the extracted goals and criteria.

[2] https://yargy.readthedocs.io/ru/latest/.
[3] https://tech.yandex.ru/mystem/.

3.4 Goal and Criteria Vectorization

Following common NLP approach [17,19], we needed to vectorize each goal and criteria, i.e. represent them in a common space of features to make further use of data mining algorithms possible. Currently, there are two major paradigms of text vectorization: namely, topic modeling [5] and distributional semantics [3], otherwise related to as word embedding models [17]. These approaches are based on a different understanding of what word similarity is: when a topic model is used, two words are similar if they share a common topic, or belong to the same domain. Word embeddings, on the other hand, use the notion of functional similarity: two words are considered similar if they are used in common contexts. We use both approaches and provide below more details on the methods and results.

Topic Modeling. Formally speaking, according to [22], a topic model of the corpus of documents D is the set topics T, the distribution of words $w_i \in V$ in topics $p(w|t)$ for all topics $t \in T$, the distribution of topics $t \in T$ in document $p(t|d)$ for all documents $d \in D$. The resulting topic model can be interpreted as soft clustering of both documents and words, where each document can belong to several topics (clusters) as well as each word can belong to several topics (clusters). Topic models are widely used in various applications such as information retrieval or text classification or as a standalone text mining tool.

We trained a topic model on the Strategic planning programs corpus. We used a popular topic modeling method, Latent Dirichlet Allocation [6], implemented in gensim[4] library, to build the topic model. We chose the number of topics to be equal to 200. The visualization of the final topic model is presented on the Fig. 2.

Although the topic model was interesting on its own and provided us with some useful insights of what are the topics and aspects of strategic planning in Russia, we used it mainly for vectorization of goals and criteria. The topic model allowed us to represent each goal and criteria as a vector with 200 dimensions, where each dimension stands for a single topic. After the topic model was trained, the parameters of distributions $p(w|t)$ and $p(t|d)$ were estimated, allowing us to determine the probability of a topic t to generate a document or a phrase, such as a goal or criteria. These probabilities formed the final topic vector for each goal and criteria.

Distributional Semantics and Word Embeddings. Word embedding models are another popular unsupervised technology in NLP. They are based on the simple observation, called "distributional hypothesis": words that occur in the same contexts tend to have similar meanings [11]. As a computational model of the distributional hypothesis so-called word-context matrices are constructed. While a word is a regular word or its lemma, a context can be defined differently. However the easiest definition of a context is based on using neighboring words of a given the

[4] https://radimrehurek.com/gensim/index.html.

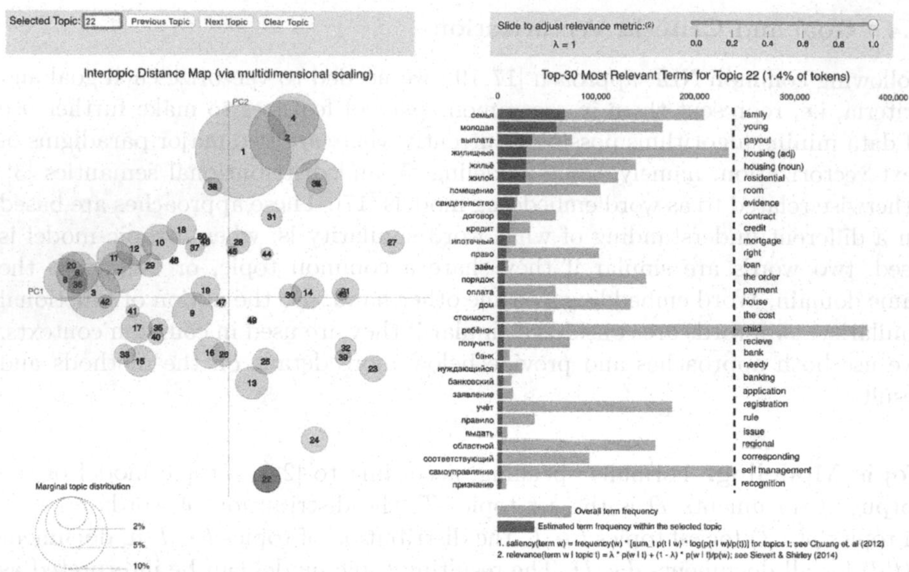

Fig. 2. Visualization of LDA topic model. Circles on the left represent topics and their relative importance, words on the right form topic # 22. The words are sorted according to their relative importance, too.

word in a window of size k, i.e., $k/2$ words to the left and the right. More complicated techniques use syntactic contexts [15]. The word embeddings are formed in the result of some form of word matrix decomposition. For example, singular value decomposition of co-occurrence word-context matrix results in a simpler kind of word embeddings, while more sophisticated trainable algorithms such as word2vec [17] (SGNS or CBOW) result in distributed word representation.

We again used gensim[5] library to train SGNS model [17] on the Strategic planning programs corpus. It is a common technique to test the quality of the word embedding model on word pairs, that are semantically related. If two words are related, they should be close in the word embeddings space; if they are not related, they should be far from each other. We manually created a set of such word pairs, that are relevant for the strategic planning domain and tested the trained word embedding models. A few examples, where the word embedding models capture the word relations correctly are presented in Fig. 3. Note that the word embeddings are trained for a single word.

To create vectors for goals and criteria using the word embedding model we exploited the following heuristic. Given a goal, we averaged embeddings of all words, which form the goal, with $tf - idf$ weights.

To compute the similarity between two vectors we, first, normed all vectors so that the length of each vector is equal to unity. Second, we used the Euclidean similarity function, which in this case is equal to the widely used cosine similarity function.

[5] https://radimrehurek.com/gensim/index.html.

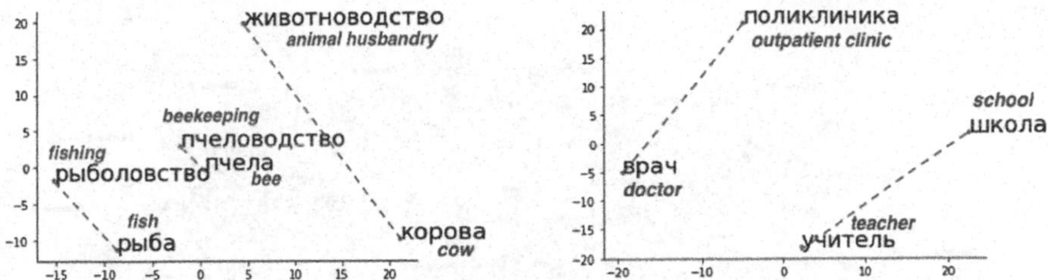

Fig. 3. An illustrative example word pair relations: (on the left) word paired "fish": "fishing", "bee": "beekeeping", "cow": "animal husbandry" lie in the same plane, however, the distance between "bee" and "beekeeping" is the shortest, most likely, because bee is the only subject to beekeeping, while there are many kinds of fishes and animals. On the right the same phenomena are illustrated.

Finally, we got two vectors for each goal and criteria: one was based on the topic model, second was based on the word embedding model. Both models were trained on Strategic planning programs corpus, which is large enough to get the models of high quality.

To sum up, there are two approaches for goal and criteria vectorization: the topic modeling based approach and the word embeddings based approach. These approaches can be compared by understanding what kind of word similarity they reveal. The first one reveals more of topical similarity (i.e. two words belong to the same domain, such as "doctor" and "hospital" belong to the same domain), while the latter reveals the functional similarity (i.e., two goals are used in similar contexts, such as "doctor" and "teacher"). To apply these vectorization approaches for goals and criteria, we need:

1. Topic modeling based approach: to use inference mode for the topic model and infer vectors for goals and criteria;
2. Word embeddings approach average embeddings of all words, which form the goal, with $tf - idf$ weights.

3.5 Goal and Criteria Clustering

Our preliminary analysis showed, that there are a lot of similar goals, such as "сбор и утилизация бытовых отходов" ("collection and disposal of household waste") and "сбор и вывоз мусора" ("garbage collection and disposal"). We used a clustering algorithm to merge such similar goals. Formally speaking, we selected goals with co-occurrence higher than some threshold and clustered corresponding word embedding vectors using K-means algorithm with K equal to 2K. The 2-dimensional visualization of goals and selected clusters is presented in Fig. 4;

Finally, we considered the centroid of each cluster as its representative. This way we reduced the number of goals to 2K and the final list of unique and most important goals extracted from the strategic planning documents.

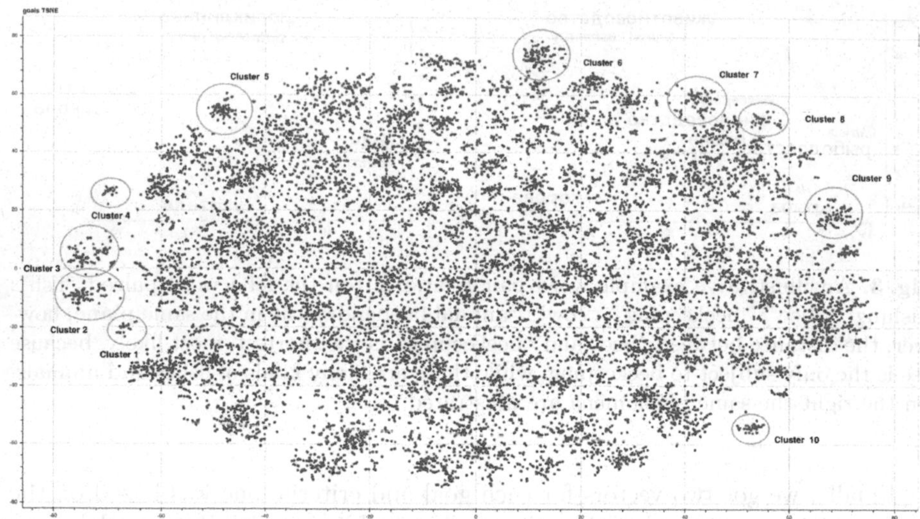

Fig. 4. t-SNE visualization of goals. **Cluster 1:** development of socially oriented non-profit organization sector; **cluster 2:** archive documents storage; **cluster 3:** preservation of library collections; **cluster 4:** creating a uniform cultural space

3.6 Goal and Criteria Matching

During the last step, we needed to match goals with criteria and form the desired ontology. The overview of the ontology is presented in Table 1. The first column stands for the ID of the LDA topic. The second column stands for the goal (the centroid of a cluster, see Subsect. 3.5), which is related to this topic. Next column presents a short list of matched criteria, while the long list is presented in the last column. The shorter version is achieved by clustering all matched criteria in $N/5$ clusters, where N is the total number of matched criteria. The fourth column presents the cluster of goals.

Table 1. The desired ontology design

Topic ID	Goal (centroid)	Criteria (centroids)	Cluster of goals	Cluster of criteria

We need to admit that exact matching between goals and criteria cannot be extracted from the original unprocessed data due to the difference in formats and technical issues of parsing the raw data. To form the desired ontology, the following steps are conducted:

1. Find up to three relevant topics for each centroid of goal clusters using the inference of the topic model;
2. Find criteria that (a) co-occur with the centroid or any other goal from the goal cluster more than three times and (b) that have high similarity using

either topic model or word embeddings model with the goal centroid; at this point, we achieve a long list of criteria, say, its length is N;
3. Cluster all criteria in $N/5$ clusters using word embeddings representation of criteria. If $N < 5$ this step is omitted.

Two illustrative examples of the entries in the resulting ontology are provided in Tables 2 and 3. For the sake of space, we omit the whole clusters of goals and centroids and provide manually chosen topic names instead of their computational IDs.

Table 2. An example of ontology entry

Topic ID	Труд, занятость (employment)
Goal (centroid)	Снижение уровня общей безработицы (Unemployment decrease)
Criteria (centroids)	Уровень безработицы (Unemployment rate), количество ярмарок вакансий (number of job fairs)

Table 3. An example of ontology entry

Topic ID	Безопасность (safety)
Goal (centroid)	Снижение гибели и травматизма людей на водных объектах (reduction of death and injuries of people on water bodies)
Criteria (centroids)	Количество обученных спасателей (number of trained rescuers), Количество оборудованных мест массового отдыха на водных объектах (the number of equipped places for mass recreation on water bodies)

The resulting ontology enumerates more than 7K entries, following the design, presented in Table 1. Thoroughly expert evaluation of the whole body of the ontology needs to be conducted as an obligatory direction for future work.

3.7 Municipal and Federal Matching

There arises another analytical task: since we got strategic goals on different levels of country division, namely, federal and municipal divisions, we were able to evaluate, whether the strategic goals of a municipal formation coincide and are consistent with the strategic goals of a federal subject. We may expect municipal formation to follow the strategy of a federal subject to a certain degree, although this is not necessary. However, even if the municipal formation follows the strategy of the regional subject, the wording of the goals still might be different. Hence we needed to exploit more sophisticated NLP techniques rather than straightforward word matching. Another reason to apply NLP techniques here is that the regional subject might set quite a broad goal, such as "развитие сельского хозяйства" ("agricultural development"), the municipal formation may choose to concentrate on the particular part of this goal, such as "развитие овцеводства" ("sheep breeding development"). Although the word2vec embeddings we calculated beforehand are not meant to capture such hierarchical relations, we still tried to use it for this task, since little end-to-end algorithms for discovery of hierarchical relations are available.

In the previous steps, we calculated goal embeddings for each municipal and federal subject. To calculate the matching between federal and municipal formation we constructed a similarity matrix in such a way that its rows represented goals of municipal formation and columns represented goals of regional subjects. The weights of the matrix represented cosine similarity (cossim) between corresponding embeddings. Further on, the following metric was used:

$$M = \frac{\sum \text{cossim of the closest goals for the current regional subject}}{\text{number of goals of the regional subject}} \times \frac{\sum \text{cossim of the closest goals for the current municipal formation}}{\text{number of goals of the municipal formation}} \quad (1)$$

By term **cossim of the closest goals for the current regional subject** we imply column-wise maximum of the matrix (row-wise respectively for municipal formations). The interpretation of this operation is to find the closest goal of municipal (regional) formation for every municipal (regional) goal. Note that the metric, defined in Eq. 1 varies between 0 and 1, which makes different regional subject-municipal formation pairs consistently comparable. The closer to unity, the more similar are the goals of the municipal formations to the goals of the regional subject, the closer to 0 – the more diverse they are.

After all, metrics are calculated, we got the list of municipal formations and corresponding regional subjects along with the similarity scores. We averaged these scores for the visualization of the whole Russian map or to plot one region as it can be seen below in Fig. 5.

Fig. 5. (On the left) Rating of Russian regions: goals consistency measure; (On the right) goals consistency measure for Vologda region. The green color indicates the values of the cosine similarity measure: the brighter the color is, the closer are the values to unity. The grey color means no data is provided.

4 Conclusions and Future Work

In this paper, we present an ongoing project on the analysis of the strategic planning documents. We explore a part of the corpus of strategic planning documents that consist of strategic planning programs only. We limit our scope to the extraction and analysis of strategic goals and criteria for achieving these goals. In this direction, the following tasks are considered:

- development of the pipeline for downloading, parsing and processing of strategic planning documents;
- extraction of keywords that stand for strategic goals and criteria (addressed throughout as goals and criteria) using rule-based NLP techniques;
- training and visualization of a topic model along with a model of word embeddings, that allow two types of goals and criteria vectorization, used further to compute the similarity measure between goals and criteria;
- construction of the ontology of the goals and criteria that presents the whole scope of strategic goal settings;
- visualization of the suggested consistency measure that shows how consistent are the goals of a municipal formation are by the goals of a federal subject.

The main contributions of the paper are the following. Firstly, we use well-known and purely computational techniques that require little manual tuning, to create an ontology of strategic goals and criteria to achieve these goals. This ontology might be of future use for those who compose strategic planning documents, as it unifies different wording of goals and criteria. Secondly, we develop a measure that is capable of capturing hierarchical semantic relations between phrases, of evaluating the consistency of planning of federal subjects and their municipal formations. This measure is visualized on a map, which provides an analytical tool to manage and evaluate the strategic planning process in municipal formations. Thirdly, our approach and pipeline can be easily adapted to any other domain, where semi-structured documents are available. In this project, we were able to avoid manual or crowd-sourcing annotation of the documents for further training of extraction algorithms due to a specific style of writing and usage of certain noun phrase patterns. In any other domain which obtains the same linguistics specifics, our approach is applicable.

The future work directions include, but are not limited to manual evaluation of the constructed ontology and the consistency measure. Each step of our pipeline can be evaluated by computing descriptive statistics, such as the number of correctly extracted/clustered/defined as similar items and the number of missed or incorrectly processed items. This evaluation is, however, rather time-consuming and requires expert knowledge, so the procedure of the evaluation is still under development.

References

1. Albarghothi, A., Saber, W., Shaalan, K.: Automatic construction of e-government services ontology from Arabic webpages. Procedia Comput. Sci. **142**, 104–113 (2018)
2. Apishev, M., Koltcov, S., Koltsova, O., Nikolenko, S., Vorontsov, K.: Mining ethnic content online with additively regularized topic models. Computacion y Sistemas **20**(3), 387–403 (2016)
3. Baroni, M., Dinu, G., Kruszewski, G.: Don't count, predict! A systematic comparison of context-counting vs. context-predicting semantic vectors. In: Proceedings of the 52nd Annual Meeting of the Association for Computational Linguistics (Volume 1: Long Papers), vol. 1, pp. 238–247 (2014)
4. Baturo, A., Dasandi, N.: What drives the international development agenda? An NLP analysis of the united nations general debate 1970–2016. In: 2017 International Conference on the Frontiers and Advances in Data Science (FADS), pp. 171–176. IEEE (2017)
5. Blei, D.M.: Probabilistic topic models. Commun. ACM **55**(4), 77–84 (2012)
6. Blei, D.M., Ng, A.Y., Jordan, M.I.: Latent dirichlet allocation. J. Mach. Learn. Res. **3**, 993–1022 (2003)
7. Chetviorkin, I., Loukachevitch, N.: Evaluating sentiment analysis systems in Russian. In: Proceedings of the 4th Biennial International Workshop on Balto-Slavic Natural Language Processing, pp. 12–17 (2013)
8. Ermilov, A., Murashkina, N., Goryacheva, V., Braslavski, P.: Stierlitz meets SVM: humor detection in Russian. In: Ustalov, D., Filchenkov, A., Pivovarova, L., Žižka, J. (eds.) AINL 2018. CCIS, vol. 930, pp. 178–184. Springer, Cham (2018). https://doi.org/10.1007/978-3-030-01204-5_17
9. Evangelopoulos, N., Visinescu, L.: Text-mining the voice of the people. Commun. ACM **55**(2), 62–69 (2012)
10. Galieva, A., Kirillivich, A., Loukachevitch, N., Nevzorova, O., Suleymanov, D., Yakubova, D.: Russian-tatar socio-political thesaurus: publishing in the linguistic linked open data cloud. Int. J. Open Inf. Technol. **5**(11), 64–73 (2017)
11. Harris, Z.S.: Distributional structure. Word **10**(2–3), 146–162 (1954)
12. Kirillovich, A., Nevzorova, O., Gimadiev, E., Loukachevitch, N.: RuThes cloud: towards a multilevel linguistic linked open data resource for Russian. In: Różewski, P., Lange, C. (eds.) KESW 2017. CCIS, vol. 786, pp. 38–52. Springer, Cham (2017). https://doi.org/10.1007/978-3-319-69548-8_4
13. Koltsova, O., Alexeeva, S., Nikolenko, S., Koltsov, M.: Measuring prejudice and ethnic tensions in user-generated content. Annu. Rev. Cybertherapy Telemed. **2017**, 76 (2017)
14. Koltsova, O., Pashakhin, S.: Agenda divergence in a developing conflict: quantitative evidence from Ukrainian and Russian TV newsfeeds. Media War Confl., 1750635219829876 (2017)
15. Levy, O., Goldberg, Y.: Dependency-based word embeddings. In: Proceedings of the 52nd Annual Meeting of the Association for Computational Linguistics (Volume 2: Short Papers), vol. 2, pp. 302–308 (2014)
16. Mikhaylov, S., Baturo, A., Dasandi, N.: United nations general debate corpus (2017). https://doi.org/10.7910/DVN/0TJX8Y
17. Mikolov, T., Sutskever, I., Chen, K., Corrado, G.S., Dean, J.: Distributed representations of words and phrases and their compositionality. In: Advances in Neural Information Processing Systems, pp. 3111–3119 (2013)

18. Rao, G.K., Dey, S.: Decision support for e-governance: a text mining approach. arXiv preprint arXiv:1108.6198 (2011)
19. Salton, G., Wong, A., Yang, C.S.: A vector space model for automatic indexing. Commun. ACM **18**(11), 613–620 (1975)
20. Shen, Y., Liu, Z., Luo, S., Fu, H., Li, Y.: Empirical research on e-government based on content mining. In: International Conference on Management of e-Commerce and e-Government. ICMECG 2009, pp. 91–94. IEEE (2009)
21. Suh, J.H., Park, C.H., Jeon, S.H.: Applying text and data mining techniques to forecasting the trend of petitions filed to e-People. Expert. Syst. Appl. **37**(10), 7255–7268 (2010)
22. Vorontsov, K., Potapenko, A.: Additive regularization of topic models. Mach. Learn. **101**(1–3), 303–323 (2015)

Regulatory Sandboxes and Experimental Legislation as the Main Instruments of Regulation in the Digital Transformation

Alexey Yefremov(✉)

Russian Academy of National Economy and Public Administration (RANEPA), Vernadskogo pr. 84, 119571 Moscow, Russia
efremov-a@ranepa.ru

Abstract. Digital transformation poses an intrinsic challenge for regulators. With the rapid development of digital technology, there is a need for new regulatory tools. Russia, like many other countries, is trying to improve its regulatory policy for digitalization and digital transformation. This paper aims comparing the possibilities and prospects for the use of regulatory sandboxes in developed countries, in Russia and in the EAEU.

The analysis demonstrates that the transition from experimental legislation to regulatory sandboxes is associated with the need for rapid adaptation of regulation to digitalization conditions. Moreover, in Russia, the full implementation of regulatory sandboxes for digital transformation is complicated by the peculiarities of the legal system and the role of the law as the main regulatory tool. In the EAEU, the introduction of regulatory sandboxes is complicated by the different approaches of states to protecting their digital sovereignty and attitudes towards virtual jurisdictions.

Based on the analysis, the new regulatory specific mechanism for the relationship between strategic planning, legal forecasting, experimentation and the formation of proactive regulation is proposed. Implementation of these recommendations would help improve legal regulation of the development of digital technologies in Russia and the EAEU. It has been demonstrated that regulatory sandboxes are one early step in a new smart—digitized and datafied—process regulatory systems.

Keywords: Digital Economy · Digital transformation · Experimental legislation · Regulation · Regulatory sandboxes

1 Introduction

For the past few years, the use of digital technologies in various fields in many countries has been accompanied by the creation of regulatory sandboxes to determine the conditions for the legal regulation of such applications.

International organizations, such as the OECD, recommend the use of regulatory sandboxes in sectors such as financial technologies (FinTech) [18], regulatory technologies (RegTech), insurance technologies (InsurTech) [20]. According to International Telecommunication Union (ITU) Global Symposium for Regulators (GSR) Best

D. A. Alexandrov et al. (Eds.): DTGS 2019, CCIS 1038, pp. 82–91, 2019.
https://doi.org/10.1007/978-3-030-37858-5_7

Practice Guidelines On New Regulatory Frontiers To Achieve Digital Transformation (2018), regulators "need to consider putting in place innovative, out-of-the-box measures such as regulatory sandboxes for enterprises wishing to test an emerging technology or innovative service without being bound by all the regulations that would normally apply" [14].

Digital transformation poses an intrinsic challenge for regulators. Regulate too early and you risk impeding innovation; wait too long and you risk a potentially over-disruptive or harmful, and widespread, innovation reaching consumers and markets. In the past, due to the incremental nature of innovation, regulators had more time to learn and adapt. Therefore, it is important to assess the possibilities and prospects for applying both traditional legal experiments (experimental legislation) and new regulatory sandboxes, to identify the problems of their application.

2 Paper Objective, Literature, Methodology and Scope

The use of new regulatory tools in the field of digitalization and digital transformation is currently only becoming the subject of scientific analysis.

If the study of experimental legislation has been going on for quite a long time both in foreign [24] and in Russian [10, 21] legal science, the issues of regulatory sandboxes have not yet received in-depth analysis.

In American and European legal science, the relationship between experimental legislation and sunset legislation is traditionally considered [5]. In Russian legal science, legal experiments and experimental legislation are not considered in relation to digitalization and digital transformation [2, 22].

Regulatory sandboxes in American [1, 13], European [3, 6, 23, 25] and Asian [15, 16], legal science are considered only in relation to financial technologies and not to digital in general. A similar situation is typical for the Russian legal science [8] there are only a few studies on the use of regulatory sandboxes for digital technologies in general [27].

However, to a large extent the analysis of the experience of using regulatory sandboxes is provided in documents of international organizations (OECD, ITU and European Union).

This paper aims comparing the possibilities and prospects for the use of regulatory sandboxes in developed countries, in Russia and in the EAEU.

For achieving the study objective, we use comparative law methodology and institutional design method.

The comparative law method is used to identify common patterns in the development of legal regulation of experiments and regulatory sandboxes in different countries, as well as supranational entities such as the EU and the EAEU. It is important that this method allowed us to identify the features of legal systems and jurisdictions that are essential for the institutional design of regulatory sandboxes in Russia and the EAEU.

The method of institutional design in this study is applied to develop proposals for the introduction of regulatory sandboxes in Russia. This method allows to identify the features of the institutional environment, the interconnection of the legal and economic systems in the country.

In the first part of the paper we will briefly review the tendency of transition from the use of experimental legislation to regulatory sandboxes in developed countries.

In the second part of this paper we will analyze the development of legal frameworks for legal experiments and regulatory sandboxes for the development of digital technologies in Russia and the EAEU.

The third part of the paper will focus on developing recommendations on the mechanism for ensuring the link between strategic planning, legal regimes for legal experiments (regulatory sandboxes) and the rule-making process in Russia and the EAEU.

The results of the study would help to identify the areas which need further research.

3 From Experimental Legislation to Regulatory Sandboxes

According to L. Mader, experimental legislation concerns 'legislation enacted for a limited period of time in order to examine if a particular legislative measure will effectively achieve certain goals. It is enacted with a prospective purpose, but from a methodological point of view it requires retrospective evaluation' [17]. Experimental laws and regulations enable regulators to gather information about the nature of the underlying problem, and test the effectiveness of new regulations on a small-scale basis for a period of time determined beforehand.

The central idea behind experimental legislation is that:

- it concerns a temporary deviation of existing laws or regulations;
- the scope of the experiment will be fixed in terms of time, place, and/or addressees;
- the effects and side effects of the rules will be evaluated; and
- in case of success, the regime will be broadened so that the experimental rules can also apply to other similar situations.

Why did the transition from experimental legislation to regulatory sandboxes occur in 2010s? This is due to the fact that the adoption of a law, even an experimental one, is a much longer process than the introduction of an experimental legal regime (the regulatory community) by a decision of the executive authority or mega regulator.

Regulatory sandboxes are designed to help governments better understand a new technology and its regulatory implications, while at the same time giving industry an opportunity to test new technology and business models in a live environment.

The "regulatory sandbox" approach was pioneered by the United Kingdom's Financial Conduct Authority (2015) to address and control the barriers to entry for Fintech firms – small and innovative firms disintermediating incumbent financial services firms with new technology – in the financial landscape. In 2016, the Authority released its "UK sandbox," which allowed innovative FinTech development without requiring a full, strict regulatory testing process. The prerequisite of a sandbox is publicly available criteria that actors need to meet as a prerequisite for entry into the sandbox (meaning that only fulfilling certain criteria they can introduce innovations in the domain) [11].

The Financial Conduct Authority in its 2017 report points out the prospects for using regulatory books for such technologies as Distributed Ledger Technology (DLT), Online platforms, Application Programme Interfaces (APIs), Biometrics, Robo-advice [12].

In early 2018, the FCA proposed the idea of a "global sandbox" in its business plan. Building on that idea, it, together with 11 other regulators and supervisors, published a consultation paper setting out a proposal for the Global Financial Innovation Network (GFIN). The consultation paper received responses from 26 jurisdictions, following which the GFIN finalised its Terms of Reference and was officially launched on 31 January 2019. The GFIN's Terms of Reference set out three primary functions:

- Regulator network: to act as a network of regulatory bodies for collaboration and exchange of experience in the field of innovation, including new technologies and business models, as well as for providing accessible regulatory contact information for firms.
- Joint RegTech: to provide a forum for RegTech collaboration and knowledge sharing/lessons learned.
- Cross-border testing: to provide firms with an environment where cross-border solutions can be tested.

The GFIN has now expanded well beyond its initial coordinating group of 12 to a network of some 29 national and international organizations.

The creation of supranational regulatory sandboxes is a challenge to national legal systems and increases competition between jurisdictions between them.

Blockchain regulatory sandboxes mostly focus on Fintech, and are being developed in countries as diverse as Australia, Canada, Indonesia, Japan, Malaysia, Switzerland, Thailand and the United Kingdom [19].

OECD recommends "to be open to creating low burden regulatory regimes for small and new entrants, or regulatory "sandboxes". In sectors such as the financial sector, more open and experimental approaches towards new industries are being encouraged by regulatory approaches with lower requirements for small and potentially innovative firms. Regulatory sandboxes provide a limited regulatory waiver or flexibility, where the limits are usually in terms of geographic space, duration or sector, and are negotiated or enabled by regulatory authorities to facilitate market-testing, experimentation and innovation" [18].

These approaches will contribute to the emergence and development of innovative technologies and business models, while maintaining a constant overview of the rules that can be quickly adjusted in case of new risks [18].

4 Legal Framework of Regulatory Sandboxes in Russia and the EAEU

Defining the legal framework for legal experiments is provided for by the Russian Program on Digital Economy 2017, the Russian National Program Digital Economy 2018.

In the EAEU, the use of regulatory sandboxes is provided by Decision of the Supreme Eurasian Economic Council "On Guidelines for the Digital Agenda of the Eurasian Economic Union" 2017 [7].

According to the Guidelines for the Digital Agenda of the Eurasian Economic Union" 2017 "regulatory sandbox" is a specially agreed upon mode of study and piloting solutions, including regulatory ones, to determine an effective interaction model and build business processes in a new field. "Regulatory sandbox" should be used to develop mechanisms and rules for regulating economic processes in the framework of digital initiatives and projects. For the successful implementation of projects, it is possible to create an environment that provides for the elaboration of digital transformation projects in the format of a regulatory sandbox. This will allow to get a significant effect in terms of the formation and accumulation of competencies, development of regulatory models, support of the processes of approbation and commercialization of projects at early stages of development, testing and prototyping solutions, collecting talented teams (teams) in projects, forming a library of process models, accelerating business development. digital asset models, collaborative solutions, and significant risk reduction. The digital agenda is implemented using the mechanisms for developing, coordinating and approving initiatives by member states (the procedure for developing initiatives submitted as part of the digital agenda, is developed based on the practice of developing initiatives), implementing projects within the digital agenda (including financial mechanisms), the use of regulatory sandboxes and other effective mechanisms.

The legal regulation of the regulatory sandboxes in the EAEU should include the general concept, the international agreement developed on its basis, amendments to the EAEU Treaty and the Regulation of the Eurasian Economic Commission.

A draft EAEU Agreement on regulatory sandboxes is currently being developed. This draft provides the principles and conditions for the introduction of uniform regulatory sandboxes for the development of digital technologies throughout the EAEU, but not all states agree to the introduction of virtual jurisdiction. EAEU states seek to preserve their digital (information) sovereignty [9] and at the same time provide the best conditions for competition of jurisdictions in relation to digitalization [26].

In a report on the regulatory policy of the Center for Strategic Research (CSR), the Russian think tank with a focus on policy and strategy and implementation in the Russian Federation, is noted that key components of regulatory policy that foster successful of the complete regulatory cycle and its assessment include:

- reduction of administrative burdens;
- implementation technical and legal tools, including regulatory sandboxes, legal experiments, plain legal writing, common commencement dates;
- of public consultations with all stakeholders;

– creating digital platforms and databases to evaluate the effects for different groups of stakeholders;
– development behavioral regulation approaches (nudging) [4].

In April 2018, the Bank of Russia announced the launch of the regulatory sandbox - the regulatory platform. The regulatory platform of the Bank of Russia is a mechanism for piloting new financial services and technologies that require changes in legal regulation. The site will be used to model the processes of applying innovative financial services, products and technologies to test hypotheses about the positive effects of their implementation.

According to the results of piloting, a financial service or technology may be approved with the subsequent formation of a plan to develop the necessary regulatory framework for their implementation, or the initiative may be deemed inappropriate. To assess the need for piloting and the impact of financial services and technologies on the financial market, as well as to prepare proposals for changes in legal regulation, an expert council with market participants and an interdepartmental expert council are created at the Bank of Russia. In addition, the interdepartmental advisory council will prepare conclusions on the results of piloting, as well as the coordination of draft action plans necessary for the introduction of financial services and technologies. Piloting on the regulatory platform can be initiated by any organization that has developed or plans to use an innovative financial service or technology. For this, the initiator company must submit an application to the Bank of Russia.

However, there are some institutional problems for using regulatory sandboxes in Russia:

– separation of rule making and law enforcement;
– most requirements are based on laws;
– exceptions can only be defined at the level of federal law.

These institutional problems do not allow direct copying of foreign models for the introduction of regulatory sandboxes.

In particular, for the suspension of federal law rules in the regulatory sandbox, it is necessary to adopt an additional federal law.

In January 2019, the draft of federal law of the Russian Federation on experimental legal regimes was submitted.

This draft of federal law provides:

– principles of using experimental legal regimes;
– powers of public authorities on their establishment;
– terms and conditions of the introduction of the experimental legal regime;
– requirements for an experimental legal regime program;
– monitoring the implementation of the experimental legal regime.

Our analysis shows, however, that this draft of federal law has a number of disadvantages:

– The subject area of regulation of this law requires clarification. In addition to the list of technologies - the possibility of implementing digital innovations in local governments, courts of the Russian Federation, other government bodies other than

those specified in it (for example, digital innovations in the field of legal proceedings, the electoral process, etc.);
- The absence of a mechanism to suspend or cancel the norms of federal laws;
- Inconsistency of powers of state and local authorities, special public law company;
- Lack of risk criteria;
- Lack of performance criteria;
- Redundancy of registries, information systems, etc.

These disadvantages will not effectively create regulatory sandboxes in Russia, and if they are formally introduced, they will not have a positive effect on the development of digital technologies and the digital economy.

To solve these problems, it is necessary to adopt a whole package of federal laws, including additions to the federal constitutional law on the Government of Russia, a set of laws on state control in various fields of application of digital technologies. It is also necessary to shape a positive attitude towards regulatory sandboxes among employees of state control bodies. Thus, staffing and organizational constraints must also be eliminated to create a positive institutional environment for regulatory sandboxes in Russia and the EAEU countries.

5 Conclusions

The analysis demonstrates that the possibilities of introducing new digital-technologies are limited by the existing rule-making mechanism, which does not provide for a single procedure and conditions for legal experiments.

Firstly, there is a need to develop a uniform procedure and conditions for conducting legal experiments in Russia. Such regulation may be formalized in federal laws on regulatory legal acts or on state administration in general. Until now, in Russia at the federal level, unlike in the regions of Russia, there is no unified federal law on normative legal regulation.

Secondly, the practice of introducing "regulatory sandboxes" is limited to individual sectors (e.g. "FinTech"), which does not allow for the identification of "cross-cutting" inter-sectoral barriers to the application of new technologies. Therefore, development of universal requirements for "regulatory sandboxes" is necessary. These requirements can also be established in a single federal law on regulatory legal acts in Russia.

Thirdly, Russian legal science lacks common approaches to the relationship between legal regimes and legal experiments and their interrelationships. An appropriate legal concept is needed that defines the general and the particular for these instruments of state regulation and their interconnection. This area is also prospective for further research.

Fourth, legislative and international regulation of regulatory sandboxes in Russia and the EAEU should include a methodology for evaluating the effectiveness of their use for the development of digital technologies and the digital economy. The formation of such a methodology and performance criteria is also a prospective area for further research.

Evaluation of the effectiveness of the introduction of regulatory sandboxes should include:

- preparation of a report on the conduct of the experiment by the regulatory body - the initiator on the basis of performance criteria, determined in accordance with federal law by a decree of the Government of the Russian Federation;
- public discussion of the report with the participants of the experiment, as well as with all interested regulatory addressees;
- finalization of the report and its presentation to the Government of the Russian Federation for further consideration in the plans of the rule-making activities of the Government of the Russian Federation and other federal executive bodies.

Last but not least, in Russia and in other countries there is no specific regulatory mechanism for the link between strategic planning, legal forecasting, experimentation and the formation of proactive regulation. It is necessary to develop this mechanism, such may include:

- identification of needs in the formation of a new legal regulation in the development of the Forecast of scientific and technological development of the Russian Federation;
- the introduction of a special legal regime for conducting a legal experiment ("regulatory sandbox") regarding the introduction and application of a new digital technology;
- according to the results of such a legal experiment, the formation of proposals to the relevant plans of the rule-making activities of public authorities;

Implementation of these recommendations would help improve legal regulation of the development of digital technologies in Russia and the EAEU.

Finally, as already noted [25] "regulatory sandboxes are but one early step in a process that will over time embrace new smart—digitized and datafied—regulatory systems".

As noted above, the creation of supranational regulatory sandboxes is a challenge to national legal systems and increases competition between jurisdictions between them. In the future, we forecast the development of competition of the jurisdiction on the axis of regulatory sandboxes not only between individual countries, but also between international organizations. The prospective areas of research include experience of using regulatory sandboxes in Russia and the EAEU after the formation of a regulatory framework for their use, the impact of regulatory sandboxes on the development of the digital economy and the competition of jurisdictions in the digital economy.

References

1. Allen, H.J.: A US Regulatory Sandbox? (2017). https://papers.ssrn.com/sol3/papers.cfm?abstract_id=3056993. Accessed 10 Feb 2019
2. Amelin, R., Channov, S., Polyakova, T.: Direct democracy: prospects for the use of information technology. In: Chugunov, A.V., Bolgov, R., Kabanov, Y., Kampis, G.,

Wimmer, M. (eds.) DTGS 2016. CCIS, vol. 674, pp. 258–268. Springer, Cham (2016). https://doi.org/10.1007/978-3-319-49700-6_24

3. Arner, D.W., Barberis, J., Buckley, R.P.: FinTech and RegTech in a nutshell, and the future in a sandbox. Res. Found. Briefs **3**(4), 1–20 (2017)
4. Center for Strategic Research, Regulatory Policy in Russia: Key Trends and the Architecture of the Future (2018). https://www.csr.ru/wp-content/uploads/2018/11/CSR_English_interactive_prefinal.pdf. Accessed 10 Feb 2019
5. Ranchordàs, S.: Constitutional Sunsets and Experimental Legislation: A Comparative Perspective. Edward Elgar, Cheltenham (2015)
6. di Castri, S., Plaitakis, A.: Going Beyond Regulatory Sandboxes to Enable FinTech Innovation in Emerging Markets (2018). https://papers.ssrn.com/sol3/papers.cfm?abstract_id=3139238. Accessed 10 Feb 2019
7. Decision of the Supreme Eurasian Economic Council No 12 "On Guidelines for the Digital Agenda of the Eurasian Economic Union", 12 October 2017. https://docs.eaeunion.org/en-us/. Accessed 10 Feb 2019
8. Dostov, V., Shoust, P., Ryabkova, E.: Regulatory sandboxes as a support tool for financial innovations. J. Digital Bank. **2**(2), 179–188 (2017)
9. Efremov, A.: Formation of the concept of information sovereignty of the state. Pravo-Zhurnal Vysshei Shkoly Ekonomiki **1**, 201–215 (2017). https://doi.org/10.17323/2072-8166.2017.1.201.215
10. Eltsov, V.N.: Legal experiments in modern Russia: efficiency assessment. TSU Bull. **11** (2008). https://cyberleninka.ru/article/n/pravovye-eksperimenty-v-sovremennoy-rossii-otsenka-effektivnosti. Accessed 10 Feb 2019
11. Financial Conduct Authority, Regulatory sandbox, London (2015). https://www.fca.org.uk/firms/regulatory-sandbox. Accessed 10 Feb 2019
12. Financial Conduct Authority, Regulatory sandbox lessons learned report, London (2017). https://www.fca.org.uk/publication/research-and-data/regulatory-sandbox-lessons-learned-report.pdf. Accessed 10 Feb 2019
13. Jenik, I., Lauer, K.: Regulatory sandboxes and financial inclusion. Working paper. CGAP, Washington, DC (2017)
14. ITU GSR-18 Best Practice Guidelines On New Regulatory Frontiers To Achieve Digital Transformation (2018). https://www.itu.int/net4/ITU-D/CDS/GSR/2018/documents/Guidelines/GSR-18_BPG_Final-E.PDF. Accessed 10 Feb 2019
15. Kálmán, J.: Ex Ante Regulation? The Legal Nature of the Regulatory Sandboxes or How to Regulate before Regulation even Exists (2018)
16. Khalida, M.B., Kunhibavab, S.: Regulatory sandbox: Malaysia's response in regulating Fintech. In: Proceedings–ICLG, p. 55 (2018)
17. Mader, L.: Evaluating the effects: a contribution to the quality of legislation. Statute Law Rev. **22**, 125 (2001)
18. OECD Maintaining competitive conditions in the era of digitalization. OECD report to G-20 Finance Ministers and Central Bank Governors, July 2018 (2018). http://www.oecd.org/g20/Maintaining-competitive-conditions-in-era-of-digitalisation-OECD.pdf. Accessed 10 Feb 2019
19. OECD Science, Technology and Innovation Outlook 2018: Adapting to Technological and Societal Disruption. OECD Publishing, Paris (2018). https://doi.org/10.1787/sti_in_outlook-2018-en. Accessed 10 Feb 2019
20. OECD Technology and innovation in the insurance sector (2017). https://www.oecd.org/pensions/Technology-and-innovation-in-the-insurance-sector.pdf. Accessed 10 Feb 2019
21. Sitvitsky, V.A., Sorokin, M.Y.: Legal experiment and the development of law. Law J. High. Sch. Econ. **4**, 15–30 (2016)

22. Tikhomirov, Y.A., Nikolay, K.N., Pomazansky, A., Pulyaeva, E.: Legal models and experiment in the field of culture. J. Russ. Law **10**(226), 19–29 (2015)
23. Treleaven, P.: Financial regulation of FinTech (2015). https://papers.ssrn.com/sol3/papers.cfm?abstract_id=3084015. Accessed 10 Feb 2019
24. van Gestel, R., van Dijck, G.: Better regulation through experimental legislation. Eur. Public Law **17**(3), 539–553 (2011)
25. Zetzsche, D., Buckley, R.P., Arner, D.W., Barberis, J.N.: Regulating a Revolution: From Regulatory Sandboxes to Smart Regulation. European Banking Institute (EBI) Research Paper Series, 11 (2017). https://doi.org/10.2139/ssrn.3018534. Accessed 10 Feb 2019
26. Yefremov, A.: Regulatory Competition in the Eurasian Economic Union (2017). http://russiancouncil.ru/papers/EAEU-Jurisdictions-Policybrief15-En.pdf. Accessed 10 Feb 2019
27. Yuzhakov, V.N., Efremov, A.A.: Directions of improvement of legal regulation in the sphere of stimulation of development of information technologies. Russ. Law Educ. Pract. Sci. **5** (101), 62–69 (2017)

A Framework for Intelligent Policy Decision Making Based on a Government Data Hub

Ali Al-Lawati[1(✉)] and Luis Barbosa[2]

[1] Information Technology Authority, Muscat, Oman
ali.allawati@ita.gov.om

[2] United Nations University Operating Unit on Policy-Driven Electronic Governance, Guimarães, Portugal
barbosa@unu.edu

Abstract. The e-Oman Integration Platform is a data hub that enables data exchanges across government in response to transactions. With millions of transactions weekly, and thereby data exchanges, we propose to investigate the potential of gathering intelligence from these linked sources to help government officials make more informed decisions. A key feature of this data is the richness and accuracy, which increases the value of the learning outcome when augmented by other big and open data sources. We consider a high-level framework within a government context, taking into account issues related to the definition of public policies, data privacy, and the potential benefits to society. A preliminary, qualitative validation of the framework in the context of e-Oman is presented. This paper lays out foundational work into an ongoing research to implement government decision-making based on big data.

Keywords: Government big data · Policy making · Data analysis · e-Oman

1 Introduction

1.1 Aims and Motivation

The increase in the amount of data generated in different forms and across different domains has presented new opportunities to make inferences that go beyond typical e-commerce applications. Recently, there has been an increasing interest in using big data to make inferences on social trends for policy decision making.

However, a key obstacle to the usage of big data for this purpose is the haphazard methods by which big data is often created. Big data in most cases is not collected in a scientifically sound process. As such, it may not be representative of the population of interest and using it without sufficient care can result in misguided inferences. The infamous case of Google Flu Trends in 2010 where the algorithm overestimated the outbreak of the flu by 100% [1] is an often cited example.

When big data is combined with linked data that is semantically query-able, the added-value can be significantly improved [2]. The e-Oman Integration Platform is a data hub that currently supports the exchange of data across many government organizations

D. A. Alexandrov et al. (Eds.): DTGS 2019, CCIS 1038, pp. 92–106, 2019.
https://doi.org/10.1007/978-3-030-37858-5_8

in real-time. In this paper, we investigate whether this data, when combined with big, open, and social data can become a valuable tool for policy-making [3].

The purpose of this paper is to analyze the challenges and considerations of performing this task by conducting a systematic literature review on big data usage for policy-making in government. Based on our findings, we present a framework for the design of data-driven applications within a governmental context.

We discuss the benefits of such an approach, as well as constraints related to privacy concerns and efficacy to the definition of public policies. The framework was motivated by the concrete need to foster the productive use of data managed by the e-Oman platform. A preliminary validation was done resorting to two key stakeholders.

This paper is structured as follows. The rest of this section describes the e-Oman Integration platform and defines the problem statement within the context of e-Oman. Section 2 details the methodology for literature review and describes an automated tool implemented to support intelligent clustering over a base of articles. A literature review follows in Sect. 3 based on the relevant themes identified. Section 4 describes the four-step framework, which is analytically validated in Sect. 5 by remote interviews with two key stakeholders of the e-Oman Integration Platform. Finally, Sect. 6 concludes and discusses future work.

1.2 Context

e-Oman is an umbrella project that aims to advance Oman into a digital society. It encompasses the enhancement of government services from traditional paper-based and manual processes into electronic and online services. A key obstacle is the exchange of data relevant to the service across different government organizations. This has been addressed with the introduction of the Integration Platform.

The e-Oman Integration Platform is a data hub through which millions of data exchanges occur every week in real-time between different government agencies. It enables the exchange of current data across government while avoiding the burden of data duplication. Since data sets may be owned by different government entities, it has enabled inter-organizational services and burden reduction on residents and businesses alike. Data exchanges within the Integration Platform occur in a response to a transaction occurring at a government entity that requires additional information from a second one. There are currently more than 12 data providers and over 35 data consumers.

1.3 Problem Statement

The vast number of data exchanges that occur on a daily basis presents many opportunities to gather intelligence that would help government officials in the decision-making process. The paper discusses how this can be utilized in practice and which sort of framework may guide the design of such data-driven applications, eventually combining different data sources.

We believe an added value to society, potentially to promote sustainable development, can arise from the smart use of data that is already being collected by governmental agencies or services, as in the case of Oman. This can be most valuable, for example, in the monitoring of population shifts, demographic changes, or development movements. Data in turn can be used by government officials to adjust budget allocations or aid in the planning process at local or national levels.

1.4 Scope

This paper is part of an ongoing research on the implementation of big data analytics for government decision making. While the problem statement spans the ultimate outcome of this research, this paper is concerned with the research work that lays the foundation for the ongoing research.

2 Methodology

2.1 Overview

Our research is sustained by a literature review that is based on systematic literature review standards. A specific approach to support paper categorization was devised for this work and implemented as an intelligent automated learning model. This system and its prototype implementation are further detailed in Subsect. 2.2.

A systematic literature review proceeds by specifying a "criterion-based selection" [4]. This establishes an objective selection method free from the biases that may emerge if the criteria are not clearly specified. In order to adhere to this definition of systematic literature review, we performed a search on "Scopus" for Journal articles where the terms "government" and "big data" appear in the title, abstract, or keywords. The choice of using "Scopus", self-proclaimed as "the largest abstract and citation database of peer-reviewed literature" [5] was motivated by the fact that Scopus has higher coverage of recent Journal articles [6]. While literature reviews often resort to keyword searches on multiple databases, restricting our search to a single database limits duplication, which might affect the performance of our learning model prototype.

Our search was limited to literature that specifically addresses the design of data-driven applications in the context of government, given our problem is specifically related to the usage of big data for the purposes of policy definition, planning, and decision making in a government context. While similar problems may have been addressed in the business sector, the mission, requirements, and challenges within a government context are different from the business sector. For example, a key challenge quite specific to this context involves collecting data from various and often competing agencies [7] all in the public sector.

Formally, only peer-reviewed journal articles were considered, which is a common standard as in [4, 8], and [9], and limits our result set to 669 articles. However, following the guidelines in [10], our evaluation was not confined to a small sample of top journals. Instead, we included all published articles that satisfied our search terms in a preliminary evaluation regardless of the field and the prominence of the journal.

Once we completed the literature review, we used the findings to define the envisaged framework for designing governmental, data-driven applications.

The last stage consisted of a preliminary validation through exposition and discussion to two senior officers from the Information Technology Authority of Oman. Although a more systematic test of the framework, through a pilot application to a concrete case study is planned, this qualitative verification provided an early, informed feedback from the real, final stakeholders, and guide subsequent developments.

2.2 The Automated Learning Model

We develop a specific method for automated support to paper evaluation in the form of a smart algorithm. This is based on a learning model that classifies each paper into a cluster of articles under a similar general theme. The system helps to summarize the literature into clusters, and structures the content, such that the most relevant are not missed. As a result, more attention is dedicated to articles most germane to the objectives fixed for this research; while objectively including literature from different domains, which is most appropriate when an interdisciplinary field such as big data is being addressed. Specifically, the purpose of the learning model is to identify the main general themes in the literature where the keys *government* and *big data* are combined. However, we realize that most such articles do span more than one theme. While we structure the literature review based on the outcome of the learning model, we consider the topics in each article related to clusters other than the one it was associated to.

Clustering is a well-known class of algorithms in machine learning whereby a set of objects are grouped in a way such that similar objects are grouped together. Clustering can be further classified into supervised clustering, and unsupervised clustering. In supervised clustering, the target clusters are defined beforehand and supplied to the algorithm, whereas in unsupervised clustering, it is up to the algorithm to define the clusters based on a pre-defined number of clusters. In the interest of not presupposing the topics in the literature, we elect to perform unsupervised clustering using a well-known algorithm: k-means.

Prior to clustering, the set of articles (dataset) gathered needs to be quantified. One method for performing this is using a bag-of-words approach combined with a scoring function such as TFIDF. While this can be an effective method in some cases, it can often provide a negative outcome, particularly where the distinction between articles is not so concrete, as it happened in our case. The bag-of-words approach fails to take context into consideration; instead it merely considers keywords and gives more weights to rare keywords [11].

Thus, we opt for paragraph vectors proposed by Le and Mikilov [11], which learns "fixed-length feature representations from variable-length pieces of texts". We generate these vectors upon a concatenation of the title, keywords, and abstract of an article.

Scopus provided training data for the paragraph vectors model. We exported a set of 26938 documents based on the search term "big data". The set was fed to the "gensim doc2vec" library which is a well-tested implementation of paragraph vectors [12].

The duration of the training was 4 min 35 s, for our training set. The model was verified by comparing inferred vectors with the training corpus. As the authors of gensim suggest in their documentation: to assess the model one can use the "training corpus as some new unseen data and then seeing how the compare with the trained model" based on self-similarity [13]. The model found that over 99.94% of documents are most similar to itself which suggests the model is "behaving in a consistent manner" [13].

The most similar and dissimilar documents for a random set of documents was analyzed and verified manually. For instance, given the article "Data Intelligence for Local Government? Assessing the Benefits and Barriers to Use of Big Data in the Public Sector", the most similar article to it based on this model is "New development: Leveraging 'big data' analytics in the public sector", and the least similar article is "A review on document image analysis techniques directly in the compressed domain".

The algorithm runs on the vector representation of the data set that meet our criterion-based selection. The elbow method is used to determine the right number of clusters most appropriate for the dataset (Fig. 1).

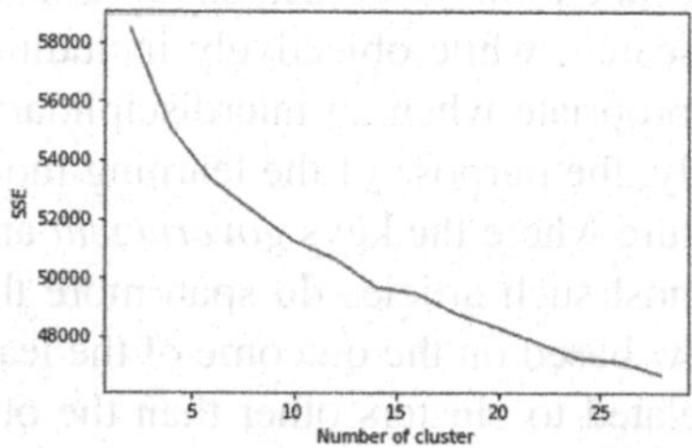

Fig. 1. The error sum of squares as a function of the number of clusters.

We selected a cluster of 10 based on the elbow method [] which establishes the optimal number of clusters. Table 1 presents the number of articles in each cluster along with a cluster name assigned to each cluster based on the prevailing topic contained articles.

Table 1. Clusters generated by the learning model and number of articles within each cluster.

Cluster	Papers
Sentiment analysis	31
High-level benefits	66
Data quality	91
Intelligent applications in the health sector	50
Big-data in government	58
Case studies of big-data in smart cities	59
Big government	106
Data privacy	72
Big data applications and strategy in the health sector	51
Policy and governance	54

Analysis was restricted to the clusters directly relevant to the objectives of this paper, although a cursory review of all other papers was also performed, including: high-level benefits, data quality, big government, big-data in government, data privacy, and policy and governance. We further reduced the list of papers based on an inspection by the authors to a set of 53 documents that is a representative sample of literature to guide our research objectives.

3 Literature Review

We present the findings from the literature review organized around five main topics.

3.1 Potential High-Level Benefits

The private sector has been leading big data research and applications in response to the increase in the amount of data generated online characterized by the three V's: variety, velocity, and volume [7]. Recently, having recognized the value of big data and its potential benefit to society, many governments around the world have invested large sums of money to aggregate and open their datasets, encourage inter-organization cooperation, and establish data analytics applications and frameworks [14].

While parallels can be drawn between the private and public sectors, the objectives of big data implementation in both sectors are different. Governments invest in big data to enable better informed policy decisions and address citizen needs [14], or, in broader terms, to transform an electronic government into a transformational government [15].

Pencheva et al. [9] also classify a body of literature under high-level benefits addressing the effectiveness, efficiency, and the legitimacy that big data applications bring to government initiatives. In particular, it has the potential to invite more participation by citizens and transform governance and decision-making.

Malomo et al. [16], provide considerable evidence on how big data exploitation can generate tangible benefits. The paper resorts to a case study linking transactions relative to students, from different government databases, provided intelligence on their needs. Several other examples of successful implementations and use of data are cited in the literature. For example, the US special force was able to find suspects in the terrorist attack at the Boston Marathon [17]. China has effectively implemented big data centers to analyze the characteristics of crime. In a different initiative, cell phone data records, analyzed in conjunction with traffic safety cameras, were able to profile drivers and identify potential violators of traffic rules.

It is believed big data has the potential to be a "new landmark" in a country's strength as an added dimension to its land, air, sea, and outer space sovereignty [18]. Big data research seems to be the next method of solving a county's toughest challenges. It helps gauge better perceptions of the present to make better decision by making possible the inspection of the granular details of a problem [19].

3.2 Data Quality

Data quality is another prevailing topic, given that big data is often the result of data exhausts – data is generated for logging and other purposes rather than being carefully constructed to guide policy-making [19]. Furthermore, since most big data is generated online, the issues of digital divide becomes prominent, i.e. this representation of samples is biased towards the citizens who are more active users of the Internet.

As a result, it is suggested that a combination of big data, open data, and linked data (BOLD) is the most effective for guiding a process of evidence-based policymaking [20, 21]. In [19], the authors note that BOLD is a better motivator of policy-decisions than citizen surveys, since it avoids the biases of optimistic and pessimistic participants, providing a more objective representation of reality.

There are, however, several issues that lead to misinterpretation of data. For instance, language can be vague, and algorithms may fail at understanding the sentiment as a result. Other issues concerning language involve the noise [19], such as spam, erroneous postings, and irrelevant comments. Moreover, when data from crowdsourcing is utilized it sometimes lack verifiability - it fails to present the context or the metadata which often limits its usability and includes bias as aforementioned [19].

Big data is, by definition, of high variety, and it can take a variety of forms. While this has the potential of enriching the insights garnered, it has the side effect of making models complex and hard to interpret. As such it is important that experiments are performed in a scientific approach, to avoid data misuse, and data omissions in favor of data which supports a favorable outcome. As such, it should be used with established and authoritative data sources to verify patterns and legitimize results [22].

3.3 Privacy Implications

Privacy is a main consideration whenever data pertaining to citizens is collected. This is of particular concern when the data accumulator is a government. There is a big worry about government shaping political opinions or setting agendas by controlling actions of citizens [23].

Actually, there is a fine line between socially beneficial uses of big data and the potential harms to privacy [24]. While laws exist in many countries to anonymize citizen data, the advent of big data has enabled reidentifying small and open data based precisely on it [25]. Shamsi et al. [26] describes 4 types of privacy violations in big data systems based on a literature survey:

1. Tracking by government: surveillance programs run by government that acquire and collect data on individuals from different sources.
2. Data from service providers: non-government organizations and private entities can utilize published government open data to collect information on individuals.
3. Re-identification attacks: correlation of different datasets can identify individuals.
4. Data breaches: security breaches can cause a leak of data.

To counteract these, laws must be drafted to ensure the privacy of individuals. However, in several instances under the pretense of national security, governments have breached these laws and violated the private lives of individuals under the cover of law. As such, it has been advocated that the laws of privacy should be establish by design rather than by choice. Technological constructions exist to anonymize data and cyber security policies should avoid, or at least limit, data breaches [26].

Conversely, it has been observed that governments are often able to purchase this information from private data collectors, such as Facebook [27]. Indeed, what information a government accumulates is already trumped by the information collected by various private corporations; fear of a big brother is not limited to governments [27].

The literature also distinguishes behavioral big data from inanimate big data [28]. Behavioral big data is data collected on human subjects and their interaction in unprecedented levels of details, and as such it has the potential of causing harm against the subject. The ease of conducting studies at a large scale involving human subjects raises many ethical and even normative questions that researchers are seldom aware of.

3.4 Policy Challenges

Technology has been utilized extensively in the delivery of public policies, namely in the form of e-government initiatives. However, it has had little success, despite of technological advances, in policy design. In [24], the authors describe ways in which big data applications can be used in each step of the policy design cycle based on their claims that it is not feasible to post-evaluate the policy using big data, rather the process of policy making needs to be transformed [24].

Within this context, Janssen et al. [2] identify four types of policy innovations based on the level of involvement of the public: co-creation-based innovation; crowdsourcing-based innovation; service innovation; and policymaking innovation. Co-creation is where data and actors outside of government evaluate government policies and has the least level of involvement, whereas the highest level of involvement policymaking innovation which is analogous to the model suggested in the previous paragraph [29].

Human resources is considered a key challenge in implementing big data based applications for government. Actually, governments often lack expertise, a handicap that can be addressed in two different ways: (1) training and hiring new staff; (2) establishing public/private partnerships. Any partnership with the private sector requires guidelines to expose private entities to big data. This is especially the case where the technical capacities are not available in the government. Indeed, big data based applications require immense data processing power and many governments lack sufficient investment in this arena.

3.5 Big Data in Government

The potential big data-driven applications for the design of public policies is enormous. Some authors, like Hotchl et al. [24] even suggest a revision of the policy cycle such that politicians approach the process of policy formation in a completely different way, entirely driven by data evidence.

Géczy et al. [30] which addresses the problem from various perspective, taking into account the data/technological, process, purpose, and economic dimensions [24].

In [31], Klievink et al. propose the big data use process as a set of activities to handling and making use of big data. In each step of the big data use process, the authors propose a list of activities that are categorizations of data activities contributed by scholars. The process is iterative: output from the last step feeds back into the first one (Fig. 2).

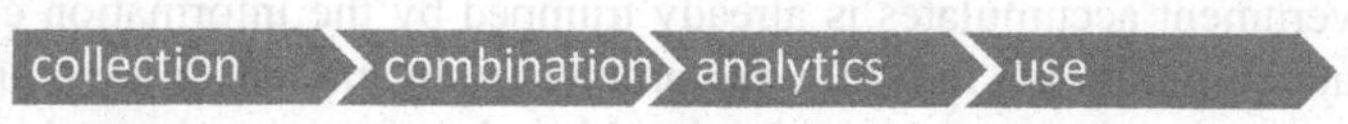

Fig. 2. Big data use process suggested by Klievink *et al.*

4 A Framework Adapted for e-Oman

4.1 Introduction

In light of the topics identified in the literature review, and the challenges of implementing big data in policymaking, we propose a framework based on the authors involvement with e-Oman. The proposed framework attempts to adapt the big data use process of Klievink et al. [31], keeping in mind, however, that this fails to address various data quality challenges identified in the literature review. As such, we propose a 4-step process as follows: *research design*, *data design*, *data analysis*, and *feedback loop*. Here, we take a look at the problem from a slightly higher level to comprehensively encompass the challenges identified in the literature.

While this framework potentially applies agnostically of the governmental or administrative context, we consider it within the context of e-Oman. As mentioned in the Introduction, our objective is to lay the foundations for the implementation of this framework within e-Oman, and as such we consider the current organizational layout and technology foundation existent within the government as an input to our framework design. In the next section, the framework is validated by two key, high-level stakeholders from agency holding the e-Oman Integration platform.

In the next four subsections, we consider each of the proposed steps in detail.

4.2 Research Design

The first step in developing a data-driven application for the governmental domain is its research design. This encompasses study design, ethical conduct and research methods [28]. The possible types of studies vary from prediction of social phenomena, to facilitating information exchange, or even promoting transparency and accountability [19].

A proper construction of the problem for which the evidence is required is thus a necessary first step. It is expected this step is performed in conjunction with the government entity who has requested the evidence. It involves their subject matter experts as well as statistical experts who understand the peculiarities of survey design. Fallacies may arise if the scenario is not properly designed, such as possible confusion between causation and correlation. An often-cited example is estimating the flu epidemic in which Google's algorithm incorrectly estimated the flu based on user searches from the tracked regions [1].

Furthermore, the step encompasses understanding the limits of what can be inferred. This involves testing assumptions and prediction of the models [20], including manual sampling to validate assumptions. It is most important to clearly establish the nature of the outcome of the study in terms of [28]:

- Causality: a relation between a certain event as a cause of a different event.
- Explanation: an understanding of why a given event occurred.
- Prediction: The usage of data to anticipate the occurrence of a given event.
- Correlation: Establishing a link between two events that share a similar stimulus.

4.3 Data Design

Assuring data quality is a major task within this step, through dataset curation which involves data cleansing, validation and anonymization. As mentioned above, big data is often a product of data exhausts [3], i.e. it was not specifically generated for the purpose of being analyzed and has to undergo processing and linkage with other data to become useful.

Equally important is getting access to the data. The datasets used will be a mix of open data, closed data, and social data. While open data is a given, social data often requires special subscriptions. However, closed data is the major obstacle. Policies of different organizations and government agencies have to be respected in terms of data sharing [32]. Request letters have to be sent and links established wherever data is not connected. A major challenge also involves knowing what data is available (Fig. 3).

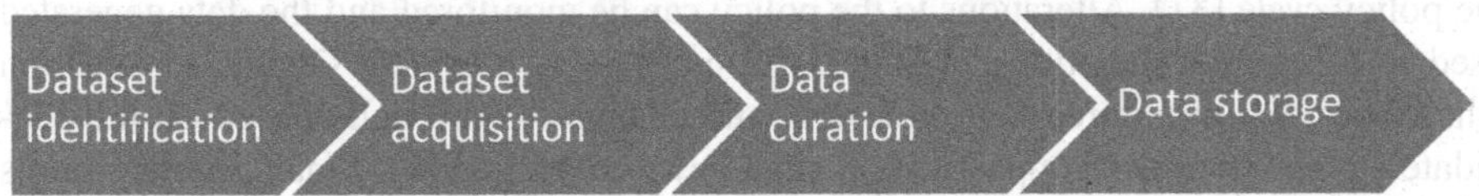

Fig. 3. Data design steps.

This step also involves data curation, a process along which data can be de-identified, summarized, etc. to maintain privacy and to prepare the data to be analyzed. Models also exist to establish the value of data sets, such as MELODA [33]. Some algorithms for inducing relationships between different datasets include: A/B testing, association rule learning, cluster analysis, neural network analysis, and visualization [3].

4.4 Data Analysis

There are many algorithms that can be implemented to analyze the data. The decision regarding the types of algorithms and data transformations to be used largely depends on the research design and data available. It is out of scope of this paper to survey such algorithms. However, the literature describes and categorizes many of the key algorithms potentially useful within a government context.

A key challenge that arises is the expertise within government organizations to perform this step. Often private public partnerships are needed for this purpose. Those should be carefully prepared and monitored. Another challenge is the storage and processing capabilities required for data analytics.

4.5 Feedback Loop

A feedback loop is a way into which the outcomes of a process are used as input to government policies [21]. Although, in some contexts, this may be considered a source of weakness of evidence-based decision-making [34], a proper feedback loop has the potential of shortening the policy design cycle.

A more accurate definition of a feedback loop is as a way to extend the reuse of the newly found data as an input to the process in a cyclical manner [31]. The two definitions are similar, but the first one cannot always fit the second if the deliverable is concrete.

We opt for the first definition such that a feedback loop is a way of presenting the findings to the policymakers or embedding them in the policy cycle whether or not such findings can be reused as input to a new iteration of the data analytics process or the proposed framework. The feedback loop can be in the form of, dashboards, data, and policy briefs/recommendations.

Dashboards [35] summarize the information that enables policy makers to make informed decisions, and when open to the public, a portal for citizens to scrutinize the government. While dashboards are a way to present data, the data can be summarized in other ways, and can be used as an input in iterations to a continuous monitoring of the policy cycle [31]. Alterations to the policy can be monitored and the data generated used to assess the alterations. A successful use case is president Obama's reelection where the team monitored key indicators and changes to the polls based on the candidate's press releases, campaign visits, and news coverage [19]. Finally, policy briefs would be most effective when external governmental or civil organizations advise policymakers based on the outcome of their application.

Figure 4 compares the steps of our approach against the approach presented by Klievink et al. [31]. As the figure illustrates, the process we propose is more comprehensive in its coverage of the process.

Nonetheless, similar to the earlier process, the proposed framework for governmental data-driven applications design is a general process by which we intend to design our ongoing research in policymaking with respect to e-Oman. The framework is intentionally abstract as the topic addressed is emergent, and the use cases cited in the literature are limited.

While the framework provides an overall process for supporting policymaking within a government context, our survey of literature suggests the work involved in developing an implementation may vary significantly in terms of type and quantity depending on the problem on hand.

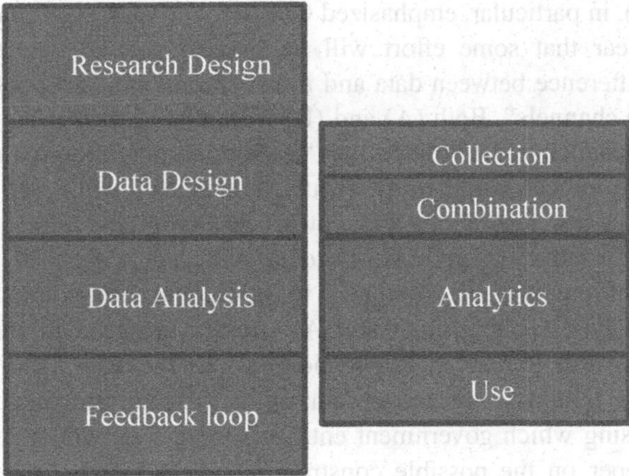

Fig. 4. A comparison between our framework and big data use process suggested by Klievink et al.

5 Preliminary Validation

5.1 Stakeholder Interviews

The proposed framework was validated through remote interview with two key stakeholders from the Information Technology Authority (ITA). They are referred in the sequel as (A), director of the e-Oman Integration Platform, and (B), the director general of Infrastructure.

The first question was rather open and intended to validate the very purpose of this work: "(1) What is the potential of the datasets linked to the ITA Integration platform, combined with open data, and social data, be used as a vehicle to verify policy and improve government decision-making?" Both stakeholders (A) and (B) were rather positive, recognizing that the government decision making process will improve due to the consolidation and proper arrangement of data. (A) exemplifies: "If there are new 1000 jobs offered in Muscat, the Ministry of Education can check how many kids they have to increase the number of classes, books, and teachers required for them. The Ministry of Health will be able to prepare its health centers to accommodate the new comers with more doctors, medicines etc." And, in broader terms, "Oman will no longer require to conduct census manually because all required data will be pulled from the already existing registered data in concerned government organizations." Stakeholder (B), on the other hand, recognizes that "there is no plan at this time to expose the data exchanged using integration platform of ITA as these data are property of other organization units". He goes on reinforcing the idea that open and combined data can be a fundamental asset "to take proper strategic decisions".

The second question addressed a major topic related to the item data design in the framework, inquiring about which laws and regulations, if any, need to be drafted to improve government policy-making based on intelligence gathered from data. Gaps on the roles and responsibilities on how to manage data in the e-Oman platform were acknowledge. (B), in particular, emphasized that "data privacy policy need to be clear", while making clear that some effort will be needed so that "government entities understand the difference between data and information, and start publishing raw data using appropriate channels". Both (A) and (B) were confident that the country will be able to meet this challenge: (A) shared that "if there are any required regulations they will be introduced to accommodate the required changes", while (B) emphasized the need to accompany new regulations with "awareness programs to the public" to foster participation in legislative design based on data evidence.

Inquired about the possible obstacles to intelligent decision-making processes based on data analytics in the Sultanate, (A) stresses the need to clarify the "incremental character" of the framework application. (B), on the other hand, called attention to two main issues, both again related to data: privacy, again, and data ownership ("it is sometimes confusing which government entities should own which data").

We went deeper on the possible constraints, asking to what extent ITA and its government partners have the necessary technical and human resources to design and implement data-driven applications. As anticipated in the framework, both stakeholders recognized the need to involve other partnerships: "We are government, not research centers. So ITA and government should rely on local companies and universities to build the analytical techniques. Another option is to buy (…) but [this] depends on local companies" (A). And "a lot of investment needs to take place to have these skills available" (B).

Finally, we inquired on the main challenges in the application of the framework to concrete projects based on e-Oman. Several factors were mentioned: overcoming the "non-ending bureaucracy" (A), data storage and location ("our main challenge will be having all government data in one location", A); and the need to raise awareness in the public ("it will be sorted out if use cases are brought to see the value of such information produced from open data", B). Security and the need for proper regulations were also mentioned. It was also suggested that the feedback stage in the framework was supported by clear auditing procedures ("a strong and thorough auditing should be implemented to insure confidentiality and integrity of the data", A).

5.2 Discussion

The stakeholders helped us to validate many of the ideas weaved into the proposed framework as discussed in the previous section.

Issues such as data storage and location, security and regulation were all identified as prerequisites. This has the potential of limiting the types of research questions that can be put forward. Drafting laws and regulations to support such an endeavor is a lengthy activity within a government context.

This increases the envisaged complexity to design the appropriate case study as planned for the future work. In particular, it may require the adoption of the project from a data-owning government entity to analyze the data exchange from a provider level as opposed to an intermediary. The problem will as such be identified in the context of the sponsor for the purpose of a case study.

6 Conclusions and Future Work

In this paper, we lay the groundwork for an application in support of policymaking within government. Our proposed framework for governmental data driven-design is a process based on the considerations put forward by experts in the field, taken within the perspective of government and analyzed in the context of the e-Oman.

The analytical validation establishes the foundation for an ongoing research based on the e-Oman integration platform as a tool to provide and facilitate the small data for policymaking within the Sultanate.

While the framework provides an overall process for supporting policymaking within a government context, our survey of literature and the challenges suggest the work involved in the implementation may vary significantly in terms of type and quantity depending on the problem on hand.

Based on the authors' association with the e-Oman project, an immediate future work is to implement a case study based on the proposed framework in the context of e-Oman and using the e-Oman Integration platform as a leading data source.

We intend to evaluate and, if needed, revise the proposed framework and report our findings to the academic community.

Another area of future work is to test our theories in other policy and social problems based on open data, big data and small data to establish a repository of case studies for the reference of interested researchers. Such a repository will help put forth a more concrete framework and tools that can generalize the common steps.

Acknowledgements. This paper is a result of the project "SmartEGOV: Harnessing EGOV for Smart Governance (Foundations, Methods, Tools)/NORTE-01-0145-FEDER-000037", supported by Norte Portugal Regional Operational Programme (NORTE 2020), under the PORTUGAL 2020 Partnership Agreement, through the European Regional Development Fund (EFDR).

References

1. Lazer, D., Kennedy, R., King, G., Vespignani, A.: The parable of Google Flu: traps in big data analysis. Science **343**, 1203–1205 (2014)
2. Janssen, M., Konopnicki, D., Snowdon, J., Ojo, A.: Driving public sector innovation using big and open linked data (BOLD). Inf. Syst. Front. **19**, 189–195 (2017)
3. Mergel, I., Rethemeyer, R., Isett, K.: Big data in public affairs. Public Adm. Rev. **76**, 928–937 (2016)
4. Ruhlandt, R.: The governance of smart cities: a systematic literature review. Cities **81**, 1–23 (2018)
5. Elsevier. https://www.elsevier.com/solutions/scopus. Accessed 29 Nov 2018
6. Chadegani, A.A., et al.: A comparison between two main academic literature collections: web of science and scopus databases. Asian Soc. Sci. **9**, 18–26 (2013)
7. Kim, G.-H., Trimi, S., Chung, J.-H.: Big-data applications in the government sector. Commun. ACM **57**, 78–85 (2014)
8. Kummitha, R., Crutzen, N.: How do we understand smart cities? An evolutionary perspective. Cities **67**, 43–52 (2017)

9. Pencheva, I., Esteve, M., Mikhaylov, S.: Big data and AI–a transformational shift for government: so, what next for research? Public Policy Adm. (2018). 0952076718780537
10. Webster, J., Watson, R.: Analyzing the past to prepare for the future: writing a literature review. MIS Q. **26**, xiii–xxiii (2002)
11. Le, Q., Mikolov, T.: Distributed representations of sentences and documents. In: International Conference on Machine Learning, pp. 1188–1196 (2014)
12. Řehůřek, R.: gensim. https://radimrehurek.com/gensim/. Accessed 12 Dec 2018
13. Doc2Vec Tutorial on the Lee Dataset. https://github.com/RaRe-Technologies/gensim/blob/develop/docs/notebooks/doc2vec-lee.ipynb. Accessed 12 Dec 2018
14. Gamage, P.: New development: leveraging 'big data' analytics in the public sector. Public Money Manag. **36**, 385–390 (2016)
15. Joseph, R., Johnson, N.: Big data and transformational government. IT Prof. **15**, 43–48 (2013)
16. Malomo, F., Sena, V.: Data intelligence for local government? Assessing the benefits and barriers to use of big data in the public sector. Policy Internet **9**, 7–27 (2017)
17. Kosorukov, A.: Digital government model: theory and practice of modern public administration. J. Legal Ethical Regul. Issues **20** (2017)
18. Jin, X., Wah, B., Cheng, X., Wang, Y.: Significance and challenges of big data research. Big Data Res. **2**, 59–64 (2015)
19. Taylor, L., Cowls, J., Schroeder, R., Meyer, E.: Big data and positive change in the developing world. Policy Internet **6**, 418–444 (2014)
20. Janssen, M., Kuk, G.: Big and open linked data (BOLD) in research, policy, and practice. J. Organ. Comput. Electron. Commer. **26**, 3–13 (2016)
21. Clarke, A., Margetts, H.: Governments and citizens getting to know each other? Open, closed, and big data in public management reform. Policy Internet **6**, 393–417 (2014)
22. Washington, A.: Government information policy in the era of big data. Rev. Policy Res. **31**, 319–325 (2014)
23. Power, D.: "Big Brother" can watch us. J. Decis. Syst. **25**, 578–588 (2016)
24. Höchtl, J., Parycek, P., Schöllhammer, R.: Big data in the policy cycle: policy decision making in the digital era. J. Organ. Comput. Electron. Commer. **26**, 147–169 (2016)
25. Hardy, K., Maurushat, A.: Opening up government data for big data analysis and public benefit. Comput. Law Secur. Rev. **33**, 30–37 (2017)
26. Shamsi, J., Khojaye, M.: Understanding privacy violations in big data systems. IT Prof. **20**, 73–81 (2018)
27. Lesk, M.: Big data, big brother, big money. IEEE Secur. Priv. **11**, 85–89 (2013)
28. Shmueli, G.: Research dilemmas with behavioral big data. Big Data **5**, 98–119 (2017)
29. Giest, S.: Big data for policymaking: fad or fasttrack? Policy Sci. **50**, 367–382 (2017)
30. Géczy, P.: Big data characteristics. Macrotheme Rev. **3**, 94–104 (2014)
31. Klievink, B., Romijn, B.-J., Cunningham, S., Bruijn, H.: Big data in the public sector: uncertainties and readiness. Inf. Syst. Front. **19**, 267–283 (2017)
32. Bertot, J., Gorham, U., Jaeger, P., Sarin, L., Choi, H.: Big data, open government and e-government: issues, policies and recommendations. Inf. Polity **19**, 5–16 (2014)
33. Abella, A., Ortiz-De-Urbina-Criado, M., De-Pablos-Heredero, C.: A model for the analysis of data-driven innovation and value generation in smart cities' ecosystems. Cities **64**, 47–53 (2017)
34. Poel, M., Meyer, E., Schroeder, R.: Big data for policymaking: great expectations, but with limited progress? Policy Internet **10**, 347–367 (2018)
35. Matheus, R., Janssen, M., Maheshwari, D.: Data science empowering the public: data-driven dashboards for transparent and accountable decision-making in smart cities. Gov. Inf. Q. (2018)

Information Technologies in G2C Communications: Cybersocial Trust Survey

Iaroslava Tensina[1], Lyudmila Vidiasova[1(✉)], and Elena Bershadskaya[2]

[1] ITMO University, Saint Petersburg, Russia
tensina.yaroslava@mail.ru, bershadskaya.lyudmila@gmail.com
[2] Penza State Technological University, Penza, Russia
bereg.50@mail.ru

Abstract. This paper presents the results of survey regarding Saint Petersburg citizens' trust in information technologies. The research was conducted on the base of Actor-network theory ideas and Social Construction of Technology (SCOT) approach. 600 respondents participated in the survey (sampling error does not exceed 4%, 95% level of confidence). The research proposed suggests an approach for studying cybersocial trust in the sphere of G2C communications found in e-government development, online services provision, e-participation in city management. The questionnaire contained the parameters for evaluation trust in new technologies used to communicate with government representatives and get public services, to solve urban problems, and to participate in city management. The survey results indicated a high level of Internet usage, as well as an increased level of trust in financial transactions through the Internet. The level of citizens' trust in getting public services online reached 45%, submitting e-applications – 41%, working with e-petitions – 38%, communicating with authorities via social networks – 15%. According to our research results, St. Petersburg citizens consider personal visit to public authorities as a more effective way to solve urban issues (19%), while the percentage of citizens who believe in the effectiveness of the Internet portals remain insignificant (5%).

Keywords: Social trust · Cybersocial trust · Information technology · Modernization · Urban studies

1 Introduction

In recent years, the process of testing and pilot implementation of complex socio-technical systems with the prefix "smart", such as "smart home", "smart city", "smart car", "smart supermarket" and other, has expanded. The elements of artificial intelligence and machine learning are used to varying degrees in these sociotechnical systems and it is assumed that some actions are carried out without the control of a human being. Social relations between people and organizations in the digital world today are subject to a "decoupling" effect, that is, technical mediation. If in interpersonal communications the work of technologies can be personally monitored and quickly

D. A. Alexandrov et al. (Eds.): DTGS 2019, CCIS 1038, pp. 107–119, 2019.
https://doi.org/10.1007/978-3-030-37858-5_9

adjusted, the contribution of technological intermediaries to institutional interactions should not be overlooked.

Recently, it has become obvious that the use of new technologies demands certain transformations of trust in the institution of public communications. In this regard, the definition of the boundaries of the possible penetration of technology into the everyday lives of individuals acquires high importance, and the problematization of cyber-social trust becomes particularly relevant. Cyber-social trust reflects the specifics of people's attitudes to the functioning of complex information systems, including elements of artificial intelligence.

For a long time, the question of proliferation and use of the Internet was understood in technological terms of digital infrastructure readiness, or in terms of the skills and knowledge that people should possess. It seemed that the problem of the "digital divide" was solved rather mechanistically, by increasing the availability of the Internet and teaching citizens how to use it. At the same time, practice shows the inadequacy of such an approach and the need to understand the "digital divide" not only in terms of the ability of citizens, but also in terms of their informed choice, one of the motives of which is trust in technology. Thus, the problem of using/not using technology turns out to be associated with problems of trust in technology, interpersonal trust, and institutional trust in the media, state institutions, business players and other actors.

In this paper we present the results of a survey of Saint Petersburg residents aimed at comparing different aspects/areas of trust as well as finding out where citizens have high and low level of trust in new technologies.

2 State of the Art

The phenomenon of trust is the object of attention in various areas of the humanities. General theoretical approaches to the study of trust were developed in the works of Baier [2], Bachmann [1], Blau [5], Gambetta [18], Giddens [19, 20], Zucker [44], Coleman [13], Kramer [24], Luhmann [29], Misztal [32], Tyler [43], Fukuyama [16], Sztompka [42].

A separate research area is represented by works in which the phenomenon of trust is investigated as a component of social and political consciousness (Belyanin and Zinchenko [3], Bodyul [6], Dankin [14], Lovell [28], Milner [31]). The problem of social and political trust was examined in the studies of Brann [7], Levis and Weigert [27], Parks [33], Seligman [40], and others. The social trust in social and political institutions, based on empirical research data, was examined in the works of Galkin [17], Levada [25], Piskotin [34] and others [10].

Stolle identifies four approaches in the Anglo-American tradition: the concept of generalized trust, the theory of rational trust, the theory of group identity or group-based trust, and the theory of moral accounts trust [41]. The concept of generalized trust comes from the hypothesis that in order to maintain sustainability in society, there must be "an abstract readiness to trust a stranger and a willingness to interact with him". The theory of rational trust considers trust as a process of social interaction, conditioned by the rational expectations of the subjects and focused on maximizing individual benefits, as a product of rational calculation in conditions with little information. The theory of group identity explains the formation of trust through an awareness of belonging to a common social group, a common sociocultural and value context. The theory of moral accounts in its constructions is based on the so-called moral argument about responsibility and the moral consciousness of the individual as the basic basis of trust.

In addition, other sources can provide with other classifications. In particular, Levi divides all concepts into cognitive and noncognitive [26]. Braun classifies approaches, identifying two dominant models of social trust: a trust model based on the social exchange paradigm and trust model built on the concept of communal trust [8]. Misztal proposes in classifications to take into account and analytically distinguish between the three main dimensions of trust: types of trust, content of trust, motives of trust and sources of trust [32].

A great contribution to the study of the problem of generalized trust in the context of modernization and democratic development was made by Inglehart, Welzel [23] and the World Values Survey project founded by them. Their analysis is based on the assumption of the modernization of society from the materialistic values of survival to the post-materialistic values of self-expression. This value shift, among other things, is associated with the growth of generalized trust, and trust, in turn, favorably affects the growth of democratic values, the development of civil society and social capital. This thinking on the relationship of trust and social capital is also reflected in the concepts of Putnam [36] and Fukuyama [16].

Most authors of the presented approaches converge in understanding trust as the confidence of some people in the actions of others, based on feelings, and not on rational understanding.

However, a fairly extensive theoretical discourse on the issue of trust does not fully cover aspects related to trust in information technologies in modern society. The impact of the Internet on people's behavior is of great interest to researchers. It is worth noting the research by Bimber [4], Grossman [21], Poster [35], Hirst and Harrison [22].

An empirical study of computer technophobia originated in the early 80s. In one of the first works on this topic, psychologist Timothy Jay identified technophobia through: (1) the behavioral component in the form of resistance to computers; (2) the emotional component in the form of fear or anxiety towards computers as complexes of rational and irrational regulators of behavior; (3) cognitive component or negative evaluation of computers. In subsequent works, the method of measuring and analyzing computer technophobia was perfected, while scientists used such synonyms as techno-stress (Brod) [9], cyberphobia (Rice) [38], computer aversion (Meier) [30], computer anxiety (Raub) [37].

The concept of adoption of innovations developed by Rogers [39] and Davis [15] also deserve special attention. Within this framework, rational factors that influence the choice of new technologies by citizens are analyzed. An expanded model of technology adaptation in the context of e-government development was proposed by Carter and Belanger [11]. They have included "trust" in their model as one of the key factors for adopting new technologies. Subsequently, analyzing the problem of adapting public electronic services, Carter and Weerakkody clarified the concept of "trust", dividing it into trust in information and communication technologies and trust in the authorities, who propose using their services in electronic form [12].

In Table 1 we summarized the areas of trust being studied in these scientific papers. The literature review found out that despite heightened attention to the phenomenon of trust, the interpretation of its nature and the factors determining it remains controversial. Trust in the modern world is becoming a structure-forming element in ensuring social communication. To date, most of the developed economic and managerial models are used to assess the effectiveness of the implementation of e-government.

Table 1. Examples of theorists within specific disciplines investigating trust

Aspect of trust	Authors
General theoretical approaches	A. Baier, R. Bachmann, P. Blau, D. Gambetta, A. Gidden, L. Zucker, J. Colema, R. Kramer, N. Luhmann, B. Miszta, T. Tyler, F. Fukuyama, P. Sztompka
Component of social and political consciousness	A.V. Belyanin and V.P. Zinchenko, V.E. Bodyul, D.M. Dankin, D.U. Lovell, B.Z. Milner
Problem of social and political trust	P. Brann, D. Levis and A. Weigert, C. Park, A. Seligman
Social trust in social and political institutions	A.A. Galkin, Yu.A. Levad, M. Piskotin
Problem of generalized trust in the context of modernization and democratic development	R. Inglehart, C. Welzel
Relationship of trust and social capital	R. Putnam and F. Fukuyama
The impact of the Internet on people's behavior	B. Bimber, L. Grossman, M. Poster, M. Hirst and J. Harrison
Adoption of innovations	E. Rogers and F. Davis
Adaptation of innovations in the context of e-government development	L. Carter, F. Belanger, V. Weerakkody

At the same time, there is no methodology for researching social and cultural differences in relation to new technologies that mediate communications in politics, economics, education and health care. The research proposed suggests an approach for studying cybersocial trust in the sphere of G2C communications found in e-government development, online services provision, e-participation in city management.

3 Research Design

3.1 Research Methodology

The study of the dynamics of citizens' attitudes toward new information technologies is advisable to develop along the lines of transformational metatoretizing, taking into account the interrelation of institutional boundaries and network structures mediated by new technologies. The task of the research is supposed to be realized based on the ideas of the Actor-network theory by Latour and the approach of Social Construction of Technology (SCOT).

The Actor-network theory will make it possible to develop an idea of the social reality that is adequate to the modern conditions of society, with an emphasis on its mutual penetration and complementarity.

Proponents of SCOT approach disputes about the linear history of scientific and technological development and the introduction of inventions into the life of a human being. They open a heterogeneous user relationship in the process of rooting innovation. This shows the interpretive flexibility of the technology and the unpredictability of its possible social effects. According to SCOT, despite some expectations as to what effects will be caused by technical innovations, the daily use of technical inventions can lead to unexpected results. Subscribing to the ideas of SCOT allows one to avoid the deterministic interpretation of computerization as a stage of objective progress of technology and to detect the features of the acculturation of new technologies in various institutional fields.

In this study, the phenomenon of trust is conceptually viewed in the institutional context of the political sphere and is expressed in assessing the trust/distrust of citizens in using information technologies to interact with government representatives through electronic petition portals, forms of electronic inquiries, receiving electronic services, e-voting, etc.

In accordance with the purpose of the study, the questions in the questionnaire were compiled in a way to obtain information on following issues:

- Trust in new technologies to communicate with government representatives and get public services;
- Trust in new technologies to solve urban problems;
- Trust in new technologies to participate in city management.

3.2 Data Collection

The conducted research aimed at identifying the level of social trust in new technologies in St. Petersburg. The data was obtained by interviewers during a personal survey of city residents. The surveys were conducted at 6 multifunctional centers (MFC) providing state and municipal services. It is important to mention that MFCs are located in densely populated districts of the city.

To calculate the sample population, data on population size, age and sex composition were used. The data was obtained on the official website of the Office of the Federal Statistical Service for St. Petersburg and the Leningrad Region. Based on the cities' population, the sample size for the survey was determined to be 600 respondents. The sampling error does not exceed 4%, the level of confidence was 95%.

The survey was conducted in November 2018. Six hundred citizens took part in the study which were divided into six age groups: 18–25 years old (15%), 26–35 years old (19%), 36–45 years old (17%), 46–55 years old (18%), 56–65 years old (16%) and over 65 years old (15%). In each age group, the percentage of men to women was calculated 43% men to 57% of women.

Analysis of the respondent's distributions by occupation showed that the majority are specialists (39%), unskilled laborers/guards/drivers (20%) and students (10%). The survey also included businessmen, senior and middle managers (6%), as well as housewives (6%) and the temporarily unemployed (3%).

4 Findings

The research findings reflect the results of the aforementioned survey regarding social trust in information technology.

4.1 Trust in the Use of New Technologies

The results of the survey showed that most of St. Petersburg residents are active Internet users. The majority of respondents noted that they use the Internet every day (42%) or are almost always online (26%). Survey results also demonstrate that most respondents define themselves as rather experienced users of information technologies, but also noted that it is difficult to master new programs on their own (32%). At the same time, 29% of respondents noted that they can easily learn new programs, applications and products.

Taking into account the high percentage of Internet and IT users, the study examined the attitude of citizens to new technologies and their use for solving urban problems and participation in city management.

The results of the survey showed that most of St. Petersburg residents primarily trust to use new technologies when there is a necessity to pay some fees through the Internet (45%) (see Fig. 1).

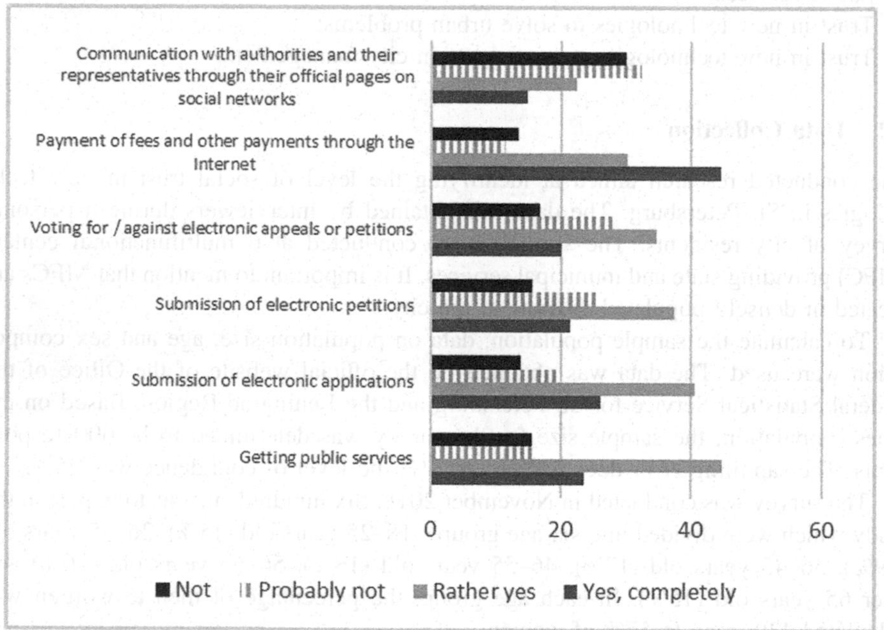

Fig. 1. Distribution of respondent's answers to the question "Do you trust information technology (Internet, mobile applications, etc.) as a tool of communication in these situations?", %

Most of these respondents belonged to "26–35 years" (25%) and "18–25 years" (24%) age groups, while part of respondents who expressed mistrust in this way of payment belonged to "over 65 years old" age group (48%) (see Table 2).

Table 2. Trust in payment of fees and other payments through the Internet by age groups

	Yes, completely	Not	Rather Yes	Rather Not
18–25 years	24%	2%	14%	3%
26–35 years	**25%**	7%	19%	9%
36–45 year	19%	5%	20%	10%
46–55 years	15%	12%	**25%**	20%
56–65 years	11%	25%	13%	22%
over 65 years	6%	**48%**	9%	**36%**

The smallest percentage of respondents indicated that they fully trust new technologies for communication with authorities and their representatives through their official pages on social networks (15%). It is worth noting that residents of St. Petersburg more often expressed their trust in getting public services through the Internet (45%), and submitting electronic applications (41%) and electronic petitions (38%).

The greatest mistrust citizens expressed was in communication with authorities and their representatives through their official pages on social networks (30%). Most of those respondents belong to the "over 65 years old" (29%) and "56–65 years" (21%) age groups. Also, respondents noted that they rather did not trust to vote for/against electronic appeals or petitions (29%).

4.2 Trust in the Use of New Technologies to Solve Urban Problems

The results of the survey demonstrate that the majority of St. Petersburg residents agreed that with the Internet expansion the authorities devote more attention to responding to citizens' requests (become more responsive to citizens, more attentive to problems of citizens) (42%) (see Fig. 2). At the same time, 1/3 of respondents disagreed with this statement (30%). It is important to mention that respondents who tend to trust in attentiveness of authorities to citizen's problem mostly belong to the young age group "26–35 years" (28%). The greatest mistrust was expressed in "65 years +" group (36%).

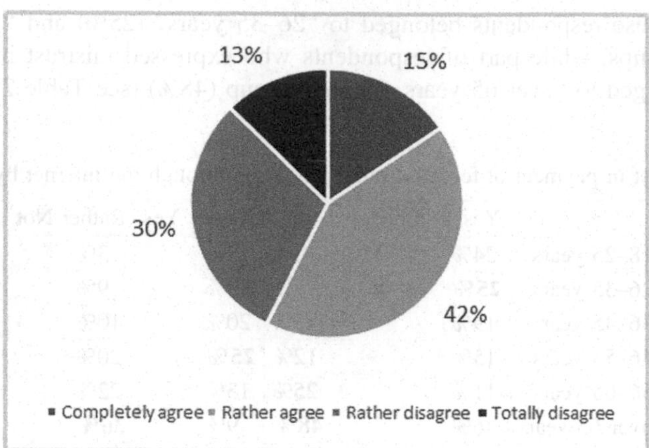

Fig. 2. Distribution of respondent's answers to the question "Do you agree with the statement «As the use of the Internet as a whole expands, the authorities devote more attention to responding to the requests of citizens»?", %

The majority of surveyed St. Petersburg residents noted that the most effective way to solve urban problems in St. Petersburg is reporting problems to the authorities by phone (27%) (see Fig. 3). Citizens consider personal visits to public authorities as a more effective way to solve problems (19%), while the percentage of citizens who trust in the effectiveness of the Internet portals remains insignificant (5%).

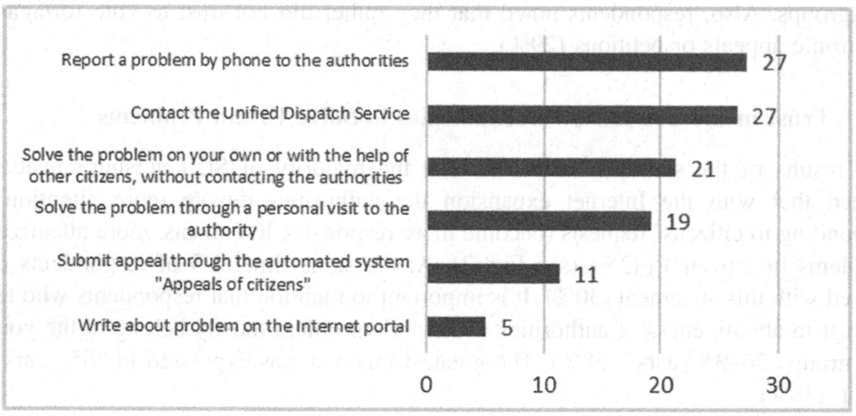

Fig. 3. Distribution of respondent's answers to the question "What is the most effective way to solve urban problems in St. Petersburg?", %

Most of the respondents noted that usually they do not have time to take any actions for solving urban problems that they notice (42%) (see Fig. 4). Most surveyed St. Petersburg residents use a phone for reporting a problem to public authorities (22%). The smallest percentage of respondents use the automated system "Appeals of citizens" (3%) and Internet portals (2%).

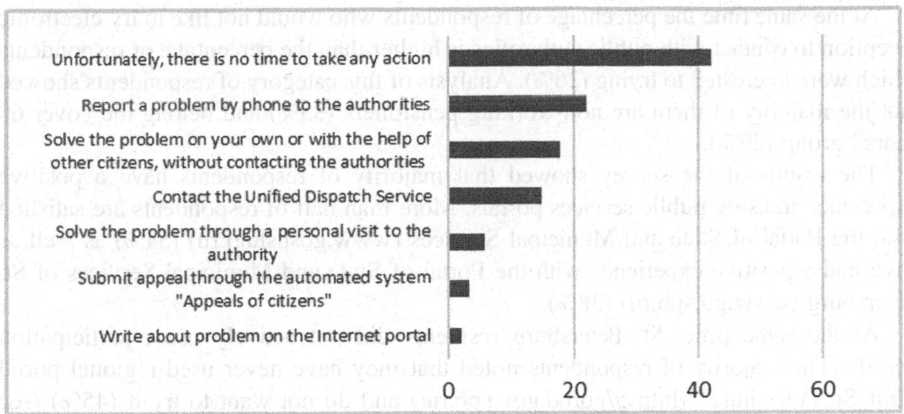

Fig. 4. Distribution of respondent's answers to the question "How do you mostly react to urban problems that you notice?", %

4.3 Trust in the Use of New Technologies to Participate in City Management

The survey results showed that most of respondents had a positive experience in contact with public authorities through electronic receptions (33%) (see Fig. 5). The percentage of respondents who had a negative experience was insignificant (5%). It is important to note that respondents who indicated having any experience all belonged to the same age group "26–35 years". Of these, 27% were satisfied with the use of electronic receptions and 34% were faced with some difficulties. The lack of experience but interest in using an electronic reception was mostly expressed by the respondents of the youngest group "18–25 years" (24%).

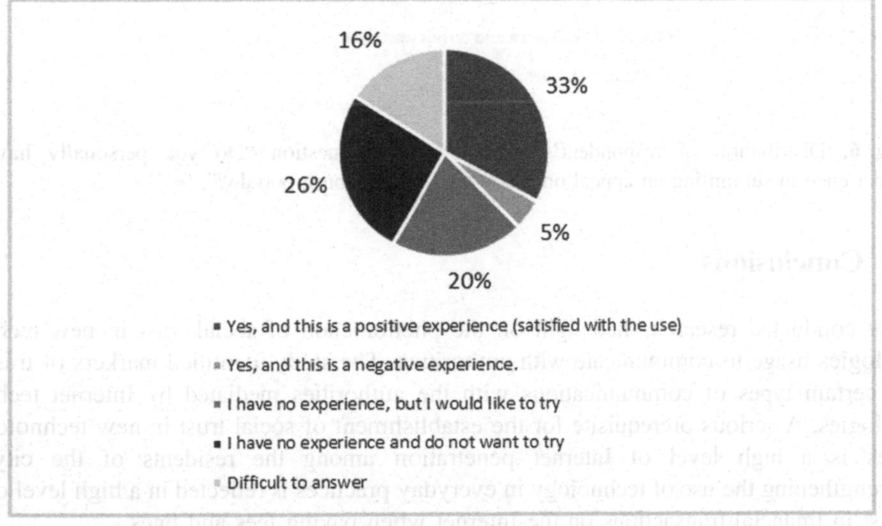

Fig. 5. Distribution of respondent's answers to the question "Do you personally have experience contacting public authorities through electronic receptions?", %

At the same time the percentage of respondents who would not like to try electronic reception to contact with public authorities is higher than the percentage of respondents which were interested to trying (26%). Analysis of this category of respondents showed that the majority of them are non-working pensioners (35%) and belong the "over 65 years" group (29%).

The results of the survey showed that majority of respondents have a positive experience in using public services portals. More than half of respondents are satisfied with the Portal of State and Municipal Services (www.gosuslugi.ru) (54%) as well as have had a positive experience with the Portal of State and Municipal Services of St. Petersburg (www.gu.spb.ru) (38%).

At the same time, St. Petersburg residents did not actively use e-participation portals. The majority of respondents noted that they have never used regional portal "Our St. Petersburg" (https://gorod.gov.spb.ru/) and do not want to try it (45%) (see Fig. 6). Similar results were obtained for portals "Change.org" (https://www.change.org/) (47%) and "Russian Public Initiative" (https://www.roi.ru/) (51%).

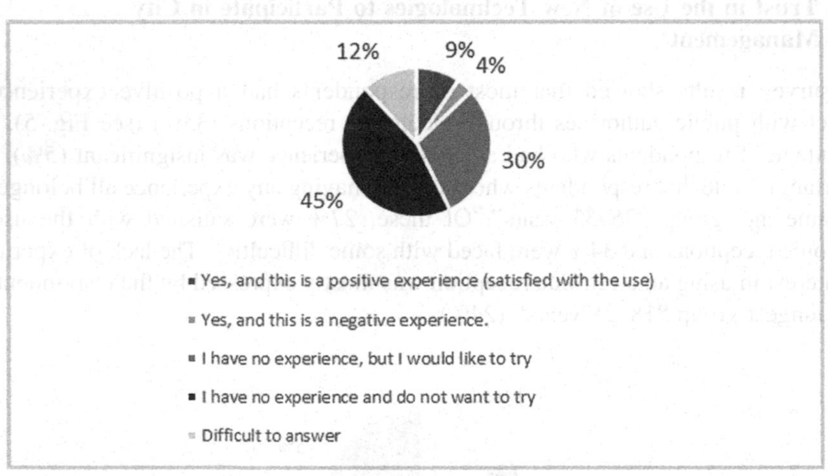

Fig. 6. Distribution of respondent's answers to the question "Do you personally have experience in submitting an appeal on the «Our St. Petersburg portal»?", %

5 Conclusions

The conducted research shed light on the phenomenon of social trust in new technologies usage to communicate with authorities. The study identified markers of trust in certain types of communications with the authorities mediated by Internet technologies. A serious prerequisite for the establishment of social trust in new technologies is a high level of Internet penetration among the residents of the city. Strengthening the use of technology in everyday practices is reflected in a high level of trust in financial transactions on the Internet when paying fees and fines.

The official channels of receiving electronic public services found a high level of endorsement from respondents. However, residents of St. Petersburg trust in communication with representatives of government on the official pages on social networks to a much lesser extent. The survey results showed that most of respondents had a positive experience in contact with public authorities through electronic receptions. At the same time the percentage of respondents who would not like to try electronic reception to contact with public authorities is higher than the percentage of respondents which were interested in trying them.

The results of the survey showed that majority of respondents have a positive experience in using public services portals. However, the respondents rated a telephone call as a more effective way to solve urban issues than web-portals.

The practical value of the study lies in the fact that it attempted to evaluate the use of electronic interaction C2G channels between citizens and the government, as well as to identify potential preferences for using and not using them, and if the respondent did not have experience in accessing them.

The limitations of the study are related to the presentation in the survey of trust as a subjective characteristic felt by the respondents personally. The wording of the questions "Do you trust in different methods of e-communication?" correlates with all-Russian public opinion polls about trust in government institutions and political leaders. Further research should be directed to the definition of a model of social trust for new technologies, including not only indicators of subjective perception, but objectively measured parameters of the manifestation of trust/distrust of communication through the Internet in various fields. Also, the research results could be contextualized with the context of other cities and countries as well.

Acknowledgements. The study was performed with financial support by the grant from the Russian Foundation for Basic Research (project №18-311-20001): "The research of cybersocial trust in the context of the use and refusal of information technology".

References

1. Bachmann, R.: Trust, power and control in transorganizational relations. Organ. Stud. **2**, 337–365 (2001)
2. Baier, A.S.: Moral Prejudices: Essays on Ethics. Harvard University Press, Cambridge (1995)
3. Belyanin, A.V., Zinchenko, V.P.: Trust in the economy and public life. Liberal Mission, 164 p. (2010)
4. Bimber, B.: The Internet and Political Transformation: Populism, Community and Accelerated Pluralism (1998)
5. Blau, P.M.: Exchange and Power in Social Life. Wiley, New York (1964)
6. Bodyul, V.E.: The problem of trust in a political leader. The problem of trust in international relations: theory and practice, pp. 75–79 (2000)
7. Brann, P., Foddy, M.: Trust and the con-sumption of a deteriorating resource. J. Conflict Resolut. **31**, 615–630 (1998)
8. Braun, D.: Politisches Vertrauen in neuen Demokratien. Springer, Wiesbaden (2013). https://doi.org/10.1007/978-3-658-01188-8. 290 p.

9. Brod, C.: Technostress: The Human Cost of the Computer Revolution. Addison-Wesley Publishing Company, Reading (1984)
10. Cappella, J.N., Jamieson, K.H.: Spiral of Cynicism: The Press and the Public Good. Oxford University Press, New York (1997). 325 p.
11. Carter, L., Belanger, F.: The utilization of e-government services: citizen trust, innovation and acceptance factor. Inf. Syst. J. **15**, 5–25 (2005)
12. Carter, L., Weerakkody, V.: E-government adoption: a cultural comparison. Inf. Syst. Front. **10**(4), 473–482 (2008)
13. Coleman, J.: Foundations of Social Theory. Belknap Press of Harvard University Press, Cambridge (1990)
14. Dankin, D.: Confidence building measures: opportunities and a framework for optimizing international relations. Secur. Eurasia **4**, 31–60 (2002)
15. Davis, F.D.: Perceived usefulness, perceived ease of use, and user acceptance of information technology. MIS Q. **13**, 319–340 (1989)
16. Fukuyama, F.: Trust: The Social Virtues and the Creation of Prosperity. Free Press, New York (1995). 457 p.
17. Galkin, A.A.: The lack of political trust and ways to overcome it. Power 10–11 (1998)
18. Gambetta, D.M.: The Price of Distrust/Trust: Making and Breaking Cooperative Relations, electronic edition, Department of Sociology, University of Oxford, chap. 10, pp. 158–175
19. Giddens, A.: Social Theory and Modern Sociology. Polity Press, Cambridge (1990)
20. Giddens, A.: The Consequences of Modernity. Polity Press, Cambridge (1992)
21. Grossmann, L.K.: The Electronic Republic: Reshaping Democracy in the Information Age. New York (1995)
22. Hirst, M., Harrison, J.: Communication and New Media: From Broadcast to Narrowcast. Oxford University Press, South Melbourne (2007)
23. Inglehart, R., Welzel, C.: Changing mass priorities: the link between modernization and democracy. Perspect. Polit. **8**(2), 551–567 (2010)
24. Kramer, R.M., Brewer, M.B., Hanna, B.: Collective trust and collective action in organizations: the decision to trust as a social decision. In: Kramer, R.M., Tyler, T.R. (eds.) Trust in Organizations: Frontiers of Theory and Research, pp. 357–389. Sage, Thousand Oaks (1996)
25. Levada, Yu.A.: Mechanisms and functions of public trust. Monit. Pub. Opin.: Econ. Soc. Changes **3**, 7–12 (2001)
26. Levi, M.: Sociology of trust. In: International Encyclopedia of the Social & Behavioral Sciences, pp. 15922–15926 (2001)
27. Levis, D., Weigert, A.J.: Trust as social reality. Soc. Forces **63**(4), 967–985 (1985)
28. Lovell, D.: Trust and politics in a post-communist society. Pro et contra **7**(3), 147–162 (2002)
29. Luhmann, N.: Trust and Power. Wiley, Chichester (1979)
30. Meier, S.T.: Computer aversion. Comput. Hum. Behav. **12**, 327–334 (1988)
31. Milner, B.Z.: The factor of confidence in the conduct of economic reforms. Questions Econ. **4**, 27–38 (1998)
32. Misztal, B.A.: Trust in Modern Societies. Blackwell, Cambridge (1996). 296 p.
33. Parks, C.D., Komorita, S.S.: Reciprocal strategies for large groups. Pers. Soc. Psychol. Rev. **1**, 314–322 (1997)
34. Piskotin, M.: The country needs bureaucracy, which deserves trust and respect. RF Today **2**, 26–28 (2002)
35. Poster, M.: The Second Media Age. Polity, Cambridge (1995)
36. Putnam, R.D.: Bowling Alone: The Collapse and Revival of American Community. Simon & Schuster, New York (2000). 541 p.

37. Raub, A: Correlates of computer anxiety in college students [unpublished doctoral dissertation], University of Pennsylvania (1982)
38. Rice, B.: Curing cyberphobia. Psychol. Today **17**(8), 79 (1983)
39. Rogers, E.M.: Diffusion of Innovations, 5th edn. Free Press, New York (2003). 551 p.
40. Seligman, A.B.: The Problem of Trust. Princeton Univ. Press, Princeton (1997). 231 p.
41. Stolle, D.: Trusting strangers – the concept of generalized trust in perspective. Aust. J. Polit. Sci. **31**(4), 397–412 (2002)
42. Sztompka, P.: Trust, distrust and two paradoxes of democracy. Eur. J. Soc. Theory **1**(1), 412 (1998)
43. Tyler, T.R., Degoey, P.: Trust in organizational authorities: the influence of motive attributions on willingness to accept decisions. In: Kramer, R.M., Tyler, T.R. (eds.) Trust in Organizations: Frontiers of theory and Research, pp. 331–357. Sage, Thousand Oaks (1996)
44. Zucker, L.G.: The production of trust: institutional sources of economic structure, 1840–1920. In: Staw, B.M., Cummings, L.L. (eds.) Research in Organizational Behavior, vol. 8, pp. 53–111. JAI Press, Greenwich (1986)

Open Government and Quality of Governance: Does OGP Make Any Difference?

Nicole Fuks and Yury Kabanov(✉)

National Research University Higher School of Economics, St. Petersburg, Russia
nikol.fuks@gmail.com, ykabanov@hse.ru

Abstract. The question if the Open Government Partnership (OGP), launched in 2011, has any impact on policies and institutions in its member-states, remains open. Despite several case studies revealing modest achievements of OGP to improve governance, little research has been done so far to explore this puzzle in general, using statistical means. Addressing this gap, this pilot study analyzes the impact of OGP membership on the quality of governance. Using policy feedback theory and Bayesian Structural Equation Modeling (BSEM), we have discovered that OGP might have an indirect influence on the governance quality via the development of civic participation, government transparency and feedback mechanisms.

Keywords: Open Government Partnership · Governance · Policy feedback · Structural equitation modeling

1 Introduction

Being for a long time a normative value, in the last decade, open government became a global innovation in public administration [14]. One of the possible factors to have affected its popularity seems to be the activity of international organizations, like the Open Government Partnership (OGP). Launched in 2011 as a multistakeholder organization, and currently having 79 member-states, this organization aims at increasing citizen participation and the use of new technologies to ultimately achieve a "more transparent, responsive, accountable and effective government".[1]

OGP has a mechanism to ensure governments follow this policy: the latter, together with the civil society organizations, should develop national action plans with commitments they are ready to make.[2] The Independent Reporting Mechanism is designed to evaluate each country's progress and affect the implementation of the actions plans.[3]

Yet, it is unclear whether OGP membership makes any difference, as countries are different in their adherence to their action plans, and the latter themselves vary according to their possible transformative impact [10]. Scholars also express quite

[1] https://www.opengovpartnership.org/process/joining-ogp/open-government-declaration/.
[2] https://www.opengovpartnership.org/tag/national-action-plan.
[3] https://www.opengovpartnership.org/about/independent-reporting-mechanism.

D. A. Alexandrov et al. (Eds.): DTGS 2019, CCIS 1038, pp. 120–129, 2019.
https://doi.org/10.1007/978-3-030-37858-5_10

moderate, if not sceptical, opinions that OGP membership has led to substantial changes in governments' performance [1, 6]. However, there are currently few papers that would evaluate impact of OGP on a larger sample, as well as unveil the mechanisms OGP membership may stimulate changes in governance. In this paper we aim at addressing the gap. We focus on one of the OGP priorities and ask the question whether OGP membership impacts the increase of the quality of government, and if yes, what the mechanisms of such impact are. Based on the policy feedback theory [11], we propose several hypotheses tested with the Bayesian Structural Equation Modeling (SEM).

The remainder of the paper is structured as follows: first, we review existing research on how OGP membership impacts member-states; secondly, we present the theoretical framework and hypotheses of the research; thirdly, we outline the empirical research design; fourthly we present and discuss the findings.

2 Impacts of the Open Government Partnership: A Review

Currently, there is not a considerable amount of research on how OGP transforms national public policies or institutions. Most of the literature here is based on case-studies or qualitative comparisons of several countries. Overall, the impact of OGP is considered to be controversial and heavily dependent on the willingness of governments to cooperate with civil society. As highlighted by Manolea and Cretu for the cases of Romania and Moldova, despite modest results, OGP membership seemed to boost the dialogue between governments, civil associations and technical experts, which might have had positive long-term results [7]. On the contrary, the lack of civil society engagement, according to Fraundorfer, became an obstacle for OGP efforts in the US, the UK and Brazil, and he believes OGP is a "smokescreen serving the governments to show off, … while in fact trying to deflect from on-going secrecy, lack of transparency, and corruption in government affairs" [1, p.622]. The same problem has been also found in Czech Republic: as argued by Laboutková, the low effect of OGP on anti-corruption policies could be explained by little civil society involvement, lack of salience and the emphasis on technical aspects, rather than substantial transformations [6]. At the same time, as shown in Wilson's analysis of the Norwegian case, there can be different direct and indirect mechanisms of policy learning and inhibition within the government agencies on the individual and organizational levels [13].

Although case studies provide valuable in-depth information, few attempts have been made so far to provide a more general analysis. Harrison and Sayogo estimated how various factors, including OGP commitment, influence transparency, participation and accountability, and found some evidence that membership in OGP positively impacts particular aspects of the dependent variables [3]. However, the level of openness in OGP countries varies substantially, which, according to Schnell and Jo, can be due structural factors, namely constraints on executives and citizens' education [12].

In sum, the review of the existing literature suggests further research on the impact of OGP membership on the internal transformations in the countries. At the same time, it gives some hints on the factors and mechanisms that facilitate or hinder successful implementation of the OGP – promoted policies, that will be tested further.

3 Theoretical Framework: Policy Feedback

Membership in OGP can be considered a sort of policy (or set of actions and commitments) potentially affecting the governmental process. Hence, the policy feedback theory by Pierson can be a valuable framework for drawing hypotheses. Pierson argues that reforms often lead to changes in socio-economic and political processes, and even to the emergence of the new institutional settings [11]. The framework highlights the main actors influenced by policies: the state elites, interest groups and the general public, - as well as the causal mechanisms of policies impact (effect): (1) the resources and incentives created by a particular policy and (2) the interpretative effect. This gives an overall of six mechanisms of the policy feedback [11]. In this study we focus on state and societal actors as influenced by OGP policy, and operationalize four possible mechanisms of OGP impact on the quality of government.

Firstly, new OGP–inspired policies may change the administrative resources within the government, as their implementation requires professionalism of bureaucracy, increase of administrative capacity and special skills [11]. For citizens, accordingly, policies produce the "lock-in effect", e.g. new forms of action within the established structures [11]. In case of open government, such effect may be seen in civic participation that the policy prioritizes [8]. New platforms are created, encouraging people to take certain actions within the new institutional structure. Hence, our hypothesis is that:

***H1*: Country membership in OGP improves the quality of government by increasing civic participation.**

Secondly, we may consider the information and interpretative effect the policy produces. In the case of the state elites, it is related to the policy learning: if the idea has proved effectiveness in one country, it may stimulate its implementation in other polities [13]. Membership in OGP, having started with only 8 and expanded to 79 countries, not to mention subnational units and civil society organization, seems to be a relevant indicator of the policy appeal to decision-makers. For the mass public, interpretation is related to the information content of the policy, helping citizens to develop political activity [11]. Pierson distinguishes two dimensions of the interpretative effect. The first one is *visibility*, i.e. citizens should observe and understand the result of the reform. Regarding the open government, such result may manifest itself in the provision of access to the open government data, as well as the overall transparency of the government. Here the second hypotheses can be formulated as follows:

***H2*: Country membership in OGP improves the quality of government by providing access to government data, as well as the ability to obtain information about government activities.**

The second effect – *traceability* - means that citizens are able to relate policy results to particular actions of government officials, as well as to express their opinion on the actions [11]. This can be associated with OGP endeavors to establish citizens participation in monitoring the quality of government. Therefore, the following research hypothesis is formulated:

***H3*: Country membership in OGP improves the quality of government by providing more opportunities for citizens to respond to the work of state actors.**

4 Data and Methods

The hypotheses formulated above presume that there are certain mechanisms (paths), through which independent and dependent variables are linked to each other. Hence, an appropriate method to analyze such interrelationship is the Structural Equation Modeling (SEM). Since our independent variable is a categorical (binary) one, we use the Bayesian structural equation modeling (BSEM). The key element of BSEM is the posterior distribution (prior distribution). A posteriori values (priors) reflect past beliefs in the probabilistic values of parameters before collecting the new data, which are formed by a theory or a previous research [9]. When a special software (e.g. AMOS) is used, these values are calculated automatically. The results are displayed in the posterior predictive p (PPP): if the value of PPP is close to 0.5, we may reject the null hypothesis and proceed with interpretation [2, p. 158-159]. We should also pay attention to the Bayesian credibility intervals of 95%, which should be interpreted as follows: if 0 falls into the lower and the upper intervals, then the relationship tested is statistically insignificant. The mean in the analysis is analogous to the regression coefficients [4, p. 785]. All calculations are performed using SPSS AMOS software.

The data sample we use for BSEM consist of 328 observations (country-year), which cover the period of 2014–2017, due to the availability of the data. Our dependent variable – *the quality of governance* – is operationalized with the data on the Government Efficiency (WGI_GE) from the World Governance Indicators by the World Bank.[4] The independent variable (OGP) of the study is binary and reflects the *membership of a country in OGP* (1 – a member, 0 – not a member). The information was collected on the official website of OGP.[5] For the mediated variables we have used the data from the Rule of Law Index by the World Justice Project,[6] which provides operationalization of our four hypotheses: (1) *civic participation* (OGI_CP) for *H1*; (2) *government bills and government data* (OGI_PLGD) and *the right to information* (OGI_RTI) for *H2* and (3) complaint mechanisms (OGI_CM) for *H3*. Descriptive statistics is presented in the Table 1.

[4] https://info.worldbank.org/governance/wgi/.

[5] https://www.opengovpartnership.org/.

[6] https://worldjusticeproject.org/.

Table 1. Descriptive Statistics of the Variables

Code	Number of cases	Minimum	Maximum	Mean	Std. Deviation
OGI_PLGD	328	,11053	,91039	,4690870	,18192122
OGI_RTI	328	,10544	,94746	,5442499	,13722368
OGI_CP	328	,16371	,94620	,5922234	,16633808
OGI_CM	328	,13575	,92617	,5732487	,14676258
WGI_GE	328	−1,67260	2,19858	,1526302	,89461254

5 Analysis

In order to get a basic overview of how variables interact with each other, we conduced a correlation analysis. The results (Table 2) suggest that the hypotheses drawn are quite relevant, as all variables correlated positively and significantly with each other. OGP member-states seem to have higher rates of openness and the governance quality, though the coefficient of correlation between OGP and WGI_GE is not very high. On the contrary, the quality of governance correlate significantly with other measurements of openness, which may speak for an indirect effect of OGP on the governance quality.

Table 2. Correlation Analysis (Spearman's rho).

	OGP	OGI_PLGD	OGI_RTI	OGI_CP	OGI_CM	WGI_GE
OGP		,330**	,422**	,473**	,427**	,245**
OGI_PLGD	,330**		,750**	,554**	,677**	,693**
OGI_RTI	,422**	,750**		,713**	,776**	,733**
OGI_CP	,473**	,554**	,713**		,756**	,582**
OGI_CM	,427**	,677**	,776**	,756**		,645**
WGI_GE	,245**	,693**	,733**	,582**	,645**	

Note: ** - correlation is significant at the 0,01 level.

We then ran several BSEM models. The first one explores the connection between OGP membership and the quality of governance via civic participation. The model has PPP of 0.5 and that allows us to proceed with interpretation. The results of the path analysis (Table 3) are significant for all cases. Quite surprisingly, the link between OGP and WGI_GE here is negative, but it is observed only in case of the direct effect: when it comes to the indirect and total effects (Table 4), the relationship turns out to be positive. As we test mostly indirect effects, which are positive and significant, we may accept the hypothesis that OGP membership positively influences the quality of governance via the increase of civic participation (H1).

The second model takes the quality and accessibility of the public laws and the government data (OGI_PLGD) as a mediated variable. The PPP value is 0.5, and the analysis (Table 5) reveals statistically significant and positive links between OGP membership and the availability of state laws and data, as well as between the latter and the government quality. At the same time, the direct link between OGP and WGI_GE is again negative and in this case insignificant (as 0 falls within the credibility intervals). But the indirect effect (Table 6) allows us to confirm H2.

Table 3. The analysis of Model 1.

Regression Weights	Mean	S. E.	S. D.	C. S.	Median	95% Lower Bound	95% Upper Bound
WGI_GE <–OGP	−0.141	0.002	0.073	1.000	−0.141	−0.285	−0.001
OGI_CP<–OGP	0.103	0.000	0.010	1.000	0.103	0.084	0.123
WGI_GE<–OGI_CP	3.717	0.011	0.368	1.000	3.708	2.999	4.453

Table 4. Standardized direct, indirect and total effect of variables from Model 1.

	OGP	OGI_CP
Direct Effect		
OGI_CP	0.616	0.000
WGI_GE	−0.156	0.689
Indirect Effect		
OGI_CP	0.000	0.000
WGI_GE	0.425	0.000
Total Effect		
OGI_CP	0.616	0.000
WGI_GE	0.269	5.689

Table 5. The analysis of Model 2.

Regression Weights	Mean	S. E.	S. D.	C. S.	Median	95% Lower Bound	95% Upper Bound
OGI_PLGD<-OGP	0.076	0.000	0.012	1.000	0.076	0.053	0.099
WGI_GE<–OGI_PLGD	3.701	0.002	0.217	1.000	3.701	3.277	2.824
WGI_GE<–OGP	−0.037	0.001	0.049	1.000	−0.037	−0.134	0.057

Table 6. Standardized direct, indirect and total effect of variables from Model 2.

	OGP	OGI_PLGD
Direct Effect		
OGI_PLGD	0.414	0.000
WGI_GE	−0.041	0.751
Indirect Effect		
OGI_PLGD	0.000	0.000
WGI_GE	0.311	0.000
Total Effect		
OGI_PLGD	0.414	0.000
WGI_GE	0.270	0.751

Another confirmation of *H2* comes from Model 3 with the right to information (OGI_RTI) as a mediated variable. The PPP value is 0.48 here, the results of the analysis are presented in Table 7. The results obtained demonstrate that all analyzed relationships of variables are significant, though, again the direct link between the independent and dependent variable is negative and not very high. The indirect effect between them is nevertheless positive (Table 8), and suggests that OGP members have a higher quality of governance due to a greater access to information for citizens, which confirms *H2*.

Table 7. The analysis of Model 3.

Regression Weights	Mean	S. E.	S. D.	C. S.	Median	95% Lower Bound	95% Upper Bound
WGI_GE <–OGP	−0.149	0.001	0.055	1.000	−0.149	−0.258	−0.042
OGI_RTI<–OGP	0.074	0.002	0.009	1.000	0.074	0.057	0.091
WGI_GE<–OGI_RTI	5.337	0.001	0.332	1.000	5.333	4.691	5.994

Table 8. Standardized direct, indirect and total effect of variables from Model 3.

	OGP	OGI_RTI
Direct Effect		
OGI_RTI	0.535	0.000
WGI_GE	-0.164	0.816
Indirect Effect		
OGI_RTI	0.000	0.000
WGI_GE	0.438	0.000
Total Effect		
OGI_RTI	0.074	0.000
WGI_GE	0.247	5.333

Finally, our fourth model tests another mediated variable – the availability of the complaint mechanism (OGP_CM). The PPP value equals 0.48. As in case of Model 2, the direct link between OGP and WGI_GE is not significant, unlike others in the model (see Table 9). The direct, indirect, and overall effects confirm the hypothesized relationship between OGP membership and the quality of governance via the availability of complaints mechanisms (*H3*) (Table 10).

Table 9. The analysis of Model 4.

Regression Weights	Mean	S. E.	S. D.	C. S.	Median	95% Lower Bound	95% Upper Bound
WGI_CM <–OGP	0.077	0.000	0.009	1.000	0.077	0.059	0.095
WGI_GE<–OGI_CM	4.632	0.003	0.308	1.000	4.629	4.029	5.246
WGI_GE<–OGP	−0.106	0.02	0.056	1.000	−0.106	−0.214	0.005

Table 10. Standardized direct, indirect and total effect of variables from Model 4.

	OGP	OGI_CM
Direct Effect		
OGI_CM	0.517	0.000
WGI_GE	−0.118	0.757
Indirect Effect		
OGI_CM	0.000	0.000
WGI_GE	0.392	0.000
Total Effect		
OGI_CM	0.077	0.000
WGI_GE	0.247	4.627

In general our results suggest that although the direct impact of OGP membership on the quality of governance is not very high, there might be an indirect effect of it via different channels, namely the rate of civic participation, availability and quality of the government information, and the development of feedback complaint mechanisms.

6 Discussion

The results of our analysis have several implications. First of all, although many scholars express their concern on OGP effectiveness [1, 6, 13], it seems to have a certain positive impact on national policies and institutional changes, which is in line with some previous findings [3], but this effect is indirect. According to the proposed framework, membership in OGP gives necessary incentives to decision-makers and non-governmental actors, stimulates policies and institution-building that allow more civic engagement and government transparency, as well as better feedback mechanisms. Such policies and institutions in-turn increase the quality of governance.

There may be alternative explanations, though. For instance, the mediated variables we used can be considered necessary prerequisites for OGP effectiveness. In order to impact national policies and institutions, OGP recommendations and national action plans should be implemented in cooperation with non-governmental actors, which is unlikely when the mechanisms of such cooperation are underdeveloped. Again, this does not contradict with the previous accounts on OGP failures in particular countries [1, 6, 13]. Another interpretation comes from the problem of causality: though BSEM helps to minimize it, there can be true that revealed relationship is due to the fact that OGP countries had already had higher rates of openness and governance quality before they joined the Partnership [12].

The existence of alternative explanations may be considered a limitation of this study, and there are several others. First of all, there is a problem of data availability, because of which, the period of analysis is short, and the use of aggregate measurements gives only a general overview. Secondly, a binary variable (OGP) that has been used does not allow estimating the intensity of a country's interaction with or commitment to OGP, only a mere fact of membership. Hence there is a necessity to perform a more rigorous analysis to differentiate between those following OGP agenda and those with nominal "smokescreen" [1] participation. Finally, the mediated variables that we have used are all related to open government measurements, and other possible structural factors that facilitate OGP impact remain unexplored, not to mention that the measurement of the governance quality might need further refinement [5]. These limitations can be overcome in future studies.

7 Conclusion

This pilot study has confirmed our hypotheses on the indirect effect of OGP membership on the quality of governance. The analysis has proved the theoretical assumptions derived from Pierson [11] that the resources and stimuli, as well as information effects (*visibility* and *traceability*) enshrined into a new policy may improve the efficiency of government, by raising civic engagement, setting new standards of transparency and building new institutions for citizen – government interaction.

At the same time, the study gives only a general overview of these relationships and paths of OGP impact. Further analysis is needed, including in-depth case studies and statistical analyses. A promising step forward here is to use more nuanced variables depicting the level of a country's attachment and commitment to OGP principles, as well as to include other mediated variables that would explore structural facilitators and barriers of the policy.

Acknowledgement. The research has been carried within the project "Strategies and mechanisms of sta-bility in multilevel political systems" within the HSE Program of Fundamental Studies (2019).

References

1. Fraundorfer, M.: The open government partnership: mere smokescreen or new paradigm? Globalizations **14**(4), 611–626 (2017). https://doi.org/10.1080/14747731.2016.1236463
2. Gelman, A., Hill, J.: Data analysis using regression and multilevel/hierarchical models. Cambridge University Press, Cambridge (2006)
3. Harrison, T.M., Sayogo, D.S.: Transparency, participation, and accountability practices in open government: a comparative study. Gov. Inf. Q. **31**(4), 513–525 (2014). https://doi.org/10.1016/j.giq.2014.08.002
4. Hox, J.J., Moerbeek, M., Van de Schoot, R.: Multilevel Analysis: Techniques and Applications. Routledge, Abingdon (2017)
5. Langbein, L., Knack, S.: The worldwide governance indicators: Six, one, or none? J. Dev. Stud. **46**(2), 350–370 (2010). https://doi.org/10.1080/00220380902952399
6. Laboutková, Š.: Open government partnership: unutilized potential in post-communist EU members?(Case of the Czech Republic). Innovation Eur. J. Soc. Sci. Res. **31**(3), 350–376 (2018). https://doi.org/10.1080/13511610.2017.1415803

7. Manolea, B., Cretu, V.: The influence of the Open Government Partnership (OGP) on the Open Data discussions. European Public Sector Information Platform. Topic Report No. 2013/10 (2013). https://www.europeandataportal.eu/sites/default/files/2013_the_influence_of_the_ogp_on_the_open_data_discussions.pdf
8. Moynihan, D.P., Soss, J.: Policy feedback and the politics of administration. Public Admin. Rev. **74**(3), 320–332 (2014). https://doi.org/10.1111/puar.12200
9. Muthén, B., Asparouhov, T.: Bayesian structural equation modeling: a more flexible representation of substantive theory. Psychol. Methods **17**(3), 7–8 (2012)
10. Open Government Partnership: Independent Reporting Mechanism. Technical Paper 1. http://www.opengovpartnership.org/wp-content/uploads/2019/07/Technical-paper-1_final.pdf
11. Pierson, P.: When effect becomes cause: policy feedback and political change. World Polit. **45**(4), 595–628 (1993). https://doi.org/10.2307/2950710
12. Schnell, S., Jo, S.: Which countries have more open governments? Assessing structural determinants of openness. The American Review of Public Administration (2019). https://doi.org/10.1177/0275074019854445
13. Wilson, C.: Multi-stakeholder initiatives, policy learning and institutionalization: the surprising failure of open government in Norway. Policy Studies, 1–20 (2019). https://doi.org/10.1080/01442872.2019.1618808
14. Yu, H., Robinson, D.G.: The new ambiguity of open government. UCLA L. Rev. Discourse **59**, 178–208 (2011)

E-Polity: Politics Online

Interaction of Authorities and Citizens: What Opportunities Does the Internet Provide (on the Example of the Yaroslavl Region)

Alexander Sokolov[(✉)] and Yuri Golovin

Demidov P.G. Yaroslavl State University, Yaroslavl, Russia
alex8119@mail.ru

Abstract. The purpose of this study was to identify the Internet potential in intersectoral interaction (authorities, non-profit organizations and population) in the Yaroslavl region. In this study, the materials of the quantitative survey conducted in January-February 2018 in the territory of the Yaroslavl region were used in comparison with the data of regular all-Russian studies. In addition, materials from two expert interviews (among representatives of regional and local authorities and among leaders and employees of non-profit organizations) were used.

It is already possible to talk about the positive impact of the Network on the dialogue between different sectors of society. Each of the parties has its advantages from the emergence and spread of the Internet: society get accessibility of services (state, local, non-profit organizations); power get simplification of procedures for regulating and controlling civil society (the ability to monitor sentiments in different territories, groups). Public receive the availability of government support measures for NGOs and civic initiatives, as well as the popularization of the non-profit organizations themselves. In the Yaroslavl region, the Internet becomes an important communication channel in the intersectoral interaction, which forms a new culture of communication, and a mechanism for consolidation. The study confirmed the hypothesis that the Internet development facilitates communication with civil society actors (obtaining information and access to power).

At the same time, it was revealed that the development of the Internet network makes it easier to control the subjects of civil society and makes the manipulation technologies more productive.

Keywords: Internet · Yaroslavl region · Communication · Interaction · Authorities · NGOs

1 Introduction

In the conditions of growing number of active citizens, public organizations, formation of new public interests, the authorities establish a dialogue and relationship with them. The authorities first started and then established a dialogue on the Internet with civil society participants since the moment the state turned its attention to a new communication tool (with its capabilities and low cost). Using the Internet in their activities,

D. A. Alexandrov et al. (Eds.): DTGS 2019, CCIS 1038, pp. 133–151, 2019.
https://doi.org/10.1007/978-3-030-37858-5_11

Russian state institutions received a means of adapting to new social processes, monitoring changes in the mood of society and the activities of non-profit organizations. For citizens and the non-profit sector, the Internet opened "doors" to the socio-political life of the country (region), and to the adoption of managerial decisions.

The Internet has expanded the capabilities of its users: it simplifies communication with civil society actors (obtaining information, access to power); reduces material and time costs, bureaucratic procedures in obtaining public services, and circulation of citizens and public organizations to the authorities. At the same time, the Internet carries potential risks. For the authorities - reducing its legitimacy, complicating the process of broadcasting positive values for the state, and sometimes facilitating their substitution. For citizens and non-commercial sector, it produce negative content materials (including those affecting the value orientations of citizens), communication risks (avoiding personal communication), cyber-risks, and consumer risks, etc.

New forms of communication, mainly the Internet, allowed citizens who want to participate in the public life of the city and region, to find contacts and opportunities for the active civic position implementation. Internet tools have made the process of including the population in the life of society quick and simple.

At the same time, it can be said that the development of intersectoral interaction in regional society has not been studied enough. There are gaps in understanding how the development of the Internet affects the openness of the work of government bodies and NPOs, and on the transformation of the nature and intensity of intersectoral interaction. The study of these processes at the regional level is particularly relevant, it can help to understand where they can acquire specific feature, lead to special results.

In this regard, the paper includes several parts. The first part is devoted to a review of the Internet opportunities for interaction of authorities and citizens. The second part demonstrates the data and methods of the author's research, the results of which are presented in paper and demonstrate the conditions and content of the Internet interaction of authorities and citizens in Yaroslavl region. The third part is devoted to a review of the revealed conditions for the development of the Internet intersectoral interaction in Yaroslavl region. The fourth part is devoted to the demonstration of the Internet role in the intersector interaction in Yaroslavl region. In the fifth part, conclusions are drawn on the research conducted and proposing a way ahead and practical recommendations for facilitating the dialogue of the citizens with authorities.

2 Internet Opportunities for Interaction of Authorities and Citizens

Modern society is characterized, on the one hand, by a decrease in the citizens' participation in traditional forms of activity (for example, elections, mass official public associations and parties [1]), and on the other, the growth of activity in new forms, the demand for greater transparency on the part of the authorities, and including citizens in decision-making process [2]. In this aspect, ICTs are a mechanism for realizing a new public request.

Rapid development and application of modern information technologies is the main world development trend in recent years. The main role in this process belongs to the

Internet, which evolved from the information base into a special communicative space. In modern conditions, the Internet has become a special type of social space, reflecting in itself many of the social interactions characteristics, while bringing in its own characteristics of virtuality.

Internet and information-communication technologies allow:

- access to alternative sources of information [3];
- create conditions for open discussions [4];
- involve youth in social and political activity [5];
- provide feedback to the authorities [6].

Thus, firstly, the Internet is a form of communication and information exchange based on the network principle and the practical equivalence of communication entities. Secondly, it acts as a driving force for the development of social networks and horizontal links, as well as their transition to a qualitatively new level, thereby contributing to the formation and development of civil society.

The development of Internet networked technologies against the background of traditional political institutions crisis leads to the fact that citizens (primarily young people) are increasingly reoriented to new channels of communication and forms of activity, which, as Joe Kane and Cathy Cohen point out, cannot be ignored [7].

It is important to note that researchers consider the Internet as:

1. A set of technologies and tools that facilitate the interaction of subjects, and allows them to form networks;
2. The environment in which new forms of participation, collective action, are being formed.
3. A new environment, a technology that allows mass participation of citizens in the decision-making process, expressing their preferences and needs [8].

In this regard, it is simultaneously a medium and an instrument of communication. Digital technologies have accelerated communication and increased opportunities for reaching the audience in space and time. At the same time, information flows are controlled by certain entities that create communication channels [9]. The speed of information dissemination will depend on whether these entities can quickly transfer information to various well-structured communities with strong internal communications. If there are no such entities between the individual communities, than the information formulated in one community will remain inside it, without going into the outside world.

The Internet development facilitated the access of the communication subject and interaction to more contacts [10]. This allowed to reduce the significance of temporary, territorial and other barriers of communication and interaction [11]. As a result, new effective mechanisms for cooperation between different actors are created [12].

The key role of the Internet is that it serves as the most important source of information [13] for each of the subjects in the process of communication and interaction, not only about the situation and the object of interaction, but also about the subjects of communication and interaction. The availability of information, the ease of its exchange, the ability to build communication and interaction through the Internet, increases the importance of citizens' activity on the Internet, requires the authorities to pay due attention to these phenomena.

It is also important to note that the Internet provides several channels for communication, which can be chosen for the interests and priorities of the communication subjects. In this case, subjects can communicate both in private channels, in which information is available only for themselves, and in public. In this regard, an important feature of the Internet is the ability to create conditions for open discussions [4], provide feedback on the government bodies' activities [14].

As a result, such communication forms a proper level of trust, forming the potential for the future [15]. The practice of confidential, operational communication gradually leads to the formation of certain group and informal norms [16].

In this regard, we should agree with S. V. Volodenkov, which indicates that the development of ICT and Internet space, their active use has significantly transformed public space and political management, significantly changing the forms and nature of interaction between the state and society [17].

At the same time, it should be noted that not everyone identifies on-line activity with off-line activity. In particular, E. Morozov, says that the actions on the Internet do not attract or are not related to actions in everyday reality [18]. They only form a sense of personal satisfaction from the perfect actions in virtual reality.

At the same time, an analysis of the practice of intersectional interaction on the Internet reveals a number of negative aspects of the development of the Internet. Among them are:

- the substitution of real communication and virtual interaction;
- anonymity of communication, fakes and bots as a side of communication, the ability to create the illusion of collective actions;
- imperfection of information security, threats of cyber-attacks and loss of confidentiality of interaction (including the safety of personal data);
- discredit the importance and potential of interaction as a constructive social institution.

In this regard, the request for research on the perception of the threats that the development of the Internet brings for constructive intersectoral interaction is being updated. It should be noted that the problem of the black sides of the Internet is recognized as relevant and is being actively investigated [19].

In the conditions of active citizens' and public organizations growth, formation of new public interests, the authorities is in need to establish a dialogue and relationship with them. Using the Internet in their activities, Russian state institutions have received a means of adapting to new social processes, monitoring changes in the mood of society and the activities of non-profit organizations. For citizens and the non-profit sector, the Internet opened "doors" to the socio-political life of the country (region), and the adoption of managerial decisions.

It is important to note that the political institutions crisis leads to the fact that young people are increasingly reoriented to new channels of communication and forms of activity, which, as noted by Joe Kane and Cathy Cohen, can not be ignored [7]. Therefore, it is important for authorities to develop communication with citizens via the Internet, create on-line platforms for discussing topical issues, and to inform and communicate through social networks, as this allows them to involve young people in sociopolitical activity [5].

3 Data and Methods

The purpose of this study was to identify the Internet potential in intersectoral interaction (authorities, non-profit organizations and population) in the Yaroslavl region. Under intersectional interaction is understood the interaction between institutional units of three different areas of the economy: government agencies, commercial enterprises and non-profit organizations, as well as the fourth subject - a simple individual (considered in the concept of intersectoral interaction as a "family"). At the same time, the study focuses on the transformation of openness and the nature of the interaction of the three actors: government agencies, non-profit organizations and individuals.

Yaroslavl region is characterized by a high degree of Internet penetration. This makes it possible to identify the influence of the Internet on various spheres of public and political life and to extrapolate these findings on processes throughout the country.

During the research, the following questions were raised: Does the development of the Internet network affect the interaction of government bodies and civil society actors (getting information, access to power)? Has the Internet simplified the mutual control over participants' activities in the intersectoral interaction? Does the development of the Internet make the state's services more accessible to civil society actors? Does the Internet services of the state and NGOs become more accessible to the population? The development of the Internet network complicates the process of broadcasting positive values for the state, and has the potential to reduce the legitimacy or not? Does the development of the Internet allow you to receive information about the government agencies activities quickly?

In order to answer these questions, the answers of all participants in the intersectoral interaction were involved and then compared. They include the answers of the population, public officials (regional and local level), managers and participants of non-profit organizations.

The main hypothesis is that the Internet development and various forms of communication on its basis stimulate the development of civil society institutions.

In this study, the materials of the quantitative survey conducted in January-February 2018 in the territory of the Yaroslavl region were used in comparison with the data of regular all-Russian studies. In addition, materials from two expert interviews (among representatives of regional and local authorities and among leaders and employees of non-profit organizations) were used.

To conduct a quantitative survey of the population, a multi-stage stratified quota sample was designed, representing the adult population of the Yaroslavl Region aged 18 years and over. The total sample size (647 respondents) is divided into quotas in accordance with the population distribution in the territory of the Yaroslavl region. Municipalities that have the status of a city district with a population of more than 100 thousand people are included in the sample as independent statistical objects. In total, the sample includes 51 towns, including Yaroslavl, Rybinsk, eight small towns of the region, and 41 rural settlements (rural settlements, urban-type villages). The sample is representative for Yaroslavl, Rybinsk and the region as a whole. The level of data reliability in the whole region is 95%, the statistical error is within the range of ±4.7%. Quantitative analysis of the data was carried out using a specialized software package SPSS.

60 employees of regional and local authorities and 64 employees and activists (including the head) of non-profit and public organizations, who have been active in the Yaroslavl region for a different period of time, were selected to conduct expert interviews.

In order to calculate the quantitative indicators, the data of the Federal State Statistics Service of the Yaroslavl Region were used [20].

Levada-Center represents the quoted all-Russian polls. The survey was conducted on December, 2017 for a representative all-Russian sample of urban and rural population among 1,600 people aged 18 and over in 137 settlements in 48 regions of the country. The respondent using a personal interview method conducts the survey at home. The distribution of answers is given as a percentage of the total number of respondents together with the data of previous surveys. The statistical error in the sample of 1600 people (with a probability of 0.95) does not exceed: 3.4% for indicators close to 50%; 2.9% for indicators close to 25%/75%; 2.0% for indicators close to 10%/90%, 1.5% for indicators close to 5%/95% [21].

4 Conditions for the Development of Internet Intersectoral Interaction in Yaroslavl Region

According to "Levada-Center" polls, as of the end of 2017, the share of users of the Network in Russia was 74%. At the same time, since the beginning of observations, the number of citizens using the Internet has grown steadily. Over the past ten years, the growth rate of Internet audience in Russia has slowed. Nevertheless, the popularity of the Internet has not yet reached its "ceiling".

In the Yaroslavl region, according to measurements, the number of Network users is slightly less than in Russia as a whole. However, more than half of the adult have become its users. The Internet audience in the Yaroslavl region in early 2018 was 580,000 people aged 18 and over. It is 55.7% of the total adult population of the region. Of course, Internet sessions have various intervals, and their duration is different.

In the regional Internet audience, socio-demographic groups are not proportionally represented. In the Yaroslavl region, there is a "digital gap" between generations: youth and the middle age group representatives, as well as residents of large cities are active users. In general, Web users are common in each of the demographic strata (except: the older age group, only 23% of Internet users).

The share of Internet users among state and municipal employees of the Yaroslavl region, according to the expert survey, was 100%. The total officials' involvement in the use of the Internet, with an average Internet penetration rate of 55.7%, can be explained by their professional activities. Today, such terms as "e-government", "electronic document management", "electronic services", etc. are used everywhere for the management practices' analysis.

95.2% of non-commercial users uses Network on its daily life and at work.

Residents of the Yaroslavl region prefer to communicate in social networks (72.5%) and entertainment (55.8%) (Table 1). Only 34.4% use the Internet to find the necessary information and only 5% for receiving state and municipal services. When analyzing the use of the Internet by the population, it should be borne in mind that communication and leisure are the basic human needs, state and municipal services are situational needs that may not arise.

Table 1. Tell me, please, for what purposes do you most often use the Internet? (you can have several answers, but not more than 5).

Statements	Residents of the region	State and municipal employees	Employees and activists of NGO
Search for background information (including official information from authorities)	34.4%	91.5%	85%
Working with e-mail	29.7%	91.5%	95%
Finding information for work/school	44.4%	69.5%	76.7%
Reading news	48.6%	79.7%	70%
Communicating in social networks	72.5%	54.2%	63.3%
Discussion in the forums	8.6%	3.4%	20%
Entertainment (music, movies, games, etc.)	55.8%	27.1%	23.3%
Search and purchase of goods and services	17.2%	27.1%	30%
Obtaining state and municipal services	5.0%	44.1%	35%
Your option/for NCOs is "working with distributors"	0.6%	0%	33.3%

While ordinary people in the Yaroslavl region use the Network for leisure and communication, the absolute majority of authorities' representatives and the non-profit sector turn to the Internet for work purposes: search for reference information (91.5% and 85.0% respectively), work with e-mail (91.5% and 95.0%), receiving state and municipal services (44.1% and 35.0%).

Thus, the number of Internet users in the Yaroslavl region already exceeds 500 thousand people (with a total adult population in the region of 1053,000 people) and this figure is steadily growing, and its influence on the vital activity of the population is also growing. This fact fully justifies the timeliness and relevance of the study.

Survey results of staff administration and NGO leaders and staff indicate that the dominant value of Internet communication is the ability to expand their horizons through meeting new perspectives on familiar things. 65.5% of officials and 70.9% of public figures chose this option.

Among the most important motives for using the Internet is communication with people with similar interests, "their own circle" (66.1%), acquaintance with the new "inaccessible" people, i.e. with people geographically separated from each other and/or people with disabilities (36.7%). Note that getting to know new people is an important aspect of Internet communication for representatives of non-profit organizations as well. However, for the absolute majority of state bodies' employees this point is not interesting (86.2%).

According to the research results, the possibilities of modern society in the field of communication have expanded many times, thanks to new information technologies. Within the framework of the society, there is the formation and dissemination of fundamentally new "channels" of interaction and information, which form a new culture of communication and dialogue. For the Yaroslavl region residents, the Internet development allows you to attract like-minded people to solve acute social problems, and to unite more citizens that are indifferent.

According to the quantitative survey, in the Yaroslavl region, the Internet today is the second most popular source of information about events in the country and the region after television (Table 2). Thus, about 49% of the Yaroslavl region adult residents learn about the news from the Network, and 70.9% from TV. Newspapers, as the main source of information about life in the country and the region, were noted by 29.7% of the participants in the mass poll. The remaining types of media are less in demand: 18.7% of the participants learn about socio-political and economic events from conversations with people. 15.6% prefer radio as the main source of information, and 3.4% read magazines.

Table 2. What is the main source of news for you about the events in the country, the Yaroslavl Region? (no more than three answers)

Source of news	%
TV	70.9%
Internet - news, analytical, official sites	35.2%
Internet - social networks, blogs	32.3%
Conversations with people	18.7%
Newspapers	29.7%
Radio	15.6%
Magazines	3.4%
None of the above	0.3%
I'm not interested in this topic, I do not follow the news	0.9%
Difficult to answer	1.9%

A more detailed analysis of the mass poll results revealed that among those for whom the Internet is the main source of information, 37% prefer to view simultaneously news sites and social networks, 32% only news sites and 30% only social networks.

In addition, it should be noted, that a significant proportion of young people and highly educated people characterizes the audience of the Internet news in the Yaroslavl region.

Not all Internet users in the region are interested about the work of regional and local authorities (34.2%), and many people try to avoid it (22.5%). Low interest in reports about the work of local officials during the survey was particularly expressed by the busiest group - representatives of the 30–39 years old group. At this age, the issues of raising children and earning money are of prime importance.

About 40% of the adult audience in the region use the Network as a source of regional and local news (according to the mass survey).

The information-oriented segment of Runet reported a lack of consensus on the regional and local authorities' work of on the Net: 32.5% met laudatory messages; slightly more than 38.6% met negative ones (the difference in the statistical error). Another 29% either did not meet such materials on the Internet, or found it difficult to answer the relevant question.

According to the research, the answers to the question "What kind of opinion about the authorities' work of the Yaroslavl region you most often meet among users of the Internet?" were dedicated to the regional authorities. Those who read unflattering reviews about the authorities, is inclined to critically evaluate their activities, rather than those who have not read such reports (notes).

Thus, on the one hand, the Internet for the nonprofessional is the prompt receipt of information on the state bodies activities and the space for freedom of expression their positions (including criticism of state bodies). On the other hand, one can speak of the real Network influence on the socio-political views of individual citizens. A large part of the regional Runet segment under no circumstances will refuse to use the Internet, if the authorities recommend it (58.7%). Even if it threatens their personal safety or the security of the state.

From the results of the research it is clear that the Internet in the Yaroslavl region not only has already affected the transportability of regional and local authorities and the degree of civil society participants activity, but has already changed the social requirements for information (efficiency, brevity, completeness), the nature of interaction between civil society actors.

Representatives of various segments (citizens, authorities, public figures) asked the same question: "How much do you agree with the following statements?" The answers of the participants to the above question were in many respects similar. Thus, it seems logical not to consider the quantitative survey results and two expert interviews separately, but to highlight several of the most important and general directions of the Internet's influence on citizens' value orientations, their welfare, socio-political mobility and awareness.

Residents, power and social activists see the global network, primarily as a space for self-realization and big (real) capacity to participate in the life of the country (region). This understanding is largely based on the practice of using the network in everyday life and work.

At the same time, the Internet carries a danger, and the inhabitants and experts differed in assessing the degree of their threat. Officials and public figures, consider a negative impact on family values and their formation as the main Internet lack. From the philistine point of view, this is the lesser evil of the Web. Of course, in society, there are those for whom the Network is a threat to family values and the demographic situation, but mostly these are elderly people who do not use the global web in everyday life (no more than 25% of the total sample). A slightly different opinion strengthened in the society today: Internet leads to depression and becomes a catalyst in the intention to commit suicide.

Another danger, which is recognized equally by the inhabitants and experts, is the Internet use by the Western countries against Russia.

In general, as the study showed, only one in four of the Runet users in the region feels safe, secure in themselves and their personal data when they visit the Internet (27.0%). Among officials, a sense of security is shared only by 6.8%, public figures - 8.5%. For the rest, the Internet is a threat, including personal data (Table 3).

Table 3. Do you feel security of yourself, your personal data when you visit the Internet?

Statements	Residents of the region	State and municipal employees	Employees and activists of NGO
Yes, I feel safe to the fullest	27.0%	6.8%	8.5%
I feel only partially self-protected, not from all threats	44.0%	59.3%	50.8%
No, I never feel secure on the Internet	26.2%	28.8%	32.2%
Difficult to answer	2.8%	5.1%	6.8%

Objective reality shows that the Internet is not safe for ordinary citizens and the state as a whole. The network has a real and quite tangible impact on the daily life of society. All this contributes to the tools implementation that guarantee security in the virtual space.

30.0% of the townsfolk are in charge of regulating Internet content, another 35.5% say, "it all depends on the type of information that is distributed." 25.8% of the Yaroslavl region population support the idea that information on the Web should be distributed freely and without censorship, (mostly young people aged 18–29 years).

Representatives of regional and municipal authorities and public figures demonstrate a greater willingness to regulate content (66.1% and 68.3% respectively) and the introduction of Internet censorship (23.7% and 33.3% respectively). In each of the expert groups, only 6% advocated full freedom of openness in RuNet (Table 4).

The degree of citizens', NGOs' and authorities' involvement in the activity on the Internet demonstrate the general conditions, the potential for the development of civil and political activity on the Internet. Significant involvement of citizens in various forms of activity on the Internet, of course, does not allow to say that they are already taking part in various forms of civil and political activity on the Internet. However, their activity on the Web is gradually forming in them the understanding that it is the same natural space of actions as off-line. This creates the potential, conditions for significant civil and political activity of citizens on the Internet in the future. Little by little, the line between off-line and on-line activities is blurred.

Therefore, it is important to monitor the penetration of the Internet into the lives of citizens, the activity of using various services on the Internet.

Table 4. You can find a variety of information on various topics on the Internet. Do you think that any information on the Internet should be distributed completely freely, without any restrictions, or is it necessary to have certain regulation (for example, state) of such dissemination of information?

Statements	Residents of the region	State and municipal employees	Employees and activists of NGO
Information on the Internet should be distributed freely and without censorship	25.8%	6.8%	6.3%
Information on the Internet needs to be regulated (censored)	30.0%	23.7%	33.3%
It all depends on the type of information that is distributed	35.5%	66.1%	68.3%
Difficult to answer	8.7%	3.4%	0%

Starting to use Internet applications that facilitate everyday life, citizens and NGOs bit by bit move to using of state and municipal services on the Internet, communication and interaction with authorities on the Internet. Thus, citizens are transferred to civil and political activity via the Internet.

5 The Internet Role in Intersector Interaction in Yaroslavl Region

Internet today in the Yaroslavl region is the third most effective means of solving personal and social problems, as well as motivating state and municipal employees to fulfill their immediate duties. The demand for online services and web pages for communication between citizens and government officials necessitates the development of information and communication tools for intersectoral interaction.

26% of the Network users used the Internet services and web sites to interact with authorities, according to a sociological survey in the Yaroslavl region. In 2017, 13.6% took advantage of the electronic appeal possibility to the authority, 8.1% on officials and deputies blogs commentaries, 7.2% on official websites drafts discussions, 6.7% on collection signatures under electronic petitions, and appeals to authorities (Table 5).

Thus, in the Yaroslavl region, the socio-political activity of the inhabitants is not reduced only to communicative activity. However, it has its own peculiarity: uneven communion of the population to the use of information technologies in a dialogue with the authorities. This is evidenced by the data of the quantitative survey. The residents of Rybinsk, small towns and rural settlements most actively use online services and web sites when they need to contact the authorities and/or a specific official. Residents of Yaroslavl, spoiled by close proximity to the buildings of public authorities, still prefer the traditional methods of dialogue with municipal and state employees.

The attitude of the Yaroslavl region officials to the actions of citizens on the Internet (petitions, on-line treatment, flash mobs, etc.) is quite serious. Absolute majority of employees recognize them as actual civic activity manifestations

Table 5. Please indicate what forms of interaction with authorities using the Internet you used? (you can have several answers, but not more than 3)

Statements	Average score
Electronic appeals to the authority	13.6%
Discussion of bills on official websites	7.2%
Comments on the blogs of officials and deputies	8.1%
Survey of citizens on official websites of authorities	2.8%
Internet-conferences with officials	2.5%
Collection of signatures under electronic petitions, appeals to the authorities	6.7%
Did not take part in such events	74.2%
Custom variant	0.8%

(comparable to traditional actions). Over the past three years, the attention of the authorities to such citizens' activity has significantly increased. If in 2016, 15.6% talked about the difference between the citizens' actions on the Internet and the actual manifestations of officials' civic activity; in 2018, it is already 36.7%. In 2016, 75.0% of experts only partially acknowledged the actions of the population on the Internet as real manifestations of civic engagement, in 2018 56.7% (Table 6).

Table 6. You can find a variety of information on various topics on the Internet. Do you think that any information on the Internet should be distributed completely freely, without any restrictions, or is it necessary to have certain regulation (for example, state) of such dissemination of information?

Statements	2016	2017	2018
Actions on the Internet FULL OF MEASURE can be perceived as actual manifestations of civil activity	15.6%	18.2%	36.7%
Actions on the Internet can be perceived as actual manifestations of civic activity	75.0%	67.3%	56.7%
Actions on the Internet can not be perceived as actual manifestations of civic engagement	9.4%	14.5%	6.7%

Officials consider conducting work with initiative actions of citizens on the Internet by methods analogous to traditional NGOs (74.4%) or by other methods (16.3%) (Table 7). Only 9.3% of state and municipal employees of the Yaroslavl region considered inappropriate to work with citizens on the Internet. Approximately in the same proportion, the responses of experts to the question of how to work with unregistered associations of citizens were distributed: 65.1% of officials consider it expedient to conduct work similar to traditional NGOs; 23.3% by other methods; 11.6% of expert officials oppose any interaction with similar structures.

This attitude of the authorities to Internet activity has had an impact on the attitude formation of some Yaroslavl region residents to electronic appeals, petitions and other

Table 7. Do you think it is necessary for the authorities to work with unregistered associations of citizens and manifestations of civil activity in the Internet in the same way as working with registered NGOs? What methods?

Statements	2017	2018
I consider it advisable to conduct work similar to traditional NGOs	65.2%	74.4%
I consider it expedient to conduct work by other methods	21.7%	16.3%
I consider it inappropriate to conduct a separate work	8.7%	9.3%
Difficult to answer	4.3%	0.0%

online services. In the minds of 27.7% of Internet users, there is an opinion about the special efficiency of the Internet in solving life problems (Table 8). Another 36.0% said that there was no dependence on the manner in which appeal was submitted. Especially often, those who at least once personally initiated an electronic appeal to the authorities, and/or the signature council under electronic petitions, and/or left their comments in the blogs of officials (deputies) held those opinions. This indicates the high effectiveness of dissemination and the communication to the authorities of their point of view on the Internet.

Table 8. In your opinion, does the interaction of citizens with authorities through the Internet make it more effective in solving problems or not?

Statements	Average score
Traditional ways of communicating with the state are more reliable and effective in solving problems of citizens	19.9%
Communicating with authorities through the Internet increases the effectiveness of solving problems of citizens	27.7%
The effectiveness of communication with authorities does not depend on the method of circulation	36.0%
Difficult to answer	16.3%

Every fifth Internet user shares the statement about the special reliability and effectiveness of "traditional ways of communicating with the state" (19.9%). Among them, most often those who are locked up on the search, receipt and consumption of information on the Internet and themselves are not ready for any initiative actions. Another 16% found it difficult to answer the relevant question.

Such officials approach facilitates the acceleration of the information introduction and communication technologies in the intersectoral interaction in the Yaroslavl region, and testifies to the convenience of this communication format for the officials themselves. Both employees and representatives of the third sector almost unanimously spoke about the fact that the Internet simplifies communication between the subjects of civil society and authorities (83.1% and 88.7% respectively).

The attitude of non-profit organizations and civil activists to representatives of power structures has always been difficult. The emergence of a new communication channel between them (the Internet) could either increase opposition and misunderstanding between them, or cause a rapprochement and growth of mutual understanding. The nature of the Network's influence on intersectoral interaction in the Yaroslavl region helped to uncover expert surveys. They give grounds to say that in the Yaroslavl region the use of the Network opportunities positively influenced the dialogue between different sectors of society. Each of the parties has its advantages from the appearance and distribution of the Internet. Consequently, the Internet has a beneficial effect on the civil society development in general.

Ordinary residents of the Yaroslavl region also recognize that the emergence of special online services positively affected the availability of state and municipal services, as well as the services of non-profit and public organizations. Those who have already applied to the authorities and to the organization of the «third sector» via the Internet, and who do not have such experience share this view.

However, 31.6% of the population are skeptical about the Network's ability to influence the availability of state and municipal services, and 48.6% about non-profit organizations' services. This point of view is prevalent, mainly among those who do not have the experience of applying to the authorities for the necessary documents and information via the Internet.

The opinion of the townsfolk about the positive impact of the Internet on the availability of state and municipal services is fully shared by representatives of government bodies and employees of non-profit organizations.

Speaking about the exceptional usefulness of the Internet for the authorities, most officials drew attention to simplifying the procedure for regulating, controlling the sphere of civil society and civic engagement. This fact during an expert interview was indicated by 60.0% of government bodies' representatives. Only 10.0% called a relatively new means of communication as the reason for the emergence of additional difficulties in the sphere of regulation and control over the situation in civil society, and citizens' activity. Explaining this by the lack of an established mechanism, blurring the responsibility for specific actions.

In addition, as recognized by the authorities, the Network simplifies interdepartmental interaction in solving problematic issues of citizens and other subjects of civil society, increases the effectiveness of information policy. At the same time, it practically does not interfere with the translation of the values necessary for the state.

The main disadvantages of the Internet, according to the authorities, are not 100% inclusion of the population in the Network, the lack of a regulated and stable algorithm of interaction with civil activists and negative content.

From the non-profit organizations and civil activists' point of view, the Internet development in the Yaroslavl region positively influenced access to government support for NGOs and civic initiatives, as well as the popularization of non-profit organizations and civil participation culture, and the inculcation of civic engagement values. During the survey, two-thirds of public opinion experts (64.5%) reported increasing importance of non-profit organizations in the procedure for making state decisions (regional, municipal).

In the Yaroslavl region, the emergence of the Internet has also affected the partnership between various non-profit organizations. In particular, it contributed to the development of cooperation and the establishment of partnerships in resolving problematic issues.

Many leaders and employees of non-profit organizations are confident that the Internet has revived the activities of government authorities. They also forced them to look for new work approaches with the non-profit sector, which positively affects the work of the latter.

It is interesting that all the above-mentioned positive aspects of the Internet influence on the intersectoral interaction in the Yaroslavl region occurred in the conditions of a lack of skills in the Network observed both among the authorities (69.4%) and employees of non-profit organizations (77.0%).

6 Discussion

A little more than half of the adult population of the Yaroslavl region (about 580 thousand people) go online. They do this with varying intensity and frequency. The network has so penetrated the consciousness of the regional society that half of its audience is not ready to give up its use in conditions of personal security, and a possible danger for the camp. In the Yaroslavl region, the Internet has become an integral part of the government bodies' work and non-profit organizations, part of their daily work. Expert polls showed that the share of Internet users among state and municipal employees of the Yaroslavl region was 100%, non-profit sector - 95.2%.

Based on research, the Internet in the Yaroslavl region on the one hand is perceived as a space of self-realization and large (real) opportunities for participation in the life of the country (region), and an important mechanism of communication in the intersectoral space. On the other hand, as a source of danger, with the inhabitants and experts dispersed in assessing the degree of their threat. Officials and public figures consider a negative impact on family values and their formation as the main lack of the Internet. From the point of view of the philistine, this is the lesser evil of the Web. In the society, there are those for whom the Network is a threat to family values and the demographic situation, but mostly these are elderly people who do not use the global web in everyday life (no more than 25% of the total sample). A slightly different opinion appears nowadays: the Internet leads to depression and becomes a catalyst in the intention to settle scores with life.

30.0% of the region population are in charge of regulating Internet content. Representatives of regional and municipal authorities and public figures demonstrate a greater willingness to regulate content (66.1% and 68.3% respectively) and the introduction of Internet censorship (23.7% and 33.3% respectively). In each of the expert groups, only 6% advocated full freedom of openness in RuNet.

Inhabitants of the Yaroslavl region, in addition to what has been said began to realize the "convenience" and effectiveness of the Internet in the process of receiving public services, and in dialogue with the authorities (solving personal and social problems). Individual users of the network saw the seriousness of the officials' attitude towards on-line appeals and citizens' activity in the areas of RuNet and social networks. In support of the above, we focus on 26% of the Network users who entered into a dialogue with officials through Internet services and websites, 13.6% left their comments on official blogs.

Even though traditional channels of communication between the population and authorities representatives began to recede into the background, but for 19.9% of the residents they are still the most preferable because of their "reliability" and "efficiency." This kind of attitude to the old means of communication will be peculiar to some part of the regional society until the Internet becomes available and/or for the absolute majority of the adult population. In addition, traditional forms will still be in demand for some time, because Internet has limitations for technical reasons.

The development of the Internet makes it possible to attract like-minded people to solve acute social problems, and to unite more citizens that are indifferent. Every fifth inhabitant of the region considers the Internet to be an effective means of communicating authorities and all stakeholders (18.5%), encouraging officials to fulfill their immediate duties (18.9%). It is considered effective both by the users of the Network, and by those who have never used it.

The research showed that 83.1% of the officials, participating in the Internet expert survey, simplifies communication between civil society actors. In the opinion of 88.7% non-profit sector representatives, the Internet facilitates communication with other subjects of civil society, authorities and citizens.

It was also revealed that the development of the Internet makes it possible to more effectively control the state decision-making, to participate in this process, to make the government more transparent: 64.5% of non-profit organizations' representatives are confident that their interaction with the state via the Internet increases the efficiency of government bodies.

At the same time, it was revealed that the development of the Internet network makes it easier to control the subjects of civil society and makes the manipulation technologies more productive. Speaking about the exceptional usefulness of the Internet for the authorities, most officials drew attention to simplify the procedure for regulating, controlling the sphere of civil society and civic engagement. This fact during an expert interview was indicated by 60.0% of government bodies' representatives.

The Network simplifies interdepartmental interaction in solving problematic issues of citizens and other civil society actors. The degree of the authorities' consent was 8.53 points (where one is the minimum degree of agreement, ten is the maximum).

The development of the Internet makes it easier to interact with the state, allowing faster delivery of problem signals, expressing disagreement with the decisions and allowing to draw attention to the 3rd sector problems. According to the population survey, approx. 26% of Network users used the Internet services and websites to interact with authorities. In 2017, they took advantage of the electronic appeal possibility to the authority - 13.6%, commentaries on blogs of officials and deputies - 8.1%, discussions on drafts on official websites - 7.2%, collection of signatures under electronic petitions, appeals to authorities - 6.7% and the like.

In the minds of 28% of Internet users, there is an opinion about the special efficiency of the Internet in solving life problems. Another 36.0% said that there was no dependence on the manner in which appeal to the authorities was submitted. Every fifth

Internet user shares the statement about the special reliability and effectiveness of "traditional communicating ways with the state" (19.9%).

The research demonstrated that the Internet has already become one of the main sources of information, both for citizens and for NGOs and government officials. The Internet has also become a tool for working for government officials and NGOs (e-mail, discussion, information retrieval). Moreover, the Internet is one of the main tools for protecting citizens' rights and interests, demonstrating existing social problems. The large-scale expansion of the Internet, the increased use of its tools allow us to say that in the future its significance will increase in the system of management and functioning of government bodies, the non-profit sector.

Citizens, starting to use the Internet for their domestic needs, will gradually form a request for electronic state and municipal services, a greater degree of openness of the public sphere. As a result, information retrieval, access to state and municipal services, and NGO services is facilitated. The activities of government bodies and NGOs become more transparent, and their activities become more controlled.

With this, the facilitation of communication on the Internet does not allow the authorities to create a monopoly in the information space, to ensure the dominance of only positive information about their activities.

The authorities should begin to perceive civil and political activity on the Internet as the classic off-line activity. Of course, not always expressed intention on the Internet is implemented, but it demonstrates the general position of the citizen.

Authorities need to think about developing convenient services for citizens on the Internet that will not only allow receiving state and municipal services via the Internet, but also influence the decision-making process of the authorities. It can be for example portals for discussing draft normative legal acts, portals "offer an idea", on-line broadcasting of meetings, on-line polls and voting on key issues. Full-scale implementation of open data technology and open government at the regional and local levels is required. This will make the government more open and accessible to citizens.

In the same time, the Internet tools alone cannot solve the problems of the effective interaction of the authorities with the population and NGOs without the authorities' readiness to take into consideration the opinion and interests of the population and NGOs. Moreover, the presence of these Internet tools without proper response to the requests received via them from the population and NGOs increases the apathy and passivity of citizens, reduces trust in the authorities and constructive civic engagement.

Therefore, the creation of these Internet tools should be accompanied with significant changes in the functioning of government bodies, increasing openness, willingness to take into consideration the proposals of citizens and NGOs.

7 Conclusions

Today it is already possible to talk about the positive impact of the Network on the dialogue between different sectors of society. Each of the parties has its advantages from the emergence and spread of the Internet: society get accessibility of services (state, local, non-profit organizations); power get simplification of procedures for regulating and controlling civil society (the ability to monitor sentiments in different territories, groups). Public receive the availability of government support measures for NGOs and civic initiatives, as well as the popularization of the non-profit organizations themselves. In the Yaroslavl region, the Internet becomes an important communication channel in the intersectoral interaction, which forms a new culture of communication, and a mechanism for consolidation.

The study confirmed the hypothesis that the Internet development facilitates communication with civil society actors (obtaining information and access to power). The development of the Internet also influenced the partnership between various non-profit organizations. In particular, it contributed to the development of cooperation and the establishment of partnerships in solving problematic issues. Almost all participants in the expert survey (representatives of the "third sector") are confident in the positive effect of the Internet on involving citizens in their activities.

However, there is an awareness not only of the opportunities provided by the Internet, but also of threats to security and basic values. This forms a request for regulation of activity on the Internet, which may become a threat to the freedom of civic activism and self-realization.

In this regard, there is a need for further monitoring of not only those aspects of the impact on the Internet that contribute to intersectoral interaction, but also those in which negative aspects are manifested by restricting rights and freedoms, the possibility of influencing the decision-making process of NGOs and citizens.

Acknowledgment. The reported study was sponsored by Russian Foundation for Humanities as part of the research project № 19-011-00268 "Transformation of civic activity in the conditions of development of information and communication technologies (on the example of the Yaroslavl region)".

References

1. Truly a World Wide Web: Globe Going Digital. Pew Global Attitudes Project. https://www.pewglobal.org. Accessed 12 Dec 2012
2. Evans, T.: Social networking sites have transformed the political landscape. In: Network Conference Studies. https://www.networkconference.netstudies.org/2010/04/social-networking-sites-havetransformed-the-political-landscape. Accessed 12 Dec 2012
3. Horrigan, J., Garrett, K., Resnick, P.: The internet and democratic debate. http://www.pewinternet.org/2004/10/27/the-internet-and-democratic-debate. Accessed 12 Dec 2017
4. Boulianne, S.: Does internet use affect engagement? A meta-analysis of research. Polit. Commun. **26**(2), 193–211 (2009)
5. Palfrey, J., Gasser, U.: Born Digital: Understanding the First Generation of Digital Natives. Basic Books, New York (2008)
6. Curran, J.: Mediations of democracy. In: Curran, J., Gurevitch, M. (eds.) Mass Media and Society. Oxford University Press, New York (2005)
7. Cohen, C., Kahne, J.: Participatory Politics: New Media and Youth Political Action. MacArthur Research Network on Youth and Participatory Politics, Chicago (2012)
8. Rodriguez, S.: Making sense of social change: observing collective action in networked cultures. Sociol. Compass **7**(12), 1053–1064 (2013)

9. Burt, R.S.: Brokerage and Closure. An Introduction to Social Capital. Oxford University Press, Oxford (2005)
10. Lovejoy, K., Saxton, G.D.: Information, community, and action: how nonprofit organizations use social media. J. Comput. Mediated Commun. **17**, 337–353 (2012)
11. Castells, M.: Networks of Outrage and Hope: Social Movements in the Internet Age. University of California Press, Berkeley (2012)
12. Shirky, C.: Cognitive Surplus: Creativity and Generosity in a Connected Age. Penguin Books, New York (2010)
13. Gil de Zuniga, H., Jung, N., Valenzuela, S.: Social media use for news and individuals' social capital, civic engagement and political participation. J. Comput. Mediated Commun. **17**, 319–336 (2012)
14. Curran, J.: Mediations of democracy. In: Curran, J., Gurevitch, M. (eds.) Mass Media and Society, 4th edn. Oxford University Press Inc., New York (2005)
15. Gilbert, E., Karahalios, K.: Predicting tie strength with social media. In: CHI 2009: Proceedings of the 27th annual SIGCHI Conference on Human Factors in Computing Systems. ACM Press, New York (2009)
16. Papacharissi, Z.: A Networked Self: Identity, Community, and Culture on Social Network Sites. Routledge, New York (2010)
17. Volodenkov, S.V.: Political communication as an instrument of power distribution in the system of "state-society" relations. Electron. Bull. **62**, 104–118 (2017). Public administration
18. Morozov, E.: The brave new world of slacktivism. Foreign Policy. http://neteffect.foreignpolicy.com/posts/2009/05/19/the_brave_new_world_of_slacktivism. Accessed 12 Oct 2015
19. Dylko, I., Dolgovb, I., Hoffman, W., Eckhart, N., Molina, M., Aaziz, O.: The dark side of technology: an experimental investigation of the influence of customizability technology on online political selective exposure. Comput. Hum. Behav. **73**, 181–190 (2017)
20. Federal State Statistics Service Homepage. http://yar.gks.ru. Accessed 25 May 2018
21. Levada-Center Homepage. https://www.levada.ru/2018/01/18/polzovanie-internetom. Accessed 20 May 2018

Political Dimension of Modern eSociety: The Case of "Gilets Jaunes" in France

Igor Chernov, Igor Ivannikov, Radomir Bolgov(✉), and Igor Barygin

Saint Petersburg State University, Saint Petersburg, Russia
igor_chernov@mail.ru, ivannikov-1968@yandex.ru,
rbolgov@yandex.ru, st007794@spbu.ru

Abstract. The study examines the main vectors of the impact of social networks on the form of political struggle, which, although partly acquiring a virtual nature, does not change its content. Based on the analysis of quantitative data of "Yellow vests" protest sites, as well as surveys on the social structure of the participants, the study deals with the technology origin and functioning of a new phenomenon of political linguistic and communicative community, acting in the social networks and is not connected with the traditional "really organized" political institutions and groups. The study focuses on the "political power" of this virtual community, i.e. limits of its influence on political decision-making at the national level.

Keywords: E-society · Yellow Vests · France · Collective action · Online community · Linguo-communicative community

1 Introduction

With the development of information and communication technologies (ICT) within the civic society, e-society is gradually developing in Western societies. Within its framework, the government is increasingly using e-democracy tools. However, while the governments consider e-democracy primarily as a tool to improve the governance and to strengthen control over citizens, protest movements develop an understanding of e-democracy as a direct plebiscite democracy, where the government just technically implements the wishes of the majority of voters expressed by Internet voting. Moreover, there is an increase in political mobility and the emergence of new opportunities for counteracting state power. There is also a partial loss of control over communication channels by state institutions. The low-cost and hard-to-control political mobilization scheme emerges instead of traditional high-cost media and political parties/trade unions.

The object of our research is the new forms of "virtual" protest political organization in the developed western countries. We analyze the case of the e-community "Gilets Jaunes"/"Yellow Vests" (GJ) in France.

Chronological framework for the study: October 2018 - January 2019.

The research question is the following: Where are the limits to growth of political influence of national political protest e-community "Gilets Jaunes", which arose within the framework of a developed Western society and social networks?

D. A. Alexandrov et al. (Eds.): DTGS 2019, CCIS 1038, pp. 152–164, 2019.
https://doi.org/10.1007/978-3-030-37858-5_12

Thus, the study does not focus on the history and does not describe this movement. It does not consider the historical and socio-economic reasons for the emergence of this protest movement. We also do not consider the use of social networks by political institutions and organizations as an additional tool to increase the political influence.

2 Theoretical Frameworks and Methodology of Research

This case study is an example of interdisciplinary research, since the whole of the social world in all its diversity is a linguo-communicative network. The online community is only the simplest model of social interaction in general. We engage sociological data, statistics (polls, surveys et al.).

Methodology of linguo-communicative analysis is based on the communicational function of the language, i.e. implies consideration of all social entities as linguo-communicative communities.

The study uses linguo-communicative approach as a new form of structural-functional approach formulated by Parsons [1]. The linguo-communicative approach as neostructuralism acts as an alternative to social constructivism [2]. If there are parallels with Lego, the society is "constructed" in any combination, but in all possible combinations, limited by number and set of parts, i.e., in our case, social reality/society. Moreover, following Giddens, the society is better to call not as a hardened structure, but as a structuration constantly changing and self-reproducing in the communication [3]. All people living in a society have a communication code (language). This code performs a cognitive and communicative function, and thus programs interpersonal interaction, underlies the emergence of linguistic and communicative networks, i.e. practically creates a society as a combination of these networks and connections. There is no "state" and "society" as objects of the physical world that are independent of people. Their reality is ensured by the communicative and cognitive functions of the language.

The emerging e-society is not only a new version of the society, which arises on basis of new communication technologies [4]. Obviously, it is neither the initial, nor the last social modification in history, which has been evolving disparately across various corners of the planet.

According to the definition by Magoulas, Lepouras and Vassilakis, "E-society is a society that consists of one or more e-Communities involved in the areas from e-Government, e-Democracy, and e-Business to e-Learning and e-Health, that use ICT in order to achieve common interests and goals… The development of e-Society is relying and depending on the development of virtual reality (VR) technologies that insure interaction between participants of an e-Society in a more acceptable and tangible way. The development of VR and consequently the e-Society is based on improvement and balancing of participants' interaction methods, hardware necessary for such interaction, content presentation and effort required for development and maintenance" [5].

Philosophy abstracts the idea of virtual reality from its technical embodiment (VR). Virtual reality can be interpreted as a set of objects modeled by real processes, the content and form of which do not coincide with these processes.

Consequently, E-Community can be regarded as: 1. A virtual community established on the World Wide Web; 2. E-Communities are one sort of communication platform on the internet, and support or initiate business processes. They are used to build constant, self-dynamic communication and interaction processes; 3. The development of shared purpose, values, and experience resulting in the formation of trust between a group of people who may be geographically dispersed and communicate mainly via electronic means.

In summary, we call the e-society a virtual set of individuals engaged in different types of relationships, exchanging information and knowledge, with technological access and use that have the potential to change the interaction and interrelations between the different actors within and between communities [6].

It is worth noting that ICT practitioners (for instance, Pistorio) are considering phenomenon of society in linguo-communicative terms: "In my views, it is a revolution in the way people interact with each other and in the way we conduct business. This revolution has been triggered by two phenomena: first, the digitalization of any form of multimedia information – be it voice, video, data or any other form of signal which can now be easily compressed and elaborated – and second the capability offered by the web of reaching in real-time any location in the world from any other location on the globe. The e-society is therefore the result of our new ability to compress almost infinitely both time and space. Today, this allow the transmission of practically unlimited amount of data in real time and where in the world. And this… implies revolutionary changes in the people interact and companies interact, with cycle times being reduced…" [7].

Parsons defined the social system as a "relational (attributed to relations) system of cooperation between the individuals and communities" [1]. Giddens (the structuration theory) presumed that the social system features "generative" (engendering) rules (and resources), rather than hard and fast frameworks" [2]. Luhmann elaborated the communications theory. In his opinion, the society consists of many systems, each performing its own function (economic, political, etc.), but all of them are intertwined with others due to the backbone system, which, basically, is a system of these systems, i.e. "a system of society", which generates and reproduces communication. According to Luhmann, "communication is an integral part of the society, however the very communication cannot exist out of touch with the society… The self-reproduction thesis via communication postulates clear distinct lines between the system and its outer world. Reproduction of communication from communications takes place in the society. All other physical, chemical, neurophysiological and mental conditions pertain to the outer world". [8] Thereby, in Luhmann's opinion, in fact the society is purely a linguistic communication.

It is obvious that all the human (social) actions are collective by nature. Therefore the second important pillar of any social research is the collective action theory. Classic concept of Olson [9] considers any protest political movement as a vertical structure. The grievances are caused by conflict characteristic for any society. However, the emergence and activity of any protest movement is possible only when there are changes in resources and opportunities for the emergence of collective action. In other words, the latent group must become institutional in order to achieve its interests, since it is the only who will cover the "costs" for the struggle, i.e. it is able to mobilize resources.

The influence of the Internet on political behavior is of great interest to researchers. It is worth mentioning here the studies of Bimber, Cornfield, Grossman, etc. [10–12].

Studies of Bimber, Flanagin and Stohl [13], devoted to the influence of ICT on collective action, complement and revise the classical theory, in which the main role in interaction, motivation and coordination is assigned to formalized organizations. So we deal with a developed version of collective action theory, which takes into account the fact that the social networks, chats, and blogs reduce communication costs and coordination, and decrease the importance of formal structures. Edelman [14] refers a horizontal connection without hierarchy. Such an organization operates basing on the principle of a swarm ("organization en essaim"). The motion of the movement is invisible, and its elements are visible only when they are collected in joint mass.

A lot of research deals with the impact of Web 2.0 technologies on society and, in particular, the impact of social media. The development of information technology over the past 20 years, and the emergence of new ways of communication have had a significant impact on the interaction between society and government, which makes it more open. Poster points out that the modern world is characterized by a decentralized communication network, which makes senders consumers, producers by consumers, manageable, breaking the logic of understanding the first media age [15]. This means that online communication can completely change the status positions of its subjects: citizens have the opportunity to apply directly to the head of state in order to receive feedback and influence a specific political decision. Hirst and Harrison note that since the days of Ancient Greece, where democracy was born, political communication has changed dramatically [16].

At the present stage of social networks development, researchers are increasingly turning to them as a source of information on a variety of issues and areas. Methods of studying the dissemination of information in social networks are largely based on the use of content analysis tools. In that regard, studies of Papacharissi are of interest [17]. Sobkowicz, Kaschesky and Bouchard used the method of automated content analysis of social media in order to identify new trends in society, the views, inclinations, moods, attitudes and expectations of interest groups and society as a whole. As a result, a model of shaping public opinion with the help of social media was presented [18].

Meijer and colleagues explored the Internet communities and social networks of emigrants who moved to the Netherlands and needs assistance in obtaining public services: registration of a residence permit, search for a place in educational institutions, receiving various benefits, etc. [19]. The study confirmed the potential impact of discussions on the Internet on the course of real social processes.

Smith, Schlozman, Brady and Verba conducted a study of the impact of communication in social media on the political activity of citizens in the U.S. [20]. Kavanaugh, Fox, Sheetz and their colleagues studied various social media and online services such as Twitter, Facebook, Flickr, YouTube, in order to identify citizens' problems in real time and respond to public security requests [21]. Linders also addresses social media in his research, assessing the role of citizens as partners and producers, and not simply as passive consumers of information on public services [22].

Tufekci writes that social networks simplify political mobilization, either events of the Arab Spring or the Occupy Wall Street movement in New York in 2011. However, the speed of online mobilization, in his opinion, has negative sides: the weakness of a long-term organization and ease of manipulation [23].

As for the genesis of "Gilets Jaunes", then, despite the novelty of this movement, the issue already covered by many articles [24, 25]. However they consider only occasional aspects of online activity, not covering the whole picture.

3 Results of Research: Case of "Gilets Jaunes" Movement

3.1 The Application of Collective Action Theory to the Statistics Analysis of "Gilets Jaunes" Political Activity in Social Networks

It is no accident that Facebook has become the digital headquarters of the "Gilets Jaunes" which turned into the leading political force of the French segment of Facebook for three months (November 2018 - January 2019). In January 2019 the group "Compteur official de gilets jaunes" numbered 2.7 million participants, while the account of French President Macron had 2.4 million subscribers, and an account of to-date most popular French politician M. Le Pen had 1.6 million subscribers. Half of Frenchmen received information from Facebook. 16.7 million Frenchmen visit other information websites every day [25]. However, this phenomenon is not unique to modern French society. The Italian political populist "Five stars movement" which supports "Gilets Jaunes" in France used the Internet platform "Rousseau" as an effective tool for its organization.

At the beginning of 2018 the policy of President Macron led to a significant growth of protest moods in French society, which spilled into the Internet. In January 2018 the first "Anger Groups" appeared. They were promoting the slogans of the future of "Gilets Jaunes". However, at the time they were small, scattered and have only a local character (i.e. on the level of French departments and "friend groups").

May 29, 2018, the distributor of cosmetics Priscillia Ludosky, living in Paris, built petition "For a drop in the fuel prices at the pump!" Change.org, which was signed by several hundred people for several months. October 10, 2018 one of the local radio stations told Ludosky that she is invited to broadcast if the petition collects at least 1,500 signatures. After the announcement about it on the Internet the right number of signatures has been collected. Ludosky was on the radio, then uploaded new petition "For a fuel price cappet at 1 euro par liter" in MesOpinion (French-language crowdsourcing site). This text became quickly spread in the network. On the same day, the chauffeur Eric Drouet, who read the petition, created a Facebook event "National Blockage Against Rising Fuel 17 November 2018". October 21, the first article about Ludosky petition appears in the French national newspaper "Le Parisien". After this issue, the topic was picked up by other national media, which led to an increase in the number of signatures from 12 000 to 850 000 in a month.

Since October 24th the movement was taken up by dozens of groups in Facebook, including Ghislain Coutard, who urged the participants of the upcoming action to put on yellow vests from their cars (it is obligatory under French law since 2008) and posted his video on Facebook where he is in a yellow vest. By early January, his video was viewed by 5.5 million users. Ludosky petition totaled 1.2 million signatures. There is an exponential growth of "Gilets Jaunes" on Facebook. For example, the group "La France en colere" gathered 340 thousand participants in January 2019. The group "Fly Rider Infos blocage", created by Maxime Nicole gathered 160 thousand participants. The group administrator "Compteur official de gilets jaunes" counted 2.7 million members of the group. Moreover, the "silent majority" of the Frenchmen already learned of "Gilets Jaunes". On January 2019 16% of French people identified themselves as "yellow vests". Moreover 44% of French people declared sympathy for them [26].

Before November 17, 2018 (the first Saturday of mass protests), hundreds of pages and groups appeared numbering from a few people to tens of thousands. Some organizers were hiding behind nicknames, representing themselves as "ordinary citizens". Local offices of anti-system political parties also came as organizers in a number of cases (for example, far left "La France insoumise"). For several days, the "Gilets Jaunes" tried to collect and centralize all the information on a single map created on Google Maps. All details of future manifestations, place, time, possibility of communication via Facebook with organizers were noted. January 22, 2019, hundreds of groups were open and active on Facebook. They gathered from several hundred to 1.8 million people. The largest group, "Le Compteur officiel de gilets jaunes", was established on November 27, 2018, and to 2019 has reached 1,8 million participants according to new Facebook counting procedure, or 3 million according to own calculations of "Gilets Jaunes".

Thus the development of "Gilets Jaunes" can be illustrated by the following graphs and diagrams, composed of quantitative data obtained with crowdtangle tool, and based on analysis of activity of 250 Facebook groups associated with "Gilets Jaunes", weekly from November 4, 2018 to January 19, 2019.

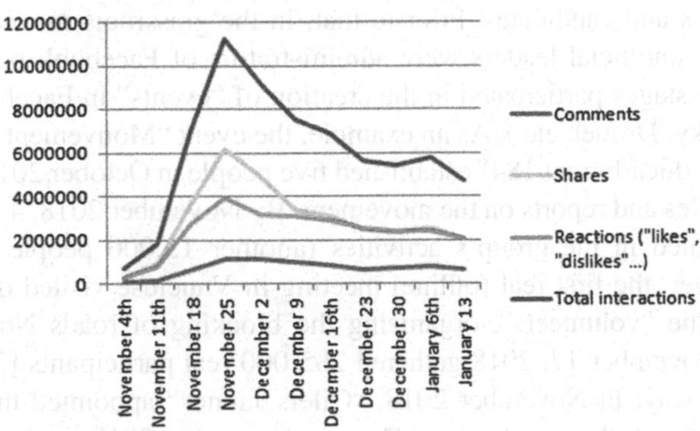

Fig. 1. Activity of "Gilets Jaunes" in Facebook from October 2018 to January 2019 [27].

Figure 1 illustrates the change in activity in groups of the "Gilets Jaunes" in Facebook from October 2018 to January 2019. The peak of activity falls on November 2018, and then there is an obvious decline in interactions of any kind.

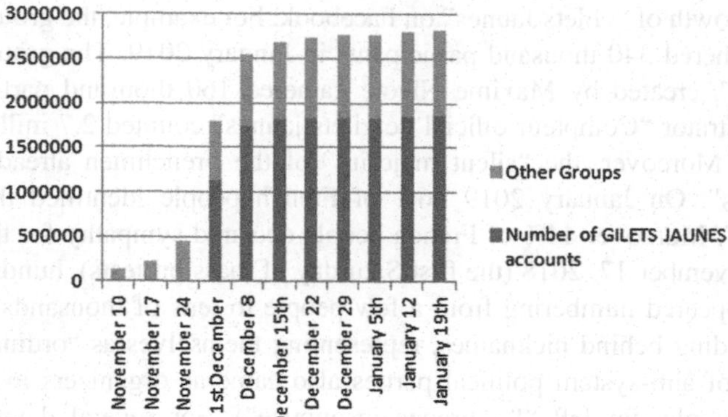

Fig. 2. Number of "Gilets Jaunes" group members in Facebook from October 2018 to January 2019 [27]

In Fig. 2, we can see a qualitative increase in the number of "Gilets Jaunes" groups during October and November 2018. After that, in December and January, there is a slowdown in growth and its stagnation. The Table 1 illustrates the same processes.

Moreover, in parallel with a slowdown in quantitative growth after the first outbreak of activity in November 2018, a gradual formalization and "monopolization" of the movement took a place. Until November 2018, the movement had neither administration nor formal structure that would define the strategy of political struggle. There were no direct connections with trade unions, associations and political parties. However, after the first mass protests "Gilets Jaunes" needed "official representatives" for negotiations with the government. It was necessary to develop a mechanism for the election of representatives and candidates. Prior to that, in the grassroots movement, arisen in social networks, unofficial leaders were administrators of Facebook pages, i.e., those who in the early stages participated in the creation of "events" in Facebook and media contacts (Ludosky, Drouet, etc.). As an example, the event "Mouvement national contre la hausse du prix ducarburant 184" established five people in October 2018. Their names appeared in articles and reports on the movement. By November 2018, 4 700 people had already participated in the group's activities (another 13 000 people had expressed interest). However, the first real (offline) meeting in Vaucluse visited only 37 people, which became the "volunteers", organizing the blocking of roads November 17. In general, Act I November 17, 2018 gathered 285 000 real participants [28].

In the same way, in November 2018, "Gilets Jaunes" appointed their representatives to negotiate with the government. Then, in December 2018, attempts began to be made to elect the "Gilets Jaunes" leadership by voting on Facebook [29]. Andre Lannee, 46-years-old car dealer from Grenoble region, proposed the following mechanism: he created pages for 13 regions of France and an additional one for all overseas regions. The threshold of legitimacy for elections from the region was determined to 30–40 thousand participants. All those who joined the group could be a candidate with uploading of their videos. In other matters, a significant number of "Gilets Jaunes" (including Priscillia Ludosky) strongly opposed the formal political organization of the movement.

Table 1. Total number of interactions of "Gilets Jaunes" groups in Facebook (per a day).

4 November 2018	11 November 2018	25 November 2018	2 December 2018	23 December 2018	13 January 2019
682 387	1 857 600	11 276 792	9 234 977	5 652 436	4 714 167

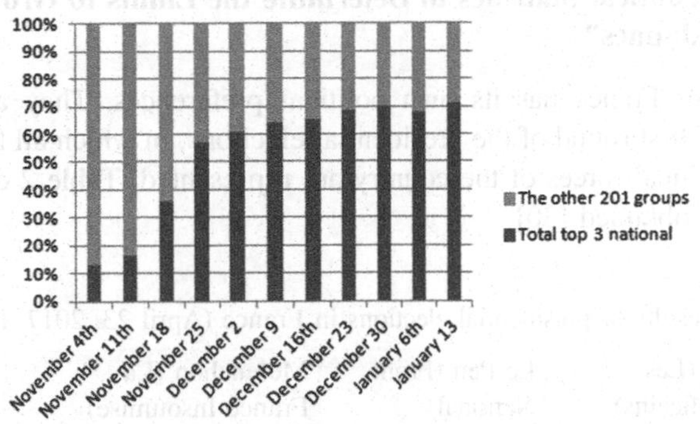

Fig. 3. The number of interactions of the three largest "Gilets Jaunes" groups relative to other groups [27].

Figure 3 demonstrates the coarsening that occurs in the "Gilets Jaunes" groups on Facebook. It is obvious that since December 2018 the activity of small groups has been dropping. The three largest groups of "Gilets Jaunes", which until November 17 represented no more than 20% of the activity of "Gilets Jaunes", as of January 2019 accounted for more than 70% of interactions.

In addition, there is a gradual changing of 'virtual' nature of the movement, accompanied by its political exit from Internet. On January 23, 2019, the first "Gilets Jaunes"'s own list was put forward for elections to the European Parliament, scheduled for May 26, 2019. The movement began to fit into the traditional scheme, but at the same time began to split into many rival groups. However for a real political influence, it is necessary not only leadership but also material (financial) resources. For example, in order to register an electoral list to European Parliament elections, the movement needs to 700–800 thousand Euros. Inevitable binding of the virtual world to the real physical and social world occured. Despite the change in the form of the protest political movement, its essence has not changed. According to the theory of collective action, this trend, illustrated by quantitative indicators, is expectable.

The collective action theory offers the following scheme for political mobilization:

Common goals (inaccessible to one person) → General motivation (to achieve a common goal) → Formation of a single community (collective subject, "we-intention" following to John Searle) → Distribution of roles (formation of a functional group structure) → functional dependence of group members from each other → coordination of individual actions (according to a specific program) → achievement of results.

Application of the collective action model suggests that the virtual linguistic and communicative political community "Gilets Jaunes" in Facebook must be organized into a traditional political movement (party), or disappear. However the large-scale participation will inevitably be lost. According to public opinion polls for the list of "Gilets Jaunes" in the elections to the European Parliament were ready to vote in January 2019 no more than 13% of voters. This is not accidental and can be explained by political and sociological statistics.

3.2 Applying Political Statistics to Determine the Limits to Growth of "Gilets Jaunes"

The population of France has its own political preferences. They are most clearly manifested in the first round of the presidential elections, in which all the systemic and anti-systemic political forces of the country are represented. Table 2 demonstrates the following results obtained [30]:

Table 2. Results of presidential elections in France (April 23, 2017, first round).

Macron	Fillon (Les Republicains)	Le Pen (Front National)	Melenchon (La France Insoumise)	Hamon (Parti Socialiste)
24,01%	20,01%	21,3%	19,58%	6,36%

However, the first round of elections 2017 was ignored by 10.5 million voters (more than 22%).

According to the results of sociological research, the participants of the "Gilets Jaunes" are divided according to their political views as follows:

Table 3. Participants of the "Gilets Jaunes" on political views (for whom they voted in the first round of the presidential elections in France) [31].

Macron	Fillon (Les Republicains)	Le Pen (Front National)	Melenchon (La France Insoumise)	Hamon (Parti Socialiste)	Boycotters
21%	31%	71%	59%	41%	54%

According to Table 3, we can see that the "Gilets Jaunes" gets support of anti-system parties, far right (Le Pen) and far left (Melenchon) who are trying to use "Gilets Jaunes" to their advantage. However, in a real political struggle, "Gilets Jaunes" will not be able to unite with each other into a single organizational structure. The people will vote for "their" traditional political organizations at the elections. Even in the case of "Gilets Jaunes" as a formalized political organization and the nomination of its own list in the European Parliament elections, the electoral losses of traditional parties will be insignificant (2–3%). The main electoral base of the "Gilets Jaunes", therefore, is potential voters who have not traditionally participated in the elections and do not trust the existing political system. They make up just over 20% of voters. Moreover, among this group, "Gilets Jaunes" support is about 54% (Table 2). Thus, potentially non-virtual "Gilets Jaunes" will get the same support of 12–15% of voters.

3.3 Application of Sociological Statistics to Determine the Limits to Growth of "Gilets Jaunes"

Table 4 shows the socio-professional structure of the "Gilets Jaunes". The highest support for the movement is observed among lower-level workers and employees, i.e. in the so-called "blue collars". However the number of blue-collar workers in France is steadily decreasing every year (see Table 5).

Table 4. Participants in the "Gilets Jaunes" by profession and education [32].

The middle class (personnel and higher intellectual professions)	Pensioners	Employees	Unemployed	Self employed	Workers
29%	50%	56%	56%	54%	62%

Table 5. The population of France by profession and education (as a percentage of the economically active population) [32].

The middle class (personnel and higher intellectual professions)	Employees	Workers
18%	26%	21%

Moreover, not all "blue collars" are ready to support the movement of "Gilets Jaunes". Moreover electoral support by these groups of the population (even at the level of 50–60% of all representatives of these "classes") will give no more than 20–25% at the national elections. Moreover, even such support is extremely unlikely, since many blue-collar workers support traditional political parties.

3.4 Assessment of the Influence of External Factors on the Growth of "Gilets Jaunes"

At the beginning of 2018 Facebook's News Feed, in response to growth of right movements which were accused at generating fake news, changed the rules of information uploading and made a decision to prioritize "news that is trustworthy, informative and local" and posts from friends and family, hoping to inspire back-and-forth discussion in the comments of posts [24]. According to Mark Zuckerberg, the goal is to enable people to freely design their communities. He introduced his new vision of the global network with 2.2 billion active users (including 38 million in France) [33] and announced "refondation" of the social network in favor of "groups". This modification was considered as an alternative to large pages that professionally disseminate information (primarily media).

The movement of "Gilets Jaunes" was an unexpected result of this policy [34]. Nevertheless, the panic fears of social networks "monster", in our opinion, are greatly exaggerated. On the one hand, since January 2019, there have been attempts to fight the protest movement within Facebook and to fit it into some kind of framework. For example, it is the change in procedure for counting the number of participants, adopted by the leadership of Facebook. It is also obvious that the control of this virtual protest movement is quite real for the one who controls the Internet providers. Moreover, the influence of Facebook on the creation of a protest political force is also somewhat exaggerated. The final word in disseminating information remains for the traditional channels of information transmission. As noted above, only October 21, 2018 after the first appearance of article about Ludosky petition in the French national newspaper "Le Parisien", there was a qualitative increase in the number of signatures on a petition from 12 000 to 850 000 signatures during a month.

4 Conclusions

E-society demonstrates its political dimension in the form of protest political e-communities. "Gilets Jaunes" is an example. However, by the beginning of 2019, the virtual movement "Gilets Jaunes" reached its maximum and began to decline. Stagnation and reduction of the virtual political activity of "Gilets Jaunes" is inevitable due to its entrance to the real political scene. Virtual linguo-communicative communities quickly arise and quickly disappear, if they do not acquire a "real structure" (like any linguo-communicative community), i.e. binding to time and place, organizational and hierarchical structures. However, with formal organization split and loss of large-scale participation are inevitable. Thus, the limits to growth of "Gilets Jaunes" are 10–25% of voters. Moreover, having emerged from the virtual space and becoming one of the organized anti-systemic forces, "Gilets Jaunes" will not be able to radically change the political balance in France. It can exist only in the conditions of political coalitions and alliances, increasingly losing the anti-systemism. Representing itself as "all of France" on the Internet and in performances on the streets of cities, "Gilets Jaunes" will not be able to become the dominant political force of the country under any circumstances. The only exceptional phenomenon characteristic of this political online movement is only the phenomenal speed of its formation.

Here we can see some of the analogies between "Gilets Jaunes" and pirate parties. Both originally appeared on the Internet. Both initially represented the "one-issue" political movements (pirate parties - against copyright, "Gilets Jaunes" - against rising gasoline prices). Then their agendas widened. Both are currently facing a choice: to remain a spontaneous movement, risking to gradually disappear, or turn into a traditional political party, risking losing their initial meaning.

Nevertheless, we can say that a new powerful tool appeared. This tool was previously used mainly by nonconformist groups to create their own performance (for example, flash mob "No pants" staged by art-group "Improv Everywhere"). Now it has become effectively applied in the traditional political struggle. However, neither society in general nor its political structure will change. Its quantitative parameters (volume of information transfer, speed, distance) but not qualitative parameters have changed. The use of social networks explains the scope of the protest political movement and partly its radicalization [33], but not its socio-economic reasons and the limits of its political influence.

The importance of language boundaries for the political e-community can also be noted. "Gilets Jaunes" groups are limited to French. It is not by chance that only French-speaking Belgium and Canada were able to create a significant own movement of "Gilets Jaunes". E-society is not global, i.e. there is no uniform communication code. Even the English language merely pretends to the global role, but it virtually confines to the role of a linguistic connection between the political, economic and scientific elites.

References

1. Parsons, T.: About social systems (2002)
2. Giddens, A.: The organization of society: an outline of the theory of structuration (2005)
3. Chernov, I.V.: Postconstructivism, or the theory of linguistic realism in international relations. Vestnik Sankt-Peterburgskogo Universiteta. Seriya 6. Mezhdunarodnyye otnosheniya (2018). (in Russian)
4. Chugunov, A.V., Bolgov, R., Kabanov, Y., Kampis, G., Wimmer, M. (eds.): DTGS 2016. CCIS, vol. 674. Springer, Cham (2016). https://doi.org/10.1007/978-3-319-49700-6. V-VI
5. Magoulas, G.D., Lepouras, G., Vassilakis, C.: Virtual reality in the e-Society. Virtual Reality **11**(2–3), 71–73 (2007)
6. Youth Forum Jeunesse. Policy Paper on the youth perspective on e-society. Adopted by the council of members. Torino, Italy, 13–14 November 2009. On the basis of Understanding e-democracy developments in Europe, Scoping Paper CAHDE 2006 2E, Council of Europe (2009)
7. Pistorio, P.: Toward the e-Society (2000)
8. Luhmann, N.: Society of Society. Logos, Moscow (2011)
9. Olson, M.: The Logic of Collective Action. Harvard University Press, Cambridge (1965)
10. Bimber, B.: The Internet and political transformation: populism, community, and accelerated pluralism. Polity **31**(1), 133–160 (1998). Fall
11. Cornfield, M.: The Internet and democratic participation. Natl. Civic Rev. **89**(3), 235–241 (2000). Fall
12. Grossman, L.: The Electronic Republic: Reshaping Democracy in the Information Age. Viking, New York (1995)
13. Bimber, B., Flanagin, A., Stohl, C.: Reconceptualising collective action in the contemporary media environment. Commun. Theory **4**(15), 365–388 (2005)
14. Edelman, M.: Social movements: changing paradigms and forms of politics. Annu. Rev. Anthropol. **30**, 285–317 (2001)
15. Poster, M.: The Second Media Age. Polity, Cambridge (1995)
16. Hirst, M., Harrison, J.: Communication and New Media: From Broadcast to Narrowcast. Oxford University Press, South Melbourne (2007)
17. Papacharissi, Z. (ed.): A Networked Self: Identity, Community and Culture on Social Networked Sites. Routledge, New York (2011)
18. Sobkowicz, P., Kaschesky, M., Bouchard, G.: Opinion mining in social media: modeling, simulating, and forecasting political opinions in the web. Gov. Inf. Q. **29**(4), 470–479 (2012)
19. Meijer, A.J., Grimmelikhuijsen, S., Brandsma, G.J.: Communities of Public Service Support: citizens engage in social learning in peer-to-peer networks. Gov. Inf. Q. **29**(1), 21–29 (2012)
20. Smith, A., Schlozman, K., Brady, H., Verba, S.: The Internet and Civic Engagement. Pew Research Center (2009). http://www.pewinternet.org/2009/09/01/the-internet-and-civic-engagement/

21. Kavanaugh, A., Fox, E., Sheetz, S., et al.: Social media use by government: from the routine to the critical. Gov. Inf. Q. **29**(4), 480–491 (2012)
22. Linders, D.: From E-Government to We-Government: defining a typology for citizen coproduction in the age of social media. Gov. Inf. Q. **29**(4), 446–454 (2012)
23. Tufekci, Z.: Twitter and Tear Gas. The Power and Fragility of Networked Protest. Yale University Press, New Haven (2017)
24. Broderick, R., Darmanin, J.: The "Yellow Jackets" Riots in France Are What Happens When Facebook Gets Involved With Local News, 6 December 2018. Buzzfeednews.com
25. Borstein, R.: En immersion numerique avec les "gilets jaunes". Fondation Jean-Jaures, 14 janvier 2019
26. Note de l'Ifop pour la Fondation Jean Jaures. Le Figaro, 23 janvier 2019
27. Sinecat, A.: Les groupes Facebook des "gilets jaunes" s'essoufflent et se restructurent. le Monde, 23 janvier 2019
28. Moulot, P.: Qui sont les porte-parole des gilets jaunes? Comment sont-ils designes? Checknews, 16 novembre 2018
29. "Gilets Jaunes": un referendum "populaire" an cours d'organisation pour elire des representants legitimes. Francinfo, 4 decembre 2018
30. Resulats des elections legislatives (2017). http://www.interieur.gouv.fr
31. #Opinion en direct. Sondage ELABE pour BFMTV, 5 decembre 2018
32. Fourquet, J., Manternach, S.: Les "Gilets Jaunes": revelateur fluorescent des fractures francaises. jean-jaures.org
33. Szadkovski, M.: Facebook, reservoir et carburant des "gilets jaunes". Le Monde, 15 decembre 2018
34. Bourdeau, T.: Facebook, mimetisme et catastrophes. RFI, 23 janvier 2019

Is Cross-Network Segregation a Factor of Political Behavior and Political Identification in the Russian Student Community?

Denis Martyanov, Galina Lukyanova(✉), and Oleg Lagutin

St. Petersburg State University, 7/9 Universitetskaya nab., St. Petersburg 199034, Russia
dsmartyanov@mail.ru, g.lukiyanova@spbu.ru, apisol@yandex.ru

Abstract. Online segregation is among the most commonly discussed phenomenon. This paper calls into question the need to focus on the dangers of echo chambers, filter bubbles; furthermore, it proposes to identify latent factors of the Internet segmentation and specify communication in homophilic communities. Thus, the current study aims to detect the mutual influence of social network choice and political behavior among Russian students. The study is based on empirical data obtained by a survey conducted in 2018 in St. Petersburg. Our research has revealed that students are a heterogeneous group. The identified four factors described as "Web-services for full-grown people," "Mobile services," "Closed silo of content," "Audiovisual services" disclose hidden relationships between quite different online services and political identification of students.

Keywords: Social networks · Cyberspace fragmentation · Political behavior · Political identity · Cross-network segregation

1 Introduction

Although the Internet is widely considered to be single cyberspace, its structure is heterogeneous. Websites, domain zones, nodes and highways form a complex hierarchy of individual network segments. Social space is formed by audiences and virtual communities that have unique characteristics for each online service. The factors that determine the differences in the audiences are, on the one hand, the specifics of the content; on the other, the technologies of the web services.

Internet segmentation is not so much a state as a process. The classic Todd Gitlin's metaphor that "public sphere, in falling, has shattered into a scatter of globules, like mercury" [10: 173], is meant to show that the Internet is falling into numerous public 'sphericules'; furthermore, the formation of these segments continues. Previous studies regarding these "sphericules" have led to understanding them as strictly isolated segments. However, far too little attention has been paid to a flexible examination of the mutual influence of network spaces on political phenomena. We argue that it is crucial to analyze web services not as separate cases, within which segregation occurs, but as interconnected routes chosen by users with similar views.

D. A. Alexandrov et al. (Eds.): DTGS 2019, CCIS 1038, pp. 165–176, 2019.
https://doi.org/10.1007/978-3-030-37858-5_13

This study aims to identify latent factors of the influence of network services on political views and political behavior in Russia. We suggested that segregation on the Internet has a cross-network nature. In particular, different types of services will specifically affect the formation of political identity and political activity. We tested this hypothesis on the students of St. Petersburg as the most active Internet users.

2 Theoretical Background

In recent years, there has been an increasing amount of literature on the social and political aspects of Internet segmentation. In political science, Internet segmentation appears to be closely linked to the foreign policy term "Cyberbalkanization." Researchers examine the fragmentation of the Internet and attempt to evaluate the impact of it on the political process within the nation states [22, 24].

The modern understanding of Cyberbalkanization is related to the governance of cyberspace [4]. A number of authors draw attention to the problems and prospects of the global political segregation of the Internet due to the increased role of the nation states in the regulation of online communication [4]. However, the main weakness of this approach is a lack of empirical research, as Cyberbalkanization is seen more as a threat rather than an empirically documentable process. In the last ten years, such use of the concept Cyberbalkanization is typical for researchers.

In the mid-2000s, the term was used to refer to network segregation or atomization, i.e., separation of individual groups from others in terms of communication [22, 24]. A great deal of published studies in political communication, including in Russia, has focused on the relationship between political views/ideological identity and network segregation [1, 5, 15]. The authors have developed several well-known concepts, such as public sphericules [10], filter bubbles [18], and echo chambers [20]. Their common area of interest is the study of homophily, i.e., the desire to communicate with people who have a similar point of view [2]. Thus, homophily becomes the most important factor of ideological segregation [9].

There are numerous empirical studies of the phenomena of network segregation, in which the researchers use both network analysis and sociological survey data to examine networks, mainly in Europe and the United States. However, the topic of network segregation remains controversial. Many attempts have been made in order to detect the signs of ideological segregation and echo chambers [6, 8, 11]. In the study investigating cross-ideological interactions in Twitter by comparing retweets and mentions, Conover concludes that "political segregation, as manifested in the topology of the retweet network, persists in spite of substantial cross-ideological interaction" [6]. Goggins and Petakovic note that "it is largely recognized that online communities influence and are influenced by offline communities" [11]. One of the factors of network segregation may be geographical separation. For instance, Duvanova explores the lack of connections between different groups in Ukraine [8].

Discussing post-truth and post-factual age, several authors raise concerns that the communication heterogeneity associated with globalization may pose a threat to the integrity of societies [3]. Specifically, group thinking may lead to the emergence of communities that are opposed to the values of society.

Nevertheless, many researchers are critical of the phenomena of echo chambers and filter bubbles. Considering the problem of fragmentation as a factor of tolerance in American and Japanese societies, Kobayashi and Ikeda conclude that "fear of a fragmented society due to selectivity in using the Internet seems to be empirically groundless." [13]. Dutton also states that the concept of echo chambers manifests sociotechnical determinism since the pattern of evidence contradicts this view [7: 9]. In Wieringa's study on ideological homophily in the Dutch Twittersphere, the author concludes that the echo chamber is a conscious choice of the users ("a kind of willful 'echo chamber'" [23]).

There are some reasons to accuse researchers studying network segregation of determinism. In our view, it would be not productive to attempt to comprehend the Internet only as a public sphere or as a sphere of echo chambers, a position typical for the early works on this problem. Ideological segregation on the Internet is a more flexible phenomenon than it seemed to be before. Ideologically oriented communities are the result of social divisions in the real world and contribute to the formation of political views in the virtual community. We assume that not only political discussion platforms but also third spaces have a latent impact on the formation of political identity. In this regard, the research should focus not so much on the dangers of echo chambers, but on the identification of latent factors of segmentation of the Internet and the specifics of communication in homophilic communities. For example, Yun et al. examine the problem of audience fragmentation in their study focused on the moderation of comments in blogs in the context of ideologically driven filtering [25].

Another significant aspect of echo chambers and filter bubbles is that these virtual communities are generally described as deviant. There is still considerable ambiguity in regard to the choice of a network resource and the factors that influence this choice. Unlike most websites of the Web 1.0 era, social networks, blogs, and applications are not sites which have specific ideologically oriented content. Probably, in most cases, the choice of social media is determined by its technological convenience, as well as social contacts that can be established by becoming a part of this network. In this case, the primary attention is drawn to the audience of social media as a factor in the formation of political attitudes. Latane states that "people will become more similar to their neighbors, leading to spatial clustering" [14: 20].

Moreover, there is still considerable controversy surrounding network migration, when changing the community involves changing the social network. Studies of network migration suffer from many methodological problems since the identification of the same user in different social media is quite a difficult task. In this regard, interesting attempts have been made in the sphere of cross-media research aimed at investigating user identity linkage [19, 21]. For instance, Nie et al. explore the dynamic changes of users in social networks [17], Newell et al. analyze network migration as in the example of a mass exodus of Reddit users [16]. In fact, as Gruzd and Wellman point out, "the articles focus only on one form of social media" [12: 1256] and fail to consider that a large number of people use several types of social media. We suppose that the reason for this is the limitations of network analysis. Despite its shortcomings, this method has been widely applied to research the Internet. At the same time, the use of traditional sociological methods seems more productive for a comprehensive examination of the impact of social networks on the political attitudes and models of political behavior.

3 Methods

In the study of cross-network segregation, traditional sociological methods were used. Empirical data were obtained as a result of sociological research conducted in February 2018 by the Center for Sociological and Internet Research at Saint-Petersburg State University. The method of collecting information was a classroom survey among students of St. Petersburg State University. The participants were asked to fill in a questionnaire. The sample size was 2,518 people. The sample was random, non-repetitive with the quotes on the following characteristics: year of studies (bachelor/master), department. The data was analyzed by the IBM SPSS program.

Constructing the factor analysis in the SPSS package, we used the procedure for calculating factor values which were then saved as additional variables with the use of the regression method. These variables were used to establish relationships for factor values. For analysis, we apply the method of dividing factor values into four percentile groups. Thus, with the use of the above procedure, each obtained factor appears as an ordinal variable expressing a strong or weak degree of influence that a particular feature has, which makes it possible to examine its connection with socio-demographic variables. Moreover, we use cluster analysis and a crosstabs procedure to identify which groups are different from the others. Adjusted residual values of more than 1.65 indicate that the number of cases in the cell is significantly larger than expected, and adjusted residuals less than −1.65 suggest the number of cases is less than expected.

4 Results

4.1 The Factors Determining the Use of Web Services

As a result of the factor analysis, four factors were identified (Table 1).

The first factor includes users of less popular social networks: Moy Mir (My world), Odnoklassniki (Classmates), LinkedIn, and Flickr, a photo-video hosting service launched in 2004. A lower percentage of regular visitors also characterizes these services among the respondents: Moy Mir (audience: 5.5%), Odnoklassniki (3.9%), LinkedIn (4.4%), and Flickr (1.9%). This factor can be labeled "Web-services for full-grown people."

The second factor also brings together quite close resources: Tumblr (7.9%), Twitter (24.6%) and Telegram (55.1%). As all of them are focused on mobile Internet and microblogging, we called this factor "Mobile services."

The third factor combines two major social networks, Vkontakte (88.6%) and Facebook (32.7%), as well as Facebook-related WhatsApp (58.5%) and Instagram (59.7%). This factor can be named with the metaphor suggested by Berners-Lee who referred to social media as "closed silo of content" because of the risk of fragmentation of the Internet. Facebook's closed nature has obviously contributed to the promotion of WhatsApp and Instagram, which are related to it and which have "inherited" Facebook's audience. Probably, this can explain the fact that these services are placed in the

Table 1. Factor matrix "The Use of Social Networks." Question: "Which social media and services do you use?" St. Petersburg, 2018

	Component			
	1	2	3	4
Moy Mir	,616			
Odnoklassniki	,602			
Flickr	,524			
LinkedIn	,486			
Tumblr		,633		
Twitter		,630		
Telegram		,598		
WhatsApp			,722	
Instagram			,553	
Facebook			,486	
Vkontakte			,402	
Skype				,783
Viber				,630
YouTube				,533

same factor. Surprisingly, Telegram, which used to be connected with Vkontakte, did not appear in the same factor alongside it, which may suggest that these popular services have slightly different audiences.

The fourth factor combines Skype (audience: 43.1%) and Viber (27.8%), used mainly for interpersonal communication, and YouTube, a video hosting service (66.1%). We called this factor "Audiovisual services."

4.2 Online Services and Offline Communication

To identify the connection of the network segregation with offline communication, we have also included the factors "Sources of information on elections," which refer to the sources trusted by the respondents. The factor analysis was composed of the following characteristics: radio; newspapers; television; advertising from candidates, leaflets, booklets; Internet; close friends (Table 2).

It can be seen from the data in Table 2 that two factors were identified: factor 1 – "Institutional sources"; factor 2 – "Social sources." The results of the construction of the factor matrices presented above (Tables 1 and 2) give us an opportunity to combine factors, which are "types of services used by students", with factors which are "sources of information on elections." Unified in terms of scaling these new features can be used together in a cluster analysis. For this purpose, we conducted a hierarchical cluster analysis with all the groups of factors. The dendrogram (Fig. 1) shows the results of the cluster analysis, and the proximity or distance reflects the factor variables as the elements of clusters.

Table 2. Factor matrix "Sources of information on elections." Question: "Do you trust the following sources of information on elections?" St. Petersburg, 2018

	Component	
	1	2
10.3. Radio	,884	
10.2. Newspapers	,862	
10.4 Television	,709	
10.6. Advertising from candidates, leaflets, booklets	,407	
10.5 Internet		,807
10.1 Close friends		,637

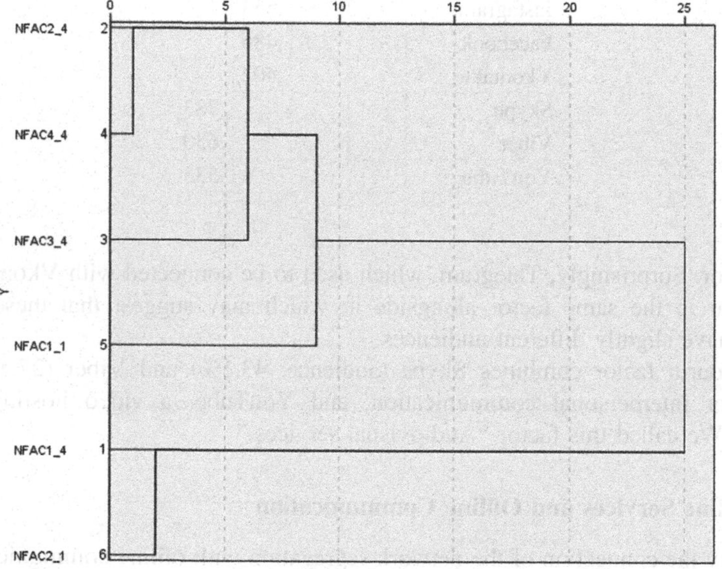

Fig. 1. Dendrogram using Ward's Linkage (Rescaled Distance Cluster Combine). Types of social networks and sources of information on elections used by young people in Russia (NFAC1_4 Web-services for full-grown people; NFAC2_4 Mobile services; NFAC3_4 Closed silo of content; NFAC4_4 Audiovisual services; NFAC1_1 Institutional sources; NFAC2_1 Social sources) St. Petersburg, 2018

As shown in Fig. 1, two clusters were formed as a result of the cluster analysis. The lower cluster formation includes the cluster "Services for full-grown people" and the cluster "Social sources," that is, the respondents who use a social network such as Moy Mir, Odnoklassniki, LinkedIn and Flickr obtain information on elections from their personal circle of contacts and Internet.

The upper cluster formation includes clusters 2, 3, 4 – "Mobile services," "Closed silo of content," and "Audiovisual services," which are not related to the information awareness in respect to the elections. The cluster "Institutional sources" is in the middle of the dendrogram, which indicates its neutral nature, and does not form clusters with any other characteristics.

4.3 The Socio-Demographic Context

Although we studied a group that is fairly homogeneous in terms of age (undergraduate and graduate students), the crosstabulation showed that age was a significant characteristic for them (Table 3).

Table 3. "Services for full-grown people" and "Age" Crosstabulation, St. Petersburg, 2018

Full years	Services for full-grown people			
	Absent	Weak	Strong	Very strong
18	**157**	114	99	**77**
	6.3%	4.5%	3.9%	**3.1%**
	4.4	,2	−1.3	**−3.3**
20	159	167	146	**131**
	6.3%	6.7%	5.8%	**5.2%**
	,7	1.3	−.5	**1.6**

As can be seen from the table above, the "Services for full-grown people" factor turns out to be interrelated with age characteristics and is the most significant for senior students. The crosstabulation shows that the "very strong" level of this factor is typical of respondents aged 20 (5.2% of the total sample with a significant adjusted residual of 1.6).

Table 4 illustrates the interrelation between "Services for full-grown people" factor and study levels. The influence of the factor for first and second-year undergraduate students is nearly absent. At the same time, undergraduate students in the third and fourth year have a strong influence on the factor under consideration (11.7%; 1.6). Moreover, for master degree students, this factor has a very strong influence (5.8%; 5.5). In other words, the older the respondent, the stronger the influence of "Services for full-grown people" factor.

The opposite pattern is typical for the factor "Mobile services." Respondents aged 18 are characterized by "strong" (5.3%; 2.4) or "very strong" (5.4; 2.3) influence of the factor. The attribute also has "strong" (11.6%; 1.9) and "very strong" (12.5%; 2.9) influence for the first and second year undergraduate students. Students in the master degree are not by the influence (5.0%; 3.5). The gender factor also plays a role here. For male respondents, the lack of influence on the "Mobile services" factor is more typical (10.2%; 2.3), whereas female respondents are more often "very strong" influenced by this factor (17.7%; 1.9).

The strong influence of the "Closed silo of content" factor is characteristic of 18-year-old students (5.1%; 1.6), and the "very strong" influence is characteristic of master level students (5.1%; 3.6). For male respondents, the lack of influence on the "Closed silo of content" factor is more typical (11.7%; 4.7), whereas female respondents are more often "strong" (17.4%; 1.6) and "very strong" (17.8%; 2.1) influenced by this factor.

Table 4. "Services for full-grown people" and "Study level" Crosstabulation, St. Petersburg, 2018

Study level	Services for full-grown people			
	Absent	Weak	Strong	Very strong
First and second-year undergraduate students	**354**	284	230	**198**
	14,1%	11,3%	**9,2%**	**7,9%**
	5,5	1,1	**−2,4**	**−4,2**
Third and fourth year undergraduate students	**218**	268	**293**	277
	8,7%	10,7%	**11,7%**	11,0%
	−2,7	,3	**1,6**	,8
Master degree students	49	72	103	**145**
	2,0%	2,9%	4,1%	**5,8%**
	−4,5	−2,1	1,0	**5,5**

The factor "Audiovisual services" has a "very strong" influence over respondents aged 20 (7.1%; 2.0) and the first and second year undergraduate students (12.3%; 2.5). Students at the master level are marked with the influence of this factor as absent (5.3%; 4.2). For female respondents, it was more typical to have a "strong" influence of this factor (17.3%; 1.7).

4.4 The Influence of Cross-Network Factors on Political Behavior

Students were asked to indicate their willingness to vote in the presidential elections of 2018. The "services for full-grown people" factor has a "very strong" degree of influence for those who are more likely to find it difficult to answer the question of their readiness to participate in elections (5.1%; 3.4), and "strong" degree for those who are likely to vote (7.1%; 1.6). Respondents who have a "weak" degree of influence of this factor decide that they would not vote in the coming elections (5.9%; 1.6).

Respondents who are "very strong" influenced by the "Mobile services" factor decide that they would definitely vote in the coming elections (6.2%; 2.0). Respondents who have no influence of this factor find it difficult to answer the question about their willingness to participate in the elections (5.6%; 4.7).

Respondents with a "strong" degree of use of "Closed silo of content" decided that they would definitely vote in the elections (6.2%; 2.1). Moreover, respondents with a "very strong" degree in "Audiovisual services" decided that they would definitely vote in the elections (6.4%; 2.4). In turn, the respondents who find it difficult to answer about their willingness to vote in the coming elections are not influenced by this factor (5.8%; 5.0).

4.5 The Influence of Cross-Network Factors on Political Identification

Obtained descriptive statistics for respondents' identification with their political views show that the most numerous groups are liberal and mixed (Fig. 2). The crosstabulation procedure reveals an interesting fact. The only stable pure ideological group characterized by network segregation turns out to be people who identify their views with liberal ideas. For this group, the absence of the influence of the factor "Services for full-grown people" is more typical (7.5%; 2.9). In turn, respondents, who are characterized by a "very strong" influence of this factor, have mixed political views (6.2%; 1.7).

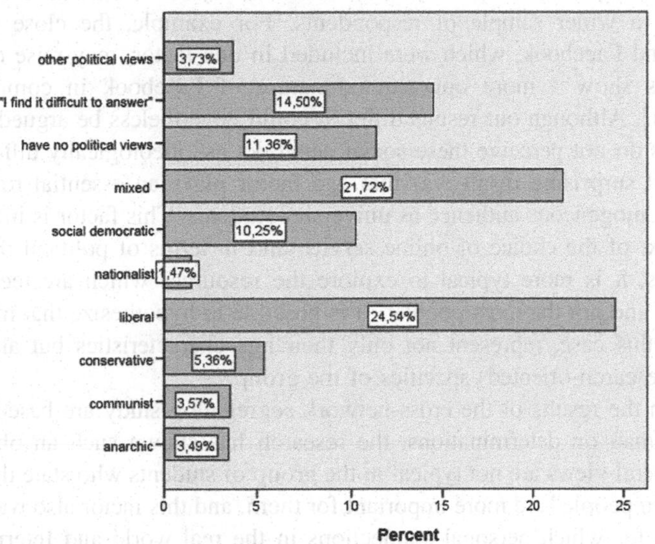

Fig. 2. Respondent's identification with their political views. Question: What political views are you closest to: anarchic, communist, conservative, liberal, nationalist, social democratic, mixed, have no political views, I find it difficult to answer, St. Petersburg, 2018

Also, respondents with liberal views have a "strong" influence of the "Mobile services" factor (7.1%; 2.4), whereas respondents who are not influenced by this factor have mixed political views (6.2%; 1.6). Moreover, respondents with liberal views have a "weak" influence of the "Audiovisual services" factor (7.5%; 2.8) or absence of it in the case of "Closed silo of content" factor (5.3%; −1.6). Thus, the factor "Services for full-grown people" is interrelated with mixed political views, whereas the "Mobile services" factor with a liberal.

5 Conclusion and Discussion

The current study was designed to determine latent factors of the influence of network services on political views and political behavior in the Russian student community. Our research confirms that students of St. Petersburg are a very heterogeneous group. The factor analysis revealed the most striking results. The identified four factors ("Web-services for full-grown people," "Mobile services," "Closed silo of content,"

"Audiovisual services") disclosed hidden relationships between quite different online services. Firstly, services that are placed in the same factor often belong to different generations of web services. Secondly, the factors include a "mix" of domestic and international services. It is plausible that a number of limitations may have influenced the obtained results. Our study is regional and covers only the student population. Further data collection is required to determine exactly whether similar trends will be identified in a wider sample of respondents. For example, the close positions of Vkontakte and Facebook, which were included in one factor, may raise questions, as some studies show a more oppositional nature of Facebook in comparison with Vkontakte [1]. Although our results differ, it could nevertheless be argued that at their age, students do not perceive these social networks as "ideologically different."

The most surprising result was that age factor plays an essential role in such a seemingly homogeneous audience as university students. This factor is important both in the context of the choice of online service and in terms of political behavior. For older cohorts, it is more typical to explore the resources which are technologically conservative and not the most popular. It is possible to hypothesize that master degree students, in this case, represent not only their age characteristics but also the "professional" (research-oriented) specifics of the group.

Although the results of the cross-network segregation study are based on correlations rather than on determinations, the research has shown such an observed relationship. Liberal views are not typical in the group of students who state that "Services for full-grown people" are more important for them, and this factor also was the closest to the group for which personal connections in the real world and Internet are main sources of information. It is crucial to note that this group, as it can be seen from the cluster analysis, is the most segregated in the Russian online environment. Moreover, "Mobile services" and "Audiovisual services," as opposed to "Services for full-grown people," are services with an audience which demonstrates more willingness to participate in the presidential election 2018.

The study of political views shows that identification with liberal views is very typical for students. At the same time, the "liberals" are the only pure ideological group for which we managed to find stable statistical dependencies. A possible explanation for this might be that liberal identification is the most intuitively clear for the youth. They are characterized by the use of "Mobile services," and ignoring "Services for full-grown people" and "Closed silo of content" (including the services related to Facebook). Taken together, these findings highlight the relationship between media choice and political consciousness, but it is too early to conclude substantial segregation of these groups of services. The cluster analysis revealed that "Mobile services," "Closed silo of content" and "Audiovisual services" represent closer factors compared to the offline media factor. However, this study has gone some way towards enhancing our understanding of the links between the choice of social networks and the political views of their users. Further research should be undertaken to investigate the social networks not as ideologically neutral spaces, but as latent factors of maintaining or forming similar political views.

Acknowledgments. For the empirical part, we utilized facilities provided by the Center for Sociological and Internet Research at Saint-Petersburg State University (project 106-9131 "The factors of absenteeism development among students in a Russian metropolis (as in the example of St. Petersburg)"). The theoretical part of the reported study was funded by RFBR and EISR according to the research project № 19-011-31551 "Manageability and discourse of virtual communities in the context of post-factual politics".

References

1. Bodrunova, S., Litvinenko, A.: Fragmentation of society and media hybridisation in today's Russia: how Facebook voices collective demands. J. Soc. Policy Stud. **14**(1), 113–124 (2016)
2. Boutyline, A., Willer, R.: The social structure of political echo chambers: variation in ideological homophily in online networks. Polit. Psychol. **38**, 551–569 (2017). https://doi.org/10.1111/pops.12337
3. Bruns, A.: Gatewatching and News Curation: Journalism, Social Media, and the Public Sphere. Peter Lang, New York (2018). https://doi.org/10.3726/b13293
4. Cattaruzza, A., Danet, D., Taillat, S., Laudrain, A.: Sovereignty in cyberspace: balkanization or democratization. In: 2016 International Conference on Cyber Conflict (CyCon U.S.), pp. 1–9. IEEE, Washington, D.C. (2016). https://doi.org/10.1109/cyconus.2016.7836628
5. Chugunov, A., Filatova, O., Misnikov, Y.: Citizens' deliberation online as will-formation: the impact of media identity on policy discourse outcomes in Russia. In: Tambouris, E., et al. (eds.) ePart 2016. LNCS, vol. 9821, pp. 67–82. Springer, Cham (2016). https://doi.org/10.1007/978-3-319-45074-2_6
6. Conover, M.D., Ratkiewicz, J., Francisco, M., Goncalves, B., Menczer, F., Flammini, A.: Political polarization on Twitter. In: Proceedings of the Fifth International AAAI Conference on Weblogs and Social Media, pp. 89–96 (2011)
7. Dutton, W.H., Reisdorf, B., Dubois, E., Blank, G.: Search and politics: the uses and impacts of search in Britain, France, Germany, Italy, Poland, Spain, and the United States. Quello Center Working Paper No. 5-1-17 (2017). https://doi.org/10.2139/ssrn.2960697
8. Duvanova, D., Nikolaev, A., Nikolsko-Rzhevskyy, A., Semenov, A.: Violent conflict and online segregation: an analysis of social network communication across Ukraine's regions. J. Comp. Econ. **44**(1), 163–181 (2016). https://doi.org/10.1016/j.jce.2015.10.003
9. Gentzkow, M., Shapiro, J.M.: Ideological segregation online and offline. Q. J. Econ. **126**(4), 1799–1839 (2011). https://doi.org/10.1093/qje/qjr044
10. Gitlin, T.: Public sphere or public sphericules? In: Liebes, T., Curran, J. (eds.) Media, Ritual and Identity, pp. 168–174. Routledge, London (1998)
11. Goggins, S., Petakovic, E.: Connecting theory to social technology platforms: a framework for measuring influence in context. Am. Behav. Sci. **58**(10), 1376–1392 (2014). https://doi.org/10.1177/0002764214527093
12. Gruzd, A., Wellman, B.: Networked influence in social media: introduction to the special issue. Am. Behav. Sci. **58**(10), 1251–1259 (2014). https://doi.org/10.1177/0002764214527087
13. Kobayashi, T., Ikeda, K.: Selective exposure in political web browsing. Inf. Commun. Soc. **12**(6), 929–953 (2009). https://doi.org/10.1080/13691180802158490
14. Latane, B.: Dynamic social impact: the creation of culture by communication. J. Commun. **46**(4), 13–25 (1996). https://doi.org/10.1111/j.1460-2466.1996.tb01501.x

15. Martyanov, D., Bykov, I.: Ideological segregation in the Russian cyberspace: evidences from St. Petersburg. In: Alexandrov, D.A., Boukhanovsky, A.V., Chugunov, A.V., Kabanov, Y., Koltsova, O. (eds.) DTGS 2017. CCIS, vol. 745, pp. 259–269. Springer, Cham (2017). https://doi.org/10.1007/978-3-319-69784-0_22
16. Newell, E., et al.: User migration in online social networks: a case study on Reddit during a period of community unrest. In: Proceedings of the Tenth International AAAI Conference on Web and Social Media (ICWSM 2016), pp. 279–288 (2016)
17. Nie, Y., Jia, Y., Li, S., Zhu, X., Li, A., Zhou, B.: Identifying users across social networks based on dynamic core interests. Neurocomputing **210**, 107–115 (2016). https://doi.org/10.1016/j.neucom.2015.10.147
18. Pariser, E.: The Filter Bubble: What the Internet is Hiding from You. The Penguin Press, New York (2011)
19. Shu, K., Wang, S., Tang, J., Zafarani, R., Liu, H.: User identity linkage across online social networks: a review. ACM SIGKDD Explor. Newsl. **18**(2), 5–17 (2017). https://doi.org/10.1145/3068777
20. Sunstein, C.R.: Republic.com 2.0. Princeton University Press, Princeton (2009)
21. Tan, S., Guan, Z., Cai, D., Qin, X., Bu, J., Chen, C.: Mapping users across networks by manifold alignment on hypergraph. In: Proceedings of the Twenty-Eighth AAAI Conference on Artificial Intelligence, pp. 159–165 (2014)
22. Van Alstyne, M., Brynjolfsson, E.: Global village or Cyber-Balkans? Modeling and measuring the integration of electronic communities. Manage. Sci. **51**(6), 851–868 (2005). https://doi.org/10.1287/mnsc.1050.0363
23. Wieringa, M.A., van Geenen, D., Schäfer, M.T., Gorzeman, L.: Political topic-communities and their framing practices in the Dutch Twittersphere. Internet Policy Rev. **7**(2) (2018). https://doi.org/10.14763/2018.2.793
24. Williams, D.: The impact of time online: social capital and Cyberbalkanization. CyberPsychol. Behav. **10**(3), 398–406 (2007). https://doi.org/10.1089/cpb.2006.9939
25. Yun, G.W., Park, S.Y., Holody, K., Yoon, K.S., Xie, S.: Selective moderation, selective responding, and balkanization of the blogosphere: a field experiment. Media Psychol. **16**(3), 295–317 (2013). https://doi.org/10.1080/15213269.2012.759462

On the Typology of the Information Ethos

Galina Nikiporets-Takigawa[1,2](✉) and Gennadiy Otiutsky[2]

[1] University of Cambridge, Sidgwick Avenue, Cambridge CB3 9DA, UK
gn254@cam.ac.uk

[2] Russian State Social University, Vilgelma Pika St. 4, 129226 Moscow, Russian Federation
{nikiporetsgiu,otjuckijgp}@rgsu.net

Abstract. The paper provides a discussion on the understanding of information ethics as a research field which scrutinizes ethical problems of social communication in close connection with the analysis of cyber informatization process. It is proposed to consider information ethics as a generic concept and interpret computer ethics as one of its types due to computer communication technologies. Historical types of information ethos and its psychological characteristics are revealed in accordance with the main types of information paradigms. The basis of this paradigm is a specific type of system 'human – information technology' and information exchange technology. In the structure of the information exchange several components can be distinguished: (a) content component, or the actual exchange of the information (content); (b) technological basis of communication which generates the ethics of technological methods of information exchange; (c) psychological aspects of information exchange which change together with each new technological method of communication. Its changes raise the specific ethical problems and form a specific type of information morality – information ethos. Ethics of information exchange and ethics of information technologies are distinguished.

Keywords: Information ethics · Information ethos · Information and communication revolutions · Computer ethics · Information paradigm

1 Statement of the Problem

Each new type of information exchange generates specific ethical problems. It is natural, therefore, that the attention of researchers is focused primarily on the ethical problems generated by the processes of cyberinformatization of modern society. At the same time, the origins of many modern ethical problems should be found in the previous types of social relations associated with information exchange and the implementation of the previous types of 'human-information technology' systems. This retrospective aspect is not considered deeply in current studies.

Meanwhile, there is a demand for the theoretical analysis of the trends in the creation and further development of the ethical relations at each historical stage of the development of information and communication. The identification of such trends will allow to introduce the methodologically fruitful forecasts for the ethical problems which appear in the process of implementation of the neural network, when the inter-action of

D. A. Alexandrov et al. (Eds.): DTGS 2019, CCIS 1038, pp. 177–186, 2019.
https://doi.org/10.1007/978-3-030-37858-5_14

'human – human', 'human – machine' will be implemented on the basis of the new neurocomputer interfaces using hybrid digital analog architectures.

One of the authors who started discussion in the 1940s–1960s over the complexity of ethical problems associated with the future integration of computers was the founder of Cybernetics Wiener [30, 31]. Introduction of the term 'information ethics' is attributed to Hauptman and Capurro [see: 19, 20], and the concept of 'computer ethics' to Maner [18].

In the last quarter of the twentieth century in western humanities and social thought the idea of information ethics was emerged, first as a situational applied knowledge – the vault of professional rules of experts in the information sector.

The direct incentive to information and ethical research was the process of computerization: in 1985, ethical problems of the use of computers were discussed in the textbook 'Computer ethics' by Johnson [11]; in Moore's paper the diversity and multiplicity of ethical problems caused by computers was noted [23]. Further, J. Moore, D. Johnson, L. Lloyd, J. van Dune, D. B. Parker, W. Manner, T. W. Bingham, J. Snapper, L. Floridi approached the analysis of computer ethics as a research filed and tried to identify its subject of study.

Most American and European researchers connect the phenomenon of information ethics only with the current stage of development of society. So, Capurro refers the impact of digital technology on society to the concept of information ethics [6, p. 7], T. W. Bingham identifies information and computer ethics [5].

Such identification is typical for Russian researchers also: Avdeeva noted 'the neighborhood of information and computer ethics' [1, p. 7]; the idea of this 'neighborhood' was reflected in the works of Koval [14], Galinsky and Panchenko [8], Filina [9]. Manzhueva and Kokina identify the history of information ethics and computer ethics [13, 19]. Dedulina directly points that 'computer ethics coincides with information ethics' [4]. Malyuk et al. write about ethics in the field of information technology, referring to modern digital technologies [17].

There are several stands in the understanding of information ethics. The first view was expressed by Johnson in 1985: ethical problems of computer use *are not something new and unknown*, and, consequently, it is not necessary to create a special theory to cope with these problems [11]. But the devices of the 1985 model are rather computers with a very narrow range of functions than the computers in their modern understanding. Therefore, many of the ethical problems generated by computers simply did not exist previously.

The second opinion is based on the novelty of the ethical situations. So, Moore formulated some of the problems generated by computer technologies in the form of 'computer invisibility'. Among them, the 'invisible fraud' is the intentional use of the invisible operations of a computer to implement unethical or criminal acts. [23, p. 266].

But for an illiterate person, the actions of the literate one whom he asked for help are also invisible, so the likelihood of creating a false document is not excluded. The conclusion is that the possibilities of negative use of information technologies ('communicative invisibilities') remain similar throughout human history, only the technologies of the possible execution of 'communicative evil' are developed.

There is also an opinion that the computerization highlights further the rationalization of human thought: 'no matter how intelligent we could make computers, there are acts of thinking that should be reserved only by human' [30, p. 40]. Thus, it is necessary to identify the *origins* of the process of rationalization and mechanization of human thinking in the previous stages of the development of the society.

All researchers associate ethical problems with the technological basis of modern cyberinformation and cybercommunication process but they do not make the next necessary step – *a comparative analysis of the stages of development of technological bases of social communication*. But if this methodological step is taken, then a pattern is revealed: each technological basis corresponds to a specific type of information ethos. We will analyze these connections in this paper.

2 Results

When comparing the considered positions on the essence of information ethics we can see, firstly, its complementarity (because they reflect the different stages of development of computer technics, and the various functions of the human and machine components of the system "human - information technics"), secondly, its onesidedness: although we are talking about ethical problems of information exchange, this exchange itself is associated only with computer technologies.

Such conclusions become inevitable when trying to answer the question *of what kind of relations* are regulated by information and computer morality. Often, researchers do not raise such a question, immediately moving to the list of the specific information problems that need moral regulation.

To answer this question we have to identify the following issues in the structure of relations of information exchange:

1. Content component, or the actual information (content) exchange. The relations of the actors at this level are governed by the general moral and psychological norms and principles that preserve stability at the different stages of the historical process (at least, in the relation to the mutual respect of communicants, prevention of false information, etc.). The theoretical justification of these norms and principles is *the universal content of information ethics*.
2. Technological basis of communication, generating *ethics of technological methods of information exchange*. It is the component of information ethics which is the most flexible and changes with the transformations in communication technologies posed by specific information and communication revolution [7, pp. 41–47].
3. Psychological aspects of information exchange, transforming together with each new technological method of communication (psychology of writing and reading, for example, has significant difference from the psychology of verbal communication). Being an 'external extension of a person', each type of communication technology makes special demands on the psychological qualities of a person. There is, for example, the division of the main types of such equipment to 'hot' (that is based on one feeling and oversaturated with information), and 'cold' – 'dispassionate' (provoking thinking and imagination, requiring active participation) [22, p. 27]. Without judging such classification, we emphasize the undoubted connection of the psychological aspects of communication with its technological aspects.

Changes in the technological basis and psychological aspects of information exchange raise the specific ethical problems and form a specific type of information morality – *information ethos*, as a set of ethical standards governing the practical use of communication technologies.

The ethics of interpersonal communication, for instance, includes a moral and psychological norm - to look into the eyes of the interlocutor. The norm is quite justified, because along with the verbal information it allows getting non-verbal information. However, the implementation of such a rule becomes impossible with the technology of the written information exchange. It becomes optional with 'smartphone' technologies, when the exchange of information between two persons sitting next to each other becomes more intense (at least in terms of the amount of information received per unit of time) in the case when each of them looks not in the eyes of the interlocutor but on the screen of his smartphone.

Thus, in the structure of media ethics we need to allocate (and share) the actual ethics of communication exchange and ethics of information technologies, or a particular technological type of information ethos: verbal ethos, the ethos of writing ('scriptoethos'), biblioethos (associated with the emergence of printed books), the ethos of electronic communication.

The computer revolution generates a new kind of information ethos, and ethics, reflecting this particular historical type of ethos, can be characterized as computer ethics. Computer ethics is a specific form of the information ethos in the era of cyberinformation and cybercommunication.

It should be specially noted that any type of information ethos includes a psychological component, as in everyday life a person often relies not on rational thoughts about the social nature of good and evil, but on an intuitive sense of 'good' and 'evil' in direct connection with the actions of a subject.

3 Discussion

Taking into account the psychological aspects of information ethos allows to critically evaluate the conclusions of some authors about the nature of information ethics, as underestimation of such aspects often leads to the methodological inaccuracies. Thus, L. Floridi intends to justify the ontocentricity of information ethics [10]. Ontocentricity is the synonym for infocentricity because L. Floridi identifies all things with the infosphere. Any entity for him is an information object, so L. Floridi 'shifts the focus of ethical reflection from the action, nature and value of the human agent to the 'evil' (harm, division, destruction), which make all in the ionosphere suffer…people, animals, organizations, plants, inanimate artifacts, digital objects in cyberspace, intellectual property articles, stones, Plato's abstractions, potential entities, disappeared civilizations, suffer' [9]. In fact, L. Floridi puts the information above the person, and the person (as an 'agent of the infosphere') loses its differences not only from other biological objects, but also from inanimate artifacts, and the concepts of good and evil lose its social nature.

L. Floridi does not notice that with this approach, he cease to explore ethics and moves on to the consideration of other social objects. Ethics is about morality; in turn, morality is 'a specific type of regulation of human relations aimed at their humanization' [16, p. 657. Highlighted by - G. N.-T., G. O.]. This regulation takes place in a special way - from the standpoint of good and evil. Therefore, *if the ethics discontinues being anthropocentric, it ceases to explore morality*.

Another thing is that social relations can develop on various occasions. Thus, political ethics analyzes and regulates relations about politics from the standpoint of dialectics of good and evil. Such ethics (which remains being ethics) can be called 'politically centered'. Ethics can study social relations mediated by various technologies, including computer-based ones ('computer-centered ethics'). But this is a special kind of centrality – centering either on the object about which ethical relations are formed, or on technologies that support this type of ethical relations. Therefore, the universal principle of information ethics is anthropocentricity, implemented through psychological mechanisms of communication based on the criteria of good and evil.

At the same time, the specifics of psychological and ethical mechanisms of information exchange are significantly influenced by communication technologies.

Two methodological concepts prove to be fruitful for further analysis:

1. The model of the "economic society" of Bell (in fact, "economic section" of the social organism), which allowed characterizing the main stages of its development [2]. Following Bell's example, a theoretical model of the 'information society' and its historical types can be built, which is considered as an 'information section' of any society;
2. The methodology used by Kuhn to study scientific revolutions [15]. He showed that 'normal' development of science is a scientific evolution within a single paradigm; the change of types of science occurs as a result of the scientific revolution, accompanied by the formation of a new paradigm of science – a new model for its functioning and development.

These are the methodological analogies which become obvious:

- the development of a particular type of information society is the gradual accumulation of existing information and communication technologies and their extensive dissemination (information evolution);
- a form of transition to a new type of information society - information and communication revolution.

It is legitimate to highlight the information paradigm as a relatively stable *algorithm for the implementation of information exchange processes* in society, determined by the technological basis of such process. Its structural components are summarized in the Table 1.

The essential components of this paradigm are protogenesis and generative situation (terms introduced by Rakitov [28, pp. 84–110]), which allowed to give a philosophical analysis of the computer revolution by the beginning of the XXI century.)

Protogenesis is associated with the formation of such social functions, which require a very specific level and quality of the information exchange. However, the achievement of such quality is impossible due to anthropological constraints (defined as biological and social nature of human) imposed on the processes of social communication conditions of a particular society.

Table 1. The structural components of the information paradigm

The components of a static structure	The components of a dynamic structure
System 'human-information technology' of a particular historical type	Specifics of redistribution of communication functions in the system 'human – information technology' between human and technical device
Technical communication devices and specific information technologies	System of information production
The protogenesis of this information and communication revolution	The rate and duration of formation of information products
Type of 'information human'	Formation and development of information strata (specific groups of information professionals)
Generative situation of this information and communication revolution	Formation and development of new information strata
Abilities and opportunities of the person and society on development of this information space	Type of the information space: intensity and method of information interconnection
Technologies of development of information time	Type of information time: duration and rhythms of the processes of information exchange
Methods of psychological and ethical interaction of subjects	Type of information ethos

The generative situation forms the technological basis for overcoming such limitations: new types of information technics and technology are created, a new type of 'human - information and communication technics' systems is formed.

Not only the technology of information exchange changes, but also the human being: new technologies often require a long – term and specialized training (for example, mastering the skills of writing and reading, and now - computer literacy). In this case, we are talking about a 'partial human' – 'information human'. This concept allows us to combine into a system those characteristics of a person that let him participate in the system of social communication, information exchange; by analogy with how the concept of 'economic human' reflects the characteristics of a person, allowing him to participate in the system of economic relations. New technologies and the new type of 'information human' also generates a new group of psychological and ethical problems of information exchange, or a *new type of information ethos*.

The influence of the information paradigms on the development of the moral and psychological norms of social communication as a specific type of information ethos can be described as the continuum of the revolutionary changes.

1. *Verbal revolution*. Its result is the formation of a specific social way of information coding, the appearance of oral speech. The first type of informational human appears - 'verbal homo'. The language forms the first type of information ethos,

which includes speech etiquette, typical for oral speech, and forms the possibility of rational understanding of ethical problems on the language basis.

2. *Revolution of literacy* forms a type of a human being who can write (scriptor) and read written texts. For the first time a mechanism of mediated psychological and ethical interaction of subjects appears, as well as the possibility of anonymous communication which reduces the threshold of ethical responsibility and creates the possibility of new types of 'information evil'. Etiquette of writing and ethics of information exchange through written texts are formed. Not only writing styles but also the types of lettering acquire ethical overtones: cursive writing, widely used in everyday life, is ethically unacceptable in official documents.
3. *The revolution of the printed word* forms the type of a human being who prints and reads printed texts: 'bibliohomo'. New ethical norms arise not only regarding the printed texts as such (only in the era of the printed word the problem of plagiarism could become ethically acute), but also about printed books as cultural artifacts.
4. *The revolution of electronic communications*, which began in the second half of the 19 century with the invention of telegraph and telephone, forms a type of 'electronic homo'. Electric and electronic mass media: telegraph, telephone, radio and television – have significantly narrowed the space-time scale of the world, have restored the dialogue of mankind on a global scale. The most important result of this revolution is the transformation of the world into one big 'global village' in which everything that happens is immediately known to all its inhabitants: 'Modern electronic communication builds a world on the model of the 'global village' [21, p. 71]. The etiquette of telegraph and telephone communication appears, and consequently – the ethics of electronic media, or 'electronic ethics'. The further development of the mediated anonymous psychological interaction gives rise to new types of ethical violations, for example, telephone hooliganism.
5. *The modern computer revolution*. The emergence of personal computers, and later - the Internet - made a real revolution in the information sphere of society, largely changed the psychology and practice of all kind of human activities. Almost all forms of coding have now digital form based on computer devices of various modifications. The digitalization of the information and communication sphere revile a special technological type – cyberinformation and cybercommunication. A new 'computer homo' and relevant to modern realities of cyberinformation and cybercommunication ethics are formed.

Alongside with these changes there is a complex of problems of network communication, of virtual reality, of information security [24, 25] and theoretical understanding of these problems leads to the avalanche-like emergence of new terms: information ethics, computer ethics, network ethics, Internet ethics, cyberethics, netiquette, virtual ethics and etc., the introduction of those is often spontaneous, and not always have adequate methodological justification.

Each of the considered information and communication revolution forms its own type of information and communication paradigm, which is the basis of a particular type of information society. The specific features of such paradigms are summarized in Table 2.

Table 2. The historical types of the information communication paradigms with transformations [26].

Type of the information paradigm	Type of the formation society and information human	Protogenesis	Generative situation	The sources of development of information ethics	Forming values of information ethics
Verbal paradigm	Verbal society; verbal human	The need for social communication; The need for constant information exchange as the basis of social relations	The emergence of language and articulate speech	Formation of oral speech, language. Formation of the first social communities	Traditions and customs are formed, basic ethical concepts are laid
Scripting paradigm	Scripting society; human - scriptor	Statogenesis and politogenesis, the need for secure social, political, legal, and ethical standards	Development of technologies for the production of writing: pottery, stone and leather processing, the invention of paper	The creation of writing; The need for a reliable fixation of social norms. Religious monopoly on writing	Rethinking the existing traditional values in the religious key and their consolidation in the moral and religious codes
Biblioparadigm	'The Gutenberg universe' (Biblio-society) Biblio- homo	The development of university education, the need for secular and religious culture in mass circulation of socially significant texts	The invention of printing, including the invention of the cash register	The invention of printing. The formation of university education. The growing weight of science. Gradual rationalization of thinking	The demarcation of traditional community customs The emergence of bourgeois individualism. Rationalization of the processes of moral choice
Electronic paradigm	Electronic society; Electronic human	The system of social requests arising from the process of globalization, the need to create a single information space	The invention of new media: telegraph, telephone, radio, TV. The forming of the technological basis of "global village"	The structure of social needs arising from the process of globalization is being transformed The need for creating of a single information space	The formation of mass culture values, the simplification of social ideals, the establishment of the ethics in the electronic media
Computer paradigm	Computer society; Computer human	The need for a new quality of social functions: management and control over production and socially significant activities, social communication, memory, improvement of material production, knowledge	The invention of the computer, the formation of Internet networks; radical transformation through computer technology of all technical means of processing, transmission and production of information – the formation of cybercommunication The digitalization of all kinds of information, the formation of cyberinformation	The formation of network and virtual spaces. The transfer of basic social concepts into the plane of cybernetic space	The appearance of cyberethics, network ethics, ethics of virtual communication The formation of professional ethics: ethics of IT-specialists, ethics of information workers

4 Conclusion

1. In the majority of the studies in the field of information ethics, this term is used to describe only the current stage of development of ethical relations. Information ethics is often unified with the computer ethics.
2. It is methodologically expedient to consider information ethics as a characteristic of the ethical and psychological side of the process of information exchange at any stage of social development.
3. The concept of 'information society' can be interpreted as a characteristic of the information 'section' of the society, which reflects the complexity of the information reality. Each historical type of information society corresponds to a specific information paradigm that characterizes a stable algorithm of information exchange process in society.
4. In the structure of the information exchange several components can be distinguished: (a) content component, or the actual exchange of the information (content); (b) technological basis of communication which generates the ethics of technological methods of information exchange; (c) psychological aspects of information exchange which change together with each new technological method of communication. Its changes raise the specific ethical problems and form a specific type of information morality – information ethos.
5. The specific historical types of information ethos groups corresponding to this information paradigm can be identified. New technologies and a new type of 'information homo' also generate an amount of psychological and ethical problems of information exchange, or a *new type of information ethos*.
6. Information ethics is a generic concept, and computer ethics is one of its types due to the computerization of information-exchange process.

References

1. Avdeeva, I.A.: Information, computer and applied ethics as theoretical components of ethics of global communicative space. Vestnik TSU **9**(137), 7–12 (2014)
2. Bell, D.: The Coming of Post-industrial Society: A Venture in Social Forecasting. Basic Books, New York (1999)
3. Bynum, T.W.: The foundation of computer ethics. Comput. Soc. **30**(2), 6–13 (2000)
4. Dedulina, M.A.: Computer ethics: philosophical understanding. Humanit. Res. **12** (2015). http://human.snauka.ru/2015/12/13416
5. Capurro, R.: Intercultural information ethics. In: Himma, K.E., Einar, K., Tavani, H. (eds.) The Handbook of Information and Computer Ethics, pp. 639–665. Wiley, Hoboken (2008)
6. Capurro, R.: Information ethics. Inf. Soc. **5**, 6–15 (2010)
7. Colin, K.K.: Fundamentals of informatics: social informatics. Akad. Project (2000)
8. Galinsky, I.L., Panchenko, A.I.: Computer ethics, information ethics, cibernetica. In: New Infocommunication Technologies in Humanities and Social Sciences and Education: International Internet Conference, 15 January–29 March 2002, pp. 112–132. Logos (2003)
9. Filina, O.A.: Social, cultural, historical and value bases of information ethics. Sci. Bull. BelSU. Ser. Philos. Sociol. Right. Issue **9**(10(65)), 232–238 (2009)

10. Floridi, L.: Information ethics: on the theoretical foundation of computer ethics. Ethics Inf. Technol. **1**(1), 37–56 (1999)
11. Johnson, D.G.: Computer Ethics, 3rd edn. Prentice Hall, Upper Saddle River (2001)
12. Khlebnikov, G.V.: Philosophy of information Luciano Floridi (2016). http://www.inion.ru/files/File/MPNI_10_02_11_Stenogramma.pdf
13. Kokina, V.M.: The history of information and computer ethics. Historical, Philosophical, Political and Law Sciences, Cultural Studies and Art History. Theory and Practice, vol. 6–1 (80), pp. 77–79 (2017)
14. Koval, E.B.: Ethics of the information society as the current stage of development of ethics. Bull. Chuvash Univ. **4**, 133–139 (2009)
15. Kuhn, T.S.: The structure of scientific revolutions. Thomas S. Kuhn; with an Introductory Essay by Ian Hacking, 4th edn. The University of Chicago Press, Chicago, London (2012)
16. Laptenok, S.D.: Morality. In: Gritsanov, A.A. (ed.) World Encyclopedia: Philosophy, p. 657. AST, Moscow (2001)
17. Malyuk, A.A., Polyanskaya, O.Y., Alekseeva, I.Y.: Ethics in the field of information technologies. Hotline-Telecom (2011)
18. Maner, W.: Starter Kit in Computer Ethics. Helvetia Press and the National Information and Resource Center for Teaching Philosophy, Hyde Park (1980)
19. Manzhueva, O.M.: On the issue of information ethics as a methodology for solving the problem of information security. In: The Collection: Social and Cultural Processes in the Conditions of Integration and Disintegration of the Materials of the All-Russian Conference with International Participation, pp. 45–47 (2017)
20. Manzhueva, O.M.: On the history of information ethics. Bull. Moscow State Reg. Univ. Ser. Philos. Sci. **3**, 65–71 (2014)
21. McLuhan, H.M.: The Gutenberg galaxy: the making of man print. Akad. project, Mir Foundation, p. 495 (2005)
22. McLuhan, H.M.: Understanding media: external expansion person, 2nd edn. Hyperborea, Kuchkovo field, p. 462 (2007)
23. Moor, J.: What is computer ethics? Metaphilosophy **16**(4), 266–275 (1985)
24. Nikiporets-Takigawa, G.Y.: On the borders of nations and national identities in the era of cybercommunities and cyberinformation. Syst. Psychol. Sociol. **1**(17), 130–137 (2016)
25. Nikiporets-Takigawa, G.: Leadership and leaders in networked social movements. Demokratizatsiya **1**, 7–22 (2017)
26. Otiutsky, G.P.: The informational paradigm as a tool for analysis of the information society. Soc. Policy Sociol. **5**(112), 192–201 (2015)
27. Otiutsky, G.P.: Information and anthropological dimension of post-industrial society. SOTIS Soc. Technol. Res. **1**(63), 64–81 (2014)
28. Rakitov, A.I. The philosophy of the computer revolution. Direct Media (2013)
29. Weizenbaum, J.: The possibility of computing machines and the human mind (from judgment to calculation). Radio and Communication (1982)
30. Wiener, N.: God & Golem Inc.: A Comment on Certain Points Where Cybernetics Impinges on Religion. MIT Press, Cambridge (1964)
31. Wiener, N.: The Human Use of Human Beings: Cybernetics and Society. Houghton Mifflin, Boston, 2nd edn. Revised; Doubleday Anchor, New York (1954)

Digitalization of Diplomacy in Global Politics on the Example of 2019 Venezuelan Presidential Crisis

Anna Sytnik(✉)

St. Petersburg State University, St. Petersburg, Russia
anna@sytnik.me

Abstract. The article explores the digitalization as the process of increasing use of digital technology in global politics. It particularly focuses on digital diplomacy as an instrument of agenda setting and presence expansion in social networks. Author investigates how state bodies and political leaders communicate on Twitter with regard to 2019 Venezuelan presidential crisis and who promotes the position more successfully. The dataset (n = 9,707,730 tweets) covers the period from December 1, 2018 to March 10, 2019. The results display the existence of phenomenon of "digital diplomacy of (non)-recognition", the importance of tweeting in native language of target audience, underestimation of the use of hashtags, and, finally, the information domination of supporters of Venezuelan opposition on Twitter. The conclusion of the research is that political communication on Twitter has become an important part of digital diplomacy in crisis situations as it delivers messages quickly and efficiently both to official departments of different countries and to wide international audience.

Keywords: Digitalization · Digital Diplomacy · Global politics · Twitter · Venezuela

1 Introduction

In recent years, various changes in all spheres of public and political life are characterized by the term "digitalization", in which digital technology is singled out as a key element. There are several interpretations of the term "digitalization". In a narrow technical sense, digitalization is perceived as the conversion of information into digital form, i.e. its digitization. In a wide public discourse, digitalization is understood as a digital transformation of organizational activity, processes, competencies, models for the effective use of digital technologies [8]. The ongoing debate on digitalization of politics is extensive and covers various aspects of political science. In the field of international relations scholars consider digitalization of diplomatic activity [13, 14], international relations [20, 21], international politics [6]. Though describing the role of digital technology, scholars rarely explore how exactly these processes transform the major concepts of international relations. This research assumes that digital technology has provoked a rethinking of the role of diplomacy in international politics. Thereby, it aims to fill the gap in existing literature by revealing the key features of the

D. A. Alexandrov et al. (Eds.): DTGS 2019, CCIS 1038, pp. 187–196, 2019.
https://doi.org/10.1007/978-3-030-37858-5_15

digitalization of diplomacy on the example of a study of Twittersphere related to 2019 Venezuelan Presidential Crisis.

The recurrent political crisis in Venezuela has been developing since January 10, 2019, when the National Assembly of Venezuela dominated by opposition declared the re-inauguration of President Maduro invalid and President of the National Assembly Guaido the acting president of the country. This case is interesting due to a broad international reaction to the events in Venezuela reproduced via Twitter. According to the knowledge of author, digital diplomacy related to 2019 Venezuelan presidential crisis hasn't yet been studied in complex. However, digital diplomacy needs to be explored in terms of identifying its presence as a phenomenon on Twitter, influential actors, discussion topics and trends. Consequently, my research question took the following form:

> RQ: To what extent and how do state bodies and political leaders use digital diplomacy with regard to 2019 Venezuelan presidential crisis and how successful is it? Who are the agenda setters and what are high-profile topics from the perspective of global politics?

2 Digitalization of Diplomacy in Global Politics

Rapid development of digital technology led to the digitalization of diplomacy and the appearance of new concepts. For the first time the use of digital technology in diplomacy was described by the term "NetDiplomacy", which appeared in the United States in 2001 and meant establishing a dialogue between the US government and foreign participants in social networks. Later, the impact of digital technology on diplomacy was captured in terms "E-diplomacy" [1, 9, 12], "Cyber Diplomacy" [2, 16], "Public Diplomacy Web 2.0" [7], "Twiplomacy" [19]. Researchers have continued to offer different definitions, though the most commonly used become the concept of "Digital Diplomacy" [15, 18]. Digital diplomacy is a set of methods for applying digital technology to achieve foreign policy goals. In most cases, digital diplomacy refers to the growing use of state social media platforms [14]; digital media (social media); digital and network technologies, including the Internet, mobile devices and social networking channels [16]; Information and Communication Technology [9].

2.1 Methodological Approaches to Digitalization of Diplomacy

The research methodology for studying the transformation of diplomacy in new digital environment has been actively developing. For the most part, it is studied in terms of effectiveness assessment of digital diplomacy, in which 2 key approaches are distinguished. The first approach is the analysis of the effectiveness of digital diplomacy on different levels, which corresponds to a specific process. The second approach examines the effectiveness of digital diplomacy in accordance with the applied strategies, considering them as evaluation parameters.

Processes of Digital Diplomacy. The effectiveness of digital diplomacy in social networks is considered at three different levels: the level of information provided to foreign audiences; level of influence; and the level of interaction with foreign audiences

[5]. According to this levels, three processes are investigated: agenda setting, presence expansion and conversation generating. As part of the study of agenda setting, the content of posts in social networks are analyzed for a selected period of time. Messages are classified by topics of discussion, frequency of their appearance, language, number, etc. The exploration of the presence expansion involves analysis of the impact of messages by counting reposts, comments, etc. In addition, scholars reveal the route of message distribution and clusters of users, i.e. carry out cluster analysis. The effectiveness assessment of the agenda setting combines the level of information with the level of influence and consists of identification of influential messages, analysis of its content and search for the causes of success [4]. For example, it was found that on Twitter, the role of messages from "ordinary" accounts (experts, civil society, citizens) is overshadowed by the important role played by media and political accounts [10]. On the level of conversation generating scholars examine the mechanism of interaction with the audience: whether digital diplomacy accounts provide feedback, correct information, write new comments. They calculate the reposts of messages from other users, comments in response to mentions, comments to the received response to their posts. Studies found that digital diplomacy is more often used to set the agenda than to generate conversations. Thus, the potential of digital diplomacy as a mechanism for interacting with the audience on social networks is not fully unlocked [4].

Strategies of Digital Diplomacy. The effectiveness of digital diplomacy is possible to assess by five parameters: listening, prioritization, hybridization, engagement, adaptation. Listening involves monitoring online discussions by using quantitative methods to track new trends or high-profile discussion topics; and qualitative methods to identify influential sites for diplomatic purposes. Prioritization is the determination of short-term and long-term goals with a constant eye on the activity in the cyberspace. Hybridization measures to what extent digital diplomacy is in line with the goals of traditional diplomacy. The key parameter in evaluating the effectiveness of digital diplomacy is involvement, because it embodies the ability to reach broad audiences in real time. The effectiveness of involvement in a short period of time is measured with quantitative methods, whilst patterns of effective interaction in the digital environment are detected by adding qualitative research methods. Finally, adaptation means that research methods for studying digital diplomacy must be flexible, i.e. adapted to the changing digital environment and actions of the target audience [3].

3 Sample and Method

3.1 Data Collection

To answer our research question, a computer program written in the programming language Python, with Beautiful Soup, a package for analyzing documents, was used to collect and analyze data obtained from the "Twitter Advanced Search" web page, which is an open and publicly available source of information about previously published tweets. The dataset comprised all accessible tweets containing a word "Venezuela" and uploaded into the database "Postgresql." I selected this particular word, first, due to its same spelling in English, Spanish, Portuguese, French, and other languages;

second, due to the frequent use of the country's name in tweets to discuss the politically tense situation there. The selection of tweets with the word "Venezuela" automatically included tweets with a similar hashtag "#Venezuela" to the dataset. The chronological framework covers the period from December 1, 2018 to March 10, 2019; this was selected related to the recurrent aggravation of the political, economic and humanitarian crisis in Venezuela and, accordingly, to the end of study. The data-coverage period is 100 days; as a result, 9,707,730 tweets that contained information related to the discussion about Venezuelan crisis were collected.

3.2 Data Processing

To compile reports of classified tweets in the MS Excel spreadsheet program, the programming language Python was used. Further, the graph shown in Fig. 1 was created to highlight the dynamics of tweets with the word "Venezuela" for the entire reviewed period.

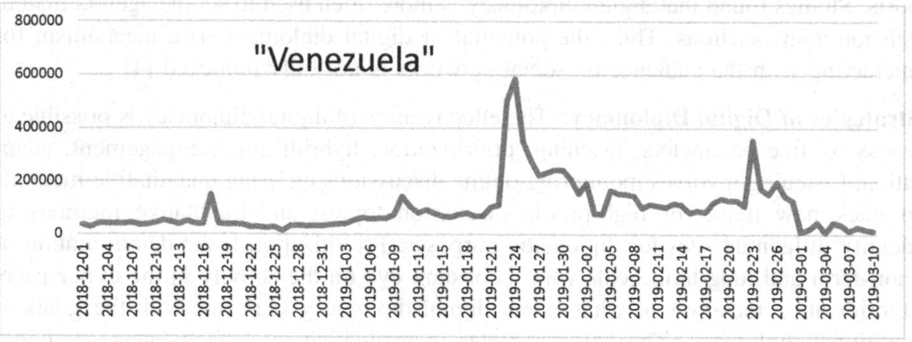

Fig. 1. The Dynamics of Tweets with the word "Venezuela" by days, December 1, 2018–March 10, 2019

Based on the data displayed in the graph, I chose the 2 most important periods for discussions about Venezuela on Twitter from the perspective of the research goals: (1) the proclamation of the Speaker of the National Assembly J. Guaido as an acting president under the Constitution of Venezuela on January 10–11; and (2) the subsequent official recognition of J. Guaido as an interim president of Venezuela by the USA and other countries on January 23.

Content Analysis of Influential Tweets. Twitter influence measures are diverse and include different metrics. In this study, the general influence classification measure "H-index" is applied in the context of Twitter. Thus, the influence index of a tweet is the sum of likes, retweets and replies [11, 17]. I used the Python programming language and the SQL query in the «Postgresql» database to classify the 50 most influential tweets with the word "Venezuela" for the 3 days: January, 10, 11 and 23. Tweets with the influence index (I.I.) less than 5000 were not considered, that's why for January 11 only 25 tweets were coded. Content analysis was applied to discover the topics of the discussion. After manually coding of tweets, for each day I identified 5 main topics. Finally, the influence indexes of all coded tweets devoted to one topic were summarized in order to identify the dominant agendas related to the crisis in Venezuela for the study period.

4 Results

4.1 Digital Diplomacy of (Non)-Recognition

Digital Diplomacy of Non-Recognition. From January 10, 2019 a group of official accounts expressing non-recognition of the legitimacy of the Maduro presidency is clearly visible. Moreover, the following discourse becomes the most influential discourse on Twitter about Venezuela (Table 1). Such digital diplomacy can be described as digital diplomacy of non-recognition, because, first, the tweets are published from official political accounts; second, they are dedicated to important international issue which were traditionally under jurisdiction of diplomatic bodies; and third, tweets are published on the same day and express a similar position. The key features of digital diplomacy of non-recognition include: indication of power vacuum in Venezuela; call for ignorance of disputed president of Venezuela Maduro; support for the National Assembly of Venezuela; and informing about severance of diplomatic relations with Venezuela. Twitter users, who applied this strategy can be divided on 3 identifiable groups: Latin American; Venezuelan Opposition; and the US group.

Table 1. Topics and authors of the most influential tweets with a word "Venezuela", January 10, 2019

No.	Content	Twitter user	I.I.
1	Non-recognition of the legitimacy of the Maduro presidency from January 10, 2019	OAS, Presidents of Chile, Colombia, Paraguay, Venezuelan Opposition, USA, etc.	410124
2	Criticism of the Maduro regime	Presidents of Argentina, Ecuador, Vice President of Colombia, Venezuelan opposition, etc.	176347
3	Criticism of Maduro supporters	Brazil activists, journalists, bloggers, online-media	115834
4	Support for Maduro	President of Venezuela N. Maduro, President of Bolivia, Blogger	78902
5	Criticism of Interventionism	Ex-Vice President of Colombia, President of the Workers' Party of Brazil	14745

Other topics on January 10 were devoted to criticism of the Maduro regime or dictatorship for the high level of inflation, hunger, violence, and violation of electoral process in Venezuela; criticism of Maduro supporters in Brazil; and, finally, support for

Maduro for the reasons of being elected by the people of Venezuela, Chavism, integration and liberation of peoples, protection of sovereignty of Venezuela.

Digital Diplomacy of Recognition. Since January 11 the digital diplomacy of non-recognition of Maduro as president of Venezuela has been smoothly replaced by digital diplomacy of recognition of Guaido as an interim president of Venezuela (Table 2). However, according to analyzed data, on January 11 Guaido was greeted as an interim president of Venezuela only by himself, OAS Secretary General, Magistrates of the Supreme Court of Venezuela (in exile), Brazilian politician, former Venezuelan mayor (in exile) and activist. Whereas, the US and the EU expressed support for National Assembly and democracy in Venezuela.

Table 2. Topics and authors of the most influential tweets with a word "Venezuela", January 11, 2019

No.	Content	Twitter user	I.I.
1	Greeting of Guaido as an Interim President of Venezuela, call to take an office	Guaido, OAS Secretary General, Journalist, Venezuelan opposition, etc.	167934
2	Criticism of the Maduro regime (usurper, suppression of demonstrations, salaries)	Guaido, Historian (Mexico), Activist (Venezuela, Cuba), Former President of Colombia, Journalist (Colombia)	65412
3	Call for the liberation of Venezuela, protest against an illegitimate regime	President of Peru, Human rights activist, Investigative Journalist	49442
4	Freedom of Venezuelans from slavery, Oil is the reason for US interest	Maduro, President of the Brazilian Workers Party, Blogger (Brazil)	28481
5	Support for National Assembly and democracy in Venezuela	US Department of State in Spanish, European Parliament	20999

The peak of digital diplomacy of recognition was on January 23, when Guaido got an official recognition as Venezuela's Interim President from a number of political leaders with total influence index 1,772,276 (Table 3). The most influential tweet on this topic was published by the official account of the US president Trump with the influence index 300,420.

It should be noted the existence of the discourse against the coup in Venezuela, adhered by the disputed President of Venezuela Maduro, President of the Brazilian Workers Party, Special Adviser to the President of Turkey and Press Secretary of the President, some Spanish and Brazilian Politicians and activists. Nevertheless, in terms of influence on Twitter they significantly lost to their active and united rivals.

Table 3. Topics and authors of the most influential tweets with a word "Venezuela", January 23, 2019

No.	Content	Twitter user	I.I.
1	Official recognition of Guaido as Venezuela's Interim President	USA, OAS, Presidents of Argentina, Paraguay, Brazil, Chile, Costa Rica, Colombia, Inter-American Development Bank, Ministry of Foreign Affairs of Peru, Venezuelan opposition	1772276
2	Support for Venezuela/Venezuelan people	Guaido (2), 3 Bloggers, Singer, Ex-President of Colombia, 2 Musicians	387376
3	Against the coup in Venezuela	Maduro, Special Adviser to the President of Turkey and Press Secretary of the President, Politician (Podemos, Spain), Politician (Brazil), TV host, Activist (Spain)	234653
4	Criticism of socialism	Journalist, Activist (USA), TV host (USA)	144404
5	Guaido and National Assembly are legitimate, unlike Maduro	President of the European Parliament, President of the European Council	72831

5 Discussion and Conclusion

The results of study of Twitter data has demonstrated the extent to which state bodies, political leaders and other actors of international politics used digital diplomacy by tweeting on the issue of 2019 Venezuelan presidential crisis. I found the information domination of supporters of Venezuelan opposition on Twitter. Moreover, having identified the agenda setters and high-profile discussion topics by applying content-analysis to the most influential tweets, I discovered some important patterns from the perspective of global politics.

First, tweets in Spanish were more influential in general comparing to tweets in English. The 2019 Venezuelan Presidential Crisis was discussed more in Spanish and Spanish-language tweets got a greater influence index. This can be explained by the following possible reasons: (a) Iberoamerican countries are more interested in the situation in Venezuela due to geographic and cultural-historical factor; (b) Venezuelan people react more actively to international tweets in their language. However, after considering not only influential, but all tweets in the dataset, I found out still a high level of the internationalization of the discussion about the situation in Venezuela. For instance, at the peak of the discussion, which fell on January 24, 393,120 tweets were published in Spanish, 99,245 - in English, and 41,578 - in Portuguese.

Second, the agenda setters on Venezuelan case are clearly polarized on 2 groups: the supporters of Maduro and the supporters of Guaido. Despite the fact that each of these groups offered similar theses and arguments, and sometimes completely similar tweets (this refers to the latter), I didn't find a strategy of using common hashtags to promote common position. In principle, world leaders resort to hashtagged discussions very rarely in their digital diplomacy, which is an interesting fact to verify and explain in future research.

A number of biases need to be considered as limitations of this study, in particular, those associated with the consideration of a relatively small number of tweets. To assess the level of distortion of results when considering only the most influential tweets, I resorted to another method by compiling a cloud of the most frequently used hashtags from all tweets from the dataset. The cloud partially confirms the conclusion, since, according to it, 2/3 of the hashtags were used to support Guaido or to criticize Maduro (Fig. 2).

Fig. 2. Influential Hashtags with a word "Venezuela", January 11, 2019

It is also worth considering that there are other classification measures for identifying influential tweets [17], the application of which could lead to different results. Another limitation is linked to the collection method of using Twitter's advanced search, which doesn't guarantee access to the complete collection of messages posted in Twitter. Finally, the chosen keyword couldn't cover complete discussions about 2019 Venezuelan Presidential Crisis on Twitter.

To conclude, the results of present study show that digital diplomacy is actively used by states bodies and politicians in crisis situations. Exploration of "small data" as distinguished from the general picture provided by "big data" displayed important trends in digitalization of global politics such as digital diplomacy of (non)-recognition. Nowadays, digital diplomacy has become a transboundary megaphone to promote the political agenda immediately and to everyone who is "listening".

References

1. Al-Muftaha, H., Weerakkodya, V., Ranab, N.P., Sivarajaha, U., Irania, Z.: Factors influencing e-diplomacy implementation: exploring causal relationships using interpretive structural modelling. Gov. Inf. Q. **35**, 502–514 (2018). https://doi.org/10.1016/j.giq.2018.03.002
2. Barston, R.P.: Modern Diplomacy. Routledge, New York (2014)
3. Bjola, C.: Getting digital diplomacy right: what quantum theory can teach us about measuring impact. Glob. Aff. **2**(3), 345–353 (2016). https://doi.org/10.1080/23340460.2016.1239388
4. Bjola, C., Jiang, L.: Social media and public diplomacy: a comparative analysis of the digital diplomatic strategies of the EU, US and Japan in China. In: Bjola, C., Holmes, M. (eds.) Digital Diplomacy: Theory and Practice, pp. 71–89. Routledge, London and New York (2015)
5. Bolgov, R., Bogdanovich, S., Yag'ya, V., Ermolina, M.: How to measure the digital diplomacy efficiency: problems and constraints. In: Chugunov, A.V., Bolgov, R., Kabanov, Y., Kampis, G., Wimmer, M. (eds.) DTGS 2016. CCIS, vol. 674, pp. 180–188. Springer, Cham (2016). https://doi.org/10.1007/978-3-319-49700-6_18
6. Bollier, D.: The rise of netpolitik: how the internet is changing international politics and diplomacy. A Report of the Eleventh Annual Aspen Institute Roundtable on Information Technology. The Aspen Institute, Washington DC (2003). http://www.bollier.org/files/aspen_reports/NETPOLITIK.PDF
7. Cull, N.: The long road to public diplomacy 2.0: the internet in US public diplomacy. Int. Stud. Rev. **15**(1), 123–139 (2013). https://doi.org/10.1111/misr.12026
8. Gobble, M.M.: Digital strategy and digital transformation. Res. Technol. Manage. **61**(5), 66–71 (2018). https://doi.org/10.1080/08956308.2018.1495969
9. Hanson, F.: Baked in and Wired: eDiplomacy@State. Foreign Policy Paper Series. No. 30: Brookings Institution, Washington DC (2012). https://www.brookings.edu/wp-content/uploads/2016/06/baked-in-hansonf-5.pdf
10. Harder, R., Sevenans, J., Van Aelst, P.: Intermedia agenda setting in the social media age: how traditional players dominate the news agenda in election times. Int. J. Press/Polit. **22**(3), 275–293 (2017). https://doi.org/10.1177/1940161217704969
11. Hirsch, J.E.: An index to quantify an individual's scientific research output that takes into account the effect of multiple coauthorship. Scientometrics **85**(3), 741–754 (2010). https://doi.org/10.1007/s11192-010-0193-9
12. Hocking, B., Melissen, J., Riordan, S., Sharp, P.: Futures for diplomacy: integrative diplomacy in the 21st century. Netherlands Institute of International Relations Clingendael. Report 1 (2012). http://www.lse.ac.uk/internationalRelations/dinamfellow/conf2012/HOCKING-Futures-of-Diplomacy.pdf
13. Jacobson, B., Höne, K., Kurbalija, J.: Data Diplomacy. Updating diplomacy to the big data era. DiploFoundation. Ministry of Foreign Affairs of Finland (2018). https://www.diplomacy.edu/sites/default/files/Data_Diplomacy_Report_2018.pdf
14. Manor, I., Segev, C.: America's selfie: how the US portrays itself on its social media accounts. In: Bjola, C., Holmes, M. (eds.) Digital Diplomacy: Theory and Practice, pp. 89–108. Routledge, London and New York (2015)
15. Olubukola, S.A.: Foreign policy in an era of digital diplomacy. Cogent Soc. Sci. **3**(1), 1297175 (2017). https://doi.org/10.1080/23311886.2017.1297175
16. Potter, E. (ed.): Cyber-Diplomacy: Managing Foreign Policy in the Twenty-First Century. McGill-Queen's University Press, Montreal (2002)

17. Riquelme, F., González-Cantergiani, P.: Measuring user influence on Twitter: a survey. Inf. Process. Manage. **52**(5), 949–975 (2016). https://doi.org/10.1016/j.ipm.2016.04.003
18. Sotiriu, S.: Digital diplomacy: between promises and reality. In: Bjola, C., Holmes, M. (eds.) Digital Diplomacy: Theory and Practice, pp. 33–51. Routledge, London and New York (2015)
19. Twiplomacy. https://twiplomacy.com
20. Verrekia, B.: Digital diplomacy and its effect on international relations. Independent Study Project (ISP) Collection (2017). https://digitalcollections.sit.edu/isp_collection/2596
21. Westcott, N.: Digital diplomacy: the impact of the internet on international relations. Oxford Internet Institute. Research Report No. 16 (2008). https://www.oii.ox.ac.uk/archive/downloads/publications/RR16.pdf

E-City: Smart Cities and Urban Planning

Adaptation of Smart City Technologies in Saint Petersburg: A Survey

Lyudmila Vidiasova(✉), Iaroslava Tensina, and Evgenii Vidiasov

ITMO University, Saint Petersburg, Russia
bershadskaya.lyudmila@gmail.com,
tensina.yaroslava@mail.ru, vidiasov@lawexp.com

Abstract. The paper describes a scientific study on the adaptation of smart city technologies in Saint Petersburg. There have been several attempts to implement the smart city concept but the adaptive capacity and the demand for new technologies by citizens remain underexplored. The research was conducted using a socio-technical approach according to which the impact of technology on society and the formation of technology by society are parallel processes. As a place for research approbation the pilot region St. Petersburg was selected. By examining a survey of city residents, this paper sheds light on an array of perceptions citizens have regarding smart cities, readiness to use new technologies and trust in the opportunity to participate in city management. The research results suggest a high level of information technologies usage and existence of the positive experience in obtaining online services. At the same time almost 1/3 of respondents didn't want to have any experience in electronic interactions with the authorities or even personal communications. The level of smart city awareness reached 11% among those respondents who clearly understood what it is and have any ideas of its implementation in Saint Petersburg. Almost 46% of the interviewed citizens could not demonstrate any knowledge on smart city concept or projects. The most frequent users of e-participation portals among the respondents from St. Petersburg are citizens aged 26–35 years. At the same time, their evaluations of such experience as positive or negative are divided almost equally. The obtained results could be used to develop recommendations for the optimal implementation of the "smart city" concept (in cooperation with the project office "Smart City of St. Petersburg" under the Administration of St. Petersburg).

Keywords: Smart City · Technologies adaptation · Information technology · Modernization · Urban studies

1 Introduction

Special attention to the phenomenon of smart cities in recent years draws mostly bright prospects about the almost limitless possibilities of using new technologies. There are a lot of works devoted to the study and development of smart city technological components and their implementation in various fields (transport infrastructure, housing and communal services, electronic public services, e-business, etc.). However, often the implementation of smart cities seriously depends on the interaction of all components and actors of this complex socio-technical system. In world practice, there are examples

D. A. Alexandrov et al. (Eds.): DTGS 2019, CCIS 1038, pp. 199–211, 2019.
https://doi.org/10.1007/978-3-030-37858-5_16

where the active introduction of new technologies has faced the following barriers: non-usage, organizational obstacles, lack of political will and users' motivation, non-transparency of benefits from using new technologies instead of traditional ones. This paper focuses on adapting users of new technologies living in existing cities and finding themselves in a digital transformation on the way to a smart city.

The paper presents the results of an urban population survey aimed to identify the level of perception of "smart cities", readiness to use new technologies and trust in the opportunity to participate in city management. The paper's structure looks as follows: state of the art section provides information on the current research achievements in the smart city field, research design demonstrates the methodology and selected approach, findings consolidate the St. Petersburg citizens' survey results on smart city adoption, discussion section opens the perspectives for future research, and conclusions summarize the revealed tendencies.

2 State of the Art

The concept of "smart city" is a new vector of studying the interaction of technological infrastructure for developing the urban environment and improving the quality of life [16]. Summarizing the research field the following directions could be found:

- issues of ICT infrastructure development and implementation [8];
- public transportation and overcoming the traffic jams barriers [11];
- environmental sustainability and ecological issues [4];
- social and cultural factors and pluralism willingness [15];
- educational issues and training options for better smart city development [7];
- healthcare system within the smart city [2];
- entrepreneurship and innovation nature and perspectives for their development [11];
- social security and cyber protection [1];
- economic issues of territory planning [14];
- information technologies in political sphere, e-services, e-governance [9];
- "smart house" system and other electronic gadgets [18];
- open government and open data [6].

The subject of "smart cities" is not new for Russian researchers as well. In particular, much attention is paid to the research of ICT infrastructure in the formation of digital cities (Khoruzhnikov, Grudinin, Zaslavsky) [10], as well as transport network infrastructure (Musautova, Nevostruev, Sidorchuk) [12] and provision of security of architectural-spatial solutions (Zhivaykin) [19].

Some research groups are engaged in studying the issues of social inclusion of various groups in the "smart cities" environment (Sergeeva, Laktukhina) [17], consolidation of joint resources and crowdsourcing (Nikiforov) [13], use of social media (Dorofeev, Markov) [3], development of human capital (Kazantsev) [5] and the emergence of a creative class (Smartyanov) [20].

The carried-out analysis of scientific research made it possible to reveal the spread of technological and economic approaches to the study of "smart cities". At the same time, focusing on technology, there is a risk of falling under the influence of technological determinism. Over the past twenty years, when studying the social effects of the diffusion and use of ICT in people's lives, a special emphasis was placed on the need to explore the digital divide and overcome it. Access to technology has long been recognized as a decisive factor in determining their use. The a priori assumption "if people have access to technology-that means they will use it" was constantly reproduced in the texts of works on social informatics. At the same time, as new technologies are disseminated and modernized (per the latest data from the FOM, the Internet audience in Russia has reached 68% of the population), there are practices of deliberate non-use of technologies with sufficient level of awareness of them and their capabilities.

This data testifies to the need to expand the scientific interpretation of the phenomenon of the "smart city" from the standpoint of social transformations taking place in society, including citizens in the management of the city, and the creation of public values. The creation of "smart cities" in foreign and domestic literature is often called a risky initiative, because at this stage there is not an abundance of unambiguous evidence confirming their effectiveness and contribution to improving the quality of life of the population.

In this paper the citizens' adaption of smart city technologies is considered to be a complex category involving:

- citizens' readiness to use new technologies;
- the level of smart city concept perception among the residents;
- citizens' willingness to participate in urban governance.

3 Research Design

3.1 Smart City Development in Saint Petersburg

Smart city development started in Saint Petersburg in 2017. In April 2017, the Governor of St. Petersburg launched the priority urban innovation program "Smart St. Petersburg" which is designed to improve the quality of citizens life and ensure the sustainable development of the city. The program is implemented through the widespread adoption of ICT in the management of urban processes and improving the efficiency of interaction between citizens, business and government representatives.

The implementation of the "smart city" system in St. Petersburg is based on the principles of timely context based streaming, providing effective G2C, B2B, B2C, G2C, IoT, short, medium and long-term planning, increasing users' motivation and trust, KPIs achievement, and resource management policy.

The development of Smart Petersburg is carried out on the basis of project management. For this purpose, a special project office and expert groups are organized, which evaluate incoming applications for projects. Criteria for the selection of projects are the following: novelty of the proposed technology, competitive advantages, presence of previously implemented analogues, the economic effect of implementation, possibilities of commercialization, form of financing, applicant's qualifications, possibility of integration into the existing infrastructure, technology efficiency indicators, compliance with the goals and objectives of the Smart City program and city development strategies, relevance of the project, social effect, the applicability of technology to improve the quality of life of citizens, public approval. The opinion of residents is reflected in the last three criteria. At the same time, the assessment of the social effect is reduced to the presence of the focus of the project on a certain category of citizens, the life situation, as well as the formation of a positive installation for living in the city. In addition, the first two blocks are evaluated by experts, and public approval is measured by the number of votes "for" the project on the site divided by the total number of votes (which does not reflect a representative sample for public opinion). Despite the active beginning of the development of the Smart City program in St. Petersburg, it is necessary to take into account the risk of social adaptation. In context of «smart city» building, orientation on citizens is necessary because without them, their trust and loyalty to modern technologies it's impossible to create an effective smart environment. Thus, one of the main issues is to identify the level of perception of "smart city" concept by citizens, readiness to use new technologies and trust of the possibility to participate in the management of the city.

3.2 Research Methodology

The research design was based on the social construction of technology (SCOT) approach. According to SCOT, the technology effective development and integration into social life is impossible without the users' activity. The users themselves create and adopt new technologies in accordance with their needs. This cycle creates an interaction of all agents and technologies, which contributes to the maintenance of the system and its optimal functioning.

The conducted research aimed at identifying the citizens' adaptation of smart city technologies in St. Petersburg. For the survey the method of questioning was used. The data was obtained by interviewers during a personal survey. As a place for conducting survey 6 multifunctional centers (MFC) providing state and municipal services were chosen. It is important to mention that MFC are located at densely populated districts of the city. Residents apply to multifunctional centers for a variety of public services. Applicants start at age 18 (with the exception of a number of services provided from age 14).

To calculate the sample population, data on population size and age and sex composition were used. The data was obtained on the official website of the Office of the Federal Statistical Service for St. Petersburg and the Leningrad Region. Based on the data on the size of the general population, the sample size for the survey was calculated - 600 respondents. The sampling error does not exceed 4% (four percent), the level of reliability was 95% (ninety-five percent).

Further, the population of St. Petersburg was divided into six age groups: 18–25 years old, 26–35 years old, 36–45 years old, 46–55 years old, 56–65 years old, and over 65 years old. In each age group, the percentage ratio of men and women was calculated.

The survey was conducted in November 2018. The respondents were asked all the questions by interviewers. Six hundred citizens took part in the study: 43% - men, 57% - women. The age structure of the expert group was as follows: 18–25 years - 15%,

26–35 years - 19%, 36–45 years - 17%, 46–55 years - 18%, 56–65 years – 16%, 65 years and over - 16%.

The majority of respondents are employees/specialists (39%), workers/guards/drivers (20%) and students (10%).

In accordance with the purpose of the study, the questions in the questionnaire were compiled in a way to obtain information on three main blocks:

- Readiness to use new technologies (indicating the overall level of technology and gadgets penetration into the daily practices of city residents);
- Level of perception of the «smart city» concept (reflecting the level of smart city awareness and understanding of its components);
- Citizens' willingness to participate in urban governance (showing willingness to participate in the smart city and its management, as well as actively use new technologies).

4 Findings

The research findings reflect the results of survey of urban population of St. Petersburg on technologies usage, awareness and practical adoption.

4.1 Readiness to Use New Technologies

The results of the survey showed that most of St. Petersburg residents are active Internet users: they use the Internet every day (42%) or almost always are online (26%). Less than half of the surveyed residents identified themselves as a rather experienced IT users which easily manage with a standard set of new programs for personal needs and work responsibilities (32%). At the same time, this part of respondents noted that it is difficult to study computer programs on their own.

Part of respondents who do not use the Internet and feel an urgent need to improve skills in this area mostly refers to "56–65 years" (29%) and "over 65 old years" age groups (46,9%).

Despite the active use of the Internet for personal and work tasks, respondents' preferences about the channels of communication with the authorities are not so straightforward. Over 40% of respondents noted the personal meeting as the preferred way to communicate with the government representatives (42%). Only 22% of respondents are ready to build communication with government authorities in fully electronic form. Some respondents chose their own answer and noted that they prefer not to interact with the authorities at all (1%).

According to the survey results, personal visits are more preferable by the respondents of the older age groups (Table 1). Fully electronic format was indicated by almost every 5–6th citizen at age 18–45 participated in the survey. Also, the study revealed the preference of telephone calls by the respondents at age 46–55 years.

Table 1. Distribution of respondent's answers by age groups

Age	Personal conversation, meeting	Electronic completion of required documents, but personal attendance upon receipt	Electronic filling out the necessary documents, talking on the phone if necessary	Communication is fully electronic
18–25	6,80%	20,13%	12,96%	27,48%
26–35	9,60%	**27,04%**	20,37%	**28,24%**
36–45	12,00%	18,24%	18,52%	22,14%
46–55	18,80%	19,50%	**29,63%**	10,69%
56–65	22,80%	10,06%	12,96%	5,34%
65 +	**30,00%**	5,03%	5,56%	6,11%

4.2 The Level of Perception of the «Smart City» Concept

The survey results demonstrate that the majority of respondents is not familiar with the term "smart city" (46%) (see Fig. 1). At the same time, some respondents heard something about "smart city" but do not have a clear understanding (33%). Only 10% of surveyed residents noted the they clearly understand what "smart city" is and how it can be implemented in St. Petersburg. Most respondents which are familiar with the concept of "smart city" belong to "36–45" (30,3%) and "18–25" (27,3%) age groups. Most of them are employees/specialists (21,2%) and students (18,2%).

Answering the question "What is smart city for you?" most respondents identified areas like smart transport, smart governance and smart ecology. It is also important to mention that for some respondents "smart city" primarily means a possibility to

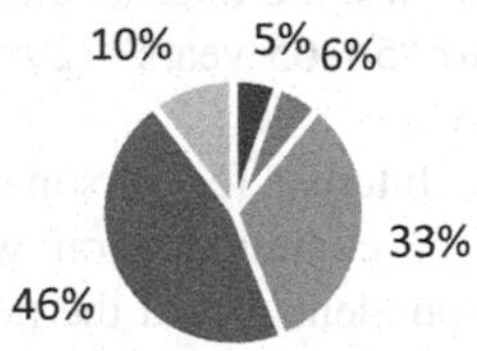

Fig. 1. Distribution of respondents' answers to the question "Are you familiar with the term «smart city»?"

participate in city life. The majority of surveyed St. Petersburg residents noted that they were ready to participate in the city management (submit appeals, take initiatives, vote for or against certain decisions on official portals) but under certain conditions (34%). At the same time, there was a large amount of respondents who were not ready to participate in city management at all (23%), while only 16% noted that they are definitely ready to take part in such activities.

Among the top-priority industries for the "smart city" project implementation, the surveyed residents of St. Petersburg identified the following areas: housing and communal services, public health, transport, social support, security and law enforcement and ecology.

4.3 Citizens' Willingness to Participate in Urban Governance

According to the survey tasks several questions were focused on the existed experience of participating in city life, communicating with the authorities through ICT channels. A large portion of the respondents indicated that they have a positive experience in contacting government representatives through electronic receptions (33%), while the portion of respondents who have had a negative experience remain insignificant (5%) (see Fig. 2). Some respondents noted that they did not have such an experience and even did not want to try (26%). At the same time, some respondents from this group expressed their interest and desire to try a new way to interact with the authorities (20%).

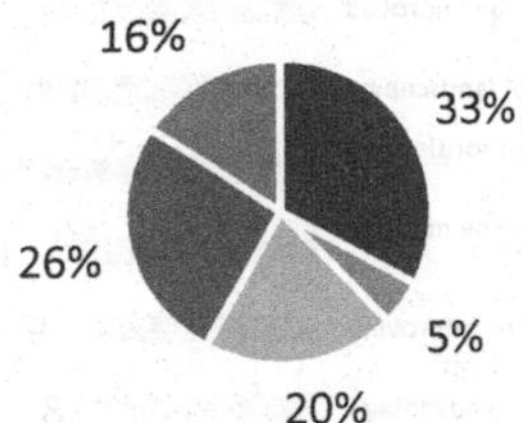

Fig. 2. Distribution of respondent's answers to the question "Do you personally have experience contacting public authorities through electronic receptions?"

As shown by the results of the survey, similar distribution is observed in relation to personal contact with government representatives. Most respondents confirmed that they have positive experience in communication with public authorities through personal meetings and conversation (36%). A slightly lower percentage of respondents noted a lack of experience and interest in interacting with the authorities (27%). The results of the survey also showed that residents of St. Petersburg have more negative experiences in personal interaction with government authorities than in electronic form (20%).

The survey results demonstrate that majority of respondents have a positive experience in using public services portals. More than half of respondents are satisfied with using the Portal of State and Municipal Services (www.gosuslugi.ru) (54%) as well as have a positive experience with the Portal of State and Municipal Services of St. Petersburg (www.gu.spb.ru) (38%).

Despite respondent's interest in participation in city management, the percentage of surveyed citizens who have an experience in using electronic participation portals remain insignificant. Most of the respondents noted that they have never used electronic participation portals "Our Petersburg" (https://gorod.gov.spb.ru/) (45%), "Russian public initiative" (https://www.roi.ru/) (51%), Change.org (https://www.change.org/) (47%) and not interested to try. The percentage of respondents who have a positive experience in using these portals varies from 5% to 13%.

Among the main benefits from the use of "smart city" technologies surveyed citizens identified increasing the quality of life, improvement of transport infrastructure, improvement of landscaping and building the productive dialogue between the authorities and citizens. Only 9% of respondents noted that they do not see any advantages from implementing "smart city" projects (see Fig. 3).

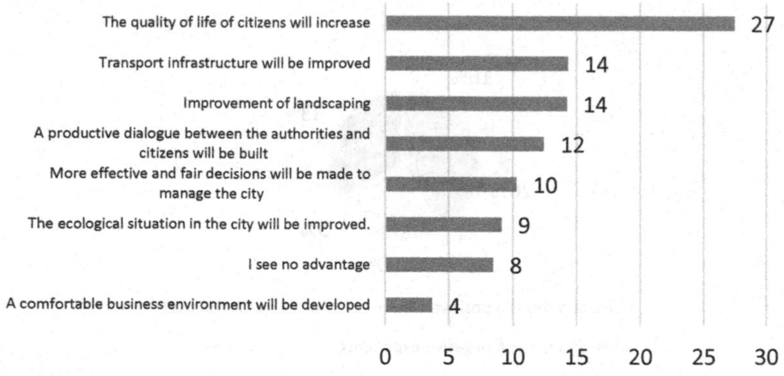

Fig. 3. Distribution of respondent's answers to the question "What benefits do you expect from using «smart city» technology?", %

Considering possible threats from the implementing of "smart city" technologies, most of the respondents noted that they do not see any threats (14%). Among defined threats citizens of St. Petersburg chose following areas: inflexibility of power, resistance to citizens' inclusion in decision-making or city management (11%); cybersecurity threats, information systems vulnerability, the emergence of hackers (11%); inequality between citizens due to different ICT competencies (10%) and public distrust of new digital technologies (9%).

5 Discussion

The presented results show, on the one hand, high rates of information technology usage and a high level of satisfaction with receiving electronic services. At the same time, the revealed level is 25–30% of respondents who do not want to have any experience in obtaining electronic services, using official portals, electronic participation sites and personal visits to the authorities. This reluctance is especially clearly expressed in representatives of the older age groups (Table 2). In addition, it was revealed that a group of residents aged 26–35 years more critically look at the quality of the provision of such services, the work of portals, etc.

Table 2. Respondents' experience with e-services portals' usage, %

	Yes, and this is a negative experience	Yes, and this is a positive experience (satisfied with the use)	Difficult to answer	I have no experience and do not want to try	I have no experience, but I would like to try
Portal of State and Municipal Services of St. Petersburg					
18–25	9,09%	19,38%	4,35%	11,11%	18,88%
26–35	**50,00%**	**23,35%**	13,04%	8,64%	21,68%
36–45	22,73%	19,82%	17,39%	7,41%	20,28%
46–55	13,64%	18,94%	19,57%	16,05%	18,88%
56–65	4,55%	13,22%	17,39%	22,22%	9,09%
65 +	0,00%	5,29%	**28,26%**	**34,57%**	11,19%
The Portal of State and Municipal Services					
18–25	13,04%	19,08%	5,26%	10,45%	15,00%
26–35	**47,83%**	**24,92%**	13,16%	5,22%	13,75%
36–45	21,74%	19,08%	18,42%	8,21%	17,50%
46–55	13,04%	17,54%	15,79%	13,43%	**30,00%**
56–65	4,35%	12,31%	15,79%	23,13%	12,50%
65 +	0,00%	7,08%	**31,58%**	**39,55%**	11,25%

In terms of experience in using e-participation sites, indicators of preferential refusal to use technologies are slightly lower. Table 3 presents the distribution of respondents by age groups in accordance with their assessment of the experience of using the "Russian Public Initiative" portal, "Change.org" petition portal, and "Our Saint Petersburg" city portal. According to the survey results, the most frequent users of e-participation portals among the respondents from St. Petersburg are citizens aged 26–35 years. At the same time, their evaluations of such experience as positive or negative are divided almost equally.

Table 3. Respondents' experience with e-participation portals' usage, %

	Yes, and this is a negative experience	Yes, and this is a positive experience	Difficult to answer	I have no experience and do not want to try	I have no experience, but I would like to try
Change.org					
18–25	24%	20%	9%	13%	19%
26–35	**37%**	26%	18%	13%	23%
36–45	17%	25%	15%	13%	20%
46–55	7%	20%	12%	18%	**24%**
56–65	7%	5%	21%	19%	9%
65 +	7%	5%	**26%**	**22%**	6%
Russian Public Initiative					
18–25	21%	23%	10%	14%	19%
26–35	**37%**	35%	18%	14%	**25%**
36–45	21%	19%	13%	14%	23%
46–55	5%	19%	14%	18%	22%
56–65	11%	3%	**23%**	17%	8%
65 +	5%	0%	22%	**23%**	3%
Our Saint Petersburg					
18–25	18%	23%	11%	14%	17%
26–35	**41%**	34%	14%	12%	**25%**
36–45	32%	21%	14%	11%	22%
46–55	5%	13%	15%	18%	22%
56–65	0%	7%	21%	20%	9%
65 +	5%	2%	**25%**	**25%**	4%

It is worth emphasizing that the evaluation of the experience of personal appeals to the authorities as a whole shows more positive responses in all age groups. At the same time, no more than 3% of respondents in each of the age groups have not had any experience with personal visits to the authorities, nor have any desire to try this method.

6 Conclusions

The research underlined a complex effect of social construction of a "smart city" phenomenon. According to survey data, information technologies are actively incorporated into social life of Saint Petersburg residents. Thus, the results of the study showed that most of the surveyed residents are active users of the Internet and modern IT technologies. This indicates that city residents are potentially ready to use "smart city" technologies implementing in St. Petersburg.

However, there is a still a question if citizens are interested in using of technologies and innovation that "smart city" could provide. As the survey results demonstrate, a huge part of St. Petersburg citizens preferred to communicate personally than using fully electronic means of communication with government representatives. It can be assumed that this indicates a decreased level of citizens' readiness to use information technologies for communication with authorities. Even if technologies are implemented, the motivation and interest of citizens to use them is necessary for the project to be successful.

The low interest in the use of new technologies may be caused by the low awareness of citizens about the possibilities of "smart cities". The survey results demonstrate that majority of surveyed respondents do not have clear understanding what smart city is and how it could be implemented in the city to improve citizen's life. At the same time, citizens identified the main areas that should be improved by using of modern technologies: housing and communal services, public health, transport, social support, security and law enforcement and ecology.

During the study, interesting results were obtained reflecting the citizens' interest to participate in the management of the city. However, even citizens are interested in these activities, most of them are ready to participate in city management only under certain conditions or entirely disinterested in trying new portals that provide them with the possibility to influence government decision. The results of the survey show that citizens of St. Petersburg are ready to use public services portals rather than e-participation portals. This can be explained by the low level of trust in such portals and their effectiveness, as well as low awareness of their functioning and examples of successful problem solving.

It should be noted that most of the surveyed citizens were able to identify the main benefits of implementing smart city technologies. Only small part of respondents noted that they do not see any advantages. This suggests that raising citizen awareness about smart city and its technologies can significantly increase their interest and motivation to use new technologies as well as increase trust in their effectiveness.

The research revealed the need to concentrate the Smart City program efforts towards different age groups of citizens in accordance with their expectations. The next research steps should be addressed to issues of conscious rejection of information technology despite their declared benefits. Identifying the causes of such rejections will help to clarify the adoption strategies in a more comprehensive way. The cross-countries analysis is also a prominent research field with a purpose to shed a light on similarities and differences in new socio-technical systems construction.

Acknowledgements. The study was performed with financial support by the grant from the Russian Science Foundation (project № 17-78-10079): "Research on adaptation models of the Smart City Concept in the conditions of modern Russian Society".

References

1. Afonso, R.A., dos Santos Brito, K., do Nascimento, C.H., Garcia, V.C., Álvaro, A.: Brazilian smart cities: using a maturity model to measure and compare inequality in cities. In: Proceedings of the 16th Annual International Conference on Digital Government Research, pp. 230–238 (2015). http://dl.acm.org/citation.cfm?id=2757426
2. Carli, R., Dotoli, M., Pellegrino, R., Ranieri, L.: Measuring and managing the smartness of cities: a framework for classifying performance indicators. In: IEEE International Conference on Systems, Man, and Cybernetics, pp. 1288–1293 (2013)
3. Dorofeev, A., Markov, A., Tsirlov, V.: Social media in identifying threats to ensure safe life in a modern city. In: Chugunov, A.V., Bolgov, R., Kabanov, Y., Kampis, G., Wimmer, M. (eds.) DTGS 2016. CCIS, vol. 674, pp. 441–449. Springer, Cham (2016). https://doi.org/10.1007/978-3-319-49700-6_44
4. Gil-Garcia, J.R., Pardo, T.A., Nam, T.: What makes a city smart? Identifying core components and proposing an integrative and comprehensive conceptualization. Inf. Polity **20**(1), 61–87 (2015). https://doi.org/10.3233/IP-150354
5. Kazantsev, N., Zakhlebin, I.: Measuring influence of internationalized universities on smart city development in terms of human capital and urban aspects. Knowl. Manage. E-Learn. **6**(4), 410–425 (2014)
6. Kuk, G., Davies, T.: The roles of agency and artifacts in assembling open data complementarities. In: ICIS (2011). https://eprints.soton.ac.uk/273064/
7. Lazaroiu Lazaroi, G.C., Roscia, M.: Definition methodology for the smart cities model. Energy **47**(1), 326–332 (2012)
8. Lee, J., Hancock, M., Hu, M.-C.: Towards an effective framework for building smart cities: lessons from Seoul and San Francisco. Technol. Forecast. Soc. Chang. **89**, 80–99 (2014)
9. Lombardi, P., Giordano, S., Farouh, H., Yousef, W.: Modelling the smart city performance. Innov. Eur. J. Soc. Sci. Res. **25**(2), 137–149 (2012)
10. Medvedev, A., Zaslavsky, A., Khoruzhnikov, S., Grudinin, V.: Reporting road problems in smart cities using OpenIoT framework. In: Podnar Žarko, I., Pripužić, K., Serrano, M. (eds.) Interoperability and Open-Source Solutions for the Internet of Things. LNCS, vol. 9001, pp. 169–182. Springer, Cham (2015). https://doi.org/10.1007/978-3-319-16546-2_13
11. Monzon, A.: Smart cities concept and challenges: bases for the assessment of smart city projects. In: Helfert, M., Krempels, K.-H., Klein, C., Donnellan, B., Gusikhin, O. (eds.) Smart Cities, Green Technologies, and Intelligent Transport Systems. CCIS, vol. 579, pp. 17–31. Springer, Cham (2015). https://doi.org/10.1007/978-3-319-27753-0_2
12. Musatova, Z., Mkhitarian, S., Nevostruev, P., Sidorchuk, R., Komleva, N.: Smart-technologies in public transport and their perception by the youth audience. Indian J. Sci. Technol. **9**(42), 164–167 (2016)
13. Nikiforov, A., Singireja, A.: Open data and crowdsourcing perspectives for smart city in the Unites States and Russia. In: ACM International Conference Proceeding Series Proceedings, pp. 171–177 (2016)
14. Perboli, G., De Marco, A., Perfetti, F., Marone, M.: A new taxonomy of smart city projects. Transp. Res. Procedia **3**, 470–478 (2014)
15. Priano, F.H., Guerra, C.F.: A framework for measuring smart cities. In: Proceedings of the 15th Annual International Conference on Digital Government Research, pp. 44–54 (2014)
16. Purnomo, F., Prabowo, H.: Smart city indicators: a systematic literature review. J. Telecommun. Electron. Comput. Eng. **3**(8), 161–164 (2016)

17. Sergeyeva, O., Laktukhina, E.: Child in "smart city": social studies review of children's mobility. In: ACM International Conference Proceeding Series Proceedings, pp. 31–34 (2016)
18. Shin, D.H., Kim, T.: Enabling the smart city. In: Proceedings of the 6th International Conference on Ubiquitous Information Management and Communication - ICUIMC 2012 (2012)
19. Zhivaykin, A.L.: The shadow of digital transformation. In: A Collection of Articles by Teachers of the IX International Scientific and Practical Conference "Modern Economy: Concepts and Models of Innovative Development", pp. 55–61 (2018)

Conceptual Big Data Processing Model for the Tasks of Smart Cities Environmental Monitoring

Dmitry Voronin(✉), Victoria Shevchenko, Olga Chengar, and Elena Mashchenko

Sevastopol State University, Sevastopol, Russia
dima@voronins.com, {VIShevchenko,OVChengar, Maschenko}@sevsu.ru

Abstract. The systems-technical analysis of the processes of collecting, storing, processing and analysing of Big Data arising in the tasks of environmental monitoring in the framework of the «Smart City» project is considered. A conceptual Big Data processing model of an environmental monitoring based on a NIST Big Data Reference Architecture is proposed.

Keywords: Smart City monitoring · Environmental monitoring · Conceptual model · Big Data processing

1 Introduction

The strategy of scientific and technological development of the Russian Federation identifies the following current areas [1]: research in the field of technological breakthrough; transition to advanced digital intelligent manufacturing technologies; Big Data, machine learning and artificial intelligence development.

The elaboration of these areas requires effective operational support, based on the use of modern information technologies that automate processes of collection, storage, processing and analysis of Big Data arising in the tasks of the Smart City concept implementation.

To implement the concept of Smart Cities, information systems and converged infrastructures are actively used. Their specific features are the following [2–4]:

- heterogeneity of equipment and technologies (server platforms, data storage systems, network equipment, cloud technologies and virtualization technologies, etc.);
- integrated management (the system is managed as a unit, rather than using separate administration tools), management is often provided as a service;
- increased requirements for information security and quality of service;
- specialization in processing and storage of continuously growing data volumes;
- ability to transfer different types of data traffic in one stream and its dynamic distribution;
- real-time data processing, which is especially important for efficient organization of the data transfer process in Smart City;

D. A. Alexandrov et al. (Eds.): DTGS 2019, CCIS 1038, pp. 212–222, 2019.
https://doi.org/10.1007/978-3-030-37858-5_17

– focus on large consumers, in particular, on regional data processing centres, providing the possibility of locating the necessary information resources, including data banks of information systems of Smart City.

As known, “Smart Environment” is one of the important directions of Smart City concept development. Moreover, the levels of monitoring systems development and environmental safety are the main metrics given in the “Indicators of Smart Cities” project [5], developed by the National Research Institute of Technologies and Communications. Consequently, the task of digital infrastructure development, used for collection, storage, processing and analysis of Big Data, arising in the tasks of environmental Smart City monitoring, is relevant.

2 Related Works

The works [6–8] are devoted to the development and study of the quality characteristics of information systems for operational processing of large amounts of data for convergent infrastructures. The focus of these papers is on the concept of composite applications. They describe CLAVIRE - the multifunctional technology platform, designed to create and to run composite applications based on distributed cloud services. Such technological platforms are the means of supporting situational centres that are useful in decision-making, especially, for various critical situations under conditions of uncertainty and incompleteness of the initial data. Based on these technologies, it is possible to build specialized decision support tools providing interactive visualization for extreme situations research. These technologies can be successfully used for Smart City operational management.

For example, the work [9] describes the use of emergency computing technologies to prevent the threat of floods in St. Petersburg. The specificity of emergency computing is that the computational architecture is formed dynamically with the choice of resources needed for solving the specific task in a limited time that is allowable for decision-making. The current capabilities of the CLAVIRE technology platform, including the distributed system construction used for Big Data streaming processing, are given in [10].

A large number of works describe various environmental monitoring tasks and the proposed solutions. The work [11] contains an overview of current progress in biological monitoring of water bodies on the Sochi coast of the Black Sea (given in order to create a unified system of water quality bioindication). The work [12] consider the conditions for sea temperature measuring using contact inertia sensors. In addition, it analyses the possibility of using algorithmic-software correction in dynamic models of focused sensors, etc. The work [14] presents organization model of monitoring system based on distributed block-type storage system. The degradation effects simulation of primary meters of the monitoring system are studied in [15].

A number of works are devoted to the Big Data processing and its application in various branches of science and economics. Thus, in [16], trends analysis in Big Data processing technologies, data storage and multi-format tools development was carried out, modern hardware platforms were discussed. In [17], the authors propose to use the concept of a functional data complex to formalize the description of an object-based data approach. In [18] the research was conducted on the acquisition and processing of Big Data in large-scale economic systems. The work [19] is devoted to developing a geo-information model to assess the natural resource potential of the specific region (Krasnodar region). The methods of pattern recognition, classification and clustering were used to search functional and logical patterns in the accumulated data. The analysis of the spectral characteristics of multi-time composites of space images is carried out. The mapping process is based on a large amount of data. The research results are used to identify the ecological status of territories to assess the degree of technogenic influence on the environment.

The classification, proposed in work [20], is oriented on data generated by the modern city, in order to highlight the information flows that can be handled using the Big Data technology. Important issues of Smart City standardization, the Internet of Things and Big Data are discussed in [21].

Of great practical importance is the publication of Federico Montori, Luca Bedogni and Luciano Bononi [22] in which, the collaborative internet of things architecture for Smart Cities and environmental monitoring is considered. The authors present a software platform for environmental monitoring data analysis, having the following features: the ability to integrate heterogeneous data sources, the implementation in the form of Web-based applications and mobile services, the ability to analyse data streams, coming from unreliable resources. However, the paper does not explicitly address the issues of Big Data analysis and the use of the cloud services.

The work [23] describes the usage of cloud technologies to analyse Big Data generated by the Smart City. The cloud service analyses the Bristol Open data by identifying correlations between selected urban environment indicators. The data pertaining to quality of life (mainly crime and safety, economy and employment) was analysed.

The Smart City architecture for real-time decision-making is proposed in the work [24]. The proposed Smart City's architecture comprises the following three levels: (1) data generation and acquisition level; (2) data management and processing level; (3) application level. In the study, the real-world dataset of Surrey (Canada) and Aarhus (Denmark) cities are analysed to derive the threshold values. The authors note that the system has been designed for specific goals and does not reflect a solution in general to every system presented in a Smart City.

It should be noted that the analysis of environmental data monitoring was not carried out by the authors of the works [23, 24] and the important features of such data processing were not considered.

Consequently, the authors of the above works do not offer a unified concept and methodology for collecting, storing, processing and analysing of Big Data in information systems and infrastructures of Smart Cities for environmental tasks monitoring.

The results of the analysis made it possible to conclude that Big Data processing is promising and relevant technology used for Smart Cities environmental monitoring. The development of a unified concept and methodology is extremely useful task for Smart City concept implementation. It will significantly prevent threats to environmental safety by increasing monitoring systems' quality. The purpose of this work is to develop a conceptual model of Big Data technologies used to solve environmental monitoring tasks in Smart Cities.

3 Big Data Processing Analysis in the Tasks of Environmental Monitoring

In accordance with Article 1 of the Federal Law «On environmental protection» [25] environmental monitoring estimates and predicts the state of the environment under the influence of natural and anthropogenic factors. Currently, a unified system of environmental monitoring is actively developing. Satellite data processing [26] is an example of monitoring data analyses (Fig. 1).

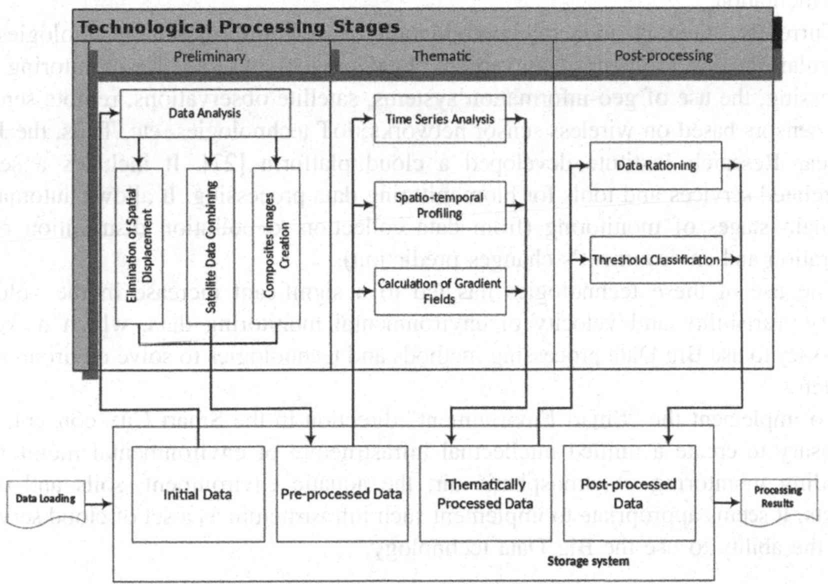

Fig. 1. Satellite data processing.

Satellite data is got from multiple satellites and is presented in a form of binary files in the size of tens or hundreds of megabytes. Such data processing needs milliards of processing cycles. The primary step is to load the analysed data into the storage system. Then, three stages of data processing are consistently implemented: preliminary processing, thematic processing and post-processing.

The pre-treatment stage includes several stages:

- Data errors identification (elimination of spatial displacement);
- Satellite data combining (combining time series of images from different satellites);
- Composites images creating (combining images in different frequency bands, etc.).

Further, at the stage of thematic processing, the following stages are implemented: time series of data analysis, spatial-temporal profiling and of gradient fields' calculation. At the final stage of post-processing, data rationing and threshold classification are carried out. Then the processing results are provided to the user.

Data processing and analysing makes it possible to study the ecological characteristics of a particular locality, to register changes occurring in the observed ecosystems under the influence of various natural and anthropogenic factors. The performance of data processing and analysis depends on the goals and objectives of data consumers, the amount of data used by the information infrastructure.

When organizing this kind of activity, it is extremely necessary to use modern information technologies efficiently. These technologies will enable high-quality and up-to-date automation of collecting, storing, processing and analysing of Big Data arising in the tasks of the digital economy, including the tasks of Smart Cities concept implementation.

Currently, there is an active introduction of new information technologies, in particular, the development of convergent cloud services and tools for monitoring data processing, the use of geo-information systems, satellite observations, remote sensing data, sensors based on wireless sensor networks, IoT technologies, etc. Thus, the Joint Nuclear Research Institute developed a cloud platform [27]. It includes a set of interrelated services and tools for biomonitoring data processing. It allows automating the main stages of monitoring (from data collection to pollution distribution maps generation and environment's changes prediction).

The use of these technologies has led to a significant increase in the volume, variety, variability and velocity of environmental monitoring data, which makes it necessary to use Big Data processing methods and technologies to solve environmental problems.

To implement the "Smart Environment" direction in the Smart City concept, it is necessary to create a unified intellectual infrastructure of environmental monitoring, including monitoring of atmospheric air, the aquatic environment, soils and other objects. It seems appropriate to implement such infrastructure as a set of cloud services with the ability to use the Big Data technology.

4 Conceptual Big Data Processing Model

To build a conceptual model of Big Data processing, adapted for the tasks of environmental monitoring, the authors propose to use: (1) the reference model of the Big Data architecture, developed in National Institute of Standards and Technology (NIST) [28, 29]; (2) IT Service Management methodology, described in IT Infrastructure Library [30, 31].

In NIST Big Data Reference Architecture (Fig. 2) the composition of the interacting components is determined, the basic relationship between the participants of the process is established. Their activities and functions can be implemented in Big Data analytics.

NIST Big Data Reference Architecture [28, 29] contains five main acting components, representing the various technical roles that exist in each Big Data system.

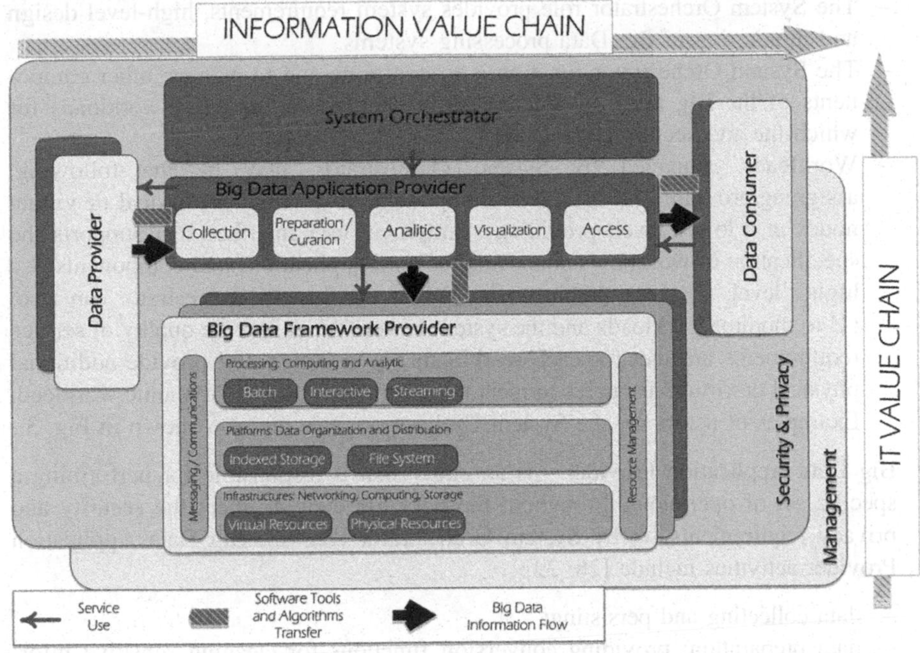

Fig. 2. NIST big data reference architecture.

1. Data Provider – is an entity that introduces new data or information flows into Big Data system through various functional interfaces. Different types of data sources are used (such as raw data or data previously converted by another system) [28, 29]. Examples of actors for the Data Provider role (adapted to the subject area of environmental monitoring), are given in Reference Architecture Taxonomy (Fig. 3): Enterprises, Monitoring Systems, Researcher and Scientist, IoT Devices, Archived environmental observations, Geographic Information Systems, Space Satellite Imagery. The standard gives the following requirements for Data Provider:
   – reliable asynchronous streaming real-time data processing got from various centralized or distributed data sources, sensors or devices;
   – batch and high-performance data transfer between data sources and compute clusters;
   – diversified data content, including data in the form of structured and unstructured text, graphics, websites, geospatial, compressed, synchronized, spatial, multimedia and other data.
2. System Orchestrator – is an entity that describes comprehensive requirements, which the system must comply, including policy, management, architecture, resources and business requirements, as well as monitoring or auditing activities to ensure that the system meets these requirements [28, 29].

- The System Orchestrator role provides system requirements, high-level design and monitoring of Big Data processing systems.
- The System Orchestrator function is to configure and to manage other components of the Big Data architecture to implement one or more workloads for which the architecture is designed.
- Workloads, managed by System Orchestrator, may be the following: assigning/providing infrastructure components to individual physical or virtual nodes at a lower level, providing a graphical user interface that supports the specification of workflows connecting several applications and components at a higher level. By using Management Fabric the System Orchestrator can also: (1) to monitor workloads and the system to verify that specific quality of service requirements are met for each workload, (2) to assign and provide additional physical or virtual resources to meet the requirements of the dynamic workload. Examples of actors for the System Orchestrator role are also shown in Fig. 3.

3. Big Data Application Provider – is an entity that is responsible for performing a specific set of operations throughout the data life cycle to meet the security and privacy requirements set by System Orchestrator (Fig. 2). Big Data Application Provider activities include [28, 29]:

   - data collecting and persisting;
   - data preparation: providing conversion functions for cleaning sensitive information; creation of metadata describing data sources, use/access policies, other relevant attributes;
   - data analytics and visualization;
   - ensuring access rights, authorization mechanisms and data access through programmable interfaces;
   - publishing the availability of the information and means to access it.

4. Data Consumer – receives and uses the results of data processing in its activities of data analytics. The actions associated with the data consumer role are as follows [28, 29]: search and data acquisition, data analysis at the local level, compilation of reports, visualization, the use of data in own business processes. The data consumer uses the interfaces or services provided by the Big Data Application Provider to access information of interest. These interfaces can include reporting, data's retrieval, rendering, and visualization. Examples of actors for the role of Data Consumers in the environmental monitoring system are the following: Research Institutes, State Organizations, Ministry of Emergency, Environmental Control, Health Care, Citizens, etc. (Fig. 3).
5. Big Data Framework Provider – an entity providing shared resources and services used by the Application Provider when creating a specific application. Big Data Framework Provider consists of one or more instances of three subcomponents: infrastructure platforms, data storage platforms, and processing environments [28, 29]. The requirements to Big Data Application Provider are the following: physical resources virtualization, flexibility providing (specialized types of data storage platforms and processing methods).

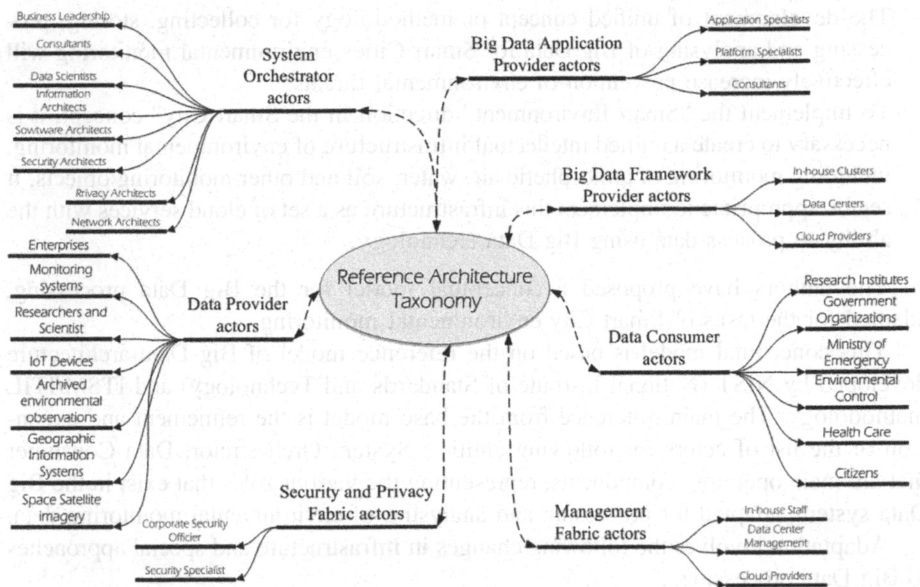

Fig. 3. Reference architecture taxonomy for big data processing.

Also in NIST Big Data Reference Architecture [28, 29] the following entities are defined to support the privacy/security policies and management tasks (Fig. 3):

- Security and Privacy Fabric interacts with System Orchestrator (for developing privacy and security policies, requirements and auditing), as well as with Big Data Application Provider and Big Data Framework Provider (for the development, deployment and operation of data analysis applications).
- Management Fabric – a management platform for configuring and managing software. It is used for performance monitoring and resources managing of Big Data analytics systems.

5 Conclusions

Analysis of the current state in the field of Big Data processing used for Smart Cities environmental monitoring showed the following:

- The modern trends are: convergent cloud services development, geoformation systems introduction, satellite observations and wireless sensor networks usage, IoT technologies development.
- The use of these technologies has led to a significant increase in the following indicators: volume, variety, variability and velocity of environmental monitoring data, which makes it necessary to use Big Data processing methods and technologies for solving environmental problems.

- The development of unified concept or methodology for collecting, storing, processing and analysing of Big Data for Smart Cities environmental monitoring will effectively increase prevention of environmental threats.
- To implement the “Smart Environment” direction in the Smart City” concept, it is necessary to create a unified intellectual infrastructure of environmental monitoring, including monitoring of atmospheric air, water, soil and other monitoring objects. It seems appropriate to implement this infrastructure as a set of cloud services with the ability to process data using Big Data technology.

The authors have proposed a conceptual model for the Big Data processing, adapted for the tasks of Smart City environmental monitoring.

This conceptual model is based on the reference model of Big Data architecture developed by NIST (National Institute of Standards and Technology) and ITSM/ITIL methodology. The main difference from the base model is the refinement and expansion of the list of actors for following entities: System Orchestrator, Data Consumer that are main operating components, representing the various roles that exist in the Big Data system, adapted for processing and analysing of environmental monitoring data.

Adaptation involves the following changes in infrastructure and special approaches to Big Data processing:

1. The development of new monitoring methods and means, for example, the usage of intelligent autonomous robots for aquatic environment’s monitoring;
2. The organization of the ETL-process using diverse specialized data sources (not only open data sets), including data on the Black Sea water area monitoring, which is a specific feature of the Sevastopol’s region. It is planned to use satellite remote sensing, waters’ monitoring performed by shore stations and measurements made by forwarding ships etc.;
3. The development of new cloud-based data analysis services that implement the necessary data analysing methods for environmental monitoring; for example, modified clustering methods for analysing air pollution’s levels by various parameters;
4. Ensuring a high degree of availability of online data processing services for a quick response to the environmental situation.

The implementation of an adapted version of the Big Data processing will result in the following: the life cycle optimization of collecting, processing and storing of environmental data, namely: (1) an increase in the volume of analysed data; (2) reduction of data loss at the stage of data collection; (3) ETL-process effective organization; (4) reducing the number of errors in the data; (5) increasing the availability of data services and processing speed; (6) organization of reliable and secure data storage.

Prospects for further research are:

- analysis and detailed description of various data processing processes in environmental monitoring systems;
- development of a unified concept and methodology for collecting, processing, storing and analysing Big Data of Smart City environmental monitoring;
- development of recommendations for decision-making on the design and deployment of intellectual infrastructure for environmental monitoring.

Acknowledgment. The study was carried out with the financial support by the Russian Foundation for Basic Research and the city of Sevastopol in the framework of a research project № 18-47-920005/18.

References

1. The strategy of scientific and technological development of the Russian Federation. http://www.consultant.ru/document/cons_doc_LAW_207967/. (in Russian)
2. Economy of convergent solutions/IT. http://www.it.ru/press_center/publications/2787/. (in Russian)
3. Convergent infrastructure Cisco и NetApp. http://www.cisco.com/c/ru_ru/about/press/press-releases/2016/03-04b.html. (in Russian)
4. Dell EMC: What is a converged infrastructure? Dell EMC Solution. https://www.emc.com/ru-ru/converged-infrastructure/definitions.htm. (in Russian)
5. Indicators of smart cities NIITS 2017. http://niitc.ru/publications/SmartCities.pdf. (in Russian)
6. Knyazkov, K., Larchenko, A.: Domain-specific technologies for developing applications in distributed environments. Izv. vuzov. Priborostroyeniye. **54**(10), 29–36 (2011). (in Russian)
7. Bukhanovsky, A., Vasiliev, V., Vinogradov, V., Smirnov, D., Sukhorukov, S., Yapparov, T.: CLAVIRE: a promising second generation cloud computing technology, **54**(10), 7–14 (2011). (in Russian)
8. Kovalchuk, S., Maslov, V.: Intellectual support of the process of designing composite applications in distributed problem-oriented environments. Izv. vuzov. Priborostroyeniye. **54** (10), 29–36 (2011). (in Russian)
9. Bukhanovsky, A., Zhitnikov, A., Petrosyan, S., Slotos, P.: High-performance emergency computing technology to prevent the threat of flooding. Izv. vuzov. Priborostroyeniye. **54** (10), 14–20 (2011). (in Russian)
10. Cloud computing of the second generation: CLAVIRE System. https://habrahabr.ru/company/spbifmo/blog/319688. (in Russian)
11. Gorbunova, T.: Bioindication in the environmental monitoring system during the transition to the sustainable development of the agglomerate of the resort city of Sochi. Environ. Control Syst. **8**(28), 47–54 (2016). (in Russian)
12. Gaysky, V., Gaysky, P.: Measuring environment temperature at sea. Environ. Control Syst. **9** (29), 36–40 (2017). (in Russian)
13. Ramazin, A.N.: Calculation of the error in determining the practical salinity based on the STP measurements. Environ. Control Syst. **9**(29), 7–18 (2017). (in Russian)
14. Skatkov, A., Shevchenko, V., Mashchenko, E., Voronin, D., Klepikov, V.: Model of the organization of the monitoring system based on a distributed block-type storage system. In: The Collection: Simulation Modeling. Theory and Practice. The Eighth All-Russian Scientific-Practical Conference on Simulation Modeling and its Application in Science and Industry, St. Petersburg, pp. 527–531 (2017). (in Russian)
15. Skatkov, A., Voronin, D., Skatkov, I.: Simulation modeling of degradation failures of primary meters of the monitoring system. Environ. Control Syst. **9**(29), 50–58 (2017). (in Russian)
16. Biktimirov, M., Elizarov, A., Scherbakov, A.: Trends in the development of big data processing technologies and tools for storing multi-format data and analytics. Electron. Libr. **19**(5), 390–407 (2016). (in Russian)

17. Yemelchenkov, E., Avdeev, D., Koparenko, E.: Big data and functional data complexes. Comput. Math. Syst. Appl. **15**, 80–81 (2014). (in Russian)
18. Kachalov, D., Farhadov, M.: Research of technologies for collecting and processing big data in large-scale economic systems. Proc. Volgograd State-Impact Tech. Univ. **15**(210), 94–98 (2017). (in Russian)
19. Arkhipova, O., Surkov, F.: Representation of big data in decision support tasks for ensuring the sustainable development of the region. Math. Methods Pattern Recogn. **18**(1), 78–79 (2017). (in Russian)
20. Nikonov, V., Miklyaev, E.: Assessment of the need to use the methods of large data in city management systems. Sci. Look Future **1**(6), 68–72 (2017). (in Russian)
21. Kupriyanovskiy, V., Kupriyanovskiy, P., Namiot, D.: Standardization of smart cities, the internet of things and big data. Considerations for practical use in Russia. Int. J. Open Inf. Technol. **4**(2), 34–39 (2016). (in Russian)
22. Montori, F., Bedogni, L., Bononi, L.: A collaborative internet of things architecture for smart cities and environmental monitoring. IEEE Internet Things J. 1–14 (2017). https://doi.org/10.1109/jiot.2017.2720855
23. Khan, Z., Anjum, A., Soomro, K., Tahir, M.A.: Towards cloud based big data analytics for smart future cities. J. Cloud Comput. Adv. Syst. Appl. **4**, 2 (2015). https://doi.org/10.1186/s13677-015-0026-8
24. Silva, B.N., Khan, M., Han, K.: Big data analytics embedded smart city architecture for performance enhancement through real-time data processing and decision-making. Wirel. Commun. Mob. Comput. **2017**, 12, Article ID 9429676 (2017). https://doi.org/10.1155/2017/9429676
25. Federal Law of January 10, 2002, No. 7-FZ (as amended on 07/29/2018) On the Protection of the Environment. http://www.consultant.ru/document/cons_doc_LAW_34823/. (in Russian)
26. Khodyaev, A., Shevyrnogov, A., Kartushinsky, A.: Satellite data processing software for environmental monitoring of world ocean waters. Bull. Siberian State Aerosp. Univ. named after academician MF Reshetnev **3**(36), 127–131 (2011). (in Russian)
27. Uzhinsky, A., Ososkov, G., Frontasyeva, M.: Management of environmental monitoring data. Open Syst. DBMS **4**, 42–43 (2017). (in Russian)
28. NIST Special Publication 1500-1r1 NIST Big Data Interoperability Framework: Volume 1, Definitions. NIST Big Data Public Working Group Definitions and Taxonomies Subgroup Version 2, June 2018. https://doi.org/10.6028/NIST.SP.1500-1r1
29. NIST Special Publication 1500-6r1. NIST Big Data Interoperability Framework: Volume 6, Reference Architecture NIST Big Data. Public Working Group Reference Architecture Subgroup, Version 2, June 2018. https://doi.org/10.6028/NIST.SP.1500-6r1
30. Bruks, P.: Metrics for IT Service Management. Alpina Business Books, Moscow (2008). (In Russian)
31. Bon, Ya.V., Kemmerling, G., Pondaman, D.: IT Service Management, Introduction. IT Expert, Moscow (2003). (In Russian)

Comparing PPGIS and LBSN Data to Measure Emotional Perception of the City

Aleksandra Nenko(✉) and Marina Petrova(✉)

ITMO University, St. Petersburg, Russia
al.nenko@itmo.ru, petromari.78@gmail.com

Abstract. Analysis of emotions has received recognition in urban studies as a mean to understand subjective quality of life. Availability of spontaneous user-generated online urban data generated by users in location based social networks broadens possibilities for such analysis as described in a number of studies. However the LBSN data is not shared deliberately by users and is not meant to be an expression of emotions, which makes its representativeness and validity questionable. Another source of data - public participation geo-information systems - helps to overcome these limitations however may have its own, such as a small and biased sample. In this paper the results of the comparative analysis of the distribution of emotions in St. Petersburg, Russia, visualized with LBSN and PPGIS data, are presented. The dataset is formed from user-generated comments on urban venues from Google Places and data from PPGIS platform Imprecity (www.imprecity.ru), where citizens deliberately share their emotions and comments about public spaces. The data samples contain 1800 emotional marks from Imprecity and 2450 geolocated comments from Google Places marked by experts and then processed with Naïve Bayes Classifier. Comparison of positive and negative emotional maps created for Imprecity and Google Places shows shared tendencies in emotional distribution, such as concentration of emotions in the city centre and collocation of positive and negative emotions. There are also differences in emotional distribution: PPGIS data shows local "emotional" islands, which correspond to pedestrian areas and green spaces. The comparative analysis appears to be insightful and capable of revealing recurring spatial tendencies in subjective perception of the city.

Keywords: Emotion analysis · Emotional geography · LBSN · PPGIS · Google Places · Imprecity

1 Introduction

In urban studies emotions people feel in urban space have been long associated with the quality of urban life (see, e.g. [1]). Urban researchers and urban planners prove that built environment is capable of making us happy or sad; people react positively towards visibility of space, greenery, availability of urban furniture and shelter from wind and rain, availability of other people, services and public arts, and they react negatively towards empty streets, broken windows and ruined buildings, garbage and mud, heavy traffic, loneliness in space [2–4]. In this context, real-time monitoring of what people feel in space becomes dramatically important. Big data coming from

D. A. Alexandrov et al. (Eds.): DTGS 2019, CCIS 1038, pp. 223–234, 2019.
https://doi.org/10.1007/978-3-030-37858-5_18

location-based social networks or rating platforms and representing human spatial behaviour and preferences can become a resource for such a system of monitoring. Analysis of urban emotions can guide us in planning public spaces [4], measuring gentrification [5], development of urban services, creating new pieces of urban art.

In studies on urban emotions big data has been extensively applied. Location based social networks (LBSN) data gives numerous options for tracing spatial behavior by GPS and geotags, for evaluating attitudes by processing verbal (comments) and non-verbal (photos, emoji) data. In terms of emotional analysis majority of this recent work focuses on processing semantic data focuses on positive and negative sentiments in text, however some studies use the concept of the 6 basic emotions by [6] which is used further in this study. Recognition of emotions such as joy, sadness, fear, anger, and surprise in user-generated comments assists exploring human perception of various characteristics of the city space. Algorithms of machine learning in recognition of emotions in small texts have become widespread and include emotion detection through specific emotion denoting words [7], "seed" words and their co-occurring terms [8], hand-coded rules [9], emotional lexicons [10]. Public participation GIS platforms are also widely used in studies on urban emotions and present another source of data - volunteered geographical information which users voluntarily share about their feelings and preferences [11].

Below the comparative analysis based on the LBSN and PPGIS datasets of emotionally loaded data generated by users in St. Petersburg, Russia, is presented. The research questions in this paper are the following. What is the structure of positive and negative emotions distribution in St. Petersburg? Do different datasets of subjective evaluations - voluntarily shared by the citizens through the PPGIS platform as "emotions" and evaluations of the places shared by people through LBSN - differ or show similar tendencies in the distribution of emotions?

2 Online User-Generated Data in Analysis of Subjective Perception of the City

Data coming from LBSN like Twitter, Instagram, Google Places and TripAdvisor posits a valuable dataset for understanding subjective perception of the city space and its further outcomes for the people's behaviour. Numerous works of late show applicability of such data. Data from LBSNs, such as Google Places, represent the people-based approach as it offers an insight into individual preferences, use and activities [12]. In [12] Google Places is used as a source to diagnose urban regeneration process. In [13] authors analyze Twitter data collected for 6 months in 2008 and demonstrate how "national mood" is changing with national events such as celebrations and elections. Analogous study has been conducted to predict results of an election campaign [14]. Antonelli and Balduini have estimated emotional reaction towards urban mega-events - Olympic Games in London in 2012, Design Week in Milan 2013 based on Twitter data [15, 16]. Bertrand has applied sentiment analysis to geolocated posts in New York social media to assess sentiments in different parts of the city [17]. Tweets are also used to define human mobility patterns [18, 19] and actual land use [20]. Mitchell has tracked dependencies between tonalities of tweets and basic indicators of subjective well-being [21]. Schweitzer has illustrated how city decision makers can receive feedback from citizens from their tweets [22]. Hollander outlines the potential of social media data in urban management [23]. Habidatum finds correlation between volume of spontaneous data generated by people in a certain place and growth in real estate prices and neighborhood satisfaction [24], while Grandi and Neri describe how to develop a city brand grounding on sentiments expressed in social networks [25].

Studies mentioned above have conducted analysis of the data mostly using sentiment analysis, also known as opinion mining, often based on machine learning techniques. The widespread approach is to define the sentiment with the help of emotional lexicons, which are lists of words indicating a certain emotion in a text [26], e.g. WordNet Affect Lexicon [27] with a few hundred words or General Inquirer [28] with 11,788 words labeled with 182 categories of word tags, including positive and negative sentiments. Such lexicons sometimes contain other affect categories, such as pleasure, arousal, feelings, and pain, but these have not been explored to a significant degree by natural language processing [29]. The most frequent emotion recognition methods are those based on rules, statistics and neural networks, such as statistical classifiers (e.g. Naive Bayes Classifier) [30], classifiers based on distributive semantics - Word2Vec [31], GloVe [32], AdaGram [33], Text2Vec, Seq 2Vec, classifiers based on neural networks [34] and pattern matching [35, 36].

Though online data generated by users in LBSN carries traces of subjective perception it has specifics. It does not present direct reflexion on the emotional state of a person, and is not necessarily linked with the place where the feeling has occurred. Strictly speaking there is now evidence that the geography of these subjective evaluations can be called "emotional geography" of the city. In this study we are interested in comparing such data with other kind of it - volunteered geographic information (VGI) on emotions. Here the source of such data is public participation GIS platform *Imprecity*.

3 Public Participation GIS Platforms in Study of Subjective Perception of the City Space

Participatory planning and public participation in urban planning has been used by few architects and urban planners since the 1960s but has gained popularity in the 1990s [37–39]. Public participation is aimed at optimization of planning results, scaling up project value for local inhabitants, increasing trust towards city administration [40, 41]. Public participation aims to integrate and create dialogue between different stakeholders and accounts for different interests [42, 43]. Last decades public participation is often mediated by ICT, in particular, public participation geoinformation systems (PPGIS), planning support systems and tools for VGI.

PPGIS tools have become widespread in studying user experience and judgements about the city space [44, 45]. PPGIS combines online interactive maps with online questionnaires and thus is convenient for both sociological and spatial analysis [11]. PPGIS platforms, such as SoftGIS, Maptionnaire, Mapita and others are frequently used in online surveys to study residents' perception of the built environment [46]. The main advantage of PPGIS as a data collection method is in deliberate sharing of local spatially defined knowledge by respondents. PPGIS platforms provide researchers with information on socio-spatial structure of the city detailed for a personal level where user's judgements and her spatial behaviour are combined together.

PPGIS has been also used to analyze emotions in the city: to collect data on personal emotions and provide user with information on emotional places and emotional routes. In other words these are online services and apps designed to build emotional maps for residents, tourists, urban explorers, and consumers of services. One of the examples, Emotion Map is a multifunctional application which gives users an opportunity to record and monitor emotions in relation to their activities and locations. In the app users place marks at locations they visit, choose their emotional label and label of their activities in that places. Marks can be shared with friends or with all app users. While travelling through the city users can check the location for interesting emotional marks created by their friends, all app users or themselves. Users can chat with each other and also receive daily reports showing personal emotional statistics [47]. Bio-mapping project by artist Christopher Nold (also see his book Emotional Cartography), though not an app, is a catchy example of emotional maps creation with the help of volunteers wired up with GPS and polygraph technology who wander around a neighbourhood area, noting feelings and reactions to their surroundings [48]. Quercia et al. have created a crowd-sourcing platform to explore pedestrian routes which people prefer to take and proving that latter are not only the shortest ones, but also beautiful, silent and happy ones [5]. ICT platform developed by Nielek et al. especially for elderly people has a simple interface and is convenient for the target group to leave emotional remarks about the city [49].

At the end of 2017 Quality of Urban Life Laboratory at ITMO University has launched Imprecity - a web-based online interactive map where citizens can share their emotions on public spaces (accessible at www.imprecity.ru) [50]. Imprecity is based on the theory of basic emotions by Paul Ekman [6]. Registered users can leave emoji of joy, anger, sadness, disgust, fear and surprise on the city map and write explanatory comments to them. Users may register with social networks Vkontakte, facebook, or Google+. Registered users can also share their private emotional map in social networks. Both registered and non-registered users can explore emotions in the city which are presented as heatmaps. Imprecity has been piloted as PPGIS in Saint-Petersburg, Russia, in frames of "Smart Saint-Petersburg" program supported by the city government, however, can be used worldwide for public campaigns and research. Imprecity has already almost 2000 entries from more than 600 unique users, the main contributors to the PPGIS platform are young active citizens interested in urbanism while Imprecity was promoted through the students and collaborators of the Institute for Design and Urban Studies at ITMO University.

Power of PPGIS in studying urban emotions is obvious: the data is voluntarily shared by the users, which helps to avoid ethical issues (arising when using data from LBSN), has precise user defined geolocation, contains user-generated semantics which signifies specific emotions and is domain specific. However there is a major drawback: PPGIS data is times less than big data derivable from LBSN: usually users interest much less in sharing their thoughts in a survey than using LBSNs. Imprecity provides a small sample which is representing only one group of citizens. Consideration of a more numerous dataset reflecting the opinions of more citizens is important. Taking into account the advantages and disadvantages of LBSN and PPGIS data we are proposing to study them in comparison.

4 Dataset and Method

The methodology of this study lies in comparison of the two datasets of geolocated emotional marks towards the city space - one received through PPGIS Imprecity and another received from LBSN Google Places for the city of Saint-Petersburg. Comparative spatial analysis is showing similarities and discrepancies in the distribution of emotions visualized with the two datasets.

Imprecity sample contains 1843 emoji from 620 unique users collected for 932 places of St. Petersburg for 2017–2019. The dataset includes user ID, date when the mark was created, geographical coordinates of the mark, the class of emotion given, the text if the commentary is given. The emotional maps are illustrated for each of the 6 emotions in the form of heatmaps at user interface (Fig. 1).

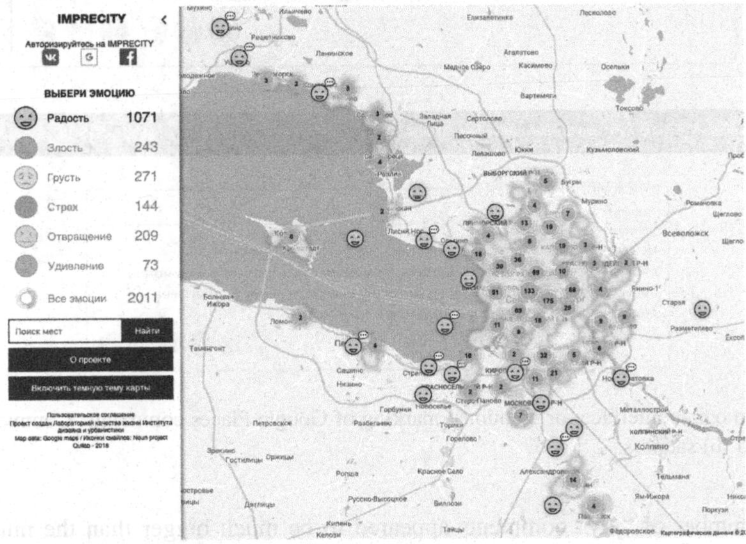

Fig. 1. Interface of *Imprecity* PPGSI in web version. The heatmap of joy in Saint-Petersburg, Russia

Google Places is a service for rating urban venues where users have the possibility to share their feedback on the level of the service in the form of comments and points, as well as photos. Each place has a profile with venue description, photos and users' ratings. The platform is used as an online marketing service as well as a peer-to-peer recommendation site.

The data for this study was collected with open Google Places API. There is a restriction for collecting data - only 5 latest comments per place can be downloaded.

The total dataset for Saint-Petersburg contains 5145 geolocated comments for 1191 unique places for the year of 2018. The dataset contains name of a venue, date when the comment was created, number of points received from a user on a 5-point scale, text of the comment, user ID.

To compare Google Places data with Imprecity data 2450 comments were marked by two experts for 6 emotions, the same ones as in Imprecity, through an online user-friendly interface (see Fig. 2).

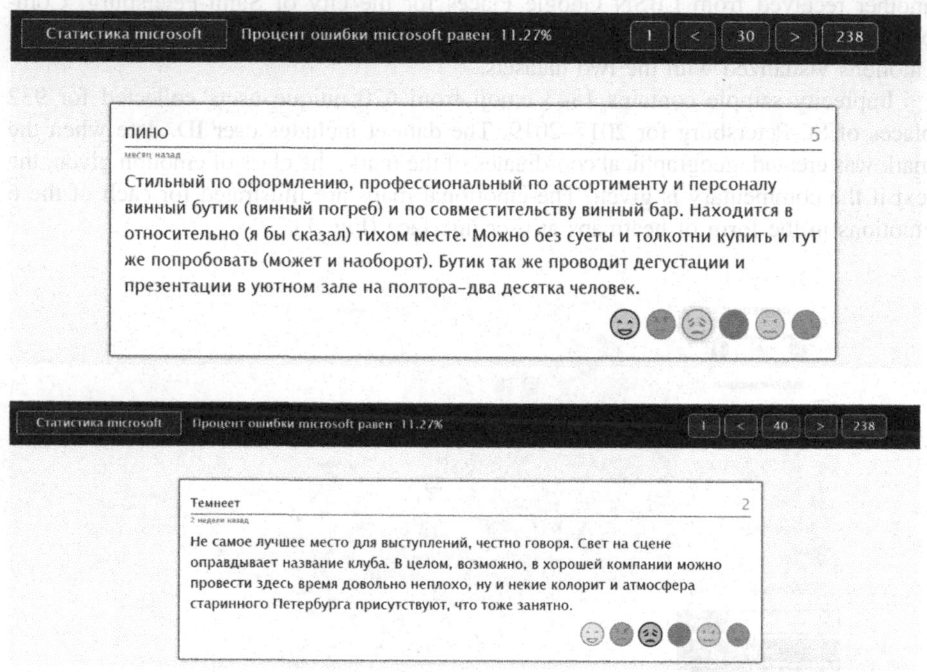

Fig. 2. An online interface for emotional marking of Google Places comments. Comments with (a) joy and (b) sadness.

The number of "joy" comments appeared to be much bigger than the number of other emotions, for this reason the sample of joy has been reduced more than twice. Then the sample was cleaned from the words other than adjectives and adverbs which are better emotional signifiers. As a machine learning technique Naïve Bayes Classifier was chosen. Naïve Bayes Classifier has low calculation complexity and optimal efficiency given the actual independence of variables. The classifier was trained on the training sample marked by experts and then used for the validation sample (see statistics in Table 1).

The results of the classification were validated with Confusion Matrix tool - a matrix of N × N size, where N is the number of emotions. The columns signify expert decisions, the rows are decisions made by the trained classifier (Fig. 3).

Table 1. Statistics of the validation dataset

Emotions classification	The number of comments in each sample	The number of words	The unique words
1 - Joy	268	1895	549
2 - Anger	172	1698	578
3 - Sadness	244	1914	625
4 - Fear	50	152	97
5 - Disgust	96	434	240
6 - Surprise	19	82	69
Total	849	6175	1269

		0,60	0,38	0,45	0,26	0,29	0,00
		1	2	3	4	5	6
0,71	1	193	20	45	1	7	4
0,45	2	32	71	32	10	11	3
0,34	3	61	60	77	7	20	0
0,24	4	16	9	2	10	4	0
0,21	5	16	24	16	10	18	0
0,00	6	2	4	1	0	2	0

Fig. 3. Confusion matrix for Naive Bayes Algorithm

The results of the validation show that percentage for classes 2–6 (all emotions except joy) is lower than 50% which is below the reliability threshold; for the emotion of surprise it is even 0 what can be explained by a small number of comments for this emotion in the dataset. However Naïve Bayes Classifier has shown over 70% accuracy for two classes of emotions - positive (joy) and negative (anger, sadness, fear, disgust, surprise) ones. For this reason it was decided to compare marked Google Places dataset and Imprecity dataset for the 2 classes of emotions until a way to increase the reliability of the classifier will be found. While the aim of this paper is to compare the two datasets this limitation is not considered crucial and comparison for 6 classes of emotions is planned for further studies.

5 Results

Comparative analysis of Imprecity and Google Places data allows to track the tendencies of geography of emotions in the city space and differences provoked by different nature of data. The positive and negative emotional geographies of Saint-Petersburg based on the two data sources are presented below in the form of heatmaps (Fig. 4).

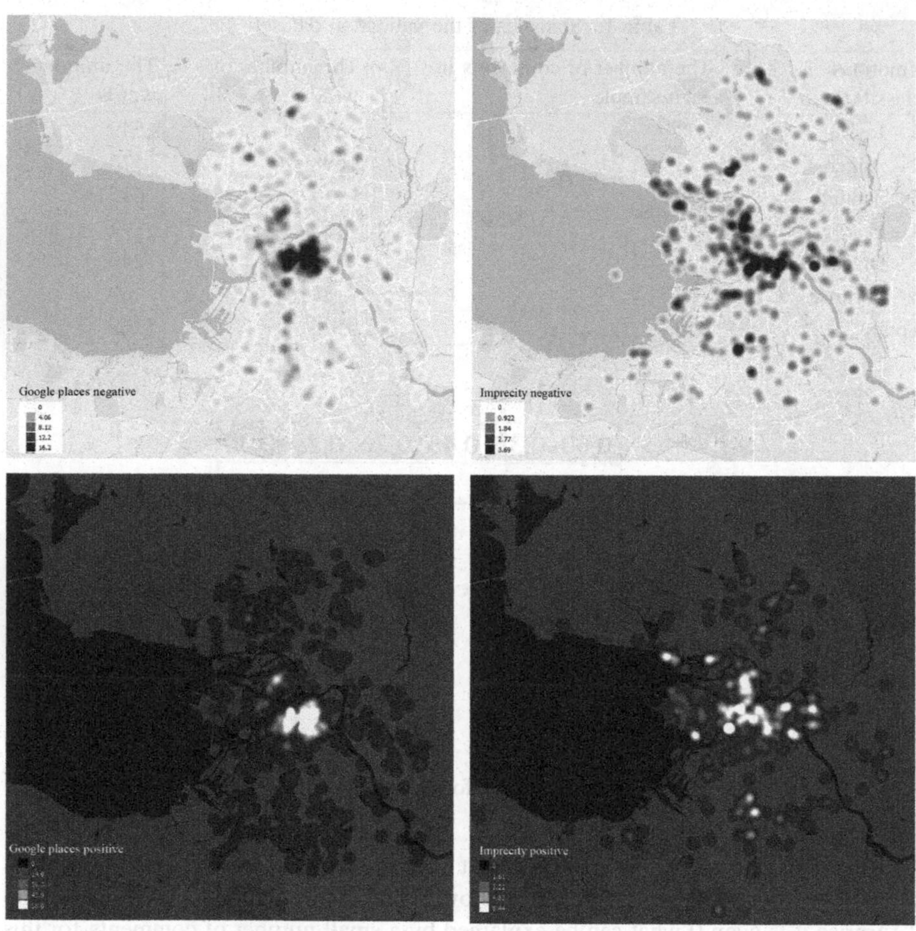

Fig. 4. Heatmaps of positive and negative emotions based on data from Imprecity and Google Places

Negative and positive emotional heatmaps for Google places sample have higher level of concentration than positive and negative heatmaps for Imprecity due to different volume of data. Moreover Google places positive and negative heatmaps are far more concentrated at the city centre while Imprecity ones are more distributed towards the city periphery. This can be explained by the nature of data: cafes, bars, shops and other urban venues which are commented on in Google Places tend to locate in the city centre, while in Imprecity people predominantly comment on public spaces close to the sites of their dwelling or regular usage. A shared trend for the both samples is the concentration of negative and positive emotions in the historic city centre at the South of the city, at the central part of the Petrogradskiy island and the western extremity of the semi-central Vasilyevskiy island. This signifies an inequality in subjective vision of urban environment - the centre takes all the positive feelings, while the periphery calls less emotions. As for the differences, the Imprecity negative heatmap has a bigger coverage than the Google Places one: it covers more spaces where people actually live, work, walk by while negative in Google Places concentrates only on the venues. Vice versa, the positive map of Google Places has a bigger coverage than the Imprecity map, however its area with highest concentration of positive emotions is lesser. Imprecity positive heatmap contains local islands of joy non-existent at the Google Places map, e.g., a cloud of joy along Moskovskiy avenue going down in southern direction, a western part of the central heat cloud at the shoreline of the Okhta river, and several heat points at the North corresponding the favourite city parks - these are areas with pedestrian routes, popular public spaces and green zones. The clouds of highest emotional concentration in Google Places positive and negative heat maps are almost identical in location and size. This signifies that the venues which people judge to be good or bad are collocated in the central areas with good accessibility. Such concentration demonstrates an unequal distribution of the venues in the city: the most visited places pile up in two areas - historical centre and sub-centre at Petrogradskiy island, while places in remote areas stay out of sight.

In the end, the comparative analysis of PPGIS platform data, such as Imprecity, and data from LBSN, such as Google Places, shows itself to be relevant and insightful for understanding the tendencies of geography of positive and negative emotions in the city space. There are recurring tendencies revealed in the data from both sources: (a) the positive and negative emotions are concentrated in the city centre and (b) are collocated. Besides the nature of data provides us with explanation of deviances from this law, for example, the PPGIS data shows us local "emotional" islands, which correspond to pedestrian areas and green spaces. Comparative analysis of the two data from two sources gives us an opportunity to receive a more accurate and valid picture on the geography of emotions in the city.

6 Discussion

The results of this study show the perspectives of comparative approach to analyse subjective perception of the city based on PPGIS and LBSN data which are both adding to each other. The Imprecity data is more accurate in view of open public spaces, while Google Places shows better picture on the venues - bars, restaurants, cafes, museums and other "closed" public spaces. The mixture of the data sources is providing a complex picture on subjective perception of the city including all its items important for the citizens. In future the LBSN dataset can be expanded through other sources such as Tripadviser and Foursquare, which will give more details on city sights and open public spaces.

In future the emotional vocabularies for machine learning algorithm can be based not only on the manual marking by the experts but also on Imprecity PPGIS semantic data which makes up vocabularies for 6 types of emotions shared by a wide number of users as lay experts. A machine learning algorithm based on a bigger training sample with 6 emotions vocabularies could be show more accuracy than the results received in this study.

During marking of Google Places data by experts it has been defined that a single comment shows itself badly as a basic unit for markup, while it can contain more than one emotion. A sentence should be considered as a basic unit, which will be used in future work.

The Naïve Bayes Classifier has shown its relevance for 2 classes of emotions - positive and negative, however for 6 emotions it is not valid. This might depend on the marking procedure, as well as the algorithm itself. In future other algorithms will be applied to compare the accuracy and choose the most precise one. In particular, we are going to use Bag of Words method. This method is a frequently used model for machine learning based on big number of unstructured words from texts (comments). The method shows fine results in classifying user comments, however is slow when the number of data is big. In further study only St. Petersburg city will be considered which limits the volume of data, and a proper cleaning of data will be carried out.

Imprecity and Google Places data provide not only geolocated emotional marks but also semantic data. The analysis of the semantics could be added into further consideration of the city emotions, for example, through aspect based semantic modelling which allows to link emotionally loaded descriptions and certain aspects of evaluated places.

References

1. Ellard, C.: Places of the Heart, The Psychogeography of Everyday Life. Bellevue Literary Press, New York (2015)
2. Gehl, J.: Cities for People. Island Press, Washington, Covelo, London (2010)
3. Whyte, W.: Social Life of Small Urban Spaces. Conservation Foundation, New York (1980)
4. Madden, K.: How to Turn a Place Around: A Handbook for Creating Successful Public Spaces. Project for Public Spaces, New York (2000)
5. Quercia, D., Schifanella, R., Aiello, L.: The shortest path to happiness: recommending beautiful, quiet, and happy routes in the city. In: Proceedings of the 25th ACM Conference on Hypertext and Social Media (HT 2014), pp. 116–125. ACM, New York (2014)
6. Ekman, P.: An argument for basic emotions. Cogn. Emot. **6**(3), 169–200 (1992)
7. Elliott, C.: The affective reasoner: a process model of emotions in a multi-agent system. Ph. D. thesis, Institute for the Learning Sciences, Northwestern University, USA (1992)
8. Read, J.: Recognising affect in text using pointwise-mutual information. Ph.D. thesis, Department of Informatics, University of Sussex, England (2004)
9. Neviarouskaya, A., Prendinger, H., Ishizuka, M.: Compositionality principle in recognition of fine-grained emotions from text. In: Proceedings of the Proceedings of the Third International Conference on Weblogs and Social Media (ICWSM 2009), pp. 278–281. AAAI Press, Menlo Park (2009)
10. Alm, C., Roth, D., Sproat, S.: Emotions from text: machine learning for text-based emotion prediction. In: Proceedings of the Joint Conference on Human Language Technology. Empirical Methods in Natural Language Processing, Vancouver, Canada, pp. 579–586 (2005)
11. Brown, G., Kyttä, M.: Key issues and research priorities for public participation GIS (PPGIS): a synthesis based on empirical research. Appl. Geogr. **46**, 126–136 (2014)
12. Martí, P., García-Mayor, C., Serrano-Estrada, L.: Identifying opportunity places for urban regeneration through LBSNs. Cities **90**, 191–206 (2019)

13. Bollen, J., Mao, H., Pepe, A.: Modeling public mood and emotion: twitter sentiment and socio-economic phenomena. In: Proceedings of the Fifth International AAAI Conference on Weblogs and Social Media, ICWSM 2011, Spain, pp. 450–453 (2011)
14. Gordon, J.: Comparative geospatial analysis of Twitter sentiment data during the 2008 and 2012 US Presidential elections. University of Oregon, USA (2013)
15. Antonelli, F.: City sensing: visualising mobile and social data about a city scale event. In: International Working Conference on Advanced Visual Interfaces, AVI 2014, Como, Italy, pp. 337–338. ACM (2014)
16. Balduini, M., Della Valle, E., Dell'Aglio, D., Tsytsarau, M., Palpanas, T., Confalonieri, C.: Social listening of city scale events using the streaming linked data framework. In: Alani, H., et al. (eds.) ISWC 2013. LNCS, vol. 8219, pp. 1–16. Springer, Heidelberg (2013). https://doi.org/10.1007/978-3-642-41338-4_1
17. Bertrand, K.: Sentiment in New York city: a high resolution spatial and temporal view, USA (2013). arXiv preprint arXiv:1308.5010
18. Cho, E., Myers, S., Leskovec, J.: Friendship and mobility: user movement in location-based social networks. In: Proceedings of the 17th ACM SIGKDD International Conference on Knowledge Discovery and Data Mining, San Diego, CA, USA, pp. 1082–1090. ACM (2011)
19. Fujisaka, T., Lee, R., Sumiya, K.: Exploring urban characteristics using movement history of mass mobile micro bloggers, pp. 13–18. ACM, New York (2010)
20. Frias-Martinez, V.: Sensing urban land use with twitter activity. Telefonica Research, Madrid, Spain (2013)
21. Mitchell, L.: The geography of happiness: connecting twitter sentiment and expression, demographics, and objective characteristics of place. PloS One **5**(8), 64–71 (2013)
22. Schweitzer, L.: Planning and social media: a case study of public transit and stigma on Twitter. J. Am. Plan. Assoc. **3**(80), 218–238 (2014)
23. Hollander, J.: The new generation of public participation: internet-based participation tools. AU - Evans-Cowley Jennifer Plan. Pract. Res. **3**(25), 397–408 (2010)
24. Value of Satisfaction. Habidatum report (2019). https://projects.habidatum.com/#value-of-satisfaction/. Accessed 19 Feb 2019
25. Grandi, R., Neri, F.: Sentiment analysis and city branding. In: Catania, B., et al. (eds.) New Trends in Databases and Information Systems. AISC, vol. 241, pp. 339–349. Springer, Cham (2014). https://doi.org/10.1007/978-3-319-01863-8_36
26. Mohammad, S., Turney, P.: Emotions evoked by common words and phrases: using mechanical turk to create an emotion lexicon. In: Proceedings of the NAACL HLT 2010 Workshop on Computational Approaches to Analysis and Generation of Emotion in Text, California, USA, pp. 26–34 (2010)
27. Strapparava, C., Valitutti, A.: WordNet-Affect: an affective extension of WordNet. Part of the Lecture Notes in Computer Science, Italy. LNCS, vol. 3784, pp. 1083–1086 (2004)
28. Stone, P., Dunphy, D., Smith, M., Ogilvie, D.: The General Inquirer: A Computer Approach to Content Analysis. The MIT Press, Cambridge (1966)
29. WordNet-Affect. http://wndomains.fbk.eu/wnaffect.html. Accessed 19 Feb 2019
30. Kotelnikov, E., Klekovkina, M.: Avtomaticheskiy analiz tonal'nosti tekstov na osnove metodov mashinnogo obucheniya [Sentiment analysis of texts based on machine learning methods]. In: Proceedings of the Conference Dialog, Vyp. 11 (18), pp. 7–10. (2012). (In Russian) = Е.В. Котельников, М.В. Клековкина. Автоматический анализ тональности текстов на основе методов машинного обучения. Компьютерная лингвистика и интеллектуальные технологии: По материалам ежегодной Международной конференции « Диалог » . Вып. 11 (18). М.: Изд-во РГГУ, с. 7–10. Москва, Россия (2012)

31. Goldberg, Y., Levy, O.: Word2vec explained: deriving Mikolov et al.'s negative-sampling word-embedding method. Cornell University, Iceland (2014). arXiv preprint arXiv:1402.3722
32. Pennington, J., Socher, R., Manning, C.: Glove: global vectors for word representation. In: Proceedings of the 2014 Conference on Empirical Methods in Natural Language Processing (EMNLP), Doha, Qatar, pp. 1532–1543 (2014)
33. Bartunov, S.: Breaking sticks and ambiguities with adaptive skip-gram. In: Artificial Intelligence and Statistics, Proceedings of the 19th International Conference on Artificial Intelligence and Statistics, PMLR, Spain, vol. 51, pp.130–138 (2016)
34. Poria, S.: Convolutional MKL based multimodal emotion recognition and sentiment analysis. In: 2016 IEEE 16th International Conference on Data Mining (ICDM), Italy, pp. 439–448. IEEE (2016)
35. Chakrabarti, S.: Scalable feature selection, classification and signature generation for organizing large text databases into hierarchical topic taxonomies. VLDB J. **7**(3), 163–178 (1998)
36. Lewis, D.: Method and apparatus for training a text classifier: Patent No. 5,675,710, 7 October 1997
37. Allmendinger, P.: Planning Theory, p. 239. Red Globe Press/Palgrave, New York (2002)
38. Friedmann, J.: Empowerment: The Politics of Alternative Development, p. 196. Blackwell, Cambridge (1992)
39. Healey, P.: Planning through debate: the communicative turn in planning theory. Town Plan. Rev. **2**(63), 143 (1992)
40. Laurian, L.: Public participation in environmental decision making: findings from communities facing toxic waste cleanup. J. Am. Plan. Assoc. **1**(70), 53–65 (2004)
41. Beierle, T., Thomas, C.: Democracy in Practice: Public Participation in Environmental Decisions. Routledge, Abingdon (2002)
42. Forrester, J.: The logistics of public participation in environmental assessment. Int. J. Environ. Pollut. **3**(11), 316 (1999)
43. Kingston, R.: Public participation in local policy decision-making: the role of web-based mapping. Cartographic J. **2**(44), 138–144 (2007)
44. Brown, G.: Public participation GIS (PPGIS) for regional and environmental planning: reflections on a decade of empirical research. J. Urban Reg. Inf. Syst. Assoc. **2**(25), 12 (2012)
45. Brown, G.: Engaging the wisdom of crowds and public judgement for land use planning using public participation geographic information systems. Aust. Planner **3**(52), 199–209 (2015)
46. Hasanzadeh, K., Laatikainen, T., Kyttä, M.: Place-based model of local activity spaces: individual place exposure and characteristics. J. Geograph. Syst. **20**, 227–252 (2018)
47. Emotion Map. https://apkpocket.pw/emotion-map/edu.syr.ischool.orange.emotionmap.apk. Accessed 10 Feb 2019
48. Nold, C.: Bio mapping: how can we use emotion to articulate cities? Livingmaps Rev. (5) (2018)
49. Nielek, R., Ciastek, M., Kopeć, W.: Emotions make cities live. Towards mapping emotions of older adults on urban space, Germany (2017)
50. Nenko, A., Petrova, M.: Emotional geography of St. Petersburg: detecting emotional perception of the city space. In: Alexandrov, D.A., Boukhanovsky, A.V., Chugunov, A.V., Kabanov, Y., Koltsova, O. (eds.) DTGS 2018. CCIS, vol. 859, pp. 95–110. Springer, Cham (2018). https://doi.org/10.1007/978-3-030-02846-6_8

Study on Interoperability of Urban Information Systems: The Case of Smart St. Petersburg

Artem V. Shiyan, Sergey A. Mityagin(✉), and Sergey I. Drozhzhin

ITMO University, Kronverkskiy pr. 49, Saint-Petersburg 197101, Russia
{avshiyan,mityagin,sergey.drojjin}@corp.ifmo.ru

Abstract. The paper discusses about interoperability mechanisms in the scale of urban IT infrastructure. It represented by a variety of interacting information systems and requirements for complex structural layers that construct urban networks. Government information systems, according to the existing legislation, automate only a certain list of priority functional services, which leads to insufficient flexibility of data exchange framework. They create a unified information space with key tools of interdepartmental interaction processes. Historical incompatibility and heterogeneity of the urban infrastructure elements prevent smart city technologies introduction, that also generating typical problems for interacting systems with each other. The long-term solution to this problem can be provided by changing requirements for technologies and interaction rules: restructuring existing government information systems, reorganizing the interaction of enabled systems, changing the architecture principles of urban infrastructure. And it's also include the advanced multi-stage study about different infrastructure levels. Based on these systems interoperability research, recommendations for the development of urban information framework are given.

Keywords: Information infrastructure · Interoperability · Information system · Smart city · System analysis

1 Introduction

Smart city involves the «smart implementation» and use complex innovative technologies in urban infrastructure. This policy planning aimed for improve quality of life and increase the processes efficiency in governmental services. Such technologies are generally defined as smart city technologies implying a significant increase of the role of information in urban processes. For the active introduction and use of smart city technologies, it is necessary to have a developed information infrastructure that meets the requirements of these technologies and the needs of the city.

Today there is no single definition about the concept of urban information infrastructure. In the ITIL (IT Infrastructure Library) standard, an IT infrastructure is generally considered as a set of hardware, software, networks, tools, and including all

D. A. Alexandrov et al. (Eds.): DTGS 2019, CCIS 1038, pp. 235–247, 2019.
https://doi.org/10.1007/978-3-030-37858-5_19

information technologies for developing, testing, monitoring and supporting an IT service [1].

Scientific publications also give different definitions to this notion. In, the information and communication infrastructure is the aggregate of territorially distributed state and corporate information systems, data networks and channels, the means of switching and managing information flows, communication lines, and organizational structures, legal and regulatory mechanisms that ensure efficient systems functioning [2].

This article considers the IT infrastructure of the city as an interrelated set of urban state information systems that provide information support for urban resource management processes. Information systems as components of the information infrastructure are an interrelated set of software and technical and mathematical maintenance, users, legal and regulatory documents.

Considering IT infrastructure as a complex system, it is important to know how much functionality, integrity (structure), organization, system quality corresponds to the current goals of the city, the tasks of urban development, the needs of the city to create and implement smart city technologies [3].

Main directions of the development of the information infrastructure in the context of the smart city are:

1. providing guaranteed for business and citizens access to high-speed Internet and the development of innovative ways to provide it;
2. development of mobile services;
3. development of digital opportunities for feedback systems with citizens and systems for discussion and support of initiatives;
4. development of «digital citizenship» (empowerment of citizens in the digital environment);
5. introduction of analytical tools in the procurement processes in the city, intelligent urban management systems to save resources;
6. development of a single data warehouse and their centralization from various public and private sources of information, ensuring the integration of diverse city data; unification of disparate information resources, providing high speed information exchange between systems;
7. using of a common data standard and the open-data platform development;
8. development of blockchain technology, and paperless electronic workflow;
9. development of low-power networks for the widespread using of Internet of things;
10. ensuring cybersecurity.

2 Challenges of Urban Information Technologies

The problems of modern IT in the city, as well as the options for their solution, are widely covered in world publications. The group of socio-economic issues in the introduction of «smart» information technologies in cities includes issues of accessibility of the Internet technologies, as well as digital inequality. It should be noted that the digital divide and digital inequality are associated with the spread of the Internet and digital technologies in general. In Western countries, the level of development reaches 80%–90%. The authors also noted that it is necessary to improve the technology to eliminate age limitations, since even in developed countries such as Switzerland, only about a quarter of the elderly are permanent users of information technology [4].

Information and communication technologies and the Internet of things are regarded as key factors for urban development. The disparity and heterogeneity of information resources, the increasing number of services, the integration and quality of data, the duplication of information, and the problem of systems interoperability can be attributed to the group of technical issues of IT implementation in the city, which are also widely covered in publications.

As noted in the survey, the heterogeneity of the ICT environment is a fundamental feature of the development of ICT. The importance of the problem of heterogeneity is confirmed in article. It is noted that this problem should be resolved as soon as possible while introducing digital technologies in smart cities. In, the intensive development of digital technologies leads to the creation of a heterogeneous environment, a significant increase in the heterogeneity of data, which is associated with information quality problems.

The quality of information is almost always far from ideal: there is inaccuracy, uncertainty, ambiguity; input of primary data is repeatedly duplicated. Therefore, they do not always correspond to the main quality indicators [5].

The creation and development of smart city technologies presupposes intensive information exchange between systems in real time. This is necessary to ensure maximum compatibility of all urban systems. Nevertheless, in many cities the exchange of information is not regulated, and unified requirements for inter-agency information exchange between systems are not applied.

The experience of creating an «electronic government» as one of the stages of the smart city in different countries shows that different level information systems are often created based on local specific administrative or functional needs. In this case, not enough attention is paid to the possibility of their subsequent use with other information systems [6].

The systems created at the city level in each case have different goals, tasks and purposes, as well as a different set of technologies and design decisions. They are often placed on various technological platforms having their own individual databases, classifiers, etc. This makes both the integration of several systems into a unified information space of the city and the introduction of new technologies a complex task. Sometimes it can be practically impossible without significant and costly modernization of city systems.

As a result, the information infrastructure becomes a set of systems that are not coordinated with each other in terms of their interaction and, hence, they are not used effectively.

In this case, the development and application of «single software platforms» is not a solution, but only a transfer of the problem to another level. Such a «decision» does not always allow to consider the functional needs of city authorities. It causes monopoly dependence on the single software platform supplier [7].

Another important problem that is solved by both individual research organizations and large international organizations such as ISO, IEC, ITU is the problem of system interoperability. Interoperability is the ability of several systems to exchange information. Obviously, for successful implementation of smart city technologies it is important to assess the interoperability of existing information systems of the city [8].

Initially, interoperability was considered exclusively at the technical level, but subsequently in the context of the development of urban IT they began to distinguish: political, legal, organizational, semantic and technical levels of interoperability. The risk of «logical conflicts» between state information systems is minimized while working with urban data, resulting in the formation of a unified information space. Therefore, a variety of methods for assessing the interoperability of information systems are the most convenient and flexible tools for identifying such conflicts.

The main symptoms of interoperability lack are:

- increased costs for the development and modernization of information systems;
- increasing the time for the providing services or information exchange between systems;
- increasing the number of operations and data conversions that are manually or with the participation of system users.

2.1 Evaluation Models for Systems Interoperability

For systems of different classes in USA/EU, systematic work has been carried out for a long time to ensure and measure interoperability for government needs. Interoperability is the basis for effective integration and is therefore important to quantify [9].

The first method of quantifying interoperability based on a fuzzy model taking into account the weights of influencing factors. It is assumed that interoperability in a distributed system or system of systems is determined by the potential ability of each component to exchange information. Use as a basis the interoperability model, allows quickly build a hierarchy of indicators with weights and evaluate parameters [10].

Method of technical interoperability calculation based on the laws of information theory. This is a formal model that allows to calculate the partial and General information entropy (measure of uncertainty), which characterizes the technical interoperability as the ability of the information system to detect data in different formats and the ability of the information system to produce correct data transformations in different formats [11].

The model quantifying of compatibility «i-score» is a six-step process. Structure key elements in this example are the interoperability matrix and multigraph. A balanced approach is to identify the number of binders in each system to form a continuously circulating data flow. This evaluates This evaluates opportunities about seamless system integration into high-performance clusters and the speed of sending request through numerous systems [12].

2.2 Determination of the Optimal Variant to Urban Systems Interoperability Assessment

After using various examples of practical results, a more relevant way of assessing interoperability was chosen. In the scientific literature it is found as a method of comparative evaluation to information systems interoperability.

The core of the technique is the methods of interval and expert weighted evaluation. The main advantage of this technique is its applicability to the evaluation of systems of different types and classes, as well as various functional purposes, as well as the ability to add and adjust a set of criteria [13].

Despite the complex calculations scalability for standards in urban information infrastructure, this approach allows a more detailed study of system relationships through the ratio of the described properties.

3 St. Petersburg IT Infrastructure Today

Nowadays, the urban interaction network is divided into four levels. The main elements are urban information systems. On the next level systems with federal status (integration in the state information space). Equally important are regional information systems, which are often complementary to urban information systems. And as the last elements of shape are a public systems (portals and data) [14].

Thus, in total, the city has an operational and strategic infrastructure complex of more than 200 daily functioning urban systems (Figs. 1, 5 and 6).

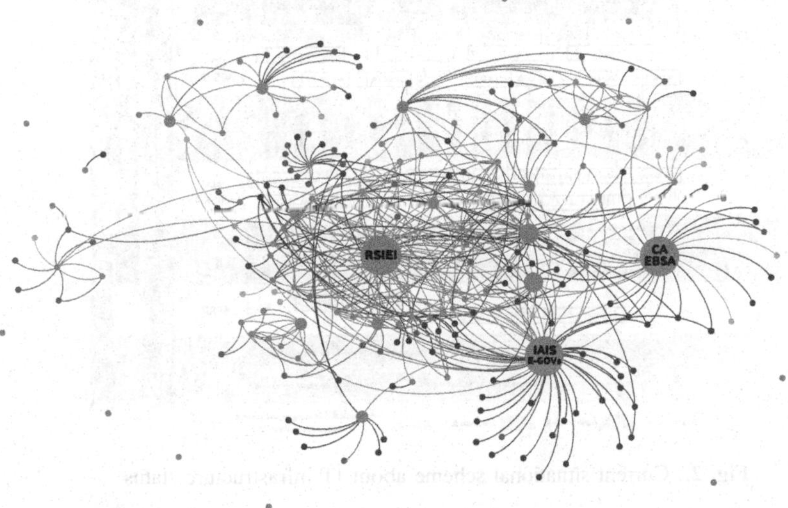

Fig. 1. Links visualization between information systems in St. Petersburg

The framework of St. Petersburg IT infrastructure consists by three key systems: RSIEI (Regional system of interdepartmental electronic interaction), IAIS E-GOVs (Interdepartmental automated information system of e-government services) and CA EBSA (Certification authority for executive bodies of state authority). That's are critical structural nodes and they aggregate majority of all network communication links. Accordingly, a significant workload of all operational urban data is circulated through these key nodes (Table 1).

Table 1. Distribution of systems by status in the urban information space

Type	Detailed data	
	Total number	Examples of the listed systems
Key node	3	RSIEI, IAIS E-GOVs, CA EBSA
System-forming node	2	TSRIS and CAIS CER
Large node	10	HSC SfC, UIRS, DU MD MIA
Standard node	201	primary network elements

3.1 The Structure of Urban Interacting Elements

Within the logic of integration processes, a structural and functional smart city model is proposed. Such a platform is an interconnected set of functional elements of the digital economy infrastructure of the city, consisting of four layers (Figs. 2 and 5).

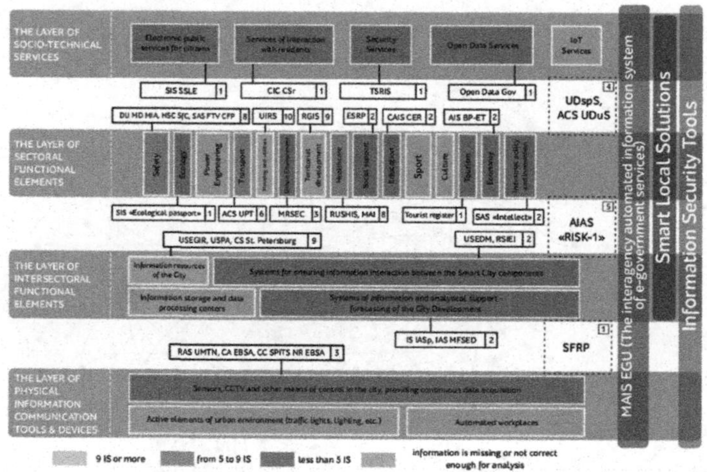

Fig. 2. Current situational scheme about IT infrastructure status

The development of elements in basic layers (physical means of information interaction and inter-sectoral functional elements) is a necessary condition for the creation of the framework of the highest-level infrastructures. This kind of distribution of the smart city architecture into layers allows to prevent the emergence of unnecessary intermediaries of interaction and to streamline the phased implementation of modules to preserve the principles of the ecosystem [15].

Layer of physical information communication tools and devices:

- hardware and software systems accompanying distributed urban processes;
- seamless integration of digital technologies into the urban environment;
- monitoring of automation objects.

Layer of intersectoral functional elements:

- ensuring smooth interaction at the applied level of all subjects of urban information space;
- aggregation of different data sources into a single urban repository;
- organization of the required level of infrastructure performance for guaranteed access to urban data.

Layer of sectoral functional elements:

- transparent coordination of urban development within the framework of the activities of the Executive authorities;
- optimization of e-government information resources;
- component implementation of modules for day-to-day management tasks.

Layer of socio-technical functional elements:

- mobility of public and municipal services;
- formation of conditions for the expansion of services in the digital profile of citizens;
- infrastructure entry points to the unified information space of the city.

3.2 Interoperability Research and Comparison of 3 Key Systems in St. Petersburg IT Infrastructure

One of the features of IT infrastructure in the cities of Russia is the prevalence of large state sectoral information systems. There are also large interdepartmental systems that automate the processes of providing services, as well as other automation systems for typical processes [17].

The main stages of the study according to the methodology include:

1. Identification of systems properties and their detailing;
2. Selection of interval values for each detailed property using fuzzy logic methods;
3. Assignment of a rank to each detailed property, for example, a direct relationship between the level of interoperability of the system and the speed of information processing.
4. Calculation of average ranks of a system.
5. Calculation of the cumulative weighted rank of the system. Experts assign weight to each property.

6. Assignment of the system to an appropriate degree of interoperability based on its cumulative weighted rank. The higher the rank, the more interoperable the system is.

Such method will optimize the management of urban IT development. Transparently defining the requirements for technical and information support systems. Moreover, common criteria for assessing interaction and adaptable to modular IT infrastructure will allow to restructure the interoperability mechanisms in a unified information space.

Despite the simplicity of the method, it can be incorporated into a more complex structured methodology (Figs. 3, 5 and 6).

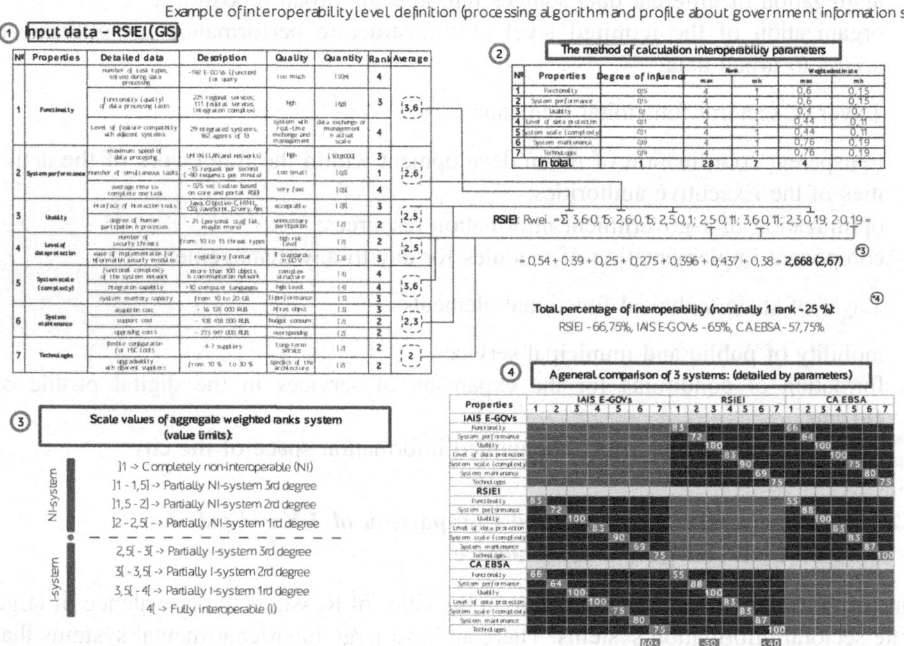

Fig. 3. Detailed report about interoperability analysis and calculation algorithm

According to the results of the study, the following conclusions can be drawn:

- the functionality and performance of the systems is ensured by a uniform technical infrastructure for all systems;
- the development uses a standard list of technologies (programming languages, DBMS, OS);
- high level of human participation in the functioning of systems;
- single approach to the creation of systems is absent;
- data processing regulation and requirements are absent;
- speed of tasks execution and information flows is not defined;

- requirements for system complexity is absent;
- threat models for each system are not sufficiently developed.

As recommendations after the conducted research it is possible to designate the following. Developed business process management systems should automate end-to-end processes associated with large chains of interaction of the state in the performance of its functions.

There is also a need for up-to-date monitoring of the main information resources. Accordingly, information systems themselves can update directories and classifiers in the background through web services. That in turn will help to design a single storage system for frequently used documents. As a result, reducing the time of information exchange between systems by transferring metadata of documents [18].

4 The Proposed Methodology for Urban Systems Interoperability

An important component of the it infrastructure of the city is the systems functioning technologies and data processing structure (Figs. 4 and 5).

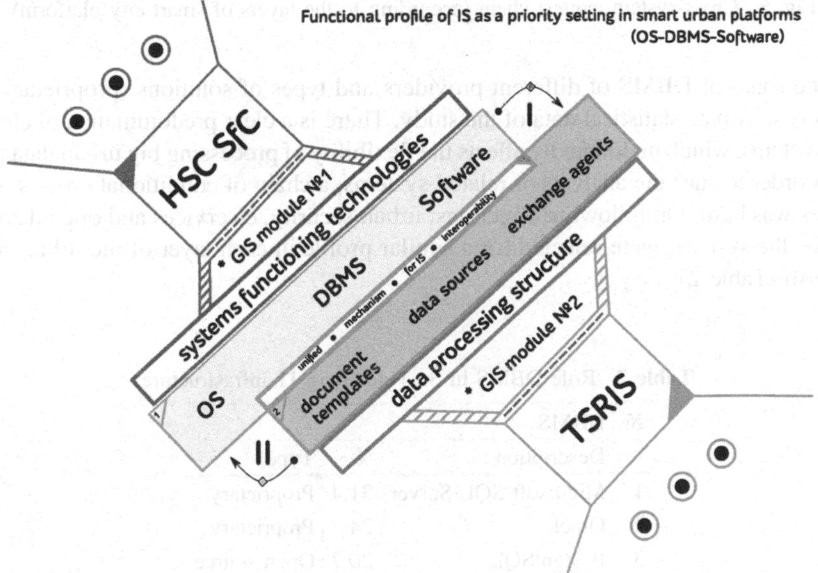

Fig. 4. Scheme of priority interoperability factors

Based on the fact that the data is processed and stored on the platform of software implementation solutions, they were taken as the basis for the analysis (OS-DBMS-Software).

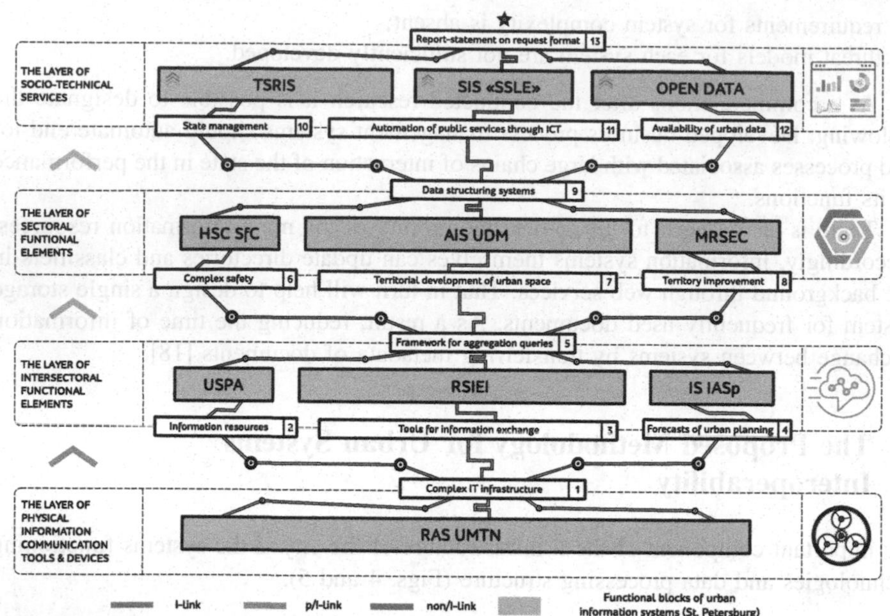

Fig. 5. Cross-system request chain (according to the layers of smart city platform)

The share of DBMS of different providers and types of solutions (proprietary and open) is shown as statistical data of the study. There is a clear predominance of closed-type systems, which undoubtedly affects the flexibility of processing big urban data [18].

In order to start the analysis of related systems, a chain of conditional cross-system queries was built. On following directions: urban security, e-services and open data. To do this, the systems were selected for a similar profile in each layer of the urban smart platform (Table 2).

Table 2. Role DBMS in St. Petersburg IT infrastructure

№	DBMS		
	Description	%	Type
1	Microsoft SQL Server	31,4	Proprietary
2	Oracle	24	Proprietary
3	PostgreSQL	20,7	Open source
4	MySQL	7,4	Open source
5	IBM DB2	4,1	Proprietary
6	Firebird	4,1	Open source
7	MongoDB	3,3	Open source
8	Clarion	2,5	Proprietary
9	MariaDB	1,7	Open source
10	dBase	0,8	Proprietary

The formation of an example query will simplify the understanding of the interoperability algorithm for everyday data exchange in government systems. Query logic from the lower layer of interaction to the final system was observed. Thus, the interoperability of two specific systems and the overall structure of the request for all participating systems is evaluated.

The step-by-step analysis allowed to detail each level and component base of the systems as much as possible. The initial data source is the urban system of St. Petersburg – Register of State Information Systems. Data analysis used on the current software and technological solutions that are used to ensure uninterrupted interaction of systems with each other (Fig. 5).

To simplify the understanding of the proposed method and detail of its calculation, a schematic visualization was chosen (Figs. 5 and 6).

The basic principle of the analysis was the comparison of technologies «1 to 1» and quantification according to the compatibility result. To eliminate the conflict in the evaluation of interoperability, a boundary parameter (0, 5) was introduced. It is used when there is insufficient data on a particular technological solution or if an additional module is required to be connected to the system for the full cycle of interaction.

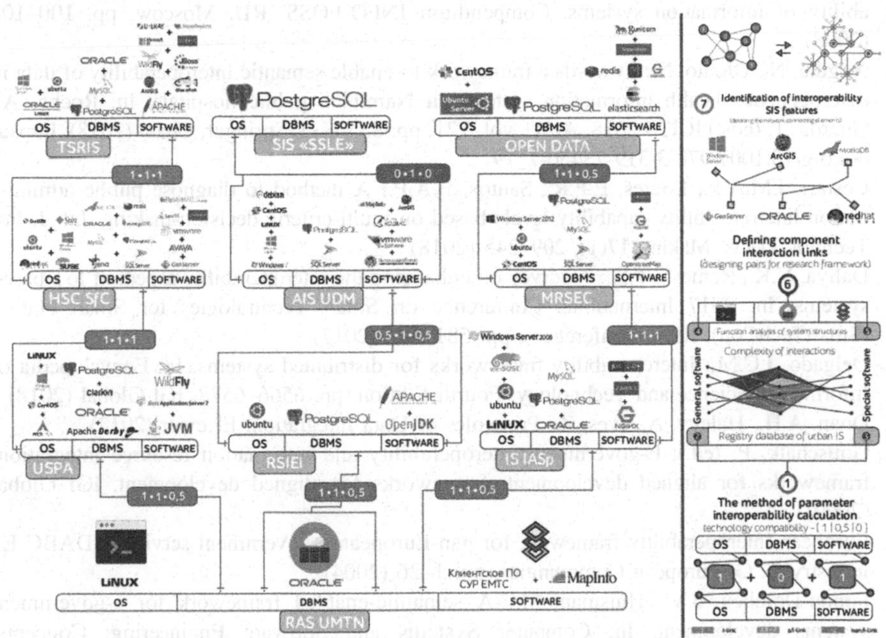

Fig. 6. Structure analysis of systems compatibility on the priority principles by «OS-DBMS-Software»

In general, according to the results of the study, almost all systems have passed the minimum level of interoperability. Some points of incompatibility associated with the heterogeneity (the presence of technologies from radically different suppliers).

The strategic prospect of creating a unified digital platform of the city involves a modular approach to the design of it infrastructure. In this regard, it is recommended to use open architectures for more flexible configuration to the scale of urban processes [17].

5 Conclusion

The article discusses the main problems of the urban information infrastructure and proposes the approach to study it. The approach is based on the qualitative comparative evaluation of systems interoperability, and it can be applied for the primary evaluation of all urban information systems. This approach can be further supplemented by quantitative methods.

The approach considered can be the basis for further urban information infrastructure modernization to implement smart city technologies.

References

1. Braude-Zolotarev, M., Grebnev, G., Yermakov, R., Rubanov, G., Serbina, E.: Interoperability of information systems. Compendium INFO-FOSS. RU, Moscow, pp. 100–108 (2008)
2. Angula, N., Dlodlo, N.: Towards a framework to enable semantic interoperability of data in heterogeneous health information systems in Namibian public hospitals. In: Rocha, Á., Guarda, T. (eds.) ICITS 2018. AISC, vol. 721, pp. 835–845. Springer, Cham (2018). https://doi.org/10.1007/978-3-319-73450-7_79
3. Cestari, J.M.A.P., Loures, E.F.R., Santos, E.A.P.: A method to diagnose public administration interoperability capability levels based on multi-criteria decision-making. Int. J. Inf. Technol. Decis. Making **17**(1), 209–245 (2018)
4. Daliya, V.K., Ramesh, T.K.: A survey on enhancing the interoperability aspect of IoT based systems. In: 2017 International Conference on Smart Technologies for Smart Nation (SmartTechCon), IEEE Conferences, pp. 581–586 (2017)
5. Delgado, J.C.M.: Interoperability frameworks for distributed systems. In: Encyclopedia of Information Science and Technology, Fourth Edition, pp. 6566–6578. IGI Global (2018)
6. Doan, A.H., Halevy, A., Ives, Z.: Principles of Data Integration. Elsevier (2012)
7. Gottschalk, P. (ed.): E-government interoperability and information resource integration: frameworks for aligned development: frameworks for aligned development. IGI Global (2009)
8. European interoperability framework for pan-European e-government services. IDABC E., Industry D. G. European Communities, pp. 1–26 (2004)
9. Fonou-Dombeu, J.V., Huisman, M.: A semantic-enabled framework for e-government systems development. In: Computer Systems and Software Engineering: Concepts, Methodologies, Tools, and Applications, pp. 501–518. IGI Global (2018)
10. Nayebpour, M.M.: The interoperability index model: improving the I-score model for interoperability measurement. Int. J. Adv. Res. Eng. Appl. Sci. **4**(11), 24–36 (2015)
11. Ford, T., et al.: Measuring system interoperability. In: Proceeding CSER (2008)
12. Guijarro, L.: Interoperability frameworks and enterprise architectures in e-government initiatives in Europe and the United States. Gov. Inf. Q. **24**(1), 89–101 (2007)

13. IEEE Standard for Interconnection and Interoperability of Distributed Energy Resources with Associated Electric Power Systems Interfaces. IEEE Std 1547–2018 (Revision of IEEE Std 1547-2003), pp. 1–138 (2018)
14. Jimenez, C.E., Solanas, A., Falcone, F.: E-government interoperability: linking open and smart government. Computer **47**(10), 22–24 (2014)
15. Grogan, P.T., De Weck, O.L.: Infrastructure system simulation interoperability using the High-Level Architecture. IEEE Syst. J. **12**(1), 103–114 (2015)
16. Brutti, A., et al.: Smart city platform specification: a modular approach to achieve interoperability in smart cities. In: Cicirelli, F., Guerrieri, A., Mastroianni, C., Spezzano, G., Vinci, A. (eds.) The Internet of Things for Smart Urban Ecosystems. IT, pp. 25–50. Springer, Cham (2019). https://doi.org/10.1007/978-3-319-96550-5_2
17. Pradhan, M., Fuchs, C., Johnsen, F.T.: A survey of applicability of military data model architectures for smart city data consumption and integration. In: 2018 IEEE 4th World Forum on Internet of Things (WF-IoT), pp. 129–134. IEEE (2018)
18. Frascella, A., et al.: A minimum set of common principles for enabling Smart City Interoperability. TECHNE-J. Technol. Archit. Environ. (1), 56–61 (2018)
19. Gabrielsen, K.R.: Interoperability in Smart Cities-Urban IoT and designing new city services. MS thesis. NTNU (2017)

Neural Network Forecasting of Traffic Congestion

Vasiliy Osipov and Dmitriy Miloserdov(✉)

St. Petersburg Institute for Informatics and Automation of Russian Academy of Sciences, 39, 14 Line, St. Petersburg 199178, Russia
osipov_vasiliy@mail.ru, dmmil94@yandex.ru

Abstract. Traffic congestions have a strong impact on the life of modern cities. Reducing congestion is one of the main concerns of private, urban and public institutions. Much effort has been devoted to the scientific research of this problem. One of the areas of these studies is the prediction of congestion. The forecast helps to distribute traffic on urban highways, thereby minimizing the congestion of individual sections and improve the road situation as a whole. There are special Internet services that analyze traffic congestion and provide users with information. They make a forecast of traffic congestions on the basis of statistics, however, as practice shows, these forecasts are not very accurate. Recently, neural network forecasting methods have been actively developing. In this paper, we investigate the possibility of recurrent neural networks with controlled synapses to predict traffic congestions. On the example of the famous Internet service "Yandex.Probki" is shown that the neural network is able to give more accurate predictions.

Keywords: Forecasting · Congestion · Neural network

1 Introduction

In order to successfully solve forecasting problems, appropriate methods are needed. One of the approaches is neural network forecasting. To date, a number of such problems are solved using neural networks of different architectures [1–7]. Various studies have used generalized regression neural network [1], long short-term memory [2], extreme learning machine with mixed core [3], probabilistic neural network [4], increasing morphological perceptron [5], deep belief nets [6], combined models [7], and others. The scope of their application is to predict the state of complex objects, for which it is almost impossible to build a sufficiently detailed mathematical model. However, the analysis of the known methods of neural network forecasting shows that they are still largely imperfect due to the lack of artificial neural networks (ANN). In recent years, there are new models of ANN, which have not yet found proper development in terms of application to the solution of forecasting problems. In particular, the problem of forecasting traffic congestions in large cities is relevant [8–14]. The article proposes to consider the applicability of recurrent neural networks (RNN) with controlled elements for predicting traffic congestions on the basis of geographic information systems (GIS).

D. A. Alexandrov et al. (Eds.): DTGS 2019, CCIS 1038, pp. 248–254, 2019.
https://doi.org/10.1007/978-3-030-37858-5_20

2 Problem Statement

In order to improve the accuracy of traffic forecasts based on the initial information of the Internet service "Yandex.Probki", the analysis of opportunities was carried out and statistics on traffic congestions in the Central district of St. Petersburg was collected. It was required to assess the possibility of obtaining more accurate forecasts with the use of the known RNN [15, 16], taking into account the interaction of traffic congestions in various points of the Central district of St. Petersburg.

3 The "Yandex.Probki" Service

The "Yandex.Probki" is one of the Internet services of the "Yandex" company, designed to inform the user about the condition and congestion of roads [17]. In large settlements, the service calculates the traffic congestion score, which characterizes the average level of congestion. Information comes from mobile devices drivers equipped with GPS. "Yandex" analyzer based on these data builds tracks and determines the speed of movement. In Moscow, St. Petersburg and other major cities the "Yandex. Probki" assess the situation on a 10-point scale (where 0 points is free movement and 10 points means that the city "stands").

4 The Features of Used RNN

The recurrent neural network with a spiral layer structure [18] was used. The investigated RNN is a two-layer structure whose layers have dimension is $N = L \times M$ of fields, where L is the length and M is the width of the layer. The layers are divided into logical fields of dimension $d \times q$ in such a way that the condition $d \times D = L$, $q \times B = M$ is satisfied, where D and B are positive integers (see Fig. 1). The distance between the layers is negligible.

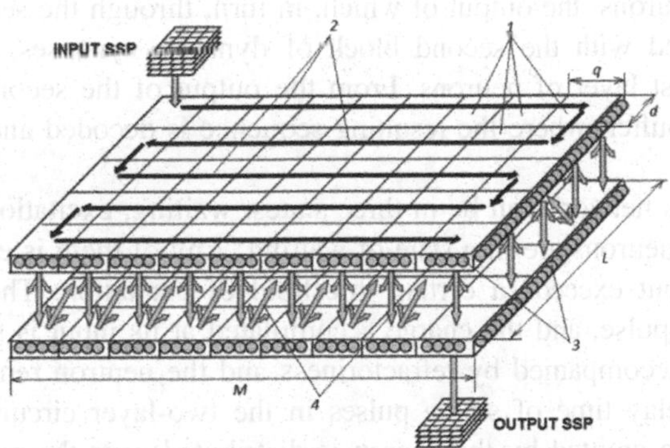

Fig. 1. Recurrent neural network with a spiral structure of layers. There 1 is a logical fields, 2 is the route of data from the input to the output network, 3 is a neurons, 4 is a synapses.

The RNN input buffer receives data and converts it into a binary sequence, which is fed to the first layer of neurons as a set of single patterns (SSP). To correctly handle the SSP needs to match the dimensionality of the fields of the RNN.

After passing through the first layer of neurons, SSP enter the unit of one-delays. Their presence is justified by the need for a time interval for the control module to make a decision on the shift of the current SSP along the layers of the neural network; the essence and meaning of the shift operation will be discussed below. After the delay, SSP arrive at the first block of dynamic synapses.

Unlike traditional RNN, the described network is endowed with so-called dynamic synapses. With their help, SSP are transmitted between layers by shifting along them depending on the current States of the latter. Such shifts can be justified in order to avoid possible conflicts of neurons in the network. Shifts are carried out by the values multiple of d and q. SSP can move through the layers from the entrance to the exit of the RNN along the given routes due to the so-called guiding synapses (see Fig. 2). Due to shifts, the neural network is endowed with a transparent logical structure, and a one-to-one correspondence is established between the elements of the input and output SSP.

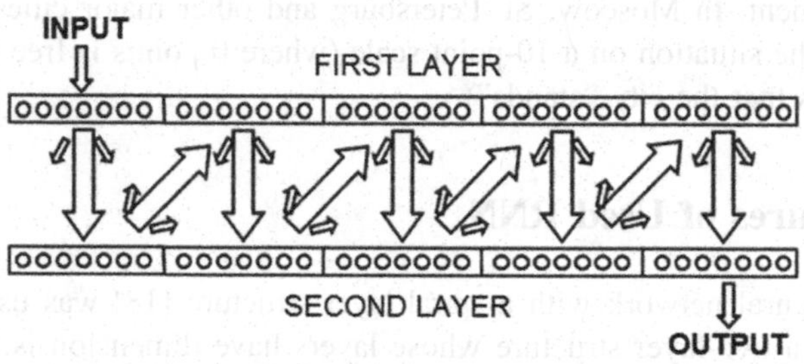

Fig. 2. The scheme of advance SSP from input to network output (view in section). Large arrows indicate the totality of the guides of the synapses.

The output of the first block of dynamic synapses is connected to the input of the second layer of neurons, the output of which, in turn, through the second unit of one-delays is associated with the second block of dynamic synapses. It outputs at the entrance of the first layer of neurons. From the output of the second layer, the data enters the output buffer, where the resulting sequence is decoded and the final results are obtained.

Neurons in this network can be in three states: waiting, excitation, and refraction. Initially, all RNN neurons are in a state of waiting. Any of them is excited if the total potential at its input exceeds a certain threshold of excitation. The excited neuron generates a single pulse, and the charge accumulated at its input is sharply absorbed. The excitation is accompanied by refractoriness and the neutron remains in this state longer than the delay time of single pulses in the two-layer circuits created by the network. The pulse emitted by the neuron is distributed over the outgoing synapses, whose weights change in accordance with the Hebbian learning principles.

5 Neural Network Forecasting Method of Traffic Congestions

In order to perform forecasting and verify the applicability of the above RNN to the solution of such problems, information on traffic congestions in the Central district of St. Petersburg was collected during two weeks from 14 to 27 February 2019. Source of information was "Yandex.Probki" Internet service. The collected data includes the speed of cars in ten selected points of the city at the time moments {09–00, 12–00, 15–00, 18–00, 21–00}. In addition to real-time data, collected and systematized forecast data "Yandex.Probki" a day before the observation for subsequent comparison with the real situation and assess the correctness of service forecasts.

The essence of the prediction method used is to use the capabilities of the neural network on the associative call information. To do this, the collected data is processed in accordance with the following algorithm.

The format of the network input data is chosen so that each SSP is a combination of m logical subfields $K_1(t)...K_{m-1}(t), K_m(t+\Delta t)$ (see Fig. 3). Each of these subfields, except $K_m(t+\Delta t)$, contains information about some criterion at a conditional time $t = 1...N$. These criteria can contain encoded information about the traffic situation at a particular point in the city. The set of obtained subfields $K_1(t)...K_{m-1}(t)$ is an associative context of the predicted criterion. The feature of the remaining subfields $K_m(t+\Delta t)$ lies in the fact that the data in it is served with some positive Δt time shift. As a result, when encoded as described above, the sequence of SSP (see Fig. 3a) RNN will be processed, on the synapses of the latter there will be memorization and binding of the context and $K_m(t+\Delta t)$ shifted parameter. Subsequently, if apply to the trained RNN incomplete (see Fig. 3b) sampling $K_1(t')...K_{m-1}(t')$ from the time interval, the last measurement of which is the closest to real time, then due to the total potential of the context, an associative call of the missing parameter will occur: $K_1(t')...K_{m-1}(t') \rightarrow P(t'+\Delta t)$. This parameter will be the forecast of K_m value on the Δt horizon.

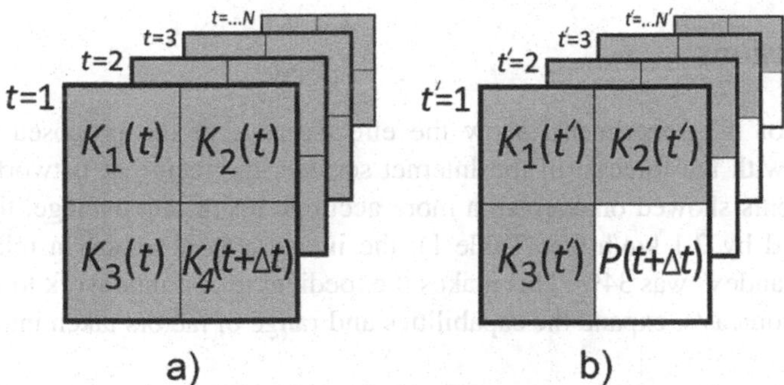

Fig. 3. The structure of the sequences of SSP supplied to the RNN in the learning process (a) and forecasting (b). For example, m = 4 is selected.

6 Forecasting Execution and Results

In the simplest case, the RNN is trained by time series shifted relative to themselves by $\Delta t = 1$ day, or 5 measurements. In this case, the number of logical subfields is two. The depth of prediction can be chosen equal to 12 days; the forecast horizon is equal to the value of the shift and in this case is 1 day. The speed values are coded with conditional codes from 1 to 8.

Training is carried out in one era. At this time, the neurons of the network is memorizing and linking information about the history of the forecast. After training, an incomplete sample is fed to the network input, and due to the memorized connections, the missing information is filled in. In this way, the forecast of traffic congestions for 10 addresses was obtained. The RMSE at the ten addresses considered by "Yandex" and the recurrent neural network are shown in Table 1.

Table 1. Forecasting efficiency.

Address	"Yandex" accuracy, km/h	RNN accuracy, km/h
Vosstaniya square	10,1	4,1
Nevskiy avenue, 158	5,5	4,4
Vladimirskiy avenue, 19	4,2	1,7
Ligovskiy avenue, 33	4,3	3,8
Marat street, 10	6,1	3,7
Vladimirskiy avenue, 10	5,5	3,5
Nevskiy avenue, 35	7,1	7,9
Vosstaniya street, 44	3,2	4,0
Nevskiy avenue, 190	12,0	4,3
2nd Sovetskaya street, 12	4,1	3,1
Average	**6,2**	**4,1**

7 Conclusions

The results of the experiments show the effectiveness of the proposed method. In comparison with the forecast of the Internet service, the recurrent network with controlled elements showed on average a more accurate result. On average, the accuracy was increased by 2.1 km/h (see Table 1); the increase in accuracy in relation to the results of "Yandex" was 34%. This makes it expedient to continue work to increase the accuracy of forecasts, expand the capabilities and range of factors taken into account in the forecast.

The disadvantages of the proposed model include the need to manually configure the global network parameters for individual forecasting cases. At the moment, work is underway to find patterns between these parameters and the efficiency of the network. However, despite the existing shortcomings, the considered RNN has the potential for solving applied problems, which was demonstrated by the results of this study.

References

1. Gheyas, I., Smith, L.: A neural network approach to time series forecasting. In: World Congress on Engineering (WCE 2009), London, U.K., vol. 2 (2009)
2. Sagheer, A., Kotb, M.: Time series forecasting of petroleum production using deep LSTM recurrent networks. Neurocomputing **323**, 203–213 (2019). https://doi.org/10.1016/j.neucom.2018.09.082
3. Chen, Y., Kloft, M., Yang, Y., Li, C., Li, L.: Mixed kernel based extreme learning machine for electric load forecasting. Neurocomputing **312**, 90–106 (2018). https://doi.org/10.1016/j.neucom.2018.05.068
4. Adeli, H., Panakkat, A.: A probabilistic neural network for earthquake magnitude prediction. Neural Netw. **22**(7), 1018–1024 (2009). https://doi.org/10.1016/j.neunet.2009.05.003
5. Araújo, R.: A morphological perceptron with gradient-based learning for Brazilian stock market forecasting. Neural Netw. **28**, 61–81 (2012). https://doi.org/10.1016/j.neunet.2011.12.004
6. Kuremoto, T., Kimura, S., Kobayashi, K., Obayashi, M.: Time series forecasting using a deep belief network with restricted Boltzmann machines. Neurocomputing **137**, 47–56 (2014). https://doi.org/10.1016/j.neucom.2013.03.047
7. Huang, L., Wang, J.: Forecasting energy fluctuation model by wavelet decomposition and stochastic recurrent wavelet neural network. Neurocomputing **309**, 70–82 (2018). https://doi.org/10.1016/j.neucom.2018.04.071
8. Marma, A., Zilys, M., Valinevicius, A.: Parking traffic jam forecast system. In: 2nd International Conference on Advances in Circuits, Electronics and Micro-Electronics, Sliema, Malta, vol. 1 (2009). https://doi.org/10.1109/cenics.2009.30
9. Daissaoui, A., Boulmakoul, A., Zineb, H.: First specifications of urban traffic-congestion forecasting models. In: 27th International Conference on Microelectronics (ICM 2015). IEEE, Casablanca (2015). https://doi.org/10.1109/icm.2015.7438035
10. Zhou, T., et al.: δ-agree AdaBoost stacked autoencoder for short-term traffic flow forecasting. Neurocomputing **247**, 31–38 (2017). https://doi.org/10.1016/j.neucom.2017.03.049
11. Moretti, F., Pizzuti, S., Panzieri, S., Annunziato, M.: Urban traffic flow forecasting through statistical and neural network bagging ensemble hybrid modeling. Neurocomputing **167**, 3–7 (2015). https://doi.org/10.1016/j.neucom.2014.08.100
12. Xia, D., Wang, B., Li, H., Li, Y., Zhang, Z.: A distributed spatial–temporal weighted model on MapReduce for short-term traffic flow forecasting. Neurocomputing **179**, 246–263 (2016). https://doi.org/10.1016/j.neucom.2015.12.013
13. Huang, M.: Intersection traffic flow forecasting based on ν-GSVR with a new hybrid evolutionary algorithm. Neurocomputing **147**, 343–349 (2015). https://doi.org/10.1016/j.neucom.2014.06.054
14. Tian, Y., Zhang, K., Li, J., Lin, X., Yang, B.: LSTM-based traffic flow prediction with missing data. Neurocomputing **318**, 297–305 (2018). https://doi.org/10.1016/j.neucom.2018.08.067
15. Osipov, V.: Neural networks with past, present and future time. Inf.-Control Syst. **4**, 30–33 (2011)
16. Osipov, V.: Neural network forecasting of events for intelligent robots. Mechatron. Autom. Control **12**, 836–840 (2015). https://doi.org/10.17587/mau.16.836-840

17. How “Yandex.Probki” Service Works. https://yandex.ru/company/technologies/yaprobki/
18. Osipov, V., Osipova, M.: Space–time signal binding in recurrent neural networks with controlled elements. Neurocomputing **308**, 194–204 (2018). https://doi.org/10.1016/j.neucom.2018.05.009

E-Economy: Online Consumers and Solutions

Personality and E-shopping: Insights from a Nationally Representative Study

John Magnus Roos[1,2,3,4](✉)

[1] Department of Social Psychology, University of Skövde, Högskolevägen 1, 541 28 Skövde, Sweden
magnus.roos@chalmers.se

[2] Division of Physical Resource Theory, Chalmers University of Technology, 412 58 Gothenburg, Sweden

[3] Centre for Consumer Research, School of Business, Economics and Law, University of Gothenburg, P.O. Box 606, 405 30 Gothenburg, Sweden

[4] Department of Business Administration and Textile Management, University of Borås, Allégatan 1, 503 32 Borås, Sweden

Abstract. According to previous research, a high degree of Openness and Neuroticism, and a low degree of Agreeableness are personality determinants of e-shopping. This study aims to explore the relationship between the Five-factor model of personality (i.e. Openness, Conscientiousness, Extraversion, Agreeableness, and Neuroticism) and e-shopping in a Swedish context. In a nationally representative sample, a questionnaire was distributed to 3400 citizens. The response rate was 53 percentage (N = 1812). The questionnaire included measures of the Five-factor model of personality (BFI-ten) and e-shopping. Multiple regression analyses were conducted to test if the Five-factor model of personality predicted e-shopping. The dependent variable was self-reported frequencies of e-shopping during the last 12 months. The first analysis showed that Openness is predicting e-shopping. However, this effect disappeared, when age, educational attainment and income were controlled for. Our conclusion is that the Five-factor model of personality is a poor predictor of e-shopping and that e-shopping frequencies are unrelated to the personality of internet users. Methodological limitations are discussed, for instance the use of a single-item for measuring e-shopping and a short-scale for measuring personality. There are difficulties comparing our findings with previous findings, since the concepts personality and e-shopping have not been defined uniformly. The analyses revealed significant variation in definitions, measurements and methodologies. Caution should also be taken in generalizing the present results to other countries and other time periods.

Keywords: Personality · E-shopping · E-buying · Online shopping

1 Introduction

The number of consumers shopping online (e-shopping), the frequencies of e-shopping per consumer, and the amount of money being spent on e-shopping is increasing in Sweden, as in several other developed economies. In 2017, the total Swedish retail

D. A. Alexandrov et al. (Eds.): DTGS 2019, CCIS 1038, pp. 257–267, 2019.
https://doi.org/10.1007/978-3-030-37858-5_21

sales was 767 billion, while the total online sales was 80 billion. Thus, e-sales accounted for 10.4% of the Swedish retail sales in 2017 [31]. The Swedish Trade Federation has estimated the e-sales to increase rapidly the coming years, and correspond to approximately 33.3% of the total retail sales in 2025 [31]. The average number of times that Swedish consumers were shopping online increased markedly during 2017 [26]. Figure 1 shows the development of frequencies in e-shopping among Swedish consumers during the period 2007–2017.

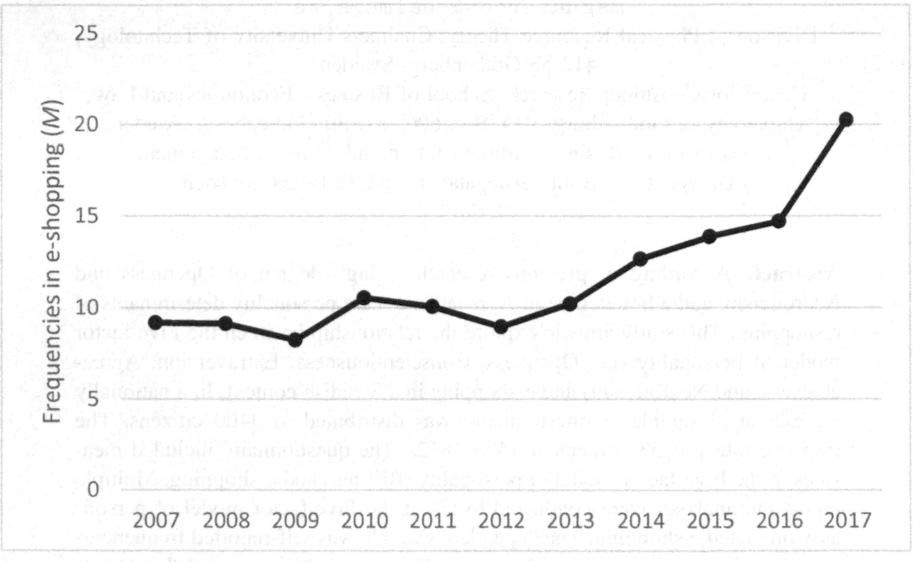

Fig. 1. The development of annual times of e-shopping among Swedish consumers during the period 2007–2017 [26, p. 27].

While several researchers are touting the unique capabilities of the online medium to provide interactivity and personalized experiences, few studies have focused systematically on mapping the personality of e-shoppers. Clearly understanding e-shoppers personality is promising, in strategy- technology- and marketing decisions, as well as web site design. Such insights might be used for effective communication or inclusive and participatory design. The purpose of the present study is to examine if personality factors (such as degree of Extraversion) influence frequencies in e-shopping.

In general, personality factors influence how people behave, how they view themselves, how they perceive and interact with the world, and how they react to external stimuli [5, 19].

Related to consumer behaviour, personality factors have been used in predicting a range of different behaviours, for instance shopping ecological goods, driving specific car brands and compulsive buying [9].

Based on early studies in the field of personality and internet use, Amichai-Hamburger stated that "personality is a highly relevant factor in determining behaviour on the Internet" [1, p. 7].

To the best of our knowledge, there are only two previous studies that have investigated the relationship between personality factors and e-shopping [i.e. 4, 21]. The present study differs from the previous two studies in several ways. The present study use a nationally representative sample (of the Swedish population), while the other two studies use less representative samples; web-panel members in Croatia and U.S students, respectively. The present study is much more up- to- date than the previous studies. The present study is based on data from 2017, while the previous two studies were published in 2006 and 2007, respectively [4, 21].

2 Theoretical Grounding: The Five-Factor Model of Personality

Many personality psychologists agree that individual differences can be usefully organized in terms of five broad, universal, bipolar factors, the Five-factor model of personality (FFM). Although different terms have been used to label the FFM we use the terms Openness, Conscientiousness, Extraversion, Agreeableness and Neuroticism [7, 8, 29]. The first letters of the FFM factors spell out the word OCEAN. For the sake of clarity, the personality factors will be presented and discussed in this order [5].

Openness is described in terms of aesthetic sensitivity, behavioural flexibility, creativity, curiosity, need for variety, novelty, unconventional attitudes, vivid imagination, and willingness to change. People high in Openness innovative, like to try new things and have broad interests, while people low in Openness tend to be more cautious, conservative, and conventional [7].

Conscientiousness is described in terms of achievement striving, competence, dutifulness, orderliness, responsibility, and self-discipline. People high in Conscientiousness are efficient, organized, and thorough, while people low in Conscientiousness are careless, hedonistic, and lazy [7].

Extraversion is characterised by high level of assertiveness, activity, excitement seeking, positive emotions, and spontaneity. People high in Extraversion are enthusiastic, excitement seeking, and sociable, while people low in Extraversion are more reserved, quiet, and withdrawn [7].

Agreeableness is described in terms of altruism, cooperativeness, good-naturedness, friendliness, tendermindedness, and tolerance. People high in Agreeableness tend to rely more on other people and they forgive people more easily than people low in Agreeableness, who tend to be more argumentative, cynical, and suspicious [7].

Neuroticism is described in terms of anxiety, distress, low self-confidence, negative emotions, tension, and vulnerability. People high in Neuroticism are anxious, nervous, and worrying, while people low in Neuroticism (i.e., emotionally stable) tend to be more calm, relaxed and self-satisfied [7].

3 Literature Review and Construction of Hypotheses

In this section we will relate the FFM to the previous literature on internet usage, especially to the literature on e-shopping. To the best of our knowledge, there are only two studies that have investigated the relationship between the FFM and e-shopping (Table 1). Based on the literature review, we will construct hypotheses for e-shopping and each of the five personality factors.

Openness is positively related to overall Internet usage and a wide variety of Internet activities related to work and leisure [15, 20]. People high in Openness are more likely to seek and test Internet activities, such as new blogs [11] and social media [6]. Openness has also been associated with willingness to buy online [4, 21]. In line with previous research, we formulate the following hypothesis:

H1: Openness is positively associated with e-shopping

A variety of findings regarding Conscientiousness and overall Internet usage were found in previous studies. According to Landers and Lounsbury [17], Conscientiousness is negatively related to overall Internet usage, while Mark and Ganzach [20] found that Conscientiousness was positively related to overall Internet usage. Regarding categories of Internet usage, some studies have found that Conscientiousness is positively related to academic activities (e.g., academic research and course participation) and information search [14, 17], while it is negatively related to leisure activities such as computer games, movies, music, and shopping [17, 28]. Our literature review leads us to assume that Conscientiousness is negatively associated with using the Internet for e-shopping:

H2: Conscientiousness is negatively associated with e-shopping

Pioneer studies on personality and Internet usage show that the Internet primarily was used by people with a low degree of Extraversion (i.e., introverts) [e.g. 1, 17]. This line of research seemed to suggest that people who were low in Extraversion were attracted to the anonymity connected to the Internet. Furthermore, researchers suggested that the Internet compensated for the need people have for social support thereby primarily benefitting introverts and people with a low degree of social support [16]. However, more recent studies have found a positive relationship between Extraversion and Internet usage [e.g. 20, 21]. Extraversion has also been shown to be positively related to using social media [6].

As the Internet is an external stimulation which seems to be more and more designed for fulfilling the extraverts' needs, we formulate the following hypothesis:

H3: Extraversion is positively associated with e-shopping

Landers and Lounsbury [17] found that Agreeableness is negatively related to overall Internet usage. However, Agreeableness was shown to be unrelated to leisure activities, including e-shopping [17]. In contrast, Bosnjak, Galesic and Tuten [4] have found that Agreeableness is negatively associated with e-shopping. People with a low degree of Agreeableness are not motivated to socialize in a physical store, instead they prefer e-shopping [34]. Thus, we propose the following hypothesis:

H4: Agreeableness is negatively associated with e-shopping

Mixed findings on Neuroticism and overall Internet usage were found in previous studies. There are studies that have shown that Neuroticism is negatively related to overall Internet usage [e.g. 33] and studies that show that Neuroticism is positive associated with overall Internet usage [e.g. 2, 12, 30]. Previous studies shows that Neuroticism is positively related to social and leisure activities, such as social media and blogs [6, 11], while it is negatively related to information and duty activities, such as searching for facts, and sending/receiving emails [28]. E-shopping may be convenient for mood-regulations among people with a high degree of Neuroticism, since the sensory stimulation is permanent accessible [18]. Previous research shows that Neuroticism is positively related to e-shopping [4, 21]. Thus, we formulate the following hypothesis:

H5: Neuroticism is positively associated with e-shopping

Table 1. Previous research on FFM and e-shopping.

Study	Sample	FFM inventory	Measurement for e-shopping	Analyses	Results: FFM relation to e-shopping
Bosnjak, Galesic and Tuten [4]	Web-panel of adult internet users in Croatia. N = 808	Twenty-two items Personality Measure, developed my Rammstedt and John [24]	An 11-point likelihood scale for measuring likelihood of online purchases	Path analysis based on a disattenuated correlation matrix	Openness (.09). Agreeablness (−.14) Neuroticism (.16). Values in parentheses are standardized path coefficients
McElroy, Hendrickson, Townsend and DeMarie [21]	MBA and senior undergraduate students from a variety of majors in USA N = 132	Revised NEO Personality Inventory (240 items)	Average of two items: Five-point scale for willingness of buying products online	1. Pearson's correlation 2. Regression analysis. Control variables: Computer-anxiety, self-efficacy, gender	1. Openness ($r = .17$, $p < .05$) 2. Neuroticism ($B = .25$, $p < .05$)

Note. r = Pearson's correlation coefficient, B = Beta, the standardized regression coefficient. P = critical value for test of significance.

4 Methodology

4.1 Sample and Procedure

The data were collected through a survey study by the SOM Institute. The SOM Institute (the Institute for Society, Opinion, and Media) is a research organization at the University of Gothenburg in Sweden. Since 1986, the institute has collected data from the Swedish population on a wide variety of issues such as consumption, demography, internet use, media use, political opinion, psychological variables (e.g. values and personality) and well-being. A postal questionnaire was sent out to 3,400 randomly selected Swedish citizens in the age rage 16–85. The data were gathered between the

September 7, 2017 and the December 31, 2017. Each participant received the survey by mail in the middle of September 2017. This was later followed up by several reminders via telephone and email [32].

4.2 Measurement Variables

The survey questions regarding e-shopping and personality factors examined in this study only made up a limited part of a more extensive survey.

The Five-factor model of personality was measured using the Big Five Inventory, BFI-ten [24], which is a ten-item inventory with two items measuring each personality factor. The BFI-ten has shown adequate levels of convergent and discriminant validity in addition to test-retest reliability [24]. Personality factor items were measured using a four-point Likert scale ranging from 1 ("strongly disagree") to 4 ("strongly agree"). The Openness factor was constructed by calculating an average of the responses to "has an active imagination" and "has few artistic interests" (reversed). The Conscientiousness factor was constructed by calculating an average of the responses to "does a thorough job" and "tends to be lazy" (reversed). The Extraversion factor was constructed by calculating an average of the responses to "is outgoing, sociable" and "is reserved" (reversed). The Agreeableness factor was constructed by calculating an average of the responses to "is generally trusting" and "tends to find fault with others" (reversed). Finally, the Neuroticism factor was constructed by calculating an average of the responses to "gets nervous easily" and "is relaxed, handles stress well" (reversed). Only respondents who had provided responses to both items of a specific factor were included in the analyses.

E-shopping was measured with "How many times have you bought products and/or services online during the last 12 months" to which the respondents were asked to indicate their frequency of shopping on a seven-point Likert scale, ranging from 1 ("never") to 7 ("daily") ($N = 1677$, $M = 3.16$, $SD = 1.37$).

We used three control variables; age, educational attainment and income. Age was asked for as an open-ended question. Educational attainment was measured by "What is your highest level of education", 1–4 (e.g., 1, pre-high school and 4, post-graduate). Income was measured by "What is your current annual household income?", 1–3 (e.g., 1, less than US $31,000 and 3, more than US $72,000).

The reason for using age as a control variable was that previous research has shown that age influence overall internet use; younger people use the Internet more than older people [13, 27]. Previous research has also shown that higher socioeconomic status in terms of educational attainment and income are positively related to overall internet use [22, 23, 27], especially for e-shopping [10].

4.3 Ethical Considerations

All procedures were in accordance with the ethical standards of the institutional and national research committee and with the 1964 Helsinki declaration and its later amendments.

5 Empirical Analysis

5.1 Descriptive Statistics

The final sample size of our study was 1812, the response rate was 53%. Among the 1812 respondents, 850 were males, 958 were females and 4 other gender (neither identified as male nor female). The mean age was 51.74 years. Of the respondents, 7.5% reported that they had not used the Internet at all during the past 12 months. Among the Internet users (N = 1676), 18.2% reported that they had not bought anything online during the past 12 months, 46.4% reported that they had bought something online at least once per month, and 19.1% reported that they had bought something online at least once per week.

5.2 Statistical Analyses

The objective was to analyze the relatedness of the Five-factor model of personality to e-shopping. First, we conducted Pearson's correlations between study variables. Table 2 contains a descriptive summary of means and standard deviations as well as the Pearson's correlations.

Table 2. Means (*M*), standard deviation (*SD*) and Pearson's correlations (*N* = 1812)

	M	*SD*	1	2	3	4	5
1. Openness	2.56	0.74					
2. Conscientiousness	3.26	0.58	−.03				
3. Extraversion	2.84	0.72	.11**	.20**			
4. Agreeableness	3.06	0.52	−.02	.21**	.19**		
5. Neuroticism	2.20	0.70	.05*	−.20**	−.26**	−.22**	
6. E-shopping	3.16	1.37	.12**	−.06*	.00	−.05	.03

Note. Significant Pearson's correlation coefficients = * $p < .05$;** $p < .01$.
Personality (1–4). E-shopping (1–7).

Second, we conducted a hierarchical regression model in three steps: In step 1, the FFM was entered, in step 2 age was entered, and in step 3 SES (i.e. educational attainment and household income) was entered. The result showed that personality factors overall counted for 2% of the variance in e-shopping. Notably, only Openness was a significant (p < .05) of e-shopping. However, the effect of Openness was markedly reduced when we controlled for age. Moreover, the effect was not significant when we also controlled for SES in terms of educational attainment and household income. The summary of results is shown in Table 3.

Table 3. Hierarchical regression models exploring how personality factors predict online shopping frequencies, controlling for age (Step 2) and SES (Step 3).

Independent variables	Step 1: personality B	Step 2: personality, age B	Step 3: personality, age, SES B
Openness	.12***	.06*	.04
Conscientiousness	−.03	.02	.01
Extraversion	.00	.00	−.02
Agreeableness	−.02	.01	.01
Neuroticism	.003	−.01	.01
Age		−.45***	−.40***
Education income			.17*** .12***
R^2	.02***	.20***	.25***

Note. B = Beta, the standardized regression coefficient. * $p < .05$;** $p < .01$; ***$p < .001$. $N = 1472$. Personality (1–4). SES = Socio-Economic-Status; Educational attainment (1–4) and Household income (1–3). Only internet users are included in the analyses.

6 Discussion

6.1 Discussion of the Empirical Findings

Based on early studies in the field of personality and internet use, Amichai-Hamburger stated that personality is a highly relevant factor in determining behavior on the Internet [1]. This might be true for some digital behaviors, but neither the present results nor the previous results [4, 21] give much empirical support to the statement of Amichai-Hamburger regarding e-shopping.

Regarding Openness, our result is in line with previous research [4, 21]; people with a high degree of Openness are shopping more frequently online (Hypothesis 1). People high on Openness might like to shop online because e-shopping offers them adventure experiences, variety and new ideas [14]. However, the effect of Openness will disappear when we include age and SES (i.e. educational attainment and household income). Previous studies [4, 21] have neither controlled for age nor SES. From the present result, it seems as the effect of Openness on e-shopping completely can be explained by higher age and higher SES in terms of educational attainment and household income. The correlation effect between Openness and e-shopping did also disappeared in the study of McElroy [21], when they controlled for computer-anxiety, self-efficacy and gender.

In contrast to the present study, previous studies have found that e-shopping is related to a high degree of Neuroticism and a low degree of Agreeableness [4, 21]. Perhaps, the FFM explained more of e-shopping in the past than nowadays? It might be that psychologists and web-designers have worked in collaborations since the previous studies and nowadays better provide e-shopping services for all kind of humans, whatever their personalities. The Internet has also become more widely used in our societies since the previous studies, which might have reduced (or even eliminated) the previous presented associations between e-shopping and certain personality factors; high degree of Openness and Neuroticism and low degree of Agreeableness.

6.2 Discussion of the Methodology

The methodological limitations this study has must be taken into account. Firstly, the cross-sectional nature of the sample only permits us to explore relations and not causal effects. However, it might be argued that personality factors cause e-shopping (like other behaviours) and not the other way around [5]. Secondly, e-shopping is measured by self-reporting and not real shopping frequencies. To estimate actual behavior from self-report surveys causes well-known problems in the field of social and personality psychology [3]. Thrirdly, e-shopping is measured by a single-item question; "How often have you bought a product or service online during the past twelve months?". We recommend further research to use an index (or battery of questions), which also might allow analyses across consumption categories, such as services versus products or non-durable goods versus durable goods. Perhaps the relationship between personality factors and e-shopping differ between buying clothes and buying food? Fourthly, the Five-factor model of personality was measured by a short scale, which have been shown to be associated with lower reliability [35]. The 240-items inventory used by McElroy et al. [21] is superior the measure in the present study, but their study suffer from other limitations, such as a small student sample ($N = 132$). Normally, there is a trade-off between the length of the scale and the number of participants. Fifthly, although our ambition was to provide a representative sample of the Swedish population in the age range 16–85, the sample is slightly underrepresented regarding males and young adults [32]. Finally, caution should also be taken in generalizing the present results to other countries and national cultures. Although the FFM has shown universal characteristics, e-shopping, and the relationship between personality factors and e-shopping, might differ across national cultures. Therefore, we do not know to what extent the present and the previous results have been influenced by national cultures, an unknown factor which makes it complicated to assess the external validity of the results.

7 Conclusion

The FFM model does account for some variance of e-shopping, but not enough to give much solace to personality researchers. Openness, the only significant factor on e-shopping, might completely be explained by other variables [Table 3; 21]. We need more empirical results in order to generalize our conclusion, especially since the field lack uniformed measurements and analyses of the FFM model and e-shopping.

References

1. Amichai-Hamburger, Y.: Internet and personality. Comput. Hum. Behav. **18**(1), 1–10 (2002)
2. Amiel, T., Sargent, S.L.: Individual differences in internet usage motives. Comput. Hum. Behav. **20**, 711–726 (2004)
3. Baumeister, R.F., Vohs, K.D., Funder, D.C.: Psychology as the science of self-reports and finger movements. Whatever happen to actual behavior? Perspect. Psychol. Sci. **2**(4), 396–403 (2007)
4. Bosnjak, M., Galesic, M., Tuten, T.: Personality determinants of online shopping: explaining online purchase intentions using a hierarchical approach. J. Bus. Res. **60**, 597–605 (2006)
5. Chamorro-Premuzic, T.: Personality and Individual Differences. BPS Blackwell, Glasgow (2012)
6. Correa, T., Hinsley, A.W., de Zúñiga, G.: Who interacts on the Web?: the intersection of users's personality and social media use. Comput. Hum. Behav. **26**(2), 247–253 (2010)
7. Costa, P.T., McCrae, R.R.: Revised NEO Personality Inventory (NEO-PI-R) and NEO Five-Factor Inventory (NEO-FFI): Professional Manual. Psychological Assessment Resources, Odessa (1992)
8. Digman, J.M.: Personality structure: emergence of the five-factor model. Annu. Rev. Psychol. **41**, 417–440 (1990)
9. Ekström, K.M., Ottosson, M., Parment, A.: Consumer behavior – classical and contemporary perspectives. Studentlitteratur, Lund (2017)
10. Farag, S., Krizek, K.J., Dijst, M.: E-shopping and its relationship with in-store shopping: empirical evidence from the Netherlands and the USA. Transp. Rev. **26**(1), 43–61 (2006)
11. Guadagno, R.E., Bradley, M.O., Cassie, A.E.: Who blogs? Personality predictors of blogging. Comput. Hum. Behav. **24**(5), 1993–2004 (2008)
12. Hamburger, Y.A., Ben-Artzi, E.: The relationship between Extraversion and Neuroticism and the different uses of the Internet. Comput. Hum. Behav. **16**(4), 441–449 (2000)
13. Hills, P., Argyle, M.: Uses of the Internet and their relationships with individual differences in personality. Comput. Hum. Behav. **19**(1), 59–70 (2003)
14. Hughes, D.J., Rowe, M., Batey, M., Lee, A.: A tale of two sites: Twitter vs. Facebook and the personality predictors of social media usage. Comput. Hum. Behav. **28**, 561–569 (2012)
15. Kim, Y., Jeong, J.S.: Personality predictors for the use of multiple Internet functions. Internet Res. **25**(3), 399–415 (2015)
16. Kraut, R., Kiesler, S., Boneva, B., Cummings, J., Helegson, V., Crawford, A.: Internet paradox revisited. J. Soc. Issues **58**(1), 49–74 (2002)
17. Landers, R.N., Lounsbury, J.W.: An investigation of Big Five and narrow personality traits in relation to Internet usage. Comput. Hum. Behav. **22**, 283–293 (2006)
18. LaRose, R., Eastin, M.S.: Is online buying out of control? Electronic commerce and consumer self-regulation. J. Broadcatsing Electron. Media **46**(4), 549–564 (2002)
19. Larsen, R.J., Buss, D.M.: Personality Psychology. Domains of Knowledge About the Human Nature. McGraw-Hill, Boston (2005)
20. Mark, G., Ganzach, Y.: Personality and Internet usage: a large-scale representative study of young adults. Comput. Hum. Behav. **36**, 274–281 (2014)
21. McElroy, J.C., Hendrickson, A.R., Townsend, A.M., DeMarie, S.M.: Dispositional factors in Internet use: personality versus cognitive style. MIS Q. **31**(4), 809–820 (2007)
22. Mocnik, D., Sirec, K.: The determinants of Internet use controlling for income level: cross-country empirical evidence. Inf. Econ. Policy **22**(3), 243–256 (2010)

23. NTIA. Falling through the net: Toward digital inclusion. A report on Americans' access to technology tools. National Telecommunication and Information Administration (NTIA), Economic and Statistics Administration, U.S. Department of Commerce. The Secretary of Commerce, Washington, DC (2000)
24. Rammstedt, B., John, O.P.: Measuring personality in one minute or less: a 10-items short version of the Big Five Inventory in English and German. J. Res. Pers. **41**(1), 2003–2012 (2007)
25. Ramstedt, B., John, O.P.: BFI-K Form S. ZUMA, Mannheim (2003)
26. Roos, J.M.: Konsumtionsrapporten: Under ytan. Centre for Consumer Research, University of Gothenburg, Gothenburg (2018)
27. Roos, J.M.: The winner takes *IT* all: Swedish digital divides in global internet usage. In: Alexandrov, D.A., Boukhanovsky, A.V., Chugunov, A.V., Kabanov, Y., Koltsova, O. (eds.) DTGS 2018. CCIS, vol. 859, pp. 3–18. Springer, Cham (2018). https://doi.org/10.1007/978-3-030-02846-6_1
28. Roos, J.M., Kazemi, A.: Personality traits and Internet usage across generation cohorts: insights from a nationally representative study. Curr. Psychol. 1–11. https://doi.org/10.1007/s12144-018-0033-2
29. Soto, C.J., John, O.P., Gosling, S.D., Potter, J.: Age differences in personality traits from 10 to 65: big five domains and facets in a large cross-sectional sample. J. Soc. Psychol. **100**(2), 330–348 (2011)
30. Swickert, R.J., Hittner, J.B., Harris, J.L., Herring, J.A.: Relationship among Internet use, personality and social support. Comput. Hum. Behav. **18**(4), 437–451 (2002)
31. The Swedish Trade Federation (Svensk Handel). Det stora detaljhandelsskiftet (2018). http://www.svenskhandel.se/globalassets/dokument/aktuellt-och-opinion/rapporter-och-foldrar/e-handelsrapporter/det-stora-detaljhandelsskiftet_2018-digital-version-08052018.pdf. Accessed 10 Feb 2019
32. Tipple, F.: Den nationella SOM-undersökningen. In: Andersson, U., Carlander, A., Lindgren, E., Oskarson, M. (eds.) Sprickor i fasaden, pp. 409–417. The SOM-Institute, University of Gothenburg, Gothenburg (2018)
33. Tuten, T., Bosnjak, M.: Understanding differences in Web usage: the role of need for cognition and the five factor model of personality. Soc. Behav. Pers. **29**(4), 391–398 (2001)
34. Wolfinbarger, M., Gilly, M.C.: Shopping online for freedom, control and fun. Calif. Manag. Rev. **43**(2), 34–55 (2001)
35. Yarkoni, T.: The abbreviation of personality, or how to measure 200 personality scales with 200 items. J. Res. Pers. **44**(2), 180–198 (2010)

Consumer Loyalty Factors in the Russian E-Commerce Market

Vera Rebiazina[1(✉)], Aigerim Stamalieva[1], and Maria Smirnova[2]

[1] National Research University Higher School of Economics, Moscow, Russia
{rebiazina, astamalieva}@hse.ru
[2] Saint-Petersburg State University, Saint Petersburg, Russia
smirnova@gsom.pu.ru

Abstract. The e-commerce market has been developing rapidly in recent years. The number of consumers making online purchases is increasing. In conditions of increasing competition in the market, a large selection of products and brands, increasing consumer power and ability to switch to competitor's products through the internet, research on consumer loyalty factors in e-commerce market becomes relevant. This paper is devoted to the study of consumer loyalty factors in the Russian e-commerce market. The findings are based on the results of an empirical research implemented in the form of an online survey of 601 consumers in the Russian e-commerce market. The main attributes and factors of consumer loyalty are highlighted in the study. As a result of factor analysis, 9 factors are identified. Based on the results of factor analysis three clusters of customers are defined. The paper contributes to studies on customer loyalty factors in Russian e-commerce market and may be used as a base for future research.

Keywords: Consumer loyalty · E-commerce · Electronic loyalty · E-loyalty · Online-shopping

1 Introduction

The Internet has become one of the main platforms for providing services and interacting with consumers. An increasing number of consumers make purchases in online stores and loyal consumers are a valuable asset; therefore, companies tend to build trustful and long-term relationships with them.

The e-commerce market is developing rapidly not only around the world, but also in Russia. According to the research "Online Trading in Russia 2018" presented by Data Insight (2018), the share of e-commerce in Russia's GDP is 2.5% and is comparable to that of the USA - 2.6%. The domestic e-commerce market in Russia in the segment of physical goods accounted for 965 billion rubles in 2017, which is 18% higher than in 2016. According to this report, the Russian e-commerce market should have reached 1.15 trillion. rub. in 2018. The size of the average check falls for the second year in a row and accounted for 3,970 rubles in 2018. The main factors behind the growth of the market was the increase in the number of new consumers and the increase in the number of orders per consumer [9]. Analysts also point out that:

D. A. Alexandrov et al. (Eds.): DTGS 2019, CCIS 1038, pp. 268–280, 2019.
https://doi.org/10.1007/978-3-030-37858-5_22

"... number of online shoppers is increasing as they gain experience of using the Internet. Those with online shopping experience shop more often and in more categories..." [9].

Development of the Russian c-commerce market is possible due to several external factors: an increase in the number of Internet users and market penetration in the regions of Russia; the growing popularity and availability of online payments; development of infrastructure for the execution of orders. Nevertheless, there are several factors specific particularly for the Russian e-commerce market that rather restrain its development: reduction in consumer incomes and marketing budgets, dynamics of the exchange currency rates, and the rise in prices for imported goods caused by overall stagnation in the economy of Russia due to foreign sanctions (Retailing in Russia, 2017).

Facing an increasing competition in the digital marketplace, firms are struggling to establish both behavioral and perceived loyalty. However, this would not be possible without understanding the drivers of loyalty in a particular market. As different points of view on consumer loyalty were developed in the literature, most of them predominantly include it is the components of behavioral and perceived loyalty. Behavioral loyalty determines the characteristics of consumer behavior, such as repeat purchases. Perceived loyalty reflects the preferences or opinions of consumers regarding company or product.

The purpose of the study is to explore the consumer loyalty factors affecting consumer decision making in the Russian e-commerce market. The study of consumer loyalty factors is one of the most important parts in building a company's marketing strategy. The study of factors will allow companies to draw attention to the strengths and weaknesses in the consumer-company relationships.

The paper consists of several parts. The first part is devoted to the study of theoretical foundations of the consumer loyalty phenomenon. Several approaches to determining loyalty are discussed and definitions of consumer loyalty in the context of e-commerce market are provided. The second part is devoted to discussion of consumer loyalty factors that most often found in the scientific literature. The third part presents the methodology used for an empirical research. The fourth part is devoted to results of factor and cluster analysis and conclusions.

2 Theoretical Framework

2.1 Consumer Loyalty in the E-Commerce Market

There are several approaches to the definition of loyalty. Cunningham [6, 7], Jones [21], Kahn, Kalvani, and Morrison [22], Kumar [23] worked on developing a first approach - a behavioral approach to loyalty. According to which, consumer behavior or consumer actions such as purchases, repeated purchases and their frequency can express consumer loyalty. The second approach was based on the consumer attitude or perception, and states that loyalty is an expression of the psychological preferences and opinions of consumers. Perceived loyalty is formed as a result of emotional assessments of the company or product by the consumer. The topic of perceived loyalty was investigated by Day [10], Lewis [25], Reichheld and Markey [28] and others. The main difference between the two approaches is that behavioral loyalty describes consumers' actions, while perceived loyalty defines consumers' emotions towards a product or a company.

Despite the sufficient elaboration of the first two approaches, Jacoby and Chestnut [18] believed that the study of consumer loyalty only on the basis of a behavioral or perceived component does not provide a complete understanding of this phenomenon. Therefore, an integrated approach to the definition of loyalty was first offered by Jacoby and Kyner [19]. They consider the importance of providing a link between behavior and perception of consumers in order to understand the causes and prerequisites of their loyalty to a particular object. Supporting this point of view Dick, Basu [11] noted that in order to understand consumer loyalty it is necessary to study behavioral and perceived loyalty simultaneously. They introduce their definition of loyalty, which takes into account both the relative perception of the brand and the repeated purchases [11].

Analysis of the existing research shows that there are differences regarding the measurement and conceptualization of traditional and electronic loyalty (e-loyalty). Gefen [15] provides the definition of electronic loyalty meaning users returning to the website and making repeated purchases. From the behavioral point of view, loyalty can be defined as the actual frequency and volume of consumer purchases, as well as the degree of positive WOM that consumers generate [14]. Srinivasan [30] determined electronic loyalty as an intention of consumers to make purchases from the same website and consumers' reluctance to switch to another website to purchase the same product. For a deeper understanding of consumer loyalty in the context of the e-commerce market, definitions are presented in Table 1.

Online loyalty as well as traditional loyalty is measured through an integrated approach that takes into account both behavioral and perceived loyalty. Behavioral online loyalty is expressed as the frequency of website visits and the time spent on the website. Perceived online loyalty is expressed as the intention to repeat a website visit, make a purchase on this website or recommend it to others.

2.2 Consumer Loyalty Factors

Based on the analysis of the existing research on consumer loyalty in the e-commerce market, the main consumer loyalty factors were derived. These factors are described below.

Online Store Reputation. Consumers perceive brands with a good reputation as a reliable indicator of high product quality [30]. A large number of players in the e-commerce market leads not only to a high competition, but also generates a large amount of information. Consumers are exposed to numerous signals and marketing campaigns from companies. To avoid information overload, consumers try to simplify the decision-making process of buying by evaluating the reputation of the brand or the online store.

Consumer Experience. This factor can also be considered as a duration of relationships between consumer and a company, particularly an online store. The company

Table 1. Definitions of consumer loyalty in the context of e-commerce market

	Author	Definition
1.	Tarafdar, Zhang [32]	Loyalty to the website is defined as the probability of repeated visits to the website by the same user
2.	Cyr [8]	Electronic loyalty is the intention to revisit the site or make a purchase in the future
3.	Doong [12]	Electronic loyalty is the intention to make purchases from the same online seller in the future
4.	Srinivasan, Anderson [30]	Electronic loyalty is a benevolent attitude of the consumer to electronic business, which manifests itself in making repeated purchases
5.	Liang [26]	Electronic loyalty is the psychological attachment of the consumer to the online seller, accompanied by the willingness of the consumer to maintain the "consumer-firm" relationship
6.	Flavian [13]	Electronic loyalty is the intention of the consumer to continue to make purchases from a certain website, without the intention to switch to other websites
7.	Wallace [33]	Consumer loyalty in relation to the online retailer is the relative and behavioral preference of the online retailer to alternatives of other suppliers
8.	Grondin [16]	Electronic loyalty is the desire of the consumer to make repeated purchases from the preferred online retailer
9.	Gefen [15]	Loyalty is the intention of the consumer to continue relationships with the same online retailer and recommend it to other consumers

should attract new consumers, while retaining the old ones. Old consumers are more loyal due to long-term cooperation and knowledge of the product. This lowers their need for consulting and assisting services from the company. Accordingly, such cooperation is beneficial for the company, since it can reduce operating costs [29]. Nevertheless, a consumer who has just come to the company can recommend it, because he is satisfied with the product and wants to share his positive impressions with others. Accordingly, there is a need to identify which of these categories of consumers would be more loyal.

Consumer Satisfaction. Understanding the key factors that lead to consumer satisfaction and loyalty is necessary to attract and retain profitable consumers in the e-commerce market. Jones and Sasser [21] have shown that the relationship between satisfaction and loyalty depends on the competition in the market. The e-commerce market is highly competitive, as competitors are closer to consumers nowadays through the power of the internet. Accordingly, companies in an online environment need to understand how they can increase consumer satisfaction and loyalty. Some researchers agree that satisfaction is a prerequisite for perceived loyalty such as providing recommendations [17]. In a situation of consumer satisfaction, recommendations and word of mouth tend to appear more often [1–3]. Yin Lam, Shankar, Erramilli [24] argue that a satisfied consumer recommends the supplier to other consumers. In their study, authors confirm the link between consumer satisfaction and perceived consumer loyalty as the willingness to recommend [24]. Anderson and Srinivasan [30] studied the effect of satisfaction on loyalty in the context of the e-commerce market. The authors define electronic satisfaction as consumer satisfaction with respect to their experience related to this firm in the e-commerce market. Scientists believe that the higher the level of satisfaction, the higher the level of loyalty in the e-commerce market [30].

Trust (vs. Risks). Trust is one of the most important drivers of loyalty; however, it is strongly affected and can be substantially deteriorated by the perceived risks, which in the digital marketplace are higher than in the traditional one. In the e-commerce market, consumers can face various risks, such as dishonest pricing, the provision of inaccurate or incomplete information about products, the distribution of personal information of consumers, the use of credit card data [15]. The existence of these risks necessitates the provision of certain guarantees from the online vendor, which can provide confidence on the part of consumers. Gefen [15] was able to prove the assumptions that consumer trust in an online vendor increases their loyalty and reduces perceived risks. The author also proved that the quality of service increases the consumer's trust in the online vendor [15].

Electronic Word of Mouth (e-wom). E-wom has a strong impact on the decision-making process and is a key factor in the online shopping market. Distribution of e-wom is possible through blogs, search engines, online communities, social networks, instant messengers. The emergence of such tools changes the format of interaction between consumers and companies - traditional personal interaction turns into informal communication in an online environment. According to several authors, e-wom is an informal type of communication between private parties about the valuation of goods or services [4, 27]. According to Hennig-Thurau, e-wom can be described as any positive or negative statement made by a potential, present or former customer of a product or company that is accessible to a large number of people and organizations via the internet [5, 17, 31]. Word of mouth communications play an important role in shaping the attitudes and behavior of potential consumers. It is assumed that consumers perceive wom as a more reliable, trustworthy type of communication. The speed and reach of the electronic wom is much higher and larger than the traditional wom, as the latter is limited in time and space [34]. Many online retailers try to encourage their consumers to generate an e-wom, as content from present consumers is more trusted by potential consumers [14, 20, 35].

3 Results of an Empirical Research

3.1 Methodology

The empirical study aims to identify consumer loyalty factors in the e-commerce market from the consumer behavior perspective. The study involved Russian consumers who purchased goods or services on the Internet at least once in the last 3 months. The criterion for the choice of respondents was the frequency and experience of making online purchases. Data was collected using the "Open Education" educational platform and respondents were participants of the online course in marketing. The survey was conducted using the questionnaire, to adopt it to the Russian language back translation procedure was used. Data collection took place from September 30 to November 18, 2018. The survey was voluntary, anonymous and did not involve any remuneration for its participants.

Operationalization. The questionnaire for the survey was developed based on scientific literature analysis and analysis of the Russian e-commerce market. Key blocks of factors were identified and defined the structure of the measurement tool. Respondents were asked to evaluate a set of 45 statements, which were evaluated on a seven-point Likert scale from 1 - absolutely disagree to 7 - absolutely agree. Over the course of analysis, 8 statements were excluded from the study.

Description of the Sample. The study involved 675 respondents. To exclude respondents without online shopping experience, the questionnaire was supplemented with two screening questions: about what online stores the respondents visit, and how often they purchase anything online or never. A preliminary analysis of the data showed that 74 respondents make purchases only in retail stores, and 16 of them have never made purchases on the Internet. Thus, the final sample included 601 respondents, the socio-demographic characteristics of which are presented in Table 2.

3.2 Factor Analysis Results

Following the exploratory nature of our study, in order to detect latent variables, a factor analysis was performed, which allows to move from a large number of indicator variables to a smaller number of factors. For carrying out the explanatory factor analysis in the SPSS software package, the following parameters were selected: the factor extraction method - the principal component method, the rotation method - varimax with Kaiser normalization.

To assess the applicability of factor analysis, it is necessary to consider the values of the Kaiser-Meier-Olkin criterion. The criterion of the adequacy of KMO is 0,914, which is more than 0,5, respectively, the data of factor analysis have a high adequacy and suitability. The Bartlett sphericity criterion with a significance of 0,000 < 0,05 indicates that the data is suitable for conducting factor analysis. As a result of factor analysis, 9 factors were identified (Table 3). Factor loadings explain the significance of each parameter in the bigger factor. The data of the full explained variance shows that the 9 factors explain 73,7% of the variance in the data.

The first factor is related to all statements regarding consumer satisfaction, particularly with satisfaction in general meaning online shopping experience meets expectations of consumers, happiness with online shopping and satisfaction with the quality of goods, services offered by online stores.

The second factor defines online store reputation. This factor is represented by a variety of variables that describe honest and truthful behavior of an online store without inflation of prices and hidden commissions.

Third factor represents the consumer experience. Consumers tend to make repeated purchases from the same online store in the future if their experience was positive. Fourth factor describes risks consumers face during online shopping such as safety of

Table 2. Description of the sample of the empirical research

Sample selection criterion	Sample characteristic	Number of respondents	Share, %
Sex	Men	120	20,0%
	Women	481	80,0%
Age	18–25	415	69,1%
	26–30	83	13,8%
	31–35	41	6,8%
	36–40	37	6,2%
	41–50	19	3,2%
	51–60	3	0,5%
Education	Secondary general education	48	8,0%
	Secondary special education	9	1,5%
	Incomplete higher education	297	49,5%
	Higher education	197	32,8%
	Two or more higher education	38	6,3%
	Present PhD/Doctor Degree	11	1,8%
Income level	Low	12	2,0%
	Middle (average)	436	72,9%
	High	150	25,1%
Marital status	Single (not married)	373	62,3%
	Married	108	18,0%
	Living together	72	12,0%
	Living apart	3	0,5%
	Divorced	9	1,5%
	Widowed	4	0,7%

personal data, credit card data etc. The fifth factor describes the ease of online shopping. The sixth factor represents client orientation of an online store. The seventh factor is related to online store competence, in particular it describes technical capabilities and the necessary competencies for doing business on the Internet. The eighth factor represents e-wom and the ninth factor describes the amount or reviews in the internet.

3.3 Cluster Analysis Results

In addition to factor analysis (see Table 3), a cluster analysis was conducted in order to identify the characteristics of consumer groups with prevailing behavioral models. The cluster analysis was carried out in two stages: at the first stage, the hierarchical clustering algorithm was applied, at the second - K-means clustering. The hierarchical clustering algorithm provides agglomeration coefficients. The analysis of the graph of the differences between agglomeration coefficients helps to identify a number of possible clusters – three (Table 4). When identifying three clusters, the differences

Table 3. Factor analysis results

Factor	Indicator	Factor loadings		
		1	2	3
Consumer satisfaction	Decision to start buying online was the right decision	,824		
	My online shopping experience meets my expectations	,794		
	I'm glad I started buying on the Internet	,784		
	I am happy with my online shopping	,753		
	I will continue to buy online	,753		
	In general, I am satisfied with the quality of goods/services offered by online stores	,680		
	If I need something, I will buy it on the Internet.	,584		
Online store reputation	Online stores behave truthfully towards consumers		,774	
	Online stores do not inflate prices at the time of sale		,762	
	Online stores behave honestly in relation to consumers		,702	
	Online stores comply with consumer commitments		,679	
	In general, prices in online stores are not too high		,671	
	Online stores respect consumers		,652	
	In general, online shopping can be trusted		,616	
Consumer experience	I will make the next purchase in the online store, where I have already bought before			,841
	I will make a purchase in the online store where I already bought before during the next year			,814
	I intend to continue to make purchases in the online store, in which I have already bought before, and I am not going to refuse from it			,787
	If I had to buy the same product again, I would buy it in the same online store			,764
Risks	I worry that my financial data may be transferred to other companies without my consent	,884		
	I worry about the safety of personal data on the Internet	,874		
	I feel uncomfortable leaving my bank card number on the Internet	,866		
	I worry about the safety of financial transactions on the Internet	,845		
	Messages sent via the Internet can be read by unauthorized people or companies without my knowledge	,745		

(*continued*)

Table 3. (*continued*)

Factor	Indicator	Factor loadings		
		1	2	3
Ease of making online purchases	It's easy for me to interact with an online store while making a purchase		,785	
	It is easy for me to perform any operations during the purchase in the online store		,771	
	It is easy for me to shop online		,769	
	In general, shopping online is easy		,762	
Customer orientation	Most online stores prove in practice that the consumer is always right			,751
	Most online stores work for clients			,731
	Most online stores demonstrate attentiveness, care, honesty and goodwill towards consumers, providing the basis for creating good relationships with them			,722
Online store competence	Most online stores have the necessary technical capabilities for doing business on the Internet	,776		
	Most online stores have the necessary competencies for doing business on the Internet	,741		
	Technological difficulties should not impede online shopping	,703		
e-wom	I write long reviews (more than 1–2 sentences)		,920	
	Over the past year I have been posting reviews online more often		,909	
Number of reviews	The more reviews, the higher the likelihood that I will choose a product and/or store to buy			,885
	I pay attention to the number of reviews when choosing a product and/or store			,877

between the behavioral characteristics of the respondents turn out to be maximal. On the contrary, when selecting four, five or six clusters, these differences are not so noticeable, therefore, three clusters are chosen as the optimal number.

The first cluster "Dedicated online shoppers" is the most numerous and includes 41% of respondents. Representatives of this cluster are satisfied with online shopping in general. As they have positive online shopping experience they plan to make repeated purchases from the same online store in the future. These consumers tend not to pay attention to e-wom and online reviews. As much as this category of consumers are professional online consumers, they still worry about the safety of financial transactions on the Internet.

Table 4. Cluster analysis results

Cluster	Share	Characteristics
"Dedicated online shoppers"	226 (41%)	Consumer satisfaction Consumer experience Online store reputation Customer orientation
"Selectively trusting" - consumers with trust to selected online stores only	172 (32%)	Online store reputation Online store competence Importance of e-wom communications and the number of reviews Ease of making online purchases Distrust for online shopping due to risks
"Conservative consumers"	148 (27%)	Dissatisfaction with online shopping Uneasy experience of making online purchases Distrust for online shopping due to risks, lack of competence and client orientation Importance of e-wom communications and the number of reviews

The second cluster ("Selectively trusting") accounts for 32% of respondents and describes consumers who are generally satisfied with their experience and who appreciate competence and reputation of online stores. The most highly evaluated indicators include those of online store competence factor such as technical capabilities and the necessary competencies for doing business on the Internet. It is easy for them to interact with an online store while making a purchase. These consumers tend to write reviews on the internet and spread e-wom. As well as the first group of consumers these clients tend to worry about that their "financial data may be transferred to other companies without their consent" or that "Messages sent via the Internet can be read by unauthorized people or companies without their knowledge".

The third cluster ("Conservative consumers") accounts for 27% of respondents and represents conservative group of consumers. These consumers are not satisfied with their experience, as it does not meet their expectations. It is not easy for them to make online purchases in general. These consumers tend to think that online stores do not have the right competencies to do online business and are not customer oriented. The highly evaluated indicators include those of e-wom and amount of reviews.

4 Conclusion

Current study aimed to investigate the specifics of consumer behavior in Russian e-commerce market with the main focus on the drivers of consumer loyalty. The identified clusters reveal three main groups of consumers according to their perception of digital marketplace, its risks and opportunities. Even with assumption that our sample included advanced internet users, only less than half of them belonged to the cluster of dedicated online shoppers. This means that the majority of respondents are well aware of the risks in the area of e-commerce, which is perceived as a limiting factor, guiding consumers to a very selected pattern of online shopping (32% of respondents) or substantially avoiders of online shopping (27%).

Following the trend of prevailing risks perception of consumers, despite numerous opportunities of obtaining additional value through online purchases, trust becomes the new currency in the internet. It is through even more careful business processes, communication and consumer service that firms might transfer consumers from the "selectively trusting" cluster to "dedicated shoppers".

It is obvious from the results of the exploratory factor analysis, that consumer satisfaction and store reputation are the guiding factors with the largest portions of explained variance of respondents' behavior online. In other words, the future consumer behavior is systematically defined through the experience and results of the previous service encounters. It is always possible to minimize online presence, however, in some areas, consumers are being truly "pushed" online as, for example, online travel agencies and services are dramatically reducing the opportunity window for traditional travel agencies. For emerging markets, like Russia, this finding means what matters for the consumers is the combination of the single service encounter with the perceived overall satisfaction with the previous encounters, in other words, combinatory efforts of market players interacting with the consumer. It is about a balance between the risks and opportunities that shapes the overall consumer perception of a digital marketplace as being trustworthy and full of opportunities or too risky.

The implications for businesses, researchers and educators, as well as policymakers are connected with educating consumers and developing their digital competencies in order to make informed choices in the digital marketplace, understand business and marketing practices, the risks and advantages of digital data collection and of the collaborative opportunities.

Acknowledgment. The paper was prepared within the working group "Sharing Economy as an Innovative Business Model" at the Faculty of Business and Management at the National Research University Higher School of Economics (HSE University) in 2019 (grant № AAAA-A19-119081290039-7) and within the framework of the Russian Academic Excellence Project «5-100».

References

1. Anderson, E.W., Mittal, V.: Strengthening the satisfaction – profit chain. J. Serv. Res. **3**(2), 107–120 (2000)
2. Anderson, E.W., Sullivan, M.W.: The antecedents and consequences of customer satisfaction for firms. Mark. Sci. **12**(2), 125–143 (1993). https://doi.org/10.1287/mksc.12.2.125
3. Anderson, R.E., Swaminathan, S.: Customer satisfaction and loyalty in e-markets: a PLS path modeling approach. J. Mark. Theory Pract. **19**(2), 221–234 (2011). https://doi.org/10.2753/MTP1069-6679190207

4. Casaló, L.V., Flavián, C., Guinalíu, M.: The role of satisfaction and website usability in developing customer loyalty and positive word-of-mouth in the e-banking services. Int. J. Bank Mark. **26**(6), 399–417 (2008)
5. Chevalier, J.A., Mayzlin, D.: The effect of word of mouth on sales: online book reviews. J. Mark. Res. **43**(3), 345–354 (2006)
6. Cunningham, R.M.: Brand loyalty – what, where, how much. Harv. Bus. Rev. **34**(1), 116–128 (1956)
7. Cunningham, R.M.: Customer loyalty to store and brand. Harv. Bus. Rev. **39**(6), 127–137 (1961)
8. Cyr, D.: Modeling web site design across cultures: relationships to trust, satisfaction, and e-loyalty. J. Manag. Inf. Syst. **24**(4), 47–72 (2008). https://doi.org/10.2753/MIS0742-1222240402
9. Data Insight research. http://datainsight.ru/ecommerce_2018
10. Day, G.S.: A two-dimensional concept of brand loyalty. In: Mathematical Models in Marketing. Lecture Notes in Economics and Mathematical Systems (Operations Research), vol. 132, pp. 89–99. Springer, Heidelberg (1976). https://doi.org/10.1007/978-3-642-51565-1_26
11. Dick, A.S., Basu, K.: Customer loyalty: toward an integrated conceptual framework. J. Acad. Mark. Sci. **22**(2), 99–113 (1994). https://doi.org/10.1177/0092070394222001
12. Doong, H.S., Wang, H.C., Shih, H.C.: Exploring loyalty intention in the electronic marketplace. Electron. Mark. **18**(2), 142–149 (2008). https://doi.org/10.1080/10196780802044792
13. Flavián, C., Guinalíu, M., Gurrea, R.: The role played by perceived usability, satisfaction and consumer trust on website loyalty. Inf. Manag. **43**(1), 1–14 (2006). https://doi.org/10.1016/j.im.2005.01.002
14. Gauri, D.K., Bhatnagar, A., Rao, R.: Role of word of mouth in online store loyalty. Commun. ACM **51**(3), 89–91 (2008). https://doi.org/10.1145/1325555.1325572
15. Gefen, D.: Customer loyalty in e-commerce. J. Assoc. Inf. Syst. **3**(1), 2 (2002). https://doi.org/10.17705/1jais.00022
16. Grondin, B.: A Framework of E-loyalty Levers. Master's thesis, Concordia University, Canada (2003)
17. Hennig-Thurau, T., Gwinner, K.P., Walsh, G., Gremler, D.D.: Electronic word-of-mouth via consumer-opinion platforms: what motivates consumers to articulate themselves on the internet? J. Interact. Mark. **18**(1), 38–52 (2004). https://doi.org/10.1002/dir.10073
18. Jacoby, J., Chestnut, R.W.: Brand loyalty: measurement and management. J. Advert. (1978). https://doi.org/10.1080/00913367.1979.10717981
19. Jacoby, J., Kyner, D.B.: Brand loyalty vs. repeat purchasing behavior. J. Mark. Res. **10**, 1–9 (1973). https://doi.org/10.2307/3149402
20. Jean Harrison-Walker, L.: E-complaining: a content analysis of an internet complaint forum. J. Serv. Mark. **15**(5), 397–412 (2001)
21. Jones, T.O., Sasser, W.E.: Why satisfied customers defect. Harv. Bus. Rev. **73**(6), 88 (1995)
22. Kahn, B.E., Kalwani, M.U., Morrison, D.G.: Measuring variety-seeking and reinforcement behaviors using panel data. J. Mark. Res. **23**(2), 89–100 (1986)
23. Kumar Roy, S., Lassar, W.M., Butaney, G.T.: The mediating impact of stickiness and loyalty on word-of-mouth promotion of retail websites: a consumer perspective. Eur. J. Mark. **48**(9/10), 1828–1849 (2014)
24. Lam, S.Y., Shankar, V., Erramilli, M.K., Murthy, B.: Customer value, satisfaction, loyalty, and switching costs: an illustration from a business-to-business service context. J. Acad. Mark. Sci. **32**(3), 293–311 (2004)

25. Lewis, M.: The influence of loyalty programs and short-term promotions on customer retention. J. Mark. Res. **41**(3), 281–292 (2004)
26. Liang, C.J., Chen, H.J., Wang, W.H.: Does online relationship marketing enhance customer retention and cross-buying? Serv. Ind. J. **28**(6), 769–787 (2008)
27. Litvin, S.W., Goldsmith, R.E., Pan, B.: Electronic word-of-mouth in hospitality and tourism management. Tour. Manag. **29**(3), 458–468 (2008)
28. Reichheld, F.F., Markey, R.: The Ultimate Question 2.0: How Net Promoter Companies Thrive in a Customer-driven World. Harvard Business Press (2011)
29. Reichheld, F.F., Teal, T., Smith, D.K.: The Loyalty Effect, vol. 1, no. 3, pp. 78–84. Harvard Business School Press, Boston (1996)
30. Srinivasan, S.S., Anderson, R., Ponnavolu, K.: Customer loyalty in e-commerce: an exploration of its antecedents and consequences. J. Retail. **78**(1), 41–50 (2002). https://doi.org/10.1016/S0022-4359(01)00065-3
31. Sun, T., Youn, S., Wu, G., Kuntaraporn, M.: Online word-of-mouth (or mouse): an exploration of its antecedents and consequences. J. Comput. Mediat. Commun. **11**(4), 1104–1127 (2006). https://doi.org/10.1111/j.1083-6101.2006.00310.x
32. Tarafdar, M., Zhang, J.: Determinants of reach and loyalty – a study of website performance and implications for website design. J. Comput. Inf. Syst. **48**(2), 16–24 (2008). https://doi.org/10.1080/08874417.2008.11646005
33. Wallace, D.W., Giese, J.L., Johnson, J.L.: Customer retailer loyalty in the context of multiple channel strategies. J. Retail. **80**(4), 249–263 (2004)
34. Yoo, C.W., Sanders, G.L., Moon, J.: Exploring the effect of E-WOM participation on E-loyalty in E-commerce. Decis. Support Syst. **55**(3), 669–678 (2013)
35. Zeithaml, V.A., Berry, L.L., Parasuraman, A.: The behavioral consequences of service quality. J. Mark., 31–46 (1996) https://doi.org/10.2307/1251929

Towards an Integrative Framework of Consumers' Digital Competences

Ksenia Golovacheva(✉) and Maria Smirnova

Graduate School of Management, Saint Petersburg State University, Volkhovsky 3, Saint Petersburg 199004, Russian Federation
{k.golovacheva, smirnova}@gsom.spbu.ru

Abstract. The paper provides an overview of existing digital competence frameworks and identifies their commonalities, differences and potential complementarities to help researchers, practitioners and policy makers develop better managerial interventions. The paper offers an integrative framework that specifies consumers' digital competences, their antecedents and consequences. A proposed approach emphasizes the need to investigate consumers' motivations, opportunities and knowledge as equally important prerequisites of effective and efficient consumer behavior in digital consumption encounters. Besides, an approach goes beyond the registration of consumers' digital behaviors, but requires estimating their efficiency. Directions for development of optimal intervention strategies to stimulate consumers' digital behaviors are proposed. The paper concludes with a set of propositions for further development of the consumers' digital competence framework.

Keywords: Digital competence · Consumers · Digital literacy

1 Introduction

Consumption-related activities such as buying products, searching for information about products, making reviews, interacting with firms after the product/service purchase are among the most popular activities that Internet users realize in their everyday life. Each activity demands different types of digital competences that relate to both general and consumption domain. Multiple frameworks to measure and track digital competences have appeared over time. Surprisingly there is still no consensus regarding what constitutes consumers' digital competences. Consequently, there is high risk that the application of any of existing frameworks without critical assessment will result in incomplete or, even worse, wrong understanding of digital development processes, which can undermine the success of public or corporate digital interventions aimed at consumers.

While the area of consumers' digital competences studies is gradually evolving, and new related concepts keep appearing (such as media literacy, digital maturity, digital engagement) [9, 15, 18], the extant literature has a number of limitations. Firstly, extant studies overemphasize technological aspects of consumers' digital competences and fail to integrate other aspects of consumer behavior that may influence how consumers think, feel and act in digital marketplace. Second, extant literature is fragmented

D. A. Alexandrov et al. (Eds.): DTGS 2019, CCIS 1038, pp. 281–291, 2019.
https://doi.org/10.1007/978-3-030-37858-5_23

and does not demonstrate how various competences are related. Hence, further development of this area requires systematization of current findings and integration of multiple viewpoints on consumers' digital competences.

The objective of this study is to develop an integrative framework of consumers' digital competences that would help researchers, practitioners and policy makers to better understand the scope of consumers' digital development trajectories. First, we reviewed existing frameworks of digital competences, their explicit declarative and denotative definitions, descriptions and measurements. Second, using interpretative content analysis, we identified their commonalities, predominant differences and potential complementarities. Finally, the model of consumers' digital competences is proposed that integrates the results of previous studies and present the list of consumer digital competences, their antecedents and consequences.

The paper is structured as follows: first, the key terms are introduced. Second, an overview of existing digital competence frameworks is presented, followed by discussion of the results of comparative analysis. Third, an integrative framework and its main elements are described. Finally, propositions for next steps have been formulated.

2 Theoretical Background

2.1 General Digital Competences

Multiple digital competence frameworks have been developed recently. Some frameworks are universal and can be applied to assess general digital competences that are necessary for individuals to realize any activities online. For instance, the European Digital Competence Framework for Citizens, known as DigComp [3], identifies five key components of digital competence – information and data literacy, communication and collaboration, digital content creation, safety, and problem solving – with 21 related competences [3]. DigComp does not include two critical areas: (i) fundamentals of familiarity with hardware and software, which is often taken for granted in mode developed countries; and (ii) career-related competences, which would help make generic competences more relevant to country contexts through practical examples of their use. As a result, UNESCO proposed a new Global Framework to Measure Digital Literacy that included previously lacking components and covered seven areas of competence [1]. Further frameworks include Digital Capability Framework (JISC), Digital Intelligence Framework (World Economic Forum) and others that contain both overlapping and distinctive characteristics of digital competences.

In parallel with the appearance of new general digital competence frameworks, further more specialized frameworks appear. For instance, new frameworks have been derived from DigComp for new contexts where digital competence is needed, the Digital Competence Framework for Consumers (DigCompConsumers) and the Digital Competence Framework for Teachers (DigCompTeach). The need for more narrow frameworks is defined by the fact that there is a variety of context-specific competences that are necessary to realize context-specific activities.

2.2 Consumers' Digital Competences

The set of competences is specific to the context where the activity is realized. Online consumer activities predominantly include consumption of information, products and services, which includes detection of significant and reliable information out of the information clutter, evaluation and interpretation of marketing claims (including misleading claims and covert tactics, consumption of offline products products/services via online channels, consumption of digital products services, replacement of offline products/services with digital products/services, adoption of innovative technologies, products and services [14]. At the same time, consumers increasingly become part of the process of production and co-production of information and products/services, which includes content generation (market mavens, opinion leaders), co-production of products/services (customization [11], lead users [13], emergent nature consumers [12], online know-how exchange [4, 5]).

Consumers' digital activities are affected by their ability to adopt, understand and use the technology, as well as understand how technology affects their choice and behavior. Lack of knowledge may lead to the cases of consumer knowledge discrimination [19]. Increasing knowledge and consumers' education can lead to increase in literacy and widen the spectrum of activities implemented in digital marketplace. On the contrary, using omnipresent digital opportunities without being sufficiently educated can lead to stimulating consumers skepticism and even result in avoidance behavior [10]. Moreover, consumers differ according the speed of digital consumption adoption, involvement in co-production of information and products/services in the digital environment.

To engage actively, safely and assertively in digital marketplace activities, consumers need specific competences. According to the Digital Competence Framework for Consumers, known as DigCompConsumers [3], these competences should help consumers make informed choices in the digital marketplace, operate safely online, understand digital marketing and advertising practices, manage online financial operations and understand the risks and advantages of digital data collection [3]. *DigCompConsumers framework* outlines 14 competences that are grouped in three main areas: pre-purchase, purchase and post-purchase. This Framework focuses exclusively on those aspects that are relevant in the context of consumers' competences in digital environments. General digital competences that consumers as users of technologies will have to acquire as a pre-requisite to function in a digital environment and consumer competences that are not specific to the digital world are not included in the framework. Moreover, these consumers' competences require regular updating in the fast-speed and turbulent environment [3].

Consumer Savvy Index [15] delineates six broad characteristics which enable consumers interact effectively with organizations: technological sophistication and innovative expertise, interpersonal network competence, online network competence, marketing literacy, complaining and specifying self-efficacy, and information flow expectations.

The aspects of consumers' ability to adopt certain patterns of digital activities according to their psychographic profile were adopted in the *Technographics model*, developed by E. Forrest who suggested that the profiling of technology consumers should be based on variables which focuses on the motivations, ownership, usage patterns, and attitudes toward information, communication and entertainment technologies as well as measures of personal values and lifestyle perspective [8]. In the context of digital technology adoption, A. Sharikov highlights four components of digital literacy – two defensive competences (protection from technological and socio-psychological threats) and two proactive competences (usage of technological and socio-communication opportunities) [22]. This model includes both proactive and defensive competencies, which might affect consumer behavior and actual consumption in the digital marketplace [6].

As an example of a framework, adopted in an emerging market context, Regional public organization "Center for Internet Technologies" (ROCIT) also developed a *Digital Literacy Index* to assess and monitor the development of digital competences of Russian citizens. Despite ROCIT Digital Literacy Index is positioned as a general literacy index, it includes a variety of competences that are relevant to the consumption context, for instance the usage of Internet for different consumptions purposes (such as search for information, financial transactions, consumption of goods and services and others) [20].

3 Methodology

In order to systematize existing knowledge ondigital competences, we critically reviewed four core existing frameworks, as well as analyzed their explicit declarative and denotative definitions, descriptions and measurements. Selected frameworks had specific focus on digital consumer competences and included: DigCompConsumers framework [3], Consumer Savvy Index [15], Technographics model by Forrester Research (e.g. [8]) and ROCIT Digital Literacy Index [20] that represents an index, developed specifically for emerging market context. Using interpretative content analysis we identified a number of characteristics that these frameworks have. As a result both overlapping and distinctive features of each framework have been revealed.

4 Results of Analysis

4.1 Comparative Analysis of Consumers' Digital Competence Frameworks

The review of four digital competence frameworks helped to identify 16 competences that are necessary to realize various consumer behaviors in 6 broader areas which are information, interaction, consumption, protection, self-responsibility and innovations. Surprisingly, there is currently no framework that simultaneously addresses all 16 competences (see Table 1).

Further analysis revealed that the four frameworks are different and limited in the number of tasks they solve (see Table 2). The explored frameworks predominantly register consumers' actual digital behavior. In other words, they focus merely on the factual usage of digital technologies for consumption purposes without specifying

Table 1. Consumers' digital competences considered in various frameworks

Consumer competence areas & competences	Consideration of competence in the framework			
	DigCompConsumers framework	Technographics model	Consumer Savvy Index	ROCIT Digital Literacy Index
Information competences				
Browsing, searching and filtering information on goods and services	√	√	√	√
Evaluating and comparing information on goods and services	√	√	√	
Recognizing and evaluating commercial communication and advertisement	√	√	√	√
Interaction competences				
Interacting in the digital marketplace to buy and sell	√	√	√	
Sharing information with other consumers in the digital marketplace	√	√	√	√
Consumption competences				
Participating in collaborative economy platforms	√	√		
Managing payments and finances through digital means	√	√		√
Understanding copyrights, licenses, and contracts of digital goods and services	√	√		√
Protection competencies				
Managing personal data and privacy	√	√	√	√
Protecting health and safety	√			√
Asserting consumer rights in the digital marketplace			√	
Self-responsibility competences				
Identifying digital consumer competence gaps and limits	√			√
Considering responsible and sustainable consumption in digital markets	√			√
Managing digital identity and profile in the digital marketplace	√	√		√
Innovative competences				
Adopting innovative products and technologies		√	√	
Co-creating products and services with companies				

whether they are used efficiently. For instance, ROCIT Digital Literacy Index simply tracks the accomplishment of different behaviors over a particular time period (e.g. making financial transactions or buying products online over last 12 months). All these online transactions are claimed to demonstrate consumers' digital literacy and proficiency. However, the mere fact of undertaking digital actions does not indicate whether these actions were realized efficiently. Some consumers might have encountered multiple troubles or spent excessive resources when undertaking those actions, while others successfully completed digital tasks efficiently using their financial, time and psychological resources. Notwithstanding, ROCIT Digital Literacy Index will refer to all consumers who eventually realized those actions as digitally literate, which definitely provides a biased estimation of digital literacy.

According to the motivation-opportunity-ability (MOA) model, effective behavior is defined by a combination of the three drivers [16, 21]. Motivation represents individual's intrinsic or external incentives to behave. Opportunity represents the combination of direct and, at least in the short run, uncontrollable factors surrounding the individual and the task environment that inhibit or enable behavior, such as the availability of time and resources. The M-O-A model has been recently successfully applied to explain consumer behavior in various contexts [17], including the context of digital marketplace: consumer virtual co-creation [2] and customer-to-customer online know-how exchange [4].

The analysis of consumers' digital competence frameworks has revealed their focus on the factual consumer behavior rather on its drivers, including their motivation behind digital behavior, technical opportunities for digital behavior, and digital knowledge. The exceptions include Consumer Savvy Index that measures consumer knowledge, Technographics model that studies consumers' motivation and develop their psychographic profile, and ROCIT Digital Literacy Index that measures the consumers' access to internet. Still, these examples are rather proving the fact that the majority of frameworks are focused on what consumers already adopted in their regular practices, and the drivers of digital behavior are addressed fragmentally.

DigCompConsumers framework provided and alternative perspective on consumer behavior in the digital marketplace and proposed that it is competences that drive efficient digital behavior. However, DigCompConsumers framework is a conceptual framework that just list consumer competences, but does not explain how they relate to motivation, opportunities and knowledge.

It is essential to highlight, that most of the existing frameworks do include both registration of the behavior and assumption that the realized behavior is and indicator of consumer competence. Alternatively, we posit that registering actual behaviors could be used only as a proxy indicator of ad-hoc ability to commit a particular behavior, but does not serve as a valid indicator of digital competence which is an ability to systematically commit a behavior effectively and efficiently.

4.2 An Integrative Framework of Consumers' Digital Competences

In order to understand the complex nature of consumers' digital behavior, there are multiple drivers of digital behavior that should be taken into account. An integrative approach to consumers' digital competences requires several steps to improve existing frameworks. First, there is a need to extend existing measurement models and monitor not only actual digital behavior components, but also their antecedents – motivation, opportunity, knowledge and competence. These are equally important prerequisites for consumer engagement into digital technology and environment. Understanding full spectrum of behavioral drivers could help develop more accurate managerial interventions. Second, there is a need to go beyond registering consumers' digital behavior, and to estimate its efficiency. Third, the spectrum of competences to be included into the integrative framework must be extended. The framework presented in the paper is specifically designed to address the specified challenges (see Fig. 1).

Table 2. Comparative analysis of tasks solved by different frameworks

Framework	Tasks					
	Identify motivation behind digital behavior	Identify technical opportunities for digital behavior	Identify digital knowledge	Assess digital competence	Register digital behavior	Estimate digital behavior efficiency
DigCompConsumers framework				√*		
Consumer Savvy Index			√		√	
Technographics model	√				√	
ROCIT Digital Literacy Index		√	√		√	
Current framework	√	√	√	√	√	√

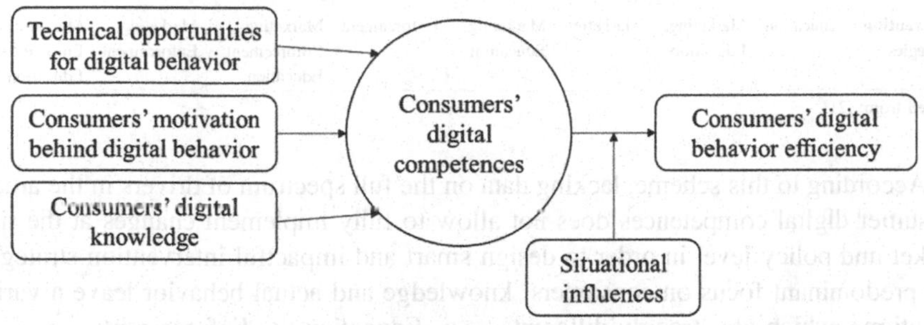

Fig. 1. An integrative framework of consumers' digital competences

An integrative framework of consumers' digital competences considers competences as a core driver of efficient digital behavior, while consumers' motivation, opportunities, and knowledge serve as drivers of competence development. The presence of consumers' digital competences does not obligatory translate into efficient digital behavior because of various situational influences (such as time constraints, cognitive load, etc.).

Finally, there is a need to link the consumers' digital competence framework with managerial instructions. According to M. Rothschild [21], there are three intervention strategies to influence digital behavior. They are metaphorically called *Education*, *Marketing* and *Enforcement*. *Education* is defined as providing messages of any type that attempt to inform and/or persuade a target to behave voluntarily in a particular manner but do not provide, on their own, direct and/or immediate reward or punishment. *Education* thus focuses on informing the user of the value of a particular behavior without explicitly promising the delivery of this value. *Marketing* entails attempts to manage behavior by offering reinforcing incentives and/or consequences in an environment that invites voluntary exchange. Both *Education & Marketing* are similar as they involve voluntary, uncoerced behavior. However, unlike *Education*, *Marketing* offers an explicit exchange of a defined benefit in return for the desired behavior, whereas *Education* only imply or identify a benefit that the person must derive on their own. *Enforcement* involves the use of coercion to achieve behavior in a nonvoluntary manner or to threaten with punishment for noncompliance or inappropriate behavior. Whereas *Marketing* relies on self-monitoring and self-sanctioning to receive the desired benefit, *Enforcement* relies on external controls to achieve the desired outcomes. Depending on the presence or absence of motivation, technical opportunities and knowledge, certain intervention strategies will provide superior results (see Table 3).

Table 3. Intervention prescriptions for different combinations of consumers' motivation (M), opportunities (O), and knowledge (K)

M	+				–			
O	+		–		+		–	
K	+	–	+	–	+	–	+	–
Intervention strategies	Education	Marketing, Education	Marketing	Marketing, Education	Enforcement	Marketing, Enforcement, Education	Marketing, Enforcement	Marketing, Enforcement, Education

Adapted from: [21].

According to this scheme, lacking data on the full spectrum of drivers in the area of consumer digital competences does not allow to fully implement changes at the firm, market and policy level in order to design smart and impactful intervention strategies. The predominant focus on consumers' knowledge and actual behavior leave a variety of options, which are strongly different – e.g. *Education* vs. *Enforcement*.

5 Discussion

Following growing attention to active development of digital marketplace, researchers and policy-makers are suggesting frameworks to evaluate what is going on in the market. Most indices illustrate how well the economies are doing in adopting the digital technologies. While economies are represented by individuals, the indices are aggregating the measures of individual competences for successful integration in the digital marketplace. As the leading area of using digital technologies affects individual consumption, the indices are either integrating the measures of consumption competences or focus specifically on the consumption angle of individual digital behavior.

There are also several directions for further development of an integrated approach specified in form of following propositions.

Proposition 1. *Consumer digital competences can be aligned with consumer decision journey stages (pre-purchase, during the purchase, after the purchase) with increasing role of consumer participation in the after-purchase stage of interaction, e.g. innovation and co-creation.*

Thus DigCompConsumers (the European Commission) represents a full spectrum of consumer activities and abilities which are conceptualized as required for a safe consumer behavior in the digital marketplace. In addition to the list of activities, competences and abilities of consumers they also apply the consumer purchase stages or consumer decision journey stages. Over the last decade the McKinsey concept of customer decision journey [7] has been integrated with the classic marketing approaches, and now the concept of consumer digital competences can be re-evaluated through these lenses.

Proposition 2. *Digital competences are to be considered in line with the psychographic or technographic profile of consumers.*

The specifics of the consumer motivation has been addressed in the Technographic model (Forrester Research), whereas the readiness and motivation of consumers to be involved in the social interaction, blogging, reviewing, e-wom can be defined as a characteristics, that can be developed, but still stays relatively stable over time. In other words, consumers who tend to be more innovative might also be flagmen in blogging and creating online content, while laggards might be involved in liking at maximum. This angle might add to understanding and conceptualizing the motivation driver of digital consumer competences.

Proposition 3. *Digital literacy should be enriched through the knowledge in the area of marketing and consumer behavior, including the concepts on consumer marketing literacy and consumer persuasion knowledge.*

As suggested by the DigCompConsumers (the European Commission) the digital literacy should increasingly include the elements, related to understanding the practices of firms in the digital marketspace. However, there is lacking interaction between the streams of research that addresses consumer digital competences and consumer marketing literacy, affecting persuasion knowledge and minimizing consumer knowledge discrimination.

Proposition 4. *The factors, affecting perceived opportunity or barriers to use the opportunity, should be included in the frameworks of consumer digital competences.*

The opportunity driver is omitted in most of the frameworks, and while included refers to the technological availability of broadband internet or social media. While these are important enablers, their presence is not enough to be considered an opportunity. On the contrary, it is consumer behavior related drivers which might turn an opportunity into a barrier when being perceived as risky or dangerous. Existing studies on consumer trust, risk perception and market skepticism can be addressed in order to enrich existing frameworks in order to include this MOA driver.

6 Conclusion

It is the main purpose of existing digital competences/literacy frameworks to structure the skills, knowledge and competences required by the consumers to be further involved in the abovementioned activities. These frameworks can be classified in (a) more general models aiming at educating wide circles of potential users of digital technologies and (b) models which specifically target consumers, in other words, account for the influences and expected outcomes of the consumption process in the digital marketplace.

The overseen frameworks have provided a basis for systematization, identification of their commonalities and differences. They serve the purpose of measuring digital activities and through them the assumed level of competences of consumers in the digital marketplace. However, the conducted analysis has revealed a strong bias of existing frameworks towards the actual behavior-based approach with lacking attention to motivation and perceived opportunities according to MOA framework. Moreover, as the stream of consumer digital competences' models appear as a separate field of investigation, the models fail to address the advances in the marketing or consumer behavior disciplines in order to provide a comprehensive approach that would not only aim for a safe and legal consumer behavior, but also to help consumers identify the desirable mode of their involvement in the digital marketspace or maybe even optimal educational trajectory in order to gain maximum value from the technology in accordance with the consumer aims, objectives, and technographic profile.

Acknowledgement. The Saint Petersburg State University's research support (project ID 40940187) is gratefully appreciated.

References

1. Antoninis, M., Montoya, S.: A global framework to measure digital literacy. http://uis.unesco.org/en/blog/global-framework-measure-digital-literacy. Accessed 10 Jan 2019
2. Bettiga, D., Lamberti, L., Noci, G.: Investigating social motivations, opportunity and ability to participate in communities of virtual co-creation. Int. J. Consum. Stud. **41**(1), 155–163 (2018)
3. Brečko, B., Ferrari, A.: The digital competence framework for consumers. Joint Research Center (JRC) Science for Policy Report, EUR28133EN (2016)
4. Briliana, V., Wahid, N.A., Fernando, Y.: The effect of motivation, opportunity, ability and social identity towards customer-to-customer online know-how exchange. Adv. Sci. Lett. **21**(4), 819–822 (2015)
5. Dessart, L., Veloutsou, C., Morgan-Thomas, A.: Capturing consumer engagement: duality, dimensionality and measurement. J. Mark. Manag. **32**(5–6), 399–426 (2016)
6. Dommeyer, C.J., Gross, B.L.: What consumers know and what they do: an investigation of consumer knowledge, awareness, and use of privacy protection strategies. J. Interact. Mark. **17**(2), 34–51 (2003)
7. Edelman, D.C., City, A.: Branding in the digital age. Harv. Bus. Rev. **88**(12), 62–69 (2010)

8. Fleming, G., Reitsma, R., Pappafotopoulos, Th., Duan, X., Birrel, R.: The state of consumers and technology: Benchmark 2017, US. Forrester Research report "North American Consumer Technographics" (2017)
9. Garnier, M., Macdonald, E.K.: The savvy French consumer: a cross-cultural replication. J. Mark. Manag. **25**(9–10), 965–986 (2009)
10. Garretson, J.A., Burton, S.: Highly coupon and sale prone consumers: benefits beyond price savings. J. Advert. Res. **43**(2), 162–172 (2003)
11. Gilmore, J.H.: The four faces of mass customization. Harv. Bus. Rev. **75**(1), 91–101 (1997)
12. Hoffman, D.L., Kopalle, P.K., Novak, T.P.: The "right" consumers for better concepts: Identifying consumers high in emergent nature to develop new product concepts. J. Mark. Res. **47**(5), 854–865 (2010)
13. Hoyer, W.D., Chandy, R., Dorotic, M., Krafft, M., Singh, S.S.: Consumer cocreation in new product development. J. Serv. Res. **13**(3), 283–296 (2010)
14. Labrecque, L.I., vor dem Esche, J., Mathwick, C., Novak, T.P., Hofacker, C.F.: Consumer power: evolution in the digital age. J. Interact. Mark. **27**(4), 257–269 (2013)
15. Macdonald, E.K., Uncles, M.D.: Consumer savvy: conceptualisation and measurement. J. Mark. Manag. **23**(5–6), 497–517 (2007)
16. MacInnis, D.J., Jaworski, B.J.: Enhancing and measuring consumers' motivation, opportunity, and ability to process brand information form ads. J. Mark. **55**(4), 32–53 (1989)
17. Nguyen, N.H.: How do customer satisfaction, confidence and knowledge in financial services affect their switching? Int. J. Econ. Res. **14**(16), 281–305 (2017)
18. Nijssen, E., Singh, J., Sirdeshmukh, D., Holzmüeller, H.: Investigating industry context effects in consumer-firm relationships: preliminary results from a dispositional approach. J. Acad. Mark. Sci. **31**(1), 46–60 (2003)
19. Pillai, K.G., Brusco, M., Goldsmith, R., Hofacker, C.: Consumer knowledge discrimination. Eur. J. Mark. **49**(9), 82–100 (2015)
20. ROCIT: Index of Digital literacy. http://цифроваяграмотность.рф. Accessed 10 Jan 2019
21. Rothschild, M.L.: Carrots, sticks, and promises: a conceptual framework for the management of public health and social issue behaviors. J. Mark. **63**, 24–37 (1999)
22. Sharikov, A.V.: On four-component model of digital literacy. J. Soc. Policy Stud. **14**(1), 87–97 (2016). (in Russian)

Digital Economy: Unemployment Risks and New Opportunities

Evgeny Itsakov[1], Nikolai Kazantsev[2,3(✉)], Soizhina Yangutova[2], Dmitry Torshin[2], and Maryia Alchykava[2]

[1] Russian Academy of National Economy and Public Administration, Moscow, Russia
eitsakov@gmail.com

[2] National Research University Higher Schools of Economics, Moscow, Russia
nicolay.kazantsev@gmail.com

[3] Alliance Manchester Business School, Manchester, UK

Abstract. In this paper we reflect on the potential employment impacts of national digital strategies. Traditional industries will be affected, and many employees will lose jobs. Ensuring their adaptation to digital economy is a responsibility co-shared between national governments, universities and employees themselves. We compare government investments into higher education and lifelong learning programs between OECD countries and state that there is a need for systematic continuous educational programs on digital skills where they are underinvested.

Keywords: Digital economy · Human capital · Digital literacy · Lifelong learning · Digital skills

1 Introduction

Digital strategies focus on the enablement of new digital capabilities[1] to speed-up economic growth [43]. However, being realized at the national levels they face disperse educational levels of citizens that brings larger time-lags before strategy realizes in a society. National digital policies often visualize new generations of workers rather than adaptation of existing ones. In order to digitalize societies all citizens regardless of age and existing education should be able to get digital skills how to use new technologies (e-Government portals, P2P digital platforms, etc.) and to work with them. Recently, the government of 1.3 mln. Estonia[2] implemented digital identification on blockchain to facilitate the access of citizens to governmental services (such as voting) from anywhere. Are citizens of larger countries being ready to use the new generation of services that digital economy brings? Which are the possibilities to obtain new skills? How to avoid risks of potential unemployment if citizens won't have the required skills? This paper considers the role of digital literacy in the realization of digital strategy [8, 9] for larger and diverse countries such as Russian Federation and proposes

[1] https://www.accenture.com/us-en/about/strategy-index (accessed 23.05.2019).

[2] E-Estonia [E-resource]. – URL: https://e-estonia.com/ (accessed 23.05.2019).

D. A. Alexandrov et al. (Eds.): DTGS 2019, CCIS 1038, pp. 292–299, 2019.
https://doi.org/10.1007/978-3-030-37858-5_24

guidelines how to diminish the potential negative effects during digital transformation. In particular, we aim at (1) exploring unemployment risks caused by digital strategies (Sect. 2); (2) reviewing national investments into digital skills and to overview the best practices of digital literacy development (Sect. 3); (3) proposing a plan to increase the digital literacy of Russian citizens (Sect. 4).

2 Digitalization and Labor Market

National digitalization influences working conditions, worker intellectual abilities and demand for digital literacy of workers [47, 50]. Further, it involves them even into a competition with machines [48, 49] that complete routine jobs better and therefore bring new unemployment risk for conventional labor [51]. Modern robotization is an obvious threat for most professions where humans cannot compete with the speed, availability, quality, flexibility and production costs of machines [52]. Table 1 lists envisioned unemployment risks caused by digital strategy to national industry sectors.

The named disadvantages could be avoided by new arising job opportunities that require specific skills [53]. In 2017, consultancies widely reported on new jobs to appear during digital transformation: Trainers/Mentors (teaching robots with sympathy and depth), Explainers/Consultants (bridging the gap between robots technologists and business leaders to increase trust in decision-making) and Sustainers/Controllers (ethical considerations, robotized action implications) [20, 36]. Therefore, there is a need for new education programs to bring such opportunities to workers and to facilitate their shifts from conventional sectors. As an example, we analyze Russian Federation where digitalization is still at lower levels compared to western countries and has not influenced the reduction of jobs yet [52] to answer research question: *how to facilitate the transition of knowledge to workers in a country such as Russia and avoid the mentioned unemployment risks?*

As the main method we used exploratory review and context analysis of academia papers (Google Scholar), consultancy reports (Accenture, IBM, others) and World Bank Reports looking at digitalization effects on industries.

3 Government Investments in Continuous Education

In 2013, Lifelong Learning UNESCO Institute has issued its 2nd Global Report on Adult Learning and Education on lifelong programs governmental spending. It reveals that the high-income countries spend 0.15% to their GDP to finance the life-long programs, while the low-income states spend almost 4 times less - 0.041% [38]. The involvement rate of the grown-up population is provided in the Table 2 below that reveals a slow adaptation pace of Russian people to digital transformation.

Table 1. Digital transformation to impact industrial changes

Industry	Substitute	Eliminated professions	Reason (advantage)	Sources
Private banking	block chain solutions	consultants	speed	[16, 17]
Investment banking	crowdfunding platforms	analysts	availability	[15]
Construction industry	industrial 3D-printers	designers, engineers	speed, quality	[37]
Projecting and prototyping	automated computer-added projecting and prototyping	designers, engineers	speed, quality	[21, 35, 41]
Web-design studios	web-site constructors, advanced infographics and animated presentation	designers	speed, quality	[32, 39]
Heavy industries	3D-printng	heavy workers	smaller consignments production, flexibility	[6, 39]
Stock and ForEx trading	e-Portals	brokers, traders	speed and robustness	[36]
Corporate consulting	self-learning algorithms and Big Data	consultants	cost cutting	[11]
FCMG, Retail	e-Commerce	employees along the supply chain	cost cutting	[1, 7]
Taxi	driverless vehicles	drivers	cost cutting	[18, 30]
Travel industry	e-Commerce	managers	Customer-orientation	[19, 27]
Corporate sales and supply	SAP Ariba and similar information systems	account managers	easiness of search	[5]
Accounting	automated pre-defined rules and policies	accountants, lawyers, judges	speed, quality	[42]
Legal services in the area of civil and tax legislation	ePay	accountants, lawyers	reduction of human labor	[12]
Classical Post	drones and automatized storage facilities	employees along the delivery chain	peer-to-peer deliveries	[4, 31]

Table 2. The adult's involvement rate into the continuous education in Russia and some countries of the EU (adults from 24 to 65 year old), year 2012 [29]

Level of education	Russia	Austria	France	Germany	UK	Spain
Lifelong educational courses, %	12	25	20	13	34	10
Self-education courses, %	21	86	46	37	–	16

Table 3 consolidates higher education and the lifelong skills between budget spending, federal budget and regional budget spending, while the Table 4 – suggests the lifelong learning governmental spending amount.

Table 3. The share of Russian spending to the continues educational programs with respect to the total spending on the education [33]

	Total spending on education in year 2016, bln. of RUR	Budget spending on the lifelong educational programs in year 2016, bln. of RUR	Lifelong learning programs share in the total educational spending, %
Consolidated budget spending	3 058,98	20,24	0,67%
Federal budget spending	564,31	7,36	1,3%
Regional budgets spending	2 521,68	13,61	0,53%

Table 4. The Russian governmental spending on lifelong learning programs (calculated based on the year 2016)

	Comparing to the low-income countries, bln. of RUR	Comparing to the middle-income countries, bln. of RUR	Comparing to the high-income countries, bln. of RUR
Suggested total spending	35,27	92,93	129,06
Suggested additional spending	15,03	72,69	108,82

In Russia, the government spending on continuing education (0.0235% of GDP in 2016 [14, 25, 28, 29, 34] is twice lower than an average for the low-income countries and seven times lower than for the high-income states. Based on these figures we derive that the lifelong education in Russia is underinvested. The retaining programs suffer from the strong underfunding even in the comparison to the low-income countries though according to the World Bank's statistics Russia belongs to the countries with income above average [40]. Russian businesses or individuals spend nearly 10 bln. USD annually on the retaining programs provided from abroad [22]. Moreover, Russian workers show little involvement in the existing lifelong learning programs, describing them as *"formal, disturbing, inefficient… and hardly implemented in the modern world"* [26]. It results that, only 60 000–70 000 employees attend such programs per year, while in South Korea all employees complete annual enrollments [24]. The presented details enforce the need of government to systematize and increase spending on continuous education of digital skills. The Russian government should focus on achieving the critical mass of the citizens with digital skills to ensure their integration into digital economy.

4 Roadmap to Continuous Digital Literacy

Training programs merge more and more with routine business responsibilities, where learning materials are aligned to the current technological trends [2, 3, 13, 26]. The leading companies spend from 2% to 10% of their salary funds to the professional development of their employees and this spending brings the significant returns [23]. Below we list the best practices found in the literature [10, 30] and propose the roadmap to better apply retaining programs (Table 4). To get new professions, workers must use digital learning tools [46], such as digital platforms developed by modern universities [44, 45] (Fig. 1).

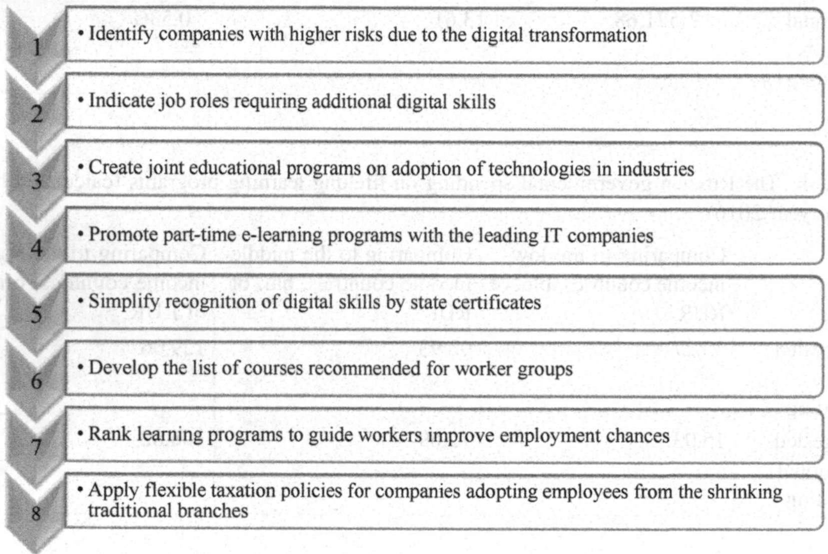

Fig. 1. List of proposed measures

The challenging task would be to make working place for the new generation professions for the Russian economy. We assume the proposed plan is a key measure aligned with governmental and business leadership. Fortunately, there are high-tech companies and universities that may work together to facilitate digital transformations of conventional industries. A key factor to success may be the willingness of Russian government to grant *carte blanche* and fiscal support to high-tech private companies leading the process of digital transformation.

5 Conclusion

In this paper we reflect on the potential negative impacts of digital strategy of the Russian Federation in terms of its effect on employment. We reveal several traditional industries will be affected by digital transformation and many employees lose jobs. Ensuring their adaptation to digital economy is a responsibility co-shared between national governments, universities and employees themselves. We conclude that there is a need for systematic continuous educational programs and offer a roadmap which targets raising digital literacy to satisfy the needs of digital economy.

References

1. Absolunet inc.: 10 Ecommerce Trends For 2017 (2017). http://10ecommercetrends.com/
2. Accenture Plc.: Making a Difference. Corporate Citizenship Report 2016 (2016). https://www.accenture.com/t20170329T044918__w__/us-en/_acnmedia/PDF-48/Accenture-2016-Corporate-Citizenship-Report.pdf#zoom=50
3. Accenture Plc.: Skills to Succeed Academy. Tackling youth unemployment in the United Kingdom through online learning (2013). https://www.accenture.com/gb-en/company-skills-succeed-academy-online-learning
4. Amazon Prime Air.: Prime Air—a delivery system from Amazon designed to safely get packages to customers in 30 min or less using unmanned aerial vehicles (2016). https://www.amazon.com/Amazon-Prime-Air/b?node=8037720011
5. Ariba Business Network: Functional capabilities review. SAP SE (2015)
6. D'Aveni, R.A.: 3-D printing will change the world. Harv. Bus. Rev. **91**, 34–35 (2013)
7. Rigby, D.K.: The future of shopping. Harv. Bus. Rev. **89**, 65–76 (2011)
8. Decree of the President of the Russian Federation from 07.07.2011 No. 899 "On the approval of priority directions for the development of science, technology and technology in the Russian Federation and a list of critical technologies of the Russian Federation" Moscow, the Kremlin (2011)
9. Decree of the President of the Russian Federation from 16.12.2015 No. 623 "On the National Center for the Development of Technologies and Basic Elements of Robotics" Moscow, the Kremlin (2015)
10. Medvedev, D.: Instructed to Discover the Ways of Blockchain Technologies Application for Russian Economy (2017). https://ria.ru/economy/20170306/1489365737.html
11. Jost, W.: Digital Business Platform 2.0. Software AG White Paper (2016)
12. ePay. Indiana Department of Revenue's electronic tax payment service (2006). http://www.in.gov/dor/4340.htm
13. European Commission. Education and Training. Lifelong Learning Programme (2006). http://ec.europa.eu/education/lifelong-learning-programme_en
14. Federal Service of State Statistics of the Russian Federation. GDP for 2016 (2016). http://www.gks.ru/wps/wcm/connect/rosstat_main/rosstat/ru/rates/46880c804a41fb53bdcebf78e6889fb6
15. Fisher, J.: Top Trends in Equity Crowdfunding. Big Things are Happening (2017). https://medium.com/crowdfund-research/top-trends-in-equity-crowdfunding-7db76efd7cae
16. German Gref Expects the Rapid Development of Blockchain Technologies (2017). https://ria.ru/economy/20170316/1490214529.html

17. German Gref: in 2–2.5 years the blockchain technologies to be everywhere in Russia (2017). https://www.vedomosti.ru/finance/news/2017/02/17/678181-gref-blokchein-rossii
18. Goldman, R.: Dubai Plans a Taxi That Skips the Driver, and the Roads. The New York Times, February 2017
19. Gui, M., Argentin, G.: Digital skills of internet natives: different forms of digital literacy in a random sample of northern Italian high school students. New Media Soc. **13**(6), 963–980 (2011)
20. Wilson, H.J., Daugherty, P., Bianzino, N.: The jobs that artificial intelligence will create. MIT Sloan Manag. Rev. **58**(4), 14 (2017)
21. Hardesty, L.: Surprisingly simple scheme for self-assembling robots (2013). http://news.mit.edu/2013/simple-scheme-for-self-assembling-robots-1004
22. International Association for Continuing Education. State of the Lifelong Education in Russia and the World (2017). http://iace-edu.com/iace/sostoyanie-dpo-v-rossii-i-mire
23. Interview ministra obrazovanija I nauki RF Fursenko A.A. Lozung "Obrazovanie na vsu zhizn" menjaetsja na "Obrazovanie v techenie vsej zhizni". Russkij mir.ru (2017). http://www.russkiymir.ru/media/magazines/article/121406/. (in Russian)
24. Kasjanov, S.V.: Chetyre uslovija nepreryvnogo obrazovanija mashinnostroitelej. Naberezhnye chelny (Tatarstan): Akkreditatsija v obrazovanii (elektronnyj zhurnal) (2013). (in Russian)
25. Mordvintsev, A.I.: O neobhodimyh izmenenijah v sistemah nepreryvnogo obrazovanija s pozitsii biznesa. Volgograd: Akkreditatsija v obrazovanii (electronnyj zhurnal) (2013). (in Russian)
26. Interview with Russian Duma deputy Shudegovym V.E. DPO: kak pokinut periferiju? Accreditatsia v obrazovanii (electronnyi zhurnal) (2013). (in Russian)
27. Itsakov, E.D.: Should the traditional tour operators fear the OTA's? Russ. Entrep. **2**(224), 145–149 (2013)
28. Kovaleva, N.V., Borodina, D.P., Kovaleva, L.E.: Spros i predlozhenie na rynke dopolnitelnogo professionalnogo obrazovanija. Dopolnitelnoe professionalnoe obrazovene strane mire **6**(6), 34–40 (2013). (in Russian)
29. Kravchenko, V.V.: Sopostavitelnyj analis otechestevennogo zapadnogoevropejskogo dopolnitelnogo obrazovanija: dissertatsija, Moscow (2012). (in Russian)
30. Lund, S., Manyika, J., Bughin, J.: Globalization is Becoming More About Data and Less About Stuff (2016). https://hbr.org/2016/03/globalization-is-becoming-more-about-data-and-less-about-stuff
31. McFarland, M.: UPS drivers may tag team deliveries with drones. CNN Money (Washington), 21 February 2017
32. MERIXSTUDIO. Web Design Trends for 2017 (2017). https://www.awwwards.com/web-design-trends-for-2017.html
33. Ministry of Education and Science of the Russian Federation. Expenses of the consolidated budget of the Russian Federation under the heading "Education" in 2016 (2017). http://fin.edu.ru/InfoPanel/min_obr1.html
34. "On the Federal Budget for 2016". Federal Law of December 14, 2015 № 359-FZ (2015)
35. Rani, P., Srinivasan, A.: Digitization of financial markets: impact and future. Int. J. Res. Finance Mark. **5**(7), 29–33 (2015)
36. Reisinger, D.: Watch a 3D-Printing Robot Construct a Building (2017). http://fortune.com/2017/04/27/mit-robot-3d-printing-building/
37. Sklar, J.: Intelligent Machines. Team Designs Robots to Build Things in Messy, Unpredictable Situations (2015). https://www.technologyreview.com/s/540156/team-designs-robots-to-build-things-in-messy-unpredictable-situations/

38. Van Deursen, A.J.A.M., Helsper, E.J., Eynon, R.: Measuring digital skills. From Digital Skills to Tangible Outcomes project report. University of Twente, London (2014)
39. World Development Indicators (2016). http://wdi.worldbank.org/tables
40. World University Rankings 2016–2017 (2016). https://www.timeshighereducation.com/world-university-rankings/2017/world-ranking#!/page/0/length/25/sort_by/rank/sort_order/asc/cols/stats
41. Zhong, Z.J.: From access to usage: the divide of self-reported digital skills among adolescents. Comput. Educ. **56**(3), 736–746 (2011)
42. "1C". Kharakteristika 1C: Bukhgalterija 8 (2016). http://v8.1c.ru/buhv8/321.htm
43. Governmental Program «Digital Economic of Russia Federation». Government of Russian Federation, Ref. 28 July 2017, №1632-p Digital Economics 2024 (2017). http://de-pm.ac.gov.ru
44. Omarova, S.K.: Sovremennye tendentsii obrazovaniya v epohu tsifrovizatsii. Tambov Gramota (zhurnal) **1**(9), 78–83 (2018). (in Russian)
45. Iafrate, F.: Digital learning (2018). https://onlinelibrary.wiley.com/doi/10.1002/9781119426653.ch2
46. Huerta, E., Sandoval-Almazán, R.: Digital literacy: problems faced by telecenter users in Mexico. Inf. Technol. Dev. **13**(3), 217–232 (2007)
47. Evangelista, R., Guerrieri, P., Meliciani, V.: The economic impact of digital technologies in Europe. Econ. Innov. New Technol. **23**(8), 802–824 (2014)
48. Lund, A., Furberg, A., Bakken, J., Engelien, K.L.: What does professional digital competence mean in teacher education? Nord. J. Digit. Liter. **9**(4), 280–298 (2014)
49. Akhmetzhanova, G.V., Bogdanova, A.V.: Informatsionno-kommunikativnaya Kompetentnost Kak Faktor Povysheniya Konkurentosposobnosti Bakalavrov Pedagogicheskogo Obrazovania. Vestink RUDN. Seria Psikhologia Pedagogika **3**, 51–55 (2011). (in Russian)
50. Degryse, C.: Digitalisation of the economy and its impact on labour markets. European Trade Union Institute (ETUI) Research Paper Series, Brussels (2016)
51. Shatilo, Yu.E., Kopkova, E.S.: Employment and unemployment in the digital economy. Mezhdunarodnyy nauchno-tekhnicheskiy zhurnal «Teoriya. Praktika. Innovatsii» (2017). (in Russian)
52. Senokosova, O.V.: Vozdeystviye tsifrovizatsii na rynok truda Rossii. Saratov J. Econ. Bus. **2** (10) (2018). (in Russian)
53. Eichhorst, W., Hinte, H., Rinne, U., Tobsch, V.: How big is the gig? Assessing the preliminary evidence on the effects of digitalization on the labor market. mrev Manag. Rev. **28**(3), 298–318 (2017). (in Russian)

Specifying the Design for Customer Learning in the Mixed Reality Experience

Jani Holopainen[1(✉)], Riikka Vehviläinen[1], Osmo Mattila[2], Essi Pöyry[1], and Petri Parvinen[1]

[1] University of Helsinki, Yliopistonkatu 4, 00100 Helsinki, Finland
jani.m.holopainen@helsinki.fi
[2] Swedish University of Agricultural Sciences, Umeå, Sweden

Abstract. Companies search for new ways of utilizing technologies such as the Mixed Reality (MR) in order to enrich their customer interactions. While more of these MR technologies are emerging to assist customer-employee interactions, there is a strategic choice related to scalability of how to organize these service encounters: face-to-face or digitally over the web. Eventually, the question is how much of these interactions can be automatized with acceptable tradeoffs for the customer experience and business outcomes. This study analyzes the influence of a MR design elements on the outcomes of a customer experience in a use case where the customer learning is focal for the service. The experiment comparing two conditions: face-to-face interactions and remote interactions over the web showed no difference in terms of customer experience and perceived learning. On the other hand, the ease-of-use of the technology as well as the familiarity with the subject and technology effected the customer learning. The results offer implications to both the customer experience management and the MR system design.

Keywords: Customer experience · Customer learning · Customer-Employee interaction · Mixed reality

1 Introduction

Customer experience and service design have emerged as key concepts in differentiating from competitors and developing services that better provide additional unique value for the customer [2]. Purchase decisions are not based only on the cognitive and rational reasons, because experiences are important factors in creating emotional bonds between customers and service providers that generate also engagement and customer loyalty [32]. Companies are required to adopt a new way of thinking the relationships with customers, since customer centricity, understanding the customer context and delivering value to individual customers, forms the core of customer experience management [21].

Service organizations are increasingly utilizing advanced communication technologies [18]. Technological development and changed customer preferences have introduced web-based e-commerce and mobile-based m-commerce as increasingly popular ways of organizing business [3]. Since customers are facing an increasing

D. A. Alexandrov et al. (Eds.): DTGS 2019, CCIS 1038, pp. 300–312, 2019.
https://doi.org/10.1007/978-3-030-37858-5_25

supply of digital services, their expectations have tightened for consistently better personalization, enjoyment, ease-of-use, and seamless fit of services as part of their daily lives without the restrictions of time and place [31].

Mixed Reality (MR) which refers to blended real and virtual environments [28] has offered tools for various fields of business to provide real-life simulations, communication mediums, and experiential marketing and learning platforms [37]. While more of these MR technologies are emerging to assist customer-employee interactions, there is a strategic choice related to scalability of how to organize these service encounters: face-to-face or digitally over the web. Eventually, the question is how much of these interactions can be automatized with acceptable tradeoffs for the customer experience and business outcomes.

This study analyzes the influence of the MR design elements on the outcomes of customer experience. The study is conducted as an experiment comparing two conditions: face-to-face interactions and remote interactions over the web. In addition, moderating effects from the previous literature are raised and analyzed: the familiarity with the subject and technology, and the ease-of-use of the technology. The customer experience is analyzed within the framework of customer learning [23], which is often the objective of the MR service encounter and the system design [37]. The results offer implications to both the customer experience management and the MR system design.

2 Customer's Virtual Experience and Learning

Experiences can be seen to form differently in offline environments and online environments. Studies on experiences in online environments have led to the formation of a variety of different concepts, such as web experience [4], online customer experience [3, 34], technology-mediated customer experience [7], and virtual experience [22]. In this study, we are experimenting two conditions: a technology-mediated customer experience, which is generated by using mixed reality in the context of timber trade and forestry services and where the service employee is present giving face-to-face instructions. The second condition is a virtual experience, where the same application is used while the service employee is giving instructions remotely over the web connection with audio and video.

Virtual experience has been presented as a form of experience alongside with direct and indirect experiences [23]. It is a form of indirect experience, but has some notable differences compared to it, mostly because of the ability of virtual experience to engage multiple senses. Virtual experience has an ability to provide part of the richness of a direct experience while still being an indirect experience.

Elements or dimensions of virtual experience can be divided into three general categories: functional factors, psychological factors and content factors [4]. The main elements of virtual experience (online experience) include trust, social presence, usability, interactivity, perceived ease-of-use, perceived usefulness, aesthetics, and enjoyment [1, 3, 15, 24, 34]. Similar features are acknowledged in the definition of virtual experience by Li et al. [21] defining individual virtual experience as vivid, involving, active, and raising affective psychological states. They also emphasize the importance of presence, involvement and enjoyment in forming the virtual experience.

Several different models have been used to assess how the design elements of virtual reality influence the outcomes of customer experience. SOR-model (stimulus, organism, response) is often used as it describes the process of how the stimulus originated from the service context is processed by an organism and leads to a response [14, 41]. The focus on stimulus (elements of service design), organism (perceived virtual experience) and response (beliefs, attitudes and intentions) can be found in many of the studies focusing on virtual experiences. Some studies have aimed at pointing out the effects of certain stimulus elements such as user interface [38] or product type [39], on the formation of the virtual experience. Others have studied the role of organism characteristics such as user goal [35] and technology-readiness [12]. In earlier studies, the effects of these factors are often assumed to be mediated by a component of virtual experience, mostly either telepresence [38, 39] or flow [13].

Most studies recognize the division of customer responses into three dimensions: cognitive, affective and conative responses [33]. BAI-model (belief, attitude, intention) represents this kind of division of the outcomes of experience into three separate constructs and variables measuring them: beliefs (e.g. information richness, learning about product attributes, usefulness), attitudes (e.g. attitude towards the contact medium, contact episode or the service provider), and intentions (e.g. purchase intention, intention to use medium again, intention to use service provider again) [7]. Another application of the BAI-model is the customer learning. The customer learning can be divided into cognitive learning, affective learning and conative learning. These dimensions of learning can be measured by product knowledge (cognitive learning), brand attitude (affective learning) and behavioral intentions, such as purchase intention (conative learning) [23].

Studies have shown that the virtual experience affects positively product knowledge, brand attitude and purchase intentions compared to indirect experiences [6]. There is also a sequential order between these outcomes. Virtual experience, through its component telepresence, has a direct effect on product knowledge and brand attitudes, but the effect on purchase intention is indirect and mediated by brand attitudes [38]. This sequential order highlights the importance of affective responses alongside with cognitive responses in order to influence behavioral responses.

The literature review on previous research shows the research gap: the different effects of the technology-mediated customer experience and the pure virtual experience on the customer experience and learning is unknown. Furthermore, there are multiple customer virtual experience moderating effects raised by the previous literature, which are not specifically studied in the field of the customer learning. Better understanding of these issues is crucial when designing the emerging MR service encounters which are inherently concentrating on the customer learning [37]. Furthermore, the study results will have implications on the automatizing of these services.

3 Research Framework and Hypotheses

We adopt the SOR-model as the research framework, where the customer experience and the outcomes are considered to result from a three-staged process including stimulus, organism and response. In terms of stimulus, we compare the effect of the technology-mediated customer experience and the pure virtual experience. In terms of MR experience interactions, from now on, the technology-mediated customer experience will be addressed as "face-to-face" and the pure virtual experience as "remote". We consider organisms such as customers' familiarity with the technology and subject as well as perceived ease-of-use of the technology. Responses are categorized following the categorization of the customer learning named product knowledge (cognitive learning), brand attitude (affective learning), and intentions (conative learning) [23], where the sequential order between these outcomes is recognized as described in the previous research [6, 38].

Interaction provides opportunities for the company to become a part of customer's activities and thus influence the creation of customer experience and value-in-use, as well as outcomes of the service encounter [9]. In addition, the personal and emotional connections that service personnel form have an important role in creating customer experiences and affect the customer responses to those experiences [42].

MR interfaces can enhance the learning of the customer by increasing both perceived and actual product knowledge compared to static interfaces [39]. It has been suggested that as MR provides the user an opportunity to explore the virtual environment by using their entire body (embodied interaction), knowledge is brought closer to the user and therefore learning is enhanced [24].

Social presence is a central concept when the role of another person is analyzed in the formation of customer experience. Social presence is defined as the capability of a communication medium to enable user to experience other people as being present [8]. Social presence has positive influence on trust, enjoyment and perceived usefulness [5].

In terms of the customer-employee interaction effect on customer experience and learning, the previous research suggests that face-to-face/remote interactions are complementary i.e. those questions that cannot be solved remotely are completed in presence [17]. Based on the previous research on customer-employee interactions and the positive effect on customer experience and learning we draw our first hypothesis:

Hypothesis 1: The face-to-face interaction has a positive impact on the customer experience and learning over the remote interaction.

The virtual experience and the object interactivity creates more vivid mental images than traditional passive contents [20, 35]. Mental images are in an important role in customer learning. Thus, customers with little previous knowledge and weak mental images, will especially benefit from mental imagery enhanced by object interactivity [35]. Also, the role of the product or service in customer's life affects their motivation to learn [29]. Thus, we propose the following hypothesis:

Hypothesis 2: Customers with little previous knowledge and weak mental images, i.e. familiarity with the subject, have more positive customer experience and enhanced learning.

The familiarity with the technology influences positively perceptions about the experience in the digital service interface as the customer feels more confident about using the technology, and thus it has an important role in online decision-making and purchases [11]. Lorenzo et al. [25] studied the role of the familiarity with online services on online decision-making and observed that the number of years the customer has used the Internet (familiarity with technology) had a significant role in the online shopping process, but the actual familiarity with the subject, i.e. the online shopping (familiarity with process), was not as important.

Hypothesis 3: The familiarity with the technology has a positive impact on the customer experience and learning.

Hernández et al. [11], in turn, suggest that the effect of familiarity with technology has more important role with the new emerging technologies, while the significance decreases as the technology becomes more conventional and people have learned how to use them. Similarly, the ease-of-use of the technology is emphasized for new users, while different utilities become more important for experienced users [11].

Hypothesis 4: The ease-of-use of the technology has a positive impact on customer experience and learning.

4 Data and Method

This study followed true experimental research design, in which research subjects are randomly assigned to treatment groups [26]. In the face-to-face condition, the service employee was physically present in the same room and it simulates a corner store customer-employee encounter. In the remote interaction, the service employee was digitally present via a Skype connection representing a digital or distant customer-employee encounter. The main idea of the experimental design is to randomly assign research subjects to an experimental and a control group, provide a treatment to the experiential group, and compare the outcomes on a dependent variable between the two groups [40].

The participants were recruited via an email invitation to participate to the experiment at the firm's service and sales point and at a forest fair. Each test lasted for 30 min that included the use of the application and answering the survey. The physical setup of the application included a computer, a HTC Vive headset (fully-immersive head-mounted display, HDM), two controllers, a screen (for service employee/observer), and virtual forest application. The content of the application was focused on demonstrating various forest management operations and teaching about them. Based on the literature and the theory frame, we develop a scale measuring the effect of the MR experience interactions, customer's familiarity with the technology and subject, and ease-of-use of the technology on the customer learning as the dependent variables (Table 1).

All the dependent variables were measured using 5-staged Likert-scale (1 = strongly disagree; 5 = strongly agree). Product knowledge (cognitive learning) was measured using a scale suggested by Li et al. [22]: product attribute attention, product attribute evaluation, product attribute association, questioning of product attributes and information seeking. Brand attitude (affective learning) was measured by using a scale for corporate reputation by Lai et al. [19]. The questions covered customer's overall perception ("In my opinion, the digital services of X provide a good user experience"), comparative perception ("In my opinion, the digital services of X are better than other similar ones"), and long-term future perception ("I believe that X will offer the best digital services in the future"). Here the company name is replaced with

Table 1. The initial scale.

Independent variables
MR interaction face-to-face/remote (Experiment, Nominal)
MR familiarity (Nominal-scale 1–3)
Easy-of-use of the technology (Nominal-scale 1–3)
Subject familiarity (Nominal-scale 1–3)
Dependent variables (Likert-scale 1–5)
Product knowledge (cognitive learning)
This kind of system would help in managing forest estate (Attention)
In my opinion, the modelled forest seemed real (Association)
In my opinion, the timber prices were reliable (Evaluation)
I learned new things on forest management (Information seeking)
I could actually apply those things that I learned on forest management (Questioning of product attributes)
Brand attitude (affective learning)
In my opinion, the digital services of X offer a good user experience (Overall perception)
In my opinion, the digital services of X are better than other similar ones (Comparative perception)
I believe that X will offer the best digital services in the future (Long-term future perception)
Intentions (conative learning)
I will be in contact with forest specialist after this experience (Interaction)
I can recommend the use of this kind of service to a friend (Interaction)
I am interested in participating in testing a similar service again (Interest)
I am ready to buy a virtual forest management plan on my own forest (Action)
Based on this experience, I am ready to sell wood (Action)

X. In terms of intentions (conative learning), we follow the suitable customer activities introduce by Kotler et al. [16]: interaction, interest and action.

In terms of independent variables, the scales were nominal as presented in the Table 1. The "VR familiarity" was surveyed with the scale (unfamiliar with MR, somewhat familiar with MR, very familiar with MR), the "ease-of-use of the technology" with the scale (easy to use, neutral to use, difficult to use) and the "subject familiarity" with the scale (very familiar with the subject, somewhat familiar with the subject, not familiar with the subject).

The Kaiser-Meyer-Olkin measure of sampling adequacy (0.773) and the Barlett's test of sphericity ($p < 0.0001$) indicated that the sample was suitable for factor analysis [27]. An exploratory factor analysis (maximum likelihood factoring) with Varimax rotation was employed (see, e.g. Hair et al. [10]). Factor eigenvalues and explanatory power of the total variance together with Cronbach's alphas were also computed for each factor in the reliability analysis. The homogeneity of variance test indicated uneven variances between the data from specific groups, hence the non-parametric analysis of variance-tests were applied. Mann-Whitney U-test was used for independent variables with two groups, and Kruskal-Wallis one-way analysis of variance was used for independent variables with more than two groups. Both tests use the ranks of the data to see whether the independent samples come from a population with the same distribution [36]. Significance level of 0.05 was used as cut-off value for significance.

5 Results

Altogether 64 people participated the experiment, out which 37 (58%) were assigned to the face-to-face and 27 (42%) to the remote condition. Other independent variable were distributed as follows: 29 (45%) unfamiliar with MR, 26 (41%) somewhat familiar with MR, 9 (14%) very familiar with MR; 38 (59%) easy to use, 12 (19%) neutral to use, 14 (22%) difficult to use; 11 (17%) very familiar with the subject, 33 (52%) somewhat familiar with the subject, 7 (11%) not familiar with the subject.

In terms of the dependent variables, the perceptions about how well the virtual forest represents real forest were almost equally divided among the participants with 56% strongly or somewhat agreeing with the statement "The forest seemed real" (M = 3.61) and 44% strongly or somewhat agreeing that the prices of wood were believable (M = 3.45). However, almost half of the participants neither agreed nor disagreed with the prices of wood. Majority (82%) of the participants agreed that the virtual forest would be a useful tool for managing forest property (M = 4.14). Learning about forest management when using the virtual forest (M = 2.48) and utilizing the learned things (M = 2.66) were perceived low by half of the participants. However, 24% of the participants strongly or somewhat agreed with the statement "I learned something new about forest management.

Majority of the participants agreed that the digital services of the firm X provide a good user experience (M = 3.94). Comparing the digital services of the firm X to other similar ones was perceived challenging as 55% did not take a stand on brand question 2 (M = 3.44). Majority of the participants agreed that the firm X will have the best digital services in the future (M = 3.89).

Majority (89%) of the participants were interested in participating in testing similar service again (M = 4.50) and 83% was willing to recommend service to a friend (M = 4.25). Almost half of the participants were ready to buy virtual forest management plan of their own forest (M = 3.27) and ready to sell wood based on the experience (M = 3.33). Intention to be in contact with forestry specialist after the experience was divided between 34% of participants strongly or somewhat agreeing and 38% strongly or somewhat disagreeing with the statement "I will probably be in contact with the forest specialist after this" (M = 2.94).

In the factor analysis, the item "Prices of wood were believable" was removed due to the low communality value (<0.25). The item "Based on this experience, I am ready to sell wood" suffered from cross-loadings, thus it was also removed from the factor solution. The two-factor solution is presented in the Table 2. The first factor comprises all the elements from the customer learning experience –model [23] e.g. product knowledge (cognitive learning), brand attitude (affective learning) and behavioral intentions (conative learning). Therefore, the first factor is named to present "customer experience". The first factor explains 46.8% of the variables' total variation. The Cronbach's alpha reliability analysis was carried out for the items of the factor showing a satisfactory value of 0.87, which is greater than a threshold value of 0.7. The second

Table 2. The two-dimensional structure of the factor analysis

Variable/Item	Factor 1	Factor 2
I can recommend the use of this kind of service to a friend	0.807	
In my opinion, the digital services of X offer a good user experience	0.707	
In my opinion, the modelled forest seemed real	0.640	
I will be in contact with forest specialist after this experience	0.639	
In my opinion, the digital services of X are better than other similar ones	0.571	
This kind of system would help in managing forest estate	0.566	
I am interested in participating in testing a similar service again	0.548	
I am ready to buy a virtual forest management plan on my own forest	0.544	
I believe that X will offer the best digital services in the future	0.540	
I learned new things on forest management		0.897
I could actually apply those things that I learned on forest management		0.878
Eigenvalue	5.15	1.55
Explained variance%	46.8	14.1
Cronbach's alpha	0.87	0.88

factor consists of items such as "I learned something new about the forest management" and "Things I learned I can utilize in managing my own forest". The second factor was named "perceived learning" as it consisted the conscious learning elements from the customer learning experience –model [23]. The second factor explains 14.1% of the variables' total variation. The Cronbach's alpha value was again satisfactory with 0.88. Together, the two-factor model accounted for 60.9% of the variance.

The one-way non-parametric ANOVA (Mann-Whitney) was run for the two-factor solution (Fig. 1). There was no statistical differences ($p > 0.05$) between the face-to-face and remote interactions and thus the hypothesis 1 "The face-to-face interaction has a positive impact on the customer experience and learning over the remote interaction" was rejected.

The hypothesis 2 "Customers familiar with the subject have more positive customer experience and enhanced learning" was accepted, but further elaborated according to the results. The ANOVA test (Kruskal–Wallis) showed that customers living close to their real estates (also having strong knowledge and mental image) had lower results in terms of "perceived learning". The same thing was found out for the customers in the other extreme living far from their forest estates and thus having weak or no previous knowledge or mental image on their forests. The customers living in the mid-range from their forests and in this regard having "little previous knowledge and weak mental images" had the highest positive score for the "perceived learning". The results suggest the acceptance of the hypothesis 2, while it should be noted that the customers with the strong previous knowledge and mental image and customers with no previous knowledge and mental image are not going to have similar positive learning experience. The familiarity with the subject and the factor "customer experience" had no statistical significance in the test.

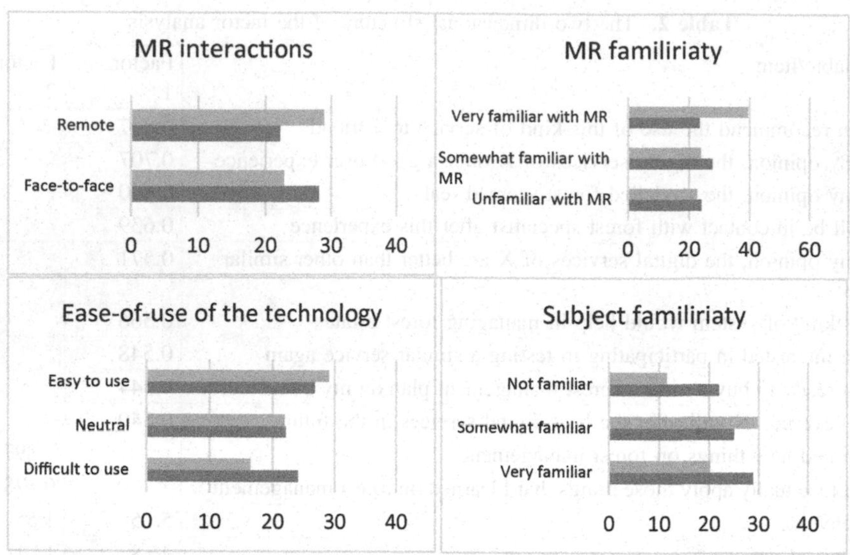

Fig. 1. Differences within dependent variable groups toward the two-factor dimensions. Factor score means ranks on the axes. (Red tile: Perceived learning; Blue tile: Customer experience) (Color figure online)

In terms of the hypothesis 3 "The familiarity with the technology has a positive impact on the customer experience and learning" was partly accepted/rejected. The factor "customer experience" and the user's familiarity with the technology had no statistical significance in the ANOVA test (Kruskal–Wallis), while the factor "perceived learning" was statistically and significantly higher for those who were more experienced with the technology. Therefore, the results suggest that no matter how experienced the customers are with the technology they can all enjoy and benefit from an experienced. However, more experienced customers with the technology can also learn more from the experience.

The hypothesis 4 showed similar results than for the hypothesis 3. The factor "customer experience" and the perceived ease-of-use of the technology showed no statistical significance, while the factor "perceived learning" was statistically and significantly higher for those who perceived the technology easy to use. The results suggest that when the technology is easy to use, the customers also perceive to learn better.

6 Discussion and Conclusions

While more immersive technologies are emerging to assist the customer-employee interactions, there is a strategic choice question of how to organize these service encounters: face-to-face or remotely over the web? The previous studies have showed the importance of face-to-face social interactions in creation of the customer experience

[42]. In addition, the face-to-face communication is considered as very rich communication form, while the remote collaboration and communication lack part of this richness of direct interaction [30]. On the other hand, the MR technologies can create high media richness and a sense embodiment bringing the knowledge closer to the user and therefore also learning can be enhanced [24].

The research task for this study was to assess, whether the social presence [8] can be created with the MR technologies. The social presence was simulated within an experimental setup consisting of two different conditions: face-to-face and remote interactions. Our results show that the MR technologies can create equal social presence whether the service is provided face-to-face or remotely over the web. Our results measured the effect of the social presence on the customer experience and learning showing equal results among the both control groups. This finding was contrary to the previous study results and our hypothesis alluding that the face-to-face interaction would have a more positive impact on the customer experience and learning over the remote interaction [17]. However, the previous results of Köhler et al. [17] suggesting that face-to-face/remote interactions are complementary i.e. those questions that cannot be solved remotely are completed in presence [17] could not be validated within this study. Our findings suggest that the area of the questions that can be solved remotely with the MR technology might be broader than with the previous communication technologies, which have been the study context for the existing theories in the field of social-presence and interactions. While we only measured the customer experience and learning, the results are limited and suggest a broader analysis of values and utilities where the MR technologies can substitute the social presence.

Our study also analyzed the familiarity with the subject as the moderating effect on the customer experience and learning. The previous studies had shown that especially the customers with little previous knowledge and weak mental images can benefit from mental imagery enhanced by the object interactivity (Schlosser, 2003) such as the MR experience [20, 24, 35]. Our results suggest that the customers with little previous knowledge and mental image may benefit the most of MR-experiences when comparing to the groups with either very high or no previous knowledge and mental image. This is also a new finding compared to the previous literature and it signifies the challenge of providing useful content and information for the users who already have high knowledge and mental image about the subject. On the other hand, for the users with no previous knowledge and mental image, the experience and perceived learning can be enhanced by adding hints such as photographs that help in understanding both context and the level of abstraction of an interactive experience such as an MR application. This finding, however, might be context specific to the forest estate visualizations, thus the result might be limited and should be tested with other research contexts as well.

As another moderating effect on the customer experience and learning, the familiarity with the technology and the ease-of-use of the technology were also analyzed. According to the previous literature, the familiarity with the technology positively influences the experience, while the effect decreases when the technology becomes more conventional [11]. Similarly, the ease-of-use of the technology is emphasized for new users, while different utilities become more important for experienced users [11]. Lorenzo et al. [25] suggest that the familiarity with the technology is more important over the familiarity with the subject. While the previous research have tested these moderators separately, our research results suggest that the moderators including familiarity with the subject and technology as well as the ease-of-use of the technology were all meaningful in creating positive learning experience, which is a new finding and a contribution to the customer learning research. Therefore, these factors should be taken into account in the design of customer-employee interactions and related systems. The major limitation of this paper is that it analyzed the perceived learning, not the actual learning results. Considering that and the relative significance of the present and other possible moderating factors on the customer learning is a promising avenue for the future research.

References

1. Algharabat, R.S.: Conceptualising and modelling virtual product experience for online retailers. Int. J. Internet Mark. Advert. **8**(4), 300–319 (2014). https://doi.org/10.1504/IJIMA.2014.067660
2. Andreassen, T., Kristensson, P., Lervik-Olsen, L., Parasuraman, A., McColl-Kennedy, J., Edvardsson, B., Colurcio, M.: Linking service design to value creation and service research. J. Serv. Manag. **27**(1), 21–29 (2016). https://doi.org/10.1108/JOSM-04-2015-0123
3. Bilgihan, A., Kandampully, J., Zhang, T.: Towards a unified customer experience in online shopping environments. Int. J. Qual. Serv. Sci. **8**(1), 102–119 (2016). https://doi.org/10.1108/IJQSS-07-2015-0054
4. Constantinides, E.: Influencing the online consumer's behavior: the web experience. Internet Res. **14**(2), 111–126 (2004). https://doi.org/10.1108/10662240410530835
5. Cyr, D., Hassanein, K., Head, M., Ivanov, A.: The Role of social presence in establishing loyalty in e-service environments. Interact. Comput. **19**(1), 43–56 (2007). https://doi.org/10.1016/j.intcom.2006.07.010
6. Daugherty, T., Li, H., Biocca, F.: Consumer learning and the effect of virtual experience relative to indirect and direct product experience. Psychol. Mark. **25**(7), 568–586 (2008). https://doi.org/10.1002/mar.20225
7. Froehle, C.M., Roth, A.V.: New measurement scales for evaluating perceptions of the technology-mediated customer service experience. J. Oper. Manag. **22**(1), 1–21 (2004). https://doi.org/10.1016/j.jom.2003.12.004
8. Gefen, D., Straub, D.W.: Consumer trust in B2C e-commerce and the importance of social presence: experiments in e-products and e-services. Omega **32**(6), 407–424 (2004). https://doi.org/10.1016/j.omega.2004.01.006
9. Grönroos, C.: A service perspective on business relationships: the value creation, interaction and marketing interface. Ind. Mark. Manag. **40**(2), 240–247 (2011). https://doi.org/10.1016/j.indmarman.2010.06.036
10. Hair, J.F., Anderson, R.E., Tatham, R.L., Black, W.C.: Multivariate Data Analysis. Prentice-Hall, Inc., New Jersey (1998)
11. Hernández, B., Jiménez, J., Martín, M.J.: Customer behavior in electronic commerce: the moderating effect of e-purchasing experience. J. Bus. Res. **63**(9–10), 964–971 (2010). https://doi.org/10.1016/j.jbusres.2009.01.019
12. Jahng, J., Jain, H.K., Ramamurthy, K.: An empirical study of the impact of product characteristics and electronic commerce interface richness on consumer attitude and purchase intentions. IEEE Trans. Syst. Man Cybern. Part A Syst. Hum. **36**(6), 1185–1201 (2006). https://doi.org/10.1109/TSMCA.2006.878977

13. Javornik, A.: It's an illusion, but it looks real!' - consumer affective, Cognitive and behavioural responses to augmented reality applications. J. Mark. Manag. **32**(9–10), 987–1011 (2016). https://doi.org/10.1080/0267257X.2016.1174726
14. Kim, H., Lennon, S.J.: E-atmosphere, emotional, cognitive, and behavioral responses. J. Fash. Mark. Manag. Int. J. **14**(3), 412–428 (2010). https://doi.org/10.1108/13612021011061861
15. Klaus, P.: The case of Amazon.com: towards a conceptual framework of online customer service experience (OCSE) using the emerging consensus technique (ECT). J. Serv. Mark. **27**(6), 443–457 (2013). https://doi.org/10.1108/JSM-02-2012-0030
16. Kotler, P., Rackham, N., Krishnaswamy, S.: Ending the war between sales & marketing. Harv. Bus. Rev. **84**(7–8), 68–78 (2006)
17. Köhler, C.F., Rohm, A.J., de Ruyter, K., Wetzels, M.: Return on interactivity: the impact of online agents on newcomer adjustment. J. Mark. **75**(2), 93–108 (2011). https://doi.org/10.1509/jm.75.2.93
18. Lai, P.C.: The literature review of technology adoption models and theories for the novelty technology. JISTEM J. Inf. Syst. Technol. Manag. **14**(1), 21–38 (2017). https://doi.org/10.4301/S1807-17752017000100002
19. Lai, C.S., Chiu, C.J., Yang, C.F., Pai, D.C.: The effects of corporate social responsibility on brand performance: the mediating effect of industrial brand equity and corporate reputation. J. Bus. Ethics **95**(3), 457–469 (2010). https://doi.org/10.1007/s10551-010-0433-1
20. Lee, K.Y.: Consumer processing of virtual experience in e-commerce: a test of an integrated framework. Comput. Hum. Behav. **28**(6), 2134–2142 (2012). https://doi.org/10.1016/j.chb.2012.06.018
21. Lemon, K.N., Verhoef, P.C.: Understanding customer experience throughout the customer journey. J. Mark. **80**(6), 69–96 (2016). https://doi.org/10.1509/jm.15.0420
22. Li, H., Daugherty, T., Biocca, F.: Characteristics of virtual experience in electronic commerce: a protocol analysis. J. Interact. Mark. **15**(3), 13–30 (2001). https://doi.org/10.1002/dir.1013
23. Li, H., Daugherty, T., Biocca, F.: The role of virtual experience in consumer learning. J. Consum. Psychol. **13**(4), 395–407 (2003). https://doi.org/10.1207/S15327663JCP1304_07
24. Lindgren, R., Tscholl, M., Wang, S., Johnson, E.: Enhancing learning and engagement through embodied interaction within a mixed reality simulation. Comput. Educ. **95**, 174–187 (2016). https://doi.org/10.1016/j.compedu.2016.01.001
25. Lorenzo, C., Constantinides, E., Geurts, P., Gómez, M.: Impact of web xperience on e-consumer responses. In: E-commerce and Web Technologies, pp. 191–200 (2007). https://doi.org/10.1007/978-3-540-74563-1_19
26. Malhotra, N.K., Birks, D.F.: Marketing research: an applied approach. Prentice Hall/Financial Times, Harlow (2003)
27. Metsämuuronen, J.: Tutkimuksen tekemisen perusteet ihmistieteissä 4 [The methods of research in human science]. Gummerus Kirjapaino Oy, Jyväskylä (2009)
28. Milgram, P., Kishino, F.: A taxonomy of mixed reality visual displays. IEICE Trans. Inf. Syst. **E77-D**(12), 1321–1329 (1994)
29. Nambisan, S., Baron, R.A.: Interactions in virtual customer environments: implications for product support and customer relationship management. J. Interact. Mark. **21**(2), 42–61 (2007). https://doi.org/10.1002/dir.20077
30. Palmer, M.T.: Interpersonal communication and virtual reality: mediating interpersonal relationships. In: Communication in the Age of Virtual Reality, pp. 277–299 (1995)

31. Parise, S., Guinan, P.J., Kafka, R.: Solving the crisis of immediacy: how digital technology can transform the customer experience. Bus. Horiz. **59**(4), 411–420 (2016). https://doi.org/10.1016/j.bushor.2016.03.004
32. Pullman, M.E., Gross, M.A.: Ability of experience design elements to elicit emotions and loyalty behaviors. Decis. Sci. **35**(3), 551–578 (2004). https://doi.org/10.1111/j.0011-7315.2004.02611.x
33. Richardson, A.: The Experiential Dimension of Psychology. University of Queensland Press, Queensland (1984)
34. Rose, S., Hair, N., Clark, M.: Online customer experience: a review of the business-to-consumer online purchase context. Int. J. Manag. Rev. **13**(1), 24–39 (2011). https://doi.org/10.1111/j.1468-2370.2010.00280.x
35. Schlosser, A.E.: Experiencing products in the virtual world: the role of goal and imagery in influencing attitudes versus purchase intentions. J. Consum. Res. **30**(2), 184–198 (2003). https://doi.org/10.1086/376807
36. Singh, K.: Quantitative Social Research Methods. SAGE Publications Pvt. Ltd., Thousand Oaks (2007). https://doi.org/10.4135/9789351507741
37. Slater, M., Sanchez-Vives, M.V.: Enhancing our lives with immersive virtual reality. Front. Robot. AI **3**, 1–47 (2016). https://doi.org/10.3389/frobt.2016.00074
38. Suh, K.S., Chang, S.: User interfaces and consumer perceptions of online stores: the role of telepresence. Behav. Inf. Technol. **25**(2), 99–113 (2006). https://doi.org/10.1080/01449290500330398
39. Suh, K.S., Lee, Y.E.: The effects of virtual reality on consumer learning: an empirical investigation. MIS Q. **29**(4), 673–697 (2005). https://doi.org/10.2307/25148705
40. Vogt, W.P.: Quantitative Research Methods for Professionals. Pearson/Allyn and Bacon, Boston (2007)
41. Zhang, H., Lu, Y., Wang, B., Wu, S.: The impacts of technological environments and co-creation experiences on customer participation. Inf. Manag. **52**(4), 468–482 (2015). https://doi.org/10.1016/j.im.2015.01.008
42. Zomerdijk, L.G., Voss, C.: Service design for experience-centric services. J. Serv. Res. **13**, 67–82 (2010)

Impact of Socio-Cultural Factors onto the National Technology Development

Evgeniya Gorlacheva(✉), Irina Omelchenko, Pavel Drogovoz, Olga Yusufova, and Vladimir Shiboldenkov

Bauman Moscow State Technical University,
Moscow 105005, Russian Federation
{egorlacheva, logistic, drogovoz, yusufova, vshiboldenkov}@bmstu.ru

Abstract. The paper proposes the empiric research of socio-cultural factors' impact on the national technology development. It is well noted that the rapid technology development gives an increase of living standards, boost country economy, and contributes substantially to the gross domestic product. Being intangible socio-cultural factors are still potential drivers to the technology development enhancement and play an important role in constituting national welfare.

The aim of the present research is to empirically investigate whether socio-cultural factors have significant impact on the national technology development and whether Hofstede's indices play a mediating role between chosen factors and the technology development. The literature review has shown that results of the similar empiric research are rather controversial. Based on a dataset from more than 100 countries we have designed and analyzed a second-order model that confirmed the impact of the chosen factors to the technology development at a national economy. The most unexpected result deals with the direct impact of the business culture (R2 = 0.92). The received results also confirmed the role of the human capital and the social capital. Hofstede's indices play a mediating role in two from three cases: between human capital and the national technology development and between business culture and the technology development.

Keywords: Technology development · Human capital · Social capital · Business culture · National economy

1 Introduction

The technology development is emerging as a hot topic among scholars and practitioners. One could single out at least two main research directions in this sphere. The first one considers the technology development at a macro level, usually at a national level and its comparison with other countries. The other one deals with the technology development at the micro level, namely at an enterprise's level. Studies at the micro level cover such research questions as concerning investments in R&D, shares of innovative products in the product mix, revenues from innovative products and linkages between innovative activity and enterprise performance [3, 16–18]. Research

D. A. Alexandrov et al. (Eds.): DTGS 2019, CCIS 1038, pp. 313–326, 2019.
https://doi.org/10.1007/978-3-030-37858-5_26

works that deal with the macro level usually focus on various antecedents and their impact to the national technology development at a national level [24, 50], the relationship between the national technology development and the gross domestic product [7, 11, 53]. Thus, in work of [7] the impact of technology border to the technology development is investigated and the authors came to a conclusion that social, economic and political conditions greatly affect the magnitude of the technology development. Empiric works seeking for an interaction between human capital and the technology development quality have shown controversial results. Barro and Romer confirmed the positive link [7, 48], Cohen rejected it [18].

Despite the relevance of this topic we could postulate that research issues of the technology development are far from their completion. One could single out the following research gaps: little attention is paid to the linkage between various factors and the technology development performance; the configuration of the selected factors might be very various; models that are used in the empiric studies mostly present first-order formative constructs; intercountry comparisons are conducted on the material of two or three countries or in regional perspective [13, 14]. Certainly we can't capture all the aspects of such multifold phenomenon as the technology development and its influencing factors, that's why we have decided to focus on investigating the link between the socio-cultural factors and the technology development, using Hofstede's indices as mediators.

The present paper extends the existing stream of research by examining impact of the chosen socio-cultural factors on the national technology development. More specifically the present study aims to examine the following research questions:

How could these factors be measured and are their overall uses linked with the technology development on the national economy?

Do Hofstede's indices play a mediating role in the relationship between socio-cultural factors and the technology development?

Can we prove our assumptions basing on the dataset from one hundred countries?

The paper is structured as follows: first, theoretical background of the research problem is provided. This is followed by the presentation of the selected studies on the technology development's indicators, socio-cultural factors. Then, the research design is presented with the subsections of the data analysis and the findings of the study. Sections with the discussion, conclusions and implications for theory and practice terminate the paper.

2 Theoretical Background

2.1 Literature Review

The importance of socio-cultural factors for the technology development and economic growth has been discussed very intensively during last two decades. The theoretical emphasis on socio-cultural factors was laid mainly by endogenous growth theory, starting with Arrow [4] and Uzawa [52]. However, despite this general, mostly theoretically driven "feeling", the empirical evidence is rather inconclusive [14, 34]. There are several studies which directly oppose the common attitude pointing at weak relationship between socio-cultural factors and the technology development, possible reversal causality or presence of omitted variables [35, 38].

Nevertheless, most of the studies are not in such direct opposition. They often emphasize unequal or asymmetrical impact of socio-cultural factors to the technology development. These studies usually come to the conclusion that the positive impact of socio-cultural factors is different for different countries. Cadil et al. [14] came to conclusion that the impact of human capital on wages and household's disposable income was found significant. Lucas [36] studied the relationship between production and human capital, both in level and in first-order differences, shows a positive and significant statistical correlation. However, Ramos et al. [46] stressed that the effect of human capital represented by education level can have even a negative effect on unemployment, connected to over-education.

The literature on this subject reveals another methodological problem: the choice of models. The models used in the literature provides the opportunity to highlight some derived limits either from the selection of the indicators used, either in their form of expression (as pace, level or logarithm) or the method of calculation [10, 23].

The literature review has shown that results received by researchers addressed to this field are various. There are two main problems what types of socio-cultural factors should be considered and how they should be measured. Mostly, the researchers consider human capital as a key determinant of the technology development. We consider three composite factors namely human capital, social capital and business culture and its link with the technology development. The problem of their indicators is presented further.

2.2 Technology Development and its Indicators

According to [24] the national technology development depends on quality of human capital. The role of intellectual resources has increased in the hierarchy of social values and high technology and growth of technological renewal has come to the fore. In modern societies the level of the human capital, together with the social capital and the business culture form an intellectual potential of a country, being a main factor, determining the national technology development [12–15].

The technology development of a country is usually characterized by technological achievements [11, 36]. Comparing the level of the technology development of different countries one can evaluate the efficiency of intellectual potential of a country and its place in the world scientific community. Nowadays there is a large amount of methods and approaches for measuring the technology development (Table 1) [5, 6].

The presented indicators are cumulative indices that determine the country level of the technological development in general terms. However only in the knowledge economy index (KEI) the social and cultural factors are taken into account [7, 11].

For each group of the technology development indicators the country is assessed in points from 1 to 10. KEI allows comparing separate indicators for each country. This index can be considered as a dependent parameter of socio-cultural factors' level. In the present paper we label it as national technology development (NTD). Let's consider the chosen independent parameters.

Table 1. Approaches in measuring the technology development at a national level.

##	Indicator	Meaning	Organization-developer
1	Competitive index	Depicts the country capabilities to produce goods worldwide competitive and increase standard of living	World economy forum/International institute of management and development
2	Technology achievement index	Is designed for the evaluation of country development in elaboration and diffusion technologies and also in forming human competencies	UNO Development program
3	Knowledge economy index	Is designed for the evaluation of knowledge economy	World Bank

2.3 Socio-Cultural Factors

Human Capital. The concept of human capital was fully embodied mainly in works of Romer [48] and Lucas [36]. Many studies and analyses focusing on human capital and growth followed – Barro [7] finds human capital to be one of key determinants of per capita income, Aghion and Howitt [1] stress the role of human capital as a factor promoting higher investment in technology with positive impact on growth. Moreover many country-specific or cross-country studies of human capital have been rising. It is also often treated as one of the possible determinants of differences and divergences in wages, productivity and income [14, 45, 46]. But the impact onto the technology development hasn't been researched enough.

In present paper we have chosen the following indicators of the human capital: total costs of education as a share of GDP (EDE); a combined indicator of the adult literacy rate and a share of people received a high education degree (EDI); the total amount of man-hours, calculated as researchers' working hours (SRI).

Social Capital. Social capital has been widely discussed since 1980s, but a precise and widely accepted definition is still not available [34]. For example, [12] define social capital as "the aggregation of actual and potential resources within a specific network, where the network is composed of relationships that involve mutual acquaintance and mutual recognition". Differently, for [19, 20] "social capital is defined by its function. It is not a single entity, but a variety of different entities having two characteristics in common: They all consist of some aspect of social structure, and they facilitate certain actions of individuals who are within the structure".

Nowadays, it is widespread recognized that social capital affects technology development in different ways. For instance, [40, 42] find that trust and norms can exert a positive effect as they reduce transaction costs and facilitate economic activities.

According to [37] the social capital is provided by the direct availability to partners' resources, social institutes, which the level of development influences the scientific and technology development of a country. The social capital, as a rule, is realized in social network providing such functions as collective activities' effectiveness; the decrease of transaction costs; the provision of necessary information diffusion, useful for economic possibilities. From the empiric perspective the social capital impact on the scientific and technology development is described in Akomak, and Weel's work [2] who, having based on 14 European regions data, have come to a conclusion about the positive correlation between the social capital and the technological development [13].

For the measuring social capital we use such indicators as the amount of international patent applications filed under the procedure of the patent cooperation treaty (WIPI); the total costs of R&D, calculated at purchasing power parity (RDE); total costs on ICT-infrastructure calculated as costs for the implementation and exploitation (ICTD).

Business Culture. Appealing to the opinion of prominent researchers [12, 38, 41] the level of business culture impacts immensely on the technology development of a country. However, the analysis of empiric works [34, 38] dealing with the intercountry comparison of cultural differences has shown that business culture differs at a country level and it should be taken into account in finding statistically significant evaluations of socio-cultural factors on the technology development [24, 26].

For measuring the business culture level we have chosen the following indicators: the combined index of the effectiveness of property rights protection, taking into account the general state of the legal environment, as well as the rights to physical and legal property (IPR); patent implementation activity, measured as the number of design applications (PSI); publication activity, measured as the share of publications of authors from a particular country in the global number of publications (STA).

2.4 Hofstede's Indices as a Mediator

Hofstede [31] has defined culture as "the collective programming of the mind which distinguishes the members of one human group from another." [31–33] has proposed six widely utilized dimensions of culture: power distance, individualism-collectiveness, masculinity-femininity, and uncertainty avoidance, long-term orientation and indulgence. Hofstede's framework has been examined empirically by many researchers in different cross-cultural studies. The purpose of this paper is to consider Hofstede's indices as mediators between chosen socio-cultural factors and the technology development.

3 Research Design

3.1 A Conceptual Model and Hypotheses' Elaboration

The technology development depends on the three chosen factors' relatedness. We also suggest that Hofstede's indices mediate the relationship between the chosen factors and the technology development in the national economy. The conceptual model is presented in Fig. 1.

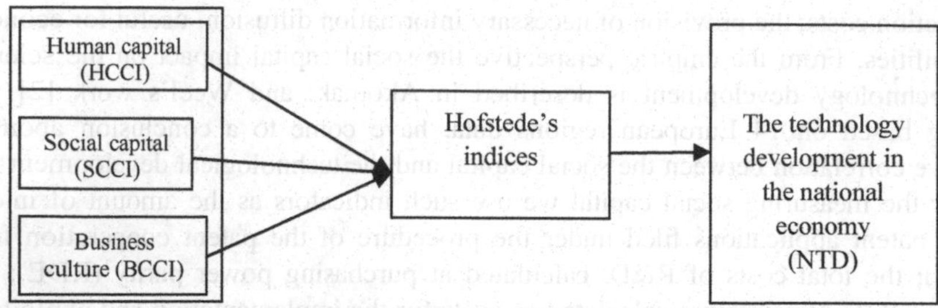

Fig. 1. Research scheme

The main hypotheses of the research are presented in the Table 2.

Table 2. Main hypotheses of the research

H	Path
H1	HCCI → NTD
H2	SCCI → NTD
H3	BCCI → NTD
H4	HCCI → HI → NTD
H5	SCCI → HI → NTD
H6	BCCI → HI → NTD

3.2 Research Methodology

The research design entails a two-stage procedure presented in Fig. 2. The first stage involves the measurement model conceptualization and item generation to form a scale for socio-cultural factors. In stage two the scale is subjected to a series of standard statistical tests. For the purpose of clarity each step within each stage is labeled in Fig. 2 using its corresponding subsection.

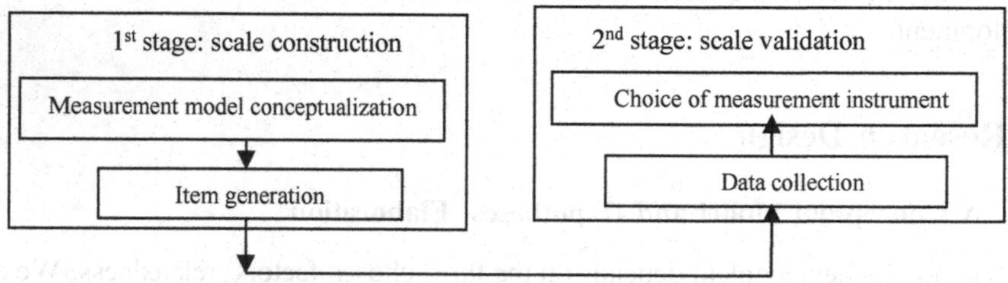

Fig. 2. Two-stage procedure of the research design

Measurement Model Conceptualization. We conceptualize the chosen socio-cultural factors as a formative second-order construct that is created by the three first-order constructs [8, 9]. In the present paper we use the terminology of a formative second-order measurement model in line with Diamantopoulos et al. [23]. This measurement structure provides the understanding of the characteristics of the key construct. According to Thorton et al. [51] a second-order formative measurement "faithfully represents all of the conceptual distinctions that the researcher believes are important and it provides the most powerful means of testing and evaluating the construct". One more evident reason of using a second-order measurement model is the transfer of uncountable notions into countable ones and the usage of official statistical data [43].

For "human capital" factor we considered three countable parameters namely education expenses as a share of gross domestic product – x_1(EDE); adult literacy – x_2(EDI); total amount of researchers – x_3(SRI).

For "social capital" factor there have been chosen such parameters as international patent applications – x_4(WIPI); expenses in R&D – x_5(RDE); expenses in implementation and exploitation of ICT – x_6(ICTD).

For "business culture" factor the parameters of intellectual property rights – x_7(IPR); amount of patent implementations – x_8(PSI) and publishing activity – x_9(STA) have been determined.

We based our conceptualization of the formative measurement model on two conceptual criteria suggested by Bollen and Bauldry [10]. Firstly, if the set of indicators is indeed casual to the latent variable then they should be "essential" to the latent variable. Secondly, a change in any indicators must also result in a change in the latent variable. From a measurement prospective each first-order construct has its unique property that is distinct from others. Indicators that describe chosen socio-cultural factors are presented in Table 3.

Item Generation. For the operationalization of the first-order measurement models we follow Churchill's scale development procedure by first generating several overlapping measurement items that capture key aspect of first-order construct to form a pool of items [21]. We have aggregated the separate parameters in composite indices.

Data Collection. In order to empirically test our conceptual model and stated hypotheses we have used a dataset of 100 countries [53]. The data of composite indices we have gathered from official statistical sources – UNESCO [54], EUROSTAT Main Indicators [22]. We used dataset for one year namely 2017 as the main idea of our research was to determine whether our conceptual model was in line with practice of intercountry comparison research.

The method of composite indices comprises the singling out of the synthetic latent parameter with the principle component method [8, 9]. In the process of the statistic transformation we have received the following meanings of composite indices:

$$HCCI = 0.49EDE + 0.33EDI + 0.17SRI \tag{1}$$

$$SCCI = 0.62WIPI + 0.29RDE + 0.01ICTD \tag{2}$$

$$BCCI = 0.5IPR + 0.32PSI + 0.18STA \tag{3}$$

Table 3. Chosen factors as composite indices

##	Abbreviation	Name	Description	Source
"Human capital" factor				
x_1	EDE	Education expenses as a share of GDP	Education expenses from all state sources	UNESCO; Federal State Statistics Service
x_2	EDI	World country rate according to Education Index	Aggregated indicator of adult literacy	UNESCO
x_3	SRI	Personal occupied in R&D	The total amount of researchers calculated by working time fund	UNESCO; Eurostat Main Indicators
"Social capital" factor				
x_4	WIPI	International patent applications	The amount of international patent applications	UNESCO; Eurostat Main Indicators
x_5	RDE	Expenses in R&D	Expenses in R&D calculated by purchasing power rate	UNESCO; Eurostat Main Indicators
x_6	ICTD	Development of ICT-infrastructure	Expenses in implementation and exploitation of ICT	UNESCO; Eurostat Main Indicators
"Business culture" factor				
x_7	IPR	The level of intellectual rights defense	Aggregated effectiveness index of intellectual rights	UNESCO; Eurostat Main Indicators
x_8	PSI	Activity of patent implementation	Amount of applications for industrial samples	UNESCO; Eurostat Main Indicators
x_9	STA	Publishing activity	Share of papers from authors of a country	UNESCO; Eurostat Main Indicators

where HCCI is labeled for human capital composite index, EDE – for education expenses as a share of GDP, EDI – education index, SRI – personnel occupied in R&D; SCCI – social capital composite index, WIPI – amount of patent applications, RDE – expenses in R&D, ICTD – development of information and communication technologies infrastructure; BCCI – business culture composite index, IPR – intellectual property rights defense, PSI – amount of patent implementations, STA – publishing activity.

A Measurement Instrument. Among the variety of measurement instruments PLS-SEM has become the most comprehensive and useful statistical approach for testing relations between dependent and independent parameters [39]. There are many methods to estimate the structural equation model such as MLE (Maximum Likelihood

Estimation), GLS (Generalized Least Square), PLS (Partial Least Square), etc. PLS has undeniable advantage compared to other methods [27, 47]. For PLS is an iterative procedure for estimating structural equation models that don't improve distributional assumptions on the data [25].

The general statistical formula has the following view:

$$NTD_{KEI} = \beta_0 + \beta_1 X_{HCCI} + \beta_2 X_{SCCI} + \beta_3 X_{BCCI} + \varepsilon \quad (4)$$

Evaluation of a suggested model starts with the evaluating indicator reliability, internal consistency (composite reliability - CR), convergent validity (average variance extracted - AVE). To meet the requirements of indicators' reliability test, the value of each indicator's loading factor must be greater than 0.5 [29, 30]. Table 4 shows that the loading factor values for all of the chosen parameters in this study are above the minimum prerequisite value. Hence it can be concluded that all parameters have been chosen correctly.

Table 4. Indicator reliability test result

Indicator	Loading factor
HCCI	0.64
SCCI	0.7
BCCI	0.65
NTD	0.61

Internal consistency testing aims to determine the level of data consistency for all indicators in this study. Internal consistency can be tested by evaluating the value of composite reliability (CR). A variable is said to be reliable if it has a value of composite reliability greater than 0.73 [29, 30]. Table 5 shows that the value of CR for all parameters except the technology development (CR = 0.49) have been with or little bit greater than the minimum value required.

Table 5. Composite reliability (CR) and convergent validity (AVE)

Indicator	HCCI	SCCI	BCCI	NTD
CR value	0.5	0.61	0.5	0.49
AVE value	0.52	0.28	0.54	0.51

Convergent validity test aims to see how far the indicators actually reflect parameters and do not reflect other parameters [29, 30]. It can be seen from the AVE of greater than 0.5. Table 5 shows that the AVE value for all parameters except social capital (AVE = 0.28) have been with the minimum value.

3.3 Evaluation of the Designed Structural Model and the Interpretation of Results

The structural model evaluation has been conducted by the examining the path coefficients and p-value, the coefficient of determination (R^2). Path coefficients examination analyzed the relationship between parameters in the structural model. Path coefficient value is deemed not significant if it is in the range −0.1 to 0.1 [28]. Table 6 shows all paths have coefficient value greater than 0.1, so that all relationship among parameters in the structural model of this research relate positively. Moreover, the significance of each relationship can be seen from the p-value. P-value describes the probability of the occurrence of errors during the hypotheses testing. In other words, a smaller p-value indicates that the hypotheses testing are significant with the low error. P-value data of this research can be seen in Table 6 and were observed by means of one-tailed.

Table 6. Hypotheses test result

H	Path	Path coeff.	p-value	Note
H1	HCCI → NTD	0.69	1,49E−05	Significant
H2	SCCI → NTD	0.43	1,28E−05	Not significant
H3	BCCI → NTD	0.62	3,77E−05	Significant
H4	HCCI → HI → NTD	0.61	3,42E−05	Significant
H5	SCCI → HI → NTD	0.35	3,29E−05	Not significant
H6	BCCI → HI → NTD	0.55	5,38E−05	Significant

Coefficient of determination R^2 is a structural model of the criteria used to measure the relationship between the variance of a particular parameter with the total variance.

According to [27–30] the value of R^2 is considered weak is it is below 0.19; is considered moderate if it is between 0.19–0.33; is considered strong if it has a value between 0.33–0.67. In our model there are parameters categorized with the strong relations, namely human capital ($R^2 = 0.78$), social capital ($R^2 = 0.48$), business culture ($R^2 = 0.92$), the technology development ($R^2 = 0.66$). R^2 results are summarized in Table 7.

Table 7. R2 values

Variable	HCCI	SCCI	BCCI	NTD
R^2 value	0.78	0.43	0.92	0.66

4 Discussion

In the present paper there has been an attempt to consider such research gaps as linkage between selected socio-cultural factors and the technology development; the combination of the selected socio-cultural factors; a second-order measurement model. In myriads of study the technology development is connected with the technological environment, national innovation systems, high technologies, etc. However, several researchers prefer to consider the technology development with requirements of the society [49]. This direction coincides with the seven technology paradigm, developed in work [44] and labeled as cognitive technology paradigm.

Another perspective that should be mentioned in the discussion is the validity and applicability of the formative measurement models. The conceptualization of the measurement model addresses two key issues highlighted in the literature. The first issue is related to the conceptualization of a formative measurement model. While some scholars argue that no construct is reflective or formative, others suggest that a construct must be either reflective or formative based on its conceptual meaning. The second key issue is that a formative measurement by nature is sensitive to its outcome variables. The path coefficients of the casual indicators and the disturbance term of the formative measurement respond to different outcome variables used.

This implies that using the same formative measurement to predict different outcome variables would to some extent change the nature of the formative construct. This has been argued as being a major hindrance for formative measurement to advance theory building.

According to Bollen [10] casual indicators should demonstrate a stable tendency toward their formative latent variable vis-a-vis different outcome variables of that formative latent variable. However, one can only realize this by subjecting to empirical test. More importantly, the validity of such a measurement model needs to be examined in future.

The last but not the least perspective that should be discussed is the choice of PLS-SEM as a measurement instrument. PLS-SEM has a quasi-standard with respect to analyzing cause-effect relationships between latent or composite variables [27–30, 47]. Its ability to model latent variables taking into account various forms of measurement error makes PLS-SEM useful for a variety of the research questions. The intrigue is whether results that we got with the PLS-SEM will coincide with results of other methods. Evidently, PLS-SEM is optimal for estimating latent or composite models with practically no limitations.

5 Conclusion

The primary objective of this study was to examine the direct impact of the chosen socio-cultural factors on technology development as well as mediating effects of Hofstede's indices on the relation between the chosen factors and technology development. The findings show that the human capital and business culture have stronger impact than the social capital. Social capital in all tests has shown weak results. Perhaps it could be explained by the chosen first-order variables.

This study has several theoretical implications for the technology development research. First of all it extends the empirical research assessing the impact of socio-cultural factors on the technology development and evaluates the mediation effect of the Hofstede's indices. Although there is a rich body of literature on the technology development and socio-cultural factors, research on the integration of the constructs is scant. And what is less understood is the mediating effect of Hostede's indices on the technology development.

Concerning the practical aspects the received results could be used at a national level while elaborating strategies of the technology development, the youth policy, the development strategies of higher education institutions; the forming budgeting in strategic directions.

At the level of the state corporations the received results could be used while elaborating corporate culture, increasing innovation activity, developing modern organization technologies. At the level of separate employees the received results shift accents for improving corporate culture, increasing labor intensity, enforcing self-reflection. The received results in total have confirmed the formulated hypothesis and correlated with the similar research, done by other authors.

The results of the conducted research allow determining the level of the and technology development in Russia in comparison with other countries, and also increase the justification of decisions that are made while elaborating strategic documents, investment programs and improving innovation potential.

We believe that our model is sound as we have tested it with the reliable survey instruments and data. Nevertheless some limitations should be reasonably admitted.

Firstly, our study has its limitations related to the conceptual model, as we consider the impact of socio-cultural factors on the technology development and it was interesting to find out how the technology development in its turn influence socio-cultural environment.

Secondly, we used data for a definite period not panel ones. It would be a challenge to use the designed model for panel data. Future work can follow this line of the research to replicate the model and thereby allow for a comparison the stability of the formative measurement model.

Thirdly, the result of our evaluations in social capital doesn't coincide with ones presented in the literature. It needs to be reproved by the further research.

References

1. Aghion, P., Howitt, P.: Endogenous Growth Theory. MIT Press, Cambridge (1997)
2. Akcomac, S., Weel, B.: Social capital, innovation and growth: evidence from Europe. Eur. Econ. Rev. **53**, 544–567 (2009)
3. Amat, O., Renart, M., Garcia, M.: Factors that determine the evolution of high-growth businesses. Intang. Cap. **9**, 379–391 (2013)
4. Arrow, K.J.: The economic implications of learning by doing. Rev. Econ. Stud. **29**, 155–173 (1962)
5. Arkhipova, M.Y., Sirotin, V.P., Sukhareva, N.A.: The elaboration of composite indicator for measuring dynamics of cyber inequality in RF. Stat. Issues **4**, 75–87 (2018)
6. Ayvazyan, S.A., Stepanov, V.S., Kozlova, M.I.: Measuring of synthetic parameters of living standards of a region and investigating of key directions of social and economic policy improvement (on the example of Samar region). Appl. Econom. **2**, 18–84 (2006)
7. Barro, R.: Economic growth in a cross section of countries. Q. J. Econ. **106**, 407–443 (1991)
8. Baxter, R.: Reflective and formative metrics of relationship value: a commentary essay. J. Bus. Res. **62**(12), 1370–1377 (2009)

9. Blalock, H.M.: Conceptualization and Measurement in the Social Sciences. Sage Publications, Beverly Hills (1982)
10. Bollen, K.A., Bauldry, S.: Three Cs in measurement models: casual indicators, composite indicators and covariates. Psychol. Methods **16**(3), 265–284 (2011)
11. Bozhechkova, A.V.: The analysis of scientific and technology progress impact on the dynamics of gross domestic product. Audit Financ. Anal. **3**, 85–94 (2011)
12. Bourdieu, P.: Forms of capital. In: Richardson, J.G. (ed.) Handbook of Theory and Research for Sociology of Education. Greenwood, New York (1986)
13. Burt, R., Hogarth, R.M., Michaud, C.: The social capital of French and American managers. Organ. Sci. **11**, 123–147 (2000)
14. Cadil, J., Petkovova, L., Blatna, D.: Human capital, economic structure and growth. Procedia Econ. Financ. **12**, 85–92 (2014)
15. Camps, S., Marques, P.: Exploring how social capital facilitates innovation: the role of innovation enablers. Technol. Forecast. Soc. Chang. **88**, 325–348 (2014)
16. Coad, A.: Exploring the processes of a firm growth: evidence from a vector autoregression. Ind. Corp. Change **19**, 1677–1703 (2010)
17. Coad, A.: Innovation and firm growth in high-technology sectors: a quantile regression approach. Res. Policy **37**(4), 633–648 (2008)
18. Cohen, D., Soto, M.: Growth and human capital: good data, good results. J. Econ. Growth **12**, 51–76 (2007)
19. Coleman, J.: Social and human capital. Soc. Sci. Mod. **3**, 122–139 (2001)
20. Coleman, J.: Social capital in the creation of human capital. Am. J. Sociol. **94**, 95–120 (1988)
21. Eurostat main indicators. https://ec.europa.eu/eurostat/web/sdi/main-tables
22. Churchill Jr., G.A.: A paradigm for developing better measures of marketing constructs. J. Mark. Res. **16**(1), 64–73 (1979)
23. Diamantopoulos, A., Riefler, P., Roth, K.P.: Advancing formative measurement models. J. Bus. Res. **61**(12), 1203–1218 (2008)
24. Drogovoz, P.A., Sadovskaya, T.G., Chursin, A.A., Shiboldenkov, V.A.: The neural network analysis of social and cultural factors impact on state innovation activity. Scientific research and development. Soc. Humanit. Res. Technol. **6**(2), 72–80 (2017)
25. Fornell, C., Bookstein, F.L.: Two structural equation models: LISREL and PLS applied to consumer exit-voice theory. J. Market. Res. **19**, 440–452 (1982)
26. Hall, E.T.: Beoynd Culture. Anchor, Garden City (1976)
27. Hair, J., Hult, G., Ringle, C., Sarstedt, M.: A Primer on Partial Least Squares Equation Modelling. Sage Publications, Thousand Oaks (2014)
28. Hair, J., Ringle, C., Sarstedt, M.: Partial least squares: the better approach to structural equation modelling? Long Range Plan. **45**(5–6), 312–319 (2012)
29. Henseler, J.: Guest editorial. Indus. Manag. Data Syst. **116**(9), 1842–1848 (2016)
30. Henseler, J., Hubona, G.S., Ray, P.A.: Using PLS path modelling in new technology research: updated guidelines. Indus. Manag. Data Syst. **116**(1), 1–19 (2016)
31. Hofstede, G.: Culture's Consequences: International Differences in Work-Related Values. Sage, Beverly Hills (1980)
32. Hofstede Insites. http://www.hofstede-insights.com/models/
33. Hofstede, G., Hofstede, G.J.: Cultures and Organizations: Software of the Mind. McGraw-Hill, New York (2005)
34. Grzegorczyk, M.: The role of culture moderated social capital in technology transfer insights from Asia and America. Technol. Forecast. Soc. Chang. **143**, 132–141 (2019)
35. Kumar, N., Rego, S.: Level of educational attainment and its impact on technology diffusion in developing countries (2009). http://dx.doi.org/10.2139/ssrn.1350187

36. Lucas, R.E.: On the mechanics of economic development. J. Monet. Econ. **22**, 3–42 (1988)
37. Landry, R., Amara, N., Lamari, M.: Does social capital determine innovation? To what extent? Technol. Forecast. Soc. Chang. **69**(7), 681–701 (2002)
38. Lockett, M.: Culture and the problems of Chinese management. Organ. Stud. **9**(4), 475–496 (1998)
39. Lowry, P.B., Gaskin, J.: Partial least squares structural equation modeling for building and testing behavioral causal theory: when to choose it and how to use it. IEEE Trans. Prof. Commun. **57**(2), 123–146 (2014)
40. Magdeeva, M.R., Zhilina, N.N., Zgidulina, T.S.: Social capital: notion and approaches to research. Econ. Manag. Probl. Solut. **1**, 18–23 (2017)
41. Mankiw, G., Romer, D., Wil, D.: A contribution to the empirics of the economic growth. Q. J. Econ. **107**, 407–437 (1992)
42. Maskell, P.: Social capital, innovation and competitiveness. In: Baron, S., Field, J., Schuller, T. (eds.) Social Capital: Critical Perspectives, pp. 111–123. Oxford University Press, New York (2000)
43. Nasledov, A.D., Morozova, S.V.: The problem of mathematical implementation in psychological research: institualization of statistic discourse. Herald Saint-Petersburg Univ. **4**, 252–261 (2010)
44. Prokhorov, I.A.: The launch of the seventh technology paradigm. http://www.energoinform.org/pointofview/prohorov/7-tech-structure.aspx
45. Queiros, M., et al.: Cross-country analysis to high-growth businesses: unveiling its determinants. J. Innov. Knowl. **4**(3), 146–153 (2017)
46. Ramos, R., Surinach, J., Artis, M.: Regional economic growth and human capital: the role of overeducation. Working papers 2009/04, Research Institute of Applied Economics (2009)
47. Rigdon, E.E.: Rethinking partial least squares path modelling: in praise of simple methods. Long Range Plan. **45**, 341–358 (2012)
48. Romer, P.: Endogenous technological change. J. Polit. Econ. **98**, 71–102 (1990)
49. Romanov, A.A., et al.: The methodology for the creation of an innovative scientific and technical reserve in the rocket and space industry. Rocket Space Ind. Device Build. Inf. Syst. **5**(2), 53–64 (2018)
50. Temple, J.: Growth effects of education and social capital in the OECD countries. OECD Econ. Stud. **33**, 57–101 (2001)
51. Thorton, S., Hennenberg, S., Naude, P.: Conceptualizing and validating organizational networking as a second-order formative construct. Ind. Mark. Manag. **43**, 951–956 (2014)
52. Usawa, H.: Optimum technical change in an aggregative model of economic growth. Int. Econ. Rev. **6**, 18–31 (1965)
53. UNESCO. http://data.uis.unesco.org
54. Humanitarian Technologies Analitical Portal. http://www.gtmarket.ru

Prospects of Blockchain-Based Information Systems for the Protection of Intellectual Property

Roman Amelin[1](✉), Vladislav Arkhipov[2](✉), Sergey Channov[3](✉), Marina Dobrobaba[4], and Victor Naumov[5](✉)

[1] National Research Saratov State University named after N. G. Chernyshevsky, 83 Astrakhanskaya Street, Saratov 410012, Russia
ame-roman@yandex.ru

[2] State of Saint Petersburg State University, 13B Universitetskaya Emb., St. Petersburg 199034, Russia
vladislav.arkhipov@dentons.com

[3] The Russian Presidential Academy of National Economy and Public Administration, 23/25 Sobornaya Street, Saratov 410031, Russia
sergeychannov@yandex.ru

[4] Kuban State University, 149 Stavropolskaya Street, Krasnodar 350040, Russia

[5] Institute of State and Law Russian Academy of Sciences, 10 Znamenka Street, Moscow 119019, Russia
victor.naumov@dentons.com

Abstract. The article analyzes the possibilities of maintaining the register of intellectual property objects using blockchain technologies. Such registries have a number of advantages in comparison with traditional methods of registration and provide more opportunities for rightholders. However, they also have certain disadvantages, primarily due to the lack of full-fledged mechanisms for resolving intellectual property disputes. This problem requires not only technical, but also organizational and legal solutions. The authors conclude that the prospects for the development of blockchain platforms for registering and managing intellectual property are linked to the possibility of dividing such registries into two types. The first one is the registries of IP objects on the permissionless blockchain platform. Information about IP objects and their authors (owners) contained in them will not be official. The second type is the registries of IP objects on the basis of permission blockchain technologies, in which superuser rights will be granted to government bodies authorized in the field of IP protection. Entries in them will be official and will have validating rights value.

Keywords: Intellectual property · Blockchain technologies · State registration · Registries · Smart contracts · Permission blockchains · Information systems

---

This work was supported by grant 17-03-00082-OГН from the Russian Foundation for Basic Research.

D. A. Alexandrov et al. (Eds.): DTGS 2019, CCIS 1038, pp. 327–337, 2019.
https://doi.org/10.1007/978-3-030-37858-5_27

1 Introduction

Most recently, blockchain technologies were perceived in many countries of the world as exotic. Currently, they are recognized as one of the most important areas of building a digital economy [1]. The main sphere of their application is still the construction of cryptocurrency systems based on them. At the same time, already in the first years of the blockchain, an understanding that this technology can be used for various purposes appeared. Currently blockchain technologies are already being used for voting, information exchange, fixing legal facts, ensuring information security, etc. [2–4]. An important direction is building decentralized distributed registries based on the blockchain. Real estate registries, vehicle registries and intellectual property (IP) registries are the most promising among them [5, 6]. Many of the most interesting problems of such application of blockchain technology lie not so much in the technical, but in the legal plane [7, 8].

Legislation of different states does not always apply to regulating IP protection issues in the same way. However, it is common to divide IP objects into two groups: (1) objects whose rights arise as a result of acts of state registration (inventions, utility models, industrial designs, etc.), (2) objects that are recognized as protected by the very fact of creation (works of literature, art, databases, phonograms, etc.).

Objects of the first group are included in certain registries maintained either by authorized state bodies (for example, Rospatent in the Russian Federation) or by international organizations (for example, the European Patent Office). Such registries can establish rights or confirm rights. At the same time, for the convenience of working with registered IP objects, the functions of maintaining their registries are often performed by other organizations, including commercial ones.

Objects of the second group do not require mandatory state registration, and there is no absolute need to include them in any registries. However, for some of them, registration with the same authorized bodies is possible, but on a voluntary basis. For example, the legislation of many countries of the world provides for the voluntary registration of computer programs and databases. In Russia, the same Rospatent carries out official registration (Article 1262 of the Civil Code of the Russian Federation). The main point of such registries is to fix the facts of creation of intellectual property objects, which makes it easier to prove in disputes about authorship or use priority (for example, for commercial designations). Other Russian organizations also maintain registers of various objects of intellectual rights (Russian copyright society, Russian Union of copyright holders, all-Russian intellectual property organization, non-profit partnership for the protection and management of rights in the field of art "MANAGIS", etc.). Inclusion in the register (which in itself is not the basis for the emergence of intellectual rights, but provides additional evidence of priority in use) may be useful for IP objects that require special registration. For example, making a record of the use of a trademark in commercial circulation in such a register at a certain point will allow a more convincing justification of the priority when registering a trademark.

Before the advent of blockchain technologies, all of these registries were conducted in traditional ways, first on paper, then on electronic data carriers. Accordingly, they existed, as a rule, in a single copy; records were made by one or several authorized subjects, etc. Blockchain and related distributed ledger technology offer new possibilities for IP protection and registration and as evidence, either at the registry stage or in court. It also promises a cost-effective way to speed up such processes. Potential use cases include: evidence of creatorship and provenance authentication, registering and clearing IP rights; controlling and tracking the distribution of (un)registered IP; providing evidence of genuine and/or first use in trade and/or commerce; digital rights management (e.g., online music sites); establishing and enforcing IP agreements, licenses or exclusive distribution networks through smart contracts; and transmitting payments in real-time to IP owners [9].

Distributed registries of IP objects based on blockchain technology have several advantages over traditional ones. These include general accessibility, cheapness (elimination of unnecessary intermediaries), efficiency, reliability (immutability of the data entered), the ability to automate the tracking of the transfer of exclusive rights and transactions for IP objects through the use of smart contracts, etc. It is logical that similar registries are already being created (PeerTracks, Bittunes, BitImage, Ujo, KODAKOne, etc.). They also appear in the Russian Federation (n'RIS, IPCHAIN, etc.).

At the same time, the use of blockchain technologies for maintaining registers of IP objects has certain disadvantages. Specialists report about them significantly less than about merits, and, if attention is paid, the emphasis is usually on purely technical problems (the high cost of blockchain technologies compared to traditional ones; "51% problem", etc.). It should be noted that some projects of registries of IP objects on the blockchain, created relatively recently, have already ceased to function (Ascribe, Binded, etc.). In our opinion, however, the massive introduction of IP registries on the blockchain requires the solution of a number of organizational and legal problems.

This article will discuss the merits of this approach (from a technical and legal point of view), the potential risks from its use, and the problems that need to be solved.

2 Review of Best Practices

First of all, it should be noted that in the past few years several dozen blockchain projects in the field of intellectual property rights management have been announced. Some of these projects have reached the implementation stage and are currently being actively tested. It is premature to say that some project claims to be a leader setting the standard in this area. Nevertheless, the review below shows that, at least technically, the creation of registers of intellectual property rights is quite possible, both on the basis of public cryptocurrency blockchains and on the original platform.

(a) Peertracks. Peertracks platform focuses exclusively on music and uses the SOUNDAC Blockchain for automated royalty payments. Copyright holders add music to SOUNDAC by going to the Rights Management Portal. During this process, they specify what is to be done with income – how the royalties should be split amongst all participants. SOUNDAC has a royalty pool from which it pays out all copyright holders. It distributes the funds based on what all users, on every streaming platform (connected to the SOUNDAC ecosystem) have been listening too. The funds go towards every song the users have been streaming. Payments are made in local currency RYLT [10].

(b) Ujo. It is also a blockchain music platform. Functions based on Ethereum. The principle of operation is approximately the same as Peertracks. Of interest is the fact that the platform announces the possibility of challenging the making of copyright records in the blockchain registry by sending claims [11].

(c) BitImage. The platform supports a wider range of intellectual property rights – audio, video, images and other digital content which are directly hosted on the platform. Buyers can purchase the content in two ways: (1) by searching through the existing digital media from the extensive collection; (2) by placing a job with any requirements and, as a result, receiving the "turn-key" content. It is possible to conclude smart contracts.

(d) Totem based on Baidu search engine. One of the largest blockchain platforms by the number of users. Allows to register only photos and other images. Provides the ability to distribute and track images and dispose of copyright. Artificial intelligence is used to assess the originality of works when downloading and identifying violators of intellectual property rights.

(e) Mediachain. Mediachain is an open, universal media library. It works with almost all works of literature, science and art. Unlike traditional DHT and blockchain-based systems, Mediachain scales efficiently when publishing billions of small records, and can accommodate use-cases like archiving high cardinality datasets or building internet-scale decentralized media applications. Mediachain pays special attention to the protection of copyright, using a special mechanism for establishing authorship [12].

(f) Blokur. The platform is used to work only with musical works. A feature of Blokur is the ability to resolve some copyright disputes in automatic mode. Blokur reconciles different sources of rights data to a single blockchain state. An algorithm resolves data conflicts automatically, eliminating labor-intensive tasks and increasing revenue for rights owners.

(g) IPCHAIN. This is the newest Russian project of registration and use of intellectual rights on the blockchain. IPCHAIN stores information on rights and objects of intellectual property, as well as atomic transactions, which are recorded by the distributed IPCHAIN registry, that are the most significant for all participants in the IP sphere and reflecting key facts types of public information records.

In general, the world at present, there are several dozens of such projects (at different stages of implementation), which indicates a certain potential of this technology in protecting IP.

3 Advantages of Blockchain Technologies in the Protection of IP Objects

Accessibility is usually referred to as the first among the advantages of building registries of IP objects using blockchain technologies. When using traditional registries, only one person or a narrow circle of authorized persons can make entries in them.

Most of the existing IP registries on the basis of blockchain technologies, as a rule, allow anyone who claims to secure his rights to an IP object to do this. Accordingly, the process of registration of IP objects not only becomes publicly available, but also significantly accelerated. The problem with conventional regulatory authorities is that their process of verifying and approving inventions is slow [13]. The exclusion of the registration authorities (no matter whether they are official or unofficial) as intermediaries allows to greatly reduce the problem.

The elimination of intermediaries has another important advantage of blockchain technologies – the cheaper process of registration of IP objects. We have already noted above that the development of registries based on blockchain technologies is more expensive. However, this rise in price at the stage of development and implementation of the system can be recouped during the period of its use. The larger the system and the more its participants, the greater the benefit. When using traditional information technologies, the increase in scale leads to a significant increase in the cost of its administration. The new member of the public network blockchain becomes both a user and a manager at the same time. Accordingly, instead of creating expensive administrative bodies, it is only necessary to reach agreement between the participants. For IP registries based on blockchain technology, the functions performed by large institutions could be carried out by simple smartphone applications. In that scenario, the cost of registering an IP right would fall considerably, thereby enabling IP right holders to register their patents and trademarks in numerous different countries via easy-to-use, blockchain-based mobile or web applications [14, p. 856].

Another major advantage of using blockchain technologies for building registries of IP objects is the immutability of registry entries. The very essence of the blockchain is that, as a general rule, after the data has been written into it, it cannot be changed. Technically, this is achieved using sequential cryptographic transformation of data about each transaction. Each entry in the transaction block is assigned a hash, which is added to the header of the record of the next transaction, and so on. As a result, the transaction hash at the top of the chain confirms data on all previous transactions [15]. Accordingly, the data on the object of intellectual property and its copyright holder will remain in the registry based on blockchain technologies forever.

Another feature of the blockchain is the ability to set time stamps. Essentially, a whole network checks the status of some data at a specific time. Thus, a decentralized network provides evidence of the presence of something (events, facts, information) at a certain time – such evidence can be used as evidence in court [16]. Accordingly, loading an IP object or information about it and its creator (copyright holder) into the blockchain registry will create a record with an exact time stamp, which will allow substantiating authorship if a dispute arises later.

The invariability of records, coupled with the establishment of time stamps, allows not only to record the fact of creation of an IP object once, but also to track its further fate in terms of the transfer of rights to this object. The blockchain could also be used by third-parties or the creator to see the complete chain of ownership of a work including licenses, sublicenses and assignments. It gives more control over the work and the content of the transactions would be easily available. Furthermore, the original creators of the work could use the blockchain technology for royalty payments. By digitally encoding the rights, royalty payments would become more reliable and efficient [17]. This, in turn, provides new opportunities at the disposal of exclusive rights, in particular, allows for the free circulation of such objects in the secondary market (sale of "second-hand" computer programs, phonograms and films in digital form, etc.) [18].

Finally, the blockchain provides the ability to set transaction rules (business logic) in relation to the transaction itself. We mean the use of so-called smart contracts – agreements concluded and executed automatically, without human intervention. Disposal of intellectual rights registered in the blockchain-registry using smart contracts is recognized as perhaps the main advantage of the blockchain [14, 19, 20], and due to its versatility and volume, it will not be considered in detail in this article.

4 Problems of Using Blockchain Technologies in the Protection of Intellectual Property

Noting the undoubted advantages of using distributed registries based on blockchain technologies for fixing rights to IP objects, scientists and specialists, as a rule, do not fix on the problematic points of their use for these purposes. Meanwhile, they are also available. The main one follows from the main advantage – the immutability of the data entered in the registry.

The above blockchain-registers of intellectual property are mainly public. They are based on the permissionless blockchain, in which there are no restrictions on users who can create blocks and perform transactions [21].

If any person can join such a registry and enter data on IP objects, it is extremely difficult to organize a mechanism for resolving disputes related to the rights to these objects. If one person created the work, and the registry entry was made to the second person, then what to do in the case when the first person subsequently proved his authorship? A rollback mechanism (in fact, a fork) for open blockchains is certainly possible, but it is due to the open nature that it is necessary to achieve user agreement. The experience of Ethereum, in which such a rollback was made (as a result of which Ethereum, among other things, split into two) testifies to the extreme complexity of this operation and its serious consequences.

Of course, in this case it is technically possible to make a new (corrective) entry in the register, in which the actual holder of rights will be indicated. However, if the open blockchain platform on which the register of IP objects operates allows you to make an unlimited number of records related to the same IP object to any user, then the question will arise: which of two or more records is correct. In addition, a number of blockchain registry services, prior to loading an IP object, carry out an automatic check for its coincidence with an object already loaded (or information from it). In this case, the usual user-copyright holder cannot make a corrective entry.

Some lawyers believe that this problem is solved without making changes to the IP registry. Thus, Inyushkin, on the basis of the premise that the blockchain registry has the legal regime of the database, indicates that the database legislation itself will protect the rights of the actual holder. "When applying the legal regime of databases to relations associated with blockchain technologies, it will be possible to use special mechanisms for bringing to responsibility for infringement of exclusive rights…

Consequently, the entry in the blockchain registry itself is not legitimate in nature, but on the contrary it gives rise to legal consequences in the form of applying liability to an attacker for violating the author's exclusive right, since the attacker made use of the work by entering it into the database under his own name" [22, p. 47].

It is difficult to argue with the fact that a record of authorship made by an inappropriate person, if this fact is subsequently proven, will not have to confirm the right or, especially, to establish the right. However, even if the present author (rightholder) is able to receive compensation from the violator of his rights through measures provided for by law, the incorrect entry in the registry of IP objects will not only prevent him from using all of the above blockchain technologies (tracking the status of the IP object and its use; through the conclusion of smart contracts, etc.), but it will also create permanent problems associated with the need to prove again and again their right to an IP object.

The problem under consideration has other facets. As noted above, there are currently many platforms that maintain registries of IP objects based on blockchain technologies. The author (rightholder) may register his IP object in one registry, and another person in a different one.

In addition, disputes about the right to IP objects may not always be associated with a deliberate violation of rights. There are situations when an object was created in collaboration, one IP object was created on the basis of another, parallel creation of similar IP objects – in all such cases, the issue of adjusting the record made earlier in the IP registry is important.

This, however, does not mean that the registries of IP objects based on permissionless blockchains have no prospects for the protection of intellectual rights. However, their role, apparently, can only be auxiliary – they will allow to form additional evidence of authorship (ownership) of the person who entered the data in the register of IP objects in the event of a dispute. Of course, IP platforms based on permissionless blockchains are also suitable for commercial and other use of IP objects, however, for the above reasons, this will be associated with certain risks.

5 The Role of Permission Blockchains in Building IP Registries

The problem of correcting information in the IP registry can be solved by using permission blockchains, in which transaction processing is carried out by a certain list of subjects (superusers). Such entities may be able to make, if necessary, additional entries in the registry, in fact, disavowing the initial ones (for example, a court decision that recognized the authorship of another person to the IP object, which was recorded earlier). With respect to these registries, a requirement must be established that the superuser's record takes precedence in case of conflict with other records; if there are several superuser entries, the last one by date is recognized as correct. At the same time, the initial records about the IP objects should be able to be entered by everyone (that is, the blockchain should not be private).

Such registries lose some of the advantages of permissionless blockchains (lack of intermediaries, simplicity, low cost). In addition, the presence of entities with the right to make corrective entries raises the question of confidence in these entities and in the registry as a whole. Thus, such an important property of the blockchain as immutability is called into question.

It seems that the prospects of creating registries of IP objects based on the permission blockchains are associated with the granting of superuser rights only to certain subjects – state (interstate) authorities or certain non-governmental organizations specializing in copyright protection, such as: European Patent Office, US Office Patents and Trademarks, United Kingdom Intellectual Property Office, Turkish Patent Office, Rospatent Russia, Russian Authors' Society, etc.

Despite the lack of some advantages compared to the registries of IP objects built on the basis of permissionless blockchain, registries using the permission blockchain will be more reliable than registries maintained by these same subjects without a blockchain. Although, as noted above, in a permission blockchain, data immutability is no longer absolute due to the admissibility of making corrective entries by the superusers, the original entries are also preserved. Due to this, it is still possible to appeal to them in case of any disputes. In addition, with respect to any registry maintained centrally, there is a risk of data loss as a result of its intentional or accidental destruction (damage). For a distributed registry, this danger is minimized. Finally, IP registries based on permission blockchains retain their advantages in tracking the status of an IP object, disposing of them through smart contracts, etc.

It appears that IP registries based on a permission blockchain, in which state authorities authorized in the field of IP protection may have superuser rights, may have official status, and the information contained in them will have legal significance by law.

This circumstance raises another issue that must be resolved in relation to these registries. There is no consensus among scientists and practitioners regarding the assignment of blockchain platforms to certain legal types of technological objects. So, some believe that by their attributes they are closest to the databases [22], others refer them to computer programs [23]. In our opinion, the blockchain registry combines both. Any blockchain platform, of course, is a database (in fact, a chain of blocks). However, they cannot function without special programs that allow these chains to form and determine which of the chains is correct.

Thus, the register of IP objects based on blockchain technologies includes both a database and programs for their processing. From the standpoint of the legislation of the Russian Federation, it thus corresponds to the legal definition of an information system (Art. 2 of the Federal Law "On Information, Information Technologies and Protection of Information"). This is important because if in the Russian Federation IP registries are created on the basis of permission blockchain technologies, in which the state authorities authorized in the field of IP protection will have the official status, they will have all the attributes of state information systems. And, therefore, all requirements for state information systems should be applied to their development and use, in particular, in relation to the development and approval of documentation, certification of software and information protection tools, preliminary and acceptance tests, etc. [24, 25].

Similar legislation on information systems exists in a number of other states, in particular, members of the CIS. In other countries, the official nature of such registries will obviously also require consideration of the special requirements of national legislation.

6 Conclusions and Perspectives

As we showed above, the advantages of using registries based on blockchain technologies are large enough compared to centralized registries, and, in general, there is no doubt that they will be in demand in protecting IP objects. Apparently, we can expect the separation of registries of IP objects based on blockchain technologies into two types.

The first type is the registries of IP objects on the permissionless blockchain platform. The information contained in them about the IP objects and their authors (right holders) will not be official. At the same time, in most cases, it can be used as a weighty proof of the priority in creating an IP object in litigations. A significant problem here is that so far many courts (and, in particular, Russian ones) are not ready to accept entries in registries based on blockchain technologies, especially established without state participation (or organizations officially specializing in the protection of intellectual rights) as evidence. From a legal perspective, the most difficult challenge to the adoption of blockchain technology for IP practice and enforcement appears to be the regulation of this technology [14]. At the same time, this problem requires solving not only at the level of changes in legislation, but also at the level of adjustments in judicial practice.

We consider it promising for the development of various permissionless blockchain platforms for IP protection to establish interaction and cooperation between them, in particular, by concluding agreements on the mutual recognition of records in registries. This will help at least reduce the possibility of abuses during the registration of IP objects in different registries by various entities, as well as increase the potential for commercial use of IP objects. In the future, the emergence of a common top-level protocol is possible, which will unite the open blockchain-platform for fixing intellectual rights.

The second type is the registries of IP objects on the basis of permission blockchain technologies, in which superuser rights will be granted to government bodies authorized in the field of IP protection. Entries in them will be official and will have validating rights value. This means that an entry in a similar registry by virtue of the law will indicate the presence of intellectual rights until otherwise proved (in the latter case, a corrective entry will be made).

At the level of individual states, a combination of both types of registers seems possible. Registries on the public blockchain platform can be used to pre-register IP objects in order to indicate priority. Official registration can be completed by entering information about an IP object into the state register on the platform of a permission blockchain. Such a two-step system seems optimal for IP objects that currently require official state registration (inventions, utility models, etc.).

Finally, in the future, it is possible to create international registries of IP objects on a permission blockchain platform with the granting of superuser rights to the World Intellectual Property Organization. In this case local governments can substitute their local national registers with the WIPO Blockchain to reduce redundancy, expenses and inefficiency [26]. Of course, this is possible only with the conclusion of relevant international agreements and amending national legislation.

References

1. Dobrolyubova, E., Alexandrov, O., Yefremov, A.: Is Russia ready for digital transformation? In: Alexandrov, D., Boukhanovsky, A., Chugunov, A., Kabanov, Y., Koltsova, O. (eds.) DTGS 2017. CCIS, vol. 745, pp. 431–444. Springer, Cham (2017). https://doi.org/10.1007/978-3-319-69784-0_36
2. Reijers, W., O'Brolchain, F., Haynes, P.: Governance in blockchain technologies and social contract theories. Ledger **1**(1), 134–151 (2016). https://doi.org/10.5915/LEDGER.2016.62
3. Clemons, E., Dewan, R., Kauffman, R., Weber, T.A.: Understanding the information-based transformation of strategy and society. J. Manag. Inf. Syst. **32**(2), 425–456 (2017)
4. Smorgunov, L.: Blockchain and a problem of procedural justice of public choice. In: Alexandrov, D., Boukhanovsky, A., Chugunov, A., Kabanov, Y., Koltsova, O. (eds.) DTGS 2018. CCIS, vol. 858, pp. 13–23. Springer, Cham (2018). https://doi.org/10.1007/978-3-030-02843-5_2
5. Zeilinger, M.: Digital art as 'monetised graphics': enforcing intellectual property on the blockchain. Philos. Technol. **3**, 15–41 (2018)
6. Zuckerman, M.: Swedish government land registry soon to conduct first blockchain property transaction. Cointelegraf (2018). https://cointelegraph.com/news/swedish-government-land-registry-soon-to-conduct-first-blockchain-property-transaction
7. De Filippi, P., Wright, A.: Blockchain and the Law: The Rule of Code. Harvard University Press, Cambridge (2018). https://doi.org/10.2307/j.ctv2867sp
8. Bulgakov, I.: Legal questions of use of blockchain technology. Law (12), 80–88 (2017). (in Russian)
9. Birgit, C.: Blockchain and IP law: a match made in crypto heaven? WIPO Mag. (1), 30–34 (2018)
10. Aitken, R.: MUSE: leveraging blockchain technology to revolutionize music industry. Forbes (2016). https://www.forbes.com/sites/rogeraitken/2016/01/23/muse-leveraging-blockchain-technology-to-revolutionize-music-industry/#5204062c2418
11. Ayton, N.: Blockchain to disrupt balance of power in TV, music and film industry. Cointelegraph (2017). https://cointelegraph.com/news/blockchain-to-disrupt-balance-of-power-in-tv-music-and-film-industry
12. About Mediachain (2018). http://docs.mediachain.io/about/about
13. How Blockchain will Disrupt Intellectual Property. Medium (2018). https://medium.com/coinmonks/how-blockchain-will-disrupt-intellectual-property-dfde59588ba7
14. Gürkaynak, G., Yılmaz, I., Yesilaltay, B., Bengi, B.: Intellectual property law and practice in the blockchain realm. Comput. Law Secur. Rev. **34**, 847–862 (2018)
15. Bambara, J., Allen, P., Iyer, K., Madsen, R., Lederer, S., Wuehler, M.: Blockchain: A Practical Guide to Developing Business, Law, and Technology Solutions. McGraw Hill Professional, New York (2018)
16. Novoselova, L., Medvedeva, T.: Blockchain for shareholder voting. Econ. Law (10), 10–21 (2017). (in Russian)
17. How can blockchain protect intellectual property rights? Mathias Avocats. https://www.avocats-mathias.com/technologies-avancees/blockchain-intellectual-property-rights
18. Saveliev, A.: Contract Law 2.0: "smart" contracts as the beginning of the end of the classical contract law. Herald Civil Law (3), 32–60 (2016). (in Russian)
19. Saveliev, A.: Some legal aspects of the use of smart contracts and blockchain technologies under Russian law. Law (5), 94–117 (2017). (in Russian)
20. Sater, S.: Tokenize the musician. Tul. J. Technol. Intell. Prop. **21**, 3–29 (2018)

21. Allaby, D.: The trust trade-off: permissioned vs permissionless blockchains. Fjord (2016). https://www.fjordnet.com/conversations/the-trust-trade-off-permissioned-vs-permissionless-blockchains/
22. Inyushkin, A.: The legal regime of databases for the use of blockchain technologies in civilian circulation. Inf. Law (1), 45–48 (2018). (in Russian)
23. Dvoinikova, D.: Technology blockchain in the field of intellectual property. Synerg. Sci. (16), 910–919 (2017). (in Russian)
24. Amelin, R.: State and municipal information systems in Russian information law: a theoretical and legal analysis. GrossMedia (2018). (in Russian)
25. Bundin, M., Martynov, A.: Russia on the way to open data. Current governmental initiatives and policy. In: Conference 2015 Digital Government and Wicked Problems: Climate Change, Urbanization, and Inequality. Arizona State University, USA, 27–30 May 2015, pp. 320–322. ACM, New York (2015)
26. Motasem, H.: Intellectual property blockchain … the future has just begun. Abu-Ghazaleh Intellectual Property (2018). http://www.agip.com/News.aspx?id=16591&group_key=news&keywords=Blockchain

Digital Business Models Transforming Support Services for Living Longer at Home

Linda Askenäs and Jan Aidemark(✉)

Linnaeus University, 531 95 Växjö, Sweden
Jan.Aidemark@lnu.se

Abstract. The rapid development of the possibilities of obtaining ubiquitous use of IT brings the digitalization of all processes, services and products to society at large. This development provides the opportunity of creating novel business models, reaching new market segments with novel products at cheaper/better and more targeted price levels. In this paper, we demonstrate the wide range of possibilities that are emerging with digitalization of a business environment in the e-health field, deriving from a process of digitalized business modelling. We discuss this approach by presenting a case of e-health in the form of an IoT solution for creating a safer home environment, and how it can be offered in different ways to its end users. The use of creative business modelling can thus be demonstrated to make emerging internet technologies available to broader segments of society. The ways that value networks interact and distribute incomes and costs create new methods of providing new services to new people, thus driving the digital transformation of society forward. The paper concludes with a set of principles for approaching creative business planning in a digitalized business reality with an e-health focus.

Keywords: Digitalization · E-health · Business model · Fall-prevention · Living at home

1 Introduction

Digitalization as a driving force for the transformation of society must be regarded as the key factor for increasing the welfare and wellbeing of citizens. There is evidence that public investment on a national level with a good basis in public policy is needed to ensure success [1]. The speed of the development in different areas of technical systems, such as internet technologies, internet of things (IoT) systems, data-driven analysis and end-user interfaces, is already high and is becoming increasingly higher. However, the actual impact, or user adoption, of these technologies might be harder to achieve, due to values that people hold or, in more general terms, to the levels of technology appreciation among citizens. Although this could, in turn, depend on or be explained by several types of logics, we here suggest perceiving it from a business model perspective. This would refer to how a technical solution is made available to a user at a certain price. The business model contains the logic for how values and costs/revenues are distributed through a network of actors who jointly create the technical service or product to the user. The business model approach to the problem of

D. A. Alexandrov et al. (Eds.): DTGS 2019, CCIS 1038, pp. 338–350, 2019.
https://doi.org/10.1007/978-3-030-37858-5_28

user adaption is to demonstrate how creative digitalized business models can form the key to delivering technical services or products to a market, and how these are perceived as valuable and priceworthy. The possibility of presenting a technical solution in different ways to the markets is seen by us as the key use of a digital business model.

Our paper approaches this problem from the point of view of the increased digitalization of the business environment with examples taken from the e-health sector. The idea of digitalization is here understood in a very broad sense, with regard to what degree the systemic environment of the products/services (e.g. the user environment, extended business network, other stakeholders and relevant external factors) is represented as information, which is then stored and made available for analysis and utilization in business planning. In short it deals with the extent to which any relevant knowledge is recorded and stored that can be of use to improve products/services by the creation of digital business models. A great deal of the information that could be used in business modelling will probably already form part of the product/service, however different formatting, store/retrieval or indexing may be needed to make it useful. In addition, it is expected that there should exist substantial sets of data that could enable applying more novel or unexpected business logics. Exploring what additional data could be created in the context of the general business process as being useful for innovative new models could be seen as a key factor for new digital business models. This could also entail extending the solution by changing or adding to it, in order to make way for more innovative aspects.

The research approach to this topic is to investigate a project of IoT solutions for “Elderly living longer at home” as an example of digital transformation in society. This is an ongoing project aiming at developing market-ready solutions that enable elderly persons to cope longer in their habitual home surroundings. These are important aims from a societal point of view, considering both the quality of life for the elderly and the burden of taking care of elderly persons in institutions, or of more sickly or fragile people in general. The purpose is to investigate more closely the nature of the meta-information needed for business modelling. A broad set of business models developed during the project are investigated both in relation to the nature of the data needed for developing the models and to the realization of the models. At the core of the project lies a general home surveillance system related to a health perspective, which can be adapted to certain situation or needs by continuously developing sensor systems, analyses and data performance levels. The information modelling processes, integrated into parts of the project, aim at providing products or services that are viable and have a positive impact on the problem area.

We wish to show the necessity of understanding business information (as made possible by digitalization) by means of a system of data sharing as well as in an openness and spirit of sharing in order to create and benefit from digitalized business models. We do this by demonstrating the possible business models of the case, such as information sets, information flow and operations, which are necessary for their realization (beyond the product/service as such). Based on this, we conclude with a number of general principles that should be considered in successful digital business model development projects during project planning.

2 Literature/Background Review

Digital transformation has always been a central theme in the introduction of information technology into business life. The way a company uses an IT system for creating, for example, wealth, competitive power or success has for long been an important condition to achieve long-term success. How to understand and approach digitalization is an ongoing challenge for companies.

The approach to building a business based on a business model is supposed to include some special properties. For example, Osterwalder et al. [2] define a business model as "a conceptual tool containing a set of objects, concepts and their relationships with the objective to express the business logic of a specific firm". The model is developed in interaction between forces including business strategy and organization and its use of information and communication technologies (ICT). However, a long set of factors need to be included, as listed by Osterwalder et al. [2], including social change, technological change, customer opinion, and the legal environment. Amit and Zott [3] focus on the need for innovation by using business model development as a key approach for a company to stay competitive. The idea of approaching the business models is not about trying to invent new products and services, but rather about finding new ways of competing and gaining revenue on current ones.

The concepts of digitalization, digital transformation or digital business strategies could be described with the words of Bharadwaj et al. [4] as follows: "digital technologies are fundamentally reshaping traditional business strategy as modular, distributed, cross functional and global business processes that enable work to be carried out across boundaries of time, distance, and function". Here it is argued that, in the future, digitalization will dominate the idea of business strategies in general. It is the richness of information exchanges that creates the condition for a digitalized business model. At the heart of the concept of digitalizing business models lies the explosion of available information that can be used for creating new ways of making businesses.

The relatively novel use of the concept of "digitalization" or "digitization" for describing the impact of IT on companies seems to stem from the degree of pervasiveness that emerging technologies have on a company and the ways the technology transforms the company, not only by providing improvements. Even though there are efforts to make distinctions between these two terms, we treat them here as referring to the same general phenomenon. Uhl and Gollenia [5] point to a number of types of novel information technology, including big data and analytics, cloud computing, mobile connectivity and social media, that drive the digitalization boom. To these can be added, for example, ubiquitous sensors, IoT systems, end user interfaces and visualization, as well as the effort of making data useful. The common feature of these innovative technologies is that they increase the scope and detail of what is possible to gather data about to a point where anything seems to be possible to capture, record and analyze.

Working with the digital business model development is open to different approaches, as no dominant method has emerged so far. Veit et al. [6] discuss the concept as a business model that has its base in digital technologies which trigger fundamental changes in how a company creates values.

Moreira et al. [7], who claim that there is a lack of structured ways of planning for production digitization, suggest an integrated approach characterized by including agile collective intelligence and a holistic view of the company and its environment. The authors argue that the digital transformation of a company forms an essential part of a development towards an industry 4.0 concept of how to compete and produce. Renmane et al. [8], who emphasize the need for a structured planning process for digitalization is needed, present a three-part framework for a working development of digital business models which includes an analysis of markets, products and services, the deconstruction of current business models, and the discovery of new configurations. To meet the need for a digitalization strategy, Matt et al. [9] suggest that such a strategy should include IT development, value creation and structural change, all of which should be scrutinized through a financial lens.

The digitalization of a business environment creates new challenges for companies, which are described by Park and El Sawy [10] as messy and complex. They argue that companies must act very interactively and perceive their approach as involving how to survive in a digitalized world. These authors present a framework where a company must configure its response by using the internal variables of "IT capabilities" and "organization size" on hand as well as the external variables of "speed of change" and "unpredictability of change".

Connor [11] points to the close interaction between customers and companies in product development and sales. Digitalization creates digital ecosystems involving a culture of collaboration with customers and other participants in the creation of new product value. In a high-speed and highly interactive network, there is constant competition to offer personalized products, which are contextualized on the basis of their location and current needs.

The process of developing new business models has to be innovative in order to utilize the powers of digital technology. Holmström [12] points to three problem areas which might hinder digital innovation as well as three principles for how to avoid these problems. He [12] sees three problems affecting the digital innovator: too much trust in the capability of the innovator, detachment between innovation and technology, and too narrow a model of digital innovation. To get a firmer grip on the innovative process, three principles are suggested including a complex and careful scrutiny of the socio-material situation, considering concrete technical solutions during the innovation, and balancing the innovation between the concrete situation and general principles. The important take-away from these principles comprises the matter of balance in planning, the balance between technology and people as well between general and concrete principles.

The user or customer side must be integrated into the innovation process by applying strategic tools for communicating and learning from those expected to benefit from the innovation and to buy into the business model. Eikebrokk et al. [13] remind us that the need for using strategic and systemic methods for this interaction points to co-creation as a possible approach. Working with customer data and user experiences within the larger context of a business network leads to value discovery, as argued by Eikebrokk et al. [13]. Fairly comprehensive and detailed check point lists have been provided to prompt a better understanding of a digital business model by, for example, Nylén and Holmström [14].

Kenney and Zysman [15] argue for the central role of digital platforms for creating a working economy and innovative business models. The platform concept includes the various aspects of data collection, storage, analysis, and end-user interfaces, applying current concepts such as big data, IoT systems, web services, analytics and cloud computing. In the new digital economy, according to Kenney and Zysman [15], the platform owners are acquiring a formidable level of power of the same scale as during the industrial revolution. Now, in the digital revolution, the platform owners can structure and decide how business is done.

From a more general and societal perspective, one important aspect in the e-health field is to accept radical changes in services and in the way institutions operate. Hining et al. [16], who discuss digital transformation from an institutional perspective, try to explain how new institutional arrangements gain approval from society. Acquiring legitimacy for digital innovations is a challenge, when structures, practices, values, and beliefs are threatened with being changed or replaced by new sets of rules of the game. Further, the particular field of health care, including the medical and care professions, is facing definite challenges. Konttila et al. [17] identify a number of areas that the care organizations must be working with in preparation for the transition brought about by digitalization. A number of areas of knowledge of digital technology and digital skills are discussed here, such as what digitalization means for providing good patient care, what new skills are needed for being social and communicate with patients, and what ethical considerations come with digitalization.

3 Theoretical Grounding and Methodology

This section presents the rationale for the choice of case and the analytic framework of the research.

3.1 Case Selection

The case of the research is a project with the focus on product development using IoT-based solutions for aiding elderly to live longer at home. The combination of human, economy and technology aspects makes it into a multifaceted case, where the possibilities and problems concerned with the digitalization of business modelling can be discussed and clarified. The basic approach of the project was to create a platform for integrating, horizontally and vertically, on all levels, aspects ranging from data collection to end-user interaction. The platform should be able to host a wide variety of applications which could in different capacities aid elderly persons to stay on living at their houses or flats instead of having to move to special living facilities or care homes. The approach to aiding the elderly was the possibility of becoming more knowledgeable about the personal situation and about how to change and adapt behaviors to new conditions. A long selection of areas could form the focus of a support system, for example home safety, nutrition, physical activity, social interaction and health care. As part of the development, a number of application areas were chosen as use cases to build the platform around. As a mainly commercial project, the productification aspect was a central and driving force. Three main areas of application were in focus: physical rehabilitation training, fall prevention and mental health training. To achieve a fully digitalized business environment, we here discuss the possibilities of innovative digitalized business models, as applied in the fall-prevention scenario. From a science and medical standpoint, fall prevention is fairly well explored, while approaching it from a product and commercial standpoint is a more open venture. Here we wish to apply the theories from the business model field, for the purpose of exploring the nature and the diverse possibilities of digitalized business models.

3.2 Data Collection

To develop different use case we used a codesign method principle 5 design workshops were conducted with 6 elderly, 4 healthcare professionals, 4 process innovators and 5 ICT specialists from different partner companies and 3 researchers. The workshops were about 4 h long each and were held from February until October. In between each of the workshops the participants tested different platforms e.g. IoT, sensors and interfaces solutions. The research have been approved by an ethical committee. The main outcome that influenced the business planning were the development of three personas.

1. Active Alice, a woman that still have a very active and social life and have little risk for falling. In this stage the need is to be aware of the risk and her own risk behaviors to be able to actively prevent the first severe fall accident.
2. Vital Hubert, a man that may have developed one chronical illness like diabetes or heart failure in the early phase and still manage to stay active and live independent at home.
3. Lifefighter Lee, hir (he/she) still living at home but manage that by help with daily life activities from spouse and relatives and care personals that visit hir regularly.

To develop the business case and business models a subproject was set up consisting with regular meetings with the managers of the partner firms within the consortium. In the first meetings the focus of the business planning was on Vital Hubert personas. Parallel to those meetings different possible costumer and partners was approached and the business approach were discussed and evaluated with them. All the meetings were documented, se summary Table 1 and analyzed with the analytical framework described in next chapter.

3.3 Analytic Framework

The choice of analytic framework was made in accordance with several criteria, the most important being the generic nature of the business force address and the lack of a direct connection to any specific technology. The framework suggested by Bharadwaj et al. [5] consists of four identified themes for analyzing the possibilities of digital business models, including changes in the scope, scale, speed and nature of value creation. After presenting an overview of these four areas of analysis we discuss some central themes for analyzing how digitalization affects business models.

(1) Scope of digital business strategy, the main idea of the scope of how a business is set up is the interconnection that digitalization offers the organization. Two themes are in focus, “digitalized products” and “digitalized business networks”. The scenario of both internal and external connections expands the possibilities for creating new products as well as for continuously changing and redeveloping them on the basis of a real-time feedback loop from customers. The process of both creating products based on real-time information externally and internally relies on extensive business networks incorporating all links in the value chain. The breaking of all forms of traditional business boundaries, including networks, ecosystems, alliances and partnerships with both competitors and customers creates possibilities that come with digitalization. It is not only the forming of these inter-organizational relations that is made possible, but also the plasticity of relations over time, i.e., the possibilities of change and reconfiguration from loosely coupled networks to tightly knit cooperation.

(2) Scale of digital business strategy, the scale of a business is the key to profits, i.e. to moving towards higher sales levels in larger markets. Four themes are mentioned: “rapid scaling”, “multi-sided platforms”, “big data” and “scaling by partnership”. Techniques such as “cloud computing”, which enable the rapid upscaling and downscaling of the scope, should be perceived as part of a company’s strategic competency. The concept of multi-sided business models is seen as central, as it shows the flexibility of creating values in different ways in different parts of the value chain. This way of perceiving a business from many angles and trying to obtain revenue from many sides increases its scope. Among the key features of digitalization is the abundance of information it creates. One strategy for dealing with this and turning it into a strategic resource is captured by concepts like “big data” or “analytics”. Advantages of scale can be achieved by creating alliances or partnerships, in other words to expand into new markets by cooperation. By combining forces, for example through increasing its presence in different parts of the world or joining different competencies in a major market offer, the scale of a business can be created.

(3) Speed of digital business strategy, four themes of how increasing the speed of information exchange can be used for deriving business advantages are discussed, including product launching, decision-making, value chain reconfiguration, and network formation. The time to market and the time for a company to react to changing demands from customers are central themes. On a more general note, the second theme regarding the speed of decision-making is actually reflected in most aspects on digitalization. More concretely, the effects on how an organization functions as a decision-making entity, in other words the number of instances of major decisions, such as new products, must take time before becoming finalized. The coordination of external business partners is of a similar character as in decision-making regarding the formation of business networks or in an ordinary value chain. How to change behavior among external business partners is a major undertaking, and to realize fast product development and time to market the whole value chain must be reconfigured at high speed.

(4) Sources of business value creation and capturing, this part of the analysis details four sources of value creation, including information, multi-sided models, the

co-creation of value in networks, and digital architectural points of control. Deriving value from information, such as direct sale, a result analysis or further refining, has already been proved to be an important source of income and is in this way able to create a multi-layered business. Finding out or inventing multi-sided models could include strategies such as when a company provides a product for free in order to be selling a service or creating multi-layered value creation. This could be achieved on a grander scale in cooperation between members of a business network, whose competencies could be combined or interact for creating new values. Taking technological control of digital architectures could provide opportunities for creating advantages over competitors or providing rallying points for cooperation.

4 Empirical Investigations: Living Longer at Home Case

Providing a sustainable business environment for digital transition in the field of e-health is a challenge. Our example, as introduced in Sect. 3.1, illustrates finding diverse digitalized business models to achieve a system for helping elderly to stay longer at home. At the core of this offer stands an internet of things (IoT) platform, which can be used to offer various services to elderly people. The developing business network responsible for the platform also develops a number of leading applications, including fall prevention, rehab training and mental training. The basic assumption about the value of the system is to improve the understanding and learning of the user and to actually perform necessary changes in lifestyle, such as training, or changing habits.

The analytic process is set out to consist of four principal steps, including scanning each item in the analytic framework for possibilities, defining themes for business models, detailing the value proposals for each of the models, and identifying sets of information, networks of information, operations on information, and the need for information analysis and the presentation of information. The last point is the most interesting, as it might mean extensions of the system for the purpose of improving business around the core product or service.

The starting point of the analysis is a set of two base-line models, "the usual suspects", so to speak. The first immediate customers are home owners, couples or single persons who feel a need of sustaining their everyday life. Integrated solutions based on sensory information are analyzed and presented to the user, to achieve a better understanding as a basis for more secure living and improved everyday habits. The second direct sale should be addressed to a governmental health care organization which sponsors medical devices to patients. The scenario could involve that a doctor prescribes a fall-prevention kit to a patient with a history of fall accidents, thus creating saving in terms of future hospital costs for renewed fall accidents. From a platform perspective, both of these could work in some combination, i.e., as both a platform and an application provider. However, as pricing would be a problem in both cases, attaining a more balanced price for these customers would require a combination of other business models. By applying a digital business modelling process, it is possible to generate alternative and multi-sided revenue streams.

Table 1. Digital business model development

Digital value source	Theme	Value proposition	Business information needs: digitalisation of product/service/process
Value of information	"AD-supported home safety systems"	Getting the user to accept looking at ads, during training. Value: revenue from system sales by having cost prepaid by an ad company, while being able to "give away" systems for free	- Analyses, patterns and predictions of future interests and needs - Matchmaking, products and user needs
Network logic	"Selling Sensors to users" Sensor partner needs the service of integration into platform	Value proposition to sensor producer. Offering sensors as electable to end users. As a multi-sided value, there will also be the value of being a data provider	- API for integration - End user interaction interfaces - Data management systems
Value of information	"Product development data"	Selling back to app developer information on how an application is working with users Value proposition to app developers to provide extra data about users from the platform	- Behavioral analysis algorithms - Data management
Network, scope	"Personalized analytics"	Developing personalized services to individual users. End users expected to be requesting specialized measures or further knowledge about issues	- Behavioral analysis algorithms - Data management
Scale	"A business platform for direct sales of products"	Offering a way of selling and buying services directly from retailers to end users. For this transaction a fee is charged	- e-shop facility
Scale	"Development apps offered on platform for direct sale"	Offering a market place for app developers where they can put their apps for sale or general distribution against a fee	- App store
Value from knowledge	"Best practice models for care processes"	Conceptualizing experiences of how to organize care processes New models for care can be productified, sold and implemented	- Packaging and standardization of e-health models, care organization can function as support
Network logic	"Test bed services for app developers"	Offering app developers to have their apps tested by the user community	- Organization of co-design - Testing software
Value knowledge	"Legal, ethical, privacy advisors for developers"	Offering developers, even those outside the platform sphere, as a service support for legal, ethical or privacy problems	- Process knowledge gathered during ethical application, certifications
Value of information	"Research result based on user behaviors"	Evaluation of new procedures and practices. Data from the platform can be used by to better	- Data quality assurance - Statistical analysis

(continued)

Table 1. (*continued*)

Digital value source	Theme	Value proposition	Business information needs: digitalisation of product/service/process
		understand effects of changes or new technology	
Platform	"Predictive analysis of technical systems"	Offering app owners to monitor the performance of apps, in order to predict possible failures or users that seem to be abandoning the app	- Analysis algorithm for system behaviors - User behavior prediction algorism
Platform	"Licensing the platform as a software package"	General market offers to license the use of the platform for other fields of business	- Packaging the platform software as a product
Network	"Co-operative development platform"	Offering membership in a cooperative platform for app developers	- Community platform for joint development and interactions

5 Results and Discussion

The problem and obstacle for effective digital transformation, as identified in this paper, concerns the delivery of the "right" services to users who perceive the values and are willing to pay for them, all in the light of new digitalized reality. In other words, it is a challenge to create new business models based on the new reality of a digitalized business environment. It is a matter of finding new products and reusing old ones, as well as re-understanding existing markets and finding new markets for the products. The solution to this problem is defined as the perception of and willingness to harness the new powers of a digitalized world. In this paper, we present an analytic model for working with the development of digitized business models. The central theme of any such model is what value to offer to a customer. The customer could be residing in any part of the value chain or extended business network. The purpose is to identify the extended information needs that would make the model possible beyond the actual need for the central product or service. All four areas of the analytic framework [5] are visible in the Table 1. In this particular case there are interesting aspects to consider in each area.

1. Scope: the digitalization of e-health care for which the IoT-platform is a solution makes up for many different levels of new products and services and for providing value to all actors throughout the value chain. The traditional supplier-buyer concept will be broken down to viewing all as potential customers instead.
2. Scale: the IoT-platform will bring more value and knowledge, depending on the number of customers involved, including end-users like elderly, relatives and health care organizations as well as the developers of, for instance, apps, analytic models or visualization tools.

3. Speed: the IoT-platform as a platform needs to provide the opportunity for multiple ways of using different business models for producing value to customers. It has to be open for new collaboration and for each actor to be at the same time both supplier or producer and customer. An elderly person is, for instance, a customer using sensors and apps but also a producer and supplier of data, while a developer is a supplier of sensors and apps but also a customer in using the data produced by end-users and other applications in the IoT framework – a two-way business.
4. Sources: in the IoT-platform there are possibilities to create value out of information on every level of the platform. Dividing creation, innovation and development into multiple collaboration networks necessitates viewing all levels of the platform as value creation, forming a business model for each level and its parts and providing value everywhere. The time frame is also important to consider, implying the use of historical data to develop a better future for both elderly and healthcare as well as for the IT organization – the value of learning in each time frame. That also includes services on best-practices to design new health care processes, tools and applications – the co-creation of innovations.

The approach of the model is of the brainstorming kind, as well as the elicitation of possibilities. Four steps are envisioned (as detailed step-by-step in Table 1), including value source (based on the analytic framework), central theme, value proposition and information analysis. As the analytic framework is general and somewhat aged, it should be further extended. Further research into current studies of digitalized business models for the purpose of combining and generalizing current best practice would be needed. The knowledge dimension, in particular, seems to be lacking in the analytic framework. The creation of spin-off services based on knowledge developed in the context of the platform could be leveraged and turned into alterative knowledge streams. The two central principles for generating alternative business models seem to be the network effect and the multi-sided platform. The multi-sided approach includes working with the reuse of evolved information for different purposes in different parts of the value chain. The network effects of forming and adopting the business eco system around the platform expand the number of actors in the network, thus increasing the potential for revenues. However, as the nature of certain values offered to some actors might put off or at least limit the interest in other actions, these two principles must be balanced against each other. Since this part of the modelling process just indicates steps towards brainstorming, further steps would include the clustering of combinations of models, finding out how they would interact, and then detailing them with traditional canvas modelling. This approach also stimulates the interaction between technical innovations by providing high-level information requirements. Since the noted split between business thinking and technical logics is a real problem, the planning approaches need to address this constructively.

Just as digitalization brings about new services and products, a new business environment emerges with a plethora of new knowledge about all aspects of the business. This amount of what might be called the users meta-data can be used to find new business models, along with new channels to share, analyze and use this data. As questions will arise of how it should be used, it could in any given situation be used for either more transparent or to more cornered and closed markets, if organizations

Table 2. General e-health business guidelines.

1.	To work with business networks that promote the open and transparent use of business meta-data produced by the digitalization of e-health solutions
2.	To give preference to open digital platforms used for open innovation, which allow independent developers to create specialized solutions, that will be building business ecosystems and creating multi-sided models
3.	To base solutions on an open standard for data management, for example Continua. Such a standard ensures the compatibility of solutions and removes the entry barrier of communicating with platforms, databases or other applications
4.	To consider the values of knowledge and information, which should be actively developed in order to facilitate the production of business meta-data
5.	To put the user at the core of the project, by creating development methods and highly use-centered processes. Co-design principles must be ensured to direct users to central elements in the technical solutions and to activate them

mastering the meta-data choose acting that way. The basic conclusion of this paper is that the use of this meta-data should be to create and enable a greater set of adaptable solutions to satisfy the needs of a market segment, i.e. sub-groups of citizens, thus facilitating the adoption of new technology and creating an environment where digitalization is available to work as a way of transforming society, some guidelines can be provided, see Table 2.

References

1. Mićić, L.: Digital transformation and its influence on GDP. Economics (Bijeljina) **5**(2), 135–147 (2017). https://doi.org/10.1515/eoik-2017-0028
2. Osterwalder, A., Pigneur, Y., Tucci, C.L.: Clarifying business models: origins, present, and future of the concept. Commun. Assoc. Inf. Syst. **16**(1), 1–25 (2005)
3. Amit, R., Zott, C.: Creating value through business model innovation. MIT Sloan Manag. Rev. **53**(3), 41–49 (2012)
4. Bharadwaj, A., El Sawy, O.A., Pavlou, P.A., Venkatraman, N.: Digital business strategy: toward a next generation of insights. MIS Q. **37**(2), 471–482 (2013)
5. Uhl, A., Gollenia, L.A.: Digital Enterprise Transformation: A Business-Driven Approach to Leveraging Innovative IT. Routledge Taylor & Francis Group, Abingdon (2016)
6. Veit, D., et al.: Business models. an information systems research agenda. Bus. Inf. Syst. Eng. **56**(1), 45–54 (2014). https://doi.org/10.1007/s11576-013-0400-4
7. Moreira, F., Ferreira, M.J., Seruca, I.: Enterprise 4.0 – the emerging digital transformed enterprise. Procedia Comput. Sci. **138**, 525–532 (2018). https://doi.org/10.1016/j.procs.2018.10.072
8. Remane, G., Hanelt, A., Nickerson, R., Kolbe, L.: Discovering digital business models in traditional industries. J. Bus. Strategy **38**(2), 41–51 (2017). https://doi.org/10.1108/JBS-10-2016-0127
9. Matt, C., Hess, T., Benlian, A.: Digital transformation strategies. Bus. Inf. Syst. Eng. **57**(5), 339–343 (2015). https://doi.org/10.1007/s12599-015-0401-5

10. Park, Y., El Sawy, O.A.: The value of configurational approaches for studying digital business strategy. In: Configurational Theory and Methods in Organizational Research, pp. 205–224 (2013)
11. Connor, M.: Creating customer value in a digitally transformed future. J. Creat. Value **1**(2), 204–213 (2015). https://doi.org/10.1177/2394964315569631
12. Holmström, J.: Recombination in digital innovation: challenges, opportunities, and the importance of a theoretical framework. Inf. Organ. **28**(2), 107–110 (2018). https://doi.org/10.1016/j.infoandorg.2018.04.002
13. Eikebrokk, T.R., Lind, E., Olsen, D.H.: Co-creation of IT-value in a cluster of small enterprises. Procedia Comput. Sci. **138**, 492–499 (2018). https://doi.org/10.1016/j.procs.2018.10.068
14. Nylén, D., Holmström, J.: Digital innovation strategy: a framework for diagnosing and improving digital product and service innovation. Bus. Horiz. **58**(1), 57–67 (2015). https://doi.org/10.1016/j.bushor.2014.09.001
15. Kenney, M., Zysman, J.: The rise of the platform economy. Issues Sci. Technol. **32**(3), 61 (2016)
16. Hinings, B., Gegenhuber, T., Greenwood, R.: Digital innovation and transformation: an institutional perspective. Inf. Organ. **28**(1), 52–61 (2018). https://doi.org/10.1016/j.infoandorg.2018.02.004
17. Konttila, J., et al.: Healthcare professionals' competence in digitalisation: a systematic review. J. Clin. Nurs. **28**(5–6), 745–761 (2018). https://doi.org/10.1111/jocn.14710

Intelligent Data Analysis and Predictive Models for Regional Labor Markets

Anna Aletdinova and Maxim Bakaev(✉)

Novosibirsk State Technical University, Novosibirsk, Russia
{aletdinova, bakaev}@corp.nstu.ru

Abstract. The digitizing economies call for new methods in studying social-economic phenomena that are often short-lived and for which no pre-identified set of indicators had been developed. In our paper we demonstrate how intelligent analysis of online data can supplement the use of more traditional methods, such as the ones relying on official statistical reports or sample surveys. We outline benefits and disadvantages for each group of methods, and also identify some challenges in joining the data obtained from the diverse sources – particularly, the classification of the data per industry sectors. The data that we used for building ARIMA models were obtained with our dedicated labor market monitoring software system, operating from 2011 and currently containing 10+ million unique data records for vacancies and resumes. We found that for average wages the official statistics data can be approximated (error 7.82%) and possibly refined by the wage levels that companies offer in the openly posted vacancies ads. Further, we constructed predictive models for the employees' demand by the companies and found positive and negative influences (Lag −2, Lag −3 and Lag −4) for several industry sectors for which online data had been collected. The data from the identified groups can be used as leading indicators to predict situation on the labor markets.

Keywords: Online data mining · Employment and wages · ARIMA models · Data mining

1 Introduction

The role of information and human capital greatly increases in post-industrial economy. A decision-maker has to constantly maintain the model of the current market situation in his or her memory. It was estimated that companies that make decisions based on business data analysis and the principles of domain-driven design "have output and productivity that is 5–6% higher than what would be expected given their other investments and information technology usage" [1].

The available official statistics data, e.g. provided by the State Committee on Statistics (Goskomstat) in Russia, are not always up-to-date. Besides, there is a problem of reverse aggregation – that is, extracting the data for a particular industry, community, etc. from the averaged data. Finally, new emerging branches of "virtual" and digital economy are not covered adequately. On the other hand, today's information and communication technologies (ICT) call for employment of diverse means for

D. A. Alexandrov et al. (Eds.): DTGS 2019, CCIS 1038, pp. 351–363, 2019.
https://doi.org/10.1007/978-3-030-37858-5_29

monitoring economic activity indexes. The emerged ability to employ Big Data methods has been creatively named "the microscope" for the labor market analysts [2], who thus obtained the tool for studying their field in much more detail.

So, researchers and engineers are faced with the mission of designing, implementing, maintaining and refining software systems for collecting and analyzing online data, as well as using them for constructing predictive models. Intelligent data analysis implies identification of the relevant data in the online environment and performing one or several of the following tasks:

- Classification (identifying the class of the object based on its properties);
- Regression analysis (constructing the function for the known properties of the object, modeling and predicting);
- Extracting associative rules (finding enduring dependencies between events or objects);
- Clustering (identification of relatively independent groups and their properties in all the data being analyzed).

The review of available intelligent data analysis tools can be found in [3] and [4], while in [5] the authors demonstrate how the online environment can be used as experimental setting to provide conclusions for the "real" economics. A recent feasible tendency is using online data to supplement statistics provided by state, municipalities, even private sector [6]. These data are freely accessible in the online environment, and although they are often poorly structured, analysts could study differences in wages, work productivity, and certain other economic indexes. Today we are facing already the "second generation" of such systems, ones that cross international borders and process semantic data in different languages (see e.g. WoLMIS labor market intelligence system [7]). The databases of such software are becoming the foundation for research in adjacent fields, e.g. analyzing labor concentration with additional related geo-data [8] or focusing on academia labor market [9]. Overall, the researchers are gaining the ability to construct long-term predictive models, undertake new experiments and monitor their results. However, there are certain challenges in employing online data for these purposes:

- Ensuring confidentiality in the data [6];
- Developing methods and rather sophisticated software tools for collecting and analyzing the data, which are semi-structured at best;
- Securing appropriate hardware and network resources for the intensive auto-collection, structuring and other processing of the data;
- Dealing with unstable output of the sources in HTML or possible limitations of API access to the database;
- Configuring and maintaining the system to work with the multitude of sources;
- Understanding both the "incompleteness" and "excessiveness" of Internet – i.e. dealing with partial and duplicate data.

Despite these complications, the advantages of automated online data collection are widely recognized: generally lower work effort, increasing the data volume, timelessness and frequency, as well as potentially better validity [10, 11]. As in any field of science and engineering, the ability to construct predictive models is essential, so our main motivation lies within this goal. In our paper, we demonstrate general applicability of intelligent analysis and labor market parameters prediction based on data collected from online sources. Our research work was performed based on statistical data provided by the Russian State Committee on Statistics (Goskomstat) and the data collected by our dedicated software system for labor market monitoring and analysis.

2 Methods and Tools

2.1 Statistical Data on the People's Working Activities

Data on the population's working activities is essential for governments, employers and employees, and subsequently to researchers. The data are used for monitoring the state of the labor market, decision-making, etc. In today's digitalizing economies the related methods and tools become quite sophisticated, but ultimately the data are obtained in one of the following principal ways:

- from statistical reports published by governmental statistics offices, which are based on population censuses, statistics forms submitted by companies, and occasional sampling surveys;
- from individual studies performed by scientific teams, rating agencies, etc.;
- by collecting available data from online sources affiliated with labor market.

The official information on the wages of employees in Russia is provided in the following sources, by and large established and run by the state: "Labor and Employment in Russia", "Russian Statistical Yearbook", "Regions of Russia. Socio-economic indicators", "Social and economic situation of federal districts", "Social and economic situation in Russia (monthly)", "Short-term economic indicators of the Russian Federation", "Information for monitoring socio-economic status of the subjects of the Russian Federation", "Past due accounts of wages", "On the differentiation of wages by professional groups". Despite the impressiveness of the list, the information is actually often duplicated in various sources. The Russian Federal State Statistics Service's website provides statistical data, particularly in its "Labor market, employment and wages" chapter. The data include operative information and results of the state statistical monitoring for wages of certain categories of workers, e.g. in social services or science, and can be used to assess the status for the labor markets. However, the nomenclature of the indexes is not always sufficient for the purposes of predicting and decision-making. Selected regional ministries of labor provide additional reports on the wages and the labor market status, but overall the traditional statistical methods have inherent disadvantages [12]:

- They still lag behind in time, even though official statistics data are increasingly becoming available for online access. However, the cutting of the time it takes for the information to arrive from its originating sources (companies, government institutions, etc.) definitely has its limits.
- The emergence of new indexes, specific for digital economies, is restricted by rather conservative official statistical bodies' methodologies and understandably inert statistical forms.

- The validity of the data is not guaranteed, as statistical forms have low priority for companies, while penalties for providing distorted data are generally minimal. Besides, a significant part of activities of organizations and individuals can be performed in the "grey", not at all transparent economy.

Further, there is an annual monitoring of economic situation and the population's well-being (RLMS-HSE) performed by Higher School of Economics, the Russian Academy of Sciences' Institute of Sociology, the University of North Carolina, etc. The method they use is based on sample survey (http://www.hse.ru/rlms), which contains questions about households' incomes, expenses and wages as well as about employees' activities: employment type, profession, major, duties and positions, job satisfaction, working conditions, compensations, professional development opportunities, and so on.

However, it is increasingly expected that advances in Business Intelligence and Analytics domains will be backed by Big Data [13] that surely cannot be obtained via sample surveys and occasional research or monitoring activities. Another daunting problem is the need to predict the effect of emerging innovations [14], while the phenomena they cause are generally short-lived and are manifested in unidentified sets of indexes. So, naturally, the modern economic analysis needs and the rapid advances in ICT lead to emergence and development of methods and tools employing online data in statistics. Already some National statistical institutes, e.g. one in the Netherlands [15], supplement their statistics with the data collected from the Internet. These new methods for obtaining the data result in new ways of selecting and constructing the indexes, in new classifications for the labor market that better match the ones used by the online data providers.

So, in today's practice three major groups of methods are used for the data collection and analysis:

- The ones based on aggregated statistics, population censuses, etc.;
- The ones based on surveys, sampling and other well-developed routines from economics and social science;
- The ones involving online data collection and mining.

2.2 Software for Labor Market Online Data Collection and Intelligent Analysis

We have designed, developed, put into operation and are now maintaining software system that is capable of collecting online data, structuring them with accordance to the specified ontological domain model, and performing the analysis. Since 2011 an instance of the system collects data on labor market for Novosibirsk and some other Siberian regions, currently containing more than 10 million processed data records. The main indexes monitored by the system are numbers of vacancies and resumes per industry sectors, proposed and requested wage levels, as well as ratios between them. The online data providers are popular job-related websites, where companies and individuals post their vacancies and resumes for open access. The architecture of our intelligent data analysis software system has three major tiers [12, p. 26]:

1. The data collection module that is responsible for accessing the online data providers' websites and grabbing data from web pages or accessing their database via API, if the corresponding mechanism is offered.
2. The processing module that is responsible for structuring the data. Currently it extracts information related to vacancies and resumes and their specified properties, as well as divides the jobs by sectors, using two thesauri to perform intelligent natural language processing.
3. The data analysis module that is responsible for decision-making support and providing capabilities for reports generation, filtering, notifications, etc. Currently it's being enhanced with modeling and predicting capabilities.

As for the data quality, the most problematic dimension in our project was completeness of the data. The online sources would occasionally introduce changes into the structure of webpages, which in some cases led to failures in the pages' processing and gaps in the data (see the approaches we considered to handle this issue in [16]). So, we introduced the newer version of the data collection mechanism based on API, which is increasingly offered by online data providers (on the contrary, HTML-based web scraping is becoming more and more constrained). Generally, for work-related source websites (e.g. HH.ru, Zarplata.ru, Trudvsem.ru) the API access has to be configured individually, while the use of HTTPS is nearly universal. Authorization is mostly performed via OAuth2, in some cases CORS technology is supported, so the data can be requested via browser from arbitrary domain (a dedicated/cors URL in API supports HEAD, GET, POST, PUT, and DELETE methods). The number of records returned for a request is limited in some cases at 10,000. At the end, all the collected data is saved into the system's database, and is checked for duplicates later, by the processing module.

The structuring of the data is straightforward in most of the cases, even without API access to a provider's database. Content fields on web pages are marked with respective id names and the implicit data model is known to us. Somehow more challenging is classification of vacancies and resumes by industry sectors, which initially differs per providers. To perform universal auto-classification of data collected from different websites, we employed a relatively simple thesaurus containing all the possible names for an industry, e.g., "IT", and "Information systems and technologies". However, in some cases collected vacancies or resumes would not specify the industry at all, so another thesaurus containing particular positions per industries, such as "System Administrator" for "IT", was also added. Understandably, maintaining it manually would be very labor-intensive, but the system is capable of self-learning by automatically adding any new position name it encounters with a properly specified sector. If auto-classification for a new data item could not be performed, the record is put into the "Others" category and can be re-processed later, with extended thesaurus.

Another important aspect in the data processing in the system is filtering out multiple copies of the same data item, e.g., collected from different sources or in different time periods. No records are deleted from the system's database, but they can be marked as "duplicates", so depending of the analysis' goals they could be removed from consideration. The first step in the intelligent filtering process is generation of hash-code for the collected HTML (pre-2017), with all the variable elements, such as counters or advertisements, removed. This approach works for most of the copies and excludes them from the subsequent structuring process, thus decreasing the system's computational load. However, for more accurate filtering on the second step, structured data are used – they are merged into a string for which we also generate a hash-code for subsequent validation and comparison. To find copies across different websites or time periods, we just need to include the source website id or the period into the merged string. Finally, items with matching hash-codes are marked as multiple copies. Though they are not removed from the system's database, they can be excluded from the data analysis. The resulting productivity of the multiple copies filtering process, even given the high volumes of data in the system, is more than satisfactory. Besides, the filtering mechanism can work as a daemon when the system load is low in the absence of data collection or processing.

The analysis described in the next chapter is based on the online data collected and processed by the software system. In the future, we plan to extend the system's analysis module with the predictive modeling functionality.

3 Results and Discussion

3.1 Structuring the Data by Industry Sectors

As we mentioned before, joining the official statistics data and the online data can be troublesome due to differences in employed classification of industry sectors with respect to the labor market activities. From Table 1 one can see that matching the data between the groups (categories) is far from trivial.

Some groups can be considered reasonably similar, e.g. *Public administration and military security, social insurance* (official statistics) and *Public service* (online data providers), but for freelance websites these groups are understandably missing. For some of the groups, like *Working professions*, *Top management* or *Temporary job*, the industry sector cannot always be inferred even from more detailed descriptions of the vacancies. Some professions do apply to nearly all industries: accountant, locksmith, technician, etc. The services are problematic as well, since they may include different sub-groups, like in *Transport and communication* vs. *Transport, auto business* vs. *Telecommunications*. On freelance job websites basically all the groups relate to services, resulting in higher detail in the classification. However, joining them all into a super-group *Services* would hinder the analysis effectiveness. On the other hand, the group *Others* already contains an outstandingly large share of data records, since it incorporates all the "unsorted" items. The unevenness in the numbers of data records for different groups is shown in Table 2 that reflects the data for 2012–2017 (6 years of data collection) in Novosibirsk. The highest number of data records was 390,657 for *Accounting, finance, banking*, while *Work at home* had only 170. Therefore, for some segments of online data appropriate analysis can be impossible and they had to be excluded from consideration.

Table 1. Different groupings for industry sectors

Official statistics	Online data providers	Freelance job websites
– Agriculture, hunting and forestry	– Insurance	– 3D graphics
– Fishery, fish farming	– Sport, beauty, health	– IT and programming; art/illustration; architecture/interior; outsourcing/consulting
– Mining	– Working professions	– Web design
– Manufacturing	– Public service	– Video
– Production and distribution of electricity, gas and water	– Retail	– Graphic design
– Building	– Wholesale	– Engineering
– Wholesale and retail trade; repair of motor vehicles, motorcycles, household products and personal items	– Restaurants, cafes, catering	– Marketing and advertising; media design/animation; management
– Hotels and restaurants	– Transport, auto business	– Music/sound; training/consultations; translations
– Transport and communication	– Non-food industry	– Polygraphic design; industrial design; development of games/graphics; advertising/presentation
– Financial activities	– Top management	– Texts; form style; flash
– Operations with real estate, renting of services	– Logistics, warehouse, purchases	– Photo
– Public administration and military security, social insurance	– Construction, architecture	
– Education	– Accounting, finance, banking	
– Health and social services	– IT and the Internet	
– Provision of other communal, social and personal services	– Marketing, advertising, PR	
	– Security and safety	
	– Medicine, pharmaceutics	
	– Office staff, ACS	
	– Real estate	
	– Jurisprudence	
	– Education, science, languages	
	– Sale of services	
	– Work for students	
	– Home care staff	
	– Food industry	
	– Telecommunications	
	– Polygraphy, publishing houses, mass media	
	– Fuel and energy complex, energy, raw materials extraction	
	– Work at home	
	– Tourism, hospitality	
	– Temporary jobs	
	– Human Resources, HR	
	– Agriculture	
	– Design, creative professions	
	– Other services	
	– Others	

Table 2. Online data records for different groups (industry sectors), collected in 2012–2017 for Novosibirsk labor market

The number of ads (vacancies + resumes)	Industry sector
More than 200,000	– Accounting, finance, banking – Office staff, ACS – Transport, auto business – Retail – IT and the Internet
100,000–200,000	– Working professions – Wholesale – Restaurants, cafes, catering – Top management
10,000–100,000	– Non-food industry – Marketing, advertising, PR – Security and safety – Medicine and pharmaceutics – Sale of services – Insurance – Sport, beauty, health – Public service – Services sector – Real estate – Jurisprudence – Education, science, languages – Work for students – Home care staff – Food industry – Telecommunications – Polygraphy, publishing houses, mass media – Tourism, hospitality – Temporary jobs – Human Resources, HR – Design, creative professions
Less than 10,000	– Fuel and energy complex, energy, raw materials extraction – Work at home – Agriculture

Online data is also more ambiguous, compared to the official statistics, in calculating average wages, since data records can be incomplete in this regard, e.g. containing intervals like "from M" or "up to N" rubles per month. For such cases we employed the following empiric rules with respect to calculating the averages:

- If left end of the wage range is not specified, the range is taken as [M; M+0.66M];
- If right end of the wage range is not specified, the range is taken as [0.66 N; N].

Obviously erroneous numbers and outliers, such as less than 3,000 rubles or 300,000 rubles per month would be removed from the analysis.

3.2 The Time Series Analysis

Auto-Regressive Integrated Moving Average (ARIMA) models are the most general class of models for forecasting a time series [17]. Lags of the stationarized series in the forecasting equation are called "autoregressive" terms, lags of the forecast errors are called "moving average" terms. The ARIMA predictive model for a stationary time series is a regression-type equation in which the predictors consist of lags of the dependent variable and/or lags of the forecast errors. A nonseasonal ARIMA model is classified as an ARIMA(p, d, q) model, where:

- p is the number of autoregressive terms,
- d is the number of nonseasonal differences needed for stationarity,
- q is the number of lagged forecast errors in the prediction equation.

The initial step in the analysis is choosing the appropriate method, for which end we need to test for non-stationary components in the time series. The results of our time series analysis for the wages suggest the presence of seasonal fluctuations (Fig. 1) and considerable differences between the averages for the official statistics and the online data.

Estimate of the average approximation error evokes the differences between the official statistics data and the online data: 7.82% for average wages in vacancies and 16.52% in resumes. In the latter case the error is unacceptable, so apparently the wages proposed by the companies in vacancies are more reasonably related to the labor market situation.

Marked seasonal fluctuations were also found for the numbers of vacancies and resumes. For example, in Fig. 2 we show the dynamics for the *Insurance* industry sector.

The seasonal component's exclusion can be performed through calculation of growth rates related to the corresponding month of the previous year [18]. Then for the residuals we construct ARIMA models relating the demand on the labor market (the number of vacancies) and the supply (the number of resumes). The relations were analyzed per industry sectors and in aggregation, the periods in consideration being 6 months. Only some of the models had significant coefficients at $\alpha = 0.05$, which we present in Table 3 (*Marketing, advertising, PR* and *Services sector* were significant at $\alpha = 0.1$).

The results of the analysis suggest that the number of vacancies published online can be used as predictive indexes for several industry sectors, up to two-year lag (Lag −4). Interestingly, the number of vacancies in the Services sector (mostly implying low qualification jobs) had negative effect on the labor market demand, which can be probably explained by its negative relation to the overall economic growth. All in all, the performed analysis demonstrates that online data can serve as leading indexes and can be used in predictive models for labor market.

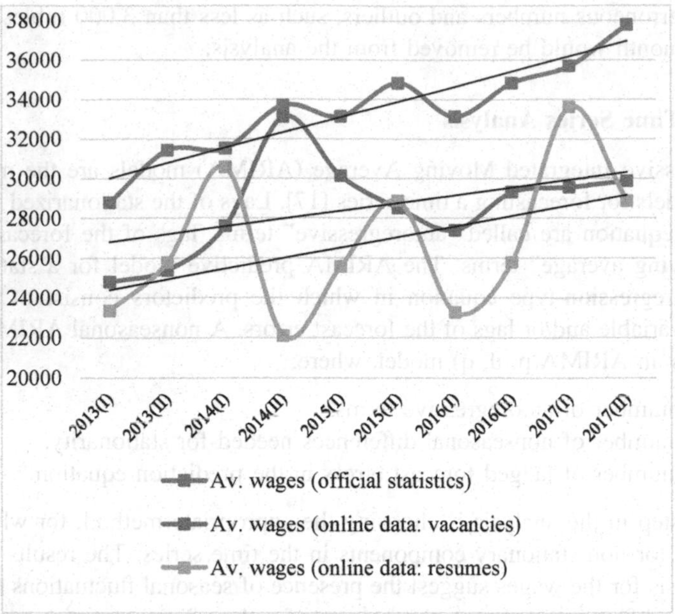

Fig. 1. Average wages in the Siberian region, per the different data sources.

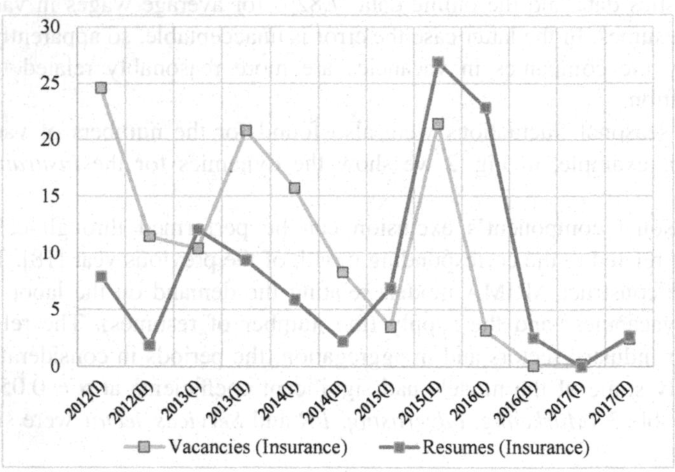

Fig. 2. Dynamics in the average weekly number of vacancies for Insurance sector in the Siberian region (per 6-months periods).

Table 3. Effects of numbers of vacancies on the officially claimed demand for employees.

Industry sector	Lag −2	Lag −3	Lag −4
Insurance			0.1651
Public service			0.0776
Retail trade			0.1004
Logistics, warehouse, purchases		0.0851	
Construction, architecture			0.0478
Accounting, finance, banks			0.0532
IT and the Internet			0.0522
Marketing, advertising, PR (significant at 0.1)			0.0790
Services sector (significant at 0.1)	−0.0478		
Security and safety			0.1030

4 Conclusions

In post-industrial economies the range of methods for monitoring wages and general situation on the labor market has extended greatly. The "traditional" methods, such as official statistics, sampling surveys, etc., are being augmented with online data. Each group of methods actually has its own benefits and disadvantages, e.g. online data collection may suffer from the need to ensure confidentiality, develop and maintain dedicated software tools, and other particulars related to the online environment.

Our current research work was based on the online data collected by specially developed software system capable of collecting, structuring, and analyzing the data from labor market-related online sources. Currently, the most intensively used mechanism for the data collection is API access to the data providers' databases. A particular challenge is intelligent classification of the data obtained from the diverse sources into industry sectors. Another notable mechanism in the system is the one that deals with duplicate and incomplete data, particularly missing values for the wages ranges.

The analysis of the classifications used by the official statistical bodies and the job-related websites identified compatibility problems. For example, freelance job websites only has categories related for services, which are quite more detailed compared to more universal job sites. A possible solution is consolidation of the groups up to economic activities tier: e.g. services, production, etc. – depending on the goal of a particular research project or business analysis. Also, the *Others* groups continues to have the highest share of vacancies and resumes (since unclassified items go here), but it complicates any detailed analyses. On the other hand, the groups that are different from the officially recognized ones allow another perspective to the labor market – for instance, researching students' and interns' work demand and supply. Another confounding aspect is large variability between the number of vacancies and resumes in the different groups. For example, the *Work at home* group only saw 170 ads during our 5 years of monitoring and is obviously not representative.

Our analysis of time series for wages, both from official statistics and the online data, found seasonal fluctuations. The identified average approximation error of 7.82% for differences in online vacancies' wages vs. official statistics was not significant.

Further, we constructed predictive models for the employees' demand by the companies, based on the online data: we found positive influence (Lag −3 and Lag −4) for *Insurance; Public service; Retail trade; Logistics, warehouse, purchases; Construction, architecture; Accounting, finance, banks; IT and the Internet; Security and safety*. On the contrary, the influence of *Services sector* was negative (Lag −2). The data from the identified groups can be used as leading indicators to predict situation on the labor markets.

We believe the results of our study, particularly the predictive models, could be applied in developing labor-related policies and contribute to mitigating disproportions on labor markets. Our future research directions include testing the models with the data obtained in 2018–2019, when the software system was transferred to the new data collection mechanism (API). We also plan to study various industries' demand for digital economy-related skills in human resources in different Russian regions.

Acknowledgement. The reported study was funded by RFBR according to the research project No. 17-32-01087 OGN a2. We would also like to thank Anastasiia Timofeeva, whose wider analysis of the online data became an inspiration for this work.

References

1. Brynjolfsson, E., Hitt, L.M., Kim, H.H.: Strength in numbers: how does data-driven decision-making affect firm performance? (2011). https://papers.ssrn.com/sol3/papers.cfm?abstract_id=1819486. Accessed 08 Feb 2019
2. Horton, J.J., Tambe, P.: Labor economists get their microscope: big data and labor market analysis. Big Data **3**(3), 130–137 (2015)
3. Larose, D.T.: Discovering Knowledge in Data: An Introduction to Data Mining. Wiley, Hoboken (2014)
4. Shmueli, G., Bruce, P.C., Yahav, I., Patel, N.R., Lichtendahl Jr., K.C.: Data Mining for Business Analytics: Concepts, Techniques, and Applications. Wiley, Hoboken (2017)
5. Horton, J.J., Rand, D.G., Zeckhauser, R.J.: The online laboratory: conducting experiments in a real labor market. Exp. Econ **14**(3), 399–425 (2011)
6. Einav, L., Levin, J.: Economics in the age of big data. Science **346**(6210), 1243089 (2014)
7. Boselli, R., et al.: WoLMIS: a labor market intelligence system for classifying web job vacancies. J. Intell. Inf. Syst. **51**(3), 477–502 (2018)
8. Azar, J.A., et al.: Concentration in US labor markets: evidence from online vacancy data. No. w24395, National Bureau of Economic Research (2018)
9. Brandas, C., Panzaru, C., Filip, F.G.: Data driven decision support systems: an application case in labour market analysis. Rom. J. Inf. Sci. Technol. **19**(1–2), 65–77 (2016)
10. European Commission: Internet as Data Source. Feasibility Study on Statistical Methods on Internet as a Source of Data Gathering. Report for the European Commission DG Communications Networks, Content & Technology, Dialogic, Netherlands, 243 p. (2012)
11. Aletdinova, A., Bakaev, M.: Human capital in the information society and the wage difference factors. In: Proceedings of the ACM International Conference Internet and Modern Society (IMS-2017), pp. 98–101 (2017)
12. Bakaev, M., Avdeenko, T.: Data extraction for decision-support systems: application in labour market monitoring and analysis. Int. J. e-Educ. e-Bus. e-Manag. e-Learn. **4**(1), 23–27 (2014)

13. Chen, H., Chiang, R.H., Storey, V.C.: Business intelligence and analytics: from big data to big impact. MIS Q. **36**(4), 1165–1188 (2012)
14. Gök, A., Waterworth, A., Shapira, P.: Use of web mining in studying innovation. Scientometrics **102**(1), 653–671 (2015)
15. Hoekstra, R., Bosch, O., Harteveld, F.: Automated data collection from web sources for official statistics: first experiences. J. Int. Assoc. Off. Stat. **28**(3–4), 99–111 (2012)
16. Giorgashvili, V.S., Bakaev, M.A.: Analysis and forecasting for labor markets based on online data. Int. J. Open Inf. Technol. **6**(12), 12–20 (2018). (in Russian)
17. Nau, R.: ARIMA models for time series forecasting. Duke University. https://people.duke.edu/~rnau/411arim.htm. Accessed 08 Feb 2019
18. Timofeeva, A.: Intelligent analysis and forecasting for regional labor markets based on online data. The Russian Foundation for Basic Research Grant Report (2018). (in Russian)

E-Society: Computational Social Science

Using Deep Learning to Predict User Behavior in the Online Discussion

Karpov Nikolay(✉) and Demidovskij Alexander

National Research University Higher School of Economics,
Bolshaya Pecherskaya Street 25/15, Nizhny Novgorod, Russia
{nkarpov,ademidovskij}@hse.ru

Abstract. Popularity of social networks makes them an attractive field for analysis of users' behavior, for example, based on the intention analysis of their posts and comments. In the linguistic theory only 25 types of intentions exist and can be joined in 5 supergroups. We use the dataset that contains directed oriented graphs which nodes store information about the author intention, text of the post in the social network "Vkontakte" etc. Each graph is split in a linked list of nodes (a sequence, 13156 sequences in our dataset) from root to each leaf so that the intention prediction becomes the sequence prediction. We have analyzed traditional and neuronet approaches that address this task and proposed to solve it with the original modifications of CNN and RNN architectures. It was decided to translate all posts to the embeddings which are then used as inputs for our neural network. According to the benchmarking experiments, we have identified that the proposed RNN architecture outperforms other alternatives. Also, predicting supergroups is done more accurately. Finally, we found out, that the context in the dialogs is lost quickly that allows to decrease the algorithm context size while keeping accuracy at the appropriate level.

Keywords: Sequence prediction · Social network analysis · Machine learning · Artificial Neural Networks

1 Introduction

In the twenty first century there is a boom around digital communications among people. It is hard to imagine modern life without social networks on the Internet. Due to this huge popularity of social networks, we can consider them as a convenient place for making research on people's behavior - analyze it and find patterns. This knowledge brings us to a broad range of directions from marketing to political manipulations over the public opinion.

In this paper we focus on people's intentions of the interlocutor. There is a notable research being done in both psychological and machine learning fields, that prove that the quantity of intentions types is finite and can be extracted from the message [4].

D. A. Alexandrov et al. (Eds.): DTGS 2019, CCIS 1038, pp. 367–377, 2019.
https://doi.org/10.1007/978-3-030-37858-5_30

However, there are still opened questions on the existence of any patterns in the dialog (sequence of messages). Would it be possible to connect motivation of the interlocutor B with the last comment from person A? Is it possible with the means of data mining and Artificial Neural Networks to find those patterns and learn to predict the intention of the next message based on previous ones?

The main contributions of this research are:

1. Representation of dialog graphs as a set of sequences of intentions;
2. Overview of the state-of-art approaches for a sequence prediction;
3. Implementation of those algorithms for the sequence prediction task;
4. Empirical accuracy estimation of the algorithms.

The rest of the paper has the following structure. Section 2 covers the mathematical formulation of the task. In Sect. 3 we give a thorough analysis of the existing methods in sequence prediction field. Section 4 is dedicated to details of the data used for experiments and in Sect. 5 we observe our neural network architectures. In Sect. 6 we present benchmarking results. Finally, the conclusions are made in Sect. 7.

2 Problem Definition

In order to start the analysis of major approaches for the sequence prediction task, it is vital to give the definition and formulate the general idea of what sequence prediction problem is.

To begin with, we define the finite alphabet $I = i_1, i_2, \ldots, i_m$ [3]. Each element of this alphabet can be either an atomic symbol or a set of elements. The main requirement is that all elements in the alphabet are unique.

Definition 1. *A sequence. A sequence is an ordered list of alphabet elements. Let $S =< i_i, i_2, \ldots, i_m >$. S be a sequence if the following condition is satisfied: $\forall s_i \in I, i \in [1, n]$.*

Accurate sequence prediction is known to require huge amount of sequences as learning data. For convenience, we denote all available sequences as $D =< S_1, S_2, \ldots, \Sigma_k >$. Therefore, the sequence prediction task implies ability to predict next element (s_{n+1}) for the given sequence $S =< i_i, i_2, \ldots, i_m >$.

3 Literature Overview

With the help of rigorous analysis of the field, we have identified the most widely used approaches such as traditional: CPT (Compact Prediction Tree) [3], CPT+ [2], PPM (Prediction by Partial Matching) [1], DG (Dependency Graph) [6], AKOM (All-Kth-Order-Model) [8], TDAG (Transition Directed Acyclic Graph) [5], CTW (Context Tree Weighting) [13], PST (Probabilistic Suffix Trees) [10]. It is necessary to highlight the approaches that use neural networks for solving the sequence prediction task: MLP (Multi Layer Perceptron), CNN (Convolutional

Neural Network), LSTM (Long Short Term Memory) [14], RNN (Recurrent Neural Network) [11], DTRNN (Discrete-Time RNN) [7] and Multi-task LSTM [12]. Further, we will examine selected algorithms due to fundamental ideas that they contain.

Compact Prediction Tree. Compact Prediction Tree (CPT) [3] - is a method, that is considered to be state-of-art when compared to other analogs. There is also an improved modification called CPT+ [2]. The latter has several optimizations, however, it does not change the basic approach. It is built around manipulations with three specific data structures: Prediction Tree (PT), Inverted Index (II), Lookup Table (LT). During the training stage, Prediction Tree is built from the set of sequences D. The tree has a root, that does not contain any element s_i and that plays a service role to build the tree. The second important structure is the Inverted Index, that is the table $II = ||ii_{kl}||$, where on the intersection of the k-th row that corresponds to the alphabet element i_k and l-th column that corresponds to the sequence S_l, there is either 1 or 0 that denotes inclusion/absence of this alphabet element in the given sequence. Finally, the third element is the Lookup Table, that connects Prediction Tree and Inverted Index and is the table that for each sequence stores the link to the leaf of Prediction Tree that corresponds to its last element. The training stage is simply a construction of these three data structures.

The prediction (inference) stage occurs when the training stage is complete. Let x be the length of the prefix (context) and S be an arbitrary sequence. The first step is to find in Inverted Index all the sequences that contain last x elements from S in the arbitrary order. This is performed by the simple intersection of rows that represent those x elements. We denote the set of such sequences as Y. For each $y \in Y$ we find the common prefix between y and S. For example, $S =< i_2, i_3, i_5, i_9, i_1 >, x = 2, y =< i_2, i_9, i_1, i_4, i_2 >$. We remove the common prefix $< i_2 >$ and for each element in the resulting subsequence $y =< i_9, i_1, i_4, i_2 >$ we create a row in a special Count Table or increase the counter in the existing row by one. As soon as elements y are over, we choose the row with the minimum value of the counter (called 'support') - this is the most probable next element.

However, if there are several rows, the second criterion is introduced that is called confidence (1). Then this criterion is used, so that the element that has a maximum value of confidence is chosen as a predicted next element for the given sequence.

$$confidence(s_i) = \frac{support(s_i)}{|y|y \in Y, s_i \in y|} \tag{1}$$

CPT as an original approach has several weaknesses that are partially solved in the optimized version of the algorithm [2]: potentially huge depth of the tree, the absence of work on cleaning the sequence from the noise signal, inability to predict the symbol that is not represented in the training data etc. Moreover, there is a question about selection rules for the maximum length of the prefix that is to this moment is solved empirically. The optimized version [2] contains several strategies on pruning the Prediction Tree via creating new alphabet elements for the recurring branches, joining branches, that do not contain further branches. However, the new CPT+ algorithm introduces new hyper-parameters such as: minimum and maximum length of subsequence, acceptable noise ratio, minimum number of Prediction Tree updates etc. Definition of these parameters appears to become a separate problem.

Prediction by Partial Matching. PPM (Prediction by Partial Matching) [1] - is the traditional approach in the sequence prediction task. The main idea is to build the Markov model of the given order k, that means usage of k elements in the context for prediction of the next element. Let $k = 2$ and the context that we predict the next element with be $<\#, a>$, where $\#$ is the space sign. For each element i_l we count number of times when the sequence $<\#, a>$ had a continuation $<\#, a, i_l>$ and denote it as $c(i_l)$. Then the probability that the next element is i_l is defined by (2).

$$p(i_l) = \frac{c(i_l)}{1 + C}, \tag{2}$$

where C is a number of times the given context appeared in the training data.

However, the important part of the model is computing the probability of the symbol that has not yet appeared in the known contexts. Its probability (called escape probabilities) is also computed, for example as in Model A in the original paper (3).

$$p(i_l) = \frac{1}{1 + C} \times \frac{1}{|I| - q}, \tag{3}$$

where q is a number of symbols that already appeared in the given context.

Regardless the simplicity of this method, there are experimental works that prove its competitiveness with other existing approaches [1,2,6,8].

Dependency Graph. DG (Dependency Graph) [6] - is an approach that was initially developed for solving the task of efficient resource pre-loading mechanism on the Internet. The aim was to predict the next resource that a user will want to visit on the base of their previous actions. Traditionally such algorithms are generic and can be used for the sequence prediction task. The core algorithm is built around the creation of data structure of the same name - Dependency Graph, so that between two nodes A and B there is the edge if those nodes appear one after another in the context - *lookahead window* - in the training data. Accordingly, the weight of the edge is the frequency that this condition is satisfied in the training data. It is important to highlight that the weight is not the same as frequency and, therefore, there is no mandatory condition on the sum of weights of outgoing edges to equal one. The inference (prediction) stage of the next element is simple. It is a selection of the element whose weight of the edge between current and the next states is maximum.

All-Kth-Order-Model. AKOM (All-Kth-Order-Model) [8] is a successor of PPM [1] and is built not around the Markov model of the given order k, but around the set of Markovian models of orders up to k-th order. In other words, the training stage consists of building such models. Prediction choice in its turn starts with the model of the order that matches the given context size with the proper fallback mechanism. It was shown in [8] that this method works well for sequences of big length and is accurate enough if we select top-10 metrics for assessing prediction accuracy of this method.

Transition Directed Acyclic Graph. As well as PPM [1] and AKOM [8], TDAG (Transition Directed Acyclic Graph) [5] is build around Markov processes. However, in this approach we build Markov trees instead of finite stochastic automata. The tree is an approximation of the Markov chain that, firstly, influences the quality of the resulting predictions and, secondly, brings at least one mandatory parameter - maximum depth of the resulting tree.

Artificial Neural Networks. Artificial Neural Networks (ANNs) [7,11,12,14] are very popular tools in solving a broad range of tasks including the sequence prediction task. Due to the fact that in [8] it was shown that prediction is accurate on long sequences and it is not taken into consideration by traditional algorithms, the usage of LSTM networks [14] brings objectively high potential for the improvement of the prediction accuracy.

Considering the structure, the state of the LSTM network C_t can be obtained via the output valve o_t. State modification is done via i_t and cleaning of the previous state C_{t-1} - *forgetting* - via f_t. Such a structure is a bit more complex than in RNN, however, it can remember long-term connections. From the accuracy perspective, according to the [14], LSTM outperforms its closest competitors: CNN (Convolutional Neural Networks) and MLP (Multi-Layer Perceptron). However, for some datasets, DG is still the most accurate approach [6].

To sum up, there is a huge variety of methods that are based either on well performing Markov chains or trees or on quick and effective data structures or on the base of neural networks, predominantly recurrent ones. In the next sections we describe the proposed approach and compare it with the existing solutions, investigated above.

4 Dataset

A dataset plays an important role in every data mining task as well as means of pre-processing this data. As the basis for our research we have used the data obtained during the following research [9] using VKMiner[1]. Data is organized as a set of graphs represented in the GML (Graph Modelling Language) format, each node of the graph contains information about author intention, text of the message, name of the author and direction of the message. GML is a hierarchical

[1] https://linis.hse.ru/soft-linis.

format of graph description based on ASCII. Intentions are represented as 25 letters of the Latin alphabet as it is shown in the Table 1. 25 types of intentions are joined into 5 super-groups (each column in the table represents one super-group).

Each graph is a post (message, image) in the social network VKontakte[2] and a chain of users answers to it. Users can answer either to the original post or to the answers, that have been already written. Therefore, the structure becomes dendritic. Moreover, long messages can contain several intentions. Visually we can build the map of the discussion as a tree of intentions. Each node in this graph is the user's intention. While building all the possible subsequences from the root to the leaves, the number of combinations is multiplied, resulting in a huge number of ways and makes the experiment too complicated. To reduce that number we have decided to use the main intention from the message and ignore all the others in case they exist. Finally, we have extracted 13156 sequences from the dataset.

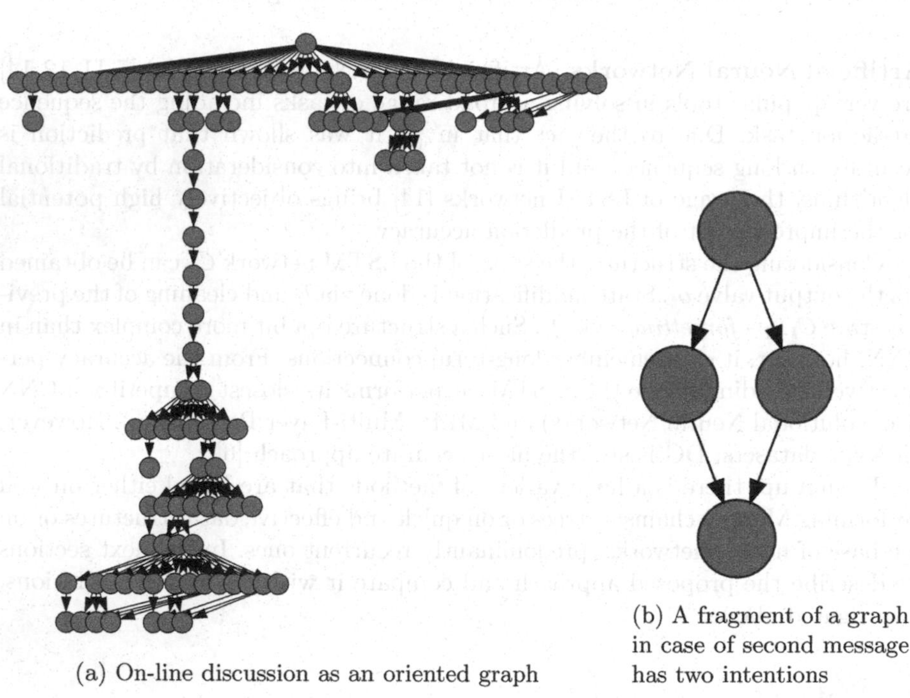

(a) On-line discussion as an oriented graph

(b) A fragment of a graph in case of second message has two intentions

Fig. 1. Training data examples

The starting point in data pre-processing is the extraction of the subsequences of intentions out of the graph from the root node to its leaves. In case the message contains two intentions it is represented by two nodes and each previous node is connected with all the next nodes (Fig. 1b).

[2] https://vk.com.

Table 1. Intention types and supertypes

Information reproducing type, To Reproduce the observable in speech		Emotionally consolidating type, Suggestion of the own world picture for cooperative collaboration		Manipulating type, Social domination, hierarchy establishment		Order-directive type, To encourage addressee to an action, make changes in the fragment of reality		Control-reactive type, To express evaluative reaction regarding the situation	
A	Surprise Question	**F**	Selfpresentation	**K**	Abusement	**P**	Inducement to a positive action/recommendation	**U**	Acceptance Accolade
B	Showing disagreement Hesitation	**G**	Attention attraction (discourse, rhetorical questions)	**L**	Frightening, threats	**Q**	Solicitation to negative	**V**	Sarkasm Malevo-lence
C	Agreement expression Support	**H**	Auditorium aussuagement Reassurance	**M**	Discredit (authority disruption)	**R**	Accusation	**W**	Criticism
D	Non-acceptance, rejection from communication	**I**	Forecasts, claims for truth	**N**	Force demon-stration (without obvious threat)	**S**	Consequences caution	**X**	Irony
E	Commiseration, sympathy	**J**	Justification (as self-justification, e.g. without accusation)	**O**	Moralisation, homily	**T**	Accusation offset (if is accused)	**Y**	Exposure

5 Neural Network Architectures

To predict next intent we use a neural network with popular architectures for the classification task. In this section, we briefly describe our choice of architectures, a regularization method and a training algorithm.

We implement 4 well known neural architectures: Multilayer Perceptron (MLP), Convolutional Neural Network (CNN), Recurrent Neural Network (RNN) and Bidirectional Recurrent Neural Network (BiRNN).

The general structure of our neural networks is presented in the Table 2.

Table 2. Structure of proposed neural networks.

Recurrent Neural Network (RNN) and Bidirectional RNN	Convolutional Neural Network (CNN)	Multilayer Perceptron (MLP)
Embedding (trainable)	Embedding (trainable)	Embedding (trainable)
LSTM (bidirectional or not)	Convolution1D	Flatten
Dropout	MaxPooling1D	FullyConnected
LSTM (bidirectional or not)	Dropout	ReLU Activation
Dropout	Convolution1D	FullyConnected
FullyConnected	MaxPooling1D	SoftMax Activation
ReLU Activation	Dropout	
FullyConnected	FullyConnected	
SoftMax Activation	ReLU Activation	
	FullyConnected	
	SoftMax Activation	

The first layer is the trainable Embedding layer in all the proposed Artificial Neural Networks. This layer maps given intention type with the embedding vector of small size (for example, 10). Then those vectors are sent either to the MLP, CNN, RNN or to the bidirectional RNN. Finally all the architectures have two fully-connected layers. The number of outputs corresponds to the number of classes, that is, to the number of intentions.

We use dropout as a regularizer to prevent our network from overfitting. Our dropout layers select 0.2 from the connections at random and turns them into zero and thus prevents co-adaptation of the features. A categorical cross-entropy cost function is optimized with the help of RMSprop algorithm.

In this paper we are not going to analyze the selection of hyper-parameters and optimal configurations of the neural networks as it goes out of the scope of current research. Instead, we have chosen the values according to the empirical engineering experience we have.

6 Computational Experiment

We have chosen a framework SPMF[3] for benchmarking different algorithms: PPM, DG, CPT+. The selection was easy as this framework was already used in numerous papers for the same reason.

On the other hand, the neural network architecture that we propose was implemented in the open-source framework Keras[4]. The open source implementation of these networks is made with the Python language in the Dialog-Intent-DL repository[5].

To assess the accuracy of those approaches the dataset was randomly split into training and testing parts (0.8 and 0.2) accordingly. The maximum length of the input sequence is 5. It is important to note that the longer is the sequence the smaller is the accuracy. Full benchmark report is presented in the Table 3.

Table 3. Prediction accuracy comparison

Algorithm	Accuracy for 25 classes	Accuracy for 5 classes
PPM	0.26	0.36
DG	0.23	0.38
CPT+	0.48	0.66
MLP	0.49	0.50
RNN	0.42	0.43
CNN	0.52	0.53
BiRNN	0.87	0.88

From the table above it is possible to make the following conclusions:

1. Algorithm CPT+ outperforms others not neural algorithms;
2. BiRNN algorithm outperforms all others with a large gap;
3. Usage of the super-groups expectedly increases the accuracy a little bit;

Figure 2 displays the evolution of accuracy depending on the epoch number. As we can see simple RNN learns very slow and has low accuracy. CNN learns faster and has higher accuracy. Bidirectional RNN is the fastest and has the better accuracy on both subplots. As we can see the simplest MLP demonstrates not bad results.

Long-term dependencies in the intentions sequences are not recognized because experiments with a smaller context as input to the algorithm produce higher accuracy.

[3] http://www.philippe-fournier-viger.com/spmf/.
[4] https://keras.io.
[5] https://github.com/demid5111/dialog-intent-dl.

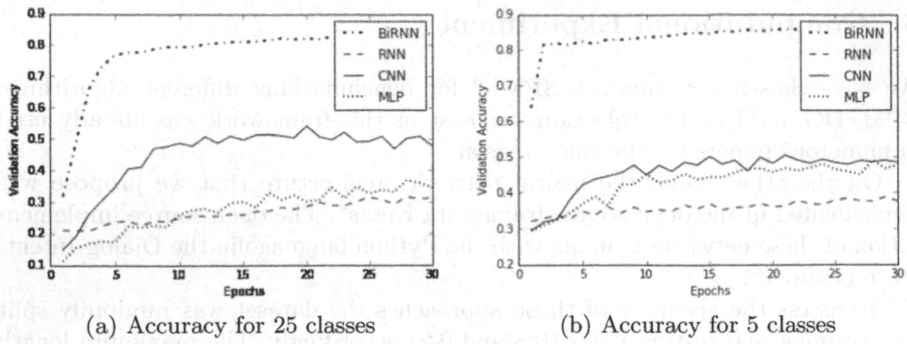

(a) Accuracy for 25 classes (b) Accuracy for 5 classes

Fig. 2. Validation accuracy over epochs

7 Conclusion

We have made the comparative analysis of the methods dedicated to the sequence prediction task and applied them to the problem of prediction of the next intention in the on-line dialog of users in the social network. Accuracy assessment is made over the original dataset that was built from the on-line dialogs as a set of graphs containing messages and their intentions.

We think that further analysis of hyperparameters can give a boost in the accuracy. Neural network architectures with attention mechanism like a Transformer could improve the accuracy a little bit. We believe that it can't affect dramatically, because we noticed only short-term dependencies in the intentions sequences. More importantly, neural methods can be easily extended via the use of additional features, like the embedding vectors for messages themselves (with the help of doc2vec) etc. The latter we consider as a direction of further research.

Acknowledgments. The paper was prepared within the framework of the Academic Fund Program at the National Research University Higher School of Economics (HSE) in 2017 (grant 17-05-0007) and by the Russian Academic Excellence Project "5-100". This work is done by partial support from RFFR grant number 19-37-90058.

References

1. Cleary, J., Witten, I.: Data compression using adaptive coding and partial string matching. IEEE Trans. Commun. **32**(4), 396–402 (1984)
2. Gueniche, T., Fournier-Viger, P., Raman, R., Tseng, V.S.: CPT+: decreasing the time/space complexity of the compact prediction tree. In: Cao, T., Lim, E.-P., Zhou, Z.-H., Ho, T.-B., Cheung, D., Motoda, H. (eds.) PAKDD 2015. LNCS (LNAI), vol. 9078, pp. 625–636. Springer, Cham (2015). https://doi.org/10.1007/978-3-319-18032-8_49
3. Gueniche, T., Fournier-Viger, P., Tseng, V.S.: Compact prediction tree: a lossless model for accurate sequence prediction. In: Motoda, H., Wu, Z., Cao, L., Zaiane, O., Yao, M., Wang, W. (eds.) ADMA 2013. LNCS (LNAI), vol. 8347, pp. 177–188. Springer, Heidelberg (2013). https://doi.org/10.1007/978-3-642-53917-6_16

4. Karpov, N., Demidovskij, A., Malafeev, A.: Development of a model to predict intention using deep learning. In: CEUR Workshop Proceedings, Supplementary Proceedings of the Sixth International Conference on Analysis of Images, Social Networks and Texts (AIST 2017), vol. 1975, pp. 69–78 (2017). http://ceur-ws.org/Vol-1975/paper8.pdf
5. Laird, P., Saul, R.: Discrete sequence prediction and its applications. Mach. Learn. **15**(1), 43–68 (1994)
6. Padmanabhan, V.N., Mogul, J.C.: Using predictive prefetching to improve world wide web latency. ACM SIGCOMM Comput. Commun. Rev. **26**(3), 22–36 (1996)
7. Pérez-Ortiz, J.A., Calera-Rubio, J., Forcada, M.L.: Online symbolic-sequence prediction with discrete-time recurrent neural networks. In: Dorffner, G., Bischof, H., Hornik, K. (eds.) ICANN 2001. LNCS, vol. 2130, pp. 719–724. Springer, Heidelberg (2001). https://doi.org/10.1007/3-540-44668-0_100
8. Pitkow, J., Pirolli, P.: Mining longest repeating subsequences to predict world wide web surfing. In: Proceedings of the 2nd Conference on USENIX Symposium on Internet Technologies and Systems - Volume 2, USITS 1999, p. 13. USENIX Association, Berkeley (1999). http://dl.acm.org/citation.cfm?id=1251480.1251493
9. Radina, N.K.: Intention analysis of online discussions (based on the example of comments on the materials of the internet portal inosmi.ru). MediaScope **4** (2016). http://www.mediascope.ru/en/2287
10. Ron, D., Singer, Y., Tishby, N.: The power of amnesia: learning probabilistic automata with variable memory length. Mach. Learn. **25**(2–3), 117–149 (1996)
11. Sun, R., Giles, C.L.: Sequence learning: from recognition and prediction to sequential decision making. IEEE Intell. Syst. **16**(4), 67–70 (2001)
12. Tax, N.: Human activity prediction in smart home environments with LSTM neural networks. In: 2018 14th International Conference on Intelligent Environments (IE), pp. 40–47. IEEE (2018)
13. Willems, F.M., Shtarkov, Y.M., Tjalkens, T.J.: The context-tree weighting method: basic properties. IEEE Trans. Inf. Theory **41**(3), 653–664 (1995)
14. Zhao, Y., Chu, S., Zhou, Y., Tu, K.: Sequence prediction using neural network classiers. In: Verwer, S., van Zaanen, M., Smetsers, R. (eds.) Proceedings of the 13th International Conference on Grammatical Inference. Proceedings of Machine Learning Research, 05–07 October 2017, vol. 57, pp. 164–169. PMLR, Delft (2017). http://proceedings.mlr.press/v57/zhao16.html

Analysis of the Dissemination of Information Through Telegram. The Case of Language Conflict in Tatarstan

Galina Gradoselskaya(✉) and Anna Korzhenko

Higher School of Economics, Moscow, Russian Federation
mss981009@mail.ru

Abstract. Messenger Telegram launched in 2013 but became popular among users in 2015. This was due to several statements that were taken for granted as absolute truth. One of such allegations was the influence of the Telegram on the information field of the country. The article discusses the dynamics of the discussion on the acute social issue - the status of the study of the national language in Tatarstan in the messenger and in the mass media. The detailed analysis of the development of an informational event in time has been carried out. We analyzed the positions of the actors included in it and their role in the dissemination of information.

Keywords: Social network analysis · On-line networks in telegram · Information propagation · Semantic networks · Discourse analysis

1 Introduction

The phenomenon of the Telegram messenger rapidly became popular after only two years of existence. From the very beginning, aggressive marketing was accompanied by loud statements and political statements that quickly spread among its users and were taken for granted.

For example, it was argued that the work of the messenger is not affected by the censorship of any countries in which it operates. They also argued that the management of the messenger does not cooperate with the special services [22].

Such an aggressive and politically oriented promotion of the Telegram ended with the introduction of restrictions by the Russian government on the work of the messenger in the country in 2018. Similar decisions were made by the governments of China and Iran [6].

Despite all the statements of a political nature, some of the myths concerning the more universal relationships of social networks and the media were formed by the messenger users. It is these commonplace statements that have become the object of our verification and research.

Thus, the messenger users concluded that the information agenda in the Telegram is more adequate than in the media. The most extreme statements reached the point that the media uses the messenger data, and in fact, are secondary to social networks.

D. A. Alexandrov et al. (Eds.): DTGS 2019, CCIS 1038, pp. 378–392, 2019.
https://doi.org/10.1007/978-3-030-37858-5_31

Therefore, in our study, we decided to check on a specific example, whether it is true that the messenger can affect the media information field. If so, we wanted to understand how it happens and what mechanisms are involved in that process.

Such a formulation of the substantive task leads to the necessity of parallel methodological research. The methodological task is to develop an algorithm for analyzing and comparing discourse between the media and Telegram channels. Thus, the analysis of discourse, its dynamics, its movement between social networks and the media becomes the main research tool.

However, the discourse does not «hang in the air» - it always has a specific author, «stuffing points» in the social network, and the structure of distribution through social networks, which also consists of actors. Therefore, in addition to discourse, it is necessary to investigate the structure of its distribution by actors and groups of actors.

Thus, if we examine the discourse on the example of the development of a particular informational event, we can assume that groups of actors are singled out in the network structure of information dissemination, including those grouped by polarity of opinions that carry out informational support for the event.

Quite a lot of attention was paid to the selection of an informational event that attracted the attention of both Telegram users and the media.

Three types of appearance and distribution of information in the messenger were considered:

- A wave of discussion about the event was raised in the Telegram-channels and went to the media;
- The informational event began to be discussed in the media and then transferred to the Telegram channels;
- The event was discussed only within the Telegram-channels.

For each type, three informational events were selected, and as a result, by the duration of the discussion, by the involvement of different types of actors, by the variety of opinions presented. However, at the time of the survey, Telegram was blocked, as described above. Due to the difficulties of a technical nature, it was decided to investigate in detail only one event.

The case study of the regional level in Tatarstan was selected for a full analysis. Despite the regional level, representatives of the federal political elites were drawn into the discussion of the language conflict in the republic, the opposition of the «Russian» and «Tatar» languages. Federal political scientists, deputies, presidential candidates, oppositionists and nationalists from both «linguistic» parties were involved. Language conflict in Tatarstan was a very long informational event: it was widely discussed from September 2017 to mid-January 2018.

2 Related Literature on Developments in Media-Space

The analysis of the communication process is dedicated to numerous studies, which involved experts from different fields: psychology, sociology, linguistics and many other scientific fields. The definition of the term «communication» is usually divided into several central meanings: firstly, communication - a tool or technology, which gives to information the ability to impact relations between the actors; secondly, communication is the process of informational influence between the subjects of communication [19]. Information interchange is understood as a set of actions necessary for the successful functioning of a communicative system. Information was first studied in mathematical and technical sciences, where it was defined as a quantitative measure of data which is distributed through technical communication channels. This approach was advocated by Shannon and Weaver [17].

The development of information and communication systems and technologies can be discernible in the transformation of models of the communication process - a schematic method of representing components of information interchange. Communicative processes can be represented by different models, which depend on the researcher`s preferences. In general, the structural representation of communication can be divided into three groups that differ in the nature of communication: linear models, circular models and semiotic models. The basic works in the first category were works of G. Lasswell, C. Shannon and W. Weaver. G. Lasswell formulated the communication model, which had five elements: source of information, information, method of information transfer, recipient of information and effect of communication [10].

The mathematical model of Shannon-Weaver, which was based on the similar principle with the model of Lasswell, became very popular among researchers. During the process of model construction, Shannon introduced the concept of entropy (noise) - external factors that distort the message and violate its integrity [17]. The Shannon-Weaver model, as well as the Lasswell model, has a significant drawback - the model does not take into account feedback. This aspect was considered in circular communication models. Schramm - the follower of C. Shannon and W. Weaver - reflected the dialogue form of communication, in which the communicator and the communicator periodically change roles [16].

One of the basic models of semiotic modeling of communication are the works of Russian scientists Jacobson [7] and Lotman [13]. Cultural sociologists made the meaning of the language code in the transmitted message more significant. Their models take into account not only the language of communication, but also the user of this language. Also important is the sociolinguistic interpretation of the communication act, which was researched by sociologists Brown and Fraser, using concepts of sociological and semiotic directions [3]. Scientists identify «circumstances» that differ in the goals and results of communication and depend on the social and situational characteristics of the participants in communication. This model proves that in various concepts of discourse the set of variables characterizing the «situation» turns out to be different - the «circumstances» are multidimensional. Although scholars now are developing new communication process models, the described linear, circular and semiotic models lie in the basis of all new inventions.

In the structure of communication gradually central mass communications (MC) and their specialized tools that have been modernized by technological advances are becoming more meaningful [12]. In a broad sense, MC could be defined as a public transfer of messages through technological channels to a large and dispersed audience [4]. Important role in the formation of the theory of mass communication played political scientist G. Lasswell. This researcher identified the main directions of sociological studies of mass communication: analysis of management of structural processes in MC, analysis of the content of messages (content analysis), analysis of the audience and analysis of the effect of communication impact [10].

Many give special attention to the audience that participates in the act of mass communication. Due to Schramm, the audience started to be viewed as heterogeneous groups influenced by different sources of information [16]. Therefore, audience began to be divided into «mass audience» and «specialized audience». Lazarsfeld and Katz suggested studying MC as a hierarchical unified system in which the most influential actors stand out. They called them «leaders of ideas» [8]. These sociologists have formed the theory of the «two-step flow of information», in which the message is first filtered by the «opinion leaders» and only after that the message reaches the audience. Lazarsfeld also studied the influence of mass media and formed the theory of the « agenda» [8]. In his opinion, the news is a socially constructed and edited reality. The media does not speak about what people think, but what they need to think about. The influence of the media was also investigated by sociologists McLuhan and Mol, who revealed the concept of the «mosaic» of culture [14] - the sociocultural situation created by the mass media and is due to the chaotic perception of heterogeneous information.

Special role in domestic studies of mass communication was occupied by studies of discourse and socio-cultural codes. The greatest contribution in this direction was made by a cultural expert and semiotician Lotman. He believed that the media is a model of how culture is «arranged» [12]. A similar opinion was supported by the German sociologist Luhmann, who believed that the mass media were able to form a new system in the mass consciousness [13]. Thus, an important aspect of mass communication is the formation and transmission of cultural concepts through text and discourse.

Of particular importance are practical and theoretical studies that consider the formation of a discursive space in the media. Such studies were reviewed by Lasswell [10] using content analysis, van Dijk [21] and Karasik [9]. These studies were performed by the method of discourse analysis. With these text analysis methods discourse content was studied. It means that scholars investigated the author's intentions and the reasons for writing the text, assessed the content of the text (tone of speech) and formulated various effects of reading the text.

The formation of open Internet content distribution platforms has contributed to the emergence of new communication practices and content distribution channels. In the article «Telegram channels: reasons for launching projects and promotion tools» the author studied the new trend of the development of the information agenda, which was concentrated in the Telegram messenger, in particular in open public groups - Telegram channels [5]. The researcher conducted a series of interviews with the owners of popular Telegram channels, as a result of which a high level of user confidence in the published content in the messenger was revealed. The articles [1, 2] show the results of a study identifying the nature of the discourse in virtual communities on a specific topic. The articles show the results of using automated tools for researching users' opinions in social media and content distribution channels, and also illustrate the use of network analysis in the assessment of key indicators in the network of communities.

3 Methods and Data Analysis of News peg Coverage in the Telegram

3.1 Data Collection of the Telegram Data

In this paper we investigated the informational event devoted to the development of the «language conflict» in Tatarstan. It developed from September 2017 until mid-January 2018.

Survey Sample Definition. To compose a selection of messages from Telegram, a program script was written in Python using the Telethon library [20]. The library simplifies accessing the messenger by using its own API (a software interface for interacting with the application server). The unloading of news publications of online mass media used the automated monitoring system «Medialogia» [15]. At the initial stages of the formation and initial verification of the sample for the study, unforeseen difficulties arose in obtaining data from the messenger.

The problem with unloading messages from the Telegram channels arose in connection with the imposition of restrictions by the Russian government on the work of the messenger in the country. The program script was automatically accessed using the application programming interface (API), but the «response» from the application service was extremely limited. The unloading of messages was hampered by the constant restrictions and blocking of the execution of a software script by the application, which were introduced by the service to reduce the load on its own capacities.

Database Formation and Research Sample. To upload messages, a list of keywords was generated taking into account the morphology and search query for both information platforms: «Tatar language», «Tatarstan», «Russian language + confrontation», «Minnikhanov» and others.

The final database of messages with references to the language conflict in Tatarstan is based on the key attributes of messages, and their coding. The following characteristics were fixed:

- the author of the Telegram channel where the post was posted;
- characteristics of the author of the channel: the number of subscribers, the name of the channel and when it was created;
- date and time of publication;
- message text;
- URL to the message;
- post views - a metric that determines how many people viewed a particular post;
- news peg and its code;
- informational event and its code.

The same characteristics were recorded for publications on the language conflict in Tatarstan in the media.

3.2 Data Analysis and Research Algorithm

It should be noted the complexity of the object of study. On the one hand, the objects were texts in the form of messages and articles, on the other hand, actors publishing posts in the Telegram, and mass media publishing materials.

Thus, the empirical base of the study is the corpus of news publications in the media and messages from Telegram channels. The final sample of messages for analysis was: 7 910 articles in the media and 414 messages of public Telegram channels.

The research algorithm can be represented as a sequence of steps:

- Uploading messages with keyword references from Telegram and media.
- Formation of a single database in Excel.
- Expert data coding.
- All event messages are encoded according to different types of information waves, which are aggregated into informational events. The same text is published in different variations by one or several authors. Such a situation is rather frequent in the information coverage of the event - this does not contradict the goal of the research, on the contrary, it is necessary to track the beginning of the formation of discourse within one information event.
- Encoding of initial data sources - analysis of who first published the text.
- Data preparation and construction of a network structure for disseminating information in the media and Telegram. To do this, use the program for statistical data processing - SPSS, graphs are visualized and analyzed using the programs Gephi and ORA.
- Sociolinguistic analysis of the dynamics of the opinions of key people about the event.
- Comparison of the discursive space between the media and Telegram.
- Interpretation of results.

4 Development of Informational Events in Telegram and Mass Media

4.1 Dynamics and Interrelation of Informational Events Coverage in the Telegram and Media

An acute social event was selected to conduct the study: «language» conflict in the Republic of Tatarstan. The reason for the long discussion was the statement by V. Putin about the inadmissibility of forcing someone to learn a non-native language: «Forcing a person to learn a language that is not native to him is just as unacceptable as is to reduce the level of teaching Russian» [18]. As a result, discussions broke out and the search for hidden meanings in the words of the president - the question of the future of the Tatar language was raised.

Formed two groups of opposing opinions. The following social groups represented one pole.

- Tatar nationalists who are trying to present the case as if it is a matter of excluding the Tatar language from among the state in the Republic of Tatarstan, and not about the abolition of the compulsory teaching of the Tatar language to children in schools at the expense of learning Russian.
- Externally neutral national majority, quietly supporting the nationalists.

At the other extreme, opponents have accumulated the study of the Tatar language in schools.

- Activists-parents of Russian origin, who initiated the whole process with the refusal of compulsory study of the Tatar language in schools after the words of the president. They began to sway the situation and provide the necessary resonance in social networks, instant messengers, and then in society.
- Parents of schoolchildren who are tired of the Tatar language, taught to their children in huge volumes by incorrect methods, often hastily trained teachers. This Russian and Tatars. It was the largest group.

Information field, in addition to the statements of the Russian President, constantly fed information accompanying events for almost half a year. Thus, during the autumn, 3 key meetings of the State Council of the Republic of Tatarstan took place in the republic, during which the fate of teaching the Tatar language was decided. Flashmobs in social networks, public meetings, permanent publications of opinions of popular people and deputies of different levels heated the situation. The dynamics of the information field in the media and in the Telegram channels is presented in Fig. 1.

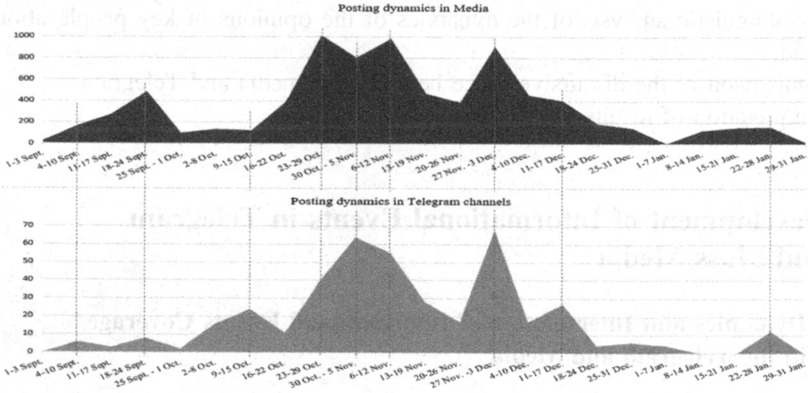

Fig. 1. Posting dynamics in Media and Telegram channels

Based on the graphs, it is possible to draw conclusions about the direct relationship between the two content distribution channels: Telegram messenger and media. The correlation coefficient between the two graphs was 0.872.

However, we still need to know whether there is a dependency and what it affects. Moreover it is significant to understand whether there is a causal relationship between the coverage of the event in the messenger and the media or not.

To test the hypothesis about the impact of the discourse of public channels on the news agenda of the media, content analysis and expert coding of messages were conducted. At first, all news publications were coded for informational waves and informational events. Then the messages from the Telegram channels correlated with the events recorded in the media. Publications were compared by date and time of appearance, determining the source of discourse formation. The following is a detailed analysis of the relationship of the information agenda in the media and Telegram channels in chronological order.

Data chronology of publications are shown below in Table 1.

Table 1. The number of publications in the Media and Telegram channels by day

Data	Media	Telegram channels
1–3 Sept.	30	0
4–10 Sept.	168	6
11–17 Sept.	271	3
18–24 Sept.	484	8
25 Sept.–1 Oct.	100	2
2–8 Oct.	133	16
9–15 Oct.	121	24
16–22 Oct.	388	11
23–29 Oct.	1013	40
30 Oct.–5 Nov.	801	64
6–12 Nov.	982	55
13–19 Nov.	472	28
20–26 Nov.	386	17
27 Nov.–3 Dec.	909	68
4–10 Dec.	458	17
11–17 Dec.	401	27
18–24 Dec.	187	4
25–31 Dec.	148	6
1–7 Jan.	6	4
8–14 Jan.	122	0
15–21 Jan.	154	0
22–28 Jan.	156	12
29–31 Jan.	19	0

To study the degree of influence of external sources on Telegram channels, the ratio of the top 10 most discussed informational events at two distribution sites of content was considered. The result of the analysis is presented in Fig. 2. Orange color highlights informational events that recur in the top 10 most popular events in the Telegram, blue color indicates events that were initiated in the media, but did not make it into the top 10 popular events of the messenger. The arrows indicate the correspondence of the position of the informational event with respect to each source, the proportion is calculated based on the ratio of mentions of the event to the total number of messages at each site.

MEDIA

Percentage	The name of the information event	№
13,6%	Publication of opinions of popular people about the situation in Tatarstan	1
5,8%	Rumors and decisions on the dismissal or retraining of teachers of the Tatar language in connection with the reduction of teaching hours	2
5,5%	The position of O. Vasilyeva on the study of the Tatar language	3
5,0%	Decisive meeting of the RT State Council on November 8	4
4,2%	The work of the Prosecutor General's Office and Rosobrnadzor at the request of V. Putin	5
4,2%	The Ministry of Education and Science of the Republic of Tajikistan has issued guidelines for schools with approximate versions of curricula.	6
3,8%	DUM RT fights for compulsory study of the Tatar language	7
3,7%	A schoolboy's mother requires 3 million from the Ministry of Science of Tatarstan	8
3,4%	31st meeting of the State Council of the Republic of Tajikistan	9
2,9%	Dismissal of the Minister of Education TR Engel Fattakhov	10

TELEGRAM CHANNELS

№	The name of the information event	Percentage
1	Publication of opinions of popular people about the situation in Tatarstan	19,1%
2	The work of the Prosecutor General's Office and Rosobrnadzor at the request of V. Putin	9,5%
3	Politicization of the ban on the study of the Tatar language	7,0%
4	Decisive meeting of the RT State Council on November 8	5,3%
5	Rumors and decisions on the dismissal or retraining of teachers of the Tatar language in connection with the reduction of teaching hours	4,5%
6	The position of O. Vasilyeva on the study of the Tatar language	4,5%
7	DUM RT fights for compulsory study of the Tatar language	4,0%
8	PR of the situation in the Telegram, social networks	3,8%
9	Rally in memory of the capture of the city by Ivan the Terrible in 1552	3,8%
10	D. Peskov: the issue of recognition of the Tatar language as the second state is not discussed	2,8%

Fig. 2. The ratio of the top 10 most discussed informational events between the Media and Telegram channels

It can be concluded that the media information agenda has a strong influence on the formation of the discursive field of Telegram channels. All events from the top 10 media are mentioned in the records of the authors of public channels.

Thus, the hypothesis about the influence of the discursive space of Telegram channels on the news agenda of the media was partially confirmed. Informational events that are formed in the messenger can be seen in media publications, but in very small quantities, while not giving any resonance or having any continuation.

4.2 Network Structure of Information Dissemination in Telegram

To study the network structure of information dissemination in the Telegram channels, relations were formed between the author of the channel and the author of the message, in which there was a mention of the event. Transforming the data from the edge form of the graph to the matrix, the data obtained were visualized in the ORA program, and the calculation of network metrics was carried out in the Gephi program. All authors who have not published their personal opinions are aggregators of the news agenda. Figure 3 shows the graph where the size of the vertices of which depends on the number of outgoing connections. Total network structure contains 95 nodes and 175 edges. Thus, key actors were computed, which bring the entire agenda in Telegram together. The more the author refers to another actor, the more strongly their link edge is colored. The larger the actor has outgoing links, the larger is its vertex size.

The actor who controls the information agenda the most is the Telegram-channel Guard. The channel is the most popular and significant (according to other channel authors) news channel. Also, a high rate of outgoing links was noted in E. Kholmogorov, who maintains a personal blog in the messenger. Kholmogorov - a publicist is an observer of «Tsargrad» - positions himself as the first «Russian conservative information and analytical channel». Also visible is a bright loop from the actor Dissident.ru, the Russian network information digest of opposition media. The official representation of the federal media - Rosbalt is also actively forming discourse.

Fig. 3. The network of actors who participated in the discussion of the information event in the Telegram

The next step in the study was the construction of networks coded by the estimated position: «support» or «against» the policy of the authorities of Tatarstan. In Fig. 4, evaluative judgments are marked with color, where: orange is «against» the policy, green is «in favor», and violet is a mixed position. The size of the graph vertices depends on the number of incoming connections.

Most of the authors who spoke out against the current situation in the republic have strong networking links. The central moderators of the counterbalance Tatar authorities information agenda were two telegram channels: «Neudashcha» and «Yedu v tatarstan». It is possible to distinguish public figures A. Venediktov and K. Potupchik. It also highlights the position of «Komsomolskaya Pravda» and two actors who reposted the publication of the newspaper.

The cluster of relatively neutral actors, who published pro and contra messages. The «Karaulny» public channel acts as an information hub and broadcasts evaluative judgments of different tonality. Not adhered to a single posting policy in the main information and analytical network publications.

Authors who advocated for the disposition of the powers of the authorities are mostly solitary. Thus, this situation shows the weak front of nationalist ideas in the Telegram channel.

The names of the actors are shown in more detail below in Table 2. The actors are ranked in descending order of betweenness centrality – top 7 shown. Reported types of actors correspond to Fig. 4.

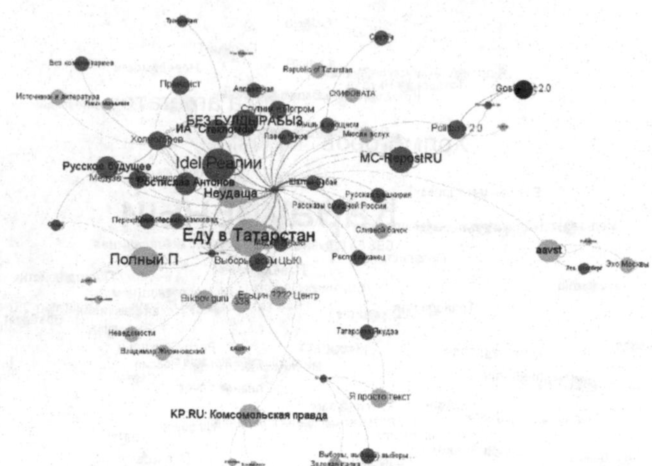

Fig. 4. A network of actors, expertly coded in relation to the policy of the authorities of Tatarstan in the language issue: orange – «against», green – «support», violet – a mixed position (Color figure online)

Table 2. Top 7 actors ranked in descending order between betweenness centrality

Channel name	Members	Author position	Betweeness centrality
Kholmogorov	3 444	Mixed	58
Neudashcha	12 172	Against	45
IA «Steklomoy»	8 095	Mixed	19
Aavst	77 498	Against	3
Politburo 2.0	16 347	Mixed	3
Tatarskaya Yakudza	3 601	Mixed	1
Mysh v ovoshchnom	27 514	Mixed	1

4.3 Network Structure of Information Dissemination in the Media

The same way were examined media sources. Figure 5 presents the online media relationship to the language issue. Relations between the media were defined in chronological order: the first published text about the informational event was considered the primary source for the rest of the actors in a single discussion. Estimated judgments are marked in color on the graph, where: raspberry is «against» the policy of the authorities of Tatarstan, green is «support», blue is a mixed position. The size of the graph vertices depends on the number of incoming connections.

In the media as well as in Telegram, one can single out the main mediators of the information agenda. The key media broadcasting nationalist ideas were the «IA Tatar-inform», the online newspaper «Business Online», «Chelninskiye izvestiya» and «Kazan 24». What is remarkable on the left side of the graph is a group of Islamist media that supported the ideology of the Muslim Spiritual Board. It also highlights the cluster of official portals of municipalities of the republic.

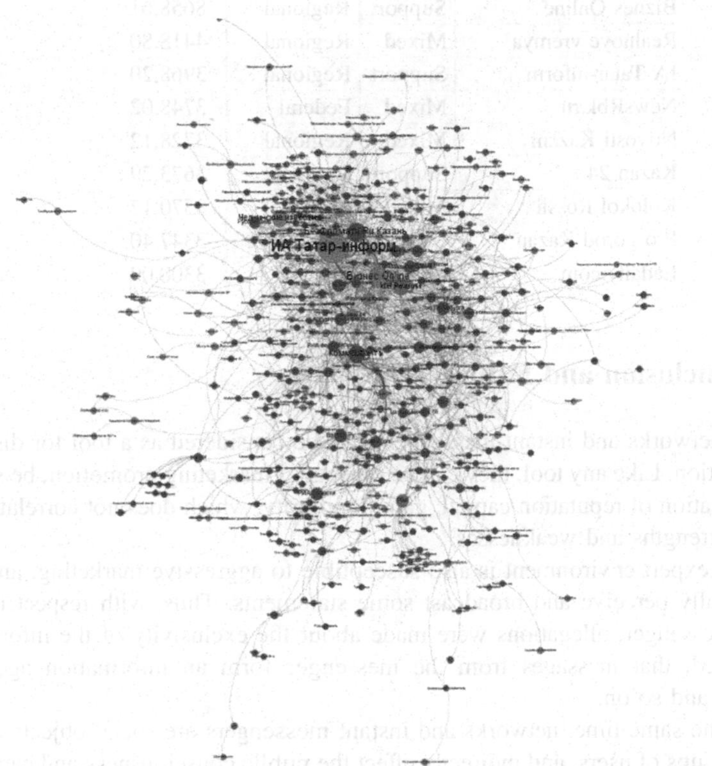

Fig. 5. A network of media expertly coded in relation to the policy of the Tatarstan authorities in the language issue: crimson – «against», green – «support», blue – mixed position (Color figure online)

The structure of the «neutral» tuned media, which projected a discourse of different evaluative segmentation, stands out especially vividly. In such media dominated two types of media: federal sites that covered various positions of Moscow and Tatar authorities, and non-informative sites that filled the agenda with duplicate articles. Such actions are not rarely taken to artificially «raise» a certain discourse in the top of large news aggregators to make the event more visible for the people.

The names of information sources are shown in more detail below in Table 3. The sources are ranked in decreasing order of centrality by betweenness centrality – top 10 shown. Reported types of actors correspond to Fig. 5.

Table 3. Top 10 actors ranked in descending order between betweenness centrality

Media level	Position	Media level	Betweeness centrality
BezFormata.Ru Kazan	Mixed	Regional	13015,06
Biznes Online	Support	Regional	8658,61
Realnoye vremya	Mixed	Regional	4418,80
IA Tatar-inform	Support	Regional	3968,20
NewsRbk.ru	Mixed	Federal	3748,02
Novosti Kazani	Mixed	Regional	3728,12
Kazan 24	Support	Regional	3673,29
Kolokol Rossii	Mixed	Regional	3570,17
Pro gorod Kazan	Support	Regional	3347,40
Eadaily.com	Mixed	Federal	3300,09

5 Conclusion and Future Work

Social networks and instant messengers can be considered as a tool for disseminating information. Like any tool, they can be objects of marketing promotion, be subjected to manipulation of reputation capital, gain popularity, which does not correlate with their actual strengths and weaknesses.

The expert environment is also susceptible to aggressive marketing, and begins to uncritically perceive and broadcast some statements. Thus, with respect to the Telegram messenger, allegations were made about the exclusivity of the information disseminated, that messages from the messenger form an information agenda in the country and so on.

At the same time, networks and instant messengers are social objects that include large groups of users, and indirectly affect the public consciousness and can potentially affect the activity of citizens of the country. Therefore, social networks and messengers that perform a crucial function in the dissemination of information, and sometimes managers of information flows, should be treated very carefully. They need to be studied in order to objectively evaluate their capabilities, with all the advantages and disadvantages.

In the light of the dual nature of the functioning of the Telegram: instrumental and social, a study was conducted of its interaction with the media using a specific example (language conflict in Tatarstan).

A thorough analytical work was carried out both with the discursive space and with the actors who disseminated information and participated in the discussion of the events in Telegam and Media.

According to the data obtained in our study, we can conclude that the expert opinion on the influence of the messenger is too overestimated.

One can judge about the formation of synergies in the nature of the dissemination of information via messenger. The media discusses the news, in parallel, a similar discourse is observed in the Telegram with materials from the media, then the media reprints the replicas and broadcasts social attitudes.

The study also examined the network practices of information dissemination in the framework of Telegram channels and the media. The hypothesis of the formation of groups of actors with opposite value judgments in the media and in the Telegram channels was proved. In addition, in the network structure of information dissemination there are groups of actors who provide general information support for the event. It is possible to mention the group of authors of Telegram channels, which are certain "mouthpieces" of the public agenda, broadcasting evaluative and analytical judgments.

In the future, it will be very exciting to carry out similar cross-platform research in other social networks, as well as compare the distribution of information from them in the mass media.

Acknowledgements. This study was funded by the Russian Academic Excellence Project "5-100".

References

1. Bershadskaya, L., Chugunov, A., Filatova, O., Trutnev, D.: e-Governance and e-Participation services: an analysis of discussions in Russian social media. In: Conference for E-Democracy and Open Governement, p. 573 (2014)
2. Bodrunova, S.S., Smoliarova, A.S., Blekanov, I.S., Litvinenko, A.A.: Content sharing in conflictual *Ad-Hoc* Twitter discussions: national patterns or universal trends? In: Alexandrov, D.A., Boukhanovsky, A.V., Chugunov, A.V., Kabanov, Y., Koltsova, O. (eds.) DTGS 2017. CCIS, vol. 745, pp. 3–15. Springer, Cham (2017). https://doi.org/10.1007/978-3-319-69784-0_1
3. Brown, P., Fraser, C.: Speech as a marker of situation. In: Social Markers in Speech, pp. 33–62. Cambridge University Press, Cambridge (1979)
4. Castells, M.: Communication, power and counter-power in the network society. Int. J. Commun. **1**(1), 29 (2007)
5. Epishkin, I.I.: Telegram channels: reasons for launching projects and promotion tools. MediaAlmanac **3**, 30–41 (2017)
6. Habr: The court decided to block Telegram in Russia (2018). https://habr.com/post/358014/. Accessed 01 Dec 2018
7. Jakobson, R., Fant, C.G., Halle, M.: Preliminaries to speech analysis: the distinctive features and their correlates. In: Linguistic Society of America, p. 481 (1951)
8. Katz, E., Lazarsfeld, P.F.: Personal Influence: The Part Played by People in the Flow of Mass Communication. Free Press, Glencoe (1955)
9. Karasik, V.I: On the types of discourse. Language personality: institutional and personal discourse. In: Sat. scientific Tr.: Change, vol. 1, pp. 5–20. Volgograd (2000)
10. Lasswell, H.: The Structure and Function of Communication in Society. The Process and Effects of Mass Communication, Chicago (1971)
11. Logan, R.K., McLuhan, M.: The Future of the Library: From Electric Media to Digital Media. Peter Lang (2016)
12. Lotman, U.M.: Semiosphere. Art St. Petersburg, St. Petersburg (2010)
13. Luhmann, N.: Social Systems. Stanford University Press, Stanford (1995)
14. McLuhan, M., Lapham, L.H.: Understanding Media: The Extensions of Man. MIT press, Cambridge (1994)

15. Medialogia - Monitoring and analysis of the media in real time. http://www.mlg.ru/. Accessed 01 Dec 2018
16. Siebert, F., Peterson, T.B., Peterson, T., Schramm, W.: Four theories of the press: the authoritarian, libertarian, social responsibility, and Soviet communist concepts of what the press should be and do. University of Illinois press, Urbana and Chicago (1956)
17. Shannon, C.E.: Communication theory of secrecy systems. Bell Syst. Tech. J. **28**(4), 656–715 (1949)
18. TASS: Putin pointed to the inadmissibility of reducing hours of learning Russian in the republics of the Russian Federation (2017). http://tass.ru/obschestvo/4428366. Accessed 01 Dec 2018
19. Tavokin, E.P.: Information as a scientific category. Soc Stud. **11**, 3–10 (2006)
20. Telegram client library - Telethon's documentation. http://telethon.readthedocs.io/en/latest/. Accessed 01 Dec 2018
21. van Dijk, T.A.: Discourse and Knowledge: A Sociocognitive Approach. Cambridge University Press, Cambridge (2014)
22. Vedomosti: FSB demanded that Telegram decipher the correspondence of users (2017). https://www.vedomosti.ru/technology/articles/2017/09/27/735506-fsb-potrebovala-telegram. Accessed 01 Dec 2018

Two Views on the 2010 Moscow Metro Bombings: Corpus-Based Contrastive Keyword Analysis

Tatiana Litvinova[1,2(✉)], Olga Litvinova[1], and Galina Zavarzina[1]

[1] Voronezh State Pedagogical University, 86 ul. Lenina, Voronezh 394043, Russia
centr_rus_yaz@mail.ru
[2] Plekhanov Russian University of Economics, Stremyanny lane 36, Moscow 117997, Russia

Abstract. The Internet has become an extremely important means of human communication. However, it is also used by extremists and terrorists who employ it to promote their ideas and recruit new members. One of the tasks facing academia and governments is detection of extremism/terrorism related content and counteracting a corresponding ideology. Analysis of linguistic features of texts from extremist sources can help to solve this task. The aim of the research is a corpus-based keyword analysis of Russian-language posts from extremist forum and texts by common Internet users on the same topic (comments on the 2010 Moscow Metro Bombings). We also used a corpus of blogs from LiveJournal as a reference corpus for deriving keywords, which is standard practice. We performed keyword analysis by means of WordSmith Tools software package and used qualitative, manual discourse analysis to identify a number of differences between texts from extremist forum and texts by common people on the same topic on lexical level.

Keywords: Extremist texts · Keyword analysis · WordSmith tool · Corpus linguistics

1 Introduction

Contemporary terrorists are making an active use of the Internet as an extremely important and highly available tool which due to its little «physical» capacity is employed for recruiting and training new members, raising funds, promoting ideas, documenting their history and mythology and organizing terrorist attacks [16, p. 36].

The analysis and understanding of extremist and terrorist ideology as it is reflected in corresponding texts is crucial for designing effective counter extremism and terrorism methods. There has mainly qualitative research into extremist and terrorist ideology and/or it was conducted on publicly available data related to extremism or terrorism. There has not been sufficient effort made to perform a quantitative analysis of the language of people who are involved in promoting the corresponding ideology.

This paper considers how automated corpus-linguistic techniques, namely keyword analysis, together with manual discourse analysis can be used to reveal differences in

D. A. Alexandrov et al. (Eds.): DTGS 2019, CCIS 1038, pp. 393–404, 2019.
https://doi.org/10.1007/978-3-030-37858-5_32

word usage and linguistics strategies by authors from Russian-language dataset which contains texts from extremist forum and common Internet users on the same topic, namely the 2010 Moscow Metro bombings. We used dataset "kavkazchat" from Dark Web Forum Portal developed by researchers from Arizona University, USA [3, 4] where texts from extremist forums are divided into topics ("threads") and languages. We also compiled a corpus of comments of Internet users on the news about this attack as well as a corpus of general usage for comparison.

«Keyword» is a «term for statistically significant lexical item which is most or least frequent in a given context (corpus) compared with other context (corpus) as a reference» [7, p. 211]. We used the Keywords module in WordSmith tools [15] to identify keywords and find word collocates that are unique to the text corpora under examination. To the best of our knowledge, this is the first corpus-based comparative study of texts from extremist forum which implies keyword analysis to reveal different views («extremist» and «non-extremist») on the same event for a better understanding of ideology, beliefs and justifications of the authors of extremist forum texts.

2 Corpus-Based Analysis of Extremist Texts

Many papers have shown that due to anonymity, quick access and urgency of different Internet platforms such as YouTube, Twitter, Instagram, Facebook, online discussion forums and blogosphere are being used by terrorists and extremists for propaganda, radicalization, recruiting members, etc. [5]. As Johansson et al. claim, «the ability to disseminate information instantaneously over vast geographical regions makes the Internet a key facilitator in the radicalisation process and preparations for terror attacks» [8, p. 375]. Extremists' use of computer-mediated communications has recently gained much attention from academia, governments and law enforcement agencies around the world. Researchers are working on understanding individuals' motivations for extremism and terrorism through language analysis. In recent years, techniques from the field of corpus-based natural language processing and text mining have been used to address these problems.

One line of research in this direction implies the study of terrorist material with the use of Linguistic Inquiry and Word Count (LIWC), content analysis software[1] which calculates the percentage of words in the entire text that matches the words in the predefined grammatical and semantic categories. For example, Pennebaker and Chung [11] analyzed Al-Qaeda transcripts from Bin Laden and Al-Zawahiri to indicate the authors' psychological state and how it develops over time.

Another line of research implies using complex corpus-linguistics tool, such as Wmatrix and WordSmith for frequency count, key word and key concept, and concordance analyses. For example, Salama [13] used WordSmith tool for the analysis of opposing discourses on Wahhabi-Saudi Islam/Wahhabism since 9/11.

With the help of WMatrix Prentice et al. [12] showed that extremists centre their rhetoric on the themes of morality, social proof, inspiration and appeals to religion and

[1] https://liwc.wpengine.com/ (last accessed 09/01/2019).

refer to the world via contrasting concepts, suggesting a polarised way of thinking compared to a general population usage.

The abovementioned studies proved the usefulness of corpus linguistics techniques for analysis of extremist texts, however most of the study has been performed using publicly available extremist materials. It is obvious that analysis of social media texts where people immediately involved in extremist ideology interact with one another is of no less importance, but access to this kind of texts is often restricted. Due to Dark Web Project [3, 4] large datasets containing texts from extremists forums in English, Arabic, French, German, and Russian became available for researchers who work in terrorism informatics and develop counter-terrorism methods. The datasets are designed so that can be used for different research purposes. Authorship analysis, sentiment analysis, name entity extraction, thematic modeling techniques were applied to the texts of terrorist forums. For example, Abbasi and Chen [1] applied authorship identification techniques to English messages obtained from a US forum that belongs to the White Knights as well as Arabic messages from the Palestinian Al-Aqsa Martyrs group.

As Baker and Vessey [2] notes, the work in the field of linguistics analysis of extremist texts to date has focused almost exclusively on English language data.

To the best of our knowledge, the only study which analyzes texts from Russian-language part of this collection ("KavkazChat" dataset) using corpus linguistic tool is one by Litvinova et al. [9]. This study makes use of WordSmith Tools software package to identify most frequent words and word clusters, build concordances and find collocates in texts retrieved from KavkazChat dataset and texts by common Internet users on the same topic. This analysis allowed authors to draw some conclusions about the characteristic features of texts by authors from extremist forum. However, in the cited work they compared two corpora and did not perform comparison with general population usage.

In current study, we aim at applying keyword analysis and manual discourse analysis to reveal lexical features characteristic of texts by authors from extremist forum in comparison to texts of common Internet users using corpus of general population usage.

3 Data and Methodology

3.1 Datasets

The material of the study are texts of the KavkazChat dataset which contains texts from a Russian-language forum with a focus on jihad in the North Caucasus. It is part of Dark Web forum portal which is a part of Dark Web collection [3]. KavkazChat was defined as extremist by Russian authorities and researchers who developed Dark Web forum portal.

KavkazChat dataset contains 699,981 posts written by 7,125 members in the period 3/21/2003–5/21/2012. These posts are organized into 16,854 «threads» (topics). As in [9], a section called «Bombings in Moscow» was chosen where the 2010 Moscow Metro bombings were discussed. The 2010 Moscow Metro bombings were suicide bombings carried out by two women during the morning rush hour of March 29, 2010, at two stations of the Moscow Metro (Lubyanka and Park Kultury). Russian officials called the incident «the deadliest and most sophisticated terrorist attack in the Russian capital in six years»[2]. On March 31, Caucasus Emirate leader Doku Umarov claimed responsibility for ordering the attacks in a video released on the Internet. He also stated that such attacks in Russia would continue unless Russia grants independence to Muslim states in the North Caucasus region[3].

This section of the forum was chosen as its topic resonates with media. The importance of the analysis of extremist rhetoric produced immediately after a terrorist attack is due to the fact that following a high-profile attack not only the character of terrorist propaganda changes but it also reaches its peak. This is in a way because of the society becoming increasingly sensitive to any information regarding terrorism.

All the posts in this topic were split into one txt file which made up the extremist corpus (also EC).

Two resources were used for compilation of the corpus for comparison. The first one were the readers' comments on the material «There have been explosions on the Moscow metro» posted by an online newspaper «The Village»[4]. The second source for comparison corpus were comments on material «Moscow metro bombings: A Chronicle of Tragedy» posted by Radio Svoboda[5]. The texts from the two sources were merged into one and made up the corpus for comparison (we called it Comment corpus, or CC). This corpus was used in the study [9].

To reveal keywords in these corpora, we need corpora of general usage (a reference corpus, or RC) [14]. To this aim, we have compiled a corpus from Livejournal with the Python Scrapy library[6]. By using the Livejournal «friend of a friend» resource (http://exampleusername.livejournal.com/data/foaf.rdf) we collected their nickname, name, date of birth and a number of the latest posts in their rss feed (http://exampleusername.livejournal.com/data/rss). The rss feed only provides up to around 25 latest posts; however, it fits our task perfectly as we are interested in presenting a variety of different authors, with no single author dominating the corpus by a large number of posts. We selected a list of users who provided their date of birth and first/last name, which allowed us to identify their age and gender. The data was divided into 6 groups of 2 gender values and 3 age intervals: 20 to 30, 30 to 40, 40–50. As we kept in mind that the corpus has to be balanced, we randomly chose 1K posts for every group, obtaining a corpus of 6K posts by 1196 unique authors, with some authors appearing in different groups, as their posts were written at different age intervals. The corpus is heterogeneous in terms of text volume and authorship. The mean age was 35 y. o. (±7.6 y.o.). The mean number of texts by a single author ranged from 1 to 24 with the mean of 5,

---

2 https://www.rt.com/news/383323-terrorist-attacks-russia-transport/ (accessed 10/01/2019).

3 https://www.rferl.org/a/Umarov_On_Video_Says_He_Ordered_Moscow_Attacks/1999257.html (accessed 10/01/2019).

4 http://www.the-village.ru/village/people/people/88720-v-moskovskom-metro-proizoshel-vzryv#comments (accessed 10/01/2019).

5 https://www.svoboda.org/a/1996131.html (accessed 10/01/2019).

6 https://scrapy.org/ (accessed 10/01/2019).

std = 4.4. The mean size of texts ranged from 76 to 5687 tokens, with the mean of 529 tokens (std = 577). This corpus was used earlier for experiments in age detection [10].

The corpus materials underwent preliminary processing. All the metadata (date, name of the author, etc.) was removed. The quotes were removed if they were responses to the previous messages. The quotes from the media, etc. were not removed. Typos were corrected. The texts of the corpus were written in Russian. The materials of the extremist forum contain occasional Chechen words written in the Cyrillic alphabet and they were not removed. All the texts were saved in the.txt format suitable for corpus analysis with the use of WordSmith software.

General statistics on the corpora used for the current study are presented in Table 1.

Table 1. Statistics of the corpora used for the study

Corpus	N of authors	N of comments	Dates of posting	Corpus size
Extremist corpus (EC)	67	466	29/03/2010–17/04/2010	274,209 characters without spaces, or 50,447 words
Comment corpus (CC)	143	1,313	30/03/2010–06/04/2010	261,874 characters without spaces, or 42,878 words
Reference corpus (RC)	1,196	6,000 posts	2014–2018	21,149,633 characters without spaces, or 3,876,801 words

Therefore the analyzed text corpora (EC and CC) which are comparable in terms of the number of texts they contain and dealing with the same topic (discussions of the explosions on the subway produced immediately following the event) were compiled to make it convenient to employ them in comparative analysis using corpus tools. It should be noted that the corpora are different in the average length of posts (108 words in the extremist forum vs. 32 in the control corpus) as well as the number of people leaving comments. We argue that the differences in the length of texts are due to the fact that extremist forum participants are involved in active propaganda and make references to religious literature, etc. to justify the attack perpetrated by deadly terrorists. The differences in the number of users can be caused by the difficulties in logging in the KavkazChat forum.

3.2 Methods

The main tool for analyzing the texts was Oxford WordSmith Tools 4.0 [15]. This is an integrated suite of programs which identifies patterns in texts. It is an internationally popular program for the work based on corpus-linguistic methodology. We used version 4.0 as it is free of charge and its functional is sufficient for the current task.

In the current study we made use of one module, namely Keywords. Keywords provide a useful way to characterize a text or a genre. The term «keyword», though it is in common use, is not defined in linguistics. Keywords are those whose frequency is unusually high in comparison with some norm. This program identifies keywords on a mechanical basis by comparing patterns of frequency.

A word is said to be «key» if

(a) it occurs in the text at least as many times as the user has specified as a Minimum Frequency;
(b) its frequency in the text when compared with its frequency in a reference corpus is such that the statistical probability as computed by an appropriate procedure is smaller than or equal to a p value specified by the user.

Keywords has proved a reliable tool for comparing language samples, be them texts or corpora [14]. The program compares two pre-existing word-lists, which must have been created using the WordList tool. One of these is assumed to be a large word-list which will act as a reference file. The other one is the word-list based on one text under investigation. The aim is to find out which words characterize the text under investigation, which is automatically assumed to be the smaller of the two texts chosen. The larger will provide background data for reference comparison (for example, Sardinha [14] supposes that RC should be at least 5 times bigger than the corpus under study). In our study, we make use of the Livejournal corpus as the reference corpus.

To compute the «keyness» of an item, the program computes its frequency in the small wordlist, the number of running words in the small wordlist, its frequency in the reference corpus, the number of running words in the reference corpus and cross-tabulates these. Statistical tests include the classic chi-square test of significance with Yates correction for a 2 × 2 table and Ted Dunning's Log Likelihood test [6]. We have chosen the latter one as it gives a better estimate of keyness, especially when contrasting long texts or a whole genre against a reference corpus (according to the program manual).

WordSmith module «Keywords» allows one not only to reveal keywords in texts ranged in accordance to their keyness, but also it constructs plots that give useful visual insights into how often and where different keywords crop up in the text. The plot is initially sorted to show which ones crop up more in the beginning (e.g. in the introduction) and then those from further in the text. This is useful for the current study as both EC and CC are arranged in the time-order manner, i.e. posts written immediately after the bombings come first.

This module also provides us with the total number of links between the keyword and other keywords in the same text, within the current collocation span (default = 5.5). That is, how many times each keyword was found within 5 words to the left or right of any of the other keywords in the plot. Column «Hits» shows how many occurrences of each keyword there were.

WordSmith Controller allows one to adjust different setting for keyword analysis. Overall, we used the following settings for our analysis. We used log likelihood statistics with the max p-value of 0.0000001 (the default level of significance), the max number of wanted keywords = 500 with the min frequency of keywords = 3.

We have designed two frequency lists individually for each text corpus. Based on the findings about the importance of analyzing function words in examining extremist discourse [11], we deliberately did not exclude such words from our analysis. Since WordSmith does not allow automatic lemmatization, we performed manual post-hoc lemmatization of the identified keywords. In addition, this data (without lemmatization) permits us to analyze statistics on the cases when particular keywords are used most frequently for additional information.

4 Results and Discussion

4.1 Keywords in Extremist Corpus

In total, 333 keywords were found in the Extremist corpus. Figure 1 shows the first 43 words with the highest keyness.

Mostly these are semantic groups associated with the contrast *мусульмане* 'Muslims' vs. *русские* 'Russians' (*русские* 'Russians', *кафиры* 'kafirs', *русня* 'a humiliating way to describe Russians'). Another word with the highest keyness is also *Вы* ('plural you in nominative case') which according to the contexts we have analyzed refers to Russians. Apart from that, the case forms of the word *Вы* (*Вас, Вам*) as well as the possessive pronoun *ваши* (*ваших*) 'yours' are frequent. The pronoun *они* 'they' is another word with a high keyness. It should be noted that the word forms *Вы, Ваши, русские, они* in the nominative case have the highest keyness, for the word *мусульмане* it is the accusative form (*мусульман*) which commonly refers to a direct object in Russia. This indicates that in the extremist texts the word *русские* is the subject and *мусульмане* is an object more often than in the corpus of blogs.

There is a distinct group of words with a high keyness which describes religion (*аллах* 'Allah', *ислам* 'Islam', *религия* 'religion', *посланник* 'messenger', *неверующий* 'atheist', *шариат* 'sharia', *кафир* 'kafir'), war (*война* 'war', *враг* 'enemy'), as well as words related to both subjects (*джихад* 'jihad, an often violent effort by some Muslim people to defend their religion against those who they believe want to destroy it') and words describing territory (*Кавказ* 'Caucasus', *земля* 'land', *территории* 'territories').

The corpus typically shows a low (compared to the reference corpus) frequency of the pronoun *я* 'I' (and case forms, a negative keyness –90.66 for the pronoun я 'I', –48.23 for the pronoun *мне* 'to me', –82.87 for the pronoun *меня* 'me').

The extremist corpus also typically has a lot of the negations *не* 'not' compared to the reference corpus.

The preposition *в* 'in' is not generally frequent compared to the general usage. It is to be noted that the word *метро* 'subway' is one of the second hundred keywords (123), which might indicate that not much attention is paid to the details of the explosion.

The analysis of the concordances allowed us to find out that the typical contexts for describing Muslims are the following: *мусульман не устраивает* 'Muslims are not happy'; *мстят за поруганную честь мусульман* 'take revenge for the honor they lost', *тысячами убивают мусульман на Кавказе* 'kill hundreds of Muslims in the Caucasus'; *козни против мусульман* 'atrocities against Muslims', *резни мусульман* 'Muslim massacres'; *праведного гнева мусульман* 'the righteous anger of Muslims', etc.

In contrast, *кафиров* ('kafirs', i.e. atheists – Authors) *надо давить* 'must be slaughtered', everything must be done *то ускорить их уход любой ценой* 'to make them perish at any cost'. *Визги кафиров* 'shrieking of kafirs', *рожи кафиров* 'shameless faces of kafirs', etc. are typical contexts.

The analysis of the concordances for the word *ислам* 'Islam' shows that for this lexeme the following contexts are typical: *ислам должен быть распространен* extremist_corpus_KW.kws

File Edit View Compute Settings Windows Help

N	Key word	Dispersion	Keyness	Links	Hits	Plot
1	QUOT	0,743	1 140,75	73	136	
2	ВЫ	0,879	875,20	251	444	
3	МУСУЛЬМАН	0,796	735,60	43	92	
4	АЛЛАХ	0,790	649,16	48	97	
5	АЛЛАХА	0,693	520,75	38	76	
6	МУСУЛЬМАНЕ	0,749	464,31	30	62	
7	КАВКАЗЕ	0,878	430,15	30	63	
8	НЕ	0,952	340,96	663	1 515	
9	ВАС	0,853	323,60	74	166	
10	КАВКАЗ	0,728	275,75	19	44	
11	КАФИРОВ	0,761	249,14	10	30	
12	КАВКАЗА	0,829	247,20	11	42	
13	ВАМ	0,877	238,55	63	145	
14	ИСЛАМ	0,658	235,68	15	35	
15	ОНИ	0,842	227,99	116	288	
16	РУССКИЕ	0,715	218,13	19	60	
17	ВАШИ	0,889	210,29	20	57	
18	РУСНИ	0,526	197,75	6	23	
19	РУССКИХ	0,691	196,72	12	60	
20	ИСЛАМА	0,827	194,65	11	28	
21	ИХ	0,865	190,08	96	256	
22	ТО	0,935	181,26	142	375	
23	РЕЛИГИИ	0,698	172,86	13	37	
24	ВОЙНА	0,809	170,75	13	54	
25	ПРОТИВ	0,796	165,98	28	83	
26	ВЗРЫВЫ	0,767	165,43	7	24	
27	ВАШИХ	0,706	163,53	13	40	
28	ЕТО	0,667	162,57	6	23	
29	МУСУЛЬМАНАМ	0,734	158,68	3	21	
30	РУСНЯ	0,385	154,23	6	20	
31	МУСУЛЬМАНАМИ	0,776	150,21	3	19	
32	МИРНЫХ	0,485	147,02	15	26	
33	КАФИРЫ	0,651	146,16	5	17	
34	ИНША	0,708	146,16	6	17	
35	ИБН	0,423	145,39	8	23	
36	МУСУЛЬМАНИН	0,550	144,03	4	20	
37	КАВКАЗЦЕВ	0,698	144,03	9	20	
38	ИСЛАМЕ	0,640	142,22	8	19	
39	НАРОД	0,847	138,27	11	56	
40	ШАРИАТ	0,681	137,57	5	16	
41	ВЗРЫВОВ	0,719	136,97	9	19	
42	ПОСЛАННИК	0,603	133,43	5	17	
43	ЖИТЬ	0,785	130,76	24	73	

KWs plot links clusters filenames notes source text

324 Type-in

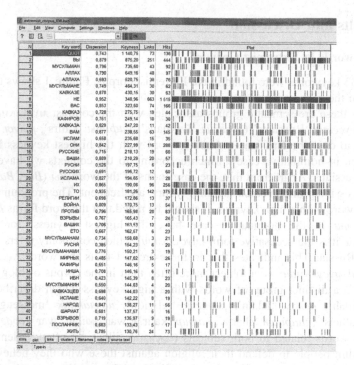

Fig. 1. Plot for keywords in Extremist corpus

'Islam should be spread further', *ислам рождает настоящих воинов* 'Islam generates real warriors', *распространяйте ислам* 'spread Islam', *ваше спасение принять ислам* 'Islam is your salvation', etc.

The concordances of the word *взрывы* 'explosions' show that according to the participants of the forum, they are *результат вашего бездействия* 'the result of your negligence', *реакция на происходящее с мусульманами* 'a reaction to what is happening to Muslims' and they *будут продолжаться* 'will go on and on', Russians *обречены увидеть новые взрывы* 'are doomed for new explosions', this is *месть за жертвы на Кавказе* 'the revenge for the casualties in the Caucasus'. Our results are in line with findings by Litvinova et al. [9] who revealed that Caucasian extremists build up a "war" discourse avoiding calling the event a terrorist attack.

The analysis of the dispersion of the words of the above groups allowed the following to be found. The number of the words describing Russians does not drop as the topic develops unlike that of the words describing Muslims (in the forum there are some users who try to grasp the extremist ideology questioning the terrorist attacks). In addition, the number of words from the groups «war», «religion» is increasing, which indicates that propaganda is on the rise with the emphasis shifting on the importance of perpetrating the attacks and blaming Russians for what happened.

4.2 Keywords in Comment Corpus

For comparison we conducted the analysis of the keywords in the corpus of comments. In total, 218 keywords were found in the Comment corpus. Figure 2 shows the statistics for keywords ranged according to their keyness. According to the analysis, the keywords with the highest keyness are distinctly those describing the location of the event (*метро* 'subway', *Москве* 'Moscow', *московском* 'Moscow' (adj)), the event itself (*взрывы* 'explosions', *взрыв* 'explosion', *теракты* 'terrorist attacks'), people involved (*террористы* 'terrorists', *погибших* 'dead', *пострадавшим* 'casualties', *люди, людей* 'people'), emotional reactions to the event (*соболезнования* 'condolence', *соболезную* 'express my condolences', *страшно* 'scared', *ужас* 'terror', *горе* 'grief') as well as authority (*ФСБ* 'FSB, The Federal Security Service of the Russian Federation', *Путин,* Путина 'Putin', *власти* 'authorities', *правительство* 'government', *спецслужбы* 'special services', *МВД* 'Ministry of Internal Affairs'), Russia and its people (*России* 'Russia', *народ* 'people', *стране* 'country').

The analysis shows that the words of different groups are distributed differently in the forum texts depending on the time when they were written. If the words describing the location of the event are distributed quite identically, those describing authority are more frequent in the posts written immediately following the explosions.

Ranging of the keywords according to their frequency also shows that a significant number of them are those naming authority (*власти* 'authorities', *ФСБ* 'FSB', *Путин* 'Putin'). The analysis of the concordances of this word group conducted using the **Concordance tool** allows us to conclude that the commentators are involved in the discussion of the authorities' (special services) responsibility for the explosions (*взрывы построил ФСБ* 'FSB is responsible for the explosions', *ФСБ забавляется* 'FSB is fooling around', *ФСБ взрывает Россию* 'FSB blows up Russia' – references to the book of the same name by A. Litvinenko and Yu. Felshtinskiy that presents a conspiracy explanation of the explosions and those responsible for the series of the terrorist attacks that happened in residential houses in Russia in the autumn of 1999 as well as the role of FSB in the Ryazan accident on September 22, 1999, *власть взрывами народ запугивает* 'the authorities are trying to scare people with the explosions', *правительство теракт заказало* 'the government started the terrorist attack', etc.).

The proportions of the most frequent words describing terrorists (the word *террорист* 'terrorist' in different cases, 0.19% of the total words in the corpus) as well as the most frequent words from the 'Chechnya topic' (*Кавказе* 'about the Caucasus' 0.04, *Кавказ* 'Caucasus' 0.02, *чеченцы* 'Chechens' 0.03, *кавказцев* 'Caucasians' 0.03, *шахидки* 'shahids' 0.02, the total of 0.14) have lower proportions than the most frequent words describing authority (*власти* 'authorities' 0.17, *власть* 'authority' 0.1, *ФСБ* 'FSB' 0.16, *Путина* 'by Putin' 0.12, *Путин* 'Putin' 0.12, *правительство* 'government' 0.07, *спецслужб* 'special services' 0.03, *КГБ* 'KGB' 0.03, the total of 0.8% of the corpus words).

Therefore the analysis of the keywords showed that the authors of the Internet comments offer their condolences to the victims' families in the first days following the attacks and express their reactions (fear, sorrow) as well as try to identify those who are responsible placing the blame primarily on the authorities and personally the president.

N	Key word	Dispersion	Keyness	Links	Hits	Plot
1	МЕТРО	0,862	647,88	54	146	
2	ВЗРЫВЫ	0,735	596,50	32	74	
3	ФСБ	0,660	384,11	25	72	
4	ТЕРРОРИСТЫ	0,735	347,06	20	48	
5	ТЕРАКТЫ	0,820	256,29	11	33	
6	ТЕРАКТОВ	0,730	252,94	7	33	
7	СОБОЛЕЗНОВАНИЯ	0,645	243,99	17	33	
8	ПОГИБШИХ	0,893	225,53	17	45	
9	ТЕРРОРИСТОВ	0,804	222,29	5	36	
10	ПУТИНА	0,657	221,28	19	55	
11	ВЗРЫВ	0,673	220,92	12	36	
12	ВЗРЫВОВ	0,821	208,75	12	27	
13	ПУТИН	0,644	181,11	25	51	
14	ВЛАСТИ	0,673	177,14	29	75	
15	КТО	0,940	169,37	61	159	
16	НЕ	0,975	167,01	384	1 171	
17	ВЫ	0,851	164,05	56	185	
18	ЛЮДИ	0,855	163,53	42	133	
19	ВЗРЫВА	0,851	158,20	5	26	
20	ТЕРАКТ	0,777	151,56	8	24	
21	ВЗОРВАЛИ	0,732	151,36	4	19	
22	ПОСТРАДАВШИМ	0,770	147,84	4	21	
23	ЛУБЯНКЕ	0,602	147,66	6	19	
24	РОССИИ	0,759	139,76	29	100	
25	НАРОД	0,793	139,54	8	53	
26	ТЕРАКТА	0,631	136,35	13	21	
27	ЛЮДЕЙ	0,846	134,20	40	118	
28	ВЫГОДНО	0,617	130,08	9	27	
29	ТЕРРАКТЫ	0,706	125,82	3	15	
30	ПОГИБШИМ	0,621	125,56	6	20	
31	CNN	0,659	124,39	4	14	
32	МОСКВЕ	0,783	122,77	10	51	
33	СТРАШНО	0,762	115,63	24	46	
34	СТРАНЕ	0,879	112,51	11	49	
35	НТТР	0,773	111,05	10	71	
36	МОСКОВСКОМ	0,748	106,64	3	22	
37	СОБОЛЕЗНОВАНИЕ	0,533	106,62	4	12	
38	ПРАВИТЕЛЬСТВО	0,694	105,69	10	31	
39	СПЕЦСЛУЖБЫ	0,692	104,25	6	18	
40	СОБОЛЕЗНУЮ	0,628	103,77	3	13	
41	МВД	0,746	102,91	10	25	
42	ЭТО	0,935	102,48	108	505	
43	КАВКАЗЕ	0,655	99,02	4	18	

Fig. 2. Plot for keywords in the Comment corpus

It can be assumed that this is the time when the users are most vulnerable to all sorts of manipulations. In the following days the number of these words is decreasing while the number of words *люди, людей* 'people' is increasing.

5 Conclusions

The comparative corpus-based analysis of one of the texts from of the KavkazChat dataset on terror attack on the Moscow subway performed with the use of keyword module from WordSmith tool 4.0 allowed us to reveal two different views on the same topic. Authors from extremist forum design a war discourse contrasting Russians and Muslims making references to religion presenting themselves as a community ('we'-discourse) paying little attention to the details of the explosions but emphasizing the responsibility of Russians, which corresponds to the previous findings by Litvinova et al. [9] which used different methodology. Commentators pay more attention to the topic of authorities, especially to Russia's president Vladimir Putin and the Federal Security Service of the Russian Federation as well as their role in the tragedy. They also express their feeling about the attack.

It should also be noted that authors of extremist forum use an increased number of words from semantic groups «war», «religion» in the course of the discussion as part of their propaganda.

Some of our results are close to the results obtained by Baker and Vessey [2] who compared English and French extremist texts and concluded that religion is a core focus of such texts; "calls for violence are consistently made based on purported devotion to and obligation deriving from divine authority; these are unfailingly supported by (mis)readings of authoritative religious figures or texts" [9, p. 274]. They also find "strong focus on othering" along with reference to reward.

A further analysis of different another threads the datasets (including discussions of the other terrorist attacks) as well as texts in other languages performed using the WordSmith software as well as other corpus linguistics and stylometric tools (LIWC, RStylo, etc.) would allow a more detailed look at extremist rhetoric.

Acknowledgment. Funding of the project "Speech portrait of the extremist: corpus-statistical research (on the material of the extremist forum "KavkazChat")" from RF President's grants for young scientists (no. MK-5718.2018.6) for T. L. and O.L. (experiment design, corpus collection, quantitative analysis) is gratefully acknowledged. Works on qualitative analysis of the data performed by G.Z. was supported by Russian Foundation for Basic Research, grant N 18-412-360006\18.

References

1. Abbasi, A., Chen, H.: Applying authorship analysis to extremist-group web forum messages. IEEE Intell. Syst. **20**(5), 67–75 (2005). https://doi.org/10.1109/MIS.2005.81
2. Baker, P., Vessey, R.: A corpus-driven comparison of English and French islamist extremist texts. Int. J. Corpus Linguist. **23**(3), 255–278 (2018). https://doi.org/10.1075/ijcl.17108.bak
3. Chen, H.: Dark Web: Exploring and Data Mining the Dark Side of the Web. Springer, New York (2012). https://doi.org/10.1007/978-1-4614-1557-2
4. Chen, H., Reid, E., Sinai, J., Silke, A., Ganor, B. (eds.): Terrorism Informatics: Knowledge Management and Data Mining for Homeland Security. Springer, New York (2008). https://doi.org/10.1007/978-0-387-71613-8
5. Correa, D., Sureka, A.: Solutions to Detect and Analyze Online Radicalization: A Survey. arXiv preprint. arXiv:1301.4916 (2013)
6. Dunning, T.: Accurate methods for the statistics of surprise and coincidence. Comput. Linguist. **19**(1), 61–74 (1993)
7. Jeon, J., Choe J.-W.: A key word analysis of english intensifying adverbs in male and female speech. In: ICE-GB. 23rd Pacific Asia Conference on Language, Information and Computation, pp. 210–219. City University of Hong Kong, Hong Kong (2009)
8. Johansson, F., Kaati, L., Sahlgren, M.: Detecting linguistic markers of violent extremism in online environments. In: Khader, M. et al. (eds.) Combating Violent Extremism and Radicalization in the Digital Era, pp. 374–390. IGI Global, Hershey, PA (2016)
9. Litvinova, T., Litvinova, O., Panicheva, P., Biryukova, E.: Using corpus linguistics tools to analyze a Russian-language Islamic extremist forum. In: Bodrunova, S. et al. (eds.) Internet Science. INSCI 2018. LNCS, vol. 11193, pp. 54–65. Springer, Cham (2018). https://doi.org/10.1007/978-3-030-01437-7_5

10. Litvinova, T., Sboev, A., Panicheva, P.: Profiling the age of Russian bloggers. In: Ustalov, D., Filchenkov, A., Pivovarova, L., Žižka, J. (eds.) Artificial Intelligence and Natural Language. AINL 2018. Communications in Computer and Information Science, vol. 930, pp. 167–177. Springer, Cham (2018). https://doi.org/10.1007/978-3-030-01204-5_16
11. Pennebaker, J., Chung, C.: Computerized text analysis of Al-Qaeda transcripts. In: Krippendorff, K., Bock, M.A. (eds.) A Content Analysis Reader, pp. 453–465. Sage, Thousand Oaks (2009)
12. Prentice, S., Rayson, P., Taylor, P.J.: The language of islamic extremism: towards an automated identification of beliefs, motivations and justifications. Int. J. Corpus Linguist. **17** (2), 259–286 (2012). https://doi.org/10.1075/ijcl.17.2.05pre
13. Salama, A.: Ideological collocation and the recontexualization of Wahhabi-Saudi Islam post-9/11: a synergy of corpus linguistics and critical discourse analysis. Discourse Soc. **22**(3), 315–342 (2011). https://doi.org/10.1177/0957926510395445
14. Sardinha, T.B.: Comparing corpora with WordSmith tools: how large must the reference corpus be? In: Proceedings of the Workshop on Comparing Corpora WCC 2000, vol. 9, pp. 7–13. ACL, Stroudsburg (2000)
15. Scott, M.: Oxford WordSmith Tools. Version 4.0. Oxford University Press, Oxford (2006)
16. Smith, A.: Words make worlds: terrorism and language. FBI Law Enforcement Bull. **76**, 12–18 (2007)

Development of a Prognostic Model of the User's Information Image Using Automated Tools for Processing Data from Social Networks

Alexandr Tropnikov[1(✉)], Anna Uglova[2(✉)], and Boris Nizomutdinov[1(✉)]

[1] St. Petersburg National Research University of Information Technologies, Mechanics and Optics (ITMO University), 199034 St. Petersburg, Russia
astropnikov@corp.ifmo.ru, boris-wels@yandex.ru

[2] The Herzen State Pedagogical University of Russia, 191186 St. Petersburg, Russia
anna.uglova@list.ru

Abstract. This article presents a first phase's results of research project, dedicated to developing prognostic models of User's Image with the automated Social Networks data processing methods. A pilot study carried out a comparative analysis of automatic methods for analyzing textual and visual data, which constituting a User's informational image. We used a correlation analysis of data, which was obtained by using parsing methods and the results of psycho diagnostic research. As a result, multiple relationships with the socio-psychological characteristics of the respondents were identified. Based on obtained data, we have concluded about acceptable predictive capabilities of automated analysis.

Keywords: Vk · Social networks · Parsing · Online communities · Psychology · Informational image

1 Introduction

The transformational processes of the information society allow the majority of people to interact daily in the network space. It leads to changes in traditional ways of communication, interaction and people behavior, fulfilling it with new meanings. The Internet is becoming a new environment for human activity, socialization and self-fulfillment. Virtuality is a new living space of a person, which determines his social and individual existence and personal development.

A huge amount of publicly available data are left by the Internet users in the network, which are actively used for political and commercial marketing aims: to monitor public opinion, to determine consumer preferences, to create targeted advertising, etc.

D. A. Alexandrov et al. (Eds.): DTGS 2019, CCIS 1038, pp. 405–413, 2019.
https://doi.org/10.1007/978-3-030-37858-5_33

Such information can be used to identify the characteristics of contemporary virtual communication, for identification of the factors that mediate intercultural and socio-political contradictions, for identification of vulnerable social groups, etc.

It should be noted that the constant interaction with the information space leads to the transformation of personal higher psychic functions, the consciousness and self-consciousness transformation phenomenon, to the complication of the mechanisms of personality identification in the conditions of informatization (Voiskounsky, Belinskaya, Yee, Peters, Hirn, Thomas, Zoelch, Kosinski, Matz etc.) [2, 5, 8–10, 13]. Thus, the question of the allocation of the phenomenon of media image and its study is being raised, primarily from the psychological point of view.

Media image is a complete structure of text and visual components of the network image of a person. The concept of "media image" is the basis for the description of both virtual personality and virtual identity and it provides an opportunity to move us to a higher methodological level of individual behavior analysis and description of virtual communities.

We focused in our research on the study of self-presentation in the social network, which is aimed at the coordination of social-perceptive and communicative processes. User constructs his desired self-presentation via media image, however, many ways of building an alternative images and manipulations of other people are opened up when usual communication channels for correcting the information don't work.

An experimental study of social and psychological characteristics of users and their media image will let identify the relevance, selectivity and semantic load of the presented characteristics of the image. The applying of automated systems will help to facilitate the process of getting of such information and to simplify the description of user's media image. The study of users' network data will allow us to create a predictive model for automated analysis of personal traits data implemented in real communicational practice and to get closer to the description of the real psychological portrait of a user.

1.1 Participants

There are some modern scientific researches that consider the possibility of developing and implementing of new methods for identifying socio-psychological characteristics of users based on the data content analysis, which would be as efficient as a traditional psycho – diagnostic researches [3, 12]. Many Russian and foreign papers are devoted to the development of various methodologies which are connected to the identification of interrelationship between data from social networks and information gained during the course of psychological testing [1, 11].

This research includes 2 approaches: classical psycho-diagnostic research and an automated collection of open data in social networks by parsing method.

We have carried out a pilot research, the purpose of which was the theoretical justification and experimental study of the predictive model of the media image on the basis of automated unloading of a different data set from the social networks profile.

The study was carried out in several stages:

At the first stage the search and analysis of foreign literature, identification of information systems used in tasks solving, comparative analysis of these systems and testing of specialized software were carried out.

At the second stage the profiles of testees were selected, the unloading of all the necessary information and processing of sorted data with the help of various services were also made. During the stage of data processing and analysis of the output information, the screening of inappropriate or inaccurate services was carried out.

During the third stage psycho-diagnostic research of the respondents with appropriate services was conducted.

At the final stage the team correlated the patterns and repeated relationships of the data with the previously performed psycho-diagnostic study, using the processed information, and created a correlation table.

It is planned to develop the algorithm, allowing to process automatically the unloaded data set and to define expected psycho-emotional features of the user in further research on the basis of this table.

The pilot study involved 25 people who are Russian Federation residents, currently in their first period of adulthood (19–32 years). All respondents were invited to participate in the study on a voluntary basis. Young people were offered to participate in the study and fill in a number of psycho-diagnostic questionnaire forms, presented in the Google form. During the stage of data processing and analysis of the output information, a screening of testees was made because of inappropriate or inaccurate services. The final sample consisted of 22 young people (10 males, 12 females; M = 24.6 years, SD = 4.12). The study participants had different level of education: 6 people (28%) with incomplete higher education and 16 people (72%) with higher education.

2 Data and Method

A questionnaire that included demographic questions and questions related to the use of social networking was used. Demographic issues: (1) Gender (2) Age, (3) Education, (4) Specialty. Questions about the using of social networks included questions about the amount of time spent in social networks, the number of used social networks, most frequently used social network. The survey also included questions about the sense of security in the social network and the conformity of the real Self and Vkontakte profile.

Value questionnaire of S. Schwartz. The questionnaire includes 57 values that must be rated on a scale of 1 to 7 and is intended for diagnoses the structure of the basic value individual's orientations (Hedonism Achievement, SocialPower, SelfDirection, Stimulation, Conformity, Prosocial, Security, Maturity, Traditio, CultureSpecific, Spiritual).

Methodology of research of self-relation by S. R. Panteleev. The methodology includes 110 statements and it is designed to identify the structure of self-relationship of the individual. The methodology includes 9 scales that allow to evaluate different internal trends of human and world interaction:

– Insularity
– Self-confidence

- Self-guidance
- Self-reflection
- Self-valuable
- Self-acceptance
- Self-attachment
- Inner-conflict
- Self-blaming

Diagnostic test of satisfaction degree of needs (Maslow's pyramid). The test includes 21 statement aimed at identifying of the basic needs in accordance with Maslow: safety needs, belongingness and Love needs, esteem needs, self-actualization needs.

The selected psycho-diagnostic toolkit helps to identify the system of valuable-semantic orientations of testee and their motivational-needs sphere and self-attitude specificities as well, which are at the basis of the formation of the self-presentation, forming an impressions about yourself for solving different adaptive purposes, including informational area. Also, at the end of the test, users were asked to enter a link to their profile in the social network VKontakte.

As a result of the implemented survey a database containing links to user pages was created. At the next step of the work the method of automated collection of publicly available information from the pages of profiles in the social network VKontakte was applied.

As a result of the parsing of personal pages, a data set was obtained, which was statistical information about the social networks user's profile.

At this stage of the study for the automated data collection about the participants the method of parsing of the pages content was used. Parsing of web-sites is an effective solution of an automatization of collection and processing of information.

The collection is carried out by a parser—a special script configured to work with vk.com.

Using the data collected on avatars, the uploading of images in to the service of image processing and face analysis was made on the Azure platform using the upload module implemented using the API.

We used the cloud-based Azure platform from Microsoft for experimental testing, that provides services of image processing and faces analysis. These services operate by using the technology of neural networks. Using pre-analyzed data from over 350,000 images, these services are able to analyze efficiently and accurately incoming images at the time of the presence of certain objects, faces, compositions, etc. In total, the neural network is able to provide information on more than 30 criteria.

Image analysis allowed us to obtain the information about the format of the image, its size, the presence of persons, the prevailing colors, existing objects and the composition. A set of tags that classify the image has been assigned to each avatar.

The face analysis service also provided data on the age, gender, facial attributes, accessories and emotions of people, captured in the image, used as an avatar.

The obtained data were processed and presented in the form of a summary table containing data on all subjects, on the basis of which the correlation analysis was carried out.

In our research, we used cluster analysis (linkage rule: Ward's method, distance measure: Euclidean distances) to classify the objects, identified on the users photos, and the description of the categories for finding interrelationships with socio-psychological characteristics.

Also Spearman's correlation coefficient was used to identify the interrelationships of socio-psychological characteristics and categories of analysis of personal data of users in social networks.

Statistical significance was established at level $p < 0.05$. In this research Statistica 10.0 software package was used for the analysis.

3 Information Extraction by Automated Methods

At the first stage of the research statistics data, obtained during the automatic upload, were combined by experts into a larger categories describing the basic components of information image of user: information about name

(name, surname, nickname, vk short address), information about age (age, date of birth), geo-localization (country, city, hometown), information about the close relationship (marital status, reference to the partner, name and surname of the partner), about professional status (current employment; company; work group; position; year of commencement of work), network association (instagram; instagram-@; instagram-link), information about education (University; year of graduation; faculty; Department; form of education; graduate status), privacy (permission to write private messages, write on the wall, add to friends), information about the number of friends, subscribers, photos, videos, audio recordings, groups, subscriptions, as well as emotions detected in users' photos (surprise, sadness, neutral expression, happiness, anger, disgust, contempt).

Cluster analysis was used to identify the main semantic categories, presented in the photos of users, received during the automatic analysis of photos. The resulting similarity tree of the analyzed objects let to trace the sequence of their integration at different levels of semantic distance and to trace the formation of the categorical structure of the photographic image of the user at different levels of generalization. There were identified 8 sub-clusters, which included 31 characteristics of the user's photo:

(1) sub-cluster (outdoor, beautiful, suit, girl, lady);
(2) sub-cluster (indoor, sitting, room, man);
(3) sub-cluster (person, standing, woman, young);
(4) sub-cluster (front, posing, "makeup", gender Female, gender Female2);
(5) sub-cluster (boy, game);
(6) sub-cluster (old, group, street);
(7) sub-cluster (illustration, colorful, Black, and, white, photography);
(8) sub-cluster (gender Male, gender Male2, "glasses", smiling).

At the third stage, correlation analysis (Spearman's correlation rate) was used to identify the personal indirectness of the information image. The results of the correlation analysis showed the presence of a statistically significant link between the components of the information image and personal characteristics of the respondents.

A large number of groups of subjects positively link with the value of tradition maintenance (correlation rate $r = 0.47$, $p < 0.05$) and culture specific values ($r = 0.46$, $p < 0.05$), need of security ($r = 0.46$, $p < 0.05$), belongingness and Love needs ($r = 0.46$, $p < 0.05$). Recognized emotions of anger* and surprising** at the user's avatar is positively correlated with the need for security ($r^* = 0.62$, $p^* < 0.05$, $r^{**} = 0.63$, $p^{**} < 0.05$) and belongingness and Love needs ($r^* = 0.67$, $p^* < 0.05$, $r^{**} = 0.64$, $p^{**} < 0.05$), also they have more expressed internal conflict ($r^* = 0.64$, $p^* < 0.05$, $r^{**} = 0.61$, $p^{**} < 0.05$) self-blaming ($r^* = 0.60$, $p^* < 0.05$, $r^{**} = 0.56$, $p^{**} < 0.05$).

The neutral face expression at the avatars is typically for those users, for whom social culture is important ($r = 0.54$, $p < 0.05$), while a happy face expression is negatively connected with this value($r = -0{,}54$, $p < 0.05$). The disgust in avatar is negatively connected with self-attachment ($r = -0{,}56$, $p < 0.05$), and contempt is positively associated with value Social Power ($r = 0{,}63$, $p < 0.05$).The more information about professional status is provided, the more important for the user are values such as maturity ($r = 0{,}45$, $p < 0.05$) and sociality ($r = 0{,}57$, $p < 0.05$).

Respondents for whom the value of power is significant, more often specify information about their close relationships and partners ($r = 0{,}46$, $p < 0.05$).

Time spent in the network is correlated positively with the number of friends ($r = 0{,}48$, $p < 0.05$), number of subscribers ($r = 0{,}48$, $p < 0.05$). A large number of friends and subscribers is positively correlated with self-value ($r = 0{,}45$, $p < 0.05$).

Categories of the photographic image, identified by the cluster analysis, also formed multiple connections.

The first sub-cluster (outdoor, beautiful, suit, girl, lady) positively connected with the value of achievement ($r = 0{,}52$, $p < 0.05$) and stimulation ($r = 0{,}49$, $p < 0.05$), self-confidence ($r = 0{,}48$, $p < 0.05$), reflected self-attitude ($r = 0{,}59$, $p < 0.05$) and connected negatively with self-blaming ($r = -0{,}60$, $p < 0.05$). The second sub-cluster (indoor, sitting, room, man) connected positively with insularity ($r = -0{,}59$, $p < 0.05$).

The third sub-cluster (person, standing, woman, young) connected positively with the value of safety ($r = 0{,}59$, $p < 0.05$) and stimulation ($r = 0{,}54$, $p < 0.05$), self-confidence ($r = 0{,}54$, $p < 0.05$), reflected self-attitude ($r = 0{,}47$, $p < 0.05$) and connected negatively with self-blaming ($r = -0{,}57$, $p < 0.05$).

The fifth sub-cluster (boy, game) connected positively with insularity ($r = 0{,}55$, $p < 0.05$) and negatively with inner-conflict ($r = -0{,}46$, $p < 0.05$).

The eight sub-cluster (gender Male, "glasses", smiling), connected negatively with the need in self-affirmation ($r = -0{,}50$, $p < 0.05$). As a result of the research, a correlation table containing the identified relationships was compiled. The part of the table that displays the most significant interconnections is shown below (Table 1).

Table 1. Sample of relationship data table

	Friends	Video	Groups	Age	Job	**Sub. 1**	**Sub. 5**
Time spend on VK	***0,48***	0,01	0,35	0,29	0,21	0,08	−0,31
Communication safety	0,29	−0,28	0,34	***0,47***	0,09	−0,09	−0,15
Achievement	0,24	***−0,44***	0,16	0,32	0,29	***0,52***	0,22
SocialPower	0,05	−0,28	−0,05	0,27	−0,13	0,18	0,18
Self Direction	−0,04	***−0,50***	0,11	0,10	0,29	***0,42***	0,14
Stimulation	0,21	−0,26	0,28	***0,51***	***0,44***	***0,49***	0,30
Prosocial	0,29	−0,18	***0,42***	−0,03	***0,57***	0,30	0,02
Security	0,39	−0,20	0,20	0,04	***0,41***	0,36	0,14
Maturity	0,25	−0,21	0,18	−0,17	***0,45***	0,32	0,22
Tradition	0,26	−0,01	***0,47***	0,25	0,32	0,10	0,11
Culture specific values	0,16	0,03	***0,46***	0,18	***0,40***	0,22	−0,05
Closedness	−0,09	0,34	−0,35	−0,18	−0,07	0,13	***0,55***
Self-assuredness	0,39	***−0,47***	−0,17	0,16	0,24	***0,48***	0,35
Reflectre self-relation	0,31	−0,20	−0,28	0,09	0,20	***0,59***	0,19
Self-worth	***0,45***	***−0,42***	−0,02	0,11	0,26	0,29	0,10
Internal conflict	−0,20	0,05	0,08	−0,27	−0,30	−0,40	***−0,46***
Self-condemnation	−0,19	0,14	0,25	−0,38	−0,14	***−0,60***	***−0,42***
Safety needs	0,23	0,07	***0,46***	0,34	0,14	−0,21	−0,32
Belongingness and Love needs	−0,05	−0,04	***0,46***	0,12	0,28	−0,17	−0,18
Esteem needs	0,31	−0,24	***0,15***	0,60	0,07	0,16	−0,09
Self-actualization needs	0,09	−0,21	0,11	0,31	0,13	0,38	0,13

4 Discussion

As we can see from the data obtained, there is a interrelationship between the motivational-need, value-semantic sphere of young people and their information image in the social network, which is consistent with modern Russian researches of Matasova, Bogdanovskaya, Lisenkova, Melnikova [4, 6, 7].

It is should be said that these authors emphasize the importance of hedonistic values for today's youth, which proved to be not significant for our respondents, it may be connected to the sample size and will be verified by us in the future research.

Obtained data are generally consistent with the results of researches of Tripathi, Xenos, Ryan, which point to the interrelationship of the number of friends and subscribers in the social network with openness, extroversion and self-worth [1, 12]. It is also worth noting that the interrelationship of the number of groups with the value of social culture is consistent with the research of Gosling, Augustine, Vazire, Holtzman, and Gaddis, which point to interrelationship of social activity of users and the number of traces in the social network (groups, records, friends) [3].

Foreign researches mainly focus on the study of the Big five, which in our research was not fully covered, and we plan to study it in future research.

It is interesting that there is a discrepancy between our research results and the work by Waterloo, Baumgartner, Peter, Valkenburg [11], who studied the norms of expression of various emotions in social networks and have proved that the expression of positive emotions is perceived as the most appropriate behavior in the information space, while in our research, the expression of happiness on the respondents' avatar is negatively associated with the value of social culture, what may be due to the cultural specificities and social norms of the residents of Russia. The specificities of identity and value orientations of Russian youth in social networks have been studied quite actively in researches of Russian scientists. However, most researches are carried out without applying of automated data analysis tools.

Applying of automated tools of data analysis in socio-psychological researches let, from the point of view of positivist methodology, to adhere to the principles of organization and construction of an experimental research of society and personality, it facilitates the procedure of checking and rechecking the data, describing large amounts of social data that determine the social context, the selection and interpretation of the facts for further research. The media image of the user analysis enable applying to several sources of information: characteristics of virtual behavior and activities of people and groups, specificities of the virtual personality (value-semantic settings, interests, preferences), analysis of human activity products. The variety of information content we have, allows us to assess the constant changes in socio-psychological phenomena, it cultural and historical conditionality. It worth to noting that the developed prognostic model is quite flexible and its form can be used within the framework of various methodological preferences for both- civil and special use.

5 Conclusion

The present work shows that the information image can be considered from the point of view of semantic regulation of personality activity - both in virtual and in real space. There is self-affirmation of the individual in an active information image is going on in social network, which is included in various communities, groups, constantly filled with new content, values and meanings. The study of the interrelationships between the components of the informational image and personal characteristics showed high predictive capabilities of automated analysis of social profile data.

Further direction of research may be associated with the expansion of the sample and analysis of data, taking into account the socio-demographic characteristics of users, as well as the peculiarities of their self-presentation in the network, the identification of the content of patterns, motives and goals as regulators of activities in the virtual environment.

References

1. Tripathi, A.K.: Personality Prediction with Social Behavior by Analyzing Social Media Data - A Survey. University of Winnipeg (2013)
2. Belinskaya, E.P., Martsinkovskaya, T.D.: Identichnost v tranzitivnom obshchestve: virtualnost i realnost. Tsifrovoye obshchestvo kak kulturno-istoricheskiy kontekst razvitiya cheloveka. Sbornik nauchnykh statey i materialov mezhdunarodnoy konferentsii. Pod obshchey redaktsiyey R.V. Ershovoy, pp. 43–48 (2018)
3. Gosling, S.D., Augustine, A.A., Vazire, S., Holtzman, N., Gaddis, S.: Manifestations of personality in online social networks: self-reported Facebook-related behaviors and observable profile information. Cyberpsychol. Behav. Soc. Netw. **14**(9), 483–488 (2011). https://doi.org/10.1089/cyber.2010.0087
4. Khodakovskaya, O.V., Bogdanovskaya, I.M., Koroleva, N.N., Alekhin, A.N., Lugovaya, V. F.: Problematic internet usage and the meaning-based regulation of activity among adolescents. In: Digital Transformation and Global Society 2018, pp. 227–238. DTGS 2018, St. Petersburg (2018). https://doi.org/10.1007/978-3-030-02846-6_18
5. Kosinski, M., Matz, S., Gosling, S., Popov, V., Stillwell, D.: Facebook as a social science research tool: opportunities, challenges, ethical considerations and practical guidelines. Am. Psychol. **70**, 543–556 (2015). https://doi.org/10.1037/a0039210
6. Lisenkova, A.A., Melnikova, A.U.: Social'nye seti kak faktor aktivnogo vliyaniya na formirovanie cennostej molodezhi. Rossijskij gumanitarnyj zhurnal **6**, 322–329 (2017)
7. Matasova, O.I.: Opredelenie cennostej sovremennyh studentov putem kontent-analiza publikacij v social'nyh setyah. In: Priority Directions of Development of Education and Science. Collection of Materials of the III International Scientific and Practical Conference, pp. 248–251. Interakiv Plus, Cheboksary (2017). https://doi.org/10.21661/r-465530
8. Peters, B.: How Not to Network a Nation: The Uneasy History of the Soviet Internet. The MIT Press, Cambridge (2016)
9. Hirn, S., Joachim, T., Zoelch, C.: The role of empathy in the development of social competence: a study of German school leavers. Int. J. Adolesc. Youth, 1–13 (2018). https://doi.org/10.1080/02673843.2018.1548361
10. Voiskounsky, A.E.: Internet addiction in the context of positive psychology. Psychol. Russia: State Art **3**, 541–549 (2010)
11. Waterloo, S.F., Baumgartner, S.E., Peter, J., Valkenburg, P.M.: Norms of online expressions of emotion: comparing Facebook, Twitter, Instagram, and WhatsApp. New Media Soc. **20**, 1813–1831 (2017). https://doi.org/10.1177/1461444817707349
12. Xenos, S., Ryan, T.: Who uses Facebook? An investigation into the relationship between the big five, shyness, narcissism, loneliness, and Facebook usage. Comput. Hum. Behav. **27**, 1658–1664 (2011). https://doi.org/10.1016/j.chb.2011.02.004
13. Yee, N.: The Proteus Paradox: How Online Games and Virtual Worlds Change Us–And How They Don't. Yale University Press (2014)

Toxic Communication on Twitch.tv. Effect of a Streamer

Roman Poyane(✉)

National Research University Higher School of Economics, Saint-Petersburg, Russia
rvpoyane@edu.hse.ru

Abstract. This paper investigates on how spectators communication is organized in chats during broadcasts on Twitch.tv with the main focus on toxic communication. The main purpose of the paper is to understand how socio-demographic characteristics of a broadcaster and channel settings which broadcaster can control affect communication in a chat. Chat logs from Twitch.tv channels were used to create a topic model of viewers discussions. The result of regression analysis indicates that socio-demographic characteristics of a broadcaster have a statistically significant effect on the type of communication, which is manifested in chat.

Keywords: Twitch.tv · Streaming · Toxic communication · Latent Dirichlet Allocation · Cumulative Link models

1 Introduction

Game streaming is a new and rapidly growing area of entertainment which still is not well-studied neither by academia nor by business practitioners. The main feature of streaming services is the chat that let the content-creators and their audience interact and communicate with each other. This paper is dedicated to studying toxic communication in the massive chats that are rather difficult to study using a purely qualitative approach.

1.1 Twitch.tv

Twitch.tv is the largest platform for broadcasting video game streams. Interaction of a streamer with the public is possible in two variations: broadcast yourself using a webcam or chat [14]. Streaming channels can be described as communities where users are constantly included in various forms of interaction both with each other and directly with a streamer (chatting, donations, participation in giveaways, etc.) according to established, but constantly changing rules [6]. All of the site users allowed to watch streams. Registration on the site is needed to participate in chat communication or to create own streaming channel.

D. A. Alexandrov et al. (Eds.): DTGS 2019, CCIS 1038, pp. 414–421, 2019.
https://doi.org/10.1007/978-3-030-37858-5_34

1.2 Twitch.tv Related Studies

Most of the papers, which explore streaming phenomena, are studying user experience [13] and user motivation [11]. Researchers also interested in investigating how the growth of Twitch.tv and its community affects the popularity of eSports in general [4].

Previous works suggest that in a way Twitch.tv can be considered a form of a 'Third Place' for its users, an informal digital meeting place where people happily congregate to enjoy a common interest and socialize with each other [6]. Researchers also state "chatrooms and multiplayer games increasingly provide the illusion of face-to-face social interaction and belonging", further reinforcing Twitch as "Third Place" [10].

1.3 Communication and Concept of 'Toxicity'

Spectators communication is another huge research topic discussed in academia. Most of the papers are focused on communication during eSports tournaments [9]. Authors found that during huge eSports tournaments streams communication type and linguistic content of messages depends on what is happening in the game - viewers try to quickly respond to what they see on their screens with short a flashy chanting. In a way, viewers behave like a roaring crowd on a stadium. Communication in chats is seen as interactions within a specific group of individuals that creates a new type of coherence, a new kind of unity [5].

Almost all of the audience traffic falls on a small proportion of large channels that produce almost the entire volume of the total number of views [15]. In this regard, communication in chat rooms of large channels is characterized by a high speed of posting messages, a large amount of spam (consisting of emoji, copy-paste and various memes) and virtually complete lack of meaningful communication [5]. However, the decrease in the total number of viewers, during the broadcast, leads to a change in the structure of communication – it changes to more meaningful communication in the audience and between the viewers and the streamer [14].

Most researchers define online toxic behavior as a combination of cyberbullying, griefing [16] and fraud, due to the use of prohibited programs that have an advantage in the game [17]. Some researchers understand those type of behaviors in four sub-dimensions [18]: (a) verbal aggression, (b) dominance, (c) entitlement, and (d) resistance to feedback. However, the scope of the definition of the toxic behavior is strongly blurred and vague, due to differences in the characteristics of the expected behavior online in each individual game or community.

As the main goal of this paper is studying toxic communication, it is needed to define it. The definition used in this paper is the following: toxic communication is the type of communication which violates social norms with the main goal of the destruction of social contact. Toxic communication consists of:

1. Offensive language, verbal abuse, mockery, trolling and flaming;
2. Unsubstantiated aggressive criticism;
3. The use of messages or rhetoric which violates Twitch.tv rules or certain channel's chat rules

Previous studies mainly considered the characteristics of the audience and stream popularity, while streamer effect on chat communication was not widely discussed in academia. Such studies lack streamer figure as some kind of medium, who can affect communication in the chat. Thus, the main purpose of this paper is to study communication in chats during personal streams and the main research question is the following: how do channel settings and streamer socio-demographic characteristics affect toxic communication?

2 Data and Method

To collect chat logs from 132 personal Dota 2 streams *twitch-chat-downloader* [7] was used. Channel characteristics were collected from *sullygnome* [12] and streamers personal data was collected from their social media. After the data collection procedure, messages were merged into documents. Each document for topic modeling consisted of 10 consecutive messages from the chat. That size allowed to construct documents large enough for proper work of Latent Dirichlet Allocation (LDA) algorithm. At the same time that allowed to avoid the situation in which documents would consist of a lot of topics with high presence level, meaning that the model would correctly assign single topic with the highest probability of manifestation to a document. Also, it allowed the LDA algorithm to work correctly and sped up the process of building topic model [2]. The *ldatuning* [8] package was used to determine the appropriate number of topics. The result shown in Fig. 1 indicated that the best suitable number of topics is 180 because test results for this number of topics are most closely related to threshold values.

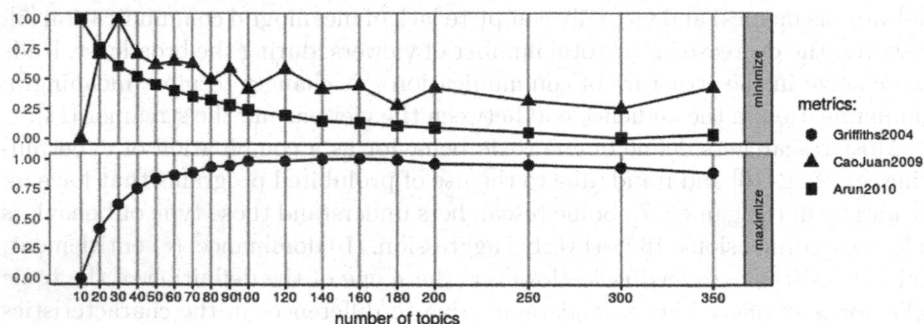

Fig. 1. Results of ldatuning

For regression analysis following categorical variables were chosen:

1. Streamer socio-demographic characteristics:
   (a) Streamers gender ('Male', 'Female')
   (b) Streamers region of origin ('Europe', 'South East Asia', 'North America', 'Middle East')

2. Stream settings:
   (a) Channels Mature Content settings ('Off', 'On')
   (b) Availability of additional broadcast of streamer webcam ('Off', 'On')

After the preprocessing stage, topic modeling using Latent Dirichlet Allocation (LDA) and regression Cumulative Link model (CLM) was applied to the data. LDA is the most common method of topic modeling in computational social science, and it is one of the most widely used methods for processing large sets of texts, which allows to conduct a quantitative text analysis [3]. For every word from the documents it shows a probability of a word occurring in each topic (per-word-per-topic probability). The most probable words for a topic form a top-words chart, which can be used to interpret content of each topic. LDA also treats every document as a mixture of topics (per-topic-per-document probability), so for every document from data it shows a probability of a topic occurring in each document. After that values of the most probable topics can be assigned to the original documents, which make it suitable for regression analysis. Ordered regression (in this case Cumulative Link model) allows to use ordered variables as a dependent, therefore it is the most suitable way to study ordered types of communication (in this case Negative, Neutral and Positive communication) [1]. The results of CLM shows probability of dependent variable being different from the baseline value, given the change in independent variables.

3 Analysis and Results

During the analysis of the collected data, the LDA model (k = 180) was built. The selected amount of topics allowed to unambiguously interpret resulting topics. After that, topics were manually labeled. Similar topics were grouped into larger themes. Themes with similar semantic meanings were assigned into semantic groups - Negative (toxic), Neutral and Positive discussions. Themes which included the empirical indicators described in the definition of toxic communication were assigned to Negative group. Themes that contained various discussions or spectator-specific behavior (such as Emoji Spam), but did not contain empirical indicators from the definition of toxic communication were assigned into Neutral group. Themes that contained an encouraging, positive reaction to the actions of the streamer or displayed the behavior of the fan → idol type were assigned into Positive group. The resulting groups are the following:

1. Positive discussions:
   (a) Greetings or Partying - messages with greetings or partying (at the beginning or end of broadcast);
   (b) Amazement or Delight - messages with expressive reaction to streamer's reaction;
   (c) Praise - messages with an expression of long-term attachment to a streamer:
   (d) Sadness - messages with the showing of empathy with a streamer:

2. Neutral discussions:
   (a) Technical Messages - messages from bots;
   (b) Neutral Copypasta - messages with different memes or not-offensive copypastas;
   (c) Music Discussion - messages with discussion of music on stream;
   (d) Stream Discussion - messages with discussion of different stream's aspects;
   (e) Offtopic - messages which are not directly linked with stream content;
   (f) Player Discussion - messages with discussion of different Dota 2 players or streamers;
   (g) Emoji Spam - messages with spam of different twitch-emojis;
   (h) Game Discussion - messages with discussion of in-game content;
3. Negative discussion:
   (a) Foreign Language - non-english messages;
   (b) Taunting - messages with trolling and mockery;
   (c) Chat Wars - messages with insults between various viewers;
   (d) Regional Insults - offensive messages towards different regions;
   (e) Insults - offensive messages;
   (f) Toxic Copypasta - messages with different offensive copypastas;
   (g) Racial Slurs - messages with expression of racism;
   (h) Boredom - messages with expression of boredom.

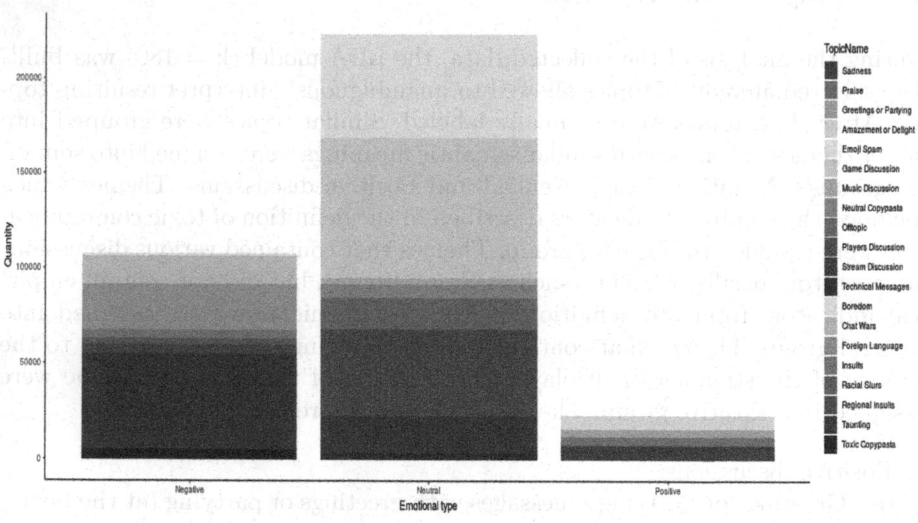

Fig. 2. Distribution of topics

The distribution of topics is shown in Fig. 2. As you can see from the plot discussion is mostly neutral, but it is worth to note that there are more Negative topics then Positive ones.

Then the regression model was built. The regression formula is following:

$$TopicEmotion_i = \beta_1\, Gender_i + \beta_2\, Webcam_i + \beta_3\, MatureContent_i + \beta_4\, Region_i + \epsilon_i$$

The results of regression analysis showed that almost all of the variables used in a model have a statistically significant effect on the type of communication ($p < .001$), with only Mature Content variable having ($p = .064$), which is slightly above the threshold. Considering the fact that all of the variables used in this research are categorical, its worth to note that the regression coefficients in CLM show how the probability of dependent variable being different from baseline value changes with the change in independent variable value from the baseline value. The regression coefficients indicate the following effects on chat discussions:

1. Positive effect:
   (a) Being female streamer rather than male streamer;
   (b) Having webcam available rather than not;
   (c) Being streamer from North America rather than from Europe;
   (d) Being streamer from the Middle East rather than from Europe;
   (e) Being streamer from South East Asia rather than from Europe.

2. Negative effect:
   (a) Having mature content settings 'On'.

Table 1. Summary of regression model

	Estimate	Std. Error	Pr(>z)	Odds Ratios
Gender:Female	0.157	0.012	<0.001***	1.170
Webcam:On	0.311	0.008	<0.001***	1.365
Mature content:On	−0.014	0.007	0.064	0.985
Region:SEA	0.078	0.009	<0.001***	1.082
Region:North America	0.103	0.014	<0.001***	1.109
Region:Middle East	0.170	0.014	<0.001***	1.186
Observations	353229			
Log Likelihood	−291943.27			
AIC	583902.54			
Note	*p < 0.05; **p < 0.01; ***p < 0.001			

However, the most important thing to analyze in CLM is Odds Ratios. Subtracting the confidence interval (which always equals 1) from the Odds Ratio value we get the chance of the dependent variable being different from baseline one, given the change in independent variables. For example, our baseline streamer is European Male with Mature settings 'Off' and Webcam 'Off'. Therefore, for female streamers, the chances of communication in chat being Neutral or Positive rather than Negative are 17% higher then for male streamers (given other variables are held constant). Adding webcam on stream have 36% chances of communication in chat being Neutral or Positive rather than Negative (given other variables are held constant). Turning mature content settings on gives 2% lower chances of communication being Neutral or Positive rather than Negative (given other variables are held constant). Being streamer from South East Asia gives 8% higher chances, being streamer from North America gives 10% higher chances, being streamer from the Middle East gives 18% higher chances of communication being Neutral or Positive rather than Negative (given other variables are held constant). Full results are shown in Table 1.

4 Conclusion

This paper presents the results of a study on how spectators communication in chat rooms of personal Dota 2 streams in Twitch.tv is organized. The study showed that the effect of streamers characteristics and stream settings on chat communication is significant. Being female and having a webcam available affects communication in chat positively. Being from South East Asia, North America and the Middle East affects communication in chat positively. Having Mature settings 'On' affects communication in chat negatively.

The following limitations of this paper should be noticed. The interpretation of the topic model should be done with the participation of several raters to interpret the content of each topic and inter-rater reliability test to confirm the level of consent among raters. It would allow lowering any possible level of bias in interpretation. Also, it would be better to use a Bayesian approach to understand which variables have more impact on the model - socio-demographic or channel size.

Acknowledgements. The author wishes to thank Viktor Karepin for his help and contribution in this work.

References

1. Agresti, A.: Categorical Data Analysis. Wiley Series in Probability and Statistics. Wiley, Hoboken (2003)
2. Blei, D.M., Ng, A.Y., Jordan, M.I.: Latent Dirichlet allocation. J. Mach. Learn. Res. **3**, 993–1022 (2003)
3. DiMaggio, P., Nag, M., Blei, D.: Exploiting affinities between topic modeling and the sociological perspective on culture: application to newspaper coverage of US government arts funding. Poetics **41**(6), 570–606 (2013)
4. Edge, N.: Evolution of the gaming experience: live video streaming and the emergence of a new web community. Elon J. Undergrad. Res. Commun. **4**(2), 33–39 (2013)
5. Ford, C., Gardner, D., Horgan, L.E., Liu, C., Nardi, B., Rickman, J.: Chat speed OP PogChamp: practices of coherence in massive twitch chat. In: Proceedings of the 2017 CHI Conference Extended Abstracts on Human Factors in Computing Systems, pp. 858–871. ACM (2017)

6. Hamilton, W.A., Garretson, O., Kerne, A.: Streaming on twitch: fostering participatory communities of play within live mixed media. In: Proceedings of the SIGCHI Conference on Human Factors in Computing Systems, pp. 1315–1324 (2014)
7. Kraabol, P.: Twitch-chat-downloader. http://github.com/PetterKraabol/Twitch-Chat-Downloader
8. Murzintcev, N.: Ldatuning: tuning of the Latent Dirichlet Allocation models parameters. R package version 0.2.0 (2016). http://CRAN.R-project.org/package=ldatuning
9. Musabirov, I., Bulygin, D., Okopny, P., Konstantinova, K.: Between an arena and a sports bar: online chats of esports spectators. arXiv preprint arXiv:1801.02862 (2018)
10. Shah, D.V., Kwak, N., Lance Holbert, R.: "Connecting" and "disconnecting" with civic life: patterns of Internet use and the production of social capital. Polit. Commun. **18**(2), 141–162 (2001)
11. Sjöblom, M., Hamari, J.: Why do people watch others play video games? An empirical study on the motivations of Twitch users. Comput. Hum. Behav. **75**, 985–996 (2017)
12. Sullygnome Homepage. http://sullygnome.com
13. Zhang, C., Liu, J.: On crowdsourced interactive live streaming: a Twitch.tv-based measurement study. In: Proceedings of the 25th ACM Workshop on Network and Operating Systems Support for Digital Audio and Video, pp. 55–60 (2015)
14. Seering, J., Kraut, R., Dabbish, L.: Shaping pro and anti-social behavior on twitch through moderation and example-setting. In: Proceedings of the 2017 ACM Conference on Computer Supported Cooperative Work and Social Computing, pp. 111–125 (2017)
15. Kaytoue, M., Silva, A., Cerf, L., Meira Jr., W., Raïssi, C.: Watch me playing, I am a professional: a first study on video game live streaming. In: Proceedings of the 21st International Conference on World Wide Web, pp. 1181–1188 (2012)
16. Foo, C.Y., Koivisto, E.M.: Defining grief play in MMORPGs: player and developer perceptions. In: Proceedings of the 2004 ACM SIGCHI International Conference on Advances in Computer Entertainment Technology, pp. 245–250 (2004)
17. Blackburn, J., et al.: Branded with a scarlet C: cheaters in a gaming social network. In: Proceedings of the 21st International Conference on World Wide Web, pp. 81–90 (2012)
18. Shen, L., LeVan, S., Quesnell, M., Tian, X.: A scale for a-holism in relational communication: concept explication, scale development, and correlates. Soc. Sci. J. **55**(4) (2018, in press)

Digital Footprint of Cultural Events: The Case of Museum Night in Russia

Aleksei Gorgadze[1,2(✉)]

[1] National Research University Higher School of Economics, Moscow, Russia
agorgadze@hse.ru
[2] Institute of Russian Literature (Pushkin House), Saint Petersburg, Russian Federation

Abstract. Numerous cultural events take place around the world every year. Visitors leave digital footprint after attending such events, which is a good source of data analysis in tourist behavior and cultural studies. This research provides mapping of festival themes associated with the annual cultural event "Museum Night" on social networking site (SNS) VKontakte (VK) most popular in Russia. All posts containing the official event hashtag in Russian (#ночьмузеев) were collected from VK. To analyse the data, more than 38 k posts spanning 2012 to 2019 are used. The results show the dynamic of the event web activity and changes over the last years.

Keywords: Cultural events · On-line social networks · User-generated content · Digital footprint · VKontakte · Museum Night

1 Introduction

The latest time is characterized by the emergence of the "Web 2.0", on-line systems that evolve thanks to "ordinary" users [1]. People fill and correct informational materials themselves. One illustrative example is the social network sites (SNS), which have significantly increased their audience and importance over the past decade. SNS users independently post data (including personal information) on their pages, blogs, portals and other on-line platforms. That is why, along with the off-line actions of event managers, it is necessary to work with the digital environment with both a communication and feedback channel and a monitoring tool.

It should be emphasized that digital marketing methods are actively used in close interaction with event management of the tourism industry. Analyzing reviews on hotel services, one can identify the main topics and the emotional coloring of each post as well as connect it with the services provided by the hotel [2]. People leave a large amount of digital data on various platforms that can be collected and analyzed. Moreover, data from different sources can partially complement each other [3].

Studies analyzing spatial patterns of mobility of people in cities show that they tend to be concentrated in specific areas of urban centers [4, 5], where the main cultural destinations (museums, parks, theaters, concert halls) are located, as well as entertainment and shopping services [6]. Not surprisingly, for example, the fact that most tourists are looking for hotels or apartments that are within walking distance of the

D. A. Alexandrov et al. (Eds.): DTGS 2019, CCIS 1038, pp. 422–431, 2019.
https://doi.org/10.1007/978-3-030-37858-5_35

main attractions of the city [7] and spend most of their time in the immediate vicinity of the hotel [8].

There are many classifications of cultural events depending on the genre, size and audience. Getz [9] proposes to attribute to cultural events various festivals, carnivals, holidays, anniversaries of any event, as well as religious events. In separate categories, he singled out entertainment events, events related to art, political events, business and commercial events, educational and scientific events, sports competitions and personal events. Cultural events are distinguished by a clear time and territorial framework, themes and objectives for the involvement of visitors to the process of consumption of cultural products.

It is also worth noting that cultural events are accompanied by a special atmosphere. A distinctive feature of the atmosphere is that it is not directly tied to a specific space and has no clear boundaries. It is expressed in the form of emotions and invisible collective appeal to space consumers [10].

Local governments are increasingly turning to event tourism as a means of economic development. The traditional view is that event-based tourism provides local economic and social benefits that outweigh their costs. Thomas and Wood [11] study the perspectives and practices of local governments and show insights into event-based tourism strategies from various UK authorities. However, in our opinion, event planning is an integral part of broader development strategies, which will also be discussed in the study.

In classical event management studies, the most popular data collection methods are surveys, interviews, and focus groups or secondary information (such as data from statistical agencies or other departments). However, such methods do not always reflect the diversity of demand in the fast-growing market for services. Field work on the collection of materials may be delayed for months, and the results obtained become obsolete. In addition, the accuracy of the analysis is directly dependent on the quality of the data collection tool and the organization of the work of many research participants (interviewers, analysts, transcribers, etc.). The use of digital footprints as an indicator of the loyalty of visitors to cultural events is an innovative approach. Modern and more efficient data collection methods are needed so that cultural event organizers can work with data more easily. An important source of information is the digital traces of visitors; they include posts on on-line forums, uploaded photos or metadata links that have been tagged on the website.

Annually, more than hundred events are held in St. Petersburg, including festivals and holidays, exhibitions and other city cultural events [12]. Museum Night (or Art Night) is an annual and most popular cultural event in Russia nowadays [13]. Event visitors tend to leave their impressions of participation on their SNS pages. The open API system [14] allows you to collect and process useful empirical data that reflects the dynamics of on-line behavior of event visitors. Thus, goal of this study is the identifying features of the night of museum visitor's digital activity on the SNS as well as identifying major changes of the event through the study of the dynamics of digital traces in order to increase the effectiveness of these events and give new impulses to event activities.

2 Data and Methodology

The source of empirical data is the social networking site VKontakte, the most popular in Russia [15]. It is most promising platform because of its open data using API methods and fullness of information about events in Russia. Using API methods, all posts containing the official hashtag of the event #ночьмузеев (*in Russian: "museum night"*) were loaded. Hashtags have many different functions such as enables visibility, aggregating tweets posted by multiple members, constructing the identity of members and etc. [16]. Several studies focuses on the hashtags as the indicator of thematic or events [17, 18]. In this paper the hashtag serves as an indicator of the event "Museum Night". The collected database contains 38 399 posts, including content text and metadata (publication date, author, number of likes, reposts, comments, views).

Collected posts can be published as regular user-visitors, and on-line groups. The on-line group were filtered and the top groups with the largest number of posts (more than 10 posts per year) for each year were manually coded according to the following parameters: group type and location (city/region). The number of subscribers and the name of the groups were also collected. Group type includes:

- Museums – all types of museums including galleries and creative space;
- Organizers – groups of event local and region organizers;
- Aggregators – on-line groups of event aggregators;
- Theaters and philharmonic including separate theatrical productions;
- Libraries;
- Other – includes services, associations, universities, events and companies or factories.

The interrelation of webometric indicators of posts (likes, reposts, comments and views) was checked using the Pearson correlation analysis.

In order to assess the value of the "Museum Night" effect on the on-line audience of cultural institutions, a second database was collected: on-line group size of museums, which take part in the "Museum Night" event. To begin with, all the URLs of on-line groups were collected. 100 museums out of 120 has on-line groups at SNS VKontakte. The main objective is to signify whether the event significantly increases the number of on-line groups subscribers. However, there is an organic increase of on-line group subscribers, so comparing the size of groups only before and after the event does not make sense. For this reason, the design of data collection includes 3 time periods for measuring the size of on-line groups: two weeks before the event (T1), one week before the event (T2) and immediately after the event (T3). Using the paired sample t-test, changes in the size of groups much before the event (T1—T2) and during the event (T2—T3) was compared.

It should be noted that one of the specifics of Internet research is that collecting data very often includes "noises" that must be removed. A necessary condition for any semantic analysis is the text lemmatization. For this task, the software "Mystem" and "Demystem" developed by the company "Yandex" will be used [19]. In addition, text data must pass other preprocessing stages (removing stopwords, punctuation, numbers, and extra white spaces as well as making all letters lowercase).

Data analyzing methods based on a normal distribution are invalid in text mining studies [20]. Therefore, parametric statistical analysis the log-likelihood (G-squared) and the log odds ratio was used to identify most common words for the sub-corpora [21–23]. The log-likelihood indicates a statistical significance which shows how much evidence we have for a difference between two corpora (sub-corpus and the rest of the corpus). The log odds ratio shows how big or important a given difference is (an effect-size statistic) [24].

3 Results

3.1 Post Analysis

The data collection involved searching and unloading posts from 2006 (the year of the SNS VKontakte founding) until June 2019. However, the first posts containing the hashtag "#ночьмузеев" appeared in 2012 (Fig. 1). The peak of publication activity was in 2017, and the last two years there has been a slight decline of this indicator.

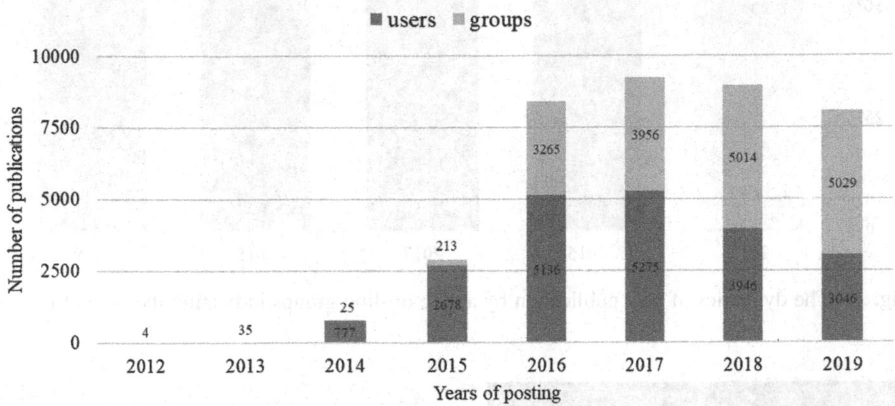

Fig. 1. Post publication dynamics

It is important to note that posts can be published by both ordinary users of SNS and on-line groups. Despite the fact that users initially published more posts than on-line groups, starting from 2018, the ratio of post authors has changed (Fig. 1). This result may indicate a change in the informational field of the event from user communication to a commercial-organizational form of interaction.

To understand the specifics of the on-line groups the top active communities were categorized into 6 groups: museums, organizers, aggregators, theaters and philharmonic, libraries and other. 2012, 2013 and 2014 years were excluded from analysis, because there was no on-line group that would publish more than 10 posts in these years. Final list of unique active groups consists 182, and the total number of posts published by this groups is 4707.

In 2015 there was only one group (event aggregator «Playbill of Novosibirsk»), which published more than 10 posts (Fig. 2). From 2016, on-line groups of museums are starting to increase the activity of publishing posts. Despite the initial large number of posts in groups of event organizers, there is an annual drop in their activity. Groups dedicated to theaters showed a small surge of activity in 2017. This year the Sverdlovsk Philharmonia (Yekaterinburg), the Baltic House Theater (St. Petersburg), the State Academic Chapel (St. Petersburg) and the Novosibirsk Music Theater (Novosibirsk) most actively published posts.

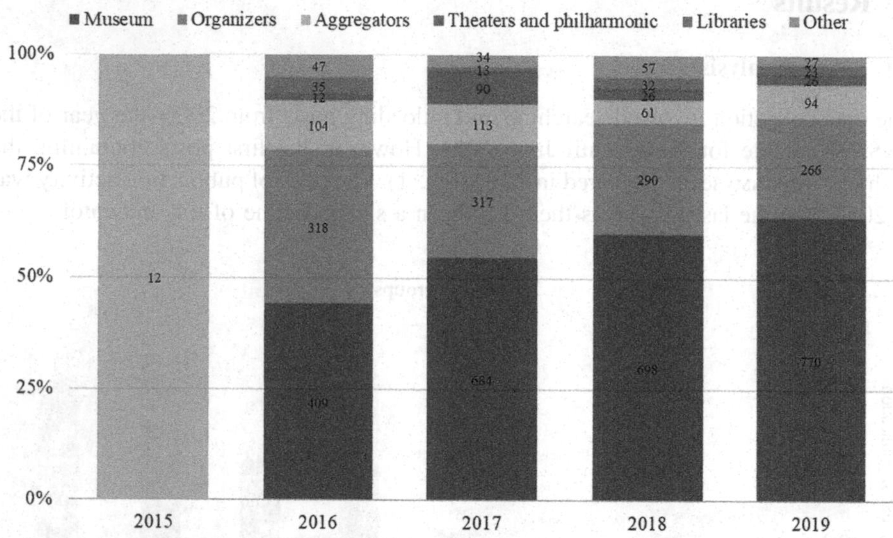

Fig. 2. The dynamics of post publication by active on-line groups indicating the type of groups

Fig. 3. The local news frame showing the organization of the "Museum Night" event at the Ural Mining and Metallurgical Company.

There were three on-line groups of industrial enterprises designated as type “other”: Ural Mining and Metallurgical Company, Ural Chemical Engineering Plant and Sredneuralsky Copper Smelter. All three enterprises are located near Ekaterinburg. In 2016 and 2017 there were special cultural programs which included excursions at industrial enterprises (Fig. 3). One of the possible reasons for the enterprise activity is that 2017 was the year of ecology in Russia.

Webometric indicators of posts such as likes, reposts, comments and views demonstrate significant correlation between them (Table 1). All variables show significant relationship (p-value < 0.01), however, the degree of the comments number coherence with other variables is very weak.

Table 1. Correlation of posts webometric indicators

	Likes	Reposts	Comments
Reposts	,596**		
Comments	,116**	,112**	
Views	,369**	,250**	,030**

** *p-value < 0.01*

While the average number of likes and reposts is gradually increasing, the number of comments has decreased dramatically since 2015 (Fig. 4). This fact demonstrates changes in the format of communication in a virtual environment. Users are less involved in discussions, but more often perform simpler actions (posts liking).

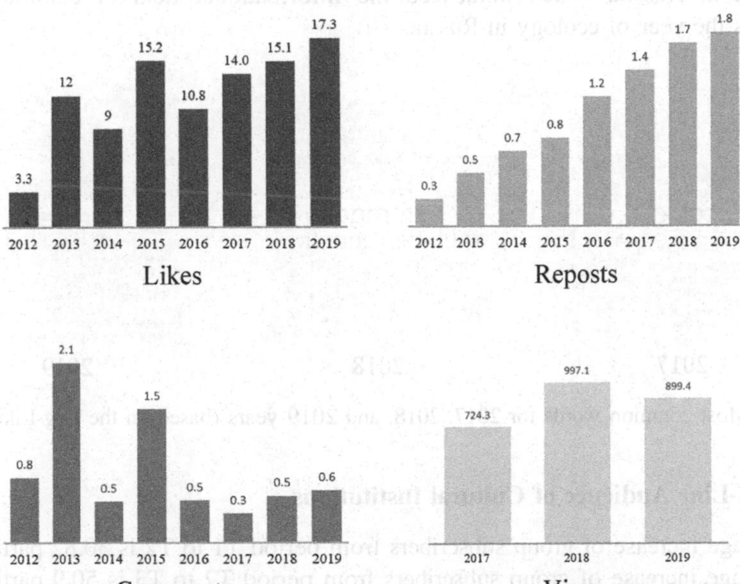

Fig. 4. Dynamics of webometric indicators

The absolute leader among the cities in the number of active groups posts is St. Petersburg (Fig. 5). Moscow, Yekaterinburg and the Republic of Karelia follow him with a big lag. Such a large gap is largely due to the vigorous activity in the digital environment of local organizers in St. Petersburg (49,4% of all active groups posts were published by Organizers).

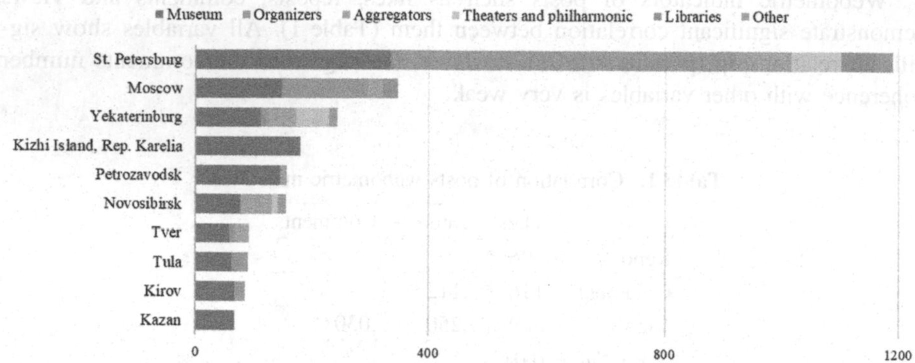

Fig. 5. Top-10 cities in the number of active groups posts

Using log-likelihood and the log odds ratio most common words for last three years were identifying (Fig. 6). The results show the most relevant topics typical of the years. The most typical words of 2019 describe the general theme of the event, which is devoted to the Mendeleev chemical elements periodic table. In 2018, the World Cup was held in Russia, which influenced the informational field of cultural events. 2017 was the year of ecology in Russia.

Fig. 6. Most common words for 2017, 2018, and 2019 years (based on the Log-Likelihood)

3.2 On-Line Audience of Cultural Institutions

The average increase of group subscribers from period T1 to T2 is 30.82 participants. The average increase of group subscribers from period T2 to T3 is 50.9 participants. The paired sample t-test showed significant (P-value < 0.05) increase of the cultural institutions on-line audiences' size (Fig. 7). This fact demonstrates the effect of cultural events in a digital environment and their important role in shaping a digital audience.

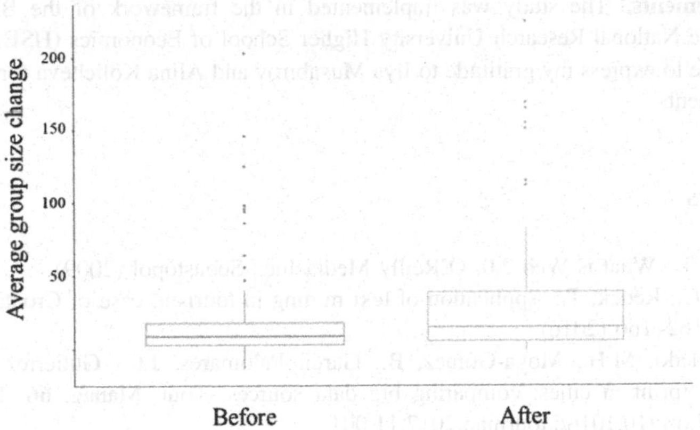

Fig. 7. The distribution of the average change in the size of the on-line groups before the event and after the event

4 Conclusion

This study demonstrates the features of the "Museum Night" visitor's digital activity on the SNS VKontakte as well as dynamics of the event digital footprint. Changing the format of communication in a virtual environment has occurred. More and more representatives of museums and cultural institutions are beginning to actively fill out the information field of the event.

In addition to this the research shows significant role of cultural event in increasing the number of cultural institutions on-line groups subscribers. However, in addition to increasing the digital audience, it is also necessary to build loyalty around the brand. This task will be considered in future studies.

The results can be used by organizations of the tourist and cultural industries to develop strategies for the development and improvement of the marketing mix (especially with regard to digital footprint). In addition, the results of the study are of particular interest to regional and city governments for assessing the performance of organizations and projects of cultural and creative industries.

5 Limitations

There are several limitations of the study. First, Internet data often contains spam, which needs to be filtered. In this study the most active spam on-line groups were filtered. However, further studies require better data cleaning. Moreover, using hashtags for data collection may severely limit the sample, which do not include posts on relevant topic. The next stage of the study should include additional channels of data collection.

Acknowledgements. The study was implemented in the framework of the Basic Research Program at the National Research University Higher School of Economics (HSE) in 2019.

I would like to express my gratitude to Ilya Musabirov and Alina Kolicheva for their for their helpful comments.

References

1. O'Reilly, T.: What is Web 2.0. O'Reilly Media Inc., Sebastopol (2009)
2. Godnov, U., Redek, T.: Application of text mining in tourism: case of Croatia. Ann. Tour. Res. **58**, 162–166 (2016)
3. Salas-Olmedo, M.H., Moya-Gómez, B., García-Palomares, J.C., Gutiérrez, J.: Tourists' digital footprint in cities: comparing big data sources. Tour. Manag. **66**, 13–25 (2018). https://doi.org/10.1016/j.tourman.2017.11.001
4. Hayllar, B., Griffin, T.: Urban tourist precincts as sites of play. In: Maciocco, G., Serreli, S. (eds.) Enhancing the City: New Perspectives for Tourism and Leisure. Urban and Landscape Perspectives, vol. 6, pp. 65–81. Springer, Dordrecht (2009). https://doi.org/10.1007/978-90-481-2419-0_4
5. Shoval, N., Raveh, A.: Categorization of tourist attractions and the modeling of tourist cities: based on the co-plot method of multivariate analysis. Tour. Manag. **25**, 741–750 (2004). https://doi.org/10.1016/j.tourman.2003.09.005
6. Pearce, J.M.: A model for stimulus generalization in Pavlovian conditioning. Psychol. Rev. **94**, 61 (1987)
7. Arbel, A., Pizam, A.: Some determinants of urban hotel location: the tourists' inclinations. J. Travel Res. **15**, 18–22 (1977)
8. Shoval, N., McKercher, B., Ng, E., Birenboim, A.: Hotel location and tourist activity in cities. Ann. Tour. Res. **38**, 1594–1612 (2011)
9. Getz, D.: Event tourism: definition, evolution, and research. Tour. Manag. **29**, 403–428 (2008)
10. Böhme, G.: Atmosphere as the fundamental concept of a new aesthetics. Thesis Eleven **36**, 113–126 (1993)
11. Thomas, R., Wood, E.: Events-based tourism: a survey of local authority strategies in the UK. Local Gov. **29**, 127–136 (2003)
12. Calendar of events. http://www.visit-petersburg.ru/calendar/
13. Museum Night is an annual event dedicated to International Museum Day | Ночь музеев, Санкт-Петербург. http://www.artnight.ru/en
14. API methods | Developers. https://vk.com/dev/methods
15. Top Websites. https://pro.similarweb.com/#/industry/topsites/Computers_Electronics_and_Technology~Social_Networks_and_Online_Communities/643/1m?webSource=Total
16. Page, R.: The linguistics of self-branding and micro-celebrity in Twitter: the role of hashtags. Discourse Commun. **6**, 181–201 (2012). https://doi.org/10.1177/1750481312437441
17. Zappavigna, M.: Ambient affiliation: a linguistic perspective on Twitter. New Media Soc. **13**, 788–806 (2011)
18. Gruzd, A., Wellman, B., Takhteyev, Y.: Imagining Twitter as an imagined community. Am. Behav. Sci. (2011). https://doi.org/10.1177/0002764211409378
19. Segalovich, I.: A fast morphological algorithm with unknown word guessing induced by a dictionary for a web search engine. In: MLMTA, pp. 273–280. Citeseer (2003)
20. Dunning, T.: Accurate methods for the statistics of surprise and coincidence. Comput. Linguist. **19**, 61–74 (1993)

21. Bradley, J.V.: Distribution-Free Statistical Tests. Prentice-Hall, Upper Saddle River (1968)
22. Mood, A.M., Graybill, F.A., Boes, D.: Introduction to the Theory of Statistics. McGraw-Hill, New York (1974)
23. DaCosta, C.J., Baenziger, J.E.: Rapid method assessing lipid protein detergent protein ratios membrane crystallization. Acta Crystallogr. Sect. D: Biol. Crystallogr. **59**, 77–83 (2003)
24. Hardie, A.: Log Ratio: An informal introduction. ESRC Centre Corpus Approaches Social Science CASS (2014)

Dr. Paper: Find Your Personal Max Planck

Tatiana Malygina[1,2](✉), Aleksandrina Shatalova[3,4], and Antonina Puchkovskaya[5]

[1] The Laboratory of Bioinformatics, ITMO University, Kronverkskiy pr. 49, St. Petersburg 197101, Russia
tanya.malygina@botkin.ai

[2] Intellogic Limited Liability Company (Intellogic LLC), office 1/334/63, building 1, 42 Bolshoi blvd., territory of Skolkovo Innovation Center, 121205 Moscow, Russia

[3] School of Biotechnology and Cryogenic Systems, ITMO University, Lomonosova Street 9, St. Petersburg 191002, Russia

[4] XEMA Company LLC, Degtyarniy lane 8-10, St. Petersburg 191144, Russia
shatalovaaleks0104@gmail.com

[5] Digital Humanities Centre, ITMO University, Lomonosova Street 9, St. Petersburg 191002, Russia
aapuchkovskaya@corp.ifmo.ru

Abstract. ITMO university has 4 megafaculties, 14 faculties, 5 institutes. It's really hard to find the great scientific supervisor in your professional field. We wanted to make the simple tool to find the right one. At this study we have collected research information associated with ITMO university from different sources, including papers from PubMed and ArXiV. We also used publicly-available information provided at ITMO University's website (which is the first thing every prospective young student might find, even if he doesn't belong to ITMO University yet). At this work we focus on exploratory analysis of the data we collected.

Keywords: Natural language processing · Text clustering · Doc2Vec

1 Introduction

In the modern world there is an incredible variety of professions because, with the development of society and the emphasis on progress, new ones are constantly added to the already existing ones. And due to the openness of the modern world, the availability of education and mobility of citizens, and it's not difficult for an emerging Internet space to master one or the other. Therefore, even from an early age, the child faces a difficult choice of profession.

To simplify this task, schools conduct various career guidance and testing. The popularity of children's career-oriented cities such as Kinberg, where the kid can try out different roles. But they are not always the right ones, because they are often based on influence of the parents, associates, friends opinions, the wage level, the prestige of the profession, fashion trends and etc. The possibility of

D. A. Alexandrov et al. (Eds.): DTGS 2019, CCIS 1038, pp. 432–438, 2019.
https://doi.org/10.1007/978-3-030-37858-5_36

obtaining an education in the profile and further employment in certain regions are also significant [3].

At young scientist's path, very important thing is supervisor personality. The level of research supervisor, his ability to maintain relations with various universities, research centers and collaborate with other colleagues, the frequency of publications and the level of journals, citation in the scientific community are significant [1,2].

2 Methods

2.1 Arxiv.org

ArXiV is a widely used server with scientific preprints, which also can be explored via API. We've made our own wrapper for arxiv REST API calls to collect papers with ITMO University affiliation. As a result, we found only 14 papers related to ITMO.

2.2 PubMed

PubMed API allows to do article search on different topics - i.e., rare genetic diseases, specific authors or institutions. For our project it is important that it allows to search papers by authors affiliations and provides the results in machine-readable form. To collect the data, we wrote the script, which uses biopython to search information on PubMed via REST API.

2.3 ACM Digital Library

For comparison, we also collected records from ACM Digital Library ITMO University's page. We used export tool. Thus, we've obtained a collection of articles written in English, with titles and with no abstracts, author names given as a string per article. We do not explore this data source in detail, we've decided to add it to show how many details are hidden at ITMO's website (and how many entries are not available at ACM Digital Library).

2.4 Openbooks Dataset

We explored ITMO University's website during November and December 2019. Probably due to attestation, some of data seemed to be missing or incomplete. That's why we gave up on idea to collect information from department[1] and specialization[2] pages.

One of the sources which seemed promising was openbooks portal. It is a collection of conference proceedings, articles, books at https://openbooks.ifmo.ru.

[1] http://edu.ifmo.ru/departments/.

[2] http://edu.ifmo.ru/specs_list/.

In Openbooks dataset, we've managed to separate different portions of data – the authors names, abstract, title, for some papers we've managed to detect if the full text download link is presented at the page; we also collected the collection of manually curated keywords associated with each article.

The Openbooks dataset is the main source of information used in data analysis, since it appeared to be the dominant data source and was the only source with information in Russian. It also contained paper abstracts which we were easily able to separate.

2.5 Teachers Dataset

The lecturer's pages[3] typically contain full name, the department, where the teacher works, the subjects he or she teaches, and a list of publications.

To collect teachers data, we used scrapy. We collected 46285 bibliography entries from 1104 teacher pages. However, some of the teachers had no bibliography entries, some of the entries were duplicated - by removing this, we've collected the last of our datasets (referred to as "Teachers's dataset").

3 Results

3.1 Comparison of Data Sources

Both PubMed and ArXiV provide information in machine-readable form, both return an information on authors affiliations, which are typically given as a list with university name, department name and address. The ACM Digital Library provides similar information, which can be used to cite the given articles. However, they alone do not help us to make really useful instrument for students and young researchers, because they provide information only in English, and this information might not contain the contact emails (unfortunately, we've also found no contact information in other data sources). Figure 1 shows relative amounts of data in all 5 data sources.

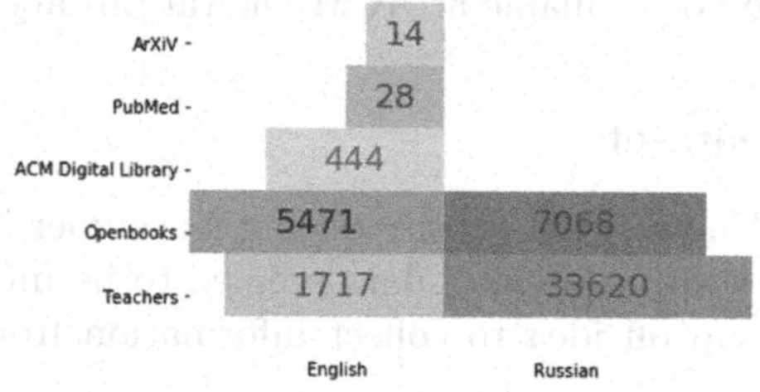

Fig. 1. The plot shows relative amounts of unique papers within different data sources (bars are drawn at logarithmic scale), written in Russian or English, the numbers indicate how many articles were found for given dataset in Russian or English.

[3] http://edu.ifmo.ru/teachers/.

As you can see from Fig. 1, our major source of information is Teachers dataset. However, it is also the most problematic: titles in bibliography entries can hardly be separated from authors list, journal name and other details, especially when this information contains typos or written partially in Russian, partially in English.

For Teachers dataset we also did basic data exploration and found out that the most part of bibliography entries are recent, and are written with Russian characters (see Fig. 2).

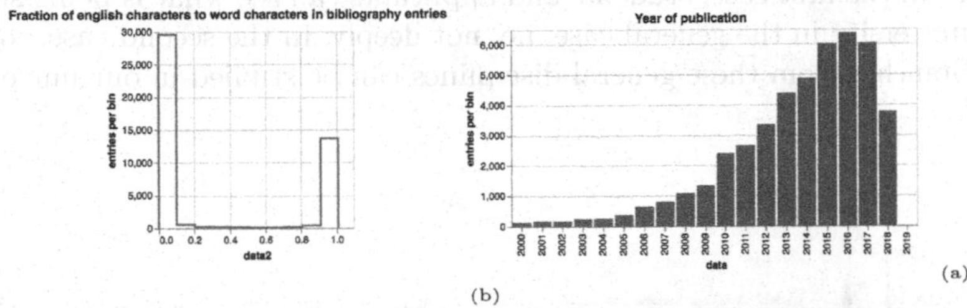

Fig. 2. (a) Plot shows what characters are used in bibliography entries from teacher pages at ITMO University website. We can see that typical bibliography uses English alphabet letters 0.2 times less frequent than Russian alphabet letters. (b) Distribution of bibliography entries per year.

3.2 Authors Map

Publication activity is the most important criterion for evaluating the effectiveness of a research practice of the teachers and their co-authors. The number of articles prepared jointly with foreign organizations may show students the ability of the supervisor to organize a worthy project, which may involve people with varying degrees of skill or from different scientific fields of activity. We try to imagine it as a big map of co-authors (shown at Fig. 3).

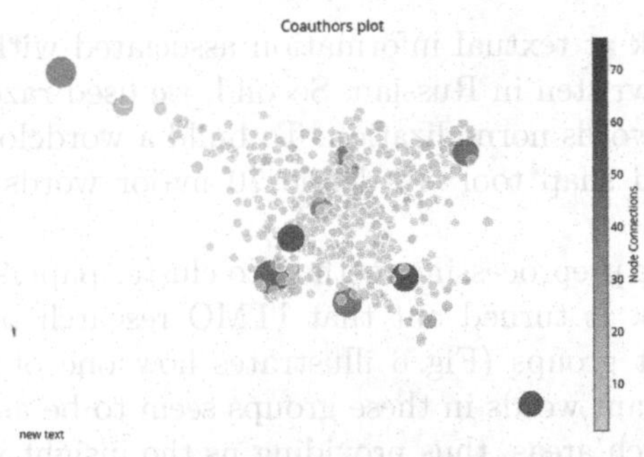

Fig. 3. We provide a co-authors map built with Openbooks dataset contents. We used extracted words to build Doc2Vec model to define relative positions between authors.

Publication activity is determined by the following key indicators:

- total number of publications for a certain period;
- distribution of publications by type of publications, by year, by co-authors;
- the average impact factor of journals in which articles are published;
- publications indexed by international scientific citation bases;
- citations.

We wanted to analyze and understand which keywords are used most often and which less. This was done in order to show main and "private" areas of research. In the first case, students and applicants can see what is being studied at the university in the general case, i.e. not deeply. In the second case, to show which branches from these general disciplines can be studied in our university.

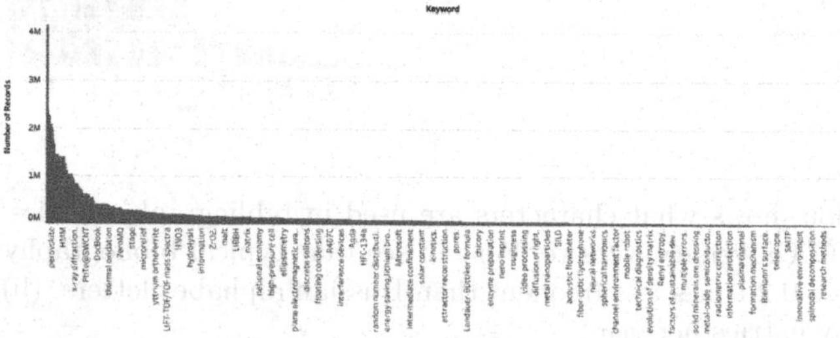

Fig. 4. Keyword usage frequencies plot.

We distinguish tags by usage frequencies (Fig. 4). For the most convenient search, we decided to "bind" tags to the articles in which they were most often used, and then to the authors of these articles. So we converted the frequency graph of the used tags (Fig. 4) into a graph that allows you to view the authors of these articles.

3.3 WordCloud and LDA Analysis

We also tried to look at textual information associated with articles. First, we picked only articles written in Russian. Second, we used razdel for tokenization and pymorphy2 for words normalization. To build a wordcloud (which is shown at Fig. 5) we've used snap tool[4] to define 70 major words in ITMO research papers.

We used the same preprocessing method to cluster papers with LDA (Latent Dirichlet Allocation). It turned out that ITMO research papers can be separated in 5–7 distinct groups (Fig. 6 illustrates how one of these groups looks like). The most relevant words in these groups seem to be associated with main megafaculties' research areas, thus providing us the insight where to search the advisor.

[4] http://snap.stanford.edu/.

Fig. 5. WordCloud with major words in ITMO research papers from Russian portion of Openbooks dataset.

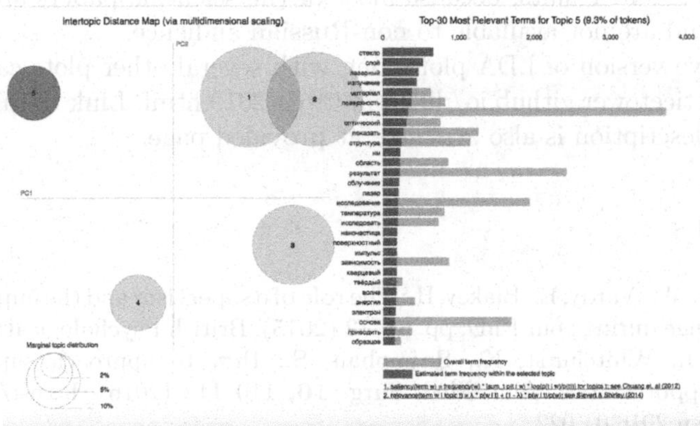

Fig. 6. An example of LDA clusters with associated words (built with pyLDAvis tool).

4 Conclusions

Our motivation to do this project was “6-handshakes”-themed assignment at ITMO University’s English course for PhD students. We wanted to make an application for potential scientific advisors or thesis reviewers search within ITMO University. Our target audience – bachelor and graduate students, who want to continue their scientific career within ITMO University, to change their research field, find new collaborations, etc. We suppose that these students might not belong to ITMO University, they might not speak English or Russian.

The main reason we gave up the idea to make an application was lack of contact information for most of the teachers. It was also hard to connect (without manual annotation and validation) most of teachers and lecturers with their research profiles. That’s why in this work we focus on exploratorial data analysis.

The University is quite large, and it is not easy to find the person who have an expertise in the research areas you dream to explore and who will help you grow, like Max Planck helped Lise Meitner by simply allowing her to attend his lectures.

There is an extensive choice of various specialties at the ITMO University. However, there is a language barrier for foreign students, since not all specialties are sufficiently covered in foreign sources. These data are necessary to create an international tag system that will be available to all students of the world, and in addition will bring our university to a new level of development.

During data analysis we noticed that articles in Russian prevail in our university, which can hide a complete picture of all research activities within ITMO from foreign students. In turn, this may affect the student exchange programs.

Our study also suggests that the world community might not have a complete picture of all the achievements of ITMO university, with the exception of ACM ICPC competitions results, because most of the scientific papers are published in Russian and are not available to non-Russian audience.

Interactive version of LDA plot along with several other plots can be found at http://latticetower.github.io/different/dtgs-2019.html. Link to initial technical project description is also available at provided page.

References

1. Griffiths, A.W., Vardy, E., Blakey, H.: The role of a supervisor and the impact of supervisory change during your PhD, pp. 68–72 (2015). British Psychological Society
2. Jafree, D.J., Whitehurst, K., Rajmohan, S.: How to approach supervisors for research opportunities. Ann. Med. Surg. **10**, 110–112 (2016). https://doi.org/10.1016/j.amsu.2016.01.022
3. Eliamani, M.P., Peter, B., Mghweno, L.R.: Access to guidance and counseling services and its influence on Students' school life and career choice. Afr. J. Guidance Counsel. **1**(1), 007–015 (2014)

Semantic Network Analysis of Ingroup and Outgroup Representations in Radical Social Movement Discourse. The Case of Russian Lesbian-Feminist Movement

Oxana Mikhailova(✉) and Galina Gradoselskaya

Higher School of Economics, Moscow, Russian Federation
oxanamikhailova@gmail.com

Abstract. This paper operationalizes ingroup and outgroup image construction in the Russian lesbian-feminist movement discourse. To investigate the speech properties which are involved in the radical social movement discourse dissemination we employed semantic network analysis. In the study were analyzed two sources of data: from 574 lesbian-feminist groups in the social network "VKontakte" and from the 18 interviews with self-identified members of Russian lesbian-feminist community. Differences in the image construction in examined environments were discovered. The methodology for the "we" and "they" representations investigation presented in this article could be applied to the study of the other radical social movement's discourses propagation.

Keywords: Semantic networks · Semantic networks analysis · Radical social movement · Discourse propagation · Lesbian feminism

1 Introduction

The radicalization of individuals and social groups, which is happening in modern society leads to a variety of social, political and psychological problems [1] and is currently one of the most popular research areas [2]. Understanding the processes that spread ideologies of radical social movements could help to prevent and resolve conflicts quicker, both at macro and micro levels. Therefore, the goal of our study was to elaborate the methodology which could help to analyze the mechanisms which spread discourses of radical social movements. These mechanisms contribute to the radical social movement identity formation. We used the definition of radical social movement proposed by Fitzgerald and Rodgers [3]. Our goal was attained with semantic network analysis. As an example of radical social movement was taken Russian lesbian feminism. In the Table 1 some of the features that characterize radical social movements are given (we did not include all of the features here, only the most relevant ones in total we dis-covered 30 characteristics on basis of which we classified radical social movements which belong to different ideological platforms).

Here are the abbreviations descriptions which were used in the Table 1.

D. A. Alexandrov et al. (Eds.): DTGS 2019, CCIS 1038, pp. 439–451, 2019.
https://doi.org/10.1007/978-3-030-37858-5_37

- "LF" – lesbian feminism.
- "GM" – gender movements (Marxist, socialist feminism).
- "A" – anarchist movements (anti-fascists, anti-militarists, tranarchism, anarcha feminism, queer anarchism, Black cross, anarcho-punks, DIY scene movements).
- "LM" – labor movement.
- "E" – environmental/or the animal rights movements.
- "NE" – new edge.
- "H" – health-oriented movements (straight edge, pro-choice, veganism).
- "AP" – emerged from anarchist practices (freegans and squatting).
- "I" – information movements ("Anonymous", free schoolers, supporters of a free university).

Although there were detected other identity creation mechanisms, in this paper we operationalized on the semantic level only one of the discursive mechanisms which lies in the basis of solidarity in radical social movement. This mechanism is called the construction of ingroup and outgroup image. The importance of this mechanism was shown both by social psychology and interdisciplinary scholarship of critical discourse analysis studies [4].

This paper starts from the brief description of problems to which semantic networks were applied previously. After that the methodological model used in our study is presented. Then the results of semantic analysis are given. In conclusion part the results of the study are summarized and future directions are allocated.

Table 1. Short list of characteristics of radical social movements

Attribute	LF	GM	A	LM	E	NE	H	AP	I
linguistic separation	+	+	+	+	+	+	+	+	+
construction of "Our" – "Their" opposition	+	+	+	+	+	-	+	+	+
separation in political system	+	+	+	+	+	+	-	+	+
separation in mass-media system	+	+	+	+	+	+	+	-	-
separation in art system	+	+	+	+	+	+	-	+	-
separation in economic system	+	+	+	-	+	+	-	+	+
existence of own written sources	+	+	+	+	+	-	+	+	-
separation in legal system	+	+	+	+	+	-	-	+	+
separation in religious system	+	+	+	+	-	+	+	-	-
separation in educational system	+	+	+	+	-	+	-	-	+
work with potential members through seminars, lectures and trainings	+	+	+	+	+	+	-	-	-
existence of organized opposition	+	+	-	-	-	+	+	-	+
existence of specific style attributes	+	+	+	-	-	+	+	-	-
concentration on deprived group	+	+	+	+	+	-	-	-	-
existence of institutes of psychological help	+	+	-	-	-	+	+	-	-
formation of need to cut all connections with outgroup members	+	-	-	-	-	+	-	-	-
communal lifestyle	+	-	-	-	-	+	-	-	-

2 Semantic Network Analysis in the Studies of the Internet Data

There is a well-developed tradition of the Internet studies in Russia [5, 6]. Many papers were written on textual analysis in online social networks. Scholars who deal with textual analysis of Internet data usually face with the need to invent new approaches to deal with increasing volumes of data. Semantic networks are one of the tools which helps to organize and structure Big Data [7]. Semantic networks are difficult to replace by the other textual data analysis approaches. The interchangeability of co-word mapping and topic modeling was studied by Leydesdorff and Nerghes [8]. The study showed that results of these types of analysis are uncorrelated, the groups which compute algorithms look totally uncorrelated, so on small sized and medium sized text samples topic modeling could not replace co-word mapping.

Currently there are two main problems to solve in semantic network analysis (SNA): sentiment analysis [9, 10] and semantic similarity measurement [11]. Complexities with the assessment of emotions are connected not only with computational algorithms but also with the presence of divergent emotion models [12]. We partly address the semantic similarity measurement problem, because we faced with the need to compare the texts from the two sources. Despite of mentioned challenges semantic networks showed their effectiveness in social sciences. To show the possible areas of application we grouped the problems which they focus on, when applied to the Internet studies in 3 categories (information propagation studies, image construction investigations and public communication inquiries) and illustrated by the studies which represent them.

First well-known application of the SNA is the inquiry of hashtags. Internet users create discursive strategies to insure the information propagation. Scholars who study such text programming mechanisms by visualizing and clustering reveal the structure of mechanisms and their origins. For instance, Eddington studied the usage of the slogan “Make America Great Again” in Trump’s presidential campaign [7]. It was found out that there were textual and conversational connections between Trump’s political campaign and hate extremist groups.

Xiong, Cho and Boatwright investigated the mobilization of #MeToo movement through Twitter [13]. In the social movement studies exchange of hashtags is often named “hashtag activism”. The authors supposed that SMO-s co-create meanings and words in social networks. SNA of ego-networks (feminism was the ego), thematic analysis and correlation tests were used. Researchers computed frequencies and degree centralities. The relationship between themes and retweets was also analyzed.

More practically oriented direction of hashtag SNA is analysis of individual accounts positioning. He and Tan applied k-core analysis method for the extraction of most catching attention topics in and when with principal component analysis computed tweet heat factor and user authority factor [14].

Second direction of analysis is the studies of communication between public actors and masses (consumers, voters ant etc.). Hong and his colleagues collected Facebook data on five technology companies [15]. They applied to the analysis dialogic communication theory and examined clusters, co-occurrence and visualized linkages between companies. Results showed that companies with the high reputation are not always more communicating with publics compared with the low reputation companies. Higher reputation was associated with more positive words, lower reputation had no prevalent type of used words. Hosseini, Diraby and Shalaby analyzed communication between transit agencies and their customer [16]. Scholars used Twitter discussions data and customer satisfaction surveys. The word frequencies were calculated, density, diameter and degree centralities distributions, percentages of labelled tweets and discrimination information divergence, sub communities based on Louvain algorithms were detected.

Third direction of semantic network analysis is the studies of the image or representations. The goal of such research is to understand the framing of perception of something. This perception could be connected with the public opinion on the selected topic. For example, Jiang, Anderton, Ronald and Barnett researched the representations of GMO [17]. The data was collected from U.S. federal websites, pages from Google search and online news. Computer-assisted SMA was applied, authors computed eigenvector centralities, found out common works in different sources, analyzed modularity. Lycarião, Alves and Santos analyzed opinion leadership in social networks, they studied creation of attitudes towards decriminalization of abortions [18]. Ego-network, which used proabortion hashtag was visually analyzed, unfortunately, network measures were not computed but conclusions about the connection of structural position and leadership were made.

This article could be placed in the third category of SNA application, because we explored the linguistic properties of Internet and offline self-presentation which are partly responsible for the construction of the image of radical social movement and the outgroup (of those who do not belong to the social movement).

3 Methods and Data Analysis of the Russian Lesbian-Feminists Discourse

The methodological model which was proposed for the analysis of radical social movement discourse dissemination involved two stages: data collection and data analysis. The scheme of the data analysis process is shown on Fig. 1. We gathered and investigated two types of discourses: habitual and internet. Habitual discourse – is the discourse produced by lesbian-feminists in the everyday life. Internet discourse – is the discourse produced by lesbian-feminists online.

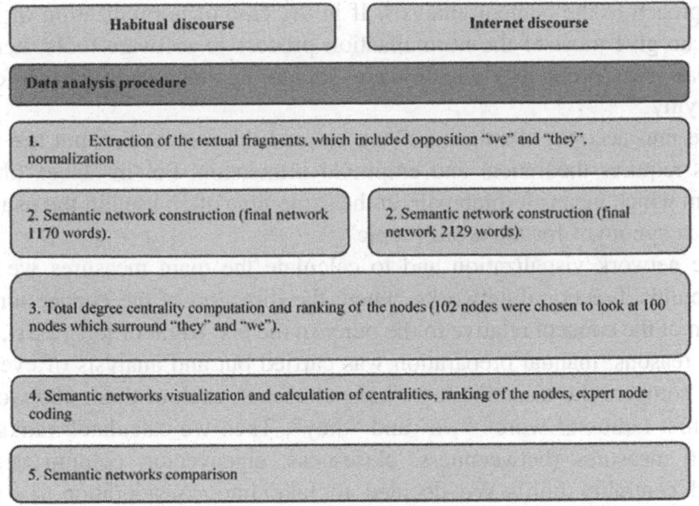

Fig. 1. Methodological model of data gathering and data analysis.

3.1 Collection Procedure of Habitual and Internet Discourses

Habitual discourse was gathered through individual semi-structured interviews with 20 women, aged from 18–35, who identified themselves as lesbian feminists. Women were recruited from the lesbian-feminist groups in the Russian social network "VK". The average length of one interview was: 1.20–2.00 h. The interviews were conducted with women who lived in 11 Russian cities and 2 European (Belgorod, Dubna, Kurgan, Minsk, Moscow, Nizhny Novgorod, Oldenburg, Orsk, Moscow region, St. Petersburg, Stavropol, Tyumen, Khabarovsk). 5 sampling techniques were used: self-selection through 4 lesbian-feminist groups and personal letters to the thought leaders of Russian lesbian feminism.

The internet discourse was obtained from the lesbian-feminists groups in "VK". Publications and comments to them were scraped from 574 groups which were posted during the period of December 2017–March 2018. This period was chosen to make the habitual and internet discourses comparable to each other. Lesbian-feminist groups were found manually by the snowball sampling method.

3.2 Data Analysis of Habitual and Internet Discourses

Whereas our purpose was to analyze the construction of "they" – "we" binary opposition, firstly, we extracted textual fragments which contained these pronouns from the internet texts and texts of the interviews. After that we performed cleaning and normalization using Automap. Normalization assumed the reduction of all nouns and adjectives to the nominative case and plural to singular. Verbs were brought to third person singular.

Content analysis in the case of analysis of radical social movements, due to the special language system that the community creates and reproduces, requires a more precise approach to the content analysis. If in the case of normalization of "ordinary" texts, we can give most of the normalization process to software tools, here we face with at least two problems, which were solved by hand-coding: (1) feminitives, (2) homonymy.

To take into account "feminitives" we created the special list, but the work with homonyms requires theoretical and empirical immersion. For instance: "theme" is a lesbian term which means lesbian pair, at the same time often used in the usual register, where it is a synonym for the word "topic".

For the network visualization and to calculate the main measures we used Ora. Automap builds directional networks, where the direction of the connection indicates the position of the concept relative to the other in the text (right or left). First, due to the mentioned reasons, manual preparation was carried out and analysis of everyday discourse. To compare the discourses, we have chosen in each of them 100 words which constitute first radius of words "we" and "they". Then we calculated ranks of words based on 6 measures (betweenness, close-ness, eigenvector, column degree, total degree and centrality hub). We decided to take into consideration six indicators, because they had different distributions and showed different leading nodes. After that, we hand-coded words which were included in 100-s and colored them in the visualizations (if you are interested in pictures and tables in color, you can write to the authors of the paper and ask them to send all materials in color). The results are shown in the Fig. 2 and in the Fig. 3, the nodes are seized according to betweenness.

4 Similarities and Differences in Semantic Networks of Ingroup and Outgroup Image Construction in Russian Lesbian Feminist Discourse

It was supposed that image of lesbian feminists is constructed through semantical spaces in the internet and in the habitual discourses and after all data analytical and data gathering stages we came up with conclusions about the similarities and differences of image construction in different discourses.

The words in both discourses were coded and we received 27 groups. In order to illustrate the created categories, we gave examples of each category in Table 2 and also included information on the existence of each category on the discourses. In the Table 2 color coding which is used in the Figs. 2 and 3 is included (h.d. – habitual discourse, i.d. – internet discourse).

4.1 General Categories Usage Comparison

From the Table 2 we see that 11 categories are endemical. This means that words connected with "violence", "plans and meetings", "material things", "feminism" and "attraction" were used to characterize ingroup and outgroup only in habitual discourse. "Plants", "money", "help", "entertainment" and "animals" were discussed only on the internet. Probably the difference in the presence of categories which frame the perception of lesbian feminists and the others is connected with the circumstances of representation which are adopted by the members of radical social movement. Internet as our qualitative part of study which is not represented in this article is usually used for the exchange of the resources and works as the main platform for the mobilization of women in different Russian regions. Therefore, it is very logical that we witnessed the usage of words "money" and "help" in the internet discourse. In habitual discourse women told their personal stories of identity formation and about their relations with different types of Others, so it is possible that in life communication they are more focused not on the promotion of lesbian feminist ideas. They solve their everyday problems which are interwoven with ideological position indirectly, from the interviews we also got to know about the troubles which women – members face when they try to demonstrate their ideology in the outlook (clothes, accessories, speech use).

We also made some general observations about the most worded categories in both discourses:

- If we look at evaluation words used in the habitual discourse, they assess Others and their community positively (Fig. 3). This could be concluded from the words "good", "best", "close", "normal", "important". The same pattern could be noticed in the internet discourse (Fig. 2), where no adjectives with "negative" meanings were not used.
- Communicative lexica in the habitual discourse is more linked to giving information "to talk", "to explain", internet discourse is more concerned with receiving "to hear", "to understand".
- "Woman images" on the internet are less heterogenous, they are neutral connected with age "woman" and "girl". In habitual discourse appears intersection of ideological standpoint and gender identity "lesbian", "feminist woman" and relational qualities "girlfriend".
- "Men images" in the internet and in habitual discourse do not significantly differ from each other. In both discourses the construction of the ingroup and outgroup images is performed with allocation of masculine sexual identity "gay" and relation "boyfriend".
- "Actions" in the habitual discourse belong to the start of doing something "to begin", "to come", "to enter". This could indicate the marginal transformational position in which are lesbian-feminists and the Others whose image they construct. On the Internet apart from "beginning" of something exist words connected with torture and disruption "to kill", to "interrupt". It is possible that these violent words are connected with the "micro-shocking" and "blatant dehumanization which happens on the Internet, that will be discussed later.
- "Cognitive operations" in the internet discourse are more active, actors "decide", "want", at the same time in the habitual discourse "they" and "we" are just bearing in mind something, they are not actively working with their information "to know", "idea", "attitude". May be the cognitive operations on the internet are more dynamic, because of collective mobilization processes which take place where.
- "Status". The same situation as with cognitive operation is happening with the statuses. On the internet ingroup and outgroup is imaged as changing their positions

"to become", "to appear". In the habitual discourse people are "leaving" and "being friends", they are static nonmoving in their life situations.

Table 2. Categories and colors.

№	Category	Existence in h. d.	Existence in i. d.	Examples
1.	women images	+	+	woman, girl, she
2.	violence	+	-	violence
3.	time	+	+	year, now, day
4.	status	+	+	to become, fall out, life
5.	quantity	+	+	one, many, quantity
6.	plants	-	+	tree, forest
7.	plans and meetings	+	-	plans, meetings
8.	places	+	+	house, Moscow, Russia
9.	people	+	+	human, people
10.	occupation	+	+	work, to work
11.	norms	+	+	law, rules
12.	money	+	+	money
13.	men images	+	+	he, man, gay, friend
14.	material things	+	-	clothes, thing
15.	help	-	+	help
16.	feminism	+	-	feminist, feminism
17.	family	+	+	mother, father, family
18.	evaluation	+	+	good, big, strongly, ready
19.	entertainment	-	+	entertainment
20.	education	+	+	information, education
21.	communication	+	+	to talk, to hear, opinion
22.	cognitive operations	+	+	to think, to calculate
23.	child	+	+	children, pregnancy
24.	body	-	+	organ, dick
25.	attraction	+	-	love, relationship
26.	animals	-	+	dog, animal
27.	actions	+	+	to sit, to interrupt, to go

4.2 Visualization of the "Ingroup" and "Outgroup" Representations

In this paper we also propose the method to visualize "we" and "they" representations (Figs. 2 and 3). We placed pronouns in the edges to make the words, which describe both of them visible. We did not change automatic layout of Ora program completely, we only moved the pronouns, so the structural relations between the words in representations did not alter. The ties between nodes in the representations were not analyzed in this paper, but they are also very informative, because they show how words organized on chains, influence each other meanings and the whole meaning of the representation.

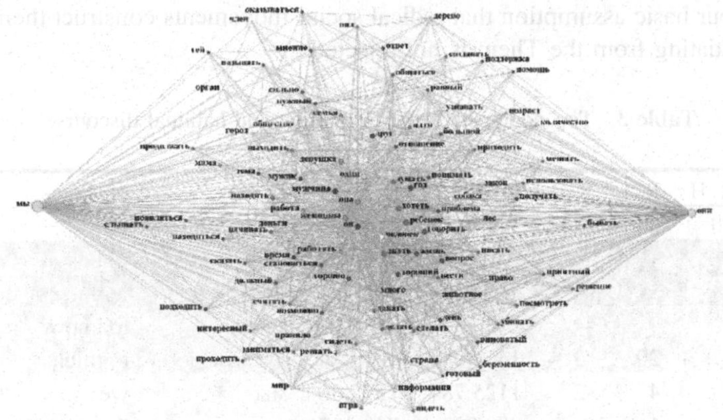

Fig. 2. Internet discourse. (Color figure online)

We colored nodes according to groups to which they belong, except the binary opposition which was painted yellow. To distinguish between discourses, we made links in the internet discourse – red and in the habitual discourse – blue.

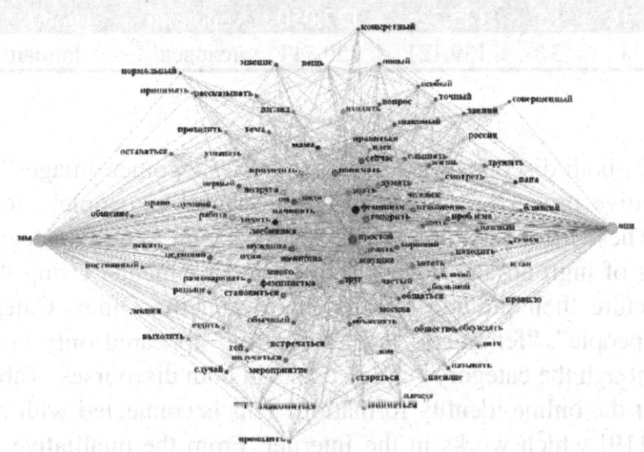

Fig. 3. Habitual discourse. (Color figure online)

4.3 Top Nodes Centralities and Ranks in Discourse Analysis

Next, we compared the discourses using centrality measures (Tables 2 and 3). R_H – rank in the habitual discourse. R_I – rank in the internet discourse, R_d – is the difference between ranks of the word used in habitual and internet discourse. B_H and B_I are betweenness centralities of words in discourses. N_Rus and N_Trans – are words in Russian and their translation in English.

In both discourses we could notice that the biggest centralities and frequencies have words "they" and "we". The leading word in these discourses is "they". This means that lesbian feminists construct their identity mostly based on the difference of the

Other, so our basic assumption that radical social movements construct their identities by differentiating from the Them is not rejected.

Table 3. Top nodes that exist in internet and habitual discourses

R_H	R_I	R_d	B_H	B_I	N_Rus	N_Trans
10	34	-24	341,988	216,499	девушка	girl
3	19	-16	279,720	192,955	говорить	to talk
9	17	-8	233,642	61,970	понимать	to understand
5	9	-4	253,267	353,102	знать	to know
17	20	-3	147,908	100,833	думать	to think
2	4	-2	1125,784	1572,06	мы	we
1	1	0	990,094	840,407	они	they
6	6	0	434,486	236,617	женщина	woman
16	13	3	249,398	263,191	мужчина	man
33	25	8	221,265	105,118	работа	work
11	2	9	181,269	217,992	он	he
21	11	10	322,824	99,233	много	many
20	8	12	169,403	205,397	хотеть	want
30	18	12	149,788	48,512	становиться	become
31	16	15	145,725	127,050	хороший	good
34	3	31	139,121	220,711	человек	human

- Categories. In both discourses are used categories "women images", "communication", "cognitive processes", "men images", "status", "people", "evaluation" and "quantity". These means that the words which belong to these categories are kernel to the mages of ingroup and outgroup in all environments. Using these categories women structure their attitude towards them and the Other. Categories "child", "animals", "people", "feminism" and "attraction" appeared only in one of the discourses. Although the category "child" exists in both discourses (Table 2) it is more important for the online identity formation. This is connected with micro-shocking mechanism [19] which works in the Internet. From the qualitative analysis of the interviews and from online ethnography we could argue that lesbian feminism creates negative framing of pregnancy and birth giving in the Internet (they post fearful images, videos and textual posts in which the childfree position is advocated).
- Ranks. The least difference between ranks of words in discourses is between "they" and "women". The largest inequality in ranks was with words "human" and "girl". In habitual discourse women tend to use more the word "girl" and this word is more meaningful to them in comparison with habitual discourse. The high usage of word "human" in the internet discourse is probably connected with the intersection of lesbian feminism with the other radical discourses. In the Internet lesbian feminists as it was argued in the interview usually recruit new members so they may be more neutral there not to "overwhelm" newbies. The collective identity work which is performed through communication on the internet is also evident because of size of

category of words connected with communication in the Internet. In the internet there is need to persuade, show the viewpoint and provide rich informative arguments (Table 4).

Table 4. Top nodes that exist only in habitual discourse

R_H	B_H	N_Rus	N_Trans
14	157,859	сейчас	now
8	242,985	начинать	to begin
15	206,339	делать	to do
18	126,029	ходить	to walk
13	159,928	лесбиянка	lesbian
24	195,740	подруга	friend
28	140,750	феминистка	feminist
26	121,655	частый	frequent
25	111,100	отношение	attitude
42	74,331	разговаривать	talk
23	108,347	нравиться	to be attractive
12	525,715	люди	people
54	50,666	общество	society
4	613,032	простой	simple
7	430,056	феминизм	feminism

We could also see that in the internet discourse man is more discussed. This is connected with the blatant dehumanization [20] of men which is performed in the specialized groups in VK. Blatant dehumanization is connected with humiliation of men, women create jokes, memes, where they compare men with “dogs”, “coks”, “wolfs” and the other animals. This blatant dehumanization is one of the mechanisms which help to strengthen the lesbian feminist identity (Table 5).

Table 5. Top nodes that exist only in internet discourse

R_I	B_I	N_Rus	N_Trans
10	175,579	год	year
41	117,628	находить	to find
5	227,335	она	she
36	175,864	собака	dog
7	237,700	один	one
28	151,262	вопрос	communication
45	194,078	друг	friend
27	148,298	работать	to work
14	308,221	ребенок	child

5 Conclusion and Future Work

In this paper we used semantic networks to investigate the discursive mechanisms connected with the representation of ingroup and outgroup in radical social movements. Sematic networks were used for the investigations of image construction and we developed discourse similarity measure based on the centralities of words in discourses.

We came to the conclusion in this article that there is difference which could be traced on the semantic level in the identity work performed online and offline. This difference is in the structure of the networks, which were analyzed visually and using centralities measures, and in the thematic categories which create meanings around "they" and "we" in analyzed discourses.

We, indeed, as it was supposed before the study, found out that the ingroup - outgroup binary opposition is reproduced in the discourse of radical social movement (this is evident from the centrality measures of "we" and "they"). Internet discourse is more mobilizing on the collective actions, the words connected with personal current life situation of ingroup and outgroup is less relevant here than in habitual discourse, where evaluative adjectives, woman images, status nouns describe the casual life of lesbian feminist.

Our study is limited because we analyzed only 100 words which are involved in ingroup – outgroup images construction. In the future we are planning to examine all words in a more detailed manner. In addition, it is significant to highlight that we studied only one case of such Russian movement and operationalized only one discursive strategy in this paper. Nevertheless, the methodological algorithm which was used in this paper could be applied to the other radical social movement's discourses. The typology of such movements was also briefly presented in this article. In the other publications we are planning to show how the spread of radical social movement discourse through such social projecting mechanisms which we found on the qualitative level of our investigation as dehumanization, mentorship, asymmetric framing, cultural appropriation, micro-shocking, ritualization, self-stigmatization could be measured on the semantic level.

References

1. Dalgaard-Nielsen, A.: Violent radicalization in Europe: what we know and what we do not know. Stud. Conflict Terrorism **33**(9), 797–814 (2010). https://doi.org/10.1080/1057610X.2010.501423
2. Dingley, J., Herman, S.: Terrorism, radicalisation and moral panics: media and academic analysis and reporting of 2016 and 2017 'terrorism'. Small Wars Insurgencies **28**(6), 996–1013 (2017). https://doi.org/10.1080/09592318.2017.1374597
3. Fitzgerald, K.J., Rodgers, D.M.: Radical social movement organizations: a theoretical model. Sociol. Q. **41**(4), 573–592 (2000). https://doi.org/10.1111/j.1533-8525.2000.tb00074.x
4. Van Dijk, T.A.: Principles of critical discourse analysis. Discourse Soc. **4**(2), 249–283 (1993)

5. Koltsova, O., Nikolenko, S., Alexeeva, S., Nagornyy, O., Koltcov, S.: Detecting interethnic relations with the data from social media. In: Alexandrov, D.A., Boukhanovsky, A.V., Chugunov, A.V., Kabanov, Y., Koltsova, O. (eds.) DTGS 2017. CCIS, vol. 745, pp. 16–30. Springer, Cham (2017). https://doi.org/10.1007/978-3-319-69784-0_2
6. Bodrunova, S.S.: When context matters. Analyzing conflicts with the use of big textual corpora from Russian and international social media. Partecipazione e conflitto **11**(2), 497–510 (2018). https://doi.org/10.1285/i20356609v11i2p497
7. Eddington, S.M.: The communicative constitution of hate organizations online: a semantic network analysis of "Make America Great Again". Soc. Media Soc. **4**(3), 205630511879076 (2018). https://doi.org/10.1177/2056305118790763
8. Leydesdorff, L., Nerghes, A.: Co-word maps and topic modeling: a comparison using small and medium-sized corpora (N < 1,000). J. Assoc. Inf. Sci. Technol. **68**(4), 1024–1035 (2017). https://doi.org/10.1002/asi.23740
9. Appel, O., et al.: A hybrid approach to the sentiment analysis problem at the sentence level. Knowl.-Based Syst. **108**, 110–124 (2016). https://doi.org/10.1016/j.knosys.2016.05.040
10. Kang, G.J., et al.: Semantic network analysis of vaccine sentiment in online social media. Vaccine **35**(29), 3621–3638 (2017). https://doi.org/10.1016/j.vaccine.2017.05.052
11. Šćepanović, S., et al.: Semantic homophily in online communication: Evidence from Twitter. Online Soc. Netw. Media **2**, 1–18 (2017). https://doi.org/10.1016/j.osnem.2017.06.001
12. Sánchez-Rada, J.F., Iglesias, C.A.: Onyx: a linked data approach to emotion representation. Inf. Process. Manage. **52**(1), 99–114 (2016). https://doi.org/10.1016/j.ipm.2015.03.007
13. Xiong, Y., et al.: Hashtag activism and message frames among social movement organizations: Semantic network analysis and thematic analysis of Twitter during the #MeToo movement. Public Relations Rev. (2018). https://doi.org/10.1016/j.pubrev.2018.10.014
14. He, Y., Tan, J.: Study on SINA micro-blog personalized recommendation based on semantic network. Expert Syst. Appl. **42**(10), 4797–4804 (2015). https://doi.org/10.1016/j.eswa.2015.01.045
15. Hong, Y.J., et al.: High/low reputation companies' dialogic communication activities and semantic networks on Facebook: a comparative study. Technol. Forecast. Soc. Chang. **110**, 78–92 (2016). https://doi.org/10.1016/j.techfore.2016.05.003
16. Hosseini, M., et al.: Supporting sustainable system adoption: Socio-semantic analysis of transit rider debates on social media. Sustain. Cities Soc. **38**, 123–136 (2018). https://doi.org/10.1016/j.scs.2017.12.025
17. Jiang, K., et al.: Semantic network analysis reveals opposing online representations of the search term "GMO". Global Challenges **2**(1), 1700082 (2018). https://doi.org/10.1002/gch2.201700082
18. Lycarião, D., dos Santos, M.A.: Bridging semantic and social network analyses: the case of the hashtag #precisamosfalarsobreaborto (we need to talk about abortion) on Twitter. Inf. Commun. Soc. **20**(3), 368–385 (2017). https://doi.org/10.1080/1369118X.2016.1168469
19. Jacobsson, K., Lindblom, J.: Emotion work in animal rights activism: a moral-sociological perspective. Acta Sociol. **56**(1), 55–68 (2013). https://doi.org/10.1177/0001699312466180
20. Kteily, N.S., Bruneau, E.: Darker demons of our nature: the need to (re)focus attention on blatant forms of dehumanization. Curr. Dir. Psychol. Sci. **26**(6), 487–494 (2017). https://doi.org/10.1177/0963721417708230

Analysis of Newcomers Activity in Communicative Posts on GitHub

Ekaterina Skriptsova(✉), Elizaveta Voronova, Elizaveta Danilova, and Alina Bakhitova

National Research University Higher School of Economics, St. Petersburg, Russia

easkriptsova@gmail.com, voronova.eliz@gmail.com, alina.bahitova@gmail.com

Abstract. GitHub is a large platform that allows developers to host repositories with code and collaborate on various projects. With the development and expansion of open-source software (OSS) many researchers focused on various aspects of such open-source communities. Due to the availability of a wide range of projects, newcomers have an opportunity to be involved in ones that differ in terms of skills and experience required. However, new developers often face some barriers during the onboarding process. The aim of the current paper is to investigate relations towards newcomers through sentiment analysis of comments they receive in issues and pull requests in repositories of top-10 open source projects by contributor count and top-10 fastest growing open source projects based on The State of the Octoverse 2018 report by GitHub. By applying sentiment analysis we focus on differences between reactions to contributions of 'old' and 'new' developers, and find that while the majority of comments is rated as neutral, the amount of negativity is slightly higher for newcomers.

Keywords: Open source software · Newcomers · Sentiment analysis

1 Introduction

Open Source is a form of interaction among software developers which provides an opportunity to work under the same projects in an open space where other, external users can also be involved into the same project, i.e. suggest new ideas or fix bugs [1].

GitHub is one of the most popular platforms where developers can collaborate on different projects. The platform has its own issue tracking system, ability to create issues and send pull requests which allow users to make commits into the existing code. Due to the availability of a wide range of projects, newcomers have an opportunity to be involved in projects that differ in terms of skills and experience required. However, new developers often face some barriers during the onboarding process [2–5]. With the development and expansion of OSS many researchers focused on various aspects of open-source communities.

In this research we aim to investigate whether communication between developers and newcomers is different in repositories from two tops of repositories based on The

D. A. Alexandrov et al. (Eds.): DTGS 2019, CCIS 1038, pp. 452–460, 2019.
https://doi.org/10.1007/978-3-030-37858-5_38

State of the Octoverse 2018 report by GitHub [18]. The research questions this paper addresses is as follows:

***RQ1**: What comments do newcomers receive for their contributions into the projects?*

According to the report, the **fastest growing** OS projects, i.e. by percent increase in contributors, are:

(1) MicrosoftDocs/azure-docs
(2) pytorch/pytorch
(3) godotengine/godot
(4) nuxt/nuxt.js
(5) ethereum/go-ethereum
(6) wix/react-native-navigation
(7) spyder-ide/spyder
(8) tensorflow/models
(9) home-assistant/home-assistant
(10) MarlinFirmware/Marlin

Top OS projects by **unique contributors count**:

(1) Microsoft/vscode
(2) facebook/react-native
(3) tensorflow/tensorflow
(4) angular/angular-cli
(5) MicrosoftDocs/azure-docs
(6) angular/angular
(7) ansible/ansible
(8) kubernetes/kubernetes
(9) npm/npm
(10) DefinitelyTyped/DefinitelyTyped

2 Related Work

This section begins with a description of the GitHub platform and its features. Then we provide an overview of the literature that examined sentiments in developers' discussions. Finally, we move to the articles about challenges that newcomers face during the onboarding process.

2.1 GitHub—a Platform for Social Coding

GitHub is a large platform that allows developers to host repositories and collaborate on various projects. Users can create repositories for their own projects or clone the existing ones and later contribute to the original. The platform provides an opportunity to submit code via pull requests, create issues that can be assigned to other users, and other software engineering interactions including code review. The development of

GitHub has prompted research from different angles. Some focused on pull requests [6], analysis of issues [7], and its social network structure [8–10], to name a few.

GitHub has not only technical features but social ones as well. Developers can stay updated about the activity of other users and repositories by following and watching them. GitHub has a feed where users can see the activity of others and updates on comments on issues and pull requests in repositories [9, 11]. Users can interact with each other by creating and commenting on issues, submitting pull requests, and forking repositories. One area of the research primarily focused on GitHub's social features. For instance, William Leibzon analyzed the structure of the developers' network and the way users collaborate and introduced a network metric to measure collaboration between the core members, which also was connected to the likelihood of the project to be successful [9].

2.2 Sentiment Analysis in Software Engineering and GitHub

Many studies focused on sentiment analysis in order to analyze the discussions of developers as emotions have a high impact on productivity, work quality, creativity, and job satisfaction [12]. For instance, Singh & Singh studied the impact of refactoring activities on the sentiments of developers in open source projects, and found that more negative than positive sentiments are expressed while performing such type of tasks [13]. Paul et al. also compared expressions of sentiments during code review between female and male developers, and in general, males use more highly offensive words [14]. Work published by Imtiaz et al. questions the reliability of such tools, and states that analyses may be unreliable as tools have a low agreement with human ratings, however, agreement of human raters is low as well [15].

Another article examined communication patterns of developers by distinguishing contributors into one-commit and multi-commit. The results showed that one-commit developers appeared to be more active and polite in comments than multi-commit developers [8].

One of the recent works presented a large scale empirical study on how emojis are used in development-related communications. The authors found that developers have emoji usage patterns, own interpretations of its meaning and the most favored emojis on GitHub are quite different from Twitter. Furthermore, usage of emojis shows a positive and supportive culture within the community, and a tendency to express positivity through emojis was also identified [16].

2.3 Newcomers

Other areas of research focus on the onboarding process of newcomers. Integration into the OSS can be a tough task due to various social and technical barriers that in many cases lead to dropouts [2–5]. Support of new developers' onboarding is crucial as many projects rely on continuous recruiting of new contributors [3, 5].

Paul et al. proved that the proportion of negative comments on the platform is bigger than positive, which is logical due to the main goal of the comments (bugs fixes) [14]. As newcomers sometimes are not experienced and skilled enough and may be unaware of community rules, we suggest that the number of negative comments for them will be higher.

***H1**: Newcomers receive more negative comments than regular developers.*

Steinmacher et al. investigated difficulties that newcomers face when making their first contribution to a project. They found that less than 20% of new developers became long-term contributors, and the decision to abandon projects was influenced by such factors as the politeness and helpfulness of answers and its author, and no evidence was found for the lack of answer [3]. However, Mendez et al. highlighted that 31% of all barriers are related to the community, including both the lack of answers and late answers. They defined such barriers as "reception issues" which mostly consists of rude and impolite or delayed answers or no answers at all [17]. Thus, such a negative experience may negatively influence the newcomers' decision to contribute. We also suggest that the amount of negativity and reaction to its receival will differ depending on whether the repository belongs to the lists of top projects by a number of contributors or by the speed of growth as they may have a different attitude towards new members. In particular, those with a high number of contributors may have a lower interest in retaining new members since there are already many developers who can contribute to the project.

***H2a**: Fast-growing projects are more open to newcomers, therefore newcomers receive less negative and continue to contribute.*

***H2b**: Projects with high number of experienced developers are more closed for newcomers, which causes more negativity in comments and, consequently, a lower retention rate.*

3 Data and Methods

Newcomers on GitHub are involved in a variety of projects that differ in terms of difficulty, skills and effort required. Some of the newcomers are skilled enough to commit into large well-known and popular projects. This research is focused on communication between developers and new members in top-10 open source projects by contributor count and top-10 fastest growing open source projects in 2018 selected based on The State of the Octoverse report by GitHub [18]. We hypothesize that it requires courage for newcomers to join projects where many things are already done by experienced developers and due to the possible complexity of the developed products. We suggest that these top-10 lists will also differ in terms of discussion participants: top fastest-growing projects may attract more new developers, while communicational posts in top projects by contributor count will include more comments from non-newbies that are aware of the existing community structure, thus, the discussion itself may differ in terms of content and sentiment. This also allows us to leave only big projects where active communication between various types of developers is present.

We define newcomers as those who contributed to the project repository less than 3 times, while he or she could have contributed to other open-source projects on GitHub.

The mean number of contributions for fastest-growing projects is 3.45, median 1, for the top by contributors count: mean 3.32, median 1.

3.1 Data

The first dataset with basic information about the repositories was collected using PyGitHub Python library which enables to manage GitHub repositories, user profiles, organizations, and access the GitHub API to collect data from these resources [19]. Data about issues and pull requests was collected using scraping due to the limitations of the GitHub API.

The following Table 1 gives a summary of parameters which were collected for repositories, issues and pull requests (communicative posts). The final dataset with comments contained 2 381 800 comments for top-10 open source projects by contributor count and 761 893 comments for top-10 fastest growing open source projects.

Table 1. Summary of parameters to be collected for repositories, issues, pull requests and users.

Type	Parameters
Repositories	Title, description, tags, forks, stargazers, watchers, collaborators full name of the repository *(owner/title)*, title of repository, description, owner, programming languages used, number of forks, number of stargazers, number of watchers, number of open issues, topics *(i.e. tags)*, list of contributors
Issues & pull requests	Repository author *(company name)*, repository title, issue/PR title, issue number, state, reviewers/assignees, labels, created at, number of participants, issue's comment number, reactions, date of comment, user's status *(contributor, author, member, collaborator)*, commentator's login, who closed an issue/PR *(if so)*, closed at, text of comment

3.2 Methods

The analysis is organized as follows. At first we provided a descriptive analysis of the dataset and identified the newcomers. Then we employed dictionary-based sentiment analysis for a deeper understanding of communication in issues and PR comments, i.e. in communicational posts. VADER sentiment analysis tool was chosen due to its appropriate detection of comments' sentiment taking into account specific narrow words, emojis and punctuation. Thus, reactions on GitHub (introduced in March 2016) [20] and emojis are included into our analysis as they can act as a complementary indicator of sentiments in developers' communication [16], and act as an indicator of positivity or negativity towards a newcomer. The original VADER lexicon was updated with words with specific meaning at GitHub, such as "bug", "ship it", "LGTM". The selected words were scored by 5 individuals independently and then averaged.

4 Results

Newcomers face a variety of difficulties during their first commits. This, in turn, influences their further contribution behaviour and overall engagement into OSS. The following Fig. 1 presents the percentage of newcomers, i.e. those who created less than 3 contributions. The indicator is higher for top-10 projects by contributors count (med. 0.89, comp. to 0.84). However, it is not surprising as the second top was selected by the number of unique contributors.

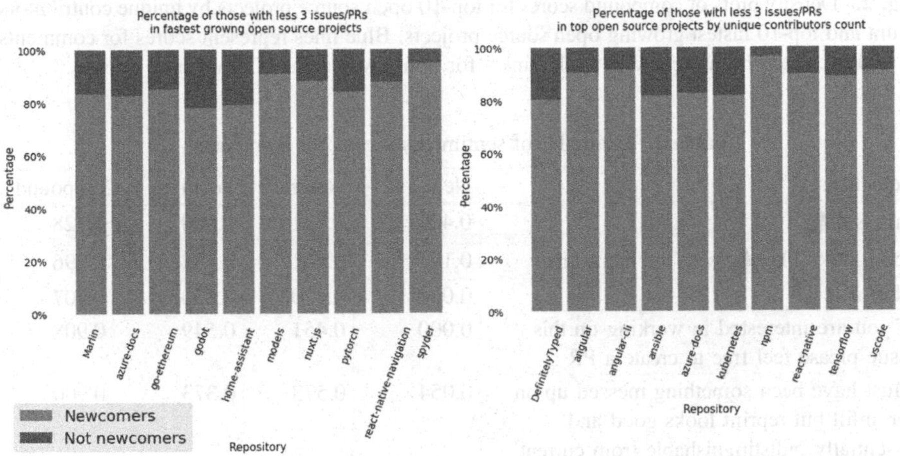

Fig. 1. Percentage of newcomers (users with 1–2 issues) for top-10 fastest growing open-source projects and for top-10 open source projects by unique contributors count. Newcomers are colored in blue, pink - non-newcomers. (Color figure online)

As the main method for this research is sentiment analysis, the next Fig. 2 presents the density of compound scores for comments depending on whether the issue or pull request was created by a newcomer or experienced developer. We hypothesized that newcomers will receive more negative comments and reactions, and the situation will differ between two tops. Based on our analysis, the major part of comments was rated as neutral for both groups of developers. The amount of negativity is slightly higher for newcomers in both tops of repositories. Distribution of compound scores for top projects by unique contributors count seem to be more different for newcomers and non-newcomers than within fastest-growing projects.

The following Table 2 shows examples of model's scores for randomly selected comments from the dataset. Overall, it detects both positivity and negativity and takes punctuation and emojis into consideration. However, some sentences (2nd example) are marked as positive while it might be considered as rather negative.

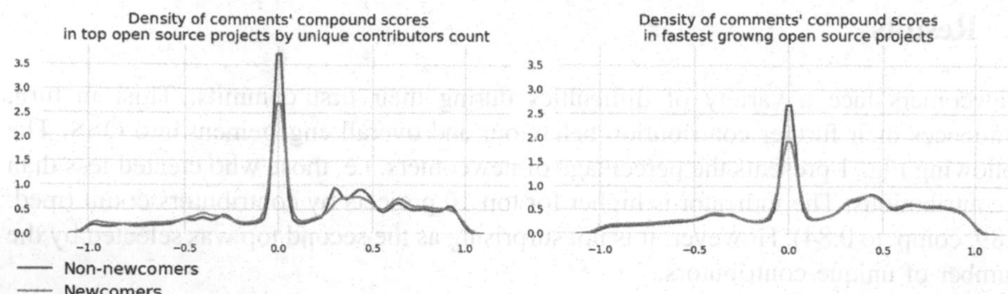

Fig. 2. Density plots of compound scores for top-10 open source projects by unique contributors count and top-10 fastest growing open source projects. Blue lines represent scores for comments to issues created by newcomers, while pink - for non-newcomers. (Color figure online)

Table 2. Examples of sentiments scores for comments.

Sentences	Negative	Neutral	Positive	Compound
This is a	0.429	0.571	0.000	−0.128
Yes - looks like with the extra line	0.197	0.461	0.342	0.296
Ship it!!!	0.000	0.170	0.830	0.707
If you are interested in working on this issue please feel free to create a PR :)	0.000	0.451	0.549	0.908
Must have been something messed up on the infill but reprint looks good and essentially indistinguishable from current LINEAR_ADV code #shipit ;)	0.054	0.573	0.373	0.900
Fault isolation is not about scalability but isolating resource consumption. For example what happens in one function eats up all threads or memory? Or if one function can cause the whole machine to be crushed?	0.195	0.805	0.000	−0.776

5 Conclusion

In this work, we analyzed the relationship towards newcomers by applying sentiment analysis to comments they receive in issues and pull requests in repositories of top-10 open source projects by contributor count and top-10 fastest growing open source projects based on The State of the Octoverse 2018 report by GitHub. Both tops of repositories have a high percentage of users who contributed less than 3 times. While the majority of comments was rated as neutral, the amount of negativity appeared to be slightly higher for newcomers in both tops of repositories. Furthermore, the distribution of compound scores between newcomers and non-newcomers in top projects by unique contributors count appeared to be higher than for newcomers and non-newcomers within fastest-growing projects.

6 Further Work

There may be a threat to the validity as it still remains a question who should be considered as a newcomer, and whether these users are active in other repositories. Thus, it will be good to examine users' overall activity outside the selected repositories, check whether and how it differs depending on the skills required in further research. The "developers" context should be examined more clearly and other lexicons may be used in order to receive sentiment scores.

References

1. Hars, A., Shaosong O.: Working for free? Motivations of participating in open source projects. In: Proceedings of the 34th Annual Hawaii International Conference on System Sciences, p. 9. IEEE (2001)
2. Steinmacher, I., Conte, T., Redmiles, D., Gerosa, M.A.: Social barriers faced by newcomers placing their first contribution in open source software projects. In: Proceedings of the 18th ACM Conference on Computer Supported Cooperative Work & Social Computing (CSCW 2015), pp. 1379–1392. Association for Computing Machinery, New York (2015)
3. Steinmacher, I., Wiese, I., Chaves, A.P., Gerosa, M.A.: Why do newcomers abandon open source software projects? In: Proceedings of the 2013 6th International Workshop on Cooperative and Human Aspects of Software Engineering, CHASE 2013. IEEE (2013)
4. Panichella, S.: Supporting newcomers in software development projects. In: 2015 IEEE International Conference on Software Maintenance and Evolution (ICSME), pp. 586–589. IEEE (2015)
5. Steinmacher, I., Wiese, I.S., Conte, T., Gerosa, M.A., Redmiles, D.: The hard life of open source software project newcomers. In: Proceedings of the 7th International Workshop on Cooperative and Human Aspects of Software Engineering - CHASE 2014, pp. 72–78. Association for Computing Machinery, New York (2014)
6. Zhang, X., et al.: How do multiple pull requests change the same code: a study of competing pull requests in GitHub. In: 2018 IEEE International Conference on Software Maintenance and Evolution (ICSME), pp. 228–239. IEEE (2018)
7. Stanik, C., Montgomery, L., Martens, D., Fucci, D., Maalej, W.: A simple NLP-based approach to support onboarding and retention in open source communities. arXiv:1806. 02592 (2018)
8. Ortu, M., Hall, T., Marchesi, M., Tonelli, R., Bowes, D., Destefanis, G.: Mining communication patterns in software development: a GitHub analysis. In: 14th International Conference on Predictive Models and data analytics in software engineering, pp. 70–79. Association for Computing Machinery, New York (2018)
9. Leibzon, W.: Social network of software development at GitHub. In: 2016 IEEE/ACM International Conference on Advances in Social Networks Analysis and Mining (ASONAM), pp. 1374–1376. IEEE (2016)
10. Thung, F., Bissyande, T.F., Lo, D., Lingxiao J.: Network structure of social coding in GitHub. In: 2013 17th European Conference on Software Maintenance and Reengineering, pp. 323–326. IEEE Computer Society, Washington (2013)
11. Saito, Y., Fujiwara, K., Igaki, H., Yoshida, N., Iida, H.: How do GitHub users feel with pull-based development? In: 2016 7th International Workshop on Empirical Software Engineering in Practice (IWESEP), pp. 7–11. IEEE (2016)

12. Guzman, E., Azócar, D., Li, Y.: Sentiment analysis of commit comments in GitHub: an empirical study. In: Proceedings of the 11th Working Conference on Mining Software Repositories, MSR 2014. Association for Computing Machinery, New York (2014)
13. Singh, N., Singh, P.: How do code refactoring activities impact software developers' sentiments? - An empirical investigation into GitHub commits. In: 2017 24th Asia-Pacific Software Engineering Conference (APSEC), pp. 648–653. IEEE (2017)
14. Paul, R., Bosu, A., Sultana, K.Z.: Expressions of Sentiments During Code Reviews: Male vs. Female. arXiv:1812.05560 (2018)
15. Imtiaz, N., Middleton, J., Girouard, P., Murphy-Hill, E.: Sentiment and politeness analysis tools on developer discussions are unreliable, but so are people. In: Proceedings of the 3rd International Workshop on Emotion Awareness in Software Engineering – SEmotion 2018, pp. 55–61. Association for Computing Machinery, New York (2018)
16. Lu, X., Cao, Y., Chen, Z., Liu, X.: A first look at emoji usage on GitHub: an empirical study. arXiv:1812.04863 (2018)
17. Mendez, C., et al.: Open source barriers to entry, revisited: a sociotechnical perspective. In: Proceedings of the 40th International Conference on Software Engineering – ICSE 2018, pp. 1004–1015. Association for Computing Machinery, New York (2018)
18. GitHub Projects. https://octoverse.github.com/projects.html
19. PyGithub 1.43.5 documentation. https://pygithub.readthedocs.io/en/latest/introduction.html
20. Add reactions to pull requests, issues, and comments. https://github.blog/2016-03-10-add-reactions-to-pull-requests-issues-and-comments/

An Approach to Automation of User's Profile Analysis

Evgeniy Budin[1(✉)], Karina Smirnova[1], Alena Suvorova[2], and Tatiana Tulupyeva[1,3]

[1] North-West Institute of Management, Branch of RANEPA, St. Petersburg, Russia
moyapochta456@gmail.com

[2] National Research University Higher School of Economics, St. Petersburg, Russia

[3] St. Petersburg Institute for Informatics and Automation of RAS, St. Petersburg, Russia

Abstract. Information from users' profiles on social networking sites is an important data source for analysis of the users' psychological characteristics. Texts, video and audio files, images, public pages can be easily accessible and analyzed. We consider the ways of estimating the users' psychological characteristics on the base of his or her profile in the social network VKontakte. We compare different machine learning models for the analysis of user's texts, such as linear regression, decision trees, random forest, support vector machine with linear, radial and sigmoidal kernels. Also we discussed the possible further stages of research including the sentiment analysis for better text description, the analysis of profile photo, and, finally, ways of combining all steps for estimating psychological characteristics of social networks users.

Keywords: Social networks · Machine learning · Text analysis · Classification · Psychological profile · Research automation

1 Introduction

Today, social networks are an inherent part of everyday life, especially among young people [4]. Most of them have accounts on social network sites such as Twitter, Facebook, VKontakte, etc. They use them to receive news, music, videos, etc., as well as to share a lot of information about themselves. Photos [30], posts [1], a list of friends [21], audio and video files [1, 8] are usually easily accessed and widely used for analysis. All this information provides wide opportunities for research about ethnic characteristics [3], migration flows [26], principles of community formation [5], protest actions [19], personal qualities of users [17] and many other areas.

Many studies are focused on exploring personal characteristics of users, how they are reflected in social media and how they influence both online and offline behavior. For example, the paper [21] discusses relationship between the user's personality traits and his/her friends' activity. First, the author measured user's personality traits according to the five-factor method (or Big Five personality traits test – extraversion,

D. A. Alexandrov et al. (Eds.): DTGS 2019, CCIS 1038, pp. 461–467, 2019.
https://doi.org/10.1007/978-3-030-37858-5_39

agreeableness, conscientiousness, neuroticism, openness to experience) and then explored associations between personality traits and data from the user's profile in social network VKontakte. So, for example, the agreeableness was weakly positively associated with the number of friends, but it was strongly associated with the number of posts and likes. The author drew attention to the fact that a large amount of likes from the user's friends was usually observed if the user had a positive attitude to extraversion, agreeableness, emotional stability and openness to experience. Thus, the author hypothesized that this effect of the association between the user's friends and the user's traits was related to the fact that "the individual with certain attitudes to the psychological traits creates a specific social environment around him, an environment with higher sympathy and more intensive participation".

In addition to information provided by the user in his or her social network profile it is possible to consider aggregated data about user's activity, for example, the level of communication activity with other members of the social network or the degree of publicity of personal information on the network. Such kind of indicators was explored in [18] to identify the personal characteristics of users. The authors' findings suggested that users with high activity showed higher levels of orientation to communication, dependence on the opinion of others, social passivity, propensity to anxiety, instability of mood, focus on experimentation, focus on self-actualization and learning new things, desire for close relationships. Users with low activity were characterized by reduced communicativeness, autonomy and conservatism, emotional stability, consciousness, restraint, independence and detachment, dominance, reduced self-actualization, avoidance of experimentation, aspiration for stability and indecisiveness, rigidity, and prevalence of "self-promotion" and "exemplarity" strategies.

Another example is a study aimed to exploring the reflection of the psychological characteristics of users in the content published in their social network accounts [27]. In the earlier phases of the study, the researchers considered the relationship between posts published by users on their pages on the social network VKontakte and the psychological characteristics of these users. To identify the characteristics, the authors developed a classification system for different post types [28, 29]. Classification was carried out by experts manually, which makes it difficult to work with large amounts of data. It is important to note that the problem of manual processing of data extracted from social networks is relevant for most of mentioned studies. It's especially noticeable in conditions of the increasing amount of analyzed information. Also, there are several studies that demonstrate the capabilities of machine learning models for processing text data, including user posts. The most popular methods include k-nearest neighbors [12, 24], decision trees [9, 11, 22], naive Bayes [13], SVM [23], latent semantic analysis [2], neural networks [10, 22, 32]. All the listed studies can solve the problem of automatic processing of textual data, but this task is significantly complicated by the specificity of the texts and initial research objectives.

The aim of the present study is to automate the steps of the above-mentioned research about the evaluation of the user's psychological characteristics based on the information in his social network account [27–29]. The set of tasks includes building users' posts classification models (according to categories specified in [27]); further exploring of associations between the types of user's posts and his or her psychological characteristics; analysis of the association between the user's profile photo and his or her psychological characteristics; analysis of the association between the user's subscription to public pages and his or her psychological characteristics. The choice of this information from user profiles is due to the fact that it is inherent to the majority of users and a number of studies indicate the associations between these features and the psychological characteristics of users [6, 14, 25, 28, 31].

2 Methods and Data

A sample of more than 2000 posts of VKontakte social network users was used for solving the first task. The sample was marked manually by experts, i.e. each post was assigned a type in each category: "information", "emotion", "action", according to the classification from [27] (Fig. 1). Note, that the sample is highly imbalanced (for example, links type posts made up about 1% of the sample) and texts are usually very short (average length of posts is 45 words). Therefore, in addition to basic approach based on "bag of words" and frequencies, we created meta-attributes for improving the accuracy of the classification, such as whether the text was a repost, the proportion of personal pronouns in the text (I, me, my, we, our, etc.), and the presence of imperatives in the text. The idea of these attributes was based on the assumption that the reposting and imperatives may be signs of "philanthropic", "sales", or "call to action" posts, while a large proportion of personal pronouns in the text indicates a "personal" type of post. Besides, oversampling has been used to correct data imbalances.

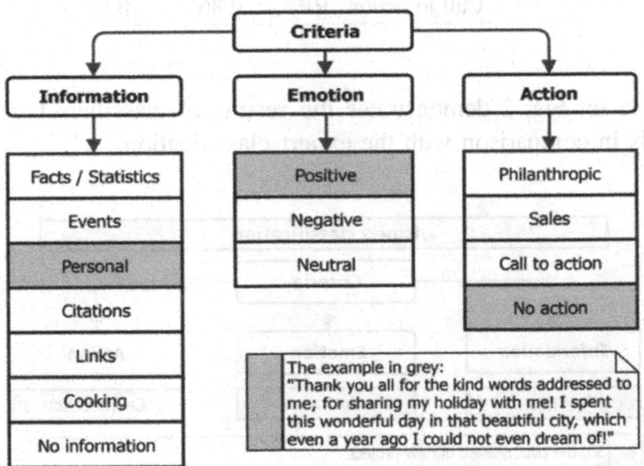

Fig. 1. Post classification system with example

All texts were pre-processed: punctuation marks, numbers, Latin letters, blank lines and stop words were removed. Words were lemmatized and their grammatical properties were extracted using MyStem from Yandex [20]. Then the method of latent Dirichlet allocation (LDA) with five topics was used and the topic per document probabilities were considered as predictors. We run several machine learning models to predict class including logistic regression, decision tree, random forest and SVM (linear, radial and sigmoid kernels). Models with the best results have been chosen to predict each type of posts.

3 Classification Results

Results are presented in the Table 1. Thus, Random Forest models showed the best results for all types of posts, except "links". The "links" were better classified by the decision tree model. It is important to note that the "cooking" and "sales" types were not included in the classification because there were only a couple such cases in the sample. We also did not classify post according to emotional criteria since the used methodology did not provide an accuracy higher than 50%.

Table 1. Best classification models measures

Criteria	Post class	Model	Accuracy	F1 score
Information	Facts	RF	0.85	0.55
	Events	RF	0.88	0.63
	Personal	RF	0.57	0.72
	Citations	RF	0.76	0.65
	Links	Tree	0.81	0.20
Action	Philanthropic	RF	0.93	0.11
	Call to action	RF	0.86	0.65

The example on Fig. 2 demonstrates the results of classifiers based on machine learning models in comparison with the expert classification.

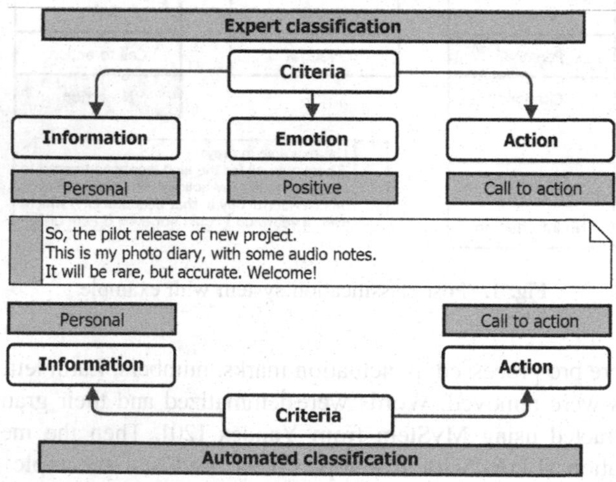

Fig. 2. Example of classification

Thus, as in earlier studies [9, 22, 23], our results showed that tree-based methods provided good prediction quality in case of working with texts. Since we used additional expert-developed text classification system, it is impossible to compare our results with other studies for predicting user psychological characteristics from social media data. But this study is an essential step for further research that can explore previously mentioned association between post classes and psychological characteristics [28]. Earlier research noted [27] that the proposed three-criteria classification provided more stable and consistent results, and it was hypothesized that such stability is related to the system's compliance with the three aspects of the study of mental processes - cognitive, affective and behavioral ones [7].

4 Further Studies

The study has several limitations worth noticing. First, the sample size is quite small, more generalizable and more stable results need larger sample: several post classes were omitted from the analysis since there were less than five positive examples of that class. Second, the LDA is a great method for topic modelling, but it has its own limitations including instability and interpretation ambiguity. Third, the present study is a part in the larger research and needs further steps described below.

The project is on its early stage and had several ways for further development. First, we plan to build a classifier for emotional criteria based on sentiment analysis using existing dictionaries. In addition, we are going to include the analysis of emoticons. Emoticons are special symbols that denote emotions in the text, so their analysis can help in determining the tonality of the posts. The role of emoticons in sentiment analysis is accented in [15, 16]. They are especially important for the analysis of texts from social networks, because texts can sometimes consist of several icons of emoticons only with no text or just a couple of words. In this case, the emotion expressed by the user is totally described by emoticons.

Second, besides the text information, as it was marked above, we plan to process the data about user's profile picture. The paper [28] accents the association between the user's psychological profile and the type of the picture. This study considers three types of a profile picture: the user's photo, a photo of user with someone (group), not the photo of user. According to that study, those users, who place not their own photo as their profile picture, demonstrate reduced social normality and courage, low diplomacy, increased independence and high displacement as a mechanism of psychological protection.

Finally, the analysis of text posts and the analysis of images will be the basis for revealing the psychological characteristics of users on the basis of the analysis of their pages in the social network VKontakte. It determines the creation of a model, based on the information obtained after the analysis of texts and images, responsible for the prediction of psychological characteristics.

References

1. Baranyuk, V., Desyatkova, A., Smirnova, O.: Approaches to defining psycho-emotional characteristics of the information image of a social network user. Int. J. Open Inf. Technol. **4** (8), 61–65 (2016)
2. Bondarchuk, D.: The use of latent semantic analysis in the tasks of classifying texts by emotional coloring. Bull. Res. Results **2**(3), 146 (2012)
3. Bonilla, Y., Rosa, J.: # Ferguson: digital protest, hashtag ethnography, and the racial politics of social media in the united states. Am. Ethnol. **42**(1), 4–17 (2015)
4. Boulianne, S.: Social media use and participation: a meta-analysis of current research. Inf. Commun. Soc. **18**(5), 524–538 (2015)
5. Centola, D., van de Rijt, A.: Choosing your network: social preferences in an online health community. Soc. Sci. Med. **125**, 19–31 (2015)
6. Dyatlova, E., Mikhina, M.: Visual images of Internet users: from photography to avatar. Bulletin of the Kostroma State University. Series: Pedagogy. Psychology. Sociokinetics **24**(4), 84–86 (2018)
7. Krylov, A.A.: Psychology. Velbi (2008)
8. Krylova (Smirnova), O., Baranyuk, V., Ishin, I.: Analysis of audio and video collections of social network users to describe their information image. Int. J. Open Inf. Technol. **5**(12), 30–38 (2017)
9. Kubarev, A., Kukushkina, O., Poddubny, V., Shevelyov, O.: Building a style sheet using text classification based on decision trees. Bull. Tomsk State Univ. Manag. Comput. Eng. Inf. **4**(21) (2012)
10. Kulikova, V.: Text classification method based on neural networks. Innov. Dev. Modern Sci. Probl. Patterns Prospects **6**, 37–40 (2017)
11. Lomotin, K., Kozlova, E., Romanov, A.: Machine learning methods application in the task of scientific text categorization on specialized texts base. Innov. Inf. Commun. Technol. **1**, 410–414 (2017)
12. Nguyen, N., Tuzovsky, A.: Classification of texts based on the assessment of semantic proximity of terms. Georesour. Eng. **320**(5). News of Tomsk Polytechnic University
13. Ovsyannikov, A., Gryzlov, I., Golubinsly, E., Smirnov, A., Vlasova, S.: Approach to automatic classification of short text messages based on modified bayes's metod. Nauchnyye vedomosti Belgorodskogo gosudarstvennogo universiteta. Seriya: Ekonomika. Informatika **8**(179), 30 (2014)
14. Obukhov, A., Churilova, E.: Modern approaches to the study of personality through narrative texts. XXI Century Teach. **4**, 331–343 (2009)
15. Read, J.: Using emoticons to reduce dependency in machine learning techniques for sentiment classification. In: Proceedings of the Student Research Workshop at the 2005 Annual Meeting of the Association for Computational Linguistics, Ann Arbor, Michigan, pp. 43–48 (2005)
16. Rubtsova, Y.: Building a body of texts to customize the tone classifier. Softw. Prod. Syst. **1**(109), 72–78 (2015)
17. Park, G., et al.: Automatic personality assessment through social media language. J. Pers. Soc. Psychol. **108**(6), 934 (2015)
18. Ryabikina, Z., Bogomolova, E.: Interrelation of personal characteristics of users of social networks of the Internet with features of their activity in the network. Polit. Netw. Electron. Sci. J. Kuban State Agrarian Univ. **109**, 1041–1057 (2015)
19. Scherman, A., Arriagada, A., Valenzuela, S.: Student and environmental protests in chile: The role of social media. Politics **35**(2), 151–171 (2015)

20. Segalovich, I., Titov, V.: Mystem [software]. https://tech.yandex.ru/mystem. Accessed 20 Mar 2019
21. Shchebetenko, S.: Settings on personality traits as a predictor of the activity of "Friends" of the user of the social network Vkontakte. Nat. Psychol. J. **4**(24), 34–44 (2016)
22. Shevelev, O., Petrakov, A.: Classification of texts using decision trees and direct propagation neural networks. Bull. Tomsk State Univ. **290**
23. Shipovskoy, V., Romanov, A.: Multi-class text classification using the support vector method. Electron. Tools Control Syst. **1–2**, 56–57 (2017)
24. Skiba, S., Loiko, V.: Data mining of users' social network profile for determination of typolgy of the consumer. part 1. Polythematic Netw. Electron. Sci. J. Kuban State Agrarian Univ. **107**
25. Slave, E.: Social and psychological characteristics of users of the social network VKontakte. Sustainable development of Russia: challenges, risks, strategies. In: Materials of the XIX International Scientific and Practical Conference: to the 25th Anniversary of the Humanitarian University, Ekaterinburg, pp. 265–270 (2016)
26. Spyratos, S., Vespe, M., Natale, F., Weber, I., Zagheni, E., Rango, M.: Migration data using social media. JRC Science Hub
27. Tulupyeva, T., Suvorova, A., Azarov, A., Tulupyev, A., Bordovskaya, N.: Computer tools in the analysis of students' digital footprints in social network: possibilities and primary results. Comput. Tools Educ. **5**
28. Tulupyeva, T., Tafintceva, A., Tulupyev, A.: An approach to the analysis of personal traits reflection in digital traces. Vestnik psikhoterapii [The Bulletin of Psychotherapy] **60**, 124–137 (2017)
29. Tulupyeva, T., Tulupyev, A., Yuschenko, N.: Social networks users value orientations expression in personal pages content (based on "vkontakte" network). Vestnik psikhoterapii [The Bulletin of Psychotherapy] **52**, 37–50 (2014)
30. Ushkin, S.: Visual images of users of the VKontakte social network. Public Opinion Monit. Econ. Soc. Change **5**(111), 159–169 (2012)
31. Voiskunsky, A.: Social perception in social networks. Bulletin of the Moscow University. Series 14: Psychology **2**, 90–104 (2014)
32. Vorobev, N., Puchkov, E.: Classification of text using convolutional neural networks. Molodoy issledovatel Dona **6**(9)

E-Society: Humanities and Education

The Use of Machine Translation System for Component Development of Adaptive Computer System for Individual Testing of Students' Knowledge

Alexander Fedosov(✉), Dina Eliseeva, and Anastasia Karnaukhova

Russian State Social University, Moscow, Russia
{alex_fedosov,eliseeva.dy}@mail.ru,
a.karnaukhova@gmail.com

Abstract. The article is devoted to the research of the modern machine translation systems as well as different aspects of their using while development and in the course of functioning of adaptive computer system for individual testing of students' knowledge. The contrastive analysis of computer-aided translation and automated translation is reported, computer-based translation in its three main modern sorts: based on rules, statistical and hybrid is estimated in the context of technological opportunities of application by both linguistics specialists and in the field of component development of learning management systems.

In the article the approaches to the problem of adaptation of computer system for individual testing of students in preparation of bachelors of engineering degrees are stated. The peculiarities of the use of machine translation systems for training course development, structuring of test material and in the process of realizing of adaptive algorithm for individual testing of students' educational progress are discussed.

Keywords: Machine translation system · Adaptive computer system · Adaptation · Computer testing

1 Introduction

Those times when a person knowing a foreign language was appreciated "as valuable as gold" whether being a member of special caste, connected by familial profession of translator, as in Carthage, or a polyglot, being proficient in several languages, as in the following centuries in Europe, recede into the past. The technologies which became habitual in the 21st century take root also into the area of the linguistic translation, bring a possibility of the modern person to the new level of development, allowing to carry out interaction by means of information and communication technologies [1].

A lot of modern researches in the field of the linguistic translation are focused on finding ways of implementation of technologies of its automation, making demands of search of practical, effective methods of implementation of the translations of large volumes of information, at the same time reducing time and financial expenditure.

D. A. Alexandrov et al. (Eds.): DTGS 2019, CCIS 1038, pp. 471–482, 2019.
https://doi.org/10.1007/978-3-030-37858-5_40

The scope of the translation by means of the software is very high: common usage of so-called "translators" in the form of various mobile applications, translation systems which became integral parts of Internet browsers, the software for professionals and the audiovisual translation with the advent of which the new era in the area of the translation activity connected, first of all, with the film industry began (in particular, the screen translation).

Computer-aided translation is a translation of texts with the help of computer technology. Translation process is carried out by a man, and the software serves as a tool helping to make a translation for smaller time and with the best quality. The main idea of this process was stated in 1980 by Martin Kay: "By taking over what is mechanical and routine, it (computer) frees human beings for what is essentially human" [2].

So-called "translation memory" gained distribution. Translation Memory is a database which contains earlier translated texts, at the same time if in the set translation phrases or sentences with exact coincidence of earlier translated text from the database, the computer automatically sets it up in the text, and if the coincidence not of 100 percent, the software suggests a translator to make adjustment. The systems of this type allowed to accelerate the translation process, provided uniformity of the translation of terminology that permitted to apply them in the field of technical translation successfully. From the most widespread Translation Memory systems it is possible to distinguish the following ones: Déjà Vu of the company Atril; OmegaT (freely extended system under the license GNU); Trados (widespread in Russia from the T-service company); Star Transit; Wordfast (a set of macros for MS Word), etc [2–5].

Machine translation systems make a translation of texts in the automatic mode without participation of a man, at the same time the following types of forming of interaction are possible:

- a translation with pre-editing that is a man prepares the original text for processing by the computer program (simplifies phrases, eliminates possible discrepancies);
- a translation with post-editing that is the computer program makes a translation of the original text, and a man proofreads;
- a translation with inter-editing that is a man interferes with the work of the translation system in difficult cases of the translation;
- a mixed translation that is the use of systems of pre-editing and post-editing;
- a computer-aided translation that is the use of computer dictionaries in process of translation by a man;
- translation systems with division of labor that is a computer program translates only rigidly structured phrases, all the rest is done by a man.

2 The Characteristics of Main Types of Machine Translation Systems

Today the problem of copyright protection in the Russian Federation is actually important more than ever. It is connected not so much with definite gaps and omissions in Russian legislation as mainly with low level of legal culture in the society in general.

It's obvious that the formation of legal culture firstly of youth is primary target, facing the system of education.

Nowadays there are three main types of machine translation systems: rule-based, statistical and hybrid.

Rule-Based Machine Translation (RBMT) implies machine translation systems on the basis of linguistic information on original and target languages. They consist of the bilingual dictionaries and grammars covering the main semantic, morphological, syntactic principles of each language [7, 8].

According to Fig. 1 [9] on the basis of these data the original text is being transformed to the target text sentence-by-sentence. Such approach to machine translation is also called classical. The principle of work of such systems is based on connection of structures of the texts (the original and conclusive result – final). These systems have several subspecies which are interlinguistic, transfer systems and the systems of the word-by-word translation.

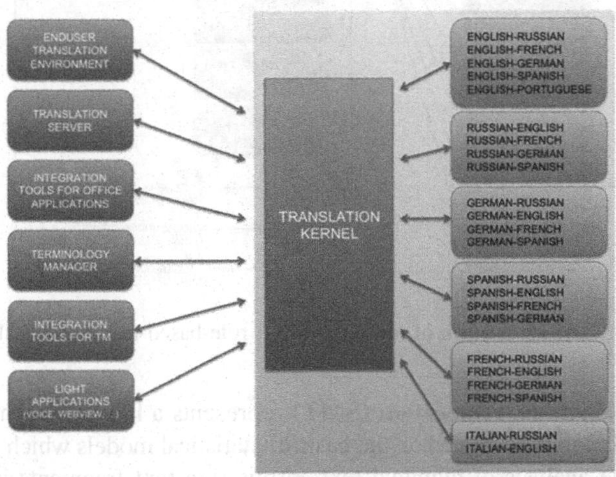

Fig. 1. The main components of rule-based machine translation

Such systems are notable for translation accuracy, they have a possibility of setting for a certain topical area, but, at the same time, demand regular updating of databases, also they are expensive at a development and introduction stage.

The component of a system unites all translation engines for all languages which are supported by a system, and provides the interface between these modules and other modules of a system by means of API and also supports work with such objects of a system as the list of reserved words, translation patterns, mechanisms of protection, etc.

Let's look at the example of the PROMT Translation Software system (Fig. 2) work of such systems where all the translation engines have similar structure and generally consist of three main components which are the following [9]:

– a linguistic database which comprises linguistic data for a language pair: dictionaries, formal description of morphology, formal description of grammar;

- an editor of the dictionary which provides access to difficult dictionary information via the interface of the program;
- a translator which provides translation process.

The computer programming language which is used for development of the software is C++. At the same time for ensuring support of development of modules which functions will work in different operating systems (such as Win32, Linux, WinCE) the technological Single Source Technology method is used.

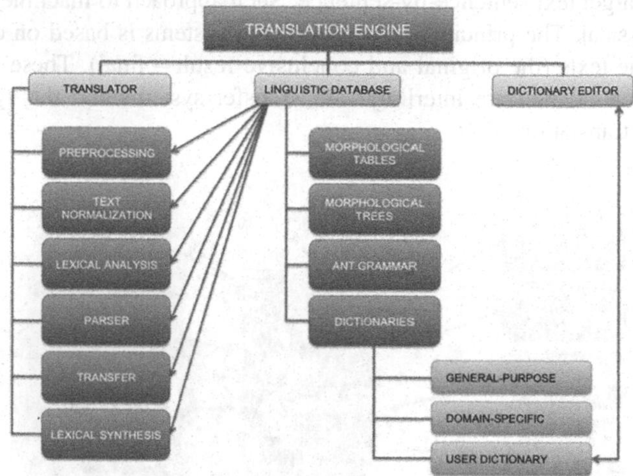

Fig. 2. The mechanism of translation into rule-based machine translation

Statistical Machine Translation (SMT) represents a kind of machine translation where the translation is generated on the basis of statistical models which parameters are derivative of the analysis of bilingual text corpus (big text fragments in original language). These systems are self-learning using at the same time earlier received statistics, and it is also not required to retrain a system introducing a new language [7, 10].

Such systems have rather simple setting for various topical areas. Besides, one of the essential advantages of statistical machine translation is rather high translation quality when performing a condition of existence of qualitative text corpuses and at long training of a system. These types of systems do not need presence of professional linguists; IT-engineer builds the system, at the same time his effort is minimized. A difficult mathematical apparatus is a disadvantage, and also for the training of a system it is necessary to have big parallel text corpuses, which essentially affects quality of the final translation. Besides training of a system takes rather long time and while integrating a new language it is necessary to carry out the analysis of a very large number of parallel corpuses.

Hybrid translation technology assumes [11]:

- use of statistical methods for development of dictionary bases in the automatic way on the basis of parallel corpuses;
- making several possible translations at the lexical level and at the level of syntactic sentence structure of a target language;
- post-editing in the automatic mode and the choice of the best (the most probable) translation from possible ones on the basis of the language model constructed on a certain corpus of a target language.

Hybrid system (Fig. 3), as well as statistical one, go through a process of training at parallel data. This process can be divided into three stages:

- a translation of an initial part of the parallel corpus in original language by a basic RBMT translation engine;
- setting of statistical model of the translation from the computer language into the human one;
- setting of statistical model on the basis of the corpus of a target language.

Hybrid systems allow to unite all advantages of rule-based machine translation and the statistical machine translation systems. The systems of hybrid translation Abbyy Compreno (from the Russian company "ABBYY"), Google Translate, Yandex. Translate became widespread.

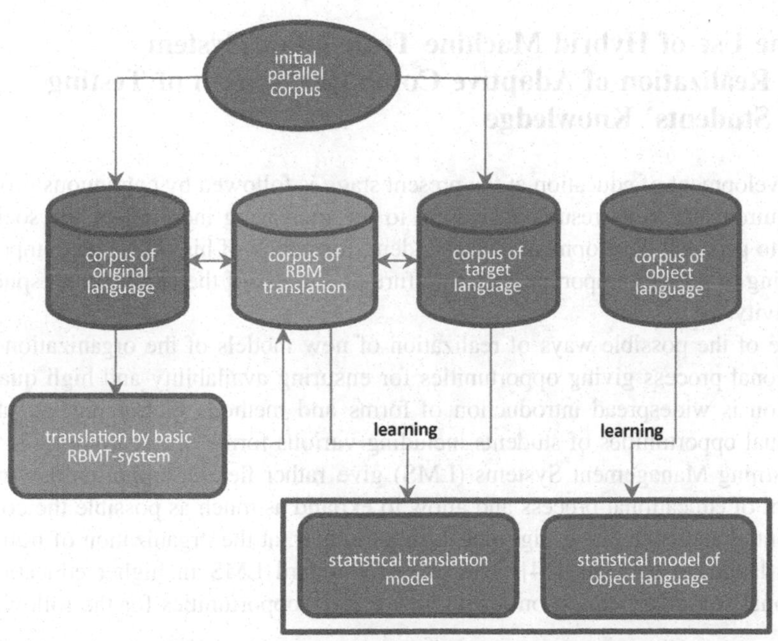

Fig. 3. The pattern of training of a hybrid system

One of successful developers in Russian market is the company PROMT. In particular, it develops the hybrid system based on introduction of statistical methods into the basic RBMT translation model. RBMT-system is complemented with two components:

- a module of statistical post-editing;
- a module of language patterns.

Statistical post-editing allows to smooth RBMT translation, bringing it closer to a natural language and at the same time keeping accurate structure of the output text. The language patterns are used for assessment of smoothness and grammatical correctness of the variants of translation generated by a hybrid system.

Having carried out the analysis of machine translation systems it is possible to draw a conclusion on existence of essential advantages of such software among which there are first of all the high speed of the linguistic translation of big texts, possibility of their use as a tool for realization of new models of teaching [1].

Besides in modern conditions at universal prevalence of the computer equipment it is possible to use such systems on various devices.

At undoubted convenience of machine translation systems the developers have good scope of work in respect of further development and technological improvement of the pointed systems. First of all the disadvantages connected with incomplete accounting of grammar rules and linguistic methods require correction which will allow to eliminate grammar and lexical errors in final texts.

3 The Use of Hybrid Machine Translation System at Realization of Adaptive Computer System of Testing of Students' Knowledge

The development of education at the present stage is followed by continuous growth of the requirements to its results answering to the increasing inquiries of the society. It relates to personal development of the student, formation of his skills and competences belonging to socially important, defining further success of the person in all spheres of his activity.

One of the possible ways of realization of new models of the organization of the educational process giving opportunities for ensuring availability and high quality of education is widespread introduction of forms and methods of training, adaptive to individual opportunities of students including various forms of e-learning [12, 13].

Learning Management Systems (LMS) give rather flexible opportunities in management of educational process and allow to expand as much as possible the coverage of potential audience that is significant, in particular, at the organization of training of foreign-language students [14]. The use of standard LMS in higher education and vocational secondary education institutions creates opportunities for the following:

- activation of educational process by means of creation of the information educational environment of modern level combining rationally organized information and testing materials with the latest information technologies;

– creation of conditions for active interaction of students with the information educational environment in addition to traditional forms of education;
– personal capacity building of students and training their skills of independent work by its rational organization at the modern level of development of information technologies.

While developing the electronic training courses realized in Learning Management Systems (LMS) and focused on studying of engineering disciplines the question of linguistic translation and structuring of educational content is exclusively relevant that assumes the solution of the following tasks.

1. The development of electronic training materials on the studied discipline in working languages with the use of functional lexis and the support on foreign-language training materials providing the necessary volume of knowledge of a subject (including an integrative component);
2. The development of test materials in working languages with the use of functional lexis on the studied discipline, providing modular check of level of the grasping both the theoretical and practical knowledge.

The disadvantage of traditional approach to the creation of information modules and their giving to the student is full copying of a teaching way when in group training each student is given the training material in the same invariable view. The modern information technologies, including means of computer linguistics by means of variable approach to creation and delivery of material are capable to consider the level of training and perception of the specific student and to align educational process with him flexibly [15].

The use of machine translation systems at realization of the electronic training courses realized in learning management systems allows:

– To activate self-study of information resources on the discipline in other languages;
– To use specific purposes dictionaries with the opportunity of their automatic configuration and connection while studying;
– To make a translation of training materials with maintaining the original structure of the initial document;
– To make a translation taking into account the topical area:
– To maintain the better translations, to create user's dictionaries;
– To create specialized glossaries on the discipline or a cycle of disciplines for the further use at machine translation.

At forming the chosen data file as training materials the information first of all has to be extremely structured. This problem is relevant because both the lack of necessary data, and a chaotic heap of the big, poorly connected among themselves information arrays are harmful to the organization of the educational process (which is especially realized in an electronic form).

The appliance of machine translation systems, in particular hybrid systems, when processing educational information in addition promotes the solution of a problem of structuring information.

For the division of information into separate components and for the establishment of necessary connections between them it is possible to use three basic types of structures:

1. parallel in which separate components are equivalent and are sorted according to any attribute;
2. hierarchic in which the treelike structure grows of a root where knots of the lower level depend only on one overlying knot;
3. network in which there can be connections between the elements of any levels.

The first principle (parallel) is logical to apply to creation of such information structures which are rather simple and also the information objects are a little or almost not connected among themselves.

The hierarchic principle along with existence of connections between the studied information objects reflects some orderliness existing between them. As the process of training is focused (directed) in time, it is the ideally most logical to organize hierarchical orderliness according to the temporary principle that is at higher level there are those objects which are studied earlier.

In real training materials the hierarchic principle should be broken in many cases, using references either between elements of one level or the reference to the previous knots, i.e. actually general structure of content is network.

All main resource materials on each studied discipline entered into LMS according to their destination usually are divided into two main units: information and testing. They can be complemented with other types of materials which play a supporting role in studying of a discipline.

The optimal structure of the information block of the training materials for a student course is the following: all block includes from 3 to 5 sections with size from 20 to 40 or 50 pages of the informative text; each section includes from 3 to 5 subsections with the size from 5 to 12 or 15 pages; each information subsection contains all necessary theoretical data and also examples of the solution of all necessary types of practical tasks. It is possible to accept as the module like an indivisible minimum unit of content the subsection or any logically finished parts [16].

As the electronic training materials are always built up on the basis of literary statement of material, for allocation of modules and sections the following agreements are offered:

1. to accept one paragraph having the independent semantic contents or several come in sequence paragraphs containing the general semantic filling as the module;
2. the information section has one chapter in which the finished part of the studied discipline or several interdependent heads come in sequence are completely opened.

The testing block is made by the control materials tied to modules. They can be generally divided into the following groups:

1. basic recitation in which knowledge of the concepts entered in the module and the main connections between them are checked;
2. advanced theoretical questions in which profound knowledge of theoretical material is checked;

3. typical tasks of the learnt material;
4. advanced tasks, etc.

In the course of individual testing it is possible to realize adaptability of the computer training system [17–19] according to the following attributes.

1. Changing of strategy of recitation depending on answers of the student. It is a traditional type of adaptability; it can be realized due to special structure of an algorithm of recitation.
2. According to the purpose the testing is divided into:
   - educational testing conducted independently for assessment of knowledge by the student himself;
   - control testing carried out under the supervision of the teacher for objective assessment of actual level of knowledge; the important special cases are progress check and final check.
3. According to the depth of recitation that is the depth of knowledge check (one-level, two-level, three-level according to the number of test tasks).
4. According to the volume of material the testing is divided into:
   - subsection (module);
   - section (in particular progress (midpoint) check) or several sections;
   - the whole discipline (in particular final check).

It is possible to realize the adaptability on the second attribute by means of a way of the choice of test material and delivery of results to a student and a teacher. During the educational testing the checked modules are "ordered" by the student himself and the results after each question are told only him. During the control assessment the checked modules are set by a teacher, the final result is told both a student and a teacher.

Here it is possible to use the results of processing of test material by machine translation systems taking into account the level of language training of the student.

It is possible to provide adaptability on the first and third signs by means of application of special separate basic algorithms considering quantity of stages of recitation at the minimum number of basic questions at one stage which are 2.

It is possible to realize adaptability on the fourth attribute by large-scale increase in numbers of tests at basic option of an algorithm. Adaptability on this attribute is also can be realized on the basis of inclusion in the checked material of the foreign-language elements and tasks of progress and final check demanding application of machine translation systems.

The offered approach and the corresponding adaptive algorithm of an examination are stated in detail in [13, 20] and in the maximum degree consider essential characteristics of computer process of knowledge check and allow to build an individual learning path of students when using various interactive means, including machine translation systems.

A skilled and experimental examination of a technique of adaptive computer testing with application of the machine translation system during the work with training materials when teaching foreign-language students on the basis of RSSU which showed increase in motivation of educational activity of students of experimental group, improvement of quality of the acquired knowledge of the studied discipline, increase in level of professional knowledge and skills of independent work with foreign-language training materials was carried out.

The positive reviews were received not only from students of experimental group, but also from the teachers training students at the subsequent related disciplines who noticed more high standard of knowledge of the students of a bachelor degree who mastered a course with use of an adaptive computer system of testing of knowledge and also increase in the general positive working spirit when studying a course of discipline by the developed technique in experimental groups was noted that was expressed in aspiration of students to assimilation of a training material of a course within studies, bigger concentration and accuracy when performing laboratory and test tasks (Fig. 4).

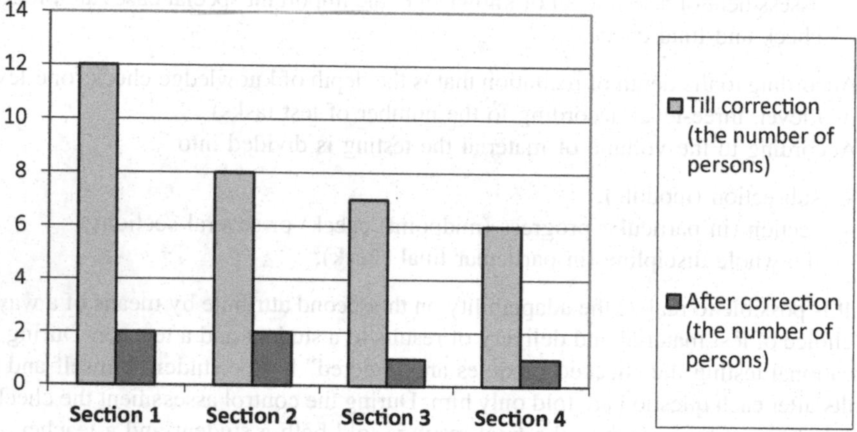

Fig. 4. Change in the number of students failing by sections of the course in the experimental group

Thus, the results of the experiment confirmed efficiency of application of adaptive computer testing of knowledge for improvement of quality of professional education of foreign-language students of a bachelor degree.

4 Conclusion and Further Research

The methodical approaches to application of an adaptive computer system for testing offered by authors gives the chance to look in a new way at a problem of development of student courses in a format of interactive training, to adapt the process of computer testing of students' knowledge at the same time according to several parameters and to reach higher educational rates when training students, building an individual learning path.

The use of machine translation systems in course of realization of electronic training courses allows to solve a problem of structuring training materials and development of test materials for realization of an adaptive algorithm of individual testing more effectively that allows to introduce it widely in process of training of students of engineering specialties including foreign-language students.

The authors see the direction of researches in further integration of machine translation systems and the adaptive computer system of individual assessment of students' knowledge as elements of the virtual educational environment of the university; introduction of machine translation systems, for example, in the form of the program agent, into various applications of educational appointment, including the applications for the automated diagnostics of students' knowledge; expansion of use of mobile platforms.

References

1. Shevchuk, V.N.: Information Technologies in Translation. Electronic Resources of the Translator-2. Zebra E, Moscow (2013). (in Russian)
2. Kay, M.: The proper place of men and machines in language translation. Mach. Transl. **12**, 3–23 (1997). https://doi.org/10.1023/A:1007911416676. Research report CSL-80-11, Xerox Palo Alto Research Center, Palo Alto, CA. It is reprinted in 1997
3. Baranov, A.N.: Introduction to Applied Linguistics. Editorial URSS, Moscow (2001). (in Russian)
4. Zubov, A.V.: Information Technologies in Linguistics. Academy, Moscow (2004). (in Russian)
5. Marchuk, Y.: Computational Linguistics. AST Vostok-Zapad, Moscow (2007). (in Russian)
6. Tissen, Y.: The internet in work of the translator. World Transl. **2**, 45–62 (2000). (in Russian)
7. Sreelekha, S., Bhattacharyya, P., Malathi, D.: Statistical vs. rule-based machine translation: a comparative study on Indian languages. In: Dash, S.S., Das, S., Panigrahi, B.K. (eds.) International Conference on Intelligent Computing and Applications. AISC, vol. 632, pp. 663–675. Springer, Singapore (2018). https://doi.org/10.1007/978-981-10-5520-1_59
8. Wilks, Y.: Machine Translation. Its Scope and Limits. Springer, Heidelberg (2009). https://doi.org/10.1007/978-0-387-72774-5
9. PROMT. Automated Translation Solutions. http://www.promt.ru
10. Koehn, P.: Statistical Machine Translation. Cambridge University Press, Cambridge (2009). https://doi.org/10.1017/CBO9780511815829
11. Xuan, H.W., Li, W., Tang, G.Y.: An advanced review of hybrid machine translation (HMT). Procedia Eng. (2012). https://doi.org/10.1016/j.proeng.2012.01.432
12. Zenkina, S.V., Sharonova, O.V.: Forms, tools and technologies of interactive educational interaction in distance learning. Inform. Educ. **4**(273), 16–19 (2016). (in Russian)
13. Eliseeva, D.Yu., Fedosov, A.Yu., Mnatsakanyan, O.L., Grigoreva, S.V., Dmitrieva, T.V.: Application of Adaptive Computer Testing as a Means of Interactive Learning for Building an Individual Educational Trajectory of a Student. In: NORDSCI Conference on Social Sciences, pp. 43–59. SALMA CONSULT LTD, Sofia, (2018). https://doi.org/10.32008/NORDSCI2018/B1/V1/4
14. Lapchik, M.P.: The thorny path of E-technologies in education. Inform. Educ. **8**(257), 3–11 (2014). (in Russian)
15. Baker, F.B., Kim, S.-H.: The Basics of Item Response Theory Using R. Springer, Heidelberg (2017). https://doi.org/10.1007/978-3-319-54205-8

16. Gdansky, N.I., Rysin, M.L., Levanov, D.N., Altimentova, DYu.: Adaptive Models of Dialogue in the Computer Training Systems: Monograph. RSSU publishing, Moscow (2013). (in Russian)
17. Olsen, J.B., Maynes, D.D., Slawson, D., Ho, K.: Comparison and equating of paper-administered, computer-administered, and computerized adaptive tests of achievement. In: Paper Presented at the Annual Meeting of the American Educational Research Association. San Francisco CA (1986)
18. Wainer, H. (ed.): Computerized Adaptive Testing: A Primer, 2nd edn. Lawrence Erlbaum, London (2000)
19. Weiss, D.J.: New Horizons in Testing: Latent Trait Test Theory and Computerized Adaptive Testing. Academic Press, New York (1983)
20. Altimentova, D.Yu., Fedosov, A.Yu.: Improvement of quality of bachelors with application of computer testing and rational modes of correction of knowledge. Pedagog. Inform. **1**, 45–53 (2017). (in Russian)

Using Virtual Reality Technology for Studying Physics

Yevgeniya Daineko(✉), Madina Ipalakova, Dana Tsoy, Zhandos Baurzhan, and Yersultanbek Yelgondy

International Information Technology University, Manas str. 34/1, Almaty, Kazakhstan
yevgeniyadaineko@gmail.com, m.ipalakova@gmail.com, danatsoy@gmail.com, zhandos.baurzhan@gmail.com, ersultan_elgondin@mail.ru

Abstract. The field of education is relatively conservative, but at the same time fast evolving sphere of human activity all around the world and in Kazakhstan as well. This is due to constant advances in all technology areas and in information technology in particular. New teaching and learning approaches, methods and techniques are introduced into the educational process, applying various technologies like artificial intelligence, computer vision, robotics, etc. And virtual reality is one of those. Virtual laboratories are one of the computer-based learning systems that can help to study various processes (physical, chemical, etc.) simulating and visualizing them on a personal computer without using the actual equipment or reagents. Moreover, with the help of such simulations it is possible to observe the process in detail, from different points or enlarge the image to a convenient size. In this paper an application that helps to study physics in secondary schools is presented. It contains a set of practical problem tasks from a number of physics sections. Each task has visualization scene with virtual reality integrated. In the article the content, architecture and interface of the application are presented along with the short review of other research in the field of application of virtual reality in education.

Keywords: Virtual reality · Education · Physics · Virtual experiments

1 Introduction

The introduction of new information technologies along with the computerization of educational institutions and the innovative activities of the academic staff are the main directions of the comprehensive modernization of education, to which the special attention is paid not only throughout the world, but in Kazakhstan as well [1–4]. As an example of this process implementation the state program "Digital Kazakhstan" can be taken, developed by the government of the Republic. One of the goals of this program is to increase the digital literacy of the population, including on secondary, higher, technical and professional levels of education, as well as within staff and professional development courses. Currently we can witness the world trend – Industry 4.0 which implies a massive introduction of cyber-physical systems, such as artificial intelligent, virtual and augmented reality, quantum computing, 3D printing, autonomous robots in

D. A. Alexandrov et al. (Eds.): DTGS 2019, CCIS 1038, pp. 483–492, 2019.
https://doi.org/10.1007/978-3-030-37858-5_41

production and everyday life, including education. The latter is also heavily influenced by information technology including not only the computerization of business processes of secondary and higher educational institutions, but introduction of new methodology and learning tools based on the modern technologies. In the latter field the computer learning systems like virtual laboratories are prominent. They allow conducting experiments without real equipment and all the processes are simulated by a computer [5, 6].

Currently, students' perceptions can be improved with the help of new visualization elements and gestures offered by modern digital technologies. In particular, with the virtual reality technology (VR – Virtual Reality), new ways of learning are coming to the fore, which make it possible to reveal the student's interest in the subject being studied, stimulate positive emotions, accelerate the learning process and help to better understand the topic. VR introduces the game principle into the learning process, which certainly has a positive effect on the students' performance.

In this article the software with a set of practical tasks and animations with virtual reality embedded for studying physics in secondary educational institutions is presented. The application is developed in the International Information Technology University (Almaty, Kazakhstan).

2 Related Works in the Field of Development and Introduction of Computer Learning Systems Based on the Virtual Reality

The level of application of various technological tools grows rapidly in all the fields of human activity and in education as well. In the past we used pen, pencils and books and now interactive technologies are available to help to deliver knowledge and understanding. In the recent years we can observe how deeply digital technologies have penetrated our lives.

Thus, in [7] the virtual environment is presented that helps students to study the tourism development issues and related impacts. VR is used to fully immerse students in the environment. The current approach is useful to provide participants with a holistic experience of real environment, which in reality is expensive, especially for groups with a large number of people. The pedagogical value is achieved through immersion in an environment based on reality, interaction with complex and ambiguous situations and information, as well as interaction with space, other students and teachers. The results demonstrate that such complex virtual learning environments can be developed, and the main problem is a high level of interactivity.

The study of algebra is accompanied by frequent problems for both students and teachers. In [8], an example of studying algebra with the help of virtual reality. The authors have developed an open educational resource Virtual Algebra Tiles, which enables students to expand their knowledge on algebra concepts using a computer. The research results showed that such a learning system for students is comfortable, and therefore the learning process becomes a more pleasant task.

In [9], a study was conducted on how gifted students perceive virtual programs. Students were enrolled in a virtual course. Data was collected through asynchronous focus groups on an interactive discussion board, using observations of synchronized activities in their virtual classroom, as well as individual interviews with participants. Studies have shown that some technical difficulties have arisen, mainly due to operator errors or non-use of available tools. From the point of view of the curriculum and pedagogy, the participants saw a slight difference between the classical and virtual classrooms. And it can be concluded that for gifted students, the quality of content and learning is more important than the reality of learning environments (virtual or actual). This information can be used further to improve the quality of on-line education or to create new software.

The article [10] is aimed at studying the perceptions of teachers regarding the introduction of virtual reality to educational process with the help of a case study in the Faculty of Information Technology (IT) at a university in the Middle East. The respondents interviewed for this study were teachers. A quantitative method was used: an adapted questionnaire was distributed among IT teachers on the Internet, which assessed their opinion on the possibility of using virtual reality as a training tool. Statistical data was used to analyze the questionnaire data. The results obtained on the basis of quantitative data revealed the willingness of teachers to use VR systems as an additional teaching tool, their intention to include them in the educational process in the future, barriers to the use of technology, and prerequisites for users. The results also showed that learning can be as effective as possible with the integration of VR technology. The article also provides recommendations for facilitating the use of VR technology as a learning tool.

A specially designed and tested virtual reality learning environment [11] can offer medical students access to educational materials and their re-learning, thus improving educational process. In addition, the use of such training tools will make medical education more accessible. The article also shows that virtual reality has a unique potential for the transformation of medical education and offers an increase in investment in technology development and the possibility of cooperation with developers.

The work [12] discusses the use of virtual reality technology to gain knowledge about evacuation, which is a key to reducing injuries and increasing survival. Serious games (SGs) based on immersion virtual reality represent an innovative approach to training and educating people in the gaming environment. This article aims to understand the development and implementation of such serious games in the context of training and research in the field of evacuation of buildings applied to various emergency situations in them, such as fire and earthquake.

In [13], the effectiveness of using immersive virtual reality for learning the effects of climate change, in particular for studying the acidity of sea water, was discussed. Studies have shown that after the experience of immersion in virtual reality, people showed a good level of knowledge, curiosity in the field of climate science, and in some cases showed a more positive attitude to the environment. The analysis also showed that immersive virtual reality is a promising additional mechanism for effective learning, since the more people explored the spatial learning environment, the more they demonstrated a high level of knowledge about environmental change.

In [14], the use of virtual reality technology to study architecture is considered. Due to its empirical nature, VR technology can be very effective in obtaining architectural education. The authors developed the LADUVR application, which users can use on the construction site to study the architectural details more closely and check what they have learned in an interactive and exciting environment. The article also presents a comparison between traditional teaching methods and the use of virtual reality technology.

The use of virtual reality technology in museums is also relevant. It allows presenting information in a more visual, interesting and memorable form, as well as attracting more visitors. The work [15] presents guidance on the development of educational games in collaboration with the museum. The authors showed that mini-educational games using virtual reality technology considerably help students in the study of artistic concepts.

In such a way, it can be concluded that the virtual reality is widely used in education for in-depth study of various courses.

3 Software Support of the Project

In this project, for the development of software, a cross-platform computer game development environment is used, the game engine Unity 3D from Unity Technologies [16]. It allows creating virtual reality applications running on personal computers, mobile devices with iOS and Android operating systems, or Web-based applications. This in turn makes applications widely available. Other benefits of Unity are:

- visual development environment, which includes not only visual modeling tools, but also an integrated environment, an assembly chain, which is aimed at increasing the productivity of developers, in particular, during the stages of prototyping and testing;
- highly qualified technical support;
- a variety of methods for manipulating physical objects, which facilitates visualization of physical processes.

Virtual reality implies a simulation in which a virtual, but realistic world is created using computer graphics. Moreover, the reproduced world is not static, but responds to the user's incoming flow (gestures, verbal commands, etc.) [17].

As a virtual reality device, the Leap Motion Controller contactless control device [18] is used, which is based on motion capture technology. To capture the projection of user's hands in space, the Leap Motion device uses two optical sensors (cameras) and an infrared light source. After connecting the device, a virtual inverted pyramid with a central vertex in the device is formed above it. The most effective range is from 25 to 600 mm above the controller with a field of view of 150°. In the area of this pyramid, Leap Motion "sees" all movements and sends them to software that converts data and signals into coordinates and messages. The software is able to recognize both simple gestures (virtual touches, clicks), and complex continuous movements: scaling, moving, rotating, and drawing various geometric shapes.

The Leap Motion Controller was chosen for the following reasons:

- Unity 3D support;
- works on mobile processors with low latency and high precision;
- hands are initialized faster and tracked better on difficult backgrounds and extreme lighting conditions.

4 Results

As a result of the project in the International Information Technology University (Almaty, Kazakhstan), a software application with a set of practical tasks and animations with virtual reality to study physics in secondary schools was developed. This application can be used not only in Kazakhstan, but also abroad, as the application menu is implemented in three languages: Kazakh, Russian and English.

The developed application gives an access to a set of physical problems from such sections of physics as kinematics, basic dynamics, static elements, conservation laws in mechanics, mechanical vibrations and waves, molecular physics and thermodynamics. Each task is implemented as a separate module, which provides a 3D visualization of the physical process studied within the problem. The interaction with the application as a whole, as well as with the visualization is realized using the Leap Motion controller.

The practical tasks were chosen in conjunction with the physics teacher from the Republican Physics and Mathematics School (Almaty, Kazakhstan). First, the topics for the tasks were selected according to the school program of the physics course. Second, the level of difficulty of the selected tasks is medium and high; the choice was made in favor of those tasks, for which additional visualization of the studied process is important in order to gain a deeper understanding and mastering of the material.

One of the distinguishing features of the presented application is that it is multilingual. The user can choose Kazakh, Russian or English language of interaction with the application. Figure 1 shows the main application menu with the Leap Motion controller integrated into it.

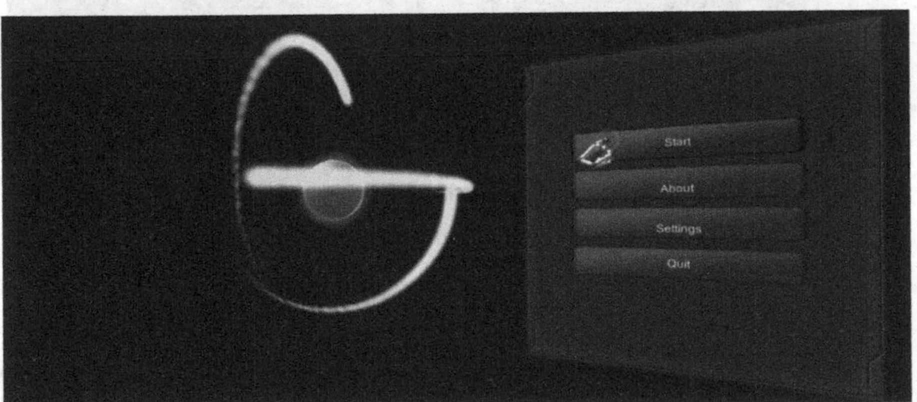

Fig. 1. Main application menu with Leap Motion

Each task contains a condition, an animated task scene and a solution. Let us consider an example of the implementation of the task with a pendulum. The problem task is as follows: will the oscillation period of the mathematical pendulum change if it is placed in water? The pendulum is ideally streamlined, so friction against water can be neglected. A demonstration of the experiment is shown in Fig. 2(a, b).

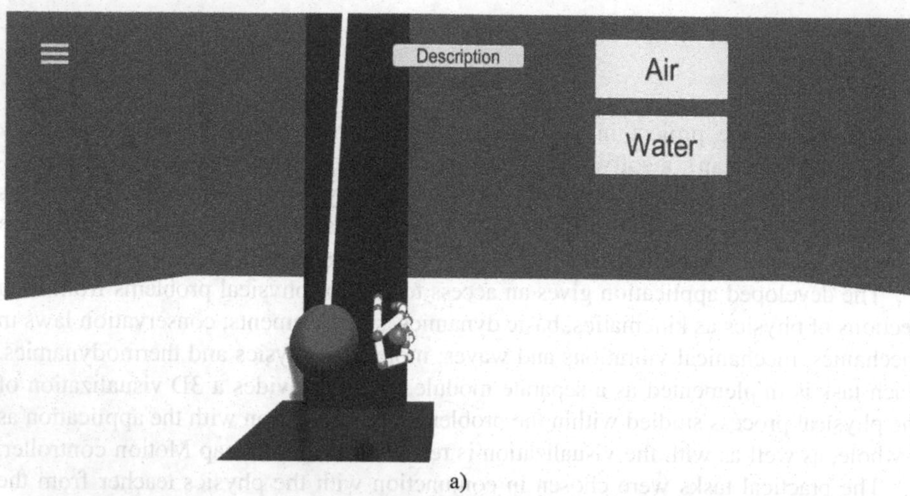

a)

b)

Fig. 2. The task example with Leap Motion

Interactive control is organized using the Leap Motion controller, keyboard and camera view (mouse control), which also allows you to rotate the 3D scene in different directions. The program also allows increasing the studied objects for a more detailed review. When changing positions and viewpoints, the dialog box is updated. Interactivity in this work is the main advantage, providing visibility and better absorption of knowledge.

In general, the work of the application can be described using the following UML diagrams. The application using Leap Motion consists of the components presented in Fig. 3. It shows the structure of the application. It consists of the Main launch, which opens the application and calls the following two modules: the tasks in the sections “Mechanics”, “Electrostatics”, etc., and the tasks with the Leap Motion controller support. A user can only see the graphical interface, but there are three more components behind them: a shared folder containing models, scripts and other necessary resources, separate folders for a specific task and a folder necessary for Leap Motion to work correctly.

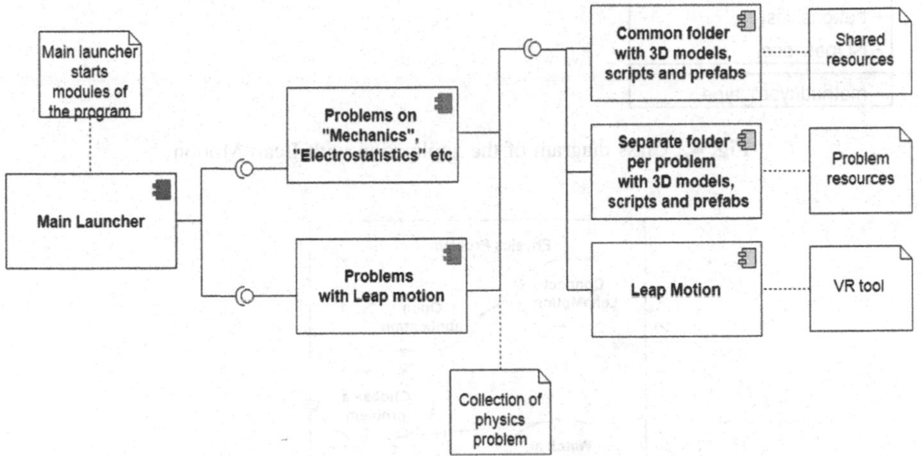

Fig. 3. Component diagram of the application with Leap Motion

The application contains three main classes: MonoBehaviour, MenuControllerScript and LeapManager. Each separate task has its own program code, which is shown as the class ProblemController in the class diagram (see Fig. 4).

User interaction with the application is described in Fig. 5. The possible actions taken by a user are described. For example, at the beginning the user must connect the controller Leap Motion. Only after that all the functionality of the application becomes available to him/her. Then, in the application he/she can select a problem, view the task and the solution, turn on the demonstration, and also change its parameters. All this happens thanks to the Menu Controller as the user interacts with the application with the help of it.

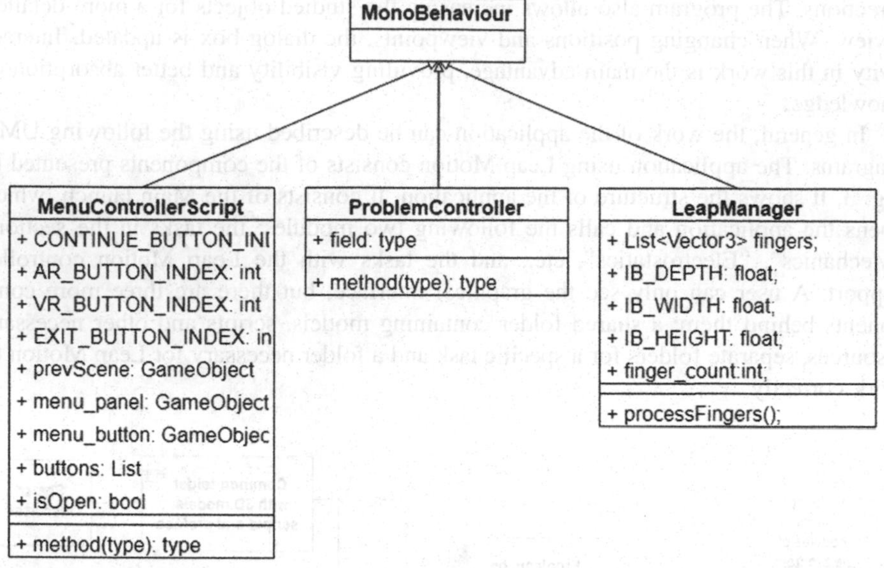

Fig. 4. Class diagram of the application with Leap Motion

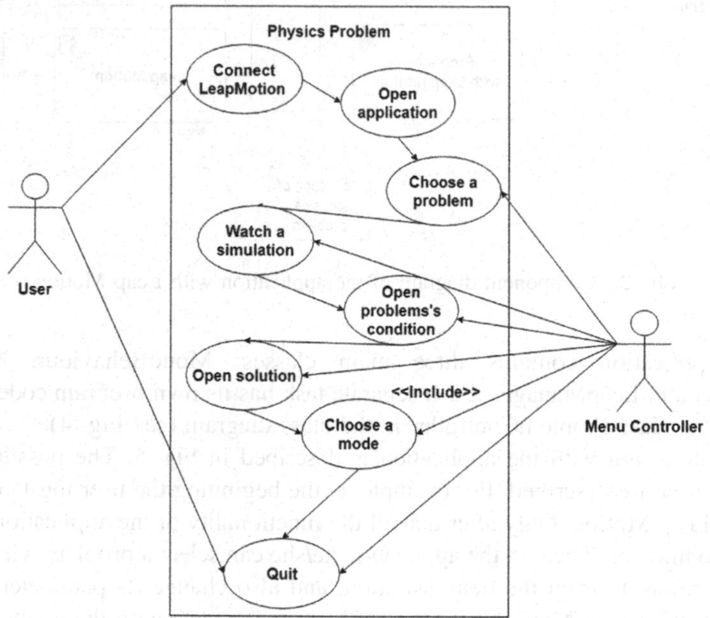

Fig. 5. Use case diagram of the application

5 Conclusion

In order to evaluate the developed virtual laboratory the students of the 9th grade of the Republican Physics and Mathematics School took part in a survey after a month of using the application. The survey consisted of 10 questions about the virtual laboratory, its functionality and the user interface. The results of the survey showed that the students were interested in the virtual laboratory in particular, and in such additional learning tools in general. They expressed their positive impression about the implementation of the application. In the comments they mentioned some points where the laboratory can be improved. And we will take into consideration their suggestions in the next versions of the application.

The teachers totally support the current project and are interested in using the virtual laboratory within classes. Also they expressed a desire to continue the collaboration and to search for new tasks and problems for visualization.

Thus, virtual reality technology opens up new perspectives in education. Along with other courses, physics has a wide potential for the development and implementation of new innovative teaching methods. This article demonstrated a software application to study physics in secondary educational institutions using virtual reality technology. We believe that this application is a good example of modern innovative computer-based learning systems of the new generation. The use of new methods and instruments in education help students to be aware of new trends in information technology field. Currently, the authors are constantly working on the development of new practical tasks as well as virtual physical laboratory works using augmented reality as well. The future work is to expand the functionality of the application by integrating into it new practical tasks from other physics sections, animations that shows the physical processes in detail and virtual physical laboratory works to conduct physical experiments.

Acknowledgments. The work was done under the funding of the Ministry of Education and Science of the Republic of Kazakhstan (No. AP05135692).

References

1. Mukhopadhyay, M., Parhar, M.: ICT in Indian higher education administration and management. In: Huang, R., Price, J.K. (eds.) ICT in Education in Global Context. LNET, pp. 263–283. Springer, Heidelberg (2014). https://doi.org/10.1007/978-3-662-43927-2_15
2. Looi, C.K., Hung, W.L.D.: ICT-in-education policies and implementation in Singapore and other Asian countries. In: Aviram, A., Richardson, J. (eds.) Upon What Does the Turtle Stand?, pp. 27–39. Springer, Dordrecht (2004). https://doi.org/10.1007/1-4020-2799-0_2
3. Efobi, U.R., Osabuohien, E.S.: Technological utilization in Africa: how do institutions matter? In: Majumdar, S., Guha, S., Marakkath, N. (eds.) Technology and Innovation for Social Change, pp. 67–84. Springer, New Delhi (2015). https://doi.org/10.1007/978-81-322-2071-8_5
4. Nour, S.M.: Overview of the use of ICT and the digital divide in Sudan. In: Nour, S.M. (ed.) Information and Communication Technology in Sudan Contributions to Economics.

Contributions to Economics, pp. 127–266. Springer, Cham (2015). https://doi.org/10.1007/978-3-319-13999-9
5. Daineko, Ye., Dmitriyev, V., Ipalakova, M.: Using virtual laboratories in teaching natural sciences: an example of physics. Comput. Appl. Eng. Educ. **25**(1), 39–47 (2017)
6. Daineko, Y.A., Ipalakova, M.T., Bolatov, Zh.Zh.: Employing information technologies based on .NET XNA framework for developing a virtual physical laboratory with elements of 3D computer modeling. Program. Comput. Softw. **43**(3), 161–171 (2017)
7. Schott, C., Marshal, S.: Virtual reality and situated experiential education: a conceptualization and exploratory trial. J. Comput. Assist. Learn. **6**(34), 843–852 (2018)
8. Garzón, J., Bautista, J.: Virtual algebra tiles: a pedagogical tool to teach and learn algebra through geometry. J. Comput. Assist. Learn. **6**(34), 876–883 (2018)
9. Potts, J.A.: Profoundly gifted students' perceptions of virtual classrooms. Gift. Child Q. **63** (1), 58–80 (2018)
10. Salsabeel, F., Alfalah, M.: Perceptions toward adopting virtual reality as a teaching aid in information technology. Educ. Inf. Technol. **23**(6), 2633–2653 (2018)
11. King, D., Tee, S., Falconer, L., Angell, C., Holley, D., Mills, A.: Virtual health education: scaling practice to transform student learning. Nurse Educ. Today **71**, 7–9 (2018)
12. Fenga, Zh., Gonzáleza, V.A., Amorb, R., Lovreglioc, R., Cabrera-Guerrerod, G.: Immersive virtual reality serious games for evacuation training and research: systematic literature review. Comput. Educ. **127**, 252–266 (2018)
13. Markowitz, D.M., Laha, R., Perone, B.P., Pea, R.D., Bailenson, J.N.: Immersive virtual reality field trips facilitate learning about climate change. Front. Psychol. **9**, 2364 (2018). https://doi.org/10.3389/fpsyg.2018.02364
14. Maghool, S.A.H., Moeini, S.H., Arefazar, Y.: An educational application based on virtual reality technology for learning architectural details: challenges and benefits. Archnet-IJAR **12**(3), 246–272 (2018)
15. Bossavit, B., Pina, A., Sanchez-Gil, I., Urtasun, A.: Educational games to enhance museum visits for schools. Educ. Technol. Soc. **21**(4), 171–186 (2018)
16. Unity 3D Homepage. https://unity3d.com/company. Accessed 09 Jan 2019
17. Burdea, G., Coiffet, P.: Virtual Reality Technology, 2nd edn. Wiley, New York (2003)
18. Leap Motion Homepage. https://leapmotion.com/. Accessed 09 Jan 2019

The Development and Implementation of M-Glossary in the System of Content and Language Integrated Learning

Liudmila Khalyapina[1] and Camila Yakhyaeva[2(✉)]

[1] Peter the Great Saint-Petersburg Polytechnic University, Saint-Petersburg, Russian Federation
lhalapina@bk.ru

[2] Saint-Petersburg State University of Civil Aviation, Saint-Petersburg, Russian Federation
yakm94@gmail.com

Abstract. The purpose of this article is to present the results of the ongoing study aimed at development and implementation of the specific mobile application – "aviation glossary" within the educational CLIL model on the basis of Saint-Petersburg State University of Civil Aviation, Saint Petersburg. The authors examined the phenomenon of content and language integrated learning, its features and components. At the same time the authors appealed to the newly-developed branch of e-learning – mobile learning, its models based on the "Bring your own device" concept and its key advantages for everyone involved in educational process. The presented article is also devoted to the description of lexicographical work of the m-glossary composition and its further usage with the "autonomous learning" model to develop students' linguistic skills, e.g. vocabulary knowledge, reading comprehension of the professionally-oriented text. The findings revealed a stable increase in the rate of students' vocabulary knowledge which is required in order to perform professional and communicational activities successfully.

Keywords: CLIL · M-learning · Mobile app · Aviation English · Non-linguistic university

1 Introduction

Reorganization of the Russian system of higher education in recent decades and international integration and development of information and telecommunication technologies, as well as growing of competition in the labor market in the era of globalization led to the need for new pedagogical technologies. In this regard, it is important to help future graduates to become a major part of a training process and form their need for constant search and professional self-development.

Taking into account the current situation, Russian and foreign scientists are looking for and trying to apply new ways of solving didactic problems, referring, in particular, to the concepts of an integrated approach.

D. A. Alexandrov et al. (Eds.): DTGS 2019, CCIS 1038, pp. 493–505, 2019.
https://doi.org/10.1007/978-3-030-37858-5_42

2 When CLIL Meets M-Learning

2.1 CLIL: Origins and Basics

The idea of combining language and subject content is not new and is directly related to one of S. Krashen's five hypotheses about the assimilation of language, implemented through meaningful "input" (comprehensive input (CI) [1]. Also, the cognitive orientation of the process of integrated learning is subordinated to the pedagogical objectives of the teaching of the higher order (analysis, synthesis, evaluation) and the theory of "BICS/CALP" in the direction from the lower order cognitive skills (knowledge, understanding, application) to the mental skills of the higher order (analysis, synthesis, evaluation). Cummins, in which "BICS" (basic interpersonal communicative skills) means the basic communication skills of everyday communication, and "CALP" (cognitive/academic language proficiency) – cognitive/academic language competence necessary in situations of professional communication [2].

The European Commission views CLIL as a concept when "a foreign language is used as a means of learning". The undeniable advantage of CLIL is the possibility of immersion in the language without the introduction of additional hours in the curriculum, which is especially important for schools of professional orientation. The European Commission also funded a large number of projects aimed at CLIL research across Europe since the early 1990s. To date, there is a tendency to generalize existing approaches (content-based learning (CBI), immersion programs, and bilingual learning (BE)). All the above-mentioned terms have been generalized by the term CLIL. According to a 2005 European Commission report, the application of CLIL guarantees the achievement of the objectives set by the European Union in the field of foreign language learning and gives pupils/students the opportunity to study subjects/disciplines in a foreign language [3].

D. Marsh, the father of the approach, gives the following definition of CLIL, which is subsequently adopted and supplemented by other authors: "CLIL refers to situations where subjects, or parts of subjects, are taught through a foreign language with dual-focused aims, namely the learning of content and the simultaneous learning of a foreign language" [4].

The design of the educational process in the framework of the integrated approach is submitted to the methodology of 4 "C" introduced by D. Coyle and includes the following components:

* content - the content of the subject discipline;
* communication - skills of oral and written professional communication;
* cognition - knowledge, i.e. the development of students' cognitive abilities in the process of simultaneous teaching a language and a special subject;
* culture - a wide range of cultural contexts aimed at forming students' civic consciousness and the ability to "integrate" into the other cultures by means of learning the language of these cultures [5].

According to the European experience of subject teaching in additional (in most cases, English) language and description of the learning process, given by Professor D. Coyle, the following models are distinguished:

Model C1: Multilingual learning. In integrated learning, more than one language is used and in teaching different disciplines during different years. This model is a "prestigious" form of education, which is designed to attract the most motivated and talented students from different countries.

Model C2: Auxiliary/supplementary integrated learning subject matter and language. Language teaching is associated with special areas, language teachers are part of the structural units for teaching specialties, their role – external support in the training of specialists. Students acquire the ability to use the CLIL language while mastering specialties.

Model C3: Substantive courses with the inclusion of language support. Training is conducted by subject teachers as well as specialists in the field of language teaching. A student even with poor knowledge of the language of instruction receives support throughout the learning process, which makes it possible to master both the subject and the language of teaching. The model is suitable for teaching students with different language and cultural backgrounds [6].

Turning to the Russian reality, for teaching foreign languages in Russian non-linguistic universities, from our point of view, the second model is characteristic, focusing on the development of General cultural and professional competence of students. Integrated teaching of special discipline and language in higher education is a developing area of theoretical and practical research, however, there is no single, universal model for each university. Using the didactic principles of content-language integrated learning in teaching professional disciplines in English to students of the international financial faculty of the Financial University under the Government of the Russian Federation", D. V. Berzin highlights such advantages as the improvement of foreign language communicative competence, as well as the possibility of using the latest authentic educational literature, which, in fact, increases the efficiency of preparation for international language and professional tests and exams. In practical classes, the author of the project also recommends applying to the translation method, especially when working with terminology, which allows students to better understand it both in Russian and in English [7].

Elements of CLIL methodology are also successfully introduced into the pedagogical practice of extracurricular work with students. On the basis of the Saratov state law Academy (SSU), within the framework of the integrated course "Legal consulting in English" is preparing law students for the international competition on legal advice in English. At the same time, E.G. Vyushkina notes the importance of the preparatory, "information and reference stage" in the two-component structure of the course, due to the need for maximum immersion in the language environment and the assimilation of the logical and grammatical basis of legal consultations [8]. As for the educational material, the author uses isolated sections of the manual "Introduction to International Legal English", as well as personal developments adapted to the language level of students.

2.2 M-Learning: Shifting the Borderlines of Higher Education

Globalization and development of the Internet provide new opportunities for professional activities and for professional education, including foreign language training. Mobile learning (m-learning), as a branch of the well-known E-learning, gives a lot of opportunities for studying via personal mobile devices and for obtaining learning materials through mobile apps. Mobile learning is not just online learning in a smaller format. Smartphones have some unique features that allow for new kinds of learning patterns. These features have been defined as the five "C's" of Mobile Learning by Clark Quinn:

Content: instructional materials that students can access anywhere, or in specific contexts.
Capture: mobile devices to capture images, video, sound, GPS coordinates, and ideas (as notes).
Communicate: the opportunity of being in touch with classmates anywhere or during specific activities.
Compute: Using devices to assist in calculating, language translating, and other computational tasks.
Combine: Using the previous four functions together in interesting ways [9].

Analysis of the works of Russian and foreign scientists [10–14] showed a stable trend in modern language education - the appeal to mobile learning or to its individual ideas and principles. This trend, for the most part, is dictated by the concept of BYOD ("Bring your own device"), which has become a "global perspective" in business, and now in the educational environment as well. The popularity of BYOD is due to the following factors:

- self-selection of the most convenient device/application;
- the possibility of combining personal, educational, and later, and working, professional tasks;
- increase in productivity/optimization of the educational process with minimal energy consumption.

An additional advantage of BYOD is the fact that in modern realities the constant development and improvement of mobile operating systems, as well as the portability of the devices themselves, makes it possible to select and combine applications, in accordance with the educational goals and objectives of a particular discipline, without departing from the conventional, traditional teaching methods. As it's noted in the study "the use of applications makes possible the unlimited use of authentic materials in a foreign language in a foreign language, training various types of speech activities and preparing students for continuous education" [15].

According to the degree of students' involvement and freedom of choice, the following educational models are distinguished:

1. The specified activity (teacher-directed) model;
2. The proposed activity (teacher-set) model;
3. The learner-driven (autonomous learning) model [16].

For the 1st model students are offered some certain educational content that is usually available on mobile devices. They can do it in and out of the classroom, individually or in a group. However, the tasks are formulated by the teacher and are mandatory. This sort of training differs from traditional e-learning practically only in the presence of its own device.

The 2nd model stands for greater freedom of the student: the proposed tasks are additional. A similar model for m-learning is focused on facilitating initiatives of the student motivates him for the future language activities.

The autonomous learning model declares almost independent learning activities. Students choose their own content in order to master a particular educational layer. They are actively discussing among themselves the difficult questions, share experiences and information. The anonymity of mobile communication encourages active discussion, even among those who are usually not involved in it. In this way, such training is extremely conducive to the socialization of students. While picking and adapting the most suitable model it should be noted, that depending on the national specifics and funding of each particular university, the methods of their implementation can vary.

Creating the online-course "A Fast Track to Professional English" for engineering and health care students in Tabula (TAMK learning platform), Metsäportti and Saarinen suggest a way to accomplish the compulsory professional English course at a faster speed within the teacher-directed model. However, the platform itself isn't as flexible as it's expected and doesn't allow any input from the students. All the discussions, forums and additional tasks are tailored by the teachers, which prevents the participants from smooth and steady communication [17, 18]. The other way to construct the m-learning system is to let the students choose what and how they want to learn and to find another online- resource. At some point social networks can serve as a tool for up-to-date, "live" communication due to quick adaptation to a specific communicative situation and practical educational aims; in addition, some moments can be clarified without breaking the authentic language environment [19, 20]. Table 1 contains the major differences of these two models, according to the study of the National Capitol Language Resource Center of the George Washington University, where their features were specified and measured [21].

Comparing the examples of the m-learning elements implementation within the integrated approach and the ideas of European researchers and weighing all pros and cons of the models mentioned above, a decision to develop the autonomous, learner-centered model was made, as it gives greater creative freedom for teachers and provides the students with opportunity to learn the basics of work with the professionally oriented texts.

It's necessary to mention a number of additional features inherent in the developed educational model: the integrative nature of the "language and content" basis, the role of language as a "tool" for the cognitive and mental abilities formation, acquisition of professional discipline and maximum immersion into the specifics of the future specialty.

Table 1. Specified activity vs Autonomous learning models. The differences.

Type of model:	Specified activity	Autonomous learning
Focusing:	On teacher/instructor	On students
Language material:	Basic lexical units and grammar structures	Language and its use in everyday life, in typical situations of communication
Instructions delivery:	The basic information is delivered by a teacher/instructor	Students communicate with one another or with a teacher/instructor, while the former models the process
Students' autonomy:	Mostly the classwork is performed by the students themselves	Students work in pairs, groups or individually, depending on the activity
Teacher's/Instructor's control:	A teacher/instructor controls each and every student utterance, correcting their mistakes	Students' speech has no constant observation; feedback/correction is provided when necessary/asked by students
Teacher's/Instructor's support:	A teacher/instructor provides their students with the information on language	Students try to find the correct answers to each other's questions, and receive teacher's/instructor's feedback if necessary
Teacher's/Instructor's evaluation:	Evaluation is provided by instructor/teacher	Besides teacher's/instructor's evaluation, students can also evaluate their progress
Choice of topics for discussion:	Topics are chosen by instructor/teacher	Students have some freedom of choice of topics
Classroom work	Usually not intense	Busy, noisy at some points

3 Methods and Procedures

3.1 Participants

The study was carried out in Saint-Petersburg State University of Civil Aviation (Saint-Petersburg). The target group consisted of the 3rd year students of the faculty of Airports and Flight Engineering, that were randomly divided into 3 experiment groups. The general number of students involved equals 42.

3.2 Procedure

As a part of our research, the use of m-learning means also involves the organization of extracurricular work of students, quality monitoring, support, and "management" of the educational process at all its stages.

We also came to the conclusion that often didactic system of work with professional vocabulary is missing or it is not given due attention. As one of its key elements, we offer a mobile Glossary and its use at the stage of consolidation of lexical material is particularly useful for students of the 3rd course of the "Organization of airport activities", for which the passage of the course "Aviation English" causes certain difficulties associated with the organization of training and selection of teaching material. The main reason for this is the specifics of the future profession, associated not only with the coordination of the work of all departments of the airport and the operation of technical means of passenger service, but also with the need to prepare technical documentation (work schedules, instructions, plans, estimates, applications for materials, equipment) and the development of projects and programs for the development of the airfield (airport) network. Thus, a question: "what are the limits of the mandatory lexical minimum that allows future graduates to perform their professional and communicative activities successfully?" was brought up. In order to meet the declared goals of the study an idea of a so-called "aviation glossary" in a form of a mobile app is born and planned to be materialized.

As an educational tool, online or e-dictionary has already been successfully implemented in the process of foreign language learning lexical competency formation [22], into extracurricular work of the engineering students and the formation of the professional vocabulary thesaurus. Work on the thesaurus of professional vocabulary, as well as set expressions, is aimed at linking speech structures and lexical units, as well as at establishing relations between words as phenomena of internal and external speech. Forms of organization of such work may differ, depending on the students' language proficiency and educational aims [23].

At the initial stage of our study all the students had to participate in a survey. The first part of the survey showed the majority of respondents obtains Intermediate level (89%), the levels of Pre-intermediate (8%) and Upper-intermediate (3%) were also registered. The vast majority of students actively use the functionality of their devices, 97% of them - in educational activities, including. According to the results of the second part of the survey, the most useful (98%) for respondents were electronic dictionaries and reference books. The situation can be explained by the specifics of the subject "Aviation English" and the peculiarities of a professionally-oriented text in English (aviation terminology, abbreviations, untranslatables, and compliance with the scientific style in translation work). Apps for learning vocabulary/grammar, as well as the possibility of accessing educational materials posted on social networks, were mentioned as effective means of training. Also, the level of students' motivation and approval (98.6%) confirmed our assumption on the need of including mobile apps in the educational process.

Then the participants were tested in order to assess their language skills, knowledge of special terminology and the understanding of the professionally-oriented text that are required for the M-glossary composition. For this purpose, we offered a text "Parts inside the Aircraft" to the students. The amount of text amounted to 1442 characters. The selected text was given with the following task "Read the text about major aircraft parts, then proceed to Step 2". It was also offered to answer the questions on the key ideas of the text. The acquisition of the reading comprehension was determined as a percentage of the number of correct answers to the total number of questions given to the text. Analysis of the data shows that the level of understanding of foreign-language special texts among the subjects is 81, 5% (out of 100% possible).

Besides testing the participants, we also studied the curriculum and the syllabus of the discipline "Aviation English" for the involved specialties to pick the modules and topic for the glossary formation. Hereafter, we faced the task of choosing the most accessible resource or mobile app for both Android and iOS supported devices. For the reason we preferred using online-service "My Efe", which combines a wide range of free services for learners: words transcription or pronunciation, "T-words" simulator, online grammar tests and flash cards. However, the most interesting part for our study is an online-dictionary and the opportunity to create your own personal dictionary or glossary up to 2000 words. Another "pro" of the resource is its flexibility, so it can be used not only on PC, but also on mobile phone. Considering "My Efe" as a major platform for the future glossary, we created a common account the students had unlimited access to.

The drafting process included the following stages:

1. Preparatory, initial
2. Text
3. Lexicographical

The initial, preparatory stage involves the search for professionally-oriented texts. The necessary number of works was selected from such bibliographic databases and scientific journals as INGENTA, DOAJ (Directory of Open Access Journals), and The High Wire Library of the Sciences and Medicine. The word count of each text did not exceed 500 words. Following the autonomous model, we described in the previous chapter, the students chose the topics of the texts which partially coincide with the syllabus. These are "Radio communication", "Air navigation (navigational aids)", "Meteorology", "Airport services" and "ICAO and its organization".

The text stage included the work with texts, searching for keywords and terms. In addition, all found units were conditionally divided into the following categories:

Aviation terminology
(absolute altitude, controlled airspace, emergency, forced landing, empennage, winglets, etc.)
Acronyms
(ATIS, ICAO, DME, VOR, ILS, METAR, VOLMET, UNICOM, etc.)
Common abbreviations
(m. (Mach number), FL (flight level), GPS, SOS, etc.)
Professionalisms
("five by five", "mishap", "bird", "fly-by-wire", "air boss", "go juice", etc.)

At the lexicographical stage, the selected lexical units are included, as well as their definitions and Russian equivalents.

After finishing the lexicographical work, we started the direct testing of the developed m-Glossary. During a few weeks all the experimental groups had "Aviation English" classes with the use of the developed Glossary as a supplement. Taking into account the results of the preparatory test, at the first stage, the subjects were asked to do several types of exercises aimed at forming reading comprehension skills, text and content analysis and the vocabulary knowledge. In addition, we had tasks for analytical reading and giving a brief summary of the texts included in order to intensify the educational process and to monitor the students' progress without invading their autonomy.

Another type of exercises was directly aimed at the formation of the linguistic skills. Prior to the text work, the students were offered to address the keywords and terms listed in the m-Glossary, according to the topics. Hereafter the following exercises were introduced: "give the equivalents to the following words and word combinations", "combine the terms with their translations", "combine the terms with their definitions". Working with these tasks teaches students not only to use special dictionaries, glossaries and other reference material, but also to search and pick the necessary information online. Moreover, some of the participants gave a positive feedback, saying these types of exercises make the learning process more interesting and efficient. After reading the key words and terms of each module, the students proceeded to reading the authentic texts taken from the above-mentioned databases. It was assumed that this work pattern integrates the theory and practice in training process making it more analytically-based. During this period the students also participated in group discussions on this or that aviation term or phenomenon.

At the end of the experiment training a test concerning the m-Glossary and its use for was conducted.

One of the challenges we faced was not only a rebuilding of the traditional structure of the lessons, but also tracking of changes within the selected criteria via regression analysis.

4 Results

As the criteria for evaluating the students' progress we took the vocabulary knowledge and the scope of reading materials (%) offered per each module to the students. As the criteria for evaluating the students' progress we took the rate of vocabulary knowledge and the scope of reading materials offered per each module (%) to the students. Figure 1 illustrates the rate of vocabulary knowledge at the initial stage of the experimental training, as well as the scope of reading materials. The line graph shows that the average of vocabulary knowledge in each of the experiment groups tends to increase throughout the training, however, at the very beginning of the training the change isn't so significant. This means that at certain point some additional means of education should be adopted in order to improve the results.

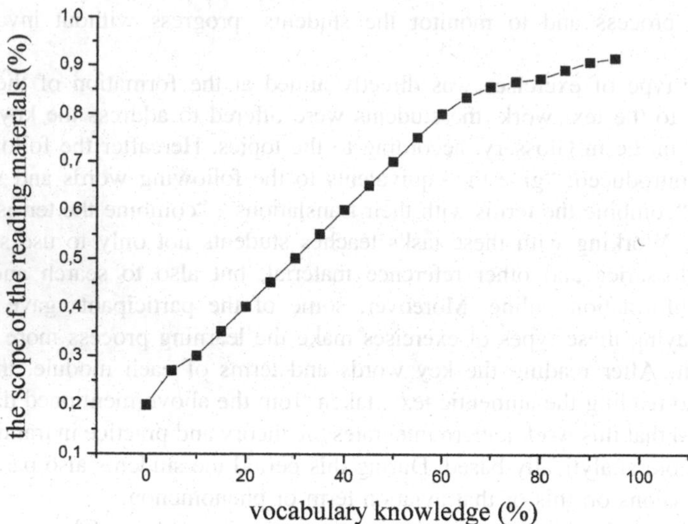

Fig. 1. The rate of vocabulary knowledge and the scope of the reading materials, the initial stage of experiment education

Figure 2 shows the change in rate of learning during the implementation of mobile "Aviation glossary" that students could use throughout the work with professionally-oriented texts and learning or revising the new or already known terminology. We can also notice some increase in the rate of vocabulary knowledge even whilst the introduction of the reading material (at 10%–40%).

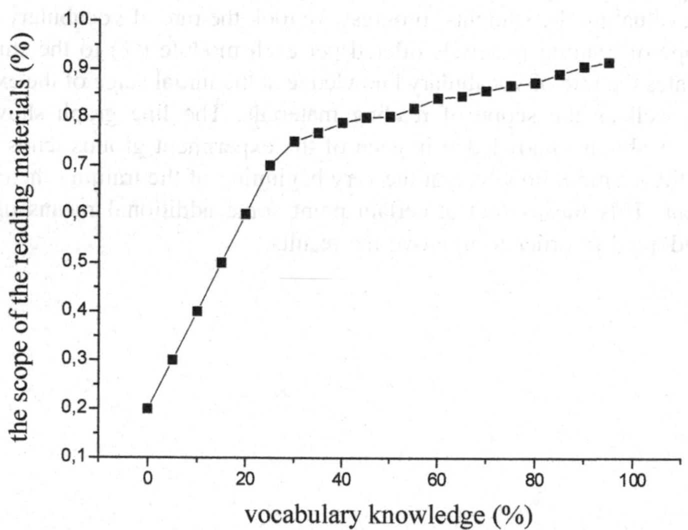

Fig. 2. The rate of vocabulary knowledge and the scope of the reading materials, the post-implementation stage

In the Fig. 3 the of learning at the initial stage and after the implementation of m-Glossary into the experimental training are compared. We can notice some considerable difference in the rate of vocabulary knowledge at the introduction and work with the reading materials. This proves the main idea of the m-Glossary - ensuring lexical and meaningful unity of aviation terms, enlarging vocabulary, developing reading comprehension skills.

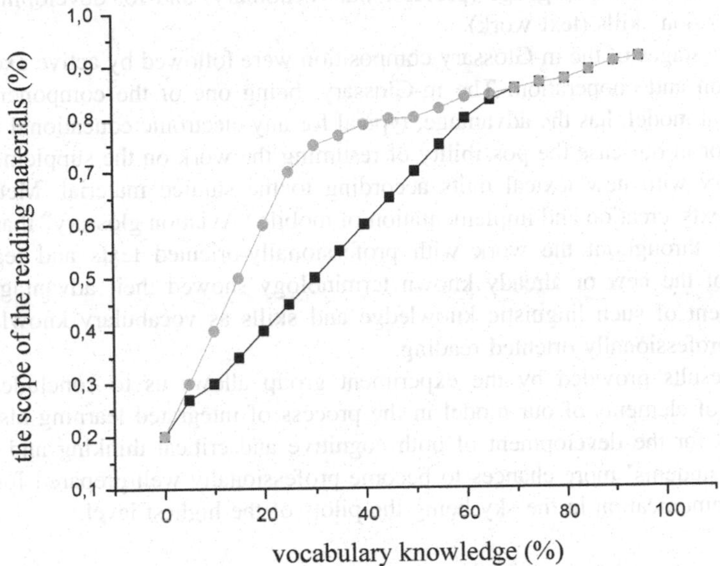

Fig. 3. The comparison of the vocabulary knowledge rate throughout the experiment learning.

Although the level achieved is still not sufficient, taking into account the positive changes in speed of learning, we can talk about some progress of students. Moreover we'd like to highlight the students' dedication to each and every stage of pedagogical experiment, their interest in acquiring the necessary skills and enthusiasm in the process of performing certain tasks.

5 Conclusion

The purpose of the above-described study was to present the intermediate results of experiment training implementation of the mobile learning elements in a form of a mobile "Aviation" glossary for the students of Saint-Petersburg State University of Civil Aviation. To meet the goals of our study we implemented the mobile learning elements in a form of a mobile "Aviation" glossary to develop the level of students' competences sufficient for the professionally-oriented language learning. We also analyzed scientific works dedicated to the CLIL researches (content and language integrated learning), didactic potential of electronic learning (E-learning), didactic values of mobile learning (M-learning) and analyzed the data of the experiment training.

We found, that despite the huge range of the mobile learning tools provided by various online sources, there are few of them that meet the actual goals and objectives of students training in a particular university. Therefore, it was decided for the students of the institute of Civil Aviation to create our own M-Glossary and special stages for the educational process, which meet the goals and objectives of teaching a particular aspect of the English language (professional vocabulary) and for developing reading comprehension skills (text work).

All the stages of the m-Glossary composition were followed by active exchange of information and cooperation. The m-Glossary, being one of the components of the educational model, has the advantage, typical for any electronic educational material - cyclicity or in our case the possibility of resuming the work on the supplement of the m-Glossary with new lexical units according to the studied material. Methodically selected texts, creation and implementation of mobile "Aviation glossary" that students could use throughout the work with professionally-oriented texts and learning or revising of the new or already known terminology showed their advantages in the development of such linguistic knowledge and skills as vocabulary knowledge and skills in professionally oriented reading.

The results provided by the experiment group allows us to conclude that the inclusion of elements of our model in the process of integrated learning also creates conditions for the development of both cognitive and critical thinking and therefore gives the students' more chances to become professionally well-prepared for international communication in the sky being the pilots of the highest level.

References

1. Krashen, S.: Principles and practice in second language acquisition. Oxford, ELT J. **37**(3), 283–285 (1983). https://doi.org/10.1093/elt/37.3.283
2. Cummins, J.: BICS and CALP: empirical and theoretical status of the distinction. In: Street, B., Hornberger, N.H. (eds.) Encyclopedia of Language and Education, pp. 71–83. Springer Science, New York (2008). http://dx.doi.org/10.1007/978-0-387-30424-3_36
3. Council of Europe: Common European Framework of Reference for Languages: Learning, Teaching, Assessment. Cambridge University Press, Cambridge (2001)
4. Marsh, D., Mehisto, P., Wolff, D., Frigols, M.J.: Framework for CLIL teacher education: a framework for the professional development of CLIL teachers European Centre for Modern Languages, Graz, Switzerland (2010)
5. Coyle, D., Hood, P., Marsh, D.: CLIL: Content and Language Integrated Learning/Do Coyle, Philip Hood, David Marsh, 173 p. Cambridge University Press, Cambridge (2010).
6. Zhorabekova, A.N.: Formation of Future Teachers' 88 words—2% Professional Competence on the Basis of Polylingual Approach: The State Analysis. International Education Studies (2015). (In Russian)
7. Berzin, D.V.: Teaching University IT-courses in English. In: Poster presentation. XI all-Russian conference "IT-teaching in Russian Federation", Voronezh (2013). (In Russian)

8. Vyushkina, E.G.: International competitions for law students: the development of communicative and professional competences. Stud. Logic Grammar Rhetoric Nr **34**(47) (2013). (In Russian)
9. Quinn, N.C.: Designing mLearning: tapping into the Mobile Revolution for Organizational Performance. Pffeider (2011). 256 p.
10. Gorbushin, A.G.: The Use of mobile technologies (BYOD technology) in the educational process, theoretical and practical aspects of psychology and pedagogy: the collective monograph under the editorship of E. V. Grishina, - Ufa: Aeterna (2014). (In Russian)
11. Shakhnov, V.A., Zinchenko, L.A., Rezchikova, E.V., Glushko, A.A., Sergeeva, N.A.: Features of BYOD trend in engineering education. Educ. Technol. Soc. **19**(4), 334–345 (2016). (In Russian)
12. Cook, T., et al.: Mobile innovation applications for the BYOD enterprise user. IBM J. Res. Dev. **57**(6), 6:1–6:10 (2013)
13. Almazova, N., Andreeva, S., Khalyapina, L.: The integration of online and offline education in the system of students' preparation for global academic mobility. In: Alexandrov, Daniel A., Boukhanovsky, A.V., Chugunov, A.V., Kabanov, Y., Koltsova, O. (eds.) DTGS 2018. CCIS, vol. 859, pp. 162–174. Springer, Cham (2018). https://doi.org/10.1007/978-3-030-02846-6_13
14. Al-Okaily, R.: Mobile learning and BYOD: implementations in an intensive English program. Learn. Teach. High. Educ. Gulf Perspect. 10(2) (2013). http://lthe.zu.ac.ae/index.php/lthehome/article/view/141/72. Accessed 21 Nov 2018
15. Baturina, N.V., Rukovishnikov, Y.S., Batunova, I.V.: Use of techniques, methods and models of the CLIL system in the process of teaching English to bachelors. Meždunarodnyj naučno-issledovatel'skij žurnal, **10**(64 Part 1), 9–13 (2017). (In Russian)
16. McFarlane, A., Roche, E., Triggs, P.: Researching mobile learning: researching mobile learning – Interim report to Becta Period: April–December 2007 – Bristol, United Kingdom: University of Bristol (2008). 31 p.
17. Metsäportti, M., Saarinen, K.: A fast track to professional english – engineering and health care students collaborating in an online course. Lang. Teach. Tomorrow **2**, 55–57 (2017)
18. Geddes, S.J.: Mobile learning in the 21st century: benefit for learners. Knowl. Tree e-J. **30** (3), 214–228 (2004). https://doi.org/10.1007/978-3-642-16607-5_17
19. Lebedeva, N.: The prospects of m-learning in the university environment. Bull. Kostroma State Univ. Ser. Pedagogy Psychol. Sociokinetics **23**(3), 6–10 (2017). (In Russian)
20. Toktarova, V.I, Blagova, A.D., Filatova, A.V., Kuzmin, N.V.: Design and implementation of mobile learning tools and resources in the modern educational environment of university. Rev. Eur. Stud. **7**(8), 318–324 (2015). Published: 29 April 2015 by Canadian Center of Science and Education in Review of European Studies Review of European Studies, vol. 7. https://doi.org/10.5539/res.v7n8p318
21. Ormrod, J.E.: Essentials of education psychology. In: Cognitive Development, pp. 283–313. Pearson Education, New Jersey (2015)
22. Zaripova, R.R., Salekhova, L., Danilov, R.L.: Interactive Web 2.0 - tools in content and language integrated learning. Higher Educ. Russia (1), 78–84 (2017). (In Russian)
23. Krylov, E.G.: Integrative Bilingual Teaching Foreign Languages and Engineering Disciplines in Technical University. Abstract of Pedagogics Doctor Dissertation Yekaterinburg (2016). 52 p. (In Russian)

Virtual Reality as a Recovering Environment - Implications for Design Principles

Antti Lähtevänoja[1(✉)], Jani Holopainen[2], Osmo Mattila[2], Ilona Södervik[2], Petri Parvinen[2], and Essi Pöyry[2]

[1] University of Jyväskylä, Seminaarinkatu 15, 40014 Jyväskylä, Finland
antti.j.lahtevanoja@student.jyu.fi

[2] University of Helsinki, Yliopistonkatu 4, 00100 Helsinki, Finland
{jani.m.holopainen, osmo.mattila}@helsinki.fi

Abstract. In this study, a simulated, VR-based environment was built and analyzed to explore if a VR environment can possess recovering effects. 61 university students tested a VR application depicting a forest and answered survey questions about the experience. The results showed that VR-environment can indeed have recovering effects. Moreover, when comparing to previous studies in real forests, the recovery effects were at similar levels. The study results suggest that as the VR-based environments can possess recovery effects, they can work as recovery environments at schools or similar environments. The study results offer implications for the designers and propose design principles to build recovering VR environments. Future research avenues to scrutinize the results in various research contexts are discussed.

Keywords: Virtual reality · Restorative environment · Directed attention fatigue · Design principles

1 Introduction

Nowadays, we live in a fast-paced world: we have to constantly process information and stimuli from various sources and decide what is crucial and what can be ignored. That is, cognitive activity is needed.

Prolonged cognitive activity can lead to mental fatigue and directed attention fatigue [14], which hinder focusing and learning [4]. Concentration and focusing problems can be seen especially in schools, as cognitive activity is at the core of learning. Learning involves multiple cognitive processes, such as absorbing, processing, remembering and retrieving information, all of which require attention [11, 21].

Recent research has showed that natural environments can decrease attention fatigue [3, 16]. Still, in urban settings, this can be a problem. Natural environments are sometimes out of reach, or people don't have the time to visit those environments, especially during a school day. Therefore, visiting VR-based recovering environment could work as a substitute for visiting natural environments and offer similar recovering experiences.

D. A. Alexandrov et al. (Eds.): DTGS 2019, CCIS 1038, pp. 506–516, 2019.
https://doi.org/10.1007/978-3-030-37858-5_43

The aim of this study is to validate whether a VR environment can possess recovery effects and thus work as a recovering environment in different contexts, like schools. Simulated, VR-based environments would make it possible to have an easy access to a restorative environment during a school day, for example. Restorative environments could help students recover from directed attention fatigue during a recess.

In addition, as previous research has indicated that VR may cause excessive cognitive load on students (e.g. [19]), we need more information if any VR environment can have recovering effects. This research aims at giving practical implications for the designers about the components and design principles to build recovering VR environments. The implications can be used to build recovering VR environments for schools or to build VR learning and education applications with less cognitive load.

2 Literature: Attention, Fatigue and Restoration

Attention is essentially defined as the ability to focus on only desired or necessary stimuli, as well as the ability to exclude unnecessary or unwanted stimuli [11]. With attention, it is possible to absorb new information through various senses and select what we pay attention and what we ignore. Furthermore, being able to direct our attention makes it possible to pay attention to the task at hand. In the case of unautomated tasks, paying attention to the task is crucial for them to be remembered, as our working memory has limits [11]. To learn, one has to hold information in the working memory and then move it to the long-term memory. To do this, we need to use attention [36]. As Miller [22] summarizes; without attention, there is no memory. Furthermore, without memory, there is no learning.

Directed attention is a mechanism which allows one to control the focus of thought and perception [15]. It allows one to block and inhibit distractions and competing stimuli during purposeful activity [12]. According to Kaplan and Berman [13], directed attention is not tied to particular stimulus patterns, unlike involuntary attention. Prolonged directed attention causes mental effort and is mentally exhaustive, and this exhausted state is called as directed attention fatigue [14]. Directed attention fatigue constitutes a substantial impairment in one's mental competence, and therefore it is important to restore from directed attention fatigue [15].

Kaplan [14] suggests that sleep itself is insufficient for recovering from directed attention fatigue (DAF). To be able to recover from DAF, one needs to find another basis for maintaining one's focus; an alternative mode of attending. This mode should render the use of directed attention temporary unnecessary [14]. One way to achieve this is to use restorative experiences. According to the attention restoration theory, ART [14], a restorative experience should have four components: fascination, being away, extent and compatibility. Fascination suggests that something in the environments fascinates people. This can be for example objects, walking in natural settings or the environment as a whole. Being away in another setting frees one's mind from the mental activity caused by the directed attention. Extent refers to the environment: it should be rich and coherent enough to constitute as a real world. Finally, compatibility suggests that the environment should fit to what one would like to try to do and would like to do [14].

Natural environments, such as parks and forests work well as restorative environments, as they involve characteristics required for restorative experience, and requires only involuntary, effortless attention [12]. Previous research has proven that restorative natural environments have indeed helped recover from directed attention fatigue, and that natural environments have generally had more restorative effects than built environments [2, 3, 8, 10, 16, 30].

Furthermore, simulated recovering environments have also been found out to have recovering effects, though not so strong as the natural environments [3, 31]. However, simulated, virtual reality - based environments with head-mounted - displays (HMD) have not been tested widely. HMD allows user to immerse completely to the simulated world, hence offering a comprehensive experience. As suggested by Nordh [23], because of the immersion, virtual reality techniques may provide more reliable results of restorativeness than photos, for example.

Based on the suggested components of restorative environment [14] and subsequent studies on recovering environments, the present study aims to build a recovering VR-based environment. The recovery effects are validated in an experiment with a survey applying contemporary scales and comparing the results with the previous recovery studies on various environments. Based on the results we propose design principles to guide designers for building recovering VR-environments.

3 Data and Methods

In this study, a simulated, VR-based forest-environment was built following the components introduced by Kaplan [14]: compatibility, being away, extent and fascination. As suggested by the previous research on recovering environments, we modeled a typical boreal forest (Fig. 1) into a VR environment. According to many studies forests are also environments that people like to visit and be oftentimes [30] complying with the compatibility as a design component. The research setup was built in the middle of a city in one of the busiest lobby areas in the city center. In addition, the data collection was done during the busiest office and teaching hours. All this was to create compatibility with another suggested design component - being away. In terms of the extent-component the modelled forest environment represented every little detail from a typical Finnish forest, in order to be rich enough to constitute as a real world [14]. In addition, as Nordh et al. [23] suggests, bushes and trees were created to create psychological distance and to support the being away-component, as well as the extent-component. The coherence with typical trees and undergrowth was validated by expert biologists. Finally, the fascination-component was built by including beautiful and pleasant elements such as flying butterflies [20], birds singing [24], sounds of gentle wind, ability to see horizon and landscape, ability to see a tree with bark and leaves very close as well as ability to see undergrowth very close [23]. In addition, a blue sky and shining sun was built to make the overall layout and the color temperature very warm, and to increase the restoration effect [27]. All the sounds were played through headphones, while the length of the sound loop was adjusted long enough that in the test use no loop was recognized. VR-environment was viewed through HTC Vive, a head-mounted display (HMD).

Fig. 1. Participant experiencing the VR-environment and screenshot from the environment.

In order to validate the possible recovery effects of the modelled VR forest environment, we followed the previous studies on perceived recovery in natural environments, the restorative outcomes, subjective vitality and emotions. These outcomes were measured in a survey before and after the treatment. VR-based environments have not been studied widely yet and therefore, the measures which has been used to evaluate the recovery and restorativeness in natural settings were applied also in this study. Restoration outcomes were measured using Restoration Outcome Scale (ROS) [17]. ROS scale consisted of six items, which measured reflected relaxation, attention restoration and clearing one's thoughts [17]. Restoration Outcome Scale (ROS) has been used to measure restoration experiences in physical surroundings such as favorite places [17]. It is based on the scales by Hartig et al. [9] and Staats et al. [26] and finalized by Korpela et al. [17]. Subjective vitality was measured using Subjective Vitality Scale (SVS) [25]. In this study, an updated and validated version of SVS scale was used [5]. The scale consisted of seven questions, which measured participant's subjective vitality (e.g. "I feel alive and vital"). Positive and negative feelings were measured with Positive and Negative affect scales Affect Schedule (PANAS) [33]. PANAS scale consisted of ten positive and ten negative affect questions (e.g. interested, excited, distressed, ashamed) [33] and has been validated by Crawford and Henry [6]. Across all questionnaires, questions were answered using a Likert scale from 1 to 7 (Fig. 2).

61 respondents participated the study. 43% of the participants were female, 54% male and 3% were else. 59% of them had used VR before. Students were asked to visit the test randomly as they passed by. All tests were made between during 8 am and

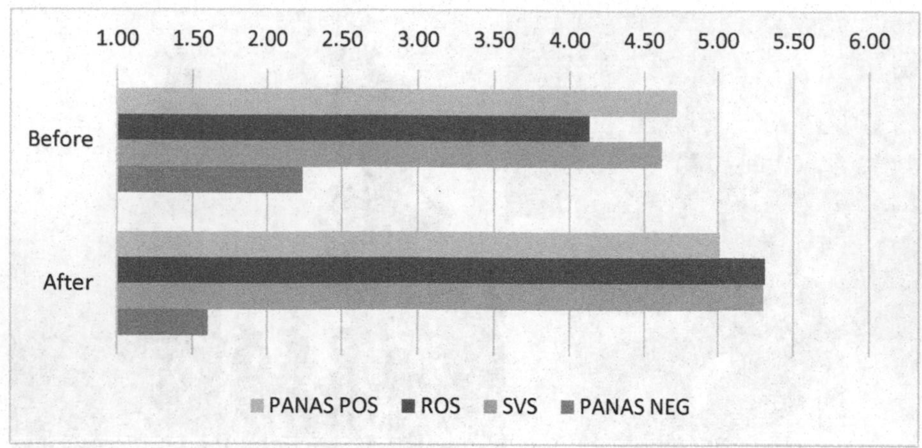

Fig. 2. Mean scores before and after the VR-based recovering experience.

4 pm, during the normal school days. All participants were Finnish speaking and the questionnaires were in Finnish.

Participants were tested individually. They started by answering the first set of ROS, SVS and PANAS questionnaires. After that, they were asked to sit down on an office chair and a researcher helped them to put on the VR-headset so they can see clearly. Participants were guided to sit down and just be in the virtual reality, and that they could spin the chair freely. A researcher told that he will tap the participant's shoulder when the experience is over. After guidance, the researcher put on the headphones for the participants. The participants stayed in the VR-environment for five minutes. After that, the researcher tapped their shoulder and helped participants to remove the headset. Participants were then asked to fill the second set of the same questionnaire. After completing the questionnaire participants were guided to leave the research space.

The reliability of each factor (SVS, PANAS, ROS) was tested by using Cronbach's alphas. For every measure, a sum variable was formulated, and a mean was calculated from sums. A paired-sample T-test was used to determine whether the mean difference of each sum variable between pre- and post-treatment was statistically significant. The one-way non-parametric ANOVA (Mann-Whitney) was used to test whether there was any of the background variables (age in 2 categories, gender, previous experience of using VR) explain the change in any of the sum variables. Analyses were completed utilizing the SPSS Statistics 25 –software.

4 Results

The scale statistics for ROS, SVS, PANAS POS and PANAS NEG are presented in the Table 1. All psychological measures had good Cronbach's α, ranging from .86 to .91. And were in line with previous studies (e.g. [30]). The mean scores and standard deviations are presented in the Table 1. When comparing the means of the sum variables (two-way), all of the results show a positive change in all the recovery results with a confidence level of 95% as follows. The mean of restoration outcomes (ROS) increased from 4.13 (SD = 1.14) to 5.31 (SD = 0.93) by 1.15 (SD = .99, t (59) = 9.01, Cl = .89, 1.4, p < .001). The mean of positive feelings increased from 4.72 (SD = 1.01) to 5.01 (SD = 0.93) by .36 (SD = .75, t(57) = 3.70, Cl = .16, .55, p < .001). The mean of negative feelings decreased from 2.24 (SD = .84) to 1.60 (SD = .69). by −.65 (SD = .59, t(59) = −8.50, Cl = −.80, −.49 p < .001). Reported vitality (SVS) increased from 4.62 (SD = 1.14) to 5.30 (SD = .87) by .65 (SD = .78, t (57) = 6.34 Cl = .44, .85, p < .001). For background variables, the one-way non-parametric ANOVA (Mann-Whitney) showed a statistically significant difference (p = 0.026) only in the increase of positive feelings (the change of PANAS POS). The mean of the positive feelings increased more for the users without any previous VR-experiences (n = 23): from 4.52 (SD = 1.01) to 5.22 (SD = 0.80) compared to the ones with previous VR-experience (n = 35): from 4.85 (SD = 1.00) to 5.00 (SD = 1.01).

Table 1. Scale statistics of all psychological measures

	Before viewing			After viewing		
	Mean	SD	Cron α	Mean	SD	Cron α
ROS	4.13	1.14	.88	5.31	0.93	.86
SVS	4.62	1.14	.91	5.30	0.87	.87
PANAS POS	4.72	1.01	.90	5.01	0.93	.90
PANAS NEG	2.24	0.84	.86	1.60	0.69	.86

5 Discussion

Results showed statistically significant changes with all psychological measures. Participant's perceived restoration outcomes, subjective vitality and positive thoughts increased, while negative thoughts decreased. These results indicate that simulated, VR-based environment can indeed have recovering effects. When comparing to previous restorative environment studies, result of VR-based simulation were as good or exceeded the results achieved from the real natural environments, such as urban woodlands [30].

Taylor and Kuo [29] proposes for schools to use nature environments in school breaks to recover students from the directed attention fatigue. Our results suggest that VR-based environments can work likewise. For example, VR-based restorative environment could be used during school day or workday to recover people from directed attention fatigue. Furthermore, our results suggest that high cognitive load, which is typically a challenge for learning environments utilizing VR (e.g. [19]), could possibly be decreased using recovery components.

Kaplan [14] suggested four-factor solution on his Attention Restoration Theory (ART): fascination, being away, extent and compatibility. These components were used to design and model a recovering VR-based environment. The Table 2 summarizes these components and derived design principles modelled and tested in this study.

These are also the proposed design principles for the designers to build recovering VR-based environments. As summarized in the Table 2, there are also several existing studies from various disciplines having aligned results with the proposed design principles. However, the proposed principles also raise several questions and need for validation by the future research. For example, among the proposed features there might be insignificant or even negative ones (causing cognitive load). Therefore, experimentation of different fascination features to discover the single feature impact and significance is suggested. In addition, experimentation on new possible features extracted from the multidisciplinary literature should be carried out. Furthermore, it is important to study environment features in many various contexts and groups. For example, some groups or contexts may emphasize one component over the another, and therefore they would benefit from a different environment.

Table 2. Proposed design principles for recovering VR-environments

Design component	Confirmed by previous research	Future research
Fascination		
Flying butterflies	Marselle et al. [20]	Experimentation of different fascination features to discover the single feature impact and significance
Singing birds	Ratcliffe et al. [24]	In addition, experimentation on new possible features extracted from the literature
Sounds of gentle wind	Abbot et al. [1]	
Ability to see horizon/landscape	Stigsdotter et al. [28]	
Ability to see close nature objects	Kaplan [14]; Nordh et al. [23]	
Blue sky	White et al. [35]	
Warm color temperature	Stone [27]	
Being away		
Contrasted environments	Tyrväinen et al. [30]	What is the effect of different contrasted environments on different user segments?
Extent		
Reflections from reality	Kaplan [14]; Erdelyi [7]	To what extend the environment needs to reflect a real and what is the effect of fantasy?
Compatibility		
Nature environments	Tyrväinen et al. [30]	Are there some other environments that might work similarly for various user segments?

Flying butterflies and singing birds have been found out to have a restorative effect in previous studies [20, 24]. Ratcliffe et al. [24] further suggest that bird singing distracts one from cognitive or affective demands, therefore connecting to the fascination-component of Kaplan's [14] ART theory. That is the case also with flying butterflies and sounds of gentle wind [1], as they direct one's attention to them. The ability to see horizon, landscape and close nature objects has also been found out to have a restorative effect [14, 23, 28], mainly through the fascination -component. In addition, the effect of seeing blue sky and the sun [27] may also be categorized to the fascination -component. As Kaplan [14] suggests, many fascinations in the nature hold the attention, but not in a dramatic fashion, and therefore has a restorative effect. With fascination component, future research could focus on determining how a single feature (e.g. flying butterflies) affects to the whole restorativeness of the environment.

In terms of the design component "being away", the effect of different contrasted environments on different user segments should be evaluated. For instance, for some segments or in some other venues the "being away" effect might be achieved by visualizing some other far-distance places than forests. Tyrväinen et al. [30] conducted a research where three different environments (built-up city centre, a city park and urban woodland) were studied. Results indicated that the perceived restorativeness was higher in the woodlands than in the urban park. It would be beneficial to study, whether this kind of differences could be found also in the context of VR environments. While there are some previous cues about the reflection of extent, realness and greenness to create psychological distance and achieve recovery [14, 23] there are also some studies showing that the fantasy can also create flow and embodiment which can be the factors for a recovering experience [7]. This gives a suggestion for the future research to explore to what extend the environment needs to reflect a real and what is the recovery effect of a fantasy in a VR-environment. Finally, as the previous research has suggested the nature environments, such as forests, to be compatible for the recovery, the possibility of some other environments having similar or better effects should be researched.

Compatibility suggests that the environment should fit what one is trying to do in the environment [14]. According to Kaplan [14], compatibility has two ways: one's purposes fit what the environment demands, and the environment gives enough information needed to meet one's purposes. Essentially, in the context of restorative VR environment this can mean that (a) the user wants to relax and recover and (b) the environment provides enough information and right setting for the user to do this. More research needs to be conducted to know what are one's purposes when viewing a restorative environment: do users want only to explore freely, or is there more purposes, for example a need to do relaxing activities? This information would be vital when designing restorative VR environments.

When talking about educational settings, many factors can cause disturbance to the recovery experience. For the future research, it would be important to consider the learner's cognitive and emotional processes, as well as the individual variance, when interacting with VR [32]. In the context of restorative environments, this can mean for example individual differences on perceiving the visual data, spatial understanding, motivation and special needs. In order to be able to design well-working restorative environments, co-operation is needed between the designers of VR-environments and the actual users, especially when designing environments for the educational field.

Furthermore, one future research avenue would be studying restorative environments and directed attention fatigue among students who need special support for their learning. More research needs to be conducted with children who possess attention deficit disorders (e.g. Attention Deficit Hyperactivity Disorder (ADHD) or Attention Deficit Disorder (ADD). It would be beneficial to know whether there is a connection between attention deficit disorders and directed attention fatigue, for example do children who possess attention deficit disorders become fatigued faster than peers who has no disorders. Symptoms of ADHD and DAF mirrors each other so closely, that the Attention Deficit Disorders Evaluation scale, which is used to measure ADHD, has also been used to measure DAF [18, 34]. Moreover, previous research has proven that natural environments has improved the concentration of children diagnosed with ADHD and ADD [18, 29]. Simulated, VR-based restorative environments would be very beneficial for children with concentration problems and/or attention deficit disorders, at best.

The results of this study are promising, but certain aspects need to be taken into account when generalizing the results. The major limitation of this study was that there was no comparison group. Therefore, more research is needed in order to investigate whether recovery components in VR learning environments could be successfully utilized in educational contexts. Moreover, future research avenues include comparing the effects of VR-Forest and real, natural forest. In addition, in future studies, physiological measures (e.g. galvanic skin response-sensors and heart rate sensors) could be used to have more data about the recovering effects.

Despite the encouraging results, the small sample size was small. Therefore, more research with a bigger sample size will be needed to validate the results in a more solid way and further, to compare the magnitude of the restoration in VR to other ways of having a break. In addition, from the results of this study, it is not clear whether only simulated, VR-based restorative experience can cause these restorative effects, or can whichever calm environment cause same kind of restorative effect. Furthermore, the proposed design principles need to be validated by the future research as suggested. Nevertheless, the results are unambiguous in terms of that VR-based environments can possess recovery effects and thus work as recovery environments at schools or these kinds of environments can be used in learning applications.

Acknowledgements. Authors of this paper would like to thank Arto Korhonen for his help with data colecting, Metsämiesten Säätiö Foundation for funding and Zoan Oy for building the modelled VR-environment.

References

1. Abbott, L.C., Taff, D., Newman, P., Benfield, J.A., Mowen, A.J.: The influence of natural sounds on attention restoration. J. Park Recreat. Adm. **34**(3), 5–15 (2016)
2. Berman, M.G., Jonides, J., Kaplan, S.: The cognitive benefits of interacting with nature. Psychol. Sci. **19**, 1207–1212 (2008). https://doi.org/10.1111/j.1467-9280.2008.02225.x
3. Berto, R.: Exposure to restorative environments helps restore attentional capacity. J. Environ. Psychol. **25**(3), 249–259 (2005)
4. Boksem, M., Meijman, T., Lorist, M.: Effects of mental fatigue on attention: an ERP study. Cogn. Brain. Res. **25**, 107–116 (2005)

5. Bostic, T.J., McGartland Rubio, D., Hood, M.: Soc. Indic. Res. **52**, 313 (2000). https://doi.org/10.1023/A:1007136110218
6. Crawford, J.R., Henry, J.D.: The positive and negative affect schedule (PANAS): construct validity, measurement properties and normative data in a large non-clinical sample. Br. J. Clin. Psychol. **43**(3), 245–265 (2004)
7. Erdelyi, M.H.: Recovery of unavailable perceptual input. Cogn. Psychol. **1**(2), 99–113 (1970)
8. Felsten, G.: Where to take a study break on the college campus: an attention restoration theory perspective. J. Environ. Psychol. **29**, 160–167 (2009). https://doi.org/10.1016/j.jenvp.2008.11.006
9. Hartig, T., Lindblom, K., Ovefelt, K.: The home and nearhome area offer restoration opportunities differentiated by gender. Scand. Hous. Plan. Res. **15**(4), 283–296 (1998)
10. Hauru, K., Lehvävirta, S., Korpela, K., Kotze, D.J.: Closure of view to the urban matrix has positive effects on perceived restorativeness in urban forests in Helsinki, Finland. Landsc. Urban Plan. **107**(4), 361–369 (2012). https://doi.org/10.1016/J.LANDURBPLAN.2012.07.002
11. Jacobson, S.: Paying Attention or Fatally Distracted? Concentration, Memory, and Multi-Tasking in a Multi-Media World, 16 Legal Writing 419 (2010)
12. Kaplan, S., Kaplan, R.: Environment and Cognition. Praeger, New York (1982)
13. Kaplan, S., Berman, M.G.: Directed attention as a common resource for executive functioning and self-regulation. Perspect. Psychol. Sci. **5**, 43–57 (2010)
14. Kaplan, S.: The restorative benefits of nature: toward an integrative framework. J. Environ. Psychol. **15**(3), 169–182 (1995)
15. Kaplan, S.: Meditation, restoration, and the management of mental fatigue. Environ. Behav. **33**, 480–506 (2001). https://doi.org/10.1177/00139160121973106
16. Kaplan, R.: The nature of the view from home: psychological benefits. Environ. Behav. **33** (4), 507–542 (2001)
17. Korpela, K., Ylén, M., Tyrväinen, L., Silvennoinen, H.: Determinants of restorative experiences in everyday favourite places. Health Place **14**, 636–652 (2008)
18. Kuo, F.E., Taylor, A.F.: A potential natural treatment for attention-deficit/hyperactivity disorder: evidence from a national study. Am. J. Public Health **94**, 1580–1586 (2004). https://doi.org/10.2105/AJPH.94.9.1580
19. Makransky, G., et al.: Adding immersive virtual reality to a science lab simulation causes more presence but less learning. Learn. Instr. **61**, 23–34 (2019). https://doi.org/10.1016/j.learninstruc.2017.12.007
20. Marselle, M.R., Irvine, K.N., Lorenzo-Arribas, A., Warber, S.L.: Does perceived restorativeness mediate the effects of perceived biodiversity and perceived naturalness on emotional well-being following group walks in nature? J. Environ. Psychol. **46**, 217–232 (2016)
21. Meyers, D.: Psychology, 9th edn. W. H. Freeman & Co., New York (2009)
22. Miller, M.: What college teachers should know about memory: a perspective from cognitive psychology. Coll. Teach. **59**, 117–122 (2011)
23. Nordh, H., Hartig, T., Hagerhall, C.M., Fry, G.: Components of small urban parks that predict the possibility for restoration. Urban For. Urban Green. **8**, 225–235 (2009)
24. Ratcliffe, E., Gatersleben, B., Sowden, P.T.: Bird sounds and their contributions to perceived attention restoration and stress recovery. J. Environ. Psychol. **36**, 221–228 (2013)
25. Ryan, R.M., Frederick, C.M.: On energy, personality, and health: subjective vitality as a dynamic reflection of well-being. J. Pers. **65**, 529–565 (1997)
26. Staats, H., Kieviet, A., Hartig, T.: Where to recover from attentional fatigue: an expectancy-value analysis of environmental preference. J. Environ. Psychol. **23**(2), 147–157 (2003)

27. Stone, N.J.: Environmental view and color for a simulated telemarketing task. J. Environ. Psychol. **23**(1), 63–78 (2003)
28. Stigsdotter, U.K., Corazon, S.S., Sidenius, U., Refshauge, A.D., Grahn, P.: Forest design for mental health promotion—using perceived sensory dimensions to elicit restorative responses. Landsc. Urban Plan. **160**, 1–15 (2017)
29. Taylor, F.A., Kuo, F.E.: Children with attention deficits concentrate better after walk in the park. J. Atten. Disord. **12**, 402–409 (2009)
30. Tyrväinen, L., Ojala, A., Korpela, K., Lanki, T., Tsunetsugu, Y., Kagawa, T.: The influence of urban green environments on stress relief measures: a field experiment. J. Environ. Psychol. **38**, 1–9 (2014)
31. Van den Berg, A., Koole, S.L., Van der Wulp, N.Y.: Environmental preference and restoration: how are they related? J. Environ. Psychol. **23**, 135–146 (2003)
32. Vesisenaho, M., et al.: Virtual reality in education: focus on the role of emotions and physiological reactivity. J. Virtual Worlds Res. **12**(1), 1–15 (2019)
33. Watson, D., Clark, L.A., Tellegen, A.: Development and validation of brief measures of positive and negative affect: the PANAS scales. J. Pers. Soc. Psychol. **54**, 1063–1070 (1988)
34. Wells, N.M.: At home with nature: effects of "greenness" on children's cognitive function. Environ. Behav. **32**, 775–795 (2000)
35. White, M., Smith, A., Humphryes, K., Pahl, S., Snelling, D., Depledge, M.: Blue space: the importance of water for preference, affect, and restorativeness ratings of natural and built scenes. J. Environ. Psychol. **30**(4), 482–493 (2010)
36. Wickens, C.D., McCarley, J.: Applied Attention Theory. Taylor & Francis, Boca Raton (2008)

LMS Moodle Interactive Exercises Sequence for Developing Linguistic Competence

Ekaterina Shostak[1(✉)], Liudmila Khalyapina[1], and Igor Khodunov[2]

[1] Peter the Great Saint-Petersburg Polytechnic University, Polytechnicheskaya 19, 194021 Saint-Petersburg, Russian Federation
ekaterinavsh@yandex.ru, lhalapina@bk.ru

[2] Ioffe Institute, Polytechnicheskaya 26, 194021 Saint-Petersburg, Russian Federation
khigand@gmail.com

Abstract. Due to the global integration processes in education (academic mobility, the increasing number of students, etc.), it has become difficult to provide a proper individual approach to each student during a class at university. Learning management systems (LMS) are viewed methodically as a means of providing this individual approach to satisfy the demands of a massive student audience. The purpose of the paper is to select the most effective interactive exercises available on Moodle platform for developing the linguistic competence and organize them in a proper sequence that would provide coherent linguistic competence development. Key notions are described in the theoretical part of the paper; the criteria determining raw data and further data analysis are provided. Quantitative methods of data analysis have been employed. The practical value of the research consists in providing the sets of interactive exercises based on objective criteria. The possible sets are presented in Appendix. A code in Python was elaborated to perform data analysis and can be used to deal with similar research problems. Researchers who are interested in the code are welcome to email the third author of the paper.

Keywords: Linguistic competence · Procedural memory · Digital exercises · LMS moodle · Interactive exercises · Working memory

1 Introduction

Nowadays higher education institutions tend to employ means of distance learning to achieve maximum result with minimum effort (and other types of resources such as time, premises, etc.) for all participants of the educational process. In this context by the word "participants" we mean not only students and educators who interact with each other directly within a course but also other university employees whose workload is implicitly related to the educational process. Due to the immense workload, which is caused by various academic mobility programs, constantly growing number of students, new subjects (which emerge on the crest of two or more previously separate scientific disciplines) and more complex tasks that every student/educator/scientist/scholar must face in their professional trajectory [1, 2], learning management systems (LMS) are

D. A. Alexandrov et al. (Eds.): DTGS 2019, CCIS 1038, pp. 517–529, 2019.
https://doi.org/10.1007/978-3-030-37858-5_44

viewed methodically as a means of providing individual approach to satisfy the demands of a massive student audience.

This research has been conducted at Peter the Great Saint-Petersburg Polytechnic University. LMS Moodle potential in relation to the development of linguistic competence in the domain of professionally-oriented language learning has been addressed.

The research aims at finding out the most relevant sequence of interactive exercises which are available on Moodle platform for developing linguistic competence. The paper's structure follows the guideline of the research stages and contains the following parts: motivation, literature overview, methods and procedure, data analysis, results and appendix.

Firstly, a literature overview on the topic of linguistic competence and working memory is presented. Secondly, linguistic competence was split into a set of abilities and skills organized in a hierarchy where the proceeding element contributes to the formation of the subsequent one. LMS Moodle interactive exercises were selected and analyzed in accordance with their potential contribution to the formation of determined elements of the linguistic competence. Based on the working memory criterion, a value of effort (made by an individual when performing a certain type of an exercise) was introduced and attributed to each exercise type when developing a certain element of the linguistic competence. The second stage of the research provided us with numerical data which was processed afterwards mathematically (the third stage). Findings of the research work are presented in the conclusion.

2 Motivation

The aim of the study is to find out the proper sequence of interactive exercises which are available on LMS Moodle platform for effective development of linguistic competence. The findings of the research bear purely practical value. The following research problem serves as a prerequisite for the study.

LMS Moodle offers a huge variety of interactive exercises which can potentially be used for building the linguistic competence. It is difficult to decide which exercises to take first; which exercises can be neglected, and how to order the exercises which finally were selected. If the probable number of combinations is to be calculated, then it will make up 4 457 400 (1), where n – the number of exercises (=15), k – the number of components that form the linguistic competence (=11).

$$C_n^k = \frac{(n+k-1)!}{k! \cdot (n-1)!} = \frac{(15+11-1)!}{11! \cdot (15-1)!} = 4\,457\,400 \qquad (1)$$

It is obvious that if some factors determining the process of learning are introduced the number will drop. Thus, we decided to select some factors, or criteria, that have a certain impact on learning process. In the study we dealt with the following criteria: exercise type, components of the linguistic competence; number of mental objects per exercise and language units (word, word combination, sentence, text).

We did not mean to give a vast theoretical overview and comparative analysis of the existing theories concerning linguistic competence; nor did we intend to compare and criticize the existing theories and concepts regarding working memory. The primary research goal for us was to obtain the resulting sequence of exercises based on selected criteria. Thus, in literature overview the basic notions related to the selected criteria are explained and essential references are provided.

3 Literature Overview

The linguistic competence is the key notion of the research and as such it needs an in-depth description. The notion of the linguistic competence is interpreted and defined in a number of ways.

Firstly, it is necessary to mention that scientists argue about the corrlation between such notions as "linguistic competence" and "communicative competence". In 1965 Chomsky emphasized the difference between linguistic competence and linguistic performance. Linguistic competence he defined as the speaker-hearer's knowledge of his language and the linguistic performance he specified as the actual use of language in concrete situations [3].

The theory of linguistic competence/performance was popular for a period of time. Thus, Wales and Marshall (1966) stated that the theory of performance describes the way we put linguistic competence to use [4]. But later on Habennas (1970) pointed out that besides the linguistic competence a speaker should also demonstrate the ability to communicate and interact which he calls communicative competence [5].

In other words, linguistic competence started to be analyzed as a part of communicative competence.

Connections between communicative competence and sociolinguistic competence was the next step in the development of the theory. Hymes (1972) stated that communicative competence should include both grammatical and sociolinguistic competences. [6]. It means that a person should not only demonstrate the ability to use grammar rules correctly in his speech, but also the person should be able to analyze sociocultural context and act in accordance with it.

All these ideas developed in different spheres of linguistics are very important for the theory of teaching foreign languages. But from methodological point of view we agree with those authors (Davis, Palmer, etc.) who consider that linguistic competence and communicative competence are different [7]. We assume that linguistic competence being part of communicative competence is the one that has to be developed first (within a class), and which cannot be developed simultaneously with the latter. Although it is obvious that within a course or a module of several classes the two competences are developed to some extent simultaneously.

If to refer to the ideas of Palmer (1979) we can see that he developed the theory of the second language experience, according to which a person can either control the formal aspects of language or control the meaning of his speech. When a speaker is focused on meaning, he or she is able to express his/her ideas well. However, in this way the choice of grammar and vocabulary (as well as the way the phrases are pronounced) is likely to be inaccurate (provided the skills have not been trained earlier) [8].

From all these we can underline two types of conclusions which are important for our research: (1) methodologically we should divide the process of teaching foreign languages into two different parts: developing linguistic competence and communicative competence; (2) at the same time we should understand that at a particular level of teaching integration of these two competences is to take the privilege part of methodology.

In order to identify the structure of linguistic competence, we need to have a clear image of the concept of a competence – what it consists of and how its elements intercorrelate. The general notion of a competence is split into several implicit components which can be presented in a hierarchy [9]:

1. **Activity** – speaking is an activity which is to some extend controlled. Activity is observable and can be performed in different ways: automatically (skill), regularly, repeatedly, etc. This component is usually measured and is referred to as **performance**.
2. **Ability** – generally it implies the individual's ability to perform the activity. Ability cannot be observed directly.
3. **Competence** – involves the individual's capacities (perceptual, cognitive, etc.), skills and abilities which are targeted (or cognitively controlled and aimed) at solving tasks (producing activities) in a particular domain. Competence cannot be observed directly; competence represents a teleonomic hierarchy. Each level has a goal against which performance (activity) can be assessed. The highest level serves as the resulting experience which states that all the previous levels have been completed (performance was positive).

In Sect. 4 we employ this teleonomic hierarchy in order to split the linguistic competence into components; these components and their disposition give us raw data to be processed afterwards with numerical methods.

There are two types of memory: procedural memory (subconscious; cannot be verbalized; content is learned through explanation) and declarative memory (conscious; can be verbalized; content is learned through explanation) [10]. Procedural memory stands for skills and automatization; whereas declarative memory stands for knowledge and "includes the capacity to activate procedural competence from a meta-level < … > in order to control the ability and to employ it responsibly" (Lehmann 2008:7). Judging by the fact, we can assume that linguistic competence is focused more on activating relative skills from procedural memory for completing a certain task (for solving the problem). Thus, for our research we need not only exercises that form skills (upload content into procedural memory) but also train our ability to activate the procedural memory (train our declarative memory) responsibly. At least, this criterion should be taken into account and is represented in Sect. 4.

The second fact, which has been proved by cognitive psychologists and neurophysiologists, is that capacities of our working memory are limited. These limitations are discussed in a number of articles [11–13]. The average number of objects that can be operated by working memory is equal to 3–4 mental objects. This factor is going to be also employed by us for attributing value to effort-consuming scale.

4 Methods and Procedure

Linguistic competence can be split into a number of components where every component corresponds to a particular type of memory (procedural or declarative). The structure is illustrated in Table 1.

Table 1. Linguistic competence split to components.

Component	Memory type
Thought **formation** using phonetic skills	Procedural memory
Thought **formation** using vocabulary skills	
Thought **formation** using grammar skills	
Thought **expression** using phonetic skills	
Thought **expression** using vocabulary skills	
Thought **expression** using grammar skills	
Ability to use the skills holistically at thought **formation** stage	Declarative memory
Ability to use the skills holistically at thought **expression** stage	

It should be noted that the structure represented in Table 1 is based on the widely accepted notion of a linguistic competence [14, 15]. A more profound insight can be obtained if every component is considered against a language unit – word, word combination, sentence and text (see Table 2).

Table 2. Linguistic competence components and language units.

Language unit	Component	Sequence number
Text (t)	Ability to use the skills holistically at thought **formation** stage	11
	Ability to use the skills holistically at thought **expression** stage	12
Sentence (s)	Thought **formation** using grammar skills	9
	Thought **expression** using grammar skills	10
Word combination (wc)	Thought **formation** using grammar skills	7
	Thought **expression** using grammar skills	8
	Thought **formation** using vocabulary skills	5
	Thought **expression** using vocabulary skills	6
Word (w)	Thought **formation** using vocabulary skills	3
	Thought **expression** using vocabulary skills	4
	Thought **formation** using phonetics skills	1
	Thought **expression** using phonetics skills	2

Thus, we get a sequence number of each component in the hierarchy of the competence. It means that component 12 is the resulting experience which states that performance at all the previous levels (1–11) should be assessed as positive.

At the next stage we selected 15 types of interactive exercises that are available on LMS Moodle platform (Hereinafter referred to as Ex. №.): **Ex. 1.** Multiple Choice; **Ex. 2.** Dialog Cards; **Ex. 3.** Drag and Drop; **Ex. 4.** Drag the Words; **Ex. 5.** Fill in the Blanks; **Ex. 6.** Find the Hotspot; **Ex. 7.** Guess the Answer; **Ex. 8.** Interactive Video; **Ex. 9.** Memory Game; **Ex. 10.** Single choice set; **Ex. 11.** Summary; **Ex. 12.** True/False Question; **Ex.13.** Image Hotspots; **Ex. 14.** Image Sequencing; **Ex. 15.** Agamotto (Image Blender). These exercises were classified in terms of their contribution to the formation of each component of the linguistic competence at each language unit level.

Table 3. The scale that measures effort expressed in the number of mental objects per exercise.

Effort	0	1	2	3	4	5
Number of mental objects per exercise	absolutely not effort-consuming	a little bit effort-consuming	relatively effort-consuming	effort-consuming	very effort-consuming	the most effort-consuming
	0–1	2	3–4	5–6	7–8	9 < …

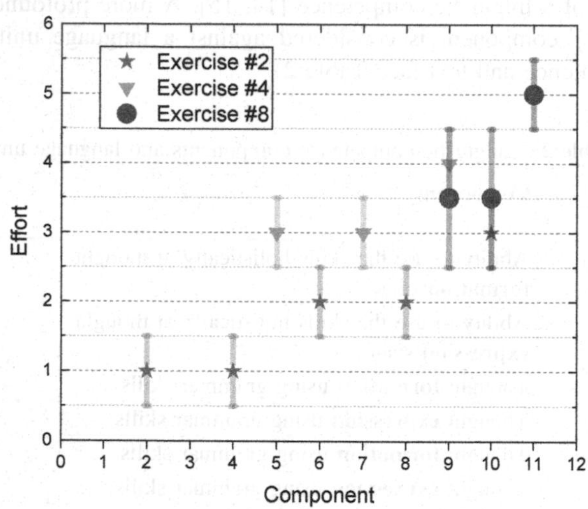

Fig. 1. Raw data presented for exercises 2, 4 and 8.

In order to evaluate effectiveness of each exercise when dealing with a certain component and a certain language unit, a new variable was introduced – effort. As the process of studying involves primarily dealing with new information (new mental objects that are meant to be acquired), it was decided to evaluate cognitive effort of working memory in relation to the number of mental objects it must operate when performing a task (see Table 3). Figure 1 illustrates the relationship between effort and component for exercises 2, 4 and 8. Due to students' psychological differences one exercise might require different effort. On Fig. 1 error bars represent estimation: accuracy of ±0.5 for exercise 4 in the estimation of effort 3 means that for all students this effort remains in the interval [2.5, 3.5]. At the next stage of the research this numerical data has been processed. Preliminary results and the steps are described in Sect. 5 with all the key graphs provided.

5 Data Analysis

At the previous stage raw data consisting of effort scale, linguistic competence components and exercise evaluation was obtained. Based on the data we make an attempt to calculate effectiveness of each exercise for each component. Effectiveness being a rather vague concept can be expressed with the following equation, where both R (result) and T (time) are considered as constants in the case and are equal to 1. This approximation is done to make calculations easier and to estimate effectiveness-to-effort dependency, where effort (which in fact comprises more elements) corresponds to the number of mental objects in the case.

$$Effectiveness = \frac{R}{T \cdot Effort} \quad (2)$$

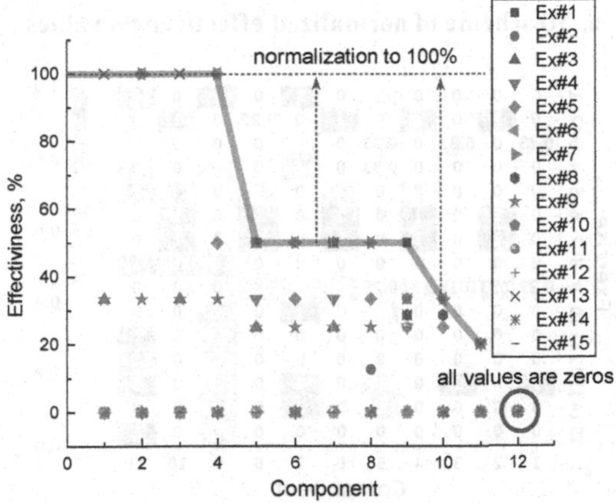

Fig. 2. Effectiveness is presented in percentage. Red dash arrows represent normalization that has be done for further analysis. Component 12 is not taken into account in further analysis. (Color figure online)

The graph depicted in Fig. 2 is sufficiently representative, as it shows the increasing level of difficulty in building components 9, 10 and 11 in comparison with the first components. The first 4 components are 2 times less effort-consuming than components 5, 6, 7, 8, 9 and 5 times less effort-consuming than component 11. Component 12 is omitted in our research as this component implies positive performance of the whole set of components; it involves speaking activity which due to limits imposed by existing technologies (it can hardly be tested automatically without assistance) is better to be measured and tested in class with the help of an instructor (a teacher).

Further, effectiveness values were brought into alignment to the maximum value for each component and projected onto the interval [0, 1] (see Fig. 3).

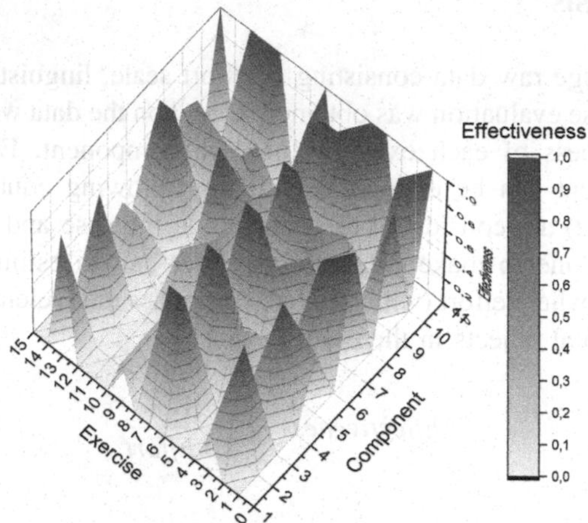

a. 3D scheme of normalized effectiveness values

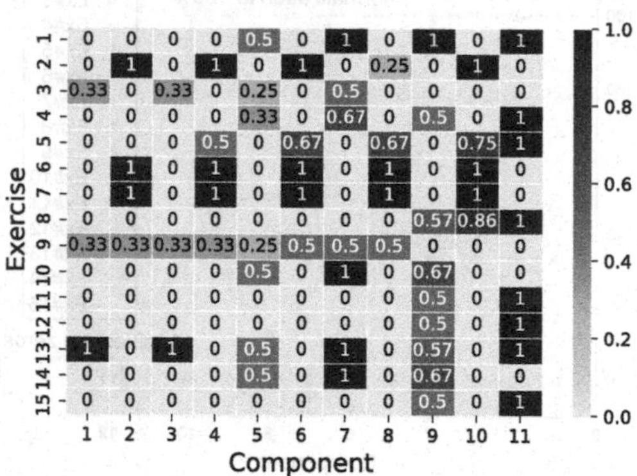

b. Heat map of normalized effectiveness values

Fig. 3. These two graphs reflect arrays of exercise, components and effectiveness data. Value of effectiveness is normalized in both plots.

Since the data set is small, due correlation analysis cannot be performed with the purpose of proving the validity of the input data. In the case significant calculation errors would occur. Therefore, to check the validity of the data, we studied value density distribution and the behaviour of the distribution function (see Fig. 4).

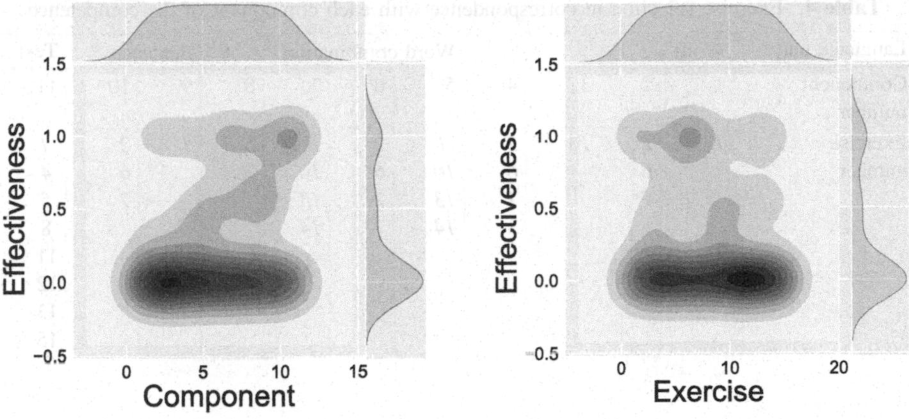

Fig. 4. Distribution functions. (Color figure online)

In both graphs along the OX axis, we can observe a distribution (located above the graph), which corresponds to a uniform distribution of the magnitude with respect to the axis. It is essential to focus on the differences between the distribution function plotted above the graph and the distribution function plotted to the right of the graph.

On the blue graph on the distribution function located to the right of the graph, we can observe two peaks with one peak reaching maximum at 0.00 (OY axis). This peak indicates that there are many exercises aimed at developing limited number of components. Also considering the density distribution, it can be noted that there are fewer exercises aimed at developing components from 2 to 5. It is also worth paying attention to the second peak of the distribution function with a maximum at 1.00 (along the OY axis). This peak indicates that there are some exercises that develop components to a maximum.

On the green graph there are two peaks in the distribution function as well: one with a maximum at 0.00 (in the OY axis) and the second one with a maximum at 1.00 (in the OY axis). These peaks and their ratio confirm the conclusions drawn from the blue graph: on the blue graph there is a poorly developed component which implies a small number of exercises; and on the green graph we see a small number of exercises which serves as a straightforward confirmation of the implication.

The study of the value density distribution and the shape of the density distribution functions for both graphs showed the discrepancies in the exercises in terms of their local focus. It illustrates that exercises 10–12 are oriented on specific components (the green graph) and components 2–5 are developed with a limited number of exercises.

Out of 4 457 400 options the following exercises have been selected as the most effective ones for a particular competence component based on the criteria stated in Sect. 4 (see Table 4).

Table 4. Exercise selection in correspondence with each component of the competence.

Language unit	Word				Word combination				Sentence		Text
Component number	1	2	3	4	5	6	7	8	9	10	11
Exercise number	*13*	2 6 7	*13*	*2* *6* *7*	*1* *10* *13* *14*	*2* *6* *7*	*1* *10* *13* *14*	*6* *7*	*1*	*2* *6* *7*	*1* *4* *5* 8 11 12 13 15

Next, we calculated the number of possible exercise sequences. It is obvious that the number of variants of sets of exercises (V) is measure of Cartesian product of 11 sets. The Cartesian power of the set $V_1 \times V_2 \times V_3 \times \ldots V_n = V^n$ or simply the length of the array of the set V is the number of sets that correspond to the Table 4. The number of sets turned out to be 20 736.

It should also be noted that the number of sets obtained also includes sets in which the same exercises are repeated with extreme cases of repetition: min - 3 times, max - 8 times.

Min repetitions (13, 2, 13, 2, 10, 2, 14, 6, 1, 7, 4). Exercise 2 occurs 3 times = 2 repetitions, exercise 13 occurs 2 times = 1 repetition. Total: 2 + 1 = 3 repetitions.

Max repetitions (13, 6, 13, 6, 1, 6, 1, 6, 1, 6, 1). Exercise 6 occurs 5 times = 4 repetitions, exercise 13 occurs 2 times = 1 repetition, exercise 1 occurs 4 times = 3 repetitions. Total 4 + 1 + 3 = 8 repetitions.

In our opinion repetitions are better to be reduced, as it seems to diversity of exercises seems to evoke more interest and to force motivation. Thus, the scenario with minimum repetitions is preferable in the case. It has been calculated that there are 1200 sets with minimum repetitions.

Afterwards sets with minimum repetitions within one block (grey, blue, yellow and red) have been calculated. In the grey block one exercise is used for component 1 and component 3, thus, there is one repetition which cannot be avoided. In the blue block the amount of repetitions was reduced, and the total number of possible sequences turned out to be 912. In the red and yellow blocks, the number of exercises remained. After matching the arrays, it was found out that they intersect only in 672 cases; which means that 672 sequences satisfy the criteria (see Fig. 5).

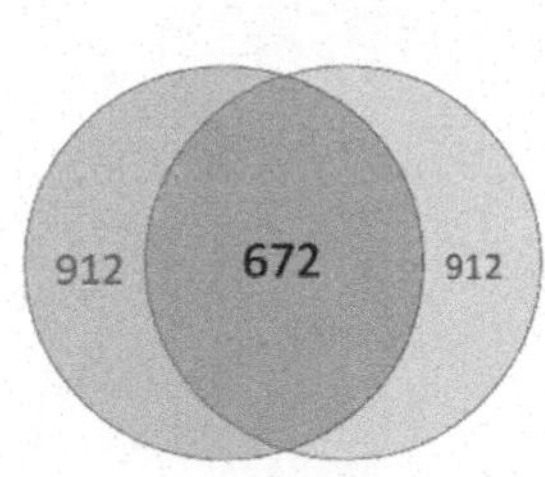

a. The last stage of selection procedure

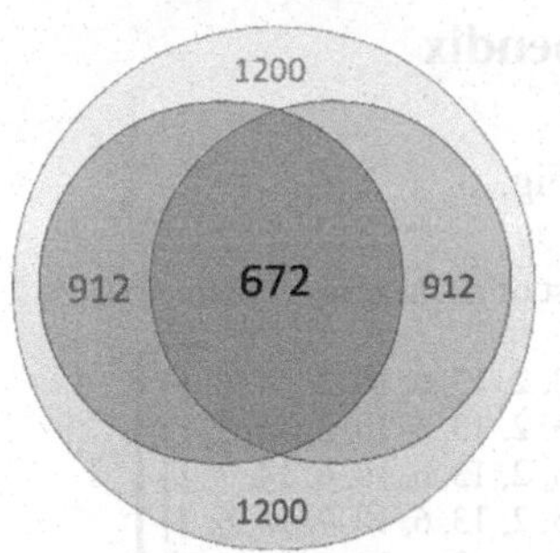

b. Full selection procedure

Fig. 5. Arrays matching.

6 Results

The purpose of the paper has been to find out the proper sequence of interactive exercises for effective development of linguistic competence. A theoretical overview on linguistic competence and working memory has been done; general notions have been introduced. Linguistic competence has been split into components and each interactive exercise available on LMS Moodle platform has been evaluated in terms of its contribution to the formation of a specific component. A value of effort (made by an individual when performing a certain type of an exercise) was introduced and attributed to each exercise type. Raw data has been processed and analyzed afterwards.

Finally, 672 sets of exercises have been selected out of 4 457 400 possible variations. In appendix the list of the 672 sets is presented. In order to find the most suitable sets of exercises, a metric should be defined. Metric implies the criteria according to which a set can be considered as suitable for a stated purpose. In our case, this criterion is the maximum number of different exercises in the course (maximum diversity). Thus, out of 672 sets it is possible to produce 11,760 pairs with a minimum of 3 repeated exercises.

When trying to find the minimum match for three sets of exercises, the value turned out to be 12 (if 3 sets are selected, then the minimum number of matched exercises is 12). Further observation shows that it is impossible to select 3 sets of exercises that would differ in 4 tasks. Taking into account this fact, we can conclude that the optimal strategy for choosing a relatively “unique” sequence of exercises for each unit (one unit needs one sequence of exercises) is the following: we can choose any two sets of exercises for Unit 1 and Unit 2 – they will have only 3 exercise that are repeated. When choosing a set of exercises for Unit 3, one should make sure that the third sequence has only 3 exercises that are repeated in Unit 2. It should also be noted that exercise 13 for component 1 and 3 is basically the same what reduces the ultimate number of exercises in a set to 10.

Appendix

See Fig. 6.

List of all the arrays obtained:

[13, 2, 13, 6, 10, 2, 14, 6, 1]
[13, 2, 13, 6, 10, 2, 14, 7, 1]
[13, 2, 13, 6, 10, 6, 14, 7, 1]
[13, 2, 13, 6, 10, 7, 14, 6, 1]
[13, 2, 13, 6, 14, 2, 10, 6, 1]
[13, 2, 13, 6, 14, 2, 10, 7, 1]
[13, 2, 13, 6, 14, 6, 10, 7, 1]
[13, 2, 13, 6, 14, 7, 10, 6, 1]
[13, 2, 13, 7, 10, 2, 14, 6, 1]
[13, 2, 13, 7, 10, 2, 14, 7, 1]
[13, 2, 13, 7, 10, 6, 14, 7, 1]
[13, 2, 13, 7, 10, 7, 14, 6, 1]
[13, 2, 13, 7, 14, 2, 10, 6, 1]
[13, 2, 13, 7, 14, 2, 10, 7, 1]
[13, 2, 13, 7, 14, 6, 10, 7, 1]
[13, 2, 13, 7, 14, 7, 10, 6, 1]
[13, 6, 13, 2, 10, 2, 14, 6, 1]
[13, 6, 13, 2, 10, 2, 14, 7, 1]
[13, 6, 13, 2, 10, 6, 14, 7, 1]
[13, 6, 13, 2, 10, 7, 14, 6, 1]
[13, 6, 13, 2, 14, 2, 10, 6, 1]
[13, 6, 13, 2, 14, 2, 10, 7, 1]
[13, 6, 13, 2, 14, 6, 10, 7, 1]
[13, 6, 13, 2, 14, 7, 10, 6, 1]
[13, 6, 13, 7, 10, 2, 14, 6, 1]
[13, 6, 13, 7, 10, 2, 14, 7, 1]
[13, 6, 13, 7, 10, 6, 14, 7, 1]
[13, 6, 13, 7, 10, 7, 14, 6, 1]
[13, 6, 13, 7, 14, 2, 10, 6, 1]
[13, 6, 13, 7, 14, 2, 10, 7, 1]
[13, 6, 13, 7, 14, 6, 10, 7, 1]
[13, 6, 13, 7, 14, 7, 10, 6, 1]
[13, 7, 13, 2, 10, 2, 14, 6, 1]
[13, 7, 13, 2, 10, 2, 14, 7, 1]
[13, 7, 13, 2, 10, 6, 14, 7, 1]
[13, 7, 13, 2, 10, 7, 14, 6, 1]
[13, 7, 13, 2, 14, 2, 10, 6, 1]
[13, 7, 13, 2, 14, 2, 10, 7, 1]
[13, 7, 13, 2, 14, 6, 10, 7, 1]
[13, 7, 13, 2, 14, 7, 10, 6, 1]
[13, 7, 13, 6, 10, 2, 14, 6, 1]
[13, 7, 13, 6, 10, 2, 14, 7, 1]
[13, 7, 13, 6, 10, 6, 14, 7, 1]
[13, 7, 13, 6, 10, 7, 14, 6, 1]
[13, 7, 13, 6, 14, 2, 10, 6, 1]
[13, 7, 13, 6, 14, 2, 10, 7, 1]
[13, 7, 13, 6, 14, 6, 10, 7, 1]
[13, 7, 13, 6, 14, 7, 10, 6, 1]

\+ [2] [6] [7] + [1] [4] [5] [8] [11] [12] [13] [15]

numbers of these two columns should be selected to have only 3 repetitions with the array

Fig. 6. Most productive sets of LMS Moodle interactive exercises for language competence.

References

1. Almazova, N., Andreeva, S., Khalyapina, L.: The integration of online and offline education in the system of students' preparation for global academic mobility. In: Alexandrov, D.A., Boukhanovsky, A.V., Chugunov, A.V., Kabanov, Y., Koltsova, O. (eds.) DTGS 2018. CCIS, vol. 859, pp. 162–174. Springer, Cham (2018). https://doi.org/10.1007/978-3-030-02846-6_13
2. Loginova, A.V.: The advantages of LMS Moodle in foreign language learning and teaching in technical departments. Vestnik nauki Sibiri **1**(1), 358–362 (2011). (in Russian)
3. Chomsky, N.: Aspects of the Theory of Syntax. MIT Press, Cambridge (1965)
4. Wales, R.J., Marshall, J.C.: Psycholinguistics papers. The proceedings of the Edinburgh conference. In: Lyons, J., Wales, R. (eds.). Edinburgh Conference 1966. Edinburgh university press, Edinburgh (1966). 268p
5. Habermas, J.: Towards a theory of communicative competence. Inquiry **13**(1–4), 360–375 (1970). https://doi.org/10.1080/00201747008601597
6. Hymes, D.: On communicative competence. In: Pride, J.B., Holmes, J. (eds.) Sociolinguistics. Part 2, pp. 269–293. Penguin, Harmondsworth (1972)
7. Davies, A.: Language teaching and linguistics: abstracts, language testing. Part II, pp. 145–159 (1978)
8. Palmer, A.S.: Compartmentalized and integrated control: an assessment of some evidence for two kinds of competence and implications for the classroom. Lang. Learn. **29**, 169–180 (1979)
9. Lehmann, C.: Linguistic competence: theory and empiry. Folia Linguist. **41**(3–4), 223–278 (2008). https://doi.org/10.1515/flin.41.3-4.223
10. Ullman, M.: The role of declarative and procedural memory in disorders of language. Linguist. Var. **13**, 133–154 (2013). https://doi.org/10.1075/lv.13.2.01ull
11. Miller, G.A.: The magical number seven, plus or minus two: some limits on our capacity for processing information. Psychol. Rev. **63**, 81–97 (1956). https://doi.org/10.1037/h0043158
12. Cowan, N.: The magical number 4 in short-term memory: a reconsideration of mental storage capacity. Behav. Brain Sci. **24**, 87–185 (2001). https://doi.org/10.1017/S0140525X01003922
13. Cowan, N., Rouder, J.N., Blume, C.L., Saults, J.S.: Models of verbal working memory capacity: what does it take to make them work? Psychol. Rev. **119**, 480–499 (2012). https://doi.org/10.1037/a0027791
14. Asimov, E.G., Shchukin, A.N.: A New Dictionary of Methodological Terms and Notions. Theory and Practice in Foreign Language Teaching. Ikar Publ., Moscow (2009). (in Russian)
15. Galskova, N., Gez, N.: Theory of Teaching Foreign Languages: Linguodidactics and Methodology. Academy, Moscow (2005). (In Russian)

Bridging the Digital Gap in Academic Writing and Information Management: The Case of Humanities Students

Yulia A. Stepanchuk(✉)

Ural Federal University, 51 Lenin av., Yekaterinburg, Russia
j.a.stepanchuk@urfu.ru

Abstract. Academic writing is a skill that increasingly attracts attention in modern university. By teaching writing skills to students, especially students in humanities, we can offset the drawbacks of today's information overloaded environment, develop students' critical thinking, clarity of thought and ability to creatively engage with textual material. This article is based on the experience of developing and teaching a master's level course that specifically focuses on note-taking as a subset of academic writing and combines digital and analogue tools in an attempt to teach students more efficient note-taking and information management skills. The data gathered through quantitative and qualitative methods help to elucidate students' note-taking and writing practices and to highlight the areas in need of further attention.

Keywords: Digital education · Higher education · Humanities · Academic writing · Writing technologies · Note-taking · Information management

1 Introduction

The issue of technology in relation to academic writing is complex and multifaceted. On the one hand, the abundance of information sources makes it easier than ever to engage in diverse research projects and access the required source materials and data. On the other hand, this abundance of sources *does not* directly translate into improved reading, interpreting and writing ability. There is a general consensus that the level of students' writing has been declining [11, 15], and a recognition that this presents a serious challenge, especially for humanities [9].

As I have argued in my previous paper [23], our digital environment presents us with a specific set of affordances that favor text consumption over text creation and actively discourage writing as a tool for thinking, memorization and analysis. Therefore, we are faced with a situation, where many skills that used to be acquired "naturally" and without clear understanding of how it happened, now need to be consciously taught.

The severe reduction of the *amount* of writing students do can be explained not only as a shift in teaching approaches [15], but also as an inadvertent consequence of the switch from paper to digital environment. It has been shown that technology in writing is often overlooked to the point of being "invisible" [10]. Consequently, the

D. A. Alexandrov et al. (Eds.): DTGS 2019, CCIS 1038, pp. 530–541, 2019.
https://doi.org/10.1007/978-3-030-37858-5_45

ways in which digital technology influences the reality of academic writing are overlooked as well. Indeed, they can be completely obscured for modern-day students who have grown up in digital environment and, therefore, have no point of comparison.

The main focus of this paper is a specific subtype of academic writing – note-taking understood as an intermediate step between text consumption and text production. Various forms of note-taking – summarization, paraphrasing, excerpting – used to be an indispensable part of paper-based intellectual culture. However, our digital tools are geared towards ease of copy and retrieval. As soon as the *need* to take notes by hand disappeared, note-taking practices experienced a sharp decline. Today students often prefer to "save time" by recording the teachers' lectures, photographing presentation slides, downloading texts and generally avoiding the need to take notes.

In this situation, note-taking becomes doubly invisible. As a form of academic activity, "note taking generally remains an area of tacit knowledge, acquired by imitation rather than formal instruction, and about which there is little explicit discussion" [4]. Meanwhile, there are good reasons to believe that note-taking constitutes an invisible foundation of academic writing, the absence of which is keenly felt even if the cause is not always understood.

2 Literature Review

Note-taking as a subtype of academic writing remains "an underresearched area" [7]; yet it has received repeated scholarly attention over the past decades. Much of the relevant research has been carried out in the fields of pedagogy and psychology; however, note-taking has been also studied within the context of literacy studies, digital tools and cultural and intellectual history.

A lot of pedagogical research focuses on note-taking as a tool to improve learning outcomes in school and university students. Such functions of note-taking as memorization, information retention and knowledge retrieval are addressed particularly often. Lecture notes are researched more often than reading notes.

Regarding memorization and recall, studies tend to show positive effects of note-taking on information recall and retention both in schoolchildren and in university students [6, 19]. The encoding effect of note-taking, however, is often less pronounced than expected [18]. It seems that simply taking notes is not enough to provide consistent reproducible benefits: a lot depends on specific practices and processes guiding such note-taking. It has been demonstrated that guided note-taking is significantly more efficient compared to unguided practices [6, 7].

As for the role of digital note-taking, it has been shown that copy-pasting has a negative effect on information retention [1]. However, not enough research exists to compare different digital applications in the context of academic note-taking.

Beyond recall, note-taking has been shown to improve comprehension [14] and possess an epistemic function that facilitates deeper learning and understanding [6]. The existing research shows high levels of variation in how a note is understood and what note-taking processes are studied [18].

Much less attention is given to the more advanced and personalized note-taking, especially as a high-level intellectual tool. Ideally, a higher-level note-taking serves not only as a recall tool, but, as Niklas Luhmann put it, “a competent partner of communication” [20] – or, to quote different authors on the same idea, as a “monologue genre of written discourse” that possesses “self-structuring quality as it establishes a dialogue with oneself” [6].

Another area that has attracted considerable interest is a history of note-taking. It has been shown that for several centuries note-taking, in form of “commonplacing”, was used as one of the dominant pedagogical tools and knowledge practices in Western culture [3]. This practice emerged within the humanistic tradition but later was adapted to the new forms of knowledge and information management [4, 24].

As a result of this research, the importance of note-taking practices in their specific cultural forms have been repeatedly re-evaluated. Among the claims proposed by different scholars, we find the assertions that note-taking formed an important part of the Renaissance cultural shift [5]; that it can be used to explain many features of early modern texts [4]; that it led to the development of European encyclopedias [25]; that it helped to manage anxiety of early modern information overload [2, 3]; and even that it facilitated, or at least contributed to, the invention of modern self [8].

This historical research demonstrates the importance of note-taking as an “invisible mediator” of knowledge practices, and the role of pedagogical techniques in establishing and transmitting culturally approved note-taking techniques.

Unfortunately, this research remains all but unknown in Russia, where academic note-taking mostly focuses on summarization (*konspektirovaniye)*, either of lectures or of reading assignments. Summarization as a pedagogical tool and an academic practice is weakly systematized and rarely researched. A simple Google Scholar search reveals over 1.6 million results for academic articles in English on “note-taking”, while the search on “konspektirovaniye” in Russian shows only 7780 results, with many of the sources simply listing it among other forms of “students’ self-guided activity” [16].

As we see, despite the existing valuable research, several areas require further development:

- much of the pedagogical research in note-taking focuses on secondary school and undergraduate levels, with not enough attention to the more advanced note-taking skills required for independent academic work;
- the proposed practical strategies for teaching note-taking are not standardized;
- different research approaches into note-taking rarely intersect;
- not enough attention is given to the specific digital tools that may facilitate or discourage good note-taking practices;
- the entire field remains largely neglected and under-researched in Russia.

The author has been trying to address these challenges in her own teaching practice by developing a course for master’s level students in humanities. The course focuses on digital tools for academic writing, with its main focus on note-taking. This article summarizes data, observation and conclusions obtained as a result of this teaching experience. Since the course is a work in progress, any data and conclusions are preliminary and require further exploration and elaboration.

3 Methods

The course is currently taught at the Ural Federal University, at the Department of Art History and Cultural Studies. It is a nearly semester-long course (24 academic hours) taught to the masters' students specializing in three different areas: Art History, Cultural Studies and Audiovisual Communications. For logistical reasons (availability of computer classes), the students' group are usually combined to create a unified teaching environment. In its current revised version, which specifically focuses on academic note-taking, the course has been taught for three semesters (1,5 years). Today the course includes several topics: (1) how to work with academic journal databases; (2) how to use a citation management software (Zotero); (3) how to take notes and create a note-taking system for academic purposes; (4) how to transition from free-form note-taking to structured academic text; (5) how to manage writing process.

In this paper, I mostly address topics 3 and 4, with some attention given to 5. While teaching the course, I have been systematically gathering information on student's note-taking practices, their approaches to information management, attitudes to various digital tools and their general attitudes regarding writing in general and academic writing in particular. The data analyzed in this article come from several sources. A quantitative set of data was obtained from a questionnaire that have been routinely handed to the students at the beginning of the course. The questionnaire was designed, first and foremost, as a teaching tool, in order to gauge students' pre-existing practices of note-taking and their levels of digital literacy. Overall, 35 questionnaires have been collected over the 3 semesters of teaching. The small sample is due to the small number of students in these specializations (on average, 6 to 10 students per an academic group).

The questionnaire has been handed out to every academic group at the beginning of the course. This provided an opportunity to better understand students' pre-existing attitudes and approaches. The questionnaire consisted of several parts. The first part contained a set of questions to elucidate students' general level of digital literacy and the digital tools they use ("What digital devices do you use on an everyday basis?", "Which of your devices you most often use for your academic work?", "What operation systems are installed on your devices?", "How you would describe your level of computer literacy?", "Do you actively organize and manage information on your devices?"). The second part of the questionnaire asked students' about their reading, writing and note-taking habits ("When you read an academic text, do you underline or highlight relevant passages?", "If yes, do you use any system for such highlights?", "Are you taking notes when reading an academic text?", "If yes, in what form?", "If you take notes, do you have a system to organize them?", "If yes, what software do you use?", "Are you satisfied with your note organization system?", "Do you use specialized note-taking applications?"). The next block of questions was used to gauge the general levels of information retention while reading. It consisted of ordinal questions that asked students to evaluate the frequency of certain situations starting from 1 (never) to 10 (constantly). Finally, the students were asked about their familiarity with online academic databases and citation management software.

The course itself focused extensively on note-taking and academic writing management. As a guiding approach, the students were offered a horizontal hypertext-like structure of notes organization loosely based on the famous Niklas Luhman's Zettelkasten. On a theoretical level, the questions "What is a note?" and "Why should we take notes?" were addressed. The instructor's own notes and note-taking approach were presented and explained, following the idea that such an example can be an effective teaching strategy [17]. The students were given a note template and asked to take their own reading notes following this template. The template, while generally freeform, included metadata (title, keywords, bibliographical data, hyperlinks to other notes); students were encouraged to fill in as much metadata as possible and to establish links with other notes. Ultimately, students had to compile and present their own sample note databases and to explain how this experience changed their attitude to academic reading and writing.

The students explored several digital solutions for organizing their notes: a note-taking tool included in Zotero, commercial applications Evernote and Microsoft OneNote, as well as a file-based organization structure. The students were encouraged to think how these tools could fit in their personal reading and writing habits and to experiment with other applications if they so desired. The topic of handwritten notes was also addressed and a general workflow combining paper-based and digital note-taking was discussed and offered for consideration. After compiling their own note databases, students were asked to create outlines based on these notes to explore transition from horizontal free-form note-taking to a linear narrative structure.

The quantitative data gathered with the help of the questionnaire were supplemented by the qualitative data obtained in classroom discussions, informal discussions after class and through the observation of students' performance while doing classroom work and assignments.

4 Results

The initial questionnaire provided valuable insights into students' approaches to reading, note-taking and information management. The first block of questions, aimed to identify general level of computer literacy, showed results that were in some part predictable. The most obvious finding was that the majority of students possess and constantly use at least two, often three digital devices, with a strong preference for mobile devices. All students possessed smartphones, and all but one had laptops. The third device could be either a desktop computer, or a tablet. Equally predictably in Russian setting, Windows and Android devices dominated, especially in the area of study and academic writing.

Next, the students were asked to self-identify their level of computer literacy. Four choices were offered: basic, average, experienced and highly experienced. To elicit more concise responses, each choice was accompanied by a short description of what each level was supposed to mean. For example, "basic" level of computer literacy was described as follows: "can use a limited number of required software; prefer default options; have difficulty changing default options; cannot install or setup new software". In answering this question, the majority of students self-identified their level of computer literacy either as "average" ("know options and applications required in day-to-day work; can change basic settings for operating system and software" – 13 students, or 37%) or "experienced" ("have a good understanding of one or more operating systems; can install or remove software; can set up operating system and software according to personal needs" – 14 students, or 40%). 5 students (14%) identified their level of computer literacy as "basic", with 3 (8%) self-identifying as "highly experienced". These self-reported levels of computer literacy generally corresponded with those subsequently observed in classroom work and assignments.

When asked to describe their attitude to general information management and organization on their devices, the majority of the students – regardless of their self-reported computer literacy – chose one of two options: either they admitted to thinking about this issue sometimes, but not knowing how to improve the situation, or they thought about it often, occasionally trying different approaches to information management. 4 students (11%) stated that they thought about information organization constantly and had a good system in place, while 6 students preferred not to think about this issue at all acting intuitively.

The next block of questions explored students' reading and writing practices: text annotation, note-taking practices and information retention. Regarding text annotation, the absolute majority of respondents stated that they routinely marked or highlighted relevant of the text while reading ("yes" – 18 students, or 52%; "sometimes" – 13 students, or 37%). Only 4 students (11%) chose "no" in answering this question. The majority of those who answered "yes" or "sometimes" (25 students, or 69%) also had some kind of text marking system in place. However, the situation changed drastically when the students were asked whether they routinely took free-form notes – summarizing and writing down their own thoughts – while reading. Here, only 7 students (20%) stated that they were "constantly" taking notes while reading, with 21 students (60%) were doing this "sometimes" and 6 students "never". Moreover, these note-taking practices were much more inconsistent than the text marking practices: the majority of respondents (25 students, or 71%) admitted to not having any note-taking and note-retrieval system in place, with only 5 (14%) having such a system. Additionally, out of 5 students who *did* report having such a system, only one felt fully satisfied with it. The methods of note-taking also varied widely: most respondents (17, or 49%) used both digital and paper notes, with 6 students (17%) using only digital tools for note-taking and 5 students (14%) preferring paper notes. It became clear in subsequent classroom discussions that among those students who took both digital and paper notes none had a clear system in place for transcribing or otherwise transferring paper notes in digital form, or for organizing and retrieving notes created in different media. The preferred approach to note-taking may be described as "whatever is at hand"/"whatever I feel like using at the moment".

Despite the prevalence of note-taking software on the market (such as Google Keep, Evernote, Microsoft OneNote and many other applications), it was not popular among the students, at least not for the academic writing purposes: 22 respondents (63%) did not use any specialized note-taking applications, with 6 students (17%) using such applications sometimes and 7 students, or 20%, never. None of the 35 students used citation management software for any purpose, and the majority did not even know what such software was supposed to do – or even that it existed.

The self-reported levels of information retention showed predictable weak points. Thus, 19 students (54%) marked their chance of "having definitely read a text yet afterwards remembering only a couple of relevant points" at a 6 to 8 level of frequency (with 6 more, or 17%, choosing level 5), while 11 students (31%) admitted to routinely being unable to find relevant notes, despite clearly remembering that they did write them down. While only 3 students (8%) reported that they had a problem of frequently completely forgetting the content of a text they had read before, 8 students (23%) faced this situation with an average (4–5) frequency. Finally, 12 students (34%) admitted that they were familiar with the situation where they "started reading a text but after some time could not remember its beginning".

After the completion of the course, the experience was discussed in classroom setting. The students were asked whether they found the course useful; whether it changed their attitudes to reading, note-taking and writing; what specific tools they incorporated in their writing practice; what difficulties they faced and what topics they would like to explore further. The discussion showed mostly positive reactions from the students. The course materials were deemed useful and relevant, with reactions varying from lukewarm to highly enthusiastic. The general opinion among students was that the course encouraged them to rethink their approaches to reading, writing and information management. Some students said that they began to take more conscious and strategic approach not only to their academic writing but to information management in general. Six students stated that they would gladly take a more in-depth workshop on academic writing and note-taking. However, many also said that they needed more guidance during the course, especially on note-linking and specific software features. Further work is required to obtain quantitative data to better measure course effectiveness and general results.

5 Discussion

5.1 General Observations: Computer Literacy and Digital Practices

The masters' students who took up the course are all specializing in humanities: art history, cultural studies and audiovisual communications. Students' self-reported level of computer literacy was either average or experienced. Students reported routinely using at least two different devices, felt confident in their ability to achieve their everyday goals on these devices and freely interacted with the online environment. However, this confidence and self-reported computer literacy in their everyday life *did not* translate into equal confidence in academic research and writing. Most strikingly, students' self-reported level of computer literacy had no correlation with their reading and note-taking practices; it also had only very weak correlation with self-reported satisfaction with their ability to manage and organize information on their devices effectively.

In classroom discussions, students specified that they preferred to use different devices for different purposes. Long-form writing was usually performed on a laptop or a desktop computer, while searching and reading could be done on both laptops and mobile devices. Smartphones were also often used to photograph or record relevant material. However, without a good system to organize written notes this approach inevitably led to knowledge fragmentation and disorganization.

Additionally, quite a few students said that they preferred to take notes and create outlines on paper. Among the reasons cited were: ease of access (pen and paper always being at hand, while a device sometimes difficult to get out, having low battery etc.), ease of writing, positive influence of paper handwriting on thought processes and organization. This intuitive preference for handwriting is particularly interesting due to its correlation with well-established research showing that writing by hand confers clear advantages for memorization and comprehension [13, 21, 22].

5.2 Note-Taking vs Highlighting: Active and Passive Reading

The questionnaire and the subsequent course experience made it clear that the majority of students took a passive approach to reading. By far the most preferred method of processing the reading material was a practice of marking or highlighting relevant parts of text while reading. It is here that the students were most organized in their reading, with the majority stating that they not only highlighted relevant passages but also had some kind of system for such highlights (color coding, etc.). Sometimes the students learned this approach at school, but more often picked it up by example or read about it online. Highlighting provided students with the subjective feeling that they were "processing" text and doing meaningful work.

However, text highlighting is only a small step towards an independent academic writing. Without active summarization, restating and meaningful engagement, there is no chance of developing individual writing style, critical approach and a necessary degree of freedom in dealing with texts. Therefore, passive marking and highlighting cannot and should not replace active note-taking. But this active written engagement with a text was largely absent from students' reading practices. Very few students took notes while reading at all, and almost none of those who did had system for their retrieval and reuse.

Even more interesting was the finding that the students' self-reported levels of computer literacy and efficiency in information management had no correlation with their approach to note-taking. Even those who stated that they often thought about data organization and experimented with different approaches, did not apply this to their reading notes. It seems that, while text marking and highlighting has been at least partially incorporated into the digital practices, note-taking largely remains in traditional "analogue" domain. Only 5 students (14%) had a system for note-taking and retrieval. Not surprisingly, students stated that they often could not find previously written notes and were forced to write relevant sections of their text from scratch.

A weak correlation has emerged showing that the students who *did* routinely take notes while reading were less likely to forget the content of the text and more likely to remember relevant points. However, this result is compounded by the small sample size and by the general haphazard approach to note-taking. That is, even the majority of those who took reading notes "constantly", reported not having any note-taking system in place, routinely losing their notes and being unable to retrieve them when needed. Unsurprisingly, such practices significantly undermined the effectiveness of note-taking in improving reading retention and comprehension.

5.3 Digital Tools or Lack of Them

Interestingly, only very few students actively used any kind of specialized note-taking software. This result was somewhat surprising: the prevalence of such applications is high, they often come in free pre-installed versions on various operation systems, and they are always included on mobile platforms. While unexpected, this finding was easily explained in subsequent classroom discussions. Most of the students were familiar with note-taking applications only on mobile platforms (Google Keep was the most popular one, since it comes pre-installed on Android platform). Some students *did* use these applications for their everyday purposes. However, they rarely used such applications when taking academic notes. Three main reasons were cited for this: (1) that the process of writing on a smartphone was generally inconvenient; (2) that such applications were better suited for short and on-point factual notes rather than for capturing free-form thoughts; (3) that it was generally difficult to organize and retrieve large number of notes using mobile applications.

As for the "senior" note-taking applications – mainly represented today by Evernote and Microsoft OneNote – they were surprisingly little known and even less popular. Classroom discussions showed that the preferred digital tool was a Microsoft Word file for writing down notes and scraps of information. Students readily admitted that such file(s) rapidly became too big and difficult to manage; however, they did not have any good solution for this problem. Many dealt with it by keeping several MS Word files for notes, which led to further fragmentation.

5.4 How Much Note-Taking Guidance?

In general, it was found that students were required much more guidance to start developing their note-taking skills than was assumed before the start of the course. This led to the redesign of course syllabus, with more time allocated to note-taking than initially deemed necessary. This generally aligns with the fact that the students had never before took a conscious approach to their note-taking and corresponds with the findings that guided note-taking works better than the unguided approach [6, 7].

However, since these were master's level students, some demonstrated considerable resistance to the idea of guided note-taking. The students at this level generally see themselves as more competent and skilled than the undergraduates; the idea of guided note-taking contradicted this self-image, and also clashed with the "romantic" ideal of creativity discussed below. The students also often possessed entrenched reading and writing habits they were reluctant to change, even when admitting that these habits were inefficient. This reinforces the idea that note-taking skills should be taught as a staged approach, with undergraduate students learning the basics as soon as possible. In this case, master's students could further develop and enrich these skills by taking more in-depth classes.

5.5 Writing Myths and Preconceptions

Writing in general, and academic writing in particular, is an activity that tends to engender a lot of confusion, myths and preconceptions. These myths and preconceptions emerged repeatedly in classroom discussions. Many of these preconceptions seem to be particularly relevant for the humanities students, since their approach to writing in general follows the more "romantic" school of thought. Indeed, humanities students tend to view writing as a creative activity, and the traditional quasi-romantic attitude to anything that involve "creativity" and "inspiration" is still very popular in Russia.

Some students demonstrated resistance to the very idea that reading or writing should be systematically organized. Their arguments coalesced into a well-known pattern of creativity vs. "the system": creative writing should be inspired, while systematic approach, note-taking routine, timing and writing goals were all seen as detrimental to a spontaneous and "free" creative process. Unsurprisingly, these romantic ideas about writing tended to correspond with the writing practices widely adopted by the students. Discussions showed that by far the most widespread method of writing academic texts was reading (with occasional disorganized note-taking), followed by writing from scratch, usually with a deadline approaching. For students strongly committed to this "romantic" ideal of writing, it was useful to emphasize the creative freedom of a well-organized note-taking system and their ability to adjust this system to suit their own needs.

This fuzzy idea of writing process means that very few students understand the amount of gradual, piecemeal work and revision required to write an academic text. Thus, the prevalence of the "blank page" approach. At the beginning of the course, students tended to regard note-taking as a waste of time and "double work", not realizing that the final text was supposed to emerge from such notes. Even after having this point explained to them, some resisted to the idea stating that such piecemeal approach somehow did not feel like "real" writing. In one memorable exchange, a student even asked: "Is it *allowed* to write like this?" This student was convinced that the only "proper" way to write a text was to start with a blank page and proceed from the beginning to end. Unsurprisingly, students readily admitted to the high levels of stress, anxiety and writer's block when dealing with writing assignments. Another function of note-taking therefore was proposed: it can help to reduce anxiety and information overload, overcome negative psychological attitudes towards writing and facilitate healthier writing management practices.

At the end of the course, students admitted that their attitude to note-taking had shifted. Some enthusiastically embraced the idea of systematic note-taking; others were more indecisive and ambivalent. These results will guide the future development of the course.

6 Conclusions

Note-taking as a subtype of academic writing often remains neglected and underappreciated skill. However, we are dealing today with a breakdown in a humanistic tradition centered on reading, analyzing and interpreting complex texts. If classical note-taking indeed helped to launch this tradition in the first place, as some researchers argue [3, 5], it is all the more important to resurrect this tradition. However, it cannot be resurrected wholesale. It needs to be adjusted to our current state of knowledge,

knowledge practices and digital tools. Writing have been shown by modern neuroscience to constitute an integral part of a cognitive loop that makes complex reasoning possible [12]. "Note-taking as a knowledge-transforming tool" [6] is a mediatory practice that bridges the gap between passive reading and production of structured academic text and between analogue and digital traditions.

Teaching note-taking skills requires a synthetic digital-analogue approach to incorporate various writing styles and individual workflows. Note-taking should be incorporated as part of academic writing instruction. Given that note-taking is a personalized mental activity, the challenge is to find a flexible enough yet structured enough approach in teaching this activity. Hypertext-like approach seems a good starting point; however, other avenues can be explored. Additionally, the question of tools should be directly addressed: students should not be left floundering and uncertain but rather presented with a set of digital tools optimized for note-taking purposes.

References

1. Bauer, A., Koedinger, K.: Pasting and encoding: note-taking in online courses. In: Sixth IEEE International Conference on Advanced Learning Technologies (ICALT 2006), pp. 789–793. IEEE (2006). https://doi.org/10.1109/ICALT.2006.1652559
2. Blair, A.: Reading strategies for coping with information overload ca. 1550-1700. J. Hist. Ideas **64**(1) (2003). https://doi.org/10.2307/3654293
3. Blair, A.: Too Much to Know: Managing Scholarly Information Before the Modern Age. Yale University Press, New Haven (2010)
4. Blair, A.: Note taking as an art of transmission. Crit. Inq. **31**(1), 85–107 (2004). https://doi.org/10.1086/427303
5. Bolgar, R.R.: The Classical Heritage and Its Beneficiaries. Cambridge University Press, Cambridge (1973). https://doi.org/10.1017/CBO9780511583735. Open WorldCat
6. Castelló, M., Monereo, C.: Students' note-taking as a knowledge-construction tool. L1-Educ. Stud. Lang. Lit. **5**(3), 265–285 (2005). https://doi.org/10.1007/s10674-005-8557-4
7. Chang, W-Ch., Ku, Y.-M.: The effects of note-taking skills instruction on elementary students' reading. J. Educ. Res. **108**(4), 278–291 (2015). https://doi.org/10.1080/00220671.2014.886175
8. Darnton, R.: Extraordinary commonplaces. The New York Review of Books, December 2000. http://www.nybooks.com/articles/2000/12/21/extraordinary-commonplaces/. Accessed 25 Nov 2018
9. Gaille, S.: The decline of college writing skills (and the rise of social media) [Gaille Energy Blog Issue 37]. https://www.linkedin.com/pulse/decline-college-writing-skills-rise-social-media-gaille-scott-gaille. Accessed 17 Apr 2018
10. Haas, C.: Writing Technology: Studies on the Materiality of Literacy. Lawrence Erlbaum Associates, Mahwah (1996)
11. Hall, S.: Practise makes perfect: developing critical thinking and writing skills in undergraduate science students. In: Proceedings of the 3rd International Conference on Higher Education Advances. Universitat Politècnica València (2017). https://doi.org/10.4995/HEAD17.2017.5512
12. Illes, J., Sahakian, B.J. (eds.): The Oxford Handbook of Neuroethics. Oxford University Press, Oxford (2011)

13. James, K.H., Engelhardt, L.: The effects of handwriting experience on functional brain development in pre-literate children. Trends Neurosci. Educ. **1**(1), 32–42 (2012). https://doi.org/10.1016/j.tine.2012.08.001
14. Faber, J.E., Morris, J.D.: The effect of note taking on ninth grade students' comprehension. Read. Psychol. **21**(3), 257–270 (2000). https://doi.org/10.1080/02702710050144377
15. Kellogg, R.T., Whiteford, A.P.: Training advanced writing skills: the case for deliberate practice. Educ. Psychol. **44**(4), 250–266 (2009). https://doi.org/10.1080/00461520903213600
16. Khlupina, N.O.: Formirovaniye obshchikh i professional'nykh kompetentsiy pri samostoyatel'noy rabote studentov. In: Professional'noye obrazovaniye v Rossii i za rubezhom, vol. 2, no. 18 (2015)
17. Kiewra, K.A.: Providing the Instructor's Notes: An Effective Addition to Student Notetaking. Educ. Psychol. **20**(1), 33–39 (1985). https://doi.org/10.1207/s15326985ep2001_5
18. Kobayashi, K.: What limits the encoding effect of note-taking? A meta-analytic examination. Contemp. Educ. Psychol. **30**(2), 242–262 (2005). https://doi.org/10.1016/j.cedpsych.2004.10.001
19. Lee, P.-L., et al.: The effects of teaching notetaking strategies on elementary students' science learning. Instr. Sci. **36**(3), 191–201 (2008). https://doi.org/10.1007/s11251-007-9027-4
20. Luhmann, N.: Communicating with Slip Boxes. http://luhmann.surge.sh/communicating-with-slip-boxes. Accessed 15 May 2019
21. McCarroll, H., Fletcher, T.: Does handwriting instruction have a place in the instructional day? The relationship between handwriting quality and academic success. Cogent Educ. **4**(1) (2017). https://doi.org/10.1080/2331186X.2017.1386427
22. Mueller, P.A., Oppenheimer, D.M.: The pen is mightier than the keyboard: advantages of longhand over laptop note taking. Psychol. Sci. **25**(6), 1159–1168 (2014). https://doi.org/10.1177/0956797614524581
23. Stepanchuk, Y.: Reading and writing in digital age: combining analogue and digital methods in teaching humanities. In: Facets of Culture in the Age of Social Transition Proceedings of the All-Russian Research Conference, pp. 216–222. KnE Engineering, knepublishing.com (2018). https://doi.org/10.18502/keg.v318.3637
24. Stolberg, M.: John Locke's 'new method of making common-place-books': tradition, innovation and epistemic effects. Early Sci. Med. **19**(5), 448–470 (2014). https://doi.org/10.1163/15733823-00195p04
25. Yeo, R., Yeo, R.: Encyclopaedic Visions: Scientific Dictionaries and Enlightenment Culture. Cambridge University Press, Cambridge (2001)

Selection Methods for Geodata Visualization of Metadata Extracted from Unstructured Digital Data for Scientific Heritage Studies

Dmitry Prokudin[1,2(✉)], Georgy Levit[3], and Uwe Hossfeld[3]

[1] St. Petersburg State University, Universitetskaya nab. 7/9, 199034 St. Petersburg, Russia
hogben.young@gmail.com
[2] ITMO University, Kronverksky pr. 49, 197101 St. Petersburg, Russia
[3] Jena University, Am Steiger 3, 07743 Jena, Germany
georgelevit@gmx.net, uwe.hossfeld@uni-jena.de

Abstract. The present study explores the methods of geodata visualization extracted from the metadata of scientific publications for use in scientific research using the scientific heritage of Georgy Gause. It is based on the results of case studies to assess the possibilities of digital information resources, metadata extraction from digital resources, and using methods for their quantitative processing. We have studied methods of extracting metadata from digital information systems that do not have export tools. Our concentration is on methods and technologies of geodata extraction, and their subsequent visualization are considered. They are considered and applied methods of a dynamic clustering of geodata markers. Based on geodata visualization, we interpreter the results. The possibility of using extracted metadata in scientific visualization systems that support standard formats is evaluated.

Keywords: Scientific information · Digital information resources · Metadata extraction · Geodata extraction · Geodata visualization · Dynamic clusterization · Digital scientific heritage · Georgy F. Gause

1 Introduction

Currently visualization technologies are widely used in various scientific disciplines. An intensively growing field in this respect is geodata visualization [2, 4, 25, 34, 48]. These methods are of special importance for big data [18, 32]. Various methods of big data processing are often employed within humanities and are part of the "digital humanities". Our objective here is to apply the methods of geodata visualization. The data was extracted from the metadata of scientific publications. As case studies, we have used the scientific heritage of a famous ecologist, Georgy Gause, to be analyzed from a science studies viewpoint. The study is based on formerly conducted research into the possibilities of using digital informational resources in the science studies [39, 40]. To do so, we have extracted metadata from digital resources and employed the methods of its quantitative evaluation [38].

D. A. Alexandrov et al. (Eds.): DTGS 2019, CCIS 1038, pp. 542–553, 2019.
https://doi.org/10.1007/978-3-030-37858-5_46

In the framework of the present study, we solved the following tasks:

- Selection of wide spread geodata visualization tools (available to every researcher, for they do not require financial investments or special computer skills)
- Extraction of data about the organizations/affiliations from the metadata of scientific publications;
- Extraction of geodata from the above data on organizations/affiliations of the publication authors;
- Ultimate visualization of the extracted information along with dynamic clusterization of markers.

2 Related Works and Literature Review

Research is currently underway in various fields related to the extraction of big data from various digital resources. Including the extracted geodata. Some digital resources for retrieval of geodata provide an API. For example, the Marketing API is used to extract geodata from Facebook [4]. The harvesting machine using the Twitter API is used to extract geodata from messages micro-blogging platform Twitter [41]. A special web application based on ArcGIS API for JavaScript technology was developed to access the geodata database of the Geophysical Center of RAS [25]. In bibliometric studies, geodata are extracted from the metadata of scientific publications placed in digital information systems (for example, the author's country) [33]. Various systems and services are being developed to extract metadata [19], including using the OAI-PMH metadata exchange Protocol [11, 17, 37]. Methods of automatic extraction of metadata from the texts of scientific articles are widely used [44, 47].

Different software platforms and software are used to visualize geodata. One popular solution is OpenStreetMap (OSM), a platform that allows users to create or edit maps using GPS-enabled devices or aerial imageries [51]. Other popular solutions include such systems as PostGIS [6, 30, 42] and GeoServer [21, 45].

When positioning geographic features, the quality of the data is an important issue. In modern studies, different approaches to the accuracy of geolocation are considered [3, 14, 29]. One solution to the quality of data in GIS is the use of metadata [9, 16, 26].

When visualizing big geodata, problems arise when using visual analysis methods. To solve this problem, clustering methods are developed that are aimed at visually combining datasets not based on their spatial localization [15]. Methods of clustering of spatial objects are increasingly used in humanitarian studies [7, 50].

3 Methods and Approaches

To solve the above tasks, several steps should be completed [22]:

- Collection of information on the objects;
- Spatial localization of the data;
- Creation of a map design;
- Selection and implementation of a visualization technology.

To implement this approach, the following methods were identified:

- Extraction of metadata from digital informational systems, which do not offer importing tools;
- Spatial identification of visualization objects;
- Mapping the objects of spatial visualization.

In addition, to meet our objectives, we investigated the methods and corresponding technologies of dynamic clusterization of spatial objects by changing map scales.

Choosing technologies for our tasks, we proceeded from the assumption that they should be available for every researcher' independently of their information technologies and computer science skills. This allow employing the suggested methods in humanities without appealing to computer scientists. We also concentrated on free software and open source technologies.

4 Information Extraction from Metadata of Scientific Publications and Its Preliminary Interpretation

To conduct our case studies, we selected a Russian-based electronic scientific library (Elibrary, http://elibrary.ru), which is the most voluminous Russian scientific information system that includes the overwhelming majority of Russian scientific journals in all scientific disciplines. Furthermore, this informational system includes full texts of scientific publications as well as detailed metadata embracing, among others, abstracts and key words. In addition, the majority of scientific publication full texts are in the open access, which allows using Elibrary in science studies. The search engine of the Elibrary offers many their options allow the filtering of information and selecting of scientific publications by apply many criteria simultaneously. Search results can be used for scientometrics. For example, one can classify publications according to their topics, key words, affiliations, authors etc. However, statistics is presented in only one window of the browser whereas the only visualization tool is a column-like diagram. Another issue of Elibrary is the lack of tools for exporting metadata and statistical calculations. This constraints the use of selected publications and the search results for further automatic processing for scientific purposes. Consequently, the first task was to extract statistical reports. For publication selection, we used the search query "Gause & the competitive exclusion principle". The search engine found 190 publications. To estimate the validity of search entries, we used statistical report "distribution by topics".

For the purposes of further processing, the extracted data was highlighted by means of operational system's standard interface tools. By using "copy-paste" technology, the results were placed into an MS Excel table, and a circular diagram was created (Fig. 1).

The majority of publications (64%) fit into the biology category; there are also publications in agriculture and forestry, medicine and health care, environmental protection, human ecology, and biotechnology, which embrace 17% of the publications. From a historical viewpoint, it these statistics that support the assumption that Georgy Gause's principle of competitive exclusion is of primary importance for general biology and will be only marginally cited in the applied science.

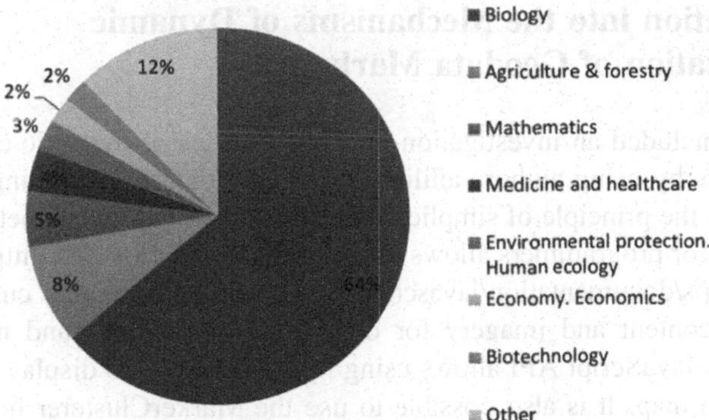

Fig. 1. Distribution of scientific publications by topics.

Using the same method as above, we imported the statistics extracted by means of the search entry "distribution by affiliations". The final list of affiliations was verified and classified into three categories: research organizations (scientific), educational organizations, and other organizations. In a special column, a type or organization was indicated along with its name. The circle diagram built on that data demonstrated the author's affiliations classified into organization types (Fig. 2).

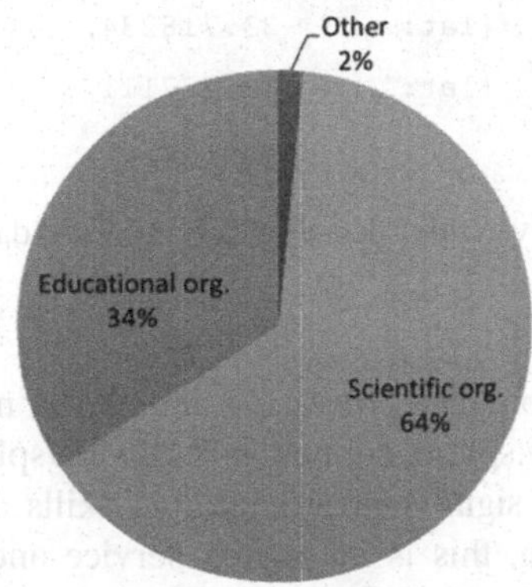

Fig. 2. Distribution of affiliations in accord with the type of organizations.

As one can see, purely research organizations dominate this diagram, that hinting to the assumption that Gause's theory was a theoretical breakthrough and is of importance for current research. To make a more precise inference, one should be able to extract purely educational publications (textbooks, published lectures) from the publications surveyed as well as consider the general index of publication activity of educational and research organizations.

5 Investigation into the Mechanisms of Dynamic Clusterization of Geodata Markers

The next step included an investigation into possibilities of dynamic clusterization of geodata markers by using authors affiliations as an indicator. By doing this, we have proceeded from the principle of simplicity and broad availability of methods and tools. Google service for programmers allows using Maps JavaScript API (https://developers.google.com/maps/documentation/javascript/tutorial), which creates customized maps with the own content and imagery for display on web pages and mobile devices. Including Maps JavaScript API allows using marker clusters to display a large number of markers on a map. It is also possible to use the MarkerClusterer library in combination with the Maps JavaScript API to combine markers of close proximity into clusters, simplifying the display of markers on the map.

This approach requires special computer skills and experience with JavaScript. Another difficulty with this method is the necessity to present geolocations considering a certain variable (Fig. 3) by manually operating with the large amount of data on geolocations.

```
var                     locations             =          [
                   {lat:      -31.563910,     lng:       147.154312},
                   {lat:      -33.718234,     lng:       150.363181},
                   {lat:      -33.727111,     lng:       150.371124},
```

Fig. 3. The structure of the variable "location" along with data on geolocation of objects (sample)

Another power tool for big data processing and cluster map designing is the service Splunk Cloud (https://www.splunk.com/en_us/software/splunk-cloud.html). This is a sophisticated tool requiring significant programmer skills and knowledge of interface commands [10]. In addition, this is not a free service and currently blocked by the embargo on the Russian federation.

Other popular free solutions for processing great amounts of geodata is PostGIS (http://geoserver.org) and GeoServer (http://postgis.net). However, to work with these one needs a very powerful computer and advanced skills in computer science [43].

We have found several other popular open source non-commercial licensing programs [20, 23, 25, 27, 35]. On this basis, Mapbox tools was selected [1, 28]. For further operation, an account in Mapbox was created.

6 Spatial Localization of Geodata and Dataset Establishing

Mapbox tool is able to process geodata in the GeoJSON format. To create a dataset of extracted organizations services, Google Maps (https://www.google.com/intl/ru_RU/maps/about/mymaps/) and Yandex Map Constructor (https://yandex.ru/map-constructor) were used. Determination of geographical coordinates of the organizations happened on the map in Maps Google service account. This was made by using organization names in the search engine. If necessary, an organization name has been proved either on the site of this organization or in other open sources.

On this stage, we have created a map with statically indicated markers of various organizations. After that, data was exported into the file in KML format [24, 31, 36, 46]. This format allowed to saving spatial coordinates of each organization (latitude and longitude). The import of geodata from this file was completed in the Yandex Map Constructor account. Doing this, we have inverted latitude and longitude, because in these two services the sequence of the presentation is different. To create a dataset, a geodata import in GeoJSON file format was made [8].

7 Establishing of a Map in the Mapbox

An account was created to work in the mapbox. Creation of the map happened in the Studio Mapbox tool in the Mapbox account. To do so, we first selected a map style "Streets", which is quite laconic and visualizes both countries and cities. After that, the data was imported from a file in a GeoJSON format. Tilesets were used to visualize markers on the map. The tileset is a collection of raster or vector data broken up into a uniform grid of square tiles at 22 preset zoom levels. Data from the dataset was imported into tileset. For the purposes of dynamic clusterization, vector type and zoom extent: z0–z10 (data will be visible above zoom 10, but may appear simplified) were selected. Then, the created style was opened in the style editor. Next, a new layer with this tileset as the source was created. On the created map, layers and styles were combined with markers.

8 Establishing the Dynamic Clusterization

To create a dynamic clusterization by changing a map scale, a method of Mapbox GL JS' built-in functions to visualize points as clusters was used [13]. In an html-code, sample corresponding locations were presented:

- An API access token to configure Mapbox GL JS, Mobile, and Mapbox web services like routing and geocoding. It was generated in the Mapbox account;
- Reference to the created map style;
- Reference to the file of GeoJSON format with dataset.

In addition, a clusterization adjustment was conducted in accordance with the number of markers and map size, which reflected the whole geographical space of Russia.

MAMP was used to visualize maps with dynamic clusterization. MAMP is a free, local server environment that can be installed under macOS and Windows with just a few clicks. MAMP provides all the tools needed for testing or development purposes, for example [5, 12, 49]. After its installation, into root directory a file with html-code and a GeoJSON format file with dataset were copied. After starting MAMP, the html-file was opened in the browser: http://localhost:8888/index.html. By alternating the map scale markers were combined into clusters (Fig. 4).

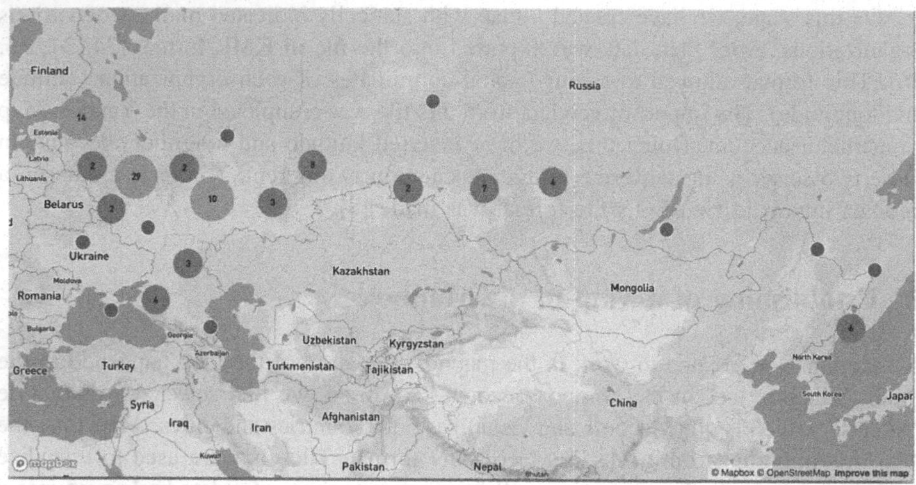

Fig. 4. Clusterization of the markers of author's affiliations.

The same approach was used for clustering publication quantities per organization. For this purpose, based on the created file with geolocations in the GeoJSON format, an analogous file was created in which an organization's geolocation was given one more time in accordance with the number of publications from Elibrary (Fig. 3). After completing these steps, we had an analogous map (Fig. 5).

Based on the extracted information one can make following conclusions:

- Major clusters of Russian organizations conducting research relevant to Gause's competitive exclusion principle are situated in Moscow, St. Petersburg, and in the Urals. To the minor extent but quite evenly affiliations are distributed in South Siberia and Far East region.
- Publication activity corresponds to the identified clusters of organizations: Moscow, St. Petersburg, and the Urals (equally), then Far East region and South Siberia.

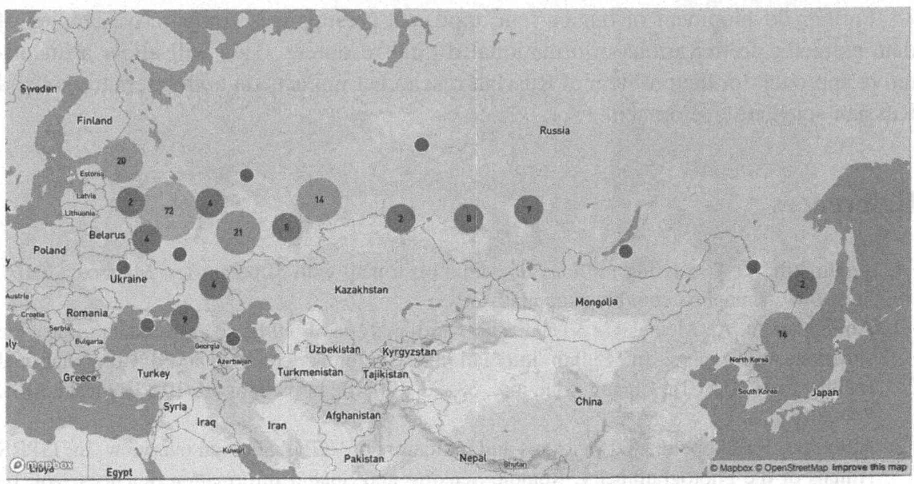

Fig. 5. Clusterization of publications markers corresponding to author's affiliations.

9 Conclusions

This study of data extracted from the online scientific library (http://elibrary.ru) allows making the following conclusions:

- Elibrary offers various tools that allow the extracting of analytical information about the publications it offers;
- The analysis of data has shown that the majority of Russian-language scientific publications is distributed in accordance with the topics of biology, ecology, medicine and its related fields;
- This completely corresponds to the research directions Gause is associated with. He is best known for his contribution into the evolutionary theory, ecology, and medicine (discovery of antibiotics);
- The metadata was extracted by means of the technology of data extraction from informational systems, which do not offer exporting tools;
- Proceeding from the principle of "open access", only widely available methods and technologies were used. Researchers without special computer skills can apply the described technologies as well. This allows recommending this approach for studies in humanities without appealing to experts in computer science;
- Methods and technologies of establishing datasets based on spatial localization of geodata were employed;
- Maps with dynamic clusterization of markers were created by using open access technologies and alternation of maps scales;
- The analysis of achieved visualization allowed the detecting of clusters of organizations and corresponding scientific publications. The visualizations reflected the appeal of researchers to the scientific heritage of Georgy Gause.

Further development of our current approach presupposes comparative studies of data extracted from various informational digital resources. This will allow a quantitative approach for the problem of Russian researcher impacts on both international and Russian science development.

References

1. Agafonkin, V.: Clustering millions of points on a map with Supercluster. Mapbox (2016). https://www.mapbox.com/blog/supercluster/
2. Amirkhanyan, A., Meinel, C.: Visualization and analysis of public social geodata to provide situational awareness. In: Eighth International Conference on Advanced Computational Intelligence (ICACI), Chiang Mai, pp. 68–73 (2016). https://doi.org/10.1109/icaci.2016.7449805
3. Antoniou, V., Skopeliti, A.: Measures and indicators of VGI quality: an overview. In: ISPRS Annals of the Photogrammetry, Remote Sensing and Spatial Information Sciences, vol. II-3/W5 (2015)
4. Araujo, M., Mejova, Y., Aupetit, M., Weber, I.: Visualizing geo-demographic urban data. In: Companion of the 2018 ACM Conference on Computer Supported Cooperative Work and Social Computing (CSCW 2018), pp. 45–48. ACM, New York (2018). https://doi.org/10.1145/3272973.3273001
5. Barnett, J.: Other ways to install drupal. In: Drupal 8 for Absolute Beginners, pp. 321–330. Apress, Berkeley (2015). https://doi.org/10.1007/978-1-4302-6467-5_19
6. Bartoszewski, D., Piorkowski, A., Lupa, M.: The comparison of processing efficiency of spatial data for PostGIS and MongoDB databases. In: Kozielski, S., Mrozek, D., Kasprowski, P., Małysiak-Mrozek, B., Kostrzewa, D. (eds.) BDAS 2019. CCIS, vol. 1018, pp. 291–302. Springer, Cham (2019). https://doi.org/10.1007/978-3-030-19093-4_22
7. Belim, S.V., Brechka, D.M., Gorbunova, T.A., Larionov, I.B., Schmidt, I.V.: Intellectual geographic information system of archaeological objects. Math. Struct. Model. **39**, 119–126 (2016). http://msm.omsu.ru/jrns/jrn39/BelimLarionovBrechka.pdf. (in Russian)
8. Butler, H., Daly, M., Doyle, A., Gillies, S., Hagen, S., Schaub, T.: The geojson format (No. RFC 7946) (2016)
9. Camara, J.H.S., Vegi, L.F.M., Pereira, R.O., Geöcze, Z.A., Lisboa-Filho, J.: ClickOnMap: a platform for development of volunteered geographic information systems. In: 12th Iberian Conference on Information Systems and Technologies (CISTI), pp. 1–6 (2017)
10. Cluster maps: Dashboards and Visualizations. Splunk Cloud Manuals. Version 7.2.3. Splunk, Inc., San Francisco (2019). https://docs.splunk.com/Documentation/SplunkCloud/7.2.3/Viz/MarkerMap
11. Corrado, E.M.: Discovery products and the open archives initiative protocol for metadata harvesting. Int. Inf. Libr. Rev. **50**(1), 47–53 (2018). https://doi.org/10.1080/10572317.2017.1422905
12. Crawford, T., Hussain, T.: A comparison of server side scripting technologies. In: Proceedings of the 15th International Conference on Software Engineering Research and Practice, Las Vegas, NV, pp. 69–76 (2017). https://csce.ucmss.com/cr/books/2017/LFS/CSREA2017/SER3291.pdf
13. Create and style clusters: Mapbox GL JS. https://docs.mapbox.com/mapbox-gl-js/example/cluster/

14. Dregossi, L.C., Albuquerque, J.P., Santos Rocha, R., Zipf, A.: A framework of quality assessment methods for crowdsourced geographic information: a systematic literature review. In: 14th International Conference on Information Systems for Crisis Response and Management, At Albi, France (2017)
15. Du, F., Zhu, A.-X., Qi, F.: Interactive visual cluster detection in large geospatial datasets based on dynamic density volume visualization. Geocarto Int. **31**(6), 597–611 (2016). https://doi.org/10.1080/10106049.2015.1073364
16. Estima, J., Painho, M.: Exploratory analysis of OpenStreetMap for land use classification. In: Proceedings of the Second ACM SIGSPATIAL International Workshop on Crowdsourced and Volunteered Geographic Information (GEOCROWD 2013), pp. 39–46. ACM, New York (2013)
17. Force, M.M., Robinson, N.J., Matthews, M., Auld, D.M., Boletta, M.: Research data in journals and repositories in the web of science: developments and recommendations. TCDL Bull. **12**(2), 27–30 (2016). https://www.ieee-tcdl.org/Bulletin/v12n1/papers/IEEE-TCDL-DC-2016_paper_3.pdf
18. Gao, S., Li, L., Li, W., Janowicz, K., Zhang, Y.: Constructing gazetteers from volunteered big geo-data based on Hadoop. Computers. Environ. Urban Syst. **61**, 172–186 (2017). https://doi.org/10.1016/j.compenvurbsys.2014.02.004
19. Garnett, A., Leahey, A., Savard, D., Towell, B., Wilson, K.: Open metadata for research data discovery in Canada. J. Libr. Metadata **17**(3–4), 201–217 (2017). https://doi.org/10.1080/19386389.2018.1443698
20. Hubert, R.B., Maguitman, A.G., Chesñevar, C.I., Malamud, M.A.: CitymisVis: a tool for the visual analysis and exploration of citizen requests and complaints. In: Baguma, R., De', R., Janowski, T. (eds.) Proceedings of the 10th International Conference on Theory and Practice of Electronic Governance (ICEGOV 2017), pp. 22–25. ACM, New York (2017). https://doi.org/10.1145/3047273.3047320
21. Jain, R., Bhatt, H., Jeevanand, N., Kumar, P.: Mapping, visualization, and digitization of the geo-referenced information: a case study on road network development in near real time. Int. Res. J. Eng. Technol. **5**(9), 845–850 (2018). https://www.irjet.net/archives/V5/i9/IRJET-V5I9153.pdf
22. Karmatsky, A.: Visualize it. Habr (2015). https://habr.com/ru/post/251755/. (in Russian)
23. Kim, D., Seo, D., Yoo, B., Ko, H.: Points of interest density based zooming interface for map exploration on smart glass. In: Yamamoto, S. (ed.) HIMI 2017. LNCS, vol. 10273, pp. 208–216. Springer, Cham (2017). https://doi.org/10.1007/978-3-319-58521-5_16
24. Kormann, M., Katsonopoulou, D., Katsarou, S., Lock, G.: Methods for developing 3D visualizations of archaeological data: a case study of the Early Bronze Age Helike Corridor House. Sci. Technol. Archaeol. Res. **3**(2), 478–489 (2017). https://doi.org/10.1080/20548923.2017.1372934
25. Krasnoperov, R.I., Soloviev, A.A., Nikolov, B.P., Zharkikh, J.I., Grudnev, A.A.: Interactive web-application for complex studying of spatial information on Earth sciences from the geodatabase of GC RAS. Geoinf. Res. Pap. **4**, BS4015 (2016). https://doi.org/10.2205/2016bs039. (in Russian)
26. Langley, S.A., Messina, J.P., Moore, N.: Using meta-quality to assess the utility of volunteered geographic information for science. Int. J. Health Geogr. **16**(1), 40 (2017)
27. Li, X., Anselin, L., Koschinsky, J.: GeoDa web: enhancing web-based mapping with spatial analytics. In: Proceedings of the 23rd SIGSPATIAL International Conference on Advances in Geographic Information Systems (SIGSPATIAL 2015). ACM, New York (2015). Article 94. https://doi.org/10.1145/2820783.2820792
28. Mapbox developers tools. https://www.mapbox.com/developers/

29. Medeiros, G., Holanda, M.: Solutions for data quality in GIS and VGI: a systematic literature review. In: Rocha, Á., Adeli, H., Reis, L.P., Costanzo, S. (eds.) WorldCIST'19 2019. AISC, vol. 930, pp. 645–654. Springer, Cham (2019). https://doi.org/10.1007/978-3-030-16181-1_61
30. Mikiewicz, D., Mackiewicz, M., Nycz, T.: Mastering PostGIS: Modern Ways to Create, Analyze, and Implement Spatial Data. Packt Publishing, Birmingham (2017)
31. Mohammadi, H., Delavar, M.R., Sharifi, M.A., Pirooz, M.D.: Spatiotemporal visualization of Tsunami waves using KML on Google Earth. Int. Arch. Photogramm. Remote. Sens. Spat. Inf. Sci. **7**, 1291–1299 (2017). https://doi.org/10.5194/isprs-archives-xlii-2-w7-1291-2017
32. Moosavi, V.: Contextual mapping: visualization of high-dimensional spatial patterns in a single geo-map. Comput. Environ. Urban Syst. **61**, 1–12 (2017). https://doi.org/10.1016/j.compenvurbsys.2016.08.005
33. Münster, S., Ioannides, M.: A scientific community of digital heritage in time and space. In: Digital Heritage, Granada, pp. 267–274 (2015). https://doi.org/10.1109/digitalheritage.2015.7419507
34. Murray, S.: Interactive Data Visualization for the Web: An Introduction to Designing with D3, 2nd edn. O'Reilly Media Inc., Sebastopol (2017)
35. Nikora, M.T.H., Hunt, T.D., Ryan, G.: CacophonyViz: Visualisation of birdsong derived ecological health indicators. J. Appl. Comput. Inf. Technol. **22**(1) (2018). http://citrenz.ac.nz/JACIT/JACIT2201/2018Nikora_CacophonyViz.html
36. Pons, X., Masó, J.: A comprehensive open package format for preservation and distribution of geospatial data and metadata. Comput. Geosci. **97**, 89–97 (2016). https://doi.org/10.1016/j.cageo.2016.09.001
37. Prabhune, A., Ansari, H., Keshav, A., Stotzka, R., Gertz, M., Hesser, J.: MetaStore: a metadata framework for scientific data repositories. In: 2016 IEEE International Conference on Big Data (Big Data), Washington, DC, pp. 3026–3035 (2016). https://doi.org/10.1109/bigdata.2016.7840956
38. Prokudin, D., Levit, G., Hossfeld, U.: Selection methods for quantitative processing of digital data for scientific heritage studies. In: Alexandrov, D.A., Boukhanovsky, A.V., Chugunov, A.V., Kabanov, Y., Koltsova, O. (eds.) DTGS 2018. CCIS, vol. 859, pp. 134–145. Springer, Cham (2018). https://doi.org/10.1007/978-3-030-02846-6_11
39. Prokudin, D., Levit, G., Hossfeld, U.: Selection methods of digital information resources for scientific heritage studies: a case study of Georgy F. Gause. In: Bolgov, R.V., Borisov, N.V., Smorgunov, L.V., Tolstikova, I.I., Zakharov, V.P. (eds.) Internet and Modern Society: Proceedings of the International Conference IMS-2017, ACM International Conference Proceeding Series, St. Petersburg, Russian Federation, 21–24 June 2017, pp. 69–74. ACM Press, New York (2017). https://doi.org/10.1145/3143699.3143739
40. Prokudin, D., Mbogo, I., Murgulets, L., Kudryavtseva, M.: The study approaches for dissemination of research results in the information society. In: Chugunov, A.V., Bolgov, R., Kabanov, Y., Kampis, G., Wimmer, M. (eds.) DTGS 2016. CCIS, vol. 674, pp. 350–362. Springer, Cham (2016). https://doi.org/10.1007/978-3-319-49700-6_33
41. Sechelea, A., Huu, T.D., Zimos, E., Deligiannis, N.: Twitter data clustering and visualization. In: 2016 23rd International Conference on Telecommunications (ICT), Thessaloniki, pp. 1–5 (2017). https://doi.org/10.1109/ict.2016.7500379
42. Sinkonde, D., Mselle, L., Shidende, N., Comai, S., Matteucci, M.: Developing an intelligent PostGIS database to support accessibility tools for urban pedestrians. Urban Sci. **2**(3), 52 (2018). https://doi.org/10.3390/urbansci2030052
43. Skorohod, M.: Clustering markers in Geoserver (2017). https://maks.live/articles/python/klasterizatsiia-markerov-v-geoserver/. (in Russian)

44. Suleymanov, R.S.: Extraction of metadata from the full-text electronic materials written in Russian using Tomita-parser. Softw. Syst. **4**, 58–62 (2016). https://doi.org/10.15827/0236-235x.116.058-062. (in Russian)
45. Sun, L., He, D., Zhao, P.: A research of publishing map technique based on GeoServer. Asian J. Appl. Sci. **8**(3), 185–195 (2015). https://doi.org/10.3923/ajaps.2015.185.195
46. Thakkar, R.C., Heffernan, I.D.: U.S. patent no. 9,703,807. U.S. Patent and Trademark Office, Washington, DC (2017)
47. Vasilev, A., Kozlov, D., Samusev, S., Shamina, O.: Izvlechenie metainformacii i bibliograficheskih ssylok iz tekstov russkojazychnyh nauchnyh statej. In: Trudy konferencii RCDL 2007, Pereslavl, vol. 1, pp. 175–181 (2007). (in Russian)
48. Vicentiy, A.V.: Adaptive visualization of geodata in social media. Naukovedenie **4**(35), 1–15 (2016). https://naukovedenie.ru/PDF/57TVN416.pdf. (in Russian)
49. West, A.W., Prettyman, S.: Create and test a database and table. In: Practical PHP 7, MySQL 8, and MariaDB Website Databases, pp. 1–31. Apress, Berkeley (2018). https://doi.org/10.1007/978-1-4842-3843-1_1
50. Zelianskaia, N.L., Baranov, D.A., Belousov, K.I.: Naive geography and topology of geomental maps. Socio Psycho Linguist. Res. **4**, 126–136 (2016). (in Russian)
51. Zhang, H., Malczewski, J.: Quality evaluation of volunteered geographic information: the case of OpenStreetMap. In: Calazans Campelo, C., Bertolotto, M., Corcoran, P. (eds.) Volunteered Geographic Information and the Future of Geospatial Data, pp. 19–46. IGI Global, Hershey (2017). https://doi.org/10.4018/978-1-5225-2446-5.ch002

News Consumption Among Russian-Speaking Immigrants in Israel from 2006 to 2018

Anna S. Smoliarova(✉) and Tamara M. Gromova

St. Petersburg State University, Saint Petersburg, Russia
a.smolyarova@spbu.ru

Abstract. The article explores the key trends in news consumption among Russian-speaking migrants in Israel in years 2006–2018, representing the first longitudinal evaluation of news consumption patterns of this social group. The analysis is based on the open data collected from 2006 to 2018 by news agency newsru.co.il, ranked by SimilarWeb as 28th of all Israeli websites. Large-scale surveys, aiming to reveal media consumption patterns among visitors of the news agency website, consisted on 25–30 closed multiple choice questions and involved circa 2000 respondents. The study highlights how the choice of media for news consumption has changed over twelve years, reveals the heavy digital character of news usage and discusses the habitual information check in high choice news environment.

Keywords: News consumption · High choice news environment · Russian Israelis · Immigration

1 Introduction

In years 2006–2018 news consumption across the world was subject to severe changes. Digital media users [1] consume news cross-medially [2, 3] and very often incidentally [4, serendipitous news consumption, e.g. 5]. Periods of news consumption became much shorter episodes that are less separated from other daily routines [1, 6, 7]. Expansion of media content options forms a high choice news environment [8] and leads to users' preference of more narrowly defined repertoires [9–11].

Media users with migration background have always attracted researchers' attention as potentially disintegrated from the host society or as more globalized and digitalized news consumers. This paper focuses on the dynamics of online and offline media consumption among Russian-speaking audience in Israel. Between 1989 and 2000 about one million immigrants from former Soviet republics moved to Israel comprising about 16% of Israel voters. Russian language media in Israel represents one of the most diverse media landscapes among other countries with Russian speaking diasporas and remains salient as news source for all generations of immigrants. The media landscape is dominated by online-only media, and three Russian language online-only news media are ranked among 50 top visited Israeli websites.

The remainder of this paper is organized as follows. The next section provides a literature review on news consumption in the age of digitalization and distinguishing features of news consumption among migrants, in particular Russian-speaking

D. A. Alexandrov et al. (Eds.): DTGS 2019, CCIS 1038, pp. 554–564, 2019.
https://doi.org/10.1007/978-3-030-37858-5_47

population in Israel. We then present our methodology (Sect. 3) and the findings of our study (Sect. 4). We conclude with a summary of our results.

2 Theoretical Framework

2.1 Transformation of News Consumption in the Age of Digitalization

Reuters Institute Digital News [12] report provides insight in trends of usage different media as news source across the globe (Table 1). One might assume that even the tendency of replacement of TV consumption by using online sources is not present in all countries. Although TV news have lost about 20% of the audience in five years in US or in Denmark, in Australia, Brazil, Canada or Hungary the share of TV news consumers among respondents remained the same, and in Italy and South Korea it has grown. The share of online news consumers seems to be quite stable, while print newspapers have taken a severe fall in the majority of the countries in this sample.

Table 1. News sources in 2013–2018

	TV		Print		Online	
	2013	2018	2013	2018	2013	2018
Australia	65	66	38	36	78	82
Brazil	75	75	50	34	90	90
Canada	71	67	36	31	75	76
Denmark	85	68	49	27	81	82
Germany	82	74	63	37	66	65
Hungary	72	70	27	20	88	87
Italy	74	82	59	39	80	78
Japan	69	65	63	37	85	59
South Korea	71	74	28	25	86	84
UK	79	66	59	36	74	74
USA	72	57	47	21	75	73

Israel has not been included in the sample covered by Reuters Institute Digital News, and we have not identified a fully comparable dataset published in a scientific publication. Therefore, we reconstruct Israeli dynamics of media usage from several sources.

In 1999 about 12% population of Israel possessed not only a computer but also had internet access [13]. In 2005 already 48,9% of households in Israel reported that they had access to the Internet, and the share of online users grew to 75,4% in 2016 [14]. More than 65% of Jewish population in 2013 read newspapers [15], and print media audience decreases quite slowly to 54,9% in the second half of 2016 [16]. 87% of Israelis watched TV at least one hour per day in 2012 [17] and in 2016 [18], and "there has not been a decrease in television viewing in the last few years" [19].

2.2 Media Consumption Among Migrants

Media consumption of migrants has been traditionally studied within three theoretical perspectives: uses and gratification theory, media effects, cultural studies [see review 20]. To some extent all three paradigms may be united by some concerns about integration. Media from host country have been opposed to the media from country of origin or minority media [21–25]. Media effects paradigm evaluates consumption of news from host country versus news from country of origin as an indicator as well as an important factor in integration process [26, 27]. Cultural studies in some part continue this logic of media influence on identity formation [28], but other researchers have also focused on multiple, liquid identities and new forms of identity created by people with migration background. Despite this criticism in a framework of "methodological nationalism", empirical studies confirm that media consumers with migration background choose news sources and consume media content according to their "differential capacities to fulfill their most urgent integration needs" [29–31]. For ex., the demand on international communication results in higher rates of Internet usage even among elder generations or subgroups with lower income. One might assume that Russian Germans should be considered as early adopters: in 2007 38% of them in comparison to 28% of Germans on average responded about the regular Internet usage, according to a survey conducted by ARD and ZDF [23]. In 2016 only 59% of Germans used Internet as news source [12], while 68% of respondents of a survey conducted among Russian-speaking population in Germany use Internet daily, and 14% at least once a week, to get information about current affairs [32].

Media habits and choices of Russian-speaking population outside Russia is well studied in the countries where Russian native speakers are eligible voters: in Germany, Israel and Baltic countries. In Estonia and Latvia they form almost a quarter of all population, according to national statistics for 2009 and 2017 accordingly, as a result of migration in Soviet times. In our paper we focus on Russian-speaking Israelis because they form the biggest Russian native speakers community with migration background in regard to general population of a country. Between 1989 and 2000 "the single largest wave of immigration in Israel's history" - about one million immigrants from former Soviet republics - "has redrawn the economic, social and political landscape" of Israel [33].

A high level of heterogeneity of media or news consumption patterns among members of an ethnic minority or a diaspora community is revealed for Russian-speaking Israelis as well. Elder generation use Internet intensively (two hours per day on average in 2012) and in varied ways [34]. Immigrants from the former Soviet Union aged 65 years and over try to enhance the quality of life with five main internet uses: (1) managing health; (2) nurturing professional interests; (3) maintaining and extending social networks; (4) appreciating the past; and (5) enjoying leisure [34]. For youngsters "Russian-language internet was the one cited more often and elaborated upon as the major source of much valued information and learning in their ongoing process of cultural and social integration" [35]. As for elder generation, for the adolescents Russian Internet became a tool for strengthen the participants' self-worth. In more recent study by Remmennick full assimilation was seen by respondents as more preferable than any bicultural integration. To some extent the share of users actively participating in Russian language mediated communication remains "compensated" by new wave of newcomers after 2013.

Therefore, in line with the long research tradition on media consumption and with the research findings on news consumption among Russian-speaking migrants, we formulate the following research questions:

RQ1. Which media have Russian-speaking Israelis been choosing as news sources from 2006 to 2018?
RQ2. How did the frequency of news consumption change from 2006 to 2018?
RQ3. Do Russian-speaking Israelis follow multiple sources of news information?
RQ4. Are social media demanded as news sources among Russian-speaking Israelis?

3 Data Sample

The data examined in the paper at hand has been gathered and published by the editorial office of news agency *newsru.co.il.* This dataset might be estimated as a unique longitudinal study of media choices done by Russian-speaking migrants. The survey has been conducted online in years 2006 [36], 2008 [37], 2009 [38], 2011 [39], 2013 [40], 2014 [41], 2016 [42] and 2018 [43]. It included 25–30 closed-ended multiple choice questions (Table 2).

Table 2. The sample of the surveys.

Year	Number of respondents
2006	1966
2009	1544
2011	2057
2013	2046
2014	1431
2016	3135
2018	1868

During the surveys the social-demographic data about the respondents has been gathered, therefore, it was possible to evaluate the capacity of this sample to represent Russian-speaking population in Israel in general. The sample doesn't fully correspond with social structure of Russian-speaking population in Israel. 69% of respondents are male, in comparison to 45% of Russian-speaking immigrants. 29% of respondents are retired, in comparison to 17% of Russian-speaking population in Israel (39% of the audience are 40–59 years of age). 69% of the audience in comparison to 49% of the Russian speaking Israelis are married and have children. In terms of level of income on average the audience of the news website is congruent with an average level of income among speaking population in Israel. Majority of the audience are non-religious (84%), they hold higher education (76%), speak Hebrew (79%) and English (57%). Still, with 13 mln total visits on desktop and mobile in autumn 2018 the news agency is ranked as 28th in the list of most popular websites in Israel, the 4th in the list of news websites and the 1st in the list of Russian-language news websites [44, 45]. Therefore, one might consider the audience of the *newsru.co.il* to be representative to the Russian-speaking news consumers in Israel.

4 Findings

RQ1. Which media have Russian-speaking Israelis been choosing as news sources from 2006 to 2018?

According to the surveys conducted by *newsru.co.il*, Russian-speaking Israelis may be described as heavy internet users (see Fig. 1). The share of TV audience has declined from 62,7% in 2006 to 29,9% in 2018. Before 2014 the number of TV viewers in the sample fluctuates around 50% and then reduces almost by half: in 2018 only 53% of those who watched TV in 2006 still choose this media as a news source. Radio in 2018 is listened only by 70% of those who followed news via radio in 2006. The most dramatic fall is revealed for the newspaper audience: percentage of respondents declined by two-thirds from 12,1% of respondents to 4,2% in 2018.

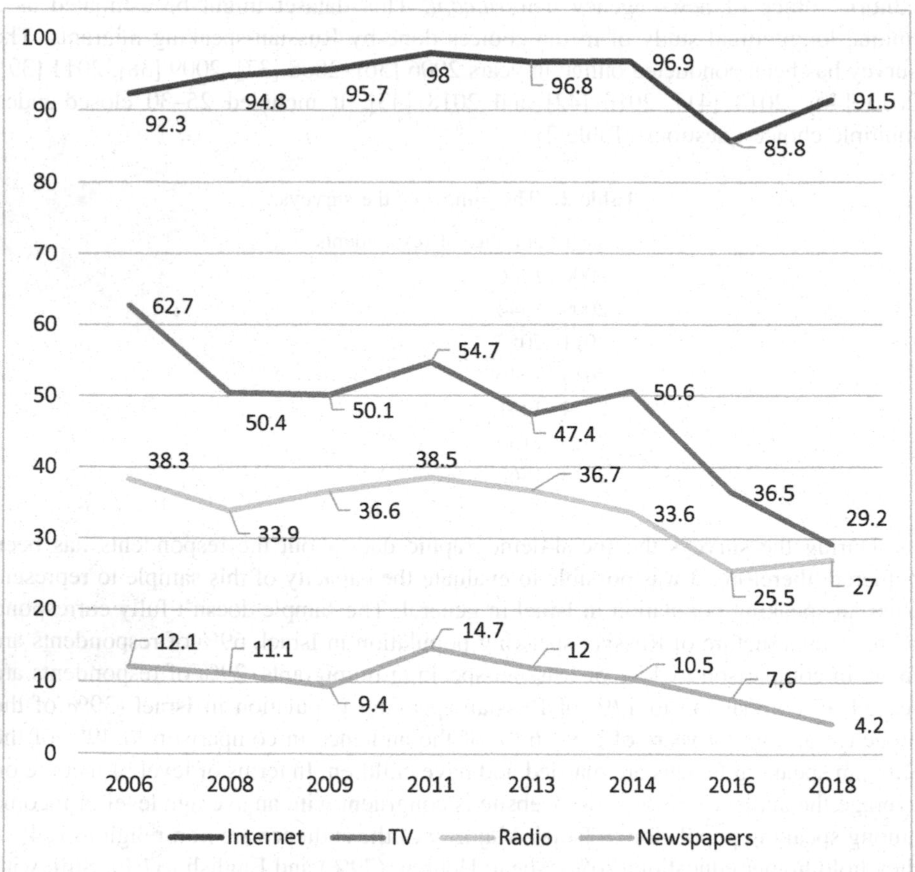

Fig. 1. News sources chosen by respondents in 2006–2018 (multiple answers were possible): *from which sources do you usually get last news?*

Internet remains the major information source during the whole period (the question was not included in the survey in 2007): from 92,3% of respondents to its maximum – 96,9% – in 2014. The decline in 2016 and 2018 may be explained by the fact that in these years the answer option has been changed. Figure 1 represents the percentage of respondents choosing “News websites”, while another suggested option – social networks – has been chosen by 42,2% in 2016 and 40,7% in 2018. 24,3% of respondents have agreed with the statement “I usually get news from Facebook or using links posted in this social network”. The share of people that get news from messengers almost tripled in two years – from 3,9% in 2016 to 10,6% in 2018.

RQ2. How did the frequency of news consumption change from 2006 to 2018?

Rapid changes have occurred in frequency of getting news (Fig. 2). While in 2006 only 20,3% of respondents have answered that they consume news constantly – one time per hour or even more often, ten years later almost one half of respondents turned to be constant news consumers. The most typical news consumption behavior in 2006 has been described with an answer “several times per day”: this pattern decreased dramatically in ten years. One might assume that a small share of these respondents moved to the group of weekly news consumers that has grown more than three times – from 1,1% in 2006 to 4,6% in 2016, while others became more news-addicted.

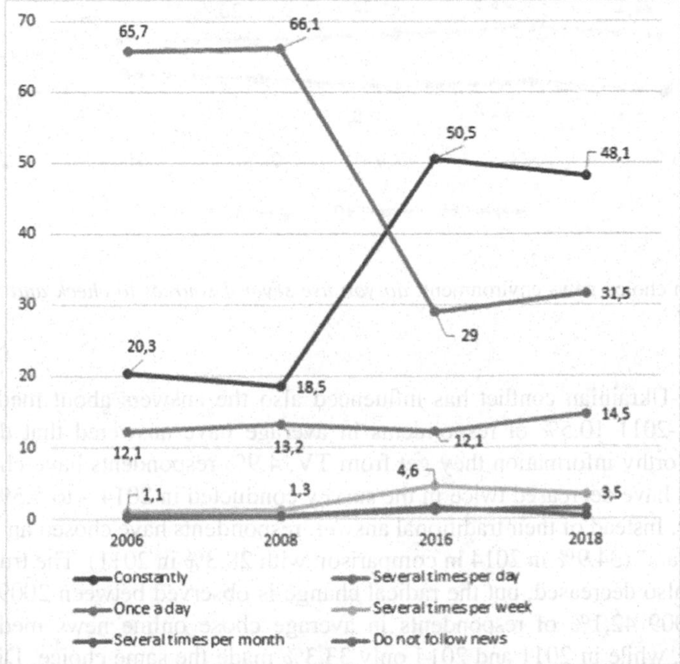

Fig. 2. Regularity of news consumption in percentage of respondents: *how often do you usually get news?*

RQ3. Do Russian-speaking Israelis follow multiple sources of news information? The question about usage of multiple news information sources has been asked from 2006 to 2014 and then in 2018 (Fig. 3). The size of three groups – multiple source users, omnivores and occasional users – does not change significantly through time, with exception for 2014, that might be explained with Russian-Ukrainian conflict that influenced profoundly Russian-speaking community in Israel. In 2014 the share of respondents who do not use several sources has grown from 8,8% in 2006 to 13,1% in 2013, decreasing rapidly to 6%; the share of multiple sources has increased of 11% in 2014.

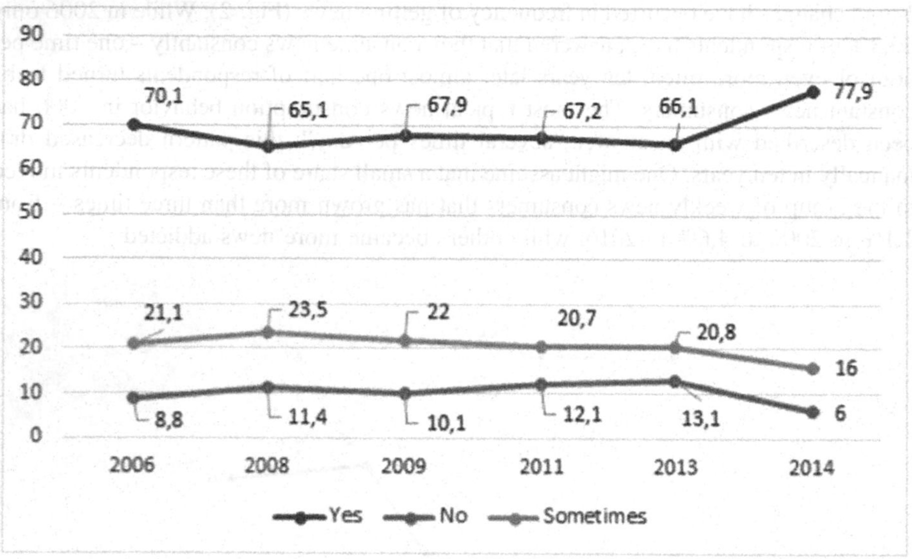

Fig. 3. High choice news environment: *do you use several sources to check and specify news information?*

Russian-Ukrainian conflict has influenced also the answers about media trust. In years 2006–2011 10,5% of respondents in average have answered that they find as most trustworthy information they get from TV, 4,9% respondents have chosen radio. Both shares have decreased twice in the survey conducted in 2014 – to 5,5% and 2,2% accordingly. Instead of their traditional answer, respondents have chosen an answer "all media are liars" (34,9% in 2014 in comparison with 28,3% in 2011). The trust to online media has also decreased, but the radical change is observed between 2009 and 2011. In 2006–2009 42,1% of respondents in average chose online news media as most trustworthy, while in 2011 and 2014 only 33,3% made the same choice. Disappointed online news users formed the first wave of respondents choosing the answer "All media are liars". In 2006–2009 19% of respondents in average chose this answer, while in 2011 already 28,3% agreed with this statement.

In 2018, respondents were asked to answer separately whether they check information they get from news websites and from social media (Table 3). The answer "only if I consider it dubious" has been added. In sum, the answers "always" and "only if I consider it dubious" for information from news websites are given by 77,5% of respondents. The trust in information from social media is lower than in news websites at first sight, but if dubious information from the news website will be checked by almost two-thirds of respondents, less than a half of them will do it for information from social media. This difference that is not compensated by respondents who "always" check information from social media might be explained by the fact that the share of social media users who hesitated to choose from three possible answers is three times bigger than news website users.

Table 3. Critical thinking in online news consumption

Do you check information that you get from…	News website	Social media
Always	15,6%	23,4%
Only if I consider it dubious	61,9%	47,4%
Never	18,1%	15,9%
Other	4,4%	13,3%

Since the question (just "check" instead of "use several sources to check and specify" and the answers ("information from news websites" instead of "news information") has been changed, the development between 2014 and 2018 cannot be interpreted properly.

RQ4. Are social media demanded as news sources among Russian-speaking Israelis?

Facebook is more popular in Israel than in many other countries: while global FB penetration does not exceed 23%, more than 43% of Israelis have an account on Facebook [Statista]. Results of the survey conducted by newsru.co.il in 2018 have shown that Facebook may be even more popular among Russian-speaking users since 64,2% of respondents confirmed the usage of this social network. Odnoklassniki, a popular social network in post-Soviet countries, ranked second in terms of popularity with 24,9% of respondents, while VK (former Vkontakte, another post-Soviet SNS) is used only by 11,8% of respondents. 21,6% answered that they do not use social media at all.

The share of respondents who regularly use social media as news source has increased almost twofold since 2011 (Table 4), while the share of occasional social media news consumers remains the same – 29%. In 2018 24, 3% of respondents agreed with the statement "I usually get news from Facebook directly or clicking on the links from this social network", and 10,7% answered "difficult to give an unambiguous answer".

Table 4. Social media as news source

Do you follow news via blogs and social media?	Yes, regularly	Yes, seldom	No	Do not understand the question
2011	17,4%	29,3%	49,9%	3,3%
2013	21,2%	27,1%	49,3%	2,4%
2014	25,9%	29,8%	42,1%	2,2%
2018	33,6%	29%	36,3%	1,1%

Among 10,6% of respondents who use messengers on the mobile phone to get news information in 2018, 47,4% prefer WhatsApp, 22% get news from Skype, 20% have chosen Facebook Messenger, 13,1% use Viber, and 8% rely on Telegram. The question does not specify whether the news are coming via interpersonal communications or from bloggers or media organizations of any kind.

5 Conclusion

The study outlined in the paper at hand addresses the dynamics of news consumption among Russian-speaking population in Israel from 2006 to 2018. For this period, cross-media media consumption forms user defined media repertoires, news consumption acts have increased in frequency and became more integrated in daily routines. Media users consume content in a high choice news environment, and the questions of quality, trustworthiness, reliability of information from different sources are widely discussed.

Analysis was based on the open data collected and published by one of the most influential Russian language news organizations in Israel, news agency *newsru.co.il*. Although its audience does not ideally represent Russian-speaking population in Israel, the website of newsru.co.il is visited by majority of news consumers who moved to Israel from post-Soviet countries. This dataset is unique in terms of a longitudinal study of media consumption among Russian-speaking migrants.

The audience of *newsru.co.il* might be described as heavy digital users who prefer to rely on "quality" media content and follow multiple sources of information. Still, almost the fifth part of respondents usually does not check news information they get, although the share of skeptical users is growing. The share of Russian speaking Israelis who regularly use social media as news source has increased almost twofold since 2011 and exceeds in 2018 the share of those who respond about relying on TV as news source. The absence of newspaper readers in comparison to the Israeli population on average may be explained by the fact that Russian language newspapers in Israel have almost vanished by 2018 as well as by challenge of reading in Hebrew. Another significant change characterizes the frequency of news consumption: in twelve years one half of respondents turned to be constant news consumers who check news updates several times per hour.

Acknowledgements. The research has been supported in full by Russian Presidential Grant for Young PhD Scientists, research grant MK-6128.2018.6.

References

1. Picone, I.: Grasping the digital news user: conceptual and methodological advances in news use studies. Digit. J. **4**(1), 125–141 (2016). https://doi.org/10.1080/21670811.2015.1096616
2. Schrøder, K.C.: Audiences are inherently cross-media: audience studies and the cross-media challenge. Commun. Manag. Q. **18**(6), 5–27 (2011)
3. Helles, R., Ørmen, J., Radil, C., Jensen, K.B.: Media audiences: the media landscapes of European audiences. Int. J. Commun. **9**, 21 (2015)
4. Yadamsuren, B., Erdelez, S.: Incidental exposure to online news. In: 73rd ASIS&T Annual Meeting on Navigating Streams in an Information Ecosystem, vol. 47, p. 22. American Society for Information Science (2010)
5. Van Damme, K., Courtois, C., Afschrift, J.: Serendipitous news consumption: a mixed-method audience-centred study on mobile devices. In: Amsterdam Conference on Social Media and the Transformation of Public Space (2014)
6. Gauntlett, D., Hill, A.: TV Living: Television. Culture and Everyday Life. Routledge, London (1999)
7. Deuze, M.: Media life and the mediatization of the lifeworld. In: Hepp, A., Krotz, F. (eds.) Mediatized Worlds: Culture and Society in a Media Age, pp. 207–220. Palgrave Macmillan, London (2014)
8. Van Damme, K., Courtois, C., Verbrugge, K., De Marez, L.: What's APPening to news? A mixed-method audience-centred study on mobile news consumption. Mob. Media Commun. **3**(2), 196–213 (2015)
9. Taneja, H., Webster, J.G., Malthouse, E.C., Ksiazek, T.B.: Media consumption across platforms: identifying user-defined repertoires. New Media Soc. **14**(6), 951–968 (2012)
10. Hasebrink, U., Popp, J.: Media repertoires as a result of selective media use. A conceptual approach to the analysis of patterns of exposure. Communications **31**(3), 369–387 (2006)
11. Hasebrink, U., Domeyer, H.: Media repertoires as patterns of behavior and as meaningful practices: a multimethod approach to media use in converging media environments. Participations **9**(2), 757–779 (2012)
12. Reuters Institute digital news report 2018. Analysis by country. http://www.digitalnewsreport.org/survey/2018/analysis-by-country-2018/
13. Adoni, H., Nossek, H.: The new media consumers: media convergence and the displacement effect. Communications **26**(1), 59–84 (2001)
14. OECD Data. https://data.oecd.org/ict/internet-access.htm
15. Nossek, H., Adoni, H., Nimrod, G.: Media audiences| is print really dying? The state of print media use in Europe. Int. J. Commun. **9**, 365–385 (2015)
16. Tucker, N.: Excess of free newspapers, led by Adelson's Israel Hayom, Choking Israel's Print Media. Haaretz (2017). https://www.haaretz.com/israel-news/business/excess-of-free-newspapers-choking-israels-print-media-1.5490749
17. Lior, G.: What do Israelis do in their free time? Ynet, 16 December 2012. https://www.ynetnews.com/articles/0,7340,L-4318880,00.html
18. Bodas, M., Siman-Tov, M., Peleg, K., Solomon, Z.: Anxiety-inducing media: the effect of constant news broadcasting on the well-being of Israeli television viewers. Psychiatry **78**(3), 265–276 (2015)
19. Nossek, H., Adoni, H.: Coexistence of 'old' and 'new' news media in a transitional media system: news repertoires in Israel. Participations **14**(2), 399–415 (2017)
20. Bonfadelli, H., Bucher, P., Piga, A.: Use of old and new media by ethnic minority youth in Europe with a special emphasis on Switzerland. Communications **32**(2), 141–170 (2007)

21. Caspi, D., Adoni, H., Cohen, A.A., Elias, N.: The red, the white and the blue: the Russian media in Israel. Gazette **64**(6), 537–556 (2002)
22. Hafez, K.: Türkische Mediennutzung in Deutschland: Hemmnis oder Chance der gesellschaftlichen Integration? Eine qualitative Studie im Auftrag des Presse- und Informationsamtes der Bundesregierung. Deutsches Orient-Institut, Hamburg (2002)
23. Simon, E.: Migranten und Medien 2007. Zielsetzung, Konzeption und Basisdaten einer repräsentativen Studie der ARD/ZDF-Medienkommission. Media Perspektiven 9/2007, pp. 426–435 (2007)
24. Johnson, M.A.: Incorporating self-categorization concepts into ethnic media research. Commun. Theory **20**(1), 106–125 (2010)
25. Elias, N.: Russian-speaking immigrants and their media: still together? Isr. Aff. **17**(1), 72–88 (2011)
26. Weiss, H.-J., Trebbe, J.: Mediennutzung und Integration der türkischen Bevölkerung in Deutschland. Ergebnisse einer Umfrage des Presse- und Informationsamtes der Bundesregierung. GöfaK Medienforschung, Potsdam (2001)
27. Geißler, R., Pöttker, H.: Integration durch Massenmedien/Mass Media-Integration. Transcript, Bielefeld (2006)
28. Peeters, A., d'Haenens, L.: Bridging or bonding? Relationships between integration and media use among ethnic minorities in the Netherlands. Communications **30**(5), 201–231 (2005)
29. Elias, N., Lemish, D.: Between three worlds. J. Fam. Issues **32**(9), 1245–1274 (2011)
30. Smoliarova, A.S.: Functional Identity of Ethnocultural Media. Mediascop (2014)
31. Viswanath, K., Arora, P.: Ethnic media in the United States: an essay on their role in integration, assimilation, and social control. Mass Commun. Soc. **3**(1), 39–56 (2000)
32. Russian-speaking Germans. Boris Nemtsov Foundation (2016). https://nemtsovfund.org/cp/wp-content/uploads/2016/12/Russians-in-Germany-v.9a_eng.pdf
33. Remmennick, L.: Twenty years together: the 'Great Aliya' and Russian Israelis in the mirror of social research. Isr. Aff. **17**, 1–6 (2011)
34. Khvorostianov, N., Elias, N., Nimrod, G.: 'Without it I am nothing': the internet in the lives of older immigrants. New Media Soc. **14**(4), 583–599 (2012)
35. Elias, N., Lemish, D.: Spinning the web of identity: the roles of the internet in the lives of immigrant adolescents. New Media Soc. **11**(4), 533–551 (2009)
36. Mass-media in life of a Russian Israeli (2006). http://newsru.co.il/info/bigpoll/smi_il.html
37. Mass-media in life of a Russian Israeli (2008). http://newsru.co.il/info/bigpoll/smi2008.html
38. Mass-media in life of Russian Israelis (2009). http://newsru.co.il/info/bigpoll/smi0309.html
39. Mass-media in life of Russian Israelis (2011). http://newsru.co.il/info/bigpoll/smi2011.html
40. Mass-media in life of Russian Israelis (2013). http://newsru.co.il/info/bigpoll/smi2013.html
41. Mass-media in life of Russian Israelis (2014). http://newsru.co.il/info/bigpoll/smi2014.html
42. Mass-media and social media in life of Russian Israelis (2016). http://newsru.co.il/info/bigpoll/smi2016.html
43. Mass-media and social media in life of Russian Israelis (2018). http://newsru.co.il/info/bigpoll/smi2018.html
44. SimilarWeb: Statistics for Newsru.co.il. https://www.similarweb.com/website/newsru.co.il
45. Alexa: Statistics for Newsru.co.il. https://www.alexa.com/siteinfo/newsru.co.il

Using the Subtask Methodology in Student Training for Demonstration Examination in "Web Design and Development" Skill

Nail Nasyrov[1(✉)], Natalia Gorlushkina[2], and Anton Uzharinskiy[3]

[1] St. Petersburg State Budget Professional Educational Organization "Radio-Engineering College", Saint Petersburg, Russia
pasdel@mail.ru

[2] ITMO University, Saint Petersburg, Russia
nagor.spb@mail.ru

[3] Federal State Budgetary Educational Institution of Higher Education "Orel State University Named After I.S. Turgenev", Orel, Russia
udjal89@mail.ru

Abstract. The final state attestation in the demonstration examination format becomes obligatory in 2020 for the educational organizations providing students with the working professions included in the list of the most demanded and perspective on the labor market. In this regard, it is necessary to develop the most effective practices to complete the demonstration exam tasks. This article discusses the approach of using subtasks and their relation to the corresponding actions in organizing students' training for the demonstration examination "Web design and development" and its successful passing.

The approach described can also be applied to training for WorldSkills standards on different levels both for "Web design and development" and other skills. The conclusions and solutions formulated in the study are the basis for the creation of the information system to support students' training for the demonstration exam.

Keywords: Subtask · Tag · Demonstration examination · WorldSkills · Web design and development · Competition · Vocational education and training · VET

1 Introduction

There have been significant changes in the process of training specialists and final assessment of the competencies obtained in the secondary vocational education in the Russian Federation. Since 2016, the approbation of the final state certification in the format of the demonstration examination is carried out in the educational organizations of professional education of Russia. Since 2020, the final state certification in the demonstration exam format becomes mandatory for educational institutions that teach students for the working professions in the top-50 list [14].

Since 2012, Russia (WorldSkills Russia) has been a member of WorldSkills International (WSI). WSI is a non-profit membership association operating worldwide

D. A. Alexandrov et al. (Eds.): DTGS 2019, CCIS 1038, pp. 565–573, 2019.
https://doi.org/10.1007/978-3-030-37858-5_48

which promotes vocational education and training (VET) in different countries. The WSI aims to develop and internationalize government and industry/business cooperation to achieve higher VET standards [10].

The demonstration exam based on WorldSkills standards is a form of the state final assessment of the graduates under the programs of secondary vocational education in educational organizations of higher and secondary vocational education, which, inter alia, provides:

- modeling of real situations from the industry to demonstrate professional competencies by the graduates;
- independent Expert evaluation of the demonstration exam performance, including experts from the enterprises;
- determination of the level of knowledge and competencies of the graduates under international requirements [1].

The WorldSkills Russia demonstration exam is conducted to determine students and graduates with the level of knowledge and skills that enable them to carry out professional activities in a particular field and perform work in a specific profession or specialty according to WorldSkills Russia standards [1].

In this regard, there is a need to develop the most effective practices to teach for the successful demonstration exam task performance and the introduction into the educational process of those that were identified during the demonstration exam testing.

The article describes the experience of the final state assessment of "Web design and development" skill at Radio-engineering College (St. Petersburg) and Orel State University (Orel) using the basic principles and techniques of WorldSkills Russia.

The relevance of the study is proved by the fact that in 2017 the representatives of the international movement WorldSkills in Iran, India, and China agreed to recognize the results of the WorldSkills Russia demonstration exam jointly. Agreements were signed with New Zealand, Mongolia, Kazakhstan, and Belarus to work together to identify the results of the students' final attestation in a demo exam format [4].

2 WorldSkills Standards Application in the Final State Assessment

Here we consider the techniques and standards of WorldSkills on the example of teaching for "Developer of Web and Multimedia Applications" profession. This profession, according to the Order of the Ministry of Labor of Russia of 02.11.2015 N831, is recognized as one of the most popular and promising in the labor market. Training in this profession can take place within the framework of mastering the basic professional educational program of secondary vocational education in the specialty 09.02.07 "Information Systems and Programming" [14].

In the Federal State Standard of this specialty, it is specified that the demonstration examination is included in the graduation qualification work or is carried out as a state examination [13].

Due to the methodological support, the development of evaluation procedures together with the rules of competitions and demonstration examinations allows building an educational process that provides a high level of training for a mid-level specialist [2].

General and organizational issues in the context of student training in other skills are described in [9, 15].

However, the WorldSkills Russia demonstration exam is a new phenomenon in education, and universal training methods have not yet been described.

Since the WorldSkills Russia demonstration exam satisfies the standards and methods of WorldSkills International, the approaches used to train participants for the competitions are also fair. For some reasons, some approaches and solutions that are used in trainings for the WorldSkills competitions do not always work correctly or are not applicable [8].

There are several significant differences:

1. usually, only several participants get ready for the competition, while the demo exam is a certification of a large number of students;
2. pieces of training are conducted only at pre-project tasks or project tasks of yesteryear. As a result, some students are not always ready to the necessary changes in Task Projects of the demonstration exam.

The current research focuses on the methodology of mass and practical training directly for the demonstration exam in "Web design and development" skill.

The developed method of tag using and subtasks is based on the Technical description, the Rules of the WorldSkills Russia demonstration exam, the Infrastructure List, and other documents regulating the activities within the WorldSkills Russia [7].

3 The Methodology Description

The applied approach is based on the idea of task project decomposition into subtasks that a participant needs to perform.

Tag is an enlarged conditional description of typical tasks within the subtask framework aimed to perform the necessary action automatically and subconsciously.

Tags in demonstration exams and subtasks descriptions allow you:

- to identify the most problematic areas of a student;
- to save time on the unnecessary repetition of actions that are well mastered by a student;
- to identify problematic combinations of typical tasks (for example, compliance with the requirements of the target audience of the website when creating design layouts and page layout).

Examples of tags that can be used are shown in Table 1.

According to the Technical Description of "Web design and development" skill, a judgment and measurement assessment of students' work performed in the framework of the WorldSkills Russia demonstration exam is provided [16].

Table 1. Examples of tags

Tag	Description	Examples, explanations
#media	Includes linked images, fonts, native files, and production file format when published	Connects and uses the provided fonts, images to correctly display the content for publishing (if possible, implements the connection in several ways). Also: relative links, features of Linux server paths
#targetAudience	Compliance of the presented solution to the target audience	Logo, fonts, colors, image styling, image selection
#jsCollision	Object Collision Handling	Includes objects of different shapes, such as a quadrilateral, two circles, a quadrilateral and a circle, etc.

4 Skill Training Model

The training process can be presented in the form of a cyclic implementation of six main stages. The general scheme of subtask application in training for the WorldSkills Russia demonstration exam is shown in Fig. 1.

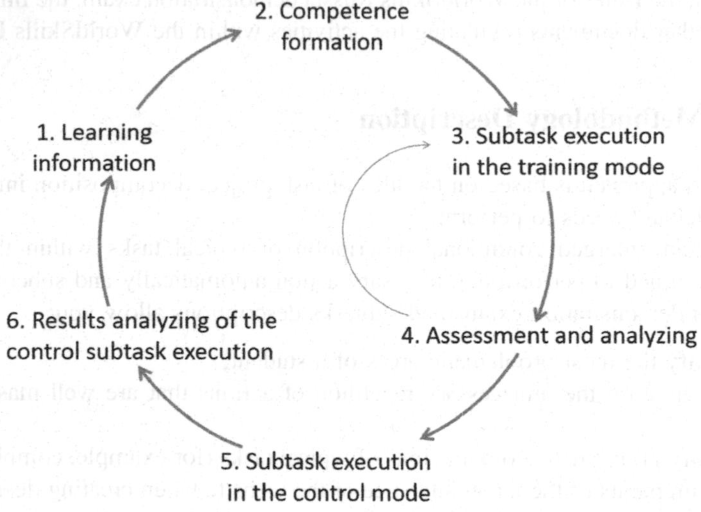

Fig. 1. General scheme of subtask application in training for the demonstration exam.

1. **Learning information.** At this stage, students learn new information. As a rule, the forms of classes are a lecture, independent work on the information provided by the teacher, independent work to study the new material using the resources of the Internet, etc.

2. **Competence formation.** The second stage is mastering the performance of the necessary actions, supported by the corresponding knowledge. The main forms are the execution of laboratory tasks and practical work, the performance of function simulators and virtual labs.
3. **Subtask execution in the training mode.** When performing subtasks in the training mode, students need to form the ability to apply knowledge in practice consciously. Reference manuals, guidelines provided by the expert, teacher help, access to the Internet, official documentation allowed at the competitions and demonstration exams and other expert approved materials are available. It is necessary to pay attention to the formation of students' competence to work with the allowed reference materials during the examination and the competition.
4. **Assessment and analyzing.** When the subtask is completed, the results of the work are evaluated. The evaluation can be carried out by an expert, by students as self-control, as well as by a group of other students. If students are involved in the process of evaluating and analyzing their works as well as works of other students, it forms an understanding of the principles and approaches that experts use when assessing the actions performed in the WorldSkills Russia demonstration exam.

One of the main tasks of this type of assessment is to teach students for professional work and a better understanding of the staff operation principles in real companies. It seems that the most promising approach is when students test themselves in various roles of the working group [3].

If necessary, a student is recommended to re-execute the subtask with a decrease in the time allotted for the assignment, as well as introducing variations in the tasks. Below is an example of a subtask for the formation of specific competencies. In this case, the corresponding tags are #authorization, #rest, #specification, variations are separated by «|» char.

Technologies: Restful, server-side
Time to complete: 15 | 10 | 8 min
Task Project: You should implement a mechanism of administrator authorization with a predetermined username and password.
The authorization API must be available by POST | GET | PUT request to {API}/auth | {API}/author | {API}/login, and accept the following required parameters:

- Login
  admin | login | root
- Password
  administrator | pA$$w0rd | dtgs-2019

If authorization is successful, the response should be returned as follows:

- status code: 200
- status text: Successful authorization | Ok
- body:
  - status - true
  - token - bearer-token to use admin API

Allowed documentation: zeal documentation (php).
You should | shouldn't use PHP framework.

The variations, for the most part, are directed to the formation of the same actions associated with the corresponding tags. However, these variations allow students to form attention to details while performing the WorldSkills Russia demonstration exam tasks.

The Task Project of the demonstration exam must differ by at least 30% from the previously published one. Therefore, making such variations in the text of the assignment contributes to the formation of students' ability to adapt to the proposed changes. This, in turn, is one of the conditions for successful passing the WorldSkills Russia demonstration exam.

In the repeated iterations, it is sometimes recommended to make changes based on the results obtained earlier in the subtask execution.

5. **Subtask execution in the control mode.** After several iterations in training mode, a participant may be prompted to complete a control task.
   When performing control tasks, the conditions are as close as possible to the test conditions: the work must be performed in a strictly allotted time and the participant can only refer to the permitted documentation. It is prohibited to use any pre-prepared fragments of the task, unless otherwise specified in advance, it is forbidden to use the resources of the Internet, etc.
6. **Results analyzing of the control subtask execution.** The results of the tasks in the control mode are analyzed and then recommendations are formed that must be considered in the study of new information. For example, an expert can refer to the work previously performed, review the results shown by students when performing complex tasks for updating the knowledge in training for learning new topics and sections, give analogy between different stacks of technologies to demonstrate relationship between various aspects of assessment.

Some features in subtask training should be noted:

1. since the preliminary tasks of the WorldSkills Russia demonstration exams are often based on the regional competition tasks, the Task Projects can be taken from these competitions;
2. the time allotted for the subtask must be specified. When re-performing a subtask in the training mode for the formation of competencies for a given tag, it is necessary to reduce the time, to accord to the demonstration exam optimal time intervals;
3. in the description of the subtasks, it is necessary to indicate what is being worked out as part of its implementation, as well as the important aspects that need to be paid attention to.
4. the available tools and media to perform the task should be specified.

It is evident that with this approach, a large amount of data on the subtask implementation and the formation of skills defined by the relevant tags is quickly formed, which can cause difficulties for the subsequent analysis of the results. To do this, as well as to improve the visibility of the statistical data and optimal planning of further activities in the subtask formation, it is recommended to use special software, for example, Microsoft Excel.

It should be noted that the essential value is not the maximum number of points a student gets for the corresponding competence but the degree of the task performance.

5 Subtasks Generation

The expert assessment, as well as the experience and teacher intuition, based on subjective opinions about the place and role of academic disciplines in the training of students, have a significant influence on the decision-making process in the field of education [5, 17]. Thus, the person, who makes the decision, bears a great responsibility for its consequences. It is necessary to use a developed specialized scientific apparatus implemented in decision support systems to make the decision-making process more objective [6].

To determine the tags that are used when generating a new subtask individually for each student, they should be classified. The algorithm uses two classes for each tag: "the tag must be used" and "the tag may not be used."

A naive Bayes classifier is used for solving the classification problem [11]. The reasons for choosing this type of classifier are:

1. conditional independence of parameters that are used when defining a tag class;
2. flexibility and adaptability with the further development of the algorithm;
3. sufficient accuracy on a small set of source data;
4. determination of the tag class, when not absolute, but relative values of the probabilities of the corresponding class are used.

The algorithm uses the following parameters of each tag: the importance of the tag, the results of measurement assessment and the results of judgment assessment in previous subtasks, the tag weight in the Task Project, and the date of subtask execution for the corresponding tag. So, tags selection for automatic generation of subtasks is carried out using the classifier [11]. Value c_{tag} determines whether to use this tag:

$$c_{tag} = \arg\max \left[logP(c) \prod_{i=1}^{n} logP(\omega_i | c) \right].$$

The weight of the tag indicates the maximum points that can be awarded to a student for the full performance of the subtask. One of the tasks of a student on the exam is to get the maximum number of points. Therefore, this metric can be used to rank tags when generating a subtask.

6 Information System to Train for the WorldSkills Russia Demonstration Exam

The technique described seems to be entirely self-sufficient to be used in the process of training for the demonstration exams and the WorldSkills Russia standards competitions in "Web design and development" skill. Based on the methodology, an information system was created that allows generating subtasks individually for each student, depending on the formation of specific skills necessary for the successful completion of the demonstration exam (https://demoskills.ru). As a result, the following is possible:

1. creation of an individual learning path based on the results demonstrated by the student;
2. optimization of the expert activities by reducing the number of routine activities;
3. resource saving while creation subtasks and aspects of the assessment;
4. determination of a more accurate selection of relevant areas for student training;
5. visualization of students' results to optimize training for the demonstration examination and, as a consequence, to improve the general level of the students' training.

7 Conclusion

In conclusion, it should be noted that such reforming of the examination practice was long overdue. In the rapidly changing modern world, it is especially essential to create a "designer" of competencies so that specialists can compete in the staff market, acquiring and developing precisely the skills that are sometimes in demand at the intersection of professions. This justifiably entails an increase in the hours of the practical part of vocational training in educational institutions, the improvement of educational standards, the creation, development, and application of new training approaches; it gives employers the opportunity to recruit personnel using a useful tool to check their level training and qualifications [12].

Within the framework of the presented study, the processes of student training for the final state certification in the form of a demonstration exam based on WorldSkills standards were described. The formulated provisions can be used to create an information system that will reduce the development time of the required number of subtasks, will individualize the training process and will improve its quality. Since the organization, procedure, and training for the demonstration exam are based on the standards of WorldSkills Russia, the above provisions of the methodology can be applied to the training process of participants for the competitions of different levels. Those provisions are based on the standards of WorldSkills Russia of "Web design and development" skill and some other skills of "Infocommunication technologies" block.

References

1. About Demonstration Exam of WorldSkills Russia. https://worldskills.ru/nashi-proektyi/demonstraczionnyij-ekzamen/obshhaya-informacziya.html. Accessed 08 Jan 2019
2. Bystrova, N.V., Frolova, N.V., Maseleno, A., Smirnova, Z.V., Vaganova, O.I., Zanfir, L.N.: WorldSkills as means of improving quality of pedagogical staff training. Int. J. Eng. Technol. (UAE) **7**(4), 4103–4108 (2018)

3. Mekhonoshin, A., Denisova, A., Gorlushkina, N.: Organization of group classes through an automated system. In: Chugunov, A.V., et al. (eds.) DTGS 2016. CCIS, vol. 674, pp. 333–343. Springer, Cham (2016). https://doi.org/10.1007/978-3-319-49700-6_31
4. Global SKILLS-PASSPORT presented in China. https://worldskills.ru/media-czentr/novosti/v-kitae-prezentovali-globalnyij-skills-passport.html. Accessed 10 Jan 2019
5. Glushchenko, A.I.: Information system of decision-making on the formation of individual curricula. In: Management of Large Systems: Proceedings, vol. 15, pp. 79–91 (2006)
6. Gorlushkina, N.N., Hlopotov, M.V., Kotsuba, I.Y.: Tasks and methods of educational data mining to support decision-making. Educ. Technol. Soc. **18**, 472–482 (2015)
7. Information for demonstration exams and different competitions on WorldSkills Russia standards. https://drive.google.com/drive/folders/1WJzf9rPLioVrYGxYHDhyWw576V-xi6zSS. Accessed 08 Jan 2019
8. Kolbina, O.V.: Formation of professional competences of students in training for the WorldSkills Russia competition in the competence of "Confectionery". In: Xth International Scientific Conference Theory and Practice of Education in the Modern World, pp. 106–108. Chita (2018)
9. Maykova, P.E.: The practice of competence-based qualification in accordance with WorldSkills standards in the framework of the intermediate evaluation. Professional education and the labour market, № 4, pp. 33–44 (2017)
10. Messenger, S., Shackleton, J., Shackleton, E.: Setting a benchmark for excellence: a case study of a Chinese and UK collaboration based on the WorldSkills international standards model. In: Global Innovation and Entrepreneurship: Challenges and Experiences from East and West, pp. 139–155 (2017)
11. Narasimha, M.M., Susheela, D.V.: Pattern Recognition: An Algorithmic Approach. Springer, London (2011). https://doi.org/10.1007/978-0-85729-495-1. ISBN 978-0857294944
12. Naumkina, V.A.: The qualification standards WorldSkills: confident access to the labour market. Professional education and the labour market, № 3, pp. 44–48 (2018)
13. Order of the Ministry of Education and Science of the Russian Federation of December 9, 2016, № 1547 "On approval of the federal State educational standard of secondary vocational education in the specialty 09.02.07 Information systems and programming". http://www.garant.ru/products/ipo/prime/doc/71477324/#ixzz5cBeRIn8h. Accessed 09 Jan 2019
14. Order of the Ministry of Labor of Russia from 02.11.2015 N 831 "On approval of the list of the 50 most demanded in the labor market, new and prospective professions requiring secondary vocational education". http://www.consultant.ru/cons/cgi/online.cgi?req=doc&base=LAW&n=188401&rnd=0F706E12B215889BF53E6C21BBC09182&dst=100009&fld=134#0738583656254327l. Accessed 09 Jan 2019
15. Petrov, E.E.: Preparation of the effective participant of the final of the national competition on the WorldSkills methodology. Professional education and the labour market, № 3, pp. 49–56 (2018)
16. Technical Description of "Web design and development" skill. https://drive.google.com/drive/folders/1x8tcr2JppoNcFXVo_d9d8DOfshmDn02e. Accessed 08 Jan 2019
17. Vorobyova, N.A., Noskov, S.I.: Software for automating the process of curriculum development. Fundamental study, no. 6(3), pp. 633–636 (2012)

The Influence of the Author's Background on the Representation of Gender Stereotypes in Soviet Children's Literature

Alexandra Vidyaeva(✉)

National Research University Higher School of Economics,
Soyuza Pechatnikov 16, 190121 Saint Petersburg, Russia
sasha305onel@gmail.com

Abstract. This paper is devoted to the problem of gender inequalities in the Soviet children's literature. There gender stereotypes are considered along with the influence of the authors' characteristics on the representation of these stereotypes in Soviet children's books. The main attention is paid to the author's generation, his/her gender and the socio-economic status of the author's family. The measurement of the socio-economic status of the author's family is provided with the coding of the author's parents' profession using the ISCO and the ISEI. This research paper highlights the main types of characters that are identified through the cluster analysis. It also discusses the characteristics of literary characters that can influence the level of the gender stereotypes representation.

Keywords: Gender stereotypes · Children's literature · Gender policy · Literature history · USSR · Education

1 Introduction

For several centuries gender inequalities could have been observed in various spheres of life. In terms of gender policy the Soviet period played a significant role in Russia. For the first time, women received the right to work on previously considered predominantly male jobs [6]. In the 50s the abolition of abortions was lifted, some benefits for certain categories of women appeared, special departments were created for political education of the female population and a special political apparatus for women (women's councils) appeared on the state arena [14]. It seems that one can characterize this period of time in the history of Russia as an attempt to transition to gender equality. However, only formally women improved their positions. Rarely it was possible to observe female representatives in higher and local authorities, sexuality was associated with reproduction. Again, after the end of World War II women were being squeezed out of areas previously owned exclusively by men [6].

The image of women in the media deserves special attention, including children's literature. Gender separation of roles is well seen in children's works. Children's literature, according to Diekman and Murnen, even which has declared itself as gender

D. A. Alexandrov et al. (Eds.): DTGS 2019, CCIS 1038, pp. 574–581, 2019.
https://doi.org/10.1007/978-3-030-37858-5_49

neutral, broadcasts male and female characters in traditionally masculine and feminine roles [5].

Such spheres of public life as religion, art, literature and educational system are the main means of forming the institution of sex. In addition, these areas of life are involved in representation of certain gender images and strengthening stereotypes prevailing in society [13].

Children's literature is considered to be one of the main agents of socialization. It promotes and plays a significant role in formation of a person, expanding his/her ideas about the world, introducing the reader to new concepts, helping to develop and acquire speech. Characters act as carriers of a particular gender in literary texts. They are endowed with such behaviors and characteristics with which their sexual status can be recognized. This is traced in the description of their speech, clothing, gestures, manners and actions [12].

In addition to the main agent, family, books as significant agents of socialization are involved in formation of gender identity on early stages of individual maturation. Formation usually occurs during preschool period and then in primary school. When gender identity is finally formed, gender constancy is created reinforced by gender-role stereotypes [4]. Children's literature gives children an idea of differences between the sexes which are accepted in society through texts and illustrations.

Concepts of masculinity and femininity, reflected on the pages of children's literature, are acquired and read by children as they mature. As children read literature, their gender identification occurs. Gender identification refers to the process at which children acquire male and female roles, skills and experience necessary for successful building of these binary roles [15].

This article is not limited to the study of gender stereotypes in the Soviet children's literature, it focuses on finding factors that can influence their representation. There are many authors who have written about gender stereotypes in literature but there is almost no research on the influence of the author's characteristics on the reflection of gender stereotypes in children's literature. Numerous studies of children's works [9], [10], [16] generally demonstrated that gender stereotypes and representative inequalities began to positively improve in the 1970s, although significant imbalances and narrow gender roles were still apparent.

The purpose of this study is to find out the influence of certain author's characteristics on the reflection of gender stereotypes in his or her texts. The research question of this work is how the author's characteristics and the representation of gender stereotypes in the Soviet children's literature are related. The research paper examines the relation of such individual author's characteristics as his or her gender, birth year and socio-economic status of the family in which the author was born to the representation of certain types of literary characters.

2 Methodology

2.1 Sample

As a criterion for the data selection, in particular children's literature, the study used the Russian Federal State Educational Standards (GEF) (https://fgos.ru/). The data contain works of Soviet children's literature, written by Soviet authors in Russian, published in separate book editions, as well as some works that are in the range of children's reading but their authors are not children's writers recommended by the GEF for primary and basic general education. The list does not include publications in periodicals. As for the subject and genre, the corpus contains works on Soviet children, written in a realistic genre. All in all, 57 books are analyzed in the current study.

In this study, 3 databases are used, which include: a list of all analyzed works of Soviet children's literature, a list of authors of all studied works with metadata about them, a list of characters with characteristics selected for analysis.

Sampling Characters. The coding of literary characters was made at the episode level of every book from the sample. The characters were coded according to the following constructed variables: sex, age, indoors (at home), outside, needy (in the sense of help), helping, brave, cowardly, aggressor, victim. The episode in this case is the context in which the literary character appears. The mentioned in the text character was added to the sample each time a new context appeared. In addition, the character characteristics considered in this paper are categorical at the episode level (for example, a character in a particular episode is/is not brave, if it is, it is assigned "1", otherwise - "0").

According to existing studies, it was decided to choose between "helper" and "needy" as one of the characteristics of literary characters for empirical analysis. Citing studies by Barnett [3], who studied a total of 1,537 picture books, boy characters are more often depicted as helping other characters, but at the same time they are more likely than other characters to receive help. This fact is related to the results of other studies, which showed that the boy characters in the books take up more space than the girls. In addition, a study in which 22 books that were awarded the Caldecott award and 19 books randomly selected from the library shelves were studied showed that men are also more often shown as "helping" others, and "needy" characters, than female characters [11].

Allen and colleagues [1], analyzing books of two periods – 1938–1940 and 1986–1988, awarded the Caldecott, noted the tendency that male characters were more often depicted outside the home than women, and such results are true for books of the period - from 1938 in 1940 and for books from 1986 to 1988. Oskamp and his colleagues did not find differences between girls and boys regarding the image outside or inside the house, however, they noted that adult male characters are more often depicted outside the home than female characters in 3: 1 ratio [7]. According to the research, it was decided to consider how the variable of the place (inside the house/outside the house) is reflected in the Soviet children's literature in relation to male and female characters.

Turner-Bowker [16], who researched 30 books from the period 1984–1994, noted that the proportion of men descriptions, as well as their presence in the headlines and pictures, was large compared to women. In addition, the researcher noted that the adjective "cowardly" was the second most common in describing women in books that were analyzed. In the current study, the variable "cowardly" and its opposite "brave" were also chosen as the characteristics of the characters.

In addition, the variables "aggressor" and "victim" were chosen as the characteristics of the characters. Although Hamilton and colleagues did not find a significant difference between the aggressive behavior of men and women, in this study it was decided to check the distribution of these characteristics regarding the children's Soviet literature.

Sampling Authors. For further analysis of variables, the frequency of occurrence of the following situational characteristics was taken into account: indoors (at home), outside, needy, helping, brave, cowardly, aggressor and victim. In total, there are 382 literary characters, of which 154 characters are children, and 228 are adults in the research. There are 44 girl characters, 110 boy characters, as for adults, women - 228, and men - 124.

The following variables were chosen as characteristics of the studied authors: the author's gender, the author's generation and his/her socio-economic status. The author's generation was determined by the writer's year of birth and the current political agenda. The socio-economic status was determined on the basis of the professions of the author's parents. At first occupational data of parents was coded based on the International Standard Classification of Occupations (http://www.harryganzeboom.nl/isco88/index.htm), then the assigned ordinal codes were translated into interval scales using the ISEI, where each number indicates a specific social status. In this paper, 26 authors are investigated, of which 22 are male authors, 4 are female. The analyzed authors were born in the interval from 1880 to 1934. Socio-economic status ranged from 20 to 85, where 20 is the lowest (orphanage, a seamstress), 85 is the highest (attorney).

2.2 Procedure

Before building a statistical model, it is important to analyze the data and explore its structure. The cluster analysis of characters was done before proceeding to the final model building. The main hypothesis at this stage: literary characters represent types where the basis for dividing into clusters are gender-related characteristics. To solve this problem, a non-hierarchical cluster analysis method, the Partitioning Around Medoids (PAM) algorithm was used. PAM is a modification of the k-means algorithm, the k-median algorithm (k-medoids). The algorithm is less sensitive to noise and outliers than the k-means algorithm, since the median is less susceptible to the effects of outliers. In addition, PAM is effective for small databases. The Gower's metric was chosen as the distance [2]. Evaluating the similarity, this distance allows the simultaneous usage of mixed data. Silhouette width was used to find the optimal number of clusters. This is the internal validation metric, which is an aggregated measure of how similar the observation is to its own cluster compared to its nearest neighboring cluster.

Besides, to test the hypothesis about the relationship of variables - "sex", "age" and other characteristics of the characters, clustering was carried out without taking into account the sex and age of literary characters.

Correspondence analysis was conducted to graphically explore relationships among qualitative variables: sex, age (coded as categorical variable) and the other characteristics of the characters in the contingency table.

The main task is to identify which variables are more prone to boy, girl, men characters and women characters. The goal of the correspondence analysis is moving from the original data matrix to a new, simpler matrix, losing as little information as possible. The correspondence analysis was carried out according to the age and sex characteristics, both for all characters in general, and for the characters of each author separately. Here the following hypothesis was put forward: all differences in the distribution of stereotypes regarding the characters of each author are quantitative. It was assumed that the characters of all studied authors will differ only in quantitative indicators regarding the studied characteristics. Certain characteristics of the characters of some writers will be more pronounced than those of other writers.

Having studied the structure of the data and conducting a descriptive analysis, the next step of the study was to build a statistical model that checks the connection of gender stereotypes of literary characters with the studied characteristics of the author. As a model, it was decided to take logistic regression, where the dependent binary variable is the presence of a gender stereotype, and the predictors are gender (nominal scale), year of birth (interval scale) and socio-economic status of the author of the work (interval scale).

3 Results

According to the results of the cluster analysis, including all the characteristics of the characters, the optimal number of clusters was "4". Interpreting the results, it can be noted that all the characters are clearly divided by gender and age (child/adult). After clustering with the exception of sex and age of characters, it can be concluded regarding the selected characteristics: there is no strong association between characters' sex, age and other studied variables (Fig. 1).

As for the correspondence analysis, the following tentative conclusions can be made: the characters of all the studied books are divided into male - and female - axis, this suggests that the variable "sex" is significant in the separation of characters, besides, the characters are divided into children - and adults - axis, which also indicates that the characters are differently reflected in the books depending on age. Regarding other characteristics chosen for the analysis of literary characters, it can be noted here that female characters are more often represented as characters inside (at home), while children's characters are described rather outside. Girl characters are often depicted as cowardly and needy, while boys are more likely brave and helpful (Fig. 2).

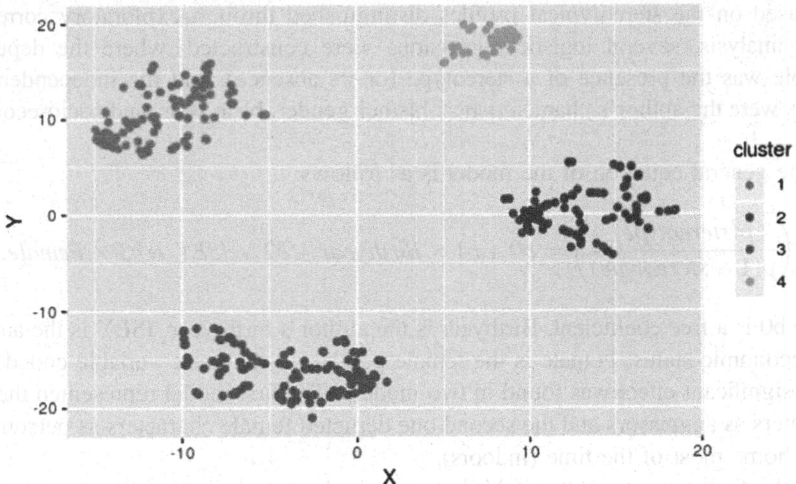

Fig. 1. Cluster analysis graph

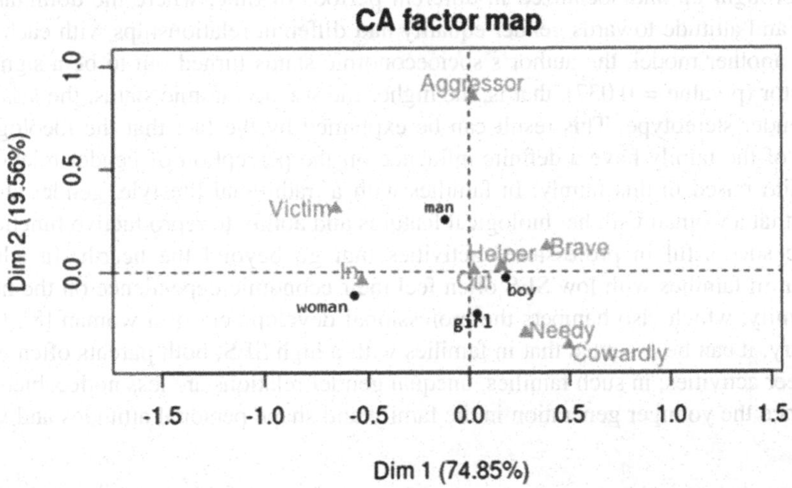

Fig. 2. Correspondence analysis graph (Color figure online)

The above graph shows the overall data trends. The rows (characters grouped by gender and age) are represented by blue dots, and the columns (character characteristics) are represented by red triangles. The distance between any points of the rows or columns gives a measure of their similarities (or differences). The points of the rows with a similar profile are located close relative to each other on the axes, the same is true for column labels.

Measurements 1 and 2, marked on the graph as Dim1 and Dim2, explain approximately 74.85% and 19.56% of the total inertia, respectively. The greater the inertia, the higher the role of this dimension.

Based on the stereotypical profiles distinguished through exploratory correspondence analysis, several logistic regressions were constructed, where the dependent variable was the presence of a stereotype (or its absence), and the independent predictors were the author's characteristics: his/her gender, birth year, and socio-economic status.

The general equation of the model is as follows:

$$\log\left(\frac{p(stereotype)}{p(1-stereotype)}\right) = b0 + b1 \times Birthyear + b2 \times ISEY + b3 \times Female, \quad (1)$$

where b0 is a free coefficient, Birthyear is the author's birth year, ISEY is the author's socioeconomic status, Female is the female gender, as the basic variable coded "0".

A significant effect was found in two models. The first model represented the male characters as aggressors and the second one depicted female characters as persons who are at home most of the time (indoors).

In the first case, the author's birth year turned out to be a significant predictor (p-value = 0.039), that is, the younger the author, the more likely the stereotype investigated in the model. This result can be partly explained by the fact that the authors were brought up and socialized in different periods of time, where the dominant ideology and attitude towards gender equality had different relationships with each other.

In another model, the author's socioeconomic status turned out to be a significant predictor (p-value = 0.037), that is, the higher the socioeconomic status, the less likely the gender stereotype. This result can be explained by the fact that the ideology and status of the family have a definite influence on the perception of gender relations by the child raised in this family. In families with a traditional lifestyle, gender attitudes argue that a woman with her biological features and ability to reproductive function can not be successful in professional activities that go beyond the hearth. In addition, women in families with low SES often feel their economic dependence on the head of the family, which also hampers the professional development of a woman [8]. On the contrary, it can be assumed that in families with a high SES, both parents often engage in career activities; in such families, unequal gender relations are less noticeable, which influence the younger generation in the family and shape personal attitudes and values.

4 Conclusion

This study plays an important role in the issue of gender inequality, which can be traced in the pages of children's literature consumed by modern schoolchildren.

The question "what to read?" addressed to modern students is acute today. Neither teachers nor parents can come to a consensus. The Ministry of Education and Science does not study the list recommended for children in schools in detail.

Depending on the goals in education, opinions on the exclusion or inclusion of one or another literature also differ. The procedure for compiling a list for reading by schoolchildren should be approached carefully, since books may have those properties and, accordingly, influence that they, at first glance, do not possess. Studies of this type can help both parents and the school educational system in the correct choice of literature for children.

References

1. Allen, A.M., Allen, D.N., Sigler, G.: Changes in sex-role stereotyping in caldecott medal award picture books 1938—1988. J. Res. Child. Educ. **7**(2), 67–73 (1993). https://doi.org/10.1080/02568549309594842
2. Barbaro, S.E., Bhulai, S., Hoogendoorn, M.: Using hierarchical clustering and Quasi-Newton methods to maximise the cophenetic correlation coefficient. 65(n.d.)
3. Barnett, M.A.: Sex bias in the helping behavior presented in children's picture books. J. Genet. Psychol. **147**(3), 343–351 (1986). https://doi.org/10.1080/00221325.1986.9914508
4. Bussey, K., Bandura, A.: Self-regulatory mechanisms governing gender development. Child Dev. **63**(5), 1236–1250 (1992)
5. Diekman, A.B., Murnen, S.K.: Learning to be little women and little men: the inequitable gender equality of nonsexist children's literature. Sex Roles **50**(5), 373–385 (2004). https://doi.org/10.1023/B:SERS.0000018892.26527.ea
6. Goldman, W.Z.: Women at the Gates: Gender and Industry in Stalin's Russia. Cambridge University Press, Cambridge (2002)
7. Hamilton, M.C., Anderson, D., Broaddus, M., Young, K.: Gender stereotyping and under-representation of female characters in 200 popular children's picture books: a twenty-first century update. Sex Roles **55**(11–12), 757–765 (2006). https://doi.org/10.1007/s11199-006-9128-6
8. Isakova, E.: Vliyanie gendernyh stereotipov na trudovuyu deyatel'nost'. Presented at the Gendernye stereotipy v sovremennoj Rossii (2006) (Исакова, Е.: Влияние гендерных стереотипов на трудовую деятельность. Presented at the Гендерные стереотипы в современной России (2006))
9. Kolbe, R., LaVoie, J.C.: Sex-role stereotyping in preschool children's picture books. Soc. Psychol. Q. **44**(4), 369–374 (1981). https://doi.org/10.2307/3033906
10. Kortenhaus, C.M., Demarest, J.: Gender role stereotyping in children's literature: an update. Sex Roles **28**(3), 219–232 (1993). https://doi.org/10.1007/BF00299282
11. McDonald, S.M.: Sex bias in the representation of male and female characters in children's picture books. J. Genet. Psychol. **150**(4), 389–401 (1989). https://doi.org/10.1080/00221325.1989.9914605
12. Kushnir, M.P.: Detskaya literatura kak translyator gendernyh stereotipov. Perspektivnye Razrabotki Nauki i Tekhniki, 10 (2010) (Кушнир, М. П.: Детская литература как транслятор гендерных стереотипов. Перспективные Разработки Науки и Техники, 10 (2010)
13. Miller, D.L.: Gender and the artist archetype: understanding gender inequality in artistic careers. Sociol. Compass **10**(2), 119–131 (2016)
14. Racioppi, L., See, K.O.: Organizing women before and after the fall: women's politics in the soviet union and post-soviet Russia. Signs **20**(4), 818–850 (1995)
15. Spence, J.T.: Gender identity and its implications for the concepts of masculinity and femininity. Nebr. Symp. Motiv. **32**, 59–95 (1984)
16. Turner-Bowker, D.M.: Gender stereotyped descriptors in children's picture books: Does "curious Jane" exist in the literature? Sex Roles **35**(7), 461–488 (1996). https://doi.org/10.1007/BF01544132

International Workshop on Internet Psychology

Exposition to Advertising Messages on Digital Media

Raquel Marques Carriço Ferreira[1(✉)] and Rita Espanha[2]

[1] Universidade Federal de Sergipe, São Cristóvão, Brazil
raquelcarrico@gmail.com
[2] CIES IUL - Instituto Universitário de Lisboa, Lisbon, Portugal
rita.espanha@iscte-iul.pt

Abstract. New technologic environments secure to their users sophisticated exit routes to intrusive publicity. There is, actually a crescent recognition about the sophistication of consumers and the complex relationship between propaganda on the digital world. Such a position is supported by 200 million users of Ad blocking software estimated throughout the world. It seems clear that relevant, smart and attractive productions are key pieces to perpetrate advertising as a business in this environment. However, how does the social networks user synthesize these concepts? What are the motives that lead users of digital media to expose themselves to advertising messages? In view of the fact that the nature of the advertisements consumption requires a high degree of interest from the audience member for their exposure, we have conducted a study in Brazil and Portugal, developed by applying the method of Grounded Theory, firmly rooted in one hundred and eighteen in-depth interviews conducted in 2016 and 2017. The text is dedicated to introduce the three most consistent motivations categories towards exposure to advertisement, A. Information/Surveillance B. Humour Management and C. Personal Integration.

Keywords: Advertising · Digital media · Selective attention · Uses and gratifications · Consumption · Exposure to propaganda

1 Introduction

To think about the reasons that lead the individual to expose himself to the advertising messages is the objective of the study undertaken, more objectively, of the young users of the Digital Media. New technological environments such as Social Networks assure its users, refined escape routes to intrusive messages, especially for young people[1], the biggest users of this environment.[2]

[1] ONU Criterion (18-24 years old).

[2] This finding can be certified by the reports of the Brazilian Media Survey researcher [1] which demonstrates that this is the most expressive group exposed to the internet in the country, and in Portugal, in the and in Portugal, in the OberCom [2] and ERC [3] which accuse the same results, young people are the most expressive group exposed to the internet.

D. A. Alexandrov et al. (Eds.): DTGS 2019, CCIS 1038, pp. 585–598, 2019.
https://doi.org/10.1007/978-3-030-37858-5_50

There is, in fact, a growing recognition of the sophistication of consumers and the complex relationship between them and advertising on the digital media. Such a statement is supported by 200 million users of ads blocking software worldwide on the web.[3]

It seems clear that relevant, interesting and attractive productions are keys to the perpetuation of Advertising as a business, but how does this audience synthesize these concepts?

Considering the fact that the nature of advertising consumption requires a high degree of interest from the audience member for their exposure, a study addressed by Grounded Theory (GT) was undertaken.

GT is a method of conducting qualitative research focused on the development of theoretical structures developed from the inductive analysis of information, which arise from the substantive data investigated. The procedures of its practice basically contemplate the 1. Simultaneous involvement in data collection and analysis; 2. The construction of analytical codes and categories arising from the data and not from the preconceived logic of deductive hypotheses; 3. The use of the constant comparative method that involves all phases of investigation; 4. sample saturation and finally 5. The conduction of the literature review that happens only after the development of an independent analysis of its data by the researcher [4].

The practices provided by the GT lead to the substantive transformation of the data into theoretical explanatory structures, bringing to light the conceptual understanding of the phenomenon under study. Along with its structure of data capture, analysis and construction of provisional portraits of reality, some fundamental methodological procedures are highlighted here. One of them is the adoption of the theoretical sample criterion that was superimposed by another, the intentional stratified sample of the urban population of Aracaju (Brazil) and Lisbon (Portugal), classified by the socioeconomic criterion and the age variation.[4]

Thus, in addition to the criterion that data should be collected until (1) no relevant data emerges and (2) the categories sought are well developed in terms of their properties and dimensions, we also take as a starting point the stratified sample of thirty-eight young people in each country to guarantee a minimum diversity of elements that could add variations on the studied phenomenon. The very choice of the research development in two different countries helped to increase the cultural variations to be considered.

With in depth interviewing, the information was collected and treated according to the indications proposed by the method, operationalized in three respective stages: open coding, axial coding and theoretical coding. The grounded analysis model was given so that the motivational categories (influencing conditions) were connected to the actions of exposure to the advertising messages.

---

[3] See 2015 global report on ad blocking in https://pagefair.com/blog/2015/ad-blocking-report.

[4] Thus the sample was subdivided into two age groups, 18–21 and 21–25; in five distinct social classes (A, B, C1, C2 and D), according to Abipeme (Brazil) and Marktest (Portugal) criteria, that applies this model of categorization based on variables adequate to capture local realities. The data collection took place through in-depth interviews with students from local universities.

In addition the German software of content analysis MAXQDA was used for the processing of the information. We present below the results and its discussion.

2 Information/Surveillance

The category identified relates to the search of receptors for information about the "market novelties" of A. specific products of immediate consumer interest, and B. vigilant interest in "market news". Although obvious in its conception, the category presents some tenuous concepts that will be elaborated here.

In the first situation, advertising is the trigger of useful information, which makes the receptor, firstly expose himself from start to finish of the advertisement information, then, seek to make sure of the best purchase options.

For example, after exposure to message, a low-price promotional ad from a perfumery store or electronics, causes the audience to begin an equitable search for advantages between the advertiser and their competitors to make a decision about buying behaviour. Such a search is a naturalized attitude due above all, "the context of the digital environment" that makes "research" too simple.

In addition, an advertising message never gives details of the attributes of the advertised object, the conditions of purchase and associated services offered. So almost always a commercial that meets the desires and needs of the group researched triggers a more refined search of the buying process:

> "(…) I watched on Facebook, I was always being bombarded (…) it's the ROCKERS, sunglasses. I ended up buying them… but of course, to check if I was really at an advantage, I researched that brand and others on the web…"

However, what really strengthens this motivational category to the exposure of advertising messages is the search for information directed to the advertised object/service that meets, at the moment of its placement, the consumer.

> "(…) Who likes advertising? There is nothing more boring … I just watch it depending on my interest at the time…"

> "(…) So all the ads I watch are the ones that go on the computer, but it's something I do not pay attention to. Propaganda information is important to me, but above all to the products that I use and I am needing…"

> "(…) There are other types of ads that pay your attention because the product matters, when I was a child, the car ads did not attract my attention, now I just think about it…"

Considering the nature of the media investigated, one cannot fail to observe two modelling conditions of the young man's exposure to advertisements in Social Networks, still characterizing this stated motivation. The algorithmic suggestions and the specialized consultancies of those who approve or recommend the product/service announced.

The Facebook algorithm, for example, is a feature used primarily to determine what appears on your user's home screen. The algorithm looks for combinations, defining what the user of this social network will be exposed to or not.

> "(…) I have Ad-blocking and I think that Facebook ends up exposing me more to the advertisements because I access them in another corner, and then, I end up getting advertising."

According to the young interviewee, he search for brands in the area of technology, games, and fitness, which would justify the appearance of commercial messages in your user account.

To Criscuolo and Pacete [5] the network prioritizes posts and shares of content made by friends and family to the detriment of the content of pages that users enjoy, this, to reduce the circulation of commercial content, which would oblige the brands to pay for their communication strategies to circulate on the network. Commercial content, however, does not seem to have diminished in the interface of network users like Facebook. According to the young people interviewed, these are numerous and insistent over a "certain time".

In this context, the content is important because somehow the brand belongs to an interest already notified by the user of the network:

> "(…) I accompany the brand NIVEA, I have already searched your site several times, mainly because I want to know about the launches (…) It's a brand that I like and use, so, also in the networks, I'm watching for the news."

> "(…) Well I follow some things from TEZENIS, I think these ads appear in my timeline because I've watched some commercials of men's underwear and bras, the products I wanted, because it is very rare for me to stop and watch the advertisements (…) I even remember that advertising in my networks."

On YouTube, business messages also follow algorithmic verification logic. The circulation of a commercial message, as the media itself puts it, considers a correspondence between the ads and the demographic characteristics of the public that accesses the network. Thus, "Advertising always appears because often you or a friend has once put a "Like" in a brand and that is following you for some time." And the exposure to the message of advertising production then happens for instrumental reasons:

> "(…) It was a young girl with a hairstyle that I liked, and had a very sharp dress shirt (…) at the same time it advertised nice prices, so I think it was that idea: OK, it's beautiful and cheap, I'll stop to watch the ad, then."

> "(…) I always remember the ads. I remember those that appear after I search anything from ZARA, OLX, probably RYANAIR, EASYJET, WTF (…) are brands that I have somehow already consumed or searched for information on the Web."

Not only are advertising messages looking for potential consumers on social networks, but "instructional" or "entertainment" content is sought out by the user, that suggests products and services. In general, these are specialized reviews of people who have some notoriety in an area of knowledge. Aesthetics subjects, food, fashion, entertainment, electronics, automobile, etc., the area of knowledge ends up involving consumption by indication and endorsement.

The search for such content is based on the experience of a prominent individual who gives greater encouragement to the experimentation of products and services:

> "(…) I get many advertisements, I can not say how many, but the amount I pay attention to is zero. When I want to buy, I go to YouTube, to watch the reviews and when I make the decision, I buy."

> "(…) And I do not care when it's a sponsored product, I end up watching because it's already inside a content that interests me… it just comes in a different packaging…. the tubers I follow make it clear the sponsorship of certain brands, it is not something veiled, even because nowadays there's no way to lie. But I prefer it to be that way, it's a nicer and deeper content than just a banner that I'm going to ignore and it's there occupying my space, slowing down my internet connection."

Thus, regardless of the order of the encounter between receptor and message,[5] content is only visualized from its immediate consumer interest.

In the second version that characterizes information/surveillance category, the receptor of the advertising message does not seek subsidy for an instrumental buying behaviour, his desire is a variant of this instrumentalisation, he wishes to be "vigilant about the novelties of the market" to perform a role of "opinion leadership", in which his peers, friends and family begin to have him as reference for instructive consultation of a certain area of knowledge that indicates the best purchase of the day.

It is a kind of detection of the productive environment and the provision of existing services or that are in the beginning of commercialization. The consumer of advertising content is vigilant to the information on the events and launches of the market of a certain specialty, and thus, he can be consulted on the best purchases to make:

> "(…) Advertising in a way keeps me ahead of news and launches… I also like to watch ads mainly in relation to smartphones because there are always friends who consult me before buying…"

> "(…) When it is one of those promotions, I usually have curiosity in checking which are the articles that are included in this promotion, be it in the case of mobile phones, accessories, tablets… so I pay attention to FNAC, WORTEN (…) because there is always someone I know who should be warned about these advantages."

Thus, in this version of exposure to advertisements, there is no instrumentalization of the individual specifically for buying behaviour, but for peer counselling on particular products and services. The objective here is to recognize the "market situation", in any specialty where the receptor becomes a reference in his social circles, acting as a watchman, counsellor, opinion leader of the buying process.

Together with the desire to search for information for deliberate buying behaviour, these two modalities of justification for exposure to advertising messages make up the motivational category Information/surveillance.

[5] In which the message reaches the receptor by algorithmic suggestion or the receptor deliberately searches for content about products and services.

3 Mood Management

Mood Management is a motivational category that is alluded to by many terms: distraction, joke, escape, aesthetic pleasure, play, fun, laught, apprehension, hobby, vicarious experience, stress relief or boredom. It is, in fact, any stimulus that helps the individual to emulate his state of mood, or even excitement, considered by the receptor as desired at the time of his exposure to the advertising message.

"(…) When it's those videos that almost look like movie trailers and you're curious, you do not even know what the product is, but the video is so smart… it's very exciting."
"(…) I watch COCA-COLA or big companies, I think the ads attract attention because they are very intense, I mean, it is mostly always a fast song, very fast and significant scenes, and people are there watching a mini-story. I get more interested because it is high-spirited (…) it is an animation and happens mirabolantes things, it is massive".

With the manipulation of mood or its management, the use of the propagandistic message is understood as consummatory and not instrumental, that is, the receptor does not make use of the message for a buying behaviour, uses publicity as a mean for the management of excitation levels/ mood at the moment of consumption:

"(…) Sometimes the stories are so clever and mysterious that it costs nothing to stay there to watch how it ends. It's like a mental game, what happens next (…)"

Zillmann is one of the leading authors of the Mood Management theory, and says that entertaining materials enable considerable excitement[6] through stimuli such as suspense, mystery, action, and humour, manifesting in the "sympathetic autonomic nervous system, and among other things, produces affective reactions" [6].

These affective reactions are reported as escape or relaxation, activation of a level of excitement considered appropriate, as individuals searching to engage with content considered to be intelligent, witty, mysterious, entertaining, calming, aesthetically charming, to leave, maintain, or even maximize their a particular state of mood, previously presented to the exhibition:

"(…) sometimes you are upset or stressed, then these advertisements help you relax, escape, for a few minutes of a problem that you have to solve … even if I'm relaxed, I want to stay relaxed watching these ads and not watch a documentary about human rights."

The attractiveness of the contents connects with the chances of them helping the receptors escape or remain emotionally from/on their respective states of undesirable/desirable excitation. In general, bored people end up exposing themselves to content that changes their initial dispositions to a more intense state, with the search for materials of action, adventure, animation, comedy, espionage, terror and suspense, or anything that subjectively provides, escape from your initial state of mind.

Likewise, receptors with high excitement levels seek to model their disposition and mood with subjectively mild, soothing contents. Such placements are relatively

[6] The entertaining material can produce considerable excitation in its receptors. Its denomination refers to a unitary force that energizes or intensifies the cortical and autonomic manifestations (stimulating in particular, affective reactions) by initiating, neutralizing or altering the receptor's mood states [7].

simplistic and so the term "mood Management" seems to fit all the concepts that have been gathered here, such as distraction, play, entertainment, joke, escape, aesthetic enchantment, play, fun, etc.…

Although the discussion of the results presented here has space in another text due to the limitations of extension, here are just a few key questions for the receptor to choose propaganda content for his "Mood Management." One of the key points for exposure to the material is its ability to involve the receptor in the mood-conditioning process:

> "(…) the ads are different … when I open a video, it is because it generated me a curiosity, or the music, the production, sometimes the light, the assembly, the cut, the unfolding of history, is something that grabs me by my stomach".

This means that it is only with engaging and enchanting productions that the receptor achieves neutralizing effects of its initial state of excitation, or maintainers of a state of disposition considered by it to be pleasurable. Thus, according to the author mentioned here, there is a great possibility of the stressed ones to choose soothing contents, as they present a romantic, fanciful, musical plot, or any other stimulus that subjectively seems appropriate to it.

Lack of engaging stimuli and excessive impact (frequency considered excessive by young people) are mitigating factors in the selection of advertising content for exposure. Propaganda is generally said to be intrusive, undesirable, and impertinent material, and only materials that prove to be exceptional are selected for assistance:

> "(…) probably the thing works while the story is current and new. If it keeps repeating itself, there is no one who wants to watch them".
> "(…) I never watch advertising, I only watch it when it's different, funny, something that catches my attention. I have not watched an advertisement for a long time. Even the YouTube banner I do not give a damn, I do not need to skip it, I just ignore it".

Some key points have been listed on what seems attractive and relevant to young people who are exposed to advertising messages, especially when the stakes are the ability to engage in such material. In a generalized way, some indications can contextualize this essential foundation. The format of Content Marketing,[7] Storytelling[8] among others as the deliberate sponsorship of formats such as series, documentaries and even films were highlighted.

[7] A variant of traditional advertising. Its characteristic is editorial content that seeks to entertain or educate, involves its own media (channel), with an interactive and captive community in which there is possibility of interaction, a qualified public that associates (subscribes, follows) for free initiative to the channel, media, and whose content is made available on the network depending on the chronology established by the content producer.

[8] Storytelling is a narrative structure usually linked to fiction. In the marketing processes of communication, we seek to attribute meanings to brands, products or technical processes in a creative context. The production of an "emotional" atmosphere for the potential consumer can stimulate involvement and sympathy for the latter. The Coca-Cola brand, often mentioned in the study, for example, uses in its campaigns motivational and aspirational elements, attaching value to the process of personal revolution, the celebration of life on the festive dates of the official calendar or random encounters.

The idea of a "non-standard" format and content is what would bring about the "attractive or interesting" effect and which appeared to be the most admired element among the contents mentioned:

> "(…) a good commercial film is a story that is well built, is unusual, is well made on a technical level, so good sound, good image, (…) and a good story, of course".
> "(…) for me a good ad appeals to aesthetics, and for a content that comes out of the standard, that surprises!".
> "(…) I like the ads that make jokes… M&M's, for example, whenever there is one, I stop to watch it … I do not consume the chocolates, but these are a guarantee of good joke, I love them (…)."

In the study, one hundred and eleven advertised brands were mentioned. For the sake of illustration, two productions cited by the interviewees will be described as representing an advertising material considered as innovative and engaging. These materials relate directly to the mood management motive for your assistance.

M&M's Inside the Cup[9] **(2016)** - (30"). A pregnant lady asks her husband to bring chocolates while watching television. The husband opens the kitchen cupboard and gets hit by edible products that are stored there. In the close image of the inner closet you watch M&M's animations in gesture of attack with other products against the man. The husband says, "Come, come to the cup!" requesting that the chocolates surrender to the cup to be served to his wife. The film closes with the signature and one of the M&M's complaining about the cup that is served to the lady.

The mixture between reference scenes of everyday life and absurd animation scenes is a feature of the brand in Portugal. The appeal is daring by its surrealistic tone, freeing itself from the demands of logic and reason, and going beyond the feasible possibilities of real life. The expression of the dream world put on the "dark humour" of chocolates struggling not to be eaten is considered unusual and comical. It reverses the very logic of the intention of the advertising film in which the chocolates should wish to be eaten by the potential buyers. Here is one of the illustrations that makes the receptor engage and manage their affective state to watch not only this but the collection of films that follow the same narrative style of the brand.

TOUS - Stories of Tenderness # 5[10] (2016) - (2'19"). The film begins with the presentation of the mark with the letterings: TOUS presents: Gwyneth Paltrow[11] in… In a typical English environment, the story is told in third person, in which two characters are introduced, Kate and Peter, each at their tables to have breakfast.

In this curious cafe, Kate and Peter are at the same time every morning, and until then, they never met each other. Kate stays in the café for only 10 min and heads home to meet her three violin pupils. Peter spends more time in the cafe, reading his newspaper carefully, before going to his studio, where he approves no more than two pairs of shoes per day (which makes us believe that he owns a women's shoe factory).

The narration continues: If they knew each other, if their eyes intertwined they would fall in love instantly. They were made for each other, but they are the only ones

---

9 https://www.YouTube.com/watch?v=dc7iwmVidZw.
10 https://www.YouTube.com/watch?v=WQIwHsluGx4.
11 North American actress well known in Brazil and Portugal.

who do not know it yet. For example, Kate's favourite shoes were designed by Peter's great-great-grandfather in 1892, on Kate's wrist is tattooed a verse of Peter's favourite song. She is learning how to grow fruits, he, to conserve them. While she puts her favourite jewellery, he chooses his favourite watch (small scene with the objects). The two named their dogs in honour of their favourite movie. But today is a different day, just as Kate gets up from her table, she notices that her right earring has fallen, the same earring that is now circulating through the cafe under the watchful eye of other customers there.

Unaware of this little adventure, Kate asks: Has anyone found an earring? Kate's dog barks and Peter's dog, too. Kate fights with her Dog: Robin! Peter too, Hood! At that moment they both looked at each other and the storyteller mentions: Robin Hood … what a wonderful coincidence, is not it? The earring of Kate will stop at Peter's foot and he hands it to Kate. The signature of the brand closes the film: TOUS, Jewellers since 1920.

The video is the number five of a discontinued series, whose theme turns to "tales of tenderness", always with the same protagonist, TOUS propaganda girl. Although the products of the brand are jewels, the pieces do not exceed values of one hundred Reais/Euros.[12] During the interview period, two promotion phases were launched, Blackfriday's and post-Christmas clearances, with a 50% drop in the current collection prices, on average. With a romantic tone in the fashion of novels, the production stands out for its impeccable aesthetic quality. Also its plot full of picturesque details, takes the receptor to climax to be revealed the expected happy ending. The unusual duration, hollywoodian production, the world-renowned protagonist, the plot that assumes a narrative of serial productions were key elements capable of engaging and enchanting their receptors in social network.

Biesenback apud Odell [8] identified some ingredients that would power the stories that steal the attention: 1. Stories that touch the emotions, "people do not respond to facts and logic as much as to emotion"; 2. A story with a representative face, "no one cares about process, but about people"; 3. Stories with appeal to universal values, "for they increase the connections between people," and 4. Stories that show, rather than just say, "Do not make claims, tell stories."[13] As an argument for the compelling power of entertaining content, the expert points out the most profitable U.S. industries are those in the entertainment business.

[12] Many of the collection's themes are juvenile.

[13] The three pillars of a good story would then be A. a character who captivates the receptor's sympathy: "It is a character in pursuit of a goal in the face of some challenge"; B. Appeal to emotions: "Emotion triggers decision making, the advertiser should not talk about what he does, but why he does it." When he makes his personal story, a process of empathy is created with the audience. "Free and passionate expression" of communication in the form of a narrative full of courageous meanings.

4 Personal Integration

The possibility of greater understanding of the social and personal world is one of the reasons for exposure to advertisements in social networks. The receptor when perceiving an advertising content whose message interprets a social situation that can "add" a knowledge, that can advise him to conduct in accordance with the collective and/or personal expectations, begins to pay attention to the content:

> "(…) I like advertising messages that leave the common place and give a new point of view for a story, something banal from day by day that can have another perspective, a new interpretation".
> "(…) The one from VODAFONE, I adore that ad, for example. It shows that technologies are increasingly present in everyone's lives including the elderly, and they show us that they also need to communicate… it is certain that it is to sell the operator, but behind this, too is the fact of technologies in society… I like the message that makes me reflect on this situation that I never thought of before, it knows how to capture a social situation and makes us sensitive to it".
> "(…) It is a lady who helps a dog on the way to work, helps an old lady, helps a flower and then is always repeating the same actions, giving money to a child who is begging on the street, and then at the end, I realized that was an ad… it said that it does not matter what your lifestyle is, what matters is to help people, after so much watching, these actions contaminate people (…)"

The reflection of the actions and customs, of the characters, of the key situations, are point out so that the receptors checks the validity and adequacy of feelings and behaviours, reinforcement of the opinions about social contexts, personal positions, and even adjustments of attitudes and practices that can be adopted at appropriate times in the daily life of the receptor. The proposal to reflect the situations brought by the advertisements would allow the verification of the values that appeared pertinent to the audience:

> "(…) this brand is creating a steady history of positivity, and these capture the attention of the person, have a important message as the world is changing (…) are important issues".
> "(…) I learn and I can see that it has to change some things, and I can perceive that it is drawing attention to problems that are real that we do not care about, and eventually opens our eyes to situations that we had not noticed before".
> "(…) basically showing the "good" of the Portuguese, I remember that because it was a very reflective piece of what it is to be a Portuguese and such".

With exposure to advertising messages, the young seizes information that makes him reflect on the representations of the consensuses of the actions and customs represented, of the meanings suggested by propaganda, social actions and practices, styles and characteristics of the personalities presented.

The appreciation of such representations would allow the verification of the values that are plausible to the audience, their affinity, identification (or not) with certain profiles, values, attitudes and behaviours. With the representations put, the receptor evaluates who he is, wants or can be, forms his opinion, reinforces or adjusts/changes his attitudes, styles or conduct in everyday situations. The exhibition for reflection, thus, has an instrumental purpose for the audience:

> "(…) I like to watch the advertisements of VICTORIA SECRETS, I really like the models thing, it calls my attention. I really like Sara Sampaio and North American Taillor Hill, which are the brand's faces in propaganda. I think they are very beautiful, I really like the beauty of

both, I really like the behaviour, the way of being… They are very close to me in age, and I dream of being something like them, I try to observe and check how can I be like them. I like to think like I could be like them".

"(…) the OLD SPICE deodorant is practically a type that represents a masculine man, and what it seems to me, is that the message is: be equal to that man, so if we use the product, we smell like the man, we approach that one ideal (…) is an ideal that inspires people."

"(…) She is a reference of beauty to me, but also behaviour, such as good mood, simplicity, lifestyle… She seems very light, relaxed and somehow I identify with her, it is because I would like to be like her. She is fun, dress herself quite well."

The observation would leads the receptor to a simple buying behaviour or behaviours that reveals traits of a desirable personality [9]. Several evidences that receptors address the content of advertising for references that emulate their appearance, behaviour, and lifestyle by a "model" given, can be found in the literature review.

For illustration purposes, two advertising films are described below as representatives of advertising assistance by young people in digital media for the sake of personal integration through counselling or learning.

Lipton AWAKE[14] (2016) - (3'05"). The film began with the daytime movement of several streets in Lisbon. The following letterings appear in the foreground: "Are we really attentive to what surrounds us?" The advertising message is characterized by the account of a social experience. In the following scenes other information are presented: "We live in a caffeinated world, always in a hurry to get somewhere". "We focus on small screens and we forget to check what really matters." "That's why we created an interactive exhibition."

There are pictures in a gallery with scenes of people who could be "helped" on the street, like an old lady carrying groceries, visibly with heavy bags, a tourist who looks lost looking at a map, someone who drops many letters on the floor. In this image there is the question on an interactive device: "Would you help?" And visitors will respond on the same device, "yes", and explain how they would help. At the end of the exhibition there is a video exhibition in which these same people are the protagonists of the street action. Without knowing that they are being filmed, they go through the same situation to which they said "I would help", but they do not realize the events around them and therefore, they do not help. Visitors when watching the video are appalled and clearly embarrassed by the dissonance of behaviour shown at the exhibits. At the end there is the LIPTON signature "Be More TEA," and other scenes follow, now with people in the experiment who have volunteered to help others on the streets.

The general idea of the advertising message in the form of a "social experiment" is to give the understanding that people who "are more tea" are more attentive and even less self-centred than those who are "caffeinated", an allusion which occurs in the form of a suggestion that "tea" would be more suitable drinks than "coffee", especially of course, those of the Lipton brand.

MISS DIOR - The new film[15] (2015) - (1'07"). Fragrance brand Christian Dior, the material-starring actress Natalie Portman, in the style of a hollywoodian super-production. In the shorter version of the video, the actress opens the door of her room

[14] https://www.YouTube.com/watch?v=L5RCYvcXRrk.

[15] https://www.YouTube.com/watch?v=52Z5ob-6jNI!t=20s.

from a luxurious hotel to the butler who hands her the bouquet of her wedding. The hotel employee has referred to the bride as the Lady, and she corrects him, claiming to be a Miss. The austere Father searches for her at the beginning of a long corridor and leads her to the altar. The girl, as she walks, shows apprehension and doubt until she arrives at the altar. She apologizes to her father and leaves the wedding scene as well as her social duties or "responsibilities." Already in another scenario she drops the wedding dress and, only on underwear, is rescued by a helicopter on the edge of a cliff, during a shower of rose petals. In the helicopter, the good hero rehearses a sensual performance on his neck and the scene closes with his most charming smile. The film closes with a landscape of Paris in which the protagonist pronounces: "Miss Dior, by Christian Dior".

In a fairy tale in reverse and *New Wave* style, the protagonist of the film gives up the highly dreamed ritual of marriage bond, a landmark of the social expectation of our culture, to embark on much less solid adventures. Although the first scenario appeared perfect and desirable, it did not match the yearning of the young lady who chooses at the very last moment to "follow her heart." The most implicit message associated with the announced fragrance is the possibility of rupture with the social conditioning imputed to the individual.

5 Discussion and Conclusions

The results presented here focused on the reasons for exposure to the advertising messages of young people, which are generally characterized by their irrelevance and impertinence, especially in a technological environment that makes them almost always intrusive: - reason why are generally ignored by this prominent public. The identification of the motivations that lead young people to the selective attention of ads is fundamental because this first behaviour has an ascendancy over the perceptions of communication, acceptance of the arguments, memorization, as well as ultimately, about the capacity to mobilize the behaviours.

The Grounded theory approach was used in research and resulted in three motivational categories: (a) Information/Surveillance; (b) Mood Management and (C) Personal Integration, concepts firmly rooted in the perspective of one hundred and eighteen young people interviewed in Aracaju (Brazil) and Lisbon (Portugal).

Information/Surveillance was characterized by the system of searching information on products and services that meet the immediate interest of the recipient. Two modelling conditions of the young man's exposure to advertisements on social networks were delineated. In the first, (A) with algorithmic suggestions in which the advertising messages reinforce the "information searches" of the receptor, modelled by their previous interests, recorded on the WEB and (B) with the exposure to specialized reviews of personalities who attest or recommend products and services. In the second with the vigilance on news and market launches for the performance of the role of "opinion leader".

Mood Management is a category that has been characterized by the search for stimuli capable of making the receptor emulate or manage its state of mind. The young who seeks to entertain himself with the propagandistic messages does not seek information for a buying behaviour; his objective is consummatory, of managing the levels of excitement at the proper moment of exposure to the chosen contents. Thus, stimuli perceived as intelligent, mysterious, entertaining, calming, aesthetically charming, maintain, maximize or minimize a particular state of mood previously presented to the consumption of the message. This purpose is the second most robust category outlined in the study.

Personal integration was the last motivational category built in the study. Here, the young user of social networks seeks to seize knowledge or advise themselves on the proposals of advertising messages for the adaptation of feelings and behaviours, reinforcement or change of opinions about social contexts, personal positions that will be integrated into their daily practices. The purpose of counselling with advertisements is instrumental: to adopt or reinforce certain opinions and behaviours, such as what to wear, with whom to socialize, what to eat, with what to worry about, and what to do. This reinforcement/adjustment can be reflected in a simple buying behaviour, but a behaviour that reveals traces of a desirable personality.

In procedural terms, exposure to advertising is initially both fortuitous and intentional (more prominently). The perception of a gratification obtained is built and constantly evaluated with the experience of new exposures. If the communicational experience is positive, more receptivity to certain brand communications is modelled. If the experience is negative or no perceived gratification is obtained, more unwillingness to new exposures to advertising messages.

In general, the process of selective attention of young people has proved to be very accurate, with little amount of content consumed, but very focused on the desired bonuses. This means that brands do not have much "margin of error" when communicating with this audience. Furthermore, given the importance of understanding the rewards expected by audience members from advertisements or advertising messages, it is important here to stress that the gratifications or motivations presented are not mutually excluding, they overlap and intertwine.

Thus, an informative communication that meets the wishes of its receptor, added to content that entertains and delineates identity postures, is interesting, pertinent and attractive. Although all this information is not necessarily contained in a single message, these are, in short, the characteristics that make them eligible for assistance.

References

1. Brazilian Media Research 2015: Habits of media consumption by the Brazilian population. Brazil Presidency of the Republic, Secretariat of Social Communication, p. 49. Secom, Brasília (2014). http://www.secom.gov.br/atuacao/pesquisa/lista-de-pesquisas-quantitativas-e-qualitativas-de-contratos-atuais/pesquisa-brasileira-de-midia-pbm-2015.pdf
2. Obercom: Network society survey p. 05 2014. The Internet in Portugal. Obercom Publications (2015). http://www.obercom.pt/content/117.cp3
3. ERC: The new dynamics of audiovisual consumption in Portugal, p. 15 (2016). http://www.erc.pt/documentos/Estudos/ConsumoAVemPT/ERC2016_AsNovasDinamicasConsumoAudioVisuais_web/assets/downloads/ERC2016_AsNovasDinamicasConsumoAudioVisuais.pdf

4. Charmaz, K.: Constructing Grounded Theory A Practical Guide Through Qualitative Analysis, p. 187. Sage Publications, London (2006)
5. Criscuolo, I., Pacete L.G.: Media and message. http://www.meioemensagem.com.br/home/midia/2016/06/30/o-impacto-da-mudanca-de-algoritmo-do-facebook.htm
6. Zillmann, D.: The Experimental Exploration of Gratifications from Media Entertainment. In: Rosengren, R.E., Wenner, L.A., Palmgreen, P. (eds.) Media Gratifications Research, pp. 225–239. Sage Publications, Beverly Hills (1985)
7. Zillmann, D.: Television viewing and physiological arousal. In: Bryant, J., Zilmann, D. (eds.) Responding to the Screen: Reception and Reaction Processes, pp. 103–134. Lawrence Publishers, New Jersey (1991)
8. Ferreira, R. M. C.: Telenovelas Brasileiras e Portuguesas: padrões de audiência e consumo, Edise, Aracaju (2015)
9. Odell, P.: How to Unleash the Power of Storytelling in Marketing. Promotional marketing. http://www.chiefmarketer.com/how-to-unleash-the-power-of-storytelling-in-marketing

YouTube Generated: Mobile Devices Usage in Primary School Children

Yuliya Proekt(✉), Valeriya Khoroshikh, Alexandra Kosheleva, Violetta Lugovaya, and Elena Piskunova

Herzen State Pedagogical University of Russia, Saint-Petersburg, Russian Federation
proekt.jl@gmail.com

Abstract. In this study authors examined a children experience of using digital devices. Previous research has shown that rapid technological changes increased access to mobile devices for preschoolers and primary school children. The new measuring tool – Icon Recognition Test – was developed by authors within the scope of the study. The psychometric properties of the test were discussed. It was shown that the experience of mobile devices usage enlarges in the context of age shifts in leading child activity from playing to active interactions with social and physical environment. The findings revealed that children have predominantly known those mobile apps which are widely used by adults.

Keywords: Primary school age · Mobile devices usage · Apps · Daily activities · Children · Adults · Social behavior

1 Introduction

Nowadays children are growing up in increasingly technology- and media-saturated environment [12, 14, 16, 23, 29, 46]. Modern children might get access to mobile devices well before they learn to walk or to speak. We could find more than 100 mobile apps for infants, toddlers, and preschooler in Russian with more than 1 million downloads on Google Play. C. Shuler has pointed out the greatest growth of popularity of learning apps for toddlers and preschoolers among top-100 selling paid apps in the Educational Category of the ITunes Store target children [44, 45]. This is an unarguable fact that children today are weaned on to use digital devices for their learning, playing, communicating with others. Moreover, some youths use mobile devices to cope with boredom, loneliness, anxiety and other negative moods [2, 13, 17, 22, 43]. Nevertheless, the main body of empirical studies was conducted with samples of school children aged 10–17 years. Preschoolers and primary school aged children were practically out of researchers' sight and their mobile devices usage (MDU) could be designated as invisible. This is not a clear picture of what do children do with digital devices and how does such kind of pastime impact social development of children. Therefore the main objective of this study was to describe an experience of using digital devices in primary school children concerning their daily activities and routines.

D. A. Alexandrov et al. (Eds.): DTGS 2019, CCIS 1038, pp. 599–610, 2019.
https://doi.org/10.1007/978-3-030-37858-5_51

Another aim of the study was to develop a new tool for measuring children's engagement in MDU.

2 Digital Technologies and Children's Lives

The sociocultural landscape of the Childhood has altered by rapid pace of technology evolution and the following changes in cultural settings. Much of the recent research has tried to define these changes in terms "Digital childhood" [52], "digitalization" [26] or "technologisation" [39] of childhood, or more as crisis of childhood [1, 11, 15, 18, 35, 37]. The nature of such definitions is associated with the increasing role of digital media as one of the most influential agents of socialization. Digital society requires new ways of development that connect common for any generation actions of social perception and communication with specific manners of virtual activities [53]. In the light of Bronfenbrenner's theory of development in its ecological context [8–10], we can say that digital technologies penetrate deep into all of the ecosystems that influence child development. They became to affect ecosystems on macrosystem level (culture, economics, and politics) but very soon spread their impact to microsystem (family, school, peers). The digital turn in ecosystems of child environment caused the need of adding a new dimension of ecosystems - the techno-microsystem "which includes child interactions with both human (e.g., communicator) and nonhuman (e.g., hardware) elements of information, communication, and recreation digital technologies" [24, p.34]. At this rate technical tools have been becoming powerful communicative mediators for children and one of the most interesting subjects of their conversations with adults and peers.

Moreover, experts tend to alarm that modern parents have reduced upbringing competence due to three conditions. The first condition is connected with an interruption of traditional ways to transfer social experience from older to younger generation. Parents haven't navigated enough in the children's digital environment and assimilated in it slower than their children [3, 39, 47, 48, 55]. The next condition reveals itself in impaired and superficial parent-child contacts [6, 31, 50]. Digital divide between generations leads to a lack of communication between the child and significant adults. By this reason, the Generalized Other is formed as a faceless media character based on screen experience of an acquaintance with the social world [55]. Through the lenses of G.H. Mead's social theory of identity the crucial role in developing of the child's Self is assigned to social interactions with parents on the first stage, other adults and peers with close emotional ties with the child later, and as a final point with the Generalized Other who is a result of social norms and values' mental representations [33]. An increasing communicative distance between children and adults reduces possibilities of the child to form an adequate image of the social world and him- or herself. Finally, there is a peculiarity in what are the parents themselves. The first generation of digital natives is not the youngest generation anymore. Now they are a new type of parents who might pay less attention to the fact that their children excessively use digital devices [20, 41, 54]. According to A. Bandura, the imitation of adult behavior is an important part of social learning [4]. That is why parents who constantly use mobile devices and the Internet set an example of behavior for their children's behavior modeling. Thus an issue of MDU' experience among daily activities and routines of primary school children might be considered as a key psychological question.

3 Method

3.1 Participants

The study involves 229 children aged between 8 and 9 (115 girls (50,2%), mean age 8,65 SD = 0,48). All of the children were within the range of normal without any disabilities or developmental delays. The children were 2nd and 3rd graders of one of Saint-Petersburg schools (Russia). The school has been chosen because its principal and teachers were interested in how to teach and bring up children in the digital age. The graders' parents also were invited to take part in this study on parent-teacher meetings. 167 participants were recruited including 20 fathers and 147 mothers (mean age 36,38; SD = 5,33). 108 parents had higher education (47,17%), 19 parents were divorced (8,3%). 5 children have families with a single parent (2.18%). In addition, 10 teachers were involved in the sample for assessment of children's social competence and their MDU engagement.

3.2 Measures

3.2.1 Engagement in MDU

This is a big methodological issue of how to measure experience of children with digital devices. It is not easy for a child to estimate the amount of time which he or she has spent using mobile devices because it demands more awareness than he or she has on this stage of mental development [51]. Usually, this kind of activity occurs spontaneously and might last a few minutes but many times a day. For the same reasons, we can't ask children to keep a time diary. Using of parents' evaluations restricted by the vulnerability of such estimates to social bias. Some parents believe that MDU is not "good thing" for their children and thus may reduce in different degrees how much time their children engage in such a type of pastime. So we have developed a new measuring tool to estimate the child experience of MDU. At the same time, we used teachers and parents' evaluations of child engagement in MDU.

Icon Recognition Test (IRT)

This test is a modified form of Author Recognition Test [49] which was adopted for the aims of the study. The authors of the original test supposed that recognition of popular writers names could be a better indicator of reading experience than self-reports. Such a way of an experience measuring can prevent social desirability bias. The logic and structure of our test version were the same. We used pictures of app icons to estimate the experience of children with mobile devices. There were three types of apps. The first type included standard icons for calling, texting, shooting and keeping photos. The second section contained icons of mobile games. The last type was composed of icons of social media apps (VKontakte, Facebook and so on). Finally, the test consists of 25 apps' icons and 25 foil pictures (companies' logos, illustrations from children books).

All of the pictures didn't have any verbal names of apps. The children were instructed to mark those pictures that they could have seen on screens of any devices. We asked them not to guess but check only those pictures that they have well known. Then we asked the child to mark where he or she had seen this picture and whose device it was. The total scores were calculated as a number of icons selected minus a number of foils selected. The test had high internal reliability (Cronbach's Alpha (standardized) $\alpha = 0.74$, split half $r = 0.76$).

Parent's Attitudes Forward Child's MDU Form

The Form includes questions about factual and desired children's age for beginning to use a computer and mobile devices, to have smartphones and tablets, children's engagement in MDU. Parents were also asked to evaluate in what degree they know about the content of their children's MDU. Ten-pointed Likert scales were suggested to evaluate children's engagement in MDU, and the degree of awareness in content of the child's MDU. Last part of the form includes questions about socio-demographic profiles of a family (children's age, gender, parent's age, gender, educational level, and family features).

Teacher's Evaluation of the Child's Engagement in MDU Scale

We asked teachers to evaluate children's engagement in MDU along a ten-pointed Likert scale (1-almost not interested in MDU; 10-excessive interested in MDU).

3.2.2 Daily Activities and Routines

Using of Time Scale (S. Ya. Rubinstein)

We used this scale to determine how parents evaluate their children's activities and routines. The Scale include a set of typical children activity (eating, sleeping, strolls, games with peers, games with adults, joint reading, being in the school, doing homework, sport, visiting entertainment places, visiting museum, theaters, circus, watching TV, using computers, tablets, smartphones and other electronic devices) [42]. Parents were asked to assess timing for each type of the child's activity in percentages of the usual week time.

Preferred Motives of Learning and Forms of Activities Survey (E.M. Bokhorsky)

The Bokhorsky survey includes two lists of attitudes concerning daily activities of primary school children [30]. The first list contains key motives of learning activity (like "to try different learning activities"; "to be friends with classmates"; "to be the best in my class" and so on). This set was used to measure the preference of different types of children's motivation (social, learning, egocentric) Children were asked to put each motive in a priority order (where the first is the most important; the last is the less important). The second list comprises typical activities in primary school age (like "reading fiction"; "playing games on a computer, smartphone, tablet"; "doing homework"; "helping parents to keep house" and so on). Three types of daily activity were revealed (learning, entertainment, and joint work with parents). Children were asked to do the same preference choices in order for what they did earlier.

Social Competence Evaluation Scale (SCES)
The Scale involves 20 items which reflect children's cognition about social life, emotion regulation in communication, social skills in sustaining contacts, achieving goals, dealing with communicative problems, coping with peer pressure [40]. The teachers were suggested to evaluate the frequency of social competence demonstration by children along a five-pointed Likert scale (1-almost never; 2-rarely; 3-sometimes; 4-often; 5-constantly). The scale contained three sub-scales (Social Interaction, Communicative Orientation, and Social Cognition).

3.3 Procedures

The data were gained from teachers, parents, and children. The study was a part of the large-scale monitoring of mental and social development of school students so parents gave permission to participate in their children earlier. On parent-teacher meetings, they were presented information about participation in the study their children, explained goals and objectives of the study, and given written form for decision-making. Then parents who agreed to participate themselves were given forms for filling at home. The data gaining from children were conducted in school during children-psychologist meetings. Each child was examined individually, apart from others in a school psychologist's office. Teachers filled the Social Competence Evaluation Scale and Evaluation of the child's engagement in MDU Scale for each child in their classes separately.

3.4 Data Analysis

In this study descriptive and comparative analysis to evaluate gender and grade level differences were conducted. The first step was performed for analyzing the data by the One Sample Kolmogorov–Smirnov Test. The results of the analysis of the Kolmogorov–Smirnov Test have shown a normal distribution ($p > 0.05$) for icon recognition (K-S $d = 0.07$), and total IRT scores (K-S $d = 0.07$). We used analysis of variance and Pearson chi-square criteria for comparative analysis, the related samples t-test for estimating differences of adults' evaluations. The next step was performed by analyzing a correlational structure of all the study variables. All analyses were calculated in Statistica v. 6.1 (StatSoft Inc.).

4 Results

The results of recognition of mobile apps icons according to gender and grades of education are shown in Table 1. The correct choices rate from 90.21% for YouTube to 12.89% for Gdz (made home-work). The mean amount of icon recognition was 57.01%. The mean number of foil picture's selection per children was 1.28 with a standard deviation of 1.42. Children have easily recognized Russian social media Vkontakte and Google maps. Those mobile apps are known as well as standard smartphone features (Phone, Photo Camera).

Table 1. Icon Recognition Test: Mobile apps and results for each icon (Note: *p < 0.05; **p < 0.01)

Mobile application	Percent identified				
	Total sample	Gender		Grade	
		Boys	Girls	2nd	3rd
YouTube	90,21	93,88	86,46	91,55	89,43
Vkontakte	81,96	82,65	81,25	71,83**	87,80**
Phone	81,44	84,69	78,13	85,92	78,86
Google Maps	80,41	80,61	80,21	78,87	81,30
Photo Camera	79,38	78,57	80,21	71,83*	83,74*
Gallery Android	77,32	75,51	79,17	73,24	79,67
Instagram	74,74	68,37*	81,25*	66,20*	79,67*
Fiksiki	73,20	68,37	78,13	84,51**	66,67**
Masha i medved' (Masha and the Bear)	70,10	67,35	72,92	80,28*	64,23*
Google Play Music	67,01	68,37	65,63	67,61	66,67
Weather	63,92	56,12*	71,88*	66,20	62,60
Tri kota (Tree cats)	62,89	58,16	67,71	77,46**	54,47**
Mult (Russian cartoon app)	62,89	59,18	66,67	67,61	60,16
LEGO® NINJAGO	62,37	68,37	56,25	64,79	60,98
Facebook	60,82	61,22	60,42	50,70*	66,67*
Minion Rush	55,15	54,08	56,25	53,52	56,10
Skype	49,48	53,06	45,83	35,21**	57,72**
Google Photos	46,91	45,92	47,92	43,66	48,78
Google-Play-Movies	39,18	41,84	36,46	33,80	42,28
Twitter	39,18	42,86	35,42	36,62	40,65
Monster Trucks racing game	31,96	29,59	34,38	36,62	29,27
Google drive	24,74	28,57	20,83	22,54	26,02
Toy Pop Cubes	19,59	19,39	19,79	18,31	20,33
Dr. Panda School	17,53	10,20**	25,00**	18,31	17,07
Gdz (made homework)	12,89	12,24	13,54	4,23**	17,89**

It was assumed that gender and grade of education might moderate an experience of MDU. The results demonstrated that 3rd graders significantly better recognized mobile apps associated with communication (VKontakte – $\chi^2 = 7.77$, $p < 0.01$; Facebook – $\chi^2 = 4.81$, $p < 0.05$; Instagram – $\chi^2 = 4.33$, $p < 0.05$; Skype – $\chi^2 = 9.12$, $p < 0.01$) and with learning (Gdz – $\chi^2 = 7.48$, $p < 0.01$). On the contrary 2nd graders significantly better recognized icons of mobile games (Masha and The Bear – $\chi^2 = 5.54$, $p < 0.05$; Fiksiki – $\chi^2 = 7.30$, $p < 0.01$; Tree cats – $\chi^2 = 10.20$, $p < 0.01$). There are not so many gender differences. Girls significantly better knew Weather app's icon ($\chi^2 = 5.22$, $p < 0.05$), Instagram icon ($\chi^2 = 4.26$, $p < 0.05$), and Dr. Panda School app's icon ($\chi^2 = 7.34$, $p < 0.01$).

Analysis of variance didn't reveal any contributions of grades or gender in IRT scores. But there are some statistically significant differences in the evaluation of children's engagement in MDU by adults. So 3rd graders' parents tend to set higher desired child age for beginning to use mobile devices than 2nd graders' parents ($F = 4.34$; $p < 0.05$). They reported that their children had begun to use mobile devices in older age than 2nd graders ($F = 28.37$; $p < 0.001$). Girls were evaluated significantly less engaged in MDU than boys by parents ($F = 3.64$, $p < 0.05$) and by teachers ($F = 30.61$; $p < 0.001$). It is interesting that there weren't any gender differences in IRT scores comparison.

Table 2. Means, Standard Deviation, Correlation coefficients between IRT scores and adults' evaluations of engagement in MDU (Note: $^{*}p < 0.05$; $^{**}p < 0.01$)

Variables	1	2	3	4	5	6	7
1. Evaluation of the child's engagement in MDU by school teachers	–						
2. Evaluation of the child's engagement in MDU by parents	0.08	–					
3. Screen time	0.06	0.24^{**}	–				
4. Desired child's age for beginning to use a computer and mobile devices	0.04	−0.01	−0.10	–			
5. Real child's age of beginning to use mobile devices	0.09	−0.38	−0.03	−0.14	–		
6. IRT icon recognition	0.18^{*}	0.04	0.02	-0.20^{*}	0.04	–	
7. IRT score	0.18^{*}	0.04	0.04	-0.17^{*}	0.01	0.95^{**}	–
Mean	3.60	7.17	5.75	6.47	6.26	14.11	12.83
Standard deviation	2.29	2.20	2.37	2.28	1.94	4.37	4.11

The findings of this study revealed disturbingly low correlation among IRT scores; teacher's and parents' evaluation of children's engagement in and experience of MDU (see Table 2). But there are connections between IRT scores and teacher's evaluation of children's engagement in MDU and parents attitudes concerning a child's age to begin MDU. The children whose parents were preferred earlier child age for MDU recognized mobile apps icons better. It is important to note that teachers tend to estimate children's engagement in MDU significantly lower than parents did ($t = 12.68$; $p < 0.001$).

Table 3 shows the relationships among different types of children's daily activities and IRT scores. The results disclose three main domains of children activities including learning, games with peers and additional out-of-school education. They take up together the most of week time. But these activities are weakly related to each other.

Table 3. Means, Standard Deviation, Correlation coefficients between IRT scores and forms of child's activities (Note: *p < 0.05; **p < 0.01)

Variables	1	2	3	4	5	6	7	8	9
1. School lessons	–								
2. Doing homework	0.45**	–							
3. Kids club and sports activities	0.15	0.14	–						
4. Visiting museums, theatres	0.22*	0.16	0.04	–					
5. Visiting entertainment places	0.12	0.10	−0.01	0.43**	–				
6. Shopping	0.19*	0.08	−0.20*	0.41**	0.48**	–			
7. Playing with adults	0.08	0.03	−0.09	0.42**	0.35**	0.23**	–		
8. Playing with children	0.16	0.01	−0.12	0.32**	0.30**	0.24**	0.46**	–	
9. Reading books	0.16	0.24**	0.06	0.38**	0.22*	0.21*	0.44**	0.46**	–
10. IRT score	0.01	0.03	0.01	0.25**	0.26**	0.18*	0.20*	0.29**	0.16
Mean	3.56	2.99	2.29	1.36	1.40	1.37	1.94	2.37	1.98
Standard deviation	0.95	1.02	1.01	0.70	0.62	0.71	0.90	0.99	1.08

The findings reveal a close connected group of activities associated with MDU (visiting museums, theatres, entertainment places, shopping, playing with adults and peers). Increasing time on these types of activities associated with better recognition of mobile apps icons. Additionally, there were appeared connection between IRT scores and egocentric motivation to learn ($r = 0.19; p < 0.05$) and preferred joint work with parents ($r = 0.18; p < 0.05$). The findings of the study didn't reveal any associations between children social competence and their IRT scores. Nevertheless, social competence correlates with adults' evaluations of children's engagement in MDU in highly controversial ways. So high teacher's evaluation of children's engagement in MDU was directly connected with higher total social competence ($r = 0.40; p < 0.01$), social interaction ($r = 0.29; p < 0.01$), communicative orientation ($r = 0.50; p < 0.001$), and social cognition ($r = 0.36; p < 0.01$). Estimated by parents screen time was inversely correlated with communicative orientation ($r = -0.25; p < 0.05$), and social cognition ($r = -0.24; p < 0.05$). Parents' evaluation of children's engagement in MDU was negatively associated with social cognition ($r = -0.25; p < 0.05$). Accordingly, parents and teachers attributed to the child opposite social skills when they estimated his or her MDU.

5 Discussion

The findings of this study help to identify an experience of primary school children with mobile devices. The landscape of the known by children mobile apps disclosed according to basic child needs. Its extension is connected to age shifts in leading types of the child's activity from playing to active interactions with social and physical environment. So the results show that 2nd-grade children have had on top of mind mobile games apps yet whereas 3rd graders have been focused on social media and learning apps. Thus we could observe the age turn in cultural space's familiarization. It is essential that children have predominantly known those mobile apps which are widely used by adults. So the parents' consumption of mobile services is becoming a behavioral model for their children. Such the results correspond to findings of previous studies which reported children's tendency to mimic parents' mobile practices and preferences [5, 25, 27, 28, 39]. Moreover, parents have actively used mobile devices in the upbringing of their children. Researchers have reported that joint mobile devices usage has been embedded in child-parent interactions since infancy [14, 19, 21]. YouTube is becoming as one of the main digital tools for such communications. This is evidenced not only by the results of this study, but other research indicated prevailing popularity of YouTube among different aged children under ten years old too [7, 32, 34]. Possibilities of YouTube to reduce the lack of children skills in reading and writing might be considered on the contrary as the Trojan horse for their further social and mental development. Even now most of the youth use YouTube for searching for information more often than other search engines. In this case, they don't need to develop reading and writing skills in light of their preference and access to audio-visual information. A similar situation is observed in relation to spatial orientation. Children get knowledge about digital navigation very early that can reduce development of their spatial orientation skills. So the findings of this study raise a set of psychological questions for further research.

In general further clarification of the psychometric properties of developing in this study IRT is required. We have tested the internal reliability of the new tool and its external validity. The test has shown satisfactory internal reliability and highly significant associations with the daily activities of children. The children who had more time for outdoor exploration of cultural environment were more successful in recognizing mobile apps icons. Although extremely weak connections of IRT scores with adults' evaluations of children engagement in MDU have been revealed we found that adults weren't "good experts" in estimating children's behavior concerning MDU. It seems that adults have to observe children MDU blindfolded. And neither parents nor teachers are able to full awareness of what children do with mobile devices and how often they use them. The attitudes of adults concerning the children's MDU were more important for their vision of the child's digital behavior. So it was expressed in previous studies based on parental self-report that adults' evaluations of children engagement in MDU might be incorrect [36, 40].

6 Conclusion

The rapid pace of changes in daily children lives induces a lot of challenges for adults concerning their possibilities and opportunities to moderate and utilize children interaction with mobile devices. In this study, we revealed the breadth and content of children experience of MDU. We found that using mobile devices is embedded in children daily activities in accordance with their needs and interests. The proposed test has certain advantages in the express estimation of children MDU. The first advantage is that the test takes only 15 min on average. In addition, it is easy for the child to report his or her experience in such a way. Furthermore, the IRT allows finding out more about preferred forms of MDU. It is significant for further studies to explore connections of the child experience of MDU with mental and social development in primary school age.

References

1. Abramenkova, V.V., Bogatyreva, A.: Deti i televizionnyj ehkran. J. Vospitanie shkol'nikov. **6**, 28–31 (2006). (in Russian)
2. Al-Saggaf, Y., MacCulloch, R., Wiener, K.: Trait boredom is a predictor of phubbing frequency. J. Technol. Behav. Sci. (2018). https://doi.org/10.1007/s41347-018-0080-4
3. Andreeva A.D. Informacionnaya sreda kak faktor social'noj situacii razvitiya sovremennogo rebenka. Nauchnyj dialog, vol. 3, 234–252 (2018). (in Russian) https://doi.org/10.24224/2227-1295-2018-3-234-252
4. Bandura, A.: Social Foundations of Thought and Action: A Social Cognitive Theory. Prentice-Hall, Englewood Cliffs (1986)
5. Bittman, M., Rutherford, L., Brown, J., Unsworth, L.: Digital natives? New and old media and children's outcomes. Aust. J. Educ. **55**(2), 161–175 (2011)
6. Bogdanovskaya, I.M., Proekt, Yu.L., Bogdanovskaya, A.B.: Rol' informacionno-kommunikacionnoj sredy v processe socializacii detej i podrostkov. Psihologicheskaya nauka i obrazovanie. № 6. S. 49–57 (2013). (in Russian)
7. Brito R., Dias, P.: 'The tablet is my BFF': Practices and perceptions of Portuguese children under 8 years old and their families. In: Pereira, I., Ramos, A., Marsh, J. (Eds) The Digital Literacy and Multimodal Practices of Young Children: Engaging with Emergent Research. Proceedings of the first Training School of COST Action IS1410, University of Minho, Braga, Portugal, June 6th–8th 2016. Centro de Investigação em Educação (CIEd), Braga. http://digilitey.eu. Accessed 2016
8. Bronfenbrenner, U.: Ecology of the family as a context for human development: research perspectives. Dev. Psychol. **22**(6), 723–742 (1986). https://doi.org/10.1037/0012-1649.22.6.723
9. Bronfenbrenner, U.: Recent advances in research on the ecology of human development. In: Silbereisen, R.K., Eyferth, K., Rudinger, G. (eds.) Development as Action in Context, pp. 287–309. Springer, Berlin (1986). https://doi.org/10.1007/978-3-662-02475-1_15
10. Bronfenbrenner, U.: The Ecology of Human Development. Experiments by Nature and Design. Harvard University Press, Cambridge (1979)
11. Buckingham, D.: After the Death of Childhood: Growing Up in the Age of Electronic Media. Polity Press, Oxford (2000)
12. Byrne, J., Kardefelt-Winther, D., Livingstone, S., Stoilova, M.: Global kids online research synthesis, 2015–2016. UNICEF Office of Research Innocenti and London School of Economics and Political Science (2016)
13. Caplan, S.: Relations among loneliness, social anxiety, and problematic Internet use. Cyberpsychol. Behav. **10**(2), 234–242 (2007). https://doi.org/10.1089/cpb.2006.9963
14. Chaudron, S., et al.: Young children (0–8) and digital technology: a qualitative exploratory study across seven countries. Publications Office of the European Union: Luxembourg, (2015). https://doi.org/10.2788/00749
15. Cordes, C., Miller, E. (eds.): Fool's Gold: A Critical Look at Computers in Childhood. Alliance for Childhood, College Park (2000)
16. Cortesi, S., Gasser, U. (eds.): Digitally Connected: Global Perspectives on Youth and Digital Media. Berkman Center Research, Harvard. (2015) https://doi.org/10.2139/ssrn.2585686
17. Elhai, J.D., Vasquez, J.K., Lustgarten, S.D., Levine, J.C., Hall, B.J.: Proneness to boredom mediates relationships between problematic smartphone use with depression and anxiety severity. Soc. Sci. Comput. Rev. 089443931774108. (2017). https://doi.org/10.1177/0894439317741087

18. Fel'dshtejn, D.I.: Glubinnye izmenenija sovremennogo Detstva i obuslovlennaja imi aktualizacija psihologo-pedagogicheskih problem razvitija obrazovanija. J. Vestnik prakticheskoj psihologii obrazovanija. **1**(26), 45–54 (2011). (in Russian)
19. Geist, E.A.: A qualitative examination of two-year-olds' interaction with tablet based interactive technology. J. Instr. Psychol. **39**, 26–35 (2012)
20. Genc, Z.: Parents' perceptions about the mobile technology use of preschool aged children. Procedia – Soc. Behav. Sci. **146**, 55–60 (2014). https://doi.org/10.1016/j.sbspro.2014.08.086
21. Harrison, E., McTavish, M.: 'Ibabies: infants' and toddlers' emergent language and literacy in a digital culture of idevices. J. Early Child. Literacy (2016). https://doi.org/10.1177/1468798416653175
22. Ihm, J.: Social implications of children's smartphone addiction: the role of support networks and social engagement. J. Behav. Addictions **7**(2), 1–9 (2018). https://doi.org/10.1556/2006.7.2018.48
23. Internet v Rossii. — M.: Tipografiya «Forvard Print» (2018)
24. Johnson, G.: Internet use and child development: the Techno-Microsystem. Aust. J. Educ. Dev. Psychol. **10**, 32–43 (2010)
25. Kucirnova, N., Sakr, M.: Child-father creative text-making at home with crayons, iPad collage and PC. Thinking Skills Creativity **17**, 59–63 (2015). https://doi.org/10.1016/j.tsc.2015.05.003
26. Lahikainen, A., Arminen, I.: Family, media, and the digitalization of childhood. In: Lahikainen, A.R., Mälkiä, T., Repo, K. (eds.) media. Family Interaction and the Digitalization of Childhood Edward Elgar, Cheltenham (2017)
27. Lauricella, A., Wartella, E., Rideout, V.: Young children's screen time: the complex role of parent and child factors. J. Appl. Dev. Psychol. **36**, 11–17 (2015). https://doi.org/10.1016/j.appdev.2014.12.001
28. Livingstone, S.: Strategies of parental regulation in the media-rich home. Comput. Hum. Behav. **23**, 920–941 (2007). https://doi.org/10.1016/j.chb.2005.08.002
29. Livingstone, S., Haddon, L., Vincent, J., Mascheroni, G., Ólafsson, K.: Net Children Go Mobile: the UK report. London School of Economics and Political Science, London (2014)
30. Lugovaya, V.F., Tregubenko, I.A.: Psihodiagnosticheskie metody i razvivayushchie programmy v deyatel'nosti shkol'noj psihologicheskoj sluzhby: Uchebno-metodicheskoe posobie. – SPb.: Izd-vo RGPU im. A.I. Gercena. (2012). (in Russian)
31. Marcinkovskaya, T.D.: Socializaciya detej doshkol'nogo vozrasta v sovremennom mire. Mir psihologii. 2015. № 4, pp. 227–238 (in Russian)
32. Marsh, J.L., Plowman, D., Yamada-Rice, J., et al.: Play and creativity in young children's use of apps. Br. J. Educ. Technol. **49**(5), 870–882 (2018). https://doi.org/10.1111/bjet.12622
33. Mead, G.H.: Mind, Self, and Society. University of Chicago Press, Chicago (1934)
34. Nevski, E., Siibak, A.: The role of parents and parental mediation on 0–3-year olds' digital play with smart devices: Estonian parents' attitudes and practices. Early Years: Int. J. **36**, 227–241 (2016). https://doi.org/10.1080/09575146.2016.1161601
35. Obuhova, L.F., Korepanova, I.A.: Sovremennyj rebenok: shagi k ponimaniju. J. Psihologicheskaja nauka i obrazovanie. **2**, 5–19 (2010). (in Russian)
36. Ogelman, H.G., Güngör, H., Körükçü, Ö., Sarkaya, H.E.: Examination of the relationship between technology use of 5–6 year-old children and their social skills and social status. J. Early child development and care (2016). https://doi.org/10.1080/03004430.2016.1208190
37. Palmer, S.: Toxic Childhood: How the Modern World is Damaging our Children and What We Can Do About it. Orion, Los Angeles (2015)
38. Plowman, L.: Researching young children's everyday uses of technology in the family home. Interact. with Comput. **27**(1), 36–46 (2014). https://doi.org/10.1093/iwc/iwu031

39. Plowman, L., McPake, J., Stephen, C.: The technologisation of childhood? Young children and technology in the home. J. Children Soc. **24**(1), 63–74 (2010). https://doi.org/10.1111/j.1099-0860.2008.00180.x
40. Proekt, Y., Kosheleva, A., Lugovaya, V., Khoroshikh, V.: Developing social competence of preschoolers in digital era: gender dimensions. In: Alexandrov, D.A., Boukhanovsky, A.V., Chugunov, A.V., Kabanov, Y., Koltsova, O. (eds.) DTGS 2017. CCIS, vol. 745, pp. 87–101. Springer, Cham (2017). https://doi.org/10.1007/978-3-319-69784-0_7
41. Rideout, V.J., Hamel, E.: The Media Family: Electronic Media in the Lives of Infants, Toddlers, Preschoolers and Their Parents. Kaiser Family Foundation, Menlo Park (2006)
42. Rubinshtejn, S.Ya.: Ispol'zovanie vremeni (fakticheskoe i zhelatel'noe) kak pokazatel' napravlennosti lichnosti. In: Portnov, A.A. (ed.) Eksperimental'nye issledovaniya v patopsihologii, pp. 245–253. Akademiya, Moskva (1976) (in Russian)
43. Samaha, M., Hawi, N.S.: Relationships among smartphone addiction, stress, academic performance, and satisfaction with life. Comput. Hum. Behav. **57**, 321–325 (2016). https://doi.org/10.1016/j.chb.2015.12.045
44. Shuler, C.: iLearn: a content analysis of the iTunes app Store's education section. In: The Joan Ganz Cooney Center at Sesame Workshop, New York (2009)
45. Shuler, C.: iLearn II: an analysis of the education category of apple's app store. In: The Joan Ganz Cooney Center at Sesame Workshop, New York (2012)
46. Soldatova, G., Rasskazova, E., Zotova, E., Lebesheva, M., Geer, M., Roggendorf, P.: Russian kids online: key findings of the EU kids online II survey in Russia. Foundation for Internet Development, Moscow (2014)
47. Soldatova, G., Nestik, T., Rasskazova, E., Zotova, E.: Cifrovaya kompetentnost' rossijskih podrostkov i roditelej: rezul'taty vserossijskogo issledovaniya. Fond Razvitiya Internet, Moskva (2013). (in Russian)
48. Soldatova, G., Zotova, E., Chekalina, A., Gostimskaya, O.: Pojmannye odnoj set'yu: social'no-psihologicheskoe issledovanie predstavlenij detej i vzroslyh ob Internete. Fond Razvitiya Internet, Moskva (2011). (in Russian)
49. Stanovich, K.E., West, R.F.: Exposure to print and orthographic processing. Reading Res. Q. **24**, 402–433 (1989). https://doi.org/10.2307/747605
50. Turkle, S.: Alone Together: Why We Expect More From Technology and Less From Each Other. Basic Books, New York (2011). https://goo.gl/E6baX
51. Vandewater, E.A., Lee, S.-J.: Measuring children's media use in the digital age: issues and challenges. Am. Behav. Sci. **52**(8), 1152–1176 (2009). https://doi.org/10.1177/0002764209331539
52. Vandewater, E.A., Rideout, V.J., Wartella, E.A., Huang, X., Lee, J.H., Shim, M.S.: Digital childhood: electronic media and technology use among infants, toddlers, and preschoolers. Pediatrics **119**, 1006–1015 (2007). https://doi.org/10.1542/peds.2006-1804
53. Voiskounsky, A.E.: Psychologiya i Internet. M.: Acropol (2010). (in Russian)
54. Xiaoming, L., Atkins, M.: Early childhood computer experience and cognitive and motor development. Pediatrics **113**(6), 172–175 (2004). https://doi.org/10.1542/peds.113.6.1715
55. Zhao, Sh: The Digital Self: Through The Looking Glass Of Telecopresent Others. Symbolic Interact. **28**(3), 387–405 (2005). https://doi.org/10.1525/si.2005.28.3.387

Developing the Way of Thinking in Pre-school Children in the Conditions of Computer Games

Yulia V. Batenova[1,2](✉)

[1] South Ural State Humanitarian Pedagogical University, Chelyabinsk, Russia
juliabatenova@gmail.com
[2] South Ural State University, Chelyabinsk, Russia

Abstract. The present article considers the impact of information technologies on the development of pre-school children, which, we believe, is relevant owing to the rise of interest showed by young children in digital technologies. Computer and mobile games firmly hold the lead among the top entertainments for children. The present study presents the theoretical and experimental basis of the idea that computer games contribute to the development of practical thinking. Drawing on the classical ideas expressed by L. S. Vygotskiy who believed that human mental processes can be changed the same way as practical activities, we analyze some modern approaches and policies aimed at the development of higher mental functions.

The article discusses the results of the educational experiment, which explored the impact of educational computer games on the development of the way of thinking in children as young as 6–7 years. The investigation consisted of three stages: the first one introduced the diagnosis of the current development, particularly, such types of thinking as conceptual speech thinking, abstract thinking, and practical thinking and constructive thinking. The second stage included the educational experiment with realization of specific programs. The selected programs are focused on the age group between 5 and 7 years, they are designed taking into account the peculiarities of the children's attention. The third stage performed a repeated control diagnosis. Comparing the data of two diagnosis allowed us tracing the changes, which happened after introduction of educational computer games.

Keywords: Computer games · Pre-school age · Theoretical thinking · Practical thinking · Developing potential

1 Introduction

At present time, human childhood is represented as not only a physiological, psychological, pedagogical, but as a complex sociocultural phenomenon. Computer games have long come into our life and are now actively being used to address the range of

The research has been performed under the financial guidance granted by The Russian Foundation for Basic Research No. 18-013-00743 A.

D. A. Alexandrov et al. (Eds.): DTGS 2019, CCIS 1038, pp. 611–621, 2019.
https://doi.org/10.1007/978-3-030-37858-5_52

educational questions, as a means of expanding the opportunities of educational and pedagogic process.

Today the speed of development of the computer games industry has risen significantly. The developers introduce series of computer games with diverse content aimed at solving tasks related to the development of mental functions and improvement of knowledge in children in various spheres of life.

Computers represent imagery type of information accessible to pre-school children who cannot read or write yet. With the help of the computer the child is offered to acquire some basic ideas about color and shape, develop their memory, the way of thinking, and speech.

To date, the interest to computer games is still relevant. Our foreign colleagues are constantly researching the issues of preoccupation with gaming tasks and the impact of this process on the episodic and prospective memory of a child [16]. The evaluation of mothers' general attitude to computer games impact on their children's development and behavior shows 90% of them indicating negative results [7]. Hock Ow, S. and Tan, C.M. point at the need to develop critical thinking in preschool children which may be done by means of computer game [5].

There are some interesting findings obtained by Schmitt, K.L., Hurwitz, L.B., Sheridan Duel, L., Nichols Linebarger, D.L. The authors of the above mentioned report, computer games hosted at a specialized educational web site effectively contribute to the development of a child's literacy [11]. They also suggest that the gaming context can act as a motivator which develops later cognitive capabilities in young children [1]. A report made by Hsiao, H.-S., Chen, J.-C. points out some benefits of using the interactive approach based on gestures to achieve high efficiency of training and develop motional skills on preschool children as compared with traditional gaming approaches to education [6].

Let us consider the question of positive impact of computer on the development of thinking. The impact of information technologies on the way of thinking of pre-school children should be studied through computer gaming. According to S. L. Novoselova, the active use of educational computer games contributes to the development of theoretical thinking: both the desired outcomes and the modes of action within the gaming environment should be necessarily perceived by an acting child. The perception of the mode of action, as well as the forecasting its outcomes and restructuring the further actions depending on those outcomes – is the first step to reflection, truly theoretical verbal-logical way of thinking, i.e. the invaluable psychological innovation for children of both pre-school and primary school age.

The authors of the "Computer and Childhood" program created in the early 1990 s believe that is relates to the specificity of operational skills where the mode of action is detached from the practical field of activity and should be perceived even before that. The absence of "direct use of hands" and the constant need to imagine what and how to do something lead to the development of abstract thinking and reflection, the possibility to forecast the result, and improve the project-oriented thinking [9].

A lot of research dedicated to the impact of computer games on the child's cognition, emphasize indisputable development of theoretical thinking, analytical skills and logic. At the same time, O. K. Tikhomirov and E. E. Lysenko performed their experiment and showed that computer games contribute not only to the development of logic thinking and cognitive activity but children's attention, as well as their volitional powers, emotional, memory, orientation skills, and the ability to compete and co-operate [13].

The research performed by I. G. Belavina says, that "In order to turn the interaction with computer into a game we need to educate the child in some specific skills of interacting, understanding of the consistency and priority of actions controlling the computer program, the impossibility of omission or replacement of one manipulating action by another one" [3].

It is stated that while playing computer games, children learn to plan, by building the logic of the element of certain events or ideas, they develop the ability to forecast the outcomes of their actions. They learn to think before they act. Objectively speaking, all that means they start to acquire the fundamentals of theoretical thinking, which is the important condition in preparing children for their schooling. At the same time, the use of computer games develops the "cognitive flexibility", i.e. the ability to find the largest number of the fundamentally differing task solutions [2, 8].

Computer games teach to act in trial and error, search for new ways of solving problems. According to most scholars, any positive moment in a game is more likely to be related to the development of the ability to progress by trials and errors, than to the hypothetical rise in IQ level. "Games are good for intuitional thinking, which is ever more necessary in this ever changing world," the children psychologist S. Tisseron says [4].

Analyzing the impact and developmental potential of computer games, we can point out that "a child playing computer games actively interacts with a certain type of a world, albeit with an artificial one. With that, he/she learns both to quickly press the buttons and build the imagery-conceptual models in their minds, which is essential to succeed in modern computer games; that demonstrates their developmental potential, and especially intellect" [12].

Our observations and research findings allow revealing particular significant aspects of the development of mental activity of preschool children who use computer gaming programs.

Objective: to reveal the characteristics of the development of thinking of pre-school children aged 5–7 years in the computer game environment. The study was conducted in Chelyabinsk. The study involved 106 preschool children with 56 of them girls and 50 boys. The lack of homework independently performed by the child at the computer is considered to be an important and essential condition of the investigation.

The hypothesis of the study sets that the development of the way of thinking in pre-school children in the conditions of computer gaming has its own peculiarities: a series of classes with computer games contributes to the development of visual-effective, and practical thinking.

2 Stages and Methods of Research

At the first stage, an ascertaining experiment was conducted, including the diagnosis of the current development. The diagnostic package included a test series "Methodology for determining school readiness" introduced by G. Yasyukova, a methodology for studying practical thinking and the diagnosis of intelligence with the help the Wechsler Intelligence Scale 15.

This stage included the following methods: intuitive visual analysis-synthesis aimed at identifying the type of pre-conceptual thinking (emotional-figurative, situational-figurative, formal-visual, syncretic thinking).

Speech Analogy. Aimed at identifying the type of pre-conceptional thinking by the connection between words or their consolidation into properties (situational-figurative, pseudo-analytical syncretic thinking).

Visual Analogy. Aimed at identifying the dominance of conceptual logical thinking.

Speech Classifications. Aimed at identifying the conceptual verbal thinking. The qualitative analysis is performed on a properly named generalizing word.

Visual Classifications. Aimed at identifying the type of conceptual figurative thinking. The qualitative analysis is performed on the division into groups (formal-visual thinking, functional-situational generalizations).

Abstract Thinking. Aimed at tracking the development of abstract thinking. The tasks for abstract thinking are accomplished by emphasizing various formal features (quantitative, interval, functional) and handling them.

Get through the Labyrinth. Methodology used to identify the level of the development of practical thinking. The qualitative analysis is performed on the time spent to get through the labyrinth, as well as on the possibility to move more precisely without touching the walls of the labyrinth.

Sequence of Pictures. (subtest VIII of the adapted edition of the Wechsler intelligence test) used to study the ability to establish a sequence of events based on the analysis of cause and effect relationship (oral narration is not required).

The Kohs Block Test. (subtest IX of the adapted edition of the Wechsler intelligence test) aimed at studying the constructive thinking of children, their ability to analyze and synthesize things at the substantive level. The child is to use cubes for creating patterns according to the samples drawn on the cards. The important thing here is the ability to transfer the elements of perception into the elements of the structure.

Paper-Folding Tasks. (subtest X of the adapted edition of the Wechsler intelligence test) aimed at studying of the ability to synthesize at the substantive level, the ability to make a whole out of the separate parts, the constructive thinking. The task is complicated by the fact that the children are given different parts of 2–3 objects at the same time.

The second stage represents the educational experiment. This introduces a learning computer program of "Unserious lessons. Educational collection". The corresponding games and levels were selected from each disc. The computer games contain scientifically reliable information; they are designed in various genres and aimed at the development of mental processes (way of thinking, memory, reaction rate, etc.).

The lessons involved older pre-school children and were held in a computer class once a week in subgroups of eight. The duration of the lesson is 30 min, with 15 min' computer training. Each lesson is structurally divided into four parts: introduction (explanation), base (playing on a computer), final (game analysis) and motion (physical exercises) - to relieve muscle tension (gymnastics for eyes, general strengthening exercises).

The third stage included the repeated control diagnosis with the same set of methodologies used at the first stage.

3 Results

By comparing the data of ascertaining and control diagnosis the study made it possible to track the changes that have occurred after the introduction of educational computer games. The diagrams below show the "before" and "after" dynamics of changes in results of the tasks completion with the use of those methodologies that showed significant shifts.

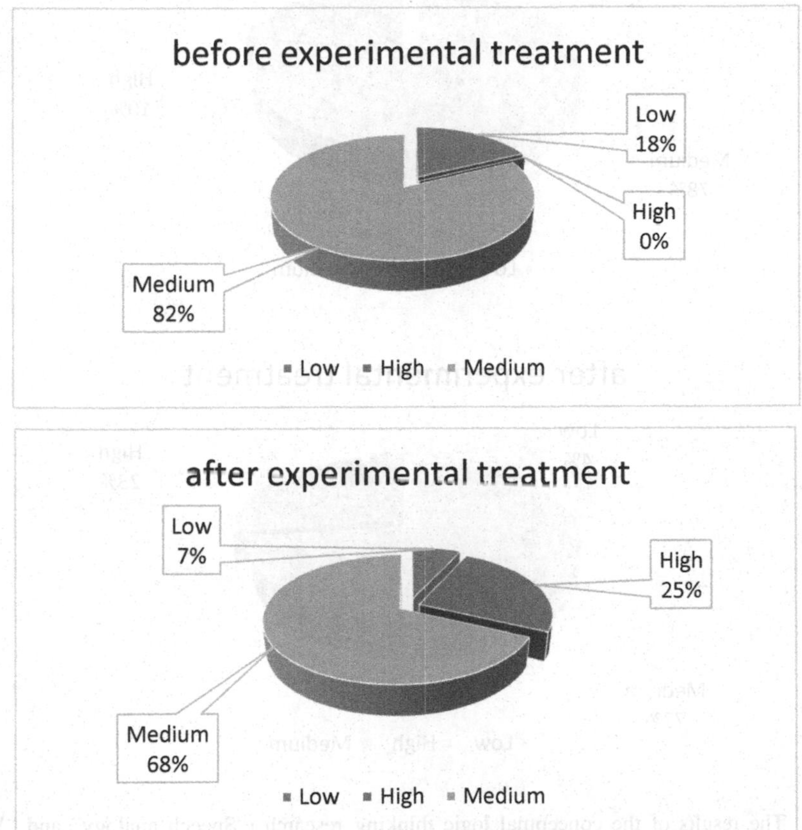

Fig. 1. The results of the conceptual intuitive thinking research ("Intuitive analysis-synthesis" method).

As the diagram shows (Fig. 1), 82% of children before the experiment showed a medium level of the development of conceptual intuitive thinking. This means that the children are able to properly generalize according to the substantial basis by complementing or forming groups and excluding inappropriate objects or words. However, they often cannot explain how they do it and why they do it in exactly this way, or they sometimes draw awkward reasoning. This happens owing to the fact that, in most cases, children operate images rather than concepts and do not support their actions with speech reflection. After the experiment, 25% of children showed high level of the development of conceptual intuitive thinking, which demonstrates the intuitively performed activity. This also indicates that the children have, albeit in their infancy, some fragmented conceptual formations.

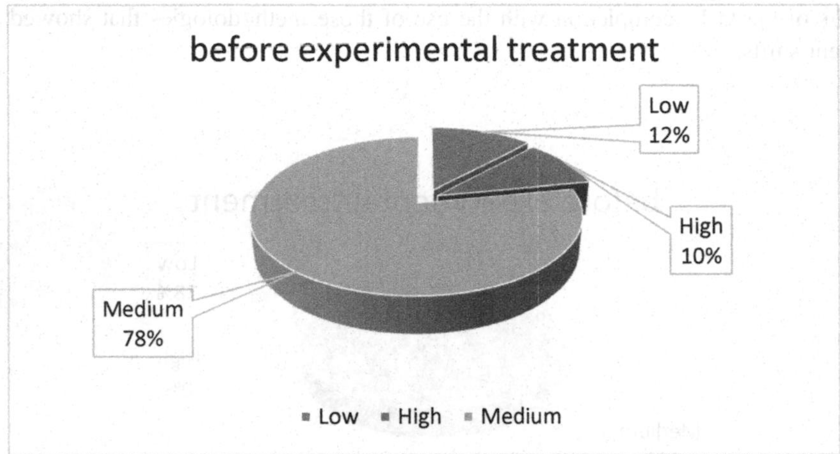

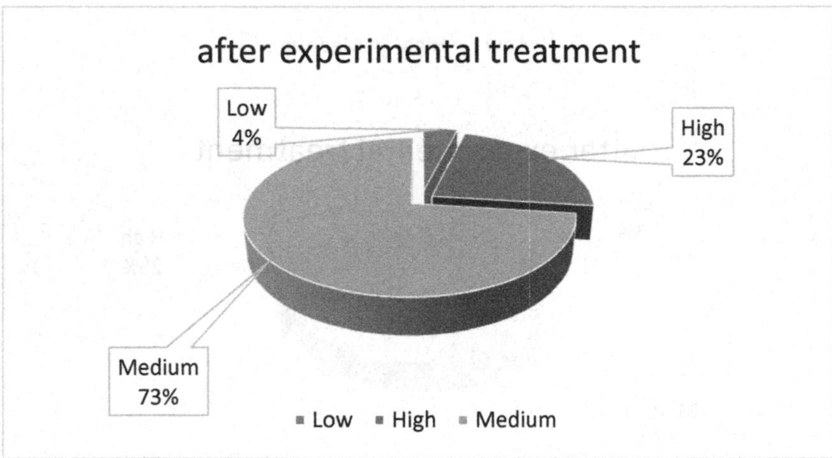

Fig. 2. The results of the conceptual logic thinking research ("Speech analogy" and "Visual analogy" methods).

Insignificant changes showed after the experimental treatment can be seen by studying the conceptual logic thinking (Fig. 2). The high rates at this parameter both "before" and "after" show that in the process of figurative comparison of pairs, the child can apply to substitution and enumeration and, having felt the equality, make the right choice. This type of work indicates the availability of conceptual structures, but the current lack of awareness and arbitrariness, i.e. the child is fully aware and able to explain his/her mode of action only after the task is completed. But understanding in the sense of "planning" does not yet precede his/her actions. The cycle of lessons with the use of the corresponding games had not showed the desired effect (neither any significant changes were revealed), however, the percentage of high marks increased by 13.

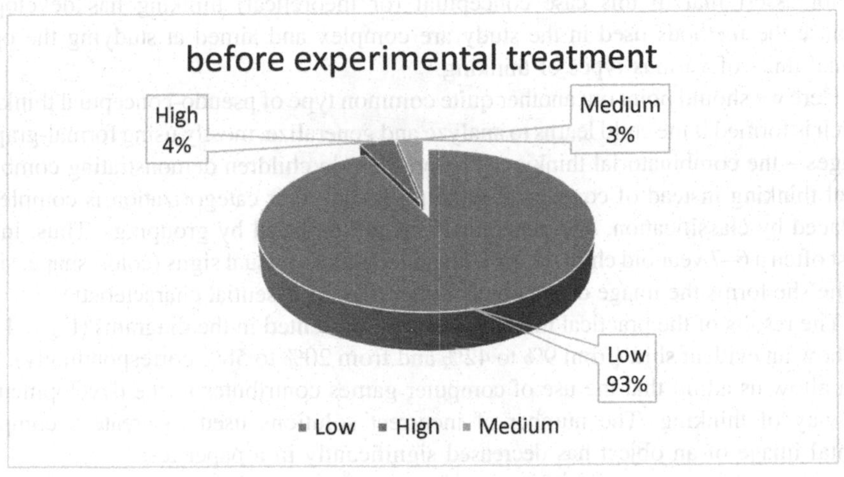

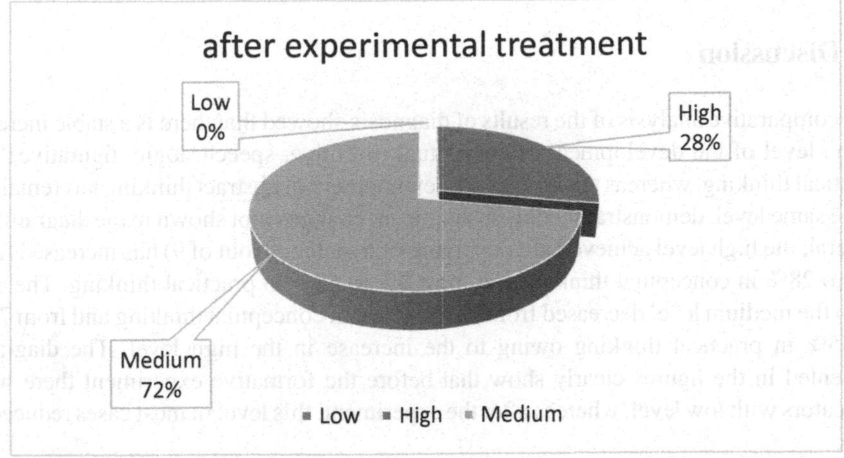

Fig. 3. The results of the conceptual imagery thinking research ("Visual classification" method).

Studying the conceptual figurative thinking allows us evaluating the ability to carry out operations that cannot be realized only on the basis of the perception process. The peculiarity of this way of thinking is it its ability to function both in the substantive-conceptual sphere, and operate with formal-graphic images. Here we see mental structuring of the simultaneously presented visual information. As the diagram shows (Fig. 3), before the experiment, almost all children showed an average result (93%). This is the norm for children 6 years. At the same time, after appropriate classes using computer gaming systems, the rate of high marks increased (28%) and low disappeared.

Analyzing the results obtained from the previous tests, it is not difficult to notice that there are improvements in the types of conceptual thinking (to a greater extent on the intuitive and figurative). As we, conceptual thinking operates with essential properties, concepts (or images that characterize these concepts and properties). But we cannot assert that in this case conceptual (or theoretical) thinking has developed, because the methods used in the study are complex and aimed at studying the operational units of various types of thinking.

Here we should point out another quite common type of pseudo-conceptual thinking, which is formed if the child learns to analyze and generalize, mostly using formal-graphic images – the combinatorial thinking. The problem in children demonstrating combinatorial thinking instead of conceptual thinking is that their categorization is completely replaced by classification, and generalizations are replaced by groupings. Thus, in the most often a 6–7 year old child thinks with general ideas, visual signs (color, shape, size), i.e. he/she forms the image of the object rather than its essential characteristic.

The results of the practical thinking research presented in the diagrams (Figs. 4 and 5) show an evident shift (from 9% to 42% and from 20% to 58% correspondingly). The data allow us admit that the use of computer games contributes to the development of the way of thinking. The number of incorrect solutions used to create a complete mental image of an object has decreased significantly in a paper test.

4 Discussion

The comparative analysis of the results of diagnosis showed that there is a stable increase in the level of the development of conceptual (intuitive, speech, logic, figurative) and practical thinking, whereas the level of the development of abstract thinking has remained at the same level, demonstrating only insignificant changes (not shown in the diagram). In general, the high level achieved after applying of 6 methods (out of 9) has increased from 0% to 28% in conceptual thinking and from 0% to 58% in practical thinking. The data from the medium level decreased from 93% to 68% in conceptual thinking and from 73% to 55% in practical thinking owing to the increase in the high level. The diagrams presented in the figures clearly show that before the formative experiment there were indicators with low level, whereas after the experiment, this level in most cases reduced to zero.

The positive dynamics can result from many factors. Firstly, since most groups are of the preparatory type, the entire curriculum (including tutors outside the computer class), in this or that way, is focused on intellectual training. Secondly, a computer game itself is a powerful means to increase academic motivation and, as a result, the efficiency of educational activity (in the present study, the computer gaming activity).

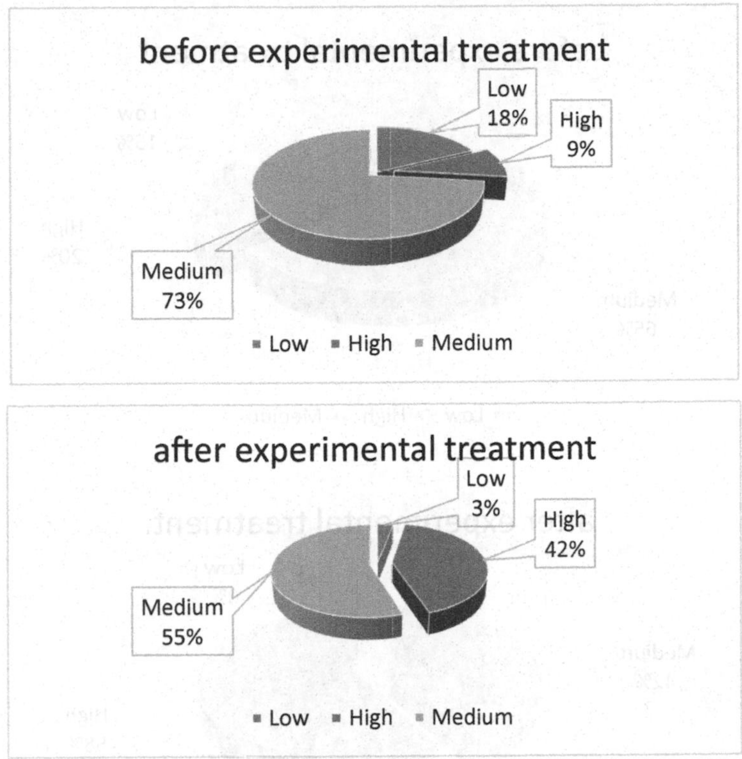

Fig. 4. The results of the practical thinking research ("Paper folding" subtest).

Despite the general positive dynamics, the monitoring of children in the process of computer studies allows us defining some trends. In particular, many children, solving various tasks, prefer to use a "mouse" instead of voice control. Thus, based on the theory of gradual formation of mental actions developed by P. Ya. Galperin, we can see the loss of one of the stages - "external speech", at which it is important to use speech for commenting on the training activities performed. What changes and transformations of the cognitive sphere will this lead to? The future research will show.

In addition, it is difficult to say whether computer is unambiguously a means of developing practical thinking, because by increasing the impact of audiovisual means, visual-figurative thinking is stimulated. However, there is lots of research that indicate a violation of the unity of the "hand-eye". The exclusion from the children's activity in the process of a computer game of the stage of direct examination of an object on the basis of hand movement along the contour of this object does not allow a purely visual analysis at a high level [11].

It is necessary to pay attention to another fairly important question: partialness, disharmony, typical for the intellectual development of a child. J. Bruner spoke about modal specificity of thinking depending on the form in which information is presented (in motor or speech form), and the existence of a special, "own" language for the implementation of relevant intellectual operations.

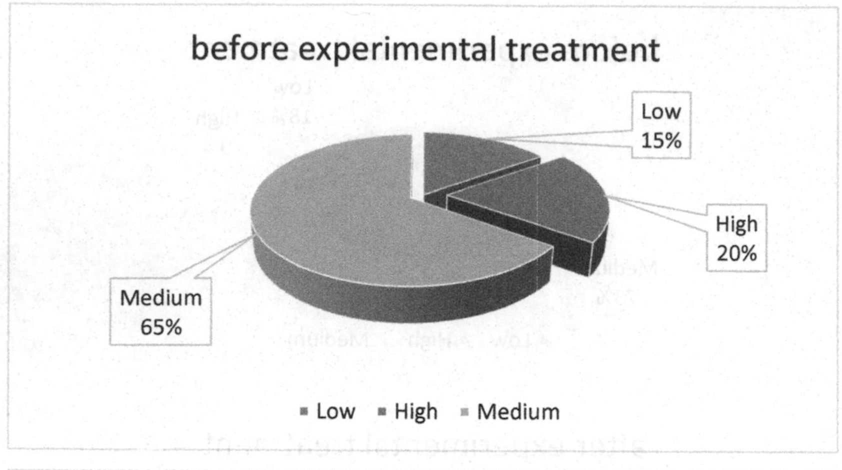

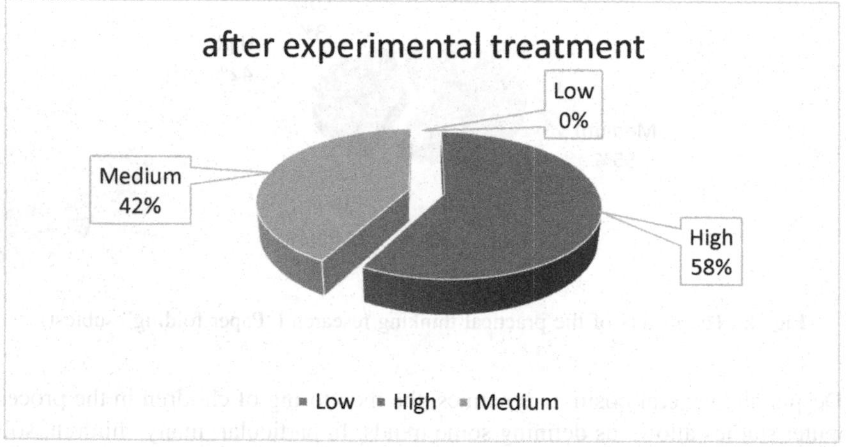

Fig. 5. The results of the practical thinking research ("Kohs Cubes" subtest).

Discussing the problem of the use of computer games we should notice that the modern interactive gaming products for preschool children have a great developing potential and improve the efficiency of education technologies. In the context of the new educational standards, computer games may be used to develop intellectual both capabilities in general and specifically some cognitive processes, and hence to improve the competitiveness of each child. For example, the virtual technologies can provide different sensor stimuli which are 'rarely achievable' in real environment of a kindergarten. That is very important for the development of cognitive and emotional capabilities of a child. Furthermore, the use of virtual gaming technologies can help to handle the correction-development challenge of education. Here, it is important to comply with the standards and requirements placed upon the use of information and communication technologies in preschool organization without any spontaneity or lack of control.

Thus, the information about changes in preschool children based on data from specific observations and experimental materials is found in many studies, although there is an evident lack of theoretically proved explanations and analysis of such changes. The results of our research suggest that in the conditions of computer gaming, the development of the way of thinking has its own characteristics: significant positive changes are revealed in practical thinking. The gradual development of children in gaming process, the increasing interest in completing the tasks, obtaining feedback on the emotional and intellectual level, and skills training could all contribute to the improvement of the performance.

References

1. Axelsson, A., Andersson, R., Gulz, A.: Scaffolding executive function capabilities via play-&-learn software for preschoolers. J. Educ. Psychol. **108**(7), 969–981 (2016)
2. Batenova, YuV: The traditional and computer game of today's preschool children: comparative analysis. Aktual'nyie problemy psikhologicheskogo znaniya **4**, 98–105 (2016)
3. Belavina, I.G.: Child's perception of a computer and computer games. Questions Psychol. **3**, 62–69 (1993)
4. Cardellan K., Gresillon G. Children of the processor. Yekaterinburg (2006)
5. Hock Ow, S., Tan, C.M.: Using a computer game to assess the critical thinking skills of preschoolers: a pilot study. In: 2017 IEEE Conference on e-Learning, e-Management and e-Services, IC3e 2017, pp. 151–156 (2018)
6. Hsiao, H.-S., Chen, J.-C.: Using a gesture interactive game-based learning approach to improve preschool children's learning performance and motor skills. Comput. Educ. **95**, 151–162 (2016)
7. Ilgar, S.M., Karakurt, C.: An investigation of the effect of preschool children's computer game playing on their development and behavior through the lens of Turkish mothers. Univ. J. Educ. Res. **6**(12), 2855–2863 (2018)
8. Khalilova F.S.: The effectiveness of computer games in the mental development of a child of senior preschool age. Culture of the peoples of the Black Sea, vol. 51, pp. 162–165. Inter-University Center "Crimea" Publ., Simferopol (2005)
9. Novoselova, S.L., Petku, G.P.: The Computer World of the Preschooler. Inter-University Center "Crimea" Publ., Moscow (1997)
10. Obukhova, L.F., Tkachenko, S.B.: Possibilities of using computer games for the development of perceptual actions. Psychol. Sci. Educ. **3**, 49–60 (2008)
11. Schmitt, K.L., Hurwitz, L.B., Sheridan Duel, L., Nichols Linebarger, D.L.: Learning through play: the impact of web-based games on early literacy development. Comput. Hum. Behav. **81**, 378–389 (2018)
12. Shmelev, A.G.: Psychodiagnosis and New Information Technologies. Computers and Cognition, Moscow (1990)
13. Tikhomirov, O.K., Lysenko, E.E.: Psychology of computer games. New Meth. Learn. Tools **1**, 30–66 (1988)
14. Voyskunsky, A.E., Avetisova, A.A.: "For" and "against" computer games. Game, training and the Internet. Moscow, pp. 5–15 (2006)
15. Yasyukova, L.A.: Methodology for determining school readiness. Prediction and prevention of problems of teaching in primary school. Tutorial guide, St. Petersburg (1999)
16. Zhang, X., Ballhausen, N., Liu, S., Kliegel, M., Wang, L.: The effects of ongoing task absorption on event-based prospective memory in preschoolers. Eur. J. Dev. Psychol. **16**(2), 123–136 (2019)

Attitudes Towards Alternative Identities in Social Networking Sites

Alexander Voiskounsky[1(✉)], Natalia Fedunina[2], Alexander Evdokimenko[3], and Olga Smyslova[4]

[1] Moscow Lomonosov State University, Moscow, Russia
vae-msu@mail.ru

[2] Moscow State University of Psychology and Education, Moscow, Russia

[3] Higher School of Economics - National Research University, Moscow, Russia

[4] UserLytics Corp., Foster City, CA, USA

Abstract. Participants of social networks experience a temptation to build multiple profiles/identities which are homomorphous (sometimes isomorphic, often contradictive) to their real-life identities. While this experience may be viewed as a masquerade, it's hard to deny psychological grounds of possessing multiple online identities. Every time a social networker owns two or more profiles, they are referred to as alternative identities, irrespective of which is 'real' Participants: 42 social networkers 15 to 25 years old, half of them females. Each was presented an Identity Dilemma, which involves issues of online identity and moral development. The dilemma was worked out as a part of the Good Play Project (Harvard Graduate School of Education), used by permission from the developers. Semi-structured interviewing procedure included putting selected questions to the participants while discussing the dilemma issues. By classification of interview narratives the following attitudes were selected, referring to alternative identities: affective, cognitive, and behavioral. Dispersion analysis and content analysis were performed to handle the data. Differences in attitudes, dependent on age, gender and identity parameters are described.

Keywords: Alternative identity · Social networking · Attitudes · Identity dilemma

1 Introduction

Social networking sites (SNS) mediate the most popular online activities nowadays. Users enjoy mobility, immersion and anonymity, they distribute behaviors and try to level up their reputation [33]. Wide availability and multi-generational involvement of SNS facilitates research on how individuals construct and explore their identities in the virtual world. Dozens of theories attempt to describe and explain virtual identity and its relationship with one's identity in a real life. Before the SNS were widely available, the Internet offered a way to users with sophisticated technical skills to explore and present to others their virtual identities [25, 30, 32].

Internet provides an individual with a variety of ways to present oneself to others: one can promote their professional skills and advertise their artwork, vocal or

D. A. Alexandrov et al. (Eds.): DTGS 2019, CCIS 1038, pp. 622–634, 2019.
https://doi.org/10.1007/978-3-030-37858-5_53

performing talents online. Numerous forums and sites allow users to share personal information about themselves and discuss their family life, values and experiences.

Recent works [2, 19, 22, 37] have demonstrated that profiles in social networks accurately enough represent any user's psychological "Self"; closeness to the true Self gives comfortable psychological outcomes [12]. Such conclusions are based on the users' digital "footprints" (such as 'likes') inalienable from the patterns of online behavior [21]. It has been estimated that almost half of all employers use Internet searches of job applicants' personal information to screen employees [17].

A significant correlation was found between the results of a personality test taken by a Facebook user and the same personality test taken by an expert representing the same user (based on the information from the user's Facebook account) [19]. In earlier studies scientists showed that the content of e-mails [10] and résumés posted online [6] can provide indications about an individual's personality. Independent experts, and later Big Data software packages are believed to be capable of tracing digital footprints left by SNS participants and evaluate their personality traits in terms of standard psychological inventories, such as "Big Five" [21, 37]. Scholars suggest that "computers are more accurate than humans in predicting personality" [13: 205].

For example, in a study with over 58, 000 volunteers who have provided researchers with an access to their Facebook "likes", their demographic profiles and the results of psychometric assessment, it was shown that records and likes from Facebook can significantly predict a number of personal attributes, including personality traits and intelligence scores [21]. Similar approach was used to analyze the data provided by Facebook status updates of 75,000 volunteers [26]. Similar accuracy was shown in predicting the individuals' age, gender, responses to personality questionnaires by analyzing about 700 million words and phrases from the Facebook content. Even more (800 million) Twitter messages expressing emotional states and fatigue were used to identify rhythms of affective behavior across seasons and weekends [7].

Not much attention has been focused upon the relationship between users' motivation for using a social network site and their self-presentations [3]. Various reports show that nearly all SNS participants create profiles first to stay in touch with friends, and second to meet new friends. When profiles replicate the real personalities the users tend to feel subjective well-being comparable to having complementary profiles with exclusively positive self-presentations. An owner of a "close to life" profile can get significant social support and encouragement through virtual friendships [18]. At the same time, young adults use to admit that their postings may contain personal information and offensive content, for example that when online they do not hesitate to mention the use of strong drinks and drugs; researchers refer these risky self-presentations with impulsiveness, self-monitoring problems and ethnic traditions [35].

2 Identities Online and Offline: A Review of Literature

2.1 How "Identity" Can Be Observed Online

The SNS users have many ways to express their personality online and to recognize the others' personalities. Probably the most helpful are the visual cues, including the avatars. A Big Data cross-cultural study (across 78 countries) of a large sample of typical wide-spread emoticons on Twitter showed [25] that within individualistic cultures (by Hofstede's scores) users prefer horizontal and mouth-oriented emoticons while within collectivistic cultures people favor vertical and eye-oriented emoticons.

The current paper is restricted to the analysis to narrative cues of identity. SNS users provide information about themselves, congruent with their own values and behavior [31]. Such claims may include some activities users engage in and/or life facts. Gathering and presenting information to others in social networks can contribute to a better integration of personality [19]. A user may reinforce the underlying traits of his or her personality by indicating personal preferences in books, music, travel, etc. The feedback from the SNS participants may contribute to one's self-perception [34].

2.2 Lies Online: The Cases and Diversity

Virtual lying stands for "intentional deception in a technologically mediated manner" [20; p. 945]. The "Munchausen by Internet" syndrome is probably the earliest deceptive online phenomenon described in medical sources [8] as an aim to get undeserved sympathies and help from members of online support groups, by pretending to have a "fictitious identity" of a heavily sick person [16]. Internet provides users and outside observers with opportunities to witness processes which rarely or never happen offline. Any identity may be created or constructed to represent oneself to other people, either known or unknown in real life. Users may save their identities, change them in no time, dissociate and multiply them. The ease of creating an online identity, together with perceived anonymity, use of avatars and the ease of self-justification due to lack of severe consequences, gives the SNS users the idea that they may present only some of their true qualities, or forge a completely different identity. The most common way to misrepresent personal qualities/characteristics is gender swapping. This is closely followed by misrepresentations related to professional life, age, or physical appearance [4]. Falsification of the information that internet users provide about themselves has been reported and discussed in many sources [14, 29].

The phenomena of deception on the internet are being intensely studied [5, 16, 30], including comparison of offline/online deception [9]. The data on gender differences has been collected by Whitty [36]. She showed that males lie more often than females when contacting other users online. Depending on their social-economic status and educational level, males let themselves change information elements in their profiles. At the same time, women (especially 21 y.o. and younger) are inclined to provide incorrect information for the sake of safety, i.e. anonymizing themselves on the net.

Utz [30] investigated the types of deception on the internet and the underlying motivations. As predicted, various types of lies presented online may be attributed to different motives of deceivers. The study focused on the following deception types: gender switching, attractiveness deception, and identity concealment. The motivations that could possibly explain the lies were privacy concerns, idealized self-presentations and malicious motivations. Protecting one's privacy by using a pseudonym or providing a false day of birth is considered a tolerable lie, while falsifications attributed to more malicious intentions are evaluated negatively [30]. Another socially accepted lie reported by about 50% of teens [23] is a bias of their birth date in order to access a website or to sign up for an online account. Diverse types of cheating, such as plagiarizing college students' homework [27, 32] have been shown to be widely accepted too. Development of new online and mobile services may create more needs and opportunities for the users to cheat or offer partially true information about themselves.

2.3 Social Networking Services as Platforms for Transformation of Identities

SNS as well as blogs offer adequate platforms to transform virtual identities. Uniting more than a billion people worldwide, Facebook is the largest non-professional, non-confessional and non-politicized network that has ever existed. Focus groups with participating teens showed that Facebook-related enthusiasm is waning due to presence of adults, excessive sharing and always good-looking pictures. Nevertheless, the use of Facebook is still an important part of socialization with peers. Newer SNS, both global (such as Twitter or LinkedIn) and local (e.g. in China, Russia or Brasil) can hardly compete with Facebook [28]. This may be a reason for about 60% of teens to keep an eye on their privacy settings on Facebook [23]. SNS participants typically publish their biographical data and inform about interests (books, music, political views, movies), post their images, and share links with "friends" or followers online. The information, pictures, and comments of a SNS user may represent his or her detailed profile, sometimes – a contradictory one. The truthfulness of profile parameters partly depends on the network's interface and mission. For example, a professional network may assist users in announcing true information on their occupation, while a social network interface in gaming environments facilitates transformations of self.

Mobile versions of various SNS, offering users to share personal information, may additionally collect and share information about users (such as geographical location and time of posting, devices used, etc.). Depending on the service, the amount of information collected and shared may be more or less obvious to users themselves. More and more users start caring that such information may be posted automatically. The awareness of the consequences of publishing information online is growing: as early as in 2012 over half of teens have decided not to post content online over reputation concerns [23]. Among the reasons teens name for not posting online are concerns: how the information may be used in the future or impact on their reputation now. More than a half of users care about privacy of their online profiles and use privacy features or post content to closed groups [3]. As many as 26% of teens have uninstalled an app because they learned it was collecting personal information, 46% teens have turned off location tracking features on their smartphone [23].

The "digital natives" may not be as Internet-savvy as people use to think. Indeed, not many of them are fully aware what information about themselves is available for others and how to maintain a good professional reputation online [12]. Those who tell lies both online and offline [9] do not care much about network reputation.

Identity transformation describes an intended partial change of person's characteristics (such as hiding or publishing bogus information) in order to create one's self-presentation. In addition to simply creating a new network identity, users make it different from the real one in many ways – including for example a new name, gender, biography, profession, usage of someone else's pictures (sometimes on a random basis). Obviously, such transformations closely relate to lying and falsification. However, Internet users tend to excuse and accept such falsifications [30].

Numerous data show that network identity is dynamic and changing, its correspondence to the real-life identity vary over time. In most cases, the virtual profile complements towards the ideal self, sometimes towards aggravation. Not discussing correspondence between virtual and real identities, we are focusing on the concept of virtual identity itself and the variety of sub-identities we suggest to call alternative.

The discussed above studies were focused on several types or issues of alternative identities (AltId). Utz [30] focused her study on three types of deceptions and investigated a limited number of motivations that may stand behind the online lies. Others collected data and investigated frequency of various types of online deception [14, 36]. It may take diverse forms and change depending on the feedback from the users who learn about lies online and what causes them: the acceptance of the fact that teens add several years to their actual age in order to be able to join a SNS may be a good example. The feedback from others, the attitudes towards AltId may offer additional ways of explaining the phenomenon. That is why studying the attitudes may shed more light on motivations behind creation/maintaining of specific AltId types.

3 Study of Attitudes Towards Alternative Identities

3.1 Methodology

We define "network identity" as the information published in users' profiles and the users' comments in other profiles or pages. The focus of our paper will be on the network identities only, as we are not trying to compare virtual and real identities.

We use a qualitative approach to focus on the alternative identity phenomenon in SNS. The **goal** is to investigate and describe attitudes towards alternative identity, age (in the youth brackets from 15 to 25 y.o.), identity parameters and gender differences in the construction and presentation of AltId by social networks users. We describe the content specifics of AltId; find out users' reactions on interacting with AltId online (specifically, cognitive, emotional and actionable reactions); classify the attitudes towards AltId; analyze motivation that drives the creation of AltId.

By permission from developers, we used the *Identity Dilemma* worked out as a part of *Project Zero* – one of the steps of *Good Play Project* [15]. Developers additionally created a structured interview methodology; it was also used in our study. The *Identity Dilemma* suggests respondents to imagine that they have suddenly found out new pieces of information about their online friend called Alex (the name refers to both a male or female). For example, imagine Alex posts something about himself or herself that is false (the respondents know this for sure) and contradicts to what was known before. The friend's online address differs from the one respondents used earlier.

Respondents (15–25 y.o., N = 42), each an active Russian SNS participant, were divided into 3 age groups: High schoolers (15–17 y.o.); College Students (18–21 y.o.); Young Adults (22–25 y.o.). The number of males and females was equal in each group. The interviews were conducted face-to-face with each participant; the length of the conversation was not limited (some interviews took over 1.5 h). The content of interviews was transcribed for further analysis; dispersion and content analyses were performed to handle the data (the latter is not described due to lack of space). Excerpts from the protocols cited below have been translated into English.

3.2 Results

Age and Gender Differences. The major data referring to age and gender specific are shown at Fig. 1. An analysis of variance of the data showed that the age factor impacts the distribution of the "Unusual Behavior" parameter in different age groups ($F = 5.812$, $p = 0.006$). Younger respondents were surprised by Alex's behavior less often than older participants. The numbers on this parameter for *High Schoolers* group were significantly lower than the results for the *College Students'* group: ($p = .008$). We did not find any difference on this parameter between males and females. (In addition, we can talk about a tendency ($p = .083$) for a difference between *Adults* and *High Schoolers* on this parameter.) A posteriori analysis showed that *High Schoolers'* scores are significantly lower than scores of both other groups. No other age/sex differences were found.

Unusual behavior, i.e. the opportunity to present personality characteristics and show off one's individuality using various methods, became the main focus of attention of the respondents when talking about alternative identity. During the interviews, the opportunity to walk in someone else's shoes (or living several lives at once) in various social contexts is considered as both a way to grow and as an obstacle in personal development. Some respondents noted the unique nature of Internet-space, its influence on creating and supporting alternative identities.

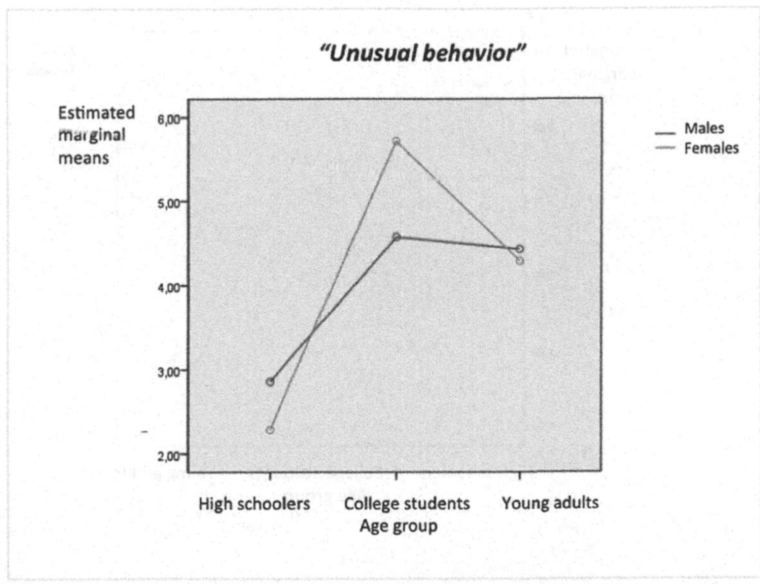

Fig. 1. "Unusual Behavior": estimated marginal means

Participants' Reported Reactions to Alternative Identities. Content analysis shows that in the interviews the following classes of reactions to the identity dilemma were observed: cognitive, emotional and actionable. Cognitive reactions were the most numerous; to present them, we are using excerpts from protocols (translated into English). The following types of cognitive reactions can be noted:

- *Reality check*, or critical evaluation: "I will try to understand to what degree it is a game or a reality, will learn if this information can be taken seriously"
- *Amnestic*: "I will recall similar cases and compare with the current case"
- *Prognostic*: "I will note to myself and be aware of such cases in the future"
- *Subject-oriented*: "I will think how this new information is related to what I already know; my understanding of this personality will change"

The analysis of variance showed a significant relationship between the respondents' age and the frequency of "reality check" reaction (F = 3.35 p = .046; Leuven criterion 2.25 p = .07). As it is shown on Fig. 2, *College Students* are more likely to check the alternative identity information for falsifications than other respondents.

On Figs. 3, 4 and 5 the resulting patterns (related with age and gender of the respondents) are presented, referring to other three cognitive reactions.

The youngest respondents have the lowest scores, male *Adults* got higher averages and the *Adults* females' scores are going down. The scores for males grow as the age of the respondents increases (Figs. 3 and 4).

Prognostic reactions (see Fig. 5) are age/gender specific. As age increases, females tend toward a prognostic reaction: keep the updated information and possibly use it.

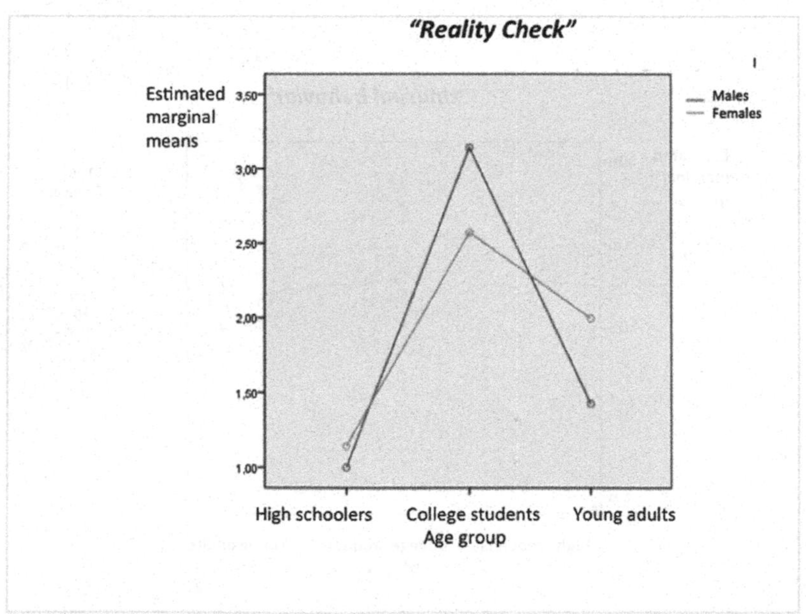

Fig. 2. "Reality Check" estimated marginal means

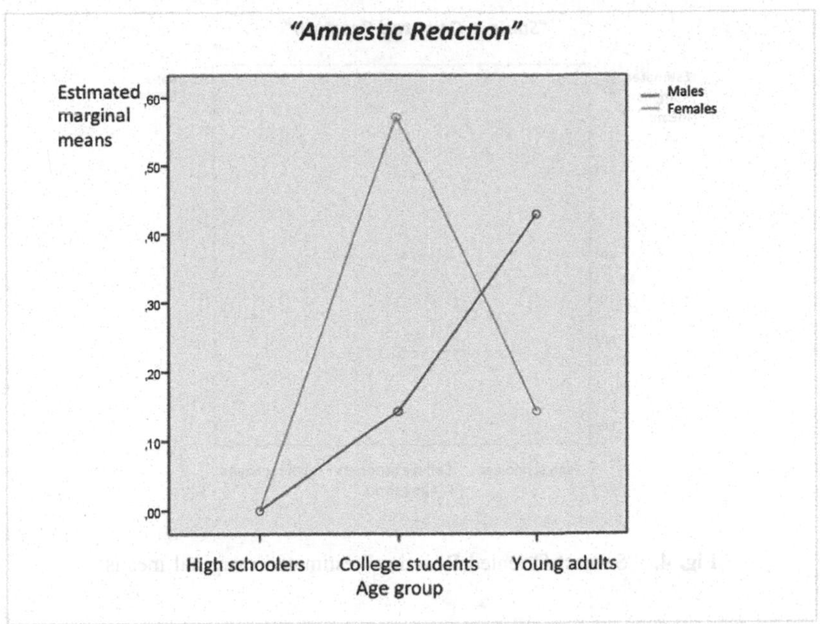

Fig. 3. "Amnestic Reaction" estimated marginal values

Emotional reactions can be divided into 3 groups: positive (happiness, respect, interest), neutral (normal, doesn't matter, calm) and negative (upset, shocking, disgust).

There are no significant differences between the age/gender groups on this parameter. Females of any age tend to elude neutral emotional reactions (see Fig. 6), while males steeply reduce the number of neutral emotional reactions in the *Adult* group.

Actionable reactions reflect a readiness to act in real life, as well as online. Analysis of variance showed that the respondents' gender impacts the parameter of "actionable reaction" (F = 5.744, significance level is .022; Leuven criterion is .79, p = .564). Females have significantly higher scores on this parameter. As the age increases, the difference grows. *Adult* females are more apt to act in real life than males (see Fig. 7).

The majority of respondents proved a connection between the readiness to act in real life and the degree of closeness to the person having an alternative identity. Few respondents reported that they would act upon such case in a real life. The majority of respondents reported that in the case when they do not know the person well enough and when the case is not urgent, they would prefer to keep online interaction with him or her. Thus they may continue searching information via SNS or other internet sources, trying to hide that they are aware of the updated information.

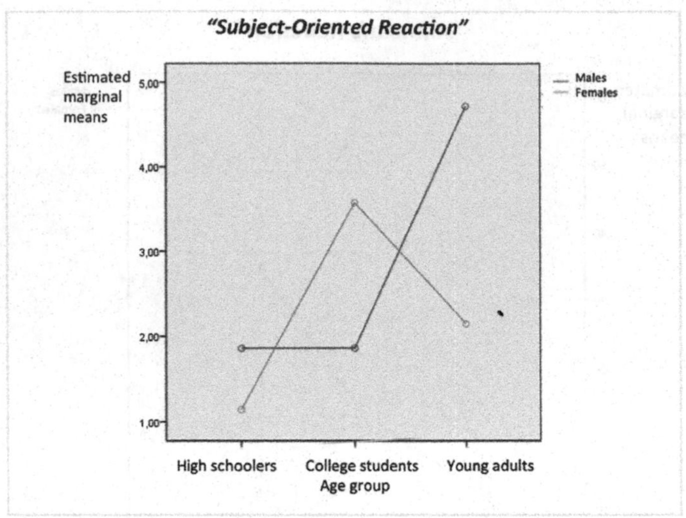

Fig. 4. "Subject-Oriented Reaction" estimated marginal means

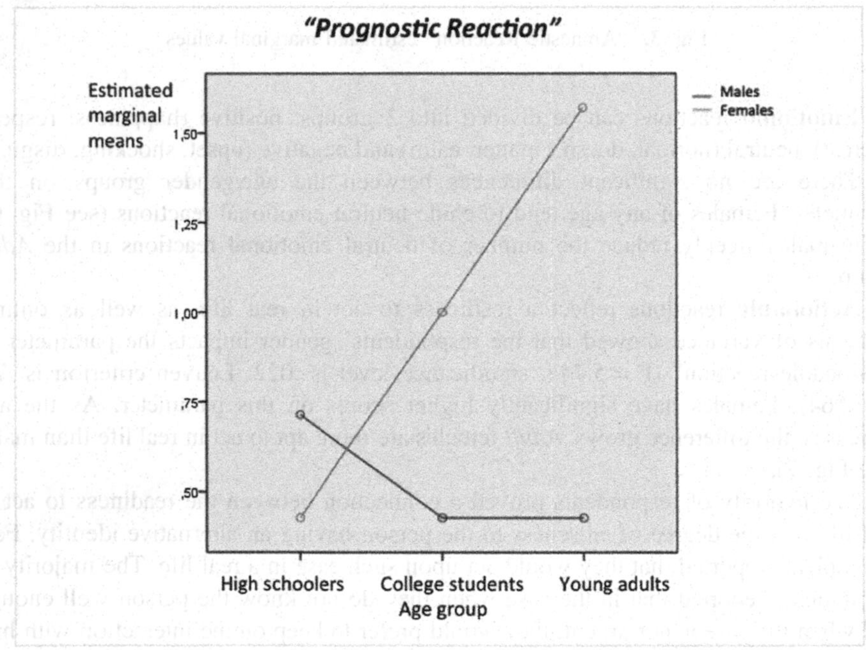

Fig. 5. "Prognostic Reaction" estimated marginal means

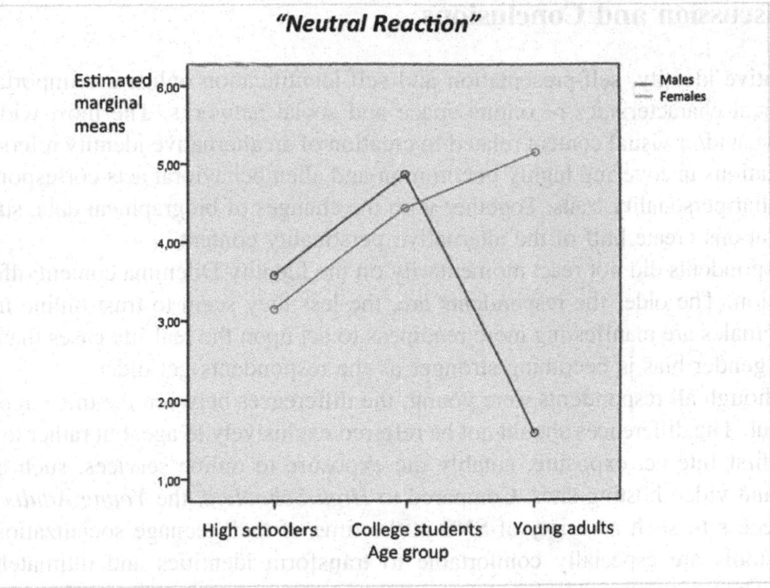

Fig. 6. "Neutral Reaction" estimated marginal means

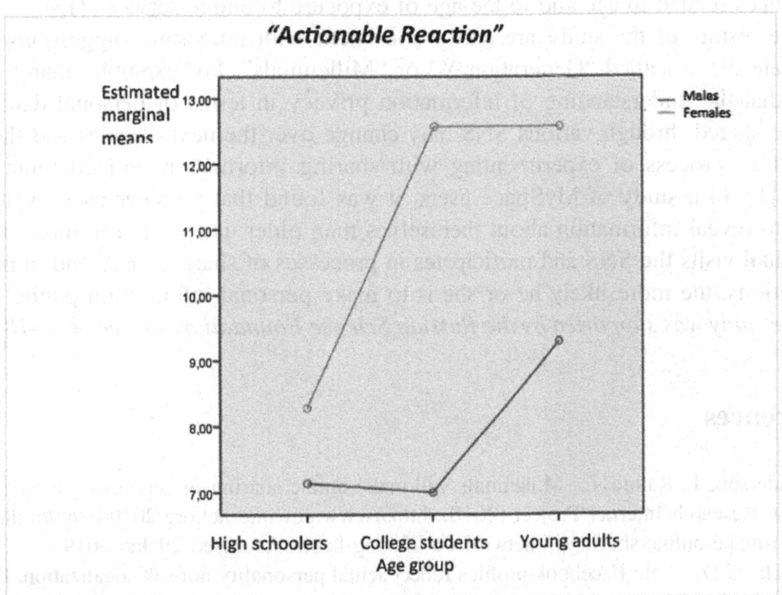

Fig. 7. "Actionable Reaction" estimated marginal means

4 Discussion and Conclusions

Alternative identity, self-presentation and self-identification online are important psychological characteristics of online space and social networks. The most widespread narrative and/or visual content related to creation of an alternative identity refers to self-presentations uncovering highly uncommon and alien behavioral acts corresponding to unfamiliar personality traits. Together with the changes of biographical data, such self-presentations create half of the alternative personality content.

Respondents did not react momentarily on the Identity Dilemma content offered for discussion. The older the respondents are, the less they seem to trust online information. Females are manifesting more readiness to act upon the real-life cases than males: such a gender bias is becoming stronger as the respondents get older.

Although all respondents were young, the differences between the three age groups stand out. The differences should not be referred exclusively to age, but rather to the age of the first Internet exposure, notably the exposure to online services, such as SNS, photo and video hosting sites. Compared to *High Schoolers,* the *Young Adults* did not have access to such a variety of SNS at the time of their teenage socialization: these online tools are especially comfortable to transform identities and ultimately build AltIds. The youngest respondents accepted the identity transformation tools and services "as given," while older respondents used to hesitate before accepting them; college-age students stayed in between. Further studies may give more clues to understanding differences related to age and to the age of exposure to online services [13].

The results of the study are partly consistent with numerous suggestions to differentiate the so-called "Generation Y" or "Millennials". For example, many experts agree that the understanding of information privacy in terms of personal data which may be shared through various SNS may change over the next decades and the "trial and error" process of experimenting with sharing information will continue in the future [1]. In a study of MySpace users, it was found that younger users were more likely to reveal information about themselves than older users [3]. The more often an individual visits the SNS and participates in processes of sharing ideas and in multiple interactions, the more likely he or she is to make personal information public.

The study was supported by the Russian Science Foundation, project # 18-18-00365

References

1. Anderson, J., Rainie, L.: Millennials will make online sharing in networks a lifelong habit. Pew Research Internet Project (2010). http://www.pewinternet.org/2010/07/09/millennials-will-make-online-sharing-in-networks-a-lifelong-habit. Accessed 29 Jan 2019
2. Back, M.D., et al.: Facebook profiles reflect actual personality not self-idealization. Psychol. Sci. **21**(3), 372–374 (2010)
3. Boyle, K., Johnson, T.J.: MySpace is your space? Examining self-presentation of MySpace users. Comput. Hum. Behav. **26**(6), 1392–1399 (2010)
4. Bruckman, A.: Gender swapping on the Internet. In: The Internet Society Proceedings, San Fransisco, California (1993). http://www.cc.gatech.edu/~asb/papers/gender-swapping.txt

5. Caspi, A., Gorsky, P.: Online deception: prevalence, motivation, and emotion. CyberPsychol. & Behav. **9**(1), 54–59 (2006)
6. Cole, M.S., Feild, H.S., Stafford, J.O.: Validity of resume reviewers' inferences concerning applicant personality based on resume evaluation. Int. J. Sel. Assess. **13**(4), 321–324 (2005)
7. Dzogang, F., Lightman, S., Cristianini, N.: Circadian mood variations in Twitter content. Brain Neurosci. Adv. **1**, 1–14 (2017)
8. Feldman, M.D., Bibby, M., Crites, S.D.: 'Virtual' factitious disorders and Munchausen by proxy. West. J. Med. **168**(6), 537–539 (1998)
9. Friend, C., Hamilton, N.F.: Deception detection: the relationship of level of trust and perspective taking in real-time online and offline communication environments. Cyberpsychol. Behav. Soc. Netw. **19**(9), 532–537 (2016)
10. Gill, A., Oberlander, J., Austin, E.: Rating e-mail personality at zero acquaintance. Personality Individ. Differ. **40**(3), 497–507 (2006)
11. Grieve, R., Watkinson, J.: The psychological benefits of being authentic on Facebook. Cyberpsychol. Behav. Soc. Netw. **19**(7), 420–425 (2016)
12. Hargittai, E.: Digital na(t)ives? variation in internet skills and uses among members of the "net generation". Sociol. Inq. **80**(1), 92–113 (2010)
13. Hinds, J., Joinson, A.: Human and computer personality prediction from digital footprints. Curr. Dir. Psychol. Sci. **28**(2), 204–211 (2019)
14. Hussain, Z., Griffiths, M.D.: Gender Swapping and socializing in cyberspace: an Exploratory Study. CyberPsychol. Behav. **11**(1), 47–53 (2008)
15. James, C., Flores, A., Francis, J.M., Pettingill, L., Rundle, M., Gardner, H.: Young People, Ethics, and the New Digital Media. The MIT Press, Cambridge (2009)
16. Joinson, A., Dietz-Uhler, B.: Explanations for the perpetration of and reactions to deception in a virtual community. Soc. Sci. Comput. Rev. **20**(3), 275–289 (2002)
17. Juffras, D.M.: Using Internet to conduct background checks on applicants for employment. Public Employ. Law Bull. **38**, 1–22 (2010)
18. Kim, J., Lee, S., Gim, W.: Culture and self-presentation: influence of social interactions in an expected social relationship. Asian J. Soc. Psychol. **14**(1), 63–74 (2011)
19. Kluemper, D.H., Rosen, P.A., Mossholder, K.W.: Social networking websites, personality ratings, and the organizational context: more than meets the eye? J. Appl. Soc. Psychol. **42** (5), 1143–1172 (2012)
20. Konecny, S.: Lying on the Internet. In: Yan, Zheng (ed.) Encyclopedia of Cyber Behavior, pp. 944–959. IGI Global Publication, Hershey (2012)
21. Kosinski, M., Stilwell, D., Graepel, T.: Private traits and attributes are predictable from digital records of human behavior. PNAS **110**(15), 5801–5805 (2013)
22. Kosinski, M., Matz, S.C., Gosling, S.D., Popov, V., Stilwell, D.: Facebook as a research tool for the social sciences: Opportunities, challenges, ethical considerations, and practical guidelines. Am. Psychol. **70**(6), 543–556 (2015)
23. Madden, M., et al.: Teens, social media, and privacy. Pew Internet Research Project (2013). http://www.pewinternet.org/2013/05/21/teens-social-media-and-privacy
24. Papacharissi, Z.: The self-online: the utility of personal home pages. J. Broadcast. Electron. Media **46**(3), 346–368 (2002)
25. Park, J., Baek, Y.M., Cha, M.: Cross-cultural comparison of nonverbal cues in emoticons on twitter: evidence from big data analysis. J. Commun. **64**(2), 333–354 (2014)
26. Schwartz, H.A., et al.: Personality, gender, and age in the language of social media: the open-vocabulary approach. PLoS ONE **8**(9), e73791 (2013). https://doi.org/10.1371/journal.pone.0073791
27. Szabo, A., Underwood, J.: Cybercheats: is information and communication technology fuelling academic dishonesty? Act. Learn. High Educ. **5**(2), 196–215 (2004)

28. Treadway, C., Smith, M.: Facebook Marketing: An Hour a Day. Wiley, Indianapolis (2010)
29. Sherry, T.: Life on the screen: identity in the age of the Internet. In: A Touchstone Book (1995)
30. Utz, S.: Types of deception and underlying motivation: what people think. Soc. Sci. Comput. Rev. **23**(1), 49–56 (2005)
31. Vazire, S., Gosling, S.D.: e-Perceptions: personality impressions based on personal websites. J. Pers. Soc. Psychol. **87**(1), 123–132 (2004)
32. Voiskounsky, A.E.: Web plagiarism: empirical study. In: Psychology in Russia: State of the Art. Scientific Yearbook, vol. 2, pp. 564–584. Russian Psychol. Soc. Publ., Moscow (2009)
33. Voiskounsky, A.: Online behavior: interdisciplinary perspectives for cyberpsychology. Ann. Rev. Cyberther. Telemed. **14**, 16–22 (2016)
34. Walther, J.B., et al.: The effect of feedback on identity shift in computer-mediated communication. Media Psychol. **14**(1), 1–26 (2011)
35. White, C.M., Cutello, C.A., Gummerum, M., Hanoch, Y.: A cross-cultural study of risky online presentations. Cyberpsychol. Behav. Soc. Netw. **21**(1), 25–31 (2018)
36. Whitty, M.T.: Liar, liar! an examination of how open, supportive and honest people are in chat rooms. Comput. Hum. Behav. **18**(4), 343–352 (2002)
37. Youyou, W., Kosinski, M., Stillwell, D.: Computer-based personality judgments are more accurate than those made by humans. PNAS **112**(4), 1036–1040 (2015)

Cyber-aggression and Problematic Behavior in Adolescence: Is There Connection?

Svetlana Antipina, Elena Bakhvalova, and Anastasia Miklyaeva

Herzen State Pedagogical University of Russia, Saint-Petersburg, Russian Federation
{sveta-anti, e.v.bakhvalova}@mail.ru, a.miklyaeva@gmail.com

Abstract. The article presents the results of a study aimed at the analysis of the relations between cyber-aggression and problematic behavior in adolescence. According to K.C. Runions's theory of cyber-aggression four types of online aggressive behavior were studied: impulsive-appetitive, impulsive-aversive, controlled-appetitive, controlled-aversive [1]. Data collection was carried out with Cyber-Aggression Typology Questionnaire, Strengths and Difficulties Questionnaire, Coping strategy indicator, Questionnaire for the assessment of the adolescents' involvement in Internet communication. The study involved 130 adolescents aged 10–16 years, 56.2% female. The results suggest that the appetitive cyber-aggression is more common in adolescence than aversive forms in spite of increasing manifestations of controlled-aversive cyber-aggression in older adolescence. Problematic behavior is a predictor of appetitive cyber-aggression only for older adolescents (15–16 years old), but these relations are not found for younger adolescents (10–12 years old). This fact is discussed according to the idea about cyber-aggression as a form of social experimentation in younger adolescence.

Keywords: Cyber-aggression · Problem behavior · Coping · Adolescence · Social experimentation

1 Introduction

The rapid Internet development creates new forms of communication. In technologically advanced countries, more than 90% of teens have a profile at least in one of social networks [2]. The results of the study "Raising children in the Internet era", which was conducted in Russia in 2016, revealed that about 92% of adolescents use Internet every day, and almost two-thirds of them are "always online". On the one hand, the expansion of online communication provides opportunities for creating and maintaining friendly contacts. On the other hand, it provokes the growth of principled new problems. One of these problems is cyber-aggression – intentional infliction of harm, the aspiration to offend other users. This behavior might take different forms (trolling, hating, flaming, etc.). Cyber-aggression is quite widespread in the communication of different aged people but it becomes particularly acute in adolescence.

D. A. Alexandrov et al. (Eds.): DTGS 2019, CCIS 1038, pp. 635–647, 2019.
https://doi.org/10.1007/978-3-030-37858-5_54

Online communication is relevant to the age-related tasks of personal development in adolescence. It allows adolescents to meet a wide range of communication needs: interacting with peers, belonging to reference social groups, acclaim. Sometimes the implementation of these needs takes the destructive forms which are expressed in self-assertion by other Internet users through aggression [3, 4]. Adolescents' cyber-aggression is a worldwide problem. It is actual for many countries of Europe [5, 6], Asia [7, 8] and America [9]. In Russia more than half of teenagers face various forms of cyber-aggression. According to Soldatova, Chigarkova, Lvova, 46% of teens witness cyber-aggression, and 44% receive aggressive messages [10]. Volkova and Volkova present similar findings: about half of Russian teenagers are involved in cyberbullying to some extent [11].

The prevalence of cyber-aggression among adolescents, as well as its negative consequences for all participants (both for "victims", "aggressors" and "witnesses"), define the relevance of studying the psychological mechanisms that determine its emergence and development. The behavior in the virtual and real world is significantly different [12], so despite large number of studies about adolescent aggression it is incorrect to use the ideas of aggressive behavior "face-to-face" to explain the cyber aggression of adolescents. In accordance with the viewpoint that cyber-aggression is a form of deviant behavior [13], our study examines the relations between cyber-aggression and various forms of emotional and behavioral problems, as well as ways to cope with them in adolescence.

2 Cyber-aggression and Problematic Behavior of Adolescents

2.1 Aggression and Cyber-aggression in Adolescence: General and Specific Characteristics

Cyber-aggression is intentional harm caused to other people by electronic means of communication [14]. Forms of cyber-aggression are diverse and include sending degrading messages, public insulting, spreading rumors, damaging personal photos, hacking into other people's accounts etc. [15]. The purpose of the cyber-aggressor is to cause harm to the victims, and the psychological meaning of his or her actions is to feel own power, to revenge the offenders and to reinforce his or her status [16, 17].

The key question that determines the psychological research of cyber-aggression in adolescence is whether cyber-aggression is a particular case of aggressive adolescent behavior similar to their interaction "face-to-face", or it is based on other psychological mechanisms?

On the one hand, a review of the literature devoted to the problem of cyber-aggression shows that cyber-aggression is directly related to aggressive actions in communication "face-to-face". Thus, the analysis of bullying and cyberbullying, which can be considered as a special cases of aggression and cyber-aggression [15], shows that the opportunity to becoming an aggressor concurrently in both contexts is quite high [1]. Empirical studies show that aggression and cyber-aggression have numerous of similar personal determinants, including low empathy [18], deficiencies of self-control [19], the low level of moral identity moral self-concept [20, 21].

On the other hand, cyber-aggression has a lot of significant differences from "face-to-face" aggression. Firstly, cyber-aggression is not limited by special time or territory [22]. Cyber-aggression might happen at any time of the day, might be initiated by the aggressor from anywhere in the world, and this features increase the possibility of its occurrence, in comparison with the aggression "face-to-face". Secondly, the anonymity of virtual communication might cause the cyber-aggressor's effect of "online disinhibition" which is manifested by permissiveness in the absence of the punishment threat, reduction of self-censorship [23]. According to Bochaver and Hlomov, the lack of direct contact between aggressor and victim may lead to distortion of the feedback in communication [24], including the cyber-aggressor's underestimation of his or her own actions and their outcomes. People usually feel less reserved and have the opportunity to express their thoughts more freely in the Internet space [23]. This contributes to aggression towards the others [25]. Therefore, it is much easier for teens to acquit their cyber-aggression, in comparison with the "face-to-face" aggression [20]. As a result, some adolescents evaluate cyber-aggression positively [26]. Thirdly the result of the cyber-aggressor's actions might be reinforced by the activity of other users, and the audience may be much wider than during simple communication [27]. Frequently just strange users make the biggest contribution to victimization by viewing aggressive content, making likes, reposting etc. Fourthly, in contrast to the aggression "face-to-face", cyber-aggression is much less regulated by adults [28, 29], and it is one more factor contributing to spread cyber-aggression among adolescents. Thus, cyber-aggression is a special form of adolescent behavior that differs from "face-to-face" aggression.

2.2 Typology of Cyber-aggression

Traditionally, there are two types of cyber-aggression: proactive and reactive [30]. Proactive aggression manifests in the use of insulting messages, provocations aimed at calling such emotions as indignation, anger, retaliatory aggression. Reactive cyber-aggression is manifested by outbursts of anger, discontent, irritation as a reply to the provocative behavior of other users. While studies show that self-reported motives of cyber-aggressors are heterogeneous and include revenge and recreation [31]. More over the roles of the aggressor and victim are less stable and may quickly replace each other [32]. Accordingly, K.C. Runions proposed the model of cyber-aggression, based on the R.C. Howard's model of aggression (2011) and contained two orthogonal dimensions: motivational goals (appetitive or aversive) and regulatory control (impulsive or controlled). This model suggests four motives of adolescent cyber-aggression: rage, revenge, rest and reward [33].

By developing this idea, Runions, Bak, and Shaw note that in this model replying cyber-aggression is represented by two forms: impulsive-aversive и controlled-aversive. The impulsive-aversive form of cyber-aggression is the reply to other users' provocations caused by the negative emotional status of the aggressor. Controlled-aversive aggression suggests actions of calculating revenge based on self-control and designed to compensate for negative emotional effects. Proactive cyber-aggression may also take impulsive and controlled forms. Impulsive-appetitive aggression manifests itself spontaneously. It is conducted without attention to long-term consequences and determined by positive emotions by current aggressive act "here-and-now" (e.g. an aggressive joke). Controlled-appetitive aggression involves proactive aggression which is aimed at achieving positive effects in the long term, e.g. receiving bonuses in relations with the significant others [34]. According to the authors of this model, these types of cyber-aggression are caused in different ways, but the empirical evidence is quite fragmentary.

2.3 Problem Behavior of Adolescents as a Determinant of Cyber-aggression

The most common approach to psychological analysis of cyber-aggression determinants is viewing cyber-aggression as a form of deviant behavior in the Internet, which is predetermined by the problematic behavior of adolescents [13]. Cyber-aggression is considered as part of adolescents' problems, which include the difficulties of school adaptation and academic performance [35], problematic Internet use [36], difficulties in interaction with peers, low level of trust with parents [37].

Due to the fact that adolescents often consider as a "target" cyber-aggression their peers, the most studied determinant of cyber-aggression is problematic relationships with peers. Most empirical studies conclude that cyber-aggression is a marker of real conflicts between adolescents [38, 39]. These studies allow to consider problematic communication with peers as one of the cyber-aggression determinants. But some another studies give an empirical evidence that the cyber-aggression does not reflect the quality of the real relations with the peers [40]. According to Pabian and colleagues, most of the negative interactions occur exclusively "face-to-face" or online, and only some of them continue in both spaces. Adolescents, who are involved in online aggression, often behave offline as if nothing happened [41]. These results once again emphasize the specifics of the cyber-aggression psychological mechanisms (in comparison with aggression in "face-to-face" communication). Also, they challenge the unambiguous relationship between cyber-aggression and problematic behavior of adolescents. According to Volkova and Volkova, cyber-aggression in adolescence can be considered as a form of social experimentation, testing communication capabilities in the virtual space, which seems more secure [11]. In addition, the results of some studies allow us to consider cyber-aggression as one of the coping mechanisms in adolescence. Soldatova and Rasskazova found that proportion of confrontational coping strategies in Internet communications increases with maturing [29]. Probably, this trend reflects the general patterns of coping-development in adolescence, which suggests consistent rising the share of problem-oriented activities. In the case when teenagers prefer reactive coping strategies, the opportunity of cyber-aggression increases [42]. Probably these facts indicate teens' lack of ability to cope with problems. Thus, information about the relationship between cyber-aggression and problematic behavior of adolescents is contradictory and require special analysis.

3 The Present Study

The aim of the present study was to analyze the relations between cyber-aggression and problematic behavior in adolescence. In our study, we used a typological approach to adolescent cyber-aggression [34]. Firstly, we predicted that in adolescence appetitive form of cyber-aggression generally prevails over the aversive form. The number of aversive aggression manifestations may increase from younger to older adolescents, but in general the proportion will be in favor of the appetitive cyber-aggression, especially if a teenager spends a lot of time for Internet-communication. Our second hypothesis posited that as the degree of awareness and self-control in adolescence consistently increases, controlled forms of cyber-aggression would rise, while the impulsive form would decline. Finally, we hypothesized that the relations between cyber-aggression, problematic behavior and coping strategies of adolescents will change in depending on the age of adolescents. Such relation may be found for older adolescents, but is unlikely in a sample of their younger peers.

3.1 Participants and Procedures

130 teenagers, pupils of secondary schools aged 10–16 took part in the study (M = 14.02; SD = 0.69, 56. 2% female). All of them were pupils, among them 60 5th-graders (aged 10–12), 46 7th-graders (aged 13–14) and 24 9th-graders (aged 15–16). The study involved adolescents from the secondary educational school of St.-Petersburg in the number of 68 students, as well as students of the secondary educational school of the Leningrad region in the amount of 62 people. The study was conducted after school hours. Adolescents had the parental consents and took part in the study voluntarily. Materials for the study were presented to participants as a set of questionnaires in paper form. It took about 30–35 min to complete the questionnaire forms.

3.2 Measures

3.2.1 Tendency to Cyber-aggression and Leading Motives

The tendency to cyber-aggression and its leading motives was evaluated by Cyber-Aggression Typology Questionnaire, CATQ (Runions, Bak, Shaw 2017). The questionnaire allows to assess the general tendency to cyber-aggression, as well as to different motives of cyber-aggressive behavior in accordance with the author's typology (impulsive-appetitive I-ap, impulsive-aversive I-av, controlled-appetitive C-ap, controlled-aversive C-av types of cyber-aggression). The questionnaire contains 29 items which are rated on a 5-point Likert scale (from 1 – "almost never" to 5 – "constantly"). We reduced the number of items in each scale of the questionnaire to 5 for the convenience of comparison (min = 5, max = 25). During the reduction of items, we considered the internal consistency of the scales by Cronbach alpha. As a result, items 1, 2, 4, 6, 10–13 and 24 were excluded from the analysis. Cronbach alpha was 0.92 for scale "Impulsive-aversive cyber-aggression", 0.78 for scale "Controlled-aversive cyber-aggression", 0.96 for scale "Controlled-appetitive cyber-aggression" and 0.96 for scale "Impulsive-appetitive cyber-aggression". The general tendency to cyber-aggression was estimated by the cumulative value of all scales (min = 20, max = 100).

3.2.2 Assessment of Problematic Behavior

Assessment of problematic behavior was carried out by the Strengths and Difficulties Questionnaire, SDQ [43] which is widely used in different countries. The Russian version of the SDQ has been adapted and validated [44]. We used a version of SDQ which suggest adolescents' self-assessment of their behavior. SDQ contains 25 items incorporated to scales "Emotional symptoms", "Behavior problems", "Hyperactivity/inattention", "Problems at communication with peers" and "Prosocial behavior". Each item was evaluated with 3-point scale (0 – "not about me", 2 – "exactly about me"). The scales consist of five items (min = 0, max = 10). As a result, the total indicator of problematic behavior is calculated, excluding the scale "Prosocial behavior" (min = 0, max = 40).

3.2.3 Assessment of Coping Behavior

Assessment of coping behavior was carried out with Coping strategy indicator, CSI [45] modified by Gretsov [46]. CSI is multidimensional questionnaire, which is defining 3 types of coping: problem solving, seeking social support, and avoidance. CSI contains 33 items evaluated with 3-point scale: "1 – not about me", "3 – exactly about me" (min = 11, max = 33).

3.2.4 Assessment of the Adolescents' Involvement in Internet Communication

The assessment of the adolescents' involvement in Internet communication was made by questionnaire. We asked adolescents to answer 5 questions: (1) How many hours a day do you spend on the Internet? (less than an hour; 1–3 h; 4–8 h; 12 h or more); (2) How many hours do you spend communicating in social networks, chats, forums? (less than an hour; 1–3 h; 4–8 h; 12 h or more); (3) How often do you demonstrate aggression during communicating on the Internet? (never; rarely; sometimes; often; constantly); (4) How often do you receive aggression from other people during communicating on the Internet? (never; rarely; sometimes; often; constantly); (5) Are you satisfied with your communication on the Internet? (not at all satisfied; not satisfied; varies; satisfied; fully satisfied).

3.3 Data Analysis

First of all, we conducted descriptive and comparative analysis to reveal age differences of Internet using and cyber-aggression by frequency analysis, analysis of variation and non-parametric comparison with Kruskel-Wallis test H and Fisher test ϕ^*. Secondly, we carried out a correlation analysis to identify the relations between cyber-aggression, problem behavior, coping strategies and adolescents' involvement in Internet communication (Spearman correlation coefficient, rs). Finally, we executed multiple regression analysis to assess the impact of adolescents' problematic behavior to cyber-aggression. Data analysis was computed by IBM SPSS Statistics.

4 Results

The results of our study show that teens consider cyber-aggression quite rare, and the most intense experience of cyber-aggression (both as an aggressor and a victim) is registered by 5th-graders, the mildest – 9th-graders.7th-graders's answers might be described as intermediate (see Table 1).

Table 1. Frequency characteristic of cyber-aggression (%)

Stage of education	Never	Seldom	Sometimes	Often	Constantly
How often do you express aggression towards other people during online-communication?					
5th grade	31.7	48.3	20.0	–	–
7th grade	26.1	52.2	19.6	2.1	–
9th grade	58.3	33.3	–	8.4	–
How often do other people express aggression towards you during online-communication?					
5th grade	36.7	35.0	23.3	5.0	–
7th grade	23.9	48.7	19.7	4.3	4.3
9th grade	41.7	33.3	12.5	12.5	–

The difference between answers' frequency in the samples of 5th-, 7th- and 9th-graders is unreliable ($p > 0.05$).

Table 2 shows the results of descriptive and comparative analysis for revealing characteristics of teens' cyber-aggression according to the stage of education.

Table 2. Means and SD of cyber-aggression characteristics

Cyber-aggression characteristics	5th grade		7th grade		9th grade	
	Mean	SD	Mean	SD	Mean	SD
Impulsive-aversive	16.22	3.26	12.26	5.14	7.46	2.92
Controlled-aversive	15.45	3.37	12.46	4.30	7.54	2.60
Controlled-appetitive	17.71	3.29	12.43	6.34	6.63	2.79
Impulsive-appetitive	17.73	2.89	12.50	5.55	7.83	2.96
Total	67.13	10.08	49.65	20.03	29.46	9.25

As shown in Table 2, the stage of education determines the intensity of teens' cyber-aggression. Cyber-aggressive manifestations are consistently reduced from 5th to 9th grade. 5th-graders demonstrated the highest rates of cyber-aggression, regardless of its type. We found the significant differences for total rate cyber-aggression and rates of its types: total rate – $H = 59.46$, $p < 0.001$, impulsive-aversive cyber-aggression – $H = 48.60$, $p < 0.001$, controlled-aversive cyber-aggression – $H = 48.63$, $p < 0.001$, controlled-appetitive cyber-aggression – $H = 55.81$, $p < 0,001$, impulsive-appetitive cyber-aggression – H = 57.62, p < 0,001. The main negative trends can be observed in appetitive types of cyber-aggression.

The analysis of problematic behavior and coping strategies did not reveal significant differences between participants of different ages (p > 0.08) except for the scale "Hyperactivity/inattention". The values of this scale consistently increase from 5 to 9 grade (H = 5.57, p < 0.02). Prosocial behavior prevails problematic behavior in each samples (M = 5.17, SD = 1.45). Next in descending order are "Hyperactivity/inattention" (M = 2.38, SD = 1.43), "Emotional problems" (M = 2.27, SD = 1.58), "Communication problems" (M = 2.05, SD = 1.21), "Behavioral problems" (M = 1.96, SD = 1.02). Adolescents in general are focused on "Problem solving" (M = 14.20, SD = 4.51) and "Seeking social support" (M = 12.31, SD = 4.88). The least common coping-strategy is "Avoidance" (M = 10.26, SD = 4.20).

Correlation analysis showed that the greatest number of significant relations between the indicators of cyber-aggression, coping strategies, and assessments of problematic behavior in adolescents are identified in the sample of 9th-graders (see Table 3).

Table 3. Correlation coefficients between indicators of cyber-aggression, coping-strategies and assessment of problems (Note: *p < 0.05; **p < 0.01)

Indicators	Cyber-aggression				
	I-av	C-av	C-ap	I-ap	Total
5th grade					
Hyperactivity	−0.26*				
Time for Internet	−0.23*	−0.25*	−0.21*		−0.22*
TimeforInternet-communication	−0.23*	−0.27*	−0.27*		−0.25*
7th grade					
Hyperactivity	−0.39*		−0.37*		−0.36*
Problematic behavior (total)			−0.33*		
Time for Internet	−0.30*				
9th grade					
Avoidance	0.50**	0.42*	0.61**	0.68**	0.67**
Prosocial behaviour	−0.42*			−0.45*	−0.44*
Behavioral problems				0.42*	
Communication problems	0.40*		0.46*	0.57**	0.50**
Problematic behavior (total)				0.45*	0.42*
Time for Internet	0.44*			0.47**	0.40*
TimeforInternet-communication	0.60**				
Proactive cyber-aggression rate	0.74**		0.62**	0.63**	0.71**

The results of the correlation analysis show that in the samples of 5th- and 7th-graders the indicators of cyber-aggression are not significantly correlated with problematic behavior (except for a few negative correlations, p < 0.05) or preferred coping-strategies. At the same time, multiple negative correlations between the indicators of cyber-aggression and time for the Internet were found ($p < 0.05$). In the sample of 9-graders the structure of correlations is much richer. Significant positive correlations of cyber-aggression with indicators of problematic behavior (first of all, behavioral problems and communication problems) ($p < 0.05$), avoidance ($p < 0.05$), time for Internet ($p < 0.01$), and negative correlation with prosocial behavior were found ($p < 0.05$). The main correlation load falls on impulsive forms of cyber-aggression.

During regression analysis we used only the total indicator of cyber-aggression as a dependent variable because of the strong correlations between the scales of the by Cyber-Aggression Typology Questionnaire ($rs > 0.61$, $p < 0.01$). We did not obtain significant results that would allow us to identify predictors of cyber-aggression for the samples of 5th-graders and 7th-graders ($r2 < 0.16$ and $r2 < 0.13$ respectively). The results for sample of 9th-graders are presented in Table 4. The is significant ($F\ (2.21) = 4.10$, $p < 0.03$). Communication problems and avoiding coping explain 45.9% (adjusted $r2 = 0.37$) of the variance in total indicator of cyber-aggression.

Table 4. Summary of multiple regression analysis for predicting cyber-aggression (total)

Variable	B	SE B (std. error)	β (beta score)	Sig. (p)
Communication problems	0.49	0.18	1.72	0.01
Avoidance	0.40	0.18	1.14	0.05

According to the results of regression analysis, problematic behavior and preferred coping strategies are not predictors of cyber-aggression for students in grades 5 and 7. In 9th grade these predictors be communication difficulties, and avoidant coping. Thus, cyber-aggression is directly related to the problem behavior of only older adolescents. In accounting to the results of correlation analysis (see Table 4), we can assume that the identified predictors have the greatest impact on the appetitive forms of cyber-aggression in older adolescents.

5 Discussion

The paper's findings partially confirmed the hypotheses of our study. Indeed, appetitive cyber-aggression is more common in adolescence than aversive form. 5th-graders are most proactive in cyber-aggression. The role of controlled-aversive aggression increases with teens' maturing. These results coincide with the conclusions of Soldatova and Rasskazova that the share of confrontational cyber-aggression, which is based on revenge on the offender, grows with maturing [29]. Despite this fact, the most pronounced form of cyber-aggression in all age groups is impulsive -appetitive cyber-aggression, which is focused on the instant achievement of a positive emotional effect.

In this regard, it is necessary to pay attention to the fact that teenagers, assessing their experience of cyber-aggression, evaluate aggressive forms of online communication as a rather rare phenomenon. Their assess contradicts the objective data which suggest that cyber-aggression in Russia is very common [10]. We assume that this is a manifestation of underestimation of cyber-aggression and its consequences. In accordance with the results of Wright, we assume that teenagers perceive aggression in online communication as a common phenomenon and cannot accurately assess the extent of its prevalence [26].

The study confirmed the hypothesis that the relationship between the tendency to cyber-aggression, problematic behavior and coping strategies of adolescents varies depending on age. Apparently, younger teenagers' cyber-aggression is not determined by problematic behavior, non-adaptive coping and real difficulties in interaction with peers. According to Volkova and Volkova [11] we conclude that, cyber-aggression is mainly a kind of "pen test" for younger adolescents, an attempt to try themselves in new social roles. This social experimentation has to consistently decline for the older adolescence in connection with the growing of mindfulness and self-regulation. Maintaining a tendency to cyber-aggression in older adolescents is really a marker of a various problems, especially difficulties in communication with peers, avoiding coping, problematic Internet use. The most alarming form of older teenagers' online behavior is appetitive cyber-aggression. Aversive cyber-aggression is probably a manifestation of active coping behavior in older adolescents, while appetitive form is a symptom of problematic behavior.

6 Conclusion

Cyber-aggression is quite widespread among adolescents, and probably its manifestations will increase with the further technological development of society. Like other forms of aggression, cyber-aggression has negative aftereffects for involved adolescents, regardless of their role in the process: "victims", "aggressors" and "witnesses". Therefore, the study about the mechanisms of cyber-aggression is an extremely important task. In the current study we examine relationships between cyber-aggression and problematic behavior in adolescence. The results showed that the determinants of cyber-aggression in adolescence are different. For younger adolescents the cyber-aggression is predicted, first of all, by testing new social roles, by the desire to explore their communicative abilities. However, in older adolescence cyber-aggression is a marker of problematic behavior and of non-adaptive coping strategies.

The findings of our study might contribute as a framework for the developing of effective programs aimed at preventing and overcoming cyber-aggression, as well as its negative aftereffects. We also expect that this study will be developed in a more detailed researches devoted to behavioral and personal predictors of cyber-aggression in adolescence.

References

1. Modecki, K.L., Minchin, J., Harbaugh, A.G., Guerra, N.G., Runions, K.C.: Bullying prevalence across contexts a meta-analysis measuring cyber and traditional bullying. J. Adolescent Health **55**(5), 602–611 (2014). https://doi.org/10.1016/j.jadohealth.2014.06.007

2. O'Neill, B., Dinh, T.: Net Children Go Mobile: Full Findings from Ireland, pp. 1–33. Dublin Institute of Technology, Dublin (2015)
3. Chen, L., Ho, S.S., Lwin, M.O.: A meta-analysis of factors predicting cyberbullying perpetration and victimization. From the social cognitive and media effects approach. New Media Soc. **19**(8), 1194–1213 (2017). https://doi.org/10.1177/1461444816634037
4. Gini, G., Card, N., Pozzoli, T.: Meta-analysis of the differential relations of traditional and cyber-victimization with internalizing problems. Aggressive Behav. **44**(2), 185–198 (2017)
5. Corcoran, L., Connolly, I., O'Moore, M.: Cyberbullying in Irish schools. An investigation of personality and self-concept. Int. J. Psychol. 153–165 (2012). doi: https://doi.org/10.1080/03033910.2012.677995
6. Gamez-Guadix, M., Orue, I., Smith, P.K., Calvete, E.: Longitudinal and reciprocal relations of cyberbullying with depression, substance use, and problematic internet use among adolescents. J. Adolesc. Health **53**, 446–452 (2013). https://doi.org/10.1016/j.jadohealth.2013.03.030
7. Kwan, G.C.E., Skoric, M.M.: Facebook bullying: an extension of battles at school. Comput. Hum. Behav. **29**, 16–25 (2013). https://doi.org/10.1016/j.chb.2012.07.014
8. Wright, M.F., Aoyama, I., Kamble, S.V., Li, Z., Soudi, S., Lei, L.: Peer Attachment and Cyber Aggression Involvement among Chinese, Indian, and Japanese Adolescents. Societies **5**, 245–255 (2015). https://doi.org/10.3390/soc5020245
9. Li, Q., Cross, D., Smith, P.K.: Cyberbullying in the Global Playground. Research from International Perspectives, p. 326. Wiley-Blackwell, Chichester (2013). https://doi.org/10.1111/camh.12037_3
10. Soldatova, G.U., Chigarkova, S.V., Lvova, E.N.: Online-aggression and adolescents: results of research among school students in Moscow and Moscow region. Epoha nauki **12**, 103–109 (2017). https://doi.org/10.1555/2409-3203-2017-0-12-103-109
11. Volkova, E.N., Volkova, I.V.: Present similar findings: about half of Russian teenagers are involved in cyberbullying to some extent. Vestneyk Mininskogo universiteta **3**(20), 17 (2017). https://doi.org/10.26795/2307-1281-2017-3-17
12. Voyskunskiy, A.E.: Behavior in cyberspace: psychological principles. Human **1**, 36–49 (2016). https://doi.org/10.24290/1029-3736-2018-24-1-52-70
13. Chibbaro, J.S.: School counselors and the cyberbully: interventions and implications. Prof SchCouns **11**, 65–67 (2007). https://doi.org/10.5330/PSC.n.2010-11.65
14. Grigg, D.W.: Cyber-aggression: definition and concept of cyberbullying. Aust. J. Guid. Counsell. **20**, 143–156 (2010). https://doi.org/10.1375/ajgc.20.2.143
15. Corcoran, L., Mc Guckin, C., Prentice, G.: Cyberbullying or cyber aggression: a review of existing definitions of cyber-based peer-to-peer. Aggression Soc. **5**, 245–255 (2015). https://doi.org/10.3390/soc5020245
16. Rafferty, R., Vander Ven, T.: I hate everything about you: a qualitative examination of cyberbullying and on-line aggression in a college sample. Deviant Behav. **35**, 364–377 (2014). https://doi.org/10.1080/1639625.2013.849171
17. Wright, M.F.: Adolescents' perceptions of popularity-motivated behaviors, characteristics, and relationships in cyberspace and cyber aggression: the role of gender. Cyber Psychol. Behav. Soc. Networking. **20**(6), 355–361 (2017). https://doi.org/10.1089/cyber.2016.0693
18. Brewer, G., Kerslake, J.: Cyberbullying, self-esteem, empathy and loneliness. Comput. Hum. Behav. **48**, 255–260 (2015). https://doi.org/10.1016/j.chb.2015.01.073
19. Vazsonyi, A.T., Machackova, H., Sevcikova, A., Smahel, D., Cerna, A.: Cyber-bullying in context. Direct and indirect effects by low self-control across 25 European countries. Eur. J. Dev. Psychol. **9**, 210–227 (2012). https://doi.org/10.1080/17405629.2011.644919

20. Pornari, C.D., Wood, J.P.: Cyber aggression in secondary school students: the role of moral disengagement, hostile attribution bias, and outcome expectancies. Aggressive Behav. **36**(2), 81–94 (2010). https://doi.org/10.1002/ab.20336
21. Chen, W.Q., Li, Y.M.: A study on the relationship between the moral self-concept and the cyber aggression behavior of college students. In: 2016 IEEE International Conference on Industrial Engineering and Engineering Management (IEEM) Bali, Indonesia pp. 1870–1874 (2016)
22. O'Moore, M., Minton, S.J.: Cyber-bullying. The Irish experience. In: Tawse, S., Quin, C. (eds.) Handbook of Aggressive Behavior Research, pp. 269–292. Nova Science Publishers Inc, New York (2009)
23. Suler, J.: The online disinhibition effect. Cyber Psychol. Behav. **7**(3), 321–326 (2004). https://doi.org/10.1089/1094931041291295
24. Bochaver, A.A., Hlomov, K.D.: Kiberbulling travlia v prostranstve sovremennyh tekhnologii. Psihologiia. Zhurnal Vysshei shkoly ekonomiki **11**(3), 178–191 (2014)
25. Espelage, D.L., Low, S., Polanin, J.R., Brown, E.C.: The impact of a middle school program to reduce aggression, victimization, and sexual violence. J. Adolesc. Health **53**, 180–186 (2013). https://doi.org/10.1016/j.jadohealth.2013.02.021
26. Wright, M.F.: Predictors of anonymous cyber aggression: the role of adolescents' beliefs about anonymity, aggression, and the permanency of digital content. Cyber Psychol. Behav. Soc. Networking **17**(7), 431–438 (2014). https://doi.org/10.1089/cyber.2013.0457
27. Kowalski, R.M., Limber, S.P., Agatston, P.W.: Cyber Bullying: Bullying in the Digital Age, pp. 180–181. Blackwell, Malden (2008). https://doi.org/10.1027/0044-3409.217.4.180
28. Goldstein, S.E.: Parental regulation of online behavior and cyber aggression: adolescents' experiences and perspectives. Cyber Psychol. J. Psychosoc. Res. Cyberspace **9**(4), 25–36 (2015). https://doi.org/10.5817/cp2015-4-2. article 2
29. Soldatova, G.U., Rasskazova, H.I.: Bezopasnost podrostkov v internete: riski, sovladanieiroditelskaiamediatciia. Natcionalnyi psihologicheskii zhurnal **3**(15), 36–48 (2014). https://doi.org/10.11621/npj.2014.0305
30. Dooley, J.J., Pyzalski, J., Cross, D.: Cyberbullying versus face to face bullying: a theoretical and conceptual review. Zeitschrift fur Psychologie **217**, 182–188 (2009). https://doi.org/10.1027/0044-3409.217.4.182
31. Raskauskas, J., Stoltz, A.D.: Involvement in traditional and electronic bullying among adolescents. Dev. Psychol. **43**, 564–575 (2007). https://doi.org/10.1037/0012-1649.43.3.564
32. Josea, P.E., Fub, K.Y.: Does receiving malicious texts predict subsequent self-harming behavior among adolescents? Comput. Hum. Behav. **89**, 328–334 (2018). https://doi.org/10.1016/j.chb.2018.08.005
33. Runions, K.C.: Toward a conceptual model of motive and self-control in cyber-aggression: Rage, revenge, reward and recreation. J. Adolesc. **42**, 751–771 (2013). https://doi.org/10.1007/s10964-013-9936-2
34. Runions, K., Bak, M., Shaw, T.: Disentangling functions of online aggression: the cyber-aggression typology questionnaire (CATQ). Aggressive Behav. **43**, 74–84 (2017). https://doi.org/10.1002/ab.21663
35. Mc Guckin, C.: School bullying amongst school pupils in Northern Ireland: how many are involved, what are the health effects, and what are the issues for school management? In: O'Moore, A.M., Stevens, P. (eds.) Bullying in Irish Education, pp. 46–64. Cork University Press, Cork (2013). ISSN 978-1-78205-043-8
36. Zhou, Z., Tang, H., Tian, Y., Wei, H., Zhang, F., Morrison, C.M.: Cyberbullying and its risk factors among Chinese high school students. Sch. Psychol. Int. **34**, 630–647 (2013). https://doi.org/10.1177/0143034313479692

37. Goldstein, S.E.: Adolescents' disclosure and secrecy about peer behavior: links with cyber aggression, relational aggression, and overt aggression. J. Child Family Stud. **25**(5), 1430–1440 (2016). https://doi.org/10.1007/s10826-015-0340-2
38. Ybarra, M.L., Diener-West, M., Leaf, P.: Examining the overlap in internet harassment and school bullying: implications for school intervention. J. Adolesc. Health **2007**(1), 42–50 (2007). https://doi.org/10.1016/j.jadohealth.2007.09.004
39. Schoffstall, C.L.: Cyber aggression. The relation between online offenders and offline social competence. Soc. Dev. **20**(3), 587–604 (2011). https://doi.org/10.1111/j.1467-9507.2011.00609
40. Washington, R., Cohen, R., Berlin, K.S., Hsueh, Y., Zhou, Z.K.: The relation of cyber aggression to peer social competence in the classroom for children in China. Soc. Dev. **27** (4), 715–731 (2018)
41. Pabian, S., et al.: Arguments online, but in school we always act normal: the embeddedness of early adolescent negative peer interactions within the whole of their offline and online peer interactions. Children Youth Serv. Rev. **86**, 1–13 (2018)
42. Kokkinos, C.M., Voulgaridou, I.: Relational and cyber aggression among adolescents: personality and emotion regulation as moderators. Comput. Hum. Behav. **68**, 528–537 (2017). https://doi.org/10.1016/j.chb.2016.11.046
43. Goodman, R.: Psychometric properties of the Strengths and Difficulties Questionnaire (SDQ). J. Am. Acad. Child Adolesc. Psychiatry **40**(11), 1337–1345 (2001). https://doi.org/10.1097/00004583-200111000-00015
44. Goodman, R., Slobodskaya, H.R., Knyazev, G.G.: Russian child mental health. A cross-sectional study of prevalence and risk factors. European Child Adolesc. Psychiatry **14**(1), 28–33 (2005). https://doi.org/10.1007/s00787-005-0420-8
45. Amirkhan, J.H.: A factor analytically derived measure of coping: the coping strategy indicator. J. Pers. Soc. Psychol. **59**, 1066–1074 (1990). https://doi.org/10.1037/0022-3514.59.5.1066
46. Gretcov, A.G., Azbel, A.A.: Uznai sebia. Psihologicheskie testy dlia podrostkov, p. 171. SPb: Peter (2006). ISBN 5-469-01385-5

Implicit Concepts of the Psychological Effects of Video Games Among Young Adult Students

Olga Khodakovskaia[1(✉)], Irina Bogdsnovskaya[2], Natalya Koroleva[2], Anatoly Alekhin[2], and Ilya Mokhnatkin[2]

[1] Saint - Petersburg State University of Culture, Dvortsovaya Emb. 2, 191186 St. Petersburg, Russia
olga-khodakovskaya@yandex.ru

[2] Herzen State Pedagogical University of Russia, Emb. of the Moika River, 48, 191186 St. Petersburg, Russian Federation

Abstract. The paper presents an implicit model of the positive and negative effects of computer games as perceived by their young adult users reconstructed from the results of psychosemantic analysis. The participants in the empirical study were 117 higher-education students in Saint Petersburg, Russia, aged between 18 and 30. To detect patterns of subjective meanings describing the effects of computer games, a repertoire array with fixed constructs was devised. Its elements were the 10 computer games most popular among young people. The constructs were formed from the results of a content analysis of the respondents' unprompted descriptions of the single-player games selected with an indication of their positive and negative effects on a person. The basic semantic constructs that shape the students' concepts of the effects of video games are "Recreation" versus "Training thinking skills" and "Immersion in the virtual reality of the game" versus "Awareness and volitional regulation of activity". Differences in concepts of the positive effects of gaming were found to depend on the amount of time respondents spent playing. A gender distinction in implicit concepts of the effects of video games was identified.

Keywords: Video games · Implicit concepts · Psychological effects · Young adult students

1 Introduction

At the present time computer games form an inseparable part of everyday human culture. The computer games industry is rightly held to be one of the most rapidly developing and most profitable branches of the economy. For example, according to a survey carried out by Mail.Ru Group in 2015, in Russia one out of every two Internet users plays computer games and the population of computer game players amounts to over 43 million people [2]. Roughly equal numbers of men and women engage in this leisure activity (52% and 48%, respectively. Commonplace conceptions about video-games are often connected with stereotypes reflecting their harmful influence on the user's personality. The results of a sociological study by the All-Russian Centre for the Study of Public Opinion (VTsIOM) show that 77% of respondents in the older

D. A. Alexandrov et al. (Eds.): DTGS 2019, CCIS 1038, pp. 648–660, 2019.
https://doi.org/10.1007/978-3-030-37858-5_55

generation and 72% of young respondents consider computer games a more significant threat than the consumption of alcohol and psychotropic drugs [20]. At the same time, videogames have a significant developmental potential and are used quite extensively in the practice of training, psychological correction and rehabilitation. Consequently, an analysis of conceptions about the positive and negative effects of young people's fascination with videogames represents a significant scientific and practical task.

2 Excessive Videogames Playing: Risks and Opportunities

Videogames and their influence on the cognitive and personality development of young people is one of the current areas of active interdisciplinary study. A whole series of studies emphasize the negative effects of attachment to a computer game on players' cognitive and personality characteristics. Those are primarily increased aggression, impulsive behavior, an inclination to risk-taking, a reduction in self-control and voluntary attention, a worsening of mnemic capabilities, a reduced capacity for work, abnormalities in neuro-psychological processes, a blocking of the capacity for creative imagination, difficulties in communication and social isolation [3, 7, 11, 14]. The risk of the development of an addiction to computer among active users is a significant problem. The results of other studies convincingly point to the positive effects of computer games on cognitive development and gamers' personality characteristics. They note such positive effects of gaming as the development of memory and attention, increased speed of information processing and cognitive control, the formation of strategic and tactical thinking and creativity, increased resistance to stress and situations of uncertainty, improved decision-making skills and social adaptation [1, 4, 9, 10, 12, 16]. The difficulty of identifying positive and negative psychological effects of computer gaming lies also in the fact that the diversity of genre and plot in the games gives rise to a differentiated character of their influence on players [4, 5]. Besides, playing preferences are to a large extent determined by the personality traits of the users. Because of this, for a deeper understanding of the psychological effects of video games it is necessary to turn to an analysis of the specifics of the gamers' subjective playing experience, their own perceptions of the positive and negative consequences of becoming drawn into the artificial reality of the game.

3 Studies of Users' Implicit Concepts About Video Games

Implicit concepts reflect a person's latent knowledge about various spheres of activity that determine the inner logic of their actions. A reconstruction of implicit concepts makes it possible to discover the full set of someone's opinions, convictions and views that act as internal criteria for the evaluation of oneself and other people, objects and phenomena in the surrounding world and as the basis for the regulation of behavior [6, 8, 13, 17, 22, 23]. For example, Voiskunskii et al. obtained an 8-factor model of gamers' implicit concepts about the playing process and its psychological characteristics, including the positive and negative consequences of becoming absorbed in the game: Control and Attention, Consequences of Playing, Interest in Playing, Self-Development,

Perception, Thinking and Memory, Self-Discovery and Game Satisfaction [24]. In the work by Hilgard, Engelhardt and Bartholow, survey results provided the basis for 9 dimensional factors reflecting the implicit attitudes and motives of video game players: Story, Violent Catharsis, Violent Reward, Social Interaction, Escapism, Loss-Aversion, Customization, Grinding/Completion, Autonomy/Exploration [15]. It should be noted that to determine the characteristics of the gamers' subjective experience the majority of studies use questionnaires and written survey. The questions devised by the researcher are, as a rule, based on particular theoretical constructs and describe the psychological characteristics of video gaming in pre-determined terms that may not coincide with the subjective components of the users' gaming experience. A psychosemantic approach envisages the description of someone's inner world, their individual experience using a unique system of characteristics intrinsic to that person and not imposed by the structure of the test. Psychosemantic methods aim at "a subjective paradigm in the analysis of data" [21], combining qualitative and quantitative analysis. Such procedures for the gathering of data are analogous to obtaining knowledge from experts. Despite a considerable number of studies devoted to the psychosemantic analysis of various substantive domains in a person's world map, there are fairly few works aimed at the reconstruction of the category structure of concepts about activities mediated by computer technologies, including video games. Voiskunskii has carried out a psychosemantic analysis of hackers' motivation. Paniukova identified the psycho semantic characteristics of various components of the modern-day information environment [19]. Monakhov et al. determined the psychosemantic characteristics of the profiles of social network users [19]. A reconstruction of the subjective semantic space of computer games was carried out in a study by Luzakov and Omel'chenko [18].

4 Research Questions

Accordingly, in the present study the following questions were asked:

(1) What are the positive and negative effects of video gaming for young adult users?
(2) What are the main semantic dimensions of an implicit model of the effects of the influence of computer gaming on cognitive and personality characteristics perceived by young adults?
(3) Are there differences in cognitive differentiation of concepts about the effects of computer gaming that are dependent on the gender of players and the time spent playing computer games?

5 Methods

5.1 Participants

At the initial stage, 117 students (25% male, 75% female) participated in the study. They were taking full-time and extra-mural courses in social sciences and the humanities at various institutions of higher education in Saint Petersburg, Russia. The choice of non-science students was a result of a desire to partially eliminate the influence of a subjects chosen educational field (precise sciences, natural sciences and technology) on conceptions of computer gaming. The sample group showed a numerical preponderance of young women, which according to the data of the Federal State Statistical Service is roughly in accordance with the gender distribution in the general overall body of students studying social sciences and the humanities [26]. Participants indicated how frequently they played video games (daily, 2–3 times a week, weekly, 2–3 times a month, once a month, less than once a month, never, respondent's own answer). Based on questionnaire, 48 women were eliminated from the survey: six had no experience of video games; eight had only played in childhood; 34 had not played for a long time (more than a year). The final size of the survey group was 49 persons (29 males, 40 females).

5.2 Measures

5.2.1 Demographic Information

Participants indicated their age (M = 21.1, SD = 2.8, range = 18–30); the age when they started playing video games (M = 10.49, SD = 2.45, range = 4–20), sex and employment status.

5.2.2 Exposure to Computer Games

Participants indicated how many hours they spent playing video games: a few hours per month; a few hours a week; about 1 h a day; 2–3 h a day; more than 5 h a day (Table 1).

Table 1. Video games exposure

Time	Female, %	Male, %
Several hours per month	67	23
Several hours a week	11	8
About 1 h a day	4	7
2–3 h a day	7	46
More than 5 h a day	11	15

5.2.3 Preferred Games

Participants were asked to list, via open response the first video games that they mastered and their favourite single-player computer games among those they were currently playing. We restricted our study to single-player games because at the present stage we were interested in analysing the respondents' individual gaming experience. Single-player gaming has some benefits: you get to proceed at your own pace; do not need to worry about maintaining an online connection; there is no need to maintain online communication with anyone; the player is able to pause the game and take frequent breaks. Altogether, the participants named 217 different games (M = 4.63, SD = 2.88, range = 1–16) that we sorted by frequency of mention and by genre. The result was a list of 10 popular single-player games that, as we confirmed, corresponds to the ratings found on various Internet sites devoted to computer gaming (ag.ru, playground.ru, igromania.ru, kanobu.ru, stopgame.ru):

1. Action-adventure/open world (GTA V); 2. Role-play/action (The Elder Scrolls V: Skyrim); 3. First-person shooter (Call of Duty: Modern Warfare 3); 4. Episodic adventure game/quest (The Walking Dead: The Game); 5. Fighting (Mortal Kombat X); 6. Simulator (The Sims 3); 7. Strategy (Starcraft 2); 8. Puzzle-platform (Portal 2); 9. Horror (Outlast); 10. Racing (Need for Speed: Most Wanted).

The list obtained does not include the arcade genre that features chiefly in console and mobile formats, since the study focussed on the personal computers segment.

5.2.4 Stages in the Construction of a Subjective Semantic Space for Computer Games

Elicitation of Concepts About the Psychological Effects of Computer Games

To elicit their concepts, the respondents were presented with ten selected single-player games (those listed in 4.2.3. Preferred games) by way of stimuli and invited to indicated in free format the positive and negative aspects of their influence on a person. In order to more clearly demonstrate the audio-visual and stylistic component of the stimuli, demonstration video clips lasting 2–3 min were put together specially for use in the study showing the stages in the process of playing the game. The respondents were also able to re-read the standard descriptions of the games in question given in Wikipedia. The answers were subjected to content analysis, with the unit taken to be words or phrases conveying a positive or negative determination of the effects of the computer game. Altogether 425 positive characteristics were elicited and 292 negative ones. Participants were asked: "To what degree does this effect apply to this game?", giving answers on a five-point Likert scale (1 – not at all; 2 – weakly; 3 – moderately; 4 – quite strongly; 5 – fully). After this assessment, the individual matrices obtained formed a "data cube": (elements) × (constructs) × (participants). The subjects' answers were consolidated into 10 larger categories (Table 2).

5.3 Data Analysis

To determine the dimensions of the semantic space for the effects of computer games, the factor analysis (principal component method) with varimax rotation and factor scores for elements computed. A test of the practicality of using factor analysis was carried out on the basis of the Kaiser-Meyer-Olkin measure of sampling adequacy (KMO). Bartlett's teste of sphericity was also carried out and indicated that a factor analysis may be useful with our data. We conducted an analysis of variance (ANOVA) in order to check how the cognitive differentiation of concepts about the effects of computer games varies in relation to two independent variables: (1) gaming habits (time spent on computer gaming ≥ 1 h a day versus time spent on computer gaming $\leq$ several hours a week); (2) the gender of participants (male versus female). Statistical significance was set at a level of $p < 0.05$. The SPSS 19.0 software package was used for analyses in this study.

Table 2. Implicit concepts, their hypothetical meanings, rating of the strength of the effects

Hypothetical meanings	Descriptions of the positive psychological effects of video games	Frequency/%	Evaluation of effects on a scale where 1 - not expressed, 5 - fully expressed	
			M	SD
Development of thinking skills	Development of logical and strategic thinking, ability to predict	105/24,7	2,43	1,46
Awareness and volitional regulation	Training cognitive functions, increased volitional regulation of concentration and self-regulation to achieve a result within the game	75/17,7	3,3	1,4
Game creativity, customization	Acquisition through playing of certain skills useful in real life, the opportunity to display one's individuality, to realize dreams, fantasies, creative urges	142/33,4	2,7	1,3
Expanding experience	Stimulating cognitive activity and existential thinking, expansion of one's range of emotions	40/9,41	2,45	1,26
Self-regulation of social behavior	Development of social intelligence, responsibility	19/4,47	1,65	1,3
Recreation	Recreation, relaxation, an outlet for negative feelings	34/8	3,75	0,9
Hypothetical meanings	Descriptions of the negative psychological effects of video games	Frequency/%	M	SD
Cruelty and destructiveness	Development of violence and aggression, psychological harm, creation of a negative emotional atmosphere	193/66,1	1,8	1,08
Escapism	Causing addiction, withdrawal from reality, inspiring wrongdoing in the real world	75/25,68	2.6	1.02
Game complexity	Difficult to play (high cost of errors, frequent restarts, little time to take decisions), time-consuming	14/4,79	1,7	0,9
Poor quality	Poor quality computer graphics, boring, no practical benefit	2,4/10	2,5	0,7

6 Results

6.1 The Factorial Structure of the Semantic Space

To identify the co-ordinate axes (dimensions) of the semantic space for computer games, the factor analysis (principal component method) with varimax rotation and factor scores for elements was computed. The Kaiser-Meyer-Olkin measure of sampling adequacy (KMO) = 0.676; in Bartlett's test of sphericity $\chi^2 = 27.33$, df = 15, $\alpha = 0.026$. Two factors were extracted with an eigenvalue greater than one. Those factors were subjected to varimax rotation. The variables with the highest factorial loading (>0.7) are shown in Table 3.

Table 3. Factor loadings

Variables	Factors	
	1	2
Development of thinking skills	−0.850	
Recreation	0.873	
Game complexity	−0.743	
Awareness and volitional regulation of activity to achieve a result within the game		−0.845
Escapism		0.801
Game creativity		0.765
Explored variance	3.5	1.3
Prp. total variance	58.6	23.4

The first factor (with 58.6% variance) contains the variable "recreation (0.83) at one pole, while the opposite pole contains "development of thinking skills (−0.85) and "game complexity" (−0.743). This factor can be regarded as one of the co-ordinate axes of the semantic space that was designated "Recreation" versus "Training thinking skills".

The second factor (with 23.4% variance) has the variables "escapism" (0.801) and "game creativity" (0.765) at one of the poles, while the opposite pole contains "awareness and volitional regulation of activity"(−0.845). This factor can be regarded as the second co-ordinate axis of the semantic space, which we designated "Immersion in the virtual reality of the game" versus "Awareness and volitional regulation of activity".

The assigned bipolar factors represent personal constructs that organize the participants' concepts of the positive and negative psychological effects of the gaming experience and serve as axes for the construction of a semantic space for computer games.

Table 4 gives the factor scores (variables calculated for each factor as the weighted sum of each item) that are taken as the coordinates of the various computer games in the semantic space.

Table 4. Computer games factor scores

Game	Factor 1	Factor 2
The Elder Scrolls V: Skyrim	−0.40	1.35
Grand Theft Auto V	1.25	0.54
Call of Duty: Modern Warfare 3	1.14	−0.95
Mortal Kombat X	0.29	−1.23
The Walking Dead: The Game	0.20	0.35
The Sims 3	−0.04	1.80
Starcraft 2	−1.79	−0.40
Portal 2	−1.12	−0.32
Outlast	−0.57	−0.88
Need for Speed: Most Wanted	1.03	−0.26

At the concluding stage of the study, the positions of the video games in the semantic space were determined. These are shown in Fig. 1. From this diagram we can see that the highest assessment on the dimension "Immersion in the virtual reality" goes to The Sims 3, a game aimed at imitating certain processes in life, and the role game The Elder Scrolls V: Skyrim. The high ratings for The Sims are most probably due to the presence of a large number of females among the players of this game. The Elder Scrolls V: Skyrim is also perceived as a game that to a certain degree activates the player's logical thinking and strategic abilities. The highest ratings on the dimension "Training thinking skills" go to the strategic game Starcraft 2 and the puzzle game Portal 2.

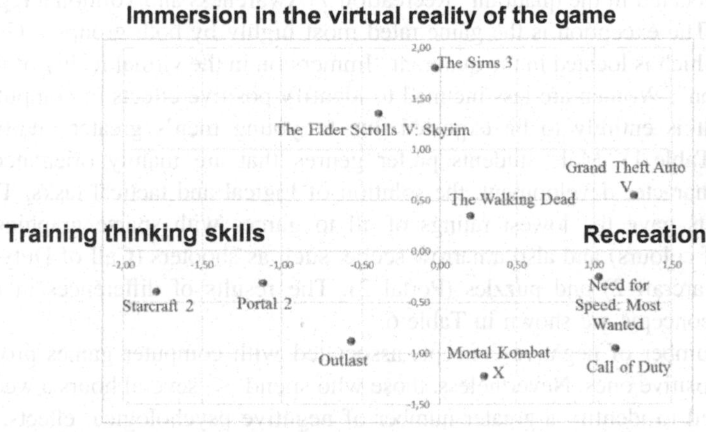

Fig. 1. Positions of video games in semantics space (factors 1 and 2)

This is a predictable result, since Starcraft 2 is concerned with improving the characteristics of one's virtual alter ego, the independent planning of game actions within the bounds of the tasks set and a large number of non-typical game situations, the onset and outcome of which need to be thought through in advance, while Portal 2 trains logic and non-standard thinking with the goal of solving logical tasks and puzzles, finding and using game objects, assembling various mechanisms, and so on.

The participants in the study also see the horror game Outlast as employing the player's predictive abilities as the most important thing in the game is search activity and calculating the outcome of previously unknown situations that are potentially dangerous for one's character. Gamers associate the stimulation of concentration and self-regulation with the fighting game Mortal Kombat X and the Call of Duty shooters that involve the need to make quick decisions, the element of reacting to rapidly changing situations and, consequently, increased reaction speed, and also volitional and non-volitional concentration. The highest rating on the "Recreation" dimension goes to the Grand Theft Auto V with a large number of characters and an elaborate plot and to Need for Speed and Call of Duty, action games with a pronounced competitive element.

6.2 Differences in the Implicit Concepts of the Effects of Video Games

From Table 5 we can see that a greater quantity of positive concepts are observed among participants who spend an hour or more a day gaming.

The heavy gamers among the study participants attribute a greater amount of positive effects to those games located in the quadrant of the semantic space formed by the dimensions "Training thinking skills" and "Awareness and volitional regulation of activity". The respondents who devote less time to gaming give a positive assessment to games located in the quadrant "Recreation"/"Awareness and volitional regulation of activity". The exception is the game rated most highly by both groups – Grand Theft Auto V, which is located in the quadrant "Immersion in the virtual reality of the game"/ "Recreation". Women are less inclined to identify positive effects of computer games. This result is entirely to be expected due to young men's greater involvement in gaming (Table 1). Male students prefer genres that are mainly orientated towards combat, character development, the solution of logical and tactical tasks. The female respondents gave the lowest ratings of all to games with sparse graphics (a small number of colours) and also a narrow scope, such as shooters (Call of Duty), strategy games (Starcraft 2) and puzzles (Portal 2). The results of differences in negatively coloured concepts are shown in Table 6.

The number of negative concepts associated with computer games proved lower than the positive ones. Nevertheless, those who spend $\leq$ several hours a week gaming are inclined to identify a greater number of negative psychological effects. The light gamers among the students were inclined to characterizes these games as violent, "sucking you in", causing addiction and creating a negative emotional atmosphere. Gender differences apply only to the strategy game *Starcraft 2*. The young women gave this game more negative characteristics, mainly connected with its complexity and awkwardness (high entry threshold), the gloominess of the graphics and its orientation towards fighting an opponent.

Table 5. Differences in the positive implicit concepts (Note: *p < 0.05; **p < 0.01; *** p < 0.001)

Game	Gaming frequency		Gender	
	≥ 1 h a day	≤ several hours a week	Female	Male
	M (SD)	M (SD)	M (SD)	M (SD)
The Elder Scrolls	1.77* (1.56)	1.00 (0.98)	1.15 (1.18)	2.79*** (1.53)
Grand Theft Auto	1.88* (1.38)	1.15 (1.12)	1.42 (1.20)	2.36** (1.60)
Call of Duty	0.71* (0.89)	0.23 (0.51)	0.42 (0.74)	1.00** (0.91)
Mortal Kombat X	1.23 (0.97)	1.12 (1.51)	1.18 (1.26)	1.21 (0.89)
The Walking Dead	0.98 (1.12)	0.73 (0.96)	0.84 (1.03)	1.08 (1.19)
The Sims 3	1.26 (1.16)	0.88 (0.82)	1.13 (1.06)	1.07 (1.07)
StarCraft 2	1.00* (1.51)	0.27 (0.60)	1.13 (1.06)	1.07 (1.07)
Portal 2	1.42** (1.56)	0.46 (0.81)	0.40 (0.74)	2.00*** (2.08)
Outlast	1.16** (1.17)	0.46 (0.76)	0.89 (1.13)	0.93 (0.92)
Need for Speed	1.39 (1.20)	1.15 (0.92)	1.22 (0.96)	1.62 (1.56)

7 Discussion

7.1 Findings

The advantage of the psychosemantic model obtained in our study is that it reflects the main directions in the construction of the respondents' gaming experience: recreation, the development of thinking skills, immersion in the world of the game, training cognitive functions. This result makes it possible to present the gamers' viewpoint with regard to interest in this or that game and the aims of individual gaming activity. The implicit model obtained coincides in part with the results obtained in the works [15, 24, 25]. It seems to us that those participants who preferred games that received high factor scores on the "Immersion in the virtual reality of the game" dimension may be at a higher risk of video game addiction. On the other hand, it may be that an enthusiasm for games of that type may point to the gamer having certain psychological problems in real life. This hypothesis could be tested in a study of the interconnection between the number of implicit concepts and students' inclination to video game addiction. It was established that the total number of concepts offered by participants depends of the amount of their gaming experience: increased time spent gaming leads to increased differentiation of perception. This result accords with Gentile's model of the multiple dimensions of video game effects [11] that identified "amount of game play" as a significant component. It is interesting that the two groups react differently to aggression within a game. The light gamers are inclined to stress the violent and aggressive character of many of the games included in the survey, while heavy gamers stressed this aspect least of all, preferring to assign aggression to the characteristics of the genre. This result might prompt ideas of a higher tolerance towards manifestations of cruelty and violence among keen gamers. The same conclusion might also be applied to the gender-dependent differences in concepts, taking into account the heavier gaming activity among male students.

Table 6. Differences in the negative implicit concepts (Note: *p < 0.05; **p < 0.01; ***p < 0.001)

Game	Gaming frequency		Gender	
	≥ 1 h a day	≤ several hours a week	Female	Male
	M (SD)	M (SD)	M (SD)	M (SD)
The Elder Scrolls	0.56 (0.73)	0.85 (0.78)	0.69 (0.77)	0.57(0.76)
Grand Theft Auto	0.33 (0.64)	0.81** (0.85)	0.55 (0.74)	0.36 (0.84)
Call of Duty	0.62 (0.73)	1.00 (0.89)	0.75 (0.84)	0.85 (0.69)
Mortal Kombat X	0.56 (0.80)	0.85 (0.78)	0.73 (0.83)	0.43 (0.65)
The Walking Dead	0.60 (0.73)	0.92 (0.93)	0.75 (0.87)	0.62 (0.65)
The Sims 3	0.56 (0.73)	0.73 (0.78)	0.62 (0.76)	0.64 (0.74)
StarCraft 2	0.53 (0.85)	1.19*** (0.85)	0.93*** (0.94)	0.21 (0.43)
Portal 2	0.37 (0.58)	0.65 (0.75)	0.55 (0.69)	0.21 (0.43)
Outlast	0.60 (0.79)	1.12* (0.91)	0.82 (0.88)	0.71 (0.83)
Need for Speed	1.60 (1.43)	1.62 (1.06)	0.32 (0.47)	0.54 (0.78)

7.2 Study Limitations and Directions for Future Research

The choice of experimental psychosemantic framework limits the applicability of the results in a more general context. The study revealed some differences, but the scale of those differences and their meaning in the general population would have to be established in a study with a larger sample consisting primarily of "serious" gamers, of whom there were fewer in this study than occasional players. Perhaps this explains the difference in the positive and negative psychological effects of video games between our psychosemantic model and those proposed by other researchers. For example, heavy gamers in our study did speak about the significance the plot of a game, its story, had for them. The factor "Story (whether game stories are important, engaging, and emotionally compelling)" is present in Hilgard, Engelhardt and Bartholow's model, but in our survey group such answers came up extremely rarely. In future research it would also be desirable to balance the sample of students in terms of their field of study, to expand the list of games to be rated and to consider not just single-player games. The second limitation is connected with the fact that the scope of the work did not allow us to focus more strongly on the specifics of the female perception of computer games. The contingent of female gamers is constantly growing so it is important to make a separate study of their gaming preferences, attitudes, motives and experience. Further study of implicit concepts of the psychological effects of video games will aid the formation of a more precise picture of a person's attitude both to specific games genres and to video games in general, what functions they perform in his or her life and what criteria govern the choice of a particular game.

8 Conclusion

In this paper psychosemantic analysis is used to develop an implicit model of the psychological effects of video games as perceived by young adult students. It shows that in the students' minds video games have greater amounts of positive effects – developing cognitive, volitional and emotional processes, encouraging creative self-realization and the revelation of individuality. The negative effect of videogames playing are less represented and in the main reflect a worsening of psychological condition, escapism, the risk of developing deviant behavior, including aggression, wrongdoing or video game addiction. Differences in concepts of the positive effects of gaming were found to depend on the amount of time respondents spent playing. Male students spend more time on video games and differentiate their positive effects to a greater extent. Heavy gamers display greater differentiation in their concepts about the positive effects, above all those associated with the development of cognitive skills and concentration on the achievement of a result. Concepts of the negative effects among those who spend little time video gaming are to a large extent founded on social stereotypes connected with the influence on video games on the mind and health. A gender distinction in implicit concepts of the effects of video games was identified.

References

1. Adachi, P.J., Willoughby, T.: More than just fun and games: the longitudinal relationships between strategic video games, self-reported problem solving skills, and academic grades. J. Youth Adolesc. **42**, 1041–1052 (2013). https://doi.org/10.1007/s10964-013-9913-9
2. Agafonov, A.G.: Social'nyj portret rossijskogo onlajn-gejmera. Social'no-politicheskie nauki **2**, 73–75 (2017). (in Russian)
3. Anderson, C.A.: An update on the effects of playing violent video games. J. Adolesc. **27**(1), 113–122 (2004). https://doi.org/10.1016/j.adolescence.2003.10.009
4. Bogacheva, N.V.: Komp'yuternye igry i psihologicheskaya specifika kognitivnoj sfery gejmerov (okonchanie). Vestnik Moskovskogo universiteta. Seriya 14: Psihologiya **1**, 94–103 (2015). (in Russian)
5. Bogacheva, N.V.: Komp'yuternye igry i psihologicheskaya specifika kognitivnoj sfery gejmerov. Vestnik Moskovskogo universiteta. Seriya 14: Psihologiya **4**, 120–130 (2014). (in Russian)
6. Bruner, J.S., Tagiuri, R.: The perception of people. In: Lindzey, G. (ed.) Handbook of Social Psychology, vol. II, pp. 634–654. Addison-Wesley, Reading (1954)
7. Burlakov, I.V.: Homo Gamer: Psihologiya komp'yuternyh igr. Klass, Moskva (2000). (in Russian)
8. Crawford, G.: Video Gamers. Routledge, London (2011)
9. Sun, D.-L., Ma, N., Bao, M., et al.: Computer games: a double-edged sword? Cyberpsychology Behav. **11**(5), 545–548 (2008). https://doi.org/10.1089/cpb.2007.0145
10. Gentile, D.A., et al.: The effects of prosocial video games on prosocial behaviors: international evidence from correlational, longitudinal, and experimental studies. Pers. Soc. Psychol. Bull. **35**(6), 752–763 (2009). https://doi.org/10.1177/0146167209333045
11. Gentile, D.A.: The multiple dimensions of video game effects. Child. Dev. Perspect. **5**(2), 75–81 (2011). https://doi.org/10.1111/j.1750-8606.2011.00159.x

12. Granic, I., Lobel, A., Engels, R.C.M.E.: The benefits of playing video games. Am. Psychol. **69**(1), 66 (2014). https://doi.org/10.1037/a0034857
13. Greenwald, A.G., Banaji, M.R.: Implicit social cognition: attitudes, self-esteem, and stereotypes. Psychol. Rev. **102**(1), 4–27 (1995)
14. Griffiths, M.D.: Computer game playing and social skills: a pilot study. Revista de psicologia, ciències de l'Educació i de l'Esport. (2010). http://www.raco.cat/index.php/Aloma/article/viewFile/216947/289580
15. Hilgard, J., Engelhardt, C.R., Bartholow, B.D.: Individual differences in motives, preferences, and pathology in video games: the gaming attitudes, motives, and experiences scales (GAMES). Front. Psychol. **4**, 608 (2013). https://doi.org/10.3389/fpsyg.2013.00608
16. Jackson, L.A., Witt, E.A., Games, A.I., et al.: Information technology use and creativity: findings from the children and technology project. Comput. Hum. Behav. **28**(2), 370–376 (2012)
17. Kelly, G.A.: The Psychology of Personal Constructs, vol. 1, p. 541. Norton, New York (1955)
18. Luzakov, A.A., Omel'chenko, N.V.: Semanticheskoe prostranstvo komp'yuternyh igr: opyt rekonstrukcii. Politematicheskij setevoj ehlektronnyj nauchnyj zhurnal Kubanskogo gosudarstvennogo agrarnogo universiteta **78**, 1377–1411 (2012). (in Russian)
19. Panyukova, Y.G.: Psihosemanticheskij analiz prostranstvennyh i temporal'nyh harakteristik raznyh vidov informacionnoj sredy. Vestnik Udmurtskogo universiteta. Seriya «Filosofiya. Psihologiya. Pedagogika» **27**(3), 339–347 (2017)
20. Pokolenie Selfie: pyat' mifov o sovremennoj molodezhi. https://wciom.ru/index.php?id=236&uid=115996. (in Russian)
21. Shmelev, A.G.: Tradicionnaya psihometrika i ehksperimental'naya psihosemantika: o"bektnaya i sub"ktnaya paradigmy analiza dannyh. Voprosy psihololgii **5**, 34–36 (1982). (in Russian)
22. Tihomirov, O.K., Lysenko, E.E.: Psihologiya komp'yuternoj igry. Novye metody i sredstva obucheniya. 1, 30–66. Moskva (1988). (in Russian)
23. Tokareva, G.V., Dorfman, L.Y.A.: Implicitnye processy i ih issledovanie v Zapadnoj psihologii. Vestnik YUzhno-Ural'skogo gosudarstvennogo universiteta. Seriya: Psihologiya **7**(1), 17–27 (2014). (in Russian)
24. Vojskunskij, A.E., Avetisova, A.A.: Tradicionnye i sovremennye issledovaniya igrovogo povedeniya. Metodologiya i istoriya psihologii **4**(4), 82–94 (2009). (in Russian)
25. Yee, N.: The demographics, motivations, and derived experiences of users of massively multi-user online graphical environments. Presence Teleop. Virt. Environ. **15**, 309–329 (2006). https://doi.org/10.1162/pres.15.3.309
26. Zhenshchiny i muzhchiny Rossii Stat.sb. Moskva, Rosstat (2016). (in Russian)

Proud and Productive Procrastination? What Do We Talk About When We Talk About #Procrastination on Twitter

Yusi Xu(✉)

University of Southern California, Los Angeles, CA 90089, USA
yusixu@usc.edu

Abstract. Procrastination is a prevalent and problematic, yet seldomly studied behavior. Twitter provides perfect examples for proud and productive procrastination through the deliberate self-representation of procrastination. Using manual coding and machine learning aided coding content analysis, this study uses 4587 tweets contained the hashtag #procrastination, and the author aims to identify the genres of tweets disclosing this behavior and further discuss the notion of value creation as sense-making [1] with this particular hashtag. Results suggested that structured procrastination was more likely associated with positive impact and it was more likely put in an ironic tone on Twitter. This finding is in line with the self-enhancement strategy when people represent themselves on social media. Data also show that people were more likely to self-reflect at critical time nodal points in a week, such as the end of weekdays and weekends. This paper offers theoretical and practical contributions to understanding the socio-cultural and psychological function of social media in the case of disclosing an arguably negative, yet prevalent behavior, procrastination.

Keywords: Procrastination · Twitter · Structured procrastination · Impact · Irony · Self-enhancement

1 Introduction

"I do my work at the same time every day: the last minute."—Unknown author

Many of us could relate to the sarcastic quote above. As a matter of fact, the tendency to delay meaningful work, or procrastination, is rather prevalent and could be dated back decades in history. In 1751, the famous English poet, Samuel Johnson, identified procrastination as "one of the general weakness which, in spite of the instruction of moralists, and the remonstrances of reason, prevail to a greater or less degree in every mind." More than two and half centuries later, procrastination is still not cured, and remains prevalent. In fact, a higher incidence rate in recent years with many people admitting to at least some degree of procrastination from time to time [2]. It is estimated that 20% of the general U.S. adults are self-reported "chronical procrastinators", without being clinically treated [3].

Despite its prevalence, most people view it as a problematic behavior and more than 95% of the procrastinators expressed wish to reduce it [4]. However, to overcome

D. A. Alexandrov et al. (Eds.): DTGS 2019, CCIS 1038, pp. 661–671, 2019.
https://doi.org/10.1007/978-3-030-37858-5_56

this bad habit is never easy. Though procrastinated behaviors may result in restless nights, high levels of stress, anxiety, withdrawal or poor performance due to lack of time, people regret delaying tasks until the last minute yet they procrastinate again [5].

In the current digital media landscape, social media seem to both contribute to and aggravate procrastination [6, 7]. On the other hand, procrastination is a heated topic of discussion on social media. Although a growing body of research has studied conversations (e.g. political and health-related) on Twitter [8], no study examines representations of procrastination on Twitter. This study focuses on the online discourse around procrastination, and aims to tentatively understand the genre, mechanism and motivations for disclosing this prevalent yet problematic behavior.

2 Literature Review and Hypotheses

2.1 Procrastination

The Latin origins of this word is procrastinus, in which pro means "forward, forth", and crustinus means tomorrow [9]. The Latin word has the meaning of to put off, delay, prolong, defer, stall, or postpone performing a task [5].

Since the word procrastination was adopted from common language to the scientific field, scholars have various definitions for it [9]. While most definitions touched upon the meaning of the Latin origins, the definition this paper used as a prevalent self-regulatory failure that alludes to deferring necessary actions required to successfully complete tasks on time, and instead engaging in activities that are more rewarding with short term over long term gains [10, 11]. At the heart of the definition is the knowingly delay of a task, and thus the delay is under control and procrastinators do so voluntarily.

Findings [12] from six nations suggest the international prevalence rates of chronic procrastination may be consistent across diverse population, despite of their distinct cultural values, norms and practices. In terms of other demographic elements, a recent epidemiological study from a global sample showed that procrastinators tend to be young, single men with less education, living in countries that normalizes lower levels of self-discipline [2].

However, apart from those epidemiological studies, scholars contended that the existing literature on procrastination could be characterized by "lack of an explicit, testable theory" [13].

2.2 Impact of Procrastination

Some scholars view procrastination as a form of self-regulatory failure [2] with serious consequences, including lower levels of academic performance, wealth, health, and well-being [9–11, 14–17].

Another line of scholars discovered the association of procrastination with higher stress and poor health in a student sample of 44 psychological students [17]. They also found procrastinators didn't perform as well as their non-procrastinating counterparts. They concluded that procrastination was a self-defeating behavior pattern marked by short-term benefit yet long-tern loss. Similarly, through a sample of 122 students, Sirios and colleagues suggested that procrastination was related to poorer health, higher perceived stress, and fewer healthy behaviors [14].

More extreme health consequences of procrastination include delaying physician appointments and putting off clinical treatment done for minor ailments, until the situation got worse and the treatment is no longer an option [11]. Other people may suffer from excessive debt, [2] lose job, drop out from school or may ruin their marriage [18].

On the other hand, other scholars argued that procrastination has adaptive or beneficial effect [3, 4]. Using a laboratory experiment, Ferrari identified procrastination as a self-handicapping strategy to serve to protect self-esteem and social-esteem [19]. According to him, students with higher ability procrastinated more than those less capable [19]. Moreover, counter-intuitively, he found that procrastination tended to increase during the course of a student's academic career, as learning became more self-regulated [13]. Some studies even suggested a positive effect of procrastination on academic performance [20].

Due to the contested impact of procrastination, the author proposes the first research question:

RQ1: Does personal post of #procrastination on Twitter report more positive or negative impact?

2.3 Twitter as a Platform for Self-representation and Self-disclosure

Shcheblanova, Bogomiagkova, and Semchenko identifies Twitter as a form of online diary in the sense that has a greater degree of publicity and openness than its prototype, a personal diary [21]. Users can express themselves as "open and sincere" as in personal diaries [21]. People also seem to disclose about themselves without worrying much about privacy, since they fear less of direct challenges or judgements than face-to-face communication with close social network [22, 23].

A recent study identified 80% of Twitter users can be classified as "me-formers", which mainly place themselves as the focus of their communications, while the other 20% are "informers" who post content targeting other users [24]. The results seem to confirm that users spontaneously share what considered the individual moments on Twitter [25]. Furthermore, to express oneself on a public platform fulfills the needs for social integration, and to relate with others in general. Hence, Twitter provides a venue for deliberate performance to create the networked self [26].

2.4 Functional Genre Theory and Its Application on Tweets Categorization

A genre is "a class of communicative events, the members of which share some set of communicative purposes" [27]. It is habitually enacted over time as a response to recurring communicative circumstances to achieve certain social purposes and is then consolidated as templates for community members to draw upon [25, 28].

Drawing upon this theory, a recent content analysis of Tweets categorized information about themselves accounted for 41% of all Tweets, the others were 25%

random thoughts, 24% opinions, and 21% information exchange [24]. This study proposed to apply this theory as the framework, and will code the dataset into four genres: Tweets with URLs, tweets about personal experiences, quotes, or unidentifiable.

2.5 Structured Procrastination and Irony

Perry coined the term "structured procrastination" to describe procrastinators' strategy to deliberately use time to complete the tasks less important in order to avoid doing the real necessary and time-sensitive duty [29]. Structured procrastination implies performing an alternative than the one intended, which is not synonymous with idleness [5, 6]. Therefore, in this sense, procrastination could be productive, since delaying doing one task often leads to doing another task instead. Hence, the articulation of structured procrastination might make a difference in the impact of procrastination. Thus, the author hypothesizes that:

H1: There is an association in personal experience Tweets between the existence of structured procrastination and certain impact of procrastination.

According to the Merriam-Webster dictionary, ironic tone was defined as "the use of words to express something other than and especially the opposite of the literal meaning" mainly for a humorous or sardonic style [30]. Due to the contradictory nature of the structured procrastination, its logic is similar to a common use of irony, as ironist employs pragmatic insincerity [31]. Pragmatic insincerity refers to the speaker's intention lies somewhere other than the usual association with that utterance [32]. Therefore, the author hypothesizes:

H2: There is an association in personal experience Tweets between the existence of structured procrastination and the use of irony.

3 Methods

3.1 Content Analysis

Data Collection. Publically available tweets that have the hashtag #procrastination were collected between May 22nd to 31st and Oct. 20th to 30th, 2017. Those Tweets with almost identical content but different automatically generated URLs were collapsed into 412 near duplicate clusters, leaving 2346 singletons that were not retweeted. The primary unit of analysis was the Tweet cluster.

Data Coding and Machine Learning Coding. Non-English tweets were first excluded from the dataset. Then the distinct tweets from the near duplicate clusters were manually coded by two coders Cohen's Kappa = 0.84) into four categories according to the content: Tweets with URLs, tweets about personal experiences, quotes, or unidentifiable. Discrepancies between two coders were resolved through discussion. Thus, a trained machine learning classifier was created, and the rest 2346 singletons were automatically classified (See Fig. 1).

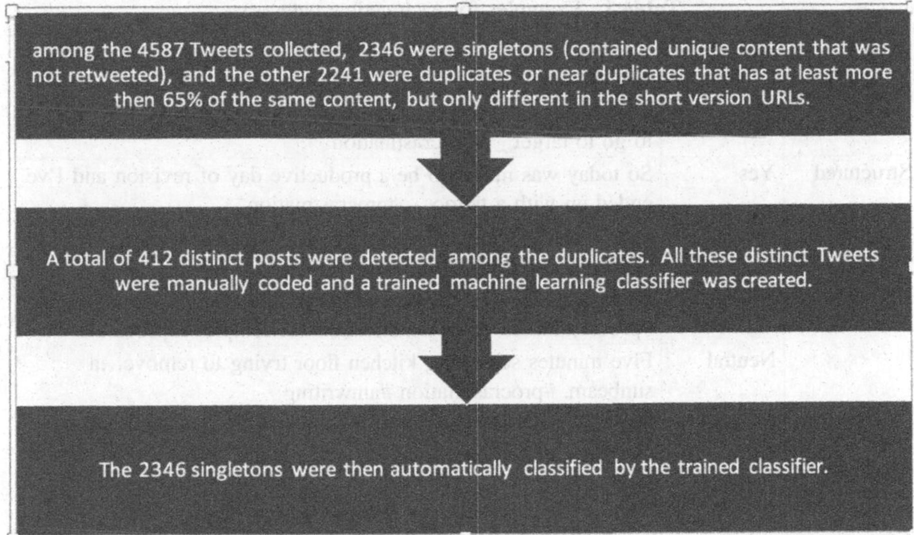

among the 4587 Tweets collected, 2346 were singletons (contained unique content that was not retweeted), and the other 2241 were duplicates or near duplicates that has at least more then 65% of the same content, but only different in the short version URLs.
A total of 412 distinct posts were detected among the duplicates. All these distinct Tweets were manually coded and a trained machine learning classifier was created.
The 2346 singletons were then automatically classified by the trained classifier.

Fig. 1. Working trajectory of data collection and coding

In the personal experience tweets subset, two coders individually coded the 100 Tweets in terms of whether they used ironic tone, whether they constitute structured procrastination, and the impact of the procrastinating behavior. The table below presents the examples of representative Tweets in each coding category.

Specifically, irony was operationalized as incongruity between the actual result of events and the normal or predictable result often has such an effect.

If a tweet mentions more than the target task, instead, it also mentions an alternative activity, it was counted as structured procrastination.

The coders also assess the affective tone of the impact from procrastination described in the tweets. If a tweet complained or blamed this behavior, then it was counted as having a negative impact. Tweets that indicate the efficient or productive results from procrastination were regarded as positive impact. Those didn't have a specific affective direction were marked as neutral (Table 1).

Statistical Testing. After checking each Tweet cluster on personal experience was not from the same IP address in order to assure independent sample, Chi-square test of independence was performed to test the hypotheses. A post hoc test was then performed to further identify the significant cells in the first hypothesis (a 2 by 3 design).

4 Results

In the manually coded near duplicates set, none English Tweets (22 tweets, accounting for 5.34% of all tweets coded) were first excluded. The remaining clusters were the manual coding sample (N = 390). 230 out of 390 (55.83%) tweets consist of URLs, which lead to an outside webpage that provides additional information. There are total

Table 1. Examples for each coding category

Irony	Yes	I'd forgotten the power of homework to get my house clean and errands run… #gradschool #procrastination
	No	I haven't packed for D.C. yet & we leave tomorrow & I still need to go to target _ #procrastination
Structured	Yes	So today was meant to be a productive day of revision and I've ended up with a tattoo… #procrastination
	No	I really need to unpack my house. I just moved here 2 years ago.. #goals #fml #procrastination
Impact	Negative	Spent way too long playing with messenger this morning! #procrastination #lackofmotivation #selfemployedproblems
	Neutral	Five minutes scrubbing kitchen floor trying to remove…a sunbeam. #procrastination #amwriting
	Positive	Just finished a 2-h test in 31 min. _ #procrastination #sadlife #whatiswrongwithme

100 personal experience clusters, accounting for 26% of the all Tweets collected (see Fig. 2).

To answer the first research question, a descriptive analysis was conducted in the personal Tweet clusters and the result showed that the majority of the personal Tweets (52%) presented procrastination to have a neutral impact, that is, no strong positive or negative influence or tone were revealed in those Tweets. Among the rest of Tweets that did have a strong sense of emotion or impact, 37% showed a negative impact from the procrastination, while the rest 11% were positive impact, including efficient use of time when avoiding the primary task or full potency was achieved in a short amount of time before the deadline.

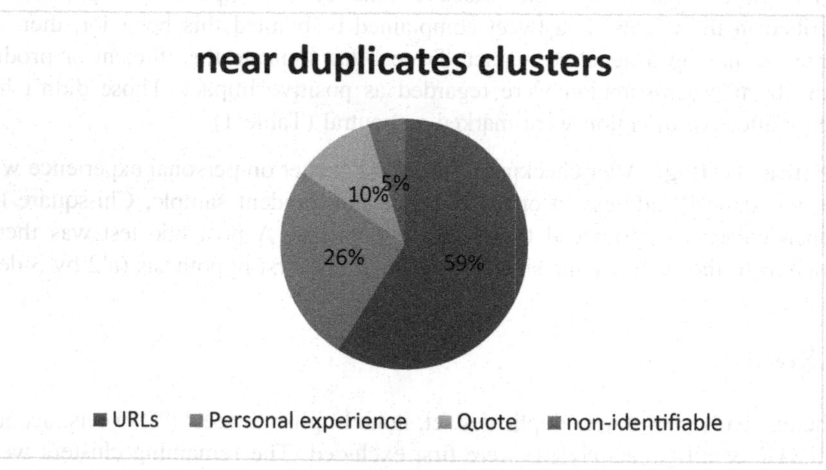

Fig. 2. Configuration of the Tweets clusters

In the personal experience Tweet set, a Chi-square test of independence was performed to examine the relations between the existence of structured procrastination and the impact of procrastination. The relation between these variables was significant, X2 (2, N = 100) = 9.1, p = .01. Hypothesis 1 was supported. Post-hoc test showed that the Tweets mentioned structured procrastination are also more likely to show a positive impact of the procrastination behavior, while the non-structured procrastination Tweets are less likely to have a positive tone (with the adjusted residual of 3.02, p < .01).

A Chi-square test of independence was performed to examine the relations between the use of ironic tone and the existence of structured procrastination. The result shows a significant association between the two variables, X2 (1, N = 100) = 14.55, p < .01. Hypothesis 2 was supported. It was confirmed that in the personal experience Tweets, the use of ironic tone was associated with the presence of structured procrastination. Specifically, Tweets indicating structured procrastination appear to be more likely to use ironies.

5 Discussion

5.1 Personal Experiences

Twitter is a space for self-expression and self-representation. From a user-centric perspective, the value creation is a process of sense making [1]. Tweets of personal experience could be viewed as creative explorations of the self and management of social relationships. In this highly connected social space, users tend present themselves as more socially-desired beings [8, 33].

Though majority (95%) viewed procrastination as a problematic behavior or a time-management failure [4] more than half of personal tweets (52%) on procrastination showed a neutral impact. As Sirois and Kitner contended, procrastination itself could be viewed as adaptive [34]. Ferrari also found procrastination to be a self-handicapping strategy to serve to protect self-esteem and social-esteem [19]. Self-enhancement might be the reason for the inconsistency between the representation of procrastination on Twitter and the common view of this behavior.

Through the representation of structured procrastination [29], many Tweets nearly validate procrastinating behavior through transforming its negativity into a positive and productive effort toward a less intended activity. The findings on the association of structured procrastination and positive impact follows the logic of self-enhancement on social media.

Moreover, for those chose to reveal their lagging behavior, self-blame was usually disguised in a self-ridicule way. In line with the psychological mechanism of self-enhancement, the use of irony in computer-mediated communication may present oneself as a humorous, sophisticated and interesting person [32]. It was not surprising to find 38% of the personal Tweets utilized an ironic tone when discussing procrastination-related topics. Moreover, scholars find that affiliative and self-enhancing humor and irony are healthy and adaptive [34]. As mentioned above, structured procrastination is an alternative way to be productive. Following the same

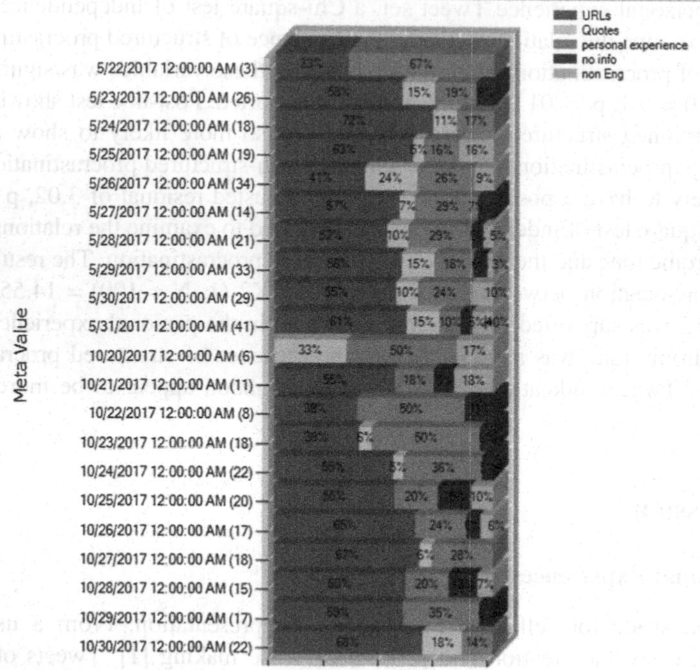

Fig. 3. Date of creation for Tweets in each category

principle, structured procrastination was associated with irony use, both serving to create a more desirable self on Twitter.

Another interesting observation is that among the 20 days the tweets were created (see Fig. 3), there were 4 days that the percentage of Tweets on personal experience particularly higher (greater than 50%). These days were either the beginning or the end of weekdays. For instance, May 22nd and Oct. 23rd, 2017 were Mondays marking the beginning of a new week; while Oct. 20th and 22nd, 2017 were respectively a Friday and Sunday, indicating the end of a week. It seems people tend to reflect on their achievement and assess their progress at critical time nodal points and then make comments about the assessment at those times.

5.2 URLs: Service or Product Promotion

Tweets with URLs are utilizing the networking nature of Twitter, and are mostly about product or service promotion. Such promotion includes: Life coach, training programs or blogs on defeating procrastination, funny videos or make-up tutorials to pass time, and other product promotion videos. Therapies and time management tips are represented in an overly excited tone that procrastination could be cured just through the whatever promotion they are launching. As shown in the chart above, Twitter seems to be a more popular platform for product or service promotion than self-representation. However, this could also due to the various motivations for respective purposes of

Tweets. From an industry perspective, social media allow economic and socio-political value creation. Such marketing purposes could be viewed as "exploitation" of the social affordances by Twitter and to increase "business revenues" [1]. Such promotions also tend to be more fervent.

5.3 Limitations and Future Direction

In the duplicated cluster set, the author used a manual coding strategy. In addition, to further code the semantic properties of the Tweets on personal experience, manual coding is especially stronger in the detection of irony [32]. However, the time and effort consumed by manual coding also confine its power in classifying large amount of data, which is made possible by many social media APIs. Other machine-aided computational methods may have better affordances in address larger dataset. For instance, the classic model of unsupervised topic modelling could be used to identify the frequent co-occurrence of words, and help us understand the emerging topics in the dataset.

The presentation of procrastination is not only understood as an individual behavior, but also as a sociocultural practice and a deliberative performance [26]. Many nuances of this behavior could not be fully uncovered through computational approach. Further discourse analysis of might help future researchers to gain an understanding of the mechanism and motivation for users to disclose about procrastination and how the users choose to represent themselves on social media concerning undesirable behaviors.

5.4 Conclusion

To the knowledge of the author, this study is the first one to empirically examine the representation or self-representation on procrastination on social media. In a nutshell, Twitter provides a space for both industry and user-centric value creation. In this study, more than half of the Tweets with the hashtag #procrastination were for marketing purpose. Among the Tweets sharing personal experience, 52% showed a neutral valence toward this behavior. A frequent theme is structured procrastination, which was more likely to be associated with positive impact and more likely to be put in an ironic tone on Twitter. These findings were in line with the self-enhancement strategy in self-representation on social media. Therefore, while Tweets are organic, generated by users, they are not always so authentic.

References

1. Bechmann, A., Lomborg, S.: Mapping actor roles in social media: different perspectives on value creation in theories of user participation. New Media Soc. **15**, 765–781 (2013)
2. Steel, P., Ferrari, J.: Sex, education and procrastination: an epidemiological study of procrastinators' characteristics from a global sample. Eur. J. Pers. **27**, 51–58 (2013)
3. Harriott, J., Ferrari, J.R.: Prevalence of procrastination among samples of adults. Psychol. Rep. **78**, 611–616 (1996)

4. O'Brien, W.K.: Applying the trans-theoretical model to academic procrastination. Unpublished doctoral dissertation, University of Houston (2002)
5. Jadidi, F., Mohammadkhani, S., Tajrishi, K.Z.: Perfectionism and academic procrastination. Procedia Soc. Behav. Sci. **30**, 534–537 (2001)
6. Schouwenburg, H.C.: Trait procrastination in academic settings: an overview of students who engage in task delays. In: Schouwenburg, H.C., Lay, C., Pylchyl, T., et al. (eds.) Counselling the Procrastinator in Academic Settings, pp. 3–18. American Psychological Association, Washington (2004)
7. Sahin, Y.L.: Comparison of user's adoption and use cases of Facebook and their academic procrastination. Digital Educ. Rev. **25**, 127–138 (2014)
8. McLaughlin, M., Hou, J., Meng, J., et al.: Propagation of information about Preexposure Prophylaxis (PrEP) for HIV prevention through Twitter. Health Commun. **31**, 998–1007 (2016)
9. Steel, P.: The nature of procrastination: a meta-analytic and theoretical review of quintessential self-regulatory failure. Psychol. Bull. **133**, 65–94 (2007)
10. Aremu, A.O., Williams, T.M., Adesina, F.T.: Influence of academic procrastination and personality types on academic achievement and efficacy of in-school adolescents in Ibadan. IFE Psychologia **19**, 93–113 (2011)
11. Abbasi, I.S., Alghamdi, N.G.: The prevalence, predictors, causes, treatment, and implications of procrastination behaviors in general, academic, and work setting. Int. J. Psychol. Stud. **7**, 59–66 (2015)
12. Ferrari, J., Díaz-Morales, J., O'Callaghan, J., et al.: Frequent behavioral delay tendencies by adults. J. Cross Cult. Psychol. **38**, 458–464 (2007)
13. Schraw, G., Wadkins, T., Olafson, L.: Doing the things we do: a grounded theory of academic procrastination. J. Educ. Psychol. **99**, 12–25 (2007)
14. Sirois, F.M., Melia-Gordon, M.L., Pychyl, T.A.: "I'll look after my health, later": an investigation of procrastination and health. Pers. Individ. Diff. **35**, 1167–1184 (2003)
15. Sirois, F.M.: "I'll look after my health, later": a replication and extension of the procrastination-health model with community-dwelling adults. Pers. Individ. Diff. **43**, 15 (2007)
16. Kim, K.R., Seo, E.H.: The relationship between procrastination and academic performance: a meta-analysis. Pers. Individ. Diff. **82**, 26–33 (2015)
17. Tice, D.M., Baumeister, R.F.: Longitudinal study of procrastination, performance, stress, and health: the costs and benefits of dawdling. Psychol. Sci. **8**, 454–458 (1997)
18. Balkis, M., Duru, E.: The evaluation of the major characteristics and aspects of the procrastination in the framework of psychological counseling and guidance. Educ. Sci. Theory Pract. **7**, 376–385 (2007)
19. Ferrari, J.R.: Self-handicapping by procrastinators: protecting self-esteem, social-esteem, or both? J. Res. Pers. **25**, 245–261 (1991)
20. Brinthaupt, T.M., Shin, C.M.: The relationship of cramming to academic flow. Coll. Student J. **35**, 457–472 (2001)
21. Shcheblanova, V., Bogomiagkova, E., Semchenko, T.: The phenomenon of the virtual youth Twitter-community in the discourses of sociological concepts and self-representations. In: Chugunov, A.V., Bolgov, R., Kabanov, Y., Kampis, G., Wimmer, M. (eds.) DTGS 2016. CCIS, vol. 674, pp. 3–13. Springer, Cham (2016). https://doi.org/10.1007/978-3-319-49700-6_1
22. Bargh, J.A., McKenna, K.Y., Fitzsimons, G.M.: Can you see the real me? Activation and expression of the "true self" on the internet. J. Soc. Issues **58**, 33–48 (2002)

23. Orehek, E., Human, L.: Self-expression on social media: do tweets present accurate and positive portraits of impulsivity, self-esteem, and attachment style? Pers. Soc. Psychol. Bull. **43**, 60–70 (2017)
24. Naaman, M., Boase, J., Lai, C.H.; Is it really about me? Message content in social awareness streams. In: Proceedings Computer Supported Cooperative Work 2010. ACM, Savanah (2010). http://infolab.stanford.edu/~mor/research/naamanCSCW10.pdf. Accessed 31 Jan 2018
25. Riemer, K., Richter, A., Seltsikas, P.: Enterprise microblogging: procrastination or productive use? In: AMCIS 2010 Proceedings, p. 506. https://aisel.aisnet.org/amcis2010/506. Accessed 31 Jan 2018
26. Papacharissi, Z.: Without you, I'm nothing: performances of the self on Twitter. Int. J. Commun. **6**, 1989–2006 (2012)
27. Swales, J.M.: Genre Analysis – English in Academic and Research Settings. Cambridge University Press, Cambridge (1990)
28. Yates, J., Orlikowski, W.J.: Genres of organizational communication: a structurational approach to studying communication and media. Acad. Manage. Rev. **17**, 299–326 (1992)
29. Perry, J.: How to procrastinate and still get things done. Chronicle High. Educ. **42**, B3 (1996)
30. Procrastinate. Merriam-Webster. https://www.merriam-webster.com/dictionary/procrastinate. Accessed 31 Jan 2018
31. Kumon-Nakamura, S., Glucksberg, S., Brown, M.: How about another piece of pie: the allusional pretense theory of discourse irony. J. Exp. Psychol. Gen. **124**, 3–21 (1995)
32. Hancock, J.: Verbal irony use in face-to-face and computer-mediated conversations. J. Lang. Soc. Psychol. **23**(4), 447–463 (2004)
33. Berger, J., Milkman, K.: What makes online content viral? J. Market. Res. **49**, 192–205 (2012)
34. Sirois, F.M., Kitner, R.: Less adaptive or more maladaptive? A meta-analytic investigation of procrastination and coping. Eur. J. Pers. **29**(4), 433–444 (2015)

The Essential Role of Innovative Technologies in Assessment and Rehabilitation Settings

Argyris V. Karapetsas(✉), Rozi M. Laskaraki, Aikaterini A. Karapetsa, Andriani G. Mitropoulou, and Maria D. Bampou

University of Thessaly, Argonafton - Filellinon Str., 382 21 Volos, Greece
akar@uth.gr

Abstract. The paper is focused on the significance of Assistive Innovative Technologies to Neuropsychological Assessment and Neurorehabilitation. The purpose of this study was to investigate the usefulness of Technology in clinical assessment and rehabilitation practice for children with Developmental Dyslexia (DD). Participants and Methods: 45 third-, and fourth-grade students with DD and a matched control group (n = 45) participated in this study. At the beginning, students underwent a clinical assessment, including both Electrophysiological [i.e. Event Related Potentials (ERPs) esp. P300 wave-form] and Neuropsychological tests, being conducted in Laboratory of Neuropsychology, at University of Thessaly, in Volos, Greece. Children with DD scored a statistically significant lower performance, compared to that of the typical readers. After assessment, a subgroup of children with dyslexia received Rehabilitation Services. The Rehabilitation Program was specifically designed for children and included digitized musical activities, being converted to sound files, via music training auditory Software programs. Results: The electrophysiological results, obtained after the rehabilitation program revealed that children had similar P300 latency values to that of the typical readers, thus children addressed their difficulties and became successful readers. Conclusions: The outcomes of the current study suggest not only that Technology plays a vital role in both Assessment and Rehabilitation approaches but also, as it continues to move forward, more and more assessment and intervention environments could be designed, providing significant benefits to individuals, thus making humans realize the new opportunities of Science and Technology.

Keywords: Innovative technologies · Dyslexia · ERPs · Rehabilitation · Music

1 Introduction: The Impact of Technology on Healthcare Practices

The paper illustrates some of the ways in which technology improves evaluation, prevents health conditions from occurring and facilitates therapy. Continuous technological developments in healthcare not only contributed to more beneficial and efficient assessment and rehabilitation practices but also improved the quality of life for individuals with disabilities. As it can be supported, Innovative Technologies give the

D. A. Alexandrov et al. (Eds.): DTGS 2019, CCIS 1038, pp. 672–679, 2019.
https://doi.org/10.1007/978-3-030-37858-5_57

means for a new era in assessment and rehabilitation strategies, techniques and interventions. Nowadays professionals are able to have access to a variety of technologies that provide tools for both assessment and clinical intervention settings.

2 Using Technology for Evaluation and Assessment

Numerous scientific data reveal that innovative technologies result in a more comprehensive assessment and a better informed diagnosis and treatment programs [1, 2]. As for the Assessment domain and indeed as for neuropsychological assessment there is clear evidence of growing interest that technological developments play a crucial role, resulting in a more accurate diagnosis. Technological advances have come about in Neuropsychology and contemporary techniques are used for basic and clinical neuroscience applications. Thus, Technology evolution led to the development of neuroimaging and electrophysiological methods used in Assessment settings, providing valuable data brain functions and dysfunctions. Indeed, the spectrum of neuroimaging and electrophysiological mapping such as FMRI, MRI, and Event Related Potentials continues to evolve, thus more and more techniques emerge as a consequence of technology contribution and revolution. Also, these methods expand our understanding not only of the underlying neural mechanisms responsible for a certain disorder but also of the possible remedial effects of rehabilitation programs, designed for certain populations [3, 4]. Indeed, as for the Event Related Potentials, a method used also in our study, scientific data confirm that this method may play a crucial role in evaluating the major deficits that individuals with dyslexia have to cope with but also in assessing the efficiency of interventions, applied to children with dyslexia [5, 6].

Also, apart from neuroimaging - electrophysiological methods and computer - administered tests, significant scientific data revealed the usage of virtual reality-based cognitive assessment which includes computerized versions of traditional paper-and-pencil based tests intergraded into a virtual environment [7]. Furthermore virtual reality has been used in the assessment of cognitive functions such memory, executive functions, attention, learning, in an attempt to better represent cognitive performance with real-world interruptions both in healthy conditions and in individuals with various cognitive disorders [8–10].

3 Modern Technology in Rehabilitation Practices

As for the Rehabilitation practices cost effective various research data support the usage of methods of Computerized rehabilitation, being actually cost effective and achieving great benefits for the patients [11]. Numerous scientific data support the use of technology-based treatment applications available for patients of various disorders [12, 13]. Recent advances in technology – particularly the development of tablet, smartphone or software applications enhance rehabilitation settings and mostly in developed countries, they are gaining ground every day in therapy sessions [14].

The significant role of innovative technologies into intervention practice is confirmed by the existence of rehabilitation robots, virtual reality environments, and software's that have been developed for treatment goals [15, 16]. Indeed, significant data revealed for interventions that use music as auditory training and as music therapy, via software's and other technological components [17–19].This option is analyzed in the current paper, as it presents a rehabilitation program including digitized musical exercises, designed for the treatment of auditory deficits for children with dyslexia.

4 Study

In the current study participated 45 third-, and fourth-grade students with Developmental Dyslexia (DD) and a matched control group (n = 45). At the beginning, the two groups underwent in a clinical assessment, including both Electrophysiological and Psychometric tests, being held in Laboratory of Neuropsychology, at University of Thessaly, in Volos, Greece.

Taking into consideration all the above mentioned data the following research hypotheses had been created:

Hypothesis 1: Children with dyslexia demonstrate cognitive deficits extend linguistic domain.

Hypothesis 2: Dyslexia deficits, as brain dysfunction deficit is able to be detected via Event Related Potentials.

Hypothesis 3: Music intervention, designed to address auditory deficits of children with dyslexia may possible be efficient and have remedial effects for these clinical population.

5 Neuropsychological Assessment

As for the psychometric tests, the following tests have been applied: (a) Raven's Progressive Matrices, (b) A neuropsychological test battery for Specific Learning Disabilities (Prof. Argyris Karapetsas, 2000), (c) Five subtests of Wechsler Intelligence Scale for Children -III (WISC- III): (a) Comprehension, (b) Similarities: (c) Vocabulary (d) Digit Span (e) Block Design, (f) PMMA - Primary Measures of Music Audiation [20] - standardized on Greek population by Stamou [21] (g) Auditory musical discrimination abilities test –A Battery For Measuring Musical Ability (Karapetsas & Laskaraki, 2013). Also, children had been assessed via Electrophysiological recordings and ERPs esp. P300 waveform recordings. The P300 brain potentials are extracted from brain electrical activities as a sign of the underlying electrophysiological brain responses to the external or internal changes and events [22]. ERPs were obtained from 3 electrode sites (both sides of temporal lobe and the center of the brain (T3, Cz, T4) according to the 10–20 International System [23]. Initial assessment's results confirmed statistically significant lower performance for students with DD, compared to the control group. Regarding the neuropsychological tests, students with DD scores indicated auditory processing deficits, working memory deficits, phonological awareness difficulties, musical abilities deficits (deficits in both pitch and rhythm processing) (see Tables 1, 2, 3 and 4). Also, as shown in Table 4, ERPs recordings revealed that students with DD scored longer P300 latencies and not normal cerebral lateralization.

Table 1. Mean values and S.D. for WISC subscales performance for the two groups (children with dyslexia and control group).

WISC subscales	Children with Dyslexia		Control group		Sig.
					p*
	Mean	S.D.	Mean	S.D.	
Similarities	12.40	4.489	16.09	3.579	.000
Block design	9.71	2.951	11.82	2.972	.001
Vocabulary	9.33	2.788	13.09	3.575	.000
Comprehension	9.27	3.564	11.13	3.739	.017
Digit span	8.13	2.793	10.44	3.381	.001

*p < .05

Table 2. Mean values and S.D. for Primary Measures of Music Audiation (PMMA) Tonal subscale performance for the two groups (children with dyslexia and control group).

Group	Mean	S.D.	Sig.
			p*
Control group	75.80	24.514	.000
Children with Dyslexia	50.64	30.206	

*p < .05

Table 3. Mean values and S.D. for Primary Measures of Music Audiation (PMMA) Rhythm subscale performance for the two groups (children with dyslexia and control group).

Group	Mean	S.D.	Sig.
			p*
Control group	70.09	22.635	.000
Children with Dyslexia	41.64	27.812	

*p < .05

Table 4. ERP's esp. P300 latency values (measured in milliseconds - msec) for the two groups (control group & children with dyslexia). ERP's were recorded from central (Cz) left temporal lobe (T3) & right temporal lobe (T4) positions.

Brain region	Children with Dyslexia		Control group		Sig.
	Mean	S.D.	Mean	S.D.	p*
Central area	370.90	9.36	326.09	3.38	.000
Left temporal lobe	378.71	4.06	303.15	10.36	.000
Right temporal lobe	372.85	3.38	318.25	10.85	.000

*p < .05

6 Rehabilitation Program

After the Neuropsychological Assessment, part of the group of children with dyslexia participated in a five – month intervention program, formed in 45-min training sessions, once a week, designed from our Laboratory and focused on auditory cognitive functions training via exercises with musical stimuli. The Auditory Music Training (AMT) included digitized musical exercises, being conducted via music software's and stored as computer sound files. The activities - games aimed to train auditory skills through the perception, discrimination and reproduction of basic music elements such as pitch, rhythm, metre and melody. It is of great significance to be reported that for the design of the auditory games we utilized digital musical instruments and music notation software's that are available and of low cost or free of charge.

7 Results

After the intervention period, children underwent a new ERPs recording for evaluating the efficacy of the intervention. Indeed, Assessment took place one month after the end of the intervention period, so to ensure that the possible observed brain activity alterations would be attributed to the remedial effects of the applied program.

Data analysis revealed that children who participated to AMT recorded shorter, almost similar, latency values to those of the control group, indicating the beneficial effects of the program applied to brain function and consequently to reading. Actually, as shown in Table 5, the two groups (children with DD & control group) achieved similar P300 latencies in all the electroencephalographic sites, being recorded. Also, another promising result was that children after participation achieved normal thus, left hemispheric lateralization, similar to that of the control group.

Table 5. ERP's esp. P300 latency values (measured in milliseconds - msec) for control group & children with dyslexia after their participation to the rehabilitation program). ERP's were recorded from central (Cz) left temporal lobe (T3) & right temporal lobe (T4) positions.

Brain region	Children with Dyslexia		Control group		Sig. *
	Mean	S.D.	Mean	S.D.	
Central area	318.16	19.69	326.09	3.38	.457
Left temporal lobe	313.77	16.37	303.15	10.36	.315
Right temporal Lobe	323.04	19.97	318.25	10.85	.688

*p > .05

Statistical research data confirmed the first research hypothesis, as children with dyslexia scored significant lower not only to linguistic but also to music ability tests that had been applied. Indeed, as for the music tests their lowest performance was in the rhythm subtest of PMMA, which also confirms the high correlation between rhythm skills and reading ability [21]. Also, as for the second research hypothesis seems to be confirmed too, based on the fact that children with dyslexia achieved longer P300 latencies and abnormal lateralization, as these measurements had been recorded via ERPs. The results support that ERPs is a significant clinical tool to evaluate reading abilities and disorders [3, 6]. Finally, as it can be suggested by the current study the third hypothesis was confirmed, as children who participated to the program dis-played normal, thus right lateralization and similar to typical readers of the control group P300 latencies in the post rehabilitation assessment. Music interventions have the potentials to address the reading deficits, and actually the auditory deficits that children with dyslexia display, contributing to alternative rehabilitation approaches for this disorder [25–27].

8 Conclusion

The present study provides evidence that children with DD can be helped by specific interventions and finally overcome their reading impairments. Brain activation profile may be altered and deficits in functional brain organization underlying dyslexia can be reversed and altered, after intensive individualized intervention [24, 25]. In addition, basic skills required for reading acquisition, such as auditory temporal processing and rhythmic skills, seem to be significantly improved through music, making it an important tool in both remediation and early intervention programs [26–29]. Also, as it is also supported by the current study, software's as well as other digital applications have been used with efficiency in rehabilitation of dyslexia and improve appropriate skills for reading [29]. It seems that the applied applications improve basic components of reading such as decoding skills - reading and comprehension [30, 31]. Also, as for music, numerous studies confirm the utilization of computer-assisted versions of musical interventions aimed to improve reading skills in children with reading disorders. Computerized – assisted interventions have the potential to accelerate progress as well as motivate children to perform their utmost ability [1, 2, 32, 33].

As a conclusion, the current paper demonstrates that apart from the social and economic benefits arise from the application of an innovative technology, more and more evidence is revealed that Innovative Technologies will play a major role in the future of both assessment and rehabilitation. Actually, it can be assumed that Innovative Technologies provide new opportunities for a new society, where disability would not be a barrier and patients will be able to cope efficiently with their life's challenges.

References

1. Saini, S., Rambli, D.R.A., Sulaiman, S., Zakaria, M.N., Shukri, S.R.M.: A low-cost game framework for a home-based stroke rehabilitation system. In: 2012 International Conference on Computer & Information Science (ICCIS), vol. 1, pp. 55–60. IEEE (2012)
2. Parsey, C.M., Schmitter-Edgecombe, M.: Applications of technology in neuropsychological assessment. Clin. Neuropsychol. **27**(8), 1328–1361 (2013)
3. Holcomb, P.J., Ackerman, P.T., Dykman, R.A.: Cognitive event-related brain potentials in children with attention and reading deficits. Psychophysiology **22**(6), 656–667 (1985)

4. Houston, R.J., Schlienz, N.J.: Event-related potentials as biomarkers of behavior change mechanisms in substance use disorder treatment. Biol. Psychiatry: Cogn. Neurosci. Neuroimaging **3**(1), 30–40 (2018)
5. Lachmann, T., Berti, S., Kujala, T., Schröger, E.: Diagnostic subgroups of developmental dyslexia have different deficits in neural processing of tones and phonemes. Int. J. Psychophysiol. **56**(2), 105–120 (2005)
6. Jucla, M., Nenert, R., Chaix, Y., Demonet, J.F.: Remediation effects on N170 and P300 in children with developmental dyslexia. Behav. Neurol. **22**(3–4), 121–129 (2010)
7. Parsons, T.D., Courtney, C.G., Arizmendi, B.J., Dawson, M.E.: Virtual reality stroop task for neurocognitive assessment. In: MMVR, pp. 433–439 (2011)
8. Elkind, J.S., Rubin, E., Rosenthal, S., Skoff, B., Prather, P.: A simulated reality scenario compared with the computerized wisconsin card sorting test: an analysis of preliminary results. CyberPsychol. Behav. **4**(4), 489–496 (2001)
9. Albani, G., et al.: Sleep dysfunctions influence decision making in undemented Parkinson's disease patients: a study in a virtual supermarket. In: MMVR, pp. 8–10 (2011)
10. Rajendran, G., Law, A.S., Logie, R.H., Van Der Meulen, M., Fraser, D., Corley, M.: Investigating multitasking in high-functioning adolescents with autism spectrum disorders using the virtual errands task. J. Autism Dev. Disord. **41**(11), 1445–1454 (2011)
11. Mousavi Hondori, H., Khademi, M.: A review on technical and clinical impact of microsoft kinect on physical therapy and rehabilitation. J. Med. Eng. (2014)
12. Koul, R., Corwin, M., Hayes, S.: Production of graphic symbol sentences by individuals with aphasia: efficacy of a computer-based augmentative and alternative communication intervention. Brain Lang. **92**(1), 58–77 (2005)
13. Kizony, R., Zeilig, G., Dudkiewicz, I., Schejter-Margalit, T., Rand, D.: Tablet apps and dexterity: comparison between 3 age groups and proof of concept for stroke re-habilitation. J. Neurol. Phys. Therapy **40**(1), 31–39 (2016)
14. Padmakar, G.S.V., Khosla, A., Chand, K.: Learn easy-android application as a technological intervention for children with dyslexia. In: Emerging Trends in the Diagnosis and Intervention of Neurodevelopmental Disorders, pp. 236–248. IGI Global (2019)
15. Correa, A.G.D., et al.: Computer assisted music therapy: a case study of an augmented reality musical system for children with cerebral palsy rehabilitation. In: Ninth IEEE International Conference on Advanced Learning Technologies. ICALT 2009. IEEE (2009)
16. Ehling, R., et al.: Successful long-term management of spasticity in patients with multiple sclerosis using a software application (APP): a pilot study. Multiple Scler. Relat. Disord. **17**, 15–21 (2017)
17. Hayes, E.A., Warrier, C.M., Nicol, T.G., Zecker, S.G., Kraus, N.: Neural plasticity following auditory training in children with learning problems. Clin. Neuro-Physiol. **114**(4), 673–684 (2003)
18. Kraus, N.: Biological impact of music and software-based auditory training. J. Commun. Disord. **45**(6), 403–410 (2012)
19. Contreras, E.C., Contreras, I.I.: Development of communication skills through auditory training software in special education. In: Advanced Methodologies and Technologies in Modern Education Delivery, pp. 263–275. IGI Global (2019)
20. Gordon, E.E.: Primary Measures of Music Audiation. GIA, Chicago (1979)
21. Stamou, L., Schmidt, C.P., Humphreys, J.T.: Standardization of the Gordon primary measures of music audiation in Greece. J. Res. Music Educ. **58**(1), 75–89 (2010)
22. Haider, A., Fazel-Rezai, R.: Application of P300 event-related potential in brain-computer interface. In: Event-Related Potentials and Evoked Potentials. InTech (2017)

23. Jasper, H.H.: Recent advances in our understanding of ascending activities of the reticular system. In: Jasper, H.H., Proctor, L.D., Knighton, R.S., Noshay, W.C., Costello, R.T. (Eds.) Reticular Formation of the Brain, Oxford, England, Little, Brown (1958)
24. Karapetsas, A.V.: Dyslexia in the child, Re-edition. Volos (2015)
25. Karapetsas, A.: Remediation effects on P300 waveform in school aged children with developmental dyslexia. Dialogues Clin. Neurosci. Ment. Health **1** (2018)
26. Flaugnacco, E., Lopez, L., Terribili, C., Montico, M., Zoia, S., Schön, D.: Music training increases phonological awareness and reading skills in developmental dyslexia: a randomized control trial. PLoS ONE **10**(9), e0138715 (2015)
27. Habib, M., Lardy, C., Desiles, T., Commeiras, C., Chobert, J., Besson, M.: Music and dyslexia: a new musical training method to improve reading and related disorders. Front. Psychol. **7**, 26 (2016)
28. Karapetsas, A.V., Laskaraki, I.R.M.: Special assessment and diagnosis techniques for reading disorders. In: Dyslexia in the Child, pp. 75–90. Re-edition, Volos (2015)
29. Karapetsas, A., Laskaraki, R.: Dyslexia: neuropsychological assessment, diagnosis and intervention. In: 1st Pan-Hellenic Conference on Neuropsychology, Athens (2018)
30. Tucci, R., Savoia, V., Bertolo, L., Vio, C., Tressoldi, P.E.: Efficacy and efficiency outcomes of a training to ameliorate developmental dyslexia using the online software Reading Trainer®. BPA-Appl. Psychol. Bull. (Bollettino di Psicologia Applicata) **63**(273) (2015)
31. Sakamat, N., Sabri, S.N., Diah, N.M.: Multimedia elements of digital storytelling for Dyslexic children. Sci. Res. J. **14**(2), 35–48 (2017)
32. Bonacina, S., Lanzi, P.L., Lorusso, M.L., Antonietti, A.: Improving reading skills in students with dyslexia: the efficacy of a sublexical training with rhythmic background. Front. Psychol. **6**, 1510 (2015)
33. Laskaraki, R., Karapetsa, A.: Neuropsychology of developmental dyslexia: assessment and rehabilitation. In: International Neuropsychological Society 2018 Mid-Year Meeting Bridging Science and Humanity, Prague, 18–20 July 2018

International Workshop on Computational Linguistics

Russian-Tatar Sociopolitical Thesaurus: Basic Structural Correspondences Between the Languages

Alfiia Galieva[1(✉)], Olga Nevzorova[1], and Yuliana Elezarova[2]

[1] Tatarstan Academy of Sciences, Kazan, Russia
amgalieva@gmail.com, onevzoro@gmail.com
[2] Saint Petersburg State University, Saint Petersburg, Russia
yuliana.elezarova@mail.ru

Abstract. The paper presents the main aspects of implementation of the Russian-Tatar Sociopolitical Thesaurus. This resource is inspired by the Russian RuThes project and is built as a hierarchical model of the sociopolitical terminology of Tatar. The thesaurus reflects the logical-semantic organization of lexical items (synonymic, generic, and other relations) on conceptual and lexical levels. Currently it comprises vocabulary related to state government, economy, social life, justice, warfare, culture, religion, sport and some other basic topics.

We developed a set of grammatical models of corresponding Russian-Tatar paired units and analyzed them in terms of semantics and structure. In this paper the main attention is paid to one-component corresponding items. The results of this work are enabling us to improve the quality of bilingual linguistic applications.

Keywords: Thesaurus · Concept · Terminology · The Russian language · The Tatar language · Sociopolitical sphere · Structural correspondences of terms

1 Introduction

Developing Tatar terminology from the viewpoint of the systemic organization of vocabulary, fixing all the variants of terms in a special resource is a task of current interest. A thesaurus reflects the logical-semantic organization of lexical items (synonymic, generic, and other relations), which allows to use formal languages for systematic description of terms. This, in its turn, provides a possibility of using thesauri for automatic text processing tasks.

Available Russian-Tatar dictionaries for special purposes [1, 7, 9, 10, 14] do not provide formal domain models, presenting merely a semantically unstructured, alphabetic list of terminological units. These dictionaries have a limited scope and do not represent the rich variety of term variants functioning in real Tatar texts, being limited to 1-2 variants of a term. Besides, the data of printed dictionaries quickly become outdated, because terminology is currently thriving. So developing an electronic Tatar Thesaurus on the data of actual text collections, with the possibility to update the data, is a topical task.

D. A. Alexandrov et al. (Eds.): DTGS 2019, CCIS 1038, pp. 683–695, 2019.
https://doi.org/10.1007/978-3-030-37858-5_58

The Russian-Tatar sociopolitical thesaurus project [15] is aimed at creating a hierarchical model of Tatar sociopolitical terminology, collecting and systematizing lexical material with succeeding fixation of items as concept names and lexical entries of the thesaurus. This paper focuses on basic structural correspondences between the languages, the main attention being paid to one-component items. Knowing structural correspondences of Russian and Tatar language units is not only of theoretical value; it allows us to improve the quality of bilingual linguistic applications.

The body of the paper is organized as follows. Section 2 explains reasons for choosing the subject domain for the thesaurus, outlines the main features of the sociopolitical sphere and the sociopolitical vocabulary. Section 3 presents the main goals, principles and methodology of compiling the Russian-Tatar Socio-Political Thesaurus. Section 4 describes basic structural correspondences between the languages using the thesaurus data. Section 5 represents quantitative assessment of the current state of the thesaurus. Section 6 lists the conclusions and outlines the prospects of future work.

2 Vocabulary Domain Selection: Sociopolitical Sphere

The sociopolitical sphere embraces politics and international relations, economics and finance, technology and industry, military relations, art, religion, sports, etc.

The sociopolitical sphere is an intermediate zone between the abstract vocabulary which is shared by any subject domain (General Lexicon), often ambiguous and hard to describe, and individual subject domains [11, 13]. The sociopolitical domain concepts are clearly manifested in news articles and news reports provided by general media sources. News articles include discussions related to a large number of specific topics; they contain a lot of domain-specific terms and nomenclature names (*criminal law, investor, inflation, legal act, Ministry of the Interior,* etc.), nevertheless news articles are intended to be apprehensible by non-professionals [5].

Sociopolitical vocabulary comprises a wide range of words denoting realities of the sociopolitical sphere, reflecting the peculiarities of the social structure of the society, ways of organizing the public life of the state, and worldviews of people. Functioning and development of this language subsystem directly or indirectly reflects a wide range of relevant social processes. Sociopolitical vocabulary as well as definitions of sociopolitical terms in dictionaries are strongly influenced by political, ideological and other factors and is historically changeable [18].

Sociopolitical vocabulary can be divided into thematic blocks according to the spheres of use. It covers the terminology of public and municipal administration, economics, law and technology, as well as comprises the most important religious, philosophical, cultural, sociological and other terms denoting realities of great social significance. For example, Dictionary of the Social Sciences, edited by Calhoun [2] is a reference work with over 1700 entries covering topics such as anthropology, sociology, economics, political science, cultural studies, human and cultural geography, and Marxism. Sociopolitical vocabulary also includes the nomenclature names of ministries and state departments, political parties and public movements, administrative and territorial entities, officials executives, etc.

The sociopolitical thesaurus may be extended into any professional subject domain; it may be embedded in various applications related to text analysis to monitor media and social networks, to search and analyze legislation texts, etc. So building a resource on sociopolitical domain for a national language is a base for a formalized description of the lexical system and various terminological subsystems of the given language. A bilingual thesaurus also provides us with an array of reliable empirical data to compare corresponding structural models of terms between the languages.

3 Principles of Designing and Methodology of Compiling the Russian-Tatar Thesaurus

The conceptual scheme of the Russian-Tatar Sociopolitical thesaurus [15], as well as the general principles and methods of modeling the lexical system are borrowed from the Russian RuThes [11, 12, 16] project. Initially, the choice of the RuThes format as the framework for a new bilingual sociopolitical thesaurus was based on the following assumptions:

1. The RuThes thesaurus contains concepts and their lexical filling basing on the Russian language data, which provides ready material for building a bilingual resource;
2. The Russian and Tatar languages are functioning in a common geopolitical space of the Russian Federation, which determines a large number of shared sociopolitical concepts;
3. The Russian language with its lexical-semantic and grammatical structures greatly impacts on present-day Tatar sociopolitical vocabulary;
4. The RuThes format provides a parallelism of conceptual structures of the languages; at the same time it permits to fix language specific features of Tatar linguistic items.

The propriety of these assumptions was proved further during the work on the Tatar part of the thesaurus and in the analysis of the thesaurus data.

The main units in RuThes are concepts (notions) designating significant classes of entities distinguished by human beings in present day social life and in the mental life of people. There are four main types of relationships between concepts in the RuTez thesaurus:

- the genus-species relationship *below-above* is a class-subclass relation, which possesses the properties of transitivity and inheritance;
- the part-whole relationship is used not merely to describe parts of physical objects, but also to denote the internal structure of the concept, including properties or roles for situations;
- the relationship of asymmetric association *asc2* - *asc1* connects two concepts whose connection cannot be described by the relations mentioned above, but neither of them could exist without the other;
- the symmetrical association of *asc* - *asc* connects, in particular, very similar concepts, which the developers did not dare to combine into one concept (for example, cases of presynonymy of items) [11].

In RuThes each concept is linked with a set of language expressions (single words or multiword expressions of different structures) which refer to the concept in texts - lexical entries. So each RuThes concept is represented as a set of synonyms or near-synonyms (plesionyms). RuThes developers use a weaker term, ontological synonyms, to designate words belonging to different parts of speech (like stabilization, to stabilize) and related to different styles and genres; idioms and even free multiword expressions which are potentially synonymous to single words are also included [12]. Ontological synonyms are the most appropriate means to represent cross-linguistic equivalents (correspondences), because such approach allows us to fix units of the same meaning ignoring surface grammatical differences. For example, Table 1 represents basic ways of translating Russian adjective + noun phrases into Tatar.

Table 1. Examples of Russian *adjective + noun* phrases and ways of translating them into Tatar

Russian unit	The structure of Russian unit	Corresponding Tatar unit	The structure of Tatar unit	English translation
графский титул	ADJ + N	граф титулы	N + N, POSS_3	Title of the count
кастовая система	ADJ + N	касталар системасы	N, PL + N, POSS_3	Caste system
авторское право	ADJ + N	авторлык хокукы	N, NMLZ +N, POSS_3	Copyright
общественная иерархия	ADJ + N	иҗтимагый иерархия	Adj + N	Social hierarchy
вооруженные силы	ADJ + N	кораллы көчләр	N, COMIT + N, PL	Military establishment

The design of the Tatar component as a whole preserves the structure of the RuThes thesaurus, i.e. the Tatar component is based on the list of concepts of the RuThes thesaurus, wherein an important step is to check up the parallelism of conceptual structures between the languages. However, the number of lexical entries of concept in Russian and Tatar can vary significantly (Table 2).

Table 2. TECHNICAL REGULATION concept in the Russian-Tatar thesaurus

Id	Concept name in Russian	Lexical entries in Russian	Concept name in Tatar	Lexical entries in Tatar
146128	ТЕХНИЧЕСКОЕ РЕГУЛИРОВАНИЕ 'technical regulation'	техническое регулирование	ТЕХНИК КӨЙЛӘҮ	техник көйләү, техник җайлау, техник яктан җайга салу, техник җайга салу, техник яктан тәртипкә салу

The project of developing the Russian-Tatar Sociopolitical Thesaurus is aimed at compiling the whole body of modern Tatar vocabulary related to the following basic domains: state government, economy, social life, justice, warfare, culture, religion, and sport.

The general methodology of creating the Tatar part of the thesaurus includes the following steps.

1. Search for equivalents (corresponding words) which are actually used in Tatar as translations of Russian words.
2. Adding new concepts representing topics which are important for the sociopolitical and cultural life of the Tatar society and which are not presented in the original RuThes.
3. Revising relations between the concepts considering the place of each new concept in the hierarchy of the existing ones and, if necessary, adding the new concepts of the intermediate level [5].

The Russian-Tatar thesaurus is mainly being compiled by manual translation of terms from the Russian RuThes into Tatar. Also the Tatar language specific concepts and their lexical entries are added, so each part of the Thesaurus – the Russian and Tatar ones - represents a unique language-internal system of lexicalizations. At the same time, the languages are interconnected so that it is possible to proceed from the concepts and words in one language to the corresponding items in the other.

Search for equivalents in the target Tatar language in many cases became a time-consuming task, because available Russian-Tatar dictionaries of general purpose [8] and special dictionaries [1, 7, 9, 10] contain obsolete lexical data.

Text collections of the following Tatar corpora [3, 17] have proved to be extremely helpful. The corpora include texts of various genres, from official documents and scientific publications to media texts, fiction, and textbooks. They are being permanently replenished, which provides a constant inflow of fresh linguistic material. The corpora have comparable volumes, each containing more than 150 million tokens, and are supplied with a system of morphological annotation [17]. The data provided by these corpora allow us to acquire reliable information on meanings, typical contextual relations and frequency of use of Tatar words, which is a necessary stage in compiling a thesaurus. If the target language units we need were not found in any source (the main reason for this is an insufficient degree of Tatar terminology development) we provided our own translation to fix the term in the Russian-Tatar thesaurus relying upon the rules and models detected during the thesaurus compilation.

To represent the lexical data consistently and in a systemic way, we developed requirements to translate concept names and lexical entries. We have worked out the following basic requirements for translating concept names:

- the meaning of the concept should be clear from its designation;
- when defining a concept, neutral and common vocabulary should be used;
- if there are options (lexical and phraseological doubles), priority should be given to the designation that reflects the concept in the most accurate way while being the most concise one, and, if this does not contradict the former conditions, a choice should be made in favor of the most frequently and officially used item.

If the concept name is ambiguous, it is provided with necessary comments in brackets (see Table 3).

Table 3. Ambiguous designations as concept names

Concept name in the Russian part of the thesaurus	Concept name in the Tatar part of the thesaurus	English translation
РОД (ГРУППА ЛЮДЕЙ)	ЫРУ	Genus (a group of people)
КУЛАК (КРЕСТЬЯНИН)	КУЛАК	Kulak (wealthy peasant using hired labor)
РУКОВОДСТВО (УЧЕБНОЕ ПОСОБИЕ)	КУЛЛАНМА	Guidance, tutorial
УЧЕНИК (НАЧИНАЮЩИЙ РАБОТНИК)	ӨЙРӘНЧЕК	Apprentice
ПРИСТАВКА (МОРФЕМА)	АЛКУШЫМЧА	Prefix

In thesaurus compilation a separate task is to build the most complete list of language units related to the same concept. We found that a distinguishing feature of contemporary Tatar lexicon is a great deal comprised of absolute synonyms which emerged due to a combination of intralinguistic and extralinguistic factors. We disclosed social and linguistic causes of the emergence of synonyms, described the main structural types of synonymous items, and presented corpus data on their frequency, with special papers elucidating this issue [4, 6].

4 Basic Structural Correspondences in the Thesaurus

The Russian-Tatar thesaurus provides us with reliable data about structural correspondences between Russian and Tatar linguistic items, which may be studied in terms of derivational and syntactic structure. We developed a set of grammatical models of corresponding Russian-Tatar and paired units and analyzed them in terms of semantics and structure. Basic ways of expressing Russian one-component items in Tatar are represented in Table 4.

The Russian-Tatar thesaurus data evidence that the option of Tatar translation is impacted by peculiarities of both semantic and grammatical systems of the target language. For example, the missing in Tatar lexical-grammatical class of collective nouns sets restrictions on the choice of Tatar equivalents; Russian collective nouns are conveyed by Plural forms in Tatar: *дворянство 'nobility, gentry'* – *дворяннар 'noblemen'*, *крестьянство 'peasantry'* – *крестьяннар 'peasants'*, *духовенство 'clergy'* – *дин әhелләре 'clerics'*, *молодежь 'youth, young people'* – *яшьләр 'young people'*.

Table 4. Basic ways of translating Russian one-component units

Russian lexeme	The structure of the Russian unit	Corresponding Tatar units	The structure of the Tatar unit
Царь 'king, tsar'	One-rooted word	*патша*	One-rooted word
Герцог 'duke'	Loanword, one-rooted word	*герцог*	Loanword, one-rooted word
Крестоносец 'crusader'	Two-rooted word	*тәре йөртүче*	calque ('cross' + 'carrier')
Женщина 'woman'	One-rooted word	*хатын-кыз*	Co-compound noun ('woman' + 'girl')
Колзозник 'collective farmer'	One-rooted word	*колхозчы*	Semicalque
Перевенец 'firstborn'	One-rooted word	*беренче бала*	Combination of words ('first' + 'child')
Глухонемой 'deaf and dumb'	Two-rooted word	*саңгырау-телсез*	Co-compound adjective ('deaf ' + 'dumb')
Домохозяйка 'housewife'	Two-rooted word	*хуҗабикә*	Two-rooted word ('owner' + 'mistress')
Ужаснуться 'to be horrified'	One-rooted word	*кот алыну*	Compound verb
Торжествовать 'to triumph'	One-rooted word	*тантана итү*	Compound verb

Russian Pluralia tantum nouns are translated by Tatar nouns without the Plural affix: качели 'teeter board' (PL) – таган 'teeter board' (SG);

брюки 'trousers, pants' (PL) – чалбар 'trousers, pants' (SG).

However in some cases there may be exceptions caused by calquing:

каникулы 'vacation' (PL) – каникуллар 'vacation' (PL), каникул 'vacation' (SG).

We distinguished classes of Russian words which correspond to compounds (two-component items) in Tatar.

1. Two-rooted Russian words, as a rule, are translated by two-word or multiword expressions:

   крестоносец 'crusader' – *тәре йөртүче*,
   первоклассник 'first-former' – *беренче сыйныф укучысы*,
   законотворчество 'lawmaking' – *закон чыгару*,
   законопроект 'bill, law project'– *закон проекты*,
   налогообложение 'taxation' – *салым салу*.

2. Russian lexical units containing a prefix, as a rule, have descriptive translation:

   вы*резать* 'to exterminate by massacre' – *кырып бетерү*,
   от*купиться* 'to pay off' – *түләп котылу*,
   об*весить 'to give short weight'* –*киметеп үлчәү*,
   до*плата* 'surcharge, extra fee' – *өстәмә түләү*,

***сверхъ**естественный* 'supernatural' – *гайре табигатле,*
***при**рожденный* 'inborn' – *тумыштан килгән,*

Prefixation is an essential way of word formation and verb inflection in Russian. The Tatar language has right-branching agglutinative morphology without any affixes placed before the stem, so Russian prefixal elements (both derivational and inflectional ones) are conveyed in Tatar by means of individual words, depending on the meaning of the Russian word's structural elements and the word's meaning as a whole.

3. Many Russian deverbal nouns are conveyed into Tatar by means of compound verbal nouns, formed by a basic notional component (most often noun) and an auxiliary verb:

   покупка 'purchase' – *сатып алу,*
   разрешение 'permission' – *рөхсәт итү,*
   извещение 'notification' – *хәбәр итү,*

4. Many Russian concepts with a rich specific meaning have no direct equivalents in the Tatar language, so they require an explicit expression:

   холеный 'soigné' – *бик каралган,*
   землистый 'earthy' – *аксыл соры, җир төсендәге,*
   рассудительный 'reasonable, judgmatical' – *уйлап эш итүчән.*

In general, at the level of concept names, the thesaurus data shows such a picture: 783 one-component Russian words are translated into Tatar as multiword items, composed of two and more components. At the same time merely 17 Tatar one-component items are translated into Russian by multiword items (for example, *игрок нападения 'attack* player*'* – *һөҗүмче, внешний облик* 'appearance' – *кыяфәт*). Such disproportion can be explained by the fact that the RuThes thesaurus represents the Russian language lexicalizations, so, in future, as we expand the original Tatar lexicon, the disproportion will be smoothed out.

We carried out a comparative study of basic word formation means of the Russian and Tatar languages. Tatar agglutinative morphology implies a greater uniformity of derivational means. A direct consequence of this is that a Tatar affix may cover a whole group of Russian word-forming suffixes. For example, the Tatar *-lık/-lek* affix that forms words of abstract meaning corresponds to a set of Russian and international suffixes. The Tatar derivational affix -çı/-çe also structurally corresponds to a number of Russian suffixes denoting persons by their activity or some specific characteristics. The Tatar -u/-ü, affix which forms names of actions, may structurally correspond to Russian suffixes building the infinitive of verbs or verbal nouns of different structures. Table 5 represents some examples of Russian and Tatar words illustrating this statement.

Table 5. Examples of Russian suffixes and corresponding Tatar derivational affixes

Russian suffixes	Tatar affix	Russian example	Tatar example	English translations
-от(а)	*-lık/-lek*	*слепота*	*сукырлык*	Blindness
-ость		*инвалидность*	*инвалидлык*	Disability
-ств(о)		*губернаторство*	*губернаторлык*	Governorship
-к(а)		*голодовка*	*ачлык (игълан итү)*	Hunger strike
null suffix		*голод*	*ачлык*	Famine
-изм		*национализм*	*милләтчелек*	Nationalism
-аж		*шпионаж*	*шпионлык*	Espionage
-чик	*-çı/-çe*	*пикетчик*	*пикетчы*	Picket participant
-щик		*погромщик*	*тетүче*	Pogrom-maker
-ник		*мятежник*	*фетнәче*	Insurgent
-тель		*законодатель*	*закон чыгаручы*	Legislator
-ист		*расисит*	*расачы*	Racist
-нер		*оппозиционер*	*оппозицияче*	Oppositionist
-тор		*арендатор*	*арендачы*	Tenant
-ир		*конвоир*	*конвойчы*	Convoy guard
-ит		*ваххабит*	*ваhhабичы*	Wahhabi
-ить	*-и/-й*	*узаконить*	*законлаштыру*	To legalize
-ниj(е)		*акционирование*	*акционерлаштыру*	Corporatization
-ация		*либерализация*	*либеральләштерү*	Liberalization
null suffix		*обыск*	*тенту*	To seek through

As we mentioned above, the RuThes thesaurus framework is based on fixing the so called ontological synonyms, which enables to designate linguistic items denoting concepts regardless of their surface realization in a language. Such an approach facilitates fixing items of different parts of speech as lexical entries of the same concept.

In Tatar, like in other Turkic languages, relative adjectives are loan words that come from different languages (Russian, Arabic, Persian, etc.), and a large number of Russian adjectives in the Tatar language have no equivalents of the same structure. So in many cases Russian *adjective + noun* phrases correspond to a grammatical pattern composed of two nouns in Tatar:

государственный контракт 'government contract' (ADJ + N) – *дәүләт контракты* (N + N, POSS_3);

детский сад 'kindergarten' (ADJ + N) – *балалар бакчасы* (N, PL + N, POSS_3).

So an approach based on finding ontological synonyms, allows us to link Russian nouns and their adjectival derivatives as the same concept. Table 6 illustrates the approach by giving examples of concepts which Russian lexical entries include as relative adjectives, whereas the corresponding Tatar items include or do not include relative adjectives.

Table 6. Russian concepts including relative adjectives and their Tatar translations

Concept name in Russian	Russian lexical entries	Concept name in Tatar	Tatar lexical entries	Presence of the Tatar relative adjective
КНЯЗЬ (ТИТУЛ) 'prince'	князь, княжеский, владетельный князь	КЕНӘЗ (ТИТУЛ)	князь, кенәз	No
РЕДАКТОР 'editor'	редактор, редакторша, редакторский	МӨХӘРРИР	Мөхәррир, редактор	No
ЕПИСКОП 'bishop'	епископ, епископский	ЕПИСКОП	епископ, әскаф	No
БУРЖУАЗИЯ 'bourgeoisie'	буржуазия, буржуазный	БУРЖУАЗИЯ	буржуазия, буржуаз	Yes
СИОНИЗМ 'Zionism'	сионизм, сионистский, сионистический	СИОНИЗМ	сионизм, сионист, сионистик	Yes

Russian two-component compound items are characterized by different ways of translating into Tatar, and ways of translating depend on the meaning of the whole compound, its structure and component's relationship both on semantic and structural levels. Ways of translating compound terms will be discussed in a separate paper.

5 Current State of the Russian-Tatar Sociopolitical Thesaurus: Quantitative Assessment

We carried out a quantitative study of the composition of the thesaurus at the level of concept names and lexical entries. Table 7 gives a brief overview of concepts and lexical entries of the Russian and Tatar parts of the thesaurus.

Table 7. Quantitative assessment of basic thesaurus units

Basic quantitative characteristics	Russian	Tatar
Number of concepts in the sample	5,490	5,490
Number of lexical entries, total	23,483	19,334
Number of words, total	38,074	38,373
Average number of lexical entries of a concept	4,277	3,552
Average length of a lexical entry, in words	1,621	1,985

The quantitative distribution of 100 most frequent word forms is also presented in Fig. 1 as a word cloud; in this case, functional words, including auxiliary verbs and participles, were not removed from the sample.

Fig. 1. The most frequently used word forms on the material of lexical entries

The Russian-Tatar Sociopolitical thesaurus contains about 10,000 concepts in the Tatar part of the thesaurus, 6000 of them provided with lists of lexical entries. Table 8 provides general information on the composition and structure of concept names in the Russian-Tatar Sociopolitical thesaurus.

Table 8. General information on concept names structure in the Russian-Tatar thesaurus

Data on concept names	Quantitative data
General number of concept names in the thesaurus	10000
Concept names containing comments in brackets, in the Russian part	959
Concept names containing comments in brackets, in the Tatar part	667
Concept names containing comments in brackets, both in the Russian and Tatar parts	459
One-component concept names, in Russian: – without comments – containing comments	3214 2269 945
One-component concept names, in Tatar: – without comments – containing comments	2520 1989 531
One component concept names in both languages	1593
Two-component concept names, in Russian: – without comments – containing comments	4024 4018 7
Two-component concept names, in Tatar: – without comments – containing comments	3995 3918 77
Multiword (three or more components) concept names in Russian	1164
Multiword concept names (three or more components) in Tatar	1723

So available thesaurus data evidences that one-component concept names in the Russian part of the thesaurus is 27.5% more than in the Tatar part, number of two component items is approximately equal, and multiword concept names prevail in the Tatar part. A significant number of Russian single terms have multiword equivalents in Tatar. Concept names containing comments in brackets, in the Russian part of the thesaurus is 30.5% more than in the Tatar part, we can assume that adding word to Tatar concept names, in many cases we disambiguate them. This question requires further research in future.

6 Conclusion

Building the Russian-Tatar Sociopolitical thesaurus is aimed at fixing all Tatar single words and multiword items related to the sociopolitical sphere, with their Russian equivalents. The bilingual resource is developed on the basis of the Russian RuThes thesaurus. Both thesauri are implemented as a hierarchy of concepts viewed as units of thinking. Each concept is linked with a set of language expressions (single words and multiword expressions) which refer to it in texts (lexical entries). The available thesaurus data provide us with reliable linguistic evidence about items related to sociopolitical sphere in the Russian and Tatar languages.

We developed a set of grammatical models of corresponding Russian-Tatar paired lexical items and analyzed them in terms of semantics and structure. We distinguished classes of Russian words which correspond to compounds (two or more component items) in Tatar. In particular, Russian lexemes composed of two stems and Russian prefixed words are, as a rule, translated into Tatar as compound words.

A comparative study of main derivational means of the Russian and Tatar languages shows that Tatar agglutinative morphology implies a greater uniformity of derivational means. So a Tatar affix covers a set of synonymous Russian word-forming suffixes. The comparative study of Russian and Tatar word formation models and derivational morphemes is to be continued.

Russian compound items are differently translated into Tatar, and ways of translating depend on the meaning of the whole multiword item, its structure and components' relationships both on semantic and structural levels. Ways of translating compound terms require further research.

The study of derivational marking of identical concepts in the Russian and Tatar languages enables to clarify the structural and typological description of the Tatar language. From a practical point of view, the result of such analysis may be used to improve bilingual Russian-Tatar linguistic applications. It should be mentioned that we used the discovered regularities and trends to replenish and improve the data of the Tatar part of the thesaurus, and the work is underway.

List of Abbreviations

ADJ adjective
COMIT Comitative
N noun

NMLZ	nominalizer
PL	Plural
POSS_3	Possessive, 3d person
SG	Singular

References

1. Amirov, K.: Russko-tatarskij yuridicheskij slovar' [Russian-Tatar Legal Dictionary]. Tatar Publishing House, Kazan (1996)
2. Calhoun, C. (ed.): Dictionary of the Social Sciences. Oxford University Press, New York (2002)
3. Corpus of Written Tatar. http://corpus.tatar/. Accessed 21 Dec 2018
4. Galieva, A.: Synonymy in modern tatar reflected by the Tatar-Russian socio-political thesaurus. In: Čibej, J., Gorjanc, V., Kosem, I., Krek, S. (eds.) Proceedings of the XVIII EURALEX International Congress: Lexicography in Global Contexts, Ljubljana, pp. 585–994 (2018)
5. Galieva, A., Kirillovich, A., Loukachevitch, N., Nevzorova, O., Suleymanov, D., Khakimov, B.: Toward domain-specific Russian-Tatar thesaurus construction. In: Bolgov, R., Borisov, N., Smorgunov, L., Tolstikova, I., Zakharov, V. (eds.) Internet and Modern Society: Proceedings of the International Conference IMS-2017 (St. Petersburg; Russian Federation, 21–24 June 2017), ACM International Conference Proceeding Series, pp. 120–124. ACM Press, New York (2017)
6. Galieva, A., Nevzorova, O., Yakubova, D.: Russian-Tatar Socio-political thesaurus: methodology, challenges, the status of the project. In: Angelova, G., et al. (eds.) International Conference Recent Advances in Natural Language Processing, pp. 245–252. INCOMA Ltd., Varna (2017)
7. Gallyamov, R.F.: Russko-tatarskij tolkovyy slovar' istoricheskikh terminov [Russian-Tatar Explanatory Dictionary of Historical Terms]. Magarif, Kazan (2006)
8. Ganiev, F. (ed.): Russko-tatarskij slovar' [Russian-Tatar Dictionary]. Insan, Moscow (1997)
9. Ganiev, F.A., Nizamov, I.M. (eds.): Russko-tatarskij obshchestvenno-politicheskij slovar'. Tatar Publishing House, Kazan (1997)
10. Garifullin, N.K.: Menedzhment: russko-tatarskij tolkovyy slovar' [Management: Russian-English-Tatar explanatory dictionary]. Magarif, Kazan (2010)
11. Loukachevitch, N.V.: Tezaurusy v zadachah informacionnogo poiska [Thesauri in information retrieval tasks]. Publishing House of Moscow State University, Moscow (2011)
12. Loukachevitch, N., Dobrov, B.: RuThes linguistic ontology vs. Russian wordnets. In: Proceedings of the Seventh Global Wordnet Conference, pp. 154–162. University of Tartu Press, Tartu (2014)
13. Loukachevitch, N., Dobrov, B.: The sociopolitical Thesaurus as a resource for automatic document processing in Russian. Terminology **21**(2), 237–262 (2015)
14. Nizamov, I.: Kratkij russko-tatarskij obshchestvenno-politicheskij slovar' [Brief Russian-Tatar Socio-Political Dictionary]. Tatar Publishing House, Kazan (1995)
15. Russian-Tatar Sociopolitical Thesaurus. http://tattez.turklang.tatar/. Accessed 21 Dec 2018
16. RuThes Linguistic Ontology. http://www.labinform.ru/pub/ruthes/index_eng.htm. Accessed 21 Dec 2018
17. Tatar National Corpus. http://tugantel.tatar/?lang=en. Accessed 21 Dec 2018
18. Veisbergs, A.: Defining political terms in lexicography: recent past and present. In: Euralex 2002 Proceedings, pp. 657–667 (2002)

Quantitative Analysis of Frequency Dynamics of Synonymic Dominants

Valery Solovyev(✉), Vladimir Bochkarev, and Anna Shevlyakova

Kazan Federal University, Kazan, Russia
maki.solovyev@mail.ru, vbochkarev@mail.ru,
anna_ling@mail.ru

Abstract. Traditionally, it is believed in linguistics that the center of any semantic field is more stable than the periphery. Quantitative testing of this hypothesis has become possible due to creation of large diachronic text corpora. The article describes the results of quantitative analysis of "central elements" (semantic dominants) of 82 synonymic sets, which were taken from a dictionary by Yu.D. Apresyan. First, we identified the most frequent words in each synonymic set. Then, we analysed the dynamics of their frequency over the two centuries, according to the Google Books Ngram corpus. It was found that the semantic dominants show a statistically significant tendency to decrease in frequency with respect to other members of the synonymic sets. It was also shown that frequency of the synonymic dominants is more stable in comparison with randomly selected words which have a close frequency.

Keywords: Corpus linguistics · Synonyms · Google Books Ngram · Prototype words · Frequency approach

1 Introduction

The use of large text corpora and methods of computational linguistics makes it possible to obtain quantitative estimates of phenomena, which were previously established at a qualitative level. Quantitative research covers a wide range of issues from sociology [1, 2] and psychology [3, 4] to historical linguistics [5, 6]. However, absence of large diachronic corpora inhibited studies of evolutionary processes.

The number of such studies has increased dramatically due to creation of the Google Books Ngram [7] corpus in 2010. This corpus has a convenient service for visualizing frequencies of words and phrases (https://books.google.com/ngrams). Recently, a number of studies on quantitative verification of the laws of evolution of vocabulary have been performed. The obtained results were questionable and even contradictory.

The law of conformity, which says that frequently used words are less prone to change in semantics was studied in [8] based on the Google Books Ngram corpus and COHA (Corpus of Historical American English) [9]. According to [8], the law of conformity is formulated as "the rate of semantic change scales with an inverse power-law of word frequency". One of the possible explanations proposed in [8] is that people can use rare words incorrectly, in wrong contexts, which can lead to a greater

D. A. Alexandrov et al. (Eds.): DTGS 2019, CCIS 1038, pp. 696–707, 2019.
https://doi.org/10.1007/978-3-030-37858-5_59

variability of their semantics. The law of conformity was indirectly confirmed in [10]. It was shown that the degree of change in the frequency of words decreases when their frequency grows. In fact, the power dependence was established between the frequency of words and the degree of variability of their frequency. However, the law of conformity was not confirmed in [11, 12]. It is said in [11, 12] that frequency of a word has almost no effect on its tendency to semantic changes.

One more law is established in [11]: "the law of innovation—independent of frequency, words that are more polysemous have higher rates of semantic change".

However, it was not confirmed in [12, 13]. The possible reason for this is difference in research methodology. In [11], a distributional semantic model was used to identify and quantify semantic change, while in [13] the WordNet thesaurus was used for these purposes (https://wordnet.princeton.edu/).

Different rate of change in semantics of words belonging to different parts of speech was described in [11]. It is stated in this paper that frequency of verbs changes faster than frequency of nouns, and frequency of nouns changes faster than that of adjectives. The opposite result was obtained in [13]: verbs change more slowly than nouns and adjectives. The results of these works were obtained using different research methods and it remains unclear which of these methods is correct.

Let us refer to another law studied in [11, 12]. It is the law of prototypicality, which says that "the degree of prototypicality of a word within its semantic cluster correlated inversely with its likelihood of change (the diachronic prototypicality effect)".

In this case, the authors of [11] indicated in a subsequent article [12] that there were methodological errors in their previous work (assumption of word independence in the regression model) and stated that the diachronic prototypicality effect was much less pronounced than they previously established.

There are some other weak points in [11, 12] that should be considered. Some study parameters were chosen arbitrarily, without any reasoning. For example, the study concerned only 6.000 of the most frequent words, and it was not explained why this number was chosen. However, this is only a very small part of the lexicon of the language. For example, the Oxford English Dictionary currently contains more than 600.000 words (http://www.oed.com/). It remains completely unclear how the prototypicality effect will manifest itself if a larger group of words is studied.

The study method is described incompletely in these works. In these papers, the selected set of words is divided into clusters with reference to the previous work by these authors [14]. However, there is no exact description of the research methodology in this work. In particular, the applied clustering algorithm was not specified. It is well known that there is no ideal clustering algorithm. Different results are obtained using different algorithms. For this reason, such results cannot be obtained again. Thus, the question of the existence and degree of the prototypicality effect remains open.

There is no generally excepted terminology and methodological consistency in this sphere of computer linguistics (see [15] for more details). It should be noted that the problem of results reproducibility exists in modern science [16]. In [17], as a result of large-scale reverifications of scientific results in psychology, it was shown that only 36% of repeated experiments showed results that coincided with the data of the primary research. All this indicates the need for increased attention to the research methodology, a detailed description of the conducted numerical experiments to ensure the verifiability of the research results.

The work objective was to develop the research method, which can be applied in further studies, and consider the effect of prototypicality from another point of view. The theory of prototype was widely developed in the 20th century. G. Lakoff introduced his own classification of prototypes. “Typical example” is one type of prototypes [18]. In our work, by “typical example” we understand a semantic dominant. The semantic dominant is the most representative word in the synonymic set, which reflects cultural realities. The dominant has the most common meaning in the synonymic set and is the most neutral lexeme, which is used more often than other words of the set and can be found in a wider range of contexts.

Synonyms form a semantic field. The semantic dominant is in the centre of this field, it is more central than other members of the synonymic set. The periphery is opposed to the centre. By periphery we understand a group of synonyms which frequency is significantly lower than that of other members of the synonymic set because they have more specific meaning. It is believed in linguistics that the centre is used more frequently and its changes are of more regular character than that of the periphery. But this theory was not confirmed since there is no reliable quantitative evidence of this effect. Therefore, we made an attempt to verify this theory using extra-large text corpora.

The study is performed on the material of the Russian language. The Google Books Ngram data were used for the analysis. There is a critical attitude to the Google Books Ngram project in a number of publications. They describe such disadvantages as lack of full texts, lack of data about text types, genres and registers. Without going into details of the discussions on these issues, we note that the absence of full texts is not essential within the framework of the methodology used in this paper, since the analysis is based on the comparison of word frequencies. Possible changes in text genre, style and composition can be a more significant problem. However, we analyze groups of close synonyms and the above-mentioned factors influence them in equal measure. Since the analysis is not based on the frequencies of the synonyms themselves, but on changing of their ratios, we expect that change in the corpus composition will not lead to a qualitative change in the conclusions.

Section 2 describes the method and provides numerical results of the experiments. The results are discussed in Sect. 3.

2 Method and Results

Methods of cluster analysis do not provide 100% reliable results. As an alternative, our work considers synonymic sets described in the most authoritative dictionary of synonyms by Apresyan [20]. The dictionary has been compiled over years by a team of recognized experts on lexical semantics and is based on classic works of Russian literature, as well as on works of contemporary writers.

It is widely used in modern linguistic studies (Google offers 145 thousand links to it). In this paper, we analyse synonymic sets from the first volume of this dictionary. Some synonymic sets were not analysed, mainly because they included homonyms. It is possible to determine a synonymic dominant by means of computer linguistics. However, it can be incorrect and goes beyond the scope of this study. As a result, 92 synonymic sets were selected, representing the following parts of speech: nouns, adjectives, verbs, adverbs, pronouns, numerals and prepositions. A complete list of synonymic sets is given in the appendix. Google Books Ngram was used to trace the evolution of synonymic sets over two centuries: from 1800 to 2008. The corpus data before 1800 are not enough for statistically significant conclusions.

We used data from the Russian sub-corpus of Google Books Ngram (version of 2012). Relative frequencies of words were calculated using the raw data obtained from the project website. We considered only vocabulary 1-grams which are words consisting of letters of the Russian alphabet and, probably, one apostrophe. In Google Books Ngram, words which differ by keyboard case are considered to be different 1-grams. However, we calculated the total relative frequency of words not taking into account case differences. Lemmatization was not used because, when calculating the average frequencies of the lemmas, distortions may occur due to homonymy.

When calculating frequencies, we considered the change in word spelling, which was due to the reform of Russian orthography held in 1918. As noted above, the synonymic dominant (prototype) is, as a rule, the most frequent element of the semantic field. The discussion concerning prototypicality and frequency was described in [19]. The study algorithm was the following. The most frequent word was determined in each synonymic raw in the interval 1800–1809 (total). This word was considered as a dominant. We formulated two null hypotheses. Hypothesis 1. Since frequency of the dominant varies insignificantly, frequencies of most dominants cannot significantly change. Hypothesis 2. If there are any changes in frequency of the synonymic dominants, these changes are random and frequencies can either increase or decrease (by 2000). This hypothesis was argued in [21]. In [21], the synonymic set {*стараться, пытаться, пробовать, силиться (starat'sja, pytat'sja, probovat', silit'sja)*} was considered. It was shown that co-occurence of the dominant of this synonymic set (the word *стараться (starat'sja)*) changes and, as a result, its frequency changes: it falls approximately 10 times (see Fig. 1).

Eighty-two synonymic sets out of ninety-two were analysed because the words belonging to the rest 10 synonymic sets were not found in the Google Books Ngram corpus at the beginning of the XIX century. The analysed sets contain 326 words. There are 2–9 words in each set (see Appendix). The percentage of use of the dominant of each synonymic set is calculated considering percentage of use of all members of the set. There can be three scenarios. 1. The percentage of use of the synonymic dominant significantly decreases. 2. The percentage of use of the synonymic dominant does not significantly change (it can vary in frequency for 10%). 3. The percentage of use of the synonymic dominant increases. Figure 2 shows examples of these scenarios.

If one analyses the graphs visually, it can be seen that the relative frequency of the centre decrease in 60% of cases, increases in 10% of cases and stays almost the same in 30% of cases. Tendency of the dominant frequencies to decrease seems obvious. However, it is required to introduce numerical characteristics of this process. Change in

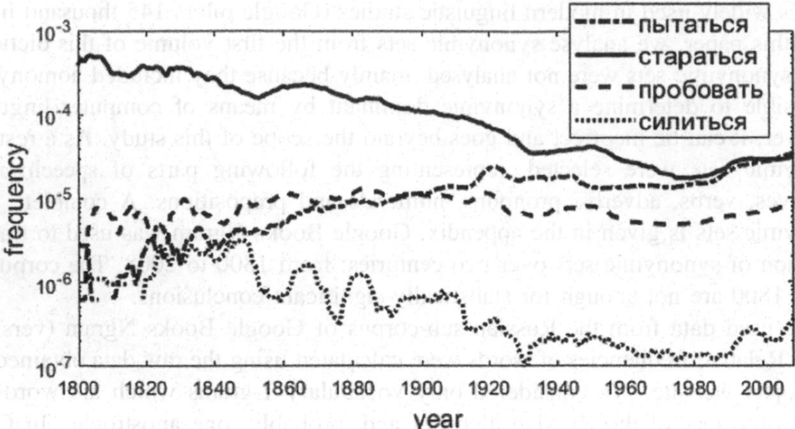

Fig. 1. Frequency decrease of the word *стараться* (starat'sja) compared to frequencies of other members of the synonymic set: *пытаться* (pytat'sja), *пробовать* (probovat'), *силиться* (silit'sja)

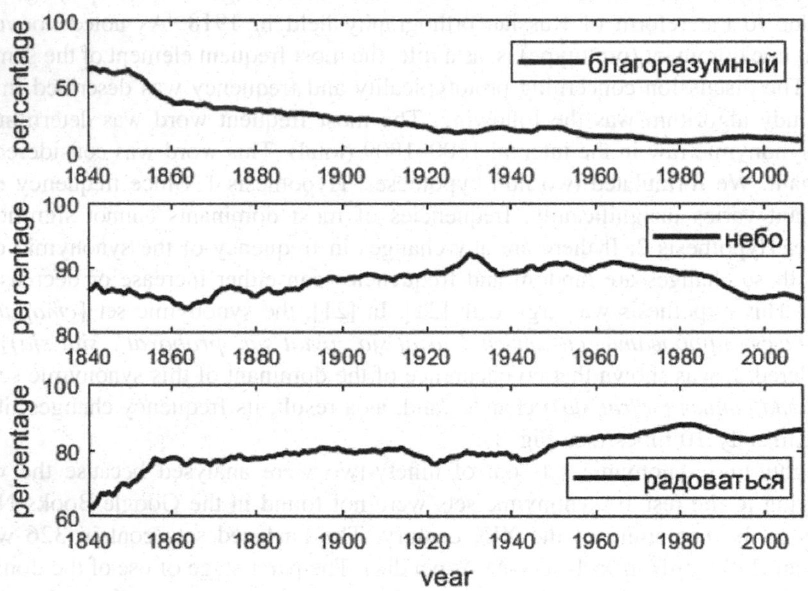

Fig. 2. Change in frequency use of the dominants благоразумный (blagorazumnyj), небо (nebo), радоваться (radovat'sja). Examples of graphs

frequency of the dominant can be due to different reasons. In the course of time, words can become outdated. Therefore, the frequency of these words and their derivatives decrease. Conversely, words can gain relevance, increasing in frequency and increasing frequency of their derivatives and synonyms. Therefore, it was necessary to compare the change in the frequency of the studied words with the change in the frequency of semantically close words, in particular synonyms. In [22], the dynamics of the frequency of the core lexicon, that is the most frequently used vocabulary, was analysed. It was shown that the total frequency of a fixed number of frequently used words decreases. Thus, the tendency to decrease in frequency prevails among high-frequency words. Since the synonymic dominants are characterised by a higher frequency compared to other words in the corresponding synonymic sets, overall tendency of the dominant to decrease in the proportion in the synonymic raw may be due to this general trend. For this reason, one should also check how typical are the changes in the frequencies of the dominants in comparison with words that have similar frequency. First, we considered how frequencies of the dominants change in comparison with the frequencies of their synonyms. Then, frequency percentage of the dominants was calculated for two 10-year periods (1800–1809 and 2000–2009). For each synonymic raw, we found the ratio of the dominant percentage values in 1800–1809 and 2000–2009. The median ratio is 0.79. Thus, the typical rate of decrease in percentage of the dominant was 21% over 200 years. Figure 3 shows the scatterplot for the frequency percentage of the dominants in these time intervals.

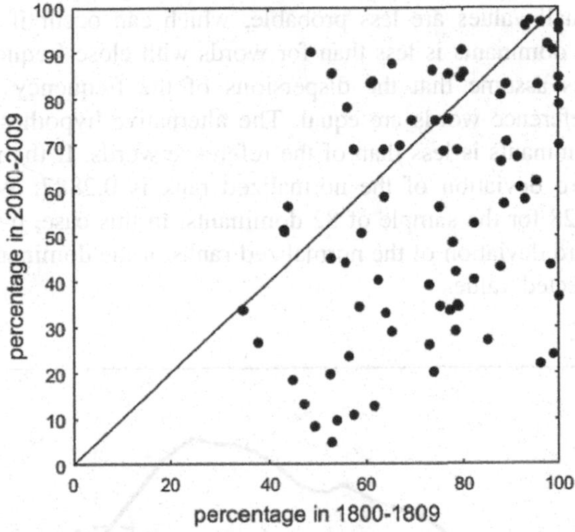

Fig. 3. Percentage change of the dominants over two centuries. The percentage scattering diagram for 1800–1809 and 2000–2009 time intervals

Of the 82 examples examined, the dominant percentage of use decreased in 60 cases (73.2%) over 200 years. Such a high excess of the frequency decrease of the dominant over its increase is a statistically significant result. Taking for the null hypothesis the assumption of equal probability of decreasing and increasing the frequency percentage, we get p-value $1.62 \cdot 10^{-5}$. For any reasonable choice of a significance level, the null hypothesis should be rejected.

Then, we analysed the dynamics of the frequencies of the dominants in comparison with the frequency dynamics of words that are close in frequency. To do this, the technique proposed in [23] was used. We made a list of words and ordered the words by frequency. Then, we selected N words located directly before and after the dominant (for each dominant). We called those words reference words. In this work N was equal to 100. For all 2N + 1 words (the considered dominant and reference words), we calculated the ratio of frequencies in two time intervals (1800–1809 and 2000–2009), and arranged them according to this parameter. We found the rank of the dominant, i.e. its position in this ordered list. It is convenient to rate the rank by the total number of words in the list. As a result, we got statistics varying from 0 to 1. If the dominants do not differ from reference words in terms of frequency variations, then the values of the normalized rank have a uniform distribution over the interval from 0 to 1.

The mathematical expectation of the normalized rank, provided that the null hypothesis is correct, is obviously 0.5. The average value of the normalized rank for 82 dominants is equal to 0.4898, which slightly differs from the expected value. This corresponds to a p-value of 0.7503. Let us consider how dispersion of frequency variation of the dominants relates to the dispersion of the frequency variations of the reference words. As can be seen in Fig. 4, the distribution of normalized ranks strongly deviates from the uniform one. In this case, the values are grouped in the middle region, and large and small values are less probable, which can occur if the dispersion of variations for the dominants is less than for words with close frequency. For the null hypothesis, let us assume that the dispersions of the frequency variations of the dominants and reference words are equal. The alternative hypothesis is that the dispersion of the dominants is less than of the reference words. If the null hypothesis is valid, the standard deviation of the normalized rank is 0.2887. We get a standard deviation of 0.2128 for the sample of 82 dominants. In this case, p-value is $1.7 \cdot 10^{-7}$, that is, the standard deviation of the normalized ranks of the dominants is significantly less than the expected value.

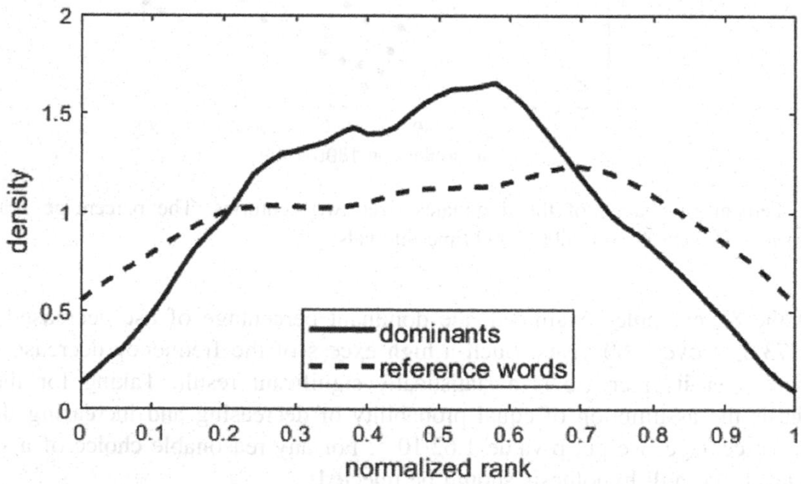

Fig. 4. Probability density function of the normalized ranks of dominants (solid line) and the words with close frequencies (dashed line)

It may be objected that the frequencies of the words, which are on the periphery of the list of reference words, can deviate from the value of the synonymic dominant frequency, which cause the observed differences. Therefore, let us also make a comparison with words that are immediate neighbours of the synonymic dominant in the ordered list of frequency (top and bottom). For them, we also determine the values of the normalized rank (in the sample of the reference words) and get a control sample of 164 words. The probability density function of the normalized ranks for words from the control sample is shown in Fig. 4 (dashed line). The Wilcoxon rank sum test shows that there are no significant differences in the median for the dominant sample and the control sample (p-value is 0.6005). To test the hypothesis of equality of dispersions, we use the Ansari-Bradley test. The main hypothesis is rejected at p-value $9.42 \cdot 10^{-5}$.

Summing up, we note that the performed analysis did not reveal differences between frequency changes of the synonymic dominants and words with close frequencies. At the same time, the variation in frequency of the synonymic dominants is lower, that is, their frequencies are more stable than those of randomly selected word with close frequencies.

3 Conclusion

It should be emphasized that our study is conducted in the time interval 1800–2008. At longer time intervals, other regularities can be observed. However, there are no text corpora of the required size for earlier centuries. We study evolution of synonymic sets only in terms of frequency variations. Another aspect of language evolution is appearance of new words and disappearance of obsolete ones. It is obvious that when neologisms appear for the first time they are on the periphery of a synonymic set because some time is required to increase their frequency. In the course of time some words become outdated, their frequency decreases, and they can be found on the periphery until they are not used anymore. Thus, it can be expected that the synonymic dominants are certainly more stable as the appearance and disappearance of words occurs on the periphery. Frequency changes of words can indicate changes occurring in a language. Therefore, they should be thoroughly studied.

Improved methods were used in our study. We analysed carefully verified synonymic sets instead of clusters of words with close meaning that are obtained automatically and are not always accurate. The obtained results show decrease in the share of uses of most synonymic dominants studied over the period 1800–2009. Frequencies of the dominants tend to decrease in comparison with frequencies of their synonyms which can indicate dynamic processes in the language caused by word competition.

To better understand this phenomenon, it was decided to check whether the difference in frequencies of the dominants and the words from the periphery of the studied synonymic sets affect the frequency change. We compared frequency dynamics of the synonymic dominants and words that are not connected with them semantically but with close frequencies (reference words). It was found that they don`t have any differences with respect to the direction of frequency changes. However, fluctuation dispersion of the frequencies of the synonymic dominants is less than that of the reference words. Thus, the second result presented in the article is that frequencies of the synonymic dominants are relatively stable (they have a smaller level of random fluctuations compared to randomly chosen words with close frequency).

Acknowledgements. This research was financially supported by the Russian Government Program of Competitive Growth of Kazan Federal University, state assignment of Ministry of Education and Science, grant agreement № 34.5517.2017/6.7 and by RFBR, grant № 17-29-09163.

Appendix. The List of Synonymic Sets

1. Беспокоить, тревожить
2. Беспокоиться, тревожиться, волноваться
3. Бороться, воевать, искоренять, изживать
4. Боязливый, пугливый, робкий, несмелый, трусливый
5. Бояться, пугаться, страшиться, спасаться, трусить, дрейфить, робеть
6. Бродяга, бомж
7. Быстрый, стремительный, быстроходный, скоростной
8. Взаимный, обоюдный, двусторонний
9. Видеть, замечать, видать, лицезреть
10. Виться, извиваться, змеиться, петлять
11. Возможный, потенциальный, вероятный, мыслимый
12. Представлять, воображать
13. Воображение, фантазия
14. Глупый, неумный, бестолковый, несмышленый
15. Голый, нагой, обнаженный
16. Гордиться, кичиться
17. Дальновидный, предусмотрительный
18. Два, двое, пара, оба
19. Для, ради, во имя, на благо
20. Добро, благо
21. Дом, здание, строение, постройка
22. Думать, полагать, усматривать
23. Дыра, дырка, дырочка, отверстие
24. Еда, снедь, яства, пища
25. Жаловаться, роптать, сетовать, плакаться, ныть, хныкать
26. Нажаловаться, наушничать, ябедничать, фискалить, кляузничать, доносить
27. Жалость, сочувствие, сострадание
28. Ждать, дожидаться, ожидать, поджидать, подождать, прождать, пережидать, выжидать
29. Заранее, заблаговременно, загодя, наперед, предварительно
30. Защитить, заступиться, вступиться
31. Избавиться, освободиться, отделаться, спастись

32. Использовать, пользоваться, употреблять, применять, прибегать, эксплуатировать
33. Куча, груда, кипа, ворох
34. Легкомысленный, беспечный, несерьезный, ветреный
35. Лень, неохота
36. Мусор, сор
37. Мысль, идея, дума
38. Надеяться, уповать, рассчитывать, полагаться
39. Намерение, умысел, замысел, задумка, прожект
40. Намеренно, нарочно, преднамеренно, умышленно, целенаправленно, сознательно
41. Напрасный, тщетный, безрезультатный, безуспешный, бесплодный, бесполезный
42. Напророчить, накаркать, накликать
43. Нарочито, подчеркнуто, демонстративно
44. Небо, небеса, небосвод, небосклон, поднебесье
45. Невольно, нечаянно, ненароком, невзначай, непроизвольно
46. Изъян, дефект, недочет
47. Нежный, ласковый
48. Необитаемый, нежилой, незаселенный, ненаселенный
49. Непонятный, неясный, непостижимый, недоступный, заумный, невразумительный
50. Обещать, сулить, клясться, обязываться
51. Оправдать, выгородить
52. Плакать, рыдать, реветь
53. Полый, пустотелый
54. Поляна, лужайка
55. Понятный, постижимый, внятный
56. Посещать, навещать, проведать, наведываться
57. Поссориться, поругаться, повздорить
58. Предсказывать, предрекать, пророчить, пророчествовать, прорицать, прогнозировать
59. Побороть, пересилить, преодолеть, превозмочь, обуздать
60. Привыкнуть, свыкнуться, притерпеться, приспособиться, адаптироваться, приноровиться, приладиться, сжиться, освоиться
61. Пристанище, приют, обиталище, обитель
62. Простить, извинить
63. Пушистый, мохнатый
64. Пытаться, стараться, пробовать, силиться
65. Радоваться, ликовать, торжествовать
66. Разговор, беседа, диалог
67. Разумный, рассудительный, благоразумный
68. Раньше, ранее, прежде, перед
69. Рассказывать, излагать, поведать, повествовать
70. Расстаться, разлучиться, распрощаться, распроститься
71. Рисовать, зарисовывать, малевать

72. Ругать, бранить, поносить, хаять, охаивать, хулить
73. Сам, самостоятельно
74. Сердить, возмущать, бесить, злить, разозлить, разъярить
75. Сердиться, возмущаться, беситься, злиться, разозлиться, разъяриться, негодовать
76. Скука, тоска
77. Слишком, чересчур, чрезмерно, непомерно, излишне, неумеренно, преувеличенно
78. Смерть, кончина, гибель
79. Сначала, вначале, сперва, поначалу, первоначально
80. Собираться, намереваться, намерен, планировать
81. Собрать, набрать
82. Советовать, рекомендовать
83. Сообразительный, смекалистый, понятливый, догадливый, находчивый
84. Сообщать, информировать, извещать, уведомлять, осведомлять, оповещать, докладывать
85. Страх, боязнь, испуг, ужас, паника
86. С трудом, насилу, еле, едва
87. Стыдиться, стесняться, смущаться, конфузиться
88. Тайна, секрет
89. Талант, одаренность, талантливость, даровитость, способности, задатки
90. Тоска, печаль, грусть
91. Ум, разум, рассудок, интеллект
92. Умный, неглупый, смышленый, мудрый, проницательный

References

1. Yeeun, L.: A corpus-driven study on the representation of marriage between 1950s and 2000s in COHA. SNU Working Papers in English Language and Linguistics, vol. 14, pp. 103–123 (2016)
2. Bochkarev, V.V., Solovyev, V.D., Shevlyakova, A.V.: The average word length dynamics as indicator of cultural changes in society. Soc. Evol. Hist. **14**(2), 153–175 (2015)
3. Généreux, M., Snejfella, B., Maslej, M.: Big data in psychology: using word embeddings to study theory-of-mind. In: 2017 IEEE International Conference on Big Data (Big Data), pp. 4747–4749. IEEE Press, Boston (2017)
4. Hellrich, J., Buechel, S., Hahn, U.: JESEME: A Website for Exploring Diachronic Changes in Word Meaning and Emotion. arXiv:1807.04148v1 [cs.CL] (2018)
5. Baranov, V., Votintsev, A., Gnutikov, R., Mironov, A., Oshchepkov, S., Romanenko, V.: Old slavic manuscript heritage: electronic publications and full-text databases. In: Electronic Imaging, the Visual Arts Conference & Beyond, Conference Proceedings, 11.1–11.8. James Hemsley, London (2004)
6. Zholobov, O.: The corpus of the Old Russian copies of the Paraenesis of Ephraem Syrus. Russ. Linguist. **35**(3), 361–380 (2011)
7. Michel, J.-B., Shen, Y.K., Aiden, A.P., Veres, A., Gray, M.K., et al.: Quantitative analysis of culture using millions of digitized books. Science **331**(6014), 176–182 (2011)

8. Hamilton, W.L., Leskovec, J., Jurafsky, D.: DiachronicWord Embeddings Reveal Statistical Laws of Semantic Change. arXiv:1605.09096v6 [cs.CL] (2018)
9. Davies, M.: Expanding horizons in historical linguistics with the 400-million word Corpus of Historical American English. Corpora **7**(2), 121–157 (2012)
10. Bochkarev, V.V., Solovyev, V.D., Wichmann, S.: Universals versus historical contingencies in lexical evolution. J. R. Soc. Interface **11**(101), 20140841 (2014)
11. Dubossarsky, H., Weinshall, D., Grossman, E.: Verbs change more than nouns: a bottom up computational approach to semantic change. Lingue e Linguaggio **15**(1), 5–25 (2016)
12. Dubossarsky, H., Grossman, E., Weinshall, D.: Outta control: laws of semantic change and inherent biases in word. Representation models. In: 2017 Conference on Empirical Methods in Natural Language Processing, Copenhagen, Denmark, pp. 1136–1145 (2017)
13. Aggelen, A., Hollink, L., Ossenbruggen, J.: Combining distributional semantics and structured data to study lexical change. In: Ciancarini, P., et al. (eds.) Knowledge Engineering and Knowledge Management, Bologna, Italy, 2016, LNAI, vol. 10180, pp. 40–49. Springer, Heidelberg (2017)
14. Dubossarsky, H., Tsvetkov, Y., Dyer, C., Grossman, E.: A bottom up approach to category mapping and meaning change. In: CEUR Workshop Proceedings, vol. 1347, pp. 66–70 (2015)
15. Kutuzov, A., Øvrelid, L., Szymanski, T., Velldal, E.: Diachronic word embeddings and semantic shifts: a survey. In: Proceedings of the 27th International Conference on Computational Linguistics, Santa Fe, New Mexico, USA, pp. 1384–1397 (2018)
16. Palus, Sh.: Science under Scrutiny: the problem of reproducibility. Sci. Am. **319**(4), 58–59 (2018)
17. Rahal, R.M.: Open science collaboration: estimating the reproducibility of psychological science. Science **349**(6251), aac4716 (2015)
18. Lakoff, G.: Classifiers as a reflection of mind. In: Noun Classes and categorization. Proceedings of a symposium on categorization and noun classification, Eugene, Oregon, October 1983, pp. 13–51. John Benjamins Publishing Company, Amsterdam (1986)
19. Rakhilina, E.V.: Kognitivnyi analiz predmetnykh imen: semantika i sochetaemost' [Cognitive analysys of subject names: semantics and co-occurence]. Russkie slovari, Moscow (2000)
20. Apresian, Yu.D., et. al.: Novyi ob"iasnitel'nyi slovar' sinonimov russkogo iazyka [New explaining dictionary of Russian synonyms]. 2nd ed. Shkola "Yazyki slavyanskoy kul'tury", Moscow (2003)
21. Solovyev, V.D.: Vozmozhnye mekhanizmy izmeneniia kognitivnoi struktury sinonimicheskikh riadov [Possible mechanisms of changing cognitive structures of symomymic sets]. In: Yazyk i mysl', pp. 478–487. Yazyki slavianskoi kul'tury, Moscow (2015)
22. Solovyev, V.D., Bochkarev, V.V., Shevlyakova, A.V.: Dynamics of core of language vocabulary. In: CEUR Workshop Proceedings, vol. 1886, pp. 122–129 (2016)
23. Bochkarev, V.V., Maslennikova, Yu.S., Svetovidov, A.A.: Semantic similarity and analysis of the word frequency dynamics. J. Phys. Conf. Ser. **936**, 012067 (2017). https://doi.org/10.1088/1742-6596/936/1/012067

Automatic Mining of Cause-Effect Discourse Connectives for Russian

Dina Pisarevskaya[1(✉)], Maria Kobozeva[1], Yulia Petukhova[2], Sergey Sedov[3], and Svetlana Toldova[4]

[1] FRC CSC RAS, Moscow, Russia
dinabpr@gmail.com, kobozeva@isa.ru

[2] Ruprecht Karl University of Heidelberg, Heidelberg, Germany
avvrik@gmail.com

[3] Moscow, Russia
sergey.sedov@gmail.com

[4] NRU Higher School of Economics, Moscow, Russia
toldova@yandex.ru

Abstract. Study of cause-effect discourse connectives can help in automated discourse processing and automatic identification of argument units. Besides conjunctions and other functional words and expressions, there are different multi-word expressions containing content-words (e.g. is etogo sleduet 'it follows that') that have the function of cause-effect connectives. We present a method for connectives mining for Russian language. Firstly, the seed list of 143 multi-word connectives was manually extracted from the Ru-RSTreebank corpus. Two Word2Vec models, trained on the news corpus, were used to detect new multi-word connectives. Before first model training, connectives from the seed list were glued to build multi-word tokens. Before second model training, in addition to it, all 3-grams in corpus, that correspond to the specific proposed patterns based on anaphoric expressions, were also glued in the same way. The method based on the second model gives a satisfactory result and lets expand connectives list for cause-effect discourse relations, after manual editing (286 new connectives).

Keywords: Rhetorical Structure Theory · Discourse connectives · Word embeddings

1 Introduction

Automated discourse analysis and discourse parsing can be used in a wide range of Natural Language Processing tasks - text summarization, coreference resolution, sentiment analysis, question-answering systems, natural language generation, argument mining etc. For the Russian language, discourse markers (connectives) can be used as features for relations extraction. The cues, that signal

This paper is partially supported by Russian Foundation for Basic Research (project No. 17-29-07033).

S. Sedov—Independent researcher.

D. A. Alexandrov et al. (Eds.): DTGS 2019, CCIS 1038, pp. 708–718, 2019.
https://doi.org/10.1007/978-3-030-37858-5_60

certain types of discourse relations, are functional words and multi-word expressions, such as conjunctions, prepositions and others that mark certain types of rhetoric relations (for example, the conjunction *poetomu* 'therefore' signals cause-effect relations). Discourse connectives are used as contextual features in discourse parsing models [16,17]. Special lists of discourse connectives exist for different languages - e.g. for German and English - DiMLex [11], Spanish [12], French [15], Arabic [13]. Some basic lists of such expressions are presented in grammars and other sources for Russian, but ready-made full lists of connectives for certain types of discourse relations do not exist yet. In the present work, we suggest the approach of creating the list of cause-effect connectives based on expanding a list of initial lexemes manually extracted from the corpus with semantically close words via word embeddings.

2 Background and Related Work

In our research, we use **the Rhetorical Structure Theory** (RST; [40]) as a framework for discourse structure representation. RST describes the relations among propositions inside a text and represents a text as a hierarchical non-projective tree where elementary discourse units (EDUs) (usually clauses) are embedded into bigger text spans. Discourse units are connected to each other by rhetorical relations, e.g. 'concession', 'cause-effect', 'elaboration' etc. Some discourse units carry more important information (nucleus) than others (satellite) do. In this research we concentrate on the 'cause-effect' relations, which concern to asymmetric relations (mononuclear), as in [Peter went home] nucleus [because he was tired]satellite [40]. The 'cause-effect' relation in discourse structure correspond to causal relations between facts, that are mainly expressed in text via verb phrases or nominalizations (c.f. *his singing yesterday...*). Some types of phrases (smaller than a finite clause) can be also treated as EDUs. This approach is used in NLP systems and in RST Treebanks annotation rules for written texts (cf. [9,38,39] and others).

Discourse relations are usually classified into explicit and implicit depending on occurrence of **discourse signals**. As analyses of the RST Signalling Corpus showed, the majority of the relations are explicit [10]. In many approaches to discourse parsing the identification of relations between coherent text spans relies on detecting lexical discourse markers. For example, the CoNLL-2015 and CoNLL-2016 shared tasks focused on shallow discourse parsing for English [18,37] and Chinese [36].

Among discourse connectives two types are distinguished - functional words enumerated in grammars, whose primary function is connecting two text spans (e.g. *iz-za* 'because of'), and secondary connectives, that are usually multi-word expressions (e.g. *eto privelo k tomu, chto* 'this led to the fact that'), not included in grammatical lexicons. Many of them are involved in the process of grammaticalization, however, at present they are not yet grammaticalized and are not included in reference grammars. That is why building a lexicon that includes secondary connectives is an essential task. Such lexicons can be constructed, for example, manually, using dictionaries and grammars [11,12,15] and available discourse corpora [13,38]. As for Russian, a theoretical approach to secondary connectives for cause-effect relations and their extraction, with basic patterns for multi-word connectives formation, was offered in [38].

Another adjacent field of studies concerns **causality extraction** irrespective of discourse analysis [33–35]. Within this research domain, the causal relations signals are usually studied. Thus, Khoo [33] distinguishes causal connectives linking two phrases, clauses or sentences (adverbial, prepositional, clauseintegrated); causative verbs; resultative and conditional constructions; causative adverbs and adjectives.

In [1] the two types of discourse connectives are highlighted. According to this work, a primary discourse connective is, morpho-syntactically, a single-word unit or a frozen multiword unit, and semantically, a predicate with two arguments referring to eventualities [1]. A secondary connective, based on research in [2], is a compositional word combination which is lexically headed by an unique core unit. Connectives of this type often allow modifications and variants. This type of connectives follows a limited number of definite templates, and each template contains unique core unit that has the strongest meaning. This core unit belongs to a closed list. On the basis of examples of causal relations, detailed templates for secondary connectives are proposed; among them there is the template of adverbial prepositional phrases [1]. It is headed by a (simple or compound) preposition (for example, *because of*), which is the lexical head of a secondary connective only if it introduces an anaphoric pronoun. Such template has, in turn, two types, according to the lexical head: the preposition or the noun [1]. The first type contains a combination of a preposition, the lexical head, and an anaphoric expression, mostly a demonstrative pronoun, like *despite/besides this, due/thanks to this, because/in spite of this*, as in the example: *I had all the necessary qualifications. Despite this, I didn't get the job* [1]. No modification is possible. The second type is the expressions lexically headed by the noun, like *for this reason, under these conditions, for this purpose*, as in the example: *We were stuck in a traffic jam. For this reason, we couldn't attend the event* [1]. Here, the noun can be modified by an adjective ('for this unbelievable reason') and inflected ('for these reasons') [1]. There is a context dependent difference between such expressions of such template (*because of this*), that referes to an abstract entity, and just free connective phrases (*because of this illness*) [1]. Another possible template, also containing an anaphoric pronoun, could be the copula template that contains a semantically weak verb, such as copula *be* [1]. According to the pattern examples, it can be built with a subject which is an anaphoric pronoun in the beginning of the next sentence, referring to the previous clause: *International flights arrived at the capital. That is the reason why the tourism industry has grown over the years* [1]. Discourse connectives of such type are inter-sentential [8].

As to identifying discourse connectives from annotated corpora, in [6] lexicon of English discourse connectives, DiMLex-Eng, is presented. It was built by merging information from two annotated corpora and an additional list of relation signals from the literature. According to this approach, free phrases such as "for this reason", that can be modified ("for this excellent reason", "for these reasons"), are not included in the lexicon. In [5], the researchers analyse methods of enriching the pre-existing resource LICO, a Lexicon of Italian Connectives retrieved from lexicographic sources, with real corpus data for connectives that mark contrast relations in text. In [3], other existing lexicon, grammars, annotated corpus, and raw corpus samples are sources for enriching German connectives lexicon. Mapping from other languages can be also used in order to create discourse connectives lexicon, as in [4].

Within another well-known discourse framework, Penn Discourse Tree Bank (PDTB) approach, connectives relate two events, states, and propositions, that can be realized mostly as clauses, nominalisations, and anaphoric expressions [7]. Thus, they are treated as two-place predicates.

In recent works, features related to discourse form and their role in argumentation were also studied in **argumentation mining**, for example, arguments which support claims [19,20,25]. According to the Rhetorics and Argumentation Theory [47,48], the persuasiveness of a message is based on the interface between discourse form (for example, hedges or connectives) and conceptual form [32]. The connection between argumentation structure and discourse structure (in terms of Rhetorical Structure Theory) is also the focus of contemporary research, as in [26].

Discourse structure of a text, namely cause-effect relations between units, could help to detect premises and conclusion. There are several main approaches to argument mining. The following scheme corresponds to the basic model: a set of statements contains three elements - a conclusion, a set of premises, and an inference from the premises to the conclusion [41]. Other models were analyzed in [44] and [43]. These models take into consideration an argument as a conclusion (or a claim) and a set of premises (also called evidence or reasons) [31]. Hence, text fragments can be classified into argumentation schemes - templates for typical arguments. Therefore, argument mining can contain the following steps: identifying argumentative segments in text [22,24,28], clustering and classifying arguments [23], determining argument structure [21,30], getting predefined argument schema [29]. Study of discourse markers (connectives) can be the initial help for automatic identification of argument units, mainly premises and conclusion.

We focus the current study on cause-effect discourse relations between adjacent clauses irrespective of sentence boundaries. For this language, the research of methods for automatic mining of cause-effect discourse relations connectives is on the initial step yet.

Ready-made lexicon of discourse connectives signaling causal relations for Russian could be used for creating features for machine learning methods that could help in understanding discourse and argumentative structure of texts of different genres, namely, news texts and science texts.

3 Dataset

For Russian, the only corpus annotated for discourse relations within the Rhetorical Structure Theory framework is the Ru-RSTreebank (http://rstreebank.ru/). It is still under development. We use the first release of it. It consists of 79 texts and is freely available. It incorporates news stories, news analytics and popular science news (5582 EDUs and 49840 tokens in total). It contains 330 examples of causal relations: 220 examples for the Cause-Effect relation and 110 for the Evidence. We manually extracted all possible causal relation connectives from this corpus and determined the basic patterns for non-grammaticalized connectives formation. Among others, these patterns include two types of patterns where a verb is a head:

1. causative verb construction (e.g. *X vedet k Y* 'X leads to Y', *X mozhno ob'jasnit Y* 'one can justify via Y')

2. light verb constructions with a content noun denoting 'cause' or 'effect' (e.g. *davat' povod* 'give rise to', *yavlyat'sya prichinoy* 'to be a cause')

We expanded these patterns basing on some work on Russian semantics [42,45] and dictionary of synonyms [46]. Finally, we got a list of 143 possible connectives - verb constructions with anaphoric elements, including combinations with modal verbs and without them. It is the initial (seed) set. All our connectives are multi-word connectives, they contain 2–4 words. Words in them are presented with their lemmas, in this research.

For model training, we used the corpus of the same genre - Russian mass media stemmed texts corpus (https://github.com/maxoodf/russian_news_corpus). This collection is free available and consists of about 1 500 000 articles from 27 top on-line sources for the period of 04.2016–03.2017 (in general about 360 000 000 words). This corpus is already lemmatized. It is crucial for the Russian language, as it lets take all possible word forms into consideration.

During preprocessing, we removed only a small number of stopwords - particles and some very frequent conjunctions (e.g. *zhe, zh, nu* 'well', *a* 'but', *dazhe* 'even', *lish* 'only', *i* 'and'). Punctuation marks and other stop-words were not removed from the articles before models training, because punctuation and functional words could show that the EDU is connected with the previous one and could be included as parts in discourse markers that contain anaphoric expressions, for example, as in the expression *eto privodit k tomu, chto* 'it causes the effect that'.

4 Experiments

The usage of the models is based on the 'distributional hypothesis' [14,49] that semantically similar words occur in similar contexts. We run two different experiments to understand if Word2Vec models could be useful in detecting multi-word connectives that are not included in the initial list. In order to do it, we apply the linguistically motivated heuristics before model training: we concatenate multi-word expressions into one token. We also glue 3-grams, situated in definite positions and containing anaphoric elements, into one token respectively, during the second experiment. Unlike simple keywords based approach, this approach lets extract complete expressions with anaphoric elements. The approach was firstly proposed, with the preliminary description, in [50].

As most of the existing pre-trained Word2Vec models for Russian (such as models from http://rusvectores.org/ru/models/) were trained without stop-words that are important for us, for both experiments we trained own Word2Vec models with specific preprocessing. Both models are CBOW models using Gensim python package, with 10 epochs.

1. In the first experiment (baseline) we performed the following step before model training: for each connective, we combined all its lemmas into one token (e.g. *potomu_chto*). Hence, this model was trained on multi-word tokens for the set of connectives and unigrams for the rest of the corpus.

2. During the second experiment (main experiment), besides concatenating multi-word connectives as in the first experiments, we also made the further step. We concatenated all 3-grams that correspond to the patterns enumerated below into multi-word tokens. After that we trained the model on this corpus.

Table 1. Results for Word2Vec models.

Model	Precision
1. Baseline model: multi-word tokens for connectives	35%
2. Main model: multi-word tokens for connectives + for patterns	53%

Table 2. Results for some seed connectives for the second model.

Connective	Precision	Precision without seed set
chto moch privodit' k 'it can lead to'	56%	13%
chto povlech za sebya 'it lead to'	47%	12%
chto privodit' k 'it lead to'	55%	13%
chto provotsirovat' 'it provoke'	36%	8%

The patterns were created on the basis of the following assumptions. It is quite often that the events themselves are expressed as nominalized constructions (cf. *ego unichtozheniye* 'his destruction'), while the 'cause-effect' relations are expressed via verbs or nouns denoting cause or effect. The names of individual events are rather rare as compared to the words expressing causal relations. Moreover, the former occur in a lot of other contexts in texts. They do not form collocations with causal expression. However, they are often substituted by the anaphoric or cataphoric expressions. Since these expressions are quite frequent in the corpus, they do form the collocations with causal words. Thus, in order to extend the list of possible content words used to express casual relations one can use anaphoric expressions for events as the core elements. To sum up, the following patterns were applied during the second experiment. They are based on content words denoting certain discourse relations that were detected using Ru-RSTreebank:

a. the construction of 3-grams is in the beginning of the sentence/after a dash/after a semicolon. It begins with lemma of *eto* 'this';

b. the construction of 3-grams is situated after a comma and begins with lemma of *chto* 'what';

c. the construction of 3-grams that contain lemma of *to* 'that'. After them there is a comma, after the comma there is lemma of *chto* 'what' or *kak* 'lit. as'.

The basic assumptions for these patterns were firstly proposed in [50].

For both models, we searched for tokens (or multi-tokens), that are semantically similar to the initial set of connectives. For results evaluation, an expert looked at top 100 most similar tokens for each connective and annotated if they could be used as cause-effect connectives. So the expert looked, for every model, at 143 lists with possible new connectives.

For each connective from the initial list, the precision was calculated as a proportion of the true positive expressions in the corresponding list of 100 most similar to it expressions. After that, the average precision was calculated. For each connective, we also calculated the precision considering as true positive the answers that were absent in the seed set.

Results for the two experiments are presented in Table 1: precision is higher for the second model experiment.

Thus, for the initial connective *chto moch privodit' k* 'it can lead to' we get 56 connectives during the second experiment, and 13 of them are new connectives not presented in the seed list. Connectives are given in lemmas, and their English translation is given not in lemmas: *chto chrevato* 'it has implications', *vesti k* 'lead to', *obuslavlivat'* 'cause', *eto proishodit' iz-za* 'happen due to', *chto proishodit' iz-za* 'happen due to', *chto sposobstvovat'* 'it leads to', *obuslavlivat'sya* 'can be caused by', *chto moch' sposobstvovat'* 'it can lead to', *eto moch' sozdavat'* 'it can create', *chto ukazavat' na* 'it points that', *chto grozit'* 'it causes threats', *chto vilivat'sya v* 'it leads to', *chto svidetel'stvovat' o* 'it has cause'. Results for some other connectives examples for the second model are in Table 2.

In general, for the second model, if we do not consider, for each connective, other expressions from the seed list as true positives, we get average precision only 53%. On the one hand, the method lets expand the general connectives list for cause-effect discourse relations. On the other hand, it shows that most of possible connectives were already got from the corpus. Hence, the method, based on the second model approach, could be useful for shorter seed sets of connectives for definite relations types. It also means that lists that we get for each connective should be cleaned in the following way: false positives (not connectives) are removed; other connectives from the seed list that are presented in this list are removed. In addition to repetitions of other connectives from the seed set, another common error is that some possible new connectives could be provided not for cause-effect relations, but for other casual-argumentative discourse relations that are close to them, such as 'purpose' or 'evidence', or could be provided for 'sequence' discourse relation type.

The proposed method lets get full, exhaustive list of connectives for a certain discourse relation, based on a smaller seed set of connectives. Such list should be edited manually, but despite rather low precision, the recall is here much more important. In the final general list of new connectives, repetitions are removed, so we get 286 new cause-effect connectives. They can be used in feature sets in automatic discourse parsing development for Russian.

Trained models, as well as discourse connectives, are available at the Ru-RSTreebank corpus page (http://rstreebank.ru/).

5 Conclusions and Discussion

The applied method gives a satisfactory result (for the second model) and lets expand connectives list for cause-effect discourse relations after manual editing a list that we get for each connective from the initial set. It uses specific patterns that include anaphoric elements that possibly can substitute discourse units. This method lets quickly get an exhaustive list of connectives for a certain relation, if there is a lack of discourse connectives lists and lexicons, although the method requires some manual work after it.

In the further studies, we plan to use the extracted connectives for developing machine learning technique for automated rhetorical relations extraction, as there are no discourse parsers for Russian yet and they could be needed for text summarization, sentiment analysis and stance detection, argumentation mining and other tasks.

We are also going to use the proposed approach, based on patterns with anaphoric elements and distributional semantic methods, to expand seed lists of connectives for elaboration, contrast, concession, preparation and other rhetorical relations. We also plan to compare causal relations markers for news texts and science texts, as the second part of the Ru-RSTreebank consists of science texts. After that we could compare discourse and argumentative structures of news texts and science texts for Russian.

References

1. Danlos, L.: Discourse and lexicons: lexemes, MWEs, grammatical constructions and compositional word combinations to signal discourse relations. In: Proceedings of the Joint Workshop on Linguistic Annotation, Multiword Expressions and Constructions (LAW-MWE-CxG-2018), Santa Fe, New Mexico, USA, pp. 30–40, 25–26 August (2018)
2. Rysova, M., Rysova, K.: The centre and periphery of discourse connectives. In: Proceedings of the 28th Pacific Asia Conference on Language, Information and Computing (PACLIC 2014), Bangkok, Thailand, pp. 452–459 (2014)
3. Scheffler, T., Stede, M.: Adding semantic relations to a large-coverage connective lexicon of German. In: Proceedings of the Eleventh International Conference on Language Resources and Evaluation (LREC-2018), pp. 1008–1013 (2018)

4. Laali, M., Kosseim, L.: Automatic mapping of french discourse connectives to PDTB discourse relations. In: Proceedings of the SIGDIAL 2017 Conference, Saarbruecken, Germany, pp. 1–6 (2017)
5. Feltracco, A., Jezek, E., Magnini, B.: Enriching a lexicon of discourse connectives with corpus-based Data. In: Proceedings of the Eleventh International Conference on Language Resources and Evaluation (LREC-2018), pp. 4327–4332 (2018)
6. Das, D., Scheffler, T., Bourgonje, P., Stede, M.: Constructing a lexicon of english discourse connectives. In: Proceedings of the SIGDIAL 2018 Conference, Melbourne, Australia, pp. 360–365 (2018)
7. Prasad, R., et al.: The Penn Discourse Treebank 2.0 Annotation Manual (2007)
8. Danlos, L., Rysova, K., Rysova, M., Stede, M.: Primary and secondary discourse connectives: definitions and lexicons. Dialogue Discourse **9**(1), 50–78 (2018)
9. Schauer, H.: From elementary discourse units to complex ones. In: Proceedings of the 1st SIGdial Workshop on Discourse and Dialogue, vol. 10, pp. 46–55. Association for Computational Linguistics (2000)
10. Das, D., Taboada, M.: RST signalling corpus: a corpus of signals of coherence relations. Lang. Resour. Eval. **52**(1), 149–184 (2018)
11. Stede, M., Umbach, C.: DiMLex: a lexicon of discourse markers for text generation and understanding. In: Proceedings of the 17th International Conference on Computational Linguistics, vol. 2, pp. 1238–1242. Association for Computational Linguistics (1998)
12. Alonso, L., Castellón, I., Gibert, K., Padró, L.: An empirical approach to discourse markers by clustering. In: Escrig, M.T., Toledo, F., Golobardes, E. (eds.) CCIA 2002. LNCS (LNAI), vol. 2504, pp. 173–183. Springer, Heidelberg (2002). https://doi.org/10.1007/3-540-36079-4_15
13. Al-Saif, A., Markert, K.: The leeds Arabic discourse treebank: annotating discourse connectives for Arabic. In: LREC, pp. 2046–2053 (2010)
14. Mikolov, T., Sutskever, I., Chen, K., Corrado, G.S., Dean, J.: Distributed representations of words and phrases and their compositionality. In: Advances in Neural Information Processing Systems, pp. 3111–3119 (2013)
15. Roze, C., Danlos, L., Muller, P.: LEXCONN: a French lexicon of discourse connectives. Discours. Revue de linguistique, psycholinguistique et informatique. J. Linguist. Psycholinguistics Comput. Linguist., no. 10 (2012)
16. Schilder, F.: Robust discourse parsing via discourse markers, topicality and position. Nat. Lang. Eng. **8**(2–3), 235–255 (2002)
17. Joty, S., Carenini, G., Ng, R.T.: Codra: a novel discriminative framework for rhetorical analysis. Comput. Linguist. **41**(3), 385–435 (2015)
18. Wang, J., Lan, M.: A refined end-to-end discourse parser. In: Proceedings of the Nineteenth Conference on Computational Natural Language Learning-Shared Task, pp. 17–24 (2015)
19. Ghosh, D., Khanam, A., Han, Y., Muresan, S.: Coarse-grained argumentation features for scoring persuasive essays. In: Proceedings of the 54th Annual Meeting of the Association for Computational Linguistics, volume 2: Short Papers, pp. 549–554. Association for Computational Linguistics (2016)
20. Habernal, I., Gurevych, I.: Which argument is more convincing? analyzing and predicting convincingness of Web arguments using bidirectional LSTM. In: Proceedings of the 54th Annual Meeting of the Association for Computational Linguistics, volume 1: Long Papers, pp. 1589–1599. Association for Computational Linguistics (2016)

21. Lawrence, J., Reed, C., Allen, C., McAlister, S., Ravenscroft, A.: Mining arguments from 19th century philosophical texts using topic based modelling. In: Proceedings of the First Workshop on Argumentation Mining, pp. 79–87. Association for Computational Linguistics (2014)
22. Levy, R., Bilu, Y., Hershcovich, D., Aharoni, E., Slonim, N.: Context dependent claim detection. In: Proceedings of COLING 2014, the 25th International Conference on Computational Linguistics: Technical Papers, pp. 1489–1500. Dublin City University and Association for Computational Linguistics (2014)
23. Misra, A., Anand, P., Fox Tree, J.E., Walker, M.: Using summarization to discover argument facets in online idealogical dialog. In: Proceedings of the 2015 Conference of the North American Chapter of the Association for Computational Linguistics: Human Language Technologies, pp. 430–440. Association for Computational Linguistics (2015)
24. Lippi, M., Torroni, P.: Context-independent claim detection for argument mining. In: Proceedings of the Twenty-Fourth International Joint Conference on Artificial Intelligence, pp. 185–191 (2015)
25. Peldszus, A., Stede, M.: An annotated corpus of argumentative microtexts. In: Argumentation and Reasoned Action: Proceedings of the 1st European Conference on Argumentation, Lisbon 2015, pp. 801–815. Association for Computational Linguistics (2016)
26. Peldszus, A., Stede, M.: Rhetorical structure and argumentation structure in monologue text. In: Proceedings of the 3rd Workshop on Argumentation Mining, pp. 103–112. Association for Computational Linguistics (2016)
27. Stab, C., Gurevych, I.: Annotating argument components and relations in persuasive essays. In: Proceedings of COLING 2014, the 25th International Conference on Computational Linguistics: Technical Papers, pp. 1501–1510. Dublin City University and Association for Computational Linguistics (2014)
28. Swanson, R., Ecker, B., Walker, M.: Argument Mining: Extracting Arguments from Online Dialogue. In: Proceedings of the 16th Annual Meeting of the Special Interest Group on Discourse and Dialogue, pp. 217–226. Association for Computational Linguistics (2015)
29. Feng, V.W., Hirst, G.: Classifying arguments by scheme. In: Proceedings of the 49th Annual Meeting of the Association for Computational Linguistics: Human Language Technologies, vol. 1, pp. 987–996. Association for Computational Linguistics (2011)
30. Ghosh, D., Muresan, S., Wacholder, N., Aakhus, M., Mitsui, M.: Analyzing argumentative discourse units in online interactions. In: Proceedings of the First Workshop on Argumentation Mining, pp. 39–48 (2014)
31. Lippi, M., Torroni, P.: Argument mining: a machine learning perspective. In: Black, E., Modgil, S., Oren, N. (eds.) TAFA 2015. LNCS (LNAI), vol. 9524, pp. 163–176. Springer, Cham (2015). https://doi.org/10.1007/978-3-319-28460-6_10
32. Hidey, C., Musi, E., Hwang, A., Muresan, S., McKeown, K.: Analyzing the semantic types of claims and premises in an online persuasive forum. In: Proceedings of the 4th Workshop on Argument Mining, pp. 11–21 (2017)
33. Khoo, C.S.G., Kornfilt, J., Oddy, R.N., Myaeng, S.H.: Automatic extraction of cause-effect information from newspaper text without knowledge-based inferencing. Literary Linguist. Comput. **13**(4), 177–186 (1998)
34. Chang, D.-S., Choi, K.-S.: Incremental cue phrase learning and bootstrapping method for causality extraction using cue phrase and word pair probabilities. Inf. Process. Manage. **42**(3), 662–678 (2006)

35. Asghar, N.: Automatic extraction of causal relations from natural language texts: a comprehensive survey. arXiv preprint arXiv:1605.07895 (2016)
36. Kang, X., Li, H., Zhou, L., Zhang, J., Zong, C.: An end-to-end Chinese discourse parser with adaptation to explicit and non-explicit relation recognition. In: Proceedings of the CoNLL-16 shared task, pp. 27–32 (2016)
37. Oepen, S., et al.: OPT: oslo-potsdam-teesside. pipelining rules, rankers, and classifier ensembles for shallow discourse parsing. In: Proceedings of the CoNLL-16 shared task, pp. 20–26 (2016)
38. Toldova, S., Pisarevskaya, D., Kobozeva, M.: The cues for rhetorical relations in Russian: "Cause-Effect" relation in Russian rhetorical structure treebank. Comput. Linguist. Intellect. Technol. **17**(24), 748–761 (2018)
39. Carlson, L., Marcu, D.: Discourse tagging reference manual. ISI Technical Report ISI-TR-545 54 (2001)
40. Mann, W.C., Thompson, S.A.: Rhetorical structure theory: toward a functional theory of text organization. Text Interdisc. J. Study Discourse **8**(3), 243–281 (1988)
41. Walton, D.: Argumentation theory: a very short introduction. In: Simari, G., Rahwan, I. (eds.) Argumentation in Artificial Intelligence, pp. 1–22. Springer, Boston (2009)
42. Glovinskaya, M.: Russkiye rechevyye akty so znacheniyem mental'nogo vozdeystviya. Logicheskiy analiz yazyka. Mental'nyye deystviya. **82–88** (1993)
43. Freeman, J.B.: Dialectics and the macrostructure of arguments: a theory of argument structure, vol. 10. Walter de Gruyter (1991)
44. Toulmin, S.E.: The Uses of Argument. Cambridge University Press, Cambridge (1958)
45. Paducheva, J.: Dinamicheskiye modeli v semantike leksiki. Litres (2017)
46. Apresyan, J., et al.: Novyy ob"yasnitel'nyy slovar' sinonimov russkogo yazyka. Vtoroy vypusk. Litres (2017)
47. Perelman, C., Olbrechts-Tyteca, L.: The new rhetoric: a treatise on argumentation. University of Notre Dame Press (1973)
48. van Eemeren F.H.: Examining argumentation in context: fifteen studies on strategic maneuvering. John Benjamins Publishing (2009)
49. Harris, Z.S.: Distributional structure. In: Harris, Z.S. (ed.) Papers in Structural and Transformational Linguistics, pp. 775–794. Springer, Dordrecht (1970). https://doi.org/10.1007/978-94-017-6059-1
50. Toldova, S., Kobozeva, M., Pisarevskaya, D.: Automatic mining of discourse connectives for Russian. In: Ustalov, D., Filchenkov, A., Pivovarova, L., Žižka, J. (eds.) AINL 2018. CCIS, vol. 930, pp. 79–87. Springer, Cham (2018). https://doi.org/10.1007/978-3-030-01204-5_8

Analytical Distribution Model for Syntactic Variables Average Values in Russian Literary Texts

Gregory Martynenko[1] and Tatiana Sherstinova[1,2](✉)

[1] Saint Petersburg State University, Universitetskaya Nab. 11, 199034 St. Petersburg, Russia
g.martynenko@spbu.ru, tsherstinova@hse.ru
[2] National Research University Higher School of Economics, St. Petersburg, Russia

Abstract. Digital technologies provide new possibilities for studying cultural heritage. Thus, literature research involving large text corpora allows to set and solve theoretical problems which previously had no prospects for their decision. For example, it has become possible to model the literary system for some definite literary period (i.e., for the Silver Age of Russian literature) and to classify prose writers according to their stylistic features. And more than that, it allows to solve more general theoretical problems. The given research was conducted on Russian literary texts of the early 20th century. The sample included 100 short stories by 100 different writers. The measurements were carried out for 5 syntactic variables. For each of these distributions, the most popular statistics were calculated. Basing on these data, we consider empirical verification of Lyapunov's central limit theorem (CLT). The article validates the effectiveness of CLT theorem and the conditions for its implementation. Besides the normal (Gaussian) function we used another analytical model—the Hausstein function. It turned out that both theoretical distributions for each of five variables do not contradict the experimental data. However, the alternative analytical model (Hausstein function) has shown even better agreement with the experimental data. The obtained results may be used in computational linguistic studies and for research of Russian literary heritage.

Keywords: Russian literary texts · Russian short stories · Digital culture · Syntax · Stylistic variables · Statistical distributions · Statistics · Normal distribution · Central limit theorem

1 Introduction

Digital technologies provide new possibilities for studying cultural heritage [1–7 et al.]. Thus, literature research involving large text corpora allows to set and solve theoretical problems which previously had no prospects for their decision [8–15 et al.]. For example, it has become possible to model the literary system for some definite literary period (i.e., for the Silver Age of Russian literature) and to classify prose writers

D. A. Alexandrov et al. (Eds.): DTGS 2019, CCIS 1038, pp. 719–731, 2019.
https://doi.org/10.1007/978-3-030-37858-5_61

according to their stylistic features. The given research was performed within the project dedicated to the study of language and style evolution of Russian fiction in the first third of the 20th century. For this purpose, literary texts are divided into a chronological sequence of stages associated with the dramatic events of the Russian history of this period [16].

The theoretical background of this study includes three main parts:

- The theory of statistical population proposed by Alexander A. Chuprov—the outstanding Russian statistician of the beginning of the 20th century [17, 18].
- The declaration for the need of mass production of Russian writers' dictionaries proposed by the famous Russian writer and scientist Andrei Bely [19].
- Systemic conceptualization of literature by an outstanding representative of the Russian formal school Yury N. Tynyanov [20].

Alexander A. Chuprov, based on the theory of communities, put forward the idea of a statistical population, the logic of which is based on collective concepts [21]. This theory is based on the idea of the community by Gustav Rümelin [22] and the idea of the coenosis by Karl Möbius [23]. Later, Chuprov's logic was applied to the concepts of text and corpus [24–27].

Andrei Bely achieved impressive results on the accent level of poetry studies. Taking into account modest technological means of his time, he did his best to reach a significant amount of observation. However, in that time, it was impossible to do it on the lexical level, although it was Andrei Bely who was first to set the important task of "producing" frequency dictionaries of Russian writers [19]. The implementation of this idea became possible only at the end of the 20th century due to the development of computer technologies.

Yury N. Tynyanov proposed the idea of the systemic nature of fiction [20], and suggested to distinguish synchronic and diachronic literary systems. By synchronic systems he understood the collection of works of a given literary era, and by diachronic ones—the sequence of successive synchronic systems.

Each literary system can be characterized through a set of statistical variables, which are used for two purposes: to solve taxonomic problems (diagnostics, clustering, typology, etc.) and to build theoretical models describing the distribution of texts and their units through a system of stylistic variables [28].

In this paper, our attention is focused on the second aspect.

2 Lyapunov's Central Limit Theorem in the Context of Linguistic and Statistic Distributions

The starting point of this study is Lyapunov's central limit theorem (CLT). From the point of view of applied statistics, its meaning was perfectly set out by the outstanding Russian expert in probability theory and mathematical statistics A. Y. Boyarsky [29]. The Lyapunov's theorem states the following. Let some large population consist of several private sets, and among these particular populations, there are none in which the average values differ sharply from those in other fragments. In this case, the distribution of mean values (not the specific values of random variables), in a sufficient number of particular populations, obeys the normal law.

The basic idea is that whatever the parameter distribution in particular population (for example, texts) is, the distribution of means for these sets will obey the normal law. Thus, the normal law arises regardless of the qualitative nature of variables and the nature of distribution in each particular population. For the emergence of the normal law, there is one essential requirement: the distribution should not contain outliers. Let us now interpret this idea in the terms of quantitative linguistics.

Let us face the task of describing the literature of some historical epoch with a variety of linguistic and stylistic variables. Then, at the input we have a quantity of writers represented by their works. It is natural to assume that the authors and their works form a single integrated system. For each variable, each text has its own probability distribution (e. g., for sentence length, paragraph length, word length, and other variables). Moreover, the probabilities for each variable obey their own distribution law and may by described by a specific mathematical model. Despite this, the distribution of means, according to Lyapunov's theorem, must obey one and the same model—the normal law.

Let us try to verify the validity of Lyapunov's hypothesis on linguistic data by using two extensive (volumetric) variables: *sentence length* and *paragraph length*, and three intensive variables: *the degree of parataxis, the degree of distantness*, and *the degree of attributeness* (the measures for these variables will be described below).

First of all, we shall consider sentence length. The study of this variable has a long history and vast literature in the Russian and European linguistic tradition [30–35 et al.]. Interestingly, sentence length was studied not only within philology, but also as part of research on theoretical statistics. In the latter case, this variable served as a model distribution demonstrating the breadth of statistics research applications [36].

Table 1 contains selected data on rank distribution of average sentence length in Russian prose of the beginning of the 20th century (1900–1917) [25]. The theoretical values are given here, too. Table 2 presents statistics for the empirical rank distribution for 100 Russian writers (one work for each author was analyzed).

Now, based on the same data, we build a normal distribution.

The sequence of steps that must be performed to obtain theoretical values is presented in Table 3. We should note that in order to obtain theoretical values it is necessary to have at our disposal just two parameters: the mean value (14.48) and the standard deviation (3.78).

When building a normal curve from empirical data, we use the following formula:

$$Y = \frac{i\sum m}{\sigma} \cdot \frac{1}{\sqrt{2\pi}} e^{-\frac{t^2}{2}},$$

where $i-$ is the interval width, $\sum m-$ is the sum of all frequencies equal to the population size, σ – standard deviation, and $t-$ centered and normalized deviation equal to $\frac{X-\bar{X}}{\sigma}$.

The value $\frac{1}{\sqrt{2\pi}}$ is tabulated and can be gained from the corresponding tables.

Table 3 also presents the values of Pearson criterion reflecting the degree of correspondence of theoretical data with the experimental ones. The probability of a criterion for a normal distribution is not small (0.262), which indicates good consistency

Table 1. The distribution of average sentence length in Russian literature in the early 20th century (1901–1917)

Rank	Writers	D_e	D_t	Rank	Writers	D_e	D_t
1	V. Bryusov	29.78	27.04	51	S. Skitalets	13.75	13.96
2	S. Auslender	24.10	24.46	52	O. Dymov	13.60	13.88
3	M. Kuzmin	22.90	23.04	53	A. Averchenko	13.57	13.80
4	V. Lidin	22.34	22.08	54	S. Eleonsky	13.56	13.72
5	W. Muizhel	22.30	21.35	55	V. Korolenko	13.50	13.64
6	L. Andreev	21.78	20.78	56	V. Lensky	13.42	13.57
7	I. Grinevskaya	20.41	20.29	57	K. Trenev	13.40	13.49
8	M. Shaginyan	20.18	19.88	58	A. Sobol	13.39	13.40
9	L. Tolstoy	19.98	19.52	59	A. Remizov	13.26	13.33
10	I. Kasatkin	19.30	19.20	60	I. Surguchev	13.24	13.26
11	D. Dalin	19.22	18.91	61	V. Vinnichenko	13.20	13.18
12	V. Brusyanin	18.94	18.64	62	A. Chapygin	13.16	13.10
13	A. Chekhov	18.90	18.40	63	N. Oliger	13.12	13.02
14	A. Kuprin	18.54	18.18	64	K. Barantsevich	13.00	12.94
15	A. Amfiteatrov	18.30	17.97	65	L. Gurevich	12.92	12.86
16	D. Mamin-Sibiryak	18.23	17.77	66	B. Sadovsky	12.90	12.78
17	M. Artsybashev	18.12	17.59	67	I. Potapenko	12.88	12.70
18	S. Elpatyevsky	17.92	17.42	68	M. Leonov	12.84	12.61
19	L. Charskaya	17.88	17.25	69	I. Volnov	12.56	12.54
20	G. Grebenshchikov	17.36	17.10	70	Z. Gippius	12.44	12.46
21	N. Teleshev	17.14	16.95	71	O. Mirtov	12.40	12.38
22	V. Nemirovich-Danchenko	17.02	16.81	72	P. Boborykin	12.04	12.29
23	M. Gorky	16.84	16.67	73	A. Serafimovich	11.98	12.20
24	A. Bogdanov	16.75	16.54	74	P. Surozhsky	11.96	12.12
25	E. Chirikov	16.44	16.41	75	V. Veresaev	11.86	12.03
26	I. Bunin	16.40	16.29	76	V. Shishkov	11.78	11.94
27	V. Iretsky	16.34	16.17	77	Yu. Belyaev	11.76	11.84
28	A. Fyodorov	16.23	16.05	78	A. Svirsky	11.74	11.76
29	N. Garin-Mikhailovsky	16.14	15.94	79	A. Budishchev	11.68	11.66
30	I. Shmelev	15.92	15.94	80	A. Bibik	11.60	11.56
31	I. Vasilevsky	15.90	15.73	81	I. Kipen	11.59	11.46
32	Yu. Slezkin	15.86	15.62	82	L. Carmen	11.58	11.36
33	B. Lazarevsky	15.64	15.52	83	A. Roslavlev	11.50	11.25
34	E. Militsyna	15.52	15.42	84	S. Kondurushkin	11.26	11.14
35	S. Yushkevich	15.50	15.32	85	D. Censor	11.23	11.02
36	D. Aizman	15.32	15.23	86	O. Olnem	11.18	10.90
37	N. Timkovsky	15.20	15.14	87	A. Kamensky	11.12	10.78
38	A. Tolstoy	15.06	15.05	88	A. Izmailov	10.68	10.71
39	S. Sergeev-Tsensky	14.92	14.96	89	S. Gusev-Orenburgsky	10.64	10.51

(continued)

Table 1. (*continued*)

Rank	Writers	D_e	D_t	Rank	Writers	D_e	D_t
40	B. Zaitsev	14.78	14.87	90	A. Neverov	10.51	10.36
41	N. Krasheninnikov	14.74	14.78	91	A. Verbitskaya	10.32	10.21
42	D. Merezhkovsky	14.62	14.70	92	E. Nagrodskaya	10.28	10.04
43	I. Nazhivin	14.61	14.61	93	S. Yesenin	9.72	9.86
44	I. Novikov	14.58	14.53	94	V. Doroshevich	9.36	9.65
45	M. Krinitsky	14.50	14.44	95	F. Sologub	9.12	9.43
46	V. Gilyarovsky	14.18	14.36	96	E. Zamyatin	8.61	9.17
47	M. Prishvin	14.10	14.28	97	I. Rukavishnikov	7.60	8.87
48	S. Podyachev	14.02	14.20	98	V. Goffman	7.33	8.50
49	G. Chulkov	13.98	14.12	99	L. Zinovyeva-Annibal	7.14	8.01
50	A. Green	13.80	14.04	100	V. Ropshin	6.36	7.25

Table 2. Statistics distribution of Russian writers by sentence length

The mean	14.482	The coefficient of variation	26.73
Geometric mean	13.988	Asymmetry	0.241
Median	13.775	Excess	0.397
Standard deviation	3.781	Rank average	43.28

Table 3. Calculation table for theoretical values of the normal law for the distribution of average sentence length

Range	Frequency	Class mark x	$x - \bar{x}$	$x - \bar{x}/\sigma$	$f(t)$	$f_m = \frac{i \cdot \sum m}{\sigma}$	Pearson criterion value
6–9	5	7.5	−6.98	1.846	0.0791	6	0.20
9–12	23	10.5	−3.98	1.653	0.2999	18	1.39
12–15	34	13.5	−0.98	0.260	0.3857	30	0.53
15–18	21	16.5	+1.52	0.534	0.3467	28	0.75
18–21	11	19.5	+4.52	1.327	0.1669	13	0.31
21–24	4	22.5	+7.52	2.120	0.053	4	0.20
24–27	1	25.5	+10.52	2.910	0.006	1	0
27–30	1	28.5	+13.52	4.150	0.0001	0	0
Sum							3.38

in the terms of χ^2-criterion. Thus, from the point of view of the Pearson criterion, the small experimental values of asymmetry and kurtosis shown in Table 2 can be considered in this situation as an error, and it can be assumed that this distribution tends to symmetry. It should be expected that with a different collection of works by the same authors, the situation may turn out to be just the same. However, this assumption needs verification.

3 Building a Haustein Function Based on Experimental Data

The Haustein function [37] in the form of a decreasing rank distribution would be:

$$k = \left(\frac{N+1}{r} - 1\right)^{\gamma} \cdot q, \tag{1}$$

where r is the rank of a member of the writers' community, k is the value of the corresponding parameter, N is the community size, and q and γ are two constant coefficients, the meaning of which we shall reveal below.

For a meaningful interpretation of the coefficients q and γ, let's take advantage of the remarkable properties of formula (1).

It is straightforward to see that with $r = \frac{N+1}{2}$, $k = q$.

This means that q is the value of the activity of the "average writer", i.e. the member of the writers's community who occupies the median position in the ranked row.

It is interesting that q is not only the median of the rank distribution, but also its geometric mean [24].

However, it should be borne in mind that the resulting formula refers to a decreasing rank distribution, when the author with the maximum average sentence length takes the first place in the table.

The rank mean of such a distribution is determined by the following formula [38]:

$$\overline{r_y} = \frac{N+1}{2} \cdot (1 - \gamma),$$

which means that

$$\gamma = 1 - \frac{2\overline{r_y}}{N+1}.$$

As for the average along the axis of the sentence length, it is equal to $\bar{k} = q \cdot \frac{\pi\gamma}{\sin\pi\gamma}$ [39].

With $\gamma \to 0$ $k \to q$. That means that coordinates of the mean tend to that of the median.

It should be noted that the coefficient q can be found by solving equation for q:

$$q = \frac{1}{\bar{k}} \cdot \frac{\pi\gamma}{\sin\pi\gamma}.$$

It also follows from this equation that the ratio $\frac{q}{k}$ (i.e., the ratio of the geometric mean to the arithmetic mean) characterizes the non-uniformity of the distribution in terms of the average sentence length.

For data presented in Table 1, γ coefficient is 0.143.

This coefficient depends only on the rank average and the size of the writers community, characterizing the degree of non-uniformity of the authors' distribution across the "levels" of the table—the closer the rank average is to the median rank (i.e., the center of the ranked series) and therefore, the closer γ to one, the less difference in sentence length between fiction writers located in the upper and lower halves of the Table 1.

Let us get down to constructing a theoretical model based on experimental data. To construct a theoretical function, we use the method of moments considering the empirical values of the parameters q and γ as theoretical. Calculated by the formula (1), theoretical values for any rank are shown in Table 1 (D_t).

From Table 1, it is clear that the agreement between theoretical and empirical data is very good. This can also be seen by referring to data in Table 4, where empirical and theoretical values of the spectral distribution (i.e., density distribution) corresponding to the rank distribution given in Table 1 are shown.

Table 4. Spectral distribution of the average sentence length in Russian short stories of the early 20th century and the correspondent theoretical values calculated with the Hausstein function

The range of average sentencc length	Empirical number of authors	Theoretical number of authors	Pearson criterion value
6–9	5	4	0.250
9–12	23	21	0.190
12–15	34	37	0.243
15–18	21	24	0.375
18–21	11	9	0.444
More than 21	6	5	0.200
Total	100		1.702

In the far right column of the table, the values of Pearson's χ^2-test are shown. They are calculated by the following formula:

$$\chi^2 = \sum \frac{(m - m^t)^2}{m^t}.$$

For our distribution, χ^2 is 1.702. Taking into account the number of degrees of freedom, which in this case is equal to $l - 1 = 6 - 3 = 3$, we refer to the Pearson criterion probability table and get the appropriate probability. It turned out to be 0.572. This probability is very high. This leads to the conclusion that the obtained theoretical values for Hausstein function do not contradict the experimental data (as it was for modeling with Gaussian function).

Theoretical graphs for the two proposed models are shown in Fig. 1.

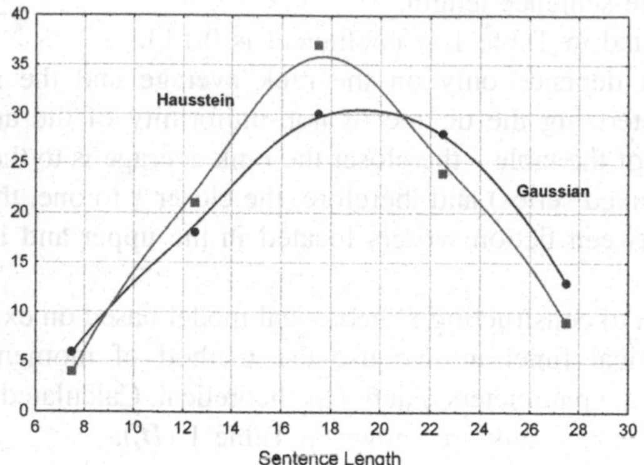

Fig. 1. Theoretical distributions of average sentence length: (1) the normal distribution, and (2) the Hausstein function

4 Distribution of Writers by Other Syntactic Variables

The described methodology was implemented for four other syntactic characteristics.

In Table 5, statistics of 5 distributions of syntactic variables are shows. The first two are the extensive (volumetric) variables. The sentence length represents the syntactic level, and the paragraph length represents the hypersyntactic level. Three other variables are intense (structural) characteristics. The first one—the number of homogeneous groups in the sentence—reflects the structural level (or, the role of composition mechanism), the second one is related with the linear orders and refers to the distantness (expressed in the number of words) between directly related syntactic components, and the third one deals with the POS-structure (in the given case, the share of adjectives).

What catches the eye in Table 5? First of all, it's the proximity of all average values (the mean, the geometric mean, and the median) for all five variables. It suggests that all presented distributions tend to the normal law. However, the excessive proximity of the geometric mean and the median against the background of noticeable asymmetry and peakedness allow to suggest that here we observe some other distribution pattern. The proximity of the median and the geometric mean is a characteristic feature of the Hausstein function, discussed above. The specific asymmetry of all five distributions is also indicated by the value of the rank mean, which is substantially less than half of the statistical population—with distribution symmetry, the rank average should be located somewhere in the median area.

Table 5. Statistics for five syntactic variables in Russian prose

Statistics	Sentence length	Paragraph length	Parataxis	Distantness	Attributeness
Mean	14.48	2.569	1.052	4.122	1.352
Geom.mean	13.99	2.463	0.990	3.952	1.312
SD	3.87	0.757	0.375	1.221	0.322
Median	13.78	2.505	1.012	3.903	1.322
Coef. of variation	26.73	29.46	35.63	29.63	23.84
Asymmetry	0.855	0.948	1.070	0.840	0.203
Excess	1.833	2.282	2.043	1.050	0.002
Rank mean	43.28	45.60	41.01	42.46	43.81

The listed statistical symptoms in aggregate suggest an idea of significant asymmetry of empirical distributions and their noticeable peakedness, which both contradict the properties of the normal distribution.

The results of testing both theoretical distributions on experimental data are presented in Table 6.

Table 6. The Pearson criterion values for 5 variables in empirical distribution modeling with the Hausstein function and the normal (Gaussian) function

Function	Sentence length	Paragraph length	Parataxis	Distantness	Attributeness
Hausstein	0.572	0.072	0.072	0.572	0.112
Gaussian	0.262	0.550	0.072	0.172	0.072

The information in Table 6 is rather interesting. Thus, the greatest impression is made by the fact that in all cases the probability of Pearson criterion value exceeds, and sometimes significantly, the value of 0.05. This means that for all variables the theoretical values obtained do not contradict the experimental data. This applies to both the Hausstein function and the normal law. At the same time, the probability values of this criterion for the Hausstein function are somewhat higher on average than that for the normal law.

On the one hand, this result confirms Lyapunov's theorem, and on the other hand, it does not reject the fact that it is possible to use another model (in our case, it is the Hausstein function), which is consistent with the experimental data, perhaps even better than the Gaussian function is. Moreover, the Hausstein function, in comparison with the normal law, has a number of remarkable properties described above.

These properties allow us to interpret empirical data more comprehensively. However, it should also be borne in mind that the Pearson criterion is decisive only in the case of small probabilities (lower than the usual values of 0.01 and 0.05). In this regard, let us refer to the opinion about the possibilities of this criterion by two classics of statistics U. Yule and M. Kendall, who wrote that χ^2 criterion determines the probability that in the random sample theoretical χ^2 value as large as its actual value may appear. If this probability is small, then one has reason to suspect a significant discrepancy between theory and experience. However, the reverse is not true, and one cannot claim that the hypothesis is correct if this probability is not small. In this case, one has only the right to say that the hypothesis does not contradict empirical data [36].

Even Pearson himself said about his criterion that it is only a criterion of "equalization goodness" of the distribution. It does not indicate the validity of the hypothesis put forward for high probabilities [40].

We should also note that for the given research we have analyzed texts by 100 writers. According to preliminary data, the general population of Russian prose writers of this period comprises at least 1000 names [41]. Expanding the field of observation may need to adjust the model in favor of peripheral authors, and this, in turn, may affect the parameters of the theoretical model and the degree of their consistency with the normal and the alternative patterns.

5 Conclusion

The paper is concerned with analytic modeling of a set of average values for syntactic/stylistic variables. The research was conducted on Russian literary texts of the early 20th century. The sample included 100 short stories by 100 different writers (each author is represented by one text). The measurements were carried out for 5 syntactic variables, for each of which the average values were calculated. All authors were ordered according to these average values, i.e., correspondent rank distributions were built, and then they were transformed into a frequency (spectral) ones. For each of these distributions, the most popular statistics were calculated.

The theoretical and statistical basis of the study is Lyapunov's Central limit theorem, one interpretation of which is that, no matter what distribution law the values of a particular random variable obey, the average values of this variable on a set of samples are subject to the normal law. We tried to find out if this is the case in linguistic reality. In addition, we included in the experimental verification another analytical model, which we previously used—the so-called Hausstein function.

Based on the experimental data for each variable, both the normal distribution and the Hausstein function were built. It turned out that from the point of view of χ^2-criterion, both theoretical distributions for each of five variables do not contradict the experimental data. In all cases, the probability value of the criterion is not small. Usually, it is considered that it is a sufficient reason to believe that such a conclusion is consistent with the hypothesis put forward, and there are no significant differences between the theoretical and empirical distributions.

But it should be mentioned that Karl Pearson himself believed that if the probability of the criterion is not small, this is only the evidence of the "goodness of alignment" [40]. Another situation is the case when the probability is low. Then, we can really conclude that the theoretical model contradicts the experimental data and the null hypothesis should be rejected. But it was not the case of our experiment.

This means that the validity of Lyapunov's theorem on the normality of means distribution is not rejected. At the same time, the alternative analytical model—the Haustein function—has shown even better agreement with the experimental data. The resolution of this issue should be concerned in future studies.

We can suppose that such uncertainty is caused by insufficient sample size. In our experiment, texts by 100 writer were analyzed. According to preliminary estimates, the number of prose writers in the beginning of the 20th century is no less than 1000 names. In current research, many peripheral authors were out of our attention. Because of that, when expanding the empirical base, we should expect some shift of average values, increase of dispersion, peakedness and asymmetry of means distribution. This may lead to a rejection of the hypothesis about the correspondence of the normal distribution to the experimental data, as well as to other "deformations" in syntactic modeling. In any case, the results of the forthcoming studies promise to be interesting and perspective. The obtained results may be used in computational linguistic studies and for research of Russian literary heritage.

Acknowledgements. The research is supported by the Russian Foundation for Basic Research, project # 17-29-09173 "The Russian language on the edge of radical historical changes: the study of language and style in prerevolutionary, revolutionary and post-revolutionary artistic prose by the methods of mathematical and computer linguistics (a corpus-based research on Russian short stories)".

References

1. Cameron, F., Kenderdine, S.: Theorizing Digital Cultural Heritage: A Critical Discourse. MIT Press, Cambridge (2007)
2. Carter, B. (ed.): Digital Humanities: Current Perspective, Practices, and Research. Emerald Publishing Limited, Bingley (2013)
3. Mosco, V.: Becoming Digital: Towards a Post-Internet Society. Emerald Publishing Limited, Bingley (2017)
4. Ridge, M.: Crowdsourcing Our Cultural Heritage. Ashgate, Burlington (2014)
5. Sandis, C.: Cultural Heritage Ethics: Between Theory and Practice. Open Book Publishers, Cambridge (2014)
6. Travis, C., von Lünen, A.: The Digital Arts and Humanities: Neogeography, Social Media and Big Data Integrations and Applications. Springer International Publishing, Cham (2016)
7. Warwick, C., Terras, M.M., Nyhan, J.: Digital Humanities in Practice. Facet Publishing in association with UCL Centre for Digital Humanities, London (2012)
8. Brockmann, S.: Literature as Virtual Reality. In: Socken, P. (ed.) The Edge of the Precipice: Why Read Literature in the Digital Age?, pp. 55–71. McGill-Queen Press, Montreal (2013)
9. Edmondson, E.: Wiki literature circles: creating digital learning communities. Engl. J. **101** (4), 43–49 (2012)
10. Hayot, E.: I/O: A comparative literature in a digital age. Comp. Lit. **57**(3), 219–226 (2005)
11. Mani, B.: Libraries without walls?: World literature in the digital century. In: Recoding World Literature: Libraries, Print Culture, and Germany's Pact with Books, pp. 215–242. Fordham University, New York (2017)

12. Martynenko, G., Sherstinova, T.: Emotional waves of a plot in literary texts: new approaches for investigation of the dynamics in digital culture. In: Alexandrov, D.A., Boukhanovsky, A. V., Chugunov, A.V., Kabanov, Y., Koltsova, O. (eds.) DTGS 2018. CCIS, vol. 859, pp. 299–309. Springer, Cham (2018). https://doi.org/10.1007/978-3-030-02846-6_24
13. Simanowski, R.: Digital literature. In: Digital Art and Meaning: Reading Kinetic Poetry, Text Machines, Mapping Art, and Interactive Installations, pp. 27–57. University of Minnesota Press (2011)
14. Svensson, P.: Three premises of big digital humanities. In: Big Digital Humanities: Imagining a Meeting Place for the Humanities and the Digital, pp. 82–130 (2016)
15. Schreibman, S.: Digital humanities: centres and peripheries. Hist. Soc. Res./Historische Sozialforschung **37**(3), 46–58 (2012)
16. Popova, T.I., Martynenko, G.Ya., Sherstinova, T.Yu., Melnik, A.G.: Metodologicheskie problemy sozdaniya Komp'yuternoj antologii russkogo rasskaza kak yazykovogo resursa dlya issledovaniya yazyka i stilya russkoj khudozhestvennoj prozy v ehpokhu revolyucionnykh peremen (pervoj treti XX veka) [Methodological problems of creating a Computer Anthology of the Russian story as a language resource for the study of the language and style of Russian artistic prose in the era revolutionary changes (first third of the 20th century)]. In: Computational Linguistics and Computational Ontologies. Issue 2 (Proceedings of the XXI International United Conference "The Internet and Modern Society, IMS-2018, St. Petersburg, 30 May 2018–2 June 2018 Collection of scientific articles"), pp. 99–104. ITMO University, St. Petersburg (2018)
17. Seneta, E.: Aleksander Aleksandrovich Chuprov (or Tschuprow). In: Heyde, C.C., Seneta, E., Crépel, P., Fienberg, S.E., Gani, J. (eds.) Statisticians of the Centuries. Springer, New York (2001). https://doi.org/10.1007/978-1-4613-0179-0_65
18. Sheynin, O.B.: A. A. Chuprov: Life, Work, Correspondence. Vandenhoeck and Ruprecht, Göttingen (1996)
19. Bely, A.: Masterstvo Gogolya [Gogol's Mastery]. OGIZ, Moscow-Leningrad (1934)
20. Tynyanov, Y.: Arkhaisty i novatory [Archaists and Innovators]. Priboj, Leningrad (1929)
21. Chuprov, A.A.: Ocherki po teorii statistiki [Essays on the Theory of Statistics]. M. and S. Sabashnikov Edition, St. Petersburg (1909)
22. Mann, B., Rümelin, G.: In: Neue Deutsche Biographie (NDB). Band 22, Duncker & Humblot, Berlin (2005)
23. Weidner, H.: Die Anfänge meeresbiologischer und ökologischer Forschung in Hamburg durch Karl Möbius (1825–1908) und Heinrich Adolph Meyer (1822–1889). Historisch-meereskundliches Jahrbuch **2**, 69–84 (1994)
24. Martynenko, G.: Osnovy stilemetrii [Fundamentals of Stylometrics]. Publishing House of Leningrad University, Leningrad (1988)
25. Martynenko, G.: Vvedenie v teoriyu chislovoj garmonii teksta [Introduction to the Theory of Numerical Harmony of Text]. Publishing House of St. Petersburg University, St. Petersburg (2009)
26. Martynenko, G., Čebanov, S.: Text as real population in Čuprov sense. J. Quant. Linguist. **5** (3), 163–166 (1998)
27. Martynenko, G.: Semiotics of statistics. J. Quant. Linguist. **10**(2), 105–115 (2003)
28. Martynenko, G.Y., Sherstinova, T.Y.: Statistical Parameterisation of Text Corpora. In: Sojka, P., Kopeček, I., Pala, K. (eds.) TSD 2000. LNCS (LNAI), vol. 1902, pp. 99–102. Springer, Heidelberg (2000). https://doi.org/10.1007/3-540-45323-7_17
29. Boyarsky, A.Y.: Zakon bol'shikh chisel [The Law of Large Numbers]. In: Boyarsky, A.Y. (ed.) Obshchaya teoriya statistiki [General Theory of Statistics], pp. 239–271. Publishing House of Moscow University, Moscow (1977)

30. Admoni, V.G.: Razmer predlozheniya i slovosochetaniya kak yavlenie sintaksicheskogo stroya [The Length of Sentences and Phrases as a Phenomenon of Syntactic Structure]. Voprosy yazykoznaniya **1966**(4), 111–118 (1966)
31. Akimova, G.N.: Razmer predlozheniya kak faktor stilistiki i grammatiki [Sentence Length as a Factor of Stylistics and Grammar]. Voprosy yazykoznaniya **1973**(2), 67–79 (1973)
32. Lesskis, G.A.: Nekotorye statisticheskie zakonomernosti kharakteristiki prostogo i slozhnogo predlozheniya v russkoj nauchnoj i khudozhestvennoj proze XVIII–XX vv. [Some Statistical Laws of the Characteristics of Simple and Compound Sentences in Russian Scientific and Fiction Texts of 18–20th centuries]. *Russkij yazyk v nacional'noj shkole* [*Russian language in the national school*] **1968**(2), 67–80 (1968)
33. Yule, G.: On sentence-length as a statistical characteristic of style in prose: with application to two cases of disputed authorship. Biometrika **30**(3/4), 363–390 (1939)
34. Huxtable, R.: Sentence length. Science **197**(4300), 208 (1977)
35. Olmsted, D.: On some axioms about sentence length. Language **43**(1), 303–305 (1967)
36. Yule, G.U., Kendall, M.G.: An Introduction to the Theory of Statistics. 14th edn. Charles Griffin & Company, London (1950). revised and enlarged
37. Hausstein, H.-D.: Prognosferfahren in der sozialistischen Wirtschaft. Verlag Die Wirtschaft, Berlin (1970)
38. Martynenko, G., Fomin, S.: Ranking moments. Nauchno-Tekhnicheskaya Informatsiya, Seriya 2, Informatsionnye Protsessy I Sistemy. Series 2 **1989**(8), 9–14 (1989)
39. Martynenko, G.: Statisticheskie kharakteristiki rangovykh raspredelenij [Statistical Characteristics of Rank Distributions]. In: Kvantitativnaya lingvistika i avtomaticheskij analiz teksta [Quantitative linguistics and automatic text analysis], **1989**(872), 50–68, Tartu (1989)
40. Karpenko, B.I.: Razvitie idej i kategorij matematicheskoj statistiki [The Development of Ideas and Categories of Mathematical Statistics]. Nauka, Moscow (1979)
41. Martynenko, G., Sherstinova, T., Popova, T., Melnik, A., Zamirayilova, E.: O principakh sozdaniya korpusa russkogo rasskaza pervoj treti XX veka [On the principles of the Creation of the Russian Short Story Corpus of the First Third of the 20th Century]. In: Proceedings of TEL Conference on Computational Linguistics-2018, vol. 1, pp. 180–198, Kazan (2019)

A Cross-Genre Morphological Tagging and Lemmatization of the Russian Poetry: Distinctive Test Sets and Evaluation

Aleksey Starchenko[1] and Olga Lyashevskaya[1,2](✉)

[1] National Research University Higher School of Economics, Moscow, Russia
amstarchenko@edu.hse.ru, olyashevskaya@hse.ru

[2] Vinogradov Institute of the Russian Language RAS, Moscow, Russia
https://www.hse.ru/org/persons/208526218,
https://www.hse.ru/en/staff/olesar

Abstract. The poetic texts pose a challenge to full morphological tagging and lemmatization since the authors seek to extend the vocabulary, employ morphologically and semantically deficient forms, go beyond standard syntactic templates, use non-projective constructions and non-standard word order, among other techniques of the creative language game. In this paper we evaluate a number of probabilistic taggers based on decision trees, CRF and neural network algorithms as well as a state-of-the-art dictionary-based tagger. The taggers were trained on prosaic texts and tested on three poetic samples of different complexity. Firstly, we suggest a method to compile the gold standard datasets for the Russian poetry. Secondly, we focus on the taggers' performance in the identification of the part of speech tags and lemmas. We reveal what kind of POS classes, paradigm classes and syntactic patterns mostly affect the quality of processing.

Keywords: NLP evaluation · Full morphology tagging · POS-tagging · Lemmatization · Russian language · Russian Poetry

1 Introduction

Poetic texts are usually processed with the help of the standard NLP tools that have been originally developed for and tested on prose. Ringger et al. [21] report a 8% drop in tagging accuracy on BNC poetry date while using a tagger trained on prosaic data. The Corpus of Russian Poetry (a part of the Russian National

The article was prepared within the framework of the Academic Fund Program at the National Research University Higher School of Economics (HSE University) in 2018–2019 (grant №18-05-0047) and within the framework of the Russian Academic Excellence Project «5–100».

D. A. Alexandrov et al. (Eds.): DTGS 2019, CCIS 1038, pp. 732–743, 2019.
https://doi.org/10.1007/978-3-030-37858-5_62

Corpus, RNC) is currently processed using Mystem [22], in which a statistical module is trained on web texts and prosaic RNC texts.

However, the distributional probabilities are different in the prosaic and poetic varieties. There are more nouns (30.3%) and adjectives (13.1%) and less verbs (14.9%) in the RNC Poetry Corpus than in the RNC Standard (prose) corpus (28.5%, 12.8%, 17.0%, respectively). The dissimilarities in lexical probabilities are even more noticeable, as the authors of poetry strive to enrich the lexicon, pick up rare gourmet rhymes, play with lacunae in grammar, be innovative in word derivation, etc., that is, to be 'creative' in the broadest sense of the term. Besides that, the rhythmic structure of poetry also affects syntactic patterns, word order, and the choice of lexical units and collocations. All these factors may challenge the cross-genre tagging and bias the prediction of the POS tags, grammatical features, and lemmas: three important constituents of the full morphological tagging.

Yet, developing a system designed specifically for poetry carries its own risks. Enhanced lexicon and more variable features such as the character and word ngrams are associated with the sparsity of language models, and using a (presumably) smaller genre-specific annotated corpus to train the new tagger is not always the best remedy in such cases. The aim of this papers is twofold. On the one hand, we discuss possible ways to compile poetic datasets as material for tagger evaluation (Sect. 2) and describe the taggers we used (Sect. 3). On the other hand, we report a preliminary experiment on the evaluation of the standard well proven tools developed for prose as a baseline for future comparison of existing and new genre-specific models (Sects. 4–6).

2 Distinctive Test Sets

The accuracy of full morphological tagging applied to modern languages is as high as 92–95% [24]. The best accuracy of POS-tagging reported for languages like English and German is close to 97%–98% [10]. With such high scores in assessment, the difference in the taggers' performance cannot be seen clearly. The idea behind the use of distinctiveness datasets (e.g. Rare Words dataset, [13]) is to provide the basis for more conservative, lower scores, taking into account only the most challenging data.

Since the low probability of a word or a word sequence is known as a bottleneck in text processing, three data sets were created: the first (Dataset A) is compiled so that it has a large percentage of out-of-vocabulary words, the second (Dataset B) includes complicated, in particular non-projective, syntactic constructions, and the third (Dataset C) contains a random poetic text as a 'general' sample.

Dataset A (750 words) is a sample drawn from the RNC Corpus of Russian Poetry [8]. It contains sentences with the high proportion of irregular forms and out-of-vocabulary words (OOV). Note that the notion of OOV words is different in dictionary-based and probabilistic tagging. If the words are not attested in the dictionary, they cannot be labeled by the dictionary-based tagger, and if the words have not been seen in the training set, they are harder to be correctly labeled by the probabilistic tagger than words which have been seen in the training data. Thus, the inventory of OOV words depends on a particular dictionary used by the tagger (cf. the grammatical dictionaries of Mystem and OpenCorpora) and on a particular training corpus and its size (cf. the RNC Standard, 6 MW, and SynTagRus, 1 MW). Still, we assume that the 'rare' words are unlikely to be present both in a dictionary and in a training collection and use the term OOV for both.

In order to compile Dataset A, we processed the word list of the Corpus of Russian Poetry by Mystem 3.1, which has an option to label the OOV words. Among the words which have been obtained, the following types are characteristic of the poetry texts:

- words with orthographic distortion and variation: *što* 'that' (cf. *čto*), *šopot* 'whisper' (cf. *šepot*), *ra-* || *zjaščee* 'smashing' (the word is divided by the line boundary);
- syllable dilation and contraction: *Zeves* 'Zeus' (cf. *Zevs*), *poln* 'full' (cf. *polon*);
- non-native names: *Io, Eol, Sal'vaterre*;
- archaic and archaic-like words: *drugi* 'friends', *oblak* 'cloud' (masculine);
- (quasi-)loan words: *mus'je* 'monsieur';
- non-standard grammatical forms: *mysliju* 'thought' (Instr. sing. noun, cf. *mysl'ju*), *uš* 'ears' (Gen. plural noun, cf. *ušej*), *ostavja* 'leaving' (Perfective gerundive, cf. *ostaviv*), *okazalasja* 'occur' (reflexive Past feminine verb, cf. *okazalas'*), *mjaučat* 'mew' (Present 3rd person plural verb, cf. *mjaukajut*).

As a next step, we inspected and ranked the OOV words from easy to difficult in terms of (a) POS identification, (b) inflectional form identification, and (c) lemma identification. For example, the short (2–3 character) words are difficult in all three aspects whereas words such as oblak are assumed to be classified correctly in terms of POS but misclassified in terms of gender labeling and lemmatization. Finally, a sample of sentences which contain at least two 'difficult' OOV words were retrieved using the frequency database of the Corpus of Russian Poetry [17]. As an instance, there are two non-standard grammatical forms in (1), and the fact that they are placed side-by-side, makes the sentence more difficult to be processed correctly.

(1) [Lanitoju] [prižavšisja] k perstu, || V ten', nedostupnuju tumanam i vetram.
lit. 'With a cheek pressing to the finger, || To the shadow, inaccessible to mists and winds'

Dataset B (850 words) is a sample of syntactically complex and non-standard sentences. We use several syntactic templates that we consider to be typical of the Russian poetry to retrieve the sentences for Dataset B:

- adjectives in the attributive position placed after their head, cf. *kisti.Noun.Gen čužoj.*Adj 'brush of someone else' in (2);
- nouns in the genitive construction where the genitive form is placed before its head, cf. *kisti.Gen kiparisy* 'cypress from one's brush' in (2);

- pre-position of the direct and indirect object, cf. (3); post-position of the subject with regard to the verb;
- verb phrases, noun phrases with one or more clause or parenthetic construction inserted inside.

(2) Kisti.Gen čužoj.Adj kiparisy i rozy. || Prosalili belyj kak vosk amvon.
lit. 'From the brush of someone else, cypress and roses || Saturated a wax white ambo.'

(3) Sveču.Acc sverkan'ju.Dat ljustr predpočitaem.
lit. '(It is) candle (that) we prefer to sparkling chandeliers.'

Dataset C (1750 words) is an excerpt drawn from the open source manually annotated UD_Russian-Taiga treebank [6]. Among other genres, this corpus includes folk poetry published on social media. Dataset C was meant to represent the 'average' level of complexity of poetic texts, although the length of the sentences appeared to be longer in Dataset C than in the Corpus of Russian Poetry in general.

3 Taggers

To date, a number of taggers have been tested on Russian (prosaic) data, both language-specific tools (Mystem, AOT [23], PyMorphy [11], NLTK4RUSSIAN [19], UDAR [20]), and general models trained on Russian data (TreeTagger [26], TnT [3], MarMoT/Lemming [18], UDpipe [25], various versions of BiLSTM taggers [1]). Evaluation of taggers on Russian prose data has been carried out within the framework of RU-EVAL 2010, MorphoRuEval 2017, SIGMORPHON 2016, CONLL 2018 shared tasks [4,14,24,29], see also evaluation experiments reported by [5,12]. In our study, we applied the following taggers to the Russian poetic material:

- Mystem-RuSyntax, an implementation of the Mystem model currently used in the annotation of the Main RNC corpus (consisting of prose texts), with the addition of context rules for POS disambiguation [7];
- Mystem 3.1, a standard implementation of Mystem provided by Mystem+ [5];
- TreeTagger (http://www.ims.uni-stuttgart.de/projekte/corplex/TreeTagger/, [26]), a tagger using automatic derivation of decision trees
- Hunpos (https://code.google.com/archive/p/hunpos/, [9]), a reimplementation of TnT tagger [3] using a trigram based HMM model;
- MarMoT (http://cistern.cis.lmu.de/marmot/, [18], a higher-order conditional random field (CRF) tagger;
- Lemming (http://cistern.cis.lmu.de/lemming/, [18], a modular log-linear tool based on the principles of a deterministic pre-extraction of edit trees, which jointly models lemmatization and tagging, an add-on to MarMoT;
- UDpipe (http://ufal.mff.cuni.cz/udpipe/, [25]), a rich feature averaged perceptron tagger, a baseline for CONLL 2018 shared task;

- Stanford POS tagger (http://nlp.stanford.edu/software/, [27]), a maximum entropy POS tagger (a bidirectional option) provided as a part of the Stanford CoreNLP Natural Language Processing Toolkit.

We use two versions of Mystem as a dictionary-based, rule-based baseline. The hypothesis builder for the OOV words in MyStem was trained on a big Yandex web collection [30], and the grammatical dictionary used is an extended version of [28]. Mystem-RuSyntax uses a model adopted to the RNC annotation guidelines [16]: unlike Mystem 3.1, it assigns separate lemmas to the perfective and the imperfective verbs and makes use of the stop list of annotations never attested in the RNC. The other taggers are probabilistic and differ in the size and type of the corpus on which the model was trained and the type of output they provide. TreeTagger, Hunpos, and MarMoT were trained on the 6MW corpus of Modern Russian prose (RNC Standard) in the framework of the Mystem+ project [5], therefore comparing their results achieved on the testing sets allows one to compare exactly the performance of the models, and not the quality of the training sample. When compared with Mystem, it should not be forgotten that the results of the comparison may change when the training sample is changed. UDpipe was trained on a 1 MW SynTagRus collection converted into UD format [6]. The Lemming model was trained by us on a 0.4 MW subcorpus of OpenCorpora prosaic texts [2]. The taggers learn from the following annotation types and therefore provide them in the output:

- Stanford POS tagger - only POS tags;
- TreeTagger, Hunpos, MarMoT - POS, grammatical features;
- Lemming - lemmas (adds lemmas to the output of MarMoT);
- UDpipe - POS, grammatical features, lemmas.

Thus, we can compare POS tagging across all models, lemmas - in Mystem, Lemming, and UDpipe, and grammatical features - across all models except Stanford and Lemming.

4 Experimental Setup

Gold Labels. All datasets were labeled with POS tags, grammatical feature tags, and lemmas. Each dataset was corrected manually by one annotator, and a small number of errors were also corrected post-hoc during evaluation stage.

Predicted Labels. The processed data were converted into the Universal Dependencies v. 2.0 standard, see Fig. 1. We followed the conversion rules of MorphoRuEval 2017 [15,24], with some adjustments. Animacy and aspect are let in evaluation, and the participle and gerundive forms are treated as forms of the verb. The predicted data were matched token by token to the gold collection. Punctuation marks, which are not returned by some taggers, and a number of frequent words known to be systematically labeled differently in different frameworks (e.g. *kotoryj* 'which') were marked off evaluation.

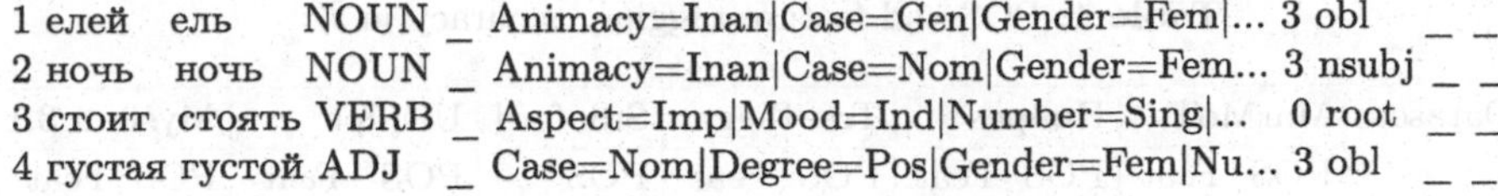
1 елей ель NOUN _ Animacy=Inan|Case=Gen|Gender=Fem|... 3 obl _ _
2 ночь ночь NOUN _ Animacy=Inan|Case=Nom|Gender=Fem... 3 nsubj _ _
3 стоит стоять VERB _ Aspect=Imp|Mood=Ind|Number=Sing|... 0 root _ _
4 густая густой ADJ _ Case=Nom|Degree=Pos|Gender=Fem|Nu... 3 obl _ _

Fig. 1. Annotations converted into UD-CONLLU format. Glossing of the clause: *елей* 'fur-NOUN.Gen.pl' *ночь* 'night-NOUN.Nom.sg' *стоит* 'stand-VERB.present.3sg' *густая* 'thick-ADJ.Nom.f.sg' 'The night of furs is thick'.

It should be noted that Mystem 3.1 does not disambiguate among possible grammatical annotations available for the identified lemma and POS and provides them all in alphabetical order. Technically, we assigned the first grammatical annotation to the token in evaluation. As a result, we cannot compare the accuracy of this tagger with the accuracy of the others, but nevertheless we can roughly compare the results of Mystem 3.1 applied to different Datasets (A, B, C).

We hypothesize that when processing Dataset B, taggers using probabilistic learning should show less stable results compared to their performance on Dataset A and C, since these taggers rely on word co-occurrence and syntax. The dictionary-based tagger Mystem should show a higher percentage of errors while parsing Dataset A, which contains a large number of non-vocabulary words. In what follows, we will analyse the results of the experiment and check if our assumptions hold.

5 POS-tagging

Table 1 shows the accuracy of POS-tagging when applied to Datasets A, B, C. Here and below, the accuracy metrics are calculated in %, with punctuation not taken into account. To compare with, the last row reports by default the results obtained on the prosaic texts in [5]. Overall, the accuracy of the best systems on the poetic texts ranges from 91.9% to 95.2% for the POS tags and from 82.4% to 92.6% for the feature tags.

Surprisingly, none of the taggers is an absolute winner: Hunpos is the best on Dataset A (OOV words), Stanford – on Dataset B (complicated syntax), POS tags, and MarMoT – on Dataset C (general). Even more surprisingly, TreeTagger, which performed best on the prosaic texts, occurs to be the least accurate on the poetic texts. The accuracy of the identification of grammatical labels does not exceed 86% (more than 10% less than the POS accuracy in winning systems) and, since Stanford does not provide this type of data, MarMoT wins the race on both Datasets B and C.

If we compare the results across datasets, we see that our assumption that the text with a complex syntactic structure is problematic for machine-based taggers has been confirmed: the scores obtained on Dataset B are certainly lower than the scores obtained on the general Dataset C. They are also lower than scores obtained on Dataset A (in both POS and feature identification tasks, the only exception is MarMoT on feature tagging).

Table 1. POS and feature tagging, accuracy in %.

Dataset	MarMoT		Hunpos		TreeTagger		Stanford	UDpipe		Mystem 3.1	
	POS	Feat	POS	Feat	POS	Feat	POS	POS	Feat	POS	Feat
A(oov)	93.1	78.6	**94.3**	**82.4**	87.4	72.2	94.1	88.9	74.3	91.7	67.7
B(order)	87.8	**82.6**	87.8	79.9	82.8	70.6	**91.9**	91.5	78.4	88.5	71.4
C(web)	**95.2**	**85.5**	94.3	83.3	90.9	77.1	93.9	92.5	78.1	91.3	65.8
Prose	96.0	—[a]	96.4	89.3	**96.9**	**92.6**	95.8[b]	98.2[b]	92.5[b]	96.4	—[a]

[a]Values not reported in [5].
[b]Models evaluated on the UD 2.3 test dataset of Russian-Syntagrus (without punctuation, 96k words).

The other hypothesis, that the accuracy will noticeably decrease with the increase in the number of non-vocabulary words, is not confirmed (compare the scores for Datasets C and A). Unlike MarMoT and TreeTagger, Hunpos and Stanford demonstrate approximately the same or slightly higher results on Dataset A. Yet, the accuracy of Marmot and TreeTagger's features decreases considerably as we move from Dataset C to Dataset A, as was expected.

Finally, Mystem, a dictionary-based tagger, shows generally uncommon results: it processes Dataset A with higher accuracy than Dataset C, even though the ratio of OOV words is higher in Dataset A. We can suggest that the tagging quality is affected by other factors which were not taken into account when we constructed the test sets. For example, there is an uneven proportion of nouns in Datasets A, B, and C: 34.2%, 30.2%, and 65.3%, respectively. As nouns usually show a greater tendency toward the grammatical ambiguity of forms, the method to get rid of homonymy we chose can lead to a greater number of errors in the case of words with ambiguous forms.

Comparing the accuracy of processing poetry vs. prose, we see that the scores are expectedly higher in the latter case, although the difference in POS tagging is not particularly noticeable. Interestingly, TreeTagger, which showed the best results in the tagging of prose, fails on poetry, demonstrating a greater bias to the type of text than the other taggers.

Table 2 summarizes the correspondence of the gold POS tags (lines) and those predicted by MarMoT/Lemming trained on a smaller 0.4 MW corpus (columns), see Sect. 6. Since its accuracy is lower compared to the accuracy of taggers described above, we can get enough error data to analyze them in more detail.

The analysis shows that words that constitute small, closed classes—i.e. conjunctions and prepositions—are most accurately identified. On the opposite side, the accuracy of processing for adverbs is low, almost close to chance. Such a low accuracy can be explained by the relative syntactic freedom of adverbs: many adverbs can appear anywhere in the sentence. In addition, a number of errors are caused by the mismatches between annotation practice in our gold data and the corpus on which Lemming was trained. Let us consider the case of predicatives.

Table 2. Confusion matrix for MarMoT: POS tags (based on Dataset A). In each cell, a number of occurrences is given; below them, the first percentage shows the ratio of the gold labels classified by the tagger as a particular POS; the second percentage is a relative frequency of the class in all cases predicted as a particular POS.

POS	adj	adp	adv	conj	det	intj	noun	num	part	pron	verb	x	Total
ADJ	67		2		1		5				2	2	79
	85%		3%		1%		6%				3%	3%	100%
	87%		9%		5%		2%				2%	6%	11%
ADP		86					1					2	89
		97%					1%					2%	100%
		99%					0%					6%	12%
ADV	2		16	3			4	1				4	30
	7%		53%	10%			13%	3%				13%	100%
	3%		70%	5%			2%	25%				11%	4%
CONJ				51					1	1		1	54
				94%					2%	2%		2%	100%
				91%					6%	2%		3%	7%
DET					20		1			3			24
					83%		4%			13%			100%
					95%		0%			7%			3%
INTJ						3						1	4
						75%						25%	100%
						100%						3%	1%
NOUN	4	1	2				230				2	15	254
	2%	0%	1%				91%				1%	6%	100%
	5%	1%	9%				89%				2%	43%	34%
NUM								3				1	4
								75%				25%	100%
								75%				3%	1%
PART							2		16		1		19
							11%		84%		5%		100%
							1%		89%		1%		3%
PRON	1			2			3		1	42			49
	2%			4%			6%		2%	86%			100%
	1%			4%			1%		6%	91%			7%
VERB	3		3				12				116	9	143
	2%		2%				8%				81%	6%	100%
	4%		13%				5%				95%	26%	19%
X							1				1		2
							50%				50%		100%
							0%				1%		0%
Total	77	87	23	56	21	3	259	4	18	46	122	35	751
	10%	12%	3%	7%	3%	0%	34%	1%	2%	6%	16%	5%	100%
	100%	100%	100%	100%	100%	100%	100%	100%	100%	100%	100%	100%	100%

This group includes words of different types: adjectival predicates ending in *-o*/ textit-e (*khorosho* 'good', *blizko* 'close to'), predicative nouns (*pora* 'it's time', *len'* 'lazy'), modal predicates (*dolžen* 'have to', *možno* 'possible'), the negative word *net* 'there is no'. If such a category is not present in the corpus tag set, the predicative words are distributed among other POS classes: adverbs, nouns, verbs. When we compared the two sets of tags, a technical decision was made (according to the practice adopted in the UD corpus from which Dataset C was taken) to label as adverbs all predicatives but the word *net*, which is considered a verb. As a result, a few predicative nouns are not labeled correctly.

The identification of some parts of speech is expectedly asymmetric. Thus, on the one hand, 95% of all verbs in the dataset are correctly identified by Lemming, which is a good result. On the other hand, Lemming also assigns the label "verb" to a number of words belonging to other parts of speech, so that its accuracy is not very high - only 80%.

6 Lemmatization

This section focuses on lemmatization. We analyze the accuracy of lemma labeling and consider a number of challenging cases. Table 3 presents the accuracy of lemmatization predicted by two lemmatizers: Lemming (probabilistic) and Mystem (hybrid, dictionary-based). Since the size of the corpus on which Lemming was trained is small (0.4 MW), the accuracy of POS and feature labels predicted by Lemming is lower than that predicted by the taggers presented above. In order to display this difference, Table 3 also summarizes data on the accuracy of the POS tagging.

Table 3. Lemmatization, accuracy in %.

Dataset	Lemming/MarMoT		Mystem	
	Lemma	POS	Lemma	POS
A	85.0	87.7	87.7	91.7
B	87.7	87.3	86.4	88.5
C	87.9	88.4	91.4	91.3

It can be seen that the quality of lemmatization by Lemming и Mystem varies weakly depending the dataset tested; we can only point out that for the dictionary-based lemmatizer, both the dataset with complex syntactic constructions (B) and the dataset with the out-of-vocabulary words (A) are problematic. At the same time, although Lemming was trained on a small data set, its accuracy is close to the accuracy of Mystem.

As for difficult cases, there is a number of OOV words with non-standard endings (*nest'* 'carry', *prinest'* 'bring', *unest'* 'carry out', instead of *nesti*, *prinesti*, *unesti*). Since no rules implemented in Mystem to support orthographic variation these infinitives are incorrectly tagged as predicatives because of their similarity with the word *nest'* 'there is no'.

Not surprisingly, Lemming often makes mistakes when applied to the cases in which the part of speech tags were incorrectly identified. In particular, when the part-tag tag cannot be chosen (that is, the tag X is selected), lemmatization is not performed: the word form is chosen as the lemma.

One more frequent type of errors is a wrong choice of the ending in the cases in which there are two words in the language with the overlapping paradigm, cf. *bank* 'bank' and *banka* 'jar'. This error is known as misclassification of the type of declension, and usually the nouns of different grammatical gender are mixed. Thus, the lemma *kos* is assigned instead of *kosa* 'braid', *kail* 'Kyle' instead of *kailo* 'pick', *platka* 'patch' instead of *platok* 'handkerchief'. This error sometimes occurs even if the morphological gender is correctly defined. The choice between two possible allomorphs can also be incorrect, cf. *khudyj* 'thin' instead of *khudoj* 'thin', *dysat'* instead of *dyshat'* 'breathing'.

7 Conclusions

We compared taggers of different types in a full morphological annotation task for poetic texts. As expected, poetry in general turns out to be difficult for processing by taggers which were designed and trained on prose, the nonstandard syntactic patterns being the most challenging. The accuracy of POS tags ranges from 91.9% to 95.2%. The drop in accuracy is more significant in the feature tagging (82.4%–85.5%), which can be explained by the complexity of the classification task itself and by some conventions of data evaluation which we followed. The case study shows that adverbs are most difficult to pars and the label verb is frequently assigned to the words of other parts of speech. As for lemmatization, it turned out that its accuracy weakly depends on the type of text and - for the selected taggers - on the type of tagger. There is no doubt that these results have to be verified in further experiments with models trained on larger data.

Overall, the distinctive test sets help to identify the gap for improvement and make it linguistically interpretable. However, since our collections are small, they do not provide enough statistics to make definitive conclusions on taggers' performance. The complexity of the structures in the poetic texts and the small amount of test data may explain the mixed results achieved with the distinctive datasets. We did not control for syntactic complexity while mining the dataset for OOV words and vice versa. None of the parameters was controlled while randomly sampling Dataset C. A more promising approach would be to annotate the word entries according to multiple parameters within one large test collection. After that, a set of additional individual metrics will be obtained by choosing a subset of the test data such as words positioned in nonstandard word order, words which have counterparts with overlapping paradigms, and other parameters of the test data profiling.

Acknowledgements. We would like to thank Lev Kazakevich who assisted with data collection for this study, and three anonymous reviewers for insightful comments on the first version of this paper.

References

1. Anastasiev, D.G., Gusev, I.O., Indenbom, E.M.: Improving part-of-speech tagging via multi-task learning and character-level word representations. In: International Conference on Computational Linguistics and Intellectual Technologies, Dialogue 2018, Moscow (2018)
2. Bocharov, V.V., Alexeeva, S.V., Granovsky, D.V., Protopopova, E.V., Stepanova, M.E., Surikov, A.V.: Crowdsourcing morphological annotation. In: Proceedings of Dialogue 2013, Moscow (2013)
3. Brants, T.: TnT - a statistical part-of-speech tagger. In: Proceedings of the 6th Applied Natural Language Processing Conference, Seattle, pp. 224–231 (2000)
4. Cotterell, R., Kirov, Ch., Sylak-Glassman, J., Yarowsky, D., Eisner, J., Hulden, M.: The SIGMORPHON 2016 shared task - morphological reinflection. In: Proceedings of the 14th SIGMORPHON Workshop on Computational Research in Phonetics, Phonology, and Morphology, pp. 10–22. ACL (2016)
5. Dereza, O.V., Kayutenko, D.A., Fenogenova, A.S.: Automatic morphological analysis for Russian: a comparative study. In: Proceedings of Dialogue 2016, Moscow (2016)
6. Droganova, K., Lyashevskaya, O., Zeman, D.: Data conversion and consistency of monolingual corpora: Russian UD treebanks. In: Proceedings of TLT 2018, Oslo (2018)
7. Droganova, K.A., Medyankin, N.S.: NLP pipeline for Russian: an easy-to-use web application for morphological and syntactic annotation. In: Proceedings of Dialogue 2016, Moscow (2016)
8. Grishina, E., Korchagin, K., Plungian, V., Sichinava, D.: Poeticheskij korpus v ramkakh Nasional'nogo korpusa russkogo yazyka: obshchaya struktura i perspektivy ispol'zovaniya [The corpus of poetry within the Russian National Corpus: a general outline and perspectives of use]. In: Natsional'nyj korpus russkogo yazyka: 2006–2008. Novye rezul'taty i perspektivy [The Russian National Corpus: 2006–2008. New results and prospects]. St. Petersburg: Nestor-Istoriya Publ. (2009)
9. Halácsy, P., Kornai, A.: Oravecz, C.: HunPos: an open source trigram tagger. In: Interactive Poster and Demonstration Sessions, ACL 2007, Stroudsburg, PA, pp. 209–212 (2007)
10. Horsmann, T., Erbs, N., Zesch, T.: Fast or accurate? - a comparative evaluation of PoS tagging models. In: GSCL 2015, Duisburg-Essen, Germany, pp. 22–30 (2015)
11. Korobov, M.: Morphological analyzer and generator for Russian and Ukrainian Languages. In: Khachay, M.Y., Konstantinova, N., Panchenko, A., Ignatov, D.I., Labunets, V.G. (eds.) AIST 2015. CCIS, vol. 542, pp. 320–332. Springer, Cham (2015). https://doi.org/10.1007/978-3-319-26123-2_31
12. Kuzmenko, E.: Morphological analysis for Russian: integration and comparison of taggers. In: Ignatov, D.I., et al. (eds.) AIST 2016. CCIS, vol. 661, pp. 162–171. Springer, Cham (2017). https://doi.org/10.1007/978-3-319-52920-2_16
13. Luong, T., Socher, R., Manning, C.: Better word representations with recursive neural networks for morphology. In: CONLL 2013, Sofia, Bulgaria, pp. 104–113 (2013)
14. Lyashevskaya, O., et al.: Ocenka metodov avtomaticheskogo analiza teksta: morfologicheskie parsery russkogo jazyka. In: Proceedings of Dialogue 2010, Moscow, pp. 318–326 (2010)
15. Lyashevskaya, O., Bocharov, V., Sorokin, A., Shavrina, T., Granovsky, D., Alexeeva, S.: Text collections for evaluation of Russian morphological taggers. Jazykovedný casopis **68**(2), 258–267 (2017)

16. Lyashevskaya, O., Plunguan, V., Sichinava, D.: O morpfologicheskom standarte Natsional'nogo korpusa russkogo jazyka [On the morphological standard of the Russian National Corpus]. In: Natsional'nyj korpus russkogo jazyka 2003–2005, pp. 111–135, Moscow (2005)
17. Lyashevskaya, O., Litvintseva, K., Vlasova, E., Sechina, E.: A Data Analysis Tool for the Corpus of Russian Poetry, Moscow, HSE University, WP BRP Linguistics (2018)
18. Müller, T., Cotterell, R., Fraser, A., Schütze, H.: Joint lemmatization and morphological tagging with lemming. In: EMNLP-2015, Lisbon, Portugal, pp. 2268–2274 (2015)
19. Panicheva, P., Protopopova, E., Mitrofanova, O., Mirzagitova, A.: Razrabotka lingvisticheskogo kompleksa dlja morfologicheskogo analiza russkojazychnykh korpusov tekstov na osnove PyMorphy i NLTK [Development of an NLP toolkit for morphological analysis of Russian text corpora based on PyMorphy and NLTK]. In: International Conference CORPORA-2015, Saint-Petersburg (2015)
20. Reynolds, R.: Russian natural language processing for computer-assisted language learning: capturing the benefits of deep morphological analysis in real-life applications. Ph.d. diss., Tromsø University of Tromsø (2016)
21. Ringger, E., et al.: Active learning for part-of-speech tagging: accelerating corpus annotation. In: Linguistic Annotation Workshop, Prague (2007)
22. Segalovich, I.: A fast morphological algorithm with unknown word guessing induced by a dictionary for a web search engine. In: MLMTA-2003, Las Vegas (2003)
23. Sokirko, A.: Morphologicheskie moduli na sajte www.aot.ru [Morphological tools on the website www.aot.ru]. In: Dialog 2004, International Conference on Computational Linguistics and Intellectual Technologies, Moscow (2004)
24. Sorokin, A., et al.: MorphoRuEval-2017: an evaluation track for the automatic morphological analysis methods for Russian. In: Proceedings of Dialog-2017, Moscow (2017)
25. Straka, M., Hajič, J., Straková, J.: UDPipe: trainable pipeline for processing CoNLL-U files performing tokenization, morphological analysis, POS tagging and parsing. In: LREC-2016, Portorož, Slovenia (2016)
26. Schmid, H.: Probabilistic part-of-speech tagging using decision trees. In: International Conference on New Methods in Language Processing, Manchester (1994)
27. Toutanova, K., Klein, D., Manning, Ch.D., Singer, Y.: Feature-rich part-of-speech tagging with a cyclic dependency network. In: NAACL, vol. 1, pp. 173–180 (2003)
28. Zaliznyak, A.A.: Grammaticheskij slovar' russkogo jazyka [The grammatical dictionary of Russian], Moscow (2003)
29. Zeman, D., et al.: CoNLL 2018 shared task: multilingual parsing from raw text to universal dependencies. In: CoNLL 2018 Shared Task: Multilingual Parsing from Raw Text to Universal Dependencies, pp. 1–21. ACL (2018)
30. Zobnin, A.I., Nosyrev, G.V.: Morfologicheskij analizator Mystem 3.0 [A morphological analyzer Mystem 3.0]. Trudy Instituta russkogo jazyka im. V. V. Vinogradova [Works of Vinogradov Institute of the Russian Language RAS] (6), 300–310 (2015)

Assessment of the Dynamics of Publication Activity in the Field of Natural Language Processing and Deep Learning

Ravil I. Mukhamedyev[1,2,4](✉), Yan Kuchin[2], Kosyakov Denis[3], Sanzhar Murzakhmetov[1,2], Adilkhan Symagulov[1,2], and Kirill Yakunin[1,2]

[1] Satbayev University (KazNRTU), 22a Satpaev Str., 050013 Almaty, Kazakhstan
ravil.muhamedyev@gmail.com

[2] Institute of Information and Computational Technologies, 050010 Almaty, Kazakhstan

[3] The State Public Scientific Technological Library of Siberian Branch of the Russian Academy of Science, Novosibirsk 630102, Russian Federation

[4] ISMA University, Riga LV1011, Latvia

Abstract. Natural language processing (NLP) is a rapidly developing field of research. In solving the problems of NLP, along with traditional methods based on a statistical model of language, machine learning methods (ML) are used. The paper considers bibliometric indicators NLP and ML. Dynamic indicators are evaluated and areas of research with the highest growth rates are identified. The indicators were calculated for the following NLP applications: Grammar Checking, Information Extraction, Text Categorization, Dialog Systems, Speech Recognition, Machine Translation, Information Retrieval, Question Answering, Opinion Mining, Smart advisors, etc. The greatest values of dynamic indicators are demonstrated by: Grammar Checking, Information Extraction, Machine Translation, Question Answering. At the same time, the following methods of solving NLP problems are developing most dynamically: Machine Learning, Deep Learning, Neural Networks and Supervised Learning. In turn, Deep Learning is used to solve a wide range of applications. Its feature is the increased requirements for the volume of data processed. The paper assesses the growth dynamics of bibliometric indicators for some Deep Learning applications. The most dynamically developing research is the field of deep learning applications to solve healthcare problems.

Keywords: Bibliometric analysis · Scientometrics · Natural language processing · Publication activity · Machine learning · Deep Learning · Dynamic indicators D1 · D2

D. A. Alexandrov et al. (Eds.): DTGS 2019, CCIS 1038, pp. 744–753, 2019.
https://doi.org/10.1007/978-3-030-37858-5_63

1 Introduction

The area of natural language processing (NLP) is characterized by a wide range of tasks and methods, some of which already have acceptable solutions in the form of software, while others require intensive research.

It may be noted that infrastructure-type tasks related to the field of morphological and syntactic analysis, the statistical model of a language are largely solved and can be included in the system being developed, for example, in the form of software as a service (SaaS) [1]. In this regard, it would be useful to identify those areas of research that are characterized by a great interest of researchers.

The number of publications, the number of citations (citation index), the number of co-authors, Hirsch index and other bibliometric indicators can be used to assess the development of a scientific field. Identification of "hot" areas in which these indicators have greater values, allows, ceteris paribus, to more clearly present the situation in the analyzed field of scientific research.

However, the number of publications is growing in many areas of natural language processing. Therefore, a simple statement of growth, for example, of number of publications, is not enough. In order to identify patterns of change in publication activity, differential indicators D1 ("speed") and D2 ("acceleration") were introduced in [2]. Differential metrics allow you to assess the dynamics of changes in the use of selected key terms by the authors of scientific publications. Thus, it is possible to more clearly reflect the growth or decline of the interest of researchers to the use of keywords that characterize the field of research.

NLP as a research field solves the problem of developing methods for the automatic analysis and presentation of the natural human language [3]. Research in this direction has been conducted since the 50s of the last century. Practical tasks of NLP include:

- automatic translation [4] and referencing
- generation of responses to user requests (Question Answering) [5, 6]
- information extraction, IE [7],
- information retrieval [9–12],
- sentiment analysis [13],
- other areas, one way or another connected with the processing of oral and written natural speech

In recent years, significant progress has been made in the areas of automatic translation (machine translation), summarization (automatic summarization), information retrieval, question answering systems, tonality analysis (sentiment analysis), information extraction (extraction) [15], author's verification (authorship verification) [16]. According to [17], the success of NLP is a consequence of the development of machine learning methods, a multiple increase in computing power, the availability of a large amount of linguistic data and the development in understanding the structure of a natural language as applied to the social context.

The need to solve practical problems of NLP served as a catalyst for the development of methods, among which we can mention machine learning and its subsections: neural networks and deep learning (DL) [14], semi-supervised learning [8] and so on.

NLP and DL as the research area are changing rapidly.

It is interesting and important to assess the dynamics of these changes by assessing the publication activity in different sections of the NLP and DL.

The idea of assessing publication activity can be attributed to the works of E. Garfield, who in [18] introduced the concept of science citation index (SCI). Later, bibliometric indicators (number of publications, citation index, number of co-authors, etc.) were widely used to assess the productivity of scientists [19, 20], fields of research [21], universities [22], the formation of research management policies [23], prediction [24, 25]. In [26, 27], the change in the Hirsch index over time is considered and the concept of the dynamic Hirsch index is proposed.

However, the main purpose of these indicators is to assess the personal contribution of a scientist. To assess the dynamics of changes in research fields, you can use the citation indicators and the number of publications.

Evaluation of changes in these indicators over time with one-year increment is not difficult, but for comparative analysis, numerical growth indicators are important. To this end, based on the differential metrics introduced in [2] for estimating the growth of research areas, the dynamic indicators of publication activity in the field of NLP and different DL applications were calculated.

The paper is organized as follow. The first section lists the analyzed NLP and DL sub-domains. In the second, we described the applied analysis technique. In the third we considered the results obtained.

The main illustrations are given in the appendix A. (https://drive.google.com/open?id=1y8vlINVmuHVEH-8GlhLLbCxVQf7zpx_T)

2 Analyzed NLP and DL Research Areas

As part of this work, we identified the following areas of publication activity for research. At first, we consider the area of NLP from the point of view of the tasks to be solved, among which [28], the following were attributed (“**NLP tasks**” or “**Tasks**” group): Grammar Checking, Information Extraction, Text Categorization, Dialog Systems, Speech Recognition, Machine Translation, Information Retrieval, Question Answering, Opinion Mining & Sentiment analysis, Smart advisors, and Automatic summarization. Secondly, the field of NLP is characterized by rapid growth of technologies and methods that contribute to the solution of the above problems. We attributed the following methods to the number of methods (“**Scientific NLP Methods**” or “**Methods**” group): Machine Learning, Neural Networks, Deep Learning, Fuzzy Logic, First order logic, Knowledge representation, Evolutionary computation & Genetic programming, Rule based system, Unsupervised learning, Clustering, Supervised learning, Statistical methods, Bayesian networks, Semantic c networks, Keyword Spotting, Lexical affinity, Ontology, Information fusion, Taxonomy.

In turn, DL has a large number of applications. The economic spheres that we have chosen for study are the mining industry, the agricultural sector, the construction industry, health care, management, and, in general, decision support. As the scientific methods of DL we considered the sequence-to-sequence, Convolutional Neural Networks, the generative adversarial network and reinforcement learning.

3 Research Methodology

To assess the dynamics of changes in publication activity, we will use, as in [2], the indicators of the compound annual growth rate (CAGR), D1 and D2, which are defined as follows:

$$CAGR = \left(\frac{Ending\ Value}{Beginnig\ Value}\right)^{\frac{1}{T-1}} - 1 \quad (1)$$

Where T is the number of periods.

$$D1_i^j(t_k) = \beta \times \frac{dn_i^j(t_k)}{dt} + \gamma \times \frac{dc_i^j(t_k)}{dt} \quad (2)$$

$$D2_i^j(t_k) = \beta' \times \frac{d(dn_i^j(t_k)/dt)}{dt} + \gamma' \times \frac{d(dc_i^j(t_k)/dt)}{dt} \quad (3)$$

Where n_i and c_i are number of publications and citations respectively, determined using search term i, β, γ, β', γ' – some empirical coefficients that regulate the “weight” of the contribution of the number of publications, the speed and acceleration of number of publications n_i and the speed and acceleration of number of citations c_i, respectively.

For the analysis of publications in English, one of the largest bibliometric databases - Science Direct, which contains about 2,500 scientific journals and 26,000 electronic books, was used [29].

To study the dynamics of publications in Russian, the leading Russian scientific electronic library eLIBRARY.ru was used. As of mid-2018, the database eLIBRARY.ru has more than 30.7 million articles, including publications of the last decades of the 20th century. According to our requests, individual publications of the mentioned period were found, but their number turned out to be extremely small, so statistics in the tables are given starting from 2005. We emphasize that although there are a lot of English-language publications from foreign editions in the eLIBRARY.ru database, we limited ourselves to queries only in Russian, since the study of English-language publications was conducted separately on the ScienceDirect database.

For each bibliometric database, corresponding search queries were formed, including the above terms in combination with NLP, NLP and ML, etc. The results of the queries were the number of publications and citations annually, starting from 2005. Data from 2018 were not used due to their incompleteness.

Based on the results obtained, for each search query, calculations of indicators CAGR, D1, D2 were performed. Constants β, γ, β’, γ’ were taken 0.8.

To assess the dynamics of changes in bibliometric indices DL, a slightly different approach was used. For each search query in Tables 9 and 10 (Appendix A) there are 14 annual values. Using this data, a polynomial regression model was constructed.

Then, 140 values are generated. Regression dependence for DL applications in agriculture is presented on Fig. 1. The obtained data was used to calculate indicators D1 and D2. The proposed method allowed calculating the values of the indicators up to 2018 inclusive (https://github.com/ravilxx/scientometrics).

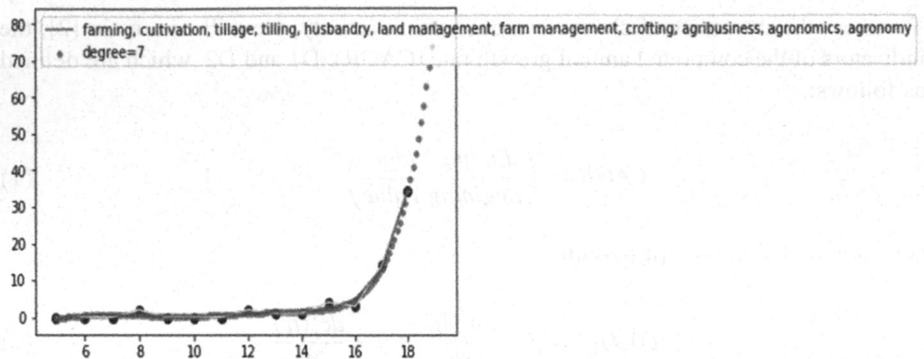

Fig. 1. Regression dependence (red) and source data (black) for data on the number of publications describing DL applications in agriculture. (Color figure online)

4 Results

Appendix A contains tables and diagrams obtained using expressions 1, 2, 3 for NLP and expressions 2 and 3 for DL. Table 1 shows the annual number of publications. Table 2 displays citations relating to the "NLP tasks" group according to Science Direct. Pictures present the dynamics of changes in the number of publications (Fig. 1A) and citations (Fig. 2A). Tables 5 and 6 show similar results for the data on eLIBRARY.ru. It should be noted that the data presented in the tables reflects only some of the existing publications in the Russian-language segment due to the peculiarities of the search queries.

In the tables relating to the Russian-speaking segment of NLP, the rows on which the dynamic indicators were calculated are highlighted in bold. The remaining rows were not used due to their non-representativeness (small amount of data). Figures 3A, 4A illustrate changes in the number of publications and citations in the "NLP tasks" group according to eLibrary.ru. Changes in publication activity in the field of applied algorithmic and mathematical methods of NLP ("scientific methods of NLP") are illustrated in Appendix A in Tables 5, 6. The change in publication activity at the intersection of machine learning and NLP (the "NLP & ML" group) is illustrated in of Table 7, 8 and Fig. 5A of Appendix A. Figure 6A shows the areas of ML use for solving NLP problems, showing a positive D2 value:

- Information Extraction
- Grammar Checking
- Machine Translation
- Question Answering

Figure 7A shows areas of joint use NLP ML and with a positive value D2:

- Machine Translation
- Question Answering
- Speech Recognition

Several NLP sections show a negative value for D2, which means a slowdown in the growth rate of the number of publications and citations (Fig. 8A):

- Automatic summarization
- Speech Recognition
- Information Retrieval
- Opinion Mining & Sentiment analysis
- Text Categorization

Note the decline in the interest of researchers to some scientific methods in NLP:

- Rule based
- Statistical methods
- Clustering
- Fuzzy logic
- Keyword spotting
- First order logic

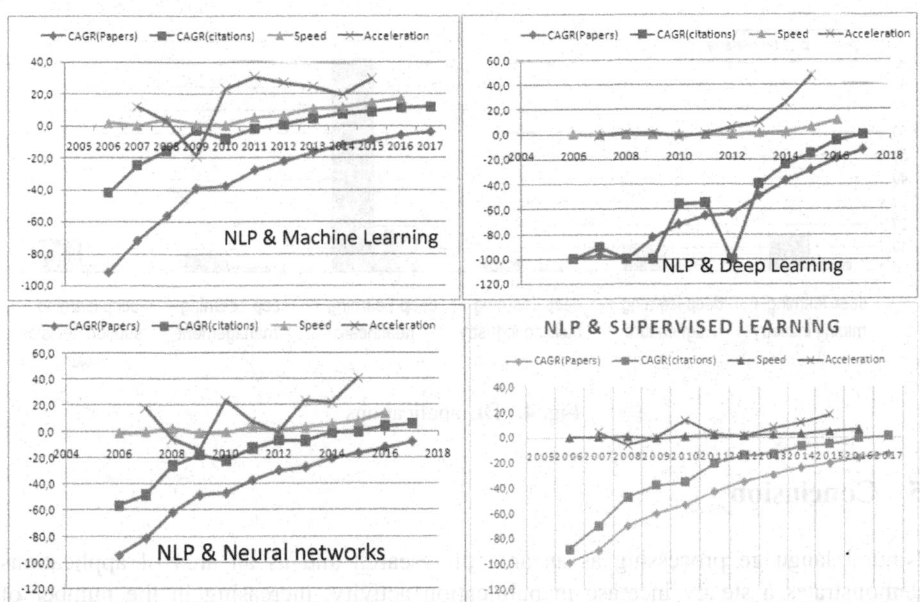

Fig. 2. The group "scientific methods of NLP", which can be attributed to the most popular, with a large and increasing positive value of D2 (acceleration)

At the same time, high positive rates of D2 are noted for ML, neural networks and in particular for DL (Fig. 2).

In the Russian-language segment, the processing of natural language seems to have reached a level of saturation, when two periods of explosive growth in the number of publications are followed by a slowdown in growth in almost all the areas of research under consideration (Fig. 11A).

For DL, the calculated values of D1 and D2 for 2018 are shown in the Figs. 3 and 4.

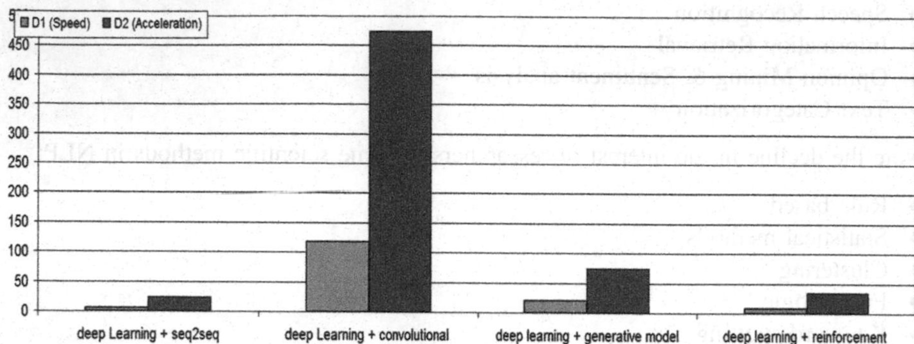

Fig. 3. Scientific methods of DL

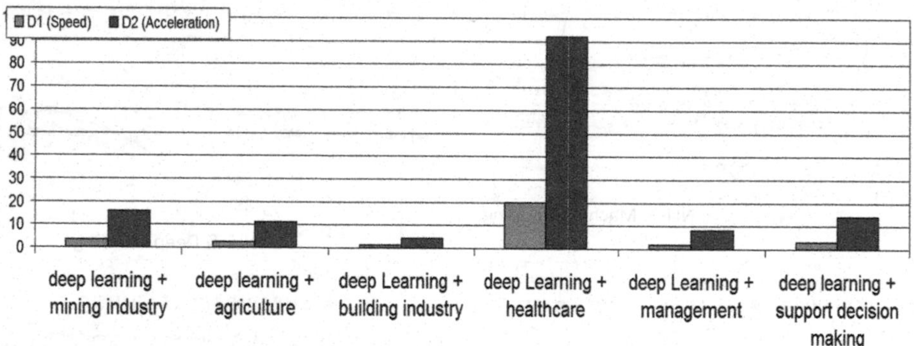

Fig. 4. DL applications

5 Conclusion

Natural language processing as an area of research and as an area of applications demonstrates a steady increase in publication activity, increasing in the number of applications and qualitative changes in the applied methods. For analysis of this growth, based on bibliometric indicators, we calculated the rates of the changes rate D1 and the acceleration of changes D2. A positive value of D2 reflects the fact of increasing the speed of growth of publications activity in research domain. A negative value, in turn, shows a slowdown of publication activity compared with previous periods. The increase in D2 over several periods indicates a sharp increase in the number of scientific papers and citations associated with the area of study. The indicators show interesting dynamics of changes for most areas, when the initial growth is replaced by a deceleration, and then repeated acceleration follows. (question answering, speech recognition). The reasons for this phenomenon could be investigated in detail in the future. However, it can be suppose that this dynamics describes, on the one hand, the intensity of development in the field of research, and on the other, the understanding of the new concepts by researchers and its practical application. Only some of the presented research areas (grammar checking, NLP & Deep Learning) show constant increase of publication activity (the D2 indicator has only positive values during entire period under consideration). Some domains of NLP research area demonstrate significant growth of publications and citations. For example, Grammar Checking, Information Extraction, Machine Translation and Question Answering are characterized positive value of D2 during last years.

As in the English segment, Russian-language publications are characterized by the dominance of information retrieval and information extraction, which are in the first and second place by the number of publications, respectively. However, unlike the English segment, the D2 indicator for extracting information has a negative value. In this way, although general tendencies characteristic of NLP are also present in the Russian-speaking sector, in recent years the growth rates have decreased. In the Russian-language segment, "natural language processing" has apparently reached the saturation level, when two periods of explosive growth in the number of publications are followed by a slowdown in growth in almost all research areas. Research areas related to machine learning (machine learning), deep learning (deep learning), neural networks (neural networks) and, as a result, the so-called supervised learning have high positive values of D2. In this case, machine learning is especially intensively used in solving speech recognition problems, automatic translation and in question-answer systems.

A comparative analysis of DL methods showed that the largest increase in publication activity is associated with convolution neural networks. Among the considered application areas for DL is health care. The choice of keywords for the selection of publications and the calculation of citations is subjective and reflects only the opinion of the authors.

The aim of further research is reducing this subjectivity when choosing the main areas of analysis using NLP methods (primarily distributive semantics) and using machine learning (primarily regression models) to calculate indicators D1 and D2.

Acknowledgments. The work was funded by a grant BR05236839 of the Ministry of Education and Science of the Republic of Kazakhstan.

References

1. Dale, R.: NLP meets the cloud. Nat. Lang. Eng. **21**(4), 653–659 (2015)
2. Muhamedyev, R.I., et al.: New bibliometric indicators for prospectivity estimation of research fields. Ann. Libr. Inf. Stud. (ALIS) **65**(1), 62–69 (2018)
3. Cambria, E., Bebo, W.: Jumping NLP curves: a review of natural language processing research. IEEE Comput. Intell. Mag. **9**(2), 48–57 (2014)
4. Sreelekha, S., Pushpak, B., Shishir, K.J., Malathi, D.: A survey report on evolution of machine translation. Int. J. Control Theory Appl. **9**(33), 233–240 (2016)
5. Höffner, K., Walter, S., Marx, E., Usbeck, R., Lehmann, J., Ngonga Ngomo, A.C.: Survey on challenges of question answering in the semantic web. Semant. Web **8**(6), 895–920 (2017)
6. Wu, Q., Damien, T., Wang, P., Shen, C., Dick, A., van den Hengel, A.: Visual question answering: a survey of methods and datasets. Comput. Vis. Image Underst. **163**, 21–40 (2017)
7. Jurafsky, D., Martin, J.H.: Speech and Language Processing, 2nd edn. Prentice-Hall Inc, Upper Saddle River (2009)
8. Niklaus, C., Cetto, M., Freitas, A., Handschuh, S.: A survey on open information extraction. arXiv preprint arXiv:1806.05599 (2018)
9. Deo, A., Jayesh, G., Shweta, G.: A survey paper on information retrieval system. Int. J. Adv. Res. Comput. Sci. **9**(1), 778–781 (2018)
10. Shokin, Y., Fedotov, A., Barakhnin, V.: Information Finding Problems. Nauka, Novosibirsk (2010)
11. Campos, R., Gaël, D., Alípio, M.J., Jatowt, A.: Survey of temporal information retrieval and related applications. ACM Comput. Surv. (CSUR) **47**(2), 1–15 (2017)
12. Purves, R.S., Clough, P., Jones, C.B., Hall, M.H., Murdock, V.: Geographic information retrieval: progress and challenges in spatial search of text. Found. Trends Inf. Retrieval **12** (3), 164–318 (2018)
13. Sun, S., Chen, L., Junyu, C.: A review of natural language processing techniques for opinion mining systems. Inf. Fusion **36**, 10–25 (2017)
14. LeCun, Y., Yoshua, B., Geoffrey, H.: Deep learning. Nature **521**(7553), 436–443 (2015)
15. Hogenboom, F., et al.: A survey of event extraction methods from text for decision support systems. Decis. Support Syst. **85**, 12–22 (2016)
16. Potthast, M., Hagen, M., Stein, B.: Author obfuscation: attacking the state of the art in authorship verification. CLEF (Working Notes), 716–749 (2016)
17. Hirschberg, J., Manning, C.D.: Advances in natural language processing. Science **349** (6245), 261–266 (2015)
18. Garfield, E.: Citation indexes for science: a new dimension in documentation through association of ideas. Science **122**, 108–111 (1955)
19. Gauthier, É.: Bibliometric analysis of scientific and technological research: a user's guide to the methodology. Canada: Science and Technology Redesign Project, Statistics Canada (1998)
20. Van Raan, A.F.J.: The use of bibliometric analysis in research performance assessment and monitoring of interdisciplinary scientific developments. Technol. Assess. Theory Pract. **1** (12), 20–29 (2003)
21. Mokhnacheva, J.V., Mitroshin, I.A.: Nanoscience and nanotechnologies at the Moscow domain: a bibliometric analysis based on «Web of Science» (Thomson Reuters). Inf. Resour. Russia **6**, 17–23 (2014)

22. Abramo, G., Ciriaco, A.D., Fabio, P.: The measurement of Italian universities' research productivity by a non parametric-bibliometric methodology. Scientometrics **76**(2), 2–25 (2008)
23. Debackere, K., Glänzel, W.: Using a bibliometric approach to support research policy making: the case of the Flemish BOF-key. Scientometrics **59**(2), 253–276 (2004)
24. Daim, T.U., Rueda, G.R., Martin, H.T.: Technology forecasting using bibliometric analysis and system dynamics. In: A Unifying Discipline for Melting the Boundaries Technology Management, pp. 112–122. IEEE, Portland (2005)
25. Daim, T.U., et al.: Forecasting emerging technologies: use of bibliometrics and patent analysis. Technol. Forecast. Soc. Chang. **73**(8), 981–1012 (2006)
26. Egghe, L.: Dynamic h-index: the hirsch index in function of time. J. Assoc. Inf. Sci. Technol. **58**(3), 452–454 (2007)
27. Rousseau, R., Fred, Y.Y.: A proposal for a dynamic h-type index. J. Assoc. Inf. Sci. Technol. **59**(11), 1853–1855 (2008)
28. Natural language Processing. https://en.wikipedia.org/wiki/Natural_language_processing. Accessed 21 Jan 2019
29. Elsevier Science Direct. https://en.wikipedia.org/wiki/Wikipedia:Elsevier_ScienceDirect. Accessed 19 Jan 2019

Russian Text Vectorization: An Approach Based on SRSTI Classifier

Yulia Solomonova(✉) and Maksim Khlopotov

ITMO University, 49 Kronverkskiy pr., lit. A, 197101 St. Petersburg, Russia
solomonovajulia@gmail.com, khlopotov@corp.ifmo.ru

Abstract. This paper presents an approach to Russian text vectorization based on SRSTI classifier. Our approach is based on using SRSTI categories as vector space dimensions. The categories are defined by lists of keywords. We explain our choice of SRSTI as a basis for vector space. We describe the keywords selection process, as well as vector calculation and comparison algorithm. We apply developed algorithm to marked-up SRSTI texts and user social profiles. We also suggest approaches to vector space improvement and evaluate them.

Keywords: Text classification · Text vectorization · Topic modelling

1 Introduction

Text vectorization is a process of representing text as a meaningful numeric vector. Numeric representation of text is used for document retrieval, web search, spam filtering, topic modeling and other fields [1].

One of the most common approaches proposed for text vectorization is representing text as a vector of word counts with the order of words being dismissed [2]. It is known as a bag of words, or bag of n-grams, depending on how many words are used as an individual term [3]. One can also create a binary vector that represents whether or not some term is present in the text.

Term Frequency and Inverse Document Frequency (TF-IDF) technique besides the information about word frequency also encapsulates information on how common the word is in all texts reviewed. Because of that, words that do not appear frequently in the text hold higher weight than commonly used words. Such an approach helps to enhance relevant words retrieval [4].

Word2vec model suggests representing words by word vectors, where each feature is a semantic property of the word, so that words space location is defined by its meaning [5]. This way, semantically close words are also close in vector space and the distance between two words signifies some semantic relationship. Another model, doc2vec, is an extension of word2vec with additional vector that holds a numeric representation of the document [6].

Skip-Thought Vectors, also called as "sentence2vec" model, use a neural network to predict the words of surrounding sentences, thus creating a sentence vector representation [7].

D. A. Alexandrov et al. (Eds.): DTGS 2019, CCIS 1038, pp. 754–764, 2019.
https://doi.org/10.1007/978-3-030-37858-5_64

There are also other popular text vectorization models, such as DSSM, InferSent, CNN, Bi-LSTM and Memory network. These models vectorize texts and use the resulting vectors for various downstream tasks [8].

In this paper, we propose an approach to Russian text vectorization based on SRSTI classifier. The values of resulting vector indicate how close thematically the source text is to a particular SRSTI category. We will also refer to this vector as a "topic profile" further in this paper.

Most of the approaches listed above are based on creating a map from words or n-grams to vector space. Our approach, however, creates a vector space based on topics that are characterized by lists of keywords.

In this perspective, our approach is closer to the field of topic modelling. However, as topic modelling is essentially word clustering, its results are hard to evaluate [9]. Moreover, Latent Dirichlet Allocation (LDA), a common topic modeling algorithm, requires a number of topics as an input parameter, which could be difficult to predict beforehand [10]. As the result of LDA fully relies on the number of topics, the model results are not sustainable.

Our approach, on the contrary, relies on SRSTI classifier that was developed by professionals in order to classify scientific and technical information and includes a fixed number of topic categories [11].

2 Basis Selection

We made a selection of topic profile basis based on GOST 7.59-2003 [12]. According to the standard, one or several following universal classification systems should be applied depending on the document type and the tasks set: Library and Bibliographic Classification (BBK), State Rubricator of Scientific and Technical Information (SRSTI), Universal Decimal Classification (UDC), Dewey Decimal Classification (DDC), Legal Acts Classifier (LAC), Interstate Classifier of Standards (ICS) or International Patent Classification (IPC).

We performed an overview analysis of listed classification systems in order to determine which of them could be used as a basis for topic profile.

Three out of seven universal classification systems considered – LAC, ICS and IPC – primarily focus on narrow fields, such as law, industry or invention. They do not include many important categories, i.e. literature, art, history and others. Because of that, we cannot use them as a basis for topic profile building.

BBK top level consists of seven categories that are described in more detail in form of subcategories at the second level. However, a significant proportion of first and second level BBK categories is useless or excessive for topic profile building. For example, first-level category "Literature of universal content" is too broad to define any concrete topic, and first-level category "Agriculture and forestry. Agricultural and Forestry Sciences" and its subcategories in too great detail describe topics that would be better presented in the form of single category. Therefore, we cannot use BBK for further work.

Ten first-level categories of UDC are not enough to form a topic profile. For example, one of the first-level categories is named "Geography. Biography.

History", but the field of geography cannot be equated with history. The next level of UDC describes some categories exceedingly redundantly (i.e., religion). Therefore, it is hard to determine which level of UDC will be sufficient for topic profile building.

The second level of the DDC contains 100 sections that can be used as a topic profile basis. However, redundancy of some of its categories (such as language or religion) and the paucity of others (such as science) may complicate further work.

SRSTI classifier has 88 categories on the first level. In this classifier much attention is paid to the distinction between different types of industry and technology. Nevertheless, the classifier does not overlook other important areas of knowledge, such as philosophy, history, art and many more. Thus, SRSTI, better than all other classifications considered, can be used as a basis for topic profile building. Therefore, we chose SRSTI as a topic profile basis for further work.

3 Data Collection and Preparation

We selected keywords to describe topic profile categories. In order to conduct an automated search for keywords it is necessary to collect a sufficient number of texts uniquely belonging to each of the classifier categories.

We chose an electronic catalog of the State Public Scientific-Technical Library of the Russian Academy of Sciences Siberian Branch (SB RAS) as a source for data collection [13]. The catalog allows to search through books based on SRSTI category. Due to the fact that the books in the library were divided into the SRSTI classifier categories by experts, we can confidently use collected data as source for keywords selection.

Since the selected electronic library system does not provide an open API, we collected data using a Python parser. We collected data on book titles and annotations (the latter is available for a small proportion of books), as well as subject headings.

Prior to keywords search, we also normalized text using morphological analyzer pymorphy2.

4 Text Vectorization Algorithm

4.1 Keywords Selection

We developed a keywords selection algorithm that consists of four main steps:

1. 50 most popular unigrams and 50 most popular bigrams lists are automatically generated based on the lists of book titles and subject headings of the selected category. The result of current step is 200 elements (unigrams and bigrams) that characterize the category in question.
2. Duplicate list items are removed.
3. Bigrams with both words present in the unigrams list are also removed.

4. We remove keywords featured in stop words list that we formed beforehand. The stop words list includes keywords that are included in many categories and are too general to characterize any of them.

Keywords selection result for category "Literature. Literary criticism. Folklore" is shown in Fig. 1.

```
"17: Литература. Литературоведение. Устное народное творчество": ["проза",
"детективный", "слово", "рассказ", "миф", "приключенческий", "язык",
"литература", "художественный", "отражение", "фантастический", "философия",
"собрание", "история", "творчество", "текст", "контекст", "стиль",
"литературоведение", "писатель", "приключение", "пушкин", "чтение",
"фольклор", "письмо", "сказка", "поэтика", "достоевский", "сочинение",
"поэт", "книга", "произведение", "филология", "литературный", "поэзия",
"роман; литература зарубежный", "зарубежный литература", "драматический
произведение", "михаил булгаков", "картина мир", "серебряный век",
"литература xviii", "сергей есенин", "плата чехов", "полка игорев",
"литературный процесс", "полный собрание", "левый толстой", "ю лермонтов",
"малое собрание", "русский зарубежье", "русский словесность"],
```

Fig. 1. Category "Literature. Literary criticism. Folklore" keywords.

Semantic incorrectness of some keywords (i.e. "Igorev shelf" and not "Lay of Igor's") is caused by text normalization using pymorphy2 morphological analyzer. However, the keywords calculation will still be completed correctly, since the source text will also be normalized using the same morphological analyzer.

We performed keywords selection for all SRSTI categories. Based on collected data we formed a JSON dictionary. The key of the dictionary is a string containing topic category name and the value is an array that stores all selected keywords.

4.2 Text Vector Calculation

The text vector is calculated as follows:

1. Number of keywords used in the text is calculated for each category in the dictionary.
2. The corresponding vector element value is set equal to the category keywords number to total words in text number ratio.
3. The vector value is normalized so that the vector elements sum is equal to one.

4.3 Vector Comparison

Vector values can be used to compare texts. Using the SciPy library, we developed a function that calculates cosine distance between vectors. Therefore, if cosine distance between two texts is close to one, then the texts in question are very close thematically. In the same way, cosine distance close to zero means that the texts in question are very distant in terms of topics.

5 Results

Examples of topic profile building algorithm result and cosine distance calculation for texts are shown in Figs. 2 and 3 respectively.

```
Блюда из рыб фугу очень популярны в Юго-Восточной Азии. Не потому, что там живет
много любителей пощекотать себе нервы, а потому что у мяса фугу приятный вкус.
Китайские ученые попытались его воссоздать и определили 12 составляющих его
веществ. Среди них оказались несколько аминокислот, в том числе глутаминовая,
нуклеотид инозинмонофосфат и ионы калия, натрия и фосфорной кислоты

учёный (1) - 00: Общественные науки в целом
учёный (1) - 12: Науковедение
число (1) - 27: Математика
вещество (1) - 31: Химия
рыба (1) - 34: Биология
азия (1) - 39: География
мясо (1) - 65: Пищевая промышленность
рыба (1) - 69: Рыбное хозяйство. Аквакультура
учёный (1) - 81: Общие и комплексные проблемы технических и прикладных наук и
отраслей народного хозяйства
```

Fig. 2. Topic profile building algorithm results.

As can be seen from Fig. 3, the calculated cosine distance value shows that the first pair of texts is very close thematically, which seems plausible because both of them are excerpts from the same article. The second pair of texts has a medium value of cosine distance. Those texts were taken from different sources; they were designed for different goals. However, they both have war as a common topic, which is reflected on the cosine distance value. The last pair of texts is very different thematically, and a small value of cosine distance reflects that.

We also developed an algorithm that loads 100 posts from each group or noteworthy page of a specific user of social networking service VK and builds a single topic profile based on all these loaded texts.

Examples of the algorithm results are presented in Table 1.

As can be seen from the Table 1, it is possible to draw a correspondence between the users activity areas and their most popular topic categories that were suggested by our algorithm.

For the purposes of evaluation, we selected articles of online library CyberLeninka as a test set [14]. For every SRSTI category we collected data on corresponding paper titles.

Then, we performed a test on whether or not the top category defined by our algorithm matches the actual SRSTI category. For every category data collected, we calculated a topic profile. Based on it we formed a list of most popular categories, or, in other words, categories that were most likely to define its topics.

The confusion matrix for our algorithm performance is presented in Fig. 4.

Текст 1	Текст 2	Косин. р-е
В армии США есть необычный вид потерь - «переутомление в бою». К этой категории относят в первую очередь тех, кто оказался в плену. Так, при высадке в Нормандии в июне 1944-го года количество «переутомленных в бою» составило около 20% от общего числа выбывших из боя. В целом, по итогам Второй мировой войны по причине «переутомления» потери США составили 929307 человек.	В последние месяцы войны немецкое командование драконовыми методами пыталось заставить войска сражаться, но тщетно. Особенно неблагоприятной была ситуация на Западном фронте. Там немецкие солдаты, зная о соблюдении Англией и США Женевской конвенции об обращении с военнопленными сдавались гораздо охотнее, чем на Востоке.	0.905
В армии США есть необычный вид потерь - «переутомление в бою». К этой категории относят в первую очередь тех, кто оказался в плену. Так, при высадке в Нормандии в июне 1944-го года количество «переутомленных в бою» составило около 20% от общего числа выбывших из боя. В целом, по итогам Второй мировой войны по причине «переутомления» потери США составили 929307 человек.	Музей Анны Ахматовой в Фонтанном доме напоминает: встреча уже послезавтра, 16 января! Во время экскурсии мы посмотрим на мемориальную экспозицию под углом страшных лет войны и блокады, расскажем о трагических страницах жизни обитателей квартиры №44. Начало в 18.00	0.623
В армии США есть необычный вид потерь - «переутомление в бою». К этой категории относят в первую очередь тех, кто оказался в плену. Так, при высадке в Нормандии в июне 1944-го года количество «переутомленных в бою» составило около 20% от общего числа выбывших из боя. В целом, по итогам Второй мировой войны по причине «переутомления» потери США составили 929307 человек.	Во вторник исполнилось 111 лет со дня рождения Льва Давидовича Ландау, нобелевского лауреата и гениального физика, который работал и читал лекции в МФТИ. Мы решили разобраться, как ученый стал легендой Физтеха, и проанализировали типичные фольклорные сюжеты о нем	0.078

Fig. 3. Cosine distance calculation for texts.

Table 1. Result of topic profile building for VK users.

VK user	Top 5 categories of built topic profile	Values
id53083705 (D.A. Medvedev, Chairman of the Government of the Russian Federation)	00: Social sciences in general	0.10528
	82: Organization and management	0.05676
	26: Complex problems of social sciences	0.05580
	81: General and complex problems of technical and applied sciences and branches of the national economy	0.04859
	10: State and law. Jurisprudence	0.04752
id4457105 (A.V. Shipulin, Russian biathlete)	00: Social sciences in general	0.17190
	26: Complex problems of social sciences	0.13843
	23: Comprehensive study of individual countries and regions	0.10909
	77: Physical education and sport	0.10289
	8: Art. Art history	0.03306
id8530294 (A.A. Vasilyev, fashion and art historian)	00: Social sciences in general	0.09988
	03: History. Historical sciences	0.09406
	26: Complex problems of social sciences	0.07475
	64: Light industry	0.07169
	18: Art. Art history	0.06710

The results of evaluation are quite promising. From 68 categories that were present in CyberLeninka library, our algorithm marked 47 of them correctly, i.e. at first place. 7 correct categories were ranked second place and 5 were ranked third place.

Taking in consideration only the first position of top categories list, we calculated overall accuracy of our algorithms performance on given test set: 0.69118.

The results of algorithms performance show that our approach has a place for improvement.

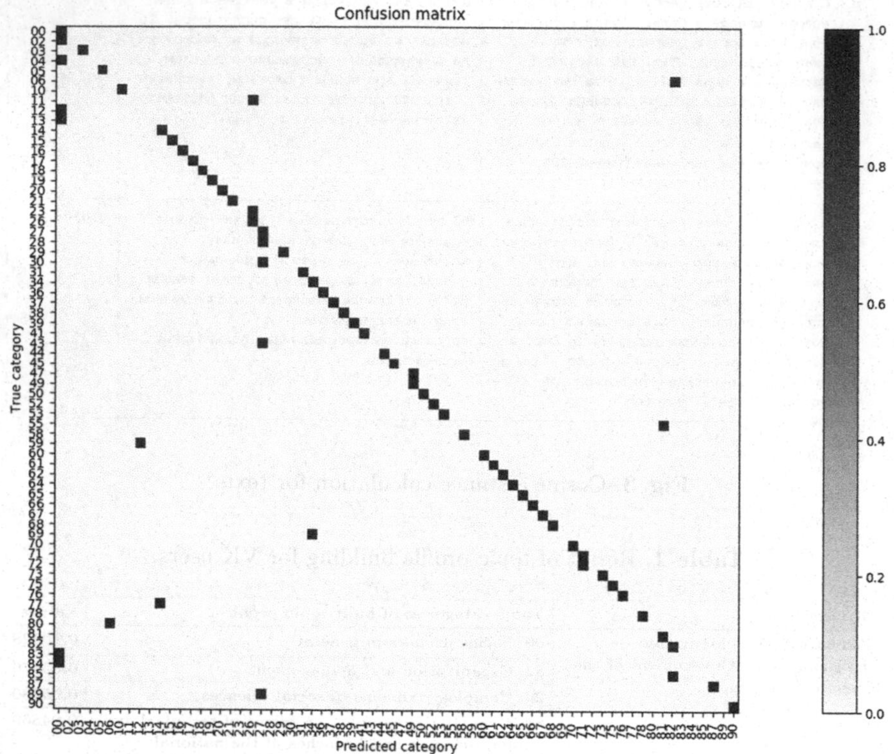

Fig. 4. Confusion matrix for evaluation results.

6 Vector Space Improvement

Evaluation results indicate that the developed vector space might be improved. As can be seen from the results, the dictionary holds a number of similar or too general categories, i.e. "00: Social sciences in general" and "26: Complex problems of social sciences". In addition, some keywords are present in many categories. For example, the keyword "scientist" is present in categories "00: Social sciences in general", "12: Science studies", "81: General and complex problems of technical and applied sciences and branches of national economy", and the keyword "physicist" appears in categories "29: Physics" and "43: General and complex problems of the natural and exact sciences".

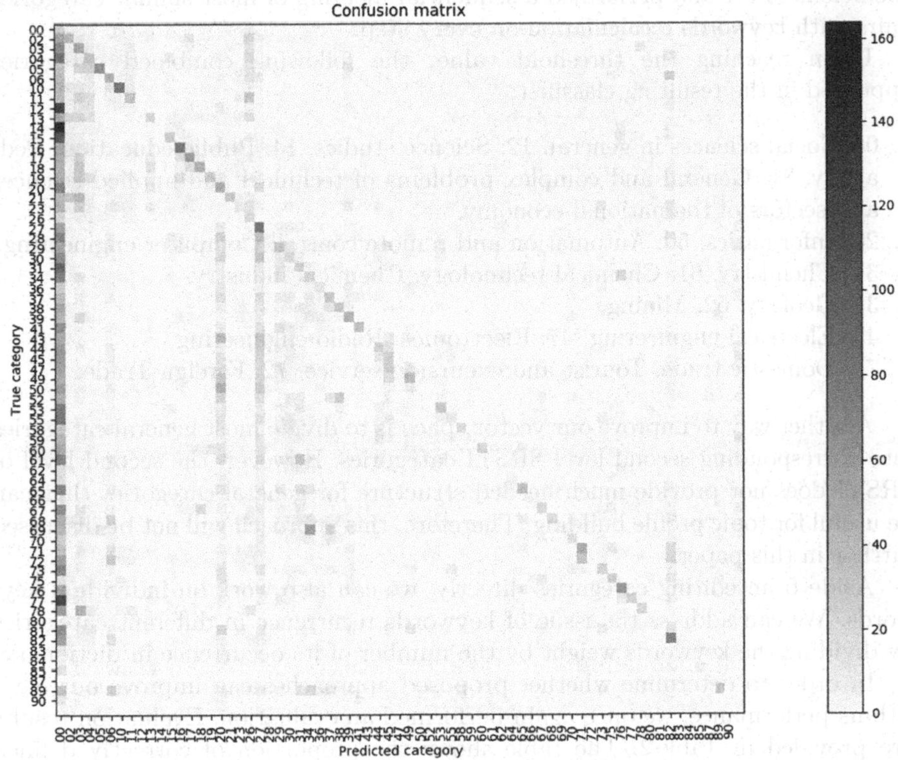

Fig. 5. Confusion matrix for individual paper titles.

In order to improve our understanding of vector space flaws, we also built confusion matrix based on our algorithm predictions for top category of individual paper titles. As can be seen from Fig. 5, while some categories were predicted correctly, our algorithm assigned category "00: Social sciences in general" to a lot of items. Other mistakenly assigned categories include "20: Computer Science", "27: Mathematics", "82: Organization and management". This issue can happen due to the fact that many papers use common math, computer science and management keywords in titles (i.e, method, technology or project), while the specific category of paper is different. These flaws can be disregarded due to the nature of test set. However, we also see that categories "45: Electrical Engineering", "47: Electronics. Radio engineering" and "49: Communication" were often mistakenly confused. Categories "34: Biology" and "69: Fisheries. Aquaculture", "38: Geology" and "52: Mining", "31: Chemistry" and "61: Chemical technology. Chemical industry" were often confused too.

There are different ways to address these issues.

We can reduce the vector space by similar categories merging. In order to do so, we formed a list of most similar categories pairs based on the pairwise calculation of the Jacquard coefficient. We set the threshold value of the Jacquard coefficient to 0.1 and performed a sequential merging of most similar categories pairs with keywords recalculation on every step.

Upon reaching the threshold value, the following combined categories appeared in the resulting classifier:

1. 00: Social sciences in general. 12: Science studies. 14: Public education. Pedagogy. 81: General and complex problems of technical and applied sciences and sectors of the national economy.
2. 20: Informatics. 50: Automation and remote control. Computer engineering.
3. 31: Chemistry. 61: Chemical technology. Chemical industry.
4. 38: Geology. 52: Mining.
5. 45: Electrical engineering. 47: Electronics. Radio engineering.
6. 71: Domestic trade. Tourist and excursion service. 72: Foreign Trade.

Another way to improve our vector space is to divide most general categories into corresponding second level SRSTI categories. However, the second level of SRSTI does not provide much needed structure for general categories that can be useful for topic profile building. Therefore, this approach will not be discussed further in this paper.

Aside from editing categories directly, we can also work on individual keywords. We can address the issue of keywords recurrence in different categories by dividing the keywords weight by the number of its occurrence in dictionary.

In order to determine whether proposed approaches can improve our algorithms performance, we once again performed an evaluation. Evaluation results are provided in Table 2. The table shows the proportion of correctly defined SRSTI categories for different number of top categories taken in consideration.

Table 2. Comparison of evaluation results for different improvement approaches.

	Original dictionary	Dictionary with united categories
Original weight calculation	Top-1: 0.69118	Top-1: 0.60294
	Top-3: 0.86765	Top-3: 0.68015
	Top-5: 0.89706	Top-5: 0.79412
Improved weight calculation	Top-1: 0.72059	Top-1: 0.64706
	Top-3: 0.88236	Top-3: 0.77941
	Top-5: 0.91176	Top-5: 0.80882

As can be seen from the Table 2, uniting similar categories does not provide any positive effects on the algorithms performance. Moreover, the results are actually getting worse. This can happen due to the merger of four categories.

New merged category will most likely be popular for many texts as its keywords cover many fields of interest. In addition, some thematically close categories were left out, i.e. categories "00: Social sciences in general" and "26: Complex problems of social sciences" still are not united. Overall, the results indicate that this approach is not successful.

Alternatively, an approach that improves weight calculation has a significant positive impact on the overall result. We plan to keep improved weight calculation in our algorithm for further work.

7 Conclusion and Future Work

In this paper, an approach to Russian text vectorization based on SRSTI classifier was presented. We described vector space basis selection and explained our choice of SRSTI classifier. We described the keywords selection process and presented the vector calculation and comparison algorithm. We applied developed algorithm to marked-up SRSTI texts and user social profiles for the purposes of evaluation. We also suggested approaches to vector space improvement and evaluated them.

As of future work, we plan to implement designed algorithm to improve a web recommender system. We are going to calculate topic profiles for authorized social media users based on text information from their profiles, i.e. user posts, noteworthy pages and groups, profile description etc. We will also calculate topic profiles for the posts on the website. By calculating these vectors, we will be able to bring the user and the posts into a single vector space, characterized by values of topic vectors. This way, based on comparison of user profile vector and post vector we will be able to form recommendations.

References

1. Shperber, G.: A gentle introduction to Doc2Vec. https://medium.com/scaleabout/a-gentle-introduction-to-doc2vec-db3e8c0cce5e. Accessed 08 Feb 2019
2. Zhang, Y., Jin, R., Zhou, Z.H.: Understanding bag-of-words model: a statistical framework. Int. J. Mach. Learn. Cybern. **1**(1–4), 43–52 (2010)
3. Le, Q., Mikolov, T.: Distributed representations of sentences and documents. In: International Conference on Machine Learning, pp. 1188–1196 (2014)
4. Ramos, J.: Using TF-IDF to determine word relevance in document queries. In: Proceedings of the First Instructional Conference on Machine Learning, pp. 133–142 (2003)
5. Mikolov, T., Chen, K., Corrado, G., Dean, J.: Efficient estimation of word representations in vector space. arXiv preprint arXiv:1301.3781 (2013)
6. Lau, J.H., Baldwin, T.: An empirical evaluation of doc2vec with practical insights into document embedding generation. arXiv preprint arXiv:1607.05368 (2016)
7. Kiros, R., et al.: Skip-thought vectors. In: Advances in Neural Information Processing Systems, pp. 3294–3302 (2015)

8. Kulkarni, R., Vintró, M., Kapetanakis, S., Sama, M.: Performance comparison of popular text vectorising models on multi-class email classification. In: Arai, K., Kapoor, S., Bhatia, R. (eds.) IntelliSys 2018. AISC, vol. 868, pp. 567–578. Springer, Cham (2019). https://doi.org/10.1007/978-3-030-01054-6_41
9. Bull, B.C., Carrier, S.R., Ezen Can, A., Mansjur, D.S.: U.S. Patent Application No. 15/888, 113 (2018)
10. Blei, D.M., Ng, A.Y., Jordan, M.I.: Latent Dirichlet allocation. J. Mach. Learn. Res. **3**, 993–1022 (2003)
11. SRSTI Homepage. http://grnti.ru/. Accessed 09 Feb 2019
12. GOST 7.59-2003 SSILP. Indexing of Documents. General Requirements for Classifying and Subject Indexing. http://docs.cntd.ru/document/1200032034. Accessed 09 Feb 2019
13. State Public Scientific-Technical Library of the Russian Academy of Sciences Siberian Branch (SB RAS). http://webirbis.spsl.nsc.ru. Accessed 10 Feb 2019
14. CyberLeninka. https://cyberleninka.ru. Accessed 10 Feb 2019

Quantum–Inspired Measure of Behavioral Semantics

Ilya A. Surov[1(✉)], Julia E. Zaytseva[2], Alexander P. Alodjants[1], and Sergey V. Khmelevsky[1]

[1] ITMO University, Birzhevaya line, 14, Saint-Petersburg, Russia
surov.i.a@yandex.ru

[2] Saint-Petersburg State University, Makarova emb, 6, Saint-Petersburg, Russia

Abstract. We propose a measure to quantify strength of semantic relation between two pairs of binary alternatives in cognition of a subject group. The measure and experimental methodology, adapted from physical toolbox for detection of quantum entanglement, allow for on-line realization when a WWW search engine functions as a model of collective cognition of its users. We demonstrate the method by quantifying culture-specific semantic relations between the archetypal living creatures and their qualities, which previously could be addressed only verbally. Methodology and state-of-the art in quantum approach to semantic modeling of human behavior are outlined.

Keywords: Quantum semantics · Quantum cognition · Contextuality · Bell inequality

1 Introduction

The human cognitive system is developed by Nature as a tool to control operation of the organism, including optimization of its behavior which demands prognosis of life processes in future. For that, cognitive system creates a worldview – a model of the world reflecting regularities which are significant for the organism [29,30]. This model is used as a template to recode and assimilate any perceived information – a process referred to as *understanding*, *comprehension*, *interpretation*, *meaning-* or *sense-making* [23,42,44,47].

The world model of an adult human involves tremendous amount of knowledge, most of which is useless at any practical situation and therefore stays inactive. Segment of that model which is invoked for understanding of a particular information block is referred to as *context*.

Contextual, meaning-oriented intelligence is a solution which nature developed for life to operate in an inexhaustible, non-axiomatizable world such as ours [52]. Same qualities are present at collective level of intelligence and behavior – a scene on which cultural, economic and other social processes unfold. Flows of human populations, businesses, goods and resources, and even ecology of the planet are eventually determined by cognitive dynamics of huge masses of people [56].

D. A. Alexandrov et al. (Eds.): DTGS 2019, CCIS 1038, pp. 765–776, 2019.
https://doi.org/10.1007/978-3-030-37858-5_65

To conduct these processes in sensible manner it is therefore critical to have a model of the relevant segment of collective cognition, for what we need a method to retrieve and quantify a structure of the collective semantic space. This is the challenge we address in the present work, suggesting a measure and an experimental technique to quantify strength of a given semantic relation in a target social group.

1.1 Quantum-Like Contextuality

Being inherently contextual, human cognition is able to address formally the same problem from uncountable different "points of view", wherein the produced decisions may differ [1]. If these contexts are mismatched with each other, then violations of rationality and Boolean logic occur. These properties contrast human cognition with classical computation, where an algorithm can proceed in a fixed number of prescribed ways. This is why the classical algorithmic approach is inappropriate to model intelligence and behavior of living systems [13,31,45].

A conceptual approach to that challenge came from the quantum theory, initially developed to describe probabilistic experiments on atom-scale physical systems [50]. Sketched in early 1980s [48,49], this approach gained moment in 2000s in works of D. Aerts, A. Khrennikov, J. Busemeyer and others [3,7,18,38]. Quantum theory showed the ability to model variety of behavioral and cognitive phenomena which compromise the classical rational logic paradigm [17,34,41].

This success of the quantum approach is a consequence of intrinsic contextuality incorporated in mathematical apparatus and conceptual structure of quantum theory [2,12,37,53]. Quantum-like cognitive models describe the observable behavior of an organism as decision making acts corresponding to results of a measurements over its cognitive system. Crucially, state of the latter is not considered as a thing in itself, but is initially defined in relation to the environment – a particular decision making situation forming the measurement context. Quantum state of a system, whether it is an electron or a human mind, can be considered as a probabilistic prognosis of the system's behavior in the set available future alternatives [17,31,50]. In this way, the concept of contextuality is a common ground for unified understanding of both quantum physical phenomena and behavior of living systems [22,24,25,32,40,46,57].

This understanding of quantum theory provides one with off-the-shelf conceptual and mathematical toolbox to address modeling problems in life sciences which are not formalized in other approaches [41]. That is the possibility which we use in the present work. Namely, we propose a cognitive application of the so-called *Bell's theorem*, originally devised by John Stuart Bell in 1964 to rigorously establish whether the quantum physical processes are locally predetermined or not [16].

1.2 Bell's Inequality

We start with the following distilled form of the Bell's theorem [21]. Consider two pairs of probabilistic quantities $A_{1,2}$ and $B_{1,2}$ each having two possible outcomes ± 1. In each experiment a pair (A_i, B_j) is randomly picked out and result of the form $(\pm 1, \pm 1)$ is recorded. Statistics of these outcomes is used to calculate the average product $\langle A_i B_j \rangle$ for each of the four possible combinations of i, j. Simple mathematical fact is that

$$\text{if} \quad \langle A_i B_j \rangle = \langle A_i \rangle \langle B_j \rangle \quad \forall i, j \tag{1}$$

$$\text{then} \quad S = \max_{\text{odd number of } +} \Big(\pm \langle A_1 B_1 \rangle \pm \langle A_1 B_2 \rangle \pm \langle A_2 B_1 \rangle \pm \langle A_2 B_2 \rangle \Big) \leq 2, \tag{2}$$

where $\langle A_i \rangle$ and $\langle B_j \rangle$ denote individual (marginal, i.e. ignoring the state of the other alternative) expectation values.

Relation (2) is known as Bell inequality with S referred to as *Bell parameter*. Maximum over odd number of plus signs reflects the ability to assign names and indices (A_i, B_j) to the measured quantities at will. That is, in (2) it is only essential that sign of any three of the summands is opposite to that of the remaining one. Inverse of the above relation

$$\text{if} \quad S > 2 \tag{3}$$

$$\text{then} \quad \langle A_i B_j \rangle \neq \langle A_i \rangle \langle B_j \rangle \quad \text{for some} \quad i, j \tag{4}$$

expresses the so-called *Bell test*.

In physics, boundary $S = 2$ is used to delimit "classical" from "quantum" phenomena. The former type, for which condition (1) holds, is associated with locally predetermined ("realistic") processes, while the latter is commonly interpreted as violation of either locality or predetermination or both [15,16,39].

Careful investigation, however, shows that interpretation of inseparability (4) as "death of local realism" [58] implicitly relies on groundless probability-theoretic assumptions. In particular, it may result from context-dependent difference between probability measures involved in formation of statistical averages $\langle \cdot \rangle$, see chapter 8 in [37]. Quantum theory, then, somehow efficiently circumvents direct description of pre-quantum physical contexts by using Hilbert space probability amplitudes and thereby produces correct statistical averages in spite of the very simplified description of the experiment [36]. This picture agrees with our view on violations of the Bell test in cognitive experiments, see chapter (2.4).

In the following, we use (3) as sufficient condition for contextuality of logic which generates the corresponding behavioral statistics.

2 Bell's Inequality in Human Cognition

2.1 Semantics of Concept Combinations

The Animal Acts. A case highly relevant to our work is the study [8]. In the experiment, concepts `The Animal` and `Acts` are incarnated in two pairs of two exemplars each corresponding to the possible values of dichotomic quantities $A_{1,2}$ and $B_{1,2}$ defined in Sect. 1.2, see Table 1. In that way a four sets of compound exemplars (A_i, B_j) were formed; for example, the compound exemplar `Horse Growls` corresponds to the quantities (A_1, B_1) both taking values $+1$.

Table 1. Compound exemplars in Bell's test of entanglement in combination of concepts `The Animal` and `Acts` [8].

i, j	Animal (A_i)	Act (B_j)
1	`Horse, Bear`	`Growls, Whinnies`
2	`Tiger, Cat`	`Snorts, Meows`

From each set (A_i, B_j), an ensemble of subjects were asked to choose a single most typical exemplar of the compound concept `The Animal Acts`. Bell's parameter calculated from statistics of these decisions as explained in Sect. 1.2 is found to be $S = 2.42$, exceeding the classical threshold $S = 2$ (Eq. 3).

This violation indicates that `The Animal` constitutes the context for choice of the `Acts`, and/or vice versa. This contextuality reflects the meaning connection between the concepts, responsible for inseparability (4) detected by Bell's test. The authors build analogy between human cognition and quantum physics, in which contextual and semantic relations between linguistic concepts correspond to *entanglement* between multipartite physical systems [8,9].

Two Different Wind Directions. Another experiment on "entanglement" in concept combinations enquires existence of the meaning connection between the concepts `One wind direction` and `Another wind direction`, expressed in the sentence `Two different wind directions` [5]. Exemplars offered for typicality assessment are composed from the two groups of directions as shown in Table 2. The obtained Bell parameter $S = 2.47$ exceeds the contextuality threshold (3).

Table 2. Compound alternatives in Bell's test of entanglement in combination of concepts `One wind direction` and `Another wind direction` [5].

i, j	First direction (A_i)	Second direction (B_j)
1	$\uparrow, \downarrow$	$\nwarrow, \searrow$
2	$\rightarrow, \leftarrow$	$\nearrow, \swarrow$

A distinguishing feature of this setup is exact correspondence with the paradigmatic Bell test in physics where two spin-1/2 particles prepared in the entangled sum-zero spin state

$$|\psi\rangle = \frac{|\uparrow\downarrow\rangle + |\downarrow\uparrow\rangle}{\sqrt{2}} \tag{5}$$

are subjected to the spin projection measurements in directions shown in Table 2 [35,58].

2.2 Internet as a Cognitive System

An intriguing version of `The animal acts` Bell test is demonstrated in [11], where decisions were made not by human subjects but by the Google Images search engine, presented with the compound query, e.g. `The horse growls`. The result page was inspected by experimenter who estimated the fraction of the returned images qualifying for the query. After appropriate normalization these fractions form the set of decision probability data required for calculation of the Bell parameter (2). The obtained value $S = 2.41$ is remarkably close to that found in the experiment with real subjects (Sect. 2.1).

Experiment [11] establishes an approach for using the Internet search engines as a model of collective cognition. This model is a distributed artificial intelligence system designed to reflect the search logic of Internet users which is calibrated in the real time by numerous search sessions. We expect this platform for social cognitive studies to become increasingly relevant in the future.

2.3 Deliberate Design of Semantics

Snow Queen. In the above experiments contextual decision making does not require from subjects any specific knowledge beyond common cognitive-linguistic skills. Experiment [19], in contrast, involves specific cognitive preparation of subjects before they are expected to produce violation of Bell inequality. During this preparation subjects study several characters by reading a fairytale (The Snow Queen by Hans Christian Andersen) and thus learn to make compound decisions with the intended semantic links. In that way a cognitive contextuality to be studied is not taken from basic cultural background but is created by experimenters at will. The proposed compound judgment alternatives are shown in the Table 3.

Table 3. Compound judgments in Bell's test of hand-crafted contextuality [19].

i, j	Character (A_i)	Characteristic (B_j)
1	`Gerda, Troll`	`Beautiful, Unattractive`
2	`Snow Queen, Old Finn Woman`	`Kind, Evil`

Experiment [19] is the first one where the observed non-signaling contextuality (Sect. 2.4). After subtracting the signaling effect the corrected Bell parameter is found to be 2.279. Uncorrected value (2) $S = 3.286$ is the largest obtained Bell parameter known to us.

Other Examples. Other successful attempts to hand-craft non-signaling contextuality are reported in Ref. [14]. This work also generalizes Bell inequality to situations containing not 4, but arbitrary number of compound questions. In particular, the first case of non-signaling contextuality with 3 compound questions is presented.

2.4 Outlook

Contrary to physics, violation of Bell's inequality in cognitive experiments summarized above does not have a ground-breaking philosophical implications; this is due to the fact that single-subject decision making does not involve spatially separated locations, as the decision making interval is long enough to allow direct communication (signaling) between any two regions of the subject's nervous system possibly responsible for decisions A and B. In fact, signaling is obvious in most of the existing cognitive Bell test violations, as indicated by dependence of the marginal statistics of outcomes A_i on the choice of the second alternative B_1/B_2, and vice versa (example calculation is given in Sect. 3.3).

Interpretation of signaling in cognitive Bell tests is open to debate [6,9,26]. In our view, it is a clear signature of meaning connection between entities A and B, realized as interaction between the corresponding patterns of neuronal excitations [10,28,43,51]. Conversely, cognitive entities which have no contextual (associative, semantic, meaning) connection between them are encoded by non-interacting neuronal patters; their activation statistics, as well as statistics of the corresponding decision making, then factorizes according to (1).

3 Bell Parameter as a Measure of Behavioral Semantics

3.1 Conception

All the studies discussed above are presented by their authors as a demonstrations of the quantum-like contextuality of behavioral data. We believe that the collected evidence is sufficient for the developed experimental and theoretical methods to be considered reliable enough for practical applications. That is the focus of the present work.

Consider an experiment "The Animal Acts" conducted in a social group ignorant of what these animals are. Members of that group would be unable to find (in their worldview) any common context carrying a meaning connection between animals and acts, which on statistical scale would produce separable decision statistics satisfying separability condition (1) and Bell inequality (2). Similarly, if the questionnaire in the "Snow Queen" experiment was not itself hinting at the right answers, then subjects ignorant of the story would be unable to match characters with their qualities, again producing separable decisions.

Comprehension of the biology course or a Snow Queen fairytale contributes to a worldview of the subjects by producing a context encompassing both sides of Tables 1, 2 and 3, allowing subjects to establish a meaning connections within the compound alternatives and produce a non-separable decision statistics possibly violating the Bell inequality[1]. Conversely, if Bell inequality is violated (3) then non-factorization (4) is unavoidable. That is, at least in one decision making task subjects assuredly produce non-separable decisions, demonstrating what we call contextuality or sensible behavior.

[1] This picture is not limited to human beings. For example, Ref. [55] reports contextual learning of mice.

We suggest that experimental and theoretical methods described above can be used for detection and quantification of cognitive-behavioral cohesion among members of the subject group. Bell parameter (2) then serves as a quantitative measure of semantic consensus regarding the considered matter – agreement in understanding of the relations between elements of the compound alternatives, producing coherent contextual decisions.

3.2 Experiment

The Bell-type experiments in cognition summarized above were performed in the US or Western Europe. As a first step in development of the proposed methodology in Russia we therefore choose to stage a testing experiment close to the seminal "The animal acts" one (Sect. 2.1). We choose to measure a semantic relations between the archetypal living creatures and their qualities, supposed to be learned in early childhood from folk fairytales, proverbs and other carriers of the national culture.

Table 4. Decision task in our experiment on quantification of semantic relations (translated from Russian). Subjects were asked to choose a single most appropriate sentence (compound alternative) from each group.

Group 1 (A_1B_1)	Group 2 (A_1B_2)	Group 3 (A_2B_1)	Group 4 (A_2B_2)
`Sparrow is fast`	`Sparrow is strong`	`Wolf is fast`	`Wolf is strong`
`Sparrow is slow`	`Sparrow is weak`	`Wolf is slow`	`Wolf is weak`
`Elephant is fast`	`Elephant is strong`	`Mosquito is fast`	`Mosquito is strong`
`Elephant is slow`	`Elephant is weak`	`Mosquito is slow`	`Mosquito is weak`

Our subjects were 310 students of Psychology Department in Saint-Petersburg State University. Subjects were asked to select a single most appropriate sentence in each of the four groups shown in the Table 4. Corresponding elements of the compound alternatives (translated from Russian) are shown in Table 5.

Table 5. Elements of the compound alternatives shown in Table 4 (translated from Russian).

i, j	Creature (A_i)	Quality (B_j)
1	`Sparrow, Elephant`	`Fast, Slow`
2	`Wolf, Mosquito`	`Strong, Weak`

3.3 Results

Raw experimental results are shown in the Fig. 1.

Mean products $\langle A_i B_j \rangle$ (Sect. 1.2) are found as sums over diagonal minus sums of non-diagonal elements of the matrices. If calculation goes in absolute numbers (in brackets) then the results are normalized by the number of subjects:

$$\langle A_1 B_1 \rangle = \frac{178 + 90 - 29 - 13}{310} = 0.73$$
$$\langle A_1 B_2 \rangle = \frac{25 + 14 - 227 - 44}{310} = -0.75$$
$$\langle A_2 B_1 \rangle = \frac{168 + 22 - 107 - 13}{310} = 0.23$$
$$\langle A_2 B_2 \rangle = \frac{232 + 43 - 25 - 10}{310} = 0.77.$$

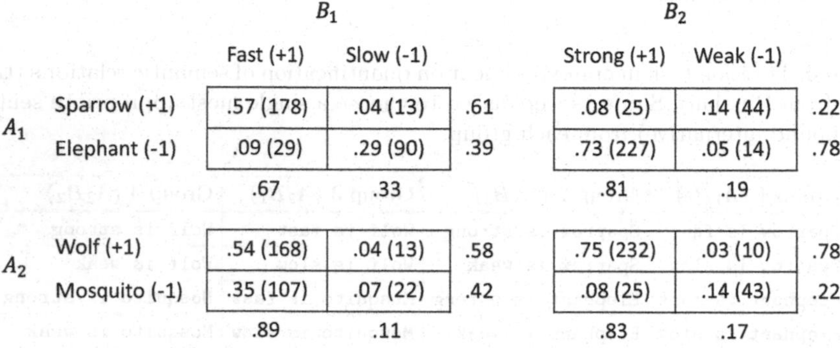

		B_1			B_2		
		Fast (+1)	Slow (-1)		Strong (+1)	Weak (-1)	
A_1	Sparrow (+1)	.57 (178)	.04 (13)	.61	.08 (25)	.14 (44)	.22
	Elephant (-1)	.09 (29)	.29 (90)	.39	.73 (227)	.05 (14)	.78
		.67	.33		.81	.19	
A_2	Wolf (+1)	.54 (168)	.04 (13)	.58	.75 (232)	.03 (10)	.78
	Mosquito (-1)	.35 (107)	.07 (22)	.42	.08 (25)	.14 (43)	.22
		.89	.11		.83	.17	

Fig. 1. Raw experimental results: statistical probabilities (absolute numbers) of choices for 16 compound alternatives combining living creatures and their qualities. For each group, probabilities and absolute numbers sum to 1 (310 subjects). Values outside the tables are marginal probabilities.

Maximum of the sum in (2) is obtained with a single minus sign for $\langle A_1 B_2 \rangle$ which gives $S = 2.47$. Statistical error is estimated by performing the same calculation for virtual random division of data by 10 groups of 31 subject each. Standard deviation of the obtained Bell parameters $\sigma = 0.45$ corresponds to the standard deviation of the mean $\sigma/\sqrt{10} = 0.14$. The reliability interval

$$S = 2.47 \pm 0.14 \tag{6}$$

is centered more than three standard deviations above the bound $S = 2$, representing a clear proof of contextually-meaningful decision making.

Value (6) quantifies a semantic relation between the archetypes of human cognition based on the Russian language and culture. Note that it falls within a remarkably narrow interval of Bell parameters obtained in different physical and cognitive Bell tests, see Sect. 2 and Ref. [6]

Signaling. In light of the Sect. 2.4 it is instructive to assess whether the observed contextuality is signaling or not.

Signaling is defined as change of the (marginal) distribution of decisions A_i in response to change of the conjoint decision alternative $B_i \rightarrow B_j$ [26]. For example, marginal distribution of A_1 in context B_1, obtained by summation of rows in the top left table in Fig. 1, constitutes of probabilities .61 and .39. Corresponding mean value of A_1 is $\langle A_1^1 \rangle = .61 - .39 = .22$. In the context B_2 analogous calculation gives $\langle A_1^2 \rangle = .22 - .78 = -.56$. Absolute difference between these means $sig(B \rightarrow A_1) = .78$ is signaling from B to A_1. All 4 possible signalings are

$$\begin{aligned}
sig(B \rightarrow A_1) &= \left|\langle A_1^2 \rangle - \langle A_1^1 \rangle\right| = |.22 + .56| = .78 \\
sig(B \rightarrow A_2) &= \left|\langle A_2^2 \rangle - \langle A_2^1 \rangle\right| = |.56 - .16| = .40 \\
sig(A \rightarrow B_1) &= \left|\langle B_1^2 \rangle - \langle B_1^1 \rangle\right| = |.78 - .34| = .44 \\
sig(A \rightarrow B_2) &= \left|\langle B_2^2 \rangle - \langle B_2^1 \rangle\right| = |.66 - .62| = .04.
\end{aligned}$$

Sum of these values 1.66 represents total amount of signaling [14,27].

4 Discussion

The ability to distinguish and take into account relevant situational factors known as contextuality is necessary for both natural and artificial intelligent systems to qualify for their intended tasks. We proposed a method to reveal this ability for contextually meaningful decision making based on the quantitative measure borrowed from the quantum theory – the Bell parameter. We conjecture that systematic application of the proposed approach to adjacent entities of cognition would allow to retrieve and quantify the structure of semantic space in a given social group.

Further development of the proposed approach to quantitative investigation of semantic structure of human cognition and behavior may start from resolving the following questions:

First is establishing the necessary condition for the contextuality, as the criterion $S > 2$ is only sufficient one. It is useless when two or more contextual relations compensate each other leading to the non-contextual range of the Bell parameter [53].

Second is whether there is any difference in semantic relations leading (i) to the signaling and non-signaling contextuality and (ii) to the Bell parameter smaller or larger than $2\sqrt{2}$, the so called Cirel'son bound [20].

Third is generalization of the Bell type methodology for systems of arbitrary number of multi-variant alternatives [33,54].

Fourth is establishing the correspondence between Bell-type semantic experiments (i) on the real social groups and (ii) on the Internet as a model of collective cognition [4,11] (Sect. 2.2). A positive conclusion would open a new page in experimental methodology of social and cognitive sciences.

References

1. Aerts, D., Broekaert, J., Gabora, L.: Intrinsic contextuality as the crux of consciousness. In: Yasue, K. (ed.) Fundamental Approaches to Consciousness. John Benjamins Publishing Company, Tokyo (2000)
2. Aerts, D.: Quantum structures: an attempt to explain the origin of their appearance in nature. Int. J. Theor. Phys. **34**(8), 1165–1186 (1995). https://doi.org/10.1007/BF00676227
3. Aerts, D.: Quantum structure in cognition. J. Math. Psychol. **53**(5), 314–348 (2009). https://doi.org/10.1016/j.jmp.2009.04.005
4. Aerts, D., et al.: Towards a quantum World Wide Web. Theor. Comput. Sci. **1**, 1–16 (2018). https://doi.org/10.1016/j.tcs.2018.03.019
5. Aerts, D., et al.: Spin and wind directions I: identifying entanglement in nature and cognition. Found. Sci. **23**(2), 323–335 (2017). https://doi.org/10.1007/s10699-017-9528-9
6. Aerts, D., et al.: Spin and wind directions II: a Bell State Quantum Model. Found. Sci. **23**(2), 337–365 (2017). https://doi.org/10.1007/s10699-017-9530-2
7. Aerts, D., Broekaert, J., Gabora, L., Sozzo, S.: Quantum Structures in Cognitive and Social Science, Frontiers Research Topics, vol. 7. Frontiers Media SA, Lausanne (2016). https://doi.org/10.3389/978-2-88919-876-4
8. Aerts, D., Sozzo, S.: Quantum structure in cognition: why and how concepts are entangled. In: Song, D., Melucci, M., Frommholz, I., Zhang, P., Wang, L., Arafat, S. (eds.) QI 2011. LNCS, vol. 7052, pp. 116–127. Springer, Heidelberg (2011). https://doi.org/10.1007/978-3-642-24971-6_12
9. Aerts, D., Sozzo, S.: Quantum entanglement in concept combinations. Int. J. Theor. Phys. **53**(10), 3587–3603 (2014). https://doi.org/10.1007/s10773-013-1946-z
10. Anokhin, K.V.: Cognitome: neural hypernetworks and percolation hypothesis of consciousness. In: The Science of Consciousness, TSC 2018 (2018)
11. Arguëlles, J.A.: The heart of an image: quantum superposition and entanglement in visual perception. Found. Sci. **23**, 757–778 (2018). https://doi.org/10.1007/s10699-018-9547-1
12. Auffèves, A., Grangier, P.: Recovering the quantum formalism from physically realist axioms. Sci. Rep. **7**(1) (2017). 43365 https://doi.org/10.1038/srep43365
13. Ball, P.: Culture crash. Nature **441**(7094), 686–688 (2006). https://doi.org/10.1038/441686a
14. Basieva, I., Cervantes, V.H., Dzhafarov, E.N., Khrennikov, A.: True contextuality beats direct influences in human decision making. J. Exp. Psychol. Gen., p. 13 (2018). https://doi.org/10.1037/xge0000585
15. Bell, J.S.: Speakable and Unspeakable in Quantum Mechanics. Cambridge University Press, Cambridge (1993)
16. Bell, J.S.: On the Einstein Podolsky Rosen paradox. Physics **1**(3), 195–200 (1964). https://doi.org/10.1002/prop.19800281202
17. Busemeyer, J.R., Bruza, P.D.: Quantum Models of Cognition and Decision. Cambridge University Press, New York (2012)
18. Busemeyer, J.R., Wang, Z.: What is quantum cognition, and how is it applied to psychology? Curr. Dir. Psychol. Sci. **24**(3), 163–169 (2015). https://doi.org/10.1177/0963721414568663
19. Cervantes, V.H., Dzhafarov, E.N.: Snow queen is evil and beautiful: experimental evidence for probabilistic contextuality in human choices. Decision **5**(3), 193–204 (2018). https://doi.org/10.1037/dec0000095

20. Cirel'son, B.S.: Quantum generalizations of Bell's inequality. Lett. Math. Phys. **4**(2), 93–100 (1980). https://doi.org/10.1007/BF00417500
21. Clauser, J.F., Horne, M.A., Shimony, A., Holt, R.A.: Proposed experiment to test local hidden-variable theories. Phys. Rev. Lett. **23**(15), 880–884 (1969). https://doi.org/10.1103/PhysRevLett.23.880
22. Davies, P.C.: Does quantum mechanics play a non-trivial role in life? BioSystems **78**(1–3), 69–79 (2004). https://doi.org/10.1016/j.biosystems.2004.07.001
23. De Jesus, P.: Thinking through enactive agency: sense-making, bio-semiosis and the ontologies of organismic worlds. Phenomenol. Cogn. Sci. **1988**, 1–27 (2018). https://doi.org/10.1007/s11097-018-9562-2
24. Deng, D.L., Li, X., Das Sarma, S.: Quantum entanglement in neural network states. Phys. Rev. X **7**(2), (2017). 021021 https://doi.org/10.1103/PhysRevX.7.021021
25. Driessen, A.: Life and quantum biology, an interdisciplinary approach. Acta Philosophica **24**(1), 69–86 (2015)
26. Dzhafarov, E.N., Kujala, J.V.: On selective influences, marginal selectivity, and Bell/CHSH inequalities. Top. Cogn. Sci. **6**(1), 121–128 (2014). https://doi.org/10.1111/tops.12060
27. Dzhafarov, E.N., Kujala, J.V., Cervantes, V.H., Zhang, R., Jones, M.: On contextuality in behavioural data. Philos. Trans. R. Soc. A **374** (2015). 20150234. https://doi.org/10.1098/rsta.2015.0099
28. Felleman, D.J., Van Essen, D.C.: Distributed hierarchical processing in the primate cerebral cortex. Cereb. Cortex **1**(1), 1–47 (1991)
29. Gabora, L., Aerts, D.: The emergence and evolution of integrated worldviews. J. Math. Psychol. **53**, 434–451 (2009)
30. Gabora, L.: Cognitive mechanisms underlying the origin and evolution of culture. Doctoral thesis, Free University of Brussels (2001). https://www.vub.ac.be/CLEA/liane/thesis_gabora.pdf
31. Gabora, L., Aerts, D.: Evolution as context-driven actualisation of potential: toward an interdisciplinary theory of change of state. Interdisc. Sci. Rev. **30**(1), 69–88 (2005). https://doi.org/10.1179/030801805X25873
32. Gershenson, C.: The world as evolving information. In: Minai, A.A., Braha, D., Bar-Yam, Y. (eds.) Unifying Themes in Complex Systems VII, pp. 100–115. Springer, Heidelberg (2012). https://doi.org/10.1007/978-3-642-18003-3_10
33. Gisin, N.: Bell inequalities: many questions, a few answers. In: Quantum Reality, Relativistic Causality, and Closing the Epistemic Circle, pp. 125–138 (2009). https://doi.org/10.1007/978-1-4020-9107-0_9
34. Haven, E., Khrennikov, A.: Quantum Social Science. Cambridge University Press, New York (2013)
35. Hensen, B., et al.: Loophole-free Bell inequality violation using electron spins separated by 1.3 kilometres. Nature **526**(7575), 682–686 (2015). https://doi.org/10.1038/nature15759
36. Hess, K., De Raedt, H., Michielsen, K.: From Boole to Leggett-Garg: epistemology of Bell-type inequalities. Adv. Math. Phys., pp. 1–7 (2016). https://doi.org/10.1155/2016/4623040
37. Khrennikov, A.: Contextual Approach to Quantum Formalism. Springer, Dordrecht (2009). https://doi.org/10.1007/978-1-4020-9593-1
38. Khrennikov, A.: Quantum-like modeling of cognition. Front. Phys. **3**(77) (2015). https://doi.org/10.3389/fphy.2015.00077
39. Khrennikov, A.: After Bell. Fortschritte der Physik **65**(6-8) (2017). 1600044 https://doi.org/10.1002/prop.201600044

40. Khrennikov, A., Basieva, I., Pothos, E.M., Yamato, I.: Quantum probability in decision making from quantum information representation of neuronal states. Sci. Rep. **8**(1) (2018). 16225 https://doi.org/10.1038/s41598-018-34531-3
41. Khrennikov, A.Y.: Ubiquitous Quantum Structure. Springer, Heidelberg (2010). https://doi.org/10.1007/978-3-642-05101-2
42. Kolchinsky, A., Wolpert, D.H.: Semantic information, autonomous agency and non-equilibrium statistical physics. Interface Focus **8**(6), (2018). 20180041 https://doi.org/10.1098/rsfs.2018.0041
43. Kumar, S., Boone, K., Tuszyński, J., Barclay, P., Simon, C.: Possible existence of optical communication channels in the brain. Sci. Rep. **6** (2016). https://doi.org/10.1038/srep36508
44. Kuznetsov, O.P.: Cognitive semantics and artificial intelligence. Sci. Tech. Inf. Process. **40**(5), 269–276 (2013). https://doi.org/10.3103/S0147688213050067
45. Lepsky, V.E., Arshinov, V.I. (eds.): On the way to post-nonclassical conceptions of public administration (in Russian). Institute of Philosophy RAS, Moscow (2005). http://www.reflexion.ru/Library/Sbornic2005.pdf
46. Maldonado, C.E., Gómez-Cruz, N.A.: Synchronicity among biological and computational levels of an organism: quantum biology and complexity. Procedia Comput. Sci. **36**(C), 177–184 (2014). https://doi.org/10.1016/j.procs.2014.09.076
47. Meijer, D.: Information: what do you mean. Syntropy J. (3), 1–49 (2013). http://www.lifeenergyscience.it/english/2013-eng-3-01.pdf
48. Orlov, Y.F.: A quantum model of doubt. Ann. N. Y. Acad. Sci. **373**, 84–92 (1981). https://doi.org/10.1111/j.1749-6632.1981.tb51134.x
49. Orlov, Y.F.: The wave logic of consciousness: a hypothesis. Int. J. Theor. Phys. **21**(1), 37–53 (1982). https://doi.org/10.1007/BF01880263
50. Peres, A.: Quantum Theory: Concepts and Methods. Kluwer Academic Publishers, New York (2002)
51. Pribram, K.H.: Quantum holography: is it relevant to brain function? Inf. Sci. **115**(1–4), 97–102 (1999). https://doi.org/10.1016/S0020-0255(98)10082-8
52. Raatikainen, P.: Gödel's Incompleteness Theorems (2015). https://plato.stanford.edu/entries/goedel-incompleteness/
53. Svozil, K.: How much contextuality? Nat. Comput. **11**(2), 261–265 (2012). https://doi.org/10.1007/s11047-012-9318-9
54. Vorob'ev, N.N.: Consistent families of measures and their extensions. Theor. Probab. Appl. **7**(2), 147–163 (1962). https://doi.org/10.1137/1107014
55. Vorob'eva, N.S., Ivashkina, O.I., Toropova, K.A., Anokhin, K.V.: Long-term contextual memory in mice: persistence and associability with reinforcement. Neurosci. Behav. Physiol. **47**(7), 780–786 (2017). https://doi.org/10.1007/s11055-017-0467-2
56. Weizsäcker, E.U., Wijkman, A.: Come On! Capitalism, Short-Termism Population and the Destruction of the Planet. Springer, New York (2018). https://doi.org/10.1007/978-1-4939-7419-1
57. Wendt, A.: Quantum Mind and Social Science. Cambridge University Press, Cambridge (2015). https://doi.org/10.1017/CBO9781107415324.004
58. Wiseman, H.: Quantum physics: death by experiment for local realism. Nature **526**, 649–650 (2015). https://doi.org/10.1038/nature15631

Author Index

Printed in the United States
By Bookmasters